CRIME IN THE UNITED STATES

CRIME IN THE UNITED STATES

2022

SIXTEENTH EDITION

EDITED BY SHANA HERTZ HATTIS

BernanPress

Lanham • Boulder • New York • London

Published by Bernan Press
An imprint of The Rowman & Littlefield Publishing Group, Inc.
4501 Forbes Boulevard, Suite 200, Lanham, Maryland 20706
www.rowman.com

86-90 Paul Street, London EC2A 4NE

ISBN 9781636710624 (hardback) | ISBN 9781636710631 (ebook)

CONTENTS

LIST OF FIGURES

SECTION I

SUMMARY OF THE UNIFORM CRIME REPORTING (UCR) PROGRAM

Bernan Press is proud to present its sixteenth edition of *Crime in the United States*. This title was formerly published by the Federal Bureau of Investigation (FBI), but is no longer available in printed form from the government. This edition contains final data from 2020, the most current year for which data is available.

This section describes the history of the UCR program and examines the best way to use the data in this publication.

Currently, the UCR program includes four data collections:

- National Incident-Based Reporting System (NIBRS) — Provides detailed incident information on 52 offenses including the victims, offenders, and property stolen, recovered, or damaged. In addition, NIBRS collects arrest data for those offenses plus 10 others.

- Summary Reporting System (SRS) — Furnishes aggregate offense counts for 10 Part I offenses and arrest data for an additional 20 offenses. The historic data collection will give way to make UCR a NIBRS-only data collection by January 1, 2021.

- Law Enforcement Officers Killed and Assaulted (LEOKA) Program — Offers information about officers who were killed or assaulted while performing their duties. The information is published and used to help agencies develop polices to improve officer safety. More information about LEOKA and the accompanying data is available in Bernan Press's *Justice Statistics: An Extended Look at Crime in the United States*.

- Hate Crime Statistics Program — Provides information on crimes motivated by offenders' bias against race, gender, gender identity, religion, disability, sexual orientation, and ethnicity. These data are also collected via NIBRS.

About the UCR Program

The UCR program's primary objective is to generate reliable information for use in law enforcement administration, operation, and management; however, over the course of the program, its data has stood out as one of the country's leading social indicators.

The UCR program is a nationwide, cooperative statistical effort of more than 18,000 city, university and college, county, state, tribal, and federal law enforcement agencies voluntarily reporting data on crimes brought to their attention. Since 1930, the FBI has administered the UCR program and continued to assess and monitor the nature and type of crime in the nation. Criminologists, sociologists, legislators, municipal planners, the media, and other students of criminal justice use the data for varied research and planning purposes.

Note for Users

It is important for UCR data users to remember that the FBI's primary objective is to generate a reliable set of crime statistics for use in law enforcement administration, operation, and management. The FBI does not provide a ranking of agencies; instead, it provides alphabetical tabulations of states, metropolitan statistical areas, cities with over 10,000 inhabitants, suburban and rural counties, and selected colleges and universities. Law enforcement officials use these data for their designed purposes. Additionally, the public relies on these data for information about the fluctuations in levels of crime from year to year, while criminologists, sociologists, legislators, city planners, media outlets, and other students of criminal justice use them for a variety of research and planning purposes. Since crime is a sociological phenomenon influenced by a variety of factors, the FBI discourages data users from ranking agencies and using the data as a measurement of the effectiveness of law enforcement.

To ensure that data are uniformly reported, the FBI provides contributing law enforcement agencies with a handbook that explains how to classify and score offenses and provides uniform crime offense definitions. Acknowledging that offense definitions may vary from state to state, the FBI cautions agencies to report offenses according to the guidelines provided in the handbook, rather than by local or state statutes. Most agencies make a good faith effort to comply with established guidelines.

The UCR program publishes the statistics most commonly requested by data users. More information regarding the availability of UCR program data is available by telephone at (304) 625-4830, or by e-mail at ucr@fbi.gov. Data requests via e-mail cannot be processed without the requester's full name, mailing address, and contact telephone number.

Variables Affecting Crime: Caution Against Ranking

Until data users examine all the variables that affect crime in a town, city, county, state, region, or college or university, they can make no meaningful comparisons. In each edition of *Crime in the United States*, many entities — including news media, tourism agencies, and other organizations with an interest in crime in the nation—use reported figures to compile rankings of cities and counties. However, these rankings are merely a quick choice made by that data user; they provide no insight into the many variables that mold the crime in a particular town, city, county, state, or region. Consequently, these rankings may lead to simplistic and/or incomplete analyses, which can create misleading perceptions and thus adversely affect cities, counties, and their residents.

Considering Other Characteristics of a Jurisdiction

To assess criminality and law enforcement's response from jurisdiction to jurisdiction, data users must consider many variables, some of which (despite having significant impact on crime) are not readily measurable or applicable among all locales. Geographic and demographic factors specific to each jurisdiction must be considered and applied in order to make an accurate and complete assessment of crime in that jurisdiction. Several sources of information are available to help the researcher explore the variables that affect crime in a particular locale. The U.S. Census Bureau data, for example, can help the user better understand the makeup of a locale's population. The transience of the population, its racial and ethnic makeup, and its composition by age and gender, educational levels, and prevalent family structures are all key factors in assessing and understanding crime.

Local chambers of commerce, planning offices, and similar entities provide information regarding the economic and cultural makeup of cities and counties. Understanding a jurisdiction's industrial/economic base, its dependence upon neighboring jurisdictions, its transportation system, its economic dependence on nonresidents (such as tourists and convention attendees), and its proximity to military installations, correctional institutions, and other types of facilities all contribute to accurately gauging and interpreting the crime known to and reported by law enforcement.

The strength (including personnel and other resources) and aggressiveness of a jurisdiction's law enforcement agency are also key factors in understanding the nature and extent of crime occurring in that area. Although information pertaining to the number of sworn and civilian employees can be found in this publication, it cannot be used alone as an assessment of the emphasis that a community places on enforcing the law. For example, one city may report more crime than another comparable city because its law enforcement agency identifies more offenses. Attitudes of citizens toward crime and their crime reporting practices—especially for minor offenses—also have an impact on the volume of crimes known to police.

Making Valid Crime Assessments

It is essential for all data users to become as well educated as possible about understanding and quantifying the nature and extent of crime in the United States and in the jurisdictions represented by law enforcement contributors to the UCR program. Valid assessments are possible only with careful study and analysis of the various unique conditions that affect each local law enforcement jurisdiction.

Some factors that are known to affect the volume and type of crime occurring from place to place are:

- Population density and degree of urbanization

- Variations in composition of population, particularly in the concentration of youth

- Stability of the population with respect to residents' mobility, commuting patterns, and transient factors

- Modes of transportation and highway systems

- Economic conditions, including median income, poverty level, and job availability

- Cultural factors and educational, recreational, and religious characteristics

- Family conditions, with respect to divorce and family cohesiveness

- Climate

- Effective strength of law enforcement agencies

- Administrative and investigative emphases of law enforcement

- Policies of other components of the criminal justice system (that is, prosecutorial, judicial, correctional, and probational policies)

- Residents' attitudes toward crime

- Crime reporting practices of residents

Although many of the listed factors equally affect the crime of a particular area, the UCR program makes no attempt to relate them to the data presented. **The data user is therefore cautioned against comparing statistical data of individual reporting units from cities, counties, metropolitan areas, states, or colleges or universities**

solely on the basis on their population coverage or student enrollment. Until data users examine all the variables that affect crime in a town, city, county, state, region, or college or university, they can make no meaningful comparisons.

Historical Background

Since 1930, the FBI has administered the UCR program; the agency continues to assess and monitor the nature and type of crime in the nation. Data users look to the UCR program for various research and planning purposes.

Recognizing a need for national crime statistics, the International Association of Chiefs of Police (IACP) formed the Committee on Uniform Crime Records in the 1920s to develop a system of uniform crime statistics. After studying state criminal codes and making an evaluation of the recordkeeping practices in use, the committee completed a plan for crime reporting that became the foundation of the UCR program in 1929. The plan included standardized offense definitions for seven main offense classifications known as Part I crimes to gauge fluctuations in the overall volume and rate of crime. Developers also instituted the Hierarchy Rule as the main reporting procedure for what is now known as the Summary Reporting System of the UCR program.

Seven main offense classifications, known as Part I crimes, were chosen to gauge the state of crime in the nation. These seven offense classifications included the violent crimes of murder and nonnegligent manslaughter, rape, robbery, and aggravated assault; also included were the property crimes of burglary, larceny-theft, and motor vehicle theft. By congressional mandate, arson was added as the eighth Part I offense category. Data collection for arson began in 1979.

During the early planning of the program, it was recognized that the differences among criminal codes precluded a mere aggregation of state statistics to arrive at a national total. Also, because of the variances in punishment for the same offenses in different states, no distinction between felony and misdemeanor crimes was possible. To avoid these problems and provide nationwide uniformity in crime reporting, standardized offense definitions were developed. Law enforcement agencies use these to submit data without regard for local statutes. UCR program offense definitions can be found in Appendix I.

In January 1930, 400 cities (representing 20 million inhabitants in 43 states) began participating in the UCR program. Congress enacted Title 28, Section 534, of the *United States Code* that same year, which authorized the attorney general to gather crime information. The attorney general, in turn, designated the FBI to serve as the national clearinghouse for the collected crime data. Since then, data based on uniform classifications and procedures for reporting have been obtained annually from the nation's law enforcement agencies.

Advisory Groups

Providing vital links between local law enforcement and the FBI for the UCR program are the Criminal Justice Information Systems Committees of the IACP and the National Sheriffs' Association (NSA). The IACP represents the thousands of police departments nationwide, as it has since the program began. The NSA encourages sheriffs throughout the country to participate fully in the program. Both committees serve the program in advisory capacities.

In 1988, a Data Providers' Advisory Policy Board was established. This board operated until 1993, when it combined with the National Crime Information Center Advisory Policy Board to form a single Advisory Policy Board (APB) to address all FBI criminal justice information services. The current APB works to ensure continuing emphasis on UCR-related issues. The Association of State Uniform Crime Reporting Programs (ASUCRP) focuses on UCR issues within individual state law enforcement associations and also promotes interest in the UCR program. These organizations foster widespread and responsible use of uniform crime statistics and lend assistance to data contributors.

Redesign of UCR

Although UCR data collection was originally conceived as a tool for law enforcement administration, the data were widely used by other entities involved in various forms of social planning by the 1980s. Recognizing the need for more detailed crime statistics, law enforcement called for a thorough evaluative study to modernize the UCR program. The FBI formulated a comprehensive three-phase redesign effort. The Bureau of Justice Statistics (BJS) agency in the Department of Justice responsible for funding criminal justice information projects, agreed to underwrite the first two phases. These phases were conducted by an independent contractor and structured to determine what, if any, changes should be made to the current program. The third phase would involve implementation of the changes identified.

The final report, the *Blueprint for the Future of the Uniform Crime Reporting Program,* was released in the summer of 1985. It specifically outlined recommendations for an expanded, improved UCR program to meet future informational needs. There were three recommended areas of enhancement to the UCR program:

- Offenses and arrests would be reported using an incident-based system

- Data would be collected on two levels. Agencies in level one would report important details about those offenses comprising the Part I crimes, their victims, and arrestees. Level two would consist of law enforcement agencies covering populations of more than 100,000 and a sampling of smaller agencies that would collect expanded detail on all significant offenses

- A quality assurance program would be introduced

In January 1986, Phase III of the redesign effort began, guided by the general recommendations set forth in the *Blueprint*. The FBI selected an experimental site to implement the redesigned program, while contractors developed new data guidelines and system specifications. Upon selecting the South Carolina Law Enforcement Division (SLED), which enlisted the cooperation of nine local law enforcement agencies, the FBI developed automated data capture specifications to adapt the SLED's state system to the national UCR program's standards, and the BJS funded the revisions. The pilot demonstration ran from March 1 through September 30, 1987, and resulted in further refinement of the guidelines and specifications.

From March 1 through March 3, 1988, the FBI held a national UCR conference to present the new system to law enforcement and to obtain feedback on its acceptability. Attendees of the conference passed three overall recommendations without dissent: first, that there be established a new, incident-based national crime reporting system; second, that the FBI manage this program, and third, that an Advisory Policy Board composed of law enforcement executives be formed to assist in directing and implementing the new program. Furthermore, attendees recommended that the implementation of national incident-based reporting proceed at a pace commensurate with the resources and limitations of contributing law enforcement agencies.

Establishing the NIBRS

From March 1988 through January 1989, the FBI developed and assumed management of the UCR program's National Incident-Based Reporting System (NIBRS), and by April 1989, the first test of NIBRS data was submitted to the national UCR program. Over the next few years, the national lUCR program published information about the redesigned program in five documents:

- *Uniform Crime Reporting Handbook*, NIBRS Edition (1992) provides a nontechnical program overview focusing on definitions, policies, and procedures of the IBRS

- *Data Submission Specifications* (May 1992) is used by local and state systems personnel, who are responsible for preparing magnetic media for submission to the FBI

- *Approaches to Implementing an Incident-Based System* (July 1992) is a guide for system designers

- *Error Message Manual* (revised December 1999) contains designations of mandatory and optional data elements, data element edits, and error messages

- *Data Collection Guidelines* (revised August 2000) contains a system overview and descriptions of the offense codes, reports, data elements, and data values used in the system

As more agencies inquired about the NIBRS, the FBI, in May 2002, made the *Handbook for Acquiring a Records Management System (RMS) That Is Compatible with the NIBRS* available to agencies considering or developing automated incident-based records management systems. The *Handbook*, developed under the sponsorship of the FBI and the BJS, provides instructions for planning and conducting a system acquisition and offers guidelines on preparing an agency for conversion to the new system and to the NIBRS.

Originally designed with 52 data elements, the redesigned NIBRS captures up to 57 data elements via 6 types of data segments: administrative, offense, victim property, offender, and arrestee. Although, in the late 1980s, the FBI committed to hold all changes to the NIBRS in abeyance until a substantial amount of contributors implemented the system, modifications have been necessary. The system's flexibility has allowed the collection of four additional pieces of information to be captured within an incident: bias-motivated offenses (1990), the presence of gang activity (1997), data for law enforcement officers killed and assaulted (2003), and data on cargo theft (2005). The system has also allowed the addition of new codes to further specify location types and property types (2010).

The FBI began accepting NIBRS data from a handful of agencies in January 1989. As more contributing law enforcement agencies become educated about the rich data available through incident-based reporting and as resources permit, more agencies are implementing the NIBRS. Based on the 2012 data submissions, 15 states submit all their data via the NIBRS and 32 state UCR Programs are certified for NIBRS participation.

Suspension of the Crime Index and the Modified Crime Index

In June 2004, the CJIS APB approved discontinuing the use of the *Crime Index* in the UCR program and its publications and directed the FBI to publish a violent crime total and a property crime total. The *Crime Index*, first published in *Crime in the United States* in 1960, was the title used for a simple aggregation of the seven main offense classifications (Part I offenses) in the Summary Reporting System. The Modified Crime Index was the number of Crime Index offenses plus arson.

For several years, the CJIS Division studied the appropriateness and usefulness of these indices and brought the matter before many advisory groups including the UCR Subcommittee of the CJIS APB, the ASUCRP, and a meeting of leading criminologists and sociologists hosted by the BJS. In short, the *Crime Index* and the *Modified Crime Index* were not true indicators of the degrees of criminality because they were always driven upward by the offense with the highest number, typically larceny-theft. The sheer volume of those offenses overshadowed more serious but less frequently committed offenses, creating a bias against a jurisdiction with a high number of larceny-thefts but a low number of other serious crimes such as murder and rape.

Recent Developments in UCR Program

In the fall of 2011, the APB recommended, and FBI Director Robert Mueller III approved, changing the definition of rape. Since 1929, in the SRS, rape had been defined as "the carnal knowledge of a female forcibly and against her will," (*UCR Handbook*, 2004, p.19). Beginning with the 2013 data collection, the SRS definition for the violent crime of rape will be: "Penetration, no matter how slight, of the vagina or anus with any body part or object, or oral penetration by a sex organ of another person, without the consent of the victim." This definition can be found in the *Summary Reporting System [SRS] User Manual*, Version 1.0, dated June 20, 2013. The FBI is developing reporting options for law enforcement agencies to meet this requirement, which will be built into the redeveloped data collection system.

In addition to approving the new definition of rape for the SRS, the APB and Director Mueller approved removing the word "forcible" from the name of the offense and also replacing the phrase "against the person's will" with "without the consent of the victim" in other sex-related offenses in the SRS, the NIBRS, the Hate Crime Statistics Program, and Cargo Theft.

In response to a directive by the U.S. Government's Office of Management and Budget, the national UCR Program has expanded its data collection categories for race from four (White, Black, American Indian or Alaska Native, and Asian or Other Pacific Islander) to five (White, Black or African American, American Indian or Alaska Native, Asian, and Native Hawaiian or Other Pacific Islander).

Also, the ethnicity categories have changed from "Hispanic" to "Hispanic or Latino" and from "Non-Hispanic" to "Not Hispanic or Latino." These changes are reflected in data presented from 2012.

The national UCR Program staff continues to develop data collection methods to comply with both the William Wilberforce Trafficking Victims Protection Reauthorization Act of 2008 and the Matthew Shepard and James Byrd, Jr. Hate Crime Prevention Act of 2009. As a result, the FBI began accepting data on human trafficking as well as data on crimes motivated by "gender and gender identity" bias and "crimes committed by, and crimes directed against, juveniles" from contributors in January 2013.

UCR Redevelopment Project Update

To streamline the program's database management and quality control activities, the FBI created the UCR Redevelopment Project (UCRRP). The UCRRP's goal is to improve the efficiency, usability, and maintainability of the UCR Program's submission processes, databases, and quality control activities. Through the UCRRP, the UCR Program will improve customer service by decreasing the time it takes to analyze data and by decreasing the time needed to release and publish crime data. The program will also enhance its external data query tool so that the public can view and analyze more published UCR data from the Internet.

Another major goal of the UCRRP is to reduce, to the point of elimination, the exchange of printed materials between submitting agencies and the FBI. Beginning with the 2013 data collections, all data was to be submitted electronically, and after July 2013, the UCR Program no longer accepted paper submissions or the electronic submission of documents (for example, Portable Document Format files). The UCRRP has begun working with agencies to help them adopt electronic submissions via the NIBRS, electronic SRS, or Extensible Markup Language.

Due to a system upgrade in 2019, the FBI now calculates rates for each offense based on the individual offenses and population that were published for each agency in tables 8-11 in Section II. (Previous to 2019, when agencies were published in tables 8-11, but they had one or two offenses removed from publication due to not meeting UCR publication guidelines, the agency's data was not used to calculate rates for this table.) This table provides the rate per 100,000 inhabitants and the number of offenses known to law enforcement for violent crimes (murder and nonnegligent manslaughter, rape, robbery, and aggravated assault) and property crimes (burglary, larceny-theft, and motor vehicle theft) nationally and by city and county groupings for law enforcement agencies submitting 12 months of publishable data for 2019. For the 2019 population estimates used in this table, the FBI computed individual rates of growth from one year to the next for every city/town and county using 2010 decennial population counts and 2011 through 2018 population estimates from the U.S. Census Bureau. Each agency's rates of growth were averaged; that average was then applied and added to its 2018 Census population estimate to derive the agency's 2019 population estimate.

Uniform Crime Reporting Program Changes Definition of Rape

For the first time in the more than 80-year history of the Uniform Crime Reporting (UCR) Program, the FBI has changed the definition of a Part 1 offense. In December 2011, then FBI Director Robert S. Mueller, III, approved revisions to the UCR Program's definition of rape as recommended by the FBI's Criminal Justice Information Services (CJIS) Division Advisory Policy Board (APB), which is made up of representatives from all facets of law enforcement.

Beginning in 2013, rape is defined for Summary UCR purposes as, "Penetration, no matter how slight, of the vagina or anus with any body part or object, or oral penetration by a sex organ of another person, without the consent of the victim." The new definition updated the 80-year-old historical definition of rape which was "carnal knowledge of a female forcibly and against her will." Effectively, the revised definition expands rape to include both male and female victims and offenders, and reflects the various forms of sexual penetration understood to be rape, especially nonconsenting acts of sodomy, and sexual assaults with objects. Beginning in 2017, only this revised definition of rape was used.

"This new, more inclusive definition will provide us with a more accurate understanding of the scope and volume of these crimes," said Attorney General Eric Holder. Proponents of the new definition and of the omission of the term "forcible" say that the changes broaden the scope of the previously narrow definitions by capturing (1) data without regard to gender, (2) the penetration of any bodily orifice, penetration by any object or body part, and (3) offenses in which physical force is not involved. Now, for example, instances in which offenders use drugs or alcohol or incidents in which offenders sodomize victims of the same gender will be counted as rape for statistical purposes.

It has long been the UCR Program's mission to collect and publish data regarding the scope and nature of crime in the nation, including those for rape. Since the FBI began collecting data using the revised definition of rape in January 2013, program officials expected that the number of reported rapes would rise. According to David Cuthbertson, former FBI Assistant Director of the CJIS Division, "As we implement this change, the FBI is confident that the number of victims of this heinous crime will be more accurately reflected in national crime statistics."

About the Editor

Shana Hertz Hattis is a consulting writer-editor for Bernan Press. She holds a master of science in education degree in from Northwestern University and a bachelor's degree in journalism from the same university. She has previously edited *Vital Statistics of the United States: Births, Life Expectancy, Deaths, and Selected Health Data* and several volumes of *Crime in the United States* for Bernan.

SECTION II

OFFENSES KNOWN TO POLICE

VIOLENT CRIME

- MURDER

- RAPE

- ROBBERY

- AGGRAVATED ASSAULT

PROPERTY CRIME

- BURGLARY

- LARCENY-THEFT

- MOTOR VEHICLE THEFT

- ARSON

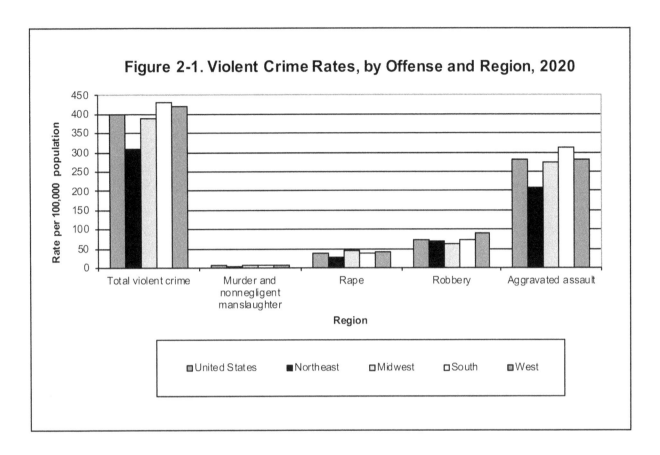

Figure 2-1. Violent Crime Rates, by Offense and Region, 2020

Definition

Violent crime consists of four offenses: murder and non-negligent manslaughter, rape, robbery, and aggravated assault. According to the Uniform Crime Reporting (UCR) program, run by the Federal Bureau of Investigation (FBI), violent crimes involve either the use of force or the threat of force.

Data Collection

The data presented in *Crime in the United States* reflect the Hierarchy Rule, which counts only the most serious offense in a multiple-offense criminal incident. In descending order of severity, the violent crimes are murder and nonnegligent manslaughter, rape, robbery, and aggravated assault; these are followed by the property crimes of burglary, larceny-theft, and motor vehicle theft. Arson is also considered a property crime, but the Hierarchy Rule does not apply to the arson offense. In cases in which arson occurs in conjunction with another violent or property crime, the arson and the additional crime are reported. More information on the expanded violent crime tables (which are available online but not included in this publication) can be found in Section I.

Important Note: Rape Data

In 2013, the FBI UCR Program began collecting rape data under a revised definition within the Summary Reporting System. Previously, offense data for forcible rape were collected under the legacy UCR definition: the carnal knowledge of a female forcibly and against her will. Beginning with the 2013 data year, the term "forcible" was removed from the offense title, and the definition was changed. The revised UCR definition of rape is: penetration, no matter how slight, of the vagina or anus with any body part or object, or oral penetration by a sex organ of another person, without the consent of the victim. Attempts or assaults to commit rape are also included in the statistics presented here; however, statutory rape and incest are excluded.

In 2017, the FBI Director approved the recommendation to discontinue the reporting of rape data using the UCR legacy definition beginning in 2019. However, to maintain the 20-year trend in Table 1, national estimates for rape under the legacy definition are provided along with estimates under the revised definition.

Important Note: COVID-19

The unprecedented conditions of the COVID-19 pandemic have undoubtedly had an effect on crimes committed, crimes cleared, arrests made, and law enforcement personnel levels. Data for 2020 should be interpreted with caution regarding the pandemic conditions, especially in comparison to previous years.

National Volume, Trends, and Rate

In 2020, an estimated 1,277,696 violent crimes occurred in the United States, an increase of 5.6 percent from the 2019 estimate. An estimated 387.8 violent crimes were committed per 100,000 inhabitants in 2020, an increase of 5.2 percent since 2019. Aggravated assaults accounted for 64.3 percent of violent crimes, the highest percentage of violent crimes reported to law enforcement. Robbery accounted for 21.0 percent of violent crimes, rape (revised definition) accounted for 11.2 percent, and murder accounted for 1.3 percent of violent crimes. (Tables 1 and 1A)

Occurrences of rape (revised definition) and robbery incidents decreased from 2019 to 2020, with rape decreasing by 11.7 percent and robbery by 9.3 percent. Murdered and nonnegligent manslaughter increased 29.4 percent and aggravated assault increased 11.7 percent. (Tables 1 and 1A)

In longer-term trends, the 2020 estimated violent crime total was 2.2 percent above the 2016 level and 5.9 percent above the 2011 level. The 5-year and 10-year trend data showed that the violent crime rate increased 0.3 percent between 2016 and 2020 and 0.2 percent between 2011 and 2020. (Tables 1 and 1A)

In 2020, offenders used firearms in 82.4 percent of the nation's murders, 45.1 percent of robberies, and 33.3 percent of aggravated assaults. (Weapons data are not collected for rape offenses.) (Expanded Homicide, Expanded Robbery, and Expanded Aggravated Assault data; see <https://crime-data-explorer.app.cloud.gov/pages/home> for more information)

Many violent crimes are committed by people in known relationships. Figure 2 shows the number of murder victims who knew their offender. In the figure, the relationship categories of husband and wife include common-law spouses and ex-spouses. The categories of mother, father, sister, brother, son, and daughter include stepparents, stepchildren, and stepsiblings. The category of "acquaintance" includes homosexual relationships and the composite category of other known-to-victim offenders.

Regional Offense Trends and Rate

The UCR program divides the United States into four regions: the Northeast, the South, the Midwest, and the West. (More details concerning geographic regions are provided in Appendix IV.) The population distribution of the regions can be found in Table 3, and the estimated volume and rate of violent crime by region are provided in Table 4.

THE NORTHEAST

The Northeast accounted for an estimated 17.0 percent of the nation's population in 2020 and an estimated 13.1 percent of its violent crimes. The estimated number of violent crimes increased 4.7 percent from 2019 to 2020. Murders increased 36.1 percent in the Northeast. Rapes decreased 13.8 percent. Robberies declined 4.2 percent. Aggravated assaults, however, rose 10.7 percent from 2019. In 2020, there were an estimated 308.4 violent crimes per 100,000 inhabitants, a 5.0 percent increase from 2019. (Tables 3 and 4)

THE MIDWEST

With an estimated 20.7 percent of the total population of the United States, the Midwest accounted for 20.2 percent of the nation's estimated number of violent crimes in 2020. The region had a 6.0 percent increase in violent crime from 2019 to 2020. The estimated number of aggravated assaults increased 13.2 percent, while the estimated number of robberies fell 6.9 percent. The estimated number of murders rose 36.2 percent. The estimated number of rapes decreased 14.0 percent. The rate of violent crime per 100,000 inhabitants in the Midwest was 387.8, an increase of 6.0 percent from 2019 to 2020. (Tables 3 and 4)

THE SOUTH

The South, the nation's most populous region, accounted for 38.4 percent of the nation's population in 2020. Approximately 41.6 percent of violent crimes in 2020 occurred in the South. Violent crime increased 6.9 percent from 2019 to 2020, while the estimated number of murders rose 26.0 percent and the estimated number of aggravated assaults rose 14.4 percent. Robberies dropped 11.0 percent, while rapes decreased by 10.1 percent. The estimated rate of violent crime in the South was 431.5 incidents per 100,000 inhabitants in 2020, a 6.1 percent increase from 2019. (Tables 3 and 4)

THE WEST

With 23.9 percent of the nation's population in 2019, the West accounted for an estimated 25.1 percent of the nation's violent crime. Violent crime in the West increased 1.4 percent from 2019 to 2020. Murders rose 26.7 percent, rapes and robberies dropped by 10.9 percent each, and aggravated assault increased 8.0 percent. The region's violent crime rate in 2020 was 418.8 per 100,000 inhabitants, a 1.0 percent rise from 2019. (Tables 3 and 4)

Community Types

The UCR program aggregates crime data into three community types: metropolitan statistical areas (MSAs), cities outside MSAs, and nonmetropolitan counties outside MSAs. Appendix IV provides additional information regarding community types. In 2020, approximately 86.1 percent of the nation's population lived in MSAs. Residents of cities outside MSAs accounted for 5.7 percent of the country's population, and residents living in nonmetropolitan counties accounted for 8.2 percent of the population. (Table 2)

In the areas reporting violent crimes to the UCR Program, approximately 85.8 percent of these crimes occurred in MSAs, while 5.2 percent occurred in cities outside MSAs and 4.0 percent occurred in nonmetropolitan counties. By community type, the violent crime rates were estimated at 414.5 incidents per 100,000 inhabitants in MSAs, 403.6 incidents per 100,000 inhabitants in cities outside MSAs, and 228.5 incidents per 100,000 inhabitants in nonmetropolitan counties. (Table 2)

Population Groups: Trends and Rates

In the UCR program, data are also aggregated into population groups; these groups are described in more detail in Appendix IV. The nation's cities had an overall increase of 4.4 percent in the estimated number of violent crimes from 2019 to 2020. By city population group, cities with under 10,000 inhabitants had the only decrease in the estimated number of violent crimes (-3.6 percent). Metropolitan counties experienced a 3.8 percent decrease in violent crimes from 2019 to 2020, while nonmetropolitan counties saw a 5.5 percent increase and suburban areas saw a 2.1 percent increase.(Table 12)

The law enforcement agencies in the nation's cities collectively reported a rate of 469.4 violent crimes per 100,000 inhabitants in 2020. Law enforcement agencies in the subset of cities with 500,000 to 999,999 inhabitants reported the highest violent crime rate, 874.7 violent crimes per 100,000 inhabitants; the violent crime rate for all cities with 250,000 or more inhabitants was 753.7 per 100,000 inhabitants. Agencies in cities with 10,000 to 24,999 inhabitants reported the lowest violent crime rate (266.8 incidents per 100,000 inhabitants). Law enforcement agencies in the nation's metropolitan counties reported a collective violent crime rate of 265.0 per 100,000 inhabitants, while agencies in nonmetropolitan counties reported a collective rate of 227.5 violent crimes per 100,000 inhabitants and suburban areas reported a violent crime rate of 250.4 violent crimes per 100,000 inhabitants. (Table 16)

Due to a system upgrade in 2019, the FBI now calculates rates for each offense based on the individual offenses and population published for each agency in tables 8-11. (Previous to 2019, when agencies were published in tables 8-11, but they had one or two offenses removed from publication due to not meeting UCR publication guidelines, the agency's data was not used to calculate rates for this table.) The FBI derived the offense rates by dividing the individual offense counts by the individual populations covered by contributing agencies for which 12 months of publishable data were supplied and then multiplying the resulting figure by 100,000. See Appendix V for the agency and population counts.

MURDER AND NONNEGLIGENT MANSLAUGHTER

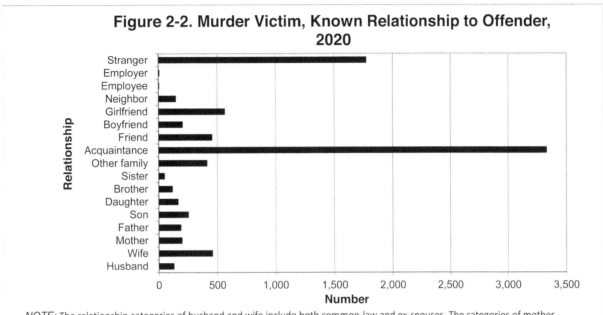

Figure 2-2. Murder Victim, Known Relationship to Offender, 2020

NOTE: The relationship categories of husband and wife include both common-law and ex-spouses. The categories of mother, father, sister, brother, son, and daughter include stepparents, stepchildren, and stepsiblings. The category of acquaintance includes homosexual relationships and the composite category of other known to victim. Approximately 9,346 victim-offender relationships were unknown.

Definition

The UCR program defines murder and non-negligent manslaughter as the willful (non-negligent) killing of one human being by another. The classification of this offense is based solely on police investigation, rather than on the determination of a court, medical examiner, coroner, jury, or other judicial body. The UCR program does not include the following situations under this offense classification: deaths caused by negligence, suicide, or accident; justifiable homicides; and attempts to murder or assaults to murder, which are considered aggravated assaults.

Important Note: COVID-19

The unprecedented conditions of the COVID-19 pandemic have undoubtedly had an effect on crimes committed, crimes cleared, arrests made, and law enforcement personnel levels. Data for 2020 should be interpreted with caution regarding the pandemic conditions, especially in comparison to previous years.

Data Collection/Supplementary Homicide Data

The UCR provides supplementary information about murder victims and offenders by age, sex, and race; the types of weapons used in the murders; the relationships of the victims to the offenders; and the circumstances surrounding the incident. Law enforcement agencies are asked to provide this data for each murder reported to the UCR program. Data can be viewed in the Expanded Homicide Data section on the FBI's Crime Explorer data page: https://crime-data-explorer.app.cloud.gov/pages/home. Highlights from these tables have been included below.

National Volume, Trends, and Rates

An estimated 21,570 persons were murdered nationwide in 2020. This number was a 29.4 percent increase from the 2019 estimate, a 23.9 percent increase from the 2016 figure, and a 47.1 percent increase from the 2011 estimate. The 2020 murder rate, 6.5 offenses per 100,000 inhabitants, was a 28.9 percent increase from the 2019 rate, a 21.6

percent increase from the 2016 rate, and a 39.1 percent increase from the 2011 rate. Murder accounted for 1.3 percent of the overall estimated number of violent crimes in 2020. (Tables 1 and 1A)

Regional Offense Trends and Rates

The UCR program divides the United States into four regions: the Northeast, the South, the Midwest, and the West. (More details concerning geographic regions are provided in Appendix IV.) In 2020, 47.1 percent of murders were reported in the South, the country's most populous region. The Midwest reported 22.3 percent of all murders, while the West reported 18.9 percent of murders and the Northeast reported 11.7 percent of murders. (Table 3)

THE NORTHEAST

In 2019, the Northeast accounted for an estimated 17.0 percent of the nation's population and 11.7 percent of its estimated number of murders. With an estimated 2,526 murders, the Northeast saw a 36.1 percent increase from its 2019 figure. The offense rate for the Northeast was 4.5 murders per 100,000 inhabitants in 2020, a 36.5 percent rise from 2019. (Tables 3 and 4)

THE MIDWEST

The Midwest accounted for an estimated 20.7 percent of the nation's total population and 22.3 percent of the country's estimated number of murders in 2020. The Midwest reported an estimated 4,803 murders in 2020 up 36.2 percent from 2019. The region experienced a rate of 7.0 murders per 100,000 inhabitants in 2020, above its 2019 rate of 5.0. (Tables 3 and 4)

THE SOUTH

The South accounted for an estimated 38.4 percent of the nation's population in 2020 and 47.1 percent of the nation's murders, the highest proportion among the four regions. The estimated 10,156 murders represented a 26.0 percent increase from the 2019 figure. The region's estimated rate of 8.0 murders per 100,000 inhabitants represented an increase of 25.0 percent from the estimated rate for 2019. (Tables 3 and 4)

THE WEST

The West accounted for an estimated 23.9 percent of the nation's population and 18.9 percent of the estimated number of murders in 2020. The West experienced an estimated 4,085 murders, a 26.7 percent increase from the 2019 estimate. The region's murder rate was 5.2 per 100,000 inhabitants, up 26.2 percent from 2019. (Tables 3 and 4)

Community Types

The UCR program aggregates data for three community types: metropolitan statistical areas (MSAs), cities outside MSAs, and nonmetropolitan counties outside MSAs. (See Appendix IV for definitions.) In 2020, MSAs accounted for 86.0 percent of the nation's population and 88.5 percent of the estimated total number of murders. MSAs experienced a rate of 5.1 murders per 100,000 inhabitants in 2020. Cities outside MSAs accounted for 5.7 percent of the U.S. population and (with an estimated 839 murders) accounted for 5.1 percent of the estimated murders in the nation. The murder rate for cities outside MSAs was 4.5 per 100,000 inhabitants. In 2020, approximately 8.3 percent of the nation's population lived in nonmetropolitan counties outside MSAs. An estimated 1,047 murders took place in these counties, accounting for 6.4 percent of the nation's estimated total. The murder rate in nonmetropolitan counties was 3.9 per 100,000 inhabitants. (Table 2)

Population Groups: Trends and Rates

The UCR program uses the following population group designations in its data presentations: cities (grouped according to population size) and counties (classified as either metropolitan or nonmetropolitan). A breakdown of these classifications is provided in Appendix IV.

From 2019 to 2020, the nation's cities experienced a 32.1 percent increase in homicides, with every group experiencing a rise in incidents. Cities with under 10,000 residents experienced the smallest increase, 3.5 percent, while cities with 1,000,000 or more residents experienced the biggest increase, 39.9 percent. Metropolitan counties experienced an increase in homicides of 17.4 percent from 2019 to 2020, while nonmetropolitan counties experienced an increase of 19.7 percent. Suburban areas experienced an increase of 20.0 percent. (Table 12)

In 2020, cities collectively had a rate of 7.4 murders per 100,000 inhabitants. Cities with 500,000 to 999,999 inhabitants had the highest murder rate (16.3 murders per 100,000 inhabitants). Cities with under 10,000 inhabitants had the lowest murder rate, with 3.6 murders per 100,000 inhabitants. The homicide rate for metropolitan counties was 4.0 murders per 100,000 inhabitants, while the rate for nonmetropolitan counties was 4.8 murders per 100,000 inhabitants. Suburban areas had a homicide rate of 3.6 per 100,000 inhabitants. (Table 16)

Due to a system upgrade in 2019, the FBI now calculates rates for each offense based on the individual offenses and population published for each agency in tables 8-11. (Previous to 2019, when agencies were published in tables 8-11, but they had one or two offenses removed from publication due to not meeting UCR publication guidelines, the agency's data was not used to calculate rates for this table.) The FBI derived the offense rates by dividing the individual offense counts by the individual populations covered by contributing agencies for which 12 months of publishable data were supplied and then multiplying the resulting figure by 100,000. See Appendix V for the agency and population counts.

Supplementary Homicide Reports Data

VICTIMS/OFFENDERS

Based on 2020 supplemental homicide data (where the ages, sexes, or races of the murder victims were identified), 84.8 percent of victims were 20 years of age or over, 14.4 percent were 19 years of age or less, and the age of 0.8 percent of the victims was unknown. Of the 17,778 murder victims represented in the 2020 expanded tables whose gender was identified, 79.8 percent were male. Concerning race among the 17,495 victims for whom race was identified, 40.3 percent of victims were White, 56.8 percent were Black or African American, and 2.9 percent were of other races. Race was unknown for 320 victims. Approximately 18.0 percent of victims were of Hispanic origin. For murders in which the gender of the offender was identified, 88.3 percent were males; the sex of offenders for 29.6 percent of homicides was unknown. For the offenders for whom race was identified, 57.2 percent were Black or African American, 39.8 percent were White, and

2.9 percent were other races; 6,612 offenders (31.4 percent) were of unknown race. Approximately 9.0 percent of offenders were of Hispanic origin. (Expanded Homicide Data)

VICTIM-OFFENDER RELATIONSHIPS

For incidents in which the victim-offender relationship was specified (including the designation of "unknown"), 10.9 percent of victims were slain by family members, 10.2 percent were murdered by strangers, and 24.0 percent were killed by someone they knew other than family members (acquaintances, neighbors, friends, employers, romantic partners, employees, etc.). The victim-offender relationship was unknown in 51.6 percent of incidents. (Expanded Homicide Data)

CIRCUMSTANCES/WEAPONS

Concerning the known circumstances surrounding murders, and including murders with unknown circumstances, 9.4 percent of victims were murdered during gang killings in 2020. Circumstances of rape, robbery, burglary, larceny-theft, motor vehicle theft, and arson accounted for 8.5 percent of murders. Circumstances were unknown for 45.6 percent of reported homicides. Of the homicides for which the type of weapon was specified, 76.7 percent involved the use of firearms. Of the identified firearms used, handguns comprised 58.8 percent of the total. (Expanded Homicide Data)

RAPE

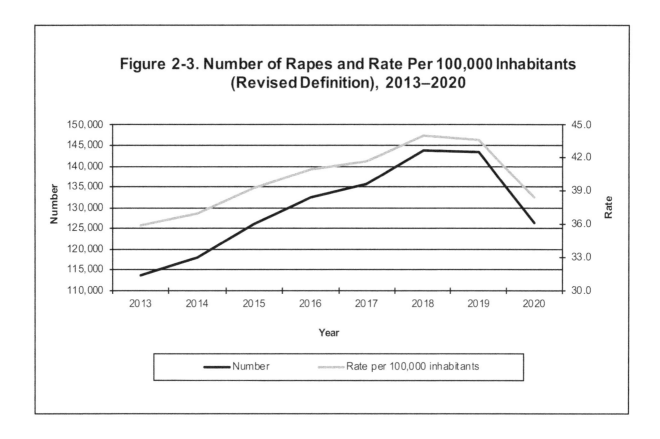

Figure 2-3. Number of Rapes and Rate Per 100,000 Inhabitants (Revised Definition), 2013–2020

Definition

In 2013, the FBI UCR Program began collecting rape data under a revised definition within the Summary Reporting System. Previously, offense data for forcible rape were collected under the legacy UCR definition: the carnal knowledge of a female forcibly and against her will. Beginning with the 2013 data year, the term "forcible" was removed from the offense title, and the definition was changed. The revised UCR definition of rape is: penetration, no matter how slight, of the vagina or anus with any body part or object, or oral penetration by a sex organ of another person, without the consent of the victim. Attempts or assaults to commit rape are also included in the statistics presented here; however, statutory rape and incest are excluded.

In 2016, the FBI Director approved the recommendation to discontinue the reporting of rape data using the UCR legacy definition beginning in 2017. However, to maintain the 20-year trend in Table 1, national estimates for rape under the legacy definition are provided along with estimates under the revised definition.

The UCR Program counts one offense for each victim of a rape, attempted rape, or assault with intent to rape, regardless of the victim's age. Non-consensual sexual relations involving a familial member is considered rape, not incest. All other crimes of a sexual nature are considered to be Part II offenses; as such, the UCR Program collects only arrest data for those crimes. The offense of statutory rape, in which no force is used but the female victim is under the age of consent, is included in the arrest total for the sex offenses category.

Important Note: COVID-19

The unprecedented conditions of the COVID-19 pandemic have undoubtedly had an effect on crimes committed, crimes cleared, arrests made, and law enforcement personnel levels. Data for 2020 should be interpreted with caution regarding the pandemic conditions, especially in comparison to previous years.

National Volume, Trends, and Rates

In 2020, the estimated number of rapes (revised definition), 126,430, decreased 11.7 percent from the 2019 estimate. The estimated volume of rapes in 2020 was 4.5 percent lower than in the 2016 estimate. (Tables 1 and 1A)

Regional Offense Trends and Rates

The UCR program divides the United States into four regions: the Northeast, the South, the Midwest, and the West. (More details concerning geographic regions are provided in Appendix IV) Regional analysis offers estimates of the volume of female rapes, the percent change from the previous year's estimate, and the rate of rape per 100,000 female inhabitants in each region.

NORTHEAST

The Northeast made up 17.0 percent of the U.S. population in 2020. An estimated 15,066 rapes—11.9 percent of the national total—occurred in the Northeast. This was an decrease of 13.8 percent from the 2019 estimated figure. The region's rate of rape occurrences—27.0 per 100,000 inhabitants—was a 13.6 percent drop from 2019. (Tables 3 and 4)

MIDWEST

The Midwest accounted for 20.7 percent of the U.S. population in 2020. Of all the rapes in the nation, 23.9 percent occurred in the Midwest in 2020. The 2020 estimate (30,157 rapes) represented a decrease of 14.0 percent from the 2019 estimate. The region's rate of rape occurrences—44.1 per 100,000 inhabitants—was a 13.9 percent drop from 2019. (Tables 3 and 4)

SOUTH

The South, the nation's most populous region, accounted for an estimated 38.4 percent of the nation's population in 2020; the region also accounted for an estimated 38.2 percent of the nation's estimated number of rapes. An estimated 48,307 victims reported rape in the South in 2020, down 10.1 percent from 2019. The region's rate of rape occurrences—38.1 per 100,000 inhabitants—was a 10.8 percent drop from 2019. (Tables 3 and 4)

WEST

The West accounted for 23.9 percent of the nation's population in 2020. The region also accounted for 26.0 percent of the nation's total number of estimated rapes with an estimated 32,900 offenses. The West saw a 10.9 percent decrease in rapes from 2019 to 2020. The region's rate of rape occurrences—41.8 per 100,000 inhabitants—was an 11.3 percent drop from 2019. (Tables 3 and 4)

Community Types

Using the U.S. Office of Management and Budget's designations, the UCR program aggregates crime data by type of community in which the offenses occur: metropolitan statistical areas (MSAs), cities outside MSAs, and nonmetropolitan counties outside MSAs. (Appendix IV provides more detailed information about community types.)

MSAS

In 2020, MSAs accounted for 86.1 percent of the nation's population and 80.7 percent of the nation's estimated number of rapes (revised definition). An estimated 107,098 victims were forcibly raped in metropolitan areas. MSAs had a rape rate of 37.8 per 100,000 inhabitants. (Table 2)

CITIES OUTSIDE MSAS

Cities outside MSAs are mostly incorporated areas that are served by city law enforcement agencies. Although accounting for only 5.7 percent of the U.S. population in 2020, cities outside MSAs accounted for 7.0 percent of the nation's estimated rapes (9,540 estimated offenses). Cities outside MSAs had a rate of 51.0 rapes per 100,000 inhabitants. (Table 2)

NONMETROPOLITAN COUNTIES

In 2020, approximately 8.2 percent of the nation's population lived in nonmetropolitan counties outside MSAs (counties made up of mostly non-incorporated areas that are served by noncity law enforcement agencies). Collectively, these areas had an estimated 9,792 rapes, representing 6.9 percent of the nation's estimated total. Nonmetropolitan counties had a rate of 36.0 rapes per 100,000 inhabitants. (Table 2)

Population Groups: Trends and Rates

The UCR program uses the following population group designations in its data presentations: cities (grouped according to population size) and counties (classified as either metropolitan or nonmetropolitan). A breakdown of these classifications is provided in Appendix IV.

From 2019 to 2020, the nation's cities experienced a 13.5 percent decrease in rapes. Cities with under 10,000 inhabitants experienced the greatest decrease (19.5 percent). Metropolitan counties experienced a 9.0 percent decrease from 2019 to 2020, while nonmetropolitan counties experienced a 9.3 percent decrease and suburban areas experienced a 10.9 percent decrease. (Table 12)

In 2020, cities collectively had a rate of 42.1 rapes per 100,000 inhabitants. Cities with 250,000 to 499,999 inhabitants had the highest rate of rape (58.5 rapes per 100,000 inhabitants). Cities with 25,000 to 49,999 inhabitants had the lowest rate, with 34.1 rapes per 100,000 inhabitants. The rape rate for metropolitan counties was

31.6 per 100,000 inhabitants, and for nonmetropolitan counties, it was 38.9 per 100,000 inhabitants. Suburban areas had a rape rate of 30.7 per 100,000 inhabitants. (Table 16)

Due to a system upgrade in 2019, the FBI now calculates rates for each offense based on the individual offenses and population published for each agency in tables 8-11. (Previous to 2019, when agencies were published in tables 8-11, but they had one or two offenses removed from publication due to not meeting UCR publication guidelines, the agency's data was not used to calculate rates for this table.) The FBI derived the offense rates by dividing the individual offense counts by the individual populations covered by contributing agencies for which 12 months of publishable data were supplied and then multiplying the resulting figure by 100,000. See Appendix V for the agency and population counts.

ROBBERY

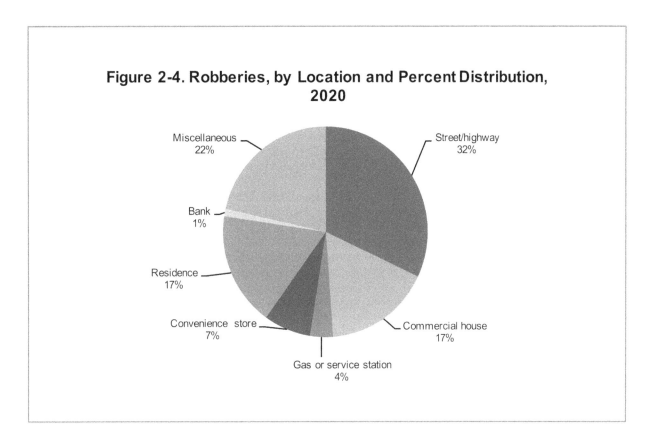

Figure 2-4. Robberies, by Location and Percent Distribution, 2020

Definition

The UCR program defines robbery as the taking or attempt to take anything of value from the care, custody, or control of a person or persons by force or threat of force or violence and/or by putting the victim in fear.

Important Note: COVID-19

The unprecedented conditions of the COVID-19 pandemic have undoubtedly had an effect on crimes committed, crimes cleared, arrests made, and law enforcement personnel levels. Data for 2020 should be interpreted with caution regarding the pandemic conditions, especially in comparison to previous years.

National Volume, Trends, and Rates

In 2020, the estimated robbery total (243,600) decreased 9.3 percent from the 2019 estimate. The 5-year robbery trend (2016 data compared with 2020 data) showed a decrease of 26.8 percent, and the decrease since 2011 (10-year estimates) was 31.3 percent. The 2020 estimated robbery rate (73.9 per 100,000 inhabitants) showed a decrease of 9.6 percent when compared with the 2019 rate. (Tables 1 and 1A)

Regional Offense Trends and Rates

The UCR program divides the United States into four regions: the Northeast, the South, the Midwest, and the West. (More details concerning geographic regions are provided in Appendix IV.)

NORTHEAST

The Northeast, with an estimated 17.0 percent of the nation's population in 2020, accounted for 15.8 percent of the nation's estimated number of robberies. The estimated number of robberies decreased 4.2 percent from 2019. The rate for this region was 69.0 robberies per 100,000 inhabitants, down from 71.6 robberies per 100,000 inhabitants in 2019. (Tables 3 and 4)

MIDWEST

The Midwest accounted for 20.7 percent of the total population of the United States and 17.8 percent of its estimated number of robberies in 2020. An estimated 43,368 robberies occurred in the Midwest in 2020, a 6.9 percent decrease from the estimated figure from 2019. The region's robbery rate was 63.5 robberies per 100,000 inhabitants in 2020, down 6.9 percent from 2019. (Tables 3 and 4)

SOUTH

The South, the nation's most highly populated region, accounted for an estimated 38.4 percent of the nation's population and 37.4 percent of the nation's estimated number of robberies in 2020. Robberies accounted for an estimated 91,100 violent crimes in this region in 2020, representing an 11.0 percent decrease from the 2019 figure. The 2020 robbery rate in the South was 71.9 per 100,000 inhabitants, down 11.7 percent from 2019. (Tables 3 and 4)

WEST

The West was home to an estimated 23.9 percent of the nation's population and accounted for 29.0 percent of the nation's estimated number of robberies in 2020. The estimated number of robberies (70,596) in the region in 2020 represented a 10.9 percent decrease from the 2019 figure. The rate of robberies per 100,000 inhabitants in the West was 89.8, an 11.3 percent decrease from the 2019 rate. (Tables 3 and 4)

Community Types

The UCR program aggregates data for three community types: metropolitan statistical areas (MSAs), cities outside MSAs, and nonmetropolitan counties outside MSAs. MSAs include a central city or urbanized area with at least 50,000 inhabitants, as well as the county that contains the principal city and other adjacent counties that have, as defined by the U.S. Office of Management and Budget, a high degree of social and economic integration as measured through commuting. Cities outside MSAs are mostly incorporated areas, and nonmetropolitan counties are made up of mostly unincorporated areas served by non-city law enforcement.

In 2020, MSAs were home to an estimated 86.1 percent of the nation's population, and 92.7 percent of the nation's estimated number of robberies took place in these areas. Robberies in MSAs occurred at a rate of 82.5 per 100,000 inhabitants. Cities outside MSAs accounted for 5.2 percent of the U.S. population and 2.2 percent of the estimated number of robberies in the nation. The robbery rate for cities outside MSAs was 33.1 per 100,000 inhabitants. Nonmetropolitan counties made up 8.2 percent of the nation's estimated population and 1.0 percent of the nation's estimated robberies, with a rate of 12.4 robberies per 100,000 inhabitants. (Table 2)

Population Groups: Trends and Rates

The national UCR program aggregates data by various population groups, which include cities, metropolitan counties, and nonmetropolitan counties. A definition of these groups can be found in Appendix IV.

The number of robberies in cities as a whole decreased by 9.6 percent between 2019 and 2020. Among the population groups and subsets labeled *city*, those cities with under 10,000 inhabitants had the greatest decrease in the number of robberies (16.3 percent). Metropolitan counties had a 10.5 percent decrease in the estimated number of robberies, and nonmetropolitan counties showed a 0.9 percent decrease. The number of robberies in suburban areas fell 10.5 percent. (Table 12)

Among the population groups, the nation's cities collectively had a rate of 97.4 robberies per 100,000 inhabitants. Of the population groups and subsets designated *city*, those with 1,000,000 or more inhabitants had the highest rate (190.6 per 100,000 inhabitants), while those with fewer than 10,000 inhabitants had the lowest rate (28.9 per 100,000 inhabitants) of robberies. Of the two county groups, metropolitan counties had a rate of 32.2 robberies per 100,000 inhabitants, while nonmetropolitan counties had a rate of 10.2 robberies per 100,000 inhabitants. Suburban areas had a robbery rate of 34.7 per 100,000 inhabitants. (Table 16)

Due to a system upgrade in 2019, the FBI now calculates rates for each offense based on the individual offenses and population published for each agency in tables 8-11. (Previous to 2019, when agencies were published in tables 8-11, but they had one or two offenses removed from publication due to not meeting UCR publication guidelines, the agency's data was not used to calculate rates for this table.) The FBI derived the offense rates by dividing the individual offense counts by the individual populations covered by contributing agencies for which 12 months of publishable data were supplied and then multiplying the resulting figure by 100,000. See Appendix V for the agency and population counts.

Offense Analysis

The UCR program collects supplemental data about robberies to document the use of weapons, the dollar loss associated with the offense, and the location types.

ROBBERY BY WEAPON

Firearms were used in 37.3 percent of robberies in 2020. Offenders used knives or cutting instruments in 9.1 percent of these crimes, strong-arm tactics in 42.6 percent of incidents, and other dangerous weapons in 11.1 percent of offenses. (Table 19)

LOSS BY DOLLAR VALUE

Based on the supplemental reports from law enforcement agencies, the average loss per robbery was $1,834. Average dollar losses were the highest for banks, which suffered an average loss of $4,339 per offense. Residences lost an average of $2,236 per offense, and gas and service stations lost an average of $1,469 per offense. Commercial houses, which include supermarkets, department stores, and restaurants, had average losses of $1,497 per offense. An average of $1,719 was taken during robberies on streets and highways. An average of $1,005 was lost in each offense against convenience stores. (Table 23)

Robbery Trends by Location

Among the location types, bank robberies had the greatest percentage decrease from 2019 to 2020, declining 29.9 percent. Robberies that occurred on streets and highways decreased 15.2 percent, while gas and service station robberies increased 8.3 percent. (Table 23)

By location type, the greatest proportion of robberies in 2020 occurred on streets and highways (32.0 percent). Robbers targeted commercial houses in 16.9 percent of offenses and struck residences in 17.5 percent of offenses. Convenience stores accounted for 7.4 percent of robberies, followed by gas and service stations (3.6 percent) and banks (1.1 percent). (Table 23)

AGGRAVATED ASSAULT

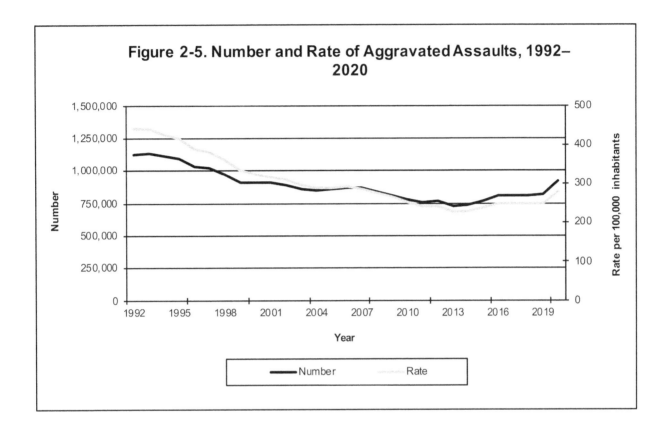

Figure 2-5. Number and Rate of Aggravated Assaults, 1992–2020

Definition

The UCR program defines aggravated assault as an unlawful attack by one person upon another for the purpose of inflicting severe or aggravated bodily injury. This type of assault is usually accompanied by the use of a weapon or by other means likely to produce death or great bodily harm. Attempted aggravated assaults that involve the display or threat of a gun, knife, or other weapon are included in this crime category because serious personal injury would likely result if these assaults were completed. When aggravated assault and larceny-theft occur together, the offense falls under the category of robbery.

Important Note: COVID-19

The unprecedented conditions of the COVID-19 pandemic have undoubtedly had an effect on crimes committed, crimes cleared, arrests made, and law enforcement personnel levels. Data for 2020 should be interpreted with caution regarding the pandemic conditions, especially in comparison to previous years.

National Volume, Trends, and Rates

In 2020, estimated occurrences of aggravated assaults totaled 921,505, a 12.1 percent increase from the 2019 figure, a 14.8 percent increase when compared with the estimate for 2016, and a 22.5 percent increase when compared to 2011. The estimated rate of aggravated assault in 2020 was 279.7 per 100,000 inhabitants, an 11.7 percent increase from 2019, a 12.6 percent increase from 2016, and a 15.8 percent increase from 2011. (Tables 1 and 1A)

Among the four types of violent crime offenses (murder, rape, robbery, and aggravated assault), aggravated assault typically has the highest rate of occurrence. This trend continued in 2020. (Table 1)

Regional Offense Trends and Rates

The UCR program divides the United States into four regions: the Northeast, the South, the Midwest, and the West. (More details concerning geographic regions are provided in Appendix IV.)

NORTHEAST

The region with the smallest proportion of the nation's population (an estimated 17.0 percent in 2020) also accounted for the smallest proportion of the nation's estimated number of aggravated assaults (12.6 percent). Occurrences of aggravated assault increased 10.7 percent from 2019 to 2020, rising to an estimated 116,092 incidents. The region continued to have the lowest aggravated assault rate in the nation, at 207.9 incidents per

100,000 inhabitants, although this represented an 11.0 percent increase from the rate in 2019. (Tables 3 and 4)

MIDWEST

With 20.7 percent of the nation's total population in 2020, the Midwest accounted for approximately 20.2 percent of the nation's estimated number of aggravated assaults. Occurrences of this offense rose 13.2 percent from the estimated total for 2019, increasing to an estimated 186,587 incidents. The region's aggravated assault rate, at 273.1 incidents per 100,000 inhabitants, represented a 13.2 percent increase from the 2019 rate. (Tables 3 and 4)

SOUTH

The South, the nation's most highly populated region, accounted for an estimated 38.4 percent of the nation's population in 2020 and the largest amount of the nation's estimated number of aggravated assaults (43.1 percent). From 2019 to 2020, the estimated number of aggravated assaults increased 14.4 percent to a total of 396,972 incidents. The rate of aggravated assaults rose 13.5 percent to 313.4 incidents per 100,000 inhabitants. (Tables 3 and 4)

WEST

In 2020, the West was home to an estimated 23.9 percent of the nation's population. The region accounted for 24.1 percent of the nation's estimated number of aggravated assaults. From 2019 to 2020, the estimated number of offenses increased 8.0 percent to a total of 221,854 incidents. The rate of aggravated assaults increased 7.6 percent to 282.1 incidents per 100,000 inhabitants. (Tables 3 and 4)

Community Types

The UCR program aggregates data for three community types: metropolitan statistical areas (MSAs), cities outside MSAs, and nonmetropolitan counties outside MSAs. MSAs include a central city or urbanized area with at least 50,000 inhabitants, as well as the county that contains the principal city and other adjacent counties that have a high degree of social and economic integration as measured through commuting. Cities outside MSAs are mostly incorporated areas, and nonmetropolitan counties are made up of mostly unincorporated areas. (For additional information about community types, see Appendix IV.)

In 2020, 86.1 percent of the nation's population lived in MSAs, where the rate of aggravated assault was an estimated 287.4 per 100,000 inhabitants. Approximately 88.5 percent of all aggravated assaults occurred in MSAs. Cities outside MSAs (with 5.7 percent of the U.S. population

and 6.4 percent of aggravated assaults) had the highest rate of aggravated assault at 313.9 offenses per 100,000 inhabitants. Nonmetropolitan counties accounted for 8.2 percent of the U.S. population and 5.2 percent of aggravated assaults. Nonmetropolitan counties had an offense rate of 175.2 aggravated assaults per 100,000 inhabitants. (Table 2)

Population Groups: Trends and Rates

Cities with 500,000 to 999,999 inhabitants experienced the greatest increase in aggravated assaults from 2019 to 2020 (16.9 percent). Cities with under 10,000 inhabitants experienced the smallest increase, 1.6 percent. The collective increase for all cities was 12.2 percent. In metropolitan counties, the number of aggravated assaults rose 9.1 percent; in nonmetropolitan counties, this number increased 9.2 percent. Aggravated assaults in suburban areas increased 7.6 percent from 2019 to 2020. (Table 12)

Aggravated assault occurred at an estimated rate of 279.7 offenses per 100,000 inhabitants nationwide. The collective rate for cities was 322.7 aggravated assaults per 100,000 inhabitants. Among city population groups and subsets, rates ranged from a high of 613.7 offenses per 100,000 inhabitants (in cities with 500,000 to 999,999 inhabitants) to a low of 191.1 offenses per 100,000 inhabitants (in cities with 25,000 to 49,999 inhabitants). The aggravated assault rate was 197.2 in metropolitan counties and 173.7 in nonmetropolitan counties. It was 181.5 in suburban areas. (Table 16)

Due to a system upgrade in 2019, the FBI now calculates rates for each offense based on the individual offenses and population published for each agency in tables 8-11. (Previous to 2019, when agencies were published in tables 8-11, but they had one or two offenses removed from publication due to not meeting UCR publication guidelines, the agency's data was not used to calculate rates for this table.) The FBI derived the offense rates by dividing the individual offense counts by the individual populations covered by contributing agencies for which 12 months of publishable data were supplied and then multiplying the resulting figure by 100,000. See Appendix V for the agency and population counts.

Offense Analysis

AGGRAVATED ASSAULT BY WEAPON

Of the aggravated assault offenses for which law enforcement agencies provided expanded data in 2020, 34.9 percent were committed with firearms; 20.2 percent involved hands, feet, and/or fists; 16.4 percent involved knives or other cutting instruments; and 28.5 percent involved other weapons. (Table 19)

PROPERTY CRIME

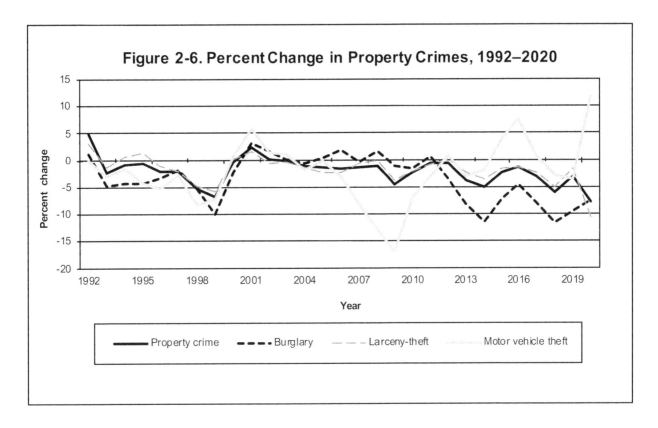

Figure 2-6. Percent Change in Property Crimes, 1992–2020

Definition

The UCR program's definition of property crime includes the offenses of burglary, larceny-theft, motor vehicle theft, and arson. The object of theft-type offenses is the taking of money or property without the use of force or threat of force against the victims. Property crime includes arson because the offense involves the destruction of property; however, arson victims may be subjected to force. Because of limited participation and the varying collection procedures conducted by local law enforcement agencies, only limited data are available for arson. More information on the expanded arson tables (which are available online but not included in this publication) can be found in Section I.

Data Collection

The data presented in *Crime in the United States* reflect the Hierarchy Rule, which counts only the most serious offense in a multiple-offense criminal incident. In descending order of severity, the violent crimes are murder and nonnegligent manslaughter, rape, robbery, and aggravated assault; these are followed by the property crimes of burglary, larceny-theft, and motor vehicle theft. The Hierarchy Rule does not apply to the offense of arson.

Important Note: COVID-19

The unprecedented conditions of the COVID-19 pandemic have undoubtedly had an effect on crimes committed, crimes cleared, arrests made, and law enforcement personnel levels. Data for 2020 should be interpreted with caution regarding the pandemic conditions, especially in comparison to previous years.

National Volume, Trends, and Rates

An estimated 6,452,038 property crimes were committed in the United States in 2020, representing a 7.8 percent decrease from the 2019 (2-year trend) estimate, an 18.6 percent decrease from the 2016 (5-year trend) estimate, and a 28.7 percent decrease from the 2011 (10-year trend) estimate. (Tables 1 and 1A)

From 2019 to 2020, motor vehicle theft increased 11.8 percent; from 2016 to 2020, it increased 5.6 percent, and from 2011 to 2020, it increased 13.1 percent. Larceny-theft decreased 25.1 percent from 2011 to 2020, 18.4 percent from 2016 to 2020, and 10.6 percent from 2019 to 2020. Burglary in 2020 declined 52.6 percent from 2011, 31.7 percent from 2016, and 7.4 percent from 2019. (Tables 1 and 1A)

The estimated property crime rate per 100,000 inhabitants in 2020 was 1,958.2 incidents per 100,000 people, an 8.1 percent decrease from the 2019 rate, a 20.1 percent decrease from the 2016 rate, and a 32.6 percent decrease from the 2011 rate. The rate of burglaries per 100,000 residents fell 55.2 percent from 2011 to 2020. The motor vehicle theft rates per 100,000 residents rose 7.0 percent from 2011 to 2020, and the larceny-theft rate declined 29.2 percent in that same timeframe. (Tables 1 and 1A)

Regional Offense Trends and Rates

The UCR program separates the United States into four regions: the Northeast, the Midwest, the South, and the West. (Geographic breakdowns can be found in Appendix IV.) Property crime data collected by the UCR program and aggregated by region reflected the following results.

NORTHEAST

The Northeast region accounted for 17.0 percent of the nation's population in 2020. The region also accounted for 11.9 percent of the nation's estimated number of property crimes in 2020. Law enforcement in the Northeast saw a 0.8 percent increase in the estimated number of property crimes from 2019 to 2020. The property crime rate for the Northeast, estimated at 1,370.6 incidents per 100,000 inhabitants, was 1.1 percent more than the 2019 rate. (Tables 3 and 4)

MIDWEST

The Midwest, with 20.7 percent of the U.S. population in 2020, accounted for 18.9 percent of the nation's estimated number of property crimes. Law enforcement in the Midwest saw the number of property crimes decrease 8.1 percent from 2019 to 2020. The rate of property crime in the Midwest in 2020, estimated at 1,785.5 incidents per 100,000 inhabitants, represented an 8.1 percent decrease from the 2019 rate. (Tables 3 and 4)

SOUTH

The South, the nation's most populous region, accounted for 38.4 percent of the U.S. population in 2020. The region also accounted for an estimated 41.4 percent of the nation's property crimes. The South experienced an 11.3 percent decrease in its estimated number of property crimes from 2019 to 2020. The 2020 property crime rate, an estimated 2,106.6 incidents per 100,000 inhabitants, dropped 12.0 percent from the 2019 rate. (Tables 3 and 4)

WEST

In 2020, the West accounted for 23.9 percent of the nation's population. The West also accounted for 27.9 percent of the nation's estimated number of property crimes. From 2019 to 2020, the estimated number of property crimes in this region decreased 5.3 percent. The estimated property crime rate in the West in 2020, 2,286.5 incidents per 100,000 inhabitants, was a 5.8 percent decrease from the 2019 rate. (Tables 3 and 4)

Community Types

The UCR program aggregates data by three community types: metropolitan statistical areas (MSAs), cities outside metropolitan areas, and nonmetropolitan counties. (Additional in-depth information regarding community types can be found in Appendix IV.) In 2020, 86.1 percent of the U.S. population lived in MSAs and had 89.0 percent of all property crimes. The property crime rate for MSAs was 2,024.6 per 100,000 inhabitants. Cities outside metropolitan areas, which accounted for 5.7 percent of the total population in 2020 and 6.7 percent of property crimes, had a property crime rate of 2,307.2 per 100,000 inhabitants. Nonmetropolitan counties, with 8.2 percent of the nation's population in 2020 and 4.3 percent of property crimes, had a property crime rate of 1,025.5 per 100,000 inhabitants. (Table 2)

Population Groups: Trends and Rates

The UCR program organizes the agencies that contribute data into population groups, which include cities, metropolitan counties, and nonmetropolitan counties. (Appendix IV provides further details about these groups.)

From 2019 to 2020, law enforcement in the nation's cities collectively reported a 7.1 percent decrease in the number of property crimes. All city groups experienced decreases in the number of property crimes; cities with under 10,000 residents had the greatest decline, 12.9 percent. Metropolitan counties also experienced a decrease of 6.4 percent from 2019 to 2020, while property crime in nonmetropolitan counties and suburban areas dropped 4.7 and 7.5 percent, respectively. (Table 12)

The nation's cities collectively had a property crime rate of 2,254.0 incidents per 100,000 inhabitants in 2020, ranging from a high of 3,483.7 per 100,000 inhabitants in cities with 500,000 to 999,999 residents to a low of 1,784.1 per 100,000 inhabitants in cities with 10,000 to 24,999 residents. Metropolitan counties had a rate of 1,289.1 incidents per 100,000 inhabitants, and nonmetropolitan counties had a rate of 991.7 incidents per 100,000 inhabitants. The rate was 1,489.8 in suburban areas. (Table 16)

Due to a system upgrade in 2019, the FBI now calculates rates for each offense based on the individual offenses and population published for each agency in tables 8-11. (Previous to 2019, when agencies were published in tables 8-11, but they had one or two offenses removed from publication due to not meeting UCR publication guidelines, the agency's data was not used to calculate rates for this table.) The FBI derived the offense rates by dividing the individual offense counts by the individual populations covered by contributing agencies for which 12 months of publishable data were supplied and then multiplying the resulting figure by 100,000. See Appendix V for the agency and population counts.

Offense Analysis

In 2020, the average dollar value per motor vehicle stolen in the United States was $9,166. The average dollar value of property taken during burglaries was $2,692, and during larceny-thefts, $1,482. (Tables 1 and 23)

BURGLARY

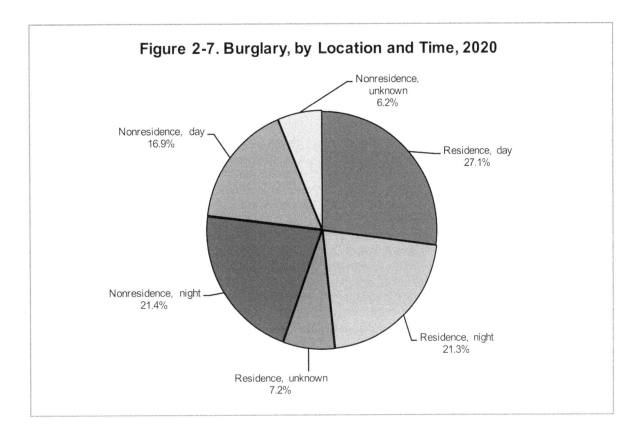

Figure 2-7. Burglary, by Location and Time, 2020

Nonresidence, unknown 6.2%

Residence, day 27.1%

Nonresidence, day 16.9%

Nonresidence, night 21.4%

Residence, night 21.3%

Residence, unknown 7.2%

Definition

The UCR program defines burglary as the unlawful entry of a structure to commit a felony or theft. To classify an offense as a burglary, the use of force to gain entry need not have occurred. The program has three subclassifications for burglary: forcible entry, unlawful entry where no force is used, and attempted forcible entry. The UCR definition of "structure" includes, but is not limited to, apartments, barns, house trailers or houseboats (when used as permanent dwellings), offices, railroad cars (but not automobiles), stables, and vessels (such as ships).

Important Note: COVID-19

The unprecedented conditions of the COVID-19 pandemic have undoubtedly had an effect on crimes committed, crimes cleared, arrests made, and law enforcement personnel levels. Data for 2020 should be interpreted with caution regarding the pandemic conditions, especially in comparison to previous years.

National Volume, Trends, and Rate

In 2020, there were an estimated 1,035,314 burglaries—a decrease of 7.4 percent when compared with 2019 data.

There was a decrease of 31.7 percent in the number of burglaries in 2020 when compared with the 2016 estimate, and a decrease of 52.6 percent when compared with the 2011 estimate. Burglary accounted for 16.0 percent of the estimated number of property crimes committed in 2020. The burglary rate for the United States in 2020 was 314.2 incidents per 100,000 inhabitants, a 7.7 percent decrease from the 2019 rate, a 33.0 percent decrease from the 2016 rate, and a 55.2 percent decrease from the 2011 rate. (Tables 1 and 1A)

Regional Offense Trends and Rates

The UCR program divides the United States into four regions: the Northeast, the Midwest, the South, and the West. (Details regarding these regions can be found in Appendix IV.) An analysis of burglary data by region showed the following details.

NORTHEAST

In 2020, 17.0 percent of the nation's population lived in the Northeast. This region accounted for 9.6 percent of the estimated total number of burglary offenses in the nation in 2020. The region's burglary rate, an estimated 178.8 offenses per 100,000 inhabitants, represented an increase of 6.2 percent from the 2019 rate. The number of incidents rose 5.9 percent to 99,884 from 2019 to 2020. (Tables 3 and 4)

MIDWEST

The Midwest accounted for 20.7 percent of the nation's population in 2020. This region accounted for 18.9 percent of the nation's estimated number of burglaries. In this region, the estimated number of burglaries dropped 9.6 percent to 195,963 from 2019 to 2020. The Midwest had a burglary rate of 286.8 offenses per 100,000 inhabitants, a 9.6 percent decrease from the 2019 rate. (Tables 3 and 4)

SOUTH

The South, the nation's most highly populated region (38.4 percent of all inhabitants), had the most burglaries in 2020 (an estimated 441,688 incidents); however, this represented an 11.4 percent drop from its estimate in 2019. This region accounted for 42.7 percent of all burglaries in the United States. The estimated rate of burglary in the South was 348.7 incidents per 100,000 inhabitants, a 12.1 percent decrease from the 2019 rate. (Tables 3 and 4)

WEST

The West accounted for 23.9 percent of the nation's population in 2020. This region accounted for an estimated 28.8 percent of the nation's burglaries. The region's burglary rate was 378.6, a 3.9 percent decrease from the 2019 rate. The total number of burglaries (297,779) represented a 3.5 percent decrease from the 2019 estimate. (Tables 3 and 4)

Community Types

The UCR program aggregates data by three community types: metropolitan statistical areas (MSAs), cities outside MSAs, and nonmetropolitan counties. (See Appendix IV for more information regarding community types.)

In 2020, 86.1 percent of the U.S. population lived in MSAs, and an estimated 80.9 percent of all burglaries occurred in this type of community. Inhabitants of cities outside MSAs accounted for 5.7 percent of the total population in 2020 and 6.6 percent of the estimated number of burglaries; nonmetropolitan counties, with 8.2 percent of the U.S. population, accounted for the remaining 6.2 percent of all burglaries. The burglary rates per 100,000 inhabitants were 311.3 in MSAs, 417.1 in cities outside MSAs, and 273.9 in nonmetropolitan counties. (Table 2)

Population Groups: Trends and Rates

In addition to analyzing data by region and community type, the UCR program aggregates crime statistics by population groups. Cities are categorized into six groups based on the number of inhabitants; counties are categorized into two groups, metropolitan and nonmetropolitan. (Appendix IV offers further details regarding these population groups.)

An examination of data from law enforcement agencies showed that the nation's cities experienced a collective 6.6 percent decrease in burglaries from 2019 to 2020. Burglaries decreased in all city groups and subsets, with cities with 10,000 to 24,999 inhabitants posting the greatest decrease (9.1 percent). The volume of burglaries decreased 11.6 percent in metropolitan counties, 10.7 percent in nonmetropolitan counties, and 10.4 percent in suburban areas. (Table 12)

The UCR program calculates burglary rates for population groups from the information provided by participating agencies that submitted all 12 months of offense data for the year. In 2020, the nation's cities had 347.1 offenses per 100,000 inhabitants. Cities with 500,000 to 999,999 inhabitants had the highest burglary rate at 582.6 incidents per 100,000 inhabitants. Cities with 25,000 to 49,999 inhabitants had the lowest burglary rate—258.2 incidents per 100,000 inhabitants. Metropolitan counties had a rate of 231.6 per 100,000 inhabitants, and nonmetropolitan counties had a rate of 272.2 per 100,000 inhabitants. The rate in suburban areas was 231.3 per 100,000 inhabitants. (Table 16)

Due to a system upgrade in 2019, the FBI now calculates rates for each offense based on the individual offenses and population published for each agency in tables 8-11. (Previous to 2019, when agencies were published in tables 8-11, but they had one or two offenses removed from publication due to not meeting UCR publication guidelines, the agency's data was not used to calculate rates for this table.) The FBI derived the offense rates by dividing the individual offense counts by the individual populations covered by contributing agencies for which 12 months of publishable data were supplied and then multiplying the resulting figure by 100,000. See Appendix V for the agency and population counts.

Offense Analysis

The UCR program requests that participating law enforcement agencies provide details regarding the nature of burglaries in their jurisdictions, such as type of entry, type of structure, time of day, and dollar loss associated with each offense.

Of all burglaries in 2020, 55.9 percent involved forcible entry, 37.5 percent were unlawful entries (without force), and 6.6 percent comprised forcible entry attempts. (Table 19)

Victims of burglary offenses suffered an estimated $5.7 billion in lost property in 2020; overall, the average dollar loss per burglary offense was $2,692. (Tables 1 and 23)

As in the past, burglars targeted residences more often than nonresidential structures. In 2020, burglaries of residential properties accounted for 55.5 percent of all burglary offenses. Of the burglaries for which time of day could be established, most burglaries of residences (48.7 percent of all reported residential burglaries) occurred during the day, while most burglaries of nonresidential structures (48.0 percent of all reported nonresidential burglaries) occurred at night. (Table 23)

LARCENY-THEFT

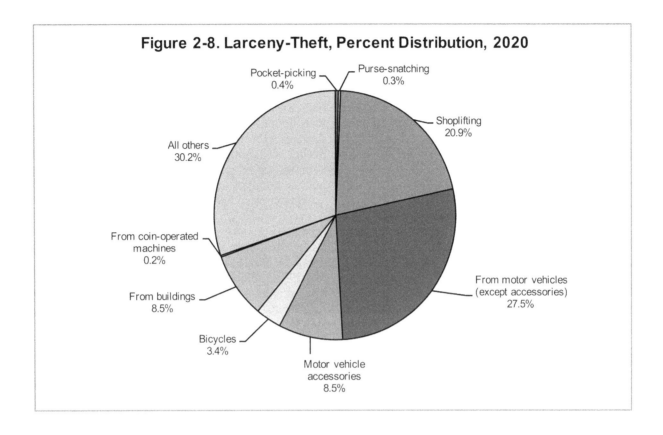

Figure 2-8. Larceny-Theft, Percent Distribution, 2020

Pocket-picking
0.4%

Purse-snatching
0.3%

Shoplifting
20.9%

All others
30.2%

From coin-operated
machines
0.2%

From buildings
8.5%

Bicycles
3.4%

Motor vehicle
accessories
8.5%

From motor vehicles
(except accessories)
27.5%

Definition

The UCR program defines larceny-theft as the unlawful taking, carrying, leading, or riding away of property from the possession or constructive possession of another. Examples are thefts of bicycles, motor vehicle parts and accessories, shoplifting, pocket picking, or the stealing of any property or article not taken by force and violence or by fraud. Attempted larcenies are included. Embezzlement, confidence games, forgery, check fraud, and so on, are excluded from this category.

Important Note: COVID-19

The unprecedented conditions of the COVID-19 pandemic have undoubtedly had an effect on crimes committed, crimes cleared, arrests made, and law enforcement personnel levels. Data for 2020 should be interpreted with caution regarding the pandemic conditions, especially in comparison to previous years.

National Volume, Trends, and Rates

Larceny-thefts accounted for an estimated 71.4 percent of property crimes in 2020, with an estimated 4,606,324 larceny-thefts nationwide. The estimated number of larceny-thefts declined 10.6 percent from 2019 to 2020. The 2020 estimate showed an 18.4 percent decline from the 2016 data and a 25.0 percent decrease from the 2011 estimate. The trend data also showed decreases in the larceny-theft rates per 100,000 inhabitants during these periods. The rate of larceny-thefts (1,398.0 per 100,000 inhabitants in 2020) declined 10.9 percent from 2019 to 2020, 19.9 percent from 2016 to 2020, and 29.2 percent from 2011 to 2020. (Tables 1 and 1A)

Regional Offense Trends and Rates

The UCR program defines four regions within the United States: the Northeast, the Midwest, the South, and the West. (See Appendix IV for a geographical description of each region.)

NORTHEAST

The Northeast was the region with the smallest proportion (17.0 percent) of the U.S. population in 2020. The region also experienced the fewest larceny-thefts in the country, accounting for only 13.1 percent of all larceny-thefts. The estimated number of offenses in 2020 (601,250) represented a 2.0 percent decline from 2019, and the estimated rate—1,076.5 incidents per 100,000 inhabitants—represented a 1.7 percent decline. (Tables 3 and 4)

MIDWEST

With 20.7 percent of the U.S. population in 2020, the Midwest accounted for an estimated 19.1 percent of the nation's larceny-thefts. The estimated number of offenses (877,996) declined 10.4 percent from the 2019 total, and the estimated rate of occurrence (1,285.2 incidents per 100,000 inhabitants) declined 10.4 percent. (Tables 3 and 4)

SOUTH

With nearly two-fifths of the U.S. population in 2020 (38.4 percent), the South had the nation's highest proportion of larceny-theft offenses: an estimated 41.9 percent. Estimated offenses in this region in 2020 totaled 1,929,682, a 13.4 percent decrease from the 2019 estimate. The South's larceny-theft rate—estimated at 1,523.5 offenses per 100,000 inhabitants—decreased 14.1 percent from the 2019 estimate. (Tables 3 and 4)

WEST

In 2020, an estimated 23.9 percent of the U.S. population lived in the West. This region was also where 26.0 percent of the nation's estimated number of larceny-thefts took place. Occurrences of larceny-theft decreased 9.9 percent from 2019 to 2020 to an estimated total of 1,197,396 offenses. The region's larceny-theft rate, estimated at 1,522.3 offenses per 100,000 inhabitants, represented a decrease of 10.4 percent from the 2019 rate. (Tables 3 and 4)

Community Types

The UCR program aggregates data for three community types: metropolitan statistical areas (MSAs), cities outside MSAs, and nonmetropolitan counties outside MSAs. MSAs include a central city or urbanized area with at least 50,000 inhabitants, as well as the county that contains the principal city and other adjacent counties that share a high degree of social and economic integration as measured through commuting. Cities outside MSAs are mostly incorporated areas, and nonmetropolitan counties are composed of unincorporated areas. (See Appendix IV for more information regarding community types.)

In 2020, MSAs were home to an estimated 86.1 percent of the nation's population and experienced 84.9 percent of the nation's larceny-theft incidents. Cities outside MSAs accounted for 5.7 percent of the U.S. population and 6.1 percent of larceny-theft offenses. Nonmetropolitan counties, which were home to 8.2 percent of the nation's population, accounted for 3.0 percent of the estimated

number of larceny-theft offenses. The larceny-theft rates per 100,000 inhabitants were 1,451.0 in MSAs, 1,712.6 in cities outside MSAs, and 628.6 in nonmetropolitan counties. (Table 2)

Population Groups: Trends and Rates

In cities, collectively, occurrences of larceny-theft decreased 10.4 percent between 2019 and 2020. Cities with under 10,000 inhabitants experienced the greatest decrease (15.7 percent). Larceny-theft continued to show decline in counties and suburban areas—metropolitan counties experienced decreased 7.6 percent, nonmetropolitan counties decreased 4.2 percent, and suburban areas decreased 9.4 percent. (Table 12)

Based on reports of larceny-theft offenses from U.S. law enforcement agencies that submitted 12 months of complete data for 2020, this offense occurred at a rate of 1,398.0 offenses per 100,000 inhabitants. The collective rate for cities was 1,686.7 offenses per 100,000 inhabitants. Among city population groups and subsets, cities with 500,000 to 999,000 inhabitants had the highest larceny-theft rate, 2,372.0 incidents per 100,000 inhabitants. Cities with 25,000 to 49,999 inhabitants had the lowest rate, at 1,435.0. In metropolitan counties, the rate was 906.9 incidents per 100,000 inhabitants; in nonmetropolitan counties, the rate was 610.5 incidents per 100,000 inhabitants. The rate in suburban areas was 1,089.1 incidents per 100,000 inhabitants. (Table 16)

Due to a system upgrade in 2019, the FBI now calculates rates for each offense based on the individual offenses and population published for each agency in tables 8-11. (Previous to 2019, when agencies were published in tables 8-11, but they had one or two offenses removed from publication due to not meeting UCR publication guidelines, the agency's data was not used to calculate rates for this table.) The FBI derived the offense rates by dividing the individual offense counts by the individual populations covered by contributing agencies for which 12 months of publishable data were supplied and then multiplying the resulting figure by 100,000. See Appendix V for the agency and population counts.

Offense Analysis

DISTRIBUTION

Table 23 provides a further breakdown of larceny-theft offenses, including shoplifting, thefts from buildings, thefts of motor vehicle accessories, thefts of bicycles, thefts from coin-operated machines, purse snatching, and pocket picking. The "all other" category, which includes the less-defined types of larceny-theft, accounted for 30.2 percent of all offenses in 2020.

LOSS BY DOLLAR VALUE

Larceny-theft offenses cost victims an estimated $6.8 billion dollars in 2020. The average value of property stolen was $1,482 per offense, $334 more than in 2019. Larceny-theft from buildings had the highest average dollar loss per offense at $1,616. Pocket picking had an average dollar loss of $1,233 per offense; thefts from motor vehicles (except accessories), $1,053; thefts of motor vehicle accessories, $873; purse snatching, $634; thefts from coin-operated machines, $816; thefts of bicycles, $724; and shoplifting, $306. (Tables 1 and 23)

Offenses in which the stolen property was valued at more than $200 accounted for 48.2 percent of all larceny-thefts in 2020. Table 23 provides further analysis, including the average dollar value per offense of all offenses in the overall category of property crime. (Table 23)

MOTOR VEHICLE THEFT

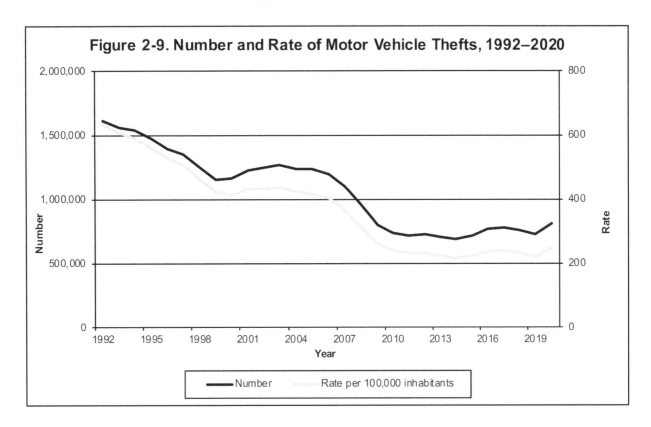

Figure 2-9. Number and Rate of Motor Vehicle Thefts, 1992–2020

Definition

The UCR program defines motor vehicle theft as the theft or attempted theft of a motor vehicle. The offense includes the stealing of automobiles, trucks, buses, motorcycles, snowmobiles, etc. The taking of a motor vehicle for temporary use by a person or persons with lawful access is excluded.

Important Note: COVID-19

The unprecedented conditions of the COVID-19 pandemic have undoubtedly had an effect on crimes committed, crimes cleared, arrests made, and law enforcement personnel levels. Data for 2020 should be interpreted with caution regarding the pandemic conditions, especially in comparison to previous years.

National Volume, Trends, and Rates

In 2020, an estimated 810,400 motor vehicle thefts took place in the United States. The estimated number of motor vehicle thefts increased 11.8 percent when compared with data from 2019, increased 5.6 percent when compared with 2016 data, and increased 13.1 percent when compared with 2011 data. (Tables 1 and 1A)

The estimated rate of motor vehicle theft in 2020 was 246.0 incidents per 100,000 inhabitants. The 2020 rate was 11.4 percent more than the 2019 rate, 3.7 percent more than the 2016 rate, and 7.0 percent more than the 2011 rate. (Tables 1 and 1A)

Regional Offense Trends and Rates

In order to analyze crime by geographic area, the UCR program divides the United States into four regions: the Northeast, the Midwest, the South, and the West. (Appendix IV provides a map delineating the regions.) This section provides a regional overview of motor vehicle theft.

NORTHEAST

The Northeast accounted for an estimated 17.0 percent of the nation's population in 2020. The region also accounted for an estimated 7.9 percent of its motor vehicle thefts. An estimated 64,344 motor vehicle thefts occurred in the Northeast in 2020, a 25.5 percent rise in occurrences from 2019. The estimated rate of 115.2 motor vehicle thefts per 100,000 inhabitants in the Northeast in 2020 represented a 25.9 percent increase from the 2019 rate. (Tables 3 and 4)

MIDWEST

An estimated 20.7 percent of the country's population resided in the Midwest in 2020. The region accounted for 18.0 percent of the nation's motor vehicle thefts. The

Midwest had an estimated 145,868 motor vehicle thefts in 2020, an increase of 11.8 percent from the previous year's total. The motor vehicle theft rate was estimated at 213.5 motor vehicles stolen per 100,000 inhabitants, an increase of 11.9 percent from the 2019 rate. (Tables 3 and 4)

SOUTH

The South, the nation's most populous region, was home to an estimated 38.4 percent of the U.S. population in 2019 and accounted for 36.6 percent of the nation's motor vehicle thefts. The estimated 296,932 motor vehicle thefts in the South represented a 5.5 percent increase from the 2019 estimate. Motor vehicles in the South were stolen at an estimated rate of 234.4 offenses per 100,000 inhabitants in 2020, a rate that was up 4.7 percent from the 2019 rate. (Tables 3 and 4)

WEST

With approximately 23.9 percent of the U.S. population in 2020, the West accounted for 37.4 percent of all motor vehicle thefts in the nation. An estimated 303,266 motor vehicle thefts occurred in this region, the most of any refion. This number represented a 15.9 percent decrease from the previous year's estimate. The region's 2020 rate of 385.6 motor vehicles stolen per 100,000 inhabitants was 15.3 percent higher than the 2019 rate. (Tables 3 and 4)

Community Types

The UCR program aggregates data by three community types: metropolitan statistical areas (MSAs), cities outside MSAs, and nonmetropolitan counties. MSAs are areas that include a principal city or urbanized area with at least 50,000 inhabitants and the county that contains the principal city and other adjacent counties that have, as defined by the U.S. Office of Management and Budget, a high degree of economic and social integration.

In 2020, the vast majority (88.5 percent) of the U.S. population resided in MSAs, where approximately 91.7 percent of motor vehicle thefts occurred. For 2020, the UCR program estimated an overall rate of 262.3 motor vehicles stolen per 100,000 MSA inhabitants. Cities outside MSAs, with 5.7 percent of the U.S. population, accounted for 3.6 percent of motor vehicle thefts, and nonmetropolitan counties, with 8.2 percent of the population, accounted for 3.5 percent of motor vehicle thefts. The UCR program estimated a 2020 rate of 177.4 motor vehicles stolen for every 100,000 inhabitants in cities outside MSAs and a rate of 123.0 motor vehicles stolen per 100,000 inhabitants in nonmetropolitan counties. (Table 2)

Population Groups: Trends and Rates

The UCR program aggregates data by various population groups, which include cities, metropolitan counties,

and nonmetropolitan counties. (A definition of these groups can be found in Appendix IV.)

In cities, collectively, the number of motor vehicle thefts increased 12.5 percent from 2019 to 2020. Occurrences rose in all groups and. subsets. Cities with 50,000 to 99,999 residents experienced the greatest increase at 15.8 percent. Metropolitan counties experienced an increase of 9.1 percent, nonmetropolitan counties experienced an increase of 5.9 percent, and suburban areas experienced an increase of 11.3 percent. (Table 12)

In 2020, cities had a collective motor vehicle theft rate of 301.8 per 100,000 inhabitants. Among the population groups and subsets, cities with 500,000 to 999,999 inhabitants experienced the highest rate of motor vehicle thefts with 529.1 motor vehicle thefts per 100,000 inhabitants. Cities with populations of under 10,000 residents had the lowest rate of motor vehicle theft with 161.2 incidents per 100,000 in population. Within the county groups, metropolitan counties had a rate of 167.4 motor vehicles stolen per 100,000 inhabitants, while nonmetropolitan counties had a rate of 125.2 incidents per 100,000 inhabitants. Suburban areas had a rate of 169.4 per 100,000 inhabitants. (Table 16)

Due to a system upgrade in 2019, the FBI now calculates rates for each offense based on the individual offenses and population published for each agency in tables 8-11. (Previous to 2019, when agencies were published in tables 8-11, but they had one or two offenses removed from publication due to not meeting UCR publication guidelines, the agency's data was not used to calculate rates for this table.) The FBI derived the offense rates by dividing the individual offense counts by the individual populations covered by contributing agencies for which 12 months of publishable data were supplied and then multiplying the resulting figure by 100,000. See Appendix V for the agency and population counts.

Offense Analysis

Based on the reports of law enforcement agencies, the UCR program estimated the combined value of motor vehicles stolen nationwide in 2020 at $7.4 billion. In 2020, the average dollar value per motor vehicle stolen in the United States was $9,166. Automobiles were, by far, the most frequently stolen vehicles, accounting for 74.0 percent of all vehicles stolen. Trucks and buses accounted for 16.9 percent of stolen vehicles, and other vehicles accounted for 9.1 percent of stolen vehicles. (Tables 1, 19, and 23)

By type of vehicle, automobiles were stolen at a rate of 177.6 cars per 100,000 inhabitants in 2020. Trucks and buses were stolen at a rate of 44.0 vehicles per 100,000 inhabitants, and other types of vehicles were stolen at a rate of 23.9 vehicles per 100,000 inhabitants. (Table 19)

ARSON

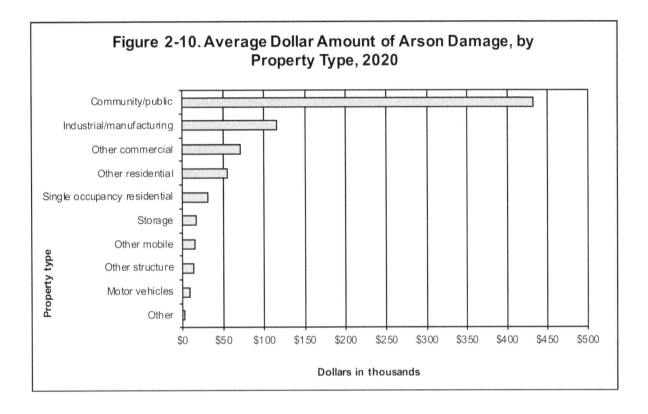

Figure 2-10. Average Dollar Amount of Arson Damage, by Property Type, 2020

Definition

The UCR program defines arson as any willful or malicious burning or attempt to burn (with or without intent to defraud) a dwelling house, public building, motor vehicle, aircraft, or personal property of another, etc.

Important Note: COVID-19

The unprecedented conditions of the COVID-19 pandemic have undoubtedly had an effect on crimes committed, crimes cleared, arrests made, and law enforcement personnel levels. Data for 2020 should be interpreted with caution regarding the pandemic conditions, especially in comparison to previous years.

Data Collection

Only fires that investigators determined were willfully set (not fires labeled as "suspicious" or "of unknown origin") are included in this arson data collection. Points to consider regarding arson statistics include:

National offense rates per 100,000 inhabitants (found in Tables 1, 2, and 4) do not include arson data; the FBI presents rates for arson separately. Arson rates are calculated

based upon data received from all law enforcement agencies that provide the UCR program with data for 12 complete months.

Arson data collection does not include estimates for arson, because the degree of reporting arson offenses varies from agency to agency. Because of this unevenness of reporting, arson offenses are excluded from Tables 1 through 7, all of which contain offense estimations.

The number of arsons reported by individual law enforcement agencies is available in Tables 8 through 11. Arson trend data (which indicate year-to-year changes) can be found in Tables 12 through 15.

Population Groups: Trends and Rates

The number of arsons reported in cities 2020 was 24.5 percent higher than the number reported in 2019. Among the population groups labeled *city,* the group with 100,000 to 249,999 inhabitants reported the largest increase (30.7 percent). Cities with under 10,000 inhabitants showed the smallest increase (12.7 percent). Agencies in the nation's metropolitan counties reported a 17.0 percent increase in the number of arsons, while those in nonmetropolitan counties reported a 20.9 percent increase from 2019 to

2020. Agencies in suburban areas reported an 18.2 percent rise in arsons. (Table 12)

Offense Analysis

The UCR program breaks down arson offenses into three property categories: structural, mobile, and other. In addition, the structural property type is broken down into seven types of structures, and the mobile property type consists of two subgroupings. The program also collects information on the estimated dollar value of the damaged property. Arson rates were based on information received from 13,159 agencies that provided 12 months of complete arson data to the UCR program.

Property Type

Arsons of structures comprised 38.5 percent of arsons, while arsons of mobile properties comprised 24.3 percent of arsons. Of arsons where location was known, 52.3 percent occurred at residences; 11.8 percent occurred on highways, alleys, streets, or sidewalks; and 6.4 percent of arsons occurred in parking garages. Approximately 0.8 percent of arsons occurred at religious buildings, such as synagogues, churches, temples, or mosques. (Table 15 and Expanded Arson Data)

Table 1. Crime in the United States, by Volume and Rate Per 100,000 Inhabitants, 2001–2020

(Number, rate per 100,000 population.)

Year	Population[1]	Violent crime[2]		Murder and nonnegligent manslaughter		Rape (revised definition)[3]		Rape (legacy definition)[4]		Robbery		Aggravated assault	
		Number	Rate	Number	Rate	Number	Rate	Number	Rate	Number	Rate	Number	Rate
2001[5]	285,317,559	1,439,480	504.5	16,037	5.6	X	X	90,863	31.8	423,557	148.5	909,023	318.6
2002	287,973,924	1,423,677	494.4	16,229	5.6	X	X	95,235	33.1	420,806	146.1	891,407	309.5
2003	290,788,976	1,383,676	475.8	16,528	5.7	X	X	93,883	32.3	414,235	142.5	859,030	295.4
2004	293,656,842	1,360,088	463.2	16,148	5.5	X	X	95,089	32.4	401,470	136.7	847,381	288.6
2005	296,507,061	1,390,745	469.0	16,740	5.6	X	X	94,347	31.8	417,438	140.8	862,220	290.8
2006	299,398,484	1,435,123	479.3	17,309	5.8	X	X	94,472	31.6	449,246	150.0	874,096	292.0
2007	301,621,157	1,422,970	471.8	17,128	5.7	X	X	92,160	30.6	447,324	148.3	866,358	287.2
2008	304,059,724	1,394,461	458.6	16,465	5.4	X	X	90,750	29.8	443,563	145.9	843,683	277.5
2009	307,006,550	1,325,896	431.9	15,399	5.0	X	X	89,241	29.1	408,742	133.1	812,514	264.7
2010	309,330,219	1,251,248	404.5	14,722	4.8	X	X	85,593	27.7	369,089	119.3	781,844	252.8
2011	311,587,816	1,206,005	387.1	14,661	4.7	X	X	84,175	27.0	354,746	113.9	752,423	241.5
2012	313,873,685	1,217,057	387.8	14,856	4.7	X	X	85,141	27.1	355,051	113.1	762,009	242.8
2013	316,497,531	1,168,298	369.1	14,319	4.5	113,695	36	82,109	25.9	345,093	109.0	726,777	229.6
2014	318,907,401	1,153,022	361.6	14,164	4.4	118,027	37.0	84,864	26.6	322,905	101.3	731,089	229.2
2015	320,896,618	1,199,310	373.7	15,883	4.9	126,134	39.3	91,261	28.4	328,109	102.2	764,057	238.1
2016	323,405,935	1,250,162	386.6	17,413	5.4	132,414	40.9	96,970	30.0	332,797	102.9	802,982	248.3
2017	325,147,121	1,247,917	383.8	17,294	5.3	135,666	41.7	99,708	30.7	320,596	98.6	810,319	249.2
2018	326,687,501	1,209,997	370.4	16,374	5.0	143,765	44.0	101,363	31.0	281,278	86.1	810,982	248.2
2019[6]	328,329,953	1,210,229	368.6	16,669	5.1	143,224	43.6	103,060	31.4	268,483	81.8	822,017	250.4
2020	329,484,123	1,277,696	387.8	21,570	6.5	126,430	38.4	91,021	27.6	243,600	73.9	921,505	279.7

Table 1. Crime in the United States, by Volume and Rate Per 100,000 Inhabitants, 2001–2020—Continued

(Number, rate per 100,000 population.)

Year	Property crime		Burglary		Larceny-theft		Motor vehicle theft	
	Number	Rate	Number	Rate	Number	Rate	Number	Rate
2001[5]	10,437,189	3,658.1	2,116,531	741.8	7,092,267	2,485.7	1,228,391	430.5
2002	10,455,277	3,630.6	2,151,252	747.0	7,057,379	2,450.7	1,246,646	432.9
2003	10,442,862	3,591.2	2,154,834	741.0	7,026,802	2,416.5	1,261,226	433.7
2004	10,319,386	3,514.1	2,144,446	730.3	6,937,089	2,362.3	1,237,851	421.5
2005	10,174,754	3,431.5	2,155,448	726.9	6,783,447	2,287.8	1,235,859	416.8
2006	10,019,601	3,346.6	2,194,993	733.1	6,626,363	2,213.2	1,198,245	400.2
2007	9,882,212	3,276.4	2,190,198	726.1	6,591,542	2,185.4	1,100,472	364.9
2008	9,774,152	3,214.6	2,228,887	733.0	6,586,206	2,166.1	959,059	315.4
2009	9,337,060	3,041.3	2,203,313	717.7	6,338,095	2,064.5	795,652	259.2
2010	9,112,625	2,945.9	2,168,459	701.0	6,204,601	2,005.8	739,565	239.1
2011	9,052,743	2,905.4	2,185,140	701.3	6,151,095	1,974.1	716,508	230.0
2012	9,001,992	2,868.0	2,109,932	672.2	6,168,874	1,965.4	723,186	230.4
2013	8,651,892	2,733.6	1,932,139	610.5	6,019,465	1,901.9	700,288	221.3
2014	8,209,010	2,574.1	1,713,153	537.2	5,809,054	1,821.5	686,803	215.4
2015	8,024,115	2,500.5	1,587,564	494.7	5,723,488	1,783.6	713,063	222.2
2016	7,928,530	2,451.6	1,516,405	468.9	5,644,835	1,745.4	767,290	237.3
2017	7,682,988	2,362.9	1,397,045	429.7	5,513,000	1,695.5	772,943	237.7
2018	7,219,084	2,209.8	1,235,013	378.0	5,232,167	1,601.6	751,904	230.2
2019[6]	6,995,235	2,130.6	1,118,096	340.5	5,152,267	1,569.2	724,872	220.8
2020	6,452,038	1,958.2	1,035,314	314.2	4,606,324	1,398.0	810,400	246.0

NOTE: Although arson data are included in the trend and clearance tables, sufficient data are not available to estimate totals for this offense. Therefore, no arson data are published in this table.

X = Not applicable.

1 Populations are U.S. Census Bureau provisional estimates as of July 1 for each year except 2000 and 2010, which are decennial census counts.   2 The violent crime figures include the offenses of murder, rape (legacy definition), robbery, and aggravated assault.   3 The figures shown in this column for the offense of rape were estimated using the revised UCR definition of rape.   4 The figures shown in this column for the offense of rape were estimated using the legacy UCR definition of rape.   5 The murder and nonnegligent homicides that occurred as a result of the events of September 11, 2001, are not included in this table.   6 The crime figures have been adjusted.

Table 1A. Crime in the United States, Percent Change in Volume and Rate Per 100,000 Inhabitants for 2 Years, 5 Years, and 10 Years, 2011–2020

(Percent change.)

Year	Violent crime[1]		Murder and nonnegligent manslaughter		Rape (revised definition)[2]		Rape (legacy definition)[3]		Robbery		Aggravated assault		Property crime		Burglary		Larceny-theft		Motor vehicle theft	
	Number	Rate	Number	Rate	Number	Rate	Number	Rate	Number	Rate	Number	Rate	Number	Rate	Number	Rate	Number	Rate	Number	Rate
2011–2020	+5.9	+0.2	+47.1	+39.1	X	X	+8.1	+2.3	-31.3	-35.1	+22.5	+15.8	-28.7	-32.6	-52.6	-55.2	-25.1	-29.2	+13.1	+7.0
2016–2020	+2.2	+0.3	+23.9	+21.6	-4.5	-6.3	-6.1	-7.9	-26.8	-28.2	+14.8	+12.6	-18.6	-20.1	-31.7	-33.0	-18.4	-19.9	+5.6	+3.7
2019–2020	+5.6	+5.2	+29.4	+28.9	-11.7	-12.0	-11.7	-12.0	-9.3	-9.6	+12.1	+11.7	-7.8	-8.1	-7.4	-7.7	-10.6	-10.9	+11.8	+11.4

X = Not applicable.
1 The violent crime figures include the offenses of murder, rape (legacy definition), robbery, and aggravated assault.   2 The figures shown in this column for the offense of rape were estimated using the revised UCR definition of rape.   3 The figures shown in this column for the offense of rape were estimated using the legacy UCR definition of rape.

Table 2. Crime, by Community Type, 2020

(Number, rate per 100,000 population, percent.)

Area	Population[1]	Violent crime[2]	Murder and nonnegligent manslaughter	Rape[3]	Robbery	Aggravated assault	Property crime	Burglary	Larceny-theft	Motor vehicle theft
United States	329,484,123	1,313,105	21,570	126,430	243,600	921,505	6,452,038	1,035,314	4,606,324	810,400
Rate per 100,000 inhabitants		398.5	6.5	38.4	73.9	279.7	1,958.2	314.2	1,398.0	246.0
Metropolitan Statistical Area	283,601,617									
Area actually reporting[4]	97.1%	1,127,195	18,499	102,090	225,756	780,850	5,463,031	837,142	3,908,491	717,398
Estimated total	100.0%	1,175,523	19,230	107,098	234,032	815,163	5,741,726	882,846	4,115,100	743,780
Rate per 100,000 inhabitants		414.5	6.8	37.8	82.5	287.4	2,024.6	311.3	1,451.0	262.3
Cities Outside Metropolitan Areas	18,709,511									
Area actually reporting[4]	91.9%	67,798	967	8,824	5,335	52,672	380,070	67,989	282,672	29,409
Estimated total	100.0%	75,504	1,042	9,540	6,185	58,737	431,657	78,030	320,428	33,199
Rate per 100,000 inhabitants		403.6	5.6	51.0	33.1	313.9	2,307.2	417.1	1,712.6	177.4
Nonmetropolitan counties	27,172,995									
Area actually reporting[4]	91.0%	53,176	1,100	8,688	2,330	41,058	232,681	63,708	140,227	28,746
Estimated total	100.0%	62,078	1,298	9,792	3,383	47,605	278,655	74,438	170,796	33,421
Rate per 100,000 inhabitants		228.5	4.8	36.0	12.4	175.2	1,025.5	273.9	628.6	123.0

Note: Although arson data are included in the trend and clearance tables, sufficient data are not available to estimate totals for this offense. Therefore, no arson data are published in this table.
[1]Population figures are U.S. Census Bureau provisional estimates as of July 1, 2020.
[2]The violent crime figures include the offenses of murder, rape (revised definition), robbery, and aggravated assault.
[3]The figures shown in this column for the offense of rape were estimated using the revised Uniform Crime Reporting definition of rape.
[4]The percentage reported under "Area actually reporting" is based upon the population covered by agencies providing 3 months or more of crime reports to the FBI.

Table 3. Crime in the United States, Population and Offense Distribution, by Region, 2020

(Percent distribution.)

Region	Population	Violent crime	Murder and nonnegligent manslaughter	Rape (revised definition)[1]	Robbery	Aggravated assault	Property crime	Burglary	Larceny-theft	Motor vehicle theft
United States[2]	100.0	100.0	100.0	100.0	100.0	100.0	100.0	100.0	100.0	100.0
Northeast	17.0	13.1	11.7	11.9	15.8	12.6	11.9	9.6	13.1	7.9
Midwest	20.7	20.2	22.3	23.9	17.8	20.2	18.9	18.9	19.1	18.0
South	38.4	41.6	47.1	38.2	37.4	43.1	41.4	42.7	41.9	36.6
West	23.9	25.1	18.9	26.0	29.0	24.1	27.9	28.8	26.0	37.4

Note: Although arson data are included in the trend and clearance tables, sufficient data are not available to estimate totals for this offense. Therefore, no arson data are published in this table.
1 The figures shown in the rape column were calculated using the revised Uniform Crime Reporting (UCR) definition of rape.   2 Because of rounding, percentages may not sum to 100.0.

Table 4. Crime in the United States,[1] by Region, Geographic Division, and State, 2019–2020

(Number, rate per 100,000 population, percent.)

Area	Population[2]	Violent crime[3]		Murder and nonnegligent manslaughter		Rape (revised definition)[4]		Robbery	
		Number	Rate	Number	Rate	Number	Rate	Number	Rate
UNITED STATES[5,6,7,8,9]									
2019	328,329,953	1,250,393	380.8	16,669	5.1	143,224	43.6	268,483	81.8
2020	329,484,123	1,313,105	398.5	21,570	6.5	126,430	38.4	243,600	73.9
Percent change		+5.0	+4.6	+29.4	+28.9	-11.7	-12.0	-9.3	-9.6
NORTHEAST[5]									
2019	56,002,934	164,411	293.6	1,856	3.3	17,487	31.2	40,222	71.8
2020	55,849,869	172,219	308.4	2,526	4.5	15,066	27.0	38,535	69.0
Percent change		+4.7	+5.0	+36.1	+36.5	-13.8	-13.6	-4.2	-3.9
New England									
2019	14,849,662	36,609	246.5	352	2.4	4,963	33.4	6,578	44.3
2020	14,847,468	34,734	233.9	380	2.6	4,093	27.6	5,898	39.7
Percent change		-5.1	-5.1	+8.0	+8.0	-17.5	-17.5	-10.3	-10.3
Connecticut									
2019	3,566,022	6,583	184.6	107	3.0	797	22.3	1,942	54.5
2020	3,557,006	6,459	181.6	140	3.9	594	16.7	2,033	57.2
Percent change		-1.9	-1.6	+30.8	+31.2	-25.5	-25.3	+4.7	+5.0
Maine									
2019	1,345,770	1,562	116.1	22	1.6	520	38.6	192	14.3
2020	1,350,141	1,466	108.6	22	1.6	486	36.0	170	12.6
Percent change		-6.1	-6.4	+0.0	-0.3	-6.5	-6.8	-11.5	-11.7
Massachusetts									
2019	6,894,883	22,662	328.7	153	2.2	2,244	32.5	3,625	52.6
2020	6,893,574	21,288	308.8	160	2.3	1,851	26.9	3,015	43.7
Percent change		-6.1	-6.0	+4.6	+4.6	-17.5	-17.5	-16.8	-16.8
New Hampshire									
2019	1,360,783	2,152	158.1	33	2.4	606	44.5	327	24.0
2020	1,366,275	2,000	146.4	12	0.9	542	39.7	280	20.5
Percent change		-7.1	-7.4	-63.6	-63.8	-10.6	-10.9	-14.4	-14.7
Rhode Island									
2019	1,058,158	2,357	222.7	26	2.5	498	47.1	421	39.8
2020	1,057,125	2,440	230.8	32	3.0	407	38.5	336	31.8
Percent change		+3.5	+3.6	+23.1	+23.2	-18.3	-18.2	-20.2	-20.1
Vermont									
2019	624,046	1,293	207.2	11	1.8	298	47.8	71	11.4
2020	623,347	1,081	173.4	14	2.2	213	34.2	64	10.3
Percent change		-16.4	-16.3	27.3	+27.4	-28.5	-28.4	-9.9	-9.8
Middle Atlantic[5]									
2019	41,153,272	127,802	310.6	1,504	3.7	12,524	30.4	33,644	81.8
2020	41,002,401	137,485	335.3	2,146	5.2	10,973	26.8	32,637	79.6
Percent change		+7.6	+8.0	+42.7	+43.2	-12.4	-12.1	-3.0	-2.6
New Jersey									
2019	8,891,258	18,382	206.7	263	3.0	1,537	17.3	5,730	64.4
2020	8,882,371	17,353	195.4	329	3.7	1,277	14.4	4,384	49.4
Percent change		-5.6	-5.5	+25.1	+25.2	-16.9	-16.8	-23.5	-23.4
New York									
2019	19,463,131	70,260	361.0	565	2.9	6,642	34.1	18,165	93.3
2020	19,336,776	70,339	363.8	808	4.2	5,468	28.3	17,525	90.6
Percent change		+0.1	+0.8	+43.0	+43.9	-17.7	-17.1	-3.5	-2.9
Pennsylvania[5]									
2019	12,798,883	39,160	306.0	676	5.3	4,345	33.9	9,749	76.2
2020	12,783,254	49,793	389.5	1,009	7.9	4,228	33.1	10,728	83.9
Percent change		+27.2	+27.3	+49.3	+49.4	-2.7	-2.6	+10.0	+10.2
MIDWEST[6,7]									
2019	68,340,091	250,007	365.8	3,527	5.2	35,056	51.3	46,597	68.2
2020	68,316,744	264,915	387.8	4,803	7.0	30,157	44.1	43,368	63.5
Percent change		+6.0	+6.0	+36.2	+36.2	-14.0	-13.9	-6.9	-6.9
East North Central[6,7]									
2019	46,903,910	173,323	369.5	2,573	5.5	24,278	51.8	35,202	75.1
2020	46,834,910	180,379	385.1	3,538	7.6	20,575	43.9	31,821	67.9
Percent change		+4.1	+4.2	+37.5	+37.7	-15.3	-15.1	-9.6	-9.5
Illinois[6]									
2019	12,667,017	52,601	415.3	851	6.7	6,161	48.6	12,660	99.9
2020	12,587,530	53,612	425.9	1,151	9.1	5,090	40.4	12,261	97.4
Percent change		+1.9	+2.6	+35.3	+36.1	-17.4	-16.9	-3.2	-2.5
Indiana									
2019	6,731,010	25,006	371.5	373	5.5	2,553	37.9	5,335	79.3
2020	6,754,953	24,161	357.7	505	7.5	2,348	34.8	4,215	62.4
Percent change		-3.4	-3.7	+35.4	+34.9	-8.0	-8.4	-21.0	-21.3
Michigan									
2019	9,984,795	43,793	438.6	576	5.8	7,356	73.7	5,352	53.6
2020	9,966,555	47,641	478.0	754	7.6	6,065	60.9	4,438	44.5
Percent change		+8.8	+9.0	+30.9	+31.1	-17.6	-17.4	-17.1	-16.9
Ohio[7]									
2019	11,696,507	34,618	296.0	584	5.0	5,850	50.0	8,861	75.8
2020	11,693,217	36,104	308.8	820	7.0	5,052	43.2	7,826	66.9
Percent change		+4.3	+4.3	+40.4	+40.5	-13.6	-13.6	-11.7	-11.7

Table 4. Crime in the United States,[1] by Region, Geographic Division, and State, 2019–2020—Continued

(Number, rate per 100,000 population, percent.)

Area	Aggravated assault		Property crime		Burglary		Larceny-theft		Motor vehicle theft	
	Number	Rate	Number	Rate	Number	Rate	Number	Rate	Number	Rate
UNITED STATES[5,6,7,8,9]										
2019	822,017	250.4	6,995,235	2,130.6	1,118,096	340.5	5,152,267	1,569.2	724,872	220.8
2020	921,505	279.7	6,452,038	1,958.2	1,035,314	314.2	4,606,324	1,398.0	810,400	246.0
Percent change	+12.1	+11.7	-7.8	-8.1	-7.4	-7.7	-10.6	-10.9	+11.8	+11.4
NORTHEAST[5]										
2019	104,846	187.2	759,192	1,355.6	94,329	168.4	613,608	1,095.7	51,255	91.5
2020	116,092	207.9	765,478	1,370.6	99,884	178.8	601,250	1,076.5	64,344	115.2
Percent change	+10.7	+11.0	+0.8	+1.1	+5.9	+6.2	-2.0	-1.7	+25.5	+25.9
New England										
2019	24,716	166.4	191,098	1,286.9	26,541	178.7	149,097	1,004.0	15,460	104.1
2020	24,363	164.1	179,648	1,210.0	23,124	155.7	137,588	926.7	18,936	127.5
Percent change	-1.4	-1.4	-6.0	-6.0	-12.9	-12.9	-7.7	-7.7	+22.5	+22.5
Connecticut										
2019	3,737	104.8	51,076	1,432.3	6,468	181.4	38,616	1,082.9	5,992	168.0
2020	3,692	103.8	55,670	1,565.1	6,656	187.1	40,592	1,141.2	8,422	236.8
Percent change	-1.2	-1.0	+9.0	+9.3	+2.9	+3.2	+5.1	+5.4	+40.6	+40.9
Maine										
2019	828	61.5	16,791	1,247.7	2,360	175.4	13,705	1,018.4	726	53.9
2020	788	58.4	15,610	1,156.2	2,009	148.8	12,739	943.5	862	63.8
Percent change	-4.8	-5.1	-7.0	-7.3	-14.9	-15.1	-7.0	-7.3	+18.7	+18.3
Massachusetts										
2019	16,640	241.3	81,399	1,180.6	12,323	178.7	62,944	912.9	6,132	88.9
2020	16,262	235.9	72,602	1,053.2	10,323	149.7	55,444	804.3	6,835	99.2
Percent change	-2.3	-2.3	-10.8	-10.8	-16.2	-16.2	-11.9	-11.9	+11.5	+11.5
New Hampshire										
2019	1,186	87.2	16,552	1,216.4	1,783	131.0	13,826	1,016.0	943	69.3
2020	1,166	85.3	15,014	1,098.9	1,412	103.3	12,558	919.1	1,044	76.4
Percent change	-1.7	-2.1	-9.3	-9.7	-20.8	-21.1	-9.2	-9.5	+10.7	+10.3
Rhode Island										
2019	1,412	133.4	16,312	1,541.5	2,321	219.3	12,628	1,193.4	1,363	128.8
2020	1,665	157.5	13,166	1,245.5	1,763	166.8	9,894	935.9	1,509	142.7
Percent change	+17.9	+18.0	-19.3	-19.2	-24.0	-24.0	-21.7	-21.6	+10.7	+10.8
Vermont										
2019	913	146.3	8,968	1,437.1	1,286	206.1	7,378	1,182.3	304	48.7
2020	790	126.7	7,586	1,217.0	961	154.2	6,361	1,020.5	264	42.4
Percent change	-13.5	-13.4	-15.4	-15.3	-25.3	-25.2	-13.8	-13.7	-13.2	-13.1
Middle Atlantic[5]										
2019	80,130	194.7	568,094	1,380.4	67,788	164.7	464,511	1,128.7	35,795	87.0
2020	91,729	223.7	585,830	1,428.8	76,760	187.2	463,662	1,130.8	45,408	110.7
Percent change	+14.5	+14.9	+3.1	+3.5	+13.2	+13.7	-0.2	+0.2	+26.9	+27.3
New Jersey										
2019	10,852	122.1	118,637	1,334.3	16,399	184.4	91,902	1,033.6	10,336	116.2
2020	11,363	127.9	102,875	1,158.2	12,983	146.2	79,614	896.3	10,278	115.7
Percent change	+4.7	+4.8	-13.3	-13.2	-20.8	-20.8	-13.4	-13.3	-0.6	-0.5
New York										
2019	44,888	230.6	269,787	1,386.1	28,065	144.2	228,672	1,174.9	13,050	67.0
2020	46,538	240.7	272,788	1,410.7	32,003	165.5	221,129	1,143.6	19,656	101.7
Percent change	+3.7	+4.4	+1.1	+1.8	+14.0	+14.8	-3.3	-2.7	+50.6	+51.6
Pennsylvania[5]										
2019	24,390	190.6	179,670	1,403.8	23,324	182.2	143,937	1,124.6	12,409	97.0
2020	33,828	264.6	210,167	1,644.1	31,774	248.6	162,919	1,274.5	15,474	121.0
Percent change	+38.7	+38.9	+17.0	+17.1	+36.2	+36.4	+13.2	+13.3	+24.7	+24.9
MIDWEST[6,7]										
2019	164,827	241.2	1,327,238	1,942.1	216,869	317.3	979,942	1,433.9	130,427	190.8
2020	186,587	273.1	1,219,817	1,785.5	195,963	286.8	877,996	1,285.2	145,858	213.5
Percent change	+13.2	+13.2	-8.1	-8.1	-9.6	-9.6	-10.4	-10.4	+11.8	+11.9
East North Central[6,7]										
2019	111,270	237.2	850,783	1,813.9	141,753	302.2	632,167	1,347.8	76,863	163.9
2020	124,445	265.7	755,390	1,612.9	123,212	263.1	547,556	1,169.1	84,622	180.7
Percent change	+11.8	+12.0	-11.2	-11.1	-13.1	-13.0	-13.4	-13.3	+10.1	+10.3
Illinois[6]										
2019	32,929	260.0	235,033	1,855.5	34,789	274.6	181,225	1,430.7	19,019	150.1
2020	35,110	278.9	196,287	1,559.4	31,020	246.4	143,935	1,143.5	21,332	169.5
Percent change	+6.6	+7.3	-16.5	-16.0	-10.8	-10.3	-20.6	-20.1	+12.2	+12.9
Indiana										
2019	16,745	248.8	131,097	1,947.7	21,586	320.7	95,745	1,422.4	13,766	204.5
2020	17,093	253.0	120,453	1,783.2	18,938	280.4	86,080	1,274.3	15,435	228.5
Percent change	+2.1	+1.7	-8.1	-8.4	-12.3	-12.6	-10.1	-10.4	+12.1	+11.7
Michigan										
2019	30,509	305.6	158,317	1,585.6	28,574	286.2	111,900	1,120.7	17,843	178.7
2020	36,384	365.1	135,633	1,360.9	23,231	233.1	94,017	943.3	18,385	184.5
Percent change	+19.3	+19.5	-14.3	-14.2	-18.7	-18.6	-16.0	-15.8	+3.0	+3.2
Ohio[7]										
2019	19,323	165.2	240,540	2,056.5	44,232	378.2	177,610	1,518.5	18,698	159.9
2020	22,406	191.6	216,363	1,850.3	37,279	318.8	159,007	1,359.8	20,077	171.7
Percent change	+16.0	+16.0	-10.1	-10.0	-15.7	-15.7	-10.5	-10.4	+7.4	+7.4

Table 4. Crime in the United States,[1] by Region, Geographic Division, and State, 2019–2020—Continued

(Number, rate per 100,000 population, percent.)

Area	Population[2]	Violent crime[3]		Murder and nonnegligent manslaughter		Rape (revised definition)[4]		Robbery	
		Number	Rate	Number	Rate	Number	Rate	Number	Rate
Wisconsin									
2019	5,824,581	17,305	297.1	189	3.2	2,358	40.5	2,994	51.4
2020	5,832,655	18,861	323.4	308	5.3	2,020	34.6	3,081	52.8
Percent change		+9.0	+8.8	63.0	+62.7	-14.3	-14.5	+2.9	+2.8
West North Central									
2019	21,436,181	76,684	357.7	954	4.5	10,778	50.3	11,395	53.2
2020	21,481,834	84,536	393.5	1,265	5.9	9,582	44.6	11,547	53.8
Percent change		+10.2	+10.0	+32.6	+32.3	-11.1	-11.3	+1.3	+1.1
Iowa[5]									
2019	3,159,596	9,086	287.6	70	2.2	1,365	43.2	919	29.1
2020	3,163,561	9,601	303.5	111	3.5	1,289	40.7	943	29.8
Percent change		+5.7	+5.5	+58.6	+58.4	-5.6	-5.7	+2.6	+2.5
Kansas									
2019	2,912,635	11,811	405.5	95	3.3	1,500	51.5	1,157	39.7
2020	2,913,805	12,385	425.0	100	3.4	1,263	43.3	928	31.8
Percent change		+4.9	+4.8	+5.3	+5.2	-15.8	-15.8	-19.8	-19.8
Minnesota									
2019	5,640,053	13,395	237.5	127	2.3	2,499	44.3	3,155	55.9
2020	5,657,342	15,698	277.5	190	3.4	2,211	39.1	3,877	68.5
Percent change		+17.2	+16.8	+49.6	+49.1	-11.5	-11.8	+22.9	+22.5
Missouri									
2019	6,140,475	30,680	499.6	576	9.4	3,019	49.2	4,995	81.3
2020	6,151,548	33,385	542.7	723	11.8	2,661	43.3	4,575	74.4
Percent change		+8.8	+8.6	+25.5	+25.3	-11.9	-12.0	-8.4	-8.6
Nebraska									
2019	1,932,571	5,887	304.6	45	2.3	1,284	66.4	795	41.1
2020	1,937,552	6,473	334.1	69	3.6	1,163	60.0	799	41.2
Percent change		+10.0	+9.7	+53.3	+52.9	-9.4	-9.7	+0.5	+0.2
North Dakota									
2019	763,724	2,302	301.4	25	3.3	464	60.8	184	24.1
2020	765,309	2,518	329.0	32	4.2	396	51.7	151	19.7
Percent change		+9.4	+9.2	+28.0	+27.7	-14.7	-14.8	-17.9	-18.1
South Dakota									
2019	887,127	3,523	397.1	16	1.8	647	72.9	190	21.4
2020	892,717	4,476	501.4	40	4.5	599	67.1	274	30.7
Percent change		+27.1	+26.3	+150.0	+148.4	-7.4	-8.0	+44.2	+43.3
SOUTH[6,7,8,9]									
2019	125,686,544	511,209	406.7	8,063	6.4	53,738	42.8	102,414	81.5
2020	126,662,754	546,535	431.5	10,156	8.0	48,307	38.1	91,100	71.9
Percent change		+6.9	+6.1	+26.0	+25.0	-10.1	-10.8	-11.0	-11.7
South Atlantic[5,8,9]									
2019	65,870,942	244,720	371.5	4,140	6.3	23,711	36.0	51,332	77.9
2020	66,392,969	258,241	389.0	5,102	7.7	21,529	32.4	44,562	67.1
Percent change		+5.5	+4.7	+23.2	+22.3	-9.2	-9.9	-13.2	-13.9
Delaware									
2019	976,668	4,128	422.7	47	4.8	329	33.7	789	80.8
2020	986,809	4,262	431.9	73	7.4	261	26.4	700	70.9
Percent change		+3.2	+2.2	+55.3	+53.7	-20.7	-21.5	-11.3	-12.2
District of Columbia[8]									
2019	708,253	7,403	1,045.2	166	23.4	345	48.7	2,714	383.2
2020	712,816	7,127	999.8	201	28.2	311	43.6	2,373	332.9
Percent change		-3.7	-4.3	+21.1	+20.3	-9.9	-10.4	-12.6	-13.1
Florida									
2019	21,492,056	81,291	378.2	1,122	5.2	8,463	39.4	16,234	75.5
2020	21,733,312	83,368	383.6	1,290	5.9	7,686	35.4	13,521	62.2
Percent change		+2.6	+1.4	+15.0	+13.7	-9.2	-10.2	-16.7	-17.6
Georgia[9]									
2019	10,628,020	34,666	326.2	605	5.7	3,005	28.3	7,488	70.5
2020	10,710,017	42,850	400.1	943	8.8	3,420	31.9	7,016	65.5
Percent change		+23.6	+22.7	+55.9	+54.7	+13.8	+12.9	-6.3	-7.0
Maryland[5]									
2019	6,054,954	27,511	454.4	545	9.0	1,944	32.1	9,215	152.2
2020	6,055,802	24,215	399.9	553	9.1	1,732	28.6	7,174	118.5
Percent change		-12.0	-12.0	+1.5	+1.5	-10.9	-10.9	-22.1	-22.2
North Carolina									
2019	10,501,384	39,773	378.7	653	6.2	3,364	32.0	7,700	73.3
2020	10,600,823	44,451	419.3	852	8.0	2,922	27.6	7,340	69.2
Percent change		+11.8	+10.7	+30.5	+29.3	-13.1	-14.0	-4.7	-5.6
South Carolina									
2019	5,157,702	26,307	510.1	455	8.8	2,528	49.0	3,325	64.5
2020	5,218,040	27,691	530.7	549	10.5	2,086	40.0	3,122	59.8
Percent change		+5.3	+4.0	+20.7	+19.3	-17.5	-18.4	-6.1	-7.2
Virginia									
2019	8,556,642	17,916	209.4	447	5.2	2,915	34.1	3,520	41.1
2020	8,590,563	17,925	208.7	524	6.1	2,279	26.5	2,947	34.3
Percent change		+0.1	-0.3	+17.2	+16.8	-21.8	-22.1	-16.3	-16.6
West Virginia									
2019	1,795,263	5,725	318.9	100	5.6	818	45.6	347	19.3
2020	1,784,787	6,352	355.9	117	6.6	832	46.6	369	20.7
Percent change		+11.0	+11.6	+17.0	+17.7	+1.7	+2.3	+6.3	+7.0

Table 4. Crime in the United States,[1] by Region, Geographic Division, and State, 2019–2020—Continued

(Number, rate per 100,000 population, percent.)

Area	Aggravated assault		Property crime		Burglary		Larceny-theft		Motor vehicle theft	
	Number	Rate	Number	Rate	Number	Rate	Number	Rate	Number	Rate
Wisconsin										
2019	11,764	202.0	85,796	1,473.0	12,572	215.8	65,687	1,127.8	7,537	129.4
2020	13,452	230.6	86,654	1,485.7	12,744	218.5	64,517	1,106.1	9,393	161.0
Percent change	+14.3	+14.2	+1.0	+0.9	+1.4	+1.2	-1.8	-1.9	+24.6	+24.5
West North Central										
2019	53,557	249.8	476,455	2,222.7	75,116	350.4	347,775	1,622.4	53,564	249.9
2020	62,142	289.3	464,427	2,162.0	72,751	338.7	330,440	1,538.2	61,236	285.1
Percent change	+16.0	+15.8	-2.5	-2.7	-3.1	-3.4	-5.0	-5.2	+14.3	+14.1
Iowa[5]										
2019	6,732	213.1	58,446	1,849.8	12,406	392.6	40,479	1,281.1	5,561	176.0
2020	7,258	229.4	53,725	1,698.2	11,739	371.1	35,751	1,130.1	6,235	197.1
Percent change	+7.8	+7.7	-8.1	-8.2	-5.4	-5.5	-11.7	-11.8	+12.1	+12.0
Kansas										
2019	9,059	311.0	66,306	2,276.5	9,996	343.2	49,420	1,696.7	6,890	236.6
2020	10,094	346.4	64,077	2,199.1	9,655	331.4	47,193	1,619.6	7,229	248.1
Percent change	+11.4	+11.4	-3.4	-3.4	-3.4	-3.5	-4.5	-4.5	+4.9	+4.9
Minnesota										
2019	7,614	135.0	117,971	2,091.7	16,026	284.1	90,685	1,607.9	11,260	199.6
2020	9,420	166.5	120,212	2,124.9	17,370	307.0	88,696	1,567.8	14,146	250.0
Percent change	+23.7	+23.3	+1.9	+1.6	+8.4	+8.1	-2.2	-2.5	+25.6	+25.2
Missouri										
2019	22,090	359.7	163,223	2,658.1	26,617	433.5	115,324	1,878.1	21,282	346.6
2020	25,426	413.3	155,698	2,531.0	23,300	378.8	108,209	1,759.1	24,189	393.2
Percent change	+15.1	+14.9	-4.6	-4.8	-12.5	-12.6	-6.2	-6.3	+13.7	+13.5
Nebraska										
2019	3,763	194.7	39,553	2,046.7	4,763	246.5	29,817	1,542.9	4,973	257.3
2020	4,442	229.3	36,991	1,909.2	4,455	229.9	27,488	1,418.7	5,048	260.5
Percent change	+18.0	+17.7	-6.5	-6.7	-6.5	-6.7	-7.8	-8.0	+1.5	+1.2
North Dakota										
2019	1,629	213.3	15,270	1,999.4	2,646	346.5	10,785	1,412.2	1,839	240.8
2020	1,939	253.4	16,256	2,124.1	3,196	417.6	10,986	1,435.5	2,074	271.0
Percent change	+19.0	+18.8	+6.5	+6.2	+20.8	+20.5	+1.9	+1.7	+12.8	+12.5
South Dakota										
2019	2,670	301.0	15,686	1,768.2	2,662	300.1	11,265	1,269.8	1,759	198.3
2020	3,563	399.1	17,468	1,956.7	3,036	340.1	12,117	1,357.3	2,315	259.3
Percent change	+33.4	+32.6	+11.4	+10.7	+14.0	+13.3	+7.6	+6.9	+31.6	+30.8
SOUTH[5,7,8,9]										
2019	346,994	276.1	3,008,909	2,394.0	498,381	396.5	2,229,081	1,773.5	281,447	223.9
2020	396,972	313.4	2,668,302	2,106.6	441,688	348.7	1,929,682	1,523.5	296,932	234.4
Percent change	+14.4	+13.5	-11.3	-12.0	-11.4	-12.1	-13.4	-14.1	+5.5	+4.7
South Atlantic[5,8,9]										
2019	165,537	251.3	1,498,001	2,274.1	223,239	338.9	1,151,490	1,748.1	123,272	187.1
2020	187,048	281.7	1,269,388	1,911.9	192,836	290.4	948,880	1,429.2	127,672	192.3
Percent change	+13.0	+12.1	-15.3	-15.9	-13.6	-14.3	-17.6	-18.2	+3.6	+2.8
Delaware										
2019	2,963	303.4	21,932	2,245.6	2,984	305.5	17,343	1,775.7	1,605	164.3
2020	3,228	327.1	19,355	1,961.4	2,508	254.2	15,182	1,538.5	1,665	168.7
Percent change	+8.9	+7.8	-11.7	-12.7	-16.0	-16.8	-12.5	-13.4	+3.7	+2.7
District of Columbia[8]										
2019	4,178	589.9	30,819	4,351.4	1,843	260.2	26,643	3,761.8	2,333	329.4
2020	4,242	595.1	24,899	3,493.0	1,964	275.5	19,536	2,740.7	3,399	476.8
Percent change	+1.5	+0.9	-19.2	-19.7	+6.6	+5.9	-26.7	-27.1	+45.7	+44.8
Florida										
2019	55,472	258.1	460,966	2,144.8	63,338	294.7	358,537	1,668.2	39,091	181.9
2020	60,871	280.1	384,556	1,769.4	52,293	240.6	293,992	1,352.7	38,271	176.1
Percent change	+9.7	+8.5	-16.6	-17.5	-17.4	-18.4	-18.0	-18.9	-2.1	-3.2
Georgia[9]										
2019	23,568	221.8	294,817	2,774.0	37,476	352.6	234,850	2,209.7	22,491	211.6
2020	31,471	293.8	214,988	2,007.4	31,139	290.7	158,343	1,478.5	25,506	238.2
Percent change	+33.5	+32.5	-27.1	-27.6	-16.9	-17.5	-32.6	-33.1	+13.4	+12.5
Maryland[5]										
2019	15,807	261.1	118,091	1,950.3	16,872	278.6	89,938	1,485.4	11,281	186.3
2020	14,756	243.7	97,487	1,609.8	15,261	252.0	71,757	1,184.9	10,469	172.9
Percent change	-6.6	-6.7	-17.4	-17.5	-9.5	-9.6	-20.2	-20.2	-7.2	-7.2
North Carolina										
2019	28,056	267.2	251,135	2,391.4	54,033	514.5	178,332	1,698.2	18,770	178.7
2020	33,337	314.5	236,026	2,226.5	49,952	471.2	165,554	1,561.7	20,520	193.6
Percent change	+18.8	+17.7	-6.0	-6.9	-7.6	-8.4	-7.2	-8.0	+9.3	+8.3
South Carolina										
2019	19,999	387.8	151,970	2,946.5	27,439	532.0	109,366	2,120.4	15,165	294.0
2020	21,934	420.3	141,987	2,721.1	23,377	448.0	103,892	1,991.0	14,718	282.1
Percent change	+9.7	+8.4	-6.6	-7.6	-14.8	-15.8	-5.0	-6.1	-2.9	-4.1
Virginia										
2019	11,034	129.0	140,944	1,647.2	13,972	163.3	116,656	1,363.3	10,316	120.6
2020	12,175	141.7	125,114	1,456.4	11,465	133.5	102,796	1,196.6	10,853	126.3
Percent change	+10.3	+9.9	-11.2	-11.6	-17.9	-18.3	-11.9	-12.2	+5.2	+4.8
West Virginia										
2019	4,460	248.4	27,327	1,522.2	5,282	294.2	19,825	1,104.3	2,220	123.7
2020	5,034	282.1	24,976	1,399.4	4,877	273.3	17,828	998.9	2,271	127.2
Percent change	+12.9	+13.5	-8.6	-8.1	-7.7	-7.1	-10.1	-9.5	+2.3	+2.9

Table 4. Crime in the United States,[1] by Region, Geographic Division, and State, 2019–2020—Continued

(Number, rate per 100,000 population, percent.)

Area	Population[2]	Violent crime[3]		Murder and nonnegligent manslaughter		Rape (revised definition)[4]		Robbery	
		Number	Rate	Number	Rate	Number	Rate	Number	Rate
East South Central[5,7]									
2019	19,188,862	83,328	434.3	1,432	7.5	7,659	39.9	13,868	72.3
2020	19,252,403	88,888	461.7	1,772	9.2	6,805	35.3	12,029	62.5
Percent change		+6.7	+6.3	+23.7	+23.3	-11.2	-11.4	-13.3	-13.5
Alabama[5]									
2019	4,907,965	24,769	504.7	390	7.9	2,119	43.2	3,922	79.9
2020	4,921,532	22,322	453.6	471	9.6	1,608	32.7	2,666	54.2
Percent change		-9.9	-10.1	+20.8	+20.4	-24.1	-24.3	-32.0	-32.2
Kentucky									
2019	4,472,345	9,872	220.7	229	5.1	1,673	37.4	2,162	48.3
2020	4,477,251	11,600	259.1	323	7.2	1,371	30.6	2,369	52.9
Percent change		+17.5	+17.4	+41.0	+40.9	-18.1	-18.1	+9.6	+9.5
Mississippi[7]									
2019	2,978,227	7,779	261.2	298	10.0	924	31.0	1,620	54.4
2020	2,966,786	8,638	291.2	315	10.6	1,148	38.7	1,419	47.8
Percent change		+11.0	+11.5	+5.7	+6.1	+24.2	+24.7	-12.4	-12.1
Tennessee									
2019	6,830,325	40,908	598.9	515	7.5	2,943	43.1	6,164	90.2
2020	6,886,834	46,328	672.7	663	9.6	2,678	38.9	5,575	81.0
Percent change		+13.2	+12.3	+28.7	+27.7	-9.0	-9.8	-9.6	-10.3
West South Central									
2019	40,626,740	183,161	450.8	2,491	6.1	22,368	55.1	37,214	91.6
2020	41,017,382	199,406	486.1	3,282	8.0	19,973	48.7	34,509	84.1
Percent change		+8.9	+7.8	+31.8	+30.5	-10.7	-11.6	-7.3	-8.2
Arkansas									
2019	3,020,985	17,547	580.8	237	7.8	2,420	80.1	1,576	52.2
2020	3,030,522	20,363	671.9	321	10.6	2,226	73.5	1,577	52.0
Percent change		+16.0	+15.7	+35.4	+35.0	-8.0	-8.3	+0.1	-0.3
Louisiana									
2019	4,658,285	26,072	559.7	547	11.7	2,282	49.0	4,129	88.6
2020	4,645,318	29,704	639.4	734	15.8	2,136	46.0	3,747	80.7
Percent change		+13.9	+14.2	+34.2	+34.6	-6.4	-6.1	-9.3	-9.0
Oklahoma									
2019	3,960,676	17,279	436.3	275	6.9	2,363	59.7	2,383	60.2
2020	3,980,783	18,255	458.6	296	7.4	2,102	52.8	2,351	59.1
Percent change		+5.6	+5.1	+7.6	+7.1	-11.0	-11.5	-1.3	-1.8
Texas									
2019	28,986,794	122,263	421.8	1,432	4.9	15,303	52.8	29,126	100.5
2020	29,360,759	131,084	446.5	1,931	6.6	13,509	46.0	26,834	91.4
Percent change		+7.2	+5.8	+34.8	+33.1	-11.7	-12.8	-7.9	-9.0
WEST[7]									
2019	78,300,384	324,766	414.8	3,223	4.1	36,943	47.2	79,250	101.2
2020	78,654,756	329,436	418.8	4,085	5.2	32,900	41.8	70,597	89.8
Percent change		+1.4	+1.0	+26.7	+26.2	-10.9	-11.3	-10.9	-11.3
Mountain									
2019	24,883,416	104,857	421.4	1,105	4.4	15,032	60.4	17,354	69.7
2020	25,213,395	110,732	439.2	1,366	5.4	13,508	53.6	16,927	67.1
Percent change		+5.6	+4.2	+23.6	+22.0	-10.1	-11.3	-2.5	-3.7
Arizona									
2019	7,291,843	32,603	447.1	397	5.4	3,650	50.1	6,305	86.5
2020	7,421,401	35,980	484.8	513	6.9	3,263	44.0	6,211	83.7
Percent change		+10.4	+8.4	+29.2	+27.0	-10.6	-12.2	-1.5	-3.2
Colorado									
2019	5,758,486	22,149	384.6	229	4.0	4,087	71.0	3,716	64.5
2020	5,807,719	24,570	423.1	294	5.1	3,652	62.9	3,964	68.3
Percent change		+10.9	+10.0	+28.4	+27.3	-10.6	-11.4	+6.7	+5.8
Idaho									
2019	1,789,060	4,162	232.6	28	1.6	918	51.3	161	9.0
2020	1,826,913	4,432	242.6	41	2.2	832	45.5	174	9.5
Percent change		+6.5	+4.3	+46.4	+43.4	-9.4	-11.2	+8.1	+5.8
Montana									
2019	1,070,123	4,472	417.9	32	3.0	679	63.5	209	19.5
2020	1,080,577	5,077	469.8	54	5.0	598	55.3	279	25.8
Percent change		+13.5	+12.4	+68.8	+67.1	-11.9	-12.8	+33.5	+32.2
Nevada									
2019	3,090,771	15,334	496.1	144	4.7	2,155	69.7	3,289	106.4
2020	3,138,259	14,445	460.3	180	5.7	1,851	59.0	2,785	88.7
Percent change		-5.8	-7.2	+25.0	+23.1	-14.1	-15.4	-15.3	-16.6
New Mexico									
2019	2,099,634	17,302	824.0	185	8.8	1,355	64.5	2,477	118.0
2020	2,106,319	16,393	778.3	164	7.8	1,170	55.5	2,086	99.0
Percent change		-5.3	-5.6	-11.4	-11.6	-13.7	-13.9	-15.8	-16.1
Utah									
2019	3,203,383	7,588	236.9	77	2.4	1,865	58.2	1,130	35.3
2020	3,249,879	8,471	260.7	102	3.1	1,809	55.7	1,362	41.9
Percent change		+11.6	+10.0	+32.5	+30.6	-3.0	-4.4	+20.5	+18.8
Wyoming									
2019	580,116	1,247	215.0	13	2.2	323	55.7	67	11.5
2020	582,328	1,364	234.2	18	3.1	333	57.2	66	11.3
Percent change		+9.4	+9.0	+38.5	+37.9	+3.1	+2.7	-1.5	-1.9

Table 4. Crime in the United States,[1] by Region, Geographic Division, and State, 2019–2020—Continued

(Number, rate per 100,000 population, percent.)

Area	Aggravated assault		Property crime		Burglary		Larceny-theft		Motor vehicle theft	
	Number	Rate	Number	Rate	Number	Rate	Number	Rate	Number	Rate
East South Central[5,7]										
2019	60,369	314.6	465,641	2,426.6	88,682	462.2	328,965	1,714.4	47,994	250.1
2020	68,282	354.7	418,860	2,175.6	76,034	394.9	293,222	1,523.0	49,604	257.7
Percent change	+13.1	+12.7	-10.0	-10.3	-14.3	-14.5	-10.9	-11.2	+3.4	+3.0
Alabama[5]										
2019	18,338	373.6	128,726	2,622.8	24,805	505.4	91,225	1,858.7	12,696	258.7
2020	17,577	357.1	105,161	2,136.8	19,660	399.5	74,575	1,515.3	10,926	222.0
Percent change	-4.1	-4.4	-18.3	-18.5	-20.7	-21.0	-18.3	-18.5	-13.9	-14.2
Kentucky										
2019	5,808	129.9	85,387	1,909.2	15,567	348.1	59,535	1,331.2	10,285	230.0
2020	7,537	168.3	79,673	1,779.5	15,407	344.1	52,769	1,178.6	11,497	256.8
Percent change	+29.8	+29.6	-6.7	-6.8	-1.0	-1.1	-11.4	-11.5	+11.8	+11.7
Mississippi[7]										
2019	4,937	165.8	69,727	2,341.2	18,341	615.8	45,665	1,533.3	5,721	192.1
2020	5,756	194.0	62,351	2,101.6	14,488	488.3	41,780	1,408.3	6,083	205.0
Percent change	+16.6	+17.0	-10.6	-10.2	-21.0	-20.7	-8.5	-8.2	+6.3	+6.7
Tennessee										
2019	31,286	458.0	181,801	2,661.7	29,969	438.8	132,540	1,940.5	19,292	282.4
2020	37,412	543.2	171,675	2,492.8	26,479	384.5	124,098	1,802.0	21,098	306.4
Percent change	+19.6	+18.6	-5.6	-6.3	-11.6	-12.4	-6.4	-7.1	+9.4	+8.5
West South Central										
2019	121,088	298.1	1,045,267	2,572.9	186,460	459.0	748,626	1,842.7	110,181	271.2
2020	141,642	345.3	980,054	2,389.4	172,818	421.3	687,580	1,676.3	119,656	291.7
Percent change	+17.0	+15.9	-6.2	-7.1	-7.3	-8.2	-8.2	-9.0	+8.6	+7.6
Arkansas										
2019	13,314	440.7	86,029	2,847.7	17,706	586.1	60,843	2,014.0	7,480	247.6
2020	16,239	535.8	79,200	2,613.4	15,854	523.1	55,413	1,828.5	7,933	261.8
Percent change	+22.0	+21.6	-7.9	-8.2	-10.5	-10.7	-8.9	-9.2	+6.1	+5.7
Louisiana										
2019	19,114	410.3	148,429	3,186.3	27,440	589.1	110,123	2,364.0	10,866	233.3
2020	23,087	497.0	133,989	2,884.4	23,698	510.1	97,891	2,107.3	12,400	266.9
Percent change	+20.8	+21.1	-9.7	-9.5	-13.6	-13.4	-11.1	-10.9	+14.1	+14.4
Oklahoma										
2019	12,258	309.5	113,504	2,865.8	26,820	677.2	73,199	1,848.1	13,485	340.5
2020	13,506	339.3	107,705	2,705.6	24,415	613.3	68,243	1,714.3	15,047	378.0
Percent change	+10.2	+9.6	-5.1	-5.6	-9.0	-9.4	-6.8	-7.2	+11.6	+11.0
Texas										
2019	76,402	263.6	697,305	2,405.6	114,494	395.0	504,461	1,740.3	78,350	270.3
2020	88,810	302.5	659,160	2,245.0	108,851	370.7	466,033	1,587.3	84,276	287.0
Percent change	+16.2	+14.8	-5.5	-6.7	-4.9	-6.1	-7.6	-8.8	+7.6	+6.2
WEST[7]										
2019	205,350	262.3	1,899,896	2,426.4	308,517	394.0	1,329,636	1,698.1	261,743	334.3
2020	221,854	282.1	1,798,441	2,286.5	297,779	378.6	1,197,396	1,522.3	303,266	385.6
Percent change	+8.0	+7.6	-5.3	-5.8	-3.5	-3.9	-9.9	-10.4	+15.9	+15.3
Mountain										
2019	71,366	286.8	591,703	2,377.9	96,771	388.9	423,075	1,700.2	71,857	288.8
2020	78,931	313.1	582,926	2,312.0	90,292	358.1	408,988	1,622.1	83,646	331.8
Percent change	+10.6	+9.2	-1.5	-2.8	-6.7	-7.9	-3.3	-4.6	+16.4	+14.9
Arizona										
2019	22,251	305.1	177,628	2,436.0	29,170	400.0	130,427	1,788.7	18,031	247.3
2020	25,993	350.2	165,323	2,227.7	24,488	330.0	122,898	1,656.0	17,937	241.7
Percent change	+16.8	+14.8	-6.9	-8.6	-16.1	-17.5	-5.8	-7.4	-0.5	-2.3
Colorado										
2019	14,117	245.2	150,564	2,614.6	20,266	351.9	108,575	1,885.5	21,723	377.2
2020	16,660	286.9	164,582	2,833.8	23,246	400.3	110,884	1,909.3	30,452	524.3
Percent change	+18.0	+17.0	+9.3	+8.4	+14.7	+13.7	+2.1	+1.3	+40.2	+39.0
Idaho										
2019	3,055	170.8	22,244	1,243.3	4,045	226.1	16,591	927.4	1,608	89.9
2020	3,385	185.3	20,313	1,111.9	3,731	204.2	14,815	810.9	1,767	96.7
Percent change	+10.8	+8.5	-8.7	-10.6	-7.8	-9.7	-10.7	-12.6	+9.9	+7.6
Montana										
2019	3,552	331.9	23,929	2,236.1	2,968	277.4	18,547	1,733.2	2,414	225.6
2020	4,146	383.7	22,917	2,120.8	2,919	270.1	17,322	1,603.0	2,676	247.6
Percent change	+16.7	+15.6	-4.2	-5.2	-1.7	-2.6	-6.6	-7.5	+10.9	+9.8
Nevada										
2019	9,746	315.3	72,028	2,330.4	15,630	505.7	45,127	1,460.1	11,271	364.7
2020	9,629	306.8	60,462	1,926.6	11,574	368.8	38,332	1,221.4	10,556	336.4
Percent change	-1.2	-2.7	-16.1	-17.3	-26.0	-27.1	-15.1	-16.3	-6.3	-7.8
New Mexico										
2019	13,285	632.7	66,744	3,178.8	14,640	697.3	42,749	2,036.0	9,355	445.6
2020	12,973	615.9	59,859	2,841.9	13,665	648.8	37,188	1,765.5	9,006	427.6
Percent change	-2.3	-2.7	-10.3	-10.6	-6.7	-7.0	-13.0	-13.3	-3.7	-4.0
Utah										
2019	4,516	141.0	69,469	2,168.6	8,658	270.3	54,078	1,688.2	6,733	210.2
2020	5,198	159.9	80,091	2,464.4	9,444	290.6	60,359	1,857.3	10,288	316.6
Percent change	+15.1	+13.5	+15.3	+13.6	+9.1	+7.5	+11.6	+10.0	+52.8	+50.6
Wyoming										
2019	844	145.5	9,097	1,568.1	1,394	240.3	6,981	1,203.4	722	124.5
2020	947	162.6	9,379	1,610.6	1,225	210.4	7,190	1,234.7	964	165.5
Percent change	+12.2	+11.8	+3.1	+2.7	-12.1	-12.5	+3.0	+2.6	+33.5	+33.0

Table 4. Crime in the United States,[1] by Region, Geographic Division, and State, 2019–2020—Continued

(Number, rate per 100,000 population, percent.)

Area	Population[2]	Violent crime[3]		Murder and nonnegligent manslaughter		Rape (revised definition)[4]		Robbery	
		Number	Rate	Number	Rate	Number	Rate	Number	Rate
Pacific[7]									
2019	53,416,968	219,909	411.7	2,118	4.0	21,911	41.0	61,896	115.9
2020	53,441,361	218,704	409.2	2,719	5.1	19,392	36.3	53,670	100.4
Percent change		-0.5	-0.6	+28.4	+28.3	-11.5	-11.5	-13.3	-13.3
Alaska									
2019	733,603	6,346	865.0	69	9.4	1,102	150.2	826	112.6
2020	731,158	6,126	837.8	49	6.7	1,132	154.8	712	97.4
Percent change		-3.5	-3.1	-29.0	-28.7	+2.7	+3.1	-13.8	-13.5
California									
2019	39,437,610	174,341	442.1	1,690	4.3	14,801	37.5	52,306	132.6
2020	39,368,078	174,026	442.0	2,203	5.6	13,449	34.2	44,728	113.6
Percent change		-0.2	*	+30.4	+30.6	-9.1	-9.0	-14.5	-14.3
Hawaii									
2019	1,415,615	3,745	264.5	37	2.6	625	44.2	1,079	76.2
2020	1,407,006	3,576	254.2	41	2.9	569	40.4	867	61.6
Percent change		-4.5	-3.9	+10.8	+11.5	-9.0	-8.4	-19.6	-19.2
Oregon[7]									
2019	4,216,116	12,382	293.7	117	2.8	1,886	44.7	2,329	55.2
2020	4,241,507	12,380	291.9	125	2.9	1,565	36.9	2,180	51.4
Percent change		*	-0.6	+6.8	+6.2	-17.0	-17.5	-6.4	-7.0
Washington									
2019	7,614,024	23,095	303.3	205	2.7	3,497	45.9	5,356	70.3
2020	7,693,612	22,596	293.7	301	3.9	2,677	34.8	5,183	67.4
Percent change		-2.2	-3.2	+46.8	+45.3	-23.4	-24.2	-3.2	-4.2
Puerto Rico									
2019	3,193,553	6,479	202.9	606	19.0	215	6.7	2,121	66.4
2020	3,159,343	5,196	164.5	529	16.7	148	4.7	1,177	37.3
Percent change		-19.8	-18.9	-12.7	-11.8	-31.2	-30.4	-44.5	-43.9

Table 4. Crime in the United States,[1] by Region, Geographic Division, and State, 2019–2020—Continued

(Number, rate per 100,000 population, percent.)

Area	Aggravated assault		Property crime		Burglary		Larceny-theft		Motor vehicle theft	
	Number	Rate	Number	Rate	Number	Rate	Number	Rate	Number	Rate
Pacific[7]										
2019	133,984	250.8	1,308,193	2,449.0	211,746	396.4	906,561	1,697.1	189,886	355.5
2020	142,923	267.4	1,215,515	2,274.5	207,487	388.3	788,408	1,475.3	219,620	411.0
Percent change	+6.7	+6.6	-7.1	-7.1	-2.0	-2.1	-13.0	-13.1	+15.7	+15.6
Alaska										
2019	4,349	592.8	21,293	2,902.5	3,558	485.0	15,118	2,060.8	2,617	356.7
2020	4,233	578.9	16,528	2,260.5	2,775	379.5	11,784	1,611.7	1,969	269.3
Percent change	-2.7	-2.3	-22.4	-22.1	-22.0	-21.7	-22.1	-21.8	-24.8	-24.5
California										
2019	105,544	267.6	921,177	2,335.8	152,551	386.8	626,865	1,589.5	141,761	359.5
2020	113,646	288.7	842,054	2,138.9	145,529	369.7	528,202	1,341.7	168,323	427.6
Percent change	+7.7	+7.9	-8.6	-8.4	-4.6	-4.4	-15.7	-15.6	+18.7	+18.9
Hawaii										
2019	2,004	141.6	40,617	2,869.2	5,534	390.9	29,878	2,110.6	5,205	367.7
2020	2,099	149.2	33,928	2,411.4	4,630	329.1	23,954	1,702.5	5,344	379.8
Percent change	+4.7	+5.4	-16.5	-16.0	-16.3	-15.8	-19.8	-19.3	+2.7	+3.3
Oregon[7]										
2019	8,050	190.9	117,567	2,788.5	15,127	358.8	86,922	2,061.7	15,518	368.1
2020	8,510	200.6	112,782	2,659.0	14,386	339.2	81,811	1,928.8	16,585	391.0
Percent change	+5.7	+5.1	-4.1	-4.6	-4.9	-5.5	-5.9	-6.4	+6.9	+6.2
Washington										
2019	14,037	184.4	207,539	2,725.7	34,976	459.4	147,778	1,940.9	24,785	325.5
2020	14,435	187.6	210,223	2,732.4	40,167	522.1	142,657	1,854.2	27,399	356.1
Percent change	+2.8	+1.8	+1.3	+0.2	+14.8	+13.7	-3.5	-4.5	+10.5	+9.4
Puerto Rico										
2019	3,537	110.8	22,441	702.7	4,291	134.4	14,483	453.5	3,667	114.8
2020	3,342	105.8	13,241	419.1	2,952	93.4	8,311	263.1	1,978	62.6
Percent change	-5.5	-4.5	-41.0	-40.4	-31.2	-30.5	-42.6	-42.0	-46.1	-45.5

NOTE: Although arson data are included in the trend and clearance tables, sufficient data are not available to estimate totals for this offense. Therefore, no arson data are published in this table.

* = Less than one-tenth of 1 percent.

1 The previous year's crime figures have been adjusted. 2 Population figures are U.S. Census Bureau provisional estimates as of July 1, 2020. 3 The violent crime figures include the offenses of murder, rape (revised definition), robbery, and aggravated assault. 4 The figures shown in this column for the offense of rape were estimated using the revised Uniform Crime Reporting (UCR) definition of rape. See chapter notes for more detail. 5 Limited data were available for Alabama, Maryland, and Pennsylvania. 6 The FBI determined that the state did not follow national UCR Program guidelines for reporting an offense. Consequently, those figures are not included in this table. The agency of Rockford submits independently and therefore includes all offenses. 7 This state's agencies submitted rape data according to the legacy UCR definition of rape. 8 Includes offenses reported by the Metro Transit Police and the District of Columbia Fire and Emergency Medical Services: Arson Investigation Unit. 9 Because of changes in the state/local agency's reporting practices, figures are not comparable to previous years' data.

Table 5. Crime in the United States, by State and Area, 2020

(Number, percent, rate per 100,000 population.)

Area	Population[1]	Violent crime[2]	Murder and nonnegligent manslaughter	Rape (revised definition)[3]	Robbery	Aggravated assault	Property crime	Burglary	Larceny-theft	Motor vehicle theft
Alabama[4]										
Metropolitan statistical area	3,750,044									
Area actually reporting	86.6%	16,638	319	1,147	2,260	12,912	75,971	13,921	53,997	8,053
Estimated total	100.0%	17,789	336	1,243	2,374	13,836	84,113	15,452	59,871	8,790
Cities outside metropolitan areas	527,001									
Area actually reporting	87.4%	2,834	73	188	204	2,369	13,407	2,276	10,061	1,070
Estimated total	100.0%	3,174	81	210	242	2,641	15,217	2,673	11,313	1,231
Nonmetropolitan counties	644,487									
Area actually reporting	71.5%	798	18	89	29	662	3,863	953	2,358	552
Estimated total	100.0%	1,359	54	155	50	1,100	5,831	1,535	3,391	905
State total	4,921,532	22,322	471	1,608	2,666	17,577	105,161	19,660	74,575	10,926
Rate per 100,000 inhabitants		453.6	9.6	32.7	54.2	357.1	2,136.8	399.5	1,515.3	222.0
Alaska										
Metropolitan statistical area	338,179									
Area actually reporting	100.0%	3,853	21	596	608	2,628	11,760	1,668	8,678	1,414
Cities outside metropolitan areas	127,563									
Area actually reporting	90.6%	900	8	266	55	571	2,147	315	1,685	147
Estimated total	100.0%	946	9	269	64	604	2,391	355	1,860	176
Nonmetropolitan counties	265,416									
Area actually reporting	100.0%	1,327	19	267	40	1,001	2,377	752	1,246	379
State total	731,158	6,126	49	1,132	712	4,233	16,528	2,775	11,784	1,969
Rate per 100,000 inhabitants		837.8	6.7	154.8	97.4	578.9	2,260.5	379.5	1,611.7	269.3
Arizona										
Metropolitan statistical area	7,066,114									
Area actually reporting	93.0%	30,068	431	2,971	6,094	20,572	152,680	21,627	114,824	16,229
Estimated total	100.0%	31,245	457	3,083	6,134	21,571	158,648	22,997	118,727	16,924
Cities outside metropolitan areas	126,679									
Area actually reporting	85.2%	4,000	37	158	57	3,748	4,253	1,012	2,625	616
Estimated total	100.0%	4,207	39	168	67	3,933	4,929	1,092	3,170	667
Nonmetropolitan counties	228,608									
Area actually reporting	73.0%	314	10	9	8	287	1,204	321	655	228
Estimated total	100.0%	528	17	12	10	489	1,746	399	1,001	346
State total	7,421,401	35,980	513	3,263	6,211	25,993	165,323	24,488	122,898	17,937
Rate per 100,000 inhabitants		484.8	6.9	44.0	83.7	350.2	2,227.7	330.0	1,656.0	241.7
Arkansas										
Metropolitan statistical area	1,927,318									
Area actually reporting	95.0%	13,909	184	1,353	1,153	11,219	53,598	10,190	37,829	5,579
Estimated total	100.0%	14,275	189	1,390	1,216	11,480	55,526	10,497	39,220	5,809
Cities outside metropolitan areas	494,464									
Area actually reporting	97.9%	3,637	91	449	228	2,869	15,072	3,329	10,673	1,070
Estimated total	100.0%	3,674	91	451	237	2,895	15,277	3,362	10,820	1,095
Nonmetropolitan counties	608,740									
Area actually reporting	79.8%	1,957	33	338	48	1,538	5,998	1,608	3,648	742
Estimated total	100.0%	2,414	41	385	124	1,864	8,397	1,995	5,373	1,029
State total	3,030,522	20,363	321	2,226	1,577	16,239	79,200	15,854	55,413	7,933
Rate per 100,000 inhabitants		671.9	10.6	73.5	52.0	535.8	2,613.4	523.1	1,828.5	261.8
California										
Metropolitan statistical area	38,539,958									
Area actually reporting	99.9%	170,104	2,158	12,997	44,286	110,663	827,403	141,667	519,418	166,318
Estimated total	100.0%	170,131	2,158	13,000	44,291	110,682	827,545	141,689	519,521	166,335
Cities outside metropolitan areas	268,242									
Area actually reporting	100.0%	1,583	9	149	281	1,144	6,887	1,501	4,407	979
Nonmetropolitan counties	559,878									
Area actually reporting	100.0%	2,312	36	300	156	1,820	7,622	2,339	4,274	1,009
State total	39,368,078	174,026	2,203	13,449	44,728	113,646	842,054	145,529	528,202	168,323
Rate per 100,000 inhabitants		442.0	5.6	34.2	113.6	288.7	2,138.9	369.7	1,341.7	427.6
Colorado										
Metropolitan statistical area	5,093,407									
Area actually reporting	99.5%	22,960	277	3,289	3,862	15,532	151,647	21,038	101,466	29,143
Estimated total	100.0%	23,015	277	3,297	3,872	15,569	152,467	21,104	102,105	29,258
Cities outside metropolitan areas	345,449									
Area actually reporting	96.4%	963	10	223	74	656	8,425	1,151	6,610	664
Estimated total	100.0%	989	10	228	75	676	8,696	1,184	6,819	693
Nonmetropolitan counties	368,863									
Area actually reporting	91.5%	523	7	118	16	382	3,103	872	1,775	456
Estimated total	100.0%	566	7	127	17	415	3,419	958	1,960	501
State total	5,807,719	24,570	294	3,652	3,964	16,660	164,582	23,246	110,884	30,452
Rate per 100,000 inhabitants		423.1	5.1	62.9	68.3	286.9	2,833.8	400.3	1,909.3	524.3
Connecticut										
Metropolitan statistical area	2,958,732									
Area actually reporting	100.0%	6,159	130	530	1,982	3,517	52,571	6,158	38,631	7,782
Cities outside metropolitan areas	111,501									
Area actually reporting	100.0%	87	1	13	24	49	1,225	124	952	149
Nonmetropolitan counties	486,773									
Area actually reporting	100.0%	213	9	51	27	126	1,874	374	1,009	491
State total	3,557,006	6,459	140	594	2,033	3,692	55,670	6,656	40,592	8,422
Rate per 100,000 inhabitants		181.6	3.9	16.7	57.2	103.8	1,565.1	187.1	1,141.2	236.8

Table 5. Crime in the United States, by State and Area, 2020—Continued

(Number, percent, rate per 100,000 population.)

Area	Population[1]	Violent crime[2]	Murder and nonnegligent manslaughter	Rape (revised definition)[3]	Robbery	Aggravated assault	Property crime	Burglary	Larceny-theft	Motor vehicle theft
Delaware										
Metropolitan statistical area	986,809									
Area actually reporting	100.0%	4,262	73	261	700	3,228	19,355	2,508	15,182	1,665
Cities outside metropolitan areas	None									
Nonmetropolitan counties	None									
State total	986,809	4,262	73	261	700	3,228	19,355	2,508	15,182	1,665
Rate per 100,000 inhabitants		431.9	7.4	26.4	70.9	327.1	1,961.4	254.2	1,538.5	168.7
District of Columbia[5]										
Metropolitan statistical area	712,816									
Area actually reporting	100.0%	7,127	201	311	2,373	4,242	24,899	1,964	19,536	3,399
Cities outside metropolitan areas	None									
Nonmetropolitan counties	None									
District total	712,816	7,127	201	311	2,373	4,242	24,899	1,964	19,536	3,399
Rate per 100,000 inhabitants		999.8	28.2	43.6	332.9	595.1	3,493.0	275.5	2,740.7	476.8
Florida										
Metropolitan statistical area	21,043,573									
Area actually reporting	99.8%	80,320	1,238	7,441	13,205	58,436	371,991	49,202	285,586	37,203
Estimated total	100.0%	80,538	1,240	7,456	13,241	58,601	373,436	49,404	286,718	37,314
Cities outside metropolitan areas	140,051									
Area actually reporting	92.0%	843	18	50	102	673	3,756	839	2,607	310
Estimated total	100.0%	885	18	54	111	702	3,983	876	2,769	338
Nonmetropolitan counties	549,688									
Area actually reporting	93.5%	1,810	30	163	145	1,472	6,423	1,900	3,989	534
Estimated total	100.0%	1,945	32	176	169	1,568	7,137	2,013	4,505	619
State total	21,733,312	83,368	1,290	7,686	13,521	60,871	384,556	52,293	293,992	38,271
Rate per 100,000 inhabitants		383.6	5.9	35.4	62.2	280.1	1,769.4	240.6	1,352.7	176.1
Georgia[6]										
Metropolitan statistical area	8,903,595									
Area actually reporting	70.7%	27,159	615	2,092	4,533	19,919	129,465	16,813	95,500	17,152
Estimated total	100.0%	37,571	855	2,843	6,496	27,377	182,131	24,901	134,357	22,873
Cities outside metropolitan areas	641,416									
Area actually reporting	61.6%	1,842	38	180	234	1,390	12,023	1,767	9,555	701
Estimated total	100.0%	2,700	47	274	353	2,026	18,207	2,740	14,355	1,112
Nonmetropolitan counties	1,165,006									
Area actually reporting	75.9%	1,905	28	244	105	1,528	10,588	2,403	7,078	1,107
Estimated total	100.0%	2,579	41	303	167	2,068	14,650	3,498	9,631	1,521
State total	10,710,017	42,850	943	3,420	7,016	31,471	214,988	31,139	158,343	25,506
Rate per 100,000 inhabitants		400.1	8.8	31.9	65.5	293.8	2,007.4	290.7	1,478.5	238.2
Hawaii										
Metropolitan statistical area	1,133,616									
Area actually reporting	14.7%	379	5	71	59	244	3,537	496	2,612	429
Estimated total	100.0%	2,769	27	401	798	1,543	28,815	3,791	20,438	4,586
Cities outside metropolitan areas	None									
Nonmetropolitan counties	273,390									
Area actually reporting	100.0%	807	14	168	69	556	5,113	839	3,516	758
State total	1,407,006	3,576	41	569	867	2,099	33,928	4,630	23,954	5,344
Rate per 100,000 inhabitants		254.2	2.9	40.4	61.6	149.2	2,411.4	329.1	1,702.5	379.8
Idaho										
Metropolitan statistical area	1,361,287									
Estimated total	99.9%	3,582	26	693	159	2,704	16,647	2,974	12,205	1,468
Area actually reporting	100.0%	3,583	26	693	159	2,705	16,653	2,975	12,210	1,468
Cities outside metropolitan areas	186,575									
Area actually reporting	96.3%	366	3	49	10	304	2,052	362	1,543	147
Estimated total	100.0%	380	3	51	10	316	2,135	380	1,603	152
Nonmetropolitan counties	279,051									
Area actually reporting	100.0%	469	12	88	5	364	1,525	376	1,002	147
State total	1,826,913	4,432	41	832	174	3,385	20,313	3,731	14,815	1,767
Rate per 100,000 inhabitants		242.6	2.2	45.5	9.5	185.3	1,111.9	204.2	810.9	96.7
Illinois[7]										
Metropolitan statistical area	11,178,842									
Area actually reporting	94.3%	48,707	1,086	4,258	11,829	31,534	170,797	25,705	125,469	19,623
Estimated total	100.0%	49,959	1,105	4,438	12,019	32,397	178,768	27,076	131,388	20,304
Cities outside metropolitan areas	800,198									
Area actually reporting	81.3%	2,047	13	380	157	1,497	11,607	2,131	8,870	606
Estimated total	100.0%	2,324	13	402	168	1,741	13,375	2,564	10,139	672
Nonmetropolitan counties	608,490									
Area actually reporting	88.9%	1,268	33	239	74	922	3,639	1,208	2,115	316
Estimated total	100.0%	1,329	33	250	74	972	4,144	1,380	2,408	356
State total	12,587,530	53,612	1,151	5,090	12,261	35,110	196,287	31,020	143,935	21,332
Rate per 100,000 inhabitants		425.9	9.1	40.4	97.4	278.9	1,559.4	246.4	1,143.5	169.5
Indiana										
Metropolitan statistical area	5,294,758									
Area actually reporting	88.2%	20,174	458	1,692	3,998	14,026	95,762	14,562	68,534	12,666
Estimated total	100.0%	21,151	464	1,812	4,104	14,771	102,523	16,051	73,029	13,443
Cities outside metropolitan areas	560,706									
Area actually reporting	55.8%	726	8	88	33	597	5,881	705	4,756	420
Estimated total	100.0%	1,345	11	176	60	1,098	11,226	1,398	9,016	812

Table 5. Crime in the United States, by State and Area, 2020—Continued

(Number, percent, rate per 100,000 population.)

Area	Population[1]	Violent crime[2]	Murder and nonnegligent manslaughter	Rape (revised definition)[3]	Robbery	Aggravated assault	Property crime	Burglary	Larceny-theft	Motor vehicle theft
Nonmetropolitan counties	899,489									
Area actually reporting	52.0%	1,133	27	211	35	860	3,491	723	2,154	614
Estimated total	100.0%	1,665	30	360	51	1,224	6,704	1,489	4,035	1,180
State total	6,754,953	24,161	505	2,348	4,215	17,093	120,453	18,938	86,080	15,435
Rate per 100,000 inhabitants		357.7	7.5	34.8	62.4	253.0	1,783.2	280.4	1,274.3	228.5
Iowa										
Metropolitan statistical area	1,947,544									
Area actually reporting	97.4%	6,581	90	774	813	4,904	39,132	8,154	26,184	4,794
Estimated total	100.0%	6,721	90	801	825	5,005	39,935	8,334	26,736	4,865
Cities outside metropolitan areas	568,224									
Area actually reporting	96.3%	1,922	14	308	100	1,500	10,086	2,145	7,080	861
Estimated total	100.0%	1,992	14	317	102	1,559	10,450	2,222	7,337	891
Nonmetropolitan counties	647,793									
Area actually reporting	98.0%	859	7	169	8	675	3,151	1,118	1,591	442
Estimated total	100.0%	888	7	171	16	694	3,340	1,183	1,678	479
State total	3,163,561	9,601	111	1,289	943	7,258	53,725	11,739	35,751	6,235
Rate per 100,000 inhabitants		303.5	3.5	40.7	29.8	229.4	1,698.2	371.1	1,130.1	197.1
Kansas										
Metropolitan statistical area	2,032,826									
Area actually reporting	79.5%	8,485	76	773	697	6,939	40,181	5,580	29,847	4,754
Estimated total	100.0%	9,430	83	881	774	7,692	47,379	6,354	35,268	5,757
Cities outside metropolitan areas	561,423									
Area actually reporting	92.4%	2,017	8	291	125	1,593	12,770	2,028	9,782	960
Estimated total	100.0%	2,205	9	310	131	1,755	13,453	2,226	10,180	1,047
Nonmetropolitan counties	319,556									
Area actually reporting	96.1%	722	8	68	23	623	3,089	1,003	1,679	407
Estimated total	100.0%	750	8	72	23	647	3,245	1,075	1,745	425
State total	2,913,805	12,385	100	1,263	928	10,094	64,077	9,655	47,193	7,229
Rate per 100,000 inhabitants		425.0	3.4	43.3	31.8	346.4	2,199.1	331.4	1,619.6	248.1
Kentucky										
Metropolitan statistical area	2,672,178									
Area actually reporting	99.9%	9,441	241	809	2,117	6,274	60,950	10,833	41,376	8,741
Estimated total	100.0%	9,446	241	809	2,119	6,277	61,003	10,841	41,415	8,747
Cities outside metropolitan areas	528,590									
Area actually reporting	99.5%	846	15	180	157	494	10,407	1,957	7,336	1,114
Estimated total	100.0%	849	15	180	157	497	10,475	1,970	7,384	1,121
Nonmetropolitan counties	1,276,483									
Area actually reporting	100.0%	1,305	67	382	93	763	8,195	2,596	3,970	1,629
State total	4,477,251	11,600	323	1,371	2,369	7,537	79,673	15,407	52,769	11,497
Rate per 100,000 inhabitants		259.1	7.2	30.6	52.9	168.3	1,779.5	344.1	1,178.6	256.8
Louisiana										
Metropolitan statistical area	3,917,340									
Area actually reporting	94.3%	24,966	626	1,774	3,312	19,254	114,133	19,428	84,040	10,665
Estimated total	100.0%	25,881	638	1,857	3,459	19,927	119,029	20,211	87,609	11,209
Cities outside metropolitan areas	264,144									
Area actually reporting	76.6%	1,757	51	68	164	1,474	7,688	1,793	5,494	401
Estimated total	100.0%	1,985	51	92	202	1,640	8,934	1,991	6,394	549
Nonmetropolitan counties	463,834									
Area actually reporting	91.1%	1,677	42	172	56	1,407	5,184	1,361	3,292	531
Estimated total	100.0%	1,838	45	187	86	1,520	6,026	1,496	3,888	642
State total	4,645,318	29,704	734	2,136	3,747	23,087	133,989	23,698	97,891	12,400
Rate per 100,000 inhabitants		639.4	15.8	46.0	80.7	497.0	2,884.4	510.1	2,107.3	266.9
Maine										
Metropolitan statistical area	803,976									
Area actually reporting	100.0%	797	11	236	119	431	9,312	1,011	7,795	506
Cities outside metropolitan areas	254,490									
Area actually reporting	100.0%	353	4	111	42	196	3,917	501	3,242	174
Nonmetropolitan counties	291,675									
Area actually reporting	100.0%	316	7	139	9	161	2,381	497	1,702	182
State total	1,350,141	1,466	22	486	170	788	15,610	2,009	12,739	862
Rate per 100,000 inhabitants		108.6	1.6	36.0	12.6	58.4	1,156.2	148.8	943.5	63.8
Maryland[4]										
Metropolitan statistical area	5,905,671									
Area actually reporting	100.0%	23,755	548	1,700	7,114	14,393	95,548	14,906	70,271	10,371
Cities outside metropolitan areas	51,424									
Area actually reporting	100.0%	349	4	18	53	274	1,323	203	1,051	69
Nonmetropolitan counties	98,707									
Area actually reporting	100.0%	111	1	14	7	89	616	152	435	29
State total	6,055,802	24,215	553	1,732	7,174	14,756	97,487	15,261	71,757	10,469
Rate per 100,000 inhabitants		399.9	9.1	28.6	118.5	243.7	1,609.8	252.0	1,184.9	172.9
Massachusetts										
Metropolitan statistical area	6,864,763									
Area actually reporting	99.2%	21,064	160	1,818	2,995	16,091	71,962	10,234	54,919	6,809
Estimated total	100.0%	21,186	160	1,837	3,012	16,177	72,225	10,289	55,107	6,829
Cities outside metropolitan areas	28,811									
Area actually reporting	100.0%	102	0	14	3	85	377	34	337	6

Table 5. Crime in the United States, by State and Area, 2020—Continued

(Number, percent, rate per 100,000 population.)

Area	Population[1]	Violent crime[2]	Murder and nonnegligent manslaughter	Rape (revised definition)[3]	Robbery	Aggravated assault	Property crime	Burglary	Larceny-theft	Motor vehicle theft
Nonmetropolitan counties										
Area actually reporting	100.0%	0	0	0	0	0	0	0	0	0
State total	6,893,574	21,288	160	1,851	3,015	16,262	72,602	10,323	55,444	6,835
Rate per 100,000 inhabitants		308.8	2.3	26.9	43.7	235.9	1,053.2	149.7	804.3	99.2
Michigan										
Metropolitan statistical area	8,171,665									
Area actually reporting	97.7%	42,329	712	4,587	4,283	32,747	116,391	19,432	80,101	16,858
Estimated total	100.0%	42,773	715	4,669	4,315	33,074	118,153	19,707	81,403	17,043
Cities outside metropolitan areas	574,930									
Area actually reporting	99.9%	1,702	14	437	83	1,168	7,910	894	6,533	483
Estimated total	100.0%	1,703	14	437	83	1,169	7,921	895	6,542	484
Nonmetropolitan counties	1,219,960									
Area actually reporting	99.0%	3,146	25	955	40	2,126	9,493	2,616	6,023	854
Estimated total	100.0%	3,165	25	959	40	2,141	9,559	2,629	6,072	858
State total	9,966,555	47,641	754	6,065	4,438	36,384	135,633	23,231	94,017	18,385
Rate per 100,000 inhabitants		478.0	7.6	60.9	44.5	365.1	1,360.9	233.1	943.3	184.5
Minnesota										
Metropolitan statistical area	4,414,276									
Area actually reporting	99.9%	13,564	170	1,792	3,773	7,829	103,367	14,521	76,020	12,826
Estimated total	100.0%	13,568	170	1,793	3,773	7,832	103,424	14,527	76,068	12,829
Cities outside metropolitan areas	575,358									
Area actually reporting	99.2%	1,385	11	270	83	1,021	11,045	1,389	8,933	723
Estimated total	100.0%	1,392	11	270	83	1,028	11,145	1,403	9,013	729
Nonmetropolitan counties	667,708									
Area actually reporting	100.0%	738	9	148	21	560	5,643	1,440	3,615	588
State total	5,657,342	15,698	190	2,211	3,877	9,420	120,212	17,370	88,696	14,146
Rate per 100,000 inhabitants		277.5	3.4	39.1	68.5	166.5	2,124.9	307.0	1,567.8	250.0
Mississippi										
Metropolitan statistical area	1,441,468									
Area actually reporting	77.5%	3,692	177	410	885	2,220	28,621	5,026	20,558	3,037
Estimated total	100.0%	4,412	186	628	938	2,660	33,213	5,817	23,818	3,578
Cities outside metropolitan areas	555,942									
Area actually reporting	49.0%	1,305	49	119	174	963	9,620	2,583	6,416	621
Estimated total	100.0%	2,370	73	213	310	1,774	18,048	5,038	11,866	1,144
Nonmetropolitan counties	969,376									
Area actually reporting	46.9%	925	32	132	94	667	5,085	1,838	2,691	556
Estimated total	100.0%	1,856	56	307	171	1,322	11,090	3,633	6,096	1,361
State total	2,966,786	8,638	315	1,148	1,419	5,756	62,351	14,488	41,780	6,083
Rate per 100,000 inhabitants		291.2	10.6	38.7	47.8	194.0	2,101.6	488.3	1,408.3	205.0
Missouri										
Metropolitan statistical area	4,621,557									
Area actually reporting	99.3%	28,401	656	2,102	4,317	21,326	125,871	17,644	87,324	20,903
Estimated total	100.0%	28,614	656	2,112	4,346	21,500	126,817	17,778	87,968	21,071
Cities outside metropolitan areas	635,377									
Area actually reporting	95.9%	2,573	35	315	146	2,077	18,815	2,949	14,378	1,488
Estimated total	100.0%	2,654	35	321	147	2,151	19,564	3,070	14,941	1,553
Nonmetropolitan counties	894,614									
Area actually reporting	95.9%	2,027	31	223	80	1,693	8,914	2,347	5,061	1,506
Estimated total	100.0%	2,117	32	228	82	1,775	9,317	2,452	5,300	1,565
State total	6,151,548	33,385	723	2,661	4,575	25,426	155,698	23,300	108,209	24,189
Rate per 100,000 inhabitants		542.7	11.8	43.3	74.4	413.3	2,531.0	378.8	1,759.1	393.2
Montana										
Metropolitan statistical area	386,281									
Area actually reporting	100.0%	2,000	21	235	194	1,550	12,719	1,597	9,723	1,399
Cities outside metropolitan areas	235,155									
Area actually reporting	98.7%	1,729	13	191	47	1,478	5,019	540	3,971	508
Estimated total	100.0%	1,747	13	194	47	1,493	5,089	547	4,027	515
Nonmetropolitan counties	459,141									
Area actually reporting	99.4%	1,323	20	169	38	1,096	5,081	770	3,552	759
Estimated total	100.0%	1,330	20	169	38	1,103	5,109	775	3,572	762
State total	1,080,577	5,077	54	598	279	4,146	22,917	2,919	17,322	2,676
Rate per 100,000 inhabitants	*	469.8	5.0	55.3	25.8	383.7	2,120.8	270.1	1,603.0	247.6
Nebraska										
Metropolitan statistical area	1,272,351									
Area actually reporting	99.0%	5,058	51	840	689	3,478	28,674	3,136	21,292	4,246
Estimated total	100.0%	5,102	51	846	695	3,510	28,866	3,165	21,422	4,279
Cities outside metropolitan areas	341,322									
Area actually reporting	93.1%	812	10	224	55	523	5,428	774	4,203	451
Estimated total	100.0%	910	10	237	71	592	5,869	855	4,542	472
Nonmetropolitan counties	323,879									
Area actually reporting	86.1%	295	8	63	5	219	1,347	293	868	186
Estimated total	100.0%	461	8	80	33	340	2,256	435	1,524	297
State total	1,937,552	6,473	69	1,163	799	4,442	36,991	4,455	27,488	5,048
Rate per 100,000 inhabitants		334.1	3.6	60.0	41.2	229.3	1,909.2	229.9	1,418.7	260.5
Nevada										
Metropolitan statistical area	2,853,689									
Area actually reporting	100.0%	13,540	155	1,741	2,709	8,935	56,841	10,635	36,142	10,064

Table 5. Crime in the United States, by State and Area, 2020—Continued

(Number, percent, rate per 100,000 population.)

Area	Population[1]	Violent crime[2]	Murder and nonnegligent manslaughter	Rape (revised definition)[3]	Robbery	Aggravated assault	Property crime	Burglary	Larceny-theft	Motor vehicle theft
Cities outside metropolitan areas	48,735									
Area actually reporting	100.0%	217	11	30	29	147	1,155	273	748	134
Nonmetropolitan counties	235,835									
Area actually reporting	100.0%	688	14	80	47	547	2,466	666	1,442	358
State total	3,138,259	14,445	180	1,851	2,785	9,629	60,462	11,574	38,332	10,556
Rate per 100,000 inhabitants		460.3	5.7	59.0	88.7	306.8	1,926.6	368.8	1,221.4	336.4
New Hampshire										
Metropolitan statistical area	862,794									
Area actually reporting	99.2%	1,274	9	306	203	756	8,897	774	7,500	623
Estimated total	100.0%	1,301	9	310	207	775	9,038	797	7,602	639
Cities outside metropolitan areas	467,654									
Area actually reporting	95.6%	568	1	206	57	304	5,264	497	4,444	323
Estimated total	100.0%	646	1	214	71	360	5,682	563	4,745	374
Nonmetropolitan counties	35,827									
Area actually reporting	92.2%	42	2	17	0	23	238	43	171	24
Estimated total	100.0%	53	2	18	2	31	294	52	211	31
State total	1,366,275	2,000	12	542	280	1,166	15,014	1,412	12,558	1,044
Rate per 100,000 inhabitants		146.4	0.9	39.7	20.5	85.3	1,098.9	103.3	919.1	76.4
New Jersey										
Metropolitan statistical area	8,882,371									
Area actually reporting	100.0%	17,353	329	1,277	4,384	11,363	102,875	12,983	79,614	10,278
Cities outside metropolitan areas	None									
Nonmetropolitan counties	None									
State total	8,882,371	17,353	329	1,277	4,384	11,363	102,875	12,983	79,614	10,278
Rate per 100,000 inhabitants		195.4	3.7	14.4	49.4	127.9	1,158.2	146.2	896.3	115.7
New Mexico										
Metropolitan statistical area	1,418,447									
Area actually reporting	100.0%	11,598	109	809	1,768	8,912	44,460	9,501	27,801	7,158
Cities outside metropolitan areas	395,987									
Area actually reporting	94.0%	2,753	29	216	262	2,246	11,207	2,802	7,250	1,155
Estimated total	100.0%	2,896	32	229	270	2,365	11,968	2,939	7,758	1,271
Nonmetropolitan counties	291,885									
Area actually reporting	96.0%	1,881	23	131	46	1,681	3,307	1,148	1,592	567
Estimated total	100.0%	1,899	23	132	48	1,696	3,431	1,225	1,629	577
State total	2,106,319	16,393	164	1,170	2,086	12,973	59,859	13,665	37,188	9,006
Rate per 100,000 inhabitants		778.3	7.8	55.5	99.0	615.9	2,841.9	648.8	1,765.5	427.6
New York										
Metropolitan statistical area	17,993,042									
Area actually reporting	99.3%	67,582	783	4,604	17,267	44,928	255,315	29,045	207,497	18,773
Estimated total	100.0%	67,805	783	4,632	17,310	45,080	257,063	29,270	208,938	18,855
Cities outside metropolitan areas	492,133									
Area actually reporting	95.3%	1,060	7	208	117	728	7,862	1,192	6,402	268
Estimated total	100.0%	1,098	7	218	119	754	8,404	1,263	6,858	283
Nonmetropolitan counties	851,601									
Area actually reporting	92.9%	1,361	14	595	56	696	7,158	1,466	5,318	374
Estimated total	100.0%	1,436	18	618	96	704	7,321	1,470	5,333	518
State total	19,336,776	70,339	808	5,468	17,525	46,538	272,788	32,003	221,129	19,656
Rate per 100,000 inhabitants		363.8	4.2	28.3	90.6	240.7	1,410.7	165.5	1,143.6	101.7
North Carolina										
Metropolitan statistical area	8,612,057									
Area actually reporting	88.8%	32,769	561	1,966	5,855	24,387	170,639	31,200	124,252	15,187
Estimated total	100.0%	36,136	615	2,248	6,444	26,829	191,181	35,707	138,329	17,145
Cities outside metropolitan areas	588,746									
Area actually reporting	78.1%	3,290	81	207	431	2,571	18,779	4,953	12,715	1,111
Estimated total	100.0%	4,113	97	245	564	3,207	23,894	6,564	15,955	1,375
Nonmetropolitan counties	1,400,020									
Area actually reporting	84.9%	3,378	113	359	267	2,639	17,352	6,346	9,329	1,677
Estimated total	100.0%	4,202	140	429	332	3,301	20,951	7,681	11,270	2,000
State total	10,600,823	44,451	852	2,922	7,340	33,337	236,026	49,952	165,554	20,520
Rate per 100,000 inhabitants		419.3	8.0	27.6	69.2	314.5	2,226.5	471.2	1,561.7	193.6
North Dakota										
Metropolitan statistical area	382,437									
Area actually reporting	100.0%	1,273	18	237	110	908	10,531	2,121	7,318	1,092
Cities outside metropolitan areas	193,373									
Area actually reporting	100.0%	1,045	12	113	32	888	4,261	734	2,818	709
Nonmetropolitan counties	189,499									
Area actually reporting	100.0%	200	2	46	9	143	1,464	341	850	273
State total	765,309	2,518	32	396	151	1,939	16,256	3,196	10,986	2,074
Rate per 100,000 inhabitants		329.0	4.2	51.7	19.7	253.4	2,124.1	417.6	1,435.5	271.0
Ohio[8]										
Metropolitan statistical area	9,394,238									
Area actually reporting	90.3%	31,161	764	3,932	7,216	19,249	167,695	29,577	121,075	17,043
Estimated total	100.0%	32,797	774	4,237	7,522	20,264	183,497	31,741	133,675	18,081
Cities outside metropolitan areas	1,012,995									
Area actually reporting	76.4%	1,350	12	338	166	834	14,656	1,943	12,103	610
Estimated total	100.0%	1,739	13	414	225	1,087	20,824	2,627	17,319	878

Table 5. Crime in the United States, by State and Area, 2020—Continued

(Number, percent, rate per 100,000 population.)

Area	Population[1]	Violent crime[2]	Murder and nonnegligent manslaughter	Rape (revised definition)[3]	Robbery	Aggravated assault	Property crime	Burglary	Larceny-theft	Motor vehicle theft
Nonmetropolitan counties	1,285,984									
Area actually reporting	85.0%	1,349	27	342	64	916	10,102	2,441	6,742	919
Estimated total	100.0%	1,568	33	401	79	1,055	12,042	2,911	8,013	1,118
State total	11,693,217	36,104	820	5,052	7,826	22,406	216,363	37,279	159,007	20,077
Rate per 100,000 inhabitants		308.8	7.0	43.2	66.9	191.6	1,850.3	318.8	1,359.8	171.7
Oklahoma										
Metropolitan statistical area	2,660,978									
Area actually reporting	100.0%	13,795	225	1,554	2,028	9,988	77,442	16,896	49,075	11,471
Cities outside metropolitan areas	731,657									
Area actually reporting	99.9%	3,247	38	382	289	2,538	22,973	5,121	15,474	2,378
Estimated total	100.0%	3,250	38	382	289	2,541	22,999	5,128	15,490	2,381
Nonmetropolitan counties	588,148									
Area actually reporting	98.0%	1,185	33	162	33	957	7,110	2,338	3,603	1,169
Estimated total	100.0%	1,210	33	166	34	977	7,264	2,391	3,678	1,195
State total	3,980,783	18,255	296	2,102	2,351	13,506	107,705	24,415	68,243	15,047
Rate per 100,000 inhabitants		458.6	7.4	52.8	59.1	339.3	2,705.6	613.3	1,714.3	378.0
Oregon[8]										
Metropolitan statistical area	3,560,965									
Area actually reporting	96.3%	10,123	96	1,227	1,975	6,825	94,922	11,466	68,855	14,601
Estimated total	100.0%	10,389	96	1,287	2,018	6,988	97,297	11,799	70,580	14,918
Cities outside metropolitan areas	315,863									
Area actually reporting	97.4%	1,020	12	174	134	700	10,030	1,399	7,802	829
Estimated total	100.0%	1,040	12	178	137	713	10,233	1,438	7,957	838
Nonmetropolitan counties	364,679									
Area actually reporting	90.3%	884	15	90	22	757	4,748	1,040	2,945	763
Estimated total	100.0%	951	17	100	25	809	5,252	1,149	3,274	829
State total	4,241,507	12,380	125	1,565	2,180	8,510	112,782	14,386	81,811	16,585
Rate per 100,000 inhabitants		291.9	2.9	36.9	51.4	200.6	2,659.0	339.2	1,928.8	391.0
Pennsylvania[4]										
Metropolitan statistical area	11,346,468									
Area actually reporting	56.3%	26,424	672	1,887	6,619	17,246	93,715	12,118	72,972	8,625
Estimated total	100.0%	45,360	943	3,753	9,972	30,692	187,212	27,994	144,943	14,275
Cities outside metropolitan areas	638,381									
Area actually reporting	63.9%	522	12	91	68	351	3,649	503	3,025	121
Estimated total	100.0%	1,397	16	174	226	981	8,237	1,239	6,364	634
Nonmetropolitan counties	798,405									
Area actually reporting	0.1%	4	0	1	0	3	10	0	10	0
Estimated total	100.0%	3,036	50	301	530	2,155	14,718	2,541	11,612	565
State total	12,783,254	49,793	1,009	4,228	10,728	33,828	210,167	31,774	162,919	15,474
Rate per 100,000 inhabitants		389.5	7.9	33.1	83.9	264.6	1,644.1	248.6	1,274.5	121.0
Puerto Rico										
Metropolitan statistical area	3,159,343									
Area actually reporting	100.0%	4,939	508	142	1,153	3,136	12,937	2,831	8,151	1,955
Cities outside metropolitan areas										
Area actually reporting	100.0%	257	21	6	24	206	304	121	160	23
Total	3,159,343	5,196	529	148	1,177	3,342	13,241	2,952	8,311	1,978
Rate per 100,000 inhabitants		164.5	16.7	4.7	37.3	105.8	419.1	93.4	263.1	62.6
Rhode Island										
Metropolitan statistical area	1,057,125									
Area actually reporting	100.0%	2,440	32	407	336	1,665	13,166	1,763	9,894	1,509
Cities outside metropolitan areas	None									
Nonmetropolitan counties	None									
State total	1,057,125	2,440	32	407	336	1,665	13,166	1,763	9,894	1,509
Rate per 100,000 inhabitants		230.8	3.0	38.5	31.8	157.5	1,245.5	166.8	935.9	142.7
South Carolina										
Metropolitan statistical area	4,482,389									
Area actually reporting	98.9%	22,153	412	1,782	2,722	17,237	119,049	18,299	88,013	12,737
Estimated total	100.0%	22,439	423	1,799	2,751	17,466	120,444	18,534	89,047	12,863
Cities outside metropolitan areas	202,374									
Area actually reporting	95.3%	2,073	56	92	189	1,736	9,021	1,804	6,683	534
Estimated total	100.0%	2,146	59	95	196	1,796	9,391	1,873	6,958	560
Nonmetropolitan counties	533,277									
Area actually reporting	95.2%	2,965	65	184	167	2,549	11,580	2,831	7,514	1,235
Estimated total	100.0%	3,106	67	192	175	2,672	12,152	2,970	7,887	1,295
State total	5,218,040	27,691	549	2,086	3,122	21,934	141,987	23,377	103,892	14,718
Rate per 100,000 inhabitants		530.7	10.5	40.0	59.8	420.3	2,721.1	448.0	1,991.0	282.1
South Dakota										
Metropolitan statistical area	432,981									
Area actually reporting	99.4%	2,270	30	336	223	1,681	11,251	1,970	7,647	1,634
Estimated total	100.0%	2,279	30	336	225	1,688	11,301	1,977	7,684	1,640
Cities outside metropolitan areas	220,585									
Area actually reporting	96.2%	1,807	7	206	21	1,573	4,399	665	3,278	456
Estimated total	100.0%	1,836	7	209	25	1,595	4,567	691	3,401	475
Nonmetropolitan counties	239,151									
Area actually reporting	85.9%	236	2	43	1	190	921	261	541	119
Estimated total	100.0%	361	3	54	24	280	1,600	368	1,032	200

Table 5. Crime in the United States, by State and Area, 2020—Continued

(Number, percent, rate per 100,000 population.)

Area	Population[1]	Violent crime[2]	Murder and nonnegligent manslaughter	Rape (revised definition)[3]	Robbery	Aggravated assault	Property crime	Burglary	Larceny-theft	Motor vehicle theft
State total	892,717	4,476	40	599	274	3,563	17,468	3,036	12,117	2,315
Rate per 100,000 inhabitants		501.4	4.5	67.1	30.7	399.1	1,956.7	340.1	1,357.3	259.3
Tennessee										
Metropolitan statistical area	5,395,999									
Area actually reporting	100.0%	40,585	602	2,198	5,346	32,439	145,547	21,208	106,428	17,911
Cities outside metropolitan areas	487,422									
Area actually reporting	100.0%	2,780	27	200	159	2,394	14,532	2,231	11,025	1,276
Nonmetropolitan counties	1,003,413									
Area actually reporting	100.0%	2,963	34	280	70	2,579	11,596	3,040	6,645	1,911
State total	6,886,834	46,328	663	2,678	5,575	37,412	171,675	26,479	124,098	21,098
Rate per 100,000 inhabitants		672.7	9.6	38.9	81.0	543.2	2,492.8	384.5	1,802.0	306.4
Texas										
Metropolitan statistical area	26,246,546									
Area actually reporting	99.8%	122,935	1,809	12,239	26,282	82,605	613,723	96,741	437,257	79,725
Estimated total	100.0%	123,092	1,809	12,258	26,293	82,732	614,731	96,947	437,942	79,842
Cities outside metropolitan areas	1,450,340									
Area actually reporting	96.3%	4,930	65	683	430	3,752	28,072	6,515	19,073	2,484
Estimated total	100.0%	5,023	65	685	432	3,841	28,809	6,732	19,494	2,583
Nonmetropolitan counties	1,663,873									
Area actually reporting	98.8%	2,934	57	561	109	2,207	15,400	5,101	8,476	1,823
Estimated total	100.0%	2,969	57	566	109	2,237	15,620	5,172	8,597	1,851
State total	29,360,759	131,084	1,931	13,509	26,834	88,810	659,160	108,851	466,033	84,276
Rate per 100,000 inhabitants		446.5	6.6	46.0	91.4	302.5	2,245.0	370.7	1,587.3	287.0
Utah										
Metropolitan statistical area	2,911,284									
Area actually reporting	92.9%	6,761	82	1,423	1,155	4,101	67,990	7,892	51,407	8,691
Estimated total	100.0%	7,667	91	1,575	1,337	4,664	75,331	8,749	56,842	9,740
Cities outside metropolitan areas	156,076									
Area actually reporting	80.7%	311	5	110	13	183	2,097	233	1,654	210
Estimated total	100.0%	390	5	138	16	231	2,592	280	2,041	271
Nonmetropolitan counties	182,519									
Area actually reporting	91.0%	376	6	84	9	277	1,953	362	1,339	252
Estimated total	100.0%	414	6	96	9	303	2,168	415	1,476	277
State total	3,249,879	8,471	102	1,809	1,362	5,198	80,091	9,444	60,359	10,288
Rate per 100,000 inhabitants		260.7	3.1	55.7	41.9	159.9	2,464.4	290.6	1,857.3	316.6
Vermont										
Metropolitan statistical area	221,248									
Area actually reporting	100.0%	439	5	115	32	287	3,561	362	3,116	83
Cities outside metropolitan areas	190,219									
Area actually reporting	100.0%	384	3	64	24	293	2,846	341	2,409	96
Nonmetropolitan counties	211,880									
Area actually reporting	100.0%	258	6	34	8	210	1,179	258	836	85
State total	623,347	1,081	14	213	64	790	7,586	961	6,361	264
Rate per 100,000 inhabitants		173.4	2.2	34.2	10.3	126.7	1,217.0	154.2	1,020.5	42.4
Virginia										
Metropolitan statistical area	7,542,652									
Area actually reporting	99.9%	15,961	438	1,905	2,814	10,804	112,733	9,615	93,273	9,845
Estimated total	100.0%	15,963	438	1,906	2,814	10,805	112,764	9,621	93,297	9,846
Cities outside metropolitan areas	242,932									
Area actually reporting	99.6%	538	22	94	45	377	5,265	581	4,384	300
Estimated total	100.0%	540	22	94	45	379	5,282	584	4,397	301
Nonmetropolitan counties	804,979									
Area actually reporting	100.0%	1,422	64	279	88	991	7,068	1,260	5,102	706
State total	8,590,563	17,925	524	2,279	2,947	12,175	125,114	11,465	102,796	10,853
Rate per 100,000 inhabitants		208.7	6.1	26.5	34.3	141.7	1,456.4	133.5	1,196.6	126.3
Washington	6,908,760									
Metropolitan statistical area	99.8%	21,080	269	2,395	5,037	13,379	195,996	36,804	133,204	25,988
Area actually reporting	100.0%	21,102	269	2,398	5,041	13,394	196,238	36,852	133,377	26,009
Estimated total	316,271									
Cities outside metropolitan areas	93.5%	859	11	160	103	585	8,375	1,539	6,061	775
Area actually reporting	100.0%	902	11	169	105	617	8,951	1,699	6,415	837
Estimated total	468,581									
Nonmetropolitan counties	100.0%	592	21	110	37	424	5,034	1,616	2,865	553
Area actually reporting	7,693,612	22,596	301	2,677	5,183	14,435	210,223	40,167	142,657	27,399
State total		293.7	3.9	34.8	67.4	187.6	2,732.4	522.1	1,854.2	356.1
Rate per 100,000 inhabitants										
West Virginia	1,152,948									
Metropolitan statistical area	83.1%	3,276	61	543	261	2,411	16,207	3,282	11,446	1,479
Area actually reporting	100.0%	4,091	68	598	313	3,112	18,269	3,640	13,024	1,605
Estimated total	172,139									
Cities outside metropolitan areas	61.5%	414	3	48	13	350	1,798	197	1,505	96
Area actually reporting	100.0%	1,094	3	59	15	1,017	3,596	365	3,018	213
Estimated total	459,700									
Nonmetropolitan counties	90.5%	1,094	40	166	40	848	2,939	820	1,688	431
Area actually reporting	100.0%	1,167	46	175	41	905	3,111	872	1,786	453
Estimated total	1,784,787	6,352	117	832	369	5,034	24,976	4,877	17,828	2,271

Table 5. Crime in the United States, by State and Area, 2020—Continued

(Number, percent, rate per 100,000 population.)

Area	Population[1]	Violent crime[2]	Murder and nonnegligent manslaughter	Rape (revised definition)[3]	Robbery	Aggravated assault	Property crime	Burglary	Larceny-theft	Motor vehicle theft
State total		355.9	6.6	46.6	20.7	282.1	1,399.4	273.3	998.9	127.2
Rate per 100,000 inhabitants										
Wisconsin	4,359,969									
Metropolitan statistical area	99.3%	16,356	270	1,541	2,960	11,585	70,961	10,348	52,276	8,337
Area actually reporting	100.0%	16,454	271	1,551	2,977	11,655	71,533	10,430	52,706	8,397
Estimated total	642,656									
Cities outside metropolitan areas	96.3%	1,359	11	297	50	1,001	9,127	743	7,900	484
Area actually reporting	100.0%	1,442	11	304	65	1,062	9,585	813	8,235	537
Estimated total	830,030									
Nonmetropolitan counties	97.2%	874	24	156	23	671	5,062	1,426	3,233	403
Area actually reporting	100.0%	965	26	165	39	735	5,536	1,501	3,576	459
State total	5,832,655	18,861	308	2,020	3,081	13,452	86,654	12,744	64,517	9,393
Rate per 100,000 inhabitants		323.4	5.3	34.6	52.8	230.6	1,485.7	218.5	1,106.1	161.0
Wyoming										
Metropolitan statistical area	181,286									
Area actually reporting	100.0%	513	7	114	45	347	4,571	547	3,512	512
Cities outside metropolitan areas	237,938									
Area actually reporting	96.4%	591	5	166	12	408	3,562	421	2,819	322
Estimated total	100.0%	621	5	167	18	431	3,736	449	2,944	343
Nonmetropolitan counties	163,104									
Area actually reporting	92.0%	210	5	49	3	153	995	205	688	102
Estimated total	100.0%	230	6	52	3	169	1,072	229	734	109
State total	582,328	1,364	18	333	66	947	9,379	1,225	7,190	964
Rate per 100,000 inhabitants		234.2	3.1	57.2	11.3	162.6	1,610.6	210.4	1,234.7	165.5

NOTE: Although arson data are included in the trend and clearance tables, sufficient data are not available to estimate totals for this offense. Therefore, no arson data are published in this table.
1 Population figures are U.S. Census Bureau provisional estimates as of July 1, 2020. 2 The violent crime figures include the offenses of murder, rape (revised definition), robbery, and aggravated assault. 3 The figures shown in this column for the offense of rape (revised definition) were estimated using the revised Uniform Crime Reporting (UCR) definition of rape. See chapter notes for further explanation. 4 Limited data for 2020 were available for Alabama, Maryland, and Pennsylvania.
5 Includes offenses reported by the Metro Transit Police and the Arson Investigation Unit of the District of Columbia Fire and Emergency Medical Services. 6 Because of changes in the state/local agency's reporting practices, figures are not comparable to previous years' data. 7 The FBI determined that the state did not follow national UCR Program guidelines for reporting an offense. Consequently, those figures are not included in this table. The agency of Rockford submits independently and therefore includes all offenses. 8 This state's agencies submitted rape data according to the legacy UCR definition of rape.

Table 6. Crime in the United States, by Selected Metropolitan Statistical Area, 2020

(Number, percent, rate per 100,000 population.)

Area	Population	Violent crime	Murder and nonnegligent manslaughter	Rape[1]	Robbery	Aggravated assault	Property crime	Burglary	Larceny-theft	Motor vehicle theft
Abilene, TX M.S.A.	172,211									
Includes Callahan, Jones, and Taylor Counties										
City of Abilene	124,061	514	3	117	63	331	2,649	435	2,013	201
Total area actually reporting	100.0%	611	6	142	64	399	3,088	568	2,269	251
Rate per 100,000 inhabitants		354.8	3.5	82.5	37.2	231.7	1,793.1	329.8	1,317.6	145.8
Akron, OH M.S.A.	702,634									
Includes Portage and Summit Counties										
City of Akron	197,433	1,797	47	215	268	1,267	6,971	1,288	4,855	828
Total area actually reporting	95.9%	2,599	55	330	347	1,867	14,557	2,315	10,999	1,243
Estimated total	100.0%	2,659	55	359	354	1,891	15,032	2,375	11,389	1,268
Rate per 100,000 inhabitants		378.4	7.8	51.1	50.4	269.1	2,139.4	338.0	1,620.9	180.5
Albany, GA M.S.A.[2]	145,715									
Includes Dougherty,[2] Lee,[2] Terrell, and Worth[2] Counties										
City of Albany[2]	71,567	1,234	19	40	132	1,043	3,148	575	2,234	339
Total area actually reporting	96.2%	1,451	23	68	147	1,213	4,200	821	2,897	482
Estimated total	100.0%	1,469	23	70	151	1,225	4,281	837	2,953	491
Rate per 100,000 inhabitants		1,008.1	15.8	48.0	103.6	840.7	2,937.9	574.4	2,026.6	337.0
Albany-Lebanon, OR M.S.A.	130,611									
Includes Linn County										
City of Albany	48,329	72	2	12	24	34	1,336	97	1,134	105
City of Lebanon	17,635	23	0	4	1	18	297	23	251	23
Total area actually reporting	100.0%	195	7	34	31	123	2,821	345	2,212	264
Rate per 100,000 inhabitants		149.3	5.4	26.0	23.7	94.2	2,159.8	264.1	1,693.6	202.1
Albany-Schenectady-Troy, NY M.S.A.	875,848									
Includes Albany, Rensselaer, Saratoga, Schenectady, and Schoharie Counties										
City of Albany	96,318	869	16	61	161	631	2,650	422	1,945	283
City of Schenectady	65,176	468	5	26	90	347	1,622	266	1,187	169
City of Troy	49,052	330	9	16	68	237	1,411	263	1,026	122
Total area actually reporting	99.7%	2,382	34	306	432	1,610	14,535	1,782	11,839	914
Estimated total	100.0%	2,386	34	307	433	1,612	14,552	1,785	11,852	915
Rate per 100,000 inhabitants		272.4	3.9	35.1	49.4	184.1	1,661.5	203.8	1,353.2	104.5
Albuquerque, NM M.S.A.	923,729									
Includes Bernalillo, Sandoval, Torrancc, and Valencia Counties										
City of Albuquerque	562,065	7,552	80	441	1,439	5,592	28,171	5,075	18,131	4,965
Total area actually reporting	100.0%	9,296	87	566	1,585	7,058	33,754	6,356	21,278	6,120
Rate per 100,000 inhabitants		1,006.4	9.4	61.3	171.6	764.1	3,654.1	688.1	2,303.5	662.5
Alexandria, LA M.S.A.	151,268									
Includes Grant and Rapides Parishes										
City of Alexandria	45,986	850	19	15	145	671	3,317	754	2,300	263
Total area actually reporting	82.1%	1,363	21	53	172	1,117	5,534	1,455	3,610	469
Estimated total	100.0%	1,464	22	62	190	1,190	6,079	1,541	4,004	534
Rate per 100,000 inhabitants		967.8	14.5	41.0	125.6	786.7	4,018.7	1,018.7	2,647.0	353.0
Amarillo, TX M.S.A.[2]	265,667									
Includes Armstrong, Carson, Oldham,[2] Potter, and Randall Counties										
City of Amarillo	200,296	1,676	15	141	241	1,279	7,369	1,400	4,903	1,066
Total area actually reporting	99.9%	1,787	18	168	249	1,352	8,082	1,561	5,353	1,168
Estimated total	100.0%	1,787	18	168	249	1,352	8,083	1,561	5,354	1,168
Rate per 100,000 inhabitants		672.6	6.8	63.2	93.7	508.9	3,042.5	587.6	2,015.3	439.6
Ames, IA M.S.A.[3]	124,033									
Includes Boone3 and Story Counties										
City of Ames	67,109	122	0	54	15	53	1,189	218	903	68
Total area actually reporting	94.6%	201	1	64	15	121			1,183	117
Estimated total	100.0%	228	1	67	19	141			1,386	128
Rate per 100,000 inhabitants		183.8	0.8	54.0	15.3	113.7			1,117.4	103.2
Anchorage, AK M.S.A.	305,257									
Includes Anchorage Municipality and Matanuska-Susitna Borough										
City of Anchorage	286,388	3,472	18	558	558	2,338	9,872	1,444	7,279	1,149
Total area actually reporting	100.0%	3,576	18	570	566	2,422	10,393	1,488	7,703	1,202
Rate per 100,000 inhabitants		1,171.5	5.9	186.7	185.4	793.4	3,404.7	487.5	2,523.4	393.8
Ann Arbor, MI M.S.A.	368,868									
Includes Washtenaw County										
City of Ann Arbor	120,647	294	1	49	38	206	1,592	153	1,358	81
Total area actually reporting	100.0%	1,521	9	233	134	1,145	4,670	569	3,698	403
Rate per 100,000 inhabitants		412.3	2.4	63.2	36.3	310.4	1,266.0	154.3	1,002.5	109.3
Appleton, WI M.S.A.	239,143									
Includes Calumet and Outagamie Counties										
City of Appleton	72,570	194	1	35	19	139	1,129	125	942	62

Table 6. Crime in the United States, by Selected Metropolitan Statistical Area, 2020—Continued

(Number, percent, rate per 100,000 population.)

Area	Population	Violent crime	Murder and nonnegligent manslaughter	Rape[1]	Robbery	Aggravated assault	Property crime	Burglary	Larceny-theft	Motor vehicle theft
Total area actually reporting	97.4%	385	3	83	28	271	2,672	299	2,228	145
Estimated total	100.0%	408	3	85	32	288	2,798	319	2,319	160
Rate per 100,000 inhabitants		170.6	1.3	35.5	13.4	120.4	1,170.0	133.4	969.7	66.9
Asheville, NC M.S.A.	467,076									
Includes Buncombe, Haywood, Henderson, and Madison Counties										
City of Asheville	93,980	761	11	54	153	543	5,395	730	4,142	523
Total area actually reporting	77.1%	1,240	20	105	207	908	10,540	2,170	7,312	1,058
Estimated total	100.0%	1,481	24	135	234	1,088	12,301	2,638	8,439	1,224
Rate per 100,000 inhabitants		317.1	5.1	28.9	50.1	232.9	2,633.6	564.8	1,806.8	262.1
Athens-Clarke County, GA M.S.A.[2]	215,827									
Includes Clarke, Madison,[2] Oconee, and Oglethorpe[2] Counties										
City of Athens-Clarke County[2]	128,152	654	4	105	102	443	3,785	597	2,837	351
Total area actually reporting	80.4%	777	4	117	105	551	4,368	732	3,221	415
Estimated total	100.0%	834	6	123	112	593	4,719	789	3,482	448
Rate per 100,000 inhabitants		386.4	2.8	57.0	51.9	274.8	2,186.5	365.6	1,613.3	207.6
Atlantic City-Hammonton, NJ M.S.A.	262,199									
Includes Atlantic County										
City of Atlantic City	37,550	309	9	28	116	156	1,013	139	785	89
City of Hammonton	13,845	23	0	0	0	23	189	37	145	7
Total area actually reporting	100.0%	665	17	55	183	410	5,054	793	3,978	283
Rate per 100,000 inhabitants		253.6	6.5	21.0	69.8	156.4	1,927.5	302.4	1,517.2	107.9
Austin-Round Rock-Georgetown, TX M.S.A.[2]	2,283,668									
Includes Bastrop, Caldwell,[2] Hays,[2] Travis,[2] and Williamson Counties										
City of Austin	1,000,276	4,671	44	478	1,101	3,048	36,322	4,774	27,481	4,067
City of Round Rock[2]	137,593	185	3	25	55	102	2,282	235	1,954	93
City of Georgetown	84,210	123	4	50	16	53	1,077	148	836	93
City of San Marcos	67,432	283	2	99	32	150	1,419	260	1,017	142
Total area actually reporting	100.0%	7,207	74	995	1,424	4,714	54,045	7,687	40,683	5,675
Rate per 100,000 inhabitants		315.6	3.2	43.6	62.4	206.4	2,366.6	336.6	1,781.5	248.5
Bakersfield, CA M.S.A.	897,941									
Includes Kern County										
City of Bakersfield	388,265	2,007	44	106	604	1,253	15,619	3,134	8,656	3,829
Total area actually reporting	100.0%	6,216	116	331	1,190	4,579	27,890	6,358	13,995	7,537
Rate per 100,000 inhabitants		692.3	12.9	36.9	132.5	509.9	3,106.0	708.1	1,558.6	839.4
Bangor, ME M.S.A.	152,409									
Includes Penobscot County										
City of Bangor	32,179	51	2	7	13	29	1,207	100	1,044	63
Total area actually reporting	100.0%	88	6	12	16	54	2,339	260	1,950	129
Rate per 100,000 inhabitants		57.7	3.9	7.9	10.5	35.4	1,534.7	170.6	1,279.5	84.6
Barnstable Town, MA M.S.A.	211,545									
Includes Barnstable County										
City of Barnstable	44,169	188	0	30	12	146	350	52	281	17
Total area actually reporting	100.0%	635	3	92	28	512	1,730	374	1,288	68
Rate per 100,000 inhabitants		300.2	1.4	43.5	13.2	242.0	817.8	176.8	608.9	32.1
Baton Rouge, LA M.S.A.[2]	855,151									
Includes Ascension, Assumption, East Baton Rouge, East Feliciana, Iberville,[2] Livingston, Pointe Coupee, St. Helena, West Baton Rouge, and West Feliciana Parishes										
City of Baton Rouge	219,245	2,087	102	55	457	1,473	10,580	1,898	7,854	828
Total area actually reporting	97.8%	4,734	143	218	653	3,720	26,001	3,884	20,343	1,774
Estimated total	100.0%	4,839	144	223	662	3,810	26,433	3,977	20,637	1,819
Rate per 100,000 inhabitants		565.9	16.8	26.1	77.4	445.5	3,091.0	465.1	2,413.3	212.7
Battle Creek, MI M.S.A	133,509									
Includes Calhoun County										
City of Battle Creek	60,479	540	8	38	30	464	1,569	335	1,066	168
Total area actually reporting	100.0%	886	14	101	48	723	3,170	574	2,326	270
Rate per 100,000 inhabitants		663.6	10.5	75.7	36.0	541.5	2,374.4	429.9	1,742.2	202.2
Bay City, MI M.S.A.	102,285									
Includes Bay County										
City of Bay City	32,485	276	0	48	25	203	500	104	331	65
Total area actually reporting	100.0%	384	3	90	32	259	1,084	206	760	118
Rate per 100,000 inhabitants		375.4	2.9	88.0	31.3	253.2	1,059.8	201.4	743.0	115.4
Beaumont-Port Arthur, TX M.S.A.[2]	391,609									
Includes Hardin,[2] Jefferson, and Orange[2] Counties										
City of Beaumont[2]	116,766	1,431	20	79	300	1,032	3,863	955	2,546	362
City of Port Arthur[2]	54,257	422	7	42	76	297	1,253	346	775	132
Total area actually reporting	99.9%	2,371	35	181	432	1,723	8,028	2,000	5,102	926
Estimated total	100.0%	2,372	35	181	432	1,724	8,036	2,002	5,107	927
Rate per 100,000 inhabitants		605.7	8.9	46.2	110.3	440.2	2,052.0	511.2	1,304.1	236.7

Table 6. Crime in the United States, by Selected Metropolitan Statistical Area, 2020—Continued

(Number, percent, rate per 100,000 population.)

Area	Population	Violent crime	Murder and nonnegligent manslaughter	Rape[1]	Robbery	Aggravated assault	Property crime	Burglary	Larceny-theft	Motor vehicle theft
Beckley, WV M.S.A	114,718									
Includes Fayette and Raleigh Counties										
City of Beckley	15,762	137	2	8	11	116	905	149	708	48
Total area actually reporting	95.3%	355	7	40	18	290	2,248	467	1,635	146
Estimated total	100.0%	433	7	44	22	360	2,269	474	1,645	150
Rate per 100,000 inhabitants		377.4	6.1	38.4	19.2	313.8	1,977.9	413.2	1,434.0	130.8
Bellingham, WA M.S.A	231,784									
Includes Whatcom County										
City of Bellingham	93,629	240	0	29	80	131	4,306	610	3,320	376
Total area actually reporting	100.0%	428	5	72	90	261	5,459	885	4,129	445
Rate per 100,000 inhabitants		184.7	2.2	31.1	38.8	112.6	2,355.2	381.8	1,781.4	192.0
Bend, OR M.S.A.	201,709									
Includes Deschutes County										
City of Bend	103,485	174	0	28	31	115	1,959	201	1,593	165
Total area actually reporting	100.0%	360	0	57	50	253	3,664	397	2,919	348
Rate per 100,000 inhabitants		178.5	0.0	28.3	24.8	125.4	1,816.5	196.8	1,447.1	172.5
Billings, MT M.S.A.	183,705									
Includes Carbon, Stillwater, and Yellowstone Counties										
City of Billings	110,157	939	14	85	125	715	5,249	717	3,715	817
Total area actually reporting	100.0%	1,152	15	103	133	901	6,378	868	4,512	998
Rate per 100,000 inhabitants		627.1	8.2	56.1	72.4	490.5	3,471.9	472.5	2,456.1	543.3
Binghamton, NY M.S.A.[2]	235,803									
Includes Broome[2] and Tioga Counties										
City of Binghamton[2]	44,083	372	1	28	50	293	1,775	294	1,380	101
Total area actually reporting	99.0%	669	4	111	79	475	4,818	711	3,875	232
Estimated total	100.0%	673	4	111	80	478	4,857	715	3,909	233
Rate per 100,000 inhabitants		285.4	1.7	47.1	33.9	202.7	2,059.8	303.2	1,657.7	98.8
Bismarck, ND M.S.A.	129,675									
Includes Burleigh, Morton, and Oliver Counties										
City of Bismarck	74,997	260	0	49	26	185	2,471	343	1,876	252
Total area actually reporting	100.0%	433	4	74	30	325	3,692	610	2,677	405
Rate per 100,000 inhabitants		333.9	3.1	57.1	23.1	250.6	2,847.1	470.4	2,064.4	312.3
Blacksburg-Christiansburg, VA M.S.A.	167,909									
Includes Giles, Montgomery, and Pulaski Counties and Radford City										
City of Blacksburg	44,422	29	0	13	2	14	310	29	266	15
City of Christiansburg	22,643	37	0	13	2	22	479	44	424	11
Total area actually reporting	100.0%	313	5	99	20	189	2,476	336	2,013	127
Rate per 100,000 inhabitants		186.4	3.0	59.0	11.9	112.6	1,474.6	200.1	1,198.9	75.6
Bloomington, IL M.S.A.[4]	170,810									
Includes McLean County4										
City of Bloomington[4]	77,386	314	1	64	23	226		144		70
Total area actually reporting	97.1%	475	1	105	44	325		289		123
Estimated total	100.0%	483	1	106	45	331		299		129
Rate per 100,000 inhabitants		282.8	0.6	62.1	26.3	193.8		175.0		75.5
Bloomington, IN M.S.A.[2]	170,127									
Includes Monroe[2] and Owen Counties										
City of Bloomington[2]	86,347	480	7	52	67	354	2,079	346	1,595	138
Total area actually reporting	83.8%	547	8	86	77	376	2,792	410	2,180	202
Estimated total	100.0%	586	8	91	79	408	3,072	467	2,372	233
Rate per 100,000 inhabitants		344.4	4.7	53.5	46.4	239.8	1,805.7	274.5	1,394.3	137.0
Boise City, ID M.S.A.	771,135									
Includes Ada, Boise, Canyon, Gem, and Owyhee Counties										
City of Boise	231,223	677	4	170	55	448	3,793	479	3,035	279
Total area actually reporting	99.9%	2,025	14	451	92	1,468	8,952	1,441	6,669	842
Estimated total	100.0%	2,026	14	451	92	1,469	8,958	1,442	6,674	842
Rate per 100,000 inhabitants		262.7	1.8	58.5	11.9	190.5	1,161.7	187.0	865.5	109.2
Boston-Cambridge-Newton, MA-NH M.S.A.[2]	4,885,414									
Includes the Metropolitan Divisions of Boston, MA; Cambridge-Newton-Framingham, MA; and Rockingham County-Strafford County, NH										
City of Boston, MA[2]	697,323	4,354	58	184	919	3,193	13,015	1,698	10,037	1,280
City of Cambridge, MA	119,938	341	1	25	67	248	2,200	202	1,917	81
City of Newton, MA	88,281	48	0	4	8	36	486	51	420	15
City of Framingham, MA	74,680	264	2	13	20	229	862	110	625	127
City of Waltham, MA	62,339	85	1	10	3	71	385	51	310	24
Total area actually reporting	99.9%	12,392	109	1,062	1,865	9,356	48,632	5,737	38,398	4,497
Estimated total	100.0%	12,399	109	1,063	1,865	9,362	48,653	5,740	38,415	4,498
Rate per 100,000 inhabitants		253.8	2.2	21.8	38.2	191.6	995.9	117.5	786.3	92.1

Table 6. Crime in the United States, by Selected Metropolitan Statistical Area, 2020—Continued

(Number, percent, rate per 100,000 population.)

Area	Population	Violent crime	Murder and nonnegligent manslaughter	Rape[1]	Robbery	Aggravated assault	Property crime	Burglary	Larceny-theft	Motor vehicle theft
Boston, MA M.D.[2]	2,037,005									
Includes Norfolk, Plymouth, and Suffolk Counties										
Total area actually reporting	99.7%	7,583	73	528	1,285	5,697	24,436	3,062	18,980	2,394
Estimated total	100.0%	7,590	73	529	1,285	5,703	24,457	3,065	18,997	2,395
Rate per 100,000 inhabitants		372.6	3.6	26.0	63.1	280.0	1,200.6	150.5	932.6	117.6
Cambridge-Newton-Framingham, MA M.D.	2,404,962									
Includes Essex and Middlesex Counties										
Total area actually reporting	100.0%	4,421	32	401	510	3,478	19,930	2,362	15,778	1,790
Rate per 100,000 inhabitants		183.8	1.3	16.7	21.2	144.6	828.7	98.2	656.1	74.4
Rockingham County-Strafford County, NH M.D.	443,447									
Includes Rockingham and Strafford Counties										
Total area actually reporting	100.0%	388	4	133	70	181	4,266	313	3,640	313
Rate per 100,000 inhabitants		87.5	0.9	30.0	15.8	40.8	962.0	70.6	820.8	70.6
Boulder, CO M.S.A.	327,747									
Includes Boulder County										
City of Boulder	106,598	343	2	31	72	238	4,019	654	2,994	371
Total area actually reporting	100.0%	961	4	177	140	640	9,046	1,328	6,723	995
Rate per 100,000 inhabitants		293.2	1.2	54.0	42.7	195.3	2,760.1	405.2	2,051.3	303.6
Bowling Green, KY M.S.A.	181,430									
Includes Allen, Butler, Edmonson, and Warren Counties										
City of Bowling Green	71,861	247	9	56	71	111	3,195	560	2,318	317
Total area actually reporting	100.0%	341	11	80	83	167	4,163	763	2,933	467
Rate per 100,000 inhabitants		188.0	6.1	44.1	45.7	92.0	2,294.5	420.5	1,616.6	257.4
Bremerton-Silverdale-Port Orchard, WA M.S.A.	272,867									
Includes Kitsap County										
City of Bremerton	41,817	143	1	16	23	103	1,342	224	945	173
City of Port Orchard	14,886	61	0	9	8	44	550	100	380	70
Total area actually reporting	100.0%	597	5	133	57	402	4,887	873	3,496	518
Rate per 100,000 inhabitants		218.8	1.8	48.7	20.9	147.3	1,791.0	319.9	1,281.2	189.8
Bridgeport-Stamford-Norwalk, CT M.S.A.[3]	928,567									
Includes Fairfield County										
City of Bridgeport	144,350	829	24	47	340	418	2,514	675	1,196	643
City of Stamford[3]	130,425	284	6	26	85	167			1,206	234
City of Norwalk	89,140	143	2	12	21	108	1,222	148	930	144
City of Danbury	85,080	98	4	9	40	45	806	81	643	82
City of Stratford	51,895	53	2	2	31	18	923	105	651	167
Total area actually reporting	100.0%	1,522	40	122	550	810			8,017	1,923
Rate per 100,000 inhabitants		163.9	4.3	13.1	59.2	87.2			863.4	207.1
Brownsville-Harlingen, TX M.S.A.	423,478									
Includes Cameron County										
City of Brownsville	183,627	738	7	83	153	495	3,394	403	2,870	121
City of Harlingen	65,014	269	3	21	67	178	2,437	315	1,999	123
Total area actually reporting	99.7%	1,526	13	176	247	1,090	8,241	1,161	6,692	388
Estimated total	100.0%	1,528	13	176	247	1,092	8,261	1,165	6,705	391
Rate per 100,000 inhabitants		360.8	3.1	41.6	58.3	257.9	1,950.8	275.1	1,583.3	92.3
Buffalo-Cheektowaga, NY M.S.A.[2]	1,119,988									
Includes Erie and Niagara[2] Counties										
City of Buffalo[2]	254,627	2,592	61	53	680	1,798	7,844	1,146	5,508	1,190
City of Cheektowaga Town	76,536	216	1	22	51	142	2,226	273	1,782	171
Total area actually reporting	100.0%	4,237	79	257	1,030	2,871	21,574	2,844	16,547	2,183
Rate per 100,000 inhabitants		378.3	7.1	22.9	92.0	256.3	1,926.3	253.9	1,477.4	194.9
Burlington, NC M.S.A.	171,665									
Includes Alamance County										
City of Burlington	55,003	527	3	43	56	425	2,391	419	1,782	190
Total area actually reporting	100.0%	820	12	65	80	663	4,070	738	2,992	340
Rate per 100,000 inhabitants		477.7	7.0	37.9	46.6	386.2	2,370.9	429.9	1,742.9	198.1
Burlington-South Burlington, VT M.S.A.	221,248									
Includes Chittenden, Franklin, and Grand Isle Counties										
City of Burlington	42,862	151	1	36	16	98	1,032	109	906	17
City of South Burlington	19,690	33	0	5	6	22	608	33	557	18
Total area actually reporting	100.0%	439	5	115	32	287	3,561	362	3,116	83
Rate per 100,000 inhabitants		198.4	2.3	52.0	14.5	129.7	1,609.5	163.6	1,408.4	37.5
California-Lexington Park, MD M.S.A.	114,031									
Includes St. Mary's County										
Total area actually reporting	100.0%	224	8	27	38	151	1,556	255	1,214	87
Rate per 100,000 inhabitants		196.4	7.0	23.7	33.3	132.4	1,364.5	223.6	1,064.6	76.3
Canton-Massillon, OH M.S.A.	396,284									
Includes Carroll and Stark Counties										

Table 6. Crime in the United States, by Selected Metropolitan Statistical Area, 2020—Continued

(Number, percent, rate per 100,000 population.)

Area	Population	Violent crime	Murder and nonnegligent manslaughter	Rape[1]	Robbery	Aggravated assault	Property crime	Burglary	Larceny-theft	Motor vehicle theft
City of Canton	70,124	1,002	14	115	154	719	3,411	708	2,350	353
City of Massillon	32,617	56	0	20	10	26	759	95	624	40
Total area actually reporting	98.0%	1,441	19	223	214	985	8,414	1,575	6,157	682
Estimated total	100.0%	1,451	19	225	216	991	8,546	1,591	6,266	689
Rate per 100,000 inhabitants		366.2	4.8	56.8	54.5	250.1	2,156.5	401.5	1,581.2	173.9
Cape Coral-Fort Myers, FL M.S.A.	787,016									
Includes Lee County										
City of Cape Coral	199,503	255	1	18	20	216	2,130	305	1,692	133
City of Fort Myers	90,380	467	9	39	67	352	1,699	193	1,359	147
Total area actually reporting	100.0%	2,100	32	239	304	1,525	8,118	1,180	6,167	771
Rate per 100,000 inhabitants		266.8	4.1	30.4	38.6	193.8	1,031.5	149.9	783.6	98.0
Cape Girardeau, MO-IL M.S.A.[2]	96,785									
Includes Alexander County,[4] IL and Bollinger and Cape Girardeau Counties, MO[2]										
City of Cape Girardeau, MO[2]	40,845	362	4	42	35	281	1,204	179	892	133
Total area actually reporting	97.9%	530	5	59	38	428	1,785	339	1,284	162
Estimated total	100.0%	532	5	59	38	430	1,811	342	1,305	164
Rate per 100,000 inhabitants		549.7	5.2	61.0	39.3	444.3	1,871.2	353.4	1,348.3	169.4
Carson City, NV M.S.A.[2]	56,250									
Includes Carson City[2]										
Total area actually reporting	100.0%	225	1	62	13	149	643	165	396	82
Rate per 100,000 inhabitants		400.0	1.8	110.2	23.1	264.9	1,143.1	293.3	704.0	145.8
Casper, WY M.S.A.[2]	80,625									
Includes Natrona County[2]										
City of Casper	58,244	124	2	59	14	49	1,659	222	1,270	167
Total area actually reporting	100.0%	183	4	71	16	92	1,954	274	1,467	213
Rate per 100,000 inhabitants		227.0	5.0	88.1	19.8	114.1	2,423.6	339.8	1,819.5	264.2
Cedar Rapids, IA M.S.A.	274,312									
Includes Benton, Jones, and Linn Counties										
City of Cedar Rapids	134,330	432	11	16	102	303	4,254	832	2,865	557
Total area actually reporting	85.6%	593	12	48	111	422	5,303	1,133	3,486	684
Estimated total	100.0%	691	12	71	116	492	5,803	1,278	3,789	736
Rate per 100,000 inhabitants		251.9	4.4	25.9	42.3	179.4	2,115.5	465.9	1,381.3	268.3
Champaign-Urbana, IL M.S.A.[3,4]	225,728									
Includes Champaign and Piatt Counties[4]										
City of Champaign[4]	89,785	827	9	60	88	670		281		191
City of Urbana[3,4]	42,211		2	41	36			137		42
Total area actually reporting	99.0%		12	139	147			613		324
Estimated total	100.0%		12	139	147			616		325
Rate per 100,000 inhabitants			5.3	61.6	65.1			272.9		144.0
Charleston, WV M.S.A.	254,717									
Includes Boone, Clay, Jackson, Kanawha, and Lincoln Counties										
City of Charleston	46,038	424	11	37	51	325	2,122	506	1,423	193
Total area actually reporting	85.3%	1,191	30	137	88	936	5,775	1,297	3,859	619
Estimated total	100.0%	1,366	30	149	95	1,092	5,873	1,332	3,910	631
Rate per 100,000 inhabitants		536.3	11.8	58.5	37.3	428.7	2,305.7	522.9	1,535.0	247.7
Charleston-North Charleston, SC M.S.A.	819,676									
Includes Berkeley, Charleston, and Dorchester Counties										
City of Charleston	139,582	650	17	54	100	479	3,218	326	2,439	453
City of North Charleston	117,503	1,345	38	90	318	899	5,998	651	4,667	680
Total area actually reporting	99.0%	3,607	91	293	648	2,575	20,056	2,492	15,247	2,317
Estimated total	100.0%	3,657	93	296	654	2,614	20,333	2,533	15,461	2,339
Rate per 100,000 inhabitants		446.2	11.3	36.1	79.8	318.9	2,480.6	309.0	1,886.2	285.4
Charlottesville, VA M.S.A.	220,388									
Includes Albemarle, Buckingham, Fluvanna, Greene, and Nelson Counties and Charlottesville City										
City of Charlottesville	47,671	189	5	25	28	131	916	79	765	72
Total area actually reporting	100.0%	415	13	83	47	272	2,849	280	2,376	193
Rate per 100,000 inhabitants		188.3	5.9	37.7	21.3	123.4	1,292.7	127.0	1,078.1	87.6
Chattanooga, TN-GA M.S.A.[2]	569,147									
Includes Catoosa,[2] Dade, and Walker Counties, GA and Hamilton, Marion, and Sequatchie Counties, TN										
City of Chattanooga, TN	184,211	2,504	33	182	268	2,021	11,709	1,173	8,435	2,101
Total area actually reporting	86.0%	3,329	40	255	322	2,712	16,606	1,994	11,791	2,821
Estimated total	100.0%	3,487	45	270	343	2,829	17,474	2,137	12,414	2,923
Rate per 100,000 inhabitants		612.7	7.9	47.4	60.3	497.1	3,070.2	375.5	2,181.2	513.6
Cheyenne, WY M.S.A.	100,661									
Includes Laramie County										

Table 6. Crime in the United States, by Selected Metropolitan Statistical Area, 2020—Continued

(Number, percent, rate per 100,000 population.)

Area	Population	Violent crime	Murder and nonnegligent manslaughter	Rape[1]	Robbery	Aggravated assault	Property crime	Burglary	Larceny-theft	Motor vehicle theft
City of Cheyenne	64,751	244	2	35	27	180	2,186	172	1,768	246
Total area actually reporting	100.0%	330	3	43	29	255	2,617	273	2,045	299
Rate per 100,000 inhabitants		327.8	3.0	42.7	28.8	253.3	2,599.8	271.2	2,031.6	297.0
Chico, CA M.S.A.	216,938									
Includes Butte County										
City of Chico	105,355	540	3	56	80	401	2,113	246	1,551	316
Total area actually reporting	100.0%	1,069	12	128	143	786	4,328	833	2,832	663
Rate per 100,000 inhabitants		492.8	5.5	59.0	65.9	362.3	1,995.0	384.0	1,305.4	305.6
Cincinnati, OH-KY-IN M.S.A.	2,227,744									
Includes Dearborn, Franklin, Ohio, and Union Counties, IN; Boone, Bracken, Campbell, Gallatin, Grant, Kenton, and Pendleton Counties, KY; and Brown, Butler, Clermont, Hamilton, and Warren Counties, OH										
City of Cincinnati, OH	304,724	2,721	92	215	750	1,664	11,224	2,322	7,396	1,506
Total area actually reporting	89.1%	4,733	123	656	1,132	2,822	32,917	5,080	24,525	3,312
Estimated total	100.0%	5,250	128	735	1,217	3,170	36,953	5,737	27,573	3,643
Rate per 100,000 inhabitants		235.7	5.7	33.0	54.6	142.3	1,658.8	257.5	1,237.7	163.5
Clarksville, TN-KY M.S.A.	311,846									
Includes Christian and Trigg Counties, KY and Montgomery and Stewart Counties, TN										
City of Clarksville, TN	161,167	983	15	84	78	806	3,615	441	2,765	409
Total area actually reporting	100.0%	1,321	21	133	117	1,050	5,777	893	4,254	630
Rate per 100,000 inhabitants		423.6	6.7	42.6	37.5	336.7	1,852.5	286.4	1,364.1	202.0
Cleveland, TN M.S.A.	125,999									
Includes Bradley and Polk Counties										
City of Cleveland	45,994	454	2	21	62	369	2,312	374	1,734	204
Total area actually reporting	100.0%	710	5	39	71	595	3,398	612	2,422	364
Rate per 100,000 inhabitants		563.5	4.0	31.0	56.3	472.2	2,696.8	485.7	1,922.2	288.9
Cleveland-Elyria, OH M.S.A.	2,042,966									
Includes Cuyahoga, Geauga, Lake, Lorain, and Medina Counties										
City of Cleveland	379,121	6,281	160	393	1,593	4,135	15,433	3,692	8,800	2,941
City of Elyria	53,677	136	7	21	26	82	785	178	546	61
Total area actually reporting	87.6%	8,616	207	664	2,100	5,645	30,659	5,749	20,511	4,399
Estimated total	100.0%	9,002	210	740	2,175	5,877	34,823	6,261	23,896	4,666
Rate per 100,000 inhabitants		440.6	10.3	36.2	106.5	287.7	1,704.5	306.5	1,169.7	228.4
Coeur d'Alene, ID M.S.A.	170,237									
Includes Kootenai County										
City of Coeur d'Alene	53,405	209	1	66	8	134	835	92	701	42
Total area actually reporting	100.0%	343	2	81	16	244	1,807	308	1,403	96
Rate per 100,000 inhabitants		201.5	1.2	47.6	9.4	143.3	1,061.5	180.9	824.1	56.4
College Station-Bryan, TX M.S.A.[2]	268,082									
Includes Brazos,[2] Burleson,[2] and Robertson Counties										
City of College Station	120,831	217	2	55	27	133	2,299	321	1,768	210
City of Bryan[2]	87,435	463	7	104	49	303	1,718	280	1,302	136
Total area actually reporting	100.0%	799	10	182	88	519	4,970	835	3,698	437
Rate per 100,000 inhabitants		298.0	3.7	67.9	32.8	193.6	1,853.9	311.5	1,379.4	163.0
Colorado Springs, CO M.S.A.	752,364									
Includes El Paso and Teller Counties										
City of Colorado Springs	485,083	2,896	36	400	376	2,084	16,394	2,588	11,374	2,432
Total area actually reporting	99.6%	3,655	47	577	440	2,591	19,859	3,100	13,880	2,879
Estimated total	100.0%	3,661	47	578	441	2,595	19,960	3,106	13,958	2,896
Rate per 100,000 inhabitants		486.6	6.2	76.8	58.6	344.9	2,653.0	412.8	1,855.2	384.9
Columbia, MO M.S.A.[2]	210,096									
Includes Boone,[2] Cooper, and Howard[2] Counties										
City of Columbia[2]	124,829	552	13	89	58	392	3,326	404	2,478	444
Total area actually reporting	98.2	739	15	132	71	521	4,522	573	3,366	583
Estimated total	100.0%	769	15	134	75	545	4,635	590	3,440	605
Rate per 100,000 inhabitants		366.0	7.1	63.8	35.7	259.4	2,206.1	280.8	1,637.3	288.0
Columbia, SC M.S.A.	847,504									
Includes Calhoun, Fairfield, Kershaw, Lexington, Richland, and Saluda Counties										
City of Columbia	131,777	991	19	86	206	680	5,898	728	4,536	634
Total area actually reporting	100.0%	4,729	78	355	644	3,652	27,730	4,335	20,161	3,234
Rate per 100,000 inhabitants		558.0	9.2	41.9	76.0	430.9	3,272.0	511.5	2,378.9	381.6
Columbus, OH M.S.A.	2,145,231									
Includes Delaware, Fairfield, Franklin, Hocking, Licking, Madison, Morrow, Perry, Pickaway, and Union Counties										
City of Columbus	911,383	5,064	174	816	1,796	2,278	28,530	5,551	19,874	3,105

Table 6. Crime in the United States, by Selected Metropolitan Statistical Area, 2020—Continued

(Number, percent, rate per 100,000 population.)

Area	Population	Violent crime	Murder and nonnegligent manslaughter	Rape[1]	Robbery	Aggravated assault	Property crime	Burglary	Larceny-theft	Motor vehicle theft
Total area actually reporting	93.8%	6,534	191	1,128	2,097	3,118	45,217	7,810	33,179	4,228
Estimated total	100.0%	6,718	192	1,164	2,131	3,231	47,407	8,082	34,972	4,353
Rate per 100,000 inhabitants		313.2	9.0	54.3	99.3	150.6	2,209.9	376.7	1,630.2	202.9
Corpus Christi, TX M.S.A.[2]	430,354									
Includes Nueces and San Patricio Counties										
City of Corpus Christi[2]	329,050	2,772	34	232	478	2,028	10,747	2,042	7,824	881
Total area actually reporting	99.9%	3,175	43	278	509	2,345	12,659	2,428	9,202	1,029
Estimated total	100.0%	3,176	43	278	509	2,346	12,668	2,430	9,208	1,030
Rate per 100,000 inhabitants		738.0	10.0	64.6	118.3	545.1	2,943.6	564.7	2,139.6	239.3
Crestview-Fort Walton Beach-Destin, FL M.S.A.	290,040									
Includes Okaloosa and Walton Counties										
City of Crestview	25,787	93	4	18	13	58	602	72	457	73
City of Fort Walton Beach	22,871	74	2	13	4	55	462	89	324	49
Total area actually reporting	100.0%	780	10	117	50	603	3,927	601	2,947	379
Rate per 100,000 inhabitants		268.9	3.4	40.3	17.2	207.9	1,354.0	207.2	1,016.1	130.7
Danville, IL M.S.A.[4]	74,737									
Includes Vermilion County[4]										
City of Danville[4]	30,208	505	8	10	59	428		399		48
Total area actually reporting	100.0%	785	13	70	87	615		658		170
Rate per 100,000 inhabitants		1,050.3	17.4	93.7	116.4	822.9		880.4		227.5
Davenport-Moline-Rock Island, IA-IL M.S.A.[4]	377,817									
Includes Henry, Mercer, and Rock Island Counties, IL[4] and Scott County, IA										
City of Davenport, IA	101,806	750	10	67	136	537	3,996	912	2,615	469
City of Moline, IL[4]	41,128	204	1	32	25	146		225		76
City of Rock Island, IL[4]	36,981	213	7	8	50	148		139		124
Total area actually reporting	96.5%	1,770	26	221	265	1,258		1,833		934
Estimated total	100.0%	1,798	26	225	269	1,278		1,866		950
Rate per 100,000 inhabitants		475.9	6.9	59.6	71.2	338.3		493.9		251.4
Decatur, IL M.S.A.[4]	102,740									
Includes Macon County[4]										
City of Decatur[4]	70,175	489	13	41	83	352		621		196
Total area actually reporting	100.0%	540	13	49	84	394		677		214
Rate per 100,000 inhabitants		525.6	12.7	47.7	81.8	383.5		658.9		208.3
Deltona-Daytona Beach-Ormond Beach, FL M.S.A.	675,651									
Includes Flagler and Volusia Counties										
City of Daytona Beach	70,084	725	14	25	77	609	2,145	274	1,668	203
City of Ormond Beach	44,271	161	1	26	23	111	1,035	166	773	96
City of DeLand	35,874	188	1	8	16	163	870	111	697	62
Total area actually reporting	100.0%	2,280	26	192	274	1,788	9,815	1,528	7,452	835
Rate per 100,000 inhabitants		337.5	3.8	28.4	40.6	264.6	1,452.7	226.2	1,102.9	123.6
Denver-Aurora-Lakewood, CO M.S.A.	2,998,046									
Includes Adams, Arapahoe, Broomfield, Clear Creek, Denver, Douglas, Elbert, Gilpin, Jefferson, and Park Counties										
City of Denver	737,709	6,329	97	670	1,218	4,344	34,294	5,223	20,662	8,409
City of Aurora	385,720	3,473	39	397	775	2,262	13,079	1,760	7,390	3,929
City of Lakewood	159,719	903	8	110	219	566	8,050	1,076	5,580	1,394
City of Centennial	112,104	144	1	6	26	111	1,979	317	1,360	302
City of Broomfield	71,795	76	0	15	13	48	2,145	222	1,654	269
City of Commerce City	62,164	298	6	73	38	181	2,051	238	1,241	572
Total area actually reporting	99.6%	14,675	183	1,970	2,811	9,711	98,712	13,268	63,475	21,969
Estimated total	100.0%	14,701	183	1,974	2,816	9,728	99,017	13,307	63,699	22,011
Rate per 100,000 inhabitants		490.4	6.1	65.8	93.9	324.5	3,302.7	443.9	2,124.7	734.2
Des Moines-West Des Moines, IA M.S.A.	709,374									
Includes Dallas, Guthrie, Jasper, Madison, Polk, and Warren Counties										
City of Des Moines	215,290	1,517	33	119	246	1,119	8,400	1,925	5,053	1,422
City of West Des Moines	69,252	93	1	27	7	58	1,140	129	893	118
Total area actually reporting	100.0%	2,402	44	247	295	1,816	14,354	3,006	9,299	2,049
Rate per 100,000 inhabitants		338.6	6.2	34.8	41.6	256.0	2,023.5	423.8	1,310.9	288.8
Detroit-Warren-Dearborn, MI M.S.A.	4,308,550									
Includes the Metropolitan Divisions of Detroit-Dearborn-Livonia and Warren-Troy-Farmington Hills										
City of Detroit	659,616	14,370	328	676	1,848	11,518	21,178	4,361	11,239	5,578
City of Warren	133,928	672	12	93	91	476	1,938	348	1,169	421
City of Dearborn	93,507	277	5	25	31	216	1,662	194	1,215	253
City of Livonia	93,342	209	0	26	12	171	1,196	115	979	102
City of Troy	84,441	86	1	9	15	61	732	46	635	51
City of Farmington Hills	80,708	84	0	11	9	64	558	65	439	54
City of Southfield	72,794	288	3	33	35	217	1,309	190	759	360
City of Taylor	60,698	371	1	25	35	310	1,108	182	790	136
City of Pontiac	59,411	840	13	50	88	689	1,096	240	743	113

Table 6. Crime in the United States, by Selected Metropolitan Statistical Area, 2020—Continued

(Number, percent, rate per 100,000 population.)

Area	Population	Violent crime	Murder and nonnegligent manslaughter	Rape[1]	Robbery	Aggravated assault	Property crime	Burglary	Larceny-theft	Motor vehicle theft
City of Novi	61,554	60	1	15	3	41	429	21	372	36
Total area actually reporting	100.0%	24,568	452	1,989	2,791	19,336	57,445	9,472	37,647	10,326
Rate per 100,000 inhabitants		570.2	10.5	46.2	64.8	448.8	1,333.3	219.8	873.8	239.7
Detroit-Warren-Dearborn, MI M.S.A.	1,736,289									
Includes Wayne County										
Total area actually reporting	100.0%	18,894	387	1,136	2,247	15,124	35,699	6,526	21,529	7,644
Rate per 100,000 inhabitants		1,088.2	22.3	65.4	129.4	871.1	2,056.1	375.9	1,239.9	440.2
Warren-Troy-Farmington Hills, MI M.D.	2,572,261									
Includes Lapeer, Livingston, Macomb, Oakland, and St. Clair Counties										
Total area actually reporting	100.0%	5,674	65	853	544	4,212	21,746	2,946	16,118	2,682
Rate per 100,000 inhabitants		220.6	2.5	33.2	21.1	163.7	845.4	114.5	626.6	104.3
Dover, DE M.S.A.	183,675									
Includes Kent County										
City of Dover	38,428	329	9	22	24	274	1,549	57	1,412	80
Total area actually reporting	100.0%	813	13	79	58	663	3,404	372	2,829	203
Rate per 100,000 inhabitants		442.6	7.1	43.0	31.6	361.0	1,853.3	202.5	1,540.2	110.5
Dubuque, IA M.S.A.	97,551									
Includes Dubuque County										
City of Dubuque	57,904	231	1	54	26	150	1,165	208	885	72
Total area actually reporting	100.0%	262	1	62	26	173	1,363	267	1,004	92
Rate per 100,000 inhabitants		268.6	1.0	63.6	26.7	177.3	1,397.2	273.7	1,029.2	94.3
Duluth, MN-WI M.S.A.[2]	287,596									
Includes Carlton,[2] Lake,[2] and St. Louis Counties, MN and Douglas County, WI[2]										
City of Duluth, MN	85,555	257	1	33	44	179	3,224	326	2,677	221
Total area actually reporting	100.0%	607	5	93	67	442	6,924	982	5,455	487
Rate per 100,000 inhabitants		211.1	1.7	32.3	23.3	153.7	2,407.5	341.5	1,896.8	169.3
Durham-Chapel Hill, NC M.S.A.	653,860									
Includes Chatham, Durham, Granville, Orange and Person Counties										
City of Durham	284,925	2,447	36	125	626	1,660	10,650	1,906	7,779	965
City of Chapel Hill	64,853	93	0	7	22	64	1,140	198	885	57
Total area actually reporting	100.0%	3,272	53	190	745	2,284	16,350	3,085	11,888	1,377
Rate per 100,000 inhabitants		500.4	8.1	29.1	113.9	349.3	2,500.5	471.8	1,818.1	210.6
Eau Claire, WI M.S.A.	170,028									
Includes Chippewa and Eau Claire Counties										
City of Eau Claire	69,086	191	2	41	38	110	1,927	334	1,494	99
Total area actually reporting	100.0%	326	3	72	42	209	2,951	558	2,227	166
Rate per 100,000 inhabitants		191.7	1.8	42.3	24.7	122.9	1,735.6	328.2	1,309.8	97.6
El Centro, CA M.S.A.	180,129									
Includes Imperial County										
City of El Centro	44,238	158	1	10	30	117	1,003	213	679	111
Total area actually reporting	96.1%	582	7	32	80	463	3,384	851	2,085	448
Estimated total	100.0%	609	7	35	85	482	3,526	873	2,188	465
Rate per 100,000 inhabitants		338.1	3.9	19.4	47.2	267.6	1,957.5	484.7	1,214.7	258.1
Elizabethtown-Fort Knox, KY M.S.A.	154,232									
Includes Hardin, Larue, and Meade Counties										
City of Elizabethtown	30,505	44	3	8	9	24	286	68	182	36
Total area actually reporting	100.0%	155	5	26	25	99	1,286	279	836	171
Rate per 100,000 inhabitants		100.5	3.2	16.9	16.2	64.2	833.8	180.9	542.0	110.9
Elmira, NY M.S.A.	82,347									
Includes Chemung County										
City of Elmira	26,820	59	2	0	25	32	812	87	684	41
Total area actually reporting	100.0%	173	3	32	28	110	1,329	131	1,131	67
Rate per 100,000 inhabitants		210.1	3.6	38.9	34.0	133.6	1,613.9	159.1	1,373.5	81.4
El Paso, TX M.S.A.[2]	845,510									
Includes El Paso[2] and Hudspeth Counties										
City of El Paso[2]	685,288	2,167	28	261	289	1,589	8,507	847	7,245	415
Total area actually reporting	100.0%	2,611	33	319	321	1,938	9,708	1,042	8,134	532
Rate per 100,000 inhabitants		308.8	3.9	37.7	38.0	229.2	1,148.2	123.2	962.0	62.9
Enid, OK M.S.A.	61,092									
Includes Garfield County										
City of Enid	49,708	233	4	35	15	179	1,420	375	948	97
Total area actually reporting	100.0%	254	4	38	15	197	1,576	430	1,039	107
Rate per 100,000 inhabitants		415.8	6.5	62.2	24.6	322.5	2,579.7	703.9	1,700.7	175.1
Evansville, IN-KY M.S.A.[2]	315,160									
Includes Posey, Vanderburgh, and Warrick Counties, IN and Henderson County, KY										
City of Evansville[2]	117,747	1,185	10	77	115	983	4,252	626	3,188	438

Table 6. Crime in the United States, by Selected Metropolitan Statistical Area, 2020—Continued

(Number, percent, rate per 100,000 population.)

Area	Population	Violent crime	Murder and nonnegligent manslaughter	Rape[1]	Robbery	Aggravated assault	Property crime	Burglary	Larceny-theft	Motor vehicle theft
Total area actually reporting	92.0%	1,563	14	119	140	1,290	6,292	1,011	4,636	645
Estimated total	100.0%	1,601	14	123	143	1,321	6,557	1,067	4,817	673
Rate per 100,000 inhabitants		508.0	4.4	39.0	45.4	419.2	2,080.5	338.6	1,528.4	213.5
Fairbanks, AK M.S.A.	32,922									
Includes Fairbanks North Star Borough										
City of Fairbanks	30,832	260	3	24	41	192	1,276	171	908	197
Total area actually reporting	100.0%	277	3	26	42	206	1,367	180	975	212
Rate per 100,000 inhabitants		841.4	9.1	79.0	127.6	625.7	4,152.2	546.7	2,961.5	643.9
Fargo, ND-MN M.S.A.	248,368									
Includes Clay County, MN and Cass County, ND										
City of Fargo, ND	126,927	584	7	107	61	409	4,403	1,016	2,922	465
Total area actually reporting	100.0%	871	14	172	82	603	7,027	1,611	4,690	726
Rate per 100,000 inhabitants		350.7	5.6	69.3	33.0	242.8	2,829.3	648.6	1,888.3	292.3
Farmington, NM M.S.A.[2]	123,608									
Includes San Juan County										
City of Farmington[2]	44,191	529	1	78	40	410	1,447	295	1,010	142
Total area actually reporting	100.0%	817	4	122	51	640	2,026	447	1,373	206
Rate per 100,000 inhabitants		661.0	3.2	98.7	41.3	517.8	1,639.1	361.6	1,110.8	166.7
Fayetteville, NC M.S.A.[2]	531,101									
Includes Cumberland, Harnett,[2] and Hoke Counties										
City of Fayetteville	212,033	2,074	30	87	262	1,695	7,210	1,327	5,418	465
Total area actually reporting	89.3%	2,811	44	145	345	2,277	11,555	2,516	8,219	820
Estimated total	100.0%	2,938	46	160	360	2,372	12,396	2,752	8,737	907
Rate per 100,000 inhabitants		553.2	8.7	30.1	67.8	446.6	2,334.0	518.2	1,645.1	170.8
Flint, MI M.S.A.	402,374									
Includes Genesee County										
City of Flint	94,842	996	44	67	83	802	1,614	406	1,004	204
Total area actually reporting	100.0%	2,324	75	260	177	1,812	5,823	1,281	3,882	660
Rate per 100,000 inhabitants		577.6	18.6	64.6	44.0	450.3	1,447.2	318.4	964.8	164.0
Florence, SC M.S.A.	205,067									
Includes Darlington and Florence Counties										
City of Florence	38,597	562	12	15	72	463	2,390	322	1,812	256
Total area actually reporting	95.7%	1,708	38	96	174	1,400	7,081	1,335	4,942	804
Estimated total	100.0%	1,764	39	100	181	1,444	7,384	1,379	5,177	828
Rate per 100,000 inhabitants		860.2	19.0	48.8	88.3	704.2	3,600.8	672.5	2,524.5	403.8
Fond du Lac, WI M.S.A.	103,517									
Includes Fond du Lac County										
City of Fond du Lac	43,295	134	1	25	9	99	878	66	776	36
Total area actually reporting	100.0%	181	2	44	10	125	1,187	130	1,003	54
Rate per 100,000 inhabitants		174.9	1.9	42.5	9.7	120.8	1,146.7	125.6	968.9	52.2
Fort Smith, AR-OK M.S.A.	250,603									
Includes Crawford, Franklin, and Sebastian Counties, AR and Sequoyah County, OK										
City of Fort Smith, AR	88,071	1,031	7	96	106	822	4,871	637	3,716	518
Total area actually reporting	99.1%	1,530	11	188	114	1,217	7,176	1,294	5,166	716
Estimated total	100.0%	1,541	11	190	115	1,225	7,224	1,303	5,199	722
Rate per 100,000 inhabitants		614.9	4.4	75.8	45.9	488.8	2,882.6	519.9	2,074.6	288.1
Fort Wayne, IN M.S.A.	415,629									
Includes Allen and Whitley Counties										
City of Fort Wayne	272,270	1,124	39	97	245	743	6,117	655	4,952	510
Total area actually reporting	94.5%	1,369	41	125	267	936	7,067	800	5,662	605
Estimated total	100.0%	1,392	41	129	269	953	7,266	851	5,782	633
Rate per 100,000 inhabitants		334.9	9.9	31.0	64.7	229.3	1,748.2	204.7	1,391.1	152.3
Fresno, CA M.S.A.	996,752									
Includes Fresno County										
City of Fresno	535,472	3,560	77	148	889	2,446	16,475	3,036	10,789	2,650
Total area actually reporting	100.0%	5,948	94	302	1,169	4,383	24,724	4,955	15,697	4,072
Rate per 100,000 inhabitants		596.7	9.4	30.3	117.3	439.7	2,480.5	497.1	1,574.8	408.5
Gainesville, FL M.S.A.	330,910									
Includes Alachua, Gilchrist, and Levy Counties										
City of Gainesville	135,076	1,042	10	128	209	695	4,297	411	3,400	486
Total area actually reporting	100.0%	2,516	17	271	356	1,872	7,414	1,120	5,513	781
Rate per 100,000 inhabitants		760.3	5.1	81.9	107.6	565.7	2,240.5	338.5	1,666.0	236.0
Gainesville, GA M.S.A.[2]	207,015									
Includes Hall County										
City of Gainesville[2]	44,398	184	0	12	38	134	1,116	140	887	89
Total area actually reporting	100.0%	479	7	58	60	354	2,631	369	2,003	259
Rate per 100,000 inhabitants		231.4	3.4	28.0	29.0	171.0	1,270.9	178.2	967.6	125.1
Glens Falls, NY M.S.A.[2]	123,934									
Includes Warren and Washington Counties										

Table 6. Crime in the United States, by Selected Metropolitan Statistical Area, 2020—Continued

(Number, percent, rate per 100,000 population.)

Area	Population	Violent crime	Murder and nonnegligent manslaughter	Rape[1]	Robbery	Aggravated assault	Property crime	Burglary	Larceny-theft	Motor vehicle theft
City of Glens Falls[2]	14,215	10	0	2	0	8	105	7	95	3
Total area actually reporting	98.0%	152	0	94	7	51	898	121	739	38
Estimated total	100.0%	156	0	95	8	53	914	124	751	39
Rate per 100,000 inhabitants		125.9	0.0	76.7	6.5	42.8	737.5	100.1	606.0	31.5
Goldsboro, NC M.S.A.	123,171									
Includes Wayne County										
City of Goldsboro	34,051	397	2	11	46	338	1,709	349	1,272	88
Total area actually reporting	97.7%	585	7	18	65	495	2,959	733	1,941	285
Estimated total	100.0%	593	7	19	65	502	3,094	758	2,045	291
Rate per 100,000 inhabitants		481.4	5.7	15.4	52.8	407.6	2,512.0	615.4	1,660.3	236.3
Grand Forks, ND-MN M.S.A.[2]	100,189									
Includes Polk County, MN2 and Grand Forks County, ND										
City of Grand Forks, ND	56,163	164	4	34	14	112	1,315	210	988	117
Total area actually reporting	100.0%	233	6	47	15	165	1,762	313	1,299	150
Rate per 100,000 inhabitants		232.6	6.0	46.9	15.0	164.7	1,758.7	312.4	1,296.5	149.7
Grand Island, NE M.S.A.	75,484									
Includes Hall, Howard, and Merrick Counties										
City of Grand Island	51,547	216	0	50	17	149	1,258	149	1,015	94
Total area actually reporting	100.0%	257	0	59	17	181	1,383	178	1,091	114
Rate per 100,000 inhabitants		340.5	0.0	78.2	22.5	239.8	1,832.2	235.8	1,445.3	151.0
Grand Junction, CO M.S.A.	154,127									
Includes Mesa County										
City of Grand Junction	64,149	348	3	43	40	262	2,966	385	2,298	283
Total area actually reporting	99.7%	563	3	89	56	415	4,546	749	3,319	478
Estimated total	100.0%	565	3	89	56	417	4,594	751	3,361	482
Rate per 100,000 inhabitants		366.6	1.9	57.7	36.3	270.6	2,980.7	487.3	2,180.7	312.7
Grand Rapids-Kentwood, MI M.S.A.	1,083,395									
Includes Ionia, Kent, Montcalm, and Ottawa Counties										
City of Grand Rapids	202,513	1,443	28	121	192	1,102	3,956	463	2,912	581
City of Kentwood	52,263	229	4	28	26	171	1,207	166	837	204
Total area actually reporting	99.9%	3,789	50	744	380	2,615	13,834	1,780	10,278	1,776
Estimated total	100.0%	3,793	50	745	380	2,618	13,853	1,783	10,293	1,777
Rate per 100,000 inhabitants		350.1	4.6	68.8	35.1	241.6	1,278.7	164.6	950.1	164.0
Grants Pass, OR M.S.A.	87,577									
Includes Josephine County										
City of Grants Pass	38,420	133	0	27	25	81	1,160	131	901	128
Total area actually reporting	100.0%	252	9	40	34	169	1,500	171	1,045	284
Rate per 100,000 inhabitants		287.7	10.3	45.7	38.8	193.0	1,712.8	195.3	1,193.2	324.3
Great Falls, MT M.S.A.	81,529									
Includes Cascade County										
City of Great Falls	58,345	266	0	43	28	195	2,999	293	2,535	171
Total area actually reporting	100.0%	359	0	55	28	276	3,261	355	2,719	187
Rate per 100,000 inhabitants		440.3	0.0	67.5	34.3	338.5	3,999.8	435.4	3,335.0	229.4
Greeley, CO M.S.A.	331,283									
Includes Weld County										
City of Greeley	110,505	470	9	53	78	330	2,722	369	1,961	392
Total area actually reporting	97.3%	1,053	16	174	130	733	6,799	819	4,781	1,199
Estimated total	100.0%	1,074	16	177	134	747	7,165	838	5,076	1,251
Rate per 100,000 inhabitants		324.2	4.8	53.4	40.4	225.5	2,162.8	253.0	1,532.2	377.6
Green Bay, WI M.S.A.	324,478									
Includes Brown, Kewaunee, and Oconto Counties										
City of Green Bay	104,649	552	6	71	45	430	1,600	206	1,279	115
Total area actually reporting	100.0%	730	8	121	52	549	3,216	475	2,554	187
Rate per 100,000 inhabitants		225.0	2.5	37.3	16.0	169.2	991.1	146.4	787.1	57.6
Greensboro-High Point, NC M.S.A.	777,379									
Includes Guilford, Randolph, and Rockingham Counties										
City of Greensboro	299,887	2,704	59	95	581	1,969	10,830	2,212	7,503	1,115
City of High Point	108,114	734	13	27	117	577	3,246	489	2442	315
Total area actually reporting	83.0%	4,124	88	195	790	3,051	18,395	3,617	12,962	1,816
Estimated total	100.0%	4,479	95	230	837	3,317	20,792	4,194	14,558	2,040
Rate per 100,000 inhabitants		576.2	12.2	29.6	107.7	426.7	2,674.6	539.5	1,872.7	262.4
Greenville, NC M.S.A.	182,129									
Includes Pitt County										
City of Greenville	94,372	415	13	26	71	305	2,481	360	2,006	115
Total area actually reporting	99.1%	659	21	33	110	495	3,588	624	2,780	184
Estimated total	100.0%	664	21	34	110	499	3,665	638	2,840	187
Rate per 100,000 inhabitants		364.6	11.5	18.7	60.4	274.0	2,012.3	350.3	1,559.3	102.7

Table 6. Crime in the United States, by Selected Metropolitan Statistical Area, 2020—Continued

(Number, percent, rate per 100,000 population.)

Area	Population	Violent crime	Murder and nonnegligent manslaughter	Rape[1]	Robbery	Aggravated assault	Property crime	Burglary	Larceny-theft	Motor vehicle theft
Hanford-Corcoran, CA M.S.A.	151,473									
Includes Kings County										
City of Hanford	58,075	321	5	17	45	254	1,119	155	755	209
City of Corcoran	21,700	112	2	11	12	87	392	82	199	111
Total area actually reporting	100.0%	777	11	63	91	612	2,506	451	1,498	557
Rate per 100,000 inhabitants		513.0	7.3	41.6	60.1	404.0	1,654.4	297.7	989.0	367.7
Harrisonburg, VA M.S.A.	135,962									
Includes Rockingham County and Harrisonburg City										
City of Harrisonburg	53,442	117	1	15	14	87	811	74	688	49
Total area actually reporting	100.0%	207	5	41	16	145	1,335	177	1,065	93
Rate per 100,000 inhabitants		152.2	3.7	30.2	11.8	106.6	981.9	130.2	783.3	68.4
Hartford-East Hartford-Middletown, CT M.S.A.	1,014,700									
Includes Hartford, Middlesex, and Tolland Counties										
City of Hartford	121,749	1,208	23	31	280	874	3,787	430	2,708	649
City of East Hartford	49,720	77	0	12	37	28	1,208	101	886	221
City of Middletown	46,106	38	3	4	7	24	597	62	477	58
Total area actually reporting	100.0%	2,211	37	175	614	1,385	21,196	2,381	16,043	2,772
Rate per 100,000 inhabitants		217.9	3.6	17.2	60.5	136.5	2,088.9	234.7	1,581.1	273.2
Hattiesburg, MS M.S.A.	168,941									
Includes Covington, Forrest, Lamar, and Perry Counties										
City of Hattiesburg	45,870	171	7	31	27	106	2,418	342	1,904	172
Total area actually reporting	80.6%	306	10	62	41	193	3,377	639	2,480	258
Estimated total	100.0%	422	10	102	43	267	3,743	720	2,705	318
Rate per 100,000 inhabitants		249.8	5.9	60.4	25.5	158.0	2,215.6	426.2	1,601.2	188.2
Hilton Head Island-Bluffton, SC M.S.A.	226,652									
Includes Beaufort and Jasper Counties										
City of Bluffton	27,549	25	0	7	2	16	199	38	145	16
Total area actually reporting	91.6%	642	16	60	61	505	3,009	435	2,356	218
Estimated total	100.0%	741	22	65	67	587	3,354	516	2,580	258
Rate per 100,000 inhabitants		326.9	9.7	28.7	29.6	259.0	1,479.8	227.7	1,138.3	113.8
Homosassa Springs, FL M.S.A.	150,189									
Includes Citrus County										
Total area actually reporting	100.0%	405	7	25	38	335	1,928	334	1,403	191
Rate per 100,000 inhabitants		269.7	4.7	16.6	25.3	223.1	1,283.7	222.4	934.2	127.2
Hot Springs, AR M.S.A.	99,763									
Includes Garland County										
City of Hot Springs	38,893	287	9	39	43	196	2,276	656	1,431	189
Total area actually reporting	100.0%	582	9	77	53	443	3,575	1,200	2,052	323
Rate per 100,000 inhabitants		583.4	9.0	77.2	53.1	444.1	3,583.5	1,202.9	2,056.9	323.8
Houston-The Woodlands-Sugar Land, TX M.S.A.[2]	7,180,258									
Includes Austin, Brazoria, Chambers, Fort Bend, Galveston, Harris, Liberty, Montgomery, and Waller Counties										
City of Houston	2,346,155	29,474	400	1,137	8,757	19,180	98,043	15,788	67,474	14,781
City of Sugar Land[2]	119,671	68	4	8	20	36	1,277	111	1,077	89
City of Baytown[2]	77,823	338	9	43	85	201	2,917	390	2,106	421
City of Conroe	94,451	175	2	35	47	91	2,336	246	1,914	176
City of Galveston[2]	50,751	327	6	80	65	176	1,694	225	1,217	252
Total area actually reporting	99.9%	45,358	662	3,206	12,057	29,433	187,868	28,857	132,143	26,868
Estimated total	100.0%	45,368	662	3,208	12,057	29,441	187,935	28,871	132,187	26,877
Rate per 100,000 inhabitants		631.8	9.2	44.7	167.9	410.0	2,617.4	402.1	1,841.0	374.3
Huntington-Ashland, WV-KY-OH M.S.A.	353,926									
Includes Boyd, Carter, and Greenup Counties, KY; Lawrence County OH; and Cabell, Putnam, and Wayne Counties, WV										
City of Huntington, WV	44,684	368	7	35	69	257	1,642	378	1,083	181
City of Ashland, KY	19,979	41	1	7	7	26	642	105	490	47
Total area actually reporting	87.3%	719	12	153	89	465	4,704	933	3,299	472
Estimated total	100.0%	850	14	164	101	571	5,213	1,015	3,697	501
Rate per 100,000 inhabitants		240.2	4.0	46.3	28.5	161.3	1,472.9	286.8	1,044.6	141.6
Idaho Falls, ID M.S.A.	154,789									
Includes Bonneville, Butte, and Jefferson Counties										
City of Idaho Falls	63,457	291	2	35	18	236	1,152	325	704	123
Total area actually reporting	100.0%	439	4	57	25	353	1,994	534	1,241	219
Rate per 100,000 inhabitants		283.6	2.6	36.8	16.2	228.1	1,288.2	345.0	801.7	141.5
Iowa City, IA M.S.A.	175,256									
Includes Johnson and Washington Counties										
City of Iowa City	75,964	151	2	21	16	112	1,335	261	934	140
Total area actually reporting	99.4%	471	3	80	26	362	2,599	501	1,880	218
Estimated total	100.0%	475	3	80	27	365	2,623	506	1,896	221
Rate per 100,000 inhabitants		271.0	1.7	45.6	15.4	208.3	1,496.7	288.7	1,081.8	126.1

Table 6. Crime in the United States, by Selected Metropolitan Statistical Area, 2020—Continued

(Number, percent, rate per 100,000 population.)

Area	Population	Violent crime	Murder and nonnegligent manslaughter	Rape[1]	Robbery	Aggravated assault	Property crime	Burglary	Larceny-theft	Motor vehicle theft
Ithaca, NY M.S.A Includes Tompkins County	101,580									
City of Ithaca	30,927	98	0	14	31	53	1,157	141	1,000	16
Total area actually reporting	100.0%	163	0	45	35	83	1,924	224	1,660	40
Rate per 100,000 inhabitants		160.5	0.0	44.3	34.5	81.7	1,894.1	220.5	1,634.2	39.4
Jackson, MI M.S.A. Includes Jackson County	157,798									
City of Jackson	32,332	350	7	47	32	264	1,001	173	722	106
Total area actually reporting	100.0%	881	14	170	44	653	2,641	392	1,984	265
Rate per 100,000 inhabitants		558.3	8.9	107.7	27.9	413.8	1,673.7	248.4	1,257.3	167.9
Jackson, TN M.S.A. Includes Chester, Crockett, Gibson, and Madison Counties	178,525									
City of Jackson	67,234	703	12	21	87	583	2,414	361	1,814	239
Total area actually reporting	100.0%	1,115	17	46	106	946	3,840	701	2,750	389
Rate per 100,000 inhabitants		624.6	9.5	25.8	59.4	529.9	2,151.0	392.7	1,540.4	217.9
Jacksonville, FL M.S.A. Includes Baker, Clay, Duval, Nassau, and St. Johns Counties	1,580,803									
City of Jacksonville	920,508	6,424	140	456	928	4,900	26,432	3,860	19,602	2,970
Total area actually reporting	100.0%	7,901	156	641	1,085	6,019	34,037	4,996	25,414	3,627
Rate per 100,000 inhabitants		499.8	9.9	40.5	68.6	380.8	2,153.1	316.0	1,607.7	229.4
Jacksonville, NC M.S.A. Includes Onslow County	199,234									
City of Jacksonville	71,842	245	3	24	23	195	1,481	263	1,153	65
Total area actually reporting	100.0%	419	4	40	40	335	3,151	720	2,236	195
Rate per 100,000 inhabitants		210.3	2.0	20.1	20.1	168.1	1,581.6	361.4	1,122.3	97.9
Janesville-Beloit, WI M.S.A. Includes Rock County	163,558									
City of Janesville	64,682	145	4	31	36	74	1,392	136	1,200	56
City of Beloit	36,921	179	2	23	34	120	1,069	117	878	74
Total area actually reporting	100.0%	381	6	63	75	237	2,916	324	2,427	165
Rate per 100,000 inhabitants		232.9	3.7	38.5	45.9	144.9	1,782.9	198.1	1,483.9	100.9
Jefferson City, MO M.S.A.[2] Includes Callaway,[2] Cole,[2] Moniteau, and Osage Counties	151,302									
City of Jefferson City	42,653	109	2	17	16	74	821	70	658	93
Total area actually reporting	97.8%	238	4	44	19	171	2,367	425	1,702	240
Estimated total	100.0%	251	4	45	20	182	2,465	436	1,775	254
Rate per 100,000 inhabitants		165.9	2.6	29.7	13.2	120.3	1,629.2	288.2	1,173.2	167.9
Johnson City, TN M.S.A. Includes Carter, Unicoi, and Washington Counties	204,189									
City of Johnson City	66,917	295	3	29	38	225	2,701	285	2,173	243
Total area actually reporting	100.0%	625	6	56	51	512	4,371	567	3,231	573
Rate per 100,000 inhabitants		306.1	2.9	27.4	25.0	250.7	2,140.7	277.7	1,582.4	280.6
Jonesboro, AR M.S.A. Includes Craighead and Poinsett Counties	135,377									
City of Jonesboro	79,702	642	12	78	55	497	2,825	1,038	1,576	211
Total area actually reporting	95.8%	871	13	130	63	665	3,847	1,339	2,193	315
Estimated total	100.0%	893	13	132	67	681	3,964	1,358	2,276	330
Rate per 100,000 inhabitants		659.6	9.6	97.5	49.5	503.0	2,928.1	1,003.1	1,681.2	243.8
Joplin, MO M.S.A.[2] Includes Jasper and Newton[2] Counties	179,903									
City of Joplin	50,935	338	9	49	67	213	3,276	379	2,528	369
Total area actually reporting	100.0%	655	11	98	91	455	6,354	868	4,761	725
Rate per 100,000 inhabitants		364.1	6.1	54.5	50.6	252.9	3,531.9	482.5	2,646.4	403.0
Kahului-Wailuku-Lahaina, HI M.S.A. Includes Maui County	167,178									
Total area actually reporting	100.0%	379	5	71	59	244	3,537	496	2,612	429
Rate per 100,000 inhabitants		226.7	3.0	42.5	35.3	146.0	2,115.7	296.7	1,562.4	256.6
Kalamazoo-Portage, MI M.S.A. Includes Kalamazoo County	265,804									
City of Kalamazoo	76,411	1,094	14	77	136	867	3,670	737	2,445	488
City of Portage	49,798	111	2	15	10	84	1,340	153	1,098	89
Total area actually reporting	100.0%	1,763	20	175	199	1,369	8,789	1,571	6,144	1,074
Rate per 100,000 inhabitants		663.3	7.5	65.8	74.9	515.0	3,306.6	591.0	2,311.5	404.1
Kankakee, IL M.S.A.[4] Includes Kankakee County[4]	108,899									
City of Kankakee[4]	25,863	244	8	23	33	180		112		52
Total area actually reporting	75.7%	340	9	50	41	240		203		93

Table 6. Crime in the United States, by Selected Metropolitan Statistical Area, 2020—Continued

(Number, percent, rate per 100,000 population.)

Area	Population	Violent crime	Murder and nonnegligent manslaughter	Rape[1]	Robbery	Aggravated assault	Property crime	Burglary	Larceny-theft	Motor vehicle theft
Estimated total	100.0%	387	10	57	52	268		250		120
Rate per 100,000 inhabitants		355.4	9.2	52.3	47.8	246.1		229.6		110.2
Kennewick-Richland, WA M.S.A.	303,959									
Includes Benton and Franklin Counties										
City of Kennewick	85,526	215	1	38	46	130	2,836	521	2,097	218
City of Richland	59,370	164	3	33	18	110	1,553	267	1,216	70
Total area actually reporting	100.0%	718	9	116	133	460	6,869	1,323	5,010	536
Rate per 100,000 inhabitants		236.2	3.0	38.2	43.8	151.3	2,259.8	435.3	1,648.2	176.3
Killeen-Temple, TX M.S.A.2,3	464,991									
Includes Bell, Coryell, and Lampasas Counties[2]										
City of Killeen[2,3]	154,417	1,033	26	87	159	761			1,851	436
City of Temple	79,878	297	8	64	29	196	2,098	302	1,460	336
Total area actually reporting	99.6%	1,750	48	216	228	1,258			5,641	1,047
Estimated total	100.0%	1,754	48	216	228	1,262			5,663	1,052
Rate per 100,000 inhabitants		377.2	10.3	46.5	49.0	271.4			1,217.9	226.2
Kingsport-Bristol, TN-VA M.S.A.	306,891									
Includes Hawkins and Sullivan Counties, TN and Scott and Washington Counties and Bristol City, VA										
City of Kingsport, TN	54,260	372	5	40	28	299	2,426	271	1,856	299
City of Bristol, TN	27,013	155	3	19	10	123	774	73	617	84
Total area actually reporting	100.0%	1,116	20	144	59	893	6,466	919	4,679	868
Rate per 100,000 inhabitants		363.6	6.5	46.9	19.2	291.0	2,106.9	299.5	1,524.6	282.8
Kingston, NY M.S.A.	175,918									
Includes Ulster County										
City of Kingston	22,682	85	3	12	17	53	455	55	378	22
Total area actually reporting	92.0%	224	5	64	25	130	1,550	178	1,303	69
Estimated total	100.0%	246	5	67	29	145	1,846	208	1,561	77
Rate per 100,000 inhabitants		139.8	2.8	38.1	16.5	82.4	1,049.4	118.2	887.3	43.8
Knoxville, TN M.S.A.	875,248									
Includes Anderson, Blount, Campbell, Knox, Loudon, Morgan, Roane, and Union Counties										
City of Knoxville	188,672	1,528	38	124	241	1,125	7,977	1,080	5,775	1,122
Total area actually reporting	100.0%	3,343	56	326	328	2,633	17,024	2,674	11,953	2,397
Rate per 100,000 inhabitants		381.9	6.4	37.2	37.5	300.8	1,945.0	305.5	1,365.7	273.9
Kokomo, IN M.S.A.[2]	82,444									
Includes Howard County[2]										
City of Kokomo[2]	58,001	437	8	25	38	366	1,152	225	838	89
Total area actually reporting	98.6%	490	8	28	40	414	1,291	267	921	103
Estimated total	100.0%	498	8	29	42	419	1,313	276	933	104
Rate per 100,000 inhabitants		604.0	9.7	35.2	50.9	508.2	1,592.6	334.8	1,131.7	126.1
La Crosse-Onalaska, WI-MN M.S.A.[2]	136,752									
Includes Houston County, MN[2] and La Crosse County, WI										
City of La Crosse, WI	51,211	131	1	34	26	70	2,236	170	1,958	108
City of Onalaska, WI	19,072	19	0	1	5	13	715	44	655	16
Total area actually reporting	100.0%	213	1	46	31	135	3,421	293	2,975	153
Rate per 100,000 inhabitants		155.8	0.7	33.6	22.7	98.7	2,501.6	214.3	2,175.5	111.9
Lafayette, LA M.S.A.	489,998									
Includes Acadia, Iberia, Lafayette, St. Martin, and Vermilion Parishes										
City of Lafayette	126,679	712	14	17	147	534	5,725	1,069	4,247	409
Total area actually reporting	84.7%	1,919	37	75	227	1,580	10,679	2,284	7,553	842
Estimated total	100.0%	2,205	41	104	276	1,784	12,188	2,523	8,644	1,021
Rate per 100,000 inhabitants		450.0	8.4	21.2	56.3	364.1	2,487.4	514.9	1,764.1	208.4
Lake Charles, LA M.S.A.[2]	210,851									
Includes Calcasieu and Cameron Parishes										
City of Lake Charles[2]	79,077	409	7	31	49	322	2,511	849	1,424	238
Total area actually reporting	95.2%	1,625	19	123	87	1,396	7,839	2,215	4,924	700
Estimated total	100.0%	1,663	19	127	94	1,423	8,041	2,247	5,070	724
Rate per 100,000 inhabitants		788.7	9.0	60.2	44.6	674.9	3,813.6	1,065.7	2,404.5	343.4
Lake Havasu City-Kingman, AZ M.S.A.[2]	214,625									
Includes Mohave County										
City of Lake Havasu City[2]	56,243	105	0	27	3	75	790	115	619	56
City of Kingman	31,351	124	2	9	17	96	1,106	136	868	102
Total area actually reporting	100.0%	490	14	50	47	379	4,643	889	3,324	430
Rate per 100,000 inhabitants		228.3	6.5	23.3	21.9	176.6	2,163.3	414.2	1,548.7	200.3
Lakeland-Winter Haven, FL M.S.A.	737,548									
Includes Polk County										
City of Lakeland	113,876	404	12	58	80	254	2,813	320	2,275	218
City of Winter Haven	46,275	171	4	19	12	136	920	125	724	71

Table 6. Crime in the United States, by Selected Metropolitan Statistical Area, 2020—Continued

(Number, percent, rate per 100,000 population.)

Area	Population	Violent crime	Murder and nonnegligent manslaughter	Rape[1]	Robbery	Aggravated assault	Property crime	Burglary	Larceny-theft	Motor vehicle theft
Total area actually reporting	100.0%	2,115	40	171	209	1,695	10,002	1,576	7,471	955
Rate per 100,000 inhabitants		286.8	5.4	23.2	28.3	229.8	1,356.1	213.7	1,013.0	129.5
Lansing-East Lansing, MI M.S.A.	550,296									
Includes Clinton, Eaton, Ingham, and Shiawassee Counties										
City of Lansing	118,651	1,699	16	121	195	1,367	3,565	1,002	1,993	570
City of East Lansing	48,098	74	0	17	13	44	817	86	568	163
Total area actually reporting	100.0%	2,741	23	385	259	2,074	9,020	1,795	6,111	1,114
Rate per 100,000 inhabitants		498.1	4.2	70.0	47.1	376.9	1,639.1	326.2	1,110.5	202.4
Laredo, TX M.S.A.[2]	278,663									
Includes Webb County[2]										
City of Laredo	265,515	859	12	90	156	601	3,836	626	2,994	216
Total area actually reporting	98.3%	924	12	95	158	659	4,093	705	3,146	242
Estimated total	100.0%	936	12	96	159	669	4,175	719	3,207	249
Rate per 100,000 inhabitants		335.9	4.3	34.5	57.1	240.1	1,498.2	258.0	1,150.9	89.4
Las Vegas-Henderson-Paradise, NV M.S.A.[2]	2,313,970									
Includes Clark County										
City of Las Vegas Metropolitan Police Department[2]	1,693,061	8,934	96	1,068	1,707	6,063	37,426	7,057	23,546	6,823
City of Henderson[2]	328,056	682	13	104	177	388	4,679	619	3,516	544
Total area actually reporting	100.0%	11,077	127	1,264	2,322	7,364	47,356	8,683	30,109	8,564
Rate per 100,000 inhabitants		478.7	5.5	54.6	100.3	318.2	2,046.5	375.2	1,301.2	370.1
Lawton, OK M.S.A.	125,862									
Includes Comanche and Cotton Counties										
City of Lawton	92,507	727	14	79	102	532	2,071	632	1,166	273
Total area actually reporting	100.0%	759	16	85	106	552	2,343	723	1,305	315
Rate per 100,000 inhabitants		603.0	12.7	67.5	84.2	438.6	1,861.6	574.4	1,036.8	250.3
Lewiston, ID-WA M.S.A.	63,436									
Includes Nez Perce County, ID and Asotin County, WA										
City of Lewiston, ID	32,886	61	1	15	4	41	767	135	582	50
Total area actually reporting	100.0%	117	3	27	7	80	1,307	254	968	85
Rate per 100,000 inhabitants		184.4	4.7	42.6	11.0	126.1	2,060.3	400.4	1,525.9	134.0
Lewiston-Auburn, ME M.S.A.[2]	108,661									
Includes Androscoggin County[2]										
City of Lewiston	36,186	97	2	26	16	53	639	81	519	39
City of Auburn	23,455	46	2	18	6	20	518	41	455	22
Total area actually reporting	100.0%	193	4	61	23	105	1,449	169	1,204	76
Rate per 100,000 inhabitants		177.6	3.7	56.1	21.2	96.6	1,333.5	155.5	1,108.0	69.9
Lexington-Fayette, KY M.S.A.	521,623									
Includes Bourbon, Clark, Fayette, Jessamine, Scott, and Woodford Counties										
City of Lexington	325,851	1,043	28	178	335	502	9,357	1,450	6,870	1,037
Total area actually reporting	100.0%	1,308	31	236	391	650	13,357	2,072	9,824	1,461
Rate per 100,000 inhabitants		250.8	5.9	45.2	75.0	124.6	2,560.7	397.2	1,883.4	280.1
Little Rock-North Little Rock-Conway, AR M.S.A.	747,089									
Includes Faulkner, Grant, Lonoke, Perry, Pulaski, and Saline Counties										
City of Little Rock	197,688	3,657	49	196	376	3,036	9,602	1,527	7,062	1,013
City of North Little Rock	66,303	665	20	12	110	523	2,433	366	1,750	317
City of Conway	68,599	359	3	45	29	282	1,915	159	1,628	128
Total area actually reporting	100.0%	7,014	98	504	664	5,748	23,746	4,039	17,116	2,591
Rate per 100,000 inhabitants		938.8	13.1	67.5	88.9	769.4	3,178.5	540.6	2,291.0	346.8
Logan, UT-ID M.S.A.[2]	143,828									
Includes Franklin County, ID and Cache County, UT[2]										
City of Logan, UT	51,899	100	0	41	6	53	592	82	472	38
Total area actually reporting	91.4%	156	1	73	6	76	993	134	756	103
Estimated total	100.0%	170	1	78	7	84	1,148	158	871	119
Rate per 100,000 inhabitants		118.2	0.7	54.2	4.9	58.4	798.2	109.9	605.6	82.7
Longview, TX M.S.A.[2]	286,379									
Includes Gregg, Harrison, Rusk, and Upshur[2] Counties										
City of Longview	81,751	276	10	62	47	157	2,362	461	1,729	172
Total area actually reporting	99.7%	891	23	142	97	629	5,916	1,258	4,062	596
Estimated total	100.0%	893	23	142	97	631	5,930	1,261	4,071	598
Rate per 100,000 inhabitants		311.8	8.0	49.6	33.9	220.3	2,070.7	440.3	1,421.5	208.8
Longview, WA M.S.A.	111,183									
Includes Cowlitz County										
City of Longview	38,629	99	0	25	20	54	1,196	214	846	136
Total area actually reporting	100.0%	208	2	60	26	120	2,224	436	1,527	261
Rate per 100,000 inhabitants		187.1	1.8	54.0	23.4	107.9	2,000.3	392.1	1,373.4	234.7

Table 6. Crime in the United States, by Selected Metropolitan Statistical Area, 2020—Continued

(Number, percent, rate per 100,000 population.)

Area	Population	Violent crime	Murder and nonnegligent manslaughter	Rape[1]	Robbery	Aggravated assault	Property crime	Burglary	Larceny-theft	Motor vehicle theft
Los Angeles-Long Beach-Anaheim, CA M.S.A.	13,124,616									
Includes the Metropolitan Divisions of Anaheim-Santa Ana-Irvine and Los Angeles-Long Beach-Glendale										
City of Los Angeles	4,000,587	28,882	351	1,983	8,013	18,535	85,932	13,773	50,990	21,169
City of Long Beach	462,654	2,343	36	242	721	1,344	12,707	2,554	7,373	2,780
City of Anaheim	351,913	1,241	16	133	412	680	8,865	1,229	5,897	1,739
City of Santa Ana	333,107	1,429	15	145	401	868	6,926	1,136	4,078	1,712
City of Irvine	297,069	152	1	36	49	66	4,452	828	3,336	288
City of Glendale	200,168	206	3	14	87	102	3,197	407	2,357	433
City of Torrance	143,421	274	3	44	105	122	2,935	378	2,060	497
City of Pasadena	141,473	414	7	51	118	238	3,021	654	2,015	352
City of Orange	138,846	180	4	14	54	108	2,396	504	1,468	424
City of Costa Mesa	113,317	488	2	64	116	306	3,581	513	2,699	369
City of Burbank	102,419	174	1	12	48	113	2,474	293	1,880	301
City of Carson	91,372	392	8	21	98	265	2,044	253	1,262	529
City of Santa Monica	90,474	541	1	38	167	335	3,852	931	2,530	391
City of Newport Beach	84,448	141	1	29	43	68	1,785	321	1,312	152
City of Tustin	79,795	148	0	13	76	59	2,131	283	1,586	262
City of Gardena	59,385	269	5	18	104	142	1,324	168	686	470
City of Arcadia	58,122	87	2	6	20	59	1,034	265	696	73
City of Fountain Valley	55,345	67	0	6	23	38	1,338	199	998	141
Total area actually reporting	100.0%	62,030	737	4,538	17,385	39,370	274,976	46,244	169,909	58,823
Rate per 100,000 inhabitants		472.6	5.6	34.6	132.5	300.0	2,095.1	352.3	1,294.6	448.2
Anaheim-Santa Ana-Irvine, CA M.D.	3,162,050									
Includes Orange County										
Total area actually reporting	100.0%	7,340	59	777	2,134	4,370	61,066	9,427	42,599	9,040
Rate per 100,000 inhabitants		232.1	1.9	24.6	67.5	138.2	1,931.2	298.1	1,347.2	285.9
Los Angeles-Long Beach-Glendale, CA M.D.	9,962,566									
Includes Los Angeles County										
Total area actually reporting	100.0%	54,690	678	3,761	15,251	35,000	213,910	36,817	127,310	49,783
Rate per 100,000 inhabitants		549.0	6.8	37.8	153.1	351.3	2,147.1	369.6	1,277.9	499.7
Lubbock, TX M.S.A.[2]	324,679									
Includes Crosby, Lubbock, and Lynn[2] Counties										
City of Lubbock	262,146	2,852	28	225	431	2,168	10,770	2,296	7,316	1,158
Total area actually reporting	98.3%	2,973	31	251	442	2,249	11,862	2,564	8,015	1,283
Estimated total	100.0%	2,985	31	252	443	2,259	11,956	2,584	8,075	1,297
Rate per 100,000 inhabitants		919.4	9.5	77.6	136.4	695.8	3,682.4	795.9	2,487.1	399.5
Lynchburg, VA M.S.A.	264,579									
Includes Amherst, Appomattox, Bedford, and Campbell Counties and Lynchburg City										
City of Lynchburg	82,871	367	3	36	51	277	1,350	177	1,047	126
Total area actually reporting	100.0%	646	9	84	64	489	3,103	378	2,446	279
Rate per 100,000 inhabitants		244.2	3.4	31.7	24.2	184.8	1,172.8	142.9	924.5	105.5
Macon-Bibb County, GA M.S.A.[2]	229,395									
Includes Bibb,[2] Crawford,[2] Jones,[2] Monroe, and Twiggs[2] Counties										
Total area actually reporting	87.5%	1,529	42	69	212	1,206	5,863	1,008	4,084	771
Estimated total	100.0%	1,624	44	78	222	1,280	6,299	1,088	4,369	842
Rate per 100,000 inhabitants		707.9	19.2	34.0	96.8	558.0	2,745.9	474.3	1,904.6	367.1
Madera, CA M.S.A.	156,466									
Includes Madera County										
City of Madera	66,351	310	4	35	69	202	1,141	200	691	250
Total area actually reporting	100.0%	578	9	61	105	403	2,132	353	1,329	450
Rate per 100,000 inhabitants		369.4	5.8	39.0	67.1	257.6	1,362.6	225.6	849.4	287.6
Madison, WI M.S.A.	671,149									
Includes Columbia, Dane, Green, and Iowa Counties										
City of Madison	262,736	842	10	74	165	593	7,301	1,307	5,346	648
Total area actually reporting	98.3%	1,310	16	157	228	909	11,885	1,914	8,980	991
Estimated total	100.0%	1,354	17	161	236	940	12,117	1,951	9,148	1,018
Rate per 100,000 inhabitants		201.7	2.5	24.0	35.2	140.1	1,805.4	290.7	1,363.0	151.7
Manchester-Nashua, NH M.S.A.	419,347									
Includes Hillsborough County										
City of Manchester	113,018	670	5	73	110	482	2,560	287	2,096	177
City of Nashua	89,671	107	0	54	12	41	818	54	710	54
Total area actually reporting	98.3%	886	5	173	133	575	4,631	461	3,860	310
Estimated total	100.0%	913	5	177	137	594	4,772	484	3,962	326
Rate per 100,000 inhabitants		217.7	1.2	42.2	32.7	141.6	1,138.0	115.4	944.8	77.7
Manhattan, KS M.S.A.[3]	130,281									
Includes Geary, Pottawatomie,[3] and Riley Counties										
Total area actually reporting	96.3%	478	6	65	20	387			1,573	151
Estimated total	100.0%	490	6	67	21	396			1,658	163
Rate per 100,000 inhabitants		376.1	4.6	51.4	16.1	304.0			1,272.6	125.1

Table 6. Crime in the United States, by Selected Metropolitan Statistical Area, 2020—Continued

(Number, percent, rate per 100,000 population.)

Area	Population	Violent crime	Murder and nonnegligent manslaughter	Rape[1]	Robbery	Aggravated assault	Property crime	Burglary	Larceny-theft	Motor vehicle theft
Mankato, MN M.S.A.[2]	102,134									
Includes Blue Earth and Nicollet[2] Counties										
City of Mankato	43,276	108	1	30	11	66	1,033	115	855	63
Total area actually reporting	100.0%	191	1	49	15	126	1,479	196	1,187	96
Rate per 100,000 inhabitants		187.0	1.0	48.0	14.7	123.4	1,448.1	191.9	1,162.2	94.0
McAllen-Edinburg-Mission, TX M.S.A.[2]	876,280									
Includes Hidalgo County[2]										
City of McAllen	144,569	123	3	43	23	54	2,791	139	2,603	49
City of Edinburg	103,491	325	6	79	36	204	2,310	281	1,966	63
City of Mission	85,052	132	1	27	14	90	1,304	133	1,096	75
Total area actually reporting	98.1%	2,363	35	419	271	1,638	15,559	2,055	12,658	846
Estimated total	100.0%	2,408	35	424	276	1,673	15,851	2,104	12,877	870
Rate per 100,000 inhabitants		274.8	4.0	48.4	31.5	190.9	1,808.9	240.1	1,469.5	99.3
Medford, OR M.S.A.	221,880									
Includes Jackson County										
City of Medford	84,016	388	2	36	94	256	3,615	296	3,012	307
Total area actually reporting	100.0%	663	3	67	122	471	6,289	698	5,058	533
Rate per 100,000 inhabitants		298.8	1.4	30.2	55.0	212.3	2,834.4	314.6	2,279.6	240.2
Memphis, TN-MS-AR M.S.A.[2]	1,348,509									
Includes Crittenden County, AR; DeSoto, Marshall, Tate, and Tunica[2] Counties, MS; and Fayette, Shelby, and Tipton Counties, TN										
City of Memphis, TN	650,937	15,310	289	411	2,131	12,479	36,197	5,831	25,924	4,442
Total area actually reporting	95.3%	18,195	324	605	2,375	14,891	49,358	7,664	35,783	5,911
Estimated total	100.0%	18,324	327	648	2,384	14,965	50,144	7,822	36,321	6,001
Rate per 100,000 inhabitants		1,358.8	24.2	48.1	176.8	1,109.7	3,718.5	580.0	2,693.4	445.0
Merced, CA M.S.A.	277,305									
Includes Merced County										
City of Merced	84,197	672	7	40	133	492	1,949	390	1,132	427
Total area actually reporting	100.0%	1,660	24	84	252	1,300	5,951	1,285	3,320	1,346
Rate per 100,000 inhabitants		598.6	8.7	30.3	90.9	468.8	2,146.0	463.4	1,197.2	485.4
Miami-Fort Lauderdale-Pompano Beach, FL M.S.A.	6,216,543									
Includes the Metropolitan Divisions of Fort Lauderdale-Pompano Beach-Sunrise, Miami-Miami Beach-Kendall, and West Palm Beach-Boca Raton-Boynton Beach										
City of Miami	476,102	2,645	61	94	610	1,880	13,092	1,453	10,017	1,622
City of Fort Lauderdale	184,347	1,158	37	91	321	709	7,662	1,074	5,681	907
City of Pompano Beach	113,545	837	19	62	244	512	3,142	434	2,237	471
City of West Palm Beach	113,268	863	18	76	231	538	3,862	452	2,967	443
City of Boca Raton	101,583	206	2	35	67	102	1,996	191	1,573	232
City of Sunrise	96,428	195	3	21	60	111	1,324	96	1,031	197
City of Miami Beach	89,017	668	5	62	200	401	5,109	444	4,244	421
City of Deerfield Beach	81,749	285	3	20	59	203	1,603	135	1,273	195
City of Boynton Beach	79,913	523	9	20	105	389	1,794	153	1,468	173
City of Delray Beach	70,487	401	5	31	67	298	2,412	245	1,929	238
City of Jupiter	67,054	83	1	10	13	59	701	99	552	50
City of Doral	68,425	63	0	9	8	46	1,238	103	986	149
City of Palm Beach Gardens	58,629	65	1	8	14	42	999	86	871	42
City of Coral Gables	50,017	51	0	7	13	31	1,167	127	959	81
Total area actually reporting	99.4%	25,744	463	1,909	5,499	17,873	135,122	13,941	106,055	15,126
Estimated total	100.0%	25,920	465	1,921	5,529	18,005	136,292	14,095	106,985	15,212
Rate per 100,000 inhabitants		417.0	7.5	30.9	88.9	289.6	2,192.4	226.7	1,721.0	244.7
Fort Lauderdale-Pompano Beach-Deerfield Beach, FL M.D.	1,970,496									
Includes Broward County										
Total area actually reporting	100.0%	7,058	150	596	1,716	4,596	40,341	4,385	30,940	5,016
Rate per 100,000 inhabitants		358.2	7.6	30.2	87.1	233.2	2,047.3	222.5	1,570.2	254.6
Miami-Miami Beach-Kendall, FL M.D.	2,733,199									
Includes Miami-Dade County										
Total area actually reporting	98.6%	13,125	224	776	2,687	9,438	66,623	6,400	52,888	7,335
Estimated total	100.0%	13,301	226	788	2,717	9,570	67,793	6,554	53,818	7,421
Rate per 100,000 inhabitants		486.6	8.3	28.8	99.4	350.1	2,480.4	239.8	1,969.0	271.5
West Palm Beach-Boca Raton-Boynton Beach, FL M.D.	1,512,848									
Includes Palm Beach County										
Total area actually reporting	100.0%	5,561	89	537	1,096	3,839	28,158	3,156	22,227	2,775
Rate per 100,000 inhabitants		367.6	5.9	35.5	72.4	253.8	1,861.3	208.6	1,469.2	183.4
Midland, MI M.S.A.	82,820									
Includes Midland County										
City of Midland	41,526	62	0	18	1	43	328	40	282	6
Total area actually reporting	100.0%	120	1	43	1	75	580	93	461	26
Rate per 100,000 inhabitants		144.9	1.2	51.9	1.2	90.6	700.3	112.3	556.6	31.4

Table 6. Crime in the United States, by Selected Metropolitan Statistical Area, 2020—Continued

(Number, percent, rate per 100,000 population.)

Area	Population	Violent crime	Murder and nonnegligent manslaughter	Rape[1]	Robbery	Aggravated assault	Property crime	Burglary	Larceny-theft	Motor vehicle theft
Midland, TX M.S.A.	187,186									
Includes Martin and Midland Counties										
City of Midland	150,529	549	10	81	50	408	3,119	404	2,249	466
Total area actually reporting	100.0%	700	13	92	55	540	4,058	532	2,838	688
Rate per 100,000 inhabitants		374.0	6.9	49.1	29.4	288.5	2,167.9	284.2	1,516.1	367.5
Milwaukee-Waukesha, WI M.S.A.[2]	1,575,891									
Includes Milwaukee, Ozaukee, Washington, and Waukesha[2] Counties										
City of Milwaukee	589,105	9,407	191	431	1,925	6,860	16,074	3,408	8,178	4,488
City of Waukesha	72,421	123	1	17	21	84	595	62	477	56
Total area actually reporting	99.5%	10,678	206	629	2,218	7,625	30,716	4,532	20,659	5,525
Estimated total	100.0%	10,688	206	631	2,219	7,632	30,821	4,540	20,751	5,530
Rate per 100,000 inhabitants		678.2	13.1	40.0	140.8	484.3	1,955.8	288.1	1,316.8	350.9
Missoula, MT M.S.A.	121,047									
Includes Missoula County										
City of Missoula	76,468	376	4	60	32	280	2,745	273	2,285	187
Total area actually reporting	100.0%	489	6	77	33	373	3,080	374	2,492	214
Rate per 100,000 inhabitants		404.0	5.0	63.6	27.3	308.1	2,544.5	309.0	2,058.7	176.8
Modesto, CA M.S.A.	549,195									
Includes Stanislaus County										
City of Modesto	216,560	1,603	16	106	281	1,200	5,340	706	3,533	1,101
Total area actually reporting	100.0%	2,823	33	185	587	2,018	10,843	1,825	6,927	2,091
Rate per 100,000 inhabitants		514.0	6.0	33.7	106.9	367.4	1,974.3	332.3	1,261.3	380.7
Monroe, LA M.S.A.	199,081									
Includes Morehouse, Ouachita, and Union Parishes										
City of Monroe	47,119	1,399	19	9	154	1,217	2,883	649	2,042	192
Total area actually reporting	91.4%	2,540	22	107	221	2,190	6,930	1,611	4,799	520
Estimated total	100.0%	2,605	23	113	233	2,236	7,275	1,665	5,049	561
Rate per 100,000 inhabitants		1,308.5	11.6	56.8	117.0	1,123.2	3,654.3	836.3	2,536.2	281.8
Morristown, TN M.S.A.	143,413									
Includes Grainger, Hamblen, and Jefferson Counties										
City of Morristown	30,330	258	1	12	22	223	1,290	177	998	115
Total area actually reporting	100.0%	519	2	39	30	448	2,686	473	1,900	313
Rate per 100,000 inhabitants		361.9	1.4	27.2	20.9	312.4	1,872 9	329.8	1,324.8	218.3
Mount Vernon-Anacortes, WA M.S.A.	130,213									
Includes Skagit County										
City of Mount Vernon	36,513	70	1	9	13	47	1,109	142	857	110
City of Anacortes	17,735	15	0	2	7	6	398	43	327	28
Total area actually reporting	100.0%	192	2	20	36	134	3,153	467	2,436	250
Rate per 100,000 inhabitants		147.5	1.5	15.4	27.6	102.9	2,421.4	358.6	1,870.8	192.0
Muskegon, MI M.S.A.	173,165									
Includes Muskegon County										
City of Muskegon	36,391	254	5	8	20	221	1,004	174	740	90
Total area actually reporting	100.0%	714	10	97	58	549	3,581	486	2,841	254
Rate per 100,000 inhabitants		412.3	5.8	56.0	33.5	317.0	2,068.0	280.7	1,640.6	146.7
Napa, CA M.S.A.	136,475									
Includes Napa County										
City of Napa	78,237	267	0	44	36	187	1,320	272	883	165
Total area actually reporting	100.0%	539	1	65	59	414	2,306	522	1,511	273
Rate per 100,000 inhabitants		394.9	0.7	47.6	43.2	303.4	1,689.7	382.5	1,107.2	200.0
Naples-Marco Island, FL M.S.A.	391,365									
Includes Collier County										
City of Naples	22,388	21	1	4	1	15	276	26	223	27
City of Marco Island	18,121	15	0	3	1	11	103	13	75	15
Total area actually reporting	100.0%	876	6	68	122	680	3,806	416	3,039	351
Rate per 100,000 inhabitants		223.8	1.5	17.4	31.2	173.8	972.5	106.3	776.5	89.7
Nashville-Davidson–Murfreesboro–Franklin, TN M.S.A.	1,969,367									
Includes Cannon, Cheatham, Davidson, Dickson, Macon, Maury, Robertson, Rutherford, Smith, Sumner, Trousdale, Williamson, and Wilson Counties										
City of Metropolitan Nashville Police Department	688,013	7,951	113	385	1,742	5,711	28,023	3,745	21,238	3,040
City of Murfreesboro	151,769	740	11	91	101	537	3,772	362	3,113	297
City of Franklin	85,722	195	1	17	14	163	792	58	685	49
Total area actually reporting	100.0%	12,137	152	757	2,097	9,131	46,329	6,307	35,206	4,816
Rate per 100,000 inhabitants		616.3	7.7	38.4	106.5	463.7	2,352.5	320.3	1,787.7	244.5
New Bern, NC M.S.A.	123,955									
Includes Craven, Jones, and Pamlico Counties										
City of New Bern	30,047	190	4	11	21	154	930	199	701	30
Total area actually reporting	89.0%	421	11	32	39	339	2,366	589	1,640	137

Table 6. Crime in the United States, by Selected Metropolitan Statistical Area, 2020—Continued

(Number, percent, rate per 100,000 population.)

Area	Population	Violent crime	Murder and nonnegligent manslaughter	Rape[1]	Robbery	Aggravated assault	Property crime	Burglary	Larceny-theft	Motor vehicle theft
Estimated total	100.0%	451	11	35	42	363	2,666	657	1,850	159
Rate per 100,000 inhabitants		363.8	8.9	28.2	33.9	292.8	2,150.8	530.0	1,492.5	128.3
New Haven-Milford, CT M.S.A.[2]	799,461									
Includes New Haven County										
City of New Haven	130,299	922	21	29	336	536	4,575	547	3,267	761
City of Milford[2]	54,968	33	0	3	25	5	1,107	109	884	114
Total area actually reporting	100.0%	2,049	49	164	745	1,091	17,342	1,843	12,726	2,773
Rate per 100,000 inhabitants		256.3	6.1	20.5	93.2	136.5	2,169.2	230.5	1,591.8	346.9
New Orleans-Metairie, LA M.S.A.[2]	1,275,017									
Includes Jefferson, Orleans, Plaquemines, St. Bernard, St. Charles,[2] St. James, St. John the Baptist, and St. Tammany Parishes										
City of New Orleans	393,779	5,215	201	712	1,106	3,196	17,876	1,994	12,358	3,524
Total area actually reporting	95.3%	7,698	272	899	1,464	5,063	33,569	3,915	25,120	4,534
Estimated total	100.0%	7,960	277	924	1,504	5,255	35,121	4,145	26,290	4,686
Rate per 100,000 inhabitants		624.3	21.7	72.5	118.0	412.2	2,754.6	325.1	2,061.9	367.5
Niles, MI M.S.A.	152,517									
Includes Berrien County										
City of Niles	11,102	74	0	16	11	47	328	42	225	61
Total area actually reporting	100.0%	1,013	8	130	58	817	2,882	566	2,030	286
Rate per 100,000 inhabitants		664.2	5.2	85.2	38.0	535.7	1,889.6	371.1	1,331.0	187.5
North Port-Sarasota-Bradenton, FL M.S.A.	850,904									
Includes Manatee and Sarasota Counties										
City of North Port	72,389	117	3	27	6	81	743	88	634	21
City of Sarasota	59,002	349	1	32	59	257	1,622	227	1,271	124
City of Bradenton	60,688	306	4	25	46	231	1,322	108	1,115	99
City of Venice	24,366	16	0	2	5	9	346	56	274	16
Total area actually reporting	100.0%	2,854	22	321	373	2,138	12,831	1,711	10,194	926
Rate per 100,000 inhabitants		335.4	2.6	37.7	43.8	251.3	1,507.9	201.1	1,198.0	108.8
Norwich-New London, CT M.S.A.	173,802									
Includes New London County										
City of Norwich	38,576	134	3	14	28	89	542	114	350	78
City of New London	26,776	67	0	7	24	36	500	79	333	88
Total area actually reporting	100.0%	313	4	42	66	201	2,210	302	1,635	273
Rate per 100,000 inhabitants		180.1	2.3	24.2	38.0	115.6	1,271.6	173.8	940.7	157.1
Ocala, FL M.S.A.	368,501									
Includes Marion County										
City of Ocala	61,275	413	3	55	61	294	1,936	161	1,663	112
Total area actually reporting	100.0%	1,557	19	184	136	1,218	6,012	1,141	4,289	582
Rate per 100,000 inhabitants		422.5	5.2	49.9	36.9	330.5	1,631.5	309.6	1,163.9	157.9
Ocean City, NJ M.S.A.	91,384									
Includes Cape May County										
City of Ocean City	10,893	8	0	1	2	5	334	39	287	8
Total area actually reporting	100.0%	154	0	19	25	110	1,856	237	1,559	60
Rate per 100,000 inhabitants		168.5	0.0	20.8	27.4	120.4	2,031.0	259.3	1,706.0	65.7
Odessa, TX M.S.A.[2]	169,268									
Includes Ector County										
City of Odessa[2]	126,288	1,020	13	107	106	794	3,163	586	2,113	464
Total area actually reporting	100.0%	1,180	19	109	160	892	5,005	859	3,270	876
Rate per 100,000 inhabitants		697.1	11.2	64.4	94.5	527.0	2,956.8	507.5	1,931.8	517.5
Ogden-Clearfield, UT M.S.A.[2]	692,112									
Includes Box Elder,[2] Davis, Morgan, and Weber Counties										
City of Ogden	88,309	446	4	79	75	288	2,915	375	2,151	389
City of Clearfield	32,358	69	1	13	10	45	525	60	413	52
Total area actually reporting	100.0%	1,197	14	354	140	689	11,454	1,580	8,686	1,188
Rate per 100,000 inhabitants		172.9	2.0	51.1	20.2	99.6	1,654.9	228.3	1,255.0	171.6
Oklahoma City, OK M.S.A.[2]	1,427,075									
Includes Canadian, Cleveland, Grady, Lincoln, Logan, McClain, and Oklahoma Counties										
City of Oklahoma City[2]	663,661	4,818	63	559	817	3,379	25,853	5,849	16,222	3,782
Total area actually reporting	100.0%	6,719	111	842	1,032	4,734	41,616	8,847	27,156	5,613
Rate per 100,000 inhabitants		470.8	7.8	59.0	72.3	331.7	2,916.2	619.9	1,902.9	393.3
Olympia-Lacey-Tumwater, WA M.S.A.	294,061									
Includes Thurston County										
City of Olympia	53,571	268	1	24	69	174	1,753	271	1,284	198
City of Lacey	53,826	83	0	13	21	49	1,386	160	1,099	127
City of Tumwater	24,493	63	0	10	13	40	613	94	453	66
Total area actually reporting	100.0%	657	3	73	127	454	5,636	990	4,029	617
Rate per 100,000 inhabitants		223.4	1.0	24.8	43.2	154.4	1,916.6	336.7	1,370.1	209.8

Table 6. Crime in the United States, by Selected Metropolitan Statistical Area, 2020—Continued

(Number, percent, rate per 100,000 population.)

Area	Population	Violent crime	Murder and nonnegligent manslaughter	Rape[1]	Robbery	Aggravated assault	Property crime	Burglary	Larceny-theft	Motor vehicle theft
Omaha-Council Bluffs, NE-IA M.S.A. Includes Harrison, Mills, and Pottawattamie Counties, IA and Cass, Douglas, Sarpy, Saunders, and Washington Counties, NE	954,892									
City of Omaha, NE	480,297	3,032	37	351	464	2,180	15,247	1,521	10,697	3,029
City of Council Bluffs, IA	62,144	574	0	36	68	470	2,976	408	2,127	441
Total area actually reporting	99.6%	4,093	44	526	570	2,953	21,718	2,423	15,293	4,002
Estimated total	100.0%	4,103	44	527	574	2,958	21,780	2,431	15,337	4,012
Rate per 100,000 inhabitants		429.7	4.6	55.2	60.1	309.8	2,280.9	254.6	1,606.2	420.2
Orlando-Kissimmee-Sanford, FL M.S.A. Includes Lake, Orange, Osceola, and Seminole Counties	2,658,987									
City of Orlando	293,363	2,524	31	169	507	1,817	11,158	1,198	8,812	1,148
City of Kissimmee	74,337	318	4	29	32	253	1,707	206	1,359	142
City of Sanford	62,342	511	3	38	84	386	1,396	210	1,084	102
Total area actually reporting	100.0%	11,347	158	1,118	1,919	8,152	49,514	7,138	37,606	4,770
Rate per 100,000 inhabitants		426.7	5.9	42.0	72.2	306.6	1,862.1	268.4	1,414.3	179.4
Oshkosh-Neenah, WI M.S.A. Includes Winnebago County	172,301									
City of Oshkosh	67,080	187	4	48	12	123	1,239	138	1,036	65
City of Neenah	26,390	57	1	12	5	39	315	21	282	12
Total area actually reporting	98.6%	322	6	75	21	220	2,233	360	1,772	101
Estimated total	100.0%	332	6	76	23	227	2,283	368	1,808	107
Rate per 100,000 inhabitants		192.7	3.5	44.1	13.3	131.7	1,325.0	213.6	1,049.3	62.1
Owensboro, KY M.S.A. Includes Daviess, Hancock, and McLean Counties	119,839									
City of Owensboro	60,430	161	5	41	45	70	2,326	404	1,638	284
Total area actually reporting	100.0%	197	6	53	51	87	2,793	539	1,903	351
Rate per 100,000 inhabitants		164.4	5.0	44.2	42.6	72.6	2,330.6	449.8	1,588.0	292.9
Oxnard-Thousand Oaks-Ventura, CA M.S.A. Includes Ventura County	839,861									
City of Oxnard	210,064	743	8	81	274	380	4,323	638	2,907	778
City of Thousand Oaks	126,823	76	1	21	23	31	1,315	189	1,027	99
City of Ventura	109,295	328	2	31	94	201	3,086	460	2,354	272
City of Camarillo	70,424	53	0	16	17	20	817	100	661	56
Total area actually reporting	100.0%	1,686	20	224	494	948	13,083	1,909	9,616	1,558
Rate per 100,000 Inhabitants		200.7	2.4	26.7	58.8	112.9	1,557.8	227.3	1,145.0	185.5
Palm Bay-Melbourne-Titusville, FL M.S.A. Includes Brevard County	606,953									
City of Palm Bay	116,897	328	3	59	39	227	1,770	241	1,380	149
City of Melbourne	83,806	757	8	74	86	589	2,531	393	1,987	151
City of Titusville	46,919	295	5	24	51	215	1,081	199	764	118
Total area actually reporting	100.0%	2,288	30	225	298	1,735	10,662	1,629	8,161	872
Rate per 100,000 inhabitants		377.0	4.9	37.1	49.1	285.9	1,756.6	268.4	1,344.6	143.7
Panama City, FL M.S.A. Includes Bay County	174,857									
City of Panama City	34,672	303	4	38	29	232	1,453	252	1,059	142
Total area actually reporting	99.4%	843	11	93	67	672	4,603	771	3,451	381
Estimated total	100.0%	847	11	93	68	675	4,626	775	3,467	384
Rate per 100,000 inhabitants		484.4	6.3	53.2	38.9	386.0	2,645.6	443.2	1,982.8	219.6
Parkersburg-Vienna, WV M.S.A. Includes Wirt and Wood Counties	88,918									
City of Parkersburg	29,096	106	2	29	23	52	1,269	265	911	93
City of Vienna	10,049	9	0	1	1	7	348	10	331	7
Total area actually reporting	100.0%	257	2	56	25	174	2,013	380	1,476	157
Rate per 100,000 inhabitants		289.0	2.2	63.0	28.1	195.7	2,263.9	427.4	1,660.0	176.6
Pensacola-Ferry Pass-Brent, FL M.S.A. Includes Escambia and Santa Rosa Counties	507,320									
City of Pensacola	53,083	327	5	26	52	244	1,543	191	1,272	80
Total area actually reporting	100.0%	2,180	38	271	395	1,476	9,849	1,911	7,084	854
Rate per 100,000 inhabitants		429.7	7.5	53.4	77.9	290.9	1,941.4	376.7	1,396.4	168.3
Peoria, IL M.S.A.[4] Includes Fulton,[4] Marshall,[4] Peoria,[4] Stark,[4] Tazewell,[4] and Woodford Counties	396,798									
City of Peoria[4]	109,924	1,084	14	72	196	802		652		430
Total area actually reporting	91.7%	1,633	22	191	227	1,193		1,380		685
Estimated total	100.0%	1,689	23	200	237	1,229		1,439		719
Rate per 100,000 inhabitants		425.7	5.8	50.4	59.7	309.7		362.7		181.2
Phoenix-Mesa-Chandler, AZ M.S.A.[2] Includes Maricopa and Pinal Counties	5,064,185									
City of Phoenix	1,708,960	13,646	187	1,068	3,278	9,113	51,089	7,406	36,254	7,429
City of Mesa[2]	527,361	1,960	19	235	380	1,326	9,737	1,597	7,124	1,016

Table 6. Crime in the United States, by Selected Metropolitan Statistical Area, 2020—Continued

(Number, percent, rate per 100,000 population.)

Area	Population	Violent crime	Murder and nonnegligent manslaughter	Rape[1]	Robbery	Aggravated assault	Property crime	Burglary	Larceny-theft	Motor vehicle theft
City of Chandler	264,071	543	9	123	104	307	4,898	505	3,956	437
City of Scottsdale	263,006	470	7	109	97	257	4,945	683	3,963	299
City of Tempe	199,935	1,100	8	155	248	689	7,124	960	5,464	700
City of Casa Grande[2]	59,822	338	1	23	38	276	1,200	150	947	103
Total area actually reporting	90.5%	22,455	288	2,145	4,722	15,300	107,047	15,453	79,187	12,407
Estimated total	100.0%	23,512	314	2,250	4,749	16,199	112,293	16,684	82,568	13,041
Rate per 100,000 inhabitants		464.3	6.2	44.4	93.8	319.9	2,217.4	329.5	1,630.4	257.5
Pine Bluff, AR M.S.A	86,540									
Includes Cleveland, Jefferson, and Lincoln Counties										
City of Pine Bluff	40,718	746	23	27	59	637	1,990	414	1,323	253
Total area actually reporting	100.0%	950	24	55	70	801	2,638	578	1,710	350
Rate per 100,000 inhabitants		1,097.8	27.7	63.6	80.9	925.6	3,048.3	667.9	1,976.0	404.4
Pittsfield, MA M.S.A.	123,599									
Includes Berkshire County										
City of Pittsfield	41,865	341	1	35	34	271	664	232	369	63
Total area actually reporting	91.7%	509	1	56	49	403	1,350	369	884	97
Estimated total	100.0%	533	1	60	53	419	1,401	380	919	102
Rate per 100,000 inhabitants		431.2	0.8	48.5	42.9	339.0	1,133.5	307.4	743.5	82.5
Pocatello, ID M.S.A.	96,729									
Includes Bannock and Power Counties										
City of Pocatello	56,900	206	0	12	11	183	1,223	291	822	110
Total area actually reporting	100.0%	260	0	14	11	235	1,747	349	1,233	165
Rate per 100,000 inhabitants		268.8	0.0	14.5	11.4	242.9	1,806.1	360.8	1,274.7	170.6
Portland-South Portland, ME M.S.A.[2]	542,906									
Includes Cumberland, Sagadahoc, and York Counties[2]										
City of Portland	66,229	129	0	28	34	67	1,143	94	991	58
City of South Portland	25,593	32	1	4	10	17	402	24	346	32
Total area actually reporting	100.0%	516	1	163	80	272	5,524	582	4,641	301
Rate per 100,000 inhabitants		95.0	0.2	30.0	14.7	50.1	1,017.5	107.2	854.8	55.4
Portland-Vancouver-Hillsboro, OR-WA M.S.A.[3]	2,511,480									
Includes Clackamas, Columbia, Multnomah,[3] Washington, and Yamhill Counties, OR and Clark and Skamania Counties, WA										
City of Portland, OR	662,941	3,465	53	262	807	2,343	31,416	3,759	21,287	6,370
City of Vancouver, WA	186,440	884	5	137	167	575	6,709	1,065	4,448	1,196
City of Hillsboro, OR	111,146	257	2	55	46	154	2,147	212	1,695	240
City of Beaverton, OR	100,085	235	1	38	47	149	2,197	255	1,693	249
City of Tigard, OR	56,377	107	1	14	24	68	1,472	161	1,170	141
Total area actually reporting	99.5%			1,029	1,505	5,104	67,067	8,584	46,657	11,826
Estimated total	100.0%			1,032	1,507	5,116	67,267	8,607	46,815	11,845
Rate per 100,000 inhabitants				41.1	60.0	203.7	2,678.4	342.7	1,864.0	471.6
Port St. Lucie, FL M.S.A.	495,563									
Includes Martin and St. Lucie Counties										
City of Port St. Lucie	206,450	264	5	35	40	184	1,666	189	1,381	96
Total area actually reporting	100.0%	1,170	23	170	167	810	5,459	679	4,362	418
Rate per 100,000 inhabitants		236.1	4.6	34.3	33.7	163.5	1,101.6	137.0	880.2	84.3
Prescott Valley-Prescott, AZ M.S.A.	239,151									
Includes Yavapai County										
City of Prescott Valley	47,459	80	0	21	10	49	374	39	317	18
City of Prescott	44,835	168	0	31	3	134	657	129	494	34
Total area actually reporting	100.0%	581	8	72	24	477	2,910	490	2,195	225
Rate per 100,000 inhabitants		242.9	3.3	30.1	10.0	199.5	1,216.8	204.9	917.8	94.1
Providence-Warwick, RI-MA M.S.A.	1,621,159									
Includes Bristol County, MA and Bristol, Kent, Newport, Providence, and Washington Counties, RI										
City of Providence, RI	179,603	873	17	66	183	607	4,337	602	3,191	544
City of Warwick, RI	80,605	66	0	21	7	38	993	92	823	78
Total area actually reporting	99.5%	4,620	41	644	610	3,325	18,780	2,756	13,972	2,052
Estimated total	100.0%	4,630	41	645	611	3,333	18,808	2,760	13,995	2,053
Rate per 100,000 inhabitants		285.6	2.5	39.8	37.7	205.6	1,160.2	170.2	863.3	126.6
Pueblo, CO M.S.A.[5]	168,374									
Includes Pueblo County[5]										
City of Pueblo	113,002	1,181	16	199	198	768	5,233	896	3,399	938
Total area actually reporting	100.0%	1,216	18	199	208	791		1,112		1,078
Rate per 100,000 inhabitants		722.2	10.7	118.2	123.5	469.8		660.4		640.2
Punta Gorda, FL M.S.A.	191,879									
Includes Charlotte County										
City of Punta Gorda	20,766	14	0	0	2	12	272	14	241	17
Total area actually reporting	100.0%	292	1	32	21	238	1,651	221	1,302	128
Rate per 100,000 inhabitants		152.2	0.5	16.7	10.9	124.0	860.4	115.2	678.6	66.7

Table 6. Crime in the United States, by Selected Metropolitan Statistical Area, 2020—Continued

(Number, percent, rate per 100,000 population.)

Area	Population	Violent crime	Murder and nonnegligent manslaughter	Rape[1]	Robbery	Aggravated assault	Property crime	Burglary	Larceny-theft	Motor vehicle theft
Racine, WI M.S.A.[2]	196,239									
Includes Racine County[2]										
City of Racine	76,573	414	2	36	86	290	1,381	321	916	144
Total area actually reporting	100.0%	540	3	54	101	382	2,437	444	1,788	205
Rate per 100,000 inhabitants		275.2	1.5	27.5	51.5	194.7	1,241.9	226.3	911.1	104.5
Raleigh-Cary, NC M.S.A.	1,422,373									
Includes Franklin, Johnston, and Wake Counties										
City of Raleigh	480,964	1,886	21	165	467	1,233	9,716	1,298	7,060	1,358
City of Cary	172,079	115	1	13	25	76	1,627	194	1,323	110
Total area actually reporting	99.3%	3,144	47	276	668	2,153	21,023	3,118	15,791	2,114
Estimated total	100.0%	3,180	47	280	673	2,180	21,397	3,194	16,068	2,135
Rate per 100,000 inhabitants		223.6	3.3	19.7	47.3	153.3	1,504.3	224.6	1,129.7	150.1
Rapid City, SD M.S.A.	143,884									
Includes Meade and Pennington Counties										
City of Rapid City	78,492	673	13	108	104	448	3,137	657	2,014	466
Total area actually reporting	100.0%	957	15	211	115	616	4,275	887	2,804	584
Rate per 100,000 inhabitants		665.1	10.4	146.6	79.9	428.1	2,971.1	616.5	1,948.8	405.9
Redding, CA M.S.A.	178,587									
Includes Shasta County										
City of Redding	92,895	513	5	67	94	347	2,323	596	1,529	198
Total area actually reporting	100.0%	977	12	99	126	740	3,430	936	2,028	466
Rate per 100,000 inhabitants		547.1	6.7	55.4	70.6	414.4	1,920.6	524.1	1,135.6	260.9
Reno, NV M.S.A.[2]	483,469									
Includes Storey and Washoe Counties										
City of Reno[2]	259,168	1,460	17	281	286	876	5,564	1,105	3,486	973
Total area actually reporting	100.0%	2,238	27	415	374	1,422	8,842	1,787	5,637	1,418
Rate per 100,000 inhabitants		462.9	5.6	85.8	77.4	294.1	1,828.9	369.6	1,165.9	293.3
Richmond, VA M.S.A.	1,303,052									
Includes Amelia, Charles City, Chesterfield, Dinwiddie, Goochland, Hanover, Henrico, King and Queen, King William, New Kent, Powhatan, Prince George, and Sussex Counties and Colonial Heights, Hopewell, Petersburg, and Richmond Cities										
City of Richmond	233,350	814	66	20	274	454	6,816	771	5,434	611
Total area actually reporting	100.0%	2,811	129	268	605	1,809	23,905	2,229	19,789	1,887
Rate per 100,000 inhabitants		215.7	9.9	20.6	46.4	138.8	1,834.5	171.1	1,518.7	144.8
Riverside-San Bernardino-Ontario, CA M.S.A.	4,651,426									
Includes Riverside and San Bernardino Counties										
City of Riverside	334,370	1,491	20	152	394	925	9,980	1,639	6,456	1,885
City of San Bernardino	216,365	3,033	68	134	730	2,101	6,059	1,201	3,149	1,709
City of Ontario	187,464	686	10	83	195	398	3,994	641	2,296	1,057
City of Corona	171,848	240	1	36	86	117	3,610	677	2,160	773
City of Temecula	116,442	148	0	12	67	69	2,262	368	1,537	357
City of Chino	96,309	335	3	31	77	224	2,075	274	1,493	308
City of Redlands	71,820	238	6	51	69	112	1,865	323	1,289	253
City of Palm Desert	53,811	125	0	5	28	92	1,564	278	1,105	181
Total area actually reporting	100.0%	20,054	335	1,296	4,281	14,142	92,307	17,140	54,945	20,222
Rate per 100,000 inhabitants		431.1	7.2	27.9	92.0	304.0	1,984.5	368.5	1,181.3	434.7
Roanoke, VA M.S.A.	313,488									
Includes Botetourt, Craig, Franklin, and Roanoke Counties and Roanoke and Salem Cities										
City of Roanoke	99,335	448	15	38	90	305	3,809	412	3,048	349
Total area actually reporting	100.0%	821	25	79	130	587	6,607	656	5,357	594
Rate per 100,000 inhabitants		261.9	8.0	25.2	41.5	187.2	2,107.6	209.3	1,708.8	189.5
Rochester, MN M.S.A.[2]	222,817									
Includes Dodge,[2] Fillmore,[2] Olmsted, and Wabasha Counties										
City of Rochester	120,336	300	5	74	44	177	2,314	332	1,828	154
Total area actually reporting	98.7%	414	6	110	47	251	2,984	522	2,248	214
Estimated total	100.0%	418	6	111	47	254	3,041	528	2,296	217
Rate per 100,000 inhabitants		187.6	2.7	49.8	21.1	114.0	1,364.8	237.0	1,030.4	97.4
Rochester, NY M.S.A.[2]	1,061,736									
Includes Livingston, Monroe,[2] Ontario, Orleans, Wayne, and Yates Counties										
City of Rochester	205,199	1,680	48	86	418	1,128	6,887	1,389	4,583	915
Total area actually reporting	94.0%	2,644	54	374	562	1,654	16,302	2,594	12,284	1,424
Estimated total	100.0%	2,782	54	388	587	1,753	17,338	2,725	13,135	1,478
Rate per 100,000 inhabitants		262.0	5.1	36.5	55.3	165.1	1,633.0	256.7	1,237.1	139.2
Rockford, IL M.S.A.[4]	332,940									
Includes Boone and Winnebago[4] Counties										
City of Rockford	144,795	2,101	30	102	238	1,731	4,104	742	2,968	394
Total area actually reporting	84.0%	2,432	34	180	280	1,938		1,000		510

Table 6. Crime in the United States, by Selected Metropolitan Statistical Area, 2020—Continued

(Number, percent, rate per 100,000 population.)

Area	Population	Violent crime	Murder and nonnegligent manslaughter	Rape[1]	Robbery	Aggravated assault	Property crime	Burglary	Larceny-theft	Motor vehicle theft
Estimated total	100.0%	2,566	36	199	297	2,034		1,132		578
Rate per 100,000 inhabitants		770.7	10.8	59.8	89.2	610.9		340.0		173.6
Sacramento-Roseville-Folsom, CA M.S.A.	2,364,420									
Includes El Dorado, Placer, Sacramento, and Yolo Counties										
City of Sacramento	519,050	3,547	42	125	879	2,501	14,248	2,834	8,903	2,511
City of Roseville	144,128	277	4	18	87	168	2,843	318	2,245	280
City of Folsom	82,427	83	0	13	21	49	1,198	223	911	64
City of Rancho Cordova	76,292	322	6	13	73	230	1,555	302	1,107	146
City of West Sacramento	54,068	211	3	22	82	104	1,505	209	1,083	213
Total area actually reporting	100.0%	8,945	113	639	2,069	6,124	47,650	8,796	32,420	6,434
Rate per 100,000 inhabitants		378.3	4.8	27.0	87.5	259.0	2,015.3	372.0	1,371.2	272.1
Saginaw, MI M.S.A.	188,889									
Includes Saginaw County										
City of Saginaw	47,767	1,029	24	57	62	886	720	225	388	107
Total area actually reporting	100.0%	1,501	33	141	93	1,234	2,410	512	1,671	227
Rate per 100,000 inhabitants		794.6	17.5	74.6	49.2	653.3	1,275.9	271.1	884.6	120.2
Salem, OR M.S.A.	436,715									
Includes Marion and Polk Counties										
City of Salem	176,632	698	2	28	148	520	6,698	678	4,911	1,109
Total area actually reporting	99.0%	1,139	7	74	224	834	12,365	1,341	8,935	2,089
Estimated total	100.0%	1,177	7	104	225	841	12,462	1,349	9,015	2,098
Rate per 100,000 inhabitants		269.5	1.6	23.8	51.5	192.6	2,853.6	308.9	2,064.3	480.4
Salinas, CA M.S.A.	431,704									
Includes Monterey County										
City of Salinas	155,984	866	8	69	233	556	3,481	790	1,779	912
Total area actually reporting	100.0%	1,480	14	175	342	949	7,728	1,463	4,736	1,529
Rate per 100,000 inhabitants		342.8	3.2	40.5	79.2	219.8	1,790.1	338.9	1,097.0	354.2
Salt Lake City, UT M.S.A.[2]	1,246,234									
Includes Salt Lake and Tooele[2] Counties										
City of Salt Lake City	202,187	1,865	17	277	487	1,084	14,865	1,545	11,128	2,192
Total area actually reporting	99.9%	4,784	60	835	961	2,928	47,548	5,350	35,415	6,783
Estimated total	100.0%	4,785	60	835	961	2,929	47,566	5,352	35,429	6,785
Rate per 100,000 inhabitants		384.0	4.8	67.0	77.1	235.0	3,816.8	429.5	2,842.9	544.4
San Angelo, TX M.S.A.[2]	122,608									
Includes Irion, Sterling, and Tom Green[2] Counties										
City of San Angelo	101,860	357	7	65	41	244	3,039	475	2,242	322
Total area actually reporting	100.0%	397	8	80	41	268	3,259	542	2,365	352
Rate per 100,000 inhabitants		323.8	6.5	65.2	33.4	218.6	2,658.1	442.1	1,928.9	287.1
San Antonio-New Braunfels, TX M.S.A.[2]	2,591,157									
Includes Atascosa, Bandera, Bexar,[2] Comal, Guadalupe, Kendall, Medina,[2] and Wilson[2] Counties										
City of San Antonio[2]	1,573,189	11,569	130	1,187	2,163	8,089	57,057	7,919	42,158	6,980
City of New Braunfels	78,610	219	6	10	25	178	1,230	206	866	158
Total area actually reporting	99.9%	13,741	170	1,555	2,391	9,625	72,724	10,939	53,056	8,729
Estimated total	100.0%	13,749	170	1,556	2,392	9,631	72,783	10,951	53,095	8,737
Rate per 100,000 inhabitants		530.6	6.6	60.1	92.3	371.7	2,808.9	422.6	2,049.1	337.2
San Diego-Chula Vista-Carlsbad, CA M.S.A.	3,331,816									
Includes San Diego County										
City of San Diego	1,437,608	5,303	56	485	1,207	3,555	24,321	3,324	16,044	4,953
City of Chula Vista	278,027	916	10	63	302	541	3,257	476	2,021	760
City of Carlsbad	116,516	224	3	24	35	162	1,841	256	1,428	157
City of Poway	49,479	53	0	4	16	33	366	84	245	37
Total area actually reporting	100.0%	11,517	114	967	2,527	7,909	49,471	7,301	32,863	9,307
Rate per 100,000 inhabitants		345.7	3.4	29.0	75.8	237.4	1,484.8	219.1	986.3	279.3
San Francisco-Oakland-Berkeley, CA M.S.A.	4,729,308									
Includes the Metropolitan Divisions of Oakland-Berkeley-Livermore, San Francisco-San Mateo-Redwood City, and San Rafael										
City of San Francisco	881,514	4,796	48	198	2,388	2,162	38,737	7,452	25,319	5,966
City of Oakland	437,923	5,653	102	362	2,479	2,710	22,622	2,537	13,373	6,712
City of Berkeley	122,346	537	6	47	274	210	5,535	797	3,933	805
City of San Mateo	105,246	274	4	41	71	158	2,306	523	1,493	290
City of Livermore	91,200	164	1	38	47	78	1,526	164	1,166	196
City of Redwood City	86,983	187	1	38	58	90	1,489	240	970	279
City of Pleasanton	83,164	94	1	11	40	42	1,188	161	937	90
City of San Ramon	76,502	54	0	11	22	21	796	104	636	56
City of Walnut Creek	70,849	91	0	3	27	61	2,063	264	1,582	217
City of South San Francisco	68,260	155	1	15	58	81	1,560	157	1,155	248
City of San Rafael	58,512	229	0	26	67	136	1,912	260	1,152	500
Total area actually reporting	100.0%	20,814	253	1,504	8,440	10,617	142,267	20,761	92,931	28,575
Rate per 100,000 inhabitants		440.1	5.3	31.8	178.5	224.5	3,008.2	439.0	1,965.0	604.2

Table 6. Crime in the United States, by Selected Metropolitan Statistical Area, 2020—Continued

(Number, percent, rate per 100,000 population.)

Area	Population	Violent crime	Murder and nonnegligent manslaughter	Rape[1]	Robbery	Aggravated assault	Property crime	Burglary	Larceny-theft	Motor vehicle theft
Oakland-Berkeley-Livermore, CA M.D.	2,826,657									
Includes Alameda and Contra Costa Counties										
Total area actually reporting	100.0%	13,515	187	967	5,307	7,054	81,991	10,295	52,093	19,603
Rate per 100,000 inhabitants		478.1	6.6	34.2	187.7	249.6	2,900.6	364.2	1,842.9	693.5
San Francisco-San Mateo-Redwood City, CA M.D.	1,645,756									
Includes San Francisco and San Mateo Counties										
Total area actually reporting	100.0%	6,676	65	485	3,010	3,116	55,003	9,668	37,150	8,185
Rate per 100,000 inhabitants		405.6	3.9	29.5	182.9	189.3	3,342.1	587.5	2,257.3	497.3
San Rafael, CA M.D.	256,895									
Includes Marin County										
Total area actually reporting	100.0%	623	1	52	123	447	5,273	798	3,688	787
Rate per 100,000 inhabitants		242.5	0.4	20.2	47.9	174.0	2,052.6	310.6	1,435.6	306.4
San Jose-Sunnyvale-Santa Clara, CA M.S.A.	1,987,878									
Includes San Benito and Santa Clara Counties										
City of San Jose	1,029,542	4,375	40	566	1,185	2,584	23,847	4,045	12,737	7,065
City of Sunnyvale	154,133	229	2	32	61	134	3,178	516	2,276	386
City of Santa Clara	131,976	206	1	39	85	81	3,301	432	2,314	555
City of Mountain View	83,745	144	0	9	52	83	2,177	422	1,566	189
City of Milpitas	86,416	111	2	16	40	53	2,103	277	1,516	310
City of Palo Alto	65,459	81	1	12	39	29	1,931	242	1,570	119
City of Cupertino	59,343	69	0	9	26	34	830	196	581	53
Total area actually reporting	100.0%	6,306	56	826	1,723	3,701	44,263	7,338	26,867	10,058
Rate per 100,000 inhabitants		317.2	2.8	41.6	86.7	186.2	2,226.6	369.1	1,351.5	506.0
San Luis Obispo-Paso Robles, CA M.S.A.	281,778									
Includes San Luis Obispo County										
City of San Luis Obispo	47,722	207	1	39	28	139	1,620	284	1,219	117
City of Paso Robles	32,428	53	3	2	8	40	363	35	295	33
Total area actually reporting	100.0%	816	7	93	79	637	4,610	868	3,381	361
Rate per 100,000 inhabitants		289.6	2.5	33.0	28.0	226.1	1,636.0	308.0	1,199.9	128.1
Santa Cruz-Watsonville, CA M.S.A.	271,608									
Includes Santa Cruz County										
City of Santa Cruz	65,073	309	2	33	76	198	2,237	267	1,734	236
City of Watsonville	54,151	299	4	27	44	224	1,132	167	655	310
Total area actually reporting	100.0%	970	12	104	172	682	6,155	905	4,252	998
Rate per 100,000 inhabitants		357.1	4.4	38.3	63.3	251.1	2,266.1	333.2	1,565.5	367.4
	444,547									
Includes Santa Barbara County										
City of Santa Maria	108,140	834	2	81	179	572	2,472	328	1,114	1,030
City of Santa Barbara	91,692	389	2	60	84	243	2,188	217	1,748	223
Total area actually reporting	100.0%	1,824	8	227	341	1,248	8,827	1,178	5,812	1,837
Rate per 100,000 inhabitants		410.3	1.8	51.1	76.7	280.7	1,985.6	265.0	1,307.4	413.2
Santa Rosa-Petaluma, CA M.S.A.	490,455									
Includes Sonoma County										
City of Santa Rosa	176,932	913	4	110	135	664	2,838	542	1,875	421
City of Petaluma	60,806	255	2	25	33	195	756	90	597	69
Total area actually reporting	100.0%	2,212	10	239	266	1,697	6,412	1,272	4,408	732
Rate per 100,000 inhabitants		451.0	2.0	48.7	54.2	346.0	1,307.4	259.4	898.8	149.2
Seattle-Tacoma-Bellevue, WA M.S.A.	4,030,255									
Includes the Metropolitan Divisions of Seattle-Bellevue-Kent and Tacoma-Lakewood										
City of Seattle	771,517	4,832	52	301	1,471	3,008	37,593	10,427	22,255	4,911
City of Tacoma	220,123	1,856	28	127	435	1,266	12,123	1,987	7,967	2,169
City of Bellevue	150,548	175	4	19	68	84	4,526	597	3,641	288
City of Kent	133,883	470	8	78	184	200	5,393	1,054	3,378	961
City of Everett	112,439	379	4	37	98	240	3,654	515	2,436	703
City of Renton	102,856	348	6	37	108	197	4,342	498	3,063	781
City of Auburn	82,779	362	10	40	121	191	3,394	584	2,150	660
City of Redmond	74,154	74	0	12	19	43	1,742	207	1,443	92
City of Lakewood	61,432	381	4	32	72	273	2,620	445	1,721	454
Total area actually reporting	100.0%	13,692	181	1,253	3,767	8,491	127,233	24,849	83,956	18,428
Rate per 100,000 inhabitants		339.7	4.5	31.1	93.5	210.7	3,156.9	616.6	2,083.1	457.2
Seattle-Bellevue-Kent, WA M.D.	3,115,239									
Includes King and Snohomish Counties										
Total area actually reporting	100.0%	9,720	128	943	2,934	5,715	97,577	19,512	64,595	13,470
Rate per 100,000 inhabitants		312.0	4.1	30.3	94.2	183.5	3,132.2	626.3	2,073.5	432.4
Tacoma-Lakewood, WA M.D.	915,016									
Includes Pierce County										
Total area actually reporting	100.0%	3,972	53	310	833	2,776	29,656	5,337	19,361	4,958
Rate per 100,000 inhabitants		434.1	5.8	33.9	91.0	303.4	3,241.0	583.3	2,115.9	541.8
Sebastian-Vero Beach, FL M.S.A.	162,048									
Includes Indian River County										
City of Sebastian	26,626	21	0	4	3	14	155	12	132	11

Table 6. Crime in the United States, by Selected Metropolitan Statistical Area, 2020—Continued

(Number, percent, rate per 100,000 population.)

Area	Population	Violent crime	Murder and nonnegligent manslaughter	Rape[1]	Robbery	Aggravated assault	Property crime	Burglary	Larceny-theft	Motor vehicle theft
City of Vero Beach	17,776	34	0	1	6	27	250	37	190	23
Total area actually reporting	100.0%	219	3	14	28	174	1,880	187	1,513	180
Rate per 100,000 inhabitants		135.1	1.9	8.6	17.3	107.4	1,160.2	115.4	933.7	111.1
Sebring-Avon Park, FL M.S.A.	106,784									
Includes Highlands County										
City of Sebring	10,664	79	3	8	15	53	389	69	302	18
Total area actually reporting	100.0%	296	8	29	39	220	1,889	333	1,405	151
Rate per 100,000 inhabitants		277.2	7.5	27.2	36.5	206.0	1,769.0	311.8	1,315.7	141.4
Sheboygan, WI M.S.A.[2]	115,218									
Includes Sheboygan County[2]										
City of Sheboygan	47,814	157	1	33	15	108	832	97	702	33
Total area actually reporting	100.0%	209	1	55	15	138	1,364	134	1,169	61
Rate per 100,000 inhabitants		181.4	0.9	47.7	13.0	119.8	1,183.8	116.3	1,014.6	52.9
Sherman-Denison, TX M.S.A.[2]	137,545									
Includes Grayson County[2]										
City of Sherman[2]	44,611	197	6	34	24	133	1,095	222	769	104
City of Denison[2]	25,858	113	1	23	9	80	484	124	276	84
Total area actually reporting	98.4%	388	9	74	40	265	2,027	445	1,331	251
Estimated total	100.0%	392	9	74	40	269	2,064	453	1,355	256
Rate per 100,000 inhabitants		285.0	6.5	53.8	29.1	195.6	1,500.6	329.3	985.1	186.1
Shreveport-Bossier City, LA M.S.A.[2]	392,827									
Includes Bossier, Caddo, and De Soto Parishes										
City of Shreveport	185,588	1,713	69	125	235	1,284	8,907	1,516	6,690	701
City of Bossier City[2]	68,869	609	8	52	77	472	3,201	400	2,472	329
Total area actually reporting	99.5%	2,675	85	196	336	2,058	14,056	2,363	10,505	1,188
Estimated total	100.0%	2,683	85	196	338	2,064	14,095	2,369	10,533	1,193
Rate per 100,000 inhabitants		683.0	21.6	49.9	86.0	525.4	3,588.1	603.1	2,681.3	303.7
Sierra Vista-Douglas, AZ M.S.A.	125,923									
Includes Cochise County										
City of Sierra Vista	42,800	82	1	4	12	65	888	85	764	39
City of Douglas	16,044	17	0	1	1	15	395	67	311	17
Total area actually reporting	91.0%	190	8	8	20	154	1,876	340	1,403	133
Estimated total	100.0%	310	8	15	33	254	2,598	479	1,925	194
Rate per 100,000 inhabitants		246.2	6.4	11.9	26.2	201.7	2,063.2	380.4	1,528.7	154.1
Sioux City, IA-NE-SD M.S.A.	144,522									
Includes Woodbury County, IA; Dakota and Dixon Counties, NE; and Union County, SD										
City of Sioux City, IA	82,628	477	9	61	75	332	2,682	479	1,933	270
Total area actually reporting	94.8%	595	9	72	79	435	3,245	552	2,357	336
Estimated total	100.0%	619	9	76	79	455	3,326	569	2,409	348
Rate per 100,000 inhabitants		428.3	6.2	52.6	54.7	314.8	2,301.4	393.7	1,666.9	240.8
Sioux Falls, SD M.S.A.	273,001									
Includes Lincoln, McCook, Minnehaha, and Turner Counties										
City of Sioux Falls	187,370	1,120	13	97	102	908	5,867	684	4,259	924
Total area actually reporting	99.3%	1,297	15	124	107	1,051	6,856	1,075	4,745	1,036
Estimated total	100.0%	1,304	15	124	109	1,056	6,891	1,080	4,771	1,040
Rate per 100,000 inhabitants		477.7	5.5	45.4	39.9	386.8	2,524.2	395.6	1,747.6	381.0
South Bend-Mishawaka, IN-MI M.S.A.[2]	323,697									
Includes St. Joseph County, IN and Cass County, MI										
City of South Bend, IN	102,119	1,765	28	78	238	1,421	3,741	659	2,511	571
City of Mishawaka, IN[2]	50,610	80	0	15	6	59	1,207	131	935	141
Total area actually reporting	87.1%	2,031	29	132	266	1,604	6,675	1,221	4,527	927
Estimated total	100.0%	2,121	30	149	274	1,668	7,031	1,302	4,773	956
Rate per 100,000 inhabitants		655.2	9.3	46.0	84.6	515.3	2,172.1	402.2	1,474.5	295.3
Spartanburg, SC M.S.A.	324,314									
Includes Spartanburg and Union Counties										
City of Spartanburg	37,469	536	4	29	94	409	2,286	434	1,595	257
Total area actually reporting	99.8%	1,642	9	90	173	1,370	7,919	1,700	5,275	944
Estimated total	100.0%	1,643	9	90	173	1,371	7,935	1,703	5,286	946
Rate per 100,000 inhabitants		506.6	2.8	27.8	53.3	422.7	2,446.7	525.1	1,629.9	291.7
Spokane-Spokane Valley, WA M.S.A.	572,842									
Includes Spokane and Stevens Counties										
City of Spokane	223,524	1,341	19	187	280	855	11,514	1,745	8,666	1,103
City of Spokane Valley	102,366	342	3	28	77	234	4,370	691	3,339	340
Total area actually reporting	100.0%	2,005	30	282	393	1,300	19,927	3,277	14,863	1,787
Rate per 100,000 inhabitants		350.0	5.2	49.2	68.6	226.9	3,478.6	572.1	2,594.6	312.0
Springfield, IL M.S.A.[4]	205,389									
Includes Menard and Sangamon[4] Counties										
City of Springfield[4]	113,912	1,078	11	101	195	771		937		254
Total area actually reporting	94.1%	1,357	12	133	215	997		1,223		357

Table 6. Crime in the United States, by Selected Metropolitan Statistical Area, 2020—Continued

(Number, percent, rate per 100,000 population.)

Area	Population	Violent crime	Murder and nonnegligent manslaughter	Rape[1]	Robbery	Aggravated assault	Property crime	Burglary	Larceny-theft	Motor vehicle theft
Estimated total	100.0%	1,369	12	134	215	1,008		1,257		366
Rate per 100,000 inhabitants		666.5	5.8	65.2	104.7	490.8		612.0		178.2
Springfield, MA M.S.A.	693,972									
Includes Franklin, Hampden and Hampshire Counties										
City of Springfield	153,084	1,480	18	70	350	1,042	3,730	618	2,616	496
Total area actually reporting	97.5%	3,163	28	272	536	2,327	10,694	1,671	7,988	1,035
Estimated total	100.0%	3,216	28	280	546	2,362	10,788	1,695	8,050	1,043
Rate per 100,000 inhabitants		463.4	4.0	40.3	78.7	340.4	1,554.5	244.2	1,160.0	150.3
Springfield, MO M.S.A.[2]	473,913									
Includes Christian, Dallas, Greene, Polk, and Webster Counties										
City of Springfield[2]	168,856	2,545	22	178	375	1,970	11,738	1,795	8,639	1,304
Total area actually reporting	97.9%	2,943	26	230	398	2,289	15,370	2,496	11,237	1,637
Estimated total	100.0%	2,993	26	232	405	2,330	15,647	2,533	11,433	1,681
Rate per 100,000 inhabitants		631.6	5.5	49.0	85.5	491.7	3,301.7	534.5	2,412.5	354.7
Springfield, OH M.S.A.	133,456									
Includes Clark County										
City of Springfield	58,696	338	8	52	107	171	3,014	619	2,060	335
Total area actually reporting	94.1%	391	9	57	110	215	3,741	767	2,611	363
Estimated total	100.0%	401	9	59	112	221	3,872	784	2,719	369
Rate per 100,000 inhabitants		300.5	6.7	44.2	83.9	165.6	2,901.3	587.5	2,037.4	276.5
Staunton, VA M.S.A.	123,568									
Includes Augusta County and Staunton and Waynesboro Cities										
City of Staunton	25,048	45	2	10	6	27	549	54	469	26
Total area actually reporting	100.0%	231	4	63	15	149	1,812	256	1,438	118
Rate per 100,000 inhabitants		186.9	3.2	51.0	12.1	120.6	1,466.4	207.2	1,163.7	95.5
St. George, UT M.S.A.	182,066									
Includes Washington County										
City of St. George	91,673	148	3	42	10	93	1,025	148	772	105
Total area actually reporting	98.4%	290	5	73	13	199	2,038	268	1,583	187
Estimated total	100.0%	294	5	74	13	202	2,118	273	1,652	193
Rate per 100,000 inhabitants		161.5	2.7	40.6	7.1	110.9	1,163.3	149.9	907.4	106.0
St. Joseph, MO-KS M.S.A.	124,927									
Includes Doniphan County, KS and Andrew, Buchanan, and DeKalb Counties, MO										
City of St. Joseph, MO	74,680	414	3	122	47	242	3,843	576	2,711	556
Total area actually reporting	99.4%	518	4	143	48	323	4,407	695	3,052	660
Estimated total	100.0%	521	4	143	48	326	4,424	698	3,063	663
Rate per 100,000 inhabitants		417.0	3.2	114.5	38.4	261.0	3,541.3	558.7	2,451.8	530.7
St. Louis, MO-IL M.S.A.[2,4]	2,802,055									
Includes Bond, Calhoun, Clinton,[4] Jersey,[4] Macoupin,[4] Madison,[4] Monroe,[4] and St. Clair Counties, IL and Franklin, Jefferson,[2] Lincoln,[2] St. Charles,[2] St. Louis,[2] and Warren Counties and St. Louis City, MO										
City of St. Louis, MO	298,422	6,017	263	234	1,242	4,278	17,399	2,552	11,626	3,221
City of St. Charles, MO	71,563	192	3	19	27	143	1,368	145	1,022	201
Total area actually reporting	95.2%	13,647	399	937	2,183	10,128		8,827		10,171
Estimated total	100.0%	13,925	402	974	2,218	10,331		9,130		10,327
Rate per 100,000 inhabitants		497.0	14.3	34.8	79.2	368.7		325.8		368.6
Stockton, CA M.S.A.	763,250									
Includes San Joaquin County										
City of Stockton	314,981	4,023	56	189	909	2,869	9,391	1,533	6,362	1,496
Total area actually reporting	100.0%	5,517	84	264	1,281	3,888	17,805	2,817	12,091	2,897
Rate per 100,000 inhabitants		722.8	11.0	34.6	167.8	509.4	2,332.8	369.1	1,584.1	379.6
Sumter, SC M.S.A.	140,399									
Includes Clarendon and Sumter Counties										
City of Sumter	39,542	491	10	9	45	427	1,459	211	1,179	69
Total area actually reporting	99.4%	1,138	28	49	88	973	3,831	738	2,809	284
Estimated total	100.0%	1,140	28	49	89	974	3,852	742	2,824	286
Rate per 100,000 inhabitants		812.0	19.9	34.9	63.4	693.7	2,743.6	528.5	2,011.4	203.7
Syracuse, NY M.S.A.	642,895									
Includes Madison, Onondaga, and Oswego Counties										
City of Syracuse	142,011	1,192	32	96	222	842	4,009	1,032	2,463	514
Total area actually reporting	100.0%	1,953	35	297	315	1,306	10,985	1,874	8,039	1,072
Rate per 100,000 inhabitants		303.8	5.4	46.2	49.0	203.1	1,708.7	291.5	1,250.4	166.7
Tallahassee, FL M.S.A.	388,159									
Includes Gadsden, Jefferson, Leon, and Wakulla Counties										

Table 6. Crime in the United States, by Selected Metropolitan Statistical Area, 2020—Continued

(Number, percent, rate per 100,000 population.)

Area	Population	Violent crime	Murder and nonnegligent manslaughter	Rape[1]	Robbery	Aggravated assault	Property crime	Burglary	Larceny-theft	Motor vehicle theft
City of Tallahassee	196,012	1,516	24	196	238	1,058	5,786	1,067	4,159	560
Total area actually reporting	97.8%	2,119	35	253	280	1,551	8,391	1,684	5,889	818
Estimated total	100.0%	2,157	35	256	285	1,581	8,643	1,728	6,075	840
Rate per 100,000 inhabitants		555.7	9.0	66.0	73.4	407.3	2,226.7	445.2	1,565.1	216.4
Tampa-St. Petersburg-Clearwater, FL M.S.A.	3,234,443									
Includes Hernando, Hillsborough, Pasco, and Pinellas Counties										
City of Tampa	407,350	2,119	41	101	325	1,652	5,561	925	3,993	643
City of St. Petersburg	267,690	1,772	15	110	275	1,372	6,841	887	5,315	639
City of Clearwater	117,859	460	0	92	87	281	2,232	249	1,850	133
City of Largo	85,594	332	4	38	60	230	1,810	154	1,505	151
City of Pinellas Park	54,114	187	0	32	47	108	1,788	185	1,484	119
Total area actually reporting	100.0%	10,159	130	1,076	1,525	7,428	44,114	5,914	34,203	3,997
Rate per 100,000 inhabitants		314.1	4.0	33.3	47.1	229.7	1,363.9	182.8	1,057.5	123.6
The Villages, FL M.S.A.	137,110									
Includes Sumter County										
Total area actually reporting	100.0%	279	3	22	20	234	967	191	666	110
Rate per 100,000 inhabitants		203.5	2.2	16.0	14.6	170.7	705.3	139.3	485.7	80.2
Toledo, OH M.S.A.	639,977									
Includes Fulton, Lucas, Ottawa, and Wood Counties										
City of Toledo	271,237	2,729	53	213	493	1,970	7,849	1,777	5,064	1,008
Total area actually reporting	92.0%	3,052	56	296	542	2,158	12,195	2,219	8,783	1,193
Estimated total	100.0%	3,108	56	306	552	2,194	12,956	2,337	9,383	1,236
Rate per 100,000 inhabitants		485.6	8.8	47.8	86.3	342.8	2,024.4	365.2	1,466.1	193.1
Trenton-Princeton, NJ M.S.A.	367,006									
Includes Mercer County										
City of Trenton	82,909	969	40	50	262	617	1,733	412	1,038	283
City of Princeton	31,458	11	0	0	3	8	196	19	161	16
Total area actually reporting	100.0%	1,316	41	101	343	831	4,910	846	3,587	477
Rate per 100,000 inhabitants		358.6	11.2	27.5	93.5	226.4	1,337.9	230.5	977.4	130.0
Tucson, AZ M.S.A.[2]	1,060,180									
Includes Pima County[2]										
City of Tucson	550,448	3,843	61	463	978	2,341	19,931	2,097	15,956	1,878
Total area actually reporting	100.0%	5,020	86	545	1,169	3,220	29,948	3,407	24,023	2,518
Rate per 100,000 inhabitants		473.5	8.1	51.4	110.3	303.7	2,824.8	321.4	2,265.9	237.5
Tulsa, OK M.S.A.[2]	1,005,482									
Includes Creek, Okmulgee, Osage, Pawnee, Rogers,[2] Tulsa, and Wagoner Counties										
City of Tulsa	402,166	4,555	72	378	741	3,364	20,557	4,407	12,246	3,904
Total area actually reporting	100.0%	5,947	94	565	873	4,415	31,267	6,704	19,185	5,378
Rate per 100,000 inhabitants		591.5	9.3	56.2	86.8	439.1	3,109.7	666.7	1,908.0	534.9
Twin Falls, ID M.S.A.[3]	113,458									
Includes Jerome and Twin Falls[3] Counties										
City of Twin Falls	50,872	259	2	36	7	214	892	100	754	38
Total area actually reporting	100.0%	435	3	71	11	350			994	90
Rate per 100,000 inhabitants		383.4	2.6	62.6	9.7	308.5			876.1	79.3
Tyler, TX M.S.A.	234,573									
Includes Smith County										
City of Tyler	108,139	472	6	53	69	344	3,296	523	2,563	210
Total area actually reporting	100.0%	869	18	104	94	653	5,092	994	3,632	466
Rate per 100,000 inhabitants		370.5	7.7	44.3	40.1	278.4	2,170.8	423.7	1,548.3	198.7
Utica-Rome, NY M.S.A.[2]	287,148									
Includes Herkimer and Oneida Counties										
City of Utica[2]	59,483	298	1	23	70	204	2,017	267	1,636	114
City of Rome[2]	31,978	65	0	8	7	50	570	70	457	43
Total area actually reporting	95.0%	625	4	138	95	388	4,594	598	3,768	228
Estimated total	100.0%	644	4	142	99	399	4,684	615	3,837	232
Rate per 100,000 inhabitants		224.3	1.4	49.5	34.5	139.0	1,631.2	214.2	1,336.2	80.8
Valdosta, GA M.S.A.[2]	147,899									
Includes Brooks,[2] Echols, Lanier,[2] and Lowndes[2] Counties										
City of Valdosta[2]	56,628	220	6	13	43	158	1,848	222	1,530	96
Total area actually reporting	96.2%	433	8	57	62	306	3,201	477	2,475	249
Estimated total	100.0%	472	9	60	68	335	3,380	503	2,608	269
Rate per 100,000 inhabitants		319.1	6.1	40.6	46.0	226.5	2,285.3	340.1	1,763.4	181.9
Vallejo, CA M.S.A.	447,025									
Includes Solano County										
City of Vallejo	122,326	1,212	27	134	315	736	4,078	1,811	1,200	1,067
Total area actually reporting	100.0%	2,350	40	275	589	1,446	10,689	2,751	5,695	2,243
Rate per 100,000 inhabitants		525.7	8.9	61.5	131.8	323.5	2,391.1	615.4	1,274.0	501.8

Table 6. Crime in the United States, by Selected Metropolitan Statistical Area, 2020—Continued

(Number, percent, rate per 100,000 population.)

Area	Population	Violent crime	Murder and nonnegligent manslaughter	Rape[1]	Robbery	Aggravated assault	Property crime	Burglary	Larceny-theft	Motor vehicle theft
Victoria, TX M.S.A.	100,050									
Includes Goliad and Victoria Counties										
City of Victoria	67,407	311	2	34	42	233	1,823	354	1,345	124
Total area actually reporting	100.0%	449	6	58	54	331	2,205	491	1,552	162
Rate per 100,000 inhabitants		448.8	6.0	58.0	54.0	330.8	2,203.9	490.8	1,551.2	161.9
Vineland-Bridgeton, NJ M.S.A.	148,593									
Includes Cumberland County										
City of Vineland	59,288	227	3	17	34	173	1,239	198	1,000	41
City of Bridgeton	24,032	234	2	11	82	139	737	158	534	45
Total area actually reporting	100.0%	669	8	39	154	468	3,192	593	2,446	153
Rate per 100,000 inhabitants		450.2	5.4	26.2	103.6	315.0	2,148.1	399.1	1,646.1	103.0
Virginia Beach-Norfolk-Newport News, VA-NC M.S.A.[2]	1,773,594									
Includes Camden, Currituck and Gates[2] Counties, NC and Gloucester, Isle of Wight, James City, Mathews, Southampton, and York Counties and Chesapeake, Franklin, Hampton, Newport News, Norfolk, Poquoson, Portsmouth, Suffolk, Virginia Beach, and Williamsburg Cities, VA										
City of Virginia Beach, VA	450,858	445	17	60	124	244	6,816	499	5,693	624
City of Norfolk, VA	242,516	1,543	49	103	259	1,132	6,591	519	5,282	790
City of Newport News, VA	178,896	1,119	25	67	104	923	3,648	416	2,896	336
City of Hampton, VA	134,082	357	24	33	95	205	3,338	301	2,765	272
City of Portsmouth, VA	94,205	867	34	26	222	585	4,277	465	3,314	498
Total area actually reporting	100.0%	6,239	183	465	1,014	4,577	34,571	3,117	28,200	3,254
Rate per 100,000 inhabitants		351.8	10.3	26.2	57.2	258.1	1,949.2	175.7	1,590.0	183.5
Visalia, CA M.S.A.	464,150									
Includes Tulare County										
City of Visalia	135,733	555	8	106	142	299	3,077	610	2,049	418
Total area actually reporting	100.0%	1,699	29	206	356	1,108	9,400	1,828	5,770	1,802
Rate per 100,000 inhabitants		366.0	6.2	44.4	76.7	238.7	2,025.2	393.8	1,243.1	388.2
Waco, TX M.S.A.	275,324									
Includes Falls and McLennan Counties										
City of Waco	140,870	905	14	80	142	669	4,854	870	3,568	416
Total area actually reporting	98.5%	1,264	16	156	178	914	7,013	1,319	5,084	610
Estimated total	100.0%	1,274	16	158	179	921	7,078	1,332	5,127	619
Rate per 100,000 inhabitants		462.7	5.8	57.4	65.0	334.5	2,570.8	483.8	1,862.2	224.8
Walla Walla, WA M.S.A.	60,767									
Includes Walla Walla County										
City of Walla Walla	32,944	83	0	21	11	51	749	126	573	50
Total area actually reporting	100.0%	129	1	26	14	88	1,267	255	920	92
Rate per 100,000 inhabitants		212.3	1.6	42.8	23.0	144.8	2,085.0	419.6	1,514.0	151.4
Watertown-Fort Drum, NY M.S.A.[2]	108,426									
Includes Jefferson County[2]										
City of Watertown	24,624	181	0	40	21	120	967	158	766	43
Total area actually reporting	100.0%	271	0	73	22	176	1,749	254	1,432	63
Rate per 100,000 inhabitants		249.9	0.0	67.3	20.3	162.3	1,613.1	234.3	1,320.7	58.1
Wausau-Weston, WI M.S.A.	163,196									
Includes Lincoln and Marathon Counties										
City of Wausau	38,492	174	0	26	14	134	560	66	435	59
Total area actually reporting	100.0%	399	3	74	20	302	1,487	227	1,144	116
Rate per 100,000 inhabitants		244.5	1.8	45.3	12.3	185.1	911.2	139.1	701.0	71.1
Wenatchee, WA M.S.A.	121,320									
Includes Chelan and Douglas Counties										
City of Wenatchee	34,525	67	0	16	6	45	570	72	448	50
Total area actually reporting	100.0%	141	1	30	16	94	1,392	239	1,029	124
Rate per 100,000 inhabitants		116.2	0.8	24.7	13.2	77.5	1,147.4	197.0	848.2	102.2
Wheeling, WV-OH M.S.A.	137,859									
Includes Belmont County, OH and Marshall and Ohio Counties, WV										
City of Wheeling, WV	26,222	330	1	31	28	270	582	180	361	41
Total area actually reporting	86.0%	525	2	82	31	410	1,140	279	782	79
Estimated total	100.0%	585	2	86	36	461	1,423	317	1,011	95
Rate per 100,000 inhabitants		424.3	1.5	62.4	26.1	334.4	1,032.2	229.9	733.4	68.9
Wichita Falls, TX M.S.A.[2]	150,700									
Includes Archer, Clay, and Wichita Counties										
City of Wichita Falls[2]	104,673	405	9	83	76	237	3,222	626	2,318	278
Total area actually reporting	95.5%	512	9	91	82	330	3,721	768	2,618	335
Estimated total	100.0%	544	9	95	83	357	3,864	809	2,702	353
Rate per 100,000 inhabitants		361.0	6.0	63.0	55.1	236.9	2,564.0	536.8	1,793.0	234.2

Table 6. Crime in the United States, by Selected Metropolitan Statistical Area, 2020—Continued

(Number, percent, rate per 100,000 population.)

Area	Population	Violent crime	Murder and nonnegligent manslaughter	Rape[1]	Robbery	Aggravated assault	Property crime	Burglary	Larceny-theft	Motor vehicle theft
Wilmington, NC M.S.A.	302,620									
Includes New Hanover and Pender Counties										
City of Wilmington	125,794	791	22	66	143	560	3,204	595	2,410	199
Total area actually reporting	80.1%	1,001	24	100	172	705	5,181	881	4,026	274
Estimated total	100.0%	1,126	26	115	186	799	6,058	1,127	4,568	363
Rate per 100,000 inhabitants		372.1	8.6	38.0	61.5	264.0	2,001.9	372.4	1,509.5	120.0
Winchester, VA-WV M.S.A.	141,877									
Includes Frederick County and Winchester City, VA and Hampshire County, WV										
City of Winchester, VA	28,279	72	2	21	10	39	586	56	495	35
Total area actually reporting	99.7%	209	5	44	16	144	1,628	185	1,316	127
Estimated total	100.0%	214	5	44	16	149	1,629	185	1,317	127
Rate per 100,000 inhabitants		150.8	3.5	31.0	11.3	105.0	1,148.2	130.4	928.3	89.5
Worcester, MA-CT M.S.A.	871,848									
Includes Windham County, CT and Worcester County, MA										
City of Worcester, MA	184,850	1,169	10	40	210	909	3,695	667	2,581	447
Total area actually reporting	98.1%	2,620	13	257	320	2,030	8,486	1,447	6,118	921
Estimated total	100.0%	2,648	13	262	322	2,051	8,555	1,460	6,169	926
Rate per 100,000 inhabitants		303.7	1.5	30.1	36.9	235.2	981.2	167.5	707.6	106.2
Yakima, WA M.S.A.	250,785									
Includes Yakima County										
City of Yakima	93,862	639	9	22	100	508	3,220	599	2,115	506
Total area actually reporting	95.5%	944	21	69	161	693	6,593	1,372	4,175	1,046
Estimated total	100.0%	966	21	72	165	708	6,835	1,420	4,348	1,067
Rate per 100,000 inhabitants		385.2	8.4	28.7	65.8	282.3	2,725.4	566.2	1,733.8	425.5
Yuba City, CA M.S.A.	174,855									
Includes Sutter and Yuba Counties										
City of Yuba City	67,165	242	4	29	70	139	1,850	264	1,275	311
Total area actually reporting	100.0%	715	7	70	139	499	4,266	727	2,500	1,039
Rate per 100,000 inhabitants		408.9	4.0	40.0	79.5	285.4	2,439.7	415.8	1,429.8	594.2
Yuma, AZ M.S.A.	216,821									
Includes Yuma County										
City of Yuma	99,096	498	11	39	43	405	1,927	330	1,412	185
Total area actually reporting	100.0%	717	20	68	54	575	3,235	653	2,184	398
Rate per 100,000 inhabitants		330.7	9.2	31.4	24.9	265.2	1,492.0	301.2	1,007.3	183.6
Aguadilla-Isabela, Puerto Rico M.S.A.	286,064									
Includes Aguada, Aguadilla, Anasco, Isabela, Lares, Moca, Rincon, San Sebastian, and Utuado Municipios										
Total area actually reporting	100.0%	372	20	16	31	305	802	234	509	59
Rate per 100,000 inhabitants		130.0	7.0	5.6	10.8	106.6	280.4	81.8	177.9	20.6
Arecibo, Puerto Rico M.S.A.	173,218									
Includes Arecibo, Camuy, Hatillo, and Quebradillas Municipios										
Total area actually reporting	100.0%	249	24	6	31	188	470	150	274	46
Rate per 100,000 inhabitants		143.7	13.9	3.5	17.9	108.5	271.3	86.6	158.2	26.6
Guayama, Puerto Rico M.S.A.	72,240									
Includes Arroyo, Guayama, and Patillas Municipios										
Total area actually reporting	100.0%	178	11	9	29	129	235	82	148	5
Rate per 100,000 inhabitants		246.4	15.2	12.5	40.1	178.6	325.3	113.5	204.9	6.9
Mayagüez, Puerto Rico M.S.A.	93,412									
Includes Hormigueros, Las Marias, and Mayaguez Municipios										
Total area actually reporting	100.0%	105	16	7	9	73	214	64	134	16
Rate per 100,000 inhabitants		112.4	17.1	7.5	9.6	78.1	229.1	68.5	143.5	17.1
Ponce, Puerto Rico M.S.A.	211,465									
Includes Adjuntas, Juana Diaz, Ponce, and Villalba Municipios										
Total area actually reporting	100.0%	287	20	8	91	168	743	166	509	68
Rate per 100,000 inhabitants		135.7	9.5	3.8	43.0	79.4	351.4	78.5	240.7	32.2
San Germán, Puerto Rico M.S.A.	120,280									
Includes Cabo Rojo, Lajas, Sabana Grande, and San German Municipios										
Total area actually reporting	100.0%	100	9	3	10	78	185	63	109	13
Rate per 100,000 inhabitants		83.1	7.5	2.5	8.3	64.8	153.8	52.4	90.6	10.8

Table 6. Crime in the United States, by Selected Metropolitan Statistical Area, 2020—Continued

(Number, percent, rate per 100,000 population.)

Area	Population	Violent crime	Murder and nonnegligent manslaughter	Rape[1]	Robbery	Aggravated assault	Property crime	Burglary	Larceny-theft	Motor vehicle theft
San Juan-Bayamón-Caguas, Puerto Rico M.S.A.	2,002,906									
Includes Aguas Buenas, Aibonito, Barceloneta, Barranquitas, Bayamon, Caguas, Canovanas, Carolina, Catano, Cayey, Ceiba, Ciales, Cidra, Comerio, Corozal, Dorado, Fajardo, Florida, Guaynabo, Gurabo, Humacao, Juncos, Las Piedras, Loiza, Luquillo, Manati, Maunabo, Morovis, Naguabo, Naranjito, Orocovis, Rio Grande, San Juan, San Lorenzo, Toa Alta, Toa Baja, Trujillo Alto, Vega Alta, Vega Baja, and Yabucoa Municipios										
Total area actually reporting	100.0%	3,510	400	91	934	2,085	10,114	2,011	6,362	1,741
Rate per 100,000 inhabitants		175.2	20.0	4.5	46.6	104.1	505.0	100.4	317.6	86.9
Yauco, Puerto Rico M.S.A.	84,112									
Includes Guanica, Guayanilla, Penuelas, and Yauco Municipios										
Total area actually reporting	100.0%	138	8	2	18	110	174	61	106	7
Rate per 100,000 inhabitants		164.1	9.5	2.4	21.4	130.8	206.9	72.5	126.0	8.3

1 The figures shown in this column for the offense of rape were reported using only the revised Uniform Crime Reporting (UCR) definition of rape. See the chapter notes for further explanation.   2 Because of changes in the state/local agency's reporting practices, figures are not comparable to previous years' data.   3 The FBI determined that the agency's data were overreported. Consequently, those data are not included in this table.   4 The FBI determined that the state did not follow national UCR Program guidelines for reporting an offense. Consequently, those figures are not included in this table.   5 The FBI determined that the agency's data were underreported. Consequently, those data are not included in this table.

Table 7. Offense Analysis, United States, 2016–2020

(Number.)

Classification	2016	2017	2018	2019[1]	2020
Murder	17,413	17,294	16,374	16,669	21,570
Rape[2]	132,414	135,666	143,765	143,224	126,430
Robbery[3]	332,797	320,596	281,278	268,483	243,600
By location					
Street/highway	129,337	119,180	102,149	94,263	77,984
Commercial house	50,785	49,654	45,148	44,210	41,139
Gas or service station	9,708	9,603	8,863	8,570	8,804
Convenience store	20,656	21,048	19,647	18,346	18,039
Residence	55,102	51,260	45,408	42,885	42,637
Bank	5,914	5,441	4,461	3,841	2,669
Miscellaneous	61,296	64,410	55,602	56,368	52,328
Burglary[3]	1,516,405	1,397,045	1,235,013	1,118,096	1,035,314
By location					
Residence (dwelling)	1,054,470	939,509	808,611	702,700	575,049
Residence, night	311,805	285,358	257,085	238,720	220,533
Residence, day	543,930	474,495	408,349	354,525	280,183
Residence, unknown	198,735	179,656	143,178	109,455	74,333
Nonresidence (store, office, etc.)	461,935	457,536	426,402	415,396	460,265
Nonresidence, night	199,741	200,859	190,817	191,731	221,126
Nonresidence, day	159,630	157,375	151,091	153,010	175,367
Nonresidence, unknown	102,564	99,302	84,493	70,654	63,772
Larceny-theft (except motor vehicle theft)[3]	5,644,835	5,513,000	5,232,167	5,152,267	4,606,324
By type					
Pocket-picking	27,648	31,026	27,326	29,865	18,910
Purse-snatching	22,671	21,961	20,113	18,810	14,101
Shoplifting	1,179,137	1,144,948	1,116,664	1,128,275	964,196
From motor vehicles (except accessories)	1,477,587	1,477,684	1,410,567	1,397,708	1,268,031
Motor vehicle accessories	415,590	407,017	324,298	330,039	393,091
Bicycles	184,546	174,803	157,042	156,013	158,157
From buildings	605,765	586,612	534,418	504,601	390,286
From coin-operated machines	12,349	12,014	11,511	11,475	8,809
All others	1,719,542	1,656,937	1,630,232	1,575,481	1,390,743
By value					
Over $200	2,561,619	2,529,654	2,445,915	2,439,300	2,219,999
$50 to $200	1,221,246	1,169,612	1,120,011	1,093,554	931,647
Under $50	1,861,970	1,813,734	1,666,185	1,619,413	1,454,678
Motor vehicle theft	767,290	772,943	751,904	724,872	810,400

1 The crime figures have been adjusted.   2 The figures shown for this offense of rape were estimated using the revised Uniform Crime Reporting (UCR) definition of rape. See chapter notes for more detail.   3 Because of rounding, the number of offenses may not add to the total.

Table 8. Offenses Known to Law Enforcement, by Selected State and City, 2020

(Number.)

State/city	Population	Violent crime	Murder and nonnegligent manslaughter	Rape[1]	Robbery	Aggravated assault	Property crime	Burglary	Larceny-theft	Motor vehicle theft	Arson[2]
ALABAMA[3]											
Cedar Bluff	1,823	4	0	0	0	4	36	7	26	3	
Centre	3,547	20	0	4	0	16	124	12	97	15	
Daleville	5,080	16	0	0	1	15	98	19	72	7	
Enterprise	28,569	128	2	17	9	100	715	97	570	48	
Eufaula	11,568	95	3	9	15	68	456	95	318	43	
Glencoe	5,063	10	0	1	0	9	41	7	32	2	
Hokes Bluff	4,254	6	0	1	0	5	33	17	15	1	
Jackson	4,583	29	1	1	1	26	83	12	68	3	
Kimberly	3,660	6	0	0	0	6	20	1	17	2	
Leesburg	1,014	2	0	0	0	2	18	8	8	2	
Leighton	754	12	0	2	0	10	36	11	20	5	
Marion	3,067	5	0	0	0	5	12	8	3	1	
Odenville	3,915	11	0	2	2	7	46	9	26	11	
Piedmont	4,501	23	0	3	0	20	92	22	59	11	
Rainbow City	9,610	6	0	2	0	4	86	17	60	9	
Rogersville	1,250	4	0	0	0	4	29	9	17	3	
Saraland	14,751	30	1	1	2	26	470	46	403	21	
Thomasville	3,799	18	0	1	0	17	112	22	82	8	
ALASKA											
Anchorage	286,388	3,472	18	558	558	2,338	9,872	1,444	7,279	1,149	73
Bethel	6,642	93	0	43	2	48	71	21	35	15	5
Bristol Bay Borough	817	4	0	0	0	4	9	5	0	4	0
Cordova	2,161	0	0	0	0	0	6	3	3	0	1
Craig	1,268	3	0	0	0	3	12	2	10	0	1
Dillingham	2,364	22	0	1	0	21	25	7	14	4	1
Fairbanks	30,832	260	3	24	41	192	1,276	171	908	197	16
Haines	2,524	5	0	1	0	4	23	5	16	2	1
Homer	6,028	17	0	1	0	16	101	11	79	11	0
Juneau	31,925	296	1	76	40	179	946	152	748	46	7
Kenai	7,885	35	1	10	1	23	148	14	128	6	2
Ketchikan	8,307	37	1	12	2	22	250	23	213	14	0
Kodiak	5,778	33	0	3	3	27	91	10	73	8	1
Kotzebue	3,249	22	2	1	0	19	6	2	3	1	0
Nome	3,900	164	2	94	5	63	72	8	56	8	0
North Pole	2,090	14	0	1	1	12	56	8	38	10	1
North Slope Borough	9,836	126	1	17	0	108	53	17	26	10	1
Palmer	7,641	18	0	2	2	14	84	10	66	8	1
Petersburg	3,259	0	0	0	0	8	84	12	70	2	0
Seward	2,806	9	0	3	1	5	59	10	41	8	0
Skagway	1,206	1	0	0	0	1	0	0	0	0	0
Soldotna	4,782	7	0	1	1	5	89	6	78	5	2
Unalaska	4,439	9	0	0	0	9	54	1	53	0	0
Valdez	3,841	7	0	2	0	5	36	3	33	0	0
Wasilla	11,228	78	0	9	5	64	341	27	285	29	0
Wrangell	2,508	2	0	1	0	1	12	3	6	3	0
ARIZONA											
Apache Junction	43,385	93	2	10	10	71	770	133	549	88	6
Avondale	89,338	310	1	14	59	236	3,025	251	2,552	222	16
Buckeye	83,608	145	1	41	18	85	1,184	141	952	91	2
Bullhead City	41,035	108	1	4	20	83	1,110	193	819	98	16
Camp Verde	11,223	39	2	0	1	36	199	46	138	15	0
Casa Grande[4]	59,822	338	1	23	38	276	1,200	150	947	103	14
Chandler	264,071	543	9	123	104	307	4,898	505	3,956	437	16
Chino Valley	12,564	24	2	0	0	22	122	23	87	12	0
Clarkdale	4,433	6	2	1	0	3	23	2	21	0	0
Colorado City	4,838	0	0	0	0	0	0	0	0	0	0
Coolidge	13,277	80	0	4	5	71	352	37	295	20	5
Cottonwood	12,380	47	1	3	8	35	478	56	392	30	7
Douglas	16,044	17	0	1	1	15	395	67	311	17	
Eagar	4,944	10	0	1	0	9	29	7	19	3	0
El Mirage	36,221	106	4	25	11	66	803	131	579	93	
Florence	27,571	25	0	0	1	24	73	12	55	6	
Gilbert	250,629	284	4	47	40	193	2,798	395	2,253	150	10
Glendale	255,468	1,123	24	83	208	808	6,956	1,273	4,924	759	67
Globe	7,328	140	1	1	6	132	469	50	382	37	
Goodyear	89,607	199	2	20	30	147	1,922	284	1,561	77	
Hayden	976	6	0	0	0	6	12	4	6	2	2
Huachuca City	1,723	1	0	1	0	0	18	2	16	0	0
Jerome	456	1	0	0	0	1	11	4	6	1	0
Kingman	31,351	124	2	9	17	96	1,106	136	868	102	13
Lake Havasu City[4]	56,243	105	0	27	3	75	790	115	619	56	7
Mammoth	1,709	4	0	0	0	4	31	10	18	3	0
Marana	50,942	39	0	6	7	26	1,165	73	1,047	45	7
Maricopa	53,165	67	0	4	9	54	615	75	478	62	0
Mesa[4]	527,361	1,960	19	235	380	1,326	9,737	1,597	7,124	1,016	22
Nogales	20,026	38	0	0	1	37	565	63	369	133	
Oro Valley[4]	46,634	27	0	3	8	16	559	40	501	18	1
Page	7,546	97	0	11	5	81	267	15	235	17	
Paradise Valley	14,859	15	0	2	2	11	216	31	175	10	
Parker[4]	3,224	7	0	0	1	6	77	24	43	10	2

Table 8. Offenses Known to Law Enforcement, by Selected State and City, 2020—Continued

(Number.)

State/city	Population	Violent crime	Murder and nonnegligent manslaughter	Rape[1]	Robbery	Aggravated assault	Property crime	Burglary	Larceny-theft	Motor vehicle theft	Arson[2]
Payson[4]	15,869	100	0	0	2	98	332	74	238	20	4
Peoria	178,486	471	3	68	73	327	2,683	431	2,037	215	9
Phoenix	1,708,960	13,646	187	1,068	3,278	9,113	51,089	7,406	36,254	7,429	297
Pima	2,580	5	0	0	0	5	21	2	16	3	
Pinetop-Lakeside	4,490	37	0	5	6	26	111	9	97	5	
Prescott	44,835	168	0	31	3	134	657	129	494	34	
Prescott Valley	47,459	80	0	21	10	49	374	39	317	18	
Sahuarita	32,053	36	1	3	4	28	273	26	236	11	0
San Luis[4]	35,574	25	0	2	2	21	323	37	201	85	0
Scottsdale	263,006	470	7	109	97	257	4,945	683	3,963	299	21
Show Low	11,527	75	0	10	1	64	313	37	259	17	2
Sierra Vista	42,800	82	1	4	12	65	888	85	764	39	
Snowflake-Taylor	10,384	66	1	0	1	64	116	26	81	9	
Somerton[4]	16,811	35	1	2	3	29	112	30	61	21	0
South Tucson	5,723	113	1	11	15	86	665	108	515	42	4
Springerville	1,979	3	0	0	1	2	5	1	1	3	0
St. Johns	3,514	16	0	9	0	7	30	9	19	2	2
Superior	3,212	15	0	1	1	13	75	26	42	7	1
Surprise[4]	144,620	209	2	34	30	143	2,006	170	1,677	159	14
Tempe	199,935	1,100	8	155	248	689	7,124	960	5,464	700	
Tolleson	7,470	90	0	4	18	68	909	200	612	97	2
Tucson	550,448	3,843	61	463	978	2,341	19,931	2,097	15,956	1,878	246
Wellton	3,062	3	0	0	0	3	26	11	15	0	0
Wickenburg	7,041	20	0	4	0	16	158	12	128	18	2
Willcox	3,509	5	0	0	0	5	138	37	88	13	
Williams	3,271	44	0	1	1	42	69	9	56	4	
Winslow	9,298	107	2	6	5	94	345	48	271	26	2
Yuma	99,096	498	11	39	43	405	1,927	330	1,412	185	25
ARKANSAS											
Alexander	3,524	41	1	7	0	33	96	37	53	6	3
Alma	5,904	20	0	9	0	11	152	30	119	3	1
Altus	726	0	0	0	0	0	6	1	4	1	0
Amity	681	0	0	0	0	0	1	0	0	1	0
Arkadelphia	10,732	48	0	1	4	43	227	35	185	7	1
Ashdown	4,367	8	2	0	1	5	110	22	76	12	0
Ash Flat	1,099	2	0	1	0	1	54	9	45	0	0
Atkins	3,040	7	0	4	0	3	72	18	52	2	1
Augusta	1,917	6	0	2	1	3	15	7	7	1	1
Austin	4,401	11	0	4	0	7	62	36	22	4	0
Bald Knob	2,864	14	1	3	0	10	105	34	67	4	1
Barling	5,076	24	0	3	0	21	75	17	54	4	0
Batesville	10,938	35	2	14	1	18	256	31	202	23	0
Bay	1,823	9	0	3	0	6	15	4	10	1	0
Beebe	8,268	29	0	8	1	20	193	38	138	17	1
Bella Vista	29,138	55	0	14	2	39	170	25	141	4	0
Benton	37,542	215	0	19	21	175	1,241	181	942	118	5
Bentonville	57,575	183	0	23	6	154	857	94	707	56	1
Berryville	5,577	12	0	1	3	8	145	23	113	9	0
Blytheville	13,239	158	18	10	21	109	705	83	600	22	1
Bono	2,517	5	0	3	0	2	19	1	15	3	1
Booneville	3,765	13	0	1	0	12	76	17	54	5	0
Bradford	734	5	0	2	0	3	7	0	6	1	0
Brinkley	2,531	19	1	0	2	16	87	21	51	15	1
Bryant	21,497	39	0	9	4	26	807	50	721	36	0
Bull Shoals	1,945	7	0	2	1	4	25	7	18	0	0
Cabot	26,593	102	0	28	10	64	372	75	253	44	1
Caddo Valley	637	2	0	0	0	2	35	7	24	4	0
Camden	10,605	114	1	5	8	100	323	87	217	19	2
Cammack Village	713	1	0	0	0	1	21	0	20	1	0
Caraway	1,283	0	0	0	0	0	13	4	8	1	2
Carlisle	2,149	2	0	1	0	1	68	15	48	5	0
Charleston	2,462	3	0	1	0	2	33	8	23	2	0
Cherokee Village	4,657	11	2	2	0	7	88	37	44	7	2
Cherry Valley	576	1	0	0	0	1	10	1	8	1	0
Clarendon	1,330	6	0	1	0	5	50	24	24	2	0
Clarksville	9,829	33	1	11	2	19	247	25	199	23	0
Clinton	2,505	4	0	0	0	4	47	8	37	2	0
Conway	68,599	359	3	45	29	282	1,915	159	1,628	128	7
Corning	3,018	6	0	1	0	5	45	9	27	9	0
Cotter	949	2	0	0	0	2	21	4	15	2	0
Crossett	4,723	33	1	3	1	28	155	47	98	10	0
Damascus	382	1	0	0	0	1	3	1	2	0	0
Danville	2,391	7	0	1	1	5	23	11	12	0	0
Dardanelle	4,520	31	0	5	3	23	77	28	48	1	0
Decatur	1,801	18	0	4	1	13	45	6	34	5	0
De Queen	6,526	26	0	4	3	19	182	59	112	11	0
Des Arc	1,568	11	0	2	0	9	13	2	10	1	0
DeWitt	2,976	19	0	2	0	17	74	16	56	2	2
Diamond City	802	0	0	0	0	0	4	4	0	0	0
Diaz	1,196	4	0	0	0	4	5	1	3	1	1
Dover	1,446	7	0	1	0	6	31	7	20	4	0
Dumas	3,984	32	0	3	5	24	31	13	18	0	0

Table 8. Offenses Known to Law Enforcement, by Selected State and City, 2020—Continued

(Number.)

State/city	Population	Violent crime	Murder and nonnegligent manslaughter	Rape[1]	Robbery	Aggravated assault	Property crime	Burglary	Larceny-theft	Motor vehicle theft	Arson[2]
Earle	2,156	16	0	1	0	15	47	12	35	0	1
El Dorado	17,523	241	8	14	24	195	794	363	377	54	7
Etowah	313	2	0	0	0	2	11	4	5	2	0
Eudora	1,866	5	1	0	0	4	24	8	16	0	6
Eureka Springs	2,110	11	0	1	0	10	73	18	50	5	0
Fairfield Bay	2,173	13	0	1	0	12	42	12	26	4	0
Farmington	7,575	18	0	7	1	10	75	18	43	14	0
Fayetteville	89,252	517	6	66	55	390	4,611	411	3,673	527	15
Flippin	1,319	5	1	3	0	1	47	7	37	3	0
Fordyce	3,646	61	0	5	3	53	146	26	112	8	0
Forrest City	13,656	223	4	13	9	197	614	95	440	79	9
Fort Smith	88,071	1,031	7	96	106	822	4,871	637	3,716	518	17
Gassville	2,168	4	0	0	0	4	46	4	41	1	0
Gentry	4,086	17	0	3	0	14	21	1	13	7	0
Gillett	680	2	0	2	0	0	6	2	4	0	0
Gravette	3,558	23	0	3	0	20	52	9	37	6	0
Greenbrier	5,779	1	0	1	0	0	14	0	12	2	0
Green Forest	2,760	36	1	11	1	23	38	7	28	3	0
Greenland	1,416	3	0	2	0	1	13	1	10	2	0
Greenwood	9,449	20	0	4	1	15	32	9	21	2	0
Gurdon	2,069	26	0	6	0	20	40	22	16	2	1
Hackett	851	1	0	1	0	0	6	0	6	0	0
Hamburg	2,574	4	0	0	0	4	15	8	7	0	0
Harrisburg	2,309	10	0	4	0	6	47	9	32	6	0
Harrison	13,096	46	0	9	1	36	237	45	175	17	2
Haskell	4,667	5	0	0	1	4	40	15	22	3	1
Hazen	1,331	10	0	0	0	10	16	9	6	1	0
Heber Springs	6,880	37	0	10	1	26	263	64	174	25	0
Helena-West Helena	10,086	165	14	6	16	129	495	143	328	24	19
Highfill	641	5	0	1	0	4	5	3	0	2	0
Highland	1,113	9	0	2	0	7	23	2	19	2	0
Hope	9,543	122	1	15	6	100	337	82	230	25	2
Hot Springs	38,893	287	9	39	43	196	2,276	656	1,431	189	7
Hoxie	2,581	12	0	1	0	11	15	4	9	2	1
Jacksonville	28,217	327	8	21	35	263	1,263	220	879	164	11
Jericho	103	1	0	0	0	1	4	1	3	0	0
Johnson	3,781	8	0	1	0	7	95	45	41	9	0
Jonesboro	79,702	642	12	78	55	497	2,825	1,038	1,576	211	13
Judsonia	1,991	12	0	2	0	10	34	14	15	5	0
Lake City	2,720	3	0	1	0	2	13	5	7	1	0
Lakeview	718	5	0	3	0	2	10	2	7	1	0
Lake Village	2,155	6	1	0	1	4	51	9	41	1	0
Leachville	1,835	13	0	4	0	9	40	17	20	3	1
Lewisville	1,097	0	0	0	0	0	9	4	3	2	0
Lincoln	2,503	5	0	1	0	4	44	7	36	1	0
Little Flock	2,816	17	0	9	0	8	38	6	30	2	0
Little Rock	197,688	3,657	49	196	376	3,036	9,602	1,527	7,062	1,013	70
Lonoke	4,178	53	0	11	4	38	155	32	119	4	0
Lowell	9,825	25	0	2	0	23	146	64	73	9	0
Luxora	1,011	1	0	0	0	1	6	2	3	1	0
Magnolia	11,434	50	2	4	8	36	406	150	249	7	0
Malvern	10,966	100	3	10	7	80	412	188	199	25	2
Mansfield	1,090	8	0	0	0	8	15	4	10	1	0
Marianna	3,325	28	4	4	3	17	113	26	80	7	2
Marion	12,285	156	0	9	10	137	364	54	279	31	1
Marked Tree	2,405	22	1	2	0	19	45	12	29	4	0
Marmaduke	1,265	12	1	5	1	5	27	7	19	1	0
Marshall	1,330	2	0	0	1	1	8	2	6	0	1
Maumelle	18,307	26	1	4	4	17	289	55	205	29	1
Mayflower	2,418	10	0	0	3	7	46	10	33	3	0
McGehee	3,631	22	1	3	1	17	51	15	29	7	0
McRae	667	0	0	0	0	0	7	0	7	0	0
Mena	5,461	14	0	7	0	7	210	20	183	7	0
Menifee	319	1	0	0	0	1	4	2	0	2	0
Mineral Springs	1,142	6	0	0	0	6	15	3	12	0	0
Monette	1,602	7	0	0	1	6	20	3	13	4	0
Monticello	9,348	45	0	5	1	39	220	50	152	18	2
Morrilton	6,631	35	0	17	4	14	221	16	196	9	1
Mountain Home	12,582	32	2	13	1	16	384	41	321	22	0
Mountain View	2,875	12	0	5	1	6	73	17	53	3	0
Mulberry	1,697	10	0	6	0	4	34	2	27	5	0
Murfreesboro	1,576	4	0	2	0	2	10	1	8	1	0
Nashville	4,360	18	0	9	2	7	116	24	92	0	2
Newport	7,423	93	0	9	3	81	436	120	301	15	5
Norfork	536	0	0	0	0	0	0	0	0	0	0
North Little Rock	66,303	665	20	12	110	523	2,433	366	1,750	317	21
Ola	1,203	2	0	0	0	2	16	3	11	2	0
Osceola	6,527	195	2	6	7	180	293	113	142	38	5
Ozark	3,583	13	0	3	1	9	66	28	31	7	1
Paragould	29,288	378	1	25	15	337	1,329	178	1,039	112	4
Paris	3,345	31	0	1	0	30	86	37	39	10	0
Patterson	385	2	0	0	0	2	6	1	4	1	0
Pea Ridge	6,398	25	0	10	0	15	77	7	68	2	0

Table 8. Offenses Known to Law Enforcement, by Selected State and City, 2020—Continued

(Number.)

State/city	Population	Violent crime	Murder and nonnegligent manslaughter	Rape[1]	Robbery	Aggravated assault	Property crime	Burglary	Larceny-theft	Motor vehicle theft	Arson[2]
Perryville	1,457	1	0	0	0	1	31	3	23	5	1
Piggott	3,494	2	0	2	0	0	33	9	24	0	0
Pine Bluff	40,718	746	23	27	59	637	1,990	414	1,323	253	42
Plumerville	768	2	0	0	0	2	10	2	7	1	0
Pocahontas	6,647	42	1	15	1	25	255	41	196	18	1
Pottsville	3,390	5	0	2	0	3	17	7	7	3	0
Prairie Grove	7,058	25	0	7	2	16	107	12	90	5	0
Prescott	2,957	10	1	2	0	7	50	9	36	5	1
Quitman	714	3	0	1	0	2	18	2	13	3	0
Ravenden	448	2	0	0	0	2	10	1	9	0	0
Redfield	1,540	8	0	1	2	5	30	9	19	2	0
Rogers	70,194	274	0	69	18	187	1,822	129	1,565	128	7
Rose Bud	488	1	0	0	0	1	13	1	8	4	0
Russellville	29,266	139	2	17	9	111	1,133	122	926	85	1
Searcy	23,742	206	7	29	27	143	983	110	769	104	2
Shannon Hills	4,098	21	0	2	1	18	64	21	32	11	1
Sheridan	4,963	11	0	3	0	8	103	27	68	8	0
Sherwood	31,636	202	3	14	14	171	847	237	525	85	2
Siloam Springs	17,332	84	0	20	11	53	449	72	329	48	2
Star City	2,005	19	0	6	1	12	19	4	13	2	0
St. Charles	210	1	0	0	0	1	2	0	2	0	0
Stuttgart	8,402	107	2	6	7	92	331	76	237	18	5
Sulphur Springs	530	2	0	1	0	1	3	0	3	0	0
Swifton	726	0	0	0	0	0	12	5	5	2	0
Texarkana	29,622	273	4	22	21	226	922	155	696	71	4
Trumann	6,934	52	0	16	1	35	370	86	257	27	2
Tuckerman	1,663	6	0	2	0	4	50	11	37	2	1
Van Buren	23,779	124	0	24	3	97	701	228	417	56	0
Vilonia	4,719	4	0	1	0	3	67	19	42	6	1
Waldron	3,344	13	1	4	0	8	135	60	65	10	0
Walnut Ridge	5,023	22	0	4	0	18	59	18	35	6	1
Ward	5,517	66	1	8	4	53	109	32	66	11	3
Warren	5,546	29	1	2	3	23	119	40	66	13	2
Weiner	669	5	0	3	0	2	24	6	12	6	0
West Fork	2,688	3	0	2	0	1	62	9	51	2	0
West Memphis	24,205	607	7	31	45	524	1,094	201	765	128	15
White Hall	4,904	13	0	1	1	11	65	26	32	7	0
Wilson	805	3	0	2	0	1	9	2	5	2	0
Wynne	7,682	103	0	9	3	91	272	46	212	14	3
CALIFORNIA											
Adelanto	34,330	274	4	12	38	220	304	82	138	84	18
Agoura Hills	20,209	23	2	0	7	14	243	42	167	34	2
Alameda	78,047	193	2	12	111	68	2,485	196	1,819	470	29
Albany	19,830	29	0	1	19	9	450	53	322	75	3
Alhambra	83,817	175	3	11	67	94	1,551	235	1,077	239	3
Aliso Viejo	51,244	28	1	1	3	23	387	56	285	46	5
Alturas	2,535	14	0	4	1	9	44	15	23	6	0
American Canyon	20,571	78	1	4	16	57	387	60	281	46	1
Anaheim	351,913	1,241	16	133	412	680	8,865	1,229	5,897	1,739	49
Anderson	10,705	70	0	10	9	51	197	34	104	59	0
Angels Camp	3,974	12	0	1	2	9	125	28	79	18	0
Antioch	112,481	591	9	40	142	400	2,719	464	1,682	573	45
Apple Valley	73,929	427	4	20	44	359	861	196	502	163	9
Arcadia	58,122	87	2	6	20	59	1,034	265	696	73	3
Arcata	18,516	77	2	6	27	42	631	125	439	67	11
Arroyo Grande	18,054	26	0	3	6	17	240	44	174	22	1
Artesia	16,610	50	4	4	15	27	306	90	165	51	1
Arvin	22,149	172	2	6	20	144	390	90	159	141	15
Atascadero	30,266	84	0	10	12	62	393	70	293	30	3
Atherton	7,162	15	0	3	2	10	142	39	99	4	1
Atwater	29,704	152	4	2	29	117	889	134	570	185	15
Auburn	14,293	32	0	8	4	20	188	29	133	26	0
Avalon	3,676	7	0	2	0	5	52	7	37	8	0
Avenal	13,321	106	1	4	4	97	97	32	45	20	2
Azusa	50,373	155	0	7	52	96	975	157	610	208	12
Bakersfield	388,265	2,007	44	106	604	1,253	15,619	3,134	8,656	3,829	599
Baldwin Park	75,233	161	2	8	36	115	862	161	425	276	6
Banning	31,392	125	4	8	20	93	543	150	213	180	0
Barstow	24,041	275	3	11	69	192	928	347	395	186	35
Bear Valley	121	7	0	1	0	6	21	3	16	2	0
Beaumont	52,884	116	3	11	20	82	874	124	575	175	9
Bell	35,526	182	2	12	34	134	502	147	238	117	0
Bellflower	76,415	348	3	27	113	205	1,799	248	1,033	518	5
Bell Gardens	42,008	150	2	8	63	77	618	74	279	265	12
Belmont	27,063	52	0	11	7	34	422	53	335	34	2
Belvedere	2,107	0	0	0	0	0	22	2	20	0	0
Benicia	28,374	25	0	6	6	13	400	63	289	48	20
Berkeley	122,346	537	6	47	274	210	5,535	797	3,933	805	52
Beverly Hills	33,776	111	0	6	48	57	1,244	263	892	89	10
Big Bear	5,305	62	1	6	3	52	91	20	66	5	1
Bishop	3,733	26	0	2	10	14	133	25	98	10	0
Blythe	19,590	118	0	5	28	85	548	166	337	45	35

Table 8. Offenses Known to Law Enforcement, by Selected State and City, 2020—Continued

(Number.)

State/city	Population	Violent crime	Murder and nonnegligent manslaughter	Rape[1]	Robbery	Aggravated assault	Property crime	Burglary	Larceny-theft	Motor vehicle theft	Arson[2]
Bradbury	1,073	0	0	0	0	0	7	3	3	1	0
Brawley	26,363	120	4	4	19	93	616	93	474	49	28
Brea	43,705	63	0	10	22	31	1,178	121	959	98	7
Brentwood	66,061	169	1	30	47	91	1,292	187	977	128	5
Brisbane	4,716	12	1	2	2	7	93	26	50	17	0
Broadmoor	4,176	20	0	1	4	15	61	14	34	13	2
Buellton	5,130	8	0	1	2	5	79	6	58	15	1
Buena Park	81,901	181	1	14	64	102	2,147	217	1,531	399	6
Burbank	102,419	174	1	12	48	113	2,474	293	1,880	301	9
Burlingame	31,126	67	0	5	21	41	1,151	131	890	130	4
Calabasas	23,897	39	0	6	14	19	255	36	184	35	2
Calexico	39,957	71	0	2	16	53	805	261	443	101	56
California City	14,286	90	0	9	9	72	231	87	100	44	7
Calimesa	9,310	21	0	0	7	14	352	78	241	33	0
Calistoga	5,255	11	0	2	1	8	91	15	64	12	0
Camarillo	70,424	53	0	16	17	20	817	100	661	56	5
Campbell	41,921	110	0	12	37	61	1,365	246	913	206	16
Canyon Lake	11,358	13	0	2	0	11	89	7	58	24	0
Capitola	10,020	22	0	5	4	13	387	40	318	29	1
Carlsbad	116,516	224	3	24	35	162	1,841	256	1,428	157	8
Carmel	3,825	15	0	3	5	7	95	20	73	2	0
Carpinteria	13,428	21	0	1	4	16	234	25	183	26	2
Carson	91,372	392	8	21	98	265	2,044	253	1,262	529	22
Cathedral City	55,417	130	5	15	32	78	651	136	325	190	3
Central Marin	34,593	40	0	6	16	18	752	196	492	64	0
Ceres	49,028	190	3	17	54	116	898	185	499	214	6
Cerritos	49,952	100	0	14	39	47	1,362	246	970	146	3
Chico	105,355	540	3	56	80	401	2,113	246	1,551	316	104
Chino	96,309	335	3	31	77	224	2,075	274	1,493	308	6
Chino Hills	84,909	112	0	6	23	83	833	184	557	92	3
Chowchilla	18,278	37	1	4	6	26	159	35	79	45	4
Chula Vista	278,027	916	10	63	302	541	3,257	476	2,021	760	67
Citrus Heights	88,314	286	3	31	72	180	2,121	341	1,511	269	18
Claremont	36,422	51	1	10	22	18	696	214	410	72	9
Clayton	12,420	1	0	0	1	0	120	5	108	7	1
Clearlake	15,268	127	0	13	31	83	382	97	179	106	24
Cloverdale	8,660	20	0	2	1	17	91	15	70	6	1
Clovis	116,809	240	1	40	39	160	2,334	306	1,826	202	8
Coachella	46,306	139	2	6	39	92	715	58	498	159	4
Coalinga	17,061	64	1	8	6	49	160	22	122	16	3
Colma	1,495	23	1	0	13	9	218	48	155	15	0
Colton	55,117	191	6	10	95	80	1,429	234	825	370	8
Colusa	6,042	16	1	2	5	8	79	22	39	18	0
Commerce	12,641	136	3	4	43	86	1,069	156	555	358	13
Compton	95,513	1,125	18	49	284	774	2,249	222	1,189	838	45
Concord	130,074	423	2	38	172	211	3,783	467	2,621	695	53
Corcoran	21,700	112	2	11	12	87	392	82	199	111	8
Corning	7,714	42	1	2	4	35	157	46	83	28	4
Corona	171,848	240	1	36	86	117	3,610	677	2,160	773	37
Coronado	23,750	17	0	3	6	8	267	32	203	32	0
Costa Mesa	113,317	488	2	64	116	306	3,581	513	2,699	369	32
Cotati	7,426	45	1	4	3	37	131	31	83	17	0
Covina	47,413	152	1	18	42	91	1,110	235	710	165	19
Crescent City	6,706	77	0	10	21	46	279	80	185	14	13
Cudahy	23,543	91	1	3	23	64	292	53	130	109	7
Culver City	39,218	196	0	5	68	123	1,600	332	1,102	166	11
Cupertino	59,343	69	0	9	26	34	830	196	581	53	14
Cypress	49,124	60	0	7	23	30	727	133	515	79	15
Daly City	106,855	192	0	31	77	84	1,460	143	1,046	271	33
Dana Point	33,604	32	0	6	8	18	450	33	383	34	1
Danville	44,800	21	0	3	8	10	239	48	182	9	0
Davis	69,853	98	0	18	30	50	2,452	386	1,918	148	14
Delano	53,625	185	7	25	38	115	856	153	451	252	54
Del Mar	4,336	8	0	3	0	5	71	21	40	10	0
Del Rey Oaks	1,657	2	0	0	1	1	53	5	40	8	0
Desert Hot Springs	29,074	218	4	13	39	162	480	143	135	202	4
Diamond Bar	55,735	62	0	7	17	38	793	236	472	85	4
Dinuba	24,807	145	0	7	18	120	439	63	304	72	13
Dixon	20,967	51	0	6	9	36	270	40	182	48	1
Dorris	892	5	0	1	0	4	19	10	7	2	0
Dos Palos	5,594	72	0	2	5	65	99	37	40	22	6
Downey	111,054	301	2	23	107	169	2,153	244	1,215	694	21
Duarte	21,263	51	0	4	10	37	348	44	247	57	0
Dublin	67,368	110	2	12	34	62	892	80	709	103	3
Dunsmuir	1,556	18	0	0	0	18	38	9	19	10	0
East Palo Alto	29,439	146	6	9	55	76	669	76	404	189	12
Eastvale	65,392	83	1	3	21	58	816	126	557	133	0
El Cajon	103,035	512	5	33	113	361	1,846	288	1,203	355	41
El Centro	44,238	158	1	10	30	117	1,003	213	679	111	8
El Cerrito	25,725	114	0	2	57	55	931	129	697	105	17
Elk Grove	177,331	398	1	50	92	255	2,380	322	1,893	165	8
El Monte	115,690	348	9	40	122	177	1,775	340	980	455	21
El Segundo	16,605	114	0	11	31	72	775	172	446	157	1

Table 8. Offenses Known to Law Enforcement, by Selected State and City, 2020—Continued

(Number.)

State/city	Population	Violent crime	Murder and nonnegligent manslaughter	Rape[1]	Robbery	Aggravated assault	Property crime	Burglary	Larceny- theft	Motor vehicle theft	Arson[2]
Emeryville	12,328	107	0	4	65	38	1,449	161	1,117	171	3
Encinitas	63,055	133	0	10	24	99	676	143	477	56	3
Escalon	7,625	24	0	3	3	18	138	32	88	18	0
Escondido	152,446	569	5	51	118	395	2,697	400	1,865	432	23
Etna	716	3	0	0	0	3	10	5	5	0	0
Eureka	26,656	182	2	23	63	94	1,041	181	690	170	34
Exeter	10,501	32	1	4	4	23	245	35	175	35	1
Fairfax	7,530	10	0	3	0	7	102	14	79	9	0
Fairfield	118,491	542	6	59	169	308	2,990	435	1,920	635	34
Farmersville	10,716	36	2	2	3	29	138	25	77	36	1
Ferndale	1,350	5	0	2	0	3	17	6	9	2	0
Fillmore	15,968	31	0	5	7	19	148	13	118	17	6
Firebaugh	8,377	22	0	1	2	19	89	25	48	16	6
Folsom	82,427	83	0	13	21	49	1,198	223	911	64	21
Fontana	216,553	666	7	74	162	423	2,504	475	1,256	773	16
Fort Bragg	7,289	21	0	1	4	16	278	42	224	12	1
Fort Jones	690	8	0	0	0	8	19	9	10	0	0
Fortuna	12,283	57	0	5	4	48	363	87	230	46	11
Foster City	34,291	41	0	9	8	24	482	41	409	32	0
Fountain Valley	55,345	67	0	6	23	38	1,338	199	998	141	4
Fowler	6,929	32	0	2	3	27	104	34	48	22	0
Fremont	244,259	407	2	28	131	246	5,722	864	3,797	1,061	33
Fresno	535,472	3,560	77	148	889	2,446	16,475	3,036	10,789	2,650	159
Fullerton	139,011	422	2	58	121	241	3,337	512	2,407	418	8
Galt	26,867	63	0	11	9	43	445	64	327	54	4
Gardena	59,385	269	5	18	104	142	1,324	168	686	470	4
Garden Grove	171,698	512	2	44	152	314	3,938	645	2,603	690	17
Gilroy	60,269	260	2	41	78	139	1,507	170	914	423	22
Glendale	200,168	206	3	14	87	102	3,197	407	2,357	433	15
Glendora	51,676	101	0	15	20	66	1,200	171	927	102	4
Goleta	30,998	60	0	5	11	44	583	91	440	52	5
Gonzales	8,321	13	0	5	2	6	63	9	39	15	0
Grand Terrace	12,643	35	0	2	1	32	211	43	121	47	1
Grass Valley	12,811	69	1	0	17	51	381	63	254	64	4
Greenfield	17,643	44	3	3	13	25	136	15	84	37	5
Gridley	7,320	20	1	1	1	17	165	18	119	28	4
Grover Beach	13,491	24	1	3	4	16	201	35	143	23	2
Guadalupe	7,865	17	0	3	1	13	89	18	40	31	1
Gustine	5,922	9	0	2	2	5	104	19	57	28	3
Hanford	58,075	321	5	17	45	254	1,119	155	755	209	4
Hawaiian Gardens	14,146	52	1	6	15	30	197	65	92	40	1
Hawthorne	86,269	675	5	25	165	480	1,631	281	837	513	10
Hayward	160,891	528	13	57	253	205	5,350	622	2,850	1,878	17
Healdsburg	11,907	25	0	0	4	21	172	26	128	18	0
Hemet	86,058	347	14	21	121	191	2,063	398	1,062	603	14
Hercules	26,524	30	0	2	12	16	238	36	163	39	2
Hermosa Beach	19,300	47	0	5	12	30	475	123	298	54	1
Hesperia	96,378	549	7	19	76	447	1,173	286	600	287	18
Hidden Hills	1,894	1	0	0	0	1	13	6	6	1	0
Highland	55,667	379	2	7	67	303	739	126	363	250	15
Hillsborough	11,447	6	0	0	1	5	99	37	57	5	0
Hollister	41,438	131	2	15	17	97	393	64	233	96	22
Holtville	6,699	9	0	0	3	6	85	21	48	16	1
Hughson	7,673	6	0	0	3	3	32	3	21	8	0
Huntington Beach	200,128	493	3	70	107	313	3,928	480	3,007	441	19
Huntington Park	57,442	421	3	25	209	184	1,720	321	751	648	32
Huron	7,343	85	0	2	12	71	72	18	37	17	31
Imperial	18,528	9	0	0	2	7	55	14	29	12	0
Imperial Beach	27,560	95	1	8	21	65	283	33	172	78	4
Indian Wells	5,527	13	1	0	1	11	111	25	76	10	0
Indio	93,219	534	7	37	97	393	1,376	281	739	356	12
Industry	201	58	0	3	28	27	794	143	517	134	4
Inglewood	107,986	679	14	43	264	358	2,495	337	1,269	889	19
Ione	8,674	13	0	2	1	10	44	10	32	2	2
Irvine	297,069	152	1	36	49	66	4,452	828	3,336	288	8
Irwindale	1,449	17	0	2	3	12	182	52	104	26	2
Isleton	848	5	0	1	0	4	12	6	5	1	0
Jackson	4,861	39	0	2	4	33	142	27	102	13	0
Jurupa Valley	111,198	286	3	8	66	209	2,347	320	1,353	674	10
Kensington	5,077	3	0	0	0	3	81	10	66	5	0
Kerman	15,478	26	0	3	7	16	276	32	215	29	1
King City	14,214	21	0	3	2	16	244	63	117	64	6
Kingsburg	12,182	17	0	1	3	13	171	45	101	25	1
La Canada Flintridge	19,982	14	0	3	4	7	262	72	170	20	3
Lafayette	26,965	15	0	1	10	4	261	32	199	30	1
Laguna Beach	22,834	89	1	4	17	67	410	61	292	57	7
Laguna Hills	31,264	57	0	6	16	35	419	73	289	57	3
Laguna Niguel	66,759	41	1	5	10	25	579	73	454	52	5
Laguna Woods	15,832	13	0	0	4	9	152	16	107	29	0
La Habra	60,672	156	1	8	42	105	1,107	161	788	158	6
La Habra Heights	6,487	3	0	1	0	2	55	17	30	8	0
Lake Elsinore	71,285	199	2	8	56	133	1,648	194	1,128	326	3
Lake Forest	86,469	95	3	9	26	57	850	124	626	100	4

Table 8. Offenses Known to Law Enforcement, by Selected State and City, 2020—Continued

(Number.)

State/city	Population	Violent crime	Murder and nonnegligent manslaughter	Rape[1]	Robbery	Aggravated assault	Property crime	Burglary	Larceny-theft	Motor vehicle theft	Arson[2]
Lakeport	5,035	29	0	7	4	18	121	31	63	27	1
Lake Shastina	2,561	5	0	0	0	5	10	1	9	0	0
Lakewood	79,222	236	1	16	86	133	1,707	238	1,202	267	9
La Mesa	59,488	181	2	16	58	105	1,036	233	649	154	21
La Mirada	48,144	92	0	6	26	60	698	105	446	147	2
Lancaster	157,689	1,198	16	84	257	841	2,690	624	1,307	759	44
La Palma	15,415	25	0	0	10	15	294	51	226	17	3
La Puente	39,589	124	1	12	38	73	387	82	183	122	6
La Quinta	42,228	46	0	1	10	35	852	119	660	73	5
La Verne	32,073	44	0	8	11	25	642	94	485	63	8
Lawndale	32,347	154	1	6	50	97	484	59	244	181	5
Lemon Grove	26,975	147	2	8	43	94	420	51	280	89	3
Lemoore	26,980	104	1	15	12	76	363	61	253	49	1
Lincoln	48,887	38	0	10	10	18	556	72	438	46	6
Lindsay	13,668	39	1	3	8	27	224	31	122	71	3
Livermore	91,200	164	1	38	47	78	1,526	164	1,166	196	14
Livingston	15,115	64	1	1	17	45	263	60	152	51	2
Lodi	68,207	225	4	12	83	126	1,262	204	823	235	14
Loma Linda	24,609	84	0	6	20	58	554	106	332	116	5
Lomita	20,327	78	4	1	14	59	319	61	209	49	3
Lompoc	42,915	239	4	25	27	183	972	175	566	231	19
Long Beach	462,654	2,343	36	242	721	1,344	12,707	2,554	7,373	2,780	198
Los Alamitos	11,400	9	0	1	3	5	224	56	125	43	2
Los Altos	30,203	23	1	2	11	9	323	81	221	21	1
Los Altos Hills	8,464	6	0	2	2	2	59	33	24	2	0
Los Angeles	4,000,587	28,882	351	1,983	8,013	18,535	85,932	13,773	50,990	21,169	2,994
Los Banos	41,631	220	9	16	35	160	933	280	494	159	20
Los Gatos	30,271	20	0	3	9	8	406	103	258	45	0
Lynwood	69,921	441	4	17	157	263	1,511	102	740	669	12
Madera	66,351	310	4	35	69	202	1,141	200	691	250	18
Malibu	11,736	40	0	9	7	24	355	67	271	17	5
Mammoth Lakes	8,236	21	0	4	4	13	96	27	61	8	0
Manhattan Beach	35,190	46	0	4	25	17	784	120	573	91	1
Manteca	84,929	217	3	16	68	130	1,429	180	1,002	247	23
Marina	23,147	47	0	14	9	24	332	49	231	52	4
Martinez	38,543	76	1	12	24	39	559	88	338	133	22
Marysville	12,519	141	0	19	15	107	463	63	205	195	17
Maywood	26,928	117	3	5	40	69	459	81	181	197	7
McFarland	15,858	57	2	6	4	45	183	42	69	72	27
Mendota	11,531	73	0	3	9	61	174	68	80	26	2
Mcnifee	96,837	139	7	11	36	85	1,659	308	1,028	323	1
Menlo Park	35,002	52	0	6	25	21	781	127	595	59	3
Merced	84,197	672	7	40	133	492	1,949	390	1,132	427	101
Mill Valley	14,297	6	0	0	1	5	311	58	239	14	1
Milpitas	86,416	111	2	16	40	53	2,103	277	1,516	310	6
Mission Viejo	94,513	71	0	5	20	46	853	112	659	82	1
Modesto	216,560	1,603	16	106	281	1,200	5,340	706	3,533	1,101	141
Monrovia	36,302	69	2	4	25	38	914	95	696	123	7
Montague	1,393	22	0	1	1	20	39	10	20	9	1
Montclair	40,473	252	4	34	78	136	1,447	409	757	281	30
Monterey	28,209	96	0	15	22	59	903	130	706	67	4
Monterey Park	59,609	113	2	11	51	49	1,230	212	781	237	15
Monte Sereno	3,438	4	0	0	0	4	15	4	9	2	0
Moorpark	36,573	17	2	3	1	11	225	27	186	12	2
Moraga	17,986	15	0	1	1	13	143	20	110	13	0
Moreno Valley	215,257	833	17	28	245	543	5,126	734	3,230	1,162	13
Morgan Hill	46,925	59	2	3	16	38	766	149	440	177	2
Morro Bay	10,577	46	1	1	3	41	159	32	120	7	2
Mountain View	83,745	144	0	9	52	83	2,177	422	1,566	189	5
Mount Shasta	3,261	15	0	2	0	13	32	4	25	3	2
Murrieta	117,639	95	0	22	29	44	1,205	181	774	250	4
Napa	78,237	267	0	44	36	187	1,320	272	883	165	8
National City	61,710	351	4	19	99	229	1,160	139	760	261	7
Needles	4,992	80	0	4	8	68	108	22	71	15	6
Nevada City	3,156	19	0	2	2	15	89	18	49	22	0
Newark	40,034	119	1	24	55	39	1,443	206	999	238	9
Newman	11,965	16	1	1	2	12	124	32	61	31	2
Newport Beach	84,448	141	1	29	43	68	1,785	321	1,312	152	3
Norco	26,536	39	0	0	15	24	605	117	381	107	1
Norwalk	103,774	437	4	22	129	282	1,771	223	1,132	416	16
Novato	55,926	238	0	9	24	205	851	80	636	135	20
Oakdale	23,926	60	1	10	15	34	310	57	193	60	9
Oakland	437,923	5,653	102	362	2,479	2,710	22,622	2,537	13,373	6,712	236
Oakley	43,385	42	0	7	14	21	478	73	306	99	6
Oceanside	176,616	717	4	73	139	501	3,180	425	2,336	419	48
Ojai	7,469	3	0	1	1	1	106	19	81	6	0
Ontario	187,464	686	10	83	195	398	3,994	641	2,296	1,057	23
Orange	138,846	180	4	14	54	108	2,396	504	1,468	424	31
Orange Cove	10,334	39	0	0	4	35	52	10	29	13	0
Orinda	20,175	6	0	0	5	1	130	44	76	10	0
Orland	7,878	22	0	2	2	18	119	29	66	24	0
Oroville	20,983	147	3	25	34	85	588	105	313	170	15
Oxnard	210,064	743	8	81	274	380	4,323	638	2,907	778	42

Table 8. Offenses Known to Law Enforcement, by Selected State and City, 2020—Continued

(Number.)

State/city	Population	Violent crime	Murder and nonnegligent manslaughter	Rape[1]	Robbery	Aggravated assault	Property crime	Burglary	Larceny-theft	Motor vehicle theft	Arson[2]
Pacifica	38,677	82	0	13	10	59	715	78	581	56	5
Pacific Grove	15,451	27	0	11	3	13	223	24	191	8	0
Palmdale	155,321	744	10	51	153	530	2,134	427	1,164	543	25
Palm Desert	53,811	125	0	5	28	92	1,564	278	1,105	181	4
Palm Springs	48,952	257	5	27	59	166	1,690	370	1,050	270	9
Palo Alto	65,459	81	1	12	39	29	1,931	242	1,570	119	22
Palos Verdes Estates	13,255	4	0	0	1	3	86	22	58	6	0
Paradise	4,072	17	0	2	1	14	99	35	39	25	0
Paramount	53,939	263	2	17	103	141	1,309	172	745	392	14
Parlier	15,734	58	2	2	10	44	161	23	83	55	36
Pasadena	141,473	414	7	51	118	238	3,021	654	2,015	352	30
Paso Robles	32,428	53	3	2	8	40	363	35	295	33	9
Patterson	22,743	49	0	3	15	31	276	46	162	68	0
Perris	80,526	306	7	9	77	213	1,890	245	1,030	615	5
Petaluma	60,806	255	2	25	33	195	756	90	597	69	8
Pico Rivera	61,925	173	3	17	56	97	1,166	180	657	329	5
Piedmont	11,184	18	0	2	7	9	367	65	235	67	1
Pinole	19,350	65	1	1	23	40	387	53	273	61	0
Pismo Beach	8,226	56	0	4	6	46	302	37	251	14	2
Pittsburg	73,673	477	4	69	108	296	1,580	284	871	425	20
Placentia	51,260	232	2	7	45	178	1,066	305	531	230	4
Placerville	11,255	41	0	3	6	32	260	58	161	41	1
Pleasant Hill	35,032	95	0	5	50	40	1,354	182	1,014	158	8
Pleasanton	83,164	94	1	11	40	42	1,188	161	937	90	5
Pomona	151,982	780	13	95	271	401	4,759	659	3,015	1,085	15
Porterville	59,757	236	3	25	42	166	1,016	223	620	173	8
Port Hueneme	21,949	58	0	7	12	39	396	43	305	48	6
Poway	49,479	53	0	4	16	33	366	84	245	37	5
Rancho Cordova	76,292	322	6	13	73	230	1,555	302	1,107	146	1
Rancho Cucamonga	178,916	551	2	45	78	426	3,265	573	2,339	353	15
Rancho Mirage	18,680	40	1	1	7	31	621	147	408	66	0
Rancho Palos Verdes	41,513	43	0	4	6	33	335	71	238	26	2
Rancho Santa Margarita	47,894	19	0	1	3	15	282	35	233	14	0
Red Bluff	14,590	144	1	33	26	84	637	113	444	80	30
Redding	92,895	513	5	67	94	347	2,323	596	1,529	198	9
Redlands	71,820	238	6	51	69	112	1,865	323	1,289	253	13
Redondo Beach	66,729	167	0	13	54	100	1,422	311	915	196	12
Redwood City	86,983	187	1	38	58	90	1,489	240	970	279	11
Reedley	25,800	127	0	11	11	105	232	60	122	50	4
Rialto	104,004	500	7	44	145	304	2,525	357	1,710	458	13
Richmond	111,367	1,074	20	33	254	767	3,679	353	1,815	1,511	66
Ridgecrest	29,120	158	1	20	19	118	320	75	200	45	14
Rio Dell	3,347	12	0	2	2	8	59	15	40	4	0
Rio Vista	10,020	24	0	4	1	19	122	30	71	21	0
Ripon	16,616	8	0	2	2	4	215	21	162	32	1
Riverbank	25,128	28	0	1	5	22	299	41	224	34	1
Riverside	334,370	1,491	20	152	394	925	9,980	1,639	6,456	1,885	96
Rocklin	70,219	70	1	23	15	31	1,135	176	851	108	4
Rohnert Park	43,572	280	1	33	33	213	709	91	515	103	7
Rolling Hills	1,843	0	0	0	0	0	6	3	3	0	0
Rolling Hills Estates	8,058	11	0	2	3	6	119	27	86	6	0
Rosemead	54,087	189	1	10	70	108	895	158	531	206	6
Roseville	144,128	277	4	18	87	168	2,843	318	2,245	280	16
Ross	2,454	1	0	0	0	1	32	2	29	1	0
Sacramento	519,050	3,547	42	125	879	2,501	14,248	2,834	8,903	2,511	260
Salinas	155,984	866	8	69	233	556	3,481	790	1,779	912	38
San Bernardino	216,365	3,033	68	134	730	2,101	6,059	1,201	3,149	1,709	98
San Bruno	42,997	100	0	13	28	59	938	86	708	144	5
San Clemente	64,665	92	1	3	30	58	866	114	655	97	4
Sand City	407	7	0	1	3	3	81	8	67	6	0
San Diego	1,437,608	5,303	56	485	1,207	3,555	24,321	3,324	16,044	4,953	222
San Dimas	33,649	83	1	8	25	49	761	104	568	89	1
San Fernando	24,399	86	1	1	27	57	254	49	117	88	4
San Francisco	881,514	4,796	48	198	2,388	2,162	38,737	7,452	25,319	5,966	377
San Gabriel	39,927	75	0	8	22	45	525	114	355	56	11
Sanger	25,457	111	2	10	18	81	371	54	241	76	2
San Jacinto	49,779	98	3	6	45	44	1,462	278	868	316	4
San Jose	1,029,542	4,375	40	566	1,185	2,584	23,847	4,045	12,737	7,065	252
San Juan Capistrano	36,074	63	1	7	17	38	303	77	183	43	0
San Leandro	89,239	462	7	22	260	173	3,416	381	1,981	1,054	10
San Luis Obispo	47,722	207	1	39	28	139	1,620	284	1,219	117	24
San Marcos	98,198	194	0	13	40	141	971	164	646	161	7
San Marino	13,042	12	0	1	2	9	238	63	166	9	1
San Mateo	105,246	274	4	41	71	158	2,306	523	1,493	290	5
San Pablo	31,164	168	2	9	76	81	854	98	450	306	29
San Rafael	58,512	229	0	26	67	136	1,912	260	1,152	500	27
San Ramon	76,502	54	0	11	22	21	796	104	636	56	3
Santa Ana	333,107	1,429	15	145	401	868	6,926	1,136	4,078	1,712	64
Santa Barbara	91,692	389	2	60	84	243	2,188	217	1,748	223	17
Santa Clara	131,976	206	1	39	85	81	3,301	432	2,314	555	15
Santa Clarita	221,932	291	2	42	71	176	2,013	359	1,366	288	9
Santa Cruz	65,073	309	2	33	76	198	2,237	267	1,734	236	45
Santa Fe Springs	17,791	92	2	3	31	56	1,039	195	635	209	1

Table 8. Offenses Known to Law Enforcement, by Selected State and City, 2020—Continued

(Number.)

State/city	Population	Violent crime	Murder and nonnegligent manslaughter	Rape[1]	Robbery	Aggravated assault	Property crime	Burglary	Larceny-theft	Motor vehicle theft	Arson[2]
Santa Maria	108,140	834	2	81	179	572	2,472	328	1,114	1,030	23
Santa Monica	90,474	541	1	38	167	335	3,852	931	2,530	391	59
Santa Paula	29,861	102	2	8	23	69	437	99	289	49	3
Santa Rosa	176,932	913	4	110	135	664	2,838	542	1,875	421	25
Santee	58,598	167	1	10	24	132	452	57	337	58	6
Saratoga	30,162	18	1	2	2	13	216	67	124	25	4
Sausalito	7,080	5	0	1	1	3	239	22	194	23	1
Scotts Valley	11,777	16	0	7	7	2	185	60	104	21	1
Seal Beach	23,873	26	0	6	8	12	561	60	459	42	3
Seaside	33,822	72	0	13	17	42	498	49	392	57	1
Sebastopol	7,697	16	1	1	7	7	179	56	114	9	3
Selma	24,982	114	1	8	17	88	533	115	318	100	2
Shafter	20,799	48	0	3	16	29	465	129	231	105	13
Sierra Madre	10,779	14	0	0	3	11	86	15	62	9	1
Signal Hill	11,467	94	0	5	24	65	738	103	502	133	4
Simi Valley	125,742	167	3	29	27	108	1,318	170	1,033	115	3
Solana Beach	13,341	14	0	1	4	9	155	44	93	18	0
Soledad	26,000	42	0	5	7	30	136	28	70	38	0
Solvang	5,909	8	0	0	1	7	65	8	54	3	0
Sonoma	11,065	22	0	4	1	17	100	25	67	8	3
Sonora	4,860	39	1	5	12	21	253	55	179	19	7
South El Monte	20,628	118	0	9	29	80	567	166	278	123	9
South Gate	93,336	637	3	19	174	441	2,946	314	1,762	870	16
South Lake Tahoe	22,286	111	0	18	20	73	427	81	312	34	6
South Pasadena	25,299	26	0	4	17	5	631	109	430	92	4
South San Francisco	68,260	155	1	15	58	81	1,560	157	1,155	248	6
Stallion Springs	2,488	2	0	0	1	1	10	5	5	0	0
Stanton	38,166	128	0	6	57	65	804	121	520	163	2
St. Helena	6,134	12	0	4	1	7	91	24	62	5	1
Stockton	314,981	4,023	56	189	909	2,869	9,391	1,533	6,362	1,496	187
Suisun City	29,842	134	1	15	27	91	585	87	409	89	20
Sunnyvale	154,133	229	2	32	61	134	3,178	516	2,276	386	27
Susanville	14,740	140	0	1	7	132	209	45	154	10	9
Sutter Creek	2,634	14	0	1	2	11	46	7	36	3	2
Taft	9,274	47	0	1	5	41	220	46	146	28	0
Tehachapi	12,873	56	0	10	16	30	335	89	206	40	0
Temecula	116,442	148	0	12	67	69	2,262	368	1,537	357	3
Temple City	35,840	49	1	3	13	32	322	68	216	38	3
Thousand Oaks	126,823	76	1	21	23	31	1,315	189	1,027	99	3
Tiburon	9,098	4	0	0	1	3	88	12	75	1	0
Torrance	143,421	274	3	44	105	122	2,935	378	2,060	497	6
Tracy	96,067	174	5	23	57	89	1,629	205	1,179	245	6
Truckee	16,800	20	0	1	1	18	109	30	67	12	2
Tulare	66,207	300	5	29	71	195	1,486	229	916	341	17
Tulelake	975	1	0	1	0	0	10	3	7	0	0
Turlock	74,183	408	5	25	90	288	2,062	377	1,308	377	35
Tustin	79,795	148	0	13	76	59	2,131	283	1,586	262	15
Twentynine Palms	26,184	141	0	8	7	126	236	94	106	36	9
Ukiah	15,992	122	0	3	12	107	270	90	132	48	52
Union City	74,625	222	0	12	65	145	1,897	234	1,219	444	19
Upland	77,511	363	1	16	109	237	1,759	363	1,118	278	0
Vacaville	101,616	247	2	36	50	159	1,760	159	1,419	182	8
Vallejo	122,326	1,212	27	134	315	736	4,078	1,811	1,200	1,067	80
Ventura	109,295	328	2	31	94	201	3,086	460	2,354	272	31
Vernon	110	48	0	3	28	17	860	186	466	208	5
Victorville	123,085	1,084	19	55	200	810	1,958	475	889	594	35
Villa Park	5,786	0	0	0	0	0	52	15	32	5	1
Visalia	135,733	555	8	106	142	299	3,077	610	2,049	418	27
Vista	102,600	345	2	29	76	238	1,203	193	740	270	9
Walnut	29,740	38	1	1	11	25	326	108	193	25	4
Walnut Creek	70,849	91	0	3	27	61	2,063	264	1,582	217	3
Waterford	9,019	24	0	0	5	19	78	8	45	25	0
Watsonville	54,151	299	4	27	44	224	1,132	167	655	310	14
Weed	2,699	9	0	0	0	9	55	11	34	10	0
West Covina	104,989	206	1	24	72	109	2,212	346	1,505	361	4
West Hollywood	36,719	205	0	29	82	94	1,205	281	822	102	9
Westlake Village	8,207	9	0	1	3	5	129	19	99	11	0
Westminster	90,741	259	0	24	114	121	2,549	480	1,727	342	14
Westmorland	2,256	14	1	0	1	12	46	9	31	6	0
West Sacramento	54,068	211	3	22	82	104	1,505	209	1,083	213	27
Wheatland	3,916	7	0	1	2	4	54	8	39	7	0
Whittier	85,074	237	6	20	80	131	1,634	257	1,065	312	3
Wildomar	37,808	58	0	6	11	41	416	53	273	90	1
Williams	5,443	21	0	4	2	15	67	23	32	12	1
Willits	4,887	41	0	2	4	35	94	29	46	19	1
Windsor	27,165	38	0	3	10	25	234	20	192	22	1
Winters	7,397	16	0	0	2	14	84	9	64	11	0
Woodlake	7,697	12	0	1	3	8	72	7	54	11	4
Woodland	61,123	227	1	15	44	167	1,376	218	972	186	32
Yorba Linda	68,017	32	0	3	7	22	573	94	425	54	1
Yountville	2,970	1	0	0	1	0	34	3	28	3	0
Yreka	7,489	40	0	0	0	40	222	26	142	54	0
Yuba City	67,165	242	4	29	70	139	1,850	264	1,275	311	12

Table 8. Offenses Known to Law Enforcement, by Selected State and City, 2020—Continued

(Number.)

State/city	Population	Violent crime	Murder and nonnegligent manslaughter	Rape[1]	Robbery	Aggravated assault	Property crime	Burglary	Larceny-theft	Motor vehicle theft	Arson[2]
Yucaipa	54,200	153	2	17	21	113	601	122	346	133	0
Yucca Valley	21,901	161	2	9	16	134	272	76	168	28	9
COLORADO											
Alamosa	9,669	73	3	12	7	51	484	69	371	44	6
Arvada	122,983	280	6	25	75	174	3,891	484	2,839	568	21
Aspen	7,478	4	0	4	0	0	133	1	132	0	0
Ault	1,913	0	0	0	0	0	1	1	0	0	0
Aurora	385,720	3,473	39	397	775	2,262	13,079	1,760	7,390	3,929	166
Avon	6,526	19	0	6	3	10	81	2	69	10	1
Basalt	4,195	0	0	0	0	0	18	5	13	0	0
Bayfield	2,731	0	0	0	0	0	34	7	23	4	0
Black Hawk	129	7	0	1	4	2	149	1	137	11	1
Blue River	929	0	0	0	0	0	2	1	1	0	0
Boulder	106,598	343	2	31	72	238	4,019	654	2,994	371	35
Breckenridge	4,991	14	1	7	0	6	116	4	109	3	0
Brighton	42,536	192	1	35	18	138	1,308	110	927	271	13
Broomfield	71,795	76	0	15	13	48	2,145	222	1,654	269	12
Brush	5,413	1	0	0	0	1	5	0	2	3	0
Buena Vista	2,902	1	0	1	0	0	51	10	34	7	0
Burlington	3,043	7	0	3	1	3	66	15	41	10	1
Calhan	840	1	0	0	0	1	10	1	9	0	1
Canon City	16,761	113	2	37	4	70	827	175	603	49	5
Carbondale	6,955	10	0	2	0	8	63	3	58	2	1
Castle Rock	71,150	45	0	14	3	28	1,183	78	1,004	101	1
Cedaredge	2,301	1	0	0	0	1	14	3	9	2	1
Centennial	112,104	144	1	6	26	111	1,979	317	1,360	302	11
Center	2,266	5	0	3	0	2	73	16	53	4	2
Cherry Hills Village	6,722	1	0	0	0	1	83	10	64	9	1
Colorado Springs	485,083	2,896	36	400	376	2,084	16,394	2,588	11,374	2,432	153
Columbine Valley	1,528	0	0	0	0	0	23	4	18	1	0
Commerce City	62,164	298	6	73	38	181	2,051	238	1,241	572	19
Cortez	8,764	49	0	13	7	29	316	43	242	31	4
Crested Butte	1,751	4	0	0	0	4	11	0	10	1	0
Cripple Creek	1,261	7	0	0	0	7	55	2	49	4	0
Dacono	6,285	2	0	2	0	0	60	2	49	9	0
Del Norte	1,556	4	0	3	0	1	23	1	21	1	0
Delta	9,011	29	0	3	2	24	399	60	306	33	4
Denver	737,709	6,329	97	670	1,218	4,344	34,294	5,223	20,662	8,409	160
Dillon	974	2	0	0	0	2	29	5	15	9	0
Dinosaur	331	0	0	0	0	0	0	0	0	0	0
Durango	19,220	68	0	13	16	39	957	115	789	53	3
Eagle	7,043	5	0	0	0	5	45	3	33	9	0
Eaton	5,911	9	0	2	0	7	48	0	39	9	0
Edgewater	5,353	17	0	8	7	2	370	35	279	56	1
Elizabeth	1,591	1	0	0	0	1	15	0	14	1	0
Empire	307	3	0	1	1	1	12	5	7	0	0
Englewood	35,464	90	1	5	15	69	2,010	165	1,452	393	21
Erie	28,198	28	0	12	2	14	326	38	257	31	3
Evans	21,515	44	2	8	24	10	430	46	286	98	4
Fairplay	797	6	0	2	0	4	16	5	9	2	0
Firestone	17,013	11	0	1	1	9	212	29	132	51	1
Florence	3,952	9	1	1	0	7	28	2	16	10	1
Fort Morgan	11,471	61	0	17	3	41	289	56	199	34	4
Fountain	31,297	129	1	25	14	89	617	72	485	60	4
Fowler	1,136	0	0	0	0	0	8	1	4	3	0
Fraser/Winter Park	2,438	6	1	3	0	2	81	6	71	4	0
Frederick	14,712	3	0	1	1	1	48	0	34	14	1
Frisco	3,231	5	0	1	1	3	73	4	60	9	0
Fruita	13,574	17	0	3	5	9	156	21	123	12	4
Georgetown	1,121	0	0	0	0	0	26	3	16	7	0
Glendale	5,243	49	1	5	16	27	904	34	720	150	4
Glenwood Springs	9,976	39	0	11	2	26	382	40	319	23	4
Golden	20,981	33	0	5	5	23	723	117	519	87	4
Granby	2,174	1	0	0	0	1	27	4	23	0	0
Grand Junction	64,149	348	3	43	40	262	2,966	385	2,298	283	32
Greeley	110,505	470	9	53	78	330	2,722	369	1,961	392	18
Green Mountain Falls	730	0	0	0	0	0	2	0	1	1	0
Gunnison	6,736	12	0	1	0	11	102	13	75	14	0
Gypsum	7,479	4	0	4	0	0	37	2	25	10	1
Haxtun	899	0	0	0	0	0	10	0	9	1	1
Hayden	1,999	2	0	0	0	2	44	12	27	5	0
Hotchkiss	929	3	0	1	0	2	21	4	14	3	0
Hudson	2,817	6	0	2	1	3	44	4	27	13	1
Hugo	782	0	0	0	0	0	5	0	3	2	0
Idaho Springs	1,793	9	0	1	0	8	76	9	54	13	0
Ignacio	914	2	0	0	0	2	11	1	7	3	0
Johnstown	15,932	26	0	5	3	18	363	29	292	42	0
Kersey	1,704	0	0	0	0	0	4	0	2	2	1
Lafayette	31,457	61	0	13	8	40	647	85	501	61	7
La Junta	6,859	33	1	5	6	21	276	56	202	18	1
Lakeside	8	1	0	0	1	0	146	1	145	0	0
Lakewood	159,719	903	8	110	219	566	8,050	1,076	5,580	1,394	47

Table 8. Offenses Known to Law Enforcement, by Selected State and City, 2020—Continued

(Number.)

State/city	Population	Violent crime	Murder and nonnegligent manslaughter	Rape[1]	Robbery	Aggravated assault	Property crime	Burglary	Larceny-theft	Motor vehicle theft	Arson[2]
Lamar	7,625	2	0	0	0	2	97	10	87	0	0
La Salle	2,389	8	0	1	0	7	49	1	37	11	0
Leadville	2,900	9	0	2	0	7	40	12	26	2	2
Limon	1,960	1	0	0	0	1	4	0	1	3	1
Littleton	48,805	72	0	24	13	35	1,176	211	745	220	12
Log Lane Village	852	4	0	0	0	4	7	1	4	2	0
Lone Tree	13,423	52	0	5	10	37	1,011	90	866	55	2
Longmont	98,545	394	2	107	48	237	2,715	313	1,974	428	44
Louisville	21,101	55	0	10	1	44	374	66	269	39	4
Mancos	1,440	0	0	0	0	0	10	1	8	1	0
Manitou Springs	5,435	13	1	3	2	7	98	9	73	16	2
Mead	4,897	15	0	6	0	9	60	9	40	11	1
Meeker	2,231	1	0	0	1	0	15	0	12	3	0
Milliken	8,509	2	0	2	0	0	36	2	26	8	1
Monte Vista	4,104	11	0	2	0	9	163	22	138	3	1
Montrose	19,864	37	0	2	2	33	630	69	518	43	4
Monument	8,361	17	0	4	2	11	127	11	102	14	0
Mountain View	540	0	0	0	0	0	19	4	14	1	0
Mountain Village	1,439	0	0	0	0	0	18	0	17	1	0
Nederland	1,543	1	0	0	0	1	14	3	9	2	0
New Castle	5,289	4	0	0	2	2	17	2	14	1	0
Northglenn	39,161	190	0	39	30	121	1,447	120	1,014	313	11
Oak Creek	966	1	0	0	0	1	9	3	5	1	0
Pagosa Springs	2,127	8	0	2	0	6	41	3	38	0	0
Palisade	2,745	5	0	2	1	2	36	1	32	3	0
Parachute	1,121	4	0	3	0	1	29	7	15	7	0
Parker	59,245	73	0	18	9	46	875	77	681	117	4
Platteville	3,905	3	0	0	1	2	61	12	34	15	0
Pueblo	113,002	1,181	16	199	198	768	5,233	896	3,399	938	59
Rangely	2,254	1	0	0	0	1	0	0	0	0	0
Ridgway	1,057	0	0	0	0	0	0	0	0	0	0
Rifle	9,747	53	0	15	2	36	277	26	218	33	0
Salida	6,183	10	0	0	0	10	220	16	178	26	0
Severance	7,040	3	0	1	0	2	20	2	17	1	0
Sheridan	6,246	35	0	9	6	20	631	47	459	125	2
Silt	3,222	1	0	0	0	1	27	1	25	1	0
Silverthorne	5,021	0	0	0	0	0	103	8	81	14	0
Simla	643	0	0	0	0	0	0	0	0	0	0
Snowmass Village	2,723	1	0	1	0	0	27	0	27	0	0
South Fork	422	0	0	0	0	0	18	1	12	5	2
Steamboat Springs	13,345	20	0	10	1	9	176	13	155	8	2
Sterling	14,459	65	0	13	3	49	531	94	399	38	5
Telluride	2,508	1	0	0	0	1	29	0	29	0	0
Thornton	144,156	415	5	150	86	174	4,538	479	3,107	952	29
Trinidad	8,114	36	1	7	9	19	305	61	221	23	4
Vail	5,450	22	0	4	0	18	197	23	163	11	0
Westminster	113,941	326	9	54	74	189	4,033	448	2,652	933	20
Wheat Ridge	31,451	173	2	35	39	97	1,674	258	1,047	369	24
Woodland Park	7,969	13	0	4	0	9	100	7	84	9	1
Wray	2,345	0	0	0	0	0	2	0	2	0	0
Yuma	3,475	8	0	1	0	7	19	2	10	7	0
CONNECTICUT											
Ansonia	18,586	36	1	7	16	12	385	34	268	83	0
Avon	18,289	6	0	3	1	2	190	18	151	21	0
Berlin	20,497	15	0	4	2	9	559	66	424	69	2
Bethel	19,932	7	1	3	1	2	128	10	97	21	1
Bloomfield	21,294	35	2	3	17	13	546	32	451	63	1
Branford	27,886	21	0	4	12	5	455	34	354	67	0
Bridgeport	144,350	829	24	47	340	418	2,514	675	1,196	643	7
Bristol	59,886	69	2	11	33	23	766	110	533	123	0
Brookfield	17,031	3	0	1	0	2	127	7	105	15	0
Canton	10,249	1	0	0	1	0	59	6	48	5	0
Cheshire	28,897	4	0	1	2	1	215	18	149	48	0
Clinton	12,890	8	0	3	1	4	327	21	288	18	0
Coventry	12,404	8	0	6	1	1	163	13	140	10	1
Cromwell	13,822	12	0	3	5	4	405	38	343	24	6
Danbury	85,080	98	4	9	40	45	806	81	643	82	0
Darien	21,840	4	0	1	0	3	369	29	295	45	0
Derby	12,281	33	0	2	14	17	369	47	250	72	0
East Hampton	12,783	1	0	0	1	0	116	10	96	10	0
East Hartford	49,720	77	0	12	37	28	1,208	101	886	221	1
East Haven	28,498	34	1	6	13	14	584	45	470	69	1
East Lyme	18,391	14	0	2	4	8	102	9	75	18	0
Easton	7,522	0	0	0	0	0	70	5	58	7	0
East Windsor	11,723	24	0	1	11	12	241	29	163	49	0
Enfield	43,551	56	0	8	13	35	799	120	609	70	1
Fairfield	62,311	26	0	2	7	17	1,179	112	952	115	0
Farmington	25,512	9	0	3	1	5	409	42	309	58	0
Glastonbury	34,487	12	0	2	2	8	523	66	377	80	0
Granby	11,531	0	0	0	0	0	117	6	97	14	0
Greenwich	63,012	8	0	0	2	6	547	34	383	130	0
Groton	8,861	23	1	3	1	18	93	18	64	11	0

Table 8. Offenses Known to Law Enforcement, by Selected State and City, 2020—Continued

(Number.)

State/city	Population	Violent crime	Murder and nonnegligent manslaughter	Rape[1]	Robbery	Aggravated assault	Property crime	Burglary	Larceny-theft	Motor vehicle theft	Arson[2]
Groton Long Point[4]	506	0	0	0	0	0	8	1	6	1	0
Groton Town	28,890	21	0	6	1	14	289	28	234	27	1
Guilford	22,106	5	0	1	4	0	243	19	205	19	0
Hamden	60,440	191	3	8	72	108	1,489	119	1,105	265	5
Hartford	121,749	1,208	23	31	280	874	3,787	430	2,708	649	55
Ledyard	14,575	8	0	1	2	5	71	8	54	9	1
Madison	18,004	1	0	0	0	1	67	4	45	18	1
Manchester[4]	57,510	96	1	11	36	48	1,719	147	1,393	179	5
Meriden	59,238	151	4	24	39	84	1,254	142	927	185	6
Middlebury	7,819	2	0	1	0	1	80	6	64	10	0
Middletown	46,106	38	3	4	7	24	597	62	477	58	1
Milford[4]	54,968	33	0	3	25	5	1,107	109	884	114	3
Monroe	19,427	4	0	4	0	0	109	6	87	16	0
Naugatuck	31,024	36	0	9	7	20	445	46	342	57	2
New Britain[4]	72,412	297	1	39	62	195	1,805	251	1,282	272	13
New Canaan	20,281	2	0	1	1	0	138	9	102	27	0
New Haven	130,299	922	21	29	336	536	4,575	547	3,267	761	30
Newington	29,957	26	0	2	10	14	849	81	677	91	1
New London	26,776	67	0	7	24	36	500	79	333	88	10
New Milford	26,668	20	1	4	4	11	183	4	153	26	0
Newtown	27,924	6	0	1	1	4	91	9	62	20	0
North Branford	14,115	5	0	2	1	2	132	15	101	16	0
North Haven	23,639	24	0	1	11	12	463	69	353	41	0
Norwalk	89,140	143	2	12	21	108	1,222	148	930	144	0
Norwich	38,576	134	3	14	28	89	542	114	350	78	9
Old Saybrook	10,042	8	0	1	1	6	85	6	71	8	0
Orange	13,922	11	1	1	8	1	408	26	335	47	0
Plainfield	15,095	20	0	8	1	11	45	2	33	10	2
Plainville	17,519	26	0	3	8	15	383	32	317	34	1
Plymouth	11,529	4	0	0	2	2	107	11	79	17	1
Portland	9,242	5	0	0	1	4	66	18	36	12	0
Putnam	9,370	21	0	11	1	9	88	14	60	14	1
Redding	9,112	2	0	1	0	1	61	6	52	3	0
Ridgefield	24,990	3	0	0	0	3	97	16	51	30	0
Rocky Hill	20,160	5	0	1	2	2	328	44	239	45	0
Seymour	16,426	11	1	3	3	4	156	21	104	31	0
Shelton	41,302	17	1	5	9	2	371	72	222	77	0
Simsbury	25,614	4	0	0	1	3	159	10	117	32	0
Southington	43,906	25	0	5	10	10	919	134	680	105	1
South Windsor	26,213	15	0	1	6	8	475	100	340	35	1
Stamford[5]	130,425	284	6	26	85	167			1,206	234	1
Stonington	18,563	12	0	5	2	5	172	19	139	14	1
Stratford	51,895	53	2	2	31	18	923	105	651	167	3
Suffield	15,820	2	0	0	0	2	89	18	44	27	0
Thomaston	7,497	5	0	0	2	3	81	12	59	10	0
Torrington	33,796	32	0	6	11	15	388	50	304	34	6
Trumbull	35,632	22	0	6	9	7	749	39	638	72	1
Vernon	29,379	9	0	1	1	7	328	70	215	43	0
Wallingford	44,236	25	1	2	7	15	312	47	240	25	1
Waterbury	107,263	400	13	44	134	209	2,843	333	1,951	559	21
Waterford	18,664	3	0	1	0	2	197	20	157	20	0
Watertown	21,475	16	0	1	2	13	312	24	236	52	0
West Hartford	62,911	30	0	4	22	4	1,715	173	1,417	125	0
West Haven	54,516	87	2	11	33	41	1,218	96	888	234	1
Weston	10,258	0	0	0	0	0	27	2	15	10	0
Westport	28,728	5	0	0	2	3	249	27	166	56	0
Wethersfield	25,936	33	0	4	17	12	529	53	392	84	0
Willimantic	17,737	21	0	7	5	9	154	28	109	17	0
Wilton	18,375	6	0	1	1	4	95	13	73	9	0
Winchester	10,536	5	0	2	3	0	123	21	93	9	2
Windsor	28,692	34	2	5	17	10	726	36	592	98	2
Windsor Locks	12,894	13	3	1	6	3	149	28	85	36	0
Wolcott	16,573	5	1	2	2	0	197	21	149	27	0
Woodbridge	8,725	8	0	1	4	3	108	18	67	23	0
DELAWARE											
Bethany Beach	1,268	0	0	0	0	0	63	4	59	0	0
Blades	1,479	1	0	0	0	1	12	0	12	0	0
Bridgeville	2,409	7	0	0	1	6	61	11	50	0	0
Camden	3,562	11	0	1	1	9	209	2	204	3	0
Cheswold	1,718	8	0	2	1	5	24	2	18	4	0
Clayton	3,577	3	0	0	0	3	19	2	16	1	1
Dagsboro	943	3	0	0	0	3	8	3	5	0	0
Delaware City	1,844	12	0	0	2	10	31	8	22	1	0
Delmar	1,850	4	0	0	1	3	47	11	36	0	1
Dewey Beach	407	5	0	1	1	3	8	1	6	1	0
Dover	38,428	329	9	22	24	274	1,549	57	1,412	80	4
Elsmere	5,851	29	1	0	4	24	110	17	70	23	0
Felton	1,429	1	0	0	0	1	13	1	12	0	0
Fenwick Island	453	0	0	0	0	0	13	1	11	1	0
Frankford	1,004	1	0	0	0	1	2	1	1	0	0
Georgetown	7,698	54	0	5	10	39	270	29	235	6	0
Greenwood	1,159	2	0	1	1	0	14	5	9	0	0

Table 8. Offenses Known to Law Enforcement, by Selected State and City, 2020—Continued

(Number.)

State/city	Population	Violent crime	Murder and nonnegligent manslaughter	Rape[1]	Robbery	Aggravated assault	Property crime	Burglary	Larceny-theft	Motor vehicle theft	Arson[2]
Harrington	3,646	25	0	2	2	21	92	19	69	4	1
Laurel	4,431	39	1	5	10	23	176	42	130	4	0
Lewes	3,378	2	0	0	0	2	36	1	35	0	0
Middletown	23,385	49	2	0	6	41	445	17	409	19	0
Milford	11,994	78	1	7	17	53	494	36	446	12	0
Millsboro	4,613	35	0	4	2	29	187	24	161	2	0
Milton	3,066	6	0	0	0	6	28	7	21	0	0
Newark	33,752	80	0	7	23	50	636	63	528	45	1
New Castle	5,420	13	0	0	4	9	183	4	168	11	0
Newport	1,035	7	0	0	0	7	29	6	18	5	0
Ocean View	2,231	2	0	0	0	2	16	3	12	1	0
Rehoboth Beach	1,573	7	0	0	0	7	99	6	93	0	0
Seaford	8,145	88	0	9	12	67	442	56	377	9	0
Selbyville	2,585	8	0	1	0	7	45	3	36	6	0
Smyrna	12,011	49	0	5	5	39	242	41	186	15	0
Wilmington	70,100	1,115	31	18	280	786	2,598	545	1,623	430	1
Wyoming	1,577	10	0	1	0	9	13	3	10	0	0
DISTRICT OF COLUMBIA											
Washington	712,816	6,828	198	307	2,208	4,115	24,459	1,963	19,126	3,370	NA
FLORIDA											
Alachua	9,998	40	0	2	3	35	251	35	188	28	0
Altamonte Springs	44,440	140	2	28	29	81	999	72	858	69	3
Altha	490	2	0	0	0	2	2	1	1	0	0
Apopka	54,842	247	1	43	41	162	1,395	259	1,040	96	1
Arcadia	8,392	49	1	2	2	44	97	36	52	9	0
Astatula	2,118	2	0	0	0	2	8	4	2	2	0
Atlantic Beach	14,012	52	1	5	5	41	250	23	206	21	0
Atlantis	2,144	3	0	0	0	3	25	1	24	0	0
Auburndale	17,046	52	0	5	6	41	504	83	398	23	0
Aventura	37,114	68	0	10	20	38	1,232	65	1,116	51	1
Bal Harbour Village	2,992	1	0	0	1	0	92	1	87	4	0
Bartow	20,507	47	0	4	9	34	419	68	322	29	2
Bay Harbor Islands	5,821	4	0	0	0	4	55	5	42	8	0
Belleair	4,297	1	0	0	0	1	42	6	34	2	0
Belleair Beach	1,610	3	0	2	0	1	5	1	4	0	0
Belleair Bluffs	2,195	0	0	0	0	0	15	1	13	1	0
Belle Glade	20,357	185	5	18	19	143	524	86	411	27	9
Belle Isle	7,392	15	0	0	2	13	92	13	57	22	0
Belleview	5,168	30	0	3	1	26	196	58	129	9	0
Biscayne Park	3,063	3	0	0	0	3	23	3	16	4	0
Blountstown	2,435	0	0	0	0	0	43	4	36	3	2
Boca Raton	101,583	206	2	35	67	102	1,996	191	1,573	232	4
Bonifay	2,698	7	0	0	0	7	28	3	21	4	0
Bowling Green	2,882	8	0	0	1	7	93	55	29	9	0
Boynton Beach	79,913	523	9	20	105	389	1,794	153	1,468	173	3
Bradenton	60,688	306	4	25	46	231	1,322	108	1,115	99	4
Bradenton Beach	1,292	1	1	0	0	0	23	3	18	2	0
Brooksville	8,663	41	0	7	4	30	236	23	201	12	1
Bunnell	2,999	30	0	3	3	24	85	10	63	12	0
Cape Coral	199,503	255	1	18	20	216	2,130	305	1,692	133	8
Casselberry	29,080	103	0	6	16	81	778	64	671	43	2
Cedar Key	719	1	0	0	0	1	4	0	4	0	0
Center Hill	1,523	4	0	1	0	3	16	5	8	3	0
Chattahoochee	3,157	33	0	0	2	31	116	21	61	34	0
Chiefland	2,181	4	0	0	0	4	97	49	48	0	0
Chipley	3,610	15	0	2	1	12	138	8	121	9	1
Clearwater	117,859	460	0	92	87	281	2,232	249	1,850	133	5
Clermont	39,932	93	0	12	15	66	612	61	517	34	0
Clewiston	8,125	34	1	0	5	28	165	43	108	14	1
Cocoa	18,769	214	3	1	51	159	1,101	120	897	84	2
Cocoa Beach	11,763	48	1	3	2	42	264	22	222	20	0
Coconut Creek	62,220	88	0	10	18	60	662	52	534	76	0
Cooper City	36,714	35	0	10	4	21	324	25	281	18	0
Coral Gables	50,017	51	0	7	13	31	1,167	127	959	81	1
Coral Springs	135,027	164	1	32	42	89	1,664	99	1,405	160	2
Crescent City	1,532	5	1	0	0	4	42	17	22	3	0
Crestview	25,787	93	4	18	13	58	602	72	457	73	3
Cross City	1,711	12	0	2	0	10	31	10	19	2	0
Cutler Bay	44,098	114	0	14	25	75	814	50	700	64	2
Dade City	7,444	47	1	5	9	32	292	41	227	24	0
Dania Beach	32,557	203	8	19	46	130	1,023	142	751	130	3
Davenport	6,516	4	0	0	0	4	95	37	52	6	0
Davie	107,988	263	2	31	38	192	2,445	267	1,918	260	4
Daytona Beach	70,084	725	14	25	77	609	2,145	274	1,668	203	16
Daytona Beach Shores	4,656	26	0	0	3	23	155	40	98	17	0
Deerfield Beach	81,749	285	3	20	59	203	1,603	135	1,273	195	1
DeFuniak Springs	7,200	32	0	7	4	21	182	25	143	14	1
DeLand	35,874	188	1	8	16	163	870	111	697	62	1
Delray Beach	70,487	401	5	31	67	298	2,412	245	1,929	238	7
Doral	68,425	63	0	9	8	46	1,238	103	986	149	0
Dunedin	36,675	53	0	6	5	42	376	57	308	11	2

Table 8. Offenses Known to Law Enforcement, by Selected State and City, 2020—Continued

(Number.)

State/city	Population	Violent crime	Murder and nonnegligent manslaughter	Rape[1]	Robbery	Aggravated assault	Property crime	Burglary	Larceny-theft	Motor vehicle theft	Arson[2]
Dunnellon	1,852	19	0	1	1	17	98	32	61	5	0
Eatonville	2,223	38	0	6	5	27	107	9	80	18	0
Edgewater	24,166	32	0	0	0	32	376	93	255	28	0
Edgewood	3,067	9	0	1	0	8	59	9	39	11	0
El Portal	2,397	3	0	0	1	2	9	2	6	1	0
Eustis	21,642	50	0	2	19	29	379	54	283	42	2
Fellsmere	5,757	8	0	0	1	7	52	8	40	4	0
Fernandina Beach	13,383	17	0	2	2	13	121	6	104	11	0
Flagler Beach	5,195	6	0	2	1	3	42	6	34	2	0
Florida City	11,826	344	3	4	66	271	657	85	521	51	0
Fort Lauderdale	184,347	1,158	37	91	321	709	7,662	1,074	5,681	907	26
Fort Myers	90,380	467	9	39	67	352	1,699	193	1,359	147	1
Fort Pierce	46,574	251	7	17	43	184	938	93	713	132	6
Fort Walton Beach	22,871	74	2	13	4	55	462	89	324	49	1
Fruitland Park	12,021	22	0	4	2	16	126	37	89	0	0
Gainesville	135,076	1,042	10	128	209	695	4,297	411	3,400	486	10
Golden Beach	934	1	0	0	0	1	8	2	4	2	0
Graceville	2,109	15	0	1	1	12	49	18	27	4	0
Greenacres City	41,518	119	1	10	29	79	711	63	597	51	2
Green Cove Springs	8,783	40	1	12	3	24	145	26	111	8	0
Gretna	1,413	8	1	0	0	7	15	6	9	0	0
Groveland	17,622	39	0	6	0	33	173	47	109	17	0
Gulf Breeze	7,037	8	0	2	0	6	82	19	61	2	0
Gulfport	12,378	31	0	6	8	17	349	30	274	45	2
Gulf Stream	995	0	0	0	0	0	26	2	13	11	0
Haines City	26,719	45	2	2	7	34	403	67	307	29	0
Hallandale Beach	40,153	200	10	16	46	128	1,047	136	763	148	7
Hialeah	234,235	447	7	27	98	315	3,851	301	3,011	539	10
Hialeah Gardens	23,667	28	0	0	3	25	463	40	389	34	1
Highland Beach	3,948	1	0	0	0	1	11	0	9	2	0
High Springs	6,285	22	0	4	2	16	59	11	45	3	0
Hillsboro Beach	2,027	1	0	0	0	1	6	1	4	1	0
Holly Hill	12,440	48	1	1	1	45	225	33	166	26	0
Hollywood	156,434	542	16	54	174	298	3,316	420	2,437	459	4
Holmes Beach	4,360	4	0	0	0	4	46	9	36	1	0
Homestead	70,538	610	3	30	214	363	1,704	202	1,376	126	9
Howey-in-the-Hills	1,191	2	0	0	0	2	7	3	3	1	0
Hypoluxo	2,868	1	0	1	0	0	40	11	29	0	0
Indialantic	2,929	5	0	0	0	5	44	5	37	2	0
Indian Creek Village	89	0	0	0	0	0	1	0	1	0	0
Indian Harbour Beach	8,602	7	0	1	1	5	108	12	87	9	0
Indian River Shores	4,363	0	0	0	0	0	17	1	15	1	0
Indian Rocks Beach	4,311	15	0	5	1	9	78	4	72	2	0
Indian Shores	3,787	4	0	1	0	3	22	1	20	1	0
Jacksonville	920,508	6,424	140	456	928	4,900	26,432	3,860	19,602	2,970	109
Jacksonville Beach	23,894	129	2	15	21	91	721	56	598	67	1
Jasper	4,127	7	0	0	1	6	50	10	34	6	0
Jay	646	1	0	1	0	0	3	0	3	0	0
Juno Beach	3,710	6	0	1	2	3	25	1	22	2	0
Jupiter	67,054	83	1	10	13	59	701	99	552	50	8
Jupiter Inlet Colony	459	0	0	0	0	0	3	0	1	2	0
Jupiter Island	942	1	0	0	0	1	4	2	2	0	0
Kenneth City	5,131	15	0	1	2	12	82	14	62	6	0
Key Biscayne	12,898	3	0	0	1	2	196	3	170	23	0
Key Colony Beach	804	0	0	0	0	0	10	2	8	0	0
Key West	24,060	106	1	23	17	65	450	43	349	58	2
Kissimmee	74,337	318	4	29	32	253	1,707	206	1,359	142	5
Lady Lake	16,255	18	0	5	4	9	141	14	110	17	0
Lake Alfred	6,425	7	0	1	1	5	39	10	27	2	0
Lake City	12,403	193	2	8	26	157	669	102	528	39	2
Lake Clarke Shores	3,653	4	0	0	2	2	35	4	29	2	0
Lake Hamilton	1,530	7	0	2	0	5	49	19	25	5	0
Lake Helen	2,822	8	0	0	0	8	15	3	9	3	0
Lakeland	113,876	404	12	58	80	254	2,813	320	2,275	218	3
Lake Mary	17,947	30	0	4	2	24	199	21	165	13	0
Lake Park	8,612	59	1	4	15	39	583	22	524	37	1
Lake Placid	2,498	10	0	0	0	10	68	5	60	3	0
Lake Wales	17,075	43	0	2	5	36	251	55	170	26	0
Lake Worth	38,945	410	3	34	140	233	1,251	164	950	137	5
Lantana	12,825	86	2	6	24	54	426	39	361	26	2
Largo	85,594	332	4	38	60	230	1,810	154	1,505	151	7
Lauderdale-by-the-Sea	6,719	14	0	3	2	9	108	12	86	10	1
Lauderdale Lakes	36,587	276	7	14	68	187	781	60	597	124	2
Lauderhill	72,421	632	7	29	94	502	1,909	276	1,412	221	18
Lawtey	725	2	0	0	0	2	7	0	7	0	0
Leesburg	24,063	159	2	17	25	115	949	164	700	85	3
Lighthouse Point	11,373	7	0	1	4	2	201	10	151	40	0
Live Oak	6,985	58	0	0	12	46	249	109	116	24	3
Longboat Key	7,342	0	0	0	0	0	75	9	64	2	0
Longwood	15,793	40	0	2	8	30	259	47	202	10	0
Loxatachee Groves	3,640	8	0	1	1	6	74	18	48	8	0
Lynn Haven	20,733	22	0	7	2	13	193	20	164	9	1
Madeira Beach	4,315	15	1	2	1	11	126	7	111	8	0

Table 8. Offenses Known to Law Enforcement, by Selected State and City, 2020—Continued

(Number.)

State/city	Population	Violent crime	Murder and nonnegligent manslaughter	Rape[1]	Robbery	Aggravated assault	Property crime	Burglary	Larceny-theft	Motor vehicle theft	Arson[2]
Maitland	17,863	29	3	4	4	18	297	45	225	27	0
Manalapan	473	0	0	0	0	0	13	2	10	1	0
Mangonia Park	2,033	37	1	1	4	31	249	27	214	8	0
Marco Island	18,121	15	0	3	1	11	103	13	75	15	0
Margate	59,449	105	0	6	34	65	675	54	548	73	2
Marianna	5,644	93	0	4	2	87	159	70	81	8	0
Mascotte	6,468	24	0	6	7	11	182	137	43	2	0
Medley	888	19	0	0	1	18	175	37	101	37	0
Melbourne	83,806	757	8	74	86	589	2,531	393	1,987	151	13
Melbourne Beach	3,321	1	0	0	0	1	37	6	29	2	0
Melbourne Village	698	0	0	0	0	0	12	0	10	2	0
Miami	476,102	2,645	61	94	610	1,880	13,092	1,453	10,017	1,622	40
Miami Beach	89,017	668	5	62	200	401	5,109	444	4,244	421	7
Miami Gardens	110,284	782	18	15	180	569	2,775	237	2,131	407	11
Miami Lakes	31,584	31	0	7	9	15	425	20	340	65	1
Miami Shores	10,358	28	1	6	10	11	540	40	471	29	2
Miami Springs	13,925	92	0	2	26	64	365	113	209	43	0
Midway	2,995	1	0	1	0	0	14	5	7	2	0
Milton	10,728	9	1	0	4	4	127	37	77	13	0
Minneola	13,001	16	0	4	1	11	92	14	65	13	0
Miramar	143,470	349	4	44	59	242	1,500	151	1,107	242	3
Monticello	2,397	15	0	1	0	14	92	24	67	1	0
Mount Dora	14,801	30	3	6	5	16	465	31	389	45	0
Naples	22,388	21	1	4	1	15	276	26	223	27	1
Neptune Beach	7,285	17	0	0	3	14	117	20	79	18	0
New Port Richey	16,954	117	0	20	21	76	434	82	316	36	1
New Smyrna Beach	28,380	75	0	0	8	67	458	81	341	36	1
Niceville	16,345	9	0	1	0	8	48	13	32	3	0
North Bay Village	8,165	16	0	2	1	13	114	7	88	19	1
North Lauderdale	44,618	192	6	19	44	123	646	72	488	86	3
North Miami	63,109	481	4	27	126	324	2,008	178	1,625	205	3
North Miami Beach	43,273	318	8	24	65	221	1,172	163	869	140	6
North Palm Beach	13,255	12	0	2	1	9	89	18	63	8	0
North Port	72,389	117	3	27	6	81	743	88	634	21	0
North Redington Beach	1,482	2	0	0	0	2	17	2	14	1	0
Oakland	3,193	18	0	0	2	16	56	24	28	4	0
Oakland Park	45,646	258	3	15	86	154	1,613	163	1,314	136	2
Ocala	61,275	413	3	55	61	294	1,936	161	1,663	112	10
Ocean Ridge	1,976	4	0	1	0	3	34	10	17	7	0
Ocoee	49,877	132	1	15	16	100	1,131	130	927	74	4
Okeechobee	5,833	10	0	0	2	8	209	19	175	15	0
Oldsmar	15,218	22	1	5	3	13	189	24	158	7	1
Orange City	12,454	36	0	4	2	30	568	48	494	26	1
Orange Park	8,864	30	0	4	7	19	165	11	134	20	0
Orlando	293,363	2,524	31	169	507	1,817	11,158	1,198	8,812	1,148	34
Ormond Beach	44,271	161	1	26	23	111	1,035	166	773	96	0
Oviedo	42,903	52	1	28	4	19	247	22	211	14	0
Pahokee	6,372	57	0	0	8	49	174	23	133	18	1
Palatka	10,436	56	6	1	11	38	552	69	445	38	0
Palm Bay	116,897	328	3	59	39	227	1,770	241	1,380	149	7
Palm Beach	8,891	3	0	0	1	2	128	20	84	24	0
Palm Beach Gardens	58,629	65	1	8	14	42	999	86	871	42	2
Palm Beach Shores	1,274	3	0	2	0	1	34	6	25	3	0
Palmetto	13,873	88	2	7	15	64	377	39	319	19	0
Palmetto Bay	24,641	30	0	5	7	18	510	55	423	32	2
Palm Springs	25,451	288	0	5	34	249	784	257	442	85	0
Panama City	34,672	303	4	38	29	232	1,453	252	1,059	142	6
Panama City Beach	12,703	131	2	12	10	107	756	56	689	11	0
Parker	4,241	9	0	1	0	8	69	16	41	12	0
Parkland	35,773	8	0	1	3	4	201	23	136	42	1
Pembroke Park	6,812	35	0	2	12	21	195	22	131	42	0
Pembroke Pines	175,757	209	4	9	57	139	2,495	184	2,074	237	9
Pensacola	53,083	327	5	26	52	244	1,543	191	1,272	80	3
Perry	6,865	70	2	2	9	57	343	149	169	25	4
Pinellas Park	54,114	187	0	32	47	108	1,788	185	1,484	119	4
Plantation	95,669	199	3	14	54	128	1,942	155	1,521	266	0
Plant City	40,330	199	3	6	36	154	906	95	724	87	7
Pompano Beach	113,545	837	19	62	244	512	3,142	434	2,237	471	13
Ponce Inlet	3,340	1	0	0	0	1	17	2	15	0	0
Port Orange	65,828	50	1	3	4	42	953	154	746	53	1
Port Richey	2,963	12	0	3	2	7	167	12	147	8	0
Port St. Joe	3,583	11	0	0	0	11	18	8	8	2	0
Port St. Lucie	206,450	264	5	35	40	184	1,666	189	1,381	96	3
Punta Gorda	20,766	14	0	0	2	12	272	14	241	17	1
Redington Beaches	1,476	0	0	0	0	0	25	2	17	6	0
Riviera Beach	35,798	428	16	23	63	326	1,174	151	909	114	9
Rockledge	28,614	60	3	7	4	46	343	50	255	38	0
Royal Palm Beach	41,142	85	1	11	10	63	637	33	569	35	0
Safety Harbor	18,144	31	0	6	2	23	211	22	166	23	3
Sanford	62,342	511	3	38	84	386	1,396	210	1,084	102	2
Sanibel	7,511	2	0	0	0	2	38	3	34	1	0
Sarasota	59,002	349	1	32	59	257	1,622	227	1,271	124	3
Satellite Beach	11,252	6	0	0	1	5	54	7	42	5	0

Table 8. Offenses Known to Law Enforcement, by Selected State and City, 2020—Continued

(Number.)

State/city	Population	Violent crime	Murder and nonnegligent manslaughter	Rape[1]	Robbery	Aggravated assault	Property crime	Burglary	Larceny-theft	Motor vehicle theft	Arson[2]
Sea Ranch Lakes	626	0	0	0	0	0	11	0	9	2	0
Sebastian	26,626	21	0	4	3	14	155	12	132	11	0
Sebring	10,664	79	3	8	15	53	389	69	302	18	0
Seminole	19,017	48	0	6	11	31	331	23	299	9	0
Sewall's Point	2,252	1	0	0	0	1	9	3	6	0	0
Shalimar	850	6	0	0	0	6	15	6	5	4	0
Sneads	1,771	5	0	0	1	4	42	14	22	6	1
South Bay	5,237	35	0	2	2	31	81	19	51	11	2
South Daytona	13,176	20	0	0	8	12	199	44	129	26	0
South Miami	11,933	50	0	6	13	31	427	90	318	19	0
South Palm Beach	1,483	2	0	1	0	1	5	0	5	0	0
South Pasadena	5,111	4	0	1	0	3	67	5	60	2	0
Southwest Ranches	8,025	18	0	2	1	15	179	13	150	16	0
Springfield	8,542	57	1	5	4	47	248	48	179	21	0
Starke	5,415	62	2	5	9	46	188	12	155	21	2
St. Augustine	15,705	76	0	11	9	56	457	43	392	22	3
St. Augustine Beach	7,101	8	0	0	0	8	72	7	61	4	0
St. Cloud	56,828	99	0	23	7	69	599	106	450	43	3
St. Pete Beach	9,616	22	0	8	0	14	190	16	166	8	0
St. Petersburg	267,690	1,772	15	110	275	1,372	6,841	887	5,315	639	34
Stuart	16,347	45	0	7	5	33	355	36	303	16	0
Sunny Isles Beach	21,907	24	0	3	4	17	212	14	178	20	0
Sunrise	96,428	195	3	21	60	111	1,324	96	1,031	197	2
Surfside	5,659	3	0	1	0	2	129	8	115	6	0
Tallahassee	196,012	1,516	24	196	238	1,058	5,786	1,067	4,159	560	9
Tamarac	67,399	146	3	20	26	97	1,009	79	788	142	1
Tampa	407,350	2,119	41	101	325	1,652	5,561	925	3,993	643	60
Tarpon Springs	25,818	109	0	23	13	73	348	34	282	32	5
Tavares	18,221	44	1	3	2	38	206	55	129	22	0
Temple Terrace	26,890	72	0	4	23	45	483	108	339	36	0
Tequesta	6,193	0	0	0	0	0	27	3	24	0	0
Titusville	46,919	295	5	24	51	215	1,081	199	764	118	6
Treasure Island	6,946	36	0	5	3	28	215	17	185	13	1
Trenton	2,179	1	0	0	0	1	11	6	5	0	0
Umatilla	3,910	1	0	1	0	0	94	13	77	4	0
Valparaiso	5,449	5	0	0	0	5	30	11	14	5	0
Venice	24,366	16	0	2	5	9	346	56	274	16	5
Vero Beach	17,776	34	0	1	6	27	250	37	190	23	0
Village of Pinecrest	19,255	17	0	2	4	11	441	45	349	47	0
Virginia Gardens	2,380	5	1	0	2	2	33	4	25	4	0
Wauchula	4,773	12	0	0	2	10	104	31	63	10	0
Welaka	718	0	0	0	0	0	7	4	3	0	0
Wellington	66,429	67	1	17	6	43	489	38	392	59	2
Westlake	1,463	2	0	2	0	0	14	1	13	0	0
West Melbourne	25,020	48	0	4	11	33	385	48	311	26	2
West Miami	9,154	12	0	1	3	8	98	14	75	9	0
Weston	71,815	36	1	10	5	20	307	30	226	51	0
West Palm Beach	113,268	863	18	76	231	538	3,862	452	2,967	443	9
West Park	15,204	98	3	7	19	69	281	43	198	40	1
White Springs	765	11	1	0	0	10	11	2	8	1	1
Wildwood	7,568	64	1	1	6	56	158	58	82	18	4
Williston	2,732	6	0	0	1	5	97	10	82	5	0
Wilton Manors	12,885	63	0	0	15	48	447	55	361	31	0
Windermere	3,619	3	2	0	0	1	20	14	6	0	0
Winter Garden	47,484	153	3	12	18	120	810	88	654	68	5
Winter Haven	46,275	171	4	19	12	136	920	125	724	71	3
Winter Park	31,183	87	1	10	25	51	685	85	550	50	1
Winter Springs	37,788	66	0	10	8	48	285	60	197	28	2
Zephyrhills	16,772	41	0	4	6	31	508	70	407	31	4
GEORGIA[4]											
Abbeville	2,654	1	0	0	0	1	3	0	1	2	0
Acworth	23,085	43	1	2	3	37	316	19	282	15	0
Adairsville	4,998	10	0	2	0	8	66	3	60	3	1
Albany	71,567	1,234	19	40	132	1,043	3,148	575	2,234	339	13
Alma	3,370	18	0	2	2	14	167	39	117	11	2
Alpharetta	68,326	151	1	6	10	134	689	82	568	39	0
Americus	14,910	161	2	11	14	134	780	89	667	24	3
Arcade	1,991	2	0	1	1	0	37	10	23	4	0
Athens-Clarke County	128,152	654	4	105	102	443	3,785	597	2,837	351	20
Bainbridge	12,006	92	3	4	10	75	446	95	333	18	5
Ball Ground	2,290	0	0	0	0	0	4	0	3	1	0
Baxley	4,655	6	0	2	0	4	123	12	99	12	0
Blackshear	3,535	13	1	1	2	9	132	41	78	13	1
Blairsville	646	2	0	0	1	1	14	1	12	1	0
Blakely	4,521	33	1	0	2	30	187	38	139	10	0
Bloomingdale	2,691	3	0	1	1	1	47	11	28	8	0
Boston	1,317	4	0	0	4	0	19	5	14	0	0
Braselton	13,758	13	0	4	1	8	155	18	119	18	1
Bremen	6,685	12	0	1	1	10	166	21	133	12	0
Brookhaven	56,248	222	2	12	81	127	1,412	159	1,085	168	6
Buchanan	1,184	1	0	0	0	1	11	3	8	0	0
Butler	1,739	4	0	0	1	3	20	6	9	5	0

Table 8. Offenses Known to Law Enforcement, by Selected State and City, 2020—Continued

(Number.)

State/city	Population	Violent crime	Murder and nonnegligent manslaughter	Rape[1]	Robbery	Aggravated assault	Property crime	Burglary	Larceny-theft	Motor vehicle theft	Arson[2]
Byron	5,304	10	0	1	3	6	144	19	86	39	1
Cairo	9,340	28	1	4	8	15	248	50	182	16	0
Calhoun	17,387	80	1	5	6	68	472	26	426	20	0
Camilla	4,981	9	2	1	0	6	51	6	43	2	0
Canon	790	1	0	0	0	1	0	0	0	0	0
Cartersville	21,995	74	1	5	10	58	414	53	320	41	5
Cave Spring	1,061	0	0	0	0	0	19	3	13	3	0
Cedartown	10,020	64	1	11	14	38	357	51	281	25	1
Centerville	7,960	17	0	1	5	11	146	30	109	7	2
Clarkston	12,697	69	2	3	28	36	260	45	164	51	0
Claxton	2,185	12	0	1	3	8	82	15	64	3	0
Cleveland	4,251	9	0	3	1	5	149	48	96	5	0
Cochran	4,984	10	0	3	2	5	60	7	47	6	1
College Park	15,204	267	10	9	72	176	934	95	626	213	7
Cordele	10,451	72	2	10	9	51	527	51	450	26	0
Covington	14,330	73	4	1	5	63	502	87	377	38	0
Dallas	14,280	37	0	4	6	27	194	35	143	16	1
Danielsville	597	1	0	0	0	1	5	0	5	0	0
Dawson	4,073	19	0	0	0	19	77	16	56	5	2
Decatur	26,473	55	0	4	15	36	473	58	384	31	3
Dillard	378	0	0	0	0	0	7	1	5	1	0
Donalsonville	2,445	10	0	0	0	10	25	4	20	1	0
Douglas	11,696	10	0	0	2	8	111	5	102	4	0
Douglasville	34,409	195	9	13	27	146	1,792	128	1,580	84	7
Duluth	29,946	50	0	4	7	39	414	48	341	25	0
Dunwoody	49,687	83	3	8	22	50	1,386	86	1,206	94	2
Eastman	5,018	46	1	5	6	34	197	34	153	10	1
Eatonton	6,753	19	0	0	1	18	153	18	131	4	0
Edison	1,380	2	0	0	0	2	4	0	1	3	0
Elberton	4,303	41	0	7	6	28	157	31	118	8	2
Ellaville	1,872	3	0	0	1	2	8	2	4	2	0
Ellijay	1,725	1	0	0	0	1	20	6	11	3	0
Emerson	1,610	8	0	1	2	5	42	6	29	7	1
Eton	903	0	0	0	0	0	4	0	4	0	0
Fairburn	17,220	38	1	4	4	29	111	8	93	10	1
Fayetteville	18,202	25	0	9	8	8	532	35	482	15	2
Fitzgerald	8,611	41	0	5	7	29	343	54	267	22	0
Flowery Branch	8,671	15	0	2	0	13	101	11	88	2	0
Folkston	5,072	7	0	0	0	7	54	10	40	4	0
Forest Park	20,202	203	2	27	46	128	877	119	634	124	4
Fort Valley	8,877	73	2	3	15	53	232	64	152	16	1
Franklin	968	2	0	1	1	0	19	3	15	1	0
Gainesville	44,398	184	0	12	38	134	1,116	140	887	89	9
Garden City	8,716	120	5	8	20	87	402	62	265	75	0
Glennville	5,004	5	0	1	0	4	90	6	66	18	0
Grantville	3,322	13	0	1	0	12	44	5	34	5	0
Gray	3,273	2	0	0	1	1	58	3	53	2	2
Greensboro	3,299	14	0	1	2	11	79	4	68	7	0
Griffin	22,773	258	7	15	23	213	1,090	169	839	82	0
Grovetown	15,650	38	0	4	5	29	109	17	84	8	0
Hahira	3,060	3	0	1	1	1	38	7	28	3	0
Hampton	8,201	7	0	1	2	4	49	4	37	8	1
Helen	565	4	0	0	0	4	63	9	50	4	0
Hiawassee	916	1	0	0	0	1	12	0	12	0	0
Hiram	4,301	23	0	2	8	13	287	11	263	13	1
Jasper	4,009	10	0	1	0	9	132	16	110	6	0
Jefferson	12,349	9	0	1	2	6	153	21	121	11	0
Johns Creek	85,408	33	3	3	5	22	384	56	309	19	3
Kingston	684	0	0	0	0	0	9	0	8	1	1
LaGrange	30,406	176	6	25	35	110	1,729	191	1,419	119	4
Lake City	2,855	3	0	1	1	1	44	1	33	10	1
Lavonia	2,204	1	0	0	0	1	71	11	52	8	0
Leesburg	3,073	6	0	1	0	5	36	8	25	3	0
Lilburn	12,941	34	1	1	13	19	276	44	200	32	0
Lookout Mountain	1,571	0	0	0	0	0	0	0	0	0	0
Louisville	2,187	8	0	0	0	8	52	4	44	4	0
Madison	4,236	7	0	0	0	7	91	10	70	11	0
Manchester	3,942	12	2	2	0	8	87	20	58	9	0
Marietta	61,348	301	4	19	68	210	1,802	176	1,418	208	3
Marshallville	1,206	1	0	1	0	0	13	5	8	0	0
McDonough	27,338	88	0	15	15	58	714	82	545	87	3
McRae-Helena	8,246	11	0	0	2	9	59	21	32	6	0
Metter	3,927	13	1	2	2	8	93	11	77	5	2
Milledgeville	18,751	141	3	4	6	128	664	86	543	35	3
Millen	2,730	16	1	2	1	12	77	15	59	3	0
Milton	40,368	15	0	5	1	9	207	32	170	5	0
Monroe	13,761	103	2	8	13	80	513	59	420	34	1
Montezuma	2,903	14	0	1	0	13	47	6	41	0	2
Morrow	7,327	38	1	3	17	17	549	21	481	47	1
Moultrie	14,199	80	0	9	13	58	535	92	412	31	2
Mount Zion	1,825	6	0	2	1	3	14	1	11	2	0
Nashville	4,839	51	0	1	7	43	229	33	188	8	0
Newington	261	1	0	0	0	1	5	0	5	0	0

Table 8. Offenses Known to Law Enforcement, by Selected State and City, 2020—Continued

(Number.)

State/city	Population	Violent crime	Murder and nonnegligent manslaughter	Rape[1]	Robbery	Aggravated assault	Property crime	Burglary	Larceny-theft	Motor vehicle theft	Arson[2]
Newnan	42,658	532	6	33	27	466	837	89	682	66	1
Oakwood	4,180	2	0	2	0	0	72	4	64	4	0
Ocilla	3,759	23	0	1	1	21	105	14	73	18	1
Oxford	2,372	0	0	0	0	0	26	2	21	3	0
Palmetto	4,890	10	2	0	3	5	65	7	53	5	2
Peachtree City	36,421	16	0	7	4	5	388	15	345	28	0
Pelham	3,420	17	2	0	5	10	113	20	81	12	3
Pine Mountain	1,430	2	0	0	1	1	27	3	23	1	0
Pooler	26,634	36	3	5	8	20	537	42	468	27	1
Port Wentworth	10,281	34	0	10	8	16	162	27	109	26	1
Reynolds	949	5	0	0	0	5	10	2	8	0	1
Richmond Hill	14,437	27	0	6	0	21	247	39	184	24	1
Rincon	10,525	24	0	3	4	17	173	34	134	5	2
Rockmart	4,458	14	0	2	1	11	244	36	197	11	0
Rossville	3,999	21	1	4	4	12	193	27	133	33	1
Roswell	95,396	357	1	23	26	307	1,079	110	873	96	3
Sandersville	5,346	12	0	0	2	10	51	6	43	2	1
Sandy Springs	111,219	164	6	12	46	100	1,539	161	1,222	156	2
Smyrna	57,317	214	9	21	34	150	1,176	140	893	143	2
Snellville	20,282	137	1	4	9	123	440	21	403	16	0
Social Circle	4,583	16	2	2	1	11	73	8	59	6	0
South Fulton	100,658	1,034	21	23	91	899	2,694	274	1,850	570	19
Springfield	4,281	5	0	1	0	4	23	4	18	1	0
Stone Mountain	6,332	23	1	3	4	15	142	11	94	37	0
Suwanee	21,633	36	2	7	7	20	247	26	204	17	1
Sylvania	2,449	8	0	0	1	7	43	11	32	0	0
Sylvester	5,732	12	0	1	0	11	96	18	77	1	0
Tallapoosa	3,186	23	0	2	3	18	65	14	46	5	0
Temple	4,832	8	0	2	0	6	109	17	83	9	0
Thunderbolt	2,634	12	0	1	1	10	29	3	23	3	0
Toccoa	8,312	23	0	9	3	11	337	43	279	15	1
Tyrone	7,575	4	0	0	1	3	42	2	33	7	0
Valdosta	56,628	220	6	13	43	158	1,848	222	1,530	96	0
Vidalia	10,398	88	3	9	9	67	159	31	126	2	0
Vienna	3,503	13	0	0	0	13	37	9	26	2	1
Villa Rica	16,296	46	0	5	7	34	390	56	317	17	1
Warner Robins	78,508	495	2	31	80	382	3,154	481	2,411	262	14
Waycross	13,363	129	3	16	24	86	758	144	571	43	3
Waynesboro	5,308	19	0	1	4	14	167	32	123	12	1
Woodstock	34,252	61	0	6	5	50	333	22	301	10	1
Zebulon	1,234	0	0	0	0	0	1	0	1	0	0
IDAHO											
Aberdeen	1,975	5	0	0	0	5	20	7	10	3	0
American Falls	4,298	8	0	0	0	8	68	16	41	11	1
Ashton	1,042	1	0	0	0	1	7	4	2	1	0
Bellevue	2,471	5	1	0	0	4	12	5	6	1	0
Blackfoot	12,036	40	0	11	2	27	266	45	201	20	3
Boise	231,223	677	4	170	55	448	3,793	479	3,035	279	35
Bonners Ferry	2,652	12	1	2	0	9	18	2	16	0	0
Buhl	4,544	10	0	1	0	9	26	3	19	4	2
Chubbuck	15,773	30	0	0	0	30	362	24	318	20	0
Coeur d'Alene	53,405	209	1	66	8	134	835	92	701	42	5
Cottonwood	944	1	0	0	0	1	2	0	2	0	0
Emmett	7,114	33	0	5	0	28	61	10	42	9	0
Filer	2,980	6	0	1	0	5	8	1	7	0	0
Fruitland	5,505	6	0	4	0	2	55	9	42	4	0
Garden City	12,084	84	1	9	2	72	241	46	176	19	1
Gooding	3,429	9	0	3	0	6	56	20	34	2	0
Hailey	8,778	14	0	1	1	12	19	4	12	3	0
Heyburn	3,489	6	0	2	0	4	44	10	31	3	0
Idaho Falls	63,457	291	2	35	18	236	1,152	325	704	123	6
Jerome	12,120	70	0	15	2	53	185	32	134	19	1
Kellogg	2,136	7	0	0	0	7	32	9	19	4	0
Ketchum	2,872	7	0	0	0	7	26	6	19	1	0
Kimberly	4,146	5	0	2	0	2	7	2	4	1	1
Lewiston	32,886	61	1	15	4	41	767	135	582	50	3
McCall	3,677	10	0	1	1	8	55	6	44	5	0
Meridian	119,203	190	1	51	7	131	1,006	160	788	58	6
Middleton	8,877	13	0	2	0	11	59	19	40	0	0
Montpelier	2,533	2	0	1	0	1	30	2	24	4	0
Moscow	25,918	10	0	1	3	6	391	51	330	10	0
Mountain Home	14,597	52	1	8	0	43	90	10	75	5	1
Nampa	101,411	319	2	98	7	212	1,666	237	1,236	193	16
Osburn	1,557	5	0	0	0	5	11	4	6	1	0
Parma	2,167	8	0	3	0	5	23	8	14	1	0
Payette	7,753	28	0	3	1	24	139	10	115	14	2
Pinehurst	1,627	1	0	0	0	1	28	1	27	0	0
Pocatello	56,900	206	0	12	11	183	1,223	291	822	110	6
Ponderay	1,170	1	0	0	0	1	27	1	25	1	0
Preston	5,592	4	0	2	0	2	59	13	46	0	0
Priest River	1,911	1	0	0	1	0	22	3	17	2	0
Rexburg	29,865	9	0	1	0	8	101	15	81	5	0

Table 8. Offenses Known to Law Enforcement, by Selected State and City, 2020—Continued

(Number.)

State/city	Population	Violent crime	Murder and nonnegligent manslaughter	Rape[1]	Robbery	Aggravated assault	Property crime	Burglary	Larceny-theft	Motor vehicle theft	Arson[2]
Rigby	4,332	1	0	0	0	1	40	6	33	1	0
Rupert	5,927	16	0	1	0	15	82	19	54	9	2
Salmon	3,171	12	0	0	0	12	23	8	15	0	0
Sandpoint	9,111	5	0	1	0	4	176	49	120	7	0
Shelley	4,470	6	0	1	0	5	53	11	39	3	0
Spirit Lake	2,610	2	0	1	0	1	32	5	26	1	1
St. Anthony	3,552	1	0	1	0	0	10	2	8	0	0
Sun Valley	1,495	1	0	0	0	1	4	2	2	0	0
Twin Falls	50,872	259	2	36	7	214	892	100	754	38	15
Wendell	2,707	4	0	2	0	2	25	6	11	8	1
Wilder	1,858	0	0	0	0	0	1	1	0	0	0
ILLINOIS[4]											
Abingdon	3,026	11	0	2	1	8		11		3	3
Addison	36,411	65	0	21	14	30		51		42	2
Albers	1,130	0	0	0	0	0		0		0	0
Alexis	771	0	0	0	0	0		0		0	0
Algonquin	30,990	27	2	8	0	17		18		13	0
Alsip	18,646	92	0	10	13	69		66		16	1
Altamont	2,341	1	0	0	0	1		5		1	0
Alton	26,027	216	2	19	27	168		164		77	14
Amboy	2,301	1	0	0	0	1		2		0	1
Annawan	849	0	0	0	0	0		0		2	0
Antioch	14,141	11	0	0	3	8		5		8	0
Arcola	2,822	4	0	0	0	4		4		1	0
Arlington Heights	74,706	43	1	9	12	21		47		26	1
Armington	320	0	0	0	0	0		0		0	0
Arthur	2,191	5	0	1	0	4		0		0	0
Ashland	1,176	1	0	1	0	0		3		1	0
Ashton	883	0	0	0	0	0		1		0	0
Assumption	1,055	0	0	0	0	0		4		0	0
Athens	1,899	0	0	0	0	0		1		0	0
Auburn	4,602	12	0	3	0	9		15		3	0
Aurora	197,709	659	11	68	78	502		225		171	32
Aviston	2,153	0	0	0	0	0		0		0	0
Bannockburn	1,508	0	0	0	0	0		1		0	0
Barrington	10,205	1	0	0	0	1		3		12	0
Barrington Hills	4,185	2	1	1	0	0		8		1	0
Bartlett	40,577	9	0	2	2	5		9		16	0
Bartonville	6,075	27	0	4	6	17		24		7	0
Batavia	26,438	18	0	2	2	14		21		18	1
Beardstown	5,372	22	0	0	0	22		24		6	0
Beecher	4,435	3	0	0	0	3		5		0	0
Belgium	364	0	0	0	0	0		0		0	0
Belleville[5]	40,537	236	2	46	35	153				112	23
Bellwood	18,629	148	1	9	42	96		73		45	0
Benton	6,826	2	0	0	0	2		4		1	0
Bethalto	9,177	4	0	1	0	3		9		4	1
Bethany	1,227	2	0	0	1	1		5		0	0
Blandinsville	589	0	0	0	0	0		0		0	0
Bloomingdale	21,746	18	0	2	4	12		18		12	1
Bloomington	77,386	314	1	64	23	226		144		70	5
Blue Mound	1,063	5	0	1	0	4		5		1	1
Bolingbrook	74,665	130	0	25	23	82		78		62	6
Bourbonnais	19,551	52	0	17	5	30		12		5	0
Braidwood	6,180	14	0	6	0	8		7		2	1
Bridgeview	16,056	40	1	3	10	26		21		16	2
Broadview	7,585	27	0	6	10	11		27		21	1
Buffalo Grove	40,380	5	0	1	1	3		12		8	0
Burbank	28,217	83	0	4	20	59		52		23	0
Burr Ridge	10,782	8	0	1	3	4		13		11	0
Byron	3,650	0	0	0	0	0		3		0	0
Cahokia	13,738	94	4	6	16	68		140		95	5
Calumet City	35,779	158	5	29	80	44		156		315	9
Cambria	1,493	3	0	2	0	1		3		3	1
Cambridge	2,069	2	0	1	0	1		0		1	0
Campton Hills	11,092	1	0	0	1	0		3		0	0
Carbondale[5]	24,933		4	31		146		128		69	6
Carlinville	5,434	29	0	16	0	13		24		8	1
Carlyle	3,174	3	0	0	0	3		5		2	0
Carol Stream	39,161	42	0	18	3	21		38		11	2
Carpentersville	37,201	27	1	13	5	8		23		9	3
Carthage	2,441	2	0	0	0	2		8		1	0
Cary	18,036	7	0	3	0	4		5		2	1
Caseyville	4,094	29	0	4	2	23		24		24	0
Catlin	1,913	3	0	0	0	3		3		0	0
Centralia	12,123	159	0	23	23	113		129			6
Champaign	89,785	827	9	60	88	670		281		191	11
Channahon	13,312	11	0	3	6	2		3		9	0
Chatham	13,152	11	0	3	0	8		15		6	0
Chenoa	3,110	0	0	0	0	0		4		3	0
Chester	8,174	10	0	1	0	9		2		2	0
Chicago	2,693,598	26,583	771	1,346	7,869	16,597		8,643		10,053	636

Table 8. Offenses Known to Law Enforcement, by Selected State and City, 2020—Continued

(Number.)

State/city	Population	Violent crime	Murder and nonnegligent manslaughter	Rape[1]	Robbery	Aggravated assault	Property crime	Burglary	Larceny-theft	Motor vehicle theft	Arson[2]
Chicago Heights	29,207	205	5	29	45	126		116		99	2
Chicago Ridge	13,885	22	0	3	11	8		8		3	3
Chillicothe	6,004	19	0	3	0	16		15		12	0
Christopher	2,703	2	0	0	0	2		5		0	1
Cicero	80,420	325	6	46	126	147		204		219	12
Clarendon Hills	8,787	3	0	1	0	2		8		2	0
Clinton	6,799	3	0	3	0	0		58		3	0
Coal City	5,378	3	0	2	0	1		4		1	0
Coal Valley	3,721	3	0	0	0	3		8		0	0
Colchester	1,277	1	0	0	0	1		2		1	0
Colfax	1,008	3	0	0	0	3		0		0	0
Cortland	4,421	5	0	1	1	3		0		0	0
Country Club Hills	16,448	42	1	17	9	15		24		81	0
Countryside	5,934	13	0	0	8	5		18		10	0
Crest Hill	20,328	57	2	16	6	33		42		16	1
Crete	7,996	17	0	2	1	14		16		6	0
Crystal Lake	39,726	37	1	11	7	18		24		14	1
Dallas City	864	0	0	0	0	0		2		0	0
Danville	30,208	505	8	10	59	428		399		48	30
Darien	21,590	8	0	2	4	2		28		4	1
Decatur	70,175	489	13	41	83	352		621		196	29
Deer Creek	659	2	0	1	0	1		0		0	0
Deerfield	18,692	3	0	2	1	0		18		17	0
DeKalb	42,710	252	4	35	40	173		114		59	9
De Soto	1,493	2	0	0	0	2		0		0	0
Des Plaines	58,950	43	0	12	14	17		79		31	4
Diamond	2,503	1	0	0	1	0		1		0	0
Dixon	15,047	15	0	14	0	1		29		2	1
Downers Grove	49,070	47	1	17	7	22		43		37	3
Dupo	3,845	5	0	0	2	3		23		17	2
Durand	1,387	3	0	0	3	0		0		1	0
East Alton	5,920	26	0	15	2	9		14		12	0
East Hazel Crest	1,492	4	0	0	0	4		10		6	0
East Moline	20,573	91	4	25	5	57		96		28	2
Edinburg	1,005	1	0	0	0	1		1		0	0
Edwardsville	25,327	8	0	0	3	5		7		9	0
Effingham	12,531	72	0	4	4	64		38		14	1
Elburn	6,043	3	0	0	0	3		2		0	0
Elgin	111,127	260	1	52	50	157		147		100	1
Elizabeth	717	0	0	0	0	0		0		0	0
Elk Grove Village	32,290	25	1	1	9	14		35		45	1
Elmhurst	47,034	39	0	7	5	27		61		32	0
Elmwood	2,002	0	0	0	0	0		1		0	0
Elmwood Park	24,011	52	1	2	13	36		39		8	6
Elwood	2,220	2	0	1	0	1		3		0	0
Energy	1,105	1	0	0	0	1		1		0	0
Erie	1,488	0	0	0	0	0		1		0	0
Eureka	5,276	27	0	3	0	24		27		2	1
Evergreen Park	19,070	65	0	3	21	41		23		5	1
Fairbury	3,602	5	0	1	3	1		8		0	0
Fairfield	4,914	26	0	4	1	21		36		4	1
Fairmont City	2,434	3	0	0	0	3		2		1	0
Fairmount	591	0	0	0	0	0		0		0	0
Fairview Heights	16,217	37	1	10	3	23		35		32	0
Farmer City	1,927	3	0	1	0	2		3		1	0
Farmington	2,200	2	0	1	0	1		5		6	0
Fisher	1,944	1	0	1	0	0		2		1	0
Fithian	445	0	0	0	0	0		0		0	0
Flora	4,829	16	0	0	2	14		9		4	1
Flossmoor	9,123	10	0	3	2	5		9		10	0
Fox Lake	10,426	24	0	8	2	14		21		16	0
Fox River Grove	4,552	2	0	1	0	1		3		3	2
Frankfort	19,551	11	0	3	2	6		20		20	1
Franklin Grove	930	0	0	0	0	0		2		0	0
Franklin Park	17,552	41	0	11	9	21		62		15	0
Freeburg	4,225	2	0	1	1	0		7		2	0
Freeport	23,583	81	5	14	16	46		75		22	0
Fulton	3,297	3	0	0	0	3		7		2	0
Galena	3,131	6	0	4	0	2		4		0	0
Galesburg	29,985	144	2	27	14	101		196		79	3
Geneva	21,831	18	0	4	1	13		19		1	0
Genoa	5,244	8	0	2	0	6		1		1	1
Georgetown	3,154	4	0	1	0	3		35		0	0
Gibson City	3,214	16	0	2	0	14		6		3	0
Gifford	1,056	0	0	0	0	0		4		0	0
Gilberts	8,218	0	0	0	0	0		2		1	0
Glen Carbon	12,842	8	0	0	2	6		6		13	0
Glencoe	8,837	6	0	2	1	3		5		16	0
Glendale Heights	33,539	50	1	12	10	27		19		20	3
Glen Ellyn	27,704	20	0	1	8	11		28		9	0
Glenview	47,601	47	1	7	10	29		97		24	5
Glenwood	8,685	11	0	0	6	5		27		40	0
Godley	775	2	0	0	1	1		0		0	0

Table 8. Offenses Known to Law Enforcement, by Selected State and City, 2020—Continued

(Number.)

State/city	Population	Violent crime	Murder and nonnegligent manslaughter	Rape[1]	Robbery	Aggravated assault	Property crime	Burglary	Larceny-theft	Motor vehicle theft	Arson[2]
Golf	493	0	0	0	0	0		0		5	0
Goodfield	1,000	3	0	1	0	2		0		0	0
Grafton	636	0	0	0	0	0		0		1	0
Grand Ridge	521	0	0	0	0	0		0		0	0
Granite City	27,982	218	2	25	20	171		180		151	18
Grantfork	342	1	0	0	0	1		0		0	0
Grant Park	1,239	0	0	0	0	0		1		2	0
Grayslake	20,688	15	0	4	1	10		24		8	0
Greenfield	979	0	0	0	0	0		2		1	0
Greenup	1,485	1	0	0	0	1		4		1	0
Greenville	6,349	5	0	0	0	5		7		4	0
Gurnee	30,281	43	0	14	6	23		40		35	1
Hainesville	3,546	4	0	1	1	2		9		0	0
Hamel	809	5	0	0	0	5		1		3	0
Hampshire	6,332	5	0	1	1	3		13		5	0
Hampton	1,732	1	0	0	0	1		6		0	0
Hanover Park	37,350	48	2	5	10	31		24		21	2
Harrisburg	8,459	53	0	4	7	42		74		20	1
Hartford	1,331	3	0	2	0	1		0		2	0
Harvard	9,019	19	0	5	2	12		1		8	0
Harwood Heights	8,302	6	0	1	2	3		8		11	0
Havana	2,954	45	0	7	1	37		11		2	1
Hawthorn Woods	8,770	1	0	0	0	1		0		2	0
Hazel Crest	13,515	44	3	4	20	17		47		120	0
Henning	232	0	0	0	0	0		0		0	0
Herrin	12,704	46	0	10	3	33		57		20	0
Hickory Hills	13,672	28	0	5	12	11		17		12	0
Highland	9,819	10	0	0	3	7		22		11	0
Highwood	5,199	3	0	1	1	1		5		1	0
Hillsboro	5,945	16	0	1	0	15		10		7	1
Hillside	7,902	31	0	3	10	18		28		13	0
Hinckley	2,048	4	0	0	0	4		2		0	0
Hinsdale	17,724	4	0	0	0	4		15		10	1
Hodgkins	1,979	2	0	0	0	2		5		7	1
Homer	1,154	0	0	0	0	0		0		0	0
Homer Glen	24,497	8	0	2	2	4		22		10	0
Homewood	18,636	39	1	8	16	14		36		49	0
Hopedale	820	3	0	0	0	3		2		0	0
Hudson	1,810	1	0	1	0	0		1		0	0
Huntley	27,566	11	0	0	0	11		17		11	0
Ina	2,273	0	0	0	0	0		0		0	0
Indianola	255	0	0	0	0	0		0		0	0
Island Lake	8,014	5	0	0	1	4		1		4	0
Itasca	9,944	4	0	2	0	2		10		5	0
Jacksonville	18,515	67	0	9	1	57		50		32	2
Jerseyville	8,172	12	0	4	0	8		22		10	0
Kankakee	25,863	244	8	23	33	180		112		52	2
Kansas	712	0	0	0	0	0		0		0	0
Kenilworth	2,471	1	0	1	0	0		2		2	0
Kildeer	4,024	1	0	0	0	1		8		2	0
Kirkland	1,727	2	0	0	0	2		0		1	0
Lacon	1,718	3	0	0	1	2		2		2	0
Ladd	1,184	0	0	0	0	0		0		0	0
La Grange	15,295	13	1	2	2	8		19		7	0
La Grange Park	13,133	7	0	0	1	6		12		4	2
La Harpe	1,134	0	0	0	0	0		5		0	0
Lake Bluff	5,548	2	0	0	2	0		4		1	0
Lake Forest	19,452	6	0	2	0	4		32		7	0
Lake in the Hills	28,598	23	0	15	1	7		9		8	0
Lake Villa	8,565	6	0	0	0	6		3		5	0
Lakewood	4,023	0	0	0	0	0		1		0	0
Lake Zurich	19,895	4	0	2	1	1		15		5	0
Lansing	27,297	116	1	12	62	41		117		202	0
La Salle	8,919	4	0	0	0	4		4		1	0
Lemont	17,432	15	0	6	2	7		18		8	1
Le Roy	3,487	8	0	1	2	5		11		4	0
Libertyville	20,181	5	0	0	3	2		13		18	0
Lincolnshire	7,962	2	0	1	1	0		9		3	0
Lincolnwood	12,207	9	0	0	4	5		23		16	0
Lindenhurst	14,174	6	0	4	1	1		3		3	0
Litchfield	6,668	8	0	2	1	5		28		11	1
Lockport	25,700	26	0	10	7	9		25		9	3
Lombard	44,392	34	1	11	9	13		53		24	1
Loves Park[4]	23,303	86	0	18	11	57		34		24	2
Lovington	1,016	6	0	1	0	5		3		1	0
Lyons	10,332	20	0	0	9	11		9		7	0
Mackinaw	1,878	2	0	0	0	2		6		0	0
Macomb	17,215	31	0	6	2	23		26		3	0
Mahomet	8,760	7	0	2	0	5		13		0	0
Manito	1,469	0	0	0	0	0		1		0	0
Maple Park	1,371	0	0	0	0	0		2		0	1
Marion	17,551	136	1	12	13	110		122		80	0
Marissa	1,788	13	0	2	0	11		18		7	1

Table 8. Offenses Known to Law Enforcement, by Selected State and City, 2020—Continued

(Number.)

State/city	Population	Violent crime	Murder and nonnegligent manslaughter	Rape[1]	Robbery	Aggravated assault	Property crime	Burglary	Larceny-theft	Motor vehicle theft	Arson[2]
Markham	12,289	74	7	5	21	41		61		102	5
Marquette Heights	2,626	2	0	0	0	2		2		0	0
Marseilles	4,804	7	0	1	1	5		18		3	1
Maryville	7,992	7	0	0	0	7		2		3	0
Mascoutah	8,045	3	0	0	1	2		0		3	0
Matteson	19,494	185	1	7	7	170		50		89	2
Mattoon	17,514	56	0	21	1	34		46		0	10
Maywood	23,055	217	16	16	92	93		62		102	3
Mazon	962	1	0	1	0	0		2		0	0
McCook	219	0	0	0	0	0		4		3	0
McHenry	27,061	34	0	8	2	24		16		9	0
McLean	791	0	0	0	0	0		0		0	0
Melrose Park	24,624	82	1	11	40	30		80		40	1
Mendota	6,954	10	0	1	1	8		15		7	0
Metropolis	5,881	33	0	7	1	25		50		4	1
Midlothian	14,294	19	0	9	5	5		38		57	1
Milan	4,969	18	0	2	2	14		33		3	0
Millstadt	3,840	2	0	1	0	1		9		1	0
Minier	1,183	0	0	0	0	0		4		0	0
Mokena	20,330	16	0	2	6	8		29		19	0
Moline	41,128	204	1	32	25	146		225		76	14
Momence	3,071	2	0	0	0	2		6		2	0
Monee	5,054	10	0	1	4	5		16		8	1
Monmouth	8,828	19	0	3	2	14		33		13	0
Montgomery	19,783	28	0	4	3	21		26		10	5
Monticello	5,532	7	0	0	1	6		11		2	0
Morris	15,216	22	0	6	4	12		30		13	1
Morrison	3,966	11	0	2	0	9		13		3	0
Morton	16,267	15	0	5	0	10		18		8	0
Morton Grove	22,746	33	1	0	15	17		78		9	0
Mount Carmel	6,971	3	1	0	1	1		8		2	0
Mount Morris	2,772	3	0	0	0	3		3		0	0
Mount Prospect	53,570	26	0	9	7	10		23		11	0
Mount Vernon	14,670	171	0	11	24	136		142		16	7
Mount Zion	5,788	10	0	1	0	9		5		1	0
Moweaqua	1,702	7	0	4	0	3		1		0	0
Mundelein	31,053	18	1	2	3	12		14		7	0
Murphysboro	7,345	45	0	5	11	29		61		11	0
Naperville	149,137	99	1	19	29	50		159		86	3
New Athens	1,865	2	0	2	0	0		5		3	0
New Baden	3,228	1	0	0	1	0		5		1	1
New Lenox	27,230	24	1	11	2	10		11		15	0
Niles	28,839	15	0	0	4	11		46		22	2
Nokomis	2,094	12	0	4	0	8		1		4	2
Normal	54,677	105	0	23	19	63		84		31	1
North Aurora	18,222	32	0	4	6	22		31		9	1
Northbrook	32,927	10	0	2	3	5		48		18	0
Northfield	5,378	2	0	0	0	2		16		8	0
Northlake	12,142	28	0	3	11	14		15		7	0
North Pekin	1,540	0	0	0	0	0		0		0	0
North Riverside	6,402	54	1	3	20	30		44		14	0
Oak Brook	8,029	13	0	4	5	4		42		12	0
Oakbrook Terrace	2,097	16	0	2	5	9		10		6	1
Oak Forest	27,084	48	0	8	15	25		37		40	0
Oak Lawn	54,836	93	0	8	28	57		55		11	3
Oak Park	52,435	194	2	17	108	67		220		85	4
Oakwood	1,473	2	0	1	0	1		4		0	0
Oblong	1,361	9	0	0	0	9		4		0	0
O'Fallon	29,672	72	0	26	10	36		57		20	4
Okawville	1,352	2	0	0	0	2		2		0	0
Olympia Fields	4,775	12	1	4	5	2		6		16	1
Onarga	1,252	1	0	1	0	0		5		0	0
Orion	1,791	3	0	0	0	3		2		2	0
Orland Park	57,993	22	0	0	5	17		12		26	0
Oswego	36,934	27	0	7	6	14		15		11	6
Ottawa	17,983	20	0	2	3	15		26		11	3
Palatine	67,358	33	0	12	6	15		12		15	1
Palestine	1,263	6	0	0	0	6		8		0	0
Palos Heights	12,520	8	0	0	3	5		5		0	0
Palos Hills	17,013	13	0	0	6	7		8		2	1
Palos Park	4,723	2	0	0	1	1		5		2	0
Paris	8,225	46	0	5	2	39		81		15	2
Park City	7,422	13	0	1	4	8		6		11	1
Park Forest	21,125	64	1	7	12	44		28		49	1
Park Ridge	36,888	19	0	3	6	10		65		10	2
Pawnee	2,628	13	0	4	1	8		0		0	0
Paxton	4,085	16	0	4	0	12		18		1	0
Peoria	109,924	1,084	14	72	196	802		652		430	75
Peoria Heights	5,748	29	0	6	2	21		14		12	0
Peotone	4,100	6	0	2	0	4		7		1	0
Peru	9,666	20	0	5	0	15		3		4	2
Petersburg	2,202	1	0	0	0	1		6		0	0
Phoenix	1,901	16	0	0	5	11		9		3	0

Table 8. Offenses Known to Law Enforcement, by Selected State and City, 2020—Continued

(Number.)

State/city	Population	Violent crime	Murder and nonnegligent manslaughter	Rape[1]	Robbery	Aggravated assault	Property crime	Burglary	Larceny-theft	Motor vehicle theft	Arson[2]
Pierron	539	0	0	0	0	0		1		0	0
Pinckneyville	5,343	5	0	4	0	1		7		0	0
Pingree Grove	10,757	7	0	4	0	3		1		1	0
Pittsfield	4,219	9	0	0	1	8		5		2	0
Plano	11,755	27	0	4	1	22		5		5	0
Pleasant Plains	790	0	0	0	0	0		0		0	0
Pontiac	11,184	34	0	4	2	28		21		6	0
Posen	5,844	18	1	0	8	9		15		28	2
Potomac	684	0	0	0	0	0		0		0	0
Princeton	7,420	10	1	0	1	8		11		4	0
Prospect Heights	15,845	21	0	2	4	15		18		6	1
Quincy	39,860	197	0	36	14	147		131		45	11
Rankin	508	0	0	0	0	0		0		0	0
Red Bud	3,457	3	0	0	0	3		4		0	0
Richmond	1,908	2	0	0	0	2		2		1	0
Richton Park	13,250	39	1	5	8	25		14		32	0
Ridge Farm	804	4	0	0	0	4		2		0	0
Riverdale	13,025	87	4	8	36	39		58		64	4
River Forest	10,776	16	0	0	11	5		17		2	0
River Grove	9,843	21	0	4	6	11		20		12	1
Riverside	8,529	14	0	3	8	3		15		1	0
Riverton	3,430	13	0	2	1	10		12		5	0
Riverwoods	3,550	1	0	1	0	0		9		0	0
Robbins	5,448	43	0	10	10	23		25		22	0
Rochelle	8,998	22	1	3	3	15		19		7	1
Rockdale	1,901	1	0	0	0	1		1		0	0
Rock Falls	8,670	32	0	14	3	15		42		21	4
Rockford[6]	144,795	2,101	30	102	238	1,731	4,104	742	2,968	394	60
Rock Island	36,981	213	7	8	50	148		139		124	23
Rolling Meadows	23,469	23	1	2	2	18		19		12	2
Roscoe[4]	10,473	15	0	4	0	11		7		5	1
Roselle	22,431	14	1	4	1	8		21		9	0
Rosemont	4,050	49	1	12	9	27		18		10	0
Rossville	1,205	5	0	0	4	1		8		0	0
Round Lake	18,069	13	0	0	4	9		18		18	0
Round Lake Heights	2,634	4	0	0	0	4		1		3	0
Round Lake Park	7,779	13	0	0	0	13		10		5	1
Roxana	1,423	4	0	3	1	0		3		7	0
Royalton	1,113	2	0	0	0	2		2		0	0
Ruma	303	0	0	0	0	0		2		0	0
Salem	6,921	26	0	6	2	18		66		14	2
Sandoval	1,207	6	0	0	0	6		13		1	16
Sandwich	7,418	10	0	0	0	10		5		0	0
San Jose	589	0	0	0	0	0		0		0	0
Sauget	167	1	1	0	0	0		9		7	0
Schaumburg	72,733	78	0	28	24	26		72		65	0
Schiller Park	11,360	21	1	1	10	9		10		25	0
Seneca	2,240	3	0	1	0	2		7		1	0
Shawneetown	1,060	7	0	0	0	7		2		0	0
Shiloh	13,701	16	0	6	0	10		9		17	2
Shorewood	17,722	17	0	11	3	3		7		8	0
Sidell	557	0	0	0	0	0		0		0	0
Silvis	7,470	28	1	3	1	23		26		10	0
Skokie	62,462	125	0	14	44	67		135		79	3
Sleepy Hollow	3,236	2	0	0	0	2		3		2	0
Smithton	3,823	0	0	0	0	0		9		0	0
South Barrington	5,044	0	0	0	0	0		15		5	0
South Beloit	7,594	17	0	3	6	8		21		12	0
South Chicago Heights	3,988	11	0	0	3	8		11		15	0
Southern View	1,560	8	0	0	0	8		3		0	0
South Holland	21,218	59	0	10	31	18		44		127	2
South Pekin	1,087	5	0	1	0	4		0		3	0
South Roxana	1,981	9	0	4	2	3		30		5	0
Springfield	113,912	1,078	11	101	195	771		937		254	39
Spring Grove	5,698	0	0	0	0	0		1		1	0
Spring Valley	5,081	11	0	4	0	7		6		1	0
Stanford	596	0	0	0	0	0		1		0	0
St. Charles	32,949	44	0	8	6	30		37		18	0
Steger	9,184	36	1	10	9	16		22		19	1
Sterling	14,361	38	3	21	3	11		62		32	1
Stickney	6,542	4	0	0	2	2		9		1	0
Stockton	1,696	2	0	1	0	1		2		0	0
Stone Park	4,812	10	2	0	3	5		21		3	0
Stonington	837	1	0	0	0	1		0		1	0
Streamwood	39,154	59	0	11	10	38		29		54	2
Streator	13,019	25	0	20	1	4		30		8	10
Sullivan	4,431	36	0	0	0	36		4		4	0
Summit	11,123	48	1	12	17	18		14		25	4
Swansea	13,323	23	0	8	3	12		29		18	0
Sycamore	18,413	13	0	4	1	8		17		7	0
Taylorville	10,264	24	0	0	3	21		29		2	1
Thayer	651	2	0	0	0	2		1		0	0
Thornton	2,403	3	0	0	1	2		6		2	0

Table 8. Offenses Known to Law Enforcement, by Selected State and City, 2020—Continued

(Number.)

State/city	Population	Violent crime	Murder and nonnegligent manslaughter	Rape[1]	Robbery	Aggravated assault	Property crime	Burglary	Larceny-theft	Motor vehicle theft	Arson[2]
Tilton	2,683	15	0	0	2	13		16		8	0
Tinley Park	55,652	38	0	5	8	25		26		31	0
Tolono	3,384	4	0	2	0	2		4		3	1
Toluca	1,254	3	0	0	0	3		3		1	0
Tonica	709	1	0	0	0	1		0		0	0
Tower Lakes	1,220	0	0	0	0	0		1		0	0
Trenton	2,576	1	0	0	0	1		7		2	0
Troy	10,422	19	0	12	1	6		4		9	0
Tuscola	4,350	7	0	0	0	7		11		5	0
University Park	6,861	19	1	0	7	11		13		23	0
Urbana[5]	42,211		2	41	36			137		42	7
Vernon Hills	26,693	21	0	5	4	12		21		5	1
Vienna	1,441	1	0	0	0	1		7		1	0
Villa Park	21,421	29	0	10	9	10		30		15	0
Viola	881	0	0	0	0	0		0		0	0
Virden	3,309	21	0	5	1	15		16		6	1
Warrensburg	1,117	3	0	1	0	2		3		1	0
Warrenville	13,172	12	0	2	3	7		19		4	0
Washington	16,662	26	2	5	1	18		22		2	0
Watseka	4,713	9	0	7	0	2		10		7	0
Waukegan	85,739	316	7	13	108	188		215		62	4
Wayne	2,427	0	0	0	0	0		5		0	0
Westchester	16,051	8	0	1	3	4		40		11	1
West Chicago	26,768	36	2	13	1	20		23		15	1
West Dundee	8,215	6	0	3	1	2		8		2	0
Western Springs	13,404	1	0	0	0	1		18		3	2
Westmont	24,416	31	0	10	3	18		40		19	2
Westville	2,918	7	0	1	0	6		11		3	0
Wheaton	52,706	46	0	9	10	27		53		19	5
Wheeling	38,753	28	1	7	7	13		26		20	1
White Hall	2,309	6	0	0	0	6		3		2	0
Williamsville	1,486	3	0	0	0	3		1		1	0
Willowbrook	8,566	21	0	4	6	11		17		8	2
Willow Springs	5,606	1	0	0	1	0		6		6	0
Winnetka	12,328	4	0	1	0	3		12		17	0
Witt	837	0	0	0	0	0		2		0	0
Wonder Lake	3,866	1	0	0	0	1		6		1	0
Wood Dale	13,588	16	0	4	4	8		12		9	0
Woodridge	33,478	33	0	7	7	19		31		28	2
Woodstock	25,283	17	0	6	2	9		6		12	1
Yates City	648	0	0	0	0	0		0		1	0
Yorkville	21,052	20	0	8	6	6		6		5	2
Zion	23,387	145	3	26	32	84		57		97	10
INDIANA											
Angola	8,748	5	0	2	1	2	241	44	175	22	0
Avon	19,377	30	1	11	5	13	376	25	328	23	1
Bargersville[4]	8,342	3	2	0	0	1	76	3	60	13	1
Bedford[4]	13,192	12	0	2	2	8	280	30	235	15	0
Bloomington[4]	86,347	480	7	52	67	354	2,079	346	1,595	138	10
Bluffton	10,173	9	0	5	2	2	132	7	120	5	0
Boonville	6,200	48	0	1	1	46	125	21	98	6	0
Brookville	2,523	6	0	0	0	6	16	1	14	1	0
Brownsburg[4]	27,621	23	0	5	5	13	266	23	215	28	0
Carmel[4]	103,100	51	1	15	15	20	605	39	508	58	1
Cedar Lake[4]	13,372	26	0	4	3	19	130	16	103	11	0
Charlestown	8,461	19	0	1	0	18	83	12	62	9	3
Chesterton	14,203	19	0	2	1	16	84	6	69	9	0
Claypool	434	1	0	1	0	0	5	2	2	1	0
Clinton	4,670	48	0	0	0	48	121	15	106	0	1
Columbia City	9,283	25	0	3	0	22	132	8	117	7	0
Cumberland[4]	6,097	17	2	3	5	7	258	26	217	15	0
Dyer[4]	15,932	1	0	0	0	1	51	0	47	4	0
Edinburgh[4]	4,603	7	0	0	1	6	64	7	51	6	0
Evansville[4]	117,747	1,185	10	77	115	983	4,252	626	3,188	438	56
Fishers[4]	97,481	64	0	9	10	45	630	23	539	68	3
Fort Wayne	272,270	1,124	39	97	245	743	6,117	655	4,952	510	87
Frankfort[4]	15,826	6	0	2	2	2	165	23	130	12	0
Franklin[4]	25,825	34	1	11	3	19	479	40	395	44	0
Greenfield	23,273	33	0	9	5	19	280	26	233	21	1
Greenwood[4]	60,460	62	1	10	15	36	1,226	42	1,071	113	4
Hartford City	5,606	12	0	0	1	11	29	5	19	5	0
Highland	22,165	18	1	1	2	14	367	30	315	22	1
Hobart[4]	27,791	48	0	14	9	25	790	51	687	52	1
Huntingburg	6,182	23	0	1	0	22	34	8	21	5	0
Huntington[4]	17,096	8	0	3	1	4	249	45	192	12	0
Indianapolis[4]	890,672	7,755	216	573	2,166	4,800	31,796	5,171	21,170	5,455	357
Jasper	15,790	51	0	2	1	48	100	6	89	5	0
Kendallville[4]	9,897	18	0	9	2	7	109	6	78	25	0
Knightsville	764	0	0	0	0	0	0	0	0	0	0
Knox[4]	3,528	32	0	4	2	26	45	8	35	2	1
Kokomo[4]	58,001	437	8	25	38	366	1,152	225	838	89	1
Lafayette	72,040	428	6	35	61	326	2,198	424	1,616	158	12

Table 8. Offenses Known to Law Enforcement, by Selected State and City, 2020—Continued

(Number.)

State/city	Population	Violent crime	Murder and nonnegligent manslaughter	Rape[1]	Robbery	Aggravated assault	Property crime	Burglary	Larceny-theft	Motor vehicle theft	Arson[2]
La Porte	21,515	70	1	14	7	48	457	89	322	46	1
Lawrence	49,865	167	4	14	75	74	972	118	697	157	5
Lebanon	16,097	71	0	1	3	67	231	22	187	22	1
Linton	5,179	7	1	2	1	3	140	7	124	9	0
Loogootee	2,700	5	0	0	0	5	3	0	3	0	0
Lowell	10,004	6	0	1	0	5	22	2	16	4	0
McCordsville	7,801	15	0	0	0	15	77	1	69	7	0
Merrillville[4]	34,774	48	7	3	16	22	472	76	310	86	2
Mishawaka[4]	50,610	80	0	15	6	59	1,207	131	935	141	4
Munster	22,357	18	0	0	8	10	259	15	215	29	0
New Albany	36,892	144	1	3	15	125	1,258	151	940	167	2
New Whiteland[4]	6,332	4	0	0	1	3	35	2	32	1	0
Noblesville[4]	66,127	60	0	23	9	28	551	37	454	60	0
North Webster	1,170	9	0	3	0	6	43	5	34	4	0
Ogden Dunes	1,086	1	0	0	0	1	9	1	6	2	0
Osceola	2,486	11	0	0	0	11	50	21	27	2	0
Pittsboro	3,698	1	0	1	0	0	11	4	7	0	0
Plainfield[4]	36,239	42	0	12	9	21	480	37	390	53	1
Plymouth	9,966	5	1	2	0	2	163	13	141	9	0
Porter	4,832	0	0	0	0	0	37	4	26	7	1
Rensselaer	5,825	10	0	3	1	6	155	30	125	0	0
Rockport	2,130	12	1	2	1	8	26	5	17	4	0
Rushville	5,973	5	0	0	1	4	135	16	113	6	0
Shelbyville[4]	19,451	121	1	4	7	109	330	51	241	38	1
Silver Lake	924	3	0	0	0	3	26	2	21	3	0
South Bend	102,119	1,765	28	78	238	1,421	3,741	659	2,511	571	47
St. John	19,289	4	0	1	0	3	79	5	65	9	1
Syracuse	2,885	17	0	1	0	16	55	2	43	10	0
Terre Haute	60,604	837	6	29	77	725	2,886	783	1,709	394	31
Vevay	1,646	13	0	0	0	13	11	2	7	2	0
Vincennes4,[5]	16,701	15	1	3	3	8			598	68	1
Warsaw	15,319	134	0	9	4	121	500	61	383	56	1
Washington	12,612	17	1	4	0	12	143	17	122	4	1
Westfield	45,469	23	0	1	4	18	340	29	297	14	2
Westville	5,852	12	0	0	0	12	18	6	11	1	0
Whitestown	10,251	21	0	1	2	18	123	10	105	8	0
Whiting[4]	4,741	7	0	0	0	7	61	8	43	10	0
Winchester	4,634	2	0	0	1	1	233	16	203	14	0
Winona Lake	4,901	16	0	3	0	13	19	4	13	2	0
Zionsville	28,824	14	0	1	1	12	86	1	76	9	0
IOWA											
Adel	5,696	14	0	2	0	12	74	23	46	5	2
Albia	3,670	18	0	2	1	15	63	20	39	4	0
Algona	5,380	17	0	0	0	17	17	0	15	2	0
Altoona	19,804	56	0	6	2	48	432	59	342	31	2
Ames	67,109	122	0	54	15	53	1,189	218	903	68	3
Ankeny	70,301	116	1	17	7	91	806	146	603	57	12
Asbury	5,909	4	0	0	0	4	20	4	12	4	0
Atlantic	6,465	15	0	3	0	12	99	17	76	6	2
Audubon	1,871	3	0	1	0	2	36	14	20	2	0
Bettendorf	36,926	37	0	10	7	20	571	114	415	42	2
Bloomfield	2,683	6	0	0	0	6	8	1	7	0	0
Burlington	24,622	121	1	22	16	82	862	142	634	86	4
Camanche	4,356	4	0	2	0	2	43	12	23	8	0
Carlisle	4,341	31	0	3	0	28	52	9	41	2	0
Carroll	9,800	8	0	2	0	6	115	16	96	3	1
Carter Lake	3,784	44	0	4	2	38	112	16	75	21	0
Cedar Rapids	134,330	432	11	16	102	303	4,254	832	2,865	557	30
Centerville	5,425	19	0	0	0	19	108	27	69	12	0
Charles City	7,269	20	0	12	3	5	75	18	52	5	3
Cherokee	4,826	13	0	2	0	11	31	5	24	2	0
Clarinda	5,343	20	0	4	0	16	79	11	54	14	0
Clarion[5]	2,695	7	0	2	0	5			10	5	0
Clear Lake	7,526	29	0	4	0	25	216	56	153	7	0
Clinton[5]	24,905	95	2	9	10	74			665	56	8
Clive	17,447	17	0	3	4	10	287	45	194	48	4
Colfax	2,061	13	0	1	2	10	28	11	16	1	1
Coralville[5]	22,699		0	9	6		571	83	456	32	0
Council Bluffs	62,144	574	0	36	68	470	2,976	408	2,127	441	17
Creston	7,701	25	0	0	0	25	185	54	114	17	4
Davenport	101,806	750	10	67	136	537	3,996	912	2,615	469	26
Decorah	7,516	2	0	1	0	1	42	0	37	5	0
Denison	8,234	10	0	2	2	6	55	14	37	4	2
Des Moines	215,290	1,517	33	119	246	1,119	8,400	1,925	5,053	1,422	69
DeWitt	5,178	5	0	2	1	2	79	17	55	7	0
Dubuque	57,904	231	1	54	26	150	1,165	208	885	72	21
Durant	1,864	1	0	1	0	0	13	3	9	1	0
Dyersville	4,357	5	0	0	0	5	31	7	24	0	0
Eldridge	6,991	3	0	0	0	3	36	9	20	7	0
Emmetsburg	3,661	3	0	0	0	3	13	2	10	1	0
Estherville	5,595	26	0	3	0	23	42	5	35	2	0
Evansdale	4,742	17	0	2	0	15	67	32	26	9	1

Table 8. Offenses Known to Law Enforcement, by Selected State and City, 2020—Continued

(Number.)

State/city	Population	Violent crime	Murder and nonnegligent manslaughter	Rape[1]	Robbery	Aggravated assault	Property crime	Burglary	Larceny-theft	Motor vehicle theft	Arson[2]
Fairfield	10,538	21	0	3	2	16	156	35	99	22	1
Forest City	4,013	15	0	0	0	15	12	3	7	2	0
Fort Dodge	23,755	180	5	9	14	152	827	130	635	62	11
Fort Madison	10,239	64	0	18	4	42	237	60	160	17	5
Glenwood	5,402	16	0	1	0	15	83	24	45	14	0
Grinnell	9,104	27	1	7	0	19	172	32	130	10	0
Hampton	4,176	5	0	0	0	5	5	2	3	0	0
Harlan	4,732	12	0	3	0	9	15	3	11	1	0
Hiawatha	7,465	48	0	3	2	43	152	39	96	17	0
Humboldt	4,577	1	0	0	0	1	41	4	30	7	1
Independence	6,141	12	0	2	2	8	91	25	59	7	0
Indianola	16,154	88	1	10	3	74	278	39	208	31	2
Iowa City	75,964	151	2	21	16	112	1,335	261	934	140	4
Iowa Falls	5,034	16	0	3	1	12	70	10	56	4	0
Jefferson	4,075	8	0	1	0	7	76	19	53	4	0
Johnston	23,252	19	0	5	0	14	230	34	158	38	3
Keokuk	10,091	68	0	8	2	58	247	63	152	32	1
Lansing	928	0	0	0	0	0	16	1	15	0	0
Le Claire	3,990	3	0	1	0	2	13	3	9	1	0
Le Mars	10,110	29	0	9	0	20	141	12	120	9	1
Manchester	4,965	17	0	1	0	16	48	16	28	4	0
Maquoketa	5,966	16	0	7	1	8	125	34	82	9	0
Marengo	2,460	13	0	2	0	11	31	2	25	4	0
Marion[5]	40,968	60	0	15	7	38			348	62	2
Marshalltown	26,564	128	3	20	7	98	470	102	326	42	7
Mason City	26,811	114	0	19	4	91	854	203	581	70	12
Missouri Valley	2,592	9	0	1	0	8	45	10	31	4	0
Monticello	3,891	12	0	1	0	11	55	12	36	7	0
Mount Pleasant	8,670	27	0	3	0	24	119	33	75	11	1
Mount Vernon	4,463	7	0	2	0	5	17	2	11	4	0
Muscatine	23,616	62	0	24	9	29	403	108	245	50	8
New Hampton	3,389	3	0	1	0	2	14	5	9	0	1
Newton	15,176	62	0	9	1	52	247	50	180	17	3
North Liberty	20,294	61	0	13	1	47	120	23	88	9	3
Norwalk[7]	12,313	6	0	2	0	4		10		3	2
Oelwein	5,846	22	0	4	0	18	95	36	55	4	0
Ogden	1,972	1	0	1	0	0	12	2	8	2	0
Onawa	2,739	6	0	0	1	5	22	6	13	3	0
Orange City	6,195	7	1	3	0	3	42	10	29	3	1
Osage	3,548	4	0	1	0	3	42	19	21	2	0
Osceola	5,275	16	0	2	0	14	104	13	85	6	5
Oskaloosa	11,505	38	0	6	0	32	193	38	135	20	5
Ottumwa	24,293	230	0	17	12	201	949	184	672	93	14
Pella[5]	10,225	27	1	12	0	14		10		7	0
Perry	7,669	17	0	3	0	14	107	21	76	10	1
Pleasant Hill	10,158	7	1	0	2	4	198	39	131	28	1
Polk City	5,165	3	0	1	0	2	26	4	20	2	1
Postville	2,034	5	0	0	1	4	36	6	24	6	0
Red Oak	5,230	14	0	3	0	11	81	21	51	9	3
Rock Valley	3,899	3	0	0	0	3	2	1	1	0	0
Sergeant Bluff	5,226	10	0	0	0	10	25	4	21	0	0
Sheldon	5,069	25	0	3	0	22	48	16	20	12	0
Shenandoah	4,786	12	0	1	0	11	32	9	18	5	0
Sioux Center	7,669	3	0	1	0	2	17	0	15	2	0
Sioux City	82,628	477	9	61	75	332	2,682	479	1,933	270	15
Spencer[5]	10,922	17	0	14	2	1			150	19	0
Spirit Lake	5,189	19	0	3	0	16	83	18	59	6	0
Storm Lake	10,282	40	0	7	1	32	157	23	124	10	4
Story City	3,307	4	0	0	0	4	52	13	33	6	1
Tama	2,717	24	0	1	0	23	22	10	10	2	0
Tipton	3,224	4	0	1	0	3	14	5	9	0	0
Toledo	2,123	13	0	0	0	13	18	9	8	1	0
Urbandale	44,959	47	1	8	5	33	458	63	336	59	3
Vinton	5,056	6	0	1	0	5	16	3	13	0	0
Washington	7,227	44	0	12	1	31	155	28	116	11	3
Waterloo	67,200	419	9	25	48	337	1,718	491	1,038	189	21
Waukee	25,590	23	0	8	1	14	237	65	155	17	2
Waukon	3,594	3	0	0	1	2	62	4	56	2	0
Waverly	10,234	47	0	6	0	41	96	15	75	6	0
West Branch	2,510	0	0	0	0	0	10	3	5	2	0
West Burlington	2,878	12	0	2	1	9	160	10	138	12	1
West Des Moines	69,252	93	1	27	7	58	1,140	129	893	118	6
West Liberty	3,768	10	0	2	1	7	23	6	13	4	0
Williamsburg	3,175	4	0	1	0	3	10	2	7	1	0
Wilton	2,828	5	0	2	1	2	11	6	3	2	0
Windsor Heights	4,798	19	0	0	3	16	185	15	161	9	0
Winterset	5,403	25	0	3	0	22	57	15	36	6	0
KANSAS											
Alta Vista	422	0	0	0	0	0	0	0	0	0	0
Andover	13,592	20	0	4	2	14	233	20	201	12	0
Anthony	2,051	7	0	0	0	7	35	9	23	3	1
Arkansas City	11,589	51	1	3	1	46	376	63	282	31	1

Table 8. Offenses Known to Law Enforcement, by Selected State and City, 2020—Continued

(Number.)

State/city	Population	Violent crime	Murder and nonnegligent manslaughter	Rape[1]	Robbery	Aggravated assault	Property crime	Burglary	Larceny-theft	Motor vehicle theft	Arson[2]
Arma	1,413	6	0	1	0	5	44	23	17	4	1
Assaria	407	0	0	0	0	0	0	0	0	0	0
Atchison	10,421	47	0	8	1	38	231	11	201	19	1
Atwood	1,221	2	0	0	0	2	6	1	3	2	0
Augusta	9,339	17	0	3	0	14	250	48	190	12	0
Basehor	6,742	5	0	1	0	4	71	9	54	8	0
Baxter Springs	3,915	17	0	6	0	11	136	40	88	8	2
Beloit	3,604	16	0	3	0	13	38	3	30	5	0
Bucklin	767	0	0	0	0	0	0	0	0	0	0
Burlington	2,530	13	0	2	0	11	31	10	19	2	1
Caney[5]	1,943	12	0	0	0	12			4	0	0
Cherryvale	2,114	3	0	0	0	3	36	11	20	5	1
Clay Center	3,944	17	0	6	0	11	115	35	60	20	1
Clearwater	2,559	4	0	1	0	3	32	8	23	1	0
Coffeyville[5]	9,171	54	0	8	8	38			288	23	5
Colby	5,365	17	0	3	0	14	92	20	66	6	2
Colony	414	0	0	0	0	0	0	0	0	0	0
Concordia	4,944	13	0	2	0	11	96	18	71	7	2
Council Grove	2,112	2	0	0	0	2	37	7	27	3	1
Derby	25,229	29	0	10	3	16	472	40	397	35	2
Dodge City	27,066	124	0	10	11	103	681	60	579	42	5
Edwardsville	4,503	27	1	1	2	23	134	15	93	26	2
El Dorado[5]	12,924	27	0	3	2	22			168	37	1
Elkhart	1,714	6	0	0	0	6	30	10	19	1	0
Ellinwood	1,923	0	0	0	0	0	22	2	19	1	0
Ellis	2,004	2	0	1	0	1	21	0	20	1	0
Ellsworth	2,943	3	0	1	0	2	35	4	29	2	0
Eudora	6,440	17	0	3	0	14	31	6	20	5	0
Fairway	3,970	3	0	2	1	0	57	8	36	13	0
Fort Scott	7,658	48	0	6	3	39	271	49	205	17	2
Frontenac	3,382	2	0	0	0	2	71	12	46	13	0
Galena	2,832	11	0	0	0	11	72	12	54	6	1
Garden City	26,360	139	2	24	15	98	904	93	741	70	15
Gardner	22,370	60	0	8	6	46	204	19	172	13	0
Garnett	3,216	10	1	2	0	7	55	17	33	5	1
Goddard	4,840	1	0	0	1	0	55	5	48	2	0
Goodland	4,397	23	0	0	1	22	79	11	58	10	1
Grandview Plaza	1,503	20	0	3	0	17	27	5	20	2	0
Great Bend[5]	14,864	79	0	13	3	63			271	26	4
Greensburg	776	3	0	1	1	1	2	2	0	0	0
Halstead	2,036	0	0	0	0	0	33	6	21	6	0
Havensville	157	0	0	0	0	0	0	0	0	0	0
Hays[5]	20,769	65	0	6	2	57			313	20	1
Haysville	11,395	38	0	4	1	33	207	35	152	20	0
Hesston	3,744	1	0	0	0	1	26	7	17	2	0
Hiawatha	3,103	10	0	4	0	6	110	19	84	7	0
Hillsboro	2,796	5	0	2	0	3	45	21	20	4	0
Hoisington	2,446	10	0	1	0	9	22	6	11	5	0
Holton	3,196	12	0	0	2	10	29	5	23	1	0
Horton	1,676	3	0	0	0	3	14	4	9	1	0
Hugoton	3,724	9	0	0	0	9	31	3	26	2	0
Independence[5]	8,405	92	2	10	6	74			318	27	2
Inman	1,328	4	0	0	1	3	9	0	8	1	0
Iola	5,220	33	0	8	1	24	215	48	160	7	3
Junction City	21,242	192	3	30	7	152	483	82	370	31	3
Kanopolis	448	0	0	0	0	0	0	0	0	0	0
Kechi	2,015	0	0	0	0	0	22	6	16	0	0
Kingman[5]	2,807	9	0	1	0	8			27	3	0
Lansing	12,023	36	0	5	2	29	121	15	89	17	0
Larned	3,632	25	0	2	0	23	123	31	88	4	2
Leavenworth[5]	36,023	294	4	29	28	233			702	146	11
Leawood	35,054	15	0	5	1	9	571	77	447	47	1
Lenexa	56,508	103	0	12	11	80	903	99	646	158	3
Lindsborg[5]	3,273	4	0	1	1	2			14	1	0
Louisburg	4,590	4	0	0	0	4	50	12	36	2	0
Lyons[5]	3,478	9	0	4	0	5			41	2	0
Maize	5,130	20	0	1	1	18	78	18	55	5	2
Marion	1,759	6	0	0	0	6	16	3	11	2	0
Marysville[5]	3,265	11	0	2	0	9			39	2	1
McPherson	13,053	28	1	5	2	20	305	42	230	33	1
Merriam	11,087	52	0	4	6	42	678	58	474	146	0
Mission[4]	9,979	43	0	5	5	33	487	35	396	56	1
Mission Hills	3,555	2	0	0	0	2	47	4	33	10	0
Montezuma	964	0	0	0	0	0	0	0	0	0	0
Mound City	676	0	0	0	0	0	0	0	0	0	0
Mulberry	521	0	0	0	0	0	7	3	4	0	0
Mulvane[5]	6,528	8	0	1	3	4			85	4	0
Neodesha	2,239	2	0	0	0	2	12	2	7	3	0
Newton	18,830	94	0	13	4	77	418	68	323	27	7
North Newton	1,761	2	0	1	0	1	12	3	9	0	0
Norton	2,705	8	0	2	0	6	59	10	43	6	0
Olathe[4]	142,228	355	2	46	22	285	1,940	155	1,550	235	11
Onaga	680	0	0	0	0	0	0	0	0	0	0

Table 8. Offenses Known to Law Enforcement, by Selected State and City, 2020—Continued

(Number.)

State/city	Population	Violent crime	Murder and nonnegligent manslaughter	Rape[1]	Robbery	Aggravated assault	Property crime	Burglary	Larceny-theft	Motor vehicle theft	Arson[2]
Osage City	2,795	9	0	2	0	7	47	9	34	4	0
Osawatomie	4,266	13	0	2	0	11	39	12	17	10	1
Oswego	1,663	1	0	0	1	0	26	18	7	1	0
Overland Park[4]	198,036	411	4	39	43	325	3,906	382	2,979	545	13
Paola	5,730	22	0	8	0	14	110	10	90	10	0
Park City	7,812	29	0	2	1	26	175	23	134	18	0
Parsons	9,373	86	1	7	11	67	381	88	281	12	7
Plainville	1,793	2	0	0	0	2	3	1	0	2	0
Pleasanton	1,157	4	0	0	0	4	14	1	10	3	0
Prairie Village	22,390	15	1	2	2	10	252	25	184	43	0
Roeland Park	6,683	13	0	0	1	12	159	15	118	26	0
Rose Hill	3,972	7	0	0	0	7	38	9	26	3	0
Russell	4,412	10	0	2	0	8	70	15	50	5	0
Sabetha	2,586	4	0	1	0	3	40	1	33	6	0
Scott City	3,738	8	0	0	0	8	20	3	14	3	0
Seneca	2,083	0	0	0	0	0	32	3	29	0	0
Shawnee	66,208	191	0	24	15	152	1,130	142	796	192	8
Spring Hill	7,572	9	0	2	0	7	102	10	78	14	1
Sterling	2,195	4	0	1	0	3	20	3	16	1	0
St. George	1,049	1	0	0	0	1	9	3	6	0	0
St. Marys	2,656	7	0	2	0	5	10	1	7	2	0
Tonganoxie	5,649	6	0	1	0	5	48	6	35	7	0
Ulysses	5,546	24	0	1	0	23	32	9	22	1	2
Valley Center	7,383	8	0	4	3	1	48	6	38	4	0
Valley Falls	1,149	1	0	0	0	1	11	1	9	1	0
Victoria	1,212	1	0	0	0	1	1	0	1	0	0
WaKeeney	1,751	10	0	0	0	10	24	4	17	3	0
Wellington	7,608	26	1	1	5	19	251	27	204	20	3
Wellsville	1,773	4	0	2	0	2	9	2	7	0	1
Westwood	1,657	2	0	0	0	2	58	3	49	6	0
Winfield	11,900	44	0	5	2	37	405	82	292	31	2
KENTUCKY											
Alexandria	9,861	4	0	1	1	2	122	7	106	9	0
Anchorage	2,431	0	0	0	0	0	14	2	11	1	0
Ashland	19,979	41	1	7	7	26	642	105	490	47	2
Auburn	1,384	0	0	0	0	0	6	1	5	0	0
Audubon Park	1,491	0	0	0	0	0	17	2	10	5	0
Augusta	1,143	2	0	0	0	2	10	5	4	1	0
Barbourville	3,018	6	0	0	1	5	65	16	37	12	0
Bardstown	13,330	26	0	3	4	19	269	59	182	28	2
Beattyville	1,212	0	0	0	0	0	9	1	2	6	0
Beaver Dam	3,578	3	0	1	0	2	21	1	19	1	1
Bellevue	5,695	3	0	2	1	0	78	8	61	9	0
Benton	4,455	5	0	2	0	3	81	17	58	6	0
Berea	16,311	16	0	4	4	8	238	47	156	35	1
Bowling Green	71,861	247	9	56	71	111	3,195	560	2,318	317	2
Brandenburg	2,898	1	0	0	0	1	14	1	11	2	0
Burkesville	1,456	0	0	0	0	0	6	1	2	3	0
Burnside	844	2	0	1	0	1	14	2	10	2	0
Cadiz	2,678	0	0	0	0	0	65	12	48	5	1
Calvert City	2,497	0	0	0	0	0	27	3	22	2	0
Campbellsville	11,559	22	1	2	8	11	347	134	176	37	0
Carlisle	1,984	4	0	1	0	3	5	0	5	0	0
Carrollton	3,763	2	0	0	0	2	25	4	17	4	0
Catlettsburg	1,734	1	0	0	0	1	25	5	17	3	0
Cave City	2,439	4	0	1	1	2	21	5	11	5	0
Central City	5,703	3	0	0	0	3	66	12	50	4	0
Clay City	1,090	2	0	0	0	2	26	2	17	7	0
Clinton	1,238	5	0	1	0	4	4	1	2	1	0
Coal Run Village	1,501	0	0	0	0	0	16	1	14	1	0
Cold Spring	6,641	5	0	2	2	1	109	10	92	7	0
Columbia	4,609	8	0	1	0	7	13	5	7	1	0
Corbin	7,190	8	0	0	4	4	141	27	97	17	2
Covington	40,324	154	1	21	63	69	1,049	157	741	151	11
Cynthiana	6,329	22	0	3	1	18	122	23	89	10	0
Danville	16,826	16	0	5	4	7	284	78	177	29	2
Dawson Springs	2,617	4	0	1	0	3	39	17	15	7	1
Dayton	5,639	8	0	3	0	5	62	13	40	9	0
Dry Ridge	2,205	0	0	0	0	0	32	3	21	8	0
Eddyville	2,544	1	0	0	0	1	15	0	14	1	0
Edgewood	8,776	4	0	1	0	3	39	2	34	3	0
Edmonton	1,593	0	0	0	0	0	11	3	7	1	0
Elizabethtown	30,505	44	3	8	9	24	286	68	182	36	3
Elkton	2,127	1	0	1	0	0	53	22	25	6	0
Elsmere	8,618	12	1	4	1	6	72	10	38	24	2
Eminence	2,591	8	0	5	0	3	48	5	40	3	0
Erlanger	23,441	22	0	9	2	11	137	23	95	19	0
Falmouth	2,091	9	0	1	2	6	61	10	45	6	0
Flatwoods	7,041	4	0	1	0	3	33	9	22	2	0
Flemingsburg	2,800	1	0	0	0	1	51	15	30	6	2
Florence	33,397	55	0	14	16	25	1,561	107	1,371	83	3
Fort Mitchell	8,249	4	0	2	0	2	71	8	51	12	0

Table 8. Offenses Known to Law Enforcement, by Selected State and City, 2020—Continued

(Number.)

State/city	Population	Violent crime	Murder and nonnegligent manslaughter	Rape[1]	Robbery	Aggravated assault	Property crime	Burglary	Larceny-theft	Motor vehicle theft	Arson[2]
Fort Thomas	16,273	6	0	3	1	2	88	14	67	7	0
Fort Wright	5,752	3	1	0	0	2	66	4	56	6	0
Frankfort	27,803	69	2	17	16	34	855	143	584	128	1
Franklin	9,072	19	1	6	7	5	247	26	202	19	0
Fulton	2,087	4	0	1	1	2	116	11	99	6	0
Georgetown	35,702	63	0	17	19	27	798	118	589	91	1
Glasgow	14,537	42	0	11	4	27	443	64	351	28	4
Graymoor-Devondale	2,956	5	0	0	3	2	46	9	29	8	0
Grayson	3,870	6	1	1	1	3	99	18	63	18	1
Greensburg	2,056	2	0	2	0	0	20	5	15	0	0
Greenup	1,105	0	0	0	0	0	6	1	3	2	0
Greenville	4,174	6	0	2	0	4	28	7	15	6	0
Guthrie	1,408	0	0	0	0	0	6	4	2	0	0
Hardinsburg	2,338	1	0	0	0	1	26	7	14	5	0
Harlan	1,480	3	0	0	1	2	14	1	13	0	2
Harrodsburg	8,553	9	0	2	1	6	127	36	81	10	0
Hartford	2,732	1	0	0	0	1	8	4	0	4	0
Hawesville	991	0	0	0	0	0	7	0	7	0	0
Hazard	4,796	11	0	2	3	6	129	16	95	18	1
Henderson	28,126	82	2	15	16	49	737	121	531	85	7
Heritage Creek	1,139	0	0	0	0	0	11	0	11	0	0
Highland Heights	7,069	5	0	0	2	3	67	10	52	5	0
Hillview	9,311	5	0	1	0	4	171	24	119	28	1
Hodgenville	3,251	4	0	2	0	2	28	11	15	2	0
Hopkinsville	30,532	89	2	17	23	47	930	173	695	62	1
Horse Cave	2,433	2	0	0	1	1	8	3	4	1	0
Hurstbourne Acres	1,899	1	0	0	1	0	26	2	22	2	0
Independence	28,957	21	0	9	3	9	130	19	94	17	0
Indian Hills	2,978	0	0	0	0	0	28	3	24	1	0
Irvine	2,279	2	0	1	0	1	13	2	6	5	0
Jackson	1,913	1	0	0	1	0	53	9	41	3	0
Jamestown	1,791	2	0	1	0	1	25	15	10	0	0
Jeffersontown	27,700	29	0	4	17	8	706	84	496	126	0
Junction City	2,312	0	0	0	0	0	8	1	5	2	0
La Center	954	0	0	0	0	0	2	1	1	0	0
La Grange	9,142	14	0	2	6	6	165	20	123	22	1
Lakeside Park-Crestview Hills	6,134	2	0	0	2	0	48	4	40	4	0
Lancaster	3,873	10	0	2	0	8	120	28	80	12	0
Lawrenceburg	11,565	6	0	1	2	3	86	21	48	17	2
Lebanon	5,726	8	1	2	1	4	82	29	36	17	0
Lebanon Junction	1,979	2	0	1	1	0	4	1	3	0	0
Leitchfield	6,880	7	0	2	1	4	141	28	102	11	1
Lewisport	1,692	0	0	0	0	0	1	1	0	0	0
Lexington	325,851	1,043	28	178	335	502	9,357	1,450	6,870	1,037	37
London	8,076	8	0	0	1	7	290	33	213	44	1
Louisa	2,313	6	0	2	1	3	27	8	9	10	0
Ludlow	4,499	2	0	1	1	0	60	4	49	7	2
Madisonville	18,494	27	2	3	3	19	197	46	111	40	4
Manchester	1,274	0	0	0	0	0	30	7	13	10	0
Marion	2,821	2	0	1	0	1	51	11	37	3	0
Mayfield	9,791	37	0	6	11	20	367	81	272	14	2
Maysville	8,695	26	0	4	8	14	278	59	185	34	3
McKee	776	0	0	0	0	0	2	1	0	1	0
Middlesboro	8,968	29	0	9	7	13	273	42	200	31	3
Middletown	7,910	5	0	0	2	3	200	23	156	21	0
Monticello	5,966	10	0	0	3	7	122	33	75	14	0
Morehead	7,644	10	0	2	1	7	122	16	91	15	0
Morganfield	3,350	1	0	0	0	1	17	4	13	0	1
Morgantown	2,429	1	0	0	0	1	11	1	6	4	0
Mount Sterling	7,268	12	0	1	4	7	376	44	307	25	0
Mount Washington	14,964	8	0	3	3	2	114	18	77	19	0
Muldraugh	991	3	0	0	0	3	29	7	12	10	0
Munfordville	1,664	2	0	0	1	1	6	2	3	1	0
Murray	19,499	28	1	10	4	13	317	45	253	19	0
Newport	14,874	52	0	12	17	23	454	68	336	50	6
Nicholasville	31,191	67	1	10	15	41	852	160	631	61	0
Oak Grove	7,299	42	2	14	7	19	235	38	169	28	0
Olive Hill	1,548	2	0	0	0	2	28	9	15	4	0
Owensboro	60,430	161	5	41	45	70	2,326	404	1,638	284	16
Owenton	1,534	1	0	0	0	1	5	0	3	2	0
Owingsville	1,580	2	0	0	0	2	8	2	5	1	0
Paducah	24,850	85	3	33	9	40	993	125	789	79	10
Paintsville	3,964	4	0	0	0	4	23	4	12	7	0
Paris	9,655	16	0	1	5	10	147	23	105	19	1
Park Hills	2,983	5	0	2	1	2	18	3	11	4	0
Pembroke	891	1	0	0	1	0	10	4	5	1	0
Pikeville	6,501	15	0	1	5	9	177	52	109	16	1
Pineville	1,709	2	0	1	0	1	24	4	17	3	0
Pioneer Village	2,967	1	0	0	0	1	23	0	15	8	0
Prestonsburg	3,500	7	0	0	1	6	33	5	19	9	0
Princeton	6,091	10	1	2	1	6	135	30	96	9	2
Prospect	4,929	0	0	0	0	0	34	3	26	5	0
Providence	2,979	0	0	0	0	0	14	6	6	2	0

Table 8. Offenses Known to Law Enforcement, by Selected State and City, 2020—Continued

(Number.)

State/city	Population	Violent crime	Murder and nonnegligent manslaughter	Rape[1]	Robbery	Aggravated assault	Property crime	Burglary	Larceny-theft	Motor vehicle theft	Arson[2]
Raceland	2,349	0	0	0	0	0	17	2	10	5	0
Radcliff	22,950	39	1	7	10	21	566	103	409	54	8
Richmond	36,691	67	1	9	18	39	950	105	770	75	3
Russell	3,208	2	0	1	0	1	31	4	25	2	0
Russell Springs	2,661	0	0	0	0	0	79	15	54	10	1
Russellville	7,125	11	0	0	5	6	224	47	158	19	1
Salyersville	1,635	12	0	0	0	12	1	0	0	1	2
Scottsville	4,576	18	0	5	1	12	127	26	91	10	0
Shelbyville	16,863	16	0	0	3	13	302	49	200	53	0
Shepherdsville	12,567	31	0	7	10	14	379	90	209	80	2
Shively	15,735	78	5	8	35	30	509	81	302	126	0
Simpsonville	2,974	2	0	0	2	0	93	3	82	8	0
Smiths Grove	807	0	0	0	0	0	18	3	12	3	0
Somerset	11,622	21	0	6	4	11	253	59	151	43	1
Southgate	4,039	9	0	1	1	7	26	3	20	3	0
South Shore	1,050	0	0	0	0	0	1	1	0	0	0
Springfield	2,980	3	0	0	1	2	35	14	18	3	0
Stanford	3,653	5	0	0	0	5	46	22	18	6	1
Stanton	2,701	3	0	1	0	2	84	18	56	10	0
St. Matthews	18,162	24	1	3	14	6	866	60	735	71	0
Taylor Mill	6,819	0	0	0	0	0	36	8	25	3	0
Taylorsville	1,322	0	0	0	0	0	10	3	4	3	0
Tompkinsville	2,242	6	1	3	0	2	5	3	1	1	0
Versailles	26,899	28	1	9	3	15	338	54	248	36	0
Villa Hills	7,478	1	0	0	1	0	68	10	56	2	0
Vine Grove	6,596	4	0	2	1	1	50	13	28	9	1
Warsaw	1,705	3	0	0	0	3	11	6	4	1	0
West Buechel	1,277	15	0	0	14	1	59	3	34	22	0
West Liberty	3,546	1	0	0	0	1	2	0	1	1	0
West Point	870	2	0	0	1	1	12	0	8	4	0
Wheelwright	462	0	0	0	0	0	0	0	0	0	0
Wilder	3,058	6	0	1	0	5	53	12	37	4	0
Williamsburg	5,287	13	0	2	3	8	25	5	13	7	1
Williamstown	3,907	4	0	0	1	3	43	10	31	2	0
Wilmore	6,496	1	0	0	0	1	33	6	26	1	1
Winchester	18,570	43	0	7	8	28	790	106	580	104	2
Woodburn	370	0	0	0	0	0	0	0	0	0	0
LOUISIANA											
Abbeville	12,018	123	3	6	8	106	309	76	231	2	0
Alexandria	45,986	850	19	15	145	671	3,317	754	2,300	263	1
Baker	13,122	80	8	4	11	57	414	59	329	26	3
Baton Rouge	219,245	2,087	102	55	457	1,473	10,580	1,898	7,854	828	146
Benton[4]	2,092	17	0	0	1	16	12	4	8	0	0
Bernice	1,583	3	0	0	0	3	24	12	12	0	0
Berwick	4,365	12	0	0	1	11	100	59	37	4	0
Bogalusa	11,427	193	16	7	15	155	494	98	355	41	1
Bossier City[4]	68,869	609	8	52	77	472	3,201	400	2,472	329	5
Breaux Bridge	8,149	66	2	0	6	58	330	51	259	20	0
Broussard	13,299	33	0	0	4	29	392	70	302	20	0
Brusly	2,619	1	0	0	0	1	20	0	20	0	0
Dixie Inn	261	3	0	1	0	2	18	0	17	1	0
Fisher	218	0	0	0	0	0	0	0	0	0	0
Franklin	6,613	70	0	2	1	67	159	28	130	1	1
French Settlement	1,201	1	0	0	1	0	13	5	5	3	0
Georgetown	319	0	0	0	0	0	1	1	0	0	0
Gonzales	11,092	73	1	6	8	58	1,086	46	1,003	37	0
Gramercy	3,260	13	0	0	0	13	67	8	55	4	0
Greenwood	3,117	13	0	0	0	13	76	26	45	5	0
Gretna	17,637	63	1	5	11	46	486	48	411	27	0
Harahan	9,249	8	1	1	3	3	75	6	63	6	0
Independence	1,908	14	0	0	2	12	71	5	59	7	1
Iowa[4]	3,184	28	0	1	0	27	102	31	60	11	0
Jena	3,397	3	1	0	0	2	5	0	5	0	0
Jennings	9,737	91	2	7	9	73	296	47	229	20	0
Kenner	66,308	178	3	29	40	106	1,781	137	1,518	126	7
Kinder	2,357	6	0	1	0	5	130	24	91	15	0
Lafayette	126,679	712	14	17	147	534	5,725	1,069	4,247	409	22
Lake Arthur	2,749	9	0	0	0	9	60	13	44	3	0
Lake Charles[4]	79,077	409	7	31	49	322	2,511	849	1,424	238	3
Lake Providence	3,375	22	0	0	1	21	4	2	2	0	0
Leesville	5,502	47	0	5	0	42	346	57	277	12	2
Mandeville	12,520	13	0	2	2	9	162	29	125	8	0
Mansfield[4]	4,587	35	1	2	0	32	72	23	47	2	1
Marksville	5,299	95	6	0	6	83	327	96	227	4	0
Minden	11,711	116	0	4	9	103	331	59	244	28	1
Monroe	47,119	1,399	19	9	154	1,217	2,883	649	2,042	192	6
Morgan City	10,576	106	0	7	7	92	431	116	283	32	0
Natchitoches	17,374	192	6	13	29	144	1,061	282	715	64	7
New Orleans	393,779	5,215	201	712	1,106	3,196	17,876	1,994	12,358	3,524	0
Opelousas	15,820	375	9	9	37	320	1,040	326	681	33	3
Pineville	14,079	133	1	14	10	108	702	140	514	48	2
Port Allen	4,695	81	1	1	2	77	144	32	98	14	0

Table 8. Offenses Known to Law Enforcement, by Selected State and City, 2020—Continued

(Number.)

State/city	Population	Violent crime	Murder and nonnegligent manslaughter	Rape[1]	Robbery	Aggravated assault	Property crime	Burglary	Larceny-theft	Motor vehicle theft	Arson[2]
Port Vincent	758	1	0	0	0	1	5	2	3	0	0
Ruston[4]	21,846	122	3	1	0	118	752	159	559	34	1
Scott	8,696	8	0	1	1	6	254	52	188	14	0
Shreveport	185,588	1,713	69	125	235	1,284	8,907	1,516	6,690	701	84
Slidell	27,669	77	0	14	14	49	878	92	754	32	1
Springhill[4]	4,720	13	0	0	0	13	52	1	49	2	0
St. Gabriel	7,553	28	1	3	2	22	82	10	70	2	0
Sulphur[4]	20,029	79	4	11	4	60	672	147	458	67	1
Thibodaux	14,418	70	1	2	0	67	602	40	516	46	0
Vinton[4]	3,216	32	0	3	1	28	149	52	82	15	2
Welsh	3,227	24	2	1	0	21	69	14	52	3	0
Westlake[4]	4,997	16	0	1	4	11	120	37	73	10	0
West Monroe	12,134	190	1	25	22	142	915	190	673	52	1
Westwego	8,303	58	0	4	0	54	165	33	112	20	0
Wilson	564	0	0	0	0	0	0	0	0	0	0
Winnfield	4,201	44	2	0	1	41	131	17	100	14	0
Youngsville	15,654	37	0	1	1	35	248	24	211	13	0
Zachary	18,283	73	3	8	4	58	429	37	378	14	1
MAINE											
Ashland	1,208	1	0	0	0	1	8	7	1	0	0
Auburn	23,455	46	2	18	6	20	518	41	455	22	1
Augusta	18,653	75	0	21	16	38	617	75	524	18	3
Baileyville	1,439	12	0	0	0	12	10	5	5	0	0
Bangor	32,179	51	2	7	13	29	1,207	100	1,044	63	0
Bar Harbor	7,716	5	0	4	0	1	40	9	31	0	0
Bath[4]	8,322	4	0	1	0	3	94	6	83	5	0
Belfast[4]	6,681	0	0	0	0	0	53	11	40	2	0
Berwick	7,944	2	0	0	0	2	61	12	45	4	1
Biddeford	21,530	50	0	15	3	32	421	37	365	19	4
Boothbay Harbor[4]	2,219	3	0	2	0	1	10	1	7	2	0
Brewer	8,988	6	0	0	0	6	212	5	203	4	0
Bridgton	5,459	5	0	3	1	1	57	7	50	0	0
Brunswick[4]	20,566	16	0	11	1	4	187	22	155	10	2
Bucksport	4,927	8	0	5	0	3	41	5	31	5	0
Buxton[4]	8,360	15	0	0	4	11	62	8	49	5	1
Calais	2,993	2	0	2	0	0	63	8	55	0	0
Camden	4,776	0	0	0	0	0	12	0	12	0	0
Cape Elizabeth	9,340	3	0	1	0	2	30	1	29	0	0
Caribou	7,532	6	0	0	0	6	146	27	102	17	0
Carrabassett Valley	788	1	0	1	0	0	19	3	16	0	0
Clinton	3,340	1	0	0	1	0	14	1	13	0	0
Cumberland[4]	8,327	3	0	1	0	2	21	0	20	1	0
Damariscotta[4]	2,144	3	0	3	0	0	39	5	33	1	0
Dexter	3,687	1	0	0	1	0	52	4	44	4	0
Dover-Foxcroft	4,018	2	0	0	0	2	35	6	29	0	0
East Millinocket	2,922	0	0	0	0	0	29	3	23	3	0
Eastport	1,258	2	0	0	0	2	24	8	16	0	0
Eliot	6,990	2	0	1	1	0	26	5	19	2	0
Ellsworth[4]	8,231	8	0	2	1	5	178	9	165	4	1
Fairfield[4]	6,531	15	0	8	1	6	84	16	66	2	2
Falmouth[4]	12,444	2	0	2	0	0	77	5	68	4	2
Farmington	7,764	9	0	4	0	5	99	8	90	1	0
Fort Fairfield	3,263	6	0	2	2	2	24	11	9	4	0
Fort Kent	3,831	3	0	0	0	3	27	2	22	3	0
Freeport	8,637	4	0	1	0	3	75	6	67	2	1
Fryeburg[4]	3,452	2	0	0	0	2	46	5	37	4	0
Gardiner	5,639	2	1	0	0	1	34	6	26	2	0
Gorham[4]	18,167	5	0	3	0	2	81	15	61	5	2
Gouldsboro	1,742	0	0	0	0	0	5	0	3	2	0
Greenville	1,599	2	1	0	0	1	6	1	5	0	0
Hallowell[4]	2,382	1	0	0	0	1	19	4	15	0	0
Hampden	7,428	0	0	0	0	0	45	4	39	2	0
Holden	3,106	2	0	2	0	0	34	7	25	2	0
Houlton	5,713	22	0	1	0	21	166	18	145	3	0
Islesboro[4]	560	0	0	0	0	0	14	5	9	0	0
Jay	4,600	6	0	3	0	3	21	2	17	2	0
Kennebunk	11,719	0	0	0	0	0	53	0	49	4	0
Kennebunkport	3,671	3	0	2	0	1	20	1	19	0	0
Kittery	9,855	6	0	5	0	1	86	4	79	3	0
Lewiston	36,186	97	2	26	16	53	639	81	519	39	14
Limestone	2,159	4	0	0	4	0	16	6	8	2	0
Lincoln[4]	4,838	6	1	1	0	4	119	20	94	5	0
Lisbon	9,004	5	0	0	0	5	95	7	83	5	1
Livermore Falls	3,154	9	0	3	0	6	27	7	19	1	0
Machias	2,007	7	0	0	0	7	28	5	21	2	0
Madawaska[4]	3,704	2	0	0	1	1	32	1	28	3	0
Mechanic Falls	2,974	8	0	4	0	4	30	7	20	3	0
Mexico	2,624	6	0	4	0	2	106	15	86	5	0
Milbridge	1,288	0	0	0	0	0	0	0	0	0	0
Millinocket	4,226	4	1	0	0	3	82	13	60	9	0
Milo	2,279	3	0	0	1	2	43	8	33	2	0
Monmouth	4,139	2	0	1	0	1	13	4	8	1	0

Table 8. Offenses Known to Law Enforcement, by Selected State and City, 2020—Continued

(Number.)

State/city	Population	Violent crime	Murder and nonnegligent manslaughter	Rape[1]	Robbery	Aggravated assault	Property crime	Burglary	Larceny-theft	Motor vehicle theft	Arson[2]
Newport[4]	3,272	2	1	1	0	0	35	12	22	1	0
North Berwick[4]	4,744	3	0	2	0	1	33	4	26	3	0
Norway	4,989	7	0	3	0	4	61	4	56	1	0
Oakland	6,317	1	0	0	0	1	42	5	31	6	0
Ogunquit[4]	932	2	0	0	0	2	21	3	18	0	0
Old Orchard Beach	9,061	22	0	12	0	10	94	13	71	10	0
Old Town	7,388	2	1	0	0	1	75	14	60	1	1
Orono	10,851	3	0	1	1	1	87	17	64	6	0
Oxford	4,095	4	0	3	0	1	116	4	110	2	0
Paris[4]	5,149	6	0	1	1	4	40	3	29	8	0
Phippsburg	2,274	0	0	0	0	0	7	1	6	0	0
Pittsfield	3,971	2	0	0	0	2	32	4	26	2	0
Portland	66,229	129	0	28	34	67	1,143	94	991	58	5
Presque Isle	8,937	16	0	7	2	7	210	29	174	7	1
Rangeley	1,153	0	0	0	0	0	9	1	8	0	0
Richmond	3,477	1	0	0	0	1	15	5	9	1	0
Rockland[4]	7,151	7	0	1	0	6	120	15	103	2	1
Rockport	3,367	0	0	0	0	0	12	0	12	0	0
Rumford	5,735	10	0	7	0	3	103	12	84	7	0
Sabattus[4]	5,054	5	0	0	0	5	25	9	15	1	0
Saco	20,133	24	0	7	1	16	301	45	230	26	2
Sanford	21,272	35	0	11	7	17	565	62	483	20	6
Scarborough	21,237	14	0	5	4	5	273	9	252	12	4
Searsport	2,635	1	0	1	0	0	17	5	11	1	0
Skowhegan	8,202	14	0	2	3	9	226	27	187	12	1
South Berwick[4]	7,605	4	0	0	2	2	43	4	36	3	0
South Portland	25,593	32	1	4	10	17	402	24	346	32	5
Southwest Harbor	1,795	0	0	0	0	0	31	2	28	1	0
Thomaston	2,741	3	0	2	0	1	90	6	77	7	1
Topsham[4]	8,891	4	0	0	0	4	71	4	60	7	0
Veazie	1,823	1	0	0	0	1	26	3	22	1	0
Waldoboro[4]	5,070	2	0	0	0	2	36	4	31	1	0
Washburn	1,526	4	0	1	0	3	29	7	21	1	0
Waterville	16,654	32	1	12	7	12	416	27	377	12	4
Wells	10,803	7	0	6	0	1	84	5	73	6	0
Westbrook	19,256	30	0	6	4	20	183	17	157	9	2
Wilton	3,944	1	0	0	0	1	7	0	7	0	0
Windham[4]	18,720	11	0	4	1	6	122	23	94	5	0
Winslow	7,599	10	0	6	0	4	90	24	62	4	0
Winter Harbor	511	0	0	0	0	0	1	0	1	0	0
Winthrop	5,983	5	1	1	1	2	59	8	49	2	0
Wiscasset[4]	3,767	5	0	0	1	4	37	2	30	5	0
Yarmouth[4]	8,617	5	0	2	1	2	54	4	49	1	0
York	13,377	7	0	3	3	1	95	9	83	3	1
MARYLAND[3]											
Bowie[4]	59,008	61	1	5	12	43	548	64	444	40	0
Ocean Pines	11,710	2	0	0	0	2	65	11	53	1	0
Takoma Park	17,831	61	2	8	27	24	469	34	402	33	0
MASSACHUSETTS											
Abington	17,306	39	0	11	5	23	110	11	87	12	0
Acton	23,728	16	0	1	1	14	128	15	109	4	2
Acushnet	10,604	16	0	4	0	12	24	4	16	4	1
Adams	7,959	14	0	6	1	7	92	16	69	7	2
Agawam	28,533	66	0	11	4	51	299	115	163	21	2
Amesbury	17,578	26	1	4	0	21	65	10	51	4	0
Amherst	40,061	62	0	20	4	38	104	18	72	14	1
Aquinnah	322	2	0	1	0	1	3	0	3	0	0
Arlington	45,582	27	0	1	2	24	136	24	98	14	1
Ashburnham	6,344	8	0	1	0	7	30	8	18	4	0
Ashby	3,217	4	0	2	0	2	21	4	15	2	0
Ashfield	1,715	0	0	0	0	0	6	0	4	2	0
Ashland	17,842	18	0	2	1	15	80	14	48	18	0
Athol	11,682	47	0	5	3	39	105	14	87	4	1
Attleboro	45,181	137	1	16	22	98	528	67	432	29	1
Auburn	16,736	26	0	1	2	23	238	21	198	19	0
Avon[4]	4,561	13	0	2	1	10	156	8	143	5	1
Ayer	8,237	8	0	0	1	7	40	6	33	1	1
Barnstable	44,169	188	0	30	12	146	350	52	281	17	9
Barre	5,568	16	1	4	0	11	9	2	6	1	0
Becket	1,709	5	0	0	0	5	7	0	5	2	0
Bedford	14,135	11	0	1	1	9	63	12	47	4	0
Belchertown	15,148	24	0	1	0	23	85	16	60	9	0
Bellingham	17,331	36	0	3	6	27	202	15	179	8	1
Belmont	26,136	16	0	2	3	11	182	86	91	5	1
Berkley	6,864	6	0	0	0	6	12	5	5	2	0
Berlin	3,266	6	0	0	1	5	13	3	9	1	0
Bernardston	2,086	5	0	0	0	5	12	1	10	1	0
Beverly	42,229	60	1	6	3	50	163	11	143	9	0
Billerica	43,473	34	1	1	1	31	178	21	133	24	1
Blackstone	9,269	8	0	1	1	6	9	1	7	1	0
Bolton	5,455	5	0	0	0	5	25	4	21	0	0

Table 8. Offenses Known to Law Enforcement, by Selected State and City, 2020—Continued

(Number.)

State/city	Population	Violent crime	Murder and nonnegligent manslaughter	Rape[1]	Robbery	Aggravated assault	Property crime	Burglary	Larceny-theft	Motor vehicle theft	Arson[2]
Boston[4]	697,323	4,354	58	184	919	3,193	13,015	1,698	10,037	1,280	34
Bourne	19,657	43	0	7	2	34	195	46	141	8	1
Boxborough	5,856	6	0	0	0	6	7	1	6	0	0
Boxford	8,328	1	0	0	0	1	21	0	21	0	0
Boylston	4,728	0	0	0	0	0	0	0	0	0	0
Braintree	37,278	85	1	1	4	79	323	37	266	20	0
Brewster	9,714	22	0	3	1	18	37	9	26	2	0
Bridgewater	8,107	25	0	3	1	21	73	14	52	7	1
Brockton	99,171	752	4	60	118	570	1,659	202	1,073	384	19
Brookfield	3,442	2	0	1	0	1	10	5	3	2	0
Brookline	59,057	63	1	1	14	47	672	35	619	18	0
Burlington	28,960	44	0	12	3	29	240	19	210	11	0
Cambridge	119,938	341	1	25	67	248	2,200	202	1,917	81	13
Canton	24,015	74	0	2	3	69	141	12	115	14	0
Carlisle	5,267	1	0	0	0	1	14	1	13	0	0
Carver	12,197	12	0	2	1	9	62	13	43	6	1
Charlton	13,720	7	0	1	0	6	44	12	24	8	0
Chatham	5,935	10	0	1	0	9	52	13	39	0	2
Chelmsford	35,369	33	0	7	2	24	302	20	260	22	0
Chelsea	39,995	249	0	18	41	190	570	98	400	72	2
Cheshire	3,118	2	0	0	1	1	5	2	2	1	0
Chesterfield	1,252	0	0	0	0	0	2	1	1	0	0
Chicopee	54,918	294	1	25	42	226	1,148	186	851	111	4
Chilmark	927	1	0	0	0	1	9	2	7	0	0
Clinton	13,967	6	0	0	0	6	9	0	9	0	0
Cohasset	8,653	9	0	1	0	8	33	5	28	0	0
Concord	18,952	14	0	3	1	10	126	10	115	1	0
Danvers	27,517	52	0	5	6	41	352	20	305	27	1
Dartmouth	33,986	72	1	12	12	47	408	37	349	22	1
Dedham	25,217	7	0	1	2	4	278	14	223	41	0
Deerfield	4,976	7	0	2	1	4	24	3	20	1	0
Dennis	13,760	51	0	8	1	42	161	36	117	8	2
Douglas	9,054	14	0	4	0	10	28	7	18	3	0
Dover	6,176	6	1	1	0	4	30	6	22	2	0
Dracut	31,708	33	0	1	4	28	272	23	215	34	2
Dudley	11,745	21	0	6	0	15	35	11	18	6	1
Dunstable	3,410	4	0	2	0	2	17	3	14	0	2
Duxbury	16,561	11	0	3	0	8	35	1	31	3	1
East Bridgewater	15,103	12	0	2	0	10	52	6	40	6	1
East Brookfield	2,200	4	0	1	0	3	2	0	1	1	2
Eastham	4,874	11	0	1	0	10	21	3	17	1	0
Easthampton	15,804	26	0	11	0	15	208	13	183	12	3
East Longmeadow	16,181	12	0	4	3	5	168	19	134	15	3
Easton	25,176	30	0	8	3	19	180	22	146	12	0
Edgartown	4,374	33	0	2	1	30	60	5	54	1	0
Erving	1,745	5	0	1	0	4	11	3	7	1	0
Essex	3,812	4	0	0	0	4	11	2	8	1	0
Everett	46,765	181	0	26	17	138	674	75	518	81	1
Fairhaven	16,014	59	0	8	4	47	199	25	166	8	2
Fall River	89,136	779	2	63	91	623	994	343	468	183	36
Falmouth	30,769	91	0	10	4	77	342	117	215	10	4
Fitchburg	40,443	221	0	19	43	159	584	108	402	74	4
Foxborough	18,539	27	0	7	4	16	125	26	86	13	1
Framingham	74,680	264	2	13	20	229	862	110	625	127	4
Franklin	34,281	6	0	1	0	5	32	7	24	1	1
Freetown	9,401	20	0	1	0	19	39	12	26	1	0
Gardner	20,629	93	2	11	4	76	258	32	207	19	0
Georgetown	8,783	5	0	0	1	4	37	6	31	0	0
Gill	1,464	0	0	0	0	0	7	1	5	1	0
Gloucester	30,445	72	0	11	4	57	96	11	76	9	1
Goshen	1,059	0	0	0	0	0	3	1	2	0	0
Grafton	18,908	10	0	2	1	7	49	3	41	5	0
Granby	6,297	8	1	2	0	5	37	5	30	2	0
Granville	1,610	0	0	0	0	0	4	1	2	1	0
Great Barrington	6,928	9	0	2	2	5	46	7	37	2	2
Groton	11,337	4	0	1	0	3	35	6	28	1	0
Groveland	6,856	0	0	0	0	0	7	0	7	0	0
Hadley	5,352	26	0	2	3	21	151	8	138	5	1
Halifax	8,207	10	0	2	1	7	54	6	42	6	1
Hamilton	8,038	5	0	0	0	5	19	1	18	0	0
Hampden	5,163	3	0	0	1	2	23	6	16	1	0
Hanover	15,143	2	0	0	1	1	50	3	46	1	0
Hanson	11,367	10	0	1	1	8	28	4	22	2	1
Hardwick	3,047	7	0	0	1	6	5	1	1	3	1
Harvard	6,595	0	0	0	0	0	24	8	14	2	0
Harwich	12,068	26	0	5	0	21	77	18	55	4	0
Hatfield	3,250	1	0	0	0	1	15	3	11	1	0
Haverhill	64,015	304	2	11	19	272	638	144	411	83	6
Hingham	25,816	50	0	5	1	44	140	24	110	6	0
Holbrook	11,035	43	0	6	3	34	144	32	99	13	1
Holden	19,412	6	0	2	0	4	21	2	16	3	3
Holland	2,473	3	0	0	0	3	10	3	7	0	0
Holliston	14,986	11	0	4	0	7	50	9	34	7	0

Table 8. Offenses Known to Law Enforcement, by Selected State and City, 2020—Continued

(Number.)

State/city	Population	Violent crime	Murder and nonnegligent manslaughter	Rape[1]	Robbery	Aggravated assault	Property crime	Burglary	Larceny-theft	Motor vehicle theft	Arson[2]
Holyoke	40,002	362	8	17	64	273	1,246	194	947	105	6
Hopedale	5,924	5	0	1	0	4	19	2	16	1	0
Hopkinton	18,806	5	0	0	0	5	29	0	27	2	0
Hudson	19,839	21	0	2	1	18	70	4	64	2	1
Hull	10,850	45	0	5	1	39	71	10	58	3	1
Ipswich	14,097	8	0	1	0	7	63	15	47	1	0
Kingston	14,481	22	0	4	1	17	93	9	79	5	1
Lakeville	12,053	24	0	3	1	20	31	14	15	2	0
Lancaster	8,040	14	0	4	2	8	31	11	17	3	0
Lawrence[4]	79,997	358	5	14	53	286	647	45	463	139	0
Lee	5,633	13	0	2	0	11	61	10	49	2	0
Leicester	11,329	18	0	2	0	16	75	14	58	3	0
Lenox	4,930	10	0	1	2	7	44	6	38	0	0
Leominster	41,598	199	0	26	24	149	697	66	587	44	3
Leverett	1,836	1	0	0	0	1	4	0	4	0	0
Lexington	33,138	12	0	0	2	10	114	23	88	3	0
Lincoln	7,092	2	0	0	0	2	20	0	20	0	0
Littleton	10,326	6	0	2	0	4	38	3	33	2	0
Longmeadow	15,640	5	0	2	0	3	129	26	93	10	0
Lowell	110,876	348	6	18	67	257	1,629	225	1,180	224	12
Ludlow	21,171	66	0	3	2	61	226	29	186	11	1
Lunenburg	11,874	24	0	2	0	22	90	11	71	8	0
Lynn	94,223	418	6	24	54	334	910	143	632	135	3
Lynnfield	13,093	7	0	2	0	5	64	1	60	3	2
Malden	60,231	162	2	6	34	120	751	98	554	99	4
Manchester-by-the-Sea	5,438	0	0	0	0	0	17	0	16	1	0
Marblehead	20,525	15	0	2	0	13	126	12	112	2	1
Marion	5,396	5	0	1	1	3	41	6	33	2	0
Marlborough	39,498	149	0	22	6	121	353	29	297	27	5
Marshfield	26,936	20	0	1	4	15	66	12	50	4	2
Mashpee	14,180	30	3	4	1	22	85	10	69	6	1
Mattapoisett	6,659	7	0	2	1	4	30	3	25	2	0
Maynard	11,420	17	0	5	0	12	51	4	39	8	1
Medfield	13,034	6	0	2	0	4	28	6	22	0	0
Medford	57,137	72	0	2	17	53	537	36	464	37	3
Melrose	27,975	26	0	1	5	20	132	17	108	7	1
Mendon	6,232	3	0	0	0	3	20	2	18	0	0
Merrimac	6,992	2	0	0	0	2	13	1	11	1	0
Methuen	50,810	62	0	5	4	53	441	55	327	59	1
Middleboro	26,606	93	2	9	5	77	176	29	130	17	1
Middleton	10,189	4	0	0	0	4	29	4	23	2	0
Milford	29,066	41	0	7	0	34	172	27	120	25	2
Millbury	13,949	20	0	3	0	17	90	8	76	6	0
Millis	8,339	10	0	2	1	7	11	2	7	2	0
Millville	3,247	1	0	0	0	1	12	3	8	1	0
Milton	27,600	8	0	6	1	1	105	9	87	9	0
Monson	8,782	16	0	2	0	14	40	11	22	7	0
Montague	8,185	45	0	2	0	43	64	16	45	3	0
Nahant	3,505	4	0	0	1	3	12	1	11	0	0
Nantucket	11,484	18	0	4	1	13	210	9	198	3	0
Natick	36,200	31	0	1	9	21	390	21	339	30	1
Needham	31,586	24	0	4	2	18	117	13	96	8	0
New Bedford	94,886	596	4	51	106	435	1,684	285	1,223	176	12
New Braintree	1,021	1	0	0	0	1	4	1	2	1	0
Newbury	7,163	15	0	0	2	13	22	6	16	0	1
Newburyport	18,288	23	0	8	0	15	91	10	72	9	1
Newton	88,281	48	0	4	8	36	486	51	420	15	0
Norfolk	12,068	2	0	0	0	2	12	1	11	0	0
North Adams	12,620	86	0	8	8	70	307	69	230	8	6
Northampton	28,428	92	0	13	10	69	469	50	403	16	5
North Andover	31,341	28	0	4	2	22	107	3	101	3	1
North Attleboro	29,280	32	0	5	4	23	312	17	288	7	0
Northborough	15,105	8	0	1	1	6	63	11	46	6	0
Northbridge	16,699	35	0	2	1	32	69	14	47	8	0
Northfield	2,950	2	0	0	0	2	29	1	27	1	0
North Reading	15,886	11	0	1	2	8	44	3	38	3	0
Norwell	11,605	9	0	0	1	8	38	3	34	1	0
Norwood	29,791	35	0	0	5	30	229	19	192	18	0
Oak Bluffs	4,677	23	0	6	0	17	43	10	31	2	1
Oakham	1,953	3	0	1	0	2	4	0	3	1	0
Orange	7,554	19	0	5	0	14	116	19	90	7	2
Orleans	5,745	12	0	4	0	8	60	9	50	1	0
Oxford	13,967	22	0	2	1	19	176	10	158	8	1
Palmer	12,200	44	0	8	1	35	108	26	78	4	1
Paxton	4,953	1	0	0	0	1	12	2	8	2	0
Peabody	52,975	114	0	14	6	94	423	37	352	34	3
Pelham	1,312	0	0	0	0	0	1	0	1	0	0
Pembroke	19,211	15	0	1	1	13	60	7	48	5	1
Pepperell	12,114	17	0	3	1	13	54	6	45	3	2
Pittsfield	41,865	341	1	35	34	271	664	232	369	63	8
Plainville	9,392	7	0	2	0	5	41	6	35	0	0
Plymouth	64,199	185	0	35	11	139	715	73	617	25	3
Plympton	3,105	5	0	2	0	3	31	6	24	1	0

Table 8. Offenses Known to Law Enforcement, by Selected State and City, 2020—Continued

(Number.)

State/city	Population	Violent crime	Murder and nonnegligent manslaughter	Rape[1]	Robbery	Aggravated assault	Property crime	Burglary	Larceny-theft	Motor vehicle theft	Arson[2]
Princeton	3,477	0	0	0	0	0	12	3	7	2	0
Provincetown	2,947	21	0	8	2	11	45	7	37	1	0
Quincy	94,519	303	1	28	37	237	1,146	198	861	87	5
Randolph	32,052	86	0	7	9	70	298	48	196	54	2
Raynham	14,512	21	0	4	4	13	146	8	130	8	0
Reading	25,417	11	0	2	0	9	109	12	86	11	0
Rehoboth	12,406	8	0	3	0	5	53	9	35	9	0
Revere	52,930	196	1	14	36	145	657	54	507	96	0
Rockland	18,652	46	0	10	1	35	41	12	25	4	0
Rockport	7,279	9	0	0	1	8	12	2	10	0	0
Rowley	6,509	8	0	2	1	5	24	7	14	3	0
Royalston	1,272	0	0	0	0	0	3	0	3	0	0
Rutland	9,000	30	0	3	1	26	14	2	10	2	0
Salem	43,154	108	1	16	16	75	650	47	565	38	6
Salisbury	9,630	20	0	6	0	14	82	19	53	10	0
Sandwich	20,008	25	0	1	1	23	68	5	62	1	0
Saugus	28,397	72	1	10	13	48	235	21	192	22	0
Scituate	19,655	11	0	3	1	7	49	3	42	4	0
Seekonk	15,927	29	0	3	2	24	298	33	244	21	0
Sharon	19,011	8	0	1	1	6	34	6	26	2	0
Shelburne	1,830	3	0	0	0	3	9	3	6	0	0
Sherborn	4,335	7	0	0	0	7	11	3	8	0	0
Shirley	7,632	21	0	4	2	15	33	7	23	3	0
Shrewsbury	38,656	4	0	1	0	3	139	5	110	24	0
Somerset	18,024	31	1	12	4	14	137	12	119	6	0
Somerville	81,552	153	1	14	17	121	966	118	758	90	2
Southampton	6,213	6	0	0	1	5	84	5	77	2	0
Southborough	10,202	23	0	8	4	11	44	8	26	10	1
Southbridge	16,805	73	0	18	1	54	191	41	131	19	3
South Hadley	17,613	41	0	6	2	33	219	46	139	34	4
Southwick	9,732	15	0	3	0	12	63	20	34	9	0
Spencer	11,896	20	0	1	0	19	79	15	46	18	0
Springfield	153,084	1,480	18	70	350	1,042	3,730	618	2,616	496	34
Sterling	8,172	5	0	1	0	4	30	5	23	2	1
Stockbridge	1,884	2	0	0	0	2	23	4	19	0	0
Stoneham	24,329	19	0	4	0	15	159	41	97	21	1
Stoughton	29,067	89	1	14	12	62	215	27	166	22	1
Stow	7,266	4	0	1	0	3	28	0	23	5	0
Sturbridge	9,585	25	0	4	0	21	102	15	70	17	2
Sudbury	19,778	14	0	0	0	14	68	7	54	7	0
Sunderland	3,622	8	0	2	0	6	11	3	7	1	0
Sutton	9,600	8	0	0	0	8	53	18	30	5	0
Swampscott	15,391	20	0	0	3	17	137	9	124	4	0
Swansea	16,854	20	0	5	2	13	115	18	86	11	0
Taunton	57,338	237	1	27	14	195	275	54	188	33	1
Templeton	8,110	7	0	1	1	5	20	7	12	1	1
Tewksbury	31,237	67	0	10	7	50	344	27	295	22	0
Tisbury	4,108	16	0	1	0	15	37	6	31	0	1
Topsfield	6,668	3	0	0	0	3	14	3	9	2	0
Townsend	9,515	18	0	0	0	18	38	7	30	1	2
Truro	1,997	4	0	0	0	4	9	1	8	0	0
Tyngsboro	12,590	8	0	3	0	5	33	3	25	5	0
Upton	8,081	7	0	1	0	6	20	2	12	6	3
Uxbridge	14,202	36	0	0	1	35	101	69	29	3	0
Wakefield	27,114	29	0	4	2	23	159	25	125	9	1
Walpole	25,273	34	0	7	3	24	209	25	182	2	0
Waltham	62,339	85	1	10	3	71	385	51	310	24	3
Ware	9,694	36	0	1	3	32	33	4	26	3	3
Wareham	23,619	89	1	13	3	72	230	49	165	16	1
Warren	5,203	19	0	2	0	17	23	8	11	4	0
Watertown	36,201	31	0	5	5	21	253	37	207	9	1
Wayland	13,859	1	0	0	0	1	0	0	0	0	0
Webster	16,876	116	0	15	7	94	182	30	137	15	3
Wellesley	28,687	10	0	6	0	4	110	19	85	6	0
Wellfleet	2,707	7	0	1	0	6	10	1	9	0	0
Wenham	5,296	3	0	1	0	2	19	0	19	0	0
Westborough	19,138	32	0	5	1	26	155	17	126	12	0
West Boylston	8,074	10	0	2	0	8	42	5	31	6	0
West Bridgewater	7,568	6	0	1	0	5	66	9	49	8	1
Westfield	41,072	84	0	24	3	57	324	45	261	18	3
Westford	25,011	4	0	0	1	3	61	3	54	4	1
Westminster	8,038	14	0	1	0	13	43	4	36	3	2
West Newbury	4,743	5	0	0	0	5	7	0	7	0	1
Weston	12,146	1	0	0	0	1	35	4	29	2	0
Westport	16,003	15	0	10	1	4	78	11	59	8	0
West Springfield	28,437	134	0	15	27	92	879	80	726	73	6
West Tisbury	2,919	9	0	0	1	8	15	2	13	0	0
Westwood	16,578	17	0	3	1	13	134	10	123	1	0
Weymouth	58,090	130	2	10	12	106	441	36	369	36	2
Whately	1,574	4	0	0	0	4	11	3	7	1	0
Whitman	15,814	19	0	4	1	14	77	13	58	6	1
Wilbraham	14,690	21	0	6	2	13	183	17	158	8	1
Williamsburg	2,464	3	0	1	0	2	14	3	10	1	0

Table 8. Offenses Known to Law Enforcement, by Selected State and City, 2020—Continued

(Number.)

State/city	Population	Violent crime	Murder and nonnegligent manslaughter	Rape[1]	Robbery	Aggravated assault	Property crime	Burglary	Larceny-theft	Motor vehicle theft	Arson[2]
Williamstown	7,397	1	0	0	0	1	33	4	26	3	0
Wilmington	23,437	31	0	2	1	28	155	16	124	15	0
Winchendon	10,908	28	0	8	1	19	96	37	55	4	1
Winchester	22,827	11	0	1	0	10	98	8	86	4	1
Winthrop	18,561	28	0	0	1	27	138	14	115	9	1
Woburn	40,142	54	1	10	7	36	394	36	313	45	2
Worcester	184,850	1,169	10	40	210	909	3,695	667	2,581	447	10
Worthington	1,177	0	0	0	0	0	2	0	2	0	0
Wrentham	12,112	9	0	1	0	8	66	5	60	1	0
Yarmouth	23,015	87	0	9	4	74	217	47	162	8	2
MICHIGAN											
Addison Township	6,638	2	0	0	1	1	16	0	15	1	0
Adrian	20,540	140	2	31	17	90	443	69	341	33	4
Adrian Township	6,237	1	0	0	0	1	5	0	5	0	0
Akron	372	1	0	0	0	1	6	2	3	1	1
Albion	8,381	99	2	6	8	83	261	55	194	12	8
Allegan	5,023	12	0	6	1	5	19	2	17	0	0
Allen Park	26,809	98	0	10	11	77	381	46	300	35	2
Alma	8,839	22	0	14	1	7	108	5	100	3	0
Almont	2,809	4	0	1	0	3	32	5	26	1	0
Alpena	9,900	41	1	12	2	26	154	27	114	13	1
Ann Arbor	120,647	294	1	49	38	206	1,592	153	1,358	81	4
Argentine Township	6,473	6	0	3	1	2	16	3	11	2	1
Armada	1,714	2	0	1	0	1	1	1	0	0	0
Auburn Hills	25,149	107	0	30	13	64	405	31	345	29	0
Au Gres	823	0	0	0	0	0	0	0	0	0	0
Augusta	900	3	0	2	0	1	13	1	12	0	0
Bad Axe	2,893	4	0	1	0	3	22	2	20	0	0
Bancroft	494	0	0	0	0	0	3	3	0	0	1
Bangor	1,827	10	0	1	0	9	29	1	25	3	0
Baraga	1,935	0	0	0	0	0	0	0	0	0	0
Baroda-Lake Township	3,890	8	0	2	0	6	37	13	20	4	0
Barryton	353	0	0	0	0	0	0	0	0	0	0
Barry Township	3,531	1	0	0	0	1	22	4	18	0	0
Bath Township	13,167	6	0	2	2	2	97	13	75	9	1
Battle Creek	60,479	540	8	38	30	464	1,569	335	1,066	168	17
Bay City	32,485	276	0	48	25	203	500	104	331	65	7
Beaverton	1,177	2	0	1	0	1	10	0	6	4	0
Belding	5,741	15	0	9	0	6	79	10	64	5	0
Bellaire	1,064	0	0	0	0	0	0	0	0	0	0
Belleville	3,887	8	0	2	3	3	34	9	23	2	0
Bellevue	1,305	0	0	0	0	0	0	0	0	0	0
Benton Harbor	9,710	310	2	13	11	284	308	66	207	35	6
Benton Township	14,251	349	5	19	24	301	631	97	469	65	4
Berkley	15,410	8	0	3	1	4	55	1	46	8	0
Berrien Springs-Oronoko Township	8,894	9	0	2	0	7	66	29	35	2	0
Beverly Hills	10,363	8	0	0	0	8	39	7	30	2	0
Big Rapids	10,355	36	0	4	1	31	97	17	75	5	1
Birch Run	1,468	4	0	1	2	1	64	8	53	3	1
Birmingham	21,536	2	0	0	0	2	120	13	97	10	0
Blackman Township	37,034	135	5	37	8	85	1,033	116	852	65	3
Blissfield	3,259	5	0	0	0	5	14	0	13	1	0
Bloomfield Hills	4,012	2	0	0	0	2	18	4	13	1	0
Bloomfield Township	42,059	10	0	4	1	5	216	18	184	14	0
Boyne City	3,729	13	0	1	0	12	38	1	36	1	0
Brandon Township	16,161	21	0	3	1	17	31	8	23	0	1
Breckenridge	1,267	0	0	0	0	0	9	3	6	0	0
Bridgeport Township	9,736	40	2	2	3	33	131	23	94	14	1
Bridgman	2,204	3	0	1	0	2	16	3	10	3	0
Brighton	7,679	4	0	1	0	3	99	7	90	2	0
Bronson	2,298	5	0	2	0	3	49	3	40	6	0
Brown City	1,242	3	0	0	0	3	15	0	15	0	0
Brownstown Township	32,255	60	0	8	2	50	210	44	137	29	2
Buchanan	4,242	12	0	4	0	8	108	15	86	7	0
Buena Vista Township	8,047	94	1	5	4	84	132	40	75	17	1
Burton	28,427	192	1	23	11	157	648	104	487	57	2
Cadillac	10,513	30	0	7	0	23	193	22	164	7	1
Cambridge Township	5,679	0	0	0	0	0	24	5	19	0	0
Canton Township	94,128	134	0	19	5	110	787	59	680	48	4
Capac	1,832	5	0	0	0	5	19	4	14	1	0
Caro	3,959	13	0	4	0	9	142	5	131	6	0
Carrollton Township	5,599	24	0	7	1	16	59	12	41	6	1
Carson City	1,111	3	0	2	0	1	4	1	3	0	1
Caseville	730	0	0	0	0	0	7	1	6	0	0
Caspian-Gaastra	1,162	3	0	0	0	3	5	3	2	0	0
Cass City	2,260	3	0	2	0	1	29	1	28	0	0
Cassopolis	1,692	2	0	1	0	1	11	3	7	1	0
Center Line	8,162	22	1	5	4	12	107	12	74	21	0
Central Lake	938	0	0	0	0	0	0	0	0	0	0
Charlevoix	2,486	6	0	2	0	4	27	1	26	0	1
Charlotte	9,091	29	0	13	2	14	169	17	140	12	0

Table 8. Offenses Known to Law Enforcement, by Selected State and City, 2020—Continued

(Number.)

State/city	Population	Violent crime	Murder and nonnegligent manslaughter	Rape[1]	Robbery	Aggravated assault	Property crime	Burglary	Larceny-theft	Motor vehicle theft	Arson[2]
Cheboygan	4,668	2	0	0	0	2	78	8	68	2	0
Chelsea	5,471	7	0	2	1	4	36	2	32	2	0
Chesaning	2,221	13	0	1	0	12	13	3	9	1	0
Chikaming Township	3,078	2	0	1	0	1	48	24	23	1	0
Chocolay Township	5,918	9	0	1	0	8	13	1	11	1	0
Clare	3,071	8	0	3	0	5	32	5	26	1	0
Clarkston	921	0	0	0	0	0	2	0	2	0	0
Clawson	11,846	8	0	1	0	7	56	7	47	2	1
Clayton Township	7,057	3	0	1	0	2	25	10	14	1	0
Clay Township	8,886	23	0	3	0	20	75	14	55	6	0
Clinton	2,285	4	0	2	0	2	9	1	7	1	0
Clinton Township	100,884	395	2	42	30	321	1,234	146	913	175	2
Clio	2,482	10	0	0	1	9	37	11	23	3	1
Coldwater	12,076	40	1	9	5	25	253	34	196	23	1
Coleman	1,199	1	0	1	0	0	10	1	8	1	0
Coloma Township	6,319	11	0	4	0	7	98	34	57	7	1
Colon	1,155	8	0	1	0	7	23	6	15	2	0
Columbia Township	7,350	11	0	6	0	5	40	5	28	7	0
Commerce Township	39,689	22	0	1	0	21	167	17	139	11	3
Constantine	2,110	6	0	3	0	3	27	9	14	4	0
Corunna	3,327	6	0	2	0	4	18	5	12	1	0
Covert Township	2,891	18	0	1	1	16	55	19	33	3	1
Croswell	2,269	8	0	2	0	6	36	5	26	5	0
Crystal Falls	1,354	2	0	0	0	2	10	5	5	0	0
Davison	4,848	17	0	5	0	12	65	15	28	22	0
Davison Township	19,197	36	0	3	2	31	180	32	132	16	1
Dearborn	93,507	277	5	25	31	216	1,662	194	1,215	253	3
Dearborn Heights	55,105	291	1	26	15	249	769	148	497	124	11
Decatur	1,724	7	0	2	1	4	54	9	43	2	0
Denton Township	5,421	2	0	1	0	1	53	1	49	3	0
Detroit	659,616	14,370	328	676	1,848	11,518	21,178	4,361	11,239	5,578	762
DeWitt	4,844	4	0	1	0	3	40	4	34	2	0
DeWitt Township	15,756	20	0	8	2	10	129	21	95	13	2
Dowagiac	5,648	49	0	6	3	40	164	13	122	29	0
Dryden Township	4,724	2	0	1	0	1	19	5	13	1	0
Durand	3,818	12	0	1	1	10	24	0	21	3	0
East Grand Rapids	12,105	2	0	1	0	1	167	16	135	16	0
East Jordan	2,348	1	0	0	0	1	53	3	45	5	0
East Lansing	48,098	74	0	17	13	44	817	86	568	163	14
Eastpointe	32,046	241	6	20	38	177	668	104	426	138	5
Eaton Rapids	5,248	34	0	5	1	28	70	9	51	10	1
Eau Claire	594	0	0	0	0	0	2	0	1	1	0
Ecorse	9,576	170	4	11	14	141	236	33	164	39	8
Elk Rapids	1,613	0	0	0	0	0	0	0	0	0	0
Elkton	743	1	0	1	0	0	5	2	3	0	0
Elsie	980	1	0	0	0	1	2	0	1	1	0
Emmett Township	11,611	31	1	5	4	21	563	34	513	16	0
Escanaba	12,111	55	0	15	0	40	291	24	262	5	2
Essexville	3,257	4	0	1	0	3	12	5	7	0	0
Evart	1,879	8	0	2	0	6	24	6	16	2	1
Fair Haven Township	1,038	0	0	0	0	0	0	0	0	0	0
Farmington	10,503	4	0	2	0	2	34	3	30	1	0
Farmington Hills	80,708	84	0	11	9	64	558	65	439	54	4
Fennville	1,433	3	0	1	0	2	7	0	7	0	0
Fenton	11,369	13	0	1	2	10	215	11	197	7	2
Ferndale	20,048	51	0	2	8	41	309	33	228	48	1
Flat Rock	10,019	27	0	3	4	20	107	8	77	22	2
Flint	94,842	996	44	67	83	802	1,614	406	1,004	204	20
Flint Township	30,178	313	6	16	35	256	1,112	144	857	111	13
Flushing	7,827	10	0	1	3	6	48	10	36	2	2
Flushing Township	10,133	1	0	1	0	0	36	9	24	3	0
Forsyth Township	6,182	12	0	4	0	8	16	1	15	0	1
Fowlerville	2,895	5	1	1	0	3	140	7	129	4	0
Frankenmuth	5,595	4	0	0	0	4	54	2	48	4	1
Frankfort	1,291	5	0	2	0	3	13	2	11	0	0
Franklin	3,256	1	0	0	0	1	18	1	17	0	0
Fraser	14,480	29	0	10	2	17	179	12	144	23	1
Fremont	4,077	8	0	2	1	5	61	4	54	3	0
Fruitport Township	14,476	23	0	2	4	17	485	15	462	8	0
Gagetown	360	0	0	0	0	0	0	0	0	0	0
Gaines Township	6,103	3	0	1	0	2	6	2	2	2	0
Galien	527	0	0	0	0	0	0	0	0	0	0
Garden City	26,282	54	0	8	12	34	204	38	134	32	0
Garfield Township	850	0	0	0	0	0	0	0	0	0	0
Gaylord	3,692	24	0	4	2	18	172	5	158	9	1
Genesee Township	20,325	112	0	10	9	93	248	70	148	30	1
Gerrish Township	2,946	2	0	1	0	1	29	4	24	1	0
Gibraltar	4,505	1	0	1	0	0	43	7	29	7	0
Gladstone	4,670	7	0	2	0	5	31	2	29	0	0
Gladwin	2,887	20	0	2	1	17	40	7	24	9	1
Grand Beach/Michiana	463	0	0	0	0	0	17	2	14	1	0
Grand Blanc	7,831	20	0	4	5	11	73	15	57	1	0
Grand Blanc Township	36,498	67	0	7	6	54	477	80	358	39	2

Table 8. Offenses Known to Law Enforcement, by Selected State and City, 2020—Continued

(Number.)

State/city	Population	Violent crime	Murder and nonnegligent manslaughter	Rape[1]	Robbery	Aggravated assault	Property crime	Burglary	Larceny-theft	Motor vehicle theft	Arson[2]
Grand Haven	11,126	25	0	4	1	20	118	7	102	9	0
Grand Ledge	7,908	9	0	6	0	3	65	9	52	4	0
Grand Rapids	202,513	1,443	28	121	192	1,102	3,956	463	2,912	581	38
Grandville	15,913	49	2	15	10	22	386	42	314	30	0
Grant	883	2	0	1	0	1	16	1	15	0	0
Grayling	1,848	10	0	1	0	9	42	4	38	0	0
Green Oak Township	19,154	10	0	3	0	7	97	17	75	5	0
Greenville	8,415	41	0	12	4	25	317	30	273	14	1
Grosse Ile Township	10,114	1	0	0	0	1	19	5	14	0	0
Grosse Pointe	5,127	4	0	0	0	4	41	1	36	4	0
Grosse Pointe Farms	9,077	3	0	0	1	2	85	15	60	10	0
Grosse Pointe Park	10,998	13	0	4	0	9	120	12	96	12	0
Grosse Pointe Shores	2,786	0	0	0	0	0	8	0	6	2	0
Grosse Pointe Woods	15,269	11	0	3	0	8	122	15	90	17	0
Hamburg Township	21,867	10	0	1	0	9	33	7	24	2	0
Hampton Township	9,354	18	0	6	1	11	85	9	71	5	0
Hamtramck	21,514	180	1	10	35	134	320	58	191	71	3
Hancock	4,487	4	0	1	0	3	25	2	22	1	0
Harbor Beach	1,575	7	0	2	0	5	27	6	18	3	0
Harbor Springs	1,207	1	0	0	0	1	5	0	5	0	0
Harper Woods	13,679	143	3	5	10	125	412	63	240	109	2
Hart	2,064	10	0	1	0	9	140	5	128	7	0
Hartford	2,582	15	0	2	0	13	19	0	18	1	0
Hastings	7,307	35	0	17	0	18	96	9	80	7	2
Hazel Park	16,340	33	1	0	6	26	215	30	165	20	0
Hesperia	927	4	0	2	0	2	19	6	12	1	3
Highland Park	10,680	205	6	13	26	160	280	51	169	60	8
Highland Township	20,281	10	0	5	0	5	59	7	41	11	0
Hillsdale	7,972	10	0	5	0	5	97	16	72	9	1
Holland	33,228	132	0	45	8	79	527	55	447	25	3
Holly	6,157	14	0	2	0	12	54	9	41	4	2
Houghton	7,760	9	0	6	0	3	102	3	99	0	1
Howell	9,620	22	0	2	1	19	79	12	59	8	1
Hudson	2,200	19	0	5	0	14	45	10	31	4	1
Huntington Woods	6,268	0	0	0	0	0	19	0	18	1	0
Huron Township	16,288	33	0	5	0	28	98	28	61	9	0
Imlay City	3,567	9	0	5	0	4	27	4	17	6	0
Independence Township	37,302	18	0	3	3	12	127	22	100	5	4
Inkster	24,173	318	10	34	24	250	543	150	294	99	13
Ionia	11,153	17	0	10	0	7	107	16	80	11	0
Iron Mountain	7,274	0	0	0	0	0	0	0	0	0	0
Iron River	2,807	7	0	0	0	7	36	6	25	5	0
Ironwood	4,816	5	0	0	0	5	30	3	21	6	0
Ishpeming	6,410	23	0	7	0	16	34	6	26	2	0
Ishpeming Township	3,513	2	0	0	0	2	2	0	2	0	0
Jackson	32,332	350	7	47	32	264	1,001	173	722	106	8
Jonesville	2,210	3	1	0	0	2	88	4	81	3	2
Kalamazoo	76,411	1,094	14	77	136	867	3,670	737	2,445	488	64
Kalamazoo Township	24,562	130	2	12	10	106	762	168	499	95	5
Kalkaska	2,103	7	0	4	0	3	20	3	17	0	0
Keego Harbor	3,431	6	0	0	0	6	13	3	10	0	0
Kentwood	52,263	229	4	28	26	171	1,207	166	837	204	4
Kinde	410	0	0	0	0	0	0	0	0	0	0
Kingsford	4,931	3	0	0	0	3	13	1	9	3	0
Kingston	406	3	0	0	0	3	6	0	3	3	0
Kinross Township	7,439	9	0	1	0	8	6	0	4	2	0
Laingsburg	1,285	0	0	0	0	0	13	1	10	2	0
Lake Angelus	308	0	0	0	0	0	1	0	1	0	0
Lake Linden	942	0	0	0	0	0	1	0	1	0	0
Lake Odessa	2,043	5	1	2	0	2	12	2	10	0	0
Lake Orion	3,206	5	0	0	1	4	15	2	13	0	0
Lakeview	1,002	1	0	0	0	1	14	0	13	1	1
L'Anse	1,824	0	0	0	0	0	0	0	0	0	0
Lansing	118,651	1,699	16	121	195	1,367	3,565	1,002	1,993	570	44
Lansing Township	8,254	57	2	6	8	41	406	41	329	36	2
Lapeer	8,505	22	0	9	2	11	162	15	142	5	1
Lapeer Township	5,017	1	0	0	0	1	11	1	10	0	0
Lathrup Village	4,090	3	0	0	2	1	13	1	10	2	0
Laurium	1,889	0	0	0	0	0	20	1	15	4	0
Lawton	1,800	7	0	1	0	6	23	5	17	1	0
Lennon	479	0	0	0	0	0	16	14	2	0	1
Leslie	1,903	0	0	0	0	0	18	2	15	1	0
Lexington	1,114	2	0	1	0	1	2	0	2	0	0
Lincoln Township	14,587	8	0	4	0	4	169	20	140	9	2
Linden	3,934	2	0	0	0	2	14	2	12	0	0
Litchfield	1,327	8	0	0	0	8	14	1	12	1	0
Livonia	93,342	209	0	26	12	171	1,196	115	979	102	8
Lowell	4,216	4	0	2	0	2	35	3	29	3	0
Ludington	8,111	31	0	16	0	15	116	11	98	7	0
Lyon Township	21,838	17	0	5	3	9	100	16	73	11	1
Mackinac Island	469	2	0	2	0	0	49	0	49	0	0
Mackinaw City	794	3	1	0	0	2	14	1	13	0	1
Madison Heights	29,906	70	2	7	14	47	458	51	343	64	1

Table 8. Offenses Known to Law Enforcement, by Selected State and City, 2020—Continued

(Number.)

State/city	Population	Violent crime	Murder and nonnegligent manslaughter	Rape[1]	Robbery	Aggravated assault	Property crime	Burglary	Larceny-theft	Motor vehicle theft	Arson[2]
Madison Township	8,229	10	0	3	0	7	178	6	167	5	0
Mancelona	1,364	0	0	0	0	0	0	0	0	0	0
Manistee	6,103	22	0	5	1	16	112	18	88	6	1
Manistique	2,923	13	0	6	0	7	42	8	31	3	0
Manton	1,588	0	0	0	0	0	0	0	0	0	0
Marenisco Township	484	0	0	0	0	0	0	0	0	0	0
Marine City	4,038	5	0	2	0	3	26	1	23	2	0
Marlette	1,755	4	0	1	0	3	7	2	4	1	0
Marquette	20,957	46	0	15	3	28	146	11	127	8	0
Marshall	6,954	19	0	3	2	14	88	8	72	8	3
Marysville	9,643	8	0	0	0	8	64	13	49	2	0
Mason	8,480	14	0	4	0	10	55	6	45	4	2
Mattawan	1,981	6	1	0	0	5	24	5	14	5	1
Mayville	878	0	0	0	0	0	5	1	4	0	0
Melvindale	10,199	101	1	7	6	87	214	32	151	31	3
Memphis	1,174	0	0	0	0	0	5	1	4	0	0
Mendon	848	0	0	0	0	0	5	1	2	2	0
Menominee	7,971	22	0	5	0	17	123	15	104	4	4
Meridian Township	43,598	95	0	18	12	65	868	85	736	47	0
Metamora Township	4,283	4	0	1	0	3	9	4	5	0	0
Metro Police Authority of Genesee County	19,883	47	1	7	3	36	221	46	144	31	0
Midland	41,682	62	0	18	1	43	329	40	283	6	1
Milan	6,065	10	0	1	0	9	56	7	47	2	0
Milford	17,038	6	0	3	1	2	59	11	45	3	0
Millington	989	1	0	0	0	1	8	1	7	0	0
Montague	2,361	1	0	0	0	1	15	1	12	2	0
Montrose Township	7,431	6	0	0	0	6	34	7	24	3	0
Morenci	2,139	4	0	1	0	3	19	2	15	2	0
Morrice	908	0	0	0	0	0	4	1	3	0	0
Mount Morris	2,822	11	0	1	0	10	61	15	42	4	0
Mount Morris Township	20,207	141	7	8	10	116	342	150	137	55	6
Mount Pleasant	24,668	46	3	9	5	29	316	26	269	21	1
Munising	2,188	1	0	0	0	1	22	1	19	2	0
Muskegon	36,391	254	5	8	20	221	1,004	174	740	90	6
Muskegon Heights	10,724	184	3	12	14	155	394	81	270	43	14
Muskegon Township	18,022	36	0	5	5	26	376	53	301	22	1
Napoleon Township	6,767	3	0	1	0	2	13	1	10	2	0
Nashville	1,691	0	0	0	0	0	14	3	10	1	0
Negaunee	4,520	4	0	1	1	2	21	4	16	1	0
Newaygo	2,076	15	0	4	0	11	48	2	43	3	1
New Baltimore	12,377	14	0	2	0	12	47	0	45	2	0
New Buffalo	1,866	3	0	3	0	0	26	4	21	1	0
New Era	439	0	0	0	0	0	1	0	1	0	0
New Lothrop	551	1	0	0	0	1	3	1	2	0	0
Niles	11,102	74	0	16	11	47	328	42	225	61	2
Northfield Township	8,720	9	0	1	1	7	65	17	44	4	0
North Muskegon	3,793	4	0	4	0	0	31	1	29	1	0
Northville	5,956	8	0	0	1	7	33	3	28	2	0
Northville Township	29,434	27	0	3	2	22	174	22	142	10	3
Norton Shores	24,742	45	0	7	10	28	537	53	441	43	0
Norway	2,736	0	0	0	0	0	0	0	0	0	0
Novi	61,554	60	1	15	3	41	429	21	372	36	3
Oakland Township	19,882	10	0	3	0	7	26	4	22	0	1
Oak Park	29,432	94	2	18	11	63	388	106	196	86	6
Olivet	1,782	3	0	2	0	1	7	1	5	1	0
Ontwa Township-Edwardsburg	6,602	13	0	4	0	9	90	18	64	8	0
Orchard Lake	2,483	3	0	0	0	3	11	1	10	0	0
Orion Township	37,125	19	0	1	1	17	135	21	100	14	1
Oscoda Township	6,741	50	0	9	0	41	77	17	59	1	0
Otisville	832	0	0	0	0	0	0	0	0	0	0
Otsego	3,997	7	0	3	0	4	42	7	31	4	1
Ovid	1,616	1	0	0	0	1	3	0	3	0	0
Owendale	222	0	0	0	0	0	0	0	0	0	0
Owosso[5]	14,363	98	0	16	3	79			124	9	3
Oxford	3,570	0	0	0	0	0	8	1	4	3	0
Oxford Township	19,592	18	0	1	1	16	66	10	52	4	0
Paw Paw	3,351	13	0	1	2	10	139	13	121	5	0
Peck	591	0	0	0	0	0	0	0	0	0	0
Pentwater	847	1	0	0	0	1	3	1	2	0	0
Perry	2,084	1	0	0	1	0	11	0	10	1	0
Petoskey	5,767	11	1	2	1	7	30	10	15	5	0
Pigeon	1,111	0	0	0	0	0	0	0	0	0	0
Pinckney	2,419	2	0	0	0	2	11	1	8	2	0
Pittsfield Township	39,400	78	1	18	12	47	535	43	440	52	2
Plainwell	3,774	9	0	4	2	3	37	2	34	1	0
Pleasant Ridge	2,423	0	0	0	0	0	11	2	9	0	0
Plymouth	9,159	7	0	3	1	3	52	9	36	7	2
Plymouth Township	26,988	15	0	6	3	6	136	11	112	13	5
Pontiac	59,411	840	13	50	88	689	1,096	240	743	113	18
Portage	49,798	111	2	15	10	84	1,340	153	1,098	89	8
Port Austin	618	2	0	0	0	2	5	0	5	0	0
Port Huron	28,602	225	1	30	18	176	631	124	467	40	12

Table 8. Offenses Known to Law Enforcement, by Selected State and City, 2020—Continued

(Number.)

State/city	Population	Violent crime	Murder and nonnegligent manslaughter	Rape[1]	Robbery	Aggravated assault	Property crime	Burglary	Larceny-theft	Motor vehicle theft	Arson[2]
Portland	3,955	7	0	1	0	6	29	6	23	0	0
Potterville	2,765	6	0	2	0	4	14	1	7	6	0
Prairieville Township	3,534	0	0	0	0	0	10	4	6	0	0
Quincy	1,614	4	0	1	0	3	23	7	15	1	0
Raisin Township	7,784	2	0	1	0	1	11	2	8	1	0
Reading	1,040	0	0	0	0	0	0	0	0	0	0
Redford Township	46,510	305	4	34	30	237	748	171	375	202	7
Reed City	2,388	20	0	5	2	13	53	10	41	2	2
Reese	1,355	1	0	0	0	1	8	0	8	0	0
Richfield Township, Genesee County	8,292	10	1	2	0	7	56	16	33	7	0
Richfield Township, Roscommon County	3,653	6	0	1	0	5	1	1	0	0	0
Richland	841	0	0	0	0	0	10	1	9	0	0
Richland Township, Saginaw County	3,904	5	0	0	0	5	22	3	17	2	0
Richmond	5,856	23	0	2	0	21	37	0	35	2	0
River Rouge	7,369	64	4	0	5	55	107	20	69	18	5
Riverview	11,986	15	0	4	0	11	70	4	58	8	1
Rochester	13,362	8	0	3	0	5	40	4	35	1	0
Rochester Hills	74,913	51	0	7	2	42	331	29	283	19	5
Rockford	6,472	11	0	8	0	3	77	7	69	1	0
Rockwood	3,145	3	0	0	1	2	17	2	14	1	0
Rogers City	2,636	9	0	7	0	2	18	4	13	1	0
Romeo	3,607	4	0	3	0	1	13	1	12	0	0
Romulus	23,533	246	3	22	16	205	474	86	303	85	3
Roosevelt Park	3,793	14	0	4	3	7	215	6	205	4	0
Roseville	46,983	217	5	49	30	133	1,138	110	902	126	7
Rothbury	448	1	0	1	0	0	3	2	1	0	0
Royal Oak	59,506	42	0	12	3	27	398	28	333	37	4
Saginaw	47,767	1,029	24	57	62	886	720	225	388	107	24
Saginaw Township	38,971	85	1	13	14	57	588	88	474	26	5
Saline	9,400	10	0	2	0	8	55	4	48	3	0
Sandusky	2,503	9	0	1	0	8	51	4	47	0	0
Saugatuck-Douglas	2,322	1	0	0	1	0	17	5	12	0	0
Sault Ste. Marie	13,340	31	0	12	3	16	176	16	154	6	1
Schoolcraft	1,554	5	0	2	0	3	19	1	17	1	0
Scottville	1,211	2	0	1	0	1	6	0	6	0	0
Sebewaing	1,618	0	0	0	0	0	7	3	4	0	0
Shelby	2,008	9	0	0	0	9	27	0	25	2	0
Shelby Township	81,416	104	0	21	8	75	406	42	323	41	2
Shepherd	1,484	0	0	0	0	0	9	0	8	1	0
Somerset Township	4,520	0	0	0	0	0	15	0	13	2	0
Southfield	72,794	288	3	33	35	217	1,309	190	759	360	7
Southgate	28,848	85	0	10	13	62	505	61	410	34	3
South Haven	4,341	28	1	4	1	22	229	19	194	16	2
South Lyon	11,877	13	1	1	0	11	43	3	38	2	0
Sparta	4,429	4	0	1	1	2	62	5	48	9	0
Spring Arbor Township	7,838	4	0	1	0	3	12	2	10	0	0
Springfield Township	14,551	7	1	3	0	3	50	9	34	7	1
Springport Township	2,156	1	0	0	0	1	6	4	2	0	0
Stanton	1,423	0	0	0	0	0	3	0	2	1	0
St. Charles	1,880	3	0	0	0	3	18	1	17	0	0
St. Clair	5,259	4	0	0	0	4	54	11	42	1	0
St. Clair Shores	58,898	103	0	12	10	81	436	60	328	48	1
Sterling Heights	132,745	233	2	33	22	176	1,140	95	891	154	4
St. Ignace	2,311	4	0	1	0	3	19	2	16	1	0
St. Johns	7,954	10	0	1	0	9	54	10	41	3	0
St. Joseph	8,313	23	0	4	0	19	100	12	81	7	0
St. Joseph Township	9,638	26	0	8	1	17	94	15	77	2	1
St. Louis	7,244	10	0	4	0	6	42	4	35	3	0
Stockbridge	1,253	7	0	1	0	6	10	3	7	0	0
Sturgis	10,831	73	1	12	6	54	260	42	173	45	2
Sumpter Township	9,348	18	4	2	0	12	51	16	33	2	0
Sylvan Lake	1,869	2	0	0	1	1	14	3	10	1	0
Tawas	4,492	9	0	2	1	6	51	9	42	0	0
Taylor	60,698	371	1	25	35	310	1,108	182	790	136	20
Tecumseh	8,392	10	0	3	1	6	42	9	28	5	1
Thetford Township	6,605	0	0	0	0	0	0	0	0	0	0
Thomas Township	11,411	15	0	3	1	11	85	12	68	5	0
Three Oaks	1,537	12	0	3	2	7	35	8	26	1	0
Three Rivers	7,604	70	1	10	5	54	283	60	194	29	0
Tittabawassee Township	10,009	9	0	2	0	7	38	4	30	4	0
Traverse City	15,855	85	0	18	5	62	211	20	174	17	2
Trenton	18,085	22	0	7	3	12	109	9	85	15	1
Troy	84,441	86	1	9	15	61	732	46	635	51	2
Tuscarora Township	2,904	3	0	0	0	3	39	4	35	0	0
Ubly	779	2	0	1	0	1	10	1	9	0	0
Unadilla Township	3,468	4	0	2	0	2	16	1	11	4	0
Union City	1,561	0	0	0	0	0	0	0	0	0	0
Utica	5,149	7	0	5	1	1	178	4	169	5	2
Van Buren Township	28,355	96	0	5	7	84	470	45	366	59	1
Vassar	2,525	12	0	0	0	12	14	3	10	1	0

Table 8. Offenses Known to Law Enforcement, by Selected State and City, 2020—Continued

(Number.)

State/city	Population	Violent crime	Murder and nonnegligent manslaughter	Rape[1]	Robbery	Aggravated assault	Property crime	Burglary	Larceny-theft	Motor vehicle theft	Arson[2]
Vernon	767	0	0	0	0	0	5	0	5	0	0
Vicksburg	3,554	4	0	2	0	2	58	10	43	5	0
Walker	25,020	48	1	9	9	29	513	51	406	56	0
Walled Lake	7,142	6	1	0	0	5	48	7	32	9	0
Warren	133,928	672	12	93	91	476	1,938	348	1,169	421	23
Waterford Township	72,735	162	2	31	15	114	557	118	367	72	5
Watersmeet Township	1,350	0	0	0	0	0	0	0	0	0	0
Watervliet	1,639	2	0	1	0	1	20	0	16	4	0
Wayland	4,241	11	0	4	1	6	33	4	27	2	0
Wayne	16,734	108	0	16	10	82	219	47	142	30	5
West Bloomfield Township	65,711	37	2	7	3	25	244	37	193	14	0
West Branch	2,042	4	0	2	0	2	27	3	24	0	1
Westland	81,244	330	4	49	30	247	883	139	647	97	18
White Cloud	1,385	3	0	2	0	1	11	4	7	0	0
Whitehall	2,846	3	0	1	0	2	23	2	20	1	0
White Lake Township	31,505	19	1	1	1	16	106	17	81	8	3
White Pigeon	1,526	1	0	0	0	1	25	4	15	6	1
Williamston	3,976	4	0	1	0	3	23	1	19	3	0
Wixom	14,110	19	0	5	3	11	178	11	150	17	0
Wolverine Lake	4,835	2	0	0	0	2	12	0	12	0	0
Woodhaven	12,427	8	0	2	0	6	141	4	112	25	0
Woodland Township	2,139	0	0	0	0	0	0	0	0	0	0
Wyoming	76,071	411	5	51	62	293	1,143	133	714	296	14
Yale	1,861	8	0	0	0	8	12	8	4	0	0
Ypsilanti	20,240	288	1	51	24	212	591	105	435	51	3
Zeeland	5,540	10	0	4	0	6	30	4	23	3	0
Zilwaukee	1,516	0	0	0	0	0	7	0	6	1	0
MINNESOTA											
Aitkin[4]	1,969	4	0	1	1	2	50	11	33	6	0
Akeley[4]	444	1	0	0	0	1	16	1	15	0	0
Albany[4]	2,787	1	0	1	0	0	6	0	6	0	1
Albert Lea	17,599	35	4	2	2	27	487	82	372	33	3
Alexandria	13,978	53	0	8	1	44	411	23	370	18	1
Annandale[4]	3,549	6	0	1	0	5	31	0	28	3	0
Anoka	17,593	58	1	9	6	42	299	40	233	26	3
Appleton	1,316	10	0	0	0	10	46	12	33	1	0
Apple Valley	55,846	60	4	21	12	23	907	68	790	49	6
Arlington[4]	2,136	1	0	0	0	1	5	0	5	0	0
Atwater[4]	1,117	0	0	0	0	0	1	0	1	0	0
Austin	25,267	70	1	9	6	54	402	59	322	21	1
Avon[4]	1,613	3	0	1	0	2	19	3	15	1	0
Babbitt[4]	1,485	4	0	1	0	3	3	1	2	0	0
Barnesville[4]	2,606	0	0	0	0	0	2	0	2	0	0
Battle Lake	935	0	0	0	0	0	1	0	1	0	0
Baxter[4]	8,447	12	0	3	1	8	349	25	321	3	1
Bayport[4]	3,799	1	0	0	0	1	27	1	22	4	0
Becker	4,997	6	0	4	0	2	31	9	20	2	1
Belgrade/Brooten[4]	1,535	0	0	0	0	0	9	0	9	0	0
Belle Plaine	7,243	8	0	2	0	6	52	6	43	3	0
Bemidji	15,567	94	1	16	7	70	1,141	87	988	66	4
Benson	3,022	3	0	0	0	3	0	0	0	0	0
Big Lake[4]	11,355	13	0	1	1	11	46	8	30	8	0
Blackduck[4]	839	1	0	0	0	1	10	1	8	1	1
Blaine	66,588	83	2	19	19	43	1,457	105	1,240	112	10
Blooming Prairie[4]	1,930	0	0	0	0	0	7	1	6	0	0
Bloomington	85,159	266	5	61	67	133	2,889	228	2,401	260	13
Blue Earth	3,087	3	0	3	0	0	20	4	14	2	0
Bovey[4]	782	1	0	0	0	1	13	1	11	1	0
Braham	1,819	2	0	1	0	1	21	2	16	3	0
Brainerd	13,417	70	0	16	3	51	489	87	359	43	4
Breckenridge[4]	3,148	4	0	0	0	4	61	10	50	1	0
Breezy Point[4]	2,424	2	0	0	0	2	8	1	6	1	0
Brooklyn Center	30,744	148	0	23	44	81	1,109	110	799	200	9
Brooklyn Park	80,897	350	3	37	95	215	2,756	286	2,125	345	9
Brownton[4]	716	0	0	0	0	0	2	0	2	0	0
Buffalo[4]	16,550	12	0	2	1	9	227	14	208	5	0
Buffalo Lake[4]	680	0	0	0	0	0	7	0	7	0	0
Burnsville[4]	61,445	150	1	14	31	104	1,560	131	1,281	148	6
Caledonia[4]	2,741	0	0	0	0	0	0	0	0	0	0
Cambridge	9,302	5	0	0	0	5	373	19	336	18	0
Canby[4]	1,658	0	0	0	0	0	3	0	3	0	0
Cannon Falls	4,046	7	0	1	0	6	96	21	69	6	0
Centennial Lakes[4]	11,704	23	0	5	1	17	149	17	127	5	0
Champlin	25,517	20	0	3	8	9	269	22	236	11	2
Chaska	27,353	11	0	0	4	7	258	24	218	16	2
Chisholm[4]	4,835	11	0	0	0	11	109	23	80	6	0
Clara City[4]	1,267	0	0	0	0	0	0	0	0	0	0
Cleveland[4]	739	0	0	0	0	0	9	5	4	0	0
Cloquet[4]	11,995	15	0	2	0	13	238	11	214	13	0
Cold Spring/Richmond[4]	5,791	2	0	0	0	2	36	1	35	0	0
Columbia Heights	21,291	100	1	10	26	63	593	71	440	82	1
Comfrey[4]	351	0	0	0	0	0	1	0	1	0	0

Table 8. Offenses Known to Law Enforcement, by Selected State and City, 2020—Continued

(Number.)

State/city	Population	Violent crime	Murder and nonnegligent manslaughter	Rape[1]	Robbery	Aggravated assault	Property crime	Burglary	Larceny-theft	Motor vehicle theft	Arson[2]
Coon Rapids	63,162	121	1	22	18	80	1,379	178	1,108	93	13
Corcoran[4]	6,352	0	0	0	0	0	23	6	12	5	0
Cottage Grove	37,940	21	0	7	8	6	570	64	470	36	7
Crookston[4]	7,749	25	1	8	0	16	104	15	85	4	0
Crosby[4]	2,316	7	0	2	0	5	15	0	15	0	0
Crosslake[4]	2,378	1	0	0	0	1	31	3	26	2	0
Crystal	22,987	62	2	15	17	28	513	48	401	64	4
Cuyuna	365	0	0	0	0	0	3	0	3	0	0
Dayton[4]	6,958	3	0	1	1	1	51	10	35	6	0
Deephaven[4]	3,963	0	0	0	0	0	20	3	17	0	0
Deer River[4]	929	8	0	0	0	8	17	0	14	3	0
Deerwood	532	0	0	0	0	0	3	0	3	0	0
Detroit Lakes	9,352	15	0	1	3	11	255	46	184	25	1
Dilworth	4,469	9	0	1	1	7	272	18	241	13	1
Duluth	85,555	257	1	33	44	179	3,224	326	2,677	221	20
Dundas[4]	1,679	2	0	0	1	1	32	2	30	0	0
Eagle Lake	3,172	2	0	0	0	2	14	6	7	1	0
East Grand Forks[4]	8,526	12	0	0	0	12	59	13	43	3	0
East Range[4]	3,558	4	0	1	1	2	20	2	15	3	0
Eden Prairie	65,353	43	0	15	8	20	921	74	785	62	5
Eden Valley[4]	1,039	0	0	0	0	0	3	0	2	1	0
Edina	53,422	43	0	10	16	17	932	162	718	52	2
Elko New Market[4]	4,855	0	0	0	0	0	22	1	19	2	0
Elk River	25,467	24	1	7	1	15	444	40	373	31	0
Elmore	611	0	0	0	0	0	3	2	1	0	0
Ely[4]	3,344	7	1	2	1	3	37	4	33	0	0
Emily	843	0	0	0	0	0	2	0	1	1	0
Eveleth[4]	3,553	13	0	2	1	10	102	30	69	3	0
Fairfax[4]	1,120	4	0	1	0	3	14	1	12	1	0
Fairmont	9,964	35	0	9	2	24	181	32	142	7	3
Faribault	23,958	61	0	15	11	35	465	78	342	45	10
Farmington[4]	23,318	26	0	6	3	17	174	27	132	15	5
Fergus Falls	13,834	38	0	11	3	24	503	69	408	26	3
Floodwood[4]	521	0	0	0	0	0	3	0	1	2	0
Foley[4]	2,678	5	0	0	0	5	50	3	44	3	1
Forest Lake	21,230	38	1	18	2	17	607	61	499	47	4
Fridley	27,892	95	0	13	32	50	1,280	117	1,024	139	3
Fulda[4]	1,197	0	0	0	0	0	12	2	10	0	0
Gaylord[4]	2,196	3	0	1	0	2	33	3	28	2	4
Gilbert[4]	1,779	1	0	0	0	1	61	5	55	1	0
Glencoe[4]	5,532	9	0	4	0	5	58	12	44	2	1
Glenwood[4]	2,617	2	0	1	0	1	25	4	21	0	0
Goodhue	1,177	0	0	0	0	0	4	2	2	0	0
Goodview[4]	4,119	5	0	1	0	4	56	6	47	3	0
Grand Rapids[4]	11,253	32	3	5	1	23	138	5	128	5	1
Granite Falls[4]	2,677	8	0	0	1	7	27	1	22	4	0
Hastings[4]	22,959	38	0	4	3	31	390	43	310	37	3
Hawley	2,213	2	0	0	0	1	10	1	7	2	0
Hector[4]	1,039	1	1	0	0	0	36	2	32	2	0
Hermantown[4]	9,661	11	0	3	0	8	454	38	403	13	0
Hibbing[4]	15,802	20	0	4	1	15	193	22	154	17	3
Hill City[4]	580	0	0	0	0	0	15	1	14	0	0
Hokah[4]	543	0	0	0	0	0	0	0	0	0	0
Hopkins	18,568	40	0	11	7	22	449	57	344	48	2
Houston[4]	963	0	0	0	0	0	2	0	2	0	0
Hutchinson[4]	13,966	20	0	6	0	14	209	12	188	9	1
International Falls[4]	5,747	16	0	2	0	14	73	21	45	7	1
Inver Grove Heights[4]	35,861	87	0	23	15	49	766	136	546	84	5
Isanti[4]	6,219	0	0	0	0	0	103	4	90	9	0
Isle[4]	801	4	0	0	1	3	30	1	29	0	0
Janesville	2,251	3	0	2	0	1	26	8	16	2	0
Jordan[4]	6,514	11	0	4	1	6	58	6	46	6	0
Kasson[4]	6,549	8	0	4	0	4	48	8	35	5	0
Kenyon	1,799	0	0	0	0	0	4	1	1	2	0
La Crescent[4]	5,016	4	0	1	0	3	82	6	72	4	0
Lake City	5,129	5	0	3	0	2	63	5	54	4	0
Lake Crystal	2,482	5	0	0	0	5	16	3	11	2	0
Lakes Area	10,000	9	0	4	1	4	145	23	109	13	0
Lake Shore[4]	1,064	1	0	0	0	1	15	2	13	0	0
Le Center[4]	2,517	0	0	0	0	0	29	0	24	5	0
Lester Prairie[4]	1,724	1	0	0	0	1	9	3	6	0	0
Le Sueur[4]	4,058	3	0	1	0	2	26	1	24	1	0
Lewiston[4]	1,539	0	0	0	0	0	14	1	12	1	0
Lino Lakes	22,337	38	1	2	1	34	221	16	196	9	1
Litchfield[4]	6,641	5	0	2	0	3	84	5	74	5	0
Little Falls[4]	8,682	19	0	5	0	14	216	14	178	24	0
Long Prairie[4]	3,284	5	0	5	0	0	42	4	36	2	0
Lonsdale[4]	4,269	2	0	1	0	1	35	10	25	0	0
Madelia[4]	2,247	2	0	2	0	0	17	5	12	0	0
Madison Lake	1,192	1	0	0	0	1	4	3	1	0	0
Mankato	43,276	108	1	30	11	66	1,033	115	855	63	6
Maple Grove	73,939	56	4	19	9	24	1,206	105	1,057	44	3
Mapleton	2,189	7	0	0	0	7	15	3	10	2	0

Table 8. Offenses Known to Law Enforcement, by Selected State and City, 2020—Continued

(Number.)

State/city	Population	Violent crime	Murder and nonnegligent manslaughter	Rape[1]	Robbery	Aggravated assault	Property crime	Burglary	Larceny-theft	Motor vehicle theft	Arson[2]
Maplewood	41,096	133	0	10	42	81	1,901	304	1,348	249	9
Marshall	13,466	19	0	4	0	15	121	23	91	7	0
McGregor[4]	360	0	0	0	0	0	0	0	0	0	0
Medina	6,952	5	0	4	0	1	75	5	66	4	0
Melrose[4]	3,663	1	0	0	0	1	30	3	27	0	0
Mendota Heights[4]	11,373	14	0	2	4	8	165	23	126	16	0
Milaca[4]	2,927	8	0	1	0	7	130	14	113	3	0
Minneapolis	435,116	5,025	79	361	1,782	2,803	19,833	3,915	11,953	3,965	125
Minnesota Lake	634	0	0	0	0	0	0	0	0	0	0
Minnetonka[4]	54,561	22	0	7	6	9	717	120	550	47	2
Minnetrista	10,738	6	0	2	0	4	49	5	42	2	0
Montevideo[4]	5,009	4	0	2	0	2	16	7	8	1	0
Montgomery[4]	3,061	1	0	1	0	0	1	0	0	1	0
Moorhead	44,132	189	3	44	16	126	1,303	290	869	144	5
Moose Lake[4]	2,815	11	0	3	0	8	14	2	12	0	0
Morris[4]	5,339	12	0	4	0	8	93	18	71	4	5
Motley[4]	658	3	0	0	0	3	29	5	23	1	0
Mounds View	13,421	27	0	4	8	15	197	23	146	28	0
Mountain Lake[4]	2,029	4	0	2	0	2	12	1	10	1	0
Nashwauk[4]	948	1	0	1	0	0	1	1	0	0	0
New Brighton	22,843	36	0	4	12	20	615	75	490	50	0
New Hope[4]	20,970	35	0	9	13	13	565	45	439	81	0
New Prague[4]	8,374	8	0	1	0	7	81	5	74	2	0
New Richland	1,179	2	0	1	0	1	27	2	24	1	0
New Ulm[4]	13,181	9	0	1	0	8	121	16	98	7	0
New York Mills	1,226	0	0	0	0	0	8	0	5	3	0
Nisswa[4]	2,112	1	0	0	0	1	2	1	1	0	0
North Branch[4]	10,841	19	0	2	0	17	211	12	179	20	2
Northfield	20,820	18	0	10	0	8	168	27	138	3	3
North Mankato	14,008	18	0	8	1	9	135	12	116	7	1
North St. Paul[4]	12,591	22	0	4	5	13	307	32	235	40	0
Oakdale	27,990	32	0	10	14	8	936	76	787	73	5
Oak Park Heights[4]	5,071	0	0	0	0	0	239	11	221	7	0
Onamia[4]	862	9	0	3	0	6	40	0	36	4	0
Orono	20,387	14	0	5	1	8	126	21	102	3	0
Osakis	1,745	0	0	0	0	0	15	1	13	1	0
Osseo[4]	2,775	3	0	0	1	2	26	1	24	1	0
Owatonna	25,720	47	0	9	1	37	398	46	306	46	2
Park Rapids[4]	4,280	16	0	3	0	13	171	22	136	13	0
Paynesville[4]	2,530	0	0	0	0	0	4	1	3	0	0
Pelican Rapids	2,563	4	0	0	0	4	1	0	0	1	0
Pequot Lakes[4]	2,315	3	0	0	0	3	13	1	11	1	0
Perham	3,724	4	1	0	0	3	7	2	2	3	1
Pierz[4]	1,362	1	0	0	0	1	22	0	22	0	1
Pillager[4]	485	0	0	0	0	0	5	0	5	0	0
Pine River[4]	925	1	0	0	0	1	62	4	55	3	0
Plainview	3,293	7	0	4	0	3	16	0	15	1	0
Plymouth	80,843	53	0	14	6	33	1,157	246	826	85	2
Preston[4]	1,285	0	0	0	0	0	12	1	9	2	0
Princeton[4]	4,728	9	0	2	0	7	174	11	148	15	0
Prior Lake	27,748	47	0	15	9	23	596	32	526	38	1
Proctor[4]	3,025	6	0	1	1	4	82	5	74	3	0
Ramsey	28,205	21	0	6	1	14	219	30	169	20	4
Red Wing	16,304	41	0	15	4	22	489	61	403	25	2
Redwood Falls	4,930	10	0	2	1	7	136	13	114	9	0
Renville[4]	1,178	3	0	0	0	3	17	1	15	1	0
Robbinsdale	14,437	64	0	8	22	34	299	67	201	31	1
Rochester	120,336	300	5	74	44	177	2,314	332	1,828	154	7
Rogers	13,769	7	0	2	0	5	305	13	270	22	0
Roseau[4]	2,677	2	0	0	0	2	10	0	10	0	0
Rosemount	25,597	7	0	2	1	4	175	19	151	5	1
Roseville	36,675	116	0	18	59	39	2,370	283	1,917	170	1
Royalton[4]	1,231	0	0	0	0	0	33	0	32	1	0
Rushford[4]	1,692	0	0	0	0	0	0	0	0	0	0
Sartell[4]	19,262	3	0	2	0	1	324	31	285	8	1
Sauk Centre[4]	4,528	6	0	2	0	4	89	11	75	3	0
Sauk Rapids	14,300	28	0	3	1	24	322	39	268	15	1
Savage	33,020	33	0	9	8	16	406	61	321	24	1
Silver Bay[4]	1,750	1	0	0	0	1	18	1	14	3	0
Sleepy Eye	3,331	11	0	2	0	9	14	2	10	2	0
South Lake Minnetonka	12,867	8	0	1	2	5	86	10	75	1	1
South St. Paul[4]	20,053	34	2	2	4	26	500	62	348	90	4
Springfield[4]	1,989	2	0	1	1	0	36	3	31	2	0
Spring Grove	1,258	1	0	0	0	1	14	1	13	0	1
Spring Lake Park	6,978	36	0	1	7	28	224	37	155	32	0
St. Anthony	9,095	18	0	2	10	6	243	30	195	18	0
Staples[4]	2,999	8	0	0	0	8	74	4	67	3	1
Starbuck[4]	1,267	4	0	0	0	4	8	1	6	1	0
St. Charles[4]	3,760	2	0	0	0	2	37	1	34	2	0
St. Francis[4]	7,997	21	0	1	2	18	95	14	74	7	4
Stillwater	19,736	17	0	6	5	6	271	36	212	23	1
St. James[4]	4,380	8	0	2	0	6	66	14	47	5	0
St. Joseph[4]	7,448	2	0	1	0	1	61	5	50	6	1

Table 8. Offenses Known to Law Enforcement, by Selected State and City, 2020—Continued

(Number.)

State/city	Population	Violent crime	Murder and nonnegligent manslaughter	Rape[1]	Robbery	Aggravated assault	Property crime	Burglary	Larceny-theft	Motor vehicle theft	Arson[2]
St. Louis Park	49,058	63	0	13	18	32	1,475	132	1,206	137	1
St. Paul	309,859	2,320	30	232	723	1,335	11,783	2,146	6,808	2,829	225
St. Paul Park[4]	5,374	6	0	1	0	5	73	18	42	13	1
St. Peter	12,041	15	0	7	1	7	110	12	95	3	2
Thief River Falls[4]	8,849	11	0	3	1	7	140	19	116	5	0
Tracy[4]	2,068	4	0	2	0	2	30	11	19	0	0
Two Harbors[4]	3,506	6	0	0	0	6	3	2	1	0	0
Virginia	8,337	45	0	5	4	36	293	41	234	18	4
Wabasha	2,468	6	0	0	0	6	33	8	23	2	0
Wadena	4,108	9	0	1	0	8	52	1	49	2	0
Waite Park[4]	7,812	26	0	6	7	13	790	44	720	26	1
Walker[4]	932	0	0	0	0	0	22	2	19	1	0
Warroad[4]	1,795	0	0	0	0	0	10	1	9	0	0
Waseca	8,805	18	0	7	0	11	174	25	144	5	0
Wayzata[4]	6,602	3	0	1	1	1	116	24	83	9	0
Wells	2,152	11	0	1	0	10	5	0	3	2	0
West Hennepin[4]	5,995	0	0	0	0	0	49	12	34	3	0
West St. Paul[4]	20,007	87	2	15	25	45	1,559	87	1,359	113	0
Wheaton[4]	1,275	4	0	0	0	4	9	0	4	5	0
White Bear Lake	26,036	36	0	8	5	23	679	96	509	74	2
Willmar	19,901	94	0	6	5	83	579	52	475	52	4
Windom[4]	4,358	13	0	1	0	12	69	3	61	5	0
Winnebago	1,330	0	0	0	0	0	2	1	0	1	0
Winona[4]	26,487	45	0	11	4	30	683	84	565	34	1
Winsted[4]	2,230	4	0	2	0	2	12	1	10	1	0
Woodbury	74,110	71	1	25	22	23	1,522	233	1,223	66	7
Worthington	13,131	33	0	12	1	20	139	28	97	14	0
Wyoming[4]	8,095	4	0	0	2	2	85	8	65	12	0
Zumbrota	3,526	0	0	0	0	0	37	2	30	5	0
MISSISSIPPI											
Ackerman[4]	1,438	2	0	0	0	2	33	7	25	1	0
Amory	6,740	7	0	2	0	5	293	66	224	3	1
Batesville[4]	7,193	27	0	2	4	21	265	35	221	9	0
Bay Springs	1,645	3	1	0	0	2	18	7	10	1	0
Bay St. Louis	14,686	18	4	2	4	8	328	122	168	38	5
Brandon	24,545	24	0	14	6	4	179	41	118	20	1
Brookhaven	11,886	50	3	3	11	33	397	200	159	38	3
Byram	11,418	27	0	2	5	20	348	30	290	28	1
Cleveland	10,944	97	2	2	16	77	678	81	538	59	6
Clinton	24,349	16	0	1	8	7	463	32	415	16	1
Corinth	14,461	68	0	6	10	52	653	270	349	34	2
Derma	969	5	2	0	1	2	5	0	5	0	0
D'Iberville[4]	14,298	12	0	1	5	6	657	41	586	30	0
Edwards	1,000	7	0	0	0	7	11	5	6	0	0
Eupora[4]	1,985	7	0	0	1	6	13	6	6	1	0
Florence[4]	4,536	10	0	3	2	5	10	2	8	0	1
Flowood[4]	9,564	25	0	7	4	14	210	12	183	15	0
Forest[5]	5,517	40	0	3	6	31			87	19	2
Fulton	3,984	9	0	3	1	5	115	35	77	3	0
Gautier[4]	18,479	42	1	7	8	26	381	39	295	47	0
Gulfport	72,142	317	10	29	44	234	3,078	464	2,355	259	29
Hattiesburg	45,870	171	7	31	27	106	2,418	342	1,904	172	4
Heidelberg	655	4	0	0	2	2	8	2	6	0	0
Hernando	16,675	11	0	4	1	6	166	10	145	11	0
Horn Lake	27,404	47	5	1	15	26	605	46	488	71	3
Iuka	2,926	7	0	0	0	7	75	17	50	8	0
Kosciusko	6,652	14	0	2	1	11	95	34	58	3	2
Laurel[4,5]	18,317		3	11	17		679	182	443	54	6
Long Beach	16,161	17	0	1	2	14	302	39	243	20	0
Lucedale	3,179	19	1	0	1	17	135	36	83	16	1
Mendenhall	2,374	4	0	2	0	2	17	9	5	3	0
Natchez	14,497	97	5	6	13	73	639	106	510	23	0
Oakland	499	0	0	0	0	0	10	3	6	1	0
Ocean Springs[4]	17,917	13	0	0	3	10	453	54	368	31	0
Olive Branch	39,566	89	3	8	17	61	862	98	666	98	4
Oxford[4]	28,866	45	0	22	7	16	609	62	534	13	4
Pascagoula[4]	21,633	65	0	12	16	37	1,196	122	1,019	55	4
Pass Christian	6,527	8	0	1	3	4	226	72	150	4	0
Petal[4]	10,652	6	0	0	3	3	41	16	21	4	0
Poplarville	2,901	4	0	1	0	3	45	8	34	3	1
Puckett	352	0	0	0	0	0	1	0	0	1	0
Richland	7,276	16	1	7	2	6	121	32	77	12	0
Ridgeland	24,080	73	0	8	12	53	527	35	454	38	0
Sandersville	728	2	0	0	0	2	24	12	10	2	0
Starkville	25,854	42	2	3	4	33	866	403	431	32	3
Summit	1,555	1	0	0	1	0	34	16	13	5	0
Tunica	847	2	0	0	1	1	42	11	27	4	0
Union	1,888	10	0	1	4	5	22	3	15	4	0
Vardaman	1,275	1	0	0	0	1	4	1	2	1	0
Vicksburg[4]	21,420	165	11	9	10	135	902	134	675	93	1
Walls	1,456	4	0	1	0	3	26	5	15	6	0
Water Valley	3,242	16	0	3	1	12	91	19	66	6	0

Table 8. Offenses Known to Law Enforcement, by Selected State and City, 2020—Continued

(Number.)

State/city	Population	Violent crime	Murder and nonnegligent manslaughter	Rape[1]	Robbery	Aggravated assault	Property crime	Burglary	Larceny-theft	Motor vehicle theft	Arson[2]
West Point	10,314	54	2	2	3	47	316	70	241	5	0
Wiggins	4,555	6	0	1	1	4	161	33	123	5	
MISSOURI											
Adrian	1,588	12	0	0	0	12	27	11	13	3	0
Advance	1,335	2	1	0	0	1	18	4	12	2	0
Alma	381	0	0	0	0	0	0	0	0	0	0
Arbyrd	457	0	0	0	0	0	2	0	0	2	0
Arcadia	555	3	0	0	0	3	1	0	1	0	0
Ashland[4]	3,996	4	0	1	0	3	64	7	56	1	0
Aurora[4]	7,441	47	0	8	0	39	285	36	227	22	1
Auxvasse	977	2	0	1	0	1	37	13	23	1	
Ava	2,852	10	0	1	0	9	90	11	77	2	0
Ballwin[4]	30,044	19	0	2	2	15	255	13	201	41	0
Battlefield[4]	6,739	8	0	1	0	7	42	9	26	7	0
Bellefontaine Neighbors[4]	10,356	206	2	2	26	176	382	80	159	143	1
Bellflower	364	0	0	0	0	0	0	0	0	0	0
Bel-Nor[4]	1,391	4	0	0	1	3	23	4	14	5	0
Belton	23,698	57	1	18	6	32	564	49	447	68	0
Bernie	1,871	0	0	0	0	0	7	4	3	0	0
Bertrand[4]	734	1	0	0	0	1	7	4	2	1	0
Billings	1,119	0	0	0	0	0	0	0	0	0	0
Birch Tree	646	2	0	0	0	2	8	5	1	2	0
Bloomfield[4]	1,822	2	0	0	0	2	26	11	12	3	0
Blue Springs[4]	56,193	119	2	14	20	83	1,311	112	1,039	160	6
Bolivar[4]	11,150	38	2	14	1	21	421	51	344	26	1
Bonne Terre	7,135	8	0	3	0	5	99	13	64	22	0
Boonville[4]	8,450	28	0	3	2	23	171	34	125	12	0
Bourbon	1,579	9	0	2	0	7	59	9	45	5	0
Bowling Green[4]	5,617	31	0	1	0	30	77	8	64	5	0
Branson	11,745	80	0	17	10	53	934	111	758	65	4
Branson West[4]	443	2	0	0	0	2	59	2	57	0	0
Breckenridge Hills[4]	4,548	43	0	2	2	39	134	16	80	38	1
Bridgeton[4]	11,521	73	3	5	15	50	811	54	663	94	1
Brookfield	4,179	7	0	3	0	4	50	11	30	9	1
Buckner[4]	3,016	6	0	1	0	5	62	9	48	5	0
Butler[4]	3,976	25	0	1	1	23	116	44	72	0	1
Byrnes Mill[4]	3,028	34	0	0	0	34	33	7	19	7	1
Cabool[4]	2,073	1	0	0	0	1	25	4	19	2	0
Camdenton	4,191	16	0	3	1	12	140	25	101	14	2
Cameron[4]	9,618	26	0	1	0	25	140	9	108	23	0
Campbell	1,788	4	0	0	0	4	44	10	31	3	0
Canalou	297	0	0	0	0	0	0	0	0	0	0
Canton[4]	2,294	0	0	0	0	0	45	12	27	6	0
Cape Girardeau[4]	40,845	362	4	42	35	281	1,204	179	892	133	16
Carthage	14,784	45	0	8	6	31	580	72	456	52	1
Caruthersville	5,268	60	2	4	3	51	147	48	83	16	3
Cassville	3,293	14	0	1	0	13	289	31	243	15	0
Centralia[4]	4,298	9	0	1	0	8	71	4	65	2	0
Chaffee	2,891	13	0	0	0	13	31	10	20	1	0
Charleston	5,422	43	1	2	3	37	88	20	60	8	0
Chesterfield[4]	47,544	43	0	5	8	30	834	118	628	88	
Chillicothe	9,735	28	0	3	1	24	139	36	88	15	2
Clarkson Valley[4]	2,603	1	0	1	0	0	13	2	9	2	0
Clarkton	1,138	0	0	0	0	0	1	0	0	1	0
Clayton[4]	16,837	19	0	0	6	13	241	27	186	28	0
Cleveland	661	0	0	0	0	0	1	1	0	0	0
Columbia[4]	124,829	552	13	89	58	392	3,326	404	2,478	444	20
Corder	400	0	0	0	0	0	3	2	0	1	0
Cottleville[4]	6,002	0	0	0	0	0	29	1	25	3	0
Country Club Hills[4]	1,244	14	1	0	7	6	32	6	18	8	0
Country Club Village	2,501	2	0	1	0	1	17	3	12	2	0
Crestwood[4]	11,829	18	0	1	8	9	197	15	163	19	0
Creve Coeur[4]	18,716	26	1	2	9	14	356	25	282	49	0
Cuba	3,286	1	0	0	0	1	132	21	103	8	0
Delta	423	0	0	0	0	0	0	0	0	0	0
Desloge[4]	4,861	21	0	3	1	17	253	17	225	11	0
Des Peres[4]	8,732	11	0	1	5	5	333	21	291	21	0
Dexter[4]	7,807	37	0	9	2	26	233	45	172	16	2
Diamond	912	2	0	0	0	2	2	0	0	2	0
Doniphan[4]	1,907	8	1	0	0	7	116	9	97	10	0
Duquesne	1,626	4	0	0	1	3	74	6	60	8	1
East Lynne	306	0	0	0	0	0	2	0	1	1	0
East Prairie	2,922	1	0	0	0	1	15	2	13	0	0
Edmundson	828	8	0	0	1	7	55	3	31	21	0
Eldon[4]	4,721	16	0	1	0	15	163	30	120	13	1
Ellisville[4]	9,927	13	0	0	0	13	105	13	77	15	1
Ellsinore	427	0	0	0	0	0	0	0	0	0	0
Eureka[4]	11,032	8	0	0	0	8	171	17	139	15	1
Excelsior Springs[4]	11,802	20	0	4	3	13	294	34	231	29	0
Exeter	769	3	0	0	0	3	0	0	0	0	0
Fairview	376	0	0	0	0	0	0	0	0	0	0
Farmington[4]	19,446	27	0	2	2	23	548	25	489	34	2

Table 8. Offenses Known to Law Enforcement, by Selected State and City, 2020—Continued

(Number.)

State/city	Population	Violent crime	Murder and nonnegligent manslaughter	Rape[1]	Robbery	Aggravated assault	Property crime	Burglary	Larceny-theft	Motor vehicle theft	Arson[2]
Fayette[4]	2,689	5	0	0	0	5	12	0	12	0	0
Ferguson	20,454	141	7	6	30	98	1,062	182	684	196	4
Festus[4]	12,085	49	0	1	1	47	199	18	146	35	0
Fleming	129	0	0	0	0	0	0	0	0	0	0
Florissant[4]	50,812	196	4	17	37	138	1,167	96	664	407	5
Fordland[4]	852	5	0	0	0	5	12	1	11	0	0
Foristell[4]	614	1	0	1	0	0	34	0	32	2	0
Frankford	313	0	0	0	0	0	0	0	0	0	0
Fredericktown	3,984	30	0	2	1	27	113	22	81	10	0
Frontenac[4]	3,839	5	0	1	0	4	92	5	72	15	0
Fulton[4]	12,578	29	0	5	2	22	433	93	302	38	0
Galena[4]	437	2	0	0	0	2	3	2	1	0	0
Gideon	960	3	0	0	0	3	5	2	2	1	0
Gladstone	27,719	130	4	18	15	93	666	81	443	142	6
Glendale	5,859	2	0	0	2	0	42	2	31	9	0
Grain Valley	14,722	19	0	3	1	15	208	19	145	44	2
Grandview	24,898	199	3	9	25	162	1,038	200	627	211	
Greenwood[4]	5,905	8	0	0	0	8	23	2	15	6	0
Hamilton[4]	1,671	5	0	0	0	5	21	3	17	1	1
Hannibal[4]	17,299	79	1	10	7	61	903	98	753	52	6
Hardin	533	0	0	0	0	0	2	0	1	1	0
Harrisonville	10,083	54	0	3	0	51	302	53	209	40	4
Hartville	605	0	0	0	0	0	5	0	4	1	0
Hawk Point	718	0	0	0	0	0	0	0	0	0	0
Hayti	2,458	37	2	5	6	24	165	35	117	13	0
Hazelwood[4]	25,051	164	6	18	28	112	789	58	456	275	2
Herculaneum[4]	4,216	15	0	3	1	11	93	3	67	23	0
Hermann[4]	2,332	5	1	1	0	3	56	6	47	3	1
Higginsville[4]	4,589	0	0	0	0	0	35	2	28	5	1
Highlandville	1,066	0	0	0	0	0	0	0	0	0	0
Hillsboro[4]	3,339	17	0	2	0	15	49	11	32	6	0
Hillsdale[4]	1,549	15	0	0	1	14	33	7	10	16	0
Holcomb	570	1	0	0	0	1	0	0	0	0	0
Holden[4]	2,234	2	0	1	0	1	37	11	25	1	1
Hollister[4]	4,613	31	1	3	3	24	76	2	66	8	0
Holts Summit[4]	5,157	5	0	2	0	3	58	11	45	2	0
Hornersville[4]	587	1	0	0	0	1	9	4	4	1	0
Houston[4]	2,081	13	0	1	1	11	122	28	86	8	0
Howardville	333	0	0	0	0	0	0	0	0	0	0
Iberia	751	0	0	0	0	0	6	4	2	0	0
Independence[4]	116,648	791	11	139	125	516	5,338	581	3,782	975	22
Jefferson City	42,653	109	2	17	16	74	821	70	658	93	7
Joplin	50,935	338	9	49	67	213	3,276	379	2,528	369	30
Kansas City	499,335	7,919	176	382	1,285	6,076	20,570	3,072	12,958	4,540	180
Kearney	11,164	5	0	4	0	1	148	7	129	12	0
Kennett[4]	10,005	90	1	12	5	72	572	129	395	48	5
Kimberling City[4]	2,286	3	0	0	0	3	20	1	14	5	1
Kirksville[4]	17,611	102	1	13	9	79	683	116	530	37	4
Kirkwood[4]	27,834	42	0	2	5	35	493	46	390	57	0
Knob Noster[4]	2,792	5	0	0	0	5	24	5	18	1	0
Ladue[4]	8,627	3	0	0	2	1	130	15	98	17	1
La Grange[4]	888	0	0	0	0	0	5	0	5	0	0
Lake Lafayette	337	3	0	2	0	1	5	4	1	0	1
Lake Lotawana	2,129	0	0	0	0	0	37	3	25	9	0
Lake Ozark	1,856	0	0	0	0	0	31	0	31	0	0
Lakeshire[4]	1,384	3	0	0	0	3	6	2	4	0	0
Lake St. Louis[4]	17,136	18	0	4	1	13	393	17	349	27	0
Lake Tapawingo[4]	718	1	0	1	0	0	1	0	1	0	0
Lake Winnebago	1,285	3	0	2	0	1	5	0	4	1	0
Lamar[4]	4,268	6	0	0	0	6	56	13	40	3	2
Laurie[4]	969	4	0	1	0	3	10	2	8	0	0
Lawson[4]	2,407	0	0	0	0	0	11	2	8	1	0
Lebanon[4]	14,829	91	0	8	3	80	768	123	592	53	2
Lee's Summit[4]	100,268	129	0	28	25	76	2,050	167	1,648	235	4
Lexington	4,513	4	0	1	0	3	89	20	63	6	2
Licking[4]	3,070	3	0	0	0	3	25	4	19	2	0
Lincoln[4]	1,194	2	0	0	0	2	11	0	7	4	0
Louisiana	3,191	10	0	1	0	9	56	8	41	7	0
Macon[4]	5,326	12	0	0	0	12	126	31	88	7	0
Mansfield	1,240	0	0	0	0	0	56	7	47	2	0
Maplewood[4]	8,096	43	0	2	10	31	443	59	341	43	0
Marble Hill	1,461	13	0	0	0	13	25	10	13	2	0
Marionville[4]	2,175	12	0	1	0	11	40	13	20	7	0
Marshall	12,817	42	0	7	3	32	222	46	161	15	2
Marshfield	7,667	7	0	0	0	7	265	44	211	10	0
Maryville[4]	11,550	6	0	1	0	5	124	24	89	11	0
Matthews	591	0	0	0	0	0	2	0	0	2	0
Mexico	11,517	11	2	2	3	4	354	24	311	19	0
Milan[4]	1,755	2	0	0	0	2	20	3	16	1	0
Miner	930	6	0	0	0	6	28	13	13	2	0
Moline Acres[4]	2,338	26	0	0	3	23	65	3	28	34	0
Monett[4]	9,150	38	0	2	2	34	333	60	250	23	0
Morehouse[4]	854	2	1	0	0	1	5	1	3	1	1

Table 8. Offenses Known to Law Enforcement, by Selected State and City, 2020—Continued

(Number.)

State/city	Population	Violent crime	Murder and nonnegligent manslaughter	Rape[1]	Robbery	Aggravated assault	Property crime	Burglary	Larceny-theft	Motor vehicle theft	Arson[2]
Mound City	1,026	0	0	0	0	0	22	1	17	4	0
Mountain View	2,641	1	0	0	1	0	51	13	34	4	1
Mount Vernon	4,502	1	0	0	1	0	111	13	89	9	0
Neosho	12,077	32	0	9	2	21	511	79	404	28	6
Nevada[4]	8,246	163	0	9	5	149	474	50	388	36	1
New Florence[4]	713	0	0	0	0	0	3	1	2	0	0
New Haven[4]	2,070	9	0	6	0	3	35	10	23	2	0
New London	987	6	0	0	0	6	10	1	8	1	0
New Madrid	2,785	27	1	1	0	25	49	11	38	0	1
Niangua[4]	429	0	0	0	0	0	0	0	0	0	0
Nixa[4]	22,924	27	1	1	0	25	198	7	178	13	0
Noel[4]	1,804	10	0	2	0	8	29	9	13	7	0
Normandy[4]	7,405	91	2	1	8	80	158	15	104	39	3
North Kansas City	4,615	39	1	4	7	27	495	24	361	110	0
Northmoor	367	1	0	0	0	1	15	7	5	3	0
Northwoods	4,350	24	1	2	2	19	98	35	40	23	0
Oak Grove	8,299	10	0	2	1	7	84	10	57	17	0
Odessa[4]	5,238	5	0	3	1	1	88	6	74	8	0
O'Fallon[4]	89,698	109	0	31	8	70	1,020	55	863	102	3
Old Monroe	290	0	0	0	0	0	2	0	2	0	0
Olivette[4]	7,829	9	1	0	3	5	138	9	120	9	0
Oregon	756	0	0	0	0	0	1	0	1	0	0
Oronogo	2,700	1	0	1	0	0	18	1	14	3	0
Orrick	800	1	0	1	0	0	4	3	1	0	0
Osage Beach[4]	4,696	22	0	6	0	16	265	35	215	15	1
Overland	15,497	84	3	6	16	59	622	51	467	104	2
Owensville	2,580	1	0	0	0	1	75	10	62	3	0
Ozark	20,788	57	0	7	4	46	355	30	301	24	0
Pacific	7,255	14	1	1	1	11	134	8	113	13	1
Pagedale[4]	3,288	54	3	0	4	47	110	11	61	38	0
Palmyra[4]	3,597	1	0	0	0	1	101	4	93	4	0
Park Hills[4]	8,504	24	0	5	1	18	235	27	171	37	1
Parkville[4]	7,369	13	0	1	1	11	143	13	116	14	0
Peculiar	5,582	6	1	1	1	3	105	19	82	4	1
Perry	696	0	0	0	0	0	2	0	2	0	0
Perryville	8,526	30	0	5	4	21	207	25	167	15	4
Pevely[4]	6,020	39	0	4	0	35	232	56	147	29	0
Piedmont	1,879	3	1	0	0	2	22	4	14	4	0
Pierce City	1,311	3	0	0	0	3	39	8	25	6	0
Pilot Grove	760	0	0	0	0	0	5	0	3	2	0
Pilot Knob[4]	712	0	0	0	0	0	6	1	5	0	0
Pineville	808	0	0	0	0	0	0	0	0	0	0
Platte City	4,987	4	0	0	2	2	48	4	29	15	1
Pleasant Hill	8,744	28	0	2	0	26	87	6	69	12	0
Pleasant Valley[4]	3,042	6	0	2	1	3	51	10	29	12	0
Poplar Bluff	16,927	85	4	10	17	54	1,109	206	745	158	0
Portageville	2,916	13	0	1	1	11	50	7	40	3	2
Potosi[4]	2,568	25	1	1	0	23	253	37	196	20	5
Queen City	628	0	0	0	0	0	0	0	0	0	0
Qulin	456	0	0	0	0	0	5	1	4	0	0
Raytown	28,922	197	3	19	47	128	1,172	254	688	230	7
Reeds Spring	863	3	0	0	0	3	2	2	0	0	0
Republic[4]	17,174	50	1	3	3	43	262	55	187	20	0
Richland[4]	1,785	4	0	2	0	2	31	2	28	1	2
Richmond	5,638	44	0	1	1	42	213	42	153	18	0
Richmond Heights[4]	8,831	34	3	1	6	24	473	20	412	41	0
Riverside[4]	3,574	22	1	1	1	19	206	15	153	38	0
Riverview[4]	2,820	45	1	1	3	40	112	26	61	25	6
Rock Hill[4]	4,615	1	0	0	0	1	55	3	47	5	0
Rogersville[4]	3,960	6	0	0	1	5	56	6	46	4	0
Rolla[4]	20,522	116	1	16	1	98	867	159	656	52	1
Rosebud[4]	405	2	0	2	0	0	11	2	9	0	0
Salem[4]	4,915	8	0	2	0	6	93	4	79	10	0
Salisbury	1,513	1	0	0	0	1	3	0	3	0	0
Sarcoxie	1,548	9	0	0	0	9	36	7	21	8	2
Savannah	5,240	5	0	1	0	4	38	5	27	6	0
Scott City[4]	4,458	9	0	1	0	8	90	10	78	2	0
Seligman[4]	841	2	0	1	0	1	19	6	9	4	0
Senath	1,595	15	0	3	1	11	6	6	0	0	1
Seneca	2,392	5	0	0	1	4	50	5	39	6	0
Seymour	2,021	6	0	1	0	5	73	15	54	4	0
Shrewsbury[4]	6,074	10	0	0	3	7	240	14	213	13	0
Sikeston[4]	15,987	135	2	9	9	115	564	89	426	49	5
Smithville	11,097	24	1	6	1	16	118	13	93	12	0
Southwest City	954	2	0	0	1	1	14	2	8	4	0
Springfield[4]	168,856	2,545	22	178	375	1,970	11,738	1,795	8,639	1,304	57
St. Ann[4]	12,586	40	0	5	5	30	260	18	187	55	0
St. Charles	71,563	192	3	19	27	143	1,368	145	1,022	201	6
St. Clair[4]	4,710	35	0	1	0	34	221	9	188	24	0
Steele	1,861	13	1	2	1	9	74	14	56	4	0
Steelville[4]	1,652	6	0	0	0	6	73	9	56	8	0
St. James[4]	4,014	18	1	2	2	13	245	21	210	14	1
St. John[4]	6,318	56	1	2	3	50	256	28	186	42	0

Table 8. Offenses Known to Law Enforcement, by Selected State and City, 2020—Continued

(Number.)

State/city	Population	Violent crime	Murder and nonnegligent manslaughter	Rape[1]	Robbery	Aggravated assault	Property crime	Burglary	Larceny-theft	Motor vehicle theft	Arson[2]
St. Joseph	74,680	414	3	122	47	242	3,843	576	2,711	556	27
St. Louis	298,422	6,017	263	234	1,242	4,278	17,399	2,552	11,626	3,221	220
Stover	1,094	13	0	3	0	10	9	0	9	0	0
St. Peters	58,849	153	1	26	8	118	1,085	95	896	94	2
Strafford[4]	2,473	4	0	1	0	3	68	13	47	8	0
St. Robert[4]	6,485	30	1	1	5	23	330	45	267	18	1
Sullivan[4]	7,128	42	0	4	4	34	385	90	266	29	1
Summersville	489	1	0	0	0	1	0	0	0	0	0
Sunrise Beach	550	1	0	0	0	1	2	1	1	0	0
Thayer[4]	2,121	8	0	2	0	6	28	8	16	4	0
Town and Country[4]	11,142	8	0	0	1	7	156	24	114	18	0
Trenton[4]	5,738	12	0	3	0	9	58	14	34	10	1
Truesdale[4]	905	0	0	0	0	0	10	1	7	2	0
Union[4]	12,195	50	0	6	4	40	544	43	429	72	8
University City[4]	34,045	146	5	6	40	95	855	89	632	134	9
Van Buren[4]	795	0	0	0	0	0	1	1	0	0	0
Velda City[4]	1,355	71	2	2	8	59	73	17	38	18	2
Verona	599	1	0	0	0	1	3	2	0	1	0
Versailles	2,477	11	0	1	1	9	63	10	49	4	1
Viburnum	648	1	0	0	0	1	5	1	0	4	0
Vinita Park	10,951	160	14	1	21	124	506	86	311	109	10
Walnut Grove[4]	794	1	0	1	0	0	5	2	3	0	0
Warrensburg	20,591	58	2	18	2	36	558	46	459	53	4
Warrenton[4]	8,450	29	0	5	3	21	268	25	222	21	1
Warson Woods	1,892	2	0	0	0	2	20	0	16	4	0
Washburn	432	0	0	0	0	0	0	0	0	0	0
Washington[4]	14,092	48	0	7	2	39	523	37	434	52	2
Waynesville[4]	5,338	10	0	4	0	6	87	5	75	7	0
Webb City	12,264	26	0	3	1	22	399	33	345	21	2
Wellsville	1,153	1	0	0	0	1	6	2	3	1	0
Wentzville	43,449	104	1	15	9	79	564	42	475	47	2
West Plains[4]	12,331	48	3	5	4	36	641	137	431	73	0
Wheaton	687	0	0	0	0	0	0	0	0	0	0
Woodson Terrace[4]	4,032	15	0	2	3	10	122	10	52	60	0
MONTANA											
Baker	1,907	3	0	3	0	0	3	0	2	1	0
Belgrade	9,762	30	2	4	0	24	220	6	202	12	1
Billings	110,157	939	14	85	125	715	5,249	717	3,715	817	23
Boulder	1,287	4	0	0	0	4	4	1	2	1	0
Bozeman	51,460	157	0	33	4	120	697	38	610	49	3
Bridger	760	2	0	0	0	2	5	1	4	0	0
Chinook	1,260	3	0	0	0	3	5	0	4	1	0
Colstrip	2,249	1	0	0	0	1	0	0	0	0	0
Columbia Falls	6,023	18	0	3	1	14	85	5	72	8	2
Columbus	2,100	4	0	1	0	3	42	12	25	5	0
Conrad	2,458	7	0	0	0	7	22	7	14	1	1
Cut Bank	3,075	23	0	3	1	19	78	8	65	5	0
Deer Lodge	2,822	3	0	0	1	2	14	0	13	1	1
Dillon	4,318	13	1	0	0	12	10	1	9	0	0
East Helena	2,113	10	0	0	0	10	50	5	40	5	0
Fort Benton	1,429	1	0	1	0	0	13	5	5	3	0
Glasgow	3,326	18	0	4	0	14	38	3	34	1	0
Glendive	4,908	6	0	1	0	5	29	10	13	6	0
Great Falls	58,345	266	0	43	28	195	2,999	293	2,535	171	25
Hamilton	4,970	17	0	5	0	12	147	12	124	11	0
Havre	9,820	70	1	9	3	57	300	38	225	37	4
Helena	33,629	216	0	50	17	149	1,227	155	974	98	13
Hot Springs	587	0	0	0	0	0	1	0	1	0	0
Kalispell	25,125	78	0	11	7	60	597	43	507	47	1
Laurel	6,732	18	0	2	2	14	149	4	126	19	2
Lewistown	5,772	21	1	6	0	14	43	1	39	3	0
Libby	2,797	4	0	1	1	2	49	2	45	2	0
Livingston	7,892	33	0	5	0	28	176	13	157	6	1
Manhattan	1,955	1	0	0	0	1	12	1	11	0	0
Miles City	8,250	19	0	3	0	16	107	13	90	4	0
Missoula	76,468	376	4	60	32	280	2,745	273	2,285	187	15
Polson	5,115	36	0	3	2	31	164	12	137	15	0
Red Lodge	2,324	3	0	1	0	2	5	0	4	1	0
Ronan City	2,141	20	0	0	0	20	66	9	49	8	0
Sidney	6,279	35	0	7	1	27	117	21	83	13	0
Stevensville	2,100	9	0	2	0	7	16	2	13	1	0
Thompson Falls	1,439	4	0	0	0	4	20	2	16	2	0
Troy	966	2	0	0	0	2	17	3	14	0	0
West Yellowstone	1,388	1	0	0	0	1	19	2	16	1	0
Whitefish	8,523	16	0	2	0	14	85	8	64	13	1
Wolf Point	2,744	33	1	2	0	30	53	12	36	5	1
NEBRASKA											
Aurora	4,554	0	0	0	0	0	28	1	23	4	0
Beatrice	12,238	39	1	14	3	21	169	24	136	9	1
Blair	7,919	11	0	6	0	5	63	6	46	11	1
Broken Bow	3,492	4	0	0	1	3	21	0	19	2	0

Table 8. Offenses Known to Law Enforcement, by Selected State and City, 2020—Continued

(Number.)

State/city	Population	Violent crime	Murder and nonnegligent manslaughter	Rape[1]	Robbery	Aggravated assault	Property crime	Burglary	Larceny-theft	Motor vehicle theft	Arson[2]
Cozad	3,708	13	0	4	0	9	25	6	18	1	0
Crete	7,009	56	0	19	0	37	105	10	85	10	1
Falls City	4,094	14	0	1	0	13	49	12	32	5	1
Gering	8,086	10	0	3	1	6	131	61	64	6	1
Gordon	1,512	6	0	0	1	5	30	5	24	1	0
Gothenburg	3,432	3	0	1	0	2	42	1	36	5	1
Grand Island	51,547	216	0	50	17	149	1,258	149	1,015	94	10
Holdrege	5,399	7	0	5	0	2	52	6	42	4	0
Kearney	34,201	122	0	32	11	79	678	83	548	47	8
La Vista	17,228	37	0	12	5	20	230	13	178	39	0
Lexington	10,103	13	0	1	2	10	169	27	135	7	2
Minden	2,954	5	0	4	0	1	32	8	23	1	0
Mitchell	1,614	2	0	2	0	0	8	1	6	1	0
Morrill	885	0	0	0	0	0	8	1	6	1	0
Nebraska City	7,292	13	1	3	0	9	179	37	130	12	1
Norfolk	24,467	29	2	14	1	12	318	34	253	31	7
North Platte	23,523	99	3	18	10	68	820	105	649	66	8
Ogallala	4,472	6	0	2	0	4	107	17	82	8	0
Omaha	480,297	3,032	37	351	464	2,180	15,247	1,521	10,697	3,029	
O'Neill[4]	3,565	1	0	1	0	0	8	3	1	4	0
Papillion	20,512	27	0	7	2	18	284	17	227	40	1
Plattsmouth	6,435	2	0	0	1	1	78	12	63	3	0
Ralston	7,422	12	0	7	0	5	114	18	75	21	0
Schuyler	6,312	2	0	0	0	2	21	6	14	1	0
Scottsbluff	15,665	60	1	14	5	40	457	65	365	27	3
Seward	7,242	2	0	1	0	1	44	6	36	2	0
Sidney	6,049	11	0	3	0	8	108	5	94	9	0
South Sioux City	12,746	50	0	4	2	44	296	22	243	31	1
Tekamah[4]	1,696	0	0	0	0	0	4	0	3	1	0
Valentine	2,704	15	0	4	0	11	20	2	16	2	0
Wahoo	4,550	5	0	1	0	4	44	3	37	4	1
West Point	3,273	1	0	1	0	0	14	1	10	3	0
NEVADA											
Boulder City[4]	16,346	23	0	1	4	18	139	26	83	30	0
Carlin4,[5]	2,268	8	0	1	0	7		10	21		0
Elko	20,697	99	5	19	18	57	609	126	401	82	
Fallon[4]	8,648	19	0	2	5	12	141	5	127	9	1
Henderson[4]	328,056	682	13	104	177	388	4,679	619	3,516	544	25
Las Vegas Metropolitan Police Department[4]	1,693,061	8,934	96	1,068	1,707	6,063	37,426	7,057	23,546	6,823	162
Lovelock	1,822	3	0	0	0	3	22	10	10	2	0
Mesquite[4]	20,290	21	0	2	1	18	226	39	173	14	1
North Las Vegas[4]	256,217	1,337	18	86	398	835	4,160	797	2,240	1,123	47
Reno[4]	259,168	1,460	17	281	286	876	5,564	1,105	3,486	973	25
Sparks[4]	106,664	446	4	83	75	284	2,087	427	1,337	323	7
West Wendover	4,258	37	0	6	4	27	74	32	37	5	0
Winnemucca	7,786	28	1	0	2	25	210	62	124	24	2
Yerington	3,256	1	0	0	0	1	1	0	1	0	0
NEW HAMPSHIRE											
Alexandria	1,618	2	0	1	0	1	11	1	9	1	0
Allenstown	4,462	4	0	3	0	1	21	3	18	0	0
Alstead	1,938	2	0	1	0	1	0	0	0	0	0
Alton	5,343	13	0	7	0	6	25	4	18	3	0
Amherst	11,414	1	0	1	0	0	74	5	65	4	2
Antrim	2,697	5	0	1	1	3	25	6	17	2	0
Ashland	2,053	7	0	2	0	5	47	8	38	1	0
Atkinson	7,196	0	0	0	0	0	18	1	17	0	0
Auburn	5,662	2	0	0	1	1	52	4	43	5	0
Barnstead	4,762	9	0	3	0	6	31	9	20	2	0
Barrington	9,358	2	0	1	0	1	45	4	40	1	0
Bartlett	2,807	3	0	2	0	1	25	6	18	1	0
Bath	1,095	0	0	0	0	0	9	0	7	2	1
Bedford	22,788	9	0	5	0	4	132	5	118	9	0
Belmont	7,342	15	0	2	0	13	127	14	101	12	2
Bennington	1,518	1	0	1	0	0	4	0	2	2	0
Berlin	10,140	14	0	3	2	9	129	12	109	8	0
Bethlehem	2,579	1	0	1	0	0	25	1	22	2	0
Boscawen	4,032	5	0	1	0	4	17	3	13	1	0
Bow	8,032	6	0	1	2	3	37	4	31	2	0
Bradford	1,714	0	0	0	0	0	10	2	8	0	0
Brentwood	4,525	3	0	0	0	3	28	7	20	1	0
Bristol	3,102	1	0	0	0	1	40	1	37	2	0
Brookline	5,506	5	0	1	0	4	20	1	16	3	1
Campton	3,297	14	0	6	0	8	34	5	27	2	0
Candia	3,970	2	0	2	0	0	22	2	18	2	2
Canterbury	2,475	1	0	0	0	1	19	2	16	1	0
Carroll	745	1	0	0	0	1	7	1	6	0	0
Center Harbor	1,099	0	0	0	0	0	8	2	6	0	0
Charlestown	5,010	3	0	0	0	3	18	7	8	3	0
Chester	5,334	3	0	2	0	1	22	1	21	0	1
Chichester	2,726	1	0	0	0	1	18	2	14	2	0

Table 8. Offenses Known to Law Enforcement, by Selected State and City, 2020—Continued

(Number.)

State/city	Population	Violent crime	Murder and nonnegligent manslaughter	Rape[1]	Robbery	Aggravated assault	Property crime	Burglary	Larceny-theft	Motor vehicle theft	Arson[2]
Claremont	12,887	14	0	6	6	2	260	16	224	20	3
Concord	43,737	84	0	24	15	45	727	61	626	40	10
Conway	10,269	23	0	14	2	7	203	12	180	11	0
Cornish	1,614	0	0	0	0	0	16	2	13	1	0
Danville	4,581	3	0	1	0	2	4	1	2	1	0
Deerfield	4,576	0	0	0	0	0	12	1	11	0	0
Deering	1,978	1	0	1	0	0	10	0	8	2	0
Derry	33,555	40	0	14	9	17	291	23	241	27	9
Dover	32,480	24	1	10	6	7	315	29	272	14	3
Dublin	1,538	1	0	0	0	1	9	0	9	0	1
Dunbarton	2,894	3	0	0	0	3	12	2	10	0	0
Durham	16,510	9	0	7	0	2	42	6	34	2	0
East Kingston	2,428	0	0	0	0	0	5	0	4	1	0
Enfield	4,526	0	0	0	0	0	17	4	11	2	1
Epping	7,115	1	0	1	0	0	42	1	40	1	1
Epsom	4,787	0	0	0	0	0	20	1	17	2	0
Exeter	15,448	16	0	7	0	9	96	5	85	6	1
Farmington	7,003	16	0	7	1	8	106	23	73	10	1
Fitzwilliam	2,367	2	0	0	1	1	18	8	9	1	0
Franconia	1,105	1	0	1	0	0	15	2	13	0	0
Franklin	8,711	9	0	3	2	4	91	5	78	8	0
Freedom	1,593	0	0	0	0	0	3	0	3	0	0
Fremont	4,764	2	0	1	0	1	18	1	16	1	0
Gilford	7,258	6	0	4	0	2	109	7	98	4	1
Gilmanton	3,779	6	0	2	0	4	30	6	20	4	1
Goffstown	18,098	11	0	6	2	3	116	6	106	4	1
Gorham	2,587	2	0	1	1	0	51	1	49	1	0
Grantham	2,942	0	0	0	0	0	6	2	4	0	0
Greenland	4,194	1	0	0	0	1	13	3	9	1	0
Hampstead	8,654	5	0	4	0	1	39	3	32	4	0
Hampton	15,570	23	0	5	0	18	133	8	115	10	0
Hampton Falls	2,437	4	0	2	0	2	19	1	16	2	1
Hancock	1,657	0	0	0	0	0	6	2	4	0	0
Hanover	11,498	5	0	4	0	1	58	9	48	1	2
Haverhill	4,551	7	0	3	0	4	71	3	61	7	0
Henniker	5,039	4	0	2	0	2	21	7	11	3	0
Hill	1,111	0	0	0	0	0	0	0	0	0	0
Hillsborough	6,001	11	0	4	1	6	56	12	40	4	0
Hinsdale	3,893	11	0	1	0	10	77	2	68	7	0
Holderness	2,106	2	0	0	0	2	15	5	10	0	1
Hollis	8,040	3	0	0	0	3	26	1	25	0	0
Hooksett	14,668	6	0	2	0	4	145	7	130	8	1
Hopkinton	5,781	0	0	0	0	0	28	2	25	1	1
Hudson	25,748	22	0	9	6	7	212	23	176	13	3
Jackson	863	0	0	0	0	0	6	0	6	0	0
Jaffrey	5,258	10	0	1	1	8	22	1	18	3	2
Keene	22,707	38	0	16	8	14	395	32	352	11	2
Kingston	6,500	2	0	1	0	1	7	1	6	0	0
Laconia	16,669	23	0	7	9	7	495	24	436	35	5
Lancaster	3,229	1	0	0	0	1	28	1	26	1	0
Lebanon	13,709	20	0	10	2	8	201	13	180	8	2
Lee	4,601	3	0	2	0	1	27	2	23	2	1
Lincoln	1,771	3	0	2	1	0	44	6	34	4	0
Lisbon	1,577	3	0	0	0	3	20	8	11	1	0
Litchfield	8,682	3	0	0	0	3	26	4	19	3	0
Littleton	5,862	15	0	6	0	9	95	4	87	4	1
Londonderry	26,812	15	0	4	2	9	170	21	133	16	1
Loudon	5,675	5	0	1	0	4	49	12	29	8	0
Lyme	1,671	0	0	0	0	0	5	1	4	0	0
Lyndeborough	1,738	0	0	0	0	0	5	0	5	0	0
Madbury	1,897	0	0	0	0	0	3	0	2	1	0
Madison	2,618	3	0	0	0	3	24	1	23	0	0
Manchester	113,018	670	5	73	110	482	2,560	287	2,096	177	12
Marlborough	2,078	3	0	1	0	2	12	0	12	0	0
Mason	1,438	0	0	0	0	0	3	0	3	0	0
Meredith	6,484	12	0	6	0	6	67	20	44	3	1
Merrimack	26,602	5	0	1	0	4	186	20	152	14	0
Middleton	1,845	2	0	0	0	2	13	1	10	2	0
Milford	16,561	10	0	4	1	5	105	11	88	6	1
Milton	4,633	3	0	2	0	1	34	8	23	3	1
Mont Vernon	2,686	0	0	0	0	0	17	0	16	1	0
Moultonborough	4,198	4	0	2	0	2	18	2	16	0	0
Nashua	89,671	107	0	54	12	41	818	54	710	54	11
New Boston	5,966	2	0	1	0	1	10	1	8	1	0
Newbury	2,246	1	0	0	0	1	14	3	11	0	0
New Durham	2,715	1	0	0	0	1	25	5	17	3	1
Newfields	1,744	2	0	1	0	1	11	0	11	0	0
New Hampton	2,231	4	0	0	0	4	21	3	16	2	0
Newington	821	1	0	0	1	0	89	4	82	3	0
New Ipswich	5,425	2	0	1	0	1	21	3	17	1	0
New London	4,300	3	0	0	0	3	37	12	25	0	0
Newmarket	9,192	7	0	1	0	6	32	1	30	1	1
Newport	6,342	9	0	6	1	2	103	9	87	7	0

Table 8. Offenses Known to Law Enforcement, by Selected State and City, 2020—Continued

(Number.)

State/city	Population	Violent crime	Murder and nonnegligent manslaughter	Rape[1]	Robbery	Aggravated assault	Property crime	Burglary	Larceny-theft	Motor vehicle theft	Arson[2]
Newton	4,969	6	1	2	0	3	14	3	9	2	0
Northfield	4,956	1	0	0	0	1	63	3	52	8	1
North Hampton	4,513	0	0	0	0	0	40	3	33	4	0
Northumberland	2,123	5	0	0	0	5	18	1	17	0	0
Northwood	4,321	2	0	2	0	0	20	1	18	1	2
Nottingham	5,182	0	0	0	0	0	28	4	23	1	0
Orford	1,308	1	0	0	0	1	13	0	13	0	0
Ossipee	4,389	10	0	4	0	6	51	5	40	6	0
Pelham	14,373	6	0	2	0	4	88	8	78	2	0
Pembroke	7,212	14	0	5	1	8	43	8	33	2	1
Peterborough	6,736	8	0	6	0	2	70	8	56	6	0
Piermont	810	3	0	2	0	1	13	3	8	2	0
Pittsburg	815	0	0	0	0	0	0	0	0	0	0
Pittsfield	4,126	9	0	2	0	7	24	5	18	1	2
Plainfield	2,404	0	0	0	0	0	11	1	8	2	0
Plaistow	7,738	5	0	0	2	3	54	4	43	7	0
Plymouth	6,850	10	0	6	0	4	91	3	83	5	0
Portsmouth	22,032	25	0	9	1	15	294	17	214	63	2
Rindge	6,100	3	0	2	1	0	47	4	41	2	25
Rochester[5]	31,762	72	1	11	25	35			807	59	7
Rollinsford	2,596	4	0	0	1	3	20	2	17	1	0
Rye	5,495	1	0	1	0	0	23	1	22	0	0
Salem	29,943	21	0	6	10	5	327	14	295	18	2
Sanbornton	3,000	3	0	1	0	2	10	0	10	0	0
Sandown	6,620	1	0	1	0	0	15	1	13	1	0
Sandwich	1,362	1	0	0	0	1	14	4	10	0	0
Seabrook	8,871	7	0	3	0	4	154	5	141	8	0
Somersworth	12,005	20	0	8	7	5	396	13	366	17	1
South Hampton	829	0	0	0	0	0	4	0	4	0	0
Springfield	1,344	0	0	0	0	0	2	1	1	0	0
Strafford	4,242	0	0	0	0	0	6	0	5	1	0
Stratham	7,521	3	1	0	0	2	27	2	25	0	1
Sunapee	3,501	3	0	2	1	0	21	1	20	0	0
Tamworth	3,101	2	0	0	0	2	30	0	26	4	0
Thornton	2,541	2	0	1	0	1	16	1	13	2	0
Tilton	3,546	10	0	3	0	7	176	14	155	7	2
Troy	2,100	1	0	0	0	1	13	0	13	0	0
Tuftonboro	2,425	4	0	2	0	2	19	0	18	1	0
Wakefield	5,799	7	0	2	0	5	45	17	25	3	0
Warner	2,931	1	0	0	0	1	24	1	22	1	0
Washington	1,101	2	0	1	0	1	2	0	2	0	0
Weare	9,124	1	0	0	0	1	21	3	18	0	0
Wentworth	972	0	0	0	0	0	7	2	5	0	0
Whitefield	2,200	2	0	1	0	1	13	2	10	1	0
Wilton	3,801	2	0	1	0	1	16	1	15	0	0
Winchester	4,213	5	0	2	0	3	39	7	27	5	2
Windham	15,017	2	0	0	2	0	52	5	46	1	2
Wolfeboro	6,433	10	1	6	1	2	28	1	25	2	0
Woodstock	1,364	0	0	0	0	0	22	3	18	1	0
NEW JERSEY											
Aberdeen Township	19,471	15	0	4	3	8	110	6	96	8	1
Absecon	8,856	25	0	2	5	18	345	44	284	17	1
Allendale	6,751	1	0	0	0	1	47	9	33	5	0
Allenhurst	482	0	0	0	0	0	9	0	9	0	0
Allentown	1,770	1	0	0	0	1	7	2	5	0	0
Alpha	2,243	1	0	0	0	1	11	0	10	1	0
Alpine	1,845	0	0	0	0	0	26	2	12	12	0
Andover Township	5,826	3	0	0	0	3	16	2	14	0	0
Asbury Park	15,331	188	1	12	48	127	525	73	437	15	2
Atlantic City	37,550	309	9	28	116	156	1,013	139	785	89	2
Atlantic Highlands	4,348	0	0	0	0	0	23	2	20	1	0
Audubon	8,608	16	0	0	6	10	281	9	268	4	1
Audubon Park	999	2	0	0	1	1	14	4	10	0	0
Avalon	1,225	7	0	0	0	7	242	17	225	0	0
Avon-by-the-Sea	1,771	0	0	0	0	0	87	8	78	1	0
Barnegat Light	588	0	0	0	0	0	6	1	5	0	0
Barnegat Township	23,998	17	0	5	3	9	119	12	105	2	3
Barrington	6,601	6	0	0	1	5	62	10	47	5	0
Bay Head	979	0	0	0	0	0	17	0	13	4	0
Bayonne	65,013	118	1	5	33	79	647	84	514	49	1
Beach Haven	1,210	0	0	0	0	0	94	5	89	0	0
Beachwood	11,357	8	0	0	1	7	42	4	38	0	0
Bedminster Township	7,963	0	0	0	0	0	32	2	26	4	0
Belleville	36,533	41	0	2	11	28	522	41	403	78	0
Bellmawr	11,318	11	0	0	1	10	177	9	159	9	0
Belmar	5,518	4	0	2	0	2	117	10	102	5	0
Belvidere	2,548	0	0	0	0	0	44	5	37	2	0
Bergenfield	27,347	13	0	0	2	11	84	8	64	12	0
Berkeley Heights Township	13,371	0	0	0	0	0	34	3	25	6	0
Berkeley Township	42,168	30	1	10	3	16	232	34	191	7	4
Berlin	7,517	9	0	1	1	7	105	10	93	2	0
Berlin Township	5,721	6	0	0	1	5	188	7	179	2	0

Table 8. Offenses Known to Law Enforcement, by Selected State and City, 2020—Continued

(Number.)

State/city	Population	Violent crime	Murder and nonnegligent manslaughter	Rape[1]	Robbery	Aggravated assault	Property crime	Burglary	Larceny-theft	Motor vehicle theft	Arson[2]
Bernards Township	27,130	0	0	0	0	0	82	9	57	16	0
Bernardsville	7,593	0	0	0	0	0	56	10	39	7	0
Beverly	2,472	21	1	1	0	19	26	8	18	0	1
Blairstown Township	5,665	9	0	2	0	7	25	5	19	1	0
Bloomfield	50,221	50	1	0	21	28	532	41	408	83	0
Bloomingdale	8,098	1	0	1	0	0	27	3	23	1	0
Bogota	8,342	0	0	0	0	0	49	3	45	1	0
Boonton	8,977	5	0	0	2	3	100	30	65	5	0
Boonton Township	4,228	2	0	2	0	0	23	6	14	3	0
Bordentown City	3,778	6	0	0	1	5	20	2	17	1	0
Bordentown Township	11,974	10	0	1	1	8	73	6	53	14	0
Bound Brook	10,174	5	0	0	0	5	94	13	76	5	1
Bradley Beach	4,131	3	0	0	0	3	83	10	71	2	0
Branchburg Township	14,526	5	0	2	0	3	76	4	67	5	0
Brick Township	76,326	61	1	9	7	44	686	112	551	23	0
Bridgeton	24,032	234	2	11	82	139	737	158	534	45	2
Bridgewater Township	44,006	6	1	0	3	2	280	47	210	23	0
Brielle	4,656	2	0	0	0	2	17	2	11	4	0
Brigantine	8,566	5	1	0	0	4	157	23	120	14	0
Brooklawn	1,892	12	0	1	7	4	150	13	130	7	0
Buena	4,250	2	0	0	2	0	39	10	26	3	0
Burlington City	9,849	32	1	0	9	22	137	21	107	9	0
Burlington Township	22,595	35	1	6	2	26	290	26	248	16	0
Butler	7,643	1	0	0	0	1	37	1	33	3	0
Byram Township	7,880	3	1	0	0	2	29	3	23	3	0
Caldwell	7,938	0	0	0	0	0	61	27	30	4	0
Califon	1,044	0	0	0	0	0	3	1	2	0	0
Camden County Police Department	73,127	1,172	23	55	222	872	1,579	252	962	365	38
Cape May	3,401	1	0	1	0	0	61	2	58	1	0
Cape May Point	273	0	0	0	0	0	6	1	5	0	0
Carlstadt	6,126	3	0	0	1	2	81	3	72	6	0
Carney's Point Township	7,632	12	0	4	3	5	87	28	44	15	0
Carteret	23,444	39	1	3	10	25	263	20	208	35	0
Cedar Grove Township	12,483	3	0	0	0	3	79	8	67	4	0
Chatham	8,586	1	0	0	1	0	61	6	47	8	3
Chatham Township	10,071	0	0	0	0	0	42	8	25	9	0
Cherry Hill Township	71,220	84	0	2	31	51	1,545	93	1,391	61	0
Chesilhurst	1,615	3	0	1	0	2	39	12	21	6	0
Chester	1,619	0	0	0	0	0	7	1	5	1	0
Chesterfield Township	7,557	0	0	0	0	0	14	3	9	2	0
Chester Township	7,640	1	0	0	0	1	34	8	22	4	0
Cinnaminson Township	16,429	10	0	0	2	8	371	27	335	9	0
Clark Township	16,026	10	0	1	1	8	137	0	125	12	0
Clayton	8,790	20	1	0	0	19	69	5	60	4	0
Clementon	4,950	4	0	0	1	3	76	22	53	1	0
Cliffside Park	26,400	15	0	2	4	9	87	4	82	1	0
Clifton	85,058	82	0	5	46	31	1,334	100	1,140	94	0
Clinton	2,684	0	0	0	0	0	7	1	6	0	0
Clinton Township	12,465	3	0	1	0	2	41	1	38	2	0
Closter	8,511	3	0	0	0	3	49	6	37	6	0
Collingswood	13,864	26	0	3	10	13	335	53	271	11	1
Colts Neck Township	9,786	2	0	0	0	2	93	6	69	18	0
Cranbury Township	4,086	1	0	0	0	1	38	3	35	0	0
Cranford Township	24,186	3	0	1	0	2	114	3	105	6	1
Cresskill	8,672	1	1	0	0	0	33	4	21	8	0
Deal	715	1	0	0	0	1	39	1	20	18	0
Delanco Township	4,448	7	0	1	1	5	27	1	25	1	0
Delaware Township	4,410	1	1	0	0	0	9	2	7	0	0
Delran Township	16,444	7	0	1	1	5	188	19	162	7	0
Demarest	4,884	1	0	0	0	1	14	1	8	5	0
Denville Township	16,400	2	0	0	1	1	56	8	41	7	0
Deptford Township	30,275	49	1	5	18	25	1,006	130	854	22	1
Dover	17,654	24	1	2	7	14	101	19	72	10	3
Dumont	17,507	7	1	0	2	4	53	5	42	6	0
Dunellen	7,192	5	0	0	0	5	107	13	91	3	0
Eastampton Township	6,156	3	0	1	2	0	73	6	62	5	0
East Brunswick Township	47,573	25	0	1	5	19	332	40	281	11	1
East Greenwich Township	10,834	3	0	1	1	1	82	4	72	6	0
East Hanover Township	10,881	2	1	1	0	1	108	8	90	10	0
East Newark	2,614	1	0	0	0	1	10	0	9	1	0
East Orange	64,320	294	6	18	76	194	810	72	566	172	6
East Rutherford	9,767	9	0	3	1	5	122	5	103	14	1
East Windsor Township	27,265	16	0	3	3	10	192	12	173	7	0
Eatontown	12,124	24	0	5	5	14	213	15	193	5	1
Edgewater	13,573	9	0	1	2	6	144	11	116	17	0
Edgewater Park Township	8,618	15	1	0	2	12	89	17	62	10	0
Edison Township	99,584	103	1	9	31	62	1,134	131	886	117	2
Egg Harbor City	4,031	15	0	2	6	7	156	30	115	11	0
Egg Harbor Township	42,110	50	4	7	6	33	795	85	672	38	1
Elizabeth	129,518	774	17	44	282	431	2,897	268	1,931	698	9
Elk Township	4,168	1	0	1	0	0	31	5	24	2	0
Elmer	1,299	0	0	0	0	0	8	4	4	0	0

Table 8. Offenses Known to Law Enforcement, by Selected State and City, 2020—Continued

(Number.)

State/city	Population	Violent crime	Murder and nonnegligent manslaughter	Rape[1]	Robbery	Aggravated assault	Property crime	Burglary	Larceny-theft	Motor vehicle theft	Arson[2]
Elmwood Park	19,994	19	0	0	10	9	259	22	211	26	1
Elsinboro Township	961	0	0	0	0	0	3	1	1	1	0
Emerson	7,610	0	0	0	0	0	28	1	24	3	0
Englewood	28,514	51	1	7	13	30	327	69	226	32	0
Englewood Cliffs	5,351	1	0	0	1	0	47	23	16	8	0
Englishtown	1,921	2	0	0	0	2	16	7	9	0	0
Essex Fells	2,083	1	0	1	0	0	26	5	11	10	0
Evesham Township	45,148	28	0	4	3	21	359	68	281	10	2
Ewing Township	36,325	49	1	6	14	28	404	49	312	43	0
Fairfield Township, Essex County	7,468	6	0	0	2	4	117	16	91	10	0
Fair Haven	5,696	1	0	0	0	1	29	3	22	4	0
Fair Lawn	32,910	12	0	2	7	3	244	15	218	11	0
Fairview	14,209	17	0	0	8	9	131	22	92	17	0
Fanwood	7,732	2	0	0	0	2	39	11	25	3	0
Far Hills	903	0	0	0	0	0	7	1	4	2	0
Fieldsboro	553	0	0	0	0	0	0	0	0	0	0
Flemington	4,577	2	0	0	0	2	50	9	38	3	0
Florence Township	12,527	13	0	4	2	7	44	4	36	4	0
Florham Park	11,455	1	0	0	0	1	67	19	45	3	0
Fort Lee	38,921	39	0	9	8	22	374	67	263	44	1
Franklin	4,684	5	0	1	0	4	37	2	34	1	1
Franklin Lakes	11,166	2	0	0	1	1	80	8	59	13	0
Franklin Township, Gloucester County	16,226	10	0	0	2	8	142	32	95	15	1
Franklin Township, Hunterdon County	3,557	0	0	0	0	0	16	0	16	0	0
Franklin Township, Somerset County	66,138	46	3	3	17	23	648	64	537	47	0
Freehold Borough	11,643	25	0	2	15	8	170	26	137	7	0
Freehold Township	34,456	25	0	2	6	17	425	37	361	27	2
Frenchtown	1,347	0	0	0	0	0	6	0	6	0	0
Galloway Township	35,444	94	0	1	4	89	408	91	295	22	0
Garfield	31,908	35	0	3	10	22	357	26	310	21	0
Garwood	4,360	0	0	0	0	0	17	1	15	1	0
Gibbsboro	2,210	2	0	0	0	2	22	4	18	0	0
Glassboro	20,461	45	3	2	6	34	267	60	186	21	0
Glen Ridge	7,574	6	0	1	1	4	94	12	74	8	0
Glen Rock	11,705	1	0	0	0	1	48	2	39	7	0
Gloucester City	11,182	15	0	0	5	10	270	40	223	7	1
Gloucester Township	63,755	54	1	11	16	26	771	54	691	26	2
Green Brook Township	7,004	1	0	0	1	0	49	6	30	13	0
Greenwich Township, Gloucester County	4,777	3	0	0	0	3	46	3	39	4	0
Greenwich Township, Warren County	5,415	2	0	0	1	1	99	9	87	3	0
Guttenberg	11,100	16	0	0	7	9	77	10	61	6	0
Hackensack	44,264	54	2	5	19	28	573	55	455	63	0
Hackettstown	9,316	6	0	0	1	5	41	4	35	2	0
Haddonfield	11,274	3	0	0	1	2	202	11	185	6	0
Haddon Heights	7,527	3	0	0	1	2	41	11	29	1	1
Haddon Township	14,510	29	1	0	4	24	273	43	223	7	0
Haledon	8,280	12	0	3	1	8	114	13	89	12	0
Hamburg	3,110	1	0	0	0	1	9	1	8	0	0
Hamilton Township, Atlantic County	25,654	29	0	4	6	19	468	50	394	24	5
Hamilton Township, Mercer County	86,805	153	0	22	49	82	1,469	252	1,145	72	3
Hammonton	13,845	23	0	0	0	23	189	37	145	7	1
Hanover Township	14,290	6	0	1	2	3	147	7	130	10	0
Harding Township	3,750	1	0	0	0	1	27	6	16	5	0
Hardyston Township	7,744	2	0	0	0	2	33	8	24	1	0
Harrington Park	4,730	0	0	0	0	0	8	1	7	0	0
Harrison	20,937	40	0	2	13	25	289	25	227	37	0
Harrison Township	13,178	8	0	1	2	5	83	13	63	7	0
Harvey Cedars	345	0	0	0	0	0	1	0	1	0	0
Hasbrouck Heights	11,988	0	0	0	0	0	29	2	27	0	0
Haworth	3,391	0	0	0	0	0	3	1	0	2	0
Hawthorne	18,728	1	0	0	1	0	163	7	148	8	0
Hazlet Township	19,593	17	0	3	3	11	226	16	191	19	0
Helmetta	2,151	0	0	0	0	0	7	1	5	1	0
High Bridge	3,385	0	0	0	0	0	12	2	9	1	1
Highland Park	13,666	5	0	3	1	1	149	21	111	17	0
Highlands	4,682	3	0	0	0	3	22	4	18	0	0
Hightstown	5,273	10	0	1	0	9	27	1	25	1	0
Hillsborough Township	40,210	19	0	8	4	7	173	31	132	10	4
Hillsdale	10,308	0	0	0	0	0	39	3	32	4	0
Hillside Township	21,995	62	1	6	21	34	535	41	423	71	0
Hi-Nella	856	3	0	0	0	3	13	2	10	1	0
Hoboken	52,902	66	1	2	13	50	774	111	626	37	1
Ho-Ho-Kus	4,058	0	0	0	0	0	28	18	7	3	0
Holland Township	5,074	1	0	0	0	1	10	2	8	0	0
Holmdel Township	16,726	9	0	0	0	9	115	16	90	9	0

Table 8. Offenses Known to Law Enforcement, by Selected State and City, 2020—Continued

(Number.)

State/city	Population	Violent crime	Murder and nonnegligent manslaughter	Rape[1]	Robbery	Aggravated assault	Property crime	Burglary	Larceny-theft	Motor vehicle theft	Arson[2]
Hopatcong	14,086	15	1	3	0	11	28	5	21	2	0
Hopewell Borough	1,901	1	0	0	0	1	5	1	3	1	0
Hopewell Township	17,641	4	0	3	0	1	76	15	57	4	0
Howell Township	52,048	36	0	7	2	27	395	43	343	9	1
Independence Township	5,386	2	0	0	0	2	9	2	6	1	0
Interlaken	786	0	0	0	0	0	8	0	7	1	0
Irvington	54,306	230	11	18	112	89	1,008	101	551	356	0
Island Heights	1,685	2	0	0	0	2	5	1	4	0	0
Jackson Township	58,120	27	1	7	3	16	211	30	170	11	0
Jamesburg	5,878	3	0	0	1	2	13	8	4	1	0
Jefferson Township	20,626	8	0	0	0	8	52	7	39	6	0
Jersey City	263,273	1,167	17	59	340	751	3,940	500	3,004	436	9
Keansburg	9,582	25	0	6	4	15	151	14	131	6	1
Kearny	41,037	45	0	2	14	29	473	29	377	67	1
Kenilworth	8,211	5	0	2	1	2	95	13	68	14	0
Keyport	6,951	9	0	1	0	8	78	4	68	6	0
Kinnelon	9,859	1	0	0	1	0	63	8	50	5	0
Lacey Township	29,524	25	1	1	4	19	163	21	137	5	0
Lake Como	1,673	2	0	1	0	1	11	2	9	0	0
Lakehurst	2,718	5	0	1	1	3	16	3	13	0	0
Lakewood Township	108,023	131	2	4	30	95	871	178	666	27	6
Lambertville	3,788	0	0	0	0	0	21	1	20	0	0
Laurel Springs	1,860	5	0	0	1	4	12	1	11	0	0
Lavallette	1,868	1	0	0	0	1	19	0	18	1	0
Lawnside	2,872	8	0	0	3	5	96	11	85	0	0
Lawrence Township, Mercer County	32,282	40	0	9	8	23	359	44	291	24	1
Lebanon Township	6,055	1	0	0	0	1	31	7	24	0	0
Leonia	9,033	3	0	0	1	2	57	2	47	8	0
Lincoln Park	10,051	5	0	0	0	5	48	6	40	2	0
Linden	42,515	142	5	15	16	106	1,106	109	888	109	3
Lindenwold	17,206	109	1	12	31	65	416	96	287	33	4
Linwood	6,612	1	0	0	0	1	25	5	20	0	0
Little Egg Harbor Township	21,928	25	0	1	0	24	233	15	216	2	0
Little Falls Township	14,463	11	0	0	2	9	95	5	82	8	0
Little Ferry	10,736	7	0	0	1	6	52	4	39	9	0
Little Silver	5,761	1	0	0	0	1	31	1	24	6	0
Livingston Township	30,372	9	0	1	0	8	245	27	193	25	1
Loch Arbour	179	0	0	0	0	0	8	2	6	0	0
Lodi	24,343	22	0	4	2	16	183	16	152	15	0
Logan Township	5,847	4	0	0	1	3	76	2	69	5	0
Long Beach Township	3,075	4	0	0	0	4	65	8	56	1	0
Long Branch	30,175	92	0	13	21	58	560	54	469	37	0
Long Hill Township	8,389	0	0	0	0	0	43	2	38	3	0
Longport	846	0	0	0	0	0	8	2	6	0	0
Lopatcong Township	8,419	1	0	0	0	1	78	10	62	6	0
Lower Alloways Creek Township	1,660	1	0	0	0	1	5	1	4	0	0
Lower Township	21,177	33	0	5	6	22	134	21	99	14	1
Lumberton Township	12,153	15	0	1	6	8	184	16	151	17	0
Lyndhurst Township	23,169	15	0	1	6	8	159	13	127	19	0
Madison	17,850	0	0	0	0	0	152	10	125	17	0
Magnolia	4,259	17	0	0	3	14	99	17	81	1	0
Mahwah Township	26,201	5	0	0	2	3	92	11	73	8	0
Manalapan Township	39,353	12	0	7	1	4	192	20	153	19	0
Manasquan	5,796	4	0	0	0	4	80	8	69	3	0
Manchester Township	43,856	14	1	3	2	8	234	46	179	9	2
Mansfield Township, Burlington County	8,527	4	0	1	0	3	60	5	32	23	0
Mansfield Township, Warren County	7,325	0	0	0	0	0	65	6	58	1	0
Mantoloking	245	0	0	0	0	0	9	1	4	4	0
Mantua Township	14,769	12	0	1	3	8	174	30	132	12	0
Manville	10,116	11	0	5	4	2	109	7	95	7	1
Maple Shade Township	18,402	48	1	12	8	27	411	53	319	39	5
Maplewood Township	25,531	14	0	1	9	4	343	11	295	37	0
Margate City	5,813	5	0	0	1	4	129	26	98	5	0
Marlboro Township	39,593	11	0	0	1	10	302	23	244	35	2
Matawan	8,613	0	0	0	0	0	6	1	4	1	0
Maywood	9,610	2	0	0	0	2	68	6	58	4	1
Medford Lakes	3,888	1	0	0	0	1	16	1	14	1	0
Medford Township	23,433	12	0	4	1	7	203	27	175	1	3
Mendham	4,825	0	0	0	0	0	31	9	15	7	0
Mendham Township	5,632	1	0	0	0	1	24	11	7	6	0
Merchantville	3,688	6	0	0	2	4	54	9	43	2	0
Metuchen	14,639	10	0	0	1	9	199	14	176	9	0
Middlesex Borough	13,669	3	0	1	0	2	75	4	62	9	4
Middle Township	18,093	35	0	6	5	24	245	36	194	15	0
Middletown Township	65,170	16	0	3	3	10	357	33	291	33	1
Midland Park	7,214	3	0	0	0	3	24	2	21	1	0
Millburn Township	20,053	2	0	0	2	0	306	25	241	40	1
Milltown	6,967	2	0	0	0	2	69	4	65	0	0
Millville	27,272	173	2	8	35	128	928	120	764	44	3

Table 8. Offenses Known to Law Enforcement, by Selected State and City, 2020—Continued

(Number.)

State/city	Population	Violent crime	Murder and nonnegligent manslaughter	Rape[1]	Robbery	Aggravated assault	Property crime	Burglary	Larceny-theft	Motor vehicle theft	Arson[2]
Mine Hill Township	3,456	1	0	0	0	1	13	1	11	1	0
Monmouth Beach	3,235	1	0	0	0	1	22	2	14	6	0
Monroe Township, Gloucester County	36,893	30	0	2	11	17	400	62	316	22	1
Monroe Township, Middlesex County	45,653	9	0	0	0	9	114	19	82	13	0
Montclair	38,621	38	0	3	14	21	267	35	211	21	1
Montgomery Township	23,268	9	0	1	0	8	84	42	35	7	0
Montvale	8,643	2	0	0	1	1	26	2	19	5	0
Montville Township	20,982	3	0	1	1	1	164	25	119	20	0
Moonachie	2,700	6	0	2	0	4	36	0	35	1	0
Moorestown Township	20,491	14	0	3	5	6	149	15	124	10	0
Morris Plains	6,335	6	0	1	1	4	54	4	48	2	0
Morristown	19,337	30	0	1	3	26	141	15	119	7	0
Morris Township	22,100	8	0	0	0	8	117	15	92	10	0
Mountain Lakes	4,224	0	0	0	0	0	44	12	26	6	0
Mountainside	6,902	0	0	0	0	0	39	6	25	8	0
Mount Arlington	5,944	4	0	0	0	4	32	4	26	2	0
Mount Ephraim	4,573	8	0	0	1	7	285	15	263	7	0
Mount Holly Township	9,546	45	0	5	5	35	105	6	98	1	0
Mount Laurel Township	41,179	58	2	14	9	33	513	26	451	36	0
Mount Olive Township	28,973	12	0	4	0	8	104	10	85	9	0
Mullica Township	5,825	7	0	0	0	7	100	26	71	3	0
National Park	2,929	5	0	0	1	4	40	11	29	0	0
Neptune City	4,573	19	0	1	4	14	124	9	111	4	1
Neptune Township	27,320	107	0	3	26	78	909	90	808	11	4
Netcong	3,116	1	0	0	1	0	13	2	11	0	0
Newark	282,242	1,492	56	116	367	953	4,567	535	2,325	1,707	29
New Brunswick	55,701	285	4	13	78	190	964	136	752	76	3
Newfield	1,536	2	0	0	2	0	3	0	2	1	0
New Hanover Township	7,859	0	0	0	0	0	3	0	3	0	0
New Milford	16,417	19	0	0	0	19	74	6	64	4	0
New Providence	13,741	3	0	0	2	1	55	0	45	10	0
Newton	8,008	6	0	4	1	1	37	6	29	2	0
North Arlington	15,695	7	0	3	0	4	106	13	84	9	0
North Bergen Township	60,567	52	0	11	11	30	305	20	229	56	0
North Brunswick Township	41,383	69	1	4	10	54	500	54	421	25	0
North Caldwell	6,666	2	0	0	1	1	24	14	6	4	0
Northfield	7,979	0	0	0	0	0	73	14	53	6	0
North Haledon	8,382	6	0	0	0	6	55	5	45	5	0
North Hanover Township	7,443	4	0	0	0	4	17	4	10	3	0
North Plainfield	21,279	25	0	2	17	6	302	23	265	14	2
Northvale	4,955	1	0	0	0	1	5	0	5	0	0
North Wildwood	3,731	12	0	1	2	9	108	5	98	5	0
Norwood	5,792	3	0	0	1	2	20	2	16	2	0
Nutley Township	28,408	21	0	0	4	17	170	16	131	23	1
Oakland	12,929	4	0	1	0	3	90	9	78	3	0
Oaklyn	3,942	4	0	0	2	2	107	14	83	10	0
Ocean City	10,893	8	0	1	2	5	334	39	287	8	1
Ocean Gate	2,042	0	0	0	0	0	19	6	13	0	0
Oceanport	5,708	5	0	0	0	5	52	11	37	4	0
Ocean Township, Monmouth County	26,462	22	0	0	14	8	541	49	466	26	2
Ocean Township, Ocean County	9,184	0	0	0	0	0	33	0	33	0	0
Ogdensburg	2,237	1	0	0	0	1	10	2	8	0	0
Old Bridge Township	65,537	26	0	2	9	15	356	52	252	52	0
Old Tappan	5,904	1	0	0	0	1	13	4	3	6	0
Oradell	8,137	3	0	1	0	2	35	17	15	3	0
Orange City	30,541	143	3	11	61	68	529	80	334	115	10
Oxford Township	2,412	0	0	0	0	0	11	1	10	0	0
Palisades Park	20,818	7	0	1	1	5	105	23	65	17	0
Palmyra	7,114	14	0	2	3	9	122	11	108	3	0
Paramus	26,222	23	0	1	2	20	455	9	420	26	0
Park Ridge	8,688	0	0	0	0	0	13	5	7	1	0
Parsippany-Troy Hills Township	51,317	26	2	2	5	17	269	32	213	24	0
Passaic	69,610	279	4	5	85	185	1,028	105	800	123	1
Paterson	144,947	1,433	27	50	426	930	2,160	566	1,342	252	15
Paulsboro	5,820	16	0	0	2	14	95	21	64	10	0
Peapack-Gladstone	2,606	0	0	0	0	0	21	7	13	1	0
Pemberton Borough	1,315	0	0	0	0	0	21	2	19	0	0
Pemberton Township	26,875	61	2	13	10	36	379	114	232	33	2
Pennington	2,575	0	0	0	0	0	4	0	4	0	0
Pennsauken Township	35,698	95	1	3	30	61	923	137	691	95	3
Penns Grove	4,721	53	5	3	9	36	199	33	148	18	4
Pennsville Township	12,315	19	0	2	7	10	260	39	209	12	3
Pequannock Township	14,887	4	0	0	1	3	67	9	49	9	0
Perth Amboy	51,384	137	1	4	23	109	508	61	393	54	1
Phillipsburg	14,136	38	0	11	8	19	234	30	189	15	2
Pine Beach	2,192	1	0	0	0	1	8	0	7	1	0
Pine Hill	10,427	32	1	2	6	23	167	35	112	20	2
Pine Valley	11	0	0	0	0	0	0	0	0	0	0
Piscataway Township	56,870	60	1	14	9	36	381	42	303	36	5

Table 8. Offenses Known to Law Enforcement, by Selected State and City, 2020—Continued

(Number.)

State/city	Population	Violent crime	Murder and nonnegligent manslaughter	Rape[1]	Robbery	Aggravated assault	Property crime	Burglary	Larceny-theft	Motor vehicle theft	Arson[2]
Pitman	8,701	7	0	0	0	7	44	1	42	1	0
Plainfield	50,333	228	7	4	75	142	733	84	582	67	3
Plainsboro Township	22,847	8	0	1	0	7	90	14	69	7	1
Pleasantville	20,135	27	2	1	20	4	266	117	124	25	1
Plumsted Township	8,598	1	0	1	0	0	40	10	28	2	0
Pohatcong Township	3,158	2	0	0	1	1	212	39	172	1	0
Point Pleasant	18,842	25	0	5	2	18	116	16	93	7	0
Point Pleasant Beach	4,543	6	0	0	0	6	84	17	55	12	0
Pompton Lakes	10,961	8	0	0	1	7	35	2	32	1	0
Princeton	31,458	11	0	0	3	8	196	19	161	16	0
Prospect Park	5,834	6	0	1	3	2	98	14	79	5	0
Rahway	30,157	43	1	2	14	26	201	27	134	40	0
Ramsey	14,904	5	0	0	1	4	86	10	66	10	0
Randolph Township	25,311	1	0	0	0	1	94	8	79	7	0
Raritan	7,888	2	0	0	0	2	60	5	48	7	0
Raritan Township	22,402	6	0	0	0	6	74	6	66	2	0
Readington Township	15,813	2	0	1	0	1	77	12	59	6	0
Red Bank	11,929	27	0	11	1	15	116	11	98	7	0
Ridgefield	11,171	3	0	0	1	2	81	20	53	8	0
Ridgefield Park	12,904	6	0	0	0	6	155	3	139	13	0
Ridgewood	25,036	8	0	2	1	5	133	9	115	9	2
Ringwood	12,177	2	0	0	0	2	25	2	22	1	0
Riverdale	4,198	0	0	0	0	0	133	2	131	0	0
River Edge	11,431	1	0	0	1	0	84	5	78	1	0
Riverside Township	7,788	16	0	2	2	12	82	16	66	0	1
Riverton	2,676	0	0	0	0	0	15	0	14	1	0
River Vale Township	10,007	0	0	0	0	0	25	2	22	1	0
Robbinsville Township	14,628	2	0	0	0	2	45	7	36	2	0
Rochelle Park Township	5,566	3	0	0	1	2	75	0	70	5	0
Rockaway	6,250	1	0	0	1	0	31	3	21	7	0
Rockaway Township	26,046	6	0	0	3	3	181	10	161	10	0
Rockleigh	528	0	0	0	0	0	0	0	0	0	0
Roseland	5,829	0	0	0	0	0	28	1	20	7	0
Roselle	21,867	34	0	1	8	25	231	23	174	34	1
Roselle Park	13,604	5	0	1	2	2	110	9	97	4	0
Roxbury Township	22,439	2	0	0	2	0	85	9	73	3	1
Rumson	6,675	0	0	0	0	0	49	0	28	21	0
Runnemede	8,273	8	1	0	3	4	161	23	131	7	0
Rutherford	18,307	10	1	4	0	5	177	18	136	23	0
Saddle Brook Township	13,533	0	0	0	0	0	188	1	182	5	0
Saddle River	3,170	3	0	0	0	3	23	8	10	5	0
Salem	4,661	96	11	11	27	47	158	53	87	18	1
Sayreville	44,282	55	0	2	11	42	260	32	192	36	0
Scotch Plains Township	24,313	5	0	1	1	3	164	67	82	15	0
Sea Bright	1,325	0	0	0	0	0	5	1	4	0	0
Sea Girt	1,758	0	0	0	0	0	13	4	6	3	0
Sea Isle City	2,019	1	0	0	0	1	114	20	94	0	0
Seaside Heights	2,917	36	0	0	11	25	194	22	165	7	0
Seaside Park	1,541	4	0	0	2	2	25	3	22	0	0
Secaucus	22,535	50	0	9	17	24	402	23	360	19	0
Ship Bottom	1,156	1	0	0	0	1	13	1	12	0	0
Shrewsbury	4,082	2	0	1	0	1	57	3	49	5	0
Somerdale	5,511	11	0	0	3	8	245	13	228	4	0
Somers Point	10,108	24	1	3	9	11	220	30	184	6	0
Somerville	12,084	2	0	0	0	2	107	5	87	15	0
South Amboy	9,235	12	1	0	0	11	73	5	63	5	0
South Bound Brook	4,526	2	0	0	1	1	30	2	27	1	0
South Brunswick Township	45,877	23	0	6	3	14	353	42	303	8	0
South Hackensack Township	2,438	9	0	0	4	5	68	4	50	14	0
South Harrison Township	3,110	0	0	0	0	0	10	0	10	0	0
South Orange Village	16,732	15	0	0	7	8	201	8	157	36	0
South Plainfield	24,100	28	0	0	6	22	288	30	247	11	1
South River	15,731	29	0	4	3	22	85	14	68	3	1
South Toms River	3,701	7	0	0	0	7	25	5	18	2	0
Sparta Township	18,467	4	0	0	0	4	18	2	14	2	0
Spotswood	8,216	6	0	0	0	6	30	7	22	1	0
Springfield Township, Burlington County	3,241	0	0	0	0	0	20	6	13	1	0
Springfield Township, Union County	17,639	13	0	1	5	7	150	17	119	14	0
Spring Lake	2,894	0	0	0	0	0	52	4	42	6	0
Spring Lake Heights	4,502	3	0	1	0	2	10	1	9	0	0
Stafford Township	28,029	13	0	3	2	8	178	14	154	10	0
Stanhope	3,275	0	0	0	0	0	12	1	9	2	0
Stone Harbor	804	2	0	1	0	1	69	9	58	2	0
Stratford	6,937	5	0	0	2	3	103	8	92	3	0
Summit	21,917	4	0	2	0	2	202	15	156	31	0
Surf City	1,203	1	0	1	0	0	19	0	15	4	0
Swedesboro	2,562	0	0	0	0	0	15	2	11	2	0
Tavistock	5	0	0	0	0	0	0	0	0	0	0
Teaneck Township	40,290	51	0	8	12	31	398	49	323	26	3
Tenafly	14,427	5	0	0	2	3	65	13	37	15	0
Teterboro	68	0	0	0	0	0	89	0	88	1	0

Table 8. Offenses Known to Law Enforcement, by Selected State and City, 2020—Continued

(Number.)

State/city	Population	Violent crime	Murder and nonnegligent manslaughter	Rape[1]	Robbery	Aggravated assault	Property crime	Burglary	Larceny-theft	Motor vehicle theft	Arson[2]
Tewksbury Township	5,754	4	0	0	0	4	33	14	12	7	0
Tinton Falls	17,388	10	0	0	3	7	238	16	217	5	0
Toms River Township	94,561	85	2	6	17	60	997	135	834	28	0
Totowa	10,777	14	0	0	3	11	184	16	136	32	0
Trenton	82,909	969	40	50	262	617	1,733	412	1,038	283	23
Tuckerton	3,396	13	0	1	0	12	14	1	11	2	0
Union Beach	5,210	6	0	0	0	6	4	3	1	0	0
Union City	68,055	203	0	10	42	151	1,185	98	1,017	70	5
Union Township	58,613	56	0	3	21	32	721	34	626	61	3
Upper Saddle River	8,199	1	0	0	0	1	34	3	21	10	0
Ventnor City	9,815	17	0	1	3	13	268	34	228	6	0
Vernon Township	21,819	1	0	0	0	1	89	11	73	5	0
Verona	13,368	1	0	1	0	0	90	7	79	4	0
Vineland	59,288	227	3	17	34	173	1,239	198	1,000	41	5
Voorhees Township	29,130	17	0	0	5	12	264	39	218	7	1
Waldwick	10,156	2	0	0	0	2	56	1	52	3	0
Wallington	11,499	11	0	0	3	8	133	6	115	12	0
Wall Township	25,489	12	0	0	4	8	226	37	172	17	0
Wanaque	11,828	5	0	0	2	3	25	1	22	2	0
Warren Township	15,689	1	0	0	1	0	57	15	30	12	0
Washington	6,446	2	0	0	0	2	53	15	37	1	1
Washington Township, Bergen County	9,171	3	0	0	2	1	19	5	12	2	0
Washington Township, Gloucester County	47,551	56	0	0	8	48	407	57	333	17	1
Washington Township, Morris County	18,086	14	0	4	1	9	73	4	64	5	0
Washington Township, Warren County	6,323	1	0	0	0	1	51	6	43	2	0
Watchung	6,018	0	0	0	0	0	271	11	257	3	0
Waterford Township	10,675	15	0	1	1	13	65	14	47	4	0
Wayne Township	53,162	54	0	0	7	47	649	64	554	31	1
Weehawken Township	14,874	20	0	2	6	12	260	33	211	16	0
Wenonah	2,202	2	0	0	0	2	19	3	15	1	0
Westampton Township	8,632	30	0	9	2	19	163	23	130	10	2
West Amwell Township	2,728	0	0	0	0	0	12	1	8	3	0
West Caldwell Township	10,841	3	0	0	1	2	62	2	56	4	0
West Cape May	1,000	1	0	0	0	1	6	0	6	0	0
West Deptford Township	20,878	16	0	0	5	11	243	61	167	15	0
Westfield	29,389	8	0	0	3	5	172	11	136	25	0
West Long Branch	7,860	2	0	1	1	0	102	4	94	4	0
West Milford Township	26,310	11	0	2	1	8	93	7	83	3	0
West New York	52,977	106	0	12	32	62	587	62	480	45	1
West Orange	47,666	59	1	11	14	33	683	89	525	69	1
Westville	4,123	9	1	0	1	7	93	18	71	4	1
West Wildwood	545	0	0	0	0	0	16	5	10	1	0
West Windsor Township	27,944	11	0	2	2	7	252	19	226	7	1
Westwood	11,079	0	0	0	0	0	56	18	37	1	0
Wharton	6,343	8	0	0	2	6	70	2	63	5	0
Wildwood	4,908	35	0	2	8	25	330	44	281	5	0
Wildwood Crest	3,024	9	0	0	0	9	94	14	77	3	1
Willingboro Township	32,048	95	2	4	22	67	174	42	115	17	1
Winfield Township	1,504	1	0	1	0	0	6	1	5	0	0
Winslow Township	38,460	72	0	2	17	53	336	57	251	28	5
Woodbridge Township	100,119	126	1	16	20	89	1,236	107	1,020	109	7
Woodbury	9,744	38	1	0	15	22	328	44	266	18	3
Woodbury Heights	2,949	1	0	0	0	1	71	8	62	1	0
Woodcliff Lake	5,845	1	0	0	0	1	21	3	15	3	0
Woodland Park	12,653	12	0	0	1	11	122	11	99	12	0
Woodlynne	2,906	13	0	0	1	12	70	7	50	13	0
Wood-Ridge	9,489	2	0	1	0	1	48	3	41	4	0
Woodstown	3,429	0	0	0	0	0	30	10	19	1	0
Woolwich Township	13,278	1	0	0	0	1	47	2	43	2	0
Wyckoff Township	16,950	2	0	0	1	1	100	13	78	9	0
NEW MEXICO											
Albuquerque	562,065	7,552	80	441	1,439	5,592	28,171	5,075	18,131	4,965	166
Angel Fire[4]	1,055	4	0	0	0	4	15	2	11	2	
Aztec[4]	6,328	25	0	2	0	23	100	28	65	7	0
Bloomfield[4]	7,633	77	1	15	6	55	121	21	91	9	1
Carlsbad[4]	30,233	195	4	18	10	163	1,039	175	708	156	7
Dexter	1,241	1	0	0	0	1	8	6	0	2	
Farmington[4]	44,191	529	1	78	40	410	1,447	295	1,010	142	20
Gallup[4]	21,460	381	5	15	84	277	912	191	623	98	
Las Vegas	12,799	56	0	3	7	46	177	41	121	15	
Logan[4]	972	2	0	1	0	1	27	11	15	1	
Sunland Park	18,437	96	0	3	3	90	115	28	72	15	2
Taos	5,917	31	0	4	3	24	289	53	209	27	
NEW YORK											
Adams Village	1,706	0	0	0	0	0	3	1	1	1	0
Addison Town and Village	2,458	6	0	0	0	6	7	0	7	0	0
Afton Village	795	0	0	0	0	0	0	0	0	0	0

Table 8. Offenses Known to Law Enforcement, by Selected State and City, 2020—Continued

(Number.)

State/city	Population	Violent crime	Murder and nonnegligent manslaughter	Rape[1]	Robbery	Aggravated assault	Property crime	Burglary	Larceny-theft	Motor vehicle theft	Arson[2]
Albany	96,318	869	16	61	161	631	2,650	422	1,945	283	21
Albion Village	5,698	24	0	3	1	20	146	23	121	2	1
Alexandria Bay Village	1,023	0	0	0	0	0	3	1	2	0	0
Alfred Village	3,970	1	0	1	0	0	17	4	13	0	0
Allegany Village	1,685	1	0	1	0	0	7	2	5	0	0
Amherst Town	121,304	153	0	18	39	96	1,865	171	1,597	97	0
Amityville Village	9,387	5	2	0	2	1	61	5	49	7	0
Amsterdam	17,675	37	0	4	9	24	281	53	213	15	3
Angelica Village	812	0	0	0	0	0	0	0	0	0	0
Arcade Village	1,919	3	0	1	0	2	14	2	12	0	0
Attica Village	2,389	0	0	0	0	0	14	0	11	3	0
Baldwinsville Village	7,895	4	0	0	1	3	50	4	45	1	1
Ballston Spa Village	5,204	0	0	0	0	0	39	9	29	1	0
Barker	504	0	0	0	0	0	0	0	0	0	0
Batavia	14,278	64	0	13	12	39	345	45	286	14	0
Beacon	13,984	15	0	1	2	12	123	22	96	5	1
Bedford Town	17,672	2	0	0	1	1	42	4	35	3	0
Bethlehem Town	35,039	26	1	7	3	15	380	25	346	9	0
Binghamton[4]	44,083	372	1	28	50	293	1,775	294	1,380	101	15
Black River	1,229	0	0	0	0	0	3	0	3	0	0
Bolton Town	2,239	0	0	0	0	0	6	0	6	0	0
Brant Town	2,056	0	0	0	0	0	15	1	12	2	0
Brewster	2,329	2	0	0	0	2	9	3	6	0	0
Briarcliff Manor Village	8,126	2	0	0	2	0	34	3	25	6	0
Brighton Town[4]	35,853	34	0	9	4	21	702	72	598	32	3
Brockport Village[4]	8,142	10	0	2	2	6	52	10	40	2	0
Brownville Village	1,076	0	0	0	0	0	2	1	1	0	0
Buchanan Village	2,233	0	0	0	0	0	12	0	12	0	0
Buffalo[4]	254,627	2,592	61	53	680	1,798	7,844	1,146	5,508	1,190	121
Cairo Town	6,390	3	0	0	0	3	39	5	33	1	1
Caledonia Village	2,083	0	0	0	0	0	2	0	2	0	0
Cambridge Village	1,803	1	0	0	1	0	17	3	13	1	0
Camden Village	2,151	0	0	0	0	0	22	1	20	1	0
Camillus Town and Village	24,098	13	0	1	2	10	265	21	229	15	1
Canajoharie Village	2,122	1	0	1	0	0	14	3	11	0	0
Canandaigua	10,112	37	1	11	5	20	219	24	186	9	1
Canastota Village	4,518	6	0	0	1	5	34	1	26	7	1
Canisteo Village	2,120	1	0	0	0	1	4	2	2	0	0
Canton Village[4]	6,516	0	0	0	0	0	13	0	13	0	0
Cape Vincent Village	689	0	0	0	0	0	1	0	1	0	0
Carmel Town	34,093	5	0	0	0	5	113	7	99	7	0
Carroll Town[4]	3,309	0	0	0	0	0	25	5	18	2	
Carthage Village	3,250	4	0	2	0	2	53	9	43	1	0
Catskill Village	3,787	6	0	1	0	5	71	5	66	0	0
Cattaraugus Village	897	0	0	0	0	0	2	1	1	0	0
Cayuga Heights Village	3,589	2	0	1	1	0	15	2	13	0	0
Cazenovia Village	2,851	2	0	0	0	2	20	6	14	0	0
Central Square Village	1,740	0	0	0	0	0	40	1	38	1	0
Centre Island Village	409	0	0	0	0	0	1	1	0	0	0
Chatham Village	1,606	0	0	0	0	0	1	0	1	0	0
Cheektowaga Town	76,536	216	1	22	51	142	2,226	273	1,782	171	11
Chester Town	8,095	0	0	0	0	0	7	1	6	0	0
Chester Village	4,108	2	0	1	0	1	13	0	12	1	0
Chittenango Village	4,826	3	0	0	0	3	19	2	16	1	0
Cicero Town	28,755	14	0	2	5	7	291	21	244	26	0
Clarkstown Town[4]	80,462	44	0	5	10	29	872	45	787	40	3
Clayton Village	1,816	0	0	0	0	0	3	0	3	0	0
Clyde Village	1,948	5	0	2	1	2	34	6	28	0	0
Cobleskill Village	4,323	19	0	0	4	15	126	11	113	2	0
Coeymans Town	7,247	8	0	0	1	7	41	6	27	8	0
Colchester Town	1,947	1	0	0	0	1	9	3	5	1	0
Cold Spring Village	1,940	0	0	0	0	0	12	1	11	0	0
Colonie Town	79,082	83	0	4	28	51	1,853	111	1,677	65	5
Cooperstown Village	1,743	0	0	0	0	0	1	1	0	0	0
Corning	10,469	33	1	9	3	20	273	68	198	7	1
Cornwall-on-Hudson Village	2,911	0	0	0	0	0	21	4	16	1	0
Cornwall Town	9,538	2	0	0	0	2	4	1	3	0	0
Cortland	18,615	49	0	13	3	33	514	74	434	6	0
Coxsackie Village	2,655	0	0	0	0	0	1	0	1	0	0
Croton-on-Hudson Village	8,097	2	0	1	0	1	40	2	36	2	0
Cuba Town	3,059	2	1	0	0	1	31	6	22	3	0
Dansville Village	4,341	2	0	0	2	0	53	7	45	1	0
Delhi Village	2,935	2	0	2	0	0	24	4	19	1	0
Depew Village	14,965	23	0	6	2	15	228	31	190	7	2
DeWitt Town	24,947	46	0	2	10	34	724	70	613	41	1
Dexter Village	992	0	0	0	0	0	2	0	2	0	0
Dobbs Ferry Village	11,037	2	0	0	1	1	96	5	85	6	0
Dolgeville Village	2,055	1	0	1	0	0	20	0	19	1	0
Dryden Village	2,066	3	0	0	1	2	57	6	51	0	0
Dunkirk[4]	11,673	27	0	0	3	24	248	57	185	6	1
Durham Town	2,648	0	0	0	0	0	1	0	1	0	0
East Aurora-Aurora Town	13,748	3	0	0	2	1	76	7	66	3	0
Eastchester Town	19,991	1	0	0	0	1	135	4	112	19	1

Table 8. Offenses Known to Law Enforcement, by Selected State and City, 2020—Continued

(Number.)

State/city	Population	Violent crime	Murder and nonnegligent manslaughter	Rape[1]	Robbery	Aggravated assault	Property crime	Burglary	Larceny-theft	Motor vehicle theft	Arson[2]
East Fishkill Town	29,578	12	0	4	2	6	137	1	126	10	0
East Greenbush Town	16,186	15	0	2	5	8	530	27	496	7	0
East Hampton Village	1,140	1	0	0	0	1	23	2	19	2	0
Eden Town	7,602	1	0	1	0	0	22	4	17	1	0
Ellicott Town[4]	4,981	11	0	1	2	8	233	21	210	2	
Ellicottville	1,563	0	0	0	0	0	20	1	19	0	0
Elmira	26,820	59	2	0	25	32	812	87	684	41	6
Elmira Heights Village	3,774	2	0	0	0	2	84	6	75	3	0
Elmira Town	5,529	0	0	0	0	0	0	0	0	0	0
Elmsford Village	5,279	1	0	0	0	1	11	0	10	1	0
Endicott Village[4]	12,443	52	0	7	8	37	397	68	312	17	2
Evans Town	16,061	23	0	8	1	14	154	18	124	12	2
Fairport Village[4]	5,300	2	0	0	0	2	28	2	23	3	0
Fishkill Village	2,153	2	0	0	0	2	30	2	28	0	0
Floral Park Village	15,844	10	0	0	3	7	61	9	41	11	0
Fort Plain Village	2,212	8	0	0	2	6	52	6	44	2	0
Frankfort Town	4,752	4	0	0	0	4	21	1	19	1	1
Frankfort Village	2,409	3	0	2	0	1	7	2	4	1	0
Franklinville Village	1,618	0	0	0	0	0	3	2	1	0	0
Fredonia Village[4]	10,205	11	0	0	1	10	298	27	271	0	
Friendship Town	1,854	0	0	0	0	0	4	1	2	1	0
Galway Village	190	0	0	0	0	0	0	0	0	0	0
Garden City Village	22,465	5	0	0	0	5	243	8	221	14	0
Gates Town	28,222	65	0	7	20	38	730	67	609	54	1
Geddes Town	10,002	6	0	1	1	4	176	10	149	17	0
Geneseo Village	8,130	1	0	0	0	1	75	4	69	2	0
Geneva	12,569	38	0	14	4	20	173	34	136	3	0
Glen Cove	27,186	3	0	0	1	2	107	13	89	5	1
Glen Park Village	469	0	0	0	0	0	1	0	1	0	0
Glens Falls[4]	14,215	10	0	2	0	8	105	7	95	3	
Glenville Town	21,609	12	0	3	2	7	312	15	288	9	1
Gloversville	14,656	79	1	14	10	54	400	57	330	13	4
Goshen Village	5,361	2	0	0	0	2	21	2	17	2	0
Gowanda Village	2,531	4	0	0	1	3	35	7	24	4	1
Granville Village	2,428	2	0	0	0	2	7	3	4	0	0
Great Neck Estates Village	2,892	1	0	0	0	1	8	3	2	3	0
Greece Town[4]	95,431	150	2	16	34	98	1,708	219	1,371	118	6
Greenburgh Town[4]	44,727	25	0	4	10	11	436	26	387	23	1
Greene Village	1,400	0	0	0	0	0	14	0	13	1	0
Greenwich Village	1,708	0	0	0	0	0	11	0	11	0	0
Greenwood Lake Village	3,080	3	0	1	0	2	19	1	16	2	0
Groton Village	2,211	0	0	0	0	0	35	3	30	2	0
Guilderland Town	34,103	25	0	7	2	16	677	54	616	7	0
Hamburg Town	46,513	51	0	0	16	35	674	83	570	21	1
Hamburg Village	9,744	6	0	0	1	5	71	14	56	1	0
Hamilton Village	4,077	0	0	0	0	0	5	1	4	0	0
Hancock Village	923	1	0	0	0	1	8	2	4	2	0
Harrison Town	29,110	6	0	0	1	5	126	12	104	10	0
Hastings-on-Hudson Village	7,853	2	0	0	1	1	94	5	84	5	0
Haverstraw Town	37,034	29	2	0	6	21	225	24	198	3	0
Hempstead Village	55,230	357	8	3	105	241	568	105	357	106	3
Herkimer Village	7,212	10	0	2	4	4	289	28	259	2	0
Highlands Town	8,329	0	0	0	0	0	0	0	0	0	0
Holley Village	1,669	1	0	0	0	1	9	3	6	0	0
Homer Village	3,081	0	0	0	0	0	1	1	0	0	0
Horseheads Village	6,325	14	0	2	2	10	97	9	81	7	0
Hudson[4]	6,004	22	0	3	2	17	154	16	136	2	4
Hudson Falls Village	7,029	7	0	3	1	3	17	3	10	4	0
Hunter Town	2,620	0	0	0	0	0	20	2	16	2	0
Huntington Bay Village	1,436	0	0	0	0	0	7	0	7	0	0
Ilion Village	7,613	28	0	6	1	21	194	22	166	6	1
Independence Town	1,130	0	0	0	0	0	3	1	2	0	0
Inlet Town	301	1	0	0	0	1	4	2	2	0	0
Irvington Village	6,478	2	0	1	1	0	29	3	24	2	0
Ithaca	30,927	98	0	14	31	53	1,157	141	1,000	16	2
Johnson City Village[4]	14,055	65	1	6	13	45	882	92	765	25	2
Johnstown	8,183	10	0	4	1	5	128	11	111	6	0
Jordan Village	1,294	0	0	0	0	0	3	1	2	0	0
Kenmore Village	14,968	37	0	0	9	28	242	27	201	14	0
Kensington Village	1,193	0	0	0	0	0	0	0	0	0	0
Kent Town	13,123	1	0	0	1	0	37	5	29	3	1
Kings Point Village	5,315	0	0	0	0	0	12	0	3	9	0
Kingston	22,682	85	3	12	17	53	455	55	378	22	5
Lackawanna	17,674	100	0	9	9	82	347	69	241	37	5
Lake Placid Village	2,339	7	0	2	0	5	16	4	12	0	0
Lake Success Village	3,161	0	0	0	0	0	14	5	5	4	0
Lakewood-Busti[4]	7,125	5	0	5	0	0	344	46	294	4	
Lancaster Town	37,633	12	0	2	1	9	347	33	298	16	0
Larchmont Village	6,112	4	0	0	0	4	82	4	73	5	0
Lewisboro Town	12,533	0	0	0	0	0	0	0	0	0	0
Liberty Village	4,182	24	1	4	4	15	150	26	120	4	0
Little Falls	4,604	12	1	2	0	9	61	17	41	3	2
Liverpool Village	2,191	0	0	0	0	0	10	0	9	1	0

Table 8. Offenses Known to Law Enforcement, by Selected State and City, 2020—Continued

(Number.)

State/city	Population	Violent crime	Murder and nonnegligent manslaughter	Rape[1]	Robbery	Aggravated assault	Property crime	Burglary	Larceny-theft	Motor vehicle theft	Arson[2]
Lloyd Harbor Village	3,655	2	0	0	0	2	12	2	7	3	0
Lloyd Town[4]	10,484	6	0	3	0	3	80	3	76	1	1
Lockport	20,212	116	0	19	26	71	490	79	385	26	1
Long Beach	33,461	13	0	0	6	7	46	4	39	3	0
Lowville Village	3,297	2	0	0	0	2	8	2	6	0	0
Lynbrook Village	19,441	15	0	0	5	10	115	10	94	11	0
Macedon Town and Village	8,856	9	0	3	1	5	87	4	79	4	1
Malone Village	5,566	32	0	5	4	23	189	33	151	5	2
Malverne Village	8,482	0	0	0	0	0	16	2	13	1	0
Mamaroneck Town	12,017	0	0	0	0	0	54	4	48	2	0
Mamaroneck Village	19,154	20	0	1	5	14	182	25	144	13	0
Manlius Town	24,139	15	0	2	1	12	259	28	211	20	2
Marcellus Village	1,707	0	0	0	0	0	7	0	7	0	0
Marlborough Town	8,579	2	0	1	0	1	19	2	17	0	0
Mechanicville	5,018	13	0	3	2	8	41	8	31	2	0
Medina Village	5,613	14	0	2	4	8	80	20	51	9	0
Menands Village	3,850	3	0	0	1	2	128	8	111	9	1
Middleport Village	1,733	1	0	0	0	1	11	0	8	3	0
Middletown	28,194	90	1	9	22	58	383	52	299	32	2
Millerton Village	2,938	0	0	0	0	0	6	2	3	1	0
Mohawk Village	2,507	2	0	0	1	1	23	4	19	0	0
Monroe Village	8,609	3	0	0	0	3	97	4	93	0	0
Montgomery Village	4,617	0	0	0	0	0	6	0	6	0	0
Monticello Village	6,338	23	0	2	5	16	82	22	58	2	1
Moravia Village	1,201	0	0	0	0	0	9	4	4	1	0
Moriah Town	4,437	0	0	0	0	0	0	0	0	0	0
Mount Hope Town	6,625	3	0	0	0	3	14	0	13	1	0
Mount Morris Village	2,765	5	0	1	0	4	51	12	35	4	0
Mount Vernon	67,339	382	7	21	84	270	879	132	615	132	15
Nassau Village	1,094	1	0	1	0	0	5	1	4	0	0
Newark Village	8,784	31	0	10	3	18	294	34	248	12	0
New Berlin Town	1,507	0	0	0	0	0	5	1	4	0	0
Newburgh	28,095	285	4	17	59	205	720	151	510	59	4
Newburgh Town	31,691	46	4	3	13	26	765	45	698	22	1
New Castle Town	17,824	0	0	0	0	0	77	2	74	1	0
New Hartford Town and Village[4]	20,173	18	0	6	5	7	467	19	444	4	0
New Windsor Town	27,980	20	0	1	4	15	298	26	264	8	1
New York	8,300,377	47,959	468	2,253	13,182	32,056	129,361	13,907	106,196	9,258	
New York Mills Village	3,200	2	0	0	0	2	43	8	32	3	1
Niagara Town[4]	8,012	1	0	0	0	1	195	18	146	31	1
Niskayuna Town	22,428	18	0	3	5	10	422	29	376	17	0
Nissequogue Village	1,730	0	0	0	0	0	10	3	7	0	0
Norfolk Town	4,380	1	0	0	0	1	1	0	1	0	0
North Castle Town	12,266	1	0	0	0	1	88	10	61	17	0
North Greenbush Town	12,264	12	0	5	1	6	179	15	156	8	0
Northport Village	7,258	0	0	0	0	0	2	0	2	0	0
North Syracuse Village	6,607	15	0	0	3	12	109	10	91	8	
North Tonawanda[4]	30,104	37	0	4	8	25	330	45	266	19	1
Norwich	6,474	28	0	12	5	11	169	24	142	3	0
Norwood Village	1,549	3	0	0	0	3	15	4	10	1	0
Ogden Town[4]	20,603	11	0	2	3	6	154	13	136	5	2
Old Brookville Village	2,196	1	0	0	0	1	47	6	23	18	0
Old Westbury Village[4]	4,603	1	0	0	0	1	20	3	11	6	1
Olean	13,334	25	0	1	1	23	242	25	204	13	1
Oneida	10,849	67	1	14	4	48	479	55	417	7	2
Orangetown Town[4]	37,320	15	1	0	7	7	289	33	241	15	0
Orchard Park Town	29,653	8	0	0	3	5	277	35	233	9	0
Oriskany Village	1,321	0	0	0	0	0	7	0	7	0	0
Ossining Village	24,786	17	0	0	7	10	196	14	176	6	1
Owego Village	3,846	15	0	2	1	12	175	32	139	4	1
Oxford Village	1,372	0	0	0	0	0	3	0	2	1	0
Oyster Bay Cove Village	4,300	0	0	0	0	0	17	3	9	5	0
Painted Post Village	1,939	1	0	0	0	1	2	0	1	1	0
Palmyra Village	3,299	0	0	0	0	0	10	2	7	1	0
Peekskill	24,371	33	3	3	14	13	176	11	156	9	1
Pelham Manor Village	5,535	1	0	0	0	1	134	20	109	5	0
Pelham Village	6,956	1	0	0	0	1	57	2	53	2	0
Penn Yan Village	4,900	3	0	2	1	0	59	6	53	0	0
Perry Village	3,471	3	0	2	0	1	49	6	42	1	0
Phoenix Village	2,226	3	0	0	0	3	7	3	4	0	0
Pine Plains Town	2,399	0	0	0	0	0	1	1	0	0	0
Plattsburgh City	19,460	27	0	3	1	23	239	26	207	6	1
Pleasantville Village	7,280	4	0	0	1	3	55	7	43	5	0
Port Byron Village	1,182	0	0	0	0	0	0	0	0	0	0
Port Chester Village	29,181	22	0	3	6	13	209	18	180	11	3
Port Jervis	8,526	22	0	6	3	13	116	10	97	9	1
Portville Village	941	0	0	0	0	0	0	0	0	0	0
Port Washington	19,391	8	0	1	2	5	115	11	102	2	0
Poughkeepsie	30,480	243	6	21	46	170	529	57	440	32	1
Poughkeepsie Town	38,934	69	0	15	20	34	892	53	799	40	
Pound Ridge Town	5,133	1	0	1	0	0	40	2	38	0	0
Pulaski Village	2,211	0	0	0	0	0	29	2	26	1	0

Table 8. Offenses Known to Law Enforcement, by Selected State and City, 2020—Continued

(Number.)

State/city	Population	Violent crime	Murder and nonnegligent manslaughter	Rape[1]	Robbery	Aggravated assault	Property crime	Burglary	Larceny-theft	Motor vehicle theft	Arson[2]
Quogue Village	1,019	1	0	0	0	1	31	4	25	2	0
Ramapo Town	95,165	73	0	21	6	46	480	51	400	29	5
Rensselaer City	9,149	19	0	6	6	7	83	6	71	6	0
Rhinebeck Village	2,554	1	0	0	0	1	18	1	17	0	0
Riverhead Town	33,461	28	0	0	8	20	475	23	440	12	4
Rochester	205,199	1,680	48	86	418	1,128	6,887	1,389	4,583	915	152
Rockville Centre Village	24,604	14	0	0	3	11	106	18	72	16	0
Rome[4]	31,978	65	0	8	7	50	570	70	457	43	0
Rotterdam Town	30,071	35	0	0	6	29	714	67	611	36	1
Rye	15,692	0	0	0	0	0	20	1	9	10	0
Rye Brook Village	9,542	0	0	0	0	0	76	4	54	18	0
Sag Harbor Village	2,296	0	0	0	0	0	0	0	0	0	0
Salamanca	5,360	18	1	3	3	11	42	12	25	5	2
Sands Point Village	2,919	1	0	1	0	0	12	2	4	6	0
Saratoga Springs	28,397	53	1	12	6	34	449	50	382	17	4
Saugerties Town	18,956	21	1	6	2	12	145	20	115	10	1
Schenectady	65,176	468	5	26	90	347	1,622	266	1,187	169	30
Schodack Town	11,617	6	0	2	0	4	47	12	33	2	0
Schoharie Village	806	0	0	0	0	0	4	0	4	0	0
Scotia Village	7,631	7	0	1	3	3	146	11	126	9	0
Seneca Falls Town[4]	8,573	15	0	6	0	9	163	12	146	5	0
Shawangunk Town[4]	13,782	3	0	2	1	0	39	6	31	2	0
Sherburne Village	1,301	3	0	0	0	3	13	1	11	1	0
Sherrill	2,964	0	0	0	0	0	18	0	18	0	0
Sidney Village	3,553	6	0	0	0	6	40	6	33	1	1
Skaneateles Village	2,466	0	0	0	0	0	21	3	18	0	0
Sleepy Hollow Village	10,064	0	0	0	0	0	24	3	15	6	3
Solvay Village	6,196	14	0	2	2	10	66	11	49	6	0
Southampton Town	51,162	38	1	3	5	29	595	54	494	47	0
Southampton Village	3,330	0	0	0	0	0	45	1	42	2	0
South Glens Falls Village	3,647	5	0	0	2	3	28	7	20	1	0
Southold Town	19,957	11	0	4	0	7	270	41	224	5	0
Spring Valley Village[4]	32,356	96	2	11	24	59	343	41	289	13	1
Stillwater Town	7,340	1	0	0	0	1	14	2	12	0	0
St. Johnsville Village	1,668	1	0	0	0	1	15	2	13	0	0
Stony Point Town[4]	15,338	3	0	0	0	3	45	10	35	0	0
Syracuse	142,011	1,192	32	96	222	842	4,009	1,032	2,463	514	48
Tarrytown Village	11,383	9	0	3	4	2	55	7	43	5	1
Theresa Village	772	0	0	0	0	0	0	0	0	0	0
Tonawanda	14,700	46	1	13	7	25	286	21	254	11	1
Troy	49,052	330	9	16	68	237	1,411	263	1,026	122	28
Trumansburg Village	1,709	0	0	0	0	0	26	2	23	1	0
Tuckahoe Village	6,554	2	0	0	0	2	21	2	16	3	0
Tuxedo Park Village	598	0	0	0	0	0	0	0	0	0	0
Ulster Town	12,626	11	0	0	1	10	155	21	131	3	0
Utica[4]	59,483	298	1	23	70	204	2,017	267	1,636	114	6
Vernon Village	1,142	3	0	0	0	3	3	0	3	0	0
Vestal Town[4]	28,639	14	0	4	0	10	466	39	414	13	3
Walden Village	6,666	1	0	0	0	1	25	1	24	0	1
Wallkill Town	29,159	49	0	6	7	36	628	39	569	20	2
Wappingers Falls Village	5,540	7	0	0	2	5	39	1	35	3	0
Warsaw Village	3,225	6	0	1	1	4	31	5	25	1	0
Warwick Town	18,459	9	0	2	1	6	72	11	61	0	0
Washingtonville Village	5,755	2	0	1	0	1	30	4	25	1	0
Waterloo Village[4]	4,842	10	1	3	0	6	35	3	30	2	0
Watertown	24,624	181	0	40	21	120	967	158	766	43	8
Wayland Village	1,753	0	0	0	0	0	3	1	2	0	0
Webb Town	1,779	0	0	0	0	0	1	0	1	0	0
Webster Town and Village[4]	45,449	27	0	1	7	19	365	39	307	19	2
Weedsport Village	1,695	0	0	0	0	0	14	0	14	0	0
Wellsville Village	4,343	9	0	3	0	6	30	3	22	5	0
West Carthage Village	1,925	1	0	0	0	1	11	1	9	1	0
Westfield Village[4]	2,941	3	0	3	0	0	10	3	5	2	0
Westhampton Beach Village	1,806	0	0	0	0	0	24	4	15	5	0
West Seneca Town	45,278	59	0	11	8	40	589	75	482	32	1
Whitestown Town	8,948	0	0	0	0	0	20	3	17	0	0
Windham Town	1,672	0	0	0	0	0	5	0	5	0	0
Woodridge Village	771	3	0	1	0	2	11	3	7	1	0
Woodstock Town	5,754	4	0	0	0	4	43	2	41	0	0
Yonkers	200,816	653	7	38	169	439	1,990	276	1,466	248	12
Yorktown Town	36,284	7	0	1	1	5	197	9	177	11	1
NORTH CAROLINA											
Aberdeen	8,189	21	0	2	6	13	278	24	245	9	3
Ahoskie	4,733	42	2	1	3	36	187	42	132	13	1
Albemarle	16,287	152	6	8	17	121	921	164	701	56	14
Apex	62,320	30	1	5	3	21	697	93	587	17	2
Archdale	11,521	24	0	2	5	17	232	42	163	27	0
Asheville	93,980	761	11	54	153	543	5,395	730	4,142	523	28
Atlantic Beach	1,513	6	0	1	0	5	116	58	55	3	0
Ayden[4]	5,155	25	3	2	2	18	91	14	69	8	0
Bailey	561	0	0	0	0	0	10	3	6	1	0
Banner Elk	1,160	0	0	0	0	0	7	0	7	0	0

Table 8. Offenses Known to Law Enforcement, by Selected State and City, 2020—Continued

(Number.)

State/city	Population	Violent crime	Murder and nonnegligent manslaughter	Rape[1]	Robbery	Aggravated assault	Property crime	Burglary	Larceny-theft	Motor vehicle theft	Arson[2]
Beaufort	4,481	6	0	1	0	5	77	14	62	1	0
Beech Mountain	325	0	0	0	0	0	16	9	7	0	0
Belhaven	1,567	1	0	0	0	1	16	3	12	1	0
Belmont	12,848	54	0	1	15	38	618	32	561	25	1
Benson	3,995	43	0	4	8	31	219	54	144	21	2
Bessemer City	5,605	18	1	0	4	13	106	20	71	15	0
Beulaville	1,292	7	0	0	1	6	62	15	44	3	0
Biltmore Forest	1,424	1	0	0	0	1	13	2	10	1	0
Biscoe	1,713	2	0	1	0	1	189	10	177	2	0
Black Mountain	8,197	13	0	4	0	9	221	63	139	19	2
Blowing Rock	1,334	3	0	0	0	3	40	27	12	1	0
Boone	19,975	23	0	6	2	15	269	24	232	13	2
Brevard	7,954	13	0	5	1	7	133	22	104	7	0
Bryson City	1,455	11	0	0	0	11	24	1	16	7	0
Bunn	390	3	1	2	0	0	16	2	14	0	0
Burgaw	4,182	14	0	5	1	8	137	11	124	2	3
Burlington	55,003	527	3	43	56	425	2,391	419	1,782	190	12
Butner	7,887	24	0	4	6	14	151	20	126	5	0
Candor	815	2	0	0	2	0	15	4	11	0	0
Canton	4,364	16	0	2	1	13	265	89	151	25	0
Cape Carteret	2,069	2	0	0	0	2	20	3	16	1	0
Carolina Beach	6,479	29	0	7	2	20	186	35	139	12	1
Carrboro	21,377	46	0	4	6	36	365	65	263	37	4
Carthage	2,582	6	0	2	0	4	92	27	60	5	1
Cary	174,441	116	1	13	25	77	1,651	197	1,342	112	6
Chadbourn	1,698	16	1	0	1	14	84	21	57	6	0
Chapel Hill	64,853	93	0	7	22	64	1,140	198	885	57	4
Charlotte-Mecklenburg	958,358	8,015	119	245	1,763	5,888	31,053	4,312	23,757	2,984	158
Cherryville	6,110	19	0	3	4	12	154	31	110	13	0
Clayton	26,087	38	2	3	4	29	597	58	517	22	1
Clinton	8,431	97	0	7	10	80	446	95	330	21	1
Columbus	998	4	0	0	2	2	75	39	34	2	1
Concord	98,411	118	6	8	25	79	1,375	111	1,140	124	3
Conover	8,567	40	0	2	3	35	394	55	317	22	0
Creedmoor	4,669	13	0	6	2	5	76	29	36	11	1
Dallas	4,835	25	2	4	6	13	140	34	93	13	1
Davidson	13,313	5	0	2	0	3	104	11	84	9	0
Drexel	1,851	1	0	0	1	0	8	2	5	1	0
Duck	398	2	0	1	0	1	15	3	12	0	0
Dunn	9,763	76	3	4	14	55	749	325	393	31	3
Durham	284,925	2,447	36	125	626	1,660	10,650	1,906	7,779	965	43
East Spencer	1,552	11	6	0	2	3	19	3	12	4	0
Eden	14,799	87	1	4	9	73	430	112	295	23	7
Edenton	4,575	47	0	3	2	42	240	139	90	11	0
Elizabeth City	17,652	72	5	6	9	52	570	172	357	41	5
Elizabethtown	3,349	32	2	1	5	24	121	33	86	2	0
Elon	12,609	10	1	1	1	7	60	23	36	1	0
Emerald Isle	3,698	11	0	0	1	10	137	37	92	8	0
Enfield	2,247	33	2	0	4	27	71	32	34	5	3
Erwin	5,227	17	0	4	1	12	127	24	97	6	4
Fair Bluff	874	0	0	0	0	0	18	8	8	2	0
Fairmont	2,585	29	0	2	0	27	85	20	64	1	1
Farmville	4,775	28	0	1	3	24	107	21	78	8	1
Fayetteville	212,033	2,074	30	87	262	1,695	7,210	1,327	5,418	465	49
Fletcher	8,508	18	0	1	1	16	172	76	72	24	0
Four Oaks	2,291	2	0	1	1	0	33	4	25	4	0
Fuquay-Varina	32,091	23	0	1	8	14	303	19	268	16	0
Garner	32,093	84	2	10	18	54	979	81	834	64	0
Gastonia	77,918	720	9	37	124	550	3,172	445	2,414	313	29
Gibsonville	7,437	15	0	5	2	8	89	29	48	12	1
Goldsboro	34,051	397	2	11	46	338	1,709	349	1,272	88	3
Graham	15,801	75	3	7	10	55	351	70	234	47	7
Granite Falls	4,654	10	0	1	2	7	269	81	173	15	2
Greensboro	299,887	2,704	59	95	581	1,969	10,830	2,212	7,503	1,115	103
Greenville	94,372	415	13	26	71	305	2,481	360	2,006	115	19
Grifton	2,689	5	0	1	1	3	23	7	11	5	0
Havelock	19,722	62	0	10	9	43	444	94	343	7	0
Haw River	2,563	7	0	0	0	7	34	6	27	1	0
Henderson	14,861	303	10	6	41	246	855	244	541	70	18
Hendersonville	14,275	57	2	9	10	36	638	171	444	23	2
Hickory	41,300	223	5	14	38	166	1,718	266	1,293	159	11
Highlands	988	2	0	0	0	2	55	14	38	3	0
High Point	113,727	773	14	28	123	608	3,417	515	2,571	331	26
Hillsborough	7,226	30	0	3	6	21	374	18	338	18	1
Holly Ridge	3,077	3	0	0	1	2	52	23	23	6	0
Holly Springs	39,600	31	1	3	0	27	370	34	330	6	0
Hudson	3,703	3	0	0	1	2	116	40	71	5	0
Huntersville	59,470	99	2	7	14	76	881	122	699	60	1
Indian Beach	119	1	0	1	0	0	20	5	14	1	0
Jacksonville	71,842	245	3	24	23	195	1,481	263	1,153	65	5
Jonesville[4]	2,207	13	0	1	1	11	78	21	56	1	0
Kannapolis	51,837	122	2	8	23	89	1,460	220	1,104	136	4
Kenansville	839	6	0	0	0	6	10	1	8	1	1

Table 8. Offenses Known to Law Enforcement, by Selected State and City, 2020—Continued

(Number.)

State/city	Population	Violent crime	Murder and nonnegligent manslaughter	Rape[1]	Robbery	Aggravated assault	Property crime	Burglary	Larceny-theft	Motor vehicle theft	Arson[2]
Kernersville	24,835	81	0	14	12	55	1,036	107	871	58	4
Kill Devil Hills	7,407	17	0	3	1	13	214	38	169	7	1
King	6,860	12	0	1	2	9	198	5	187	6	0
Kings Mountain	11,015	25	1	7	1	16	299	67	190	42	2
Kinston[4]	19,862	235	7	13	21	194	1,206	270	875	61	22
Kitty Hawk	3,606	9	0	2	0	7	120	10	105	5	0
Knightdale	18,735	48	0	0	10	38	354	39	283	32	0
Laurinburg	14,905	266	9	10	19	228	692	401	246	45	12
Lenoir	17,880	50	0	11	6	33	607	154	366	87	1
Lexington	18,933	105	3	5	16	81	596	127	408	61	2
Lincolnton	11,300	59	4	6	3	46	486	56	396	34	1
Long View	4,936	15	1	3	3	8	179	40	111	28	1
Louisburg	3,641	30	0	1	4	25	117	19	94	4	1
Lowell	3,738	5	0	1	2	2	58	19	23	16	0
Madison	2,103	17	1	7	1	8	70	17	51	2	2
Maggie Valley	1,247	6	0	0	0	6	80	24	49	7	0
Marion	7,861	15	1	3	1	10	439	111	283	45	1
Marshville	2,825	10	1	1	0	8	91	29	56	6	1
Matthews	33,860	61	5	7	20	29	1,082	129	897	56	4
Maxton	2,335	8	0	0	8	0	85	26	52	7	3
Mayodan	2,372	5	0	4	1	0	109	17	85	7	0
Mebane	16,894	46	0	4	3	39	578	37	521	20	1
Middlesex	826	0	0	0	0	0	17	0	16	1	0
Mint Hill	28,209	59	0	6	7	46	361	75	266	20	1
Monroe	35,836	364	2	30	57	275	1,736	265	1,344	127	7
Mooresville	39,692	80	0	10	14	56	972	78	828	66	6
Morehead City	9,729	40	0	9	1	30	354	39	302	13	1
Morrisville	30,264	24	0	1	13	10	639	57	540	42	1
Mount Olive	4,573	12	0	0	2	10	106	25	69	12	0
Murfreesboro	2,978	6	0	1	1	4	61	15	40	6	0
Nags Head	2,999	4	0	0	0	4	107	15	90	2	1
New Bern	30,047	190	4	11	21	154	930	199	701	30	1
Newland	684	1	0	0	1	0	13	2	8	3	1
Newport	4,646	4	0	1	1	2	88	30	54	4	0
Newton	13,204	43	0	1	3	39	443	116	297	30	1
North Topsail Beach	743	2	0	0	0	2	28	11	16	1	0
North Wilkesboro	4,192	12	0	0	0	12	191	115	62	14	1
Oak Island	8,581	16	1	2	0	13	162	57	93	12	1
Oxford	8,934	91	1	1	13	76	216	37	163	16	1
Pembroke	2,940	14	1	3	5	5	190	60	116	14	0
Pinehurst	16,837	19	1	2	1	15	133	43	81	9	0
Pine Knoll Shores	1,325	1	0	0	0	1	28	15	13	0	0
Pine Level	2,059	3	0	0	2	1	16	8	7	1	0
Pineville	9,214	61	1	4	17	39	954	129	760	65	1
Pittsboro	4,440	15	0	3	2	10	74	6	64	4	0
Plymouth	3,311	39	1	2	3	33	85	28	53	4	3
Princeton	1,423	0	0	0	0	0	12	1	11	0	0
Raeford	4,990	20	1	3	1	15	138	54	79	5	0
Raleigh	482,264	1,891	21	165	468	1,237	9,745	1,302	7,081	1,362	50
Red Springs	3,282	33	1	2	7	23	276	142	119	15	4
Reidsville	13,936	138	6	5	12	115	689	111	526	52	0
Richlands	1,726	1	0	1	0	0	12	1	9	2	0
Roanoke Rapids	14,178	149	7	7	35	100	598	125	453	20	9
Robersonville	1,328	11	1	1	3	6	48	12	33	3	0
Rockingham	8,567	66	4	6	14	42	410	110	284	16	0
Rockwell	2,164	3	0	2	0	1	33	8	22	3	0
Rocky Mount	53,520	615	13	16	90	496	1,564	366	1,101	97	13
Rolesville	9,304	5	0	0	0	5	37	5	30	2	0
Rowland	987	9	0	0	1	8	38	11	25	2	1
Roxboro	8,304	79	1	2	7	69	287	66	214	7	2
Salisbury	34,045	251	7	10	46	188	1,218	165	951	102	8
Saluda	695	2	0	2	0	0	3	0	3	0	0
Scotland Neck	1,819	19	0	0	6	13	157	125	27	5	1
Selma	7,218	47	1	1	8	37	199	47	133	19	2
Siler City	8,267	57	0	5	6	46	326	65	239	22	4
Smithfield	13,215	65	0	1	17	47	487	73	397	17	5
Snow Hill	1,503	5	1	0	1	3	26	5	20	1	0
Southern Pines	14,924	66	1	8	11	46	285	59	217	9	4
Southern Shores	2,986	1	0	1	0	0	31	7	24	0	0
Spencer	3,256	9	0	3	0	6	72	13	52	7	2
Stallings	16,426	9	0	2	0	7	172	35	124	13	1
Stantonsburg	778	5	0	1	0	4	19	3	16	0	0
Star	846	2	0	1	0	1	17	1	16	0	0
Surf City	2,537	17	0	0	1	16	118	13	104	1	1
Swansboro	3,425	4	0	1	0	3	135	17	115	3	0
Tabor City	4,181	14	0	1	2	11	104	16	77	11	0
Taylorsville	2,167	1	0	0	0	1	113	32	73	8	0
Taylortown	867	4	0	1	0	3	27	5	20	2	0
Thomasville	26,631	118	2	3	23	90	735	162	470	103	5
Trent Woods	4,005	0	0	0	0	0	14	3	11	0	0
Troutman	2,806	5	0	3	0	2	55	4	50	1	0
Troy	3,194	25	0	1	2	22	130	35	84	11	0
Valdese	4,416	12	0	5	0	7	54	14	33	7	0

Table 8. Offenses Known to Law Enforcement, by Selected State and City, 2020—Continued

(Number.)

State/city	Population	Violent crime	Murder and nonnegligent manslaughter	Rape[1]	Robbery	Aggravated assault	Property crime	Burglary	Larceny-theft	Motor vehicle theft	Arson[2]
Wadesboro	5,221	124	3	5	19	97	365	118	225	22	2
Wake Forest	47,738	66	1	2	8	55	519	57	436	26	0
Washington	9,459	124	1	5	12	106	374	69	300	5	4
Waxhaw	18,222	9	0	4	1	4	172	27	140	5	1
Waynesville	10,174	54	1	5	4	44	758	131	594	33	5
Weaverville	4,065	5	0	2	1	2	178	3	164	11	0
Weldon	1,452	17	0	2	4	11	62	17	37	8	0
Wendell	8,951	12	0	1	4	7	104	25	70	9	0
West Jefferson	1,313	4	0	2	1	1	71	7	58	6	0
Whispering Pines	3,451	1	0	0	0	1	14	1	13	0	0
Williamston	5,145	66	0	3	11	52	297	106	183	8	2
Wilmington	125,794	791	22	66	143	560	3,204	595	2,410	199	27
Wilson	49,486	270	7	9	41	213	1,439	251	1,068	120	9
Windsor	3,353	3	1	1	0	1	35	8	24	3	0
Winterville	10,010	9	0	0	3	6	68	16	48	4	1
Woodland	693	3	0	0	1	2	22	18	2	2	1
Wrightsville Beach	2,563	6	0	1	0	5	92	15	75	2	0
Yadkinville	2,865	13	1	4	2	6	80	17	62	1	0
Youngsville	1,402	3	0	0	2	1	30	5	25	0	0
Zebulon	6,104	31	0	1	7	23	286	54	223	9	1
NORTH DAKOTA											
Belfield	1,039	2	0	0	0	2	17	4	13	0	0
Berthold	483	1	0	0	0	1	5	0	5	0	0
Beulah	3,141	0	0	0	0	0	21	5	14	2	0
Bismarck	74,997	260	0	49	26	185	2,471	343	1,876	252	12
Bowman	1,594	0	0	0	0	0	14	1	11	2	0
Burlington	1,218	0	0	0	0	0	1	0	1	0	0
Carrington	1,971	1	0	0	0	1	16	5	8	3	1
Cavalier	1,226	0	0	0	0	0	10	0	10	0	0
Devils Lake	7,339	27	0	8	2	17	269	31	201	37	2
Dickinson	23,801	39	1	4	1	33	456	51	346	59	1
Ellendale	1,232	4	0	3	0	1	11	2	9	0	0
Emerado	451	1	0	1	0	0	7	3	3	1	0
Fargo	126,927	584	7	107	61	409	4,403	1,016	2,922	465	25
Grafton	4,143	9	0	1	0	8	63	12	41	10	1
Grand Forks	56,163	164	4	34	14	112	1,315	210	988	117	1
Harvey	1,630	2	0	0	0	2	12	2	9	1	0
Hazen	2,298	0	0	0	0	0	5	0	5	0	0
Jamestown	15,044	35	0	6	0	29	354	55	261	38	2
Kenmare	1,013	0	0	0	0	0	9	4	4	1	0
Killdeer	1,202	0	0	0	0	0	12	1	9	2	0
Lamoure	883	0	0	0	0	0	2	1	1	0	0
Lincoln	4,006	6	0	1	0	5	18	3	11	4	0
Lisbon	2,041	4	0	2	0	2	12	2	9	1	0
Mandan	23,221	83	1	17	4	61	980	212	656	112	4
Medora	131	0	0	0	0	0	0	0	0	0	0
Minot	48,108	155	7	45	9	94	800	152	495	153	5
Napoleon	747	0	0	0	0	0	6	0	6	0	0
New Town	2,677	2	0	1	0	1	10	0	9	1	0
Northwood	890	0	0	0	0	0	4	1	3	0	0
Oakes	1,685	1	0	0	0	1	1	1	0	0	0
Powers Lake	285	0	0	0	0	0	1	0	1	0	0
Rolla	1,249	1	0	0	0	1	63	10	40	13	0
Rugby	2,561	1	0	0	0	1	37	10	24	3	0
Stanley	2,868	5	0	0	0	5	6	0	3	3	0
Steele	711	3	0	1	0	2	3	0	3	0	0
Surrey	1,452	0	0	0	0	0	1	1	0	0	0
Tioga	1,348	6	0	1	0	5	22	0	20	2	0
Valley City	6,288	15	0	1	0	14	124	20	86	18	2
Wahpeton	7,731	28	0	3	3	22	204	41	143	20	1
Watford City	9,309	19	0	1	0	18	95	17	66	12	0
West Fargo	38,561	55	0	15	4	36	730	184	483	63	5
Williston	31,046	116	2	10	8	96	725	99	563	63	5
Wishek	880	1	0	0	0	1	9	1	8	0	0
OHIO											
Ada	5,500	5	0	0	0	5	43	1	42	0	0
Akron	197,433	1,797	47	215	268	1,267	6,971	1,288	4,855	828	94
Alliance	21,356	47	0	10	5	32	544	61	444	39	9
American Township	12,017	4	0	1	0	3	71	9	59	3	0
Amherst	12,244	6	0	1	5	0	116	6	108	2	0
Archbold	4,319	1	0	1	0	0	39	1	37	1	0
Ashland	20,247	23	0	12	1	10	315	25	280	10	0
Ashville	4,425	3	0	0	1	2	59	11	42	6	0
Athens	24,570	19	0	1	7	11	541	82	440	19	0
Aurora	16,430	5	0	0	1	4	116	11	101	4	0
Austintown	34,688	64	1	11	9	43	542	78	453	11	0
Avon Lake	24,724	4	0	0	0	4	53	6	43	4	0
Barberton	25,890	65	2	18	8	37	651	126	480	45	3
Barnesville	3,977	0	0	0	0	0	5	0	3	2	0
Batavia	1,989	2	0	1	0	1	36	3	32	1	0

Table 8. Offenses Known to Law Enforcement, by Selected State and City, 2020—Continued

(Number.)

State/city	Population	Violent crime	Murder and nonnegligent manslaughter	Rape[1]	Robbery	Aggravated assault	Property crime	Burglary	Larceny-theft	Motor vehicle theft	Arson[2]
Bath Township, Summit County	9,635	6	0	0	1	5	115	6	103	6	0
Bay Village	15,135	6	0	1	0	5	126	6	102	18	0
Bazetta Township	5,494	3	0	0	2	1	299	9	288	2	0
Beachwood	11,547	19	0	3	7	9	364	14	331	19	0
Beavercreek	48,029	24	0	10	6	8	989	62	870	57	0
Beaver Township	6,358	1	0	1	0	0	76	25	47	4	0
Bellaire	3,985	5	0	2	0	3	22	1	21	0	0
Bellbrook	7,387	2	0	0	1	1	32	4	27	1	0
Bellefontaine	13,240	9	0	3	1	5	184	23	150	11	1
Bellville	1,933	4	0	0	0	4	11	1	9	1	1
Belpre	6,381	12	0	6	0	6	74	9	61	4	0
Berea[4]	18,539	24	0	2	9	13	140	16	118	6	1
Bethel	2,823	5	0	1	1	3	48	7	39	2	0
Blanchester	4,264	13	0	1	2	10	81	10	63	8	0
Blue Ash	12,405	22	0	7	2	13	204	12	183	9	0
Botkins	1,157	0	0	0	0	0	17	0	17	0	1
Bowling Green	31,621	14	1	4	5	4	436	19	405	12	1
Brecksville	13,591	2	0	0	0	2	57	2	50	5	0
Bridgeport	1,716	2	0	1	0	1	8	1	7	0	0
Brimfield Township	10,324	8	0	3	1	4	331	21	299	11	0
Broadview Heights	19,059	2	0	0	0	2	19	1	14	4	0
Brooklyn[4]	10,584	9	0	0	5	4	482	29	423	30	0
Bucyrus	11,698	23	0	4	2	17	220	34	177	9	0
Burton	1,451	0	0	0	0	0	4	0	3	1	0
Butler Township	7,816	23	1	6	3	13	568	19	519	30	2
Canal Fulton	5,406	2	0	0	0	2	50	10	39	1	0
Canfield	7,138	1	0	1	0	0	25	3	22	0	0
Canton	70,124	1,002	14	115	154	719	3,411	708	2,350	353	16
Carey	3,541	2	0	0	0	2	9	2	7	0	1
Centerville	23,670	17	0	10	2	5	280	35	231	14	0
Chardon	5,160	5	0	0	1	4	84	3	79	2	2
Cheviot	8,195	15	0	1	7	7	228	37	165	26	0
Cincinnati[7]	304,724	2,721	92	215	750	1,664	11,224	2,322	7,396	1,506	
Circleville	14,113	33	1	16	4	12	549	88	433	28	3
Clayton	13,219	1	0	0	1	0	105	18	77	10	0
Clay Township, Montgomery County	4,236	3	0	0	0	3	18	3	14	1	0
Clearcreek Township	16,312	2	0	0	0	2	33	3	30	0	1
Cleveland	379,121	6,281	160	393	1,593	4,135	15,433	3,692	8,800	2,941	168
Cleveland Heights	43,725	115	7	10	16	82	527	56	403	68	6
Clinton Township	4,102	19	0	1	9	9	161	19	131	11	0
Clyde	6,141	2	0	0	0	2	65	11	54	0	0
Coitsville Township	1,309	3	0	0	1	2	17	4	10	3	0
Coldwater	4,579	1	0	1	0	0	31	2	29	0	0
Colerain Township	59,307	103	3	4	19	77	1,062	118	870	74	5
Columbiana	6,233	3	0	0	0	3	27	0	25	2	0
Columbus[7]	911,383	5,064	174	816	1,796	2,278	28,530	5,551	19,874	3,105	
Commercial Point	1,687	1	0	0	0	1	11	2	8	1	0
Conneaut	12,498	19	1	3	2	13	133	26	99	8	1
Copley Township	17,280	12	1	4	2	5	226	23	182	21	0
Cortland	6,729	6	0	1	1	4	48	6	41	1	0
Cuyahoga Falls	49,061	37	1	14	6	16	961	99	829	33	0
Dayton	140,193	1,523	46	132	300	1,045	5,391	1,370	3,234	787	8
Defiance	16,576	25	0	4	1	20	235	21	206	8	1
Delaware	42,064	57	0	31	4	22	367	75	276	16	11
Delhi Township	29,831	14	0	3	3	8	283	28	239	16	2
Delphos[4,8]	6,917		0		0	0	67	9	56	2	1
Dennison	2,588	5	0	2	0	3	1	0	1	0	1
Dover	12,707	5	0	2	1	2	79	25	46	8	1
Dublin	49,954	22	1	10	4	7	372	53	288	31	1
Eastlake[4]	17,982	34	0	6	9	19	265	18	226	21	0
East Liverpool	10,539	8	0	3	1	4	154	27	123	4	0
East Palestine	4,392	5	2	0	0	3	55	8	46	1	0
Eaton	8,118	14	0	7	0	7	214	21	182	11	1
Elyria	53,677	136	7	21	26	82	785	178	546	61	3
Englewood	13,435	11	0	2	2	7	272	17	249	6	5
Euclid	46,272	240	4	20	55	161	1,327	195	916	216	3
Fairborn	33,951	100	0	22	8	70	529	103	391	35	6
Fairfax	1,701	1	0	0	0	1	154	2	152	0	0
Fairfield Township	22,978	24	1	5	3	15	367	25	315	27	0
Fairview Park	16,081	7	0	0	3	4	97	8	86	3	1
Fayette	1,237	2	0	0	0	2	16	4	12	0	0
Findlay	41,237	65	0	27	10	28	777	83	665	29	3
Forest Park	18,571	43	1	3	15	24	352	62	263	27	1
Fremont[8]	15,841		0		6	16	545	57	473	15	0
Gahanna	35,738	60	1	15	11	33	615	62	506	47	7
Gallipolis	3,546	9	0	3	0	6	282	18	252	12	0
Georgetown	4,215	10	1	1	0	8	77	16	56	5	1
Germantown	5,517	2	0	2	0	0	45	11	32	2	0
Goshen Township, Clermont County	16,407	7	0	2	1	4	111	12	94	5	0

Table 8. Offenses Known to Law Enforcement, by Selected State and City, 2020—Continued

(Number.)

State/city	Population	Violent crime	Murder and nonnegligent manslaughter	Rape[1]	Robbery	Aggravated assault	Property crime	Burglary	Larceny-theft	Motor vehicle theft	Arson[2]
Goshen Township, Mahoning County	3,075	3	0	0	0	3	58	7	47	4	0
Grafton	5,628	2	0	0	0	2	21	5	16	0	0
Grandview Heights	8,566	4	1	0	0	3	169	29	130	10	0
Granville	5,943	4	0	3	0	1	69	6	62	1	0
Greenfield	4,546	7	0	3	0	4	46	8	20	18	0
Greenhills	3,563	2	0	1	0	1	10	0	10	0	0
Green Township	59,142	60	0	10	14	36	902	151	706	45	1
Greenville	12,549	28	0	4	2	22	186	27	145	14	2
Grove City	42,551	80	1	4	26	49	1,054	52	925	77	6
Groveport	5,649	14	0	0	4	10	95	5	89	1	0
Harrison	12,133	2	0	0	0	2	151	7	138	6	0
Hartville	3,093	2	0	0	0	2	37	2	34	1	0
Heath	11,015	27	0	7	7	13	447	60	368	19	0
Highland Hills	945	1	0	1	0	0	1	0	0	1	0
Hilliard	37,585	24	0	6	11	7	265	37	211	17	2
Hillsboro	6,549	0	0	0	0	0	69	8	50	11	1
Hinckley Township[4]	8,117	5	1	0	1	3	24	5	15	4	2
Holland	1,650	3	0	0	2	1	419	11	406	2	0
Howland Township	16,318	11	0	1	1	9	201	25	168	8	0
Hubbard	7,370	12	0	3	0	9	84	7	72	5	0
Huber Heights	38,158	67	0	24	11	32	682	77	542	63	5
Hudson	22,234	5	0	1	0	4	147	21	126	0	0
Hunting Valley[4]	716	0	0	0	0	0	3	2	1	0	0
Huron	6,840	4	0	3	0	1	76	9	65	2	0
Independence	7,173	18	0	3	6	9	127	5	109	13	0
Indian Hill	5,795	0	0	0	0	0	30	7	22	1	0
Ironton	10,469	22	0	5	2	15	105	28	67	10	0
Jackson	6,211	6	0	2	0	4	188	28	148	12	1
Jackson Township, Stark County	40,270	55	2	15	6	32	851	127	696	28	5
Jamestown	2,148	2	0	0	0	2	51	19	31	1	1
Kent	29,732	27	0	0	8	19	452	62	369	21	1
Kenton	8,163	24	0	9	3	12	232	63	167	2	2
Kirtland	6,807	10	0	0	1	9	26	1	24	1	0
Kirtland Hills[8]	644	0	0	0	0	0	0	0	0	0	0
Lakemore	3,072	4	1	0	0	3	50	7	40	3	0
Lakewood	49,389	64	1	9	29	25	744	62	592	90	3
Lancaster	40,700	101	0	26	20	55	1,212	112	1,028	72	9
Lawrence Township	8,278	5	0	3	0	2	58	13	44	1	0
Lebanon	20,720	30	0	3	2	25	282	21	250	11	1
Lexington	4,670	0	0	0	0	0	12	0	12	0	0
Lisbon	2,620	0	0	0	0	0	7	0	7	0	0
Lithopolis	1,893	2	0	0	0	2	13	2	10	1	0
Lockland	3,440	24	2	2	6	14	46	8	31	7	0
Lodi	2,915	3	0	1	0	2	8	2	5	1	0
Logan	7,007	13	0	6	4	3	329	61	245	23	1
London	10,378	12	0	3	1	8	141	11	124	6	0
Lorain	63,831	323	2	32	60	229	1,510	323	1,096	91	14
Lordstown	3,241	2	0	0	0	2	27	5	19	3	1
Loudonville	2,614	2	0	2	0	0	23	2	17	4	0
Louisville	9,370	5	0	0	1	4	84	11	71	2	0
Loveland	13,265	10	0	7	0	3	83	7	73	3	1
Lyndhurst	13,291	22	1	3	5	13	145	11	110	24	1
Macedonia	12,098	9	0	0	2	7	200	7	185	8	0
Madeira	9,303	2	0	1	0	1	50	5	41	4	0
Madison Township, Franklin County	19,828	27	0	5	6	16	157	32	100	25	0
Madison Township, Lake County	15,570	9	0	2	0	7	186	9	174	3	0
Maple Heights	21,953	125	1	6	31	87	186	52	74	60	2
Mariemont	3,524	0	0	0	0	0	23	2	20	1	0
Marietta	13,281	15	0	2	4	9	163	16	140	7	1
Martins Ferry	6,475	10	0	7	0	3	60	11	45	4	2
Massillon	32,617	56	0	20	10	26	759	95	624	40	3
Maumee	13,605	17	0	3	6	8	291	16	264	11	1
McArthur	1,637	5	0	1	0	4	46	12	30	4	0
McConnelsville	1,746	1	0	0	0	1	31	5	25	1	0
Mechanicsburg	1,586	3	0	3	0	0	40	4	32	4	0
Medina	25,882	21	2	8	2	9	196	17	173	6	3
Mentor	47,275	63	0	14	1	48	616	65	515	36	5
Mentor-on-the-Lake	7,385	5	1	1	1	2	44	3	37	4	0
Miamisburg	20,140	41	0	16	11	14	262	49	185	28	2
Miami Township, Clermont County	42,931	24	0	14	1	9	414	31	362	21	0
Miami Township, Montgomery County	29,125	61	4	15	11	31	679	67	576	36	5
Middletown	48,814	147	3	11	28	105	1,170	182	889	99	2
Mifflin Township	2,609	17	1	0	3	13	67	15	42	10	0
Milford	6,872	11	1	1	0	9	172	12	152	8	2
Mogadore	3,816	1	0	0	0	1	40	14	24	2	0
Monroe	16,663	17	2	3	1	11	296	11	273	12	0
Montgomery	10,929	6	0	2	1	3	79	4	71	4	0

Table 8. Offenses Known to Law Enforcement, by Selected State and City, 2020—Continued

(Number.)

State/city	Population	Violent crime	Murder and nonnegligent manslaughter	Rape[1]	Robbery	Aggravated assault	Property crime	Burglary	Larceny-theft	Motor vehicle theft	Arson[2]
Montpelier	3,910	16	0	9	0	7	138	14	116	8	1
Montville Township	11,971	4	0	0	1	3	60	9	47	4	0
Moraine	6,478	43	0	5	7	31	428	51	346	31	2
Mount Healthy	6,729	70	0	4	10	56	257	75	170	12	2
Mount Orab	3,418	13	0	1	0	12	54	5	47	2	0
Munroe Falls	5,064	1	0	0	1	0	26	6	20	0	0
Napoleon	8,148	19	0	5	0	14	225	29	192	4	0
Navarre	1,804	2	0	0	0	2	19	7	10	2	0
Nelsonville	5,102	19	0	3	4	12	165	33	113	19	0
New Albany	11,330	4	0	2	0	2	108	12	91	5	0
Newark	50,625	139	3	35	26	75	1,748	251	1,363	134	35
New Boston	2,080	11	1	0	4	6	230	13	214	3	0
New Bremen	2,959	0	0	0	0	0	31	3	28	0	0
New Franklin	14,125	9	0	3	2	4	86	19	60	7	1
New Lebanon	3,983	4	0	1	1	2	63	15	45	3	2
New Lexington	4,665	10	0	1	1	8	103	20	74	9	1
New Philadelphia	17,423	7	0	0	1	6	105	2	101	2	0
New Richmond	2,710	4	0	0	0	4	12	2	9	1	0
New Straitsville	709	0	0	0	0	0	25	7	15	3	0
Newton Falls	4,442	17	0	2	0	15	42	5	33	4	0
Newtown	2,671	0	0	0	0	0	6	0	6	0	0
New Waterford	1,174	3	0	1	0	2	10	4	6	0	0
Niles	18,070	40	0	9	9	22	500	80	402	18	1
North Baltimore	3,558	5	0	0	0	5	16	4	12	0	0
North Canton	17,142	21	2	9	5	5	254	24	217	13	2
North College Hill	9,269	19	2	1	8	8	237	28	192	17	1
Northfield	3,662	9	0	3	2	4	45	1	39	5	0
North Olmsted	31,176	13	1	4	5	3	371	28	306	37	1
North Royalton	30,007	13	0	4	2	7	155	21	121	13	1
Northwood	5,458	11	0	4	3	4	136	22	106	8	0
Norton	11,951	10	0	2	1	7	218	41	162	15	0
Norwalk	16,843	41	0	8	1	32	192	17	169	6	5
Oak Harbor	2,701	2	0	0	0	2	15	1	14	0	0
Oak Hill	1,518	1	0	0	0	1	17	2	15	0	0
Oberlin	8,178	10	0	8	1	1	72	19	52	1	2
Olmsted Township[4]	13,478	0	0	0	0	0	36	5	28	3	0
Ontario	6,068	1	0	0	1	0	220	2	215	3	0
Oregon	20,026	43	0	13	4	26	578	45	509	24	1
Orrville	8,427	16	1	5	3	7	65	11	52	2	0
Ottawa Hills	4,491	1	0	0	0	1	33	3	21	9	0
Oxford Township	2,210	0	0	0	0	0	14	2	12	0	0
Parma	77,684	135	0	26	26	83	688	106	506	76	9
Peninsula	554	0	0	0	0	0	21	0	21	0	0
Pepper Pike	6,367	1	0	0	0	1	38	5	29	4	0
Perrysburg	21,723	13	0	9	2	2	181	12	168	1	0
Perrysburg Township	13,011	2	0	0	1	1	81	11	65	5	0
Perry Township, Columbiana County	4,259	0	0	0	0	0	5	0	3	2	0
Perry Township, Franklin County	3,761	1	0	0	0	1	37	4	32	1	0
Perry Township, Stark County	28,005	79	1	19	14	45	531	124	367	40	1
Pickerington	22,631	22	1	10	7	4	197	32	146	19	1
Pierce Township	11,789	9	0	5	1	3	161	22	133	6	1
Piketon	2,135	1	0	1	0	0	35	4	25	6	0
Pioneer	1,402	0	0	0	0	0	15	3	12	0	0
Plain City	4,628	2	0	0	0	2	4	0	4	0	0
Poland Township	11,772	4	0	1	0	3	31	8	22	1	0
Poland Village	2,363	0	0	0	0	0	9	3	6	0	0
Port Clinton	6,159	13	0	11	0	2	66	11	51	4	0
Portsmouth	20,151	140	1	19	18	102	940	177	699	64	3
Powell	13,593	0	0	0	0	0	78	17	55	6	0
Reading	11,024	22	0	4	5	13	269	33	222	14	1
Reminderville	4,658	5	0	0	0	5	22	0	22	0	0
Reynoldsburg	38,600	137	1	16	34	86	950	115	749	86	4
Rio Grande	766	0	0	0	0	0	2	1	0	1	0
Riverside	25,128	48	2	11	3	32	340	70	214	56	4
Rocky River	19,951	11	0	1	1	9	55	4	47	4	0
Sabina	2,576	3	0	0	0	3	71	13	57	1	0
Sagamore Hills	10,917	0	0	0	0	0	30	6	23	1	0
Salem	11,538	16	0	4	2	10	327	16	304	7	0
Salineville	1,209	3	0	2	1	0	23	1	22	0	0
Sandusky	24,422	38	0	10	12	16	722	138	565	19	3
Sebring	4,163	9	0	4	0	5	97	11	82	4	1
Seven Hills	11,561	4	0	1	0	3	54	9	23	22	1
Shawnee Township	12,044	9	0	3	0	6	117	17	96	4	4
Sheffield Lake	8,892	2	0	1	1	0	66	12	54	0	1
Shelby	9,002	26	0	9	0	17	128	16	110	2	0
Sidney	20,372	100	2	34	10	54	589	84	474	31	6
Solon	22,703	7	0	2	1	4	144	14	127	3	0
South Bloomfield	2,000	0	0	0	0	0	29	3	18	8	0
South Euclid	21,179	59	0	6	19	34	497	35	428	34	0
Spencerville	2,154	0	0	0	0	0	22	7	12	3	0
Springdale	11,160	55	1	11	13	30	319	22	258	39	0

Table 8. Offenses Known to Law Enforcement, by Selected State and City, 2020—Continued

(Number.)

State/city	Population	Violent crime	Murder and nonnegligent manslaughter	Rape[1]	Robbery	Aggravated assault	Property crime	Burglary	Larceny-theft	Motor vehicle theft	Arson[2]
Springfield	58,696	338	8	52	107	171	3,014	619	2,060	335	53
Springfield Township, Hamilton County	35,947	63	0	3	12	48	451	65	341	45	2
Springfield Township, Mahoning County	6,352	4	0	2	0	2	56	13	38	5	1
Springfield Township, Summit County	14,507	56	0	12	10	34	679	100	543	36	5
St. Clair Township	7,436	7	0	0	0	7	120	2	118	0	0
St. Marys	8,142	4	0	0	0	4	85	10	70	5	0
Stow	34,781	18	0	8	4	6	485	44	430	11	0
Strasburg	2,697	4	0	0	0	4	10	0	9	1	0
Streetsboro	16,527	6	0	0	1	5	203	17	176	10	0
Strongsville	44,623	19	0	1	14	4	608	29	555	24	2
Struthers	10,048	13	0	3	1	9	93	20	64	9	0
Sugarcreek Township	8,484	4	0	3	0	1	151	4	140	7	1
Swanton	3,860	0	0	0	0	0	29	10	19	0	0
Sylvania	19,337	11	0	2	4	5	133	11	120	2	1
Sylvania Township	29,711	31	1	3	8	19	519	36	457	26	2
Tallmadge	17,517	20	0	11	4	5	318	66	228	24	8
Tiffin	17,543	8	0	4	1	3	237	36	197	4	0
Toledo[9]	271,237	2,729	53	213	493	1,970	7,849	1,777	5,064	1,008	
Toronto	4,883	3	0	0	0	3	15	3	11	1	0
Trotwood	24,399	158	1	16	28	113	595	129	380	86	11
Twinsburg[4]	18,895	16	1	0	2	13	126	6	102	18	1
Uhrichsville	5,304	8	0	4	0	4	47	17	25	5	0
Uniontown	3,309	3	0	0	1	2	58	3	50	5	0
University Heights	12,711	29	0	5	13	11	161	15	120	26	1
Upper Arlington	35,557	11	0	0	9	2	336	44	285	7	0
Upper Sandusky	6,423	10	0	7	0	3	108	9	99	0	1
Urbana	11,351	18	0	4	0	14	243	30	212	1	1
Utica	2,273	4	0	1	0	3	10	4	6	0	0
Van Wert	10,659	30	1	5	4	20	253	44	203	6	2
Vienna Township	3,761	7	0	2	1	4	46	8	31	7	0
Village of Leesburg	1,324	0	0	0	0	0	19	1	17	1	0
Wadsworth	24,324	16	1	6	1	8	311	18	287	6	2
Wapakoneta	9,680	13	0	3	2	8	112	13	95	4	0
Warren	38,462	173	10	30	42	91	1,073	267	747	59	10
Warren Township	5,144	7	0	2	1	4	59	12	34	13	2
Washington Court House	14,076	38	0	9	6	23	377	54	300	23	0
Waterville	5,543	3	0	0	0	3	39	3	35	1	0
Wauseon	7,411	9	0	4	1	4	127	6	119	2	1
Waverly	4,217	10	0	1	1	8	92	4	84	4	0
Weathersfield	7,965	15	1	2	1	11	97	19	71	7	2
Wellston	5,489	16	1	2	1	12	135	22	99	14	1
West Carrollton	12,833	33	1	9	6	17	204	32	145	27	2
West Chester Township	62,685	66	1	24	14	27	946	88	820	38	0
Westerville	41,652	39	0	6	5	28	685	35	618	32	5
Whitehall	19,014	157	2	10	50	95	842	118	642	82	8
Whitehouse	4,932	5	0	2	0	3	10	1	9	0	0
Wickliffe	12,743	25	0	4	4	17	157	18	129	10	1
Willard	5,993	10	0	0	1	9	122	13	106	3	0
Williamsburg	2,579	4	0	2	0	2	39	8	24	7	0
Willoughby	23,058	13	0	4	6	3	358	33	297	28	2
Wilmington	12,353	30	0	9	6	15	349	37	304	8	1
Wintersville	3,642	3	0	0	0	3	66	7	57	2	0
Woodlawn	3,410	5	0	1	1	3	64	6	57	1	0
Wooster	26,424	70	0	20	11	39	661	91	550	20	4
Worthington	14,822	12	0	3	6	3	194	19	166	9	0
Wyoming	8,578	3	0	0	2	1	58	9	43	6	0
Xenia	27,095	75	0	22	4	49	588	72	491	25	8
Yellow Springs	3,771	4	0	2	0	2	67	8	56	3	0
Zanesville	25,136	81	2	15	17	47	874	123	721	30	6
OKLAHOMA											
Achille	545	0	0	0	0	0	2	2	0	0	0
Ada	17,278	89	1	15	10	63	640	165	405	70	6
Adair	809	0	0	0	0	0	12	3	8	1	0
Allen	925	1	0	0	0	1	23	9	11	3	0
Altus	18,184	31	1	2	3	25	400	107	245	48	1
Alva	4,944	2	0	0	0	2	50	20	29	1	0
Amber	487	1	0	0	0	1	5	3	1	1	0
Anadarko	6,473	60	0	2	4	54	325	82	216	27	14
Antlers	2,308	9	0	0	0	9	33	9	15	9	0
Apache	1,387	3	0	1	0	2	29	10	16	3	0
Arcadia	273	1	0	0	0	1	1	0	0	1	0
Ardmore[4]	24,718	215	0	17	12	186	1,123	322	715	86	5
Arkoma	1,889	3	0	0	0	3	8	0	3	5	0
Atoka	3,019	12	0	0	0	12	139	55	70	14	1
Avant	306	0	0	0	0	0	4	2	2	0	0
Barnsdall	1,140	0	0	0	0	0	13	6	7	0	0
Bartlesville	36,183	88	1	13	10	64	1,144	251	791	102	9
Beaver	1,387	0	0	0	0	0	13	1	10	2	0
Beggs	1,233	4	0	1	1	2	16	9	3	4	0

Table 8. Offenses Known to Law Enforcement, by Selected State and City, 2020—Continued

(Number.)

State/city	Population	Violent crime	Murder and nonnegligent manslaughter	Rape[1]	Robbery	Aggravated assault	Property crime	Burglary	Larceny-theft	Motor vehicle theft	Arson[2]
Bernice	581	0	0	0	0	0	6	2	4	0	0
Bethany	19,239	83	4	9	18	52	626	132	419	75	5
Big Cabin	248	0	0	0	0	0	6	1	5	0	0
Binger	628	0	0	0	0	0	1	0	1	0	0
Bixby	28,840	20	0	3	0	17	373	71	234	68	0
Blackwell	6,508	17	0	6	0	11	119	40	61	18	1
Blanchard	9,090	8	0	2	0	6	91	16	60	15	2
Boise City	1,067	3	0	0	0	3	17	6	8	3	0
Bokchito	694	0	0	0	0	0	10	3	6	1	0
Bokoshe	496	2	0	0	1	1	0	0	0	0	0
Boley	1,173	0	0	0	0	0	1	1	0	0	0
Boswell	679	4	0	0	0	4	9	1	5	3	1
Bristow	4,196	10	0	1	0	9	97	30	52	15	0
Broken Arrow	111,488	192	2	35	30	125	2,158	273	1,630	255	2
Broken Bow	4,081	27	0	2	2	23	217	50	150	17	2
Burns Flat	1,885	4	0	0	0	4	2	0	2	0	0
Butler	296	0	0	0	0	0	0	0	0	0	0
Cache	2,810	3	0	0	0	3	32	12	16	4	1
Caddo	1,115	3	0	0	0	3	6	2	3	1	0
Calera	2,393	7	0	1	1	5	39	12	23	4	0
Calvin	273	0	0	0	0	0	1	0	1	0	1
Caney	197	2	0	1	0	1	8	0	7	1	0
Canton	585	4	0	0	1	3	13	5	8	0	0
Carnegie	1,636	6	0	1	0	5	24	13	10	1	0
Carney	620	0	0	0	0	0	1	0	1	0	0
Cashion	879	2	0	0	0	2	3	2	1	0	0
Catoosa	6,930	49	1	5	3	40	248	27	181	40	3
Chandler	3,084	7	0	0	0	7	43	4	30	9	2
Chattanooga	451	0	0	0	0	0	0	0	0	0	0
Checotah	3,069	8	0	1	0	7	94	27	58	9	1
Chelsea	1,899	3	0	2	0	1	30	5	19	6	0
Cherokee	1,489	3	0	0	1	2	27	8	17	2	0
Chickasha	16,478	80	5	3	5	67	586	150	396	40	5
Choctaw	12,850	12	1	3	1	7	168	33	120	15	0
Chouteau	2,090	3	0	1	1	1	63	7	42	14	0
Claremore[4]	18,757	31	1	7	2	21	565	64	471	30	5
Clayton	782	8	0	0	0	8	6	4	2	0	0
Cleveland[4]	3,112	13	0	1	0	12	41	4	30	7	0
Clinton	9,094	31	0	4	6	21	236	63	142	31	3
Coalgate	1,774	10	0	1	0	9	12	3	3	6	0
Colbert	1,264	18	0	0	0	18	5	0	3	2	0
Colcord	852	4	0	1	0	3	28	6	18	4	1
Collinsville	7,441	17	1	4	2	10	102	19	67	16	1
Comanche	1,547	9	0	1	1	7	21	6	15	0	0
Cordell	2,715	2	0	0	0	2	28	6	19	3	0
Covington	534	0	0	0	0	0	6	3	3	0	0
Coweta	10,109	36	0	3	0	33	161	37	103	21	0
Crescent	1,577	1	0	0	0	1	5	2	3	0	0
Cushing	7,592	33	0	7	1	25	244	38	176	30	0
Cyril	1,006	0	0	0	0	0	12	8	3	1	1
Davenport	806	5	0	0	1	4	7	2	5	0	0
Davis	2,921	21	0	0	0	21	96	19	64	13	2
Del City	21,750	216	4	14	25	173	792	133	540	119	0
Depew	479	1	0	0	0	1	7	1	3	3	0
Dewar	848	0	0	0	0	0	5	2	3	0	0
Dewey	3,381	6	1	1	0	4	67	13	46	8	0
Dibble	868	0	0	0	0	0	10	3	5	2	0
Dickson	1,252	3	0	0	0	3	28	7	18	3	0
Disney	302	0	0	0	0	0	3	1	2	0	0
Drumright	2,827	2	0	0	0	2	67	31	32	4	0
Duncan	22,226	42	1	4	7	30	895	226	612	57	4
Durant	19,007	40	2	7	5	26	559	135	377	47	1
Edmond	95,571	139	1	26	11	101	1,484	184	1,169	131	3
Eldorado	402	0	0	0	0	0	3	2	0	1	0
Elgin	3,313	0	0	0	0	0	7	1	5	1	0
Elk City	11,571	16	0	2	1	13	290	65	192	33	2
Elmore City	712	4	0	1	0	3	18	2	16	0	0
El Reno	20,348	35	2	7	4	22	349	78	220	51	5
Enid	49,708	233	4	35	15	179	1,420	375	948	97	2
Erick	993	0	0	0	0	0	7	2	3	2	0
Eufaula	2,849	11	1	0	0	10	60	16	33	11	0
Fairfax	1,253	2	0	0	0	2	16	6	6	4	0
Fairland	1,028	3	0	0	0	3	8	1	5	2	0
Fairview	2,596	9	0	1	0	8	32	12	17	3	0
Fletcher	1,138	3	0	0	0	3	5	1	3	1	1
Fort Cobb	605	0	0	0	0	0	2	0	1	1	0
Fort Towson	487	3	0	0	0	3	22	5	14	3	4
Frederick	3,504	21	0	5	2	14	95	30	62	3	7
Gans	299	0	0	0	0	0	0	0	0	0	0
Geary	1,263	5	0	0	0	5	33	9	17	7	0
Glenpool	14,319	51	0	4	4	43	255	42	181	32	0
Goodwell	1,267	1	0	0	0	1	19	5	12	2	0
Gore	948	5	0	1	0	4	23	7	16	0	0

Table 8. Offenses Known to Law Enforcement, by Selected State and City, 2020—Continued

(Number.)

State/city	Population	Violent crime	Murder and nonnegligent manslaughter	Rape[1]	Robbery	Aggravated assault	Property crime	Burglary	Larceny-theft	Motor vehicle theft	Arson[2]
Grandfield	922	2	0	1	0	1	20	6	9	5	0
Granite	1,946	2	0	0	0	2	7	2	4	1	0
Grove	7,210	27	0	2	2	23	258	31	199	28	1
Guthrie	11,829	24	1	2	3	18	234	65	147	22	1
Guymon	10,939	24	1	7	3	13	149	44	84	21	1
Harrah	6,681	17	0	1	0	16	109	25	73	11	2
Hartshorne	1,944	9	0	0	0	9	60	30	28	2	2
Haskell	1,922	11	0	0	0	11	27	7	15	5	1
Healdton	2,671	13	0	1	0	12	40	9	19	12	2
Heavener	3,286	19	0	1	0	18	59	23	32	4	2
Hennessey	2,233	1	0	0	0	1	8	2	5	1	0
Henryetta	5,527	12	0	3	0	9	169	65	78	26	0
Hinton	3,221	0	0	0	0	0	19	1	13	5	0
Hobart	3,393	18	0	0	0	18	78	26	43	9	0
Holdenville	5,470	17	0	2	2	13	155	51	83	21	5
Hollis	1,853	5	0	1	0	4	27	6	19	2	0
Hominy	3,370	9	0	1	0	8	26	11	13	2	0
Hooker	1,835	2	0	1	0	1	15	4	8	3	0
Howe	787	1	0	1	0	0	11	2	6	3	0
Hugo	5,067	31	1	5	4	21	235	45	164	26	8
Hulbert	581	0	0	0	0	0	1	0	1	0	0
Hydro	933	0	0	0	0	0	8	0	7	1	0
Idabel	6,827	65	3	7	11	44	436	102	320	14	4
Inola	1,804	1	0	0	0	1	8	3	5	0	0
Jay	2,546	12	0	1	1	10	68	11	44	13	1
Jenks	24,639	26	0	3	6	17	262	42	187	33	0
Jennings	353	0	0	0	0	0	4	0	2	2	1
Jones	3,225	9	2	1	0	6	55	19	31	5	3
Kansas	801	2	0	1	0	1	25	15	7	3	0
Kellyville	1,146	1	0	0	1	0	14	3	5	6	0
Keota	547	1	0	0	0	1	2	1	0	1	0
Kiefer	2,053	2	0	0	0	2	33	6	16	11	0
Kingfisher	4,939	18	0	3	0	15	82	14	57	11	0
Kingston	1,683	0	0	0	0	0	4	1	0	3	0
Kiowa	670	5	0	0	0	5	12	4	6	2	1
Konawa	1,186	10	0	1	0	9	71	20	47	4	5
Krebs	1,933	3	0	0	1	2	50	17	27	6	2
Lamont	389	0	0	0	0	0	0	0	0	0	0
Langley	821	0	0	0	0	0	19	6	11	2	1
Langston	1,872	1	0	1	0	0	7	4	1	2	0
Laverne	1,327	0	0	0	0	0	3	0	3	0	0
Lawton	92,507	727	14	79	102	532	2,071	632	1,166	273	0
Lexington	2,188	6	0	3	0	3	33	7	26	0	0
Lindsay	2,770	16	0	3	0	13	113	29	76	8	1
Locust Grove	1,392	10	0	0	0	10	71	20	34	17	0
Lone Grove	5,153	8	0	0	1	7	79	27	42	10	0
Luther	1,829	1	0	0	0	1	12	4	4	4	0
Madill	4,063	4	0	1	2	1	141	32	101	8	1
Mangum	2,667	12	0	0	1	11	20	8	11	1	0
Mannford	3,207	6	2	1	1	2	37	9	16	12	0
Marietta	2,785	4	0	0	0	4	68	20	37	11	1
Marlow	4,393	8	0	0	1	7	111	30	73	8	1
Maud	1,061	0	0	0	0	0	19	6	13	0	0
Maysville	1,202	3	0	0	0	3	33	7	21	5	0
McAlester[4]	17,752	57	3	8	7	39	560	113	386	61	1
McCurtain	500	2	0	0	0	2	2	0	2	0	0
McLoud	4,767	7	0	1	3	3	75	13	54	8	1
Medford	932	1	0	1	0	0	4	1	2	1	0
Medicine Park	460	1	0	0	1	0	2	1	1	0	0
Meeker	1,140	2	0	0	0	2	8	1	5	2	0
Miami	13,032	55	0	10	4	41	351	83	240	28	6
Midwest City	57,730	183	9	19	44	111	1,632	262	1,192	178	8
Minco	1,650	1	0	1	0	0	13	2	10	1	1
Moore	62,840	131	3	22	23	83	1,452	232	1,083	137	4
Mooreland	1,165	0	0	0	0	0	6	2	3	1	0
Morris	1,414	1	0	0	0	1	2	1	1	0	3
Mounds	1,273	7	0	0	0	7	20	5	13	2	0
Mountain View	729	0	0	0	0	0	8	2	3	3	0
Muldrow	3,228	9	0	1	0	8	51	16	28	7	0
Muskogee	36,884	446	3	33	43	367	1,291	341	810	140	7
Mustang	23,658	48	0	9	1	38	243	22	193	28	1
Nash	193	0	0	0	0	0	0	0	0	0	0
Newcastle	11,038	13	1	5	0	7	190	36	112	42	0
Newkirk	2,155	6	0	0	0	6	42	12	25	5	0
Nichols Hills	3,966	4	0	1	0	3	56	19	32	5	0
Nicoma Park	2,473	6	0	0	0	6	54	13	35	6	1
Ninnekah	1,052	0	0	0	0	0	3	0	2	1	0
Noble	7,117	13	0	3	1	9	140	25	95	20	0
Norman	126,480	366	5	43	49	269	3,261	475	2,379	407	6
North Enid	928	2	0	1	0	1	5	2	3	0	0
Nowata	3,533	15	1	2	1	11	64	10	48	6	0
Oilton	1,014	6	0	0	0	6	23	9	10	4	1
Okarche	1,344	0	0	0	0	0	12	3	8	1	0

Table 8. Offenses Known to Law Enforcement, by Selected State and City, 2020—Continued

(Number.)

State/city	Population	Violent crime	Murder and nonnegligent manslaughter	Rape[1]	Robbery	Aggravated assault	Property crime	Burglary	Larceny-theft	Motor vehicle theft	Arson[2]
Okeene	1,131	1	0	0	0	1	16	4	11	1	0
Okemah	3,120	13	0	1	2	10	103	26	67	10	0
Oklahoma City[4]	663,661	4,818	63	559	817	3,379	25,853	5,849	16,222	3,782	121
Okmulgee	11,627	68	3	6	12	47	498	99	359	40	3
Olustee	549	0	0	0	0	0	3	0	3	0	0
Oologah	1,179	0	0	0	0	0	1	1	0	0	0
Owasso	37,815	78	2	12	13	51	703	76	571	56	1
Paoli	613	0	0	0	0	0	0	0	0	0	0
Pauls Valley	6,111	42	1	5	4	32	269	93	156	20	1
Pawhuska	3,386	15	0	3	0	12	127	48	72	7	1
Pawnee	2,096	15	0	4	1	10	57	20	26	11	0
Perkins	2,815	8	0	1	1	6	77	38	31	8	0
Perry	4,807	11	0	1	0	10	67	25	38	4	1
Piedmont	8,931	7	0	0	0	7	44	13	29	2	2
Pocola	4,128	13	0	1	1	11	28	9	15	4	0
Ponca City[4]	23,484	181	2	19	34	126	1,037	279	661	97	8
Pond Creek	831	0	0	0	0	0	3	1	2	0	0
Porum	698	1	0	0	0	1	5	0	4	1	0
Poteau	8,899	57	2	1	4	50	328	57	255	16	0
Prague	2,365	10	0	3	0	7	67	12	43	12	1
Pryor Creek	9,361	63	0	10	0	53	251	64	142	45	1
Purcell	6,445	24	0	7	2	15	231	54	154	23	0
Quinton	978	5	0	1	0	4	18	9	6	3	2
Rattan	295	0	0	0	0	0	3	1	2	0	0
Roland	3,998	12	0	1	0	11	45	6	31	8	0
Rush Springs	1,259	1	0	1	0	0	35	9	24	2	0
Salina	1,393	7	0	3	0	4	26	6	13	7	0
Sallisaw	8,448	22	0	4	0	18	242	42	190	10	5
Sand Springs	20,026	19	0	6	6	7	902	117	649	136	0
Savanna	641	2	0	0	0	2	18	4	12	2	0
Sawyer	312	3	0	0	0	3	4	2	1	1	0
Sayre	4,500	3	0	0	2	1	51	12	32	7	1
Seiling	855	0	0	0	0	0	0	0	0	0	0
Seminole	6,994	21	0	8	3	10	213	48	134	31	1
Shady Point	996	1	0	0	0	1	3	2	1	0	0
Shattuck	1,247	0	0	0	0	0	21	1	19	1	0
Shawnee	31,606	155	1	19	16	119	1,340	219	933	188	5
Skiatook	8,135	22	0	3	2	17	206	73	118	15	3
Snyder	1,265	7	0	2	1	4	17	6	11	0	0
South Coffeyville	729	1	0	0	0	1	14	2	12	0	0
Sparks	171	0	0	0	0	0	2	0	2	0	0
Spencer	3,973	13	1	1	1	10	84	28	38	18	0
Sperry	1,354	11	1	1	0	9	39	9	19	11	1
Sportsmen Acres	307	0	0	0	0	0	0	0	0	0	0
Stigler	2,680	10	0	1	0	9	48	21	24	3	0
Stillwater	50,831	146	0	39	11	96	1,248	229	934	85	12
Stilwell	4,070	19	0	3	2	14	104	13	76	15	1
Stratford	1,525	2	0	0	0	2	14	2	10	2	0
Stringtown	401	0	0	0	0	0	1	0	0	1	0
Stroud	2,701	6	0	0	2	4	64	22	35	7	1
Sulphur	5,055	9	0	0	2	7	110	19	79	12	0
Tahlequah	16,936	31	2	4	3	22	456	51	383	22	0
Talala	279	0	0	0	0	0	2	1	1	0	0
Talihina	1,078	3	0	0	0	3	26	5	15	6	1
Tecumseh	6,652	19	0	3	0	16	210	54	125	31	1
Texhoma	898	0	0	0	0	0	0	0	0	0	0
Thackerville	520	0	0	0	0	0	1	0	1	0	0
The Village	9,632	24	0	4	3	17	227	21	189	17	0
Thomas	1,200	0	0	0	0	0	10	3	6	1	0
Tipton	750	1	0	0	0	1	16	5	9	2	0
Tishomingo	3,085	5	0	0	0	5	28	10	13	5	0
Tonkawa	2,956	7	0	2	0	5	88	25	58	5	1
Tulsa	402,166	4,555	72	378	741	3,364	20,557	4,407	12,246	3,904	253
Tupelo	300	0	0	0	0	0	6	2	4	0	0
Tushka	388	2	0	0	0	2	10	3	5	2	0
Tuttle	7,768	11	0	4	0	7	63	11	42	10	1
Tyrone	738	1	0	0	0	1	1	1	0	0	1
Union City	2,221	4	1	1	0	2	13	3	6	4	2
Valley Brook	770	3	0	1	1	1	20	7	13	0	1
Valliant	736	1	0	0	1	0	5	3	2	0	0
Velma	592	0	0	0	0	0	6	5	1	0	0
Verden	538	1	0	0	0	1	2	1	1	0	1
Verdigris	4,669	6	0	2	0	4	47	5	37	5	0
Vian	1,356	7	0	1	0	6	49	24	22	3	0
Vici	705	0	0	0	0	0	2	0	2	0	0
Vinita	5,264	15	0	3	0	12	85	19	50	16	0
Wagoner	9,283	21	1	2	3	15	189	60	110	19	3
Wakita	324	0	0	0	0	0	0	0	0	0	0
Walters	2,334	0	0	0	0	0	34	13	15	6	0
Warner	1,584	1	0	0	0	1	12	0	9	3	0
Warr Acres	10,140	42	1	6	7	28	426	163	221	42	2
Washington	605	0	0	0	0	0	4	3	1	0	0
Watonga	2,820	18	0	2	1	15	58	13	42	3	1

Table 8. Offenses Known to Law Enforcement, by Selected State and City, 2020—Continued

(Number.)

State/city	Population	Violent crime	Murder and nonnegligent manslaughter	Rape[1]	Robbery	Aggravated assault	Property crime	Burglary	Larceny-theft	Motor vehicle theft	Arson[2]
Watts	312	2	0	0	0	2	0	0	0	0	0
Waukomis	1,297	0	0	0	0	0	16	5	10	1	0
Waurika	1,867	0	0	0	0	0	17	4	11	2	0
Waynoka	912	4	0	0	0	4	13	2	11	0	0
Weatherford	12,155	21	2	2	3	14	232	47	161	24	1
Weleetka	949	4	0	0	0	4	6	2	3	1	0
Wellston	772	1	0	0	0	1	3	0	2	1	1
West Siloam Springs	862	1	0	0	0	1	47	5	33	9	0
Westville	1,542	3	0	0	0	3	58	16	30	12	1
Wetumka	1,193	5	0	0	1	4	33	5	19	9	1
Wewoka	3,202	11	0	1	1	9	93	42	37	14	1
Wilburton	2,512	4	0	2	1	1	64	19	41	4	0
Wilson	1,692	1	0	0	0	1	19	7	8	4	1
Woodward	12,143	31	0	10	1	20	312	82	212	18	1
Wyandotte	323	0	0	0	0	0	0	0	0	0	0
Wynnewood	2,201	1	0	0	0	1	21	7	8	6	0
Wynona	434	0	0	0	0	0	1	0	1	0	0
Yale	1,222	0	0	0	0	0	10	3	5	2	3
Yukon	28,735	33	0	5	4	24	583	66	492	25	0
OREGON											
Albany	55,926	83	2	14	28	39	1,545	112	1,312	121	22
Ashland	21,419	41	1	8	7	25	510	44	431	35	6
Astoria	10,076	60	0	12	8	40	318	49	237	32	4
Baker City	9,808	29	1	9	5	14	348	55	284	9	3
Banks	2,063	3	0	2	0	1	20	2	16	2	0
Beaverton	100,085	235	1	38	47	149	2,197	255	1,693	249	27
Bend	103,485	174	0	28	31	115	1,959	201	1,593	165	37
Boardman	3,811	3	0	2	0	1	47	2	38	7	0
Brookings	6,495	21	0	1	2	18	96	14	78	4	3
Burns	2,794	5	0	3	0	2	31	4	27	0	0
Carlton	2,202	0	0	0	0	0	32	3	27	2	0
Central Point	19,032	50	0	10	2	38	353	26	295	32	7
Columbia City	2,030	2	0	0	0	2	17	4	7	6	0
Coos Bay	16,403	84	0	14	18	52	784	183	548	53	39
Cornelius	12,925	53	0	13	11	29	272	35	211	26	3
Cottage Grove	10,556	30	0	5	4	21	183	21	127	35	9
Dallas	17,265	32	0	4	1	27	381	51	305	25	1
Eagle Point	9,681	22	0	2	2	18	122	8	98	16	2
Enterprise	2,002	3	0	2	0	1	29	2	26	1	0
Eugene	174,513	681	2	107	163	409	6,980	1,073	5,187	720	90
Florence	9,228	10	0	2	0	8	218	17	193	8	3
Forest Grove	26,065	56	0	10	3	43	526	86	403	37	3
Gaston	732	2	0	0	0	2	6	1	4	1	2
Gervais	2,795	10	0	2	0	8	42	5	18	19	0
Gladstone	12,418	28	0	10	7	11	229	25	168	36	4
Grants Pass	38,420	133	0	27	25	81	1,160	131	901	128	17
Gresham	109,767	510	5	70	120	315	3,078	421	1,751	906	36
Hermiston	17,896	37	1	7	8	21	435	54	341	40	4
Hillsboro	111,146	257	2	55	46	154	2,147	212	1,695	240	20
Hood River	7,863	12	0	0	4	8	277	30	226	21	2
Hubbard	3,615	6	0	1	1	4	55	7	41	7	0
Independence	10,477	13	0	3	0	10	145	10	122	13	1
Jacksonville	2,912	7	0	0	0	7	71	4	61	6	1
Junction City	6,333	16	0	2	3	11	134	12	111	11	0
Keizer	40,087	70	1	3	12	54	758	68	585	105	4
King City	4,512	8	0	3	0	5	43	4	31	8	0
Klamath Falls	22,693	135	1	9	20	105	670	103	470	97	22
La Grande	13,674	20	0	1	1	18	323	51	240	32	3
Lake Oswego	40,171	27	0	8	3	16	659	116	493	50	3
Lebanon	17,635	23	0	4	1	18	297	23	251	23	4
Lincoln City[5]	9,275			11	5	29	365	53	293	19	3
Madras	7,140	10	0	0	2	8	293	33	229	31	1
McMinnville	35,040	95	0	27	4	64	782	95	629	58	9
Medford	84,016	388	2	36	94	256	3,615	296	3,012	307	76
Milton-Freewater	7,075	15	1	4	3	7	115	21	72	22	2
Milwaukie	21,040	30	0	4	5	21	312	33	213	66	4
Molalla	9,351	19	0	4	2	13	104	16	78	10	0
Monmouth	10,708	11	0	3	2	6	116	7	103	6	2
Mount Angel	3,647	7	0	0	0	7	33	3	23	7	0
Myrtle Creek	3,493	3	0	0	1	2	166	25	119	22	0
Newport	10,950	26	0	7	1	18	302	23	263	16	6
North Bend	9,778	14	0	2	4	8	281	33	230	18	2
North Plains	2,231	1	0	0	0	1	57	7	46	4	0
Ontario	10,952	72	1	5	5	61	634	54	536	44	7
Oregon City	37,892	114	0	14	19	81	593	78	457	58	11
Pendleton	16,804	37	1	8	6	22	534	82	411	41	15
Philomath	5,805	5	0	1	0	4	76	8	63	5	0
Phoenix	4,680	10	0	0	2	8	227	16	196	15	0
Pilot Rock	1,510	6	0	1	0	5	24	6	14	4	1
Portland	662,941	3,465	53	262	807	2,343	31,416	3,759	21,287	6,370	295
Prineville	10,919	33	0	11	0	22	198	16	169	13	2
Rainier	2,021	0	0	0	0	0	43	2	39	2	1

Table 8. Offenses Known to Law Enforcement, by Selected State and City, 2020—Continued

(Number.)

State/city	Population	Violent crime	Murder and nonnegligent manslaughter	Rape[1]	Robbery	Aggravated assault	Property crime	Burglary	Larceny-theft	Motor vehicle theft	Arson[2]
Redmond	33,198	88	0	14	10	64	1,055	94	853	108	6
Reedsport	4,111	15	0	2	1	12	131	13	105	13	1
Rockaway Beach	1,429	5	0	0	1	4	45	15	29	1	2
Rogue River	2,355	5	0	0	4	1	71	5	62	4	0
Roseburg	23,551	78	0	16	18	44	1,383	162	1,101	120	8
Salem	176,632	698	2	28	148	520	6,698	678	4,911	1,109	111
Scappoose	7,666	12	0	3	0	9	117	10	96	11	0
Seaside	6,938	23	0	4	2	17	138	12	117	9	2
Sherwood	20,052	11	0	1	4	6	261	16	220	25	0
Silverton	10,782	14	0	3	2	9	241	38	178	25	6
Springfield	63,666	194	2	33	22	137	1,760	160	1,426	174	24
Stayton	8,364	18	0	1	2	15	243	9	209	25	0
St. Helens	13,818	35	0	10	0	25	191	44	118	29	1
Sunriver	1,393	3	0	0	0	3	54	21	30	3	0
Sutherlin	8,223	21	0	2	2	17	205	26	153	26	5
Sweet Home	10,099	24	3	2	0	19	328	26	275	27	7
Talent	6,671	6	0	0	2	4	105	18	80	7	1
The Dalles	15,849	48	0	15	8	25	590	100	441	49	7
Tigard	56,377	107	1	14	24	68	1,472	161	1,170	141	11
Tillamook	5,392	13	0	1	3	9	208	28	169	11	1
Toledo	3,665	8	0	2	0	6	40	5	34	1	0
Tualatin	28,030	64	0	13	19	32	726	65	587	74	4
Umatilla	7,366	15	0	2	0	13	88	12	66	10	2
Vernonia	2,294	4	0	1	0	3	16	1	11	4	1
Warrenton	5,823	27	0	2	4	21	373	29	335	9	3
West Linn	26,916	12	0	2	3	7	314	27	266	21	2
Winston	5,528	13	2	2	2	7	145	18	110	17	0
Woodburn	26,521	87	1	22	19	45	872	79	533	260	8
Yamhill	1,187	0	0	0	0	0	12	1	11	0	0
PENNSYLVANIA[3]											
Adams Township, Cambria County	5,474	2	0	0	0	2	8	1	6	1	1
Aliquippa	8,780	38	2	4	8	24	101	23	64	14	1
Cherry Tree	335	0	0	0	0	0	0	0	0	0	0
Derry Township, Dauphin County	25,313	39	0	5	3	31	280	23	246	11	0
DuBois	7,319	17	0	4	0	13	114	3	107	4	0
East Earl Township	6,934	1	0	0	0	1	41	3	35	3	0
Harrisburg	49,244	422	23	30	102	267	876	173	579	124	21
Jermyn	2,041	5	0	0	0	5	33	3	29	1	0
Kiskiminetas Township	4,440	1	0	1	0	0	23	2	21	0	1
Kittanning	3,692	6	0	2	3	1	145	30	112	3	0
Larksville	4,376	1	1	0	0	0	11	1	9	1	0
Shippensburg	5,570	0	0	0	0	0	6	1	5	0	0
St. Clair Boro	2,811	0	0	0	0	0	71	0	71	0	0
Stonycreek Township	2,558	2	0	1	1	0	52	9	38	5	0
Tower City	1,270	0	0	0	0	0	0	0	0	0	
Upper Providence Township, Montgomery County	24,725	9	0	3	3	3	179	9	165	5	1
Vandergrift	4,840	19	0	0	1	18	9	2	7	0	0
West Mead Township	4,994	8	0	1	0	7	7	1	6	0	0
Wilkins Township	6,109	10	0	0	0	10	76	5	66	5	2
RHODE ISLAND											
Barrington	15,986	3	0	2	0	1	120	15	103	2	1
Bristol	21,748	5	0	1	0	4	69	6	61	2	3
Burrillville	16,904	15	0	2	2	11	65	6	54	5	2
Central Falls	19,530	89	2	14	15	58	245	33	169	43	6
Charlestown	7,803	8	0	4	0	4	37	7	25	5	0
Coventry	34,740	43	0	15	2	26	252	27	209	16	2
Cranston	81,313	111	2	27	13	69	858	86	685	87	12
Cumberland	35,357	28	0	8	3	17	217	48	158	11	5
East Greenwich	13,084	5	0	1	0	4	92	6	69	17	2
East Providence	47,542	112	1	17	9	85	349	42	270	37	5
Foster	4,747	7	0	2	1	4	33	8	22	3	0
Glocester	10,358	8	0	1	0	7	19	7	9	3	0
Hopkinton	8,025	4	0	3	0	1	37	6	25	6	0
Jamestown	5,493	3	0	3	0	0	20	3	17	0	0
Johnston	29,458	37	0	7	3	27	366	61	257	48	4
Lincoln	22,029	34	0	8	6	20	226	33	167	26	0
Little Compton	3,463	5	0	0	0	5	9	0	7	2	0
Middletown	15,817	40	0	3	0	37	102	10	85	7	0
Narragansett	15,248	10	0	6	0	4	80	10	62	8	1
Newport	24,202	74	0	14	4	56	370	50	295	25	4
New Shoreham	1,025	0	0	0	0	0	18	2	16	0	0
North Kingstown	26,221	26	0	8	3	15	221	16	196	9	2
North Providence	32,652	51	0	6	6	39	193	31	122	40	3
North Smithfield	12,616	10	0	3	2	5	177	11	153	13	0
Pawtucket	72,017	288	4	41	36	207	1,496	217	1,066	213	13
Portsmouth	17,162	9	0	1	2	6	57	13	38	6	3
Providence	179,603	873	17	66	183	607	4,337	602	3,191	544	8
Richmond	7,724	3	0	0	1	2	28	6	20	2	0

Table 8. Offenses Known to Law Enforcement, by Selected State and City, 2020—Continued

(Number.)

State/city	Population	Violent crime	Murder and nonnegligent manslaughter	Rape[1]	Robbery	Aggravated assault	Property crime	Burglary	Larceny-theft	Motor vehicle theft	Arson[2]
Scituate	10,739	3	0	0	0	3	35	7	25	3	0
Smithfield	21,893	21	0	2	7	12	143	10	123	10	0
South Kingstown	30,238	15	0	4	1	10	135	22	106	7	0
Warren	10,469	18	0	5	1	12	93	8	83	2	2
Warwick	80,605	66	0	21	7	38	993	92	823	78	17
Westerly	22,277	18	1	9	0	8	292	21	244	27	0
West Greenwich	6,399	3	0	1	0	2	43	6	30	7	0
West Warwick	28,831	61	0	14	3	44	221	55	138	28	6
Woonsocket	41,693	209	4	45	24	136	756	156	500	100	11
SOUTH CAROLINA											
Abbeville	4,990	22	0	4	2	16	151	20	115	16	0
Aiken	31,007	250	5	9	33	203	1,493	146	1,248	99	3
Allendale	2,870	59	3	2	7	47	105	28	61	16	0
Atlantic Beach	459	11	0	2	0	9	20	6	11	3	0
Aynor	1,025	0	0	0	0	0	9	1	5	3	0
Bamberg	3,147	28	0	2	7	19	137	34	96	7	0
Barnwell	4,241	102	2	3	2	95	193	47	133	13	0
Batesburg-Leesville	5,419	30	0	0	1	29	197	25	160	12	0
Beaufort	13,561	66	0	6	5	55	477	47	411	19	0
Belton	4,488	11	0	0	1	10	153	19	105	29	2
Bennettsville	7,591	91	1	2	5	83	241	28	203	10	2
Bethune	352	0	0	0	0	0	7	4	3	0	0
Bishopville	2,971	40	2	1	1	36	170	36	120	14	2
Blackville	2,166	12	2	2	1	7	41	13	25	3	0
Bluffton	27,549	25	0	7	2	16	199	38	145	16	0
Bowman	880	4	0	0	0	4	13	2	11	0	0
Branchville	946	2	0	1	0	1	26	1	24	1	0
Burnettown	2,762	2	0	0	0	2	34	6	26	2	0
Calhoun Falls	1,892	22	0	1	0	21	36	17	18	1	0
Camden	7,264	88	2	2	7	77	357	58	282	17	3
Cayce	14,117	94	3	5	10	76	659	78	499	82	1
Central	5,407	3	0	0	1	2	106	4	94	8	0
Chapin	1,657	3	0	0	1	2	57	12	39	6	0
Charleston	139,582	650	17	54	100	479	3,218	326	2,439	453	19
Cheraw	5,529	33	3	0	3	27	362	33	311	18	1
Chesnee	969	4	0	2	0	2	38	4	29	5	0
Chester	5,354	65	3	3	4	55	196	22	159	15	3
Chesterfield	1,409	2	0	0	0	2	44	16	26	2	0
Clemson	17,951	26	0	3	1	22	359	36	249	74	1
Clinton	8,363	78	2	13	4	59	301	52	217	32	2
Clover	6,693	26	0	2	6	18	140	15	115	10	1
Columbia	131,777	991	19	86	206	680	5,898	728	4,536	634	17
Conway	27,120	110	3	15	18	74	683	74	563	46	3
Coward	773	1	0	0	0	1	24	2	20	2	0
Cowpens	2,450	8	0	1	1	6	48	7	37	4	0
Darlington	5,895	94	1	2	8	83	374	38	312	24	0
Denmark	2,876	27	0	0	3	24	94	38	51	5	0
Due West	1,200	1	0	1	0	0	25	3	21	1	0
Duncan	3,679	11	0	4	1	6	65	7	47	11	0
Easley	21,512	90	1	7	6	76	1,028	100	843	85	3
Edgefield	4,816	2	0	0	1	1	32	9	16	7	0
Edisto Beach	405	1	0	0	0	1	11	1	8	2	0
Elgin	1,616	2	0	1	0	1	78	5	72	1	0
Elloree	635	5	0	0	1	4	15	3	12	0	0
Florence	38,597	562	12	15	72	463	2,390	322	1,812	256	2
Forest Acres	10,283	41	0	5	6	30	586	62	483	41	0
Fort Mill	23,966	32	1	3	4	24	231	19	195	17	4
Fountain Inn	10,820	62	0	18	6	38	226	32	166	28	1
Gaston	1,706	3	0	0	2	1	72	10	51	11	0
Georgetown	8,697	108	7	1	10	90	490	54	407	29	1
Greenville	72,014	502	7	29	85	381	2,929	320	2,371	238	8
Greenwood	23,422	298	4	22	32	240	1,247	268	940	39	14
Greer	34,320	97	1	16	20	60	1,051	86	879	86	6
Hampton	2,474	19	0	1	0	18	136	18	106	12	0
Hanahan	28,143	61	1	4	15	41	326	61	233	32	1
Hardeeville	7,970	48	4	3	10	31	175	26	137	12	1
Hartsville	7,519	88	4	8	6	70	450	68	364	18	3
Hemingway	388	2	1	0	1	0	17	3	10	4	0
Holly Hill	1,168	4	0	0	1	3	55	8	43	4	0
Honea Path	3,857	22	0	1	5	16	204	29	153	22	3
Irmo	12,639	41	0	3	4	34	461	97	335	29	1
Isle of Palms	4,385	7	0	4	0	3	57	4	46	7	0
Iva	1,335	7	0	3	0	4	49	15	28	6	0
Jackson	1,812	3	0	0	2	1	20	4	14	2	1
Johnsonville	1,484	0	0	0	0	0	11	4	4	3	0
Jonesville	831	6	0	0	0	6	10	3	4	3	0
Kingstree	3,035	24	0	1	1	22	160	28	124	8	1
Lake View	752	9	0	1	1	7	35	9	20	6	0
Landrum	2,713	16	0	1	1	14	68	10	54	4	0
Latta	1,275	15	3	0	1	11	75	9	64	2	0
Lexington	22,592	47	2	7	13	25	493	43	419	31	0
Liberty	3,143	10	1	0	3	6	86	11	68	7	1

Table 8. Offenses Known to Law Enforcement, by Selected State and City, 2020—Continued

(Number.)

State/city	Population	Violent crime	Murder and nonnegligent manslaughter	Rape[1]	Robbery	Aggravated assault	Property crime	Burglary	Larceny-theft	Motor vehicle theft	Arson[2]
Loris	2,804	22	0	1	0	21	82	10	66	6	1
Lyman	3,768	15	0	1	2	12	75	15	52	8	0
Manning	3,869	61	4	2	3	52	359	43	303	13	1
Marion	6,268	79	4	3	9	63	314	64	232	18	3
Mauldin	25,662	67	4	6	7	50	506	68	392	46	0
McCormick	2,310	9	0	0	0	9	57	13	44	0	0
Moncks Corner	12,580	53	1	3	6	43	451	40	380	31	1
Mount Pleasant	94,704	94	0	14	12	68	1,257	95	1,023	139	3
Mullins	4,196	52	1	1	5	45	158	53	99	6	2
Myrtle Beach	35,658	492	6	57	87	342	3,108	258	2,617	233	6
Newberry	10,181	103	2	1	5	95	392	105	273	14	1
New Ellenton	2,164	4	0	0	2	2	37	4	28	5	0
Ninety Six	2,042	7	0	0	1	6	44	5	37	2	0
North	702	4	0	0	1	3	49	4	44	1	0
North Augusta	24,139	48	1	11	12	24	722	58	623	41	2
North Charleston	117,503	1,345	38	90	318	899	5,998	651	4,667	680	27
North Myrtle Beach	17,183	99	0	13	6	80	997	90	844	63	3
Orangeburg	12,529	217	4	7	29	177	822	184	573	65	4
Pamplico	1,219	2	0	0	0	2	13	5	7	1	0
Pawleys Island	109	0	0	0	0	0	10	1	8	1	0
Pelion	714	7	0	1	1	5	29	3	22	4	0
Pickens	3,177	19	0	2	0	17	162	13	139	10	0
Port Royal	13,553	37	1	2	8	26	203	23	172	8	1
Quinby	922	0	0	0	0	0	0	0	0	0	0
Ridgeland	3,788	7	1	0	2	4	67	5	56	6	0
Ridge Spring	749	7	0	1	3	3	27	6	20	1	1
Scranton	863	0	0	0	0	0	8	1	7	0	0
Seneca	8,581	85	3	7	3	72	233	38	175	20	2
Simpsonville	24,960	84	1	13	14	56	816	76	660	80	1
Spartanburg	37,469	536	4	29	94	409	2,286	434	1,595	257	15
Springdale	2,745	15	1	1	3	10	113	19	82	12	0
Sullivans Island	1,939	0	0	0	0	0	32	4	26	2	0
Summerville	53,711	183	4	22	24	133	1,497	120	1,267	110	1
Sumter	39,542	491	10	9	45	427	1,459	211	1,179	69	7
Surfside Beach	4,608	16	0	1	1	14	116	9	101	6	0
Tega Cay	11,813	5	0	3	0	2	225	15	210	0	0
Travelers Rest	5,435	2	0	0	1	1	213	14	192	7	0
Union	7,565	79	2	4	5	68	447	70	347	30	0
Wagener	841	0	0	0	0	0	1	0	1	0	0
Walhalla	4,498	8	0	2	0	6	33	6	26	1	1
Walterboro	5,387	39	0	1	6	32	373	22	333	18	1
Ware Shoals	2,152	14	0	1	5	8	122	31	81	10	0
Wellford	2,754	4	0	0	1	3	28	4	22	2	1
West Columbia	18,143	141	2	16	27	96	1,454	121	1,211	122	1
Westminster	2,609	14	0	1	0	13	70	27	36	7	0
West Pelzer	954	0	0	0	0	0	21	3	15	3	0
Whitmire	1,455	5	0	0	2	3	30	9	20	1	0
Williamston	4,294	34	0	2	2	30	106	23	74	9	0
Williston	2,902	22	3	3	5	11	128	39	80	9	0
York	8,486	79	0	5	11	63	416	61	334	21	2
SOUTH DAKOTA											
Aberdeen	28,494	159	1	31	5	122	666	151	468	47	1
Avon	590	0	0	0	0	0	0	0	0	0	0
Belle Fourche	5,712	14	0	2	0	12	105	16	84	5	0
Beresford	2,028	5	0	1	0	4	18	3	15	0	0
Box Elder	10,402	59	1	14	4	40	292	52	199	41	0
Brandon	10,205	5	0	1	0	4	31	8	19	4	0
Brookings	24,682	38	0	12	2	24	232	37	187	8	1
Canton	3,615	9	0	0	0	9	56	7	40	9	0
Chamberlain	2,364	16	0	3	0	13	76	13	55	8	0
Clark	1,053	1	0	0	0	1	3	1	2	0	0
Deadwood	1,293	1	0	0	0	1	1	0	1	0	0
Eagle Butte	1,349	0	0	0	0	0	4	2	2	0	0
Elk Point	1,860	0	0	0	0	0	1	1	0	0	0
Faith	410	0	0	0	0	0	0	0	0	0	0
Flandreau	2,314	6	0	2	0	4	54	3	42	9	0
Freeman	1,272	5	0	0	0	5	11	2	9	0	0
Gettysburg	1,070	2	0	1	0	1	2	0	0	2	0
Groton	1,477	0	0	0	0	0	0	0	0	0	0
Hermosa	428	0	0	0	0	0	0	0	0	0	0
Hot Springs	3,477	14	0	2	1	11	13	3	10	0	0
Huron	13,469	43	0	2	0	41	288	29	242	17	0
Jefferson	507	1	0	1	0	0	5	0	4	1	0
Kimball	670	0	0	0	0	0	11	4	7	0	0
Lead	2,923	4	0	0	0	4	30	2	24	4	0
Lennox	2,520	6	0	1	0	5	12	3	8	1	0
Madison	7,357	5	0	1	0	4	69	13	52	4	0
Martin	1,042	13	0	3	0	10	58	15	39	4	0
Menno	615	0	0	0	0	0	0	0	0	0	0
Miller	1,318	0	0	0	0	0	5	3	2	0	0
Mitchell	15,726	73	2	19	2	50	520	66	379	75	8
Mobridge	3,442	13	0	0	0	13	30	10	16	4	1

Table 8. Offenses Known to Law Enforcement, by Selected State and City, 2020—Continued

(Number.)

State/city	Population	Violent crime	Murder and nonnegligent manslaughter	Rape[1]	Robbery	Aggravated assault	Property crime	Burglary	Larceny-theft	Motor vehicle theft	Arson[2]
Murdo	432	10	0	0	0	10	5	1	4	0	0
North Sioux City	2,975	5	0	0	1	4	56	1	45	10	0
Parkston	1,473	0	0	0	0	0	0	0	0	0	0
Philip	764	0	0	0	0	0	0	0	0	0	0
Pierre	13,888	128	0	18	2	108	413	56	319	38	0
Platte	1,261	1	0	1	0	0	2	1	0	1	0
Rapid City	78,492	673	13	108	104	448	3,137	657	2,014	466	12
Rosholt	430	0	0	0	0	0	0	0	0	0	0
Scotland	800	0	0	0	0	0	0	0	0	0	0
Sioux Falls	187,370	1,120	13	97	102	908	5,867	684	4,259	924	41
Sisseton	2,392	2	0	1	0	1	8	0	8	0	0
Spearfish	11,902	35	0	6	2	27	307	35	262	10	1
Springfield	1,915	0	0	0	0	0	0	0	0	0	0
Sturgis	6,955	16	0	2	0	14	185	38	137	10	1
Summerset	2,769	1	0	0	0	1	58	5	50	3	0
Tea	6,340	17	0	0	0	17	54	16	34	4	0
Tripp	621	0	0	0	0	0	1	0	0	1	0
Tyndall	1,017	0	0	0	0	0	0	0	0	0	0
Vermillion	10,969	19	1	5	0	13	209	13	176	20	0
Wagner	1,544	4	0	2	0	2	17	0	17	0	0
Watertown	22,248	56	1	15	2	38	412	62	320	30	2
Winner	2,813	7	0	1	1	5	70	12	52	6	0
Yankton	14,712	83	0	24	2	57	474	56	386	32	3
TENNESSEE											
Adamsville	2,161	4	0	0	1	3	17	4	9	4	1
Alamo	2,268	20	0	0	0	20	69	15	49	5	0
Alcoa	10,174	61	0	10	4	47	437	28	369	40	2
Alexandria	1,017	4	0	0	0	4	7	2	2	3	0
Algood	4,584	8	0	2	1	5	97	8	82	7	0
Ardmore	1,221	0	0	0	0	0	32	5	21	6	0
Ashland City	4,785	27	0	1	1	25	217	27	181	9	0
Athens	14,059	131	1	5	14	111	799	104	621	74	9
Atoka	9,632	6	0	2	0	4	72	11	54	7	0
Baileyton	454	4	0	0	1	3	6	1	4	1	0
Bartlett	59,714	153	0	7	9	137	1,156	115	968	73	1
Baxter	1,551	2	0	0	0	2	30	4	21	5	0
Bean Station	3,098	7	0	0	0	7	40	5	28	7	0
Belle Meade	2,854	0	0	0	0	0	31	3	27	1	0
Bells	2,439	13	0	1	0	12	23	1	19	3	0
Benton	1,268	1	0	0	0	1	14	1	12	1	0
Berry Hill	505	10	0	0	2	8	146	28	114	4	0
Big Sandy	519	0	0	0	0	0	2	1	1	0	0
Blaine	1,861	2	0	0	0	2	20	2	14	4	0
Bluff City	1,667	1	0	0	0	1	32	1	24	7	0
Bolivar	4,892	110	2	3	6	99	209	55	141	13	1
Bradford	970	2	0	0	0	2	10	2	7	1	0
Brentwood	43,454	19	0	3	3	13	332	66	249	17	1
Brighton	2,911	0	0	0	0	0	2	0	2	0	0
Bristol	27,013	155	3	19	10	123	774	73	617	84	5
Bruceton	1,387	1	0	1	0	0	16	6	9	1	0
Burns	1,467	1	0	0	0	1	4	2	2	0	0
Calhoun	501	0	0	0	0	0	3	0	3	0	0
Camden	3,637	0	0	0	0	0	7	0	7	0	0
Carthage	2,343	7	0	0	1	6	40	5	34	1	2
Caryville	2,130	7	0	0	2	5	29	0	25	4	0
Celina	1,412	4	0	0	0	4	14	2	10	2	0
Centerville	3,533	12	0	2	1	9	50	11	31	8	1
Chapel Hill	1,548	3	0	0	1	2	10	1	7	2	0
Charleston	703	1	0	0	0	1	5	1	4	0	0
Chattanooga	184,211	2,504	33	182	268	2,021	11,709	1,173	8,435	2,101	38
Church Hill	6,655	4	0	0	0	4	10	4	4	2	0
Clarksburg	378	0	0	0	0	0	0	0	0	0	0
Clarksville	161,167	983	15	84	78	806	3,615	441	2,765	409	10
Cleveland	45,994	454	2	21	62	369	2,312	374	1,734	204	7
Clifton	2,651	4	0	0	0	4	6	3	2	1	1
Clinton	10,111	46	0	8	4	34	307	38	229	40	1
Collegedale	11,750	13	0	4	0	9	139	10	120	9	1
Collierville	51,677	91	0	6	8	77	637	72	522	43	1
Collinwood	940	2	0	0	0	2	5	0	4	1	0
Columbia	41,013	303	2	25	29	247	1,289	202	972	115	6
Coopertown	4,621	6	0	0	2	4	33	11	17	5	1
Cornersville	1,307	1	0	0	0	1	5	1	3	1	0
Covington	8,818	130	0	7	3	120	451	56	368	27	2
Cowan	1,650	6	0	0	0	6	24	4	16	4	0
Cross Plains	1,841	0	0	0	0	0	3	1	2	0	0
Crossville	11,885	23	1	6	2	14	532	94	395	43	2
Cumberland City	306	1	0	0	0	1	5	0	5	0	0
Dandridge	3,229	7	0	0	0	7	90	14	61	15	2
Dayton	7,367	22	0	1	2	19	204	29	143	32	0
Decatur	1,668	12	0	1	2	9	40	6	28	6	0
Decaturville	862	1	0	0	1	0	3	2	0	1	0
Decherd	2,374	25	1	1	1	22	93	18	63	12	0

Table 8. Offenses Known to Law Enforcement, by Selected State and City, 2020—Continued

(Number.)

State/city	Population	Violent crime	Murder and nonnegligent manslaughter	Rape[1]	Robbery	Aggravated assault	Property crime	Burglary	Larceny-theft	Motor vehicle theft	Arson[2]
Dickson	15,680	133	0	8	5	120	560	55	459	46	2
Dover	1,562	4	0	0	0	4	5	0	5	0	0
Dresden	2,921	8	0	0	1	7	31	8	22	1	0
Dunlap	5,214	34	0	1	0	33	137	25	81	31	0
Dyer	2,195	6	0	0	0	6	23	0	22	1	0
Dyersburg	16,226	207	1	7	21	178	1,103	190	857	56	3
Eagleville	779	3	0	0	0	3	4	0	3	1	0
East Ridge	21,202	119	2	7	16	94	684	100	502	82	4
Elkton	522	2	0	0	0	2	4	1	3	0	0
Englewood	1,535	8	0	1	0	7	21	4	10	7	0
Erin	1,274	1	0	1	0	0	20	3	16	1	0
Erwin	5,901	14	0	1	0	13	67	8	45	14	0
Estill Springs	2,035	21	0	2	0	19	22	2	16	4	0
Ethridge	488	2	0	0	0	2	3	0	3	0	0
Etowah	3,495	25	0	1	0	24	79	15	53	11	1
Fairview	9,300	20	0	0	1	19	114	12	92	10	0
Fayetteville	7,077	36	1	0	2	33	239	44	181	14	1
Franklin	85,722	195	1	17	14	163	792	58	685	49	2
Friendship	662	0	0	0	0	0	9	0	8	1	0
Gadsden	463	1	0	0	0	1	3	0	2	1	0
Gainesboro	960	1	0	0	0	1	2	0	1	1	0
Gallatin	44,584	137	1	10	11	115	439	75	332	32	3
Gallaway	644	4	0	0	0	4	6	0	4	2	0
Gates	607	1	0	0	0	1	5	2	2	1	0
Gatlinburg	3,846	22	0	2	0	20	153	16	126	11	0
Germantown	39,264	42	0	3	4	35	531	27	465	39	0
Gibson	383	0	0	0	0	0	0	0	0	0	0
Gleason	1,368	5	0	0	0	5	28	9	16	3	0
Goodlettsville	16,896	48	0	2	16	30	475	75	343	57	1
Gordonsville	1,249	0	0	0	0	0	11	1	8	2	0
Grand Junction	267	0	0	0	0	0	1	0	1	0	0
Graysville	1,587	7	0	0	0	7	32	2	30	0	0
Greenbrier	6,896	15	0	1	0	14	44	10	26	8	0
Greeneville	14,875	71	1	3	1	66	482	59	370	53	1
Greenfield	2,074	10	0	0	0	10	24	3	17	4	0
Halls	2,047	13	0	1	1	11	53	13	34	6	0
Harriman	6,110	30	0	9	1	20	171	30	121	20	2
Henderson	6,361	32	0	0	1	31	83	25	49	9	0
Hendersonville	58,901	95	1	2	8	84	585	91	460	34	3
Henry	448	0	0	0	0	0	4	4	0	0	0
Hohenwald	3,822	18	0	1	0	17	171	9	157	5	0
Hollow Rock	677	1	0	0	0	1	3	0	2	1	0
Hornbeak	467	0	0	0	0	0	3	0	2	1	0
Humboldt	8,116	62	0	7	4	51	217	52	145	20	4
Huntingdon	3,818	2	0	0	0	2	30	1	27	2	0
Huntland	841	0	0	0	0	0	0	0	0	0	0
Jacksboro	2,060	4	0	0	0	4	72	0	69	3	0
Jackson	67,234	703	12	21	87	583	2,414	361	1,814	239	11
Jamestown	2,123	8	0	0	0	8	59	4	49	6	0
Jasper	3,459	9	0	0	0	9	43	3	30	10	0
Jefferson City	8,188	12	0	3	1	8	170	21	139	10	0
Jellico	2,148	2	0	0	0	2	32	5	22	5	0
Johnson City	67,293	296	3	29	38	226	2,717	287	2,186	244	14
Jonesborough	5,675	15	0	1	1	13	102	16	69	17	0
Kenton	1,185	1	0	0	0	1	23	0	22	1	0
Kimball	1,452	3	0	0	0	3	43	2	33	8	0
Kingsport	54,260	372	5	40	28	299	2,426	271	1,856	299	8
Kingston	5,998	3	0	1	0	2	38	7	27	4	0
Kingston Springs	2,726	2	0	0	0	2	11	0	8	3	0
Knoxville	188,672	1,528	38	124	241	1,125	7,977	1,080	5,775	1,122	14
Lafayette	5,428	12	0	2	3	7	128	31	85	12	1
La Follette	6,606	41	0	2	3	36	190	44	123	23	0
La Vergne	36,067	187	2	14	21	150	619	124	404	91	2
Lawrenceburg	11,093	47	0	5	1	41	297	51	218	28	2
Lebanon	37,832	216	0	19	26	171	1,059	149	832	78	2
Lenoir City	9,404	65	1	5	4	55	268	26	216	26	1
Lewisburg	12,515	68	0	7	2	59	217	28	167	22	1
Lexington	7,915	29	0	4	1	24	202	18	159	25	1
Livingston	4,046	13	0	0	0	13	82	18	59	5	2
Lookout Mountain	1,892	0	0	0	0	0	17	2	7	8	0
Loretto	1,780	2	0	1	0	1	18	2	14	2	0
Loudon	5,953	2	0	0	0	2	65	15	40	10	0
Madisonville	5,031	22	0	0	2	20	214	36	154	24	1
Manchester	11,145	75	1	2	4	68	349	48	283	18	1
Martin	10,380	35	0	2	1	32	246	37	206	3	0
Maryville	30,006	64	0	2	1	61	324	30	272	22	1
Mason	1,525	1	0	0	0	1	5	1	4	0	0
Maury City	657	1	1	0	0	0	18	11	7	0	0
Maynardville	2,435	3	0	0	1	2	27	6	17	4	0
McEwen	1,731	0	0	0	0	0	16	5	9	2	0
McKenzie	5,323	14	0	1	1	12	105	34	59	12	1
Medina	4,365	13	0	1	0	12	34	9	25	0	0
Memphis	650,937	15,310	289	411	2,131	12,479	36,197	5,831	25,924	4,442	357

Table 8. Offenses Known to Law Enforcement, by Selected State and City, 2020—Continued

(Number.)

State/city	Population	Violent crime	Murder and nonnegligent manslaughter	Rape[1]	Robbery	Aggravated assault	Property crime	Burglary	Larceny-theft	Motor vehicle theft	Arson[2]
Metropolitan Nashville Police Department	688,013	7,951	113	385	1,742	5,711	28,023	3,745	21,238	3,040	103
Middleton	627	0	0	0	0	0	0	0	0	0	0
Milan	7,585	56	1	3	1	51	179	50	113	16	2
Millersville	6,811	34	0	1	1	32	52	12	33	7	2
Millington	10,626	87	0	8	12	67	559	90	421	48	0
Minor Hill	532	0	0	0	0	0	0	0	0	0	0
Monteagle	1,231	8	0	0	1	7	43	12	22	9	1
Monterey	2,906	10	0	1	1	8	43	3	34	6	0
Morristown	30,330	258	1	12	22	223	1,290	177	998	115	3
Moscow	553	3	0	0	0	3	5	0	5	0	0
Mountain City	2,429	5	0	0	1	4	19	2	17	0	0
Mount Carmel	5,284	10	0	1	0	9	52	9	30	13	0
Mount Juliet	38,685	71	0	8	3	60	636	54	542	40	1
Mount Pleasant	4,934	25	0	2	2	21	83	13	56	14	1
Munford	6,134	12	0	4	0	8	85	20	59	6	0
Murfreesboro	151,769	740	11	91	101	537	3,772	362	3,113	297	9
Newbern	3,289	21	1	2	0	18	70	10	55	5	0
New Johnsonville	1,868	3	0	0	0	3	15	3	12	0	0
New Market	1,379	1	0	0	0	1	11	1	10	0	0
Newport	6,880	65	0	9	2	54	494	57	382	55	1
New Tazewell	2,707	4	0	1	0	3	51	4	46	1	0
Niota	735	6	0	2	0	4	17	4	12	1	1
Nolensville	10,665	9	0	1	1	7	51	5	42	4	0
Norris	1,603	0	0	0	0	0	9	0	6	3	0
Oakland	8,558	6	0	0	0	6	60	8	48	4	0
Oak Ridge	29,139	168	0	24	14	130	621	81	495	45	3
Obion	1,032	1	0	0	0	1	8	1	7	0	0
Oliver Springs	3,416	6	0	0	1	5	47	6	28	13	0
Oneida	3,696	13	0	1	0	12	96	17	74	5	2
Paris	10,047	34	1	1	0	32	310	47	249	14	0
Parsons	2,283	5	0	0	0	5	13	4	6	3	1
Petersburg	571	1	0	0	0	1	5	0	5	0	0
Pigeon Forge	6,311	48	1	9	6	32	280	47	195	38	1
Pikeville	1,756	1	0	1	0	0	21	1	14	6	0
Piperton	2,057	1	0	0	0	1	20	5	12	3	0
Pittman Center	578	0	0	0	0	0	1	0	0	1	0
Plainview	2,160	0	0	0	0	0	8	3	3	2	0
Pleasant View	4,874	10	0	0	0	10	38	1	30	7	0
Portland	13,208	65	1	10	2	52	225	43	168	14	3
Pulaski	7,571	42	0	4	8	30	269	38	215	16	0
Puryear	662	0	0	0	0	0	2	0	2	0	0
Red Bank	11,861	42	0	5	3	34	303	61	191	51	1
Red Boiling Springs	1,135	1	0	0	0	1	4	1	2	1	0
Ridgely	1,605	20	0	0	2	18	40	10	22	8	0
Ripley	7,686	132	5	6	5	116	273	58	191	24	3
Rockwood	5,410	34	0	3	0	31	293	43	235	15	1
Rocky Top	1,774	10	0	0	0	10	116	11	86	19	0
Rogersville	4,368	13	0	1	1	11	188	24	150	14	2
Rossville	1,003	1	0	0	0	1	5	2	3	0	0
Rutherford	1,058	0	0	0	0	0	8	3	5	0	0
Rutledge	1,362	0	0	0	0	0	32	6	24	2	0
Saltillo	536	0	0	0	0	0	1	1	0	0	0
Savannah	6,928	65	0	6	1	58	361	57	284	20	3
Scotts Hill	978	2	0	0	0	2	8	4	2	2	0
Selmer	4,289	27	0	3	0	24	108	19	81	8	1
Sevierville	17,395	109	2	8	3	96	698	62	567	69	0
Sharon	911	2	0	0	0	2	10	4	5	1	0
Shelbyville	22,306	192	2	14	8	168	561	68	431	62	3
Signal Mountain	8,644	1	0	0	0	1	57	4	44	9	0
Smithville	4,929	22	0	1	1	20	112	17	92	3	3
Smyrna	52,984	204	2	10	34	158	1,242	155	980	107	4
Soddy-Daisy	13,697	22	1	0	3	18	358	72	252	34	2
Somerville	3,282	27	0	0	1	26	51	8	39	4	0
South Carthage	1,408	5	0	0	1	4	15	4	7	4	0
South Fulton	2,195	8	0	2	1	5	39	12	24	3	0
South Pittsburg	3,022	6	0	0	0	6	17	4	10	3	0
Sparta	4,960	6	0	0	0	6	149	21	117	11	2
Spencer	1,700	1	0	0	0	1	11	1	9	1	0
Spring City	1,850	8	1	1	1	5	39	9	24	6	0
Springfield	17,372	121	3	5	18	95	386	25	319	42	2
Spring Hill	45,765	75	3	12	3	57	389	35	340	14	0
St. Joseph	833	1	0	0	0	1	8	3	3	2	0
Surgoinsville	1,755	0	0	0	0	0	15	2	10	3	0
Sweetwater	5,904	40	0	0	1	39	267	46	189	32	0
Tazewell	2,281	11	0	1	0	10	61	11	43	7	0
Tellico Plains	915	1	0	0	0	1	4	2	2	0	0
Tiptonville	3,920	8	0	0	1	7	28	10	15	3	1
Toone	330	6	0	0	0	6	1	0	1	0	1
Townsend	467	4	0	0	0	4	15	4	10	1	0
Tracy City	1,391	2	0	1	0	1	33	1	23	9	1
Trenton	4,168	46	0	3	4	39	143	11	121	11	0
Trezevant	834	0	0	0	0	0	3	2	0	1	0

Table 8. Offenses Known to Law Enforcement, by Selected State and City, 2020—Continued

(Number.)

State/city	Population	Violent crime	Murder and nonnegligent manslaughter	Rape[1]	Robbery	Aggravated assault	Property crime	Burglary	Larceny-theft	Motor vehicle theft	Arson[2]
Trimble	609	0	0	0	0	0	3	2	0	1	0
Troy	1,313	2	0	0	0	2	12	5	6	1	0
Tullahoma	19,664	139	2	9	6	122	527	81	413	33	7
Tusculum	2,692	3	0	1	1	1	14	2	11	1	1
Unicoi	3,592	2	0	0	0	2	20	3	13	4	0
Union City	10,263	95	1	10	6	78	463	75	346	42	3
Vonore	1,559	16	0	1	1	14	53	9	38	6	1
Wartburg	924	2	0	0	0	2	15	7	8	0	0
Wartrace	700	0	0	0	0	0	1	1	0	0	0
Watertown	1,528	0	0	0	0	0	0	0	0	0	0
Waverly	4,154	14	0	0	0	14	45	5	34	6	0
Waynesboro	2,417	4	0	0	0	4	21	5	11	5	0
Westmoreland	2,421	2	0	0	0	2	5	1	2	2	0
White Bluff	3,706	9	0	0	1	8	31	5	23	3	0
White House	12,936	26	0	5	2	19	138	15	110	13	2
White Pine	2,353	3	0	0	0	3	50	4	42	4	0
Whiteville	4,436	14	1	1	0	12	25	8	15	2	0
Whitwell	1,731	5	0	0	0	5	34	3	20	11	0
Winchester	9,029	44	0	2	1	41	289	47	228	14	2
Woodbury	2,919	5	0	0	1	4	18	4	12	2	0
TEXAS											
Abernathy[4]	2,694	3	1	0	1	1	11	3	5	3	1
Abilene	124,061	514	3	117	63	331	2,649	435	2,013	201	10
Addison[4]	16,778	72	0	9	20	43	1,018	116	687	215	0
Alamo	20,078	109	2	18	6	83	733	100	588	45	0
Alamo Heights[4]	8,807	6	0	0	1	5	194	21	160	13	1
Alba	550	0	0	0	0	0	4	4	0	0	1
Alice	18,634	113	0	15	10	88	801	194	565	42	9
Allen	108,218	105	1	24	19	61	996	82	859	55	0
Alton[4]	18,632	103	2	5	8	88	195	34	145	16	2
Alvarado[4]	4,626	23	1	3	5	14	85	15	59	11	0
Alvin[4]	27,015	83	0	18	13	52	731	70	603	58	3
Amarillo	200,296	1,676	15	141	241	1,279	7,369	1,400	4,903	1,066	32
Andrews[4]	14,487	53	0	11	1	41	258	31	206	21	2
Angleton[4]	19,500	38	0	15	4	19	299	18	259	22	3
Anna[4]	16,036	14	0	1	1	12	164	26	124	14	0
Anson	2,283	3	0	0	0	3	25	6	17	2	0
Anthony[4]	5,389	4	0	1	0	3	67	6	54	7	0
Aransas Pass[4]	8,414	58	3	6	2	47	342	87	231	24	2
Archer City	1,687	1	0	0	0	1	15	4	9	2	0
Arcola[4]	2,811	3	0	0	2	1	41	9	27	5	
Argyle[4]	4,527	1	0	0	0	1	22	5	17	0	0
Arlington	402,700	2,142	23	244	361	1,514	10,271	1,211	7,796	1,264	33
Arp	1,037	2	0	0	1	1	8	0	5	3	0
Athens	12,757	36	1	6	9	20	224	51	142	31	1
Atlanta	5,451	18	0	3	1	14	149	35	101	13	1
Aubrey[4]	5,274	5	2	1	0	2	44	25	14	5	0
Austin	1,000,276	4,671	44	478	1,101	3,048	36,322	4,774	27,481	4,067	134
Azle[4]	13,660	32	0	4	2	26	182	34	128	20	1
Baird	1,485	3	0	0	0	3	30	9	11	10	1
Balch Springs	25,189	180	0	7	41	132	822	93	520	209	3
Balcones Heights	3,362	50	1	3	6	40	203	24	147	32	0
Ballinger	3,629	13	0	1	1	11	71	38	28	5	0
Bangs	1,518	1	0	0	0	1	0	0	0	0	11
Bartonville[4]	1,810	0	0	0	0	0	14	1	10	3	0
Bastrop[4]	9,479	50	0	7	9	34	296	18	247	31	0
Bay City	17,505	91	7	18	11	55	614	101	490	23	14
Baytown[4]	77,823	338	9	43	85	201	2,917	390	2,106	421	6
Beaumont[4]	116,766	1,431	20	79	300	1,032	3,863	955	2,546	362	21
Bedford	49,274	122	2	22	11	87	1,096	93	887	116	0
Bee Cave	7,255	10	0	1	1	8	184	22	144	18	0
Beeville	12,788	45	0	0	6	39	394	89	294	11	6
Bellmead	10,835	114	2	18	16	78	559	68	436	55	3
Bells	1,528	1	0	1	0	0	13	4	8	1	0
Bellville	4,233	17	1	0	1	15	47	12	30	5	0
Belton	23,435	47	2	19	7	19	563	56	476	31	0
Benbrook	23,766	41	0	9	13	19	326	37	259	30	2
Bertram[4]	1,491	2	0	0	0	2	16	6	7	3	0
Big Sandy[4]	1,418	0	0	0	0	0	7	3	4	0	0
Big Spring	28,294	141	2	6	11	122	805	140	556	109	3
Bishop	3,048	4	1	0	1	2	44	10	28	6	0
Blanco	2,103	4	0	1	1	2	22	10	7	5	0
Blue Mound	2,450	1	0	0	0	1	22	3	8	11	0
Boerne	19,342	31	0	7	3	21	272	33	201	38	0
Bogata[4]	1,053	2	0	1	0	1	30	10	14	6	0
Bonham	10,416	16	0	5	2	9	100	12	80	8	0
Borger	12,318	33	0	6	1	26	354	100	219	35	0
Bovina	1,768	8	0	0	0	8	3	1	2	0	0
Brady	5,280	14	0	2	0	12	68	35	23	10	1
Brazoria	3,059	6	0	0	1	5	39	5	28	6	0
Breckenridge	5,386	17	0	1	1	15	119	21	88	10	2
Bremond	971	3	0	0	1	2	19	9	8	2	1

Table 8. Offenses Known to Law Enforcement, by Selected State and City, 2020—Continued

(Number.)

State/city	Population	Violent crime	Murder and nonnegligent manslaughter	Rape[1]	Robbery	Aggravated assault	Property crime	Burglary	Larceny-theft	Motor vehicle theft	Arson[2]
Brenham	18,106	51	0	16	5	30	308	37	253	18	0
Bridge City[4]	7,864	13	0	5	0	8	80	13	57	10	0
Bridgeport	6,732	10	3	0	0	7	69	10	51	8	0
Brookshire	5,948	18	1	3	1	13	67	13	46	8	2
Brookside Village	1,583	3	0	1	1	1	16	5	9	2	0
Brownfield	9,324	28	0	4	0	24	250	36	47	167	1
Brownsboro	1,309	0	0	0	0	0	0	0	0	0	0
Brownsville	183,627	738	7	83	153	495	3,394	403	2,870	121	14
Brownwood	18,367	86	0	17	12	57	595	109	451	35	5
Bruceville-Eddy	1,705	4	0	0	0	4	21	11	5	5	0
Bryan[4]	87,435	463	7	104	49	303	1,718	280	1,302	136	6
Buda[4]	18,531	37	0	4	9	24	277	31	227	19	0
Bullard	3,900	3	0	0	0	3	19	7	10	2	0
Bulverde	5,370	6	0	1	1	4	86	6	74	6	0
Burkburnett	11,321	20	0	4	2	14	155	36	106	13	0
Burleson[4]	49,660	108	1	18	6	83	671	67	519	85	2
Burnet	6,455	18	0	6	0	12	74	15	49	10	2
Cactus	3,250	6	0	2	0	4	41	5	25	11	0
Caddo Mills[4]	1,739	9	0	0	0	9	16	3	7	6	0
Cameron	5,458	16	0	2	1	13	88	46	37	5	1
Canton	3,895	7	1	0	2	4	71	5	61	5	0
Canyon	16,263	14	0	7	2	5	132	9	117	6	0
Carthage	6,395	24	0	5	1	18	180	23	149	8	2
Castle Hills	4,509	11	0	0	6	5	271	24	213	34	1
Castroville	3,159	6	0	1	1	4	41	12	26	3	1
Cedar Hill[4]	48,352	69	4	12	12	41	920	80	744	96	0
Cedar Park[4]	82,653	83	1	33	13	36	1,059	171	797	91	0
Celina	18,165	19	1	7	0	11	130	13	116	1	0
Center	5,157	15	0	2	1	12	91	13	76	2	1
Chandler[4]	3,233	2	0	0	1	1	28	8	20	0	0
Childress	6,039	8	0	1	0	7	35	11	17	7	0
Cibolo[4]	32,777	37	0	8	4	25	271	43	209	19	0
Cisco	3,774	16	0	3	3	10	73	32	32	9	1
Clarksville	3,042	2	0	0	0	2	16	5	9	2	0
Cleburne	31,486	104	1	22	11	70	522	90	370	62	3
Cleveland	8,285	48	3	0	3	42	346	48	261	37	0
Clifton[4]	3,446	3	1	0	0	2	15	4	10	1	0
Clyde	3,838	4	0	0	0	4	42	18	24	0	1
College Station	120,831	217	2	55	27	133	2,299	321	1,768	210	2
Colleyville[4]	27,602	8	0	2	3	3	154	13	137	4	0
Collinsville[4]	2,000	2	0	1	0	1	1	1	0	0	0
Columbus	3,646	11	0	0	5	6	57	5	47	5	0
Comanche[4]	4,183	8	0	2	1	5	110	20	84	6	2
Combes[4]	3,002	8	0	2	0	6	38	7	24	7	0
Conroe	94,451	175	2	35	47	91	2,336	246	1,914	176	2
Coppell[4]	41,807	29	0	5	5	19	632	65	536	31	0
Copperas Cove	33,333	144	4	1	12	127	712	113	553	46	1
Corinth[4]	22,367	13	0	1	4	8	223	37	164	22	0
Corpus Christi[4]	329,050	2,772	34	232	478	2,028	10,747	2,042	7,824	881	88
Corrigan	1,613	3	1	0	1	1	19	2	13	4	0
Crandall[4]	4,147	18	0	1	3	14	158	33	112	13	0
Crowley[4]	16,909	47	1	4	3	39	417	47	346	24	0
Crystal City	7,158	7	0	0	0	7	28	13	15	0	0
Cuero	8,237	43	0	4	1	38	167	34	113	20	2
Cumby	800	0	0	0	0	0	0	0	0	0	0
Cuney	140	0	0	0	0	0	0	0	0	0	0
Daingerfield[4]	2,362	25	0	1	0	24	45	9	32	4	0
Dalhart[4]	8,349	23	1	4	1	17	148	39	100	9	1
Dallas	1,363,028	11,514	236	569	3,292	7,417	46,974	9,917	26,656	10,401	180
Dalworthington Gardens[4]	2,382	3	0	0	1	2	28	2	23	3	0
Dawson	800	0	0	0	0	0	18	4	12	2	0
Dayton	8,510	9	0	1	1	7	170	26	123	21	2
Decatur	7,220	12	0	5	1	6	306	10	282	14	1
Deer Park[4]	33,631	45	0	13	7	25	573	63	466	44	0
De Leon	2,193	4	0	2	0	2	26	8	15	3	0
Del Rio	35,733	58	1	21	12	24	563	139	388	36	2
Denison[4]	25,858	113	1	23	9	80	484	124	276	84	1
Denver City	4,964	1	0	0	0	1	32	7	23	2	1
DeSoto[4]	53,515	189	2	17	44	126	1,177	224	757	196	0
Devine	4,883	6	0	0	0	6	115	4	101	10	0
Diboll[4]	5,182	3	0	0	0	3	42	16	20	6	0
Dickinson[4]	21,364	76	1	13	13	49	408	118	242	48	1
Dilley	4,559	3	1	0	0	2	72	42	27	3	0
Dimmitt4,[5]	4,065		0	0	0		20	6	13	1	0
Donna	16,400	172	1	14	22	135	545	80	428	37	3
Double Oak	3,089	1	0	1	0	0	6	0	6	0	0
Dublin[4]	3,546	5	0	3	0	2	16	11	4	1	0
Dumas	13,729	33	0	8	1	24	283	30	209	44	0
Duncanville[4]	38,847	140	1	14	74	51	866	110	549	207	1
Eagle Lake	3,793	9	0	0	1	8	87	51	27	9	0
Eagle Pass	30,029	43	2	0	4	37	553	138	370	45	0
Early	3,205	10	0	3	0	7	62	14	46	2	1
Eastland	3,836	4	0	2	0	2	67	16	42	9	0

Table 8. Offenses Known to Law Enforcement, by Selected State and City, 2020—Continued

(Number.)

State/city	Population	Violent crime	Murder and nonnegligent manslaughter	Rape[1]	Robbery	Aggravated assault	Property crime	Burglary	Larceny-theft	Motor vehicle theft	Arson[2]
Edinburg	103,491	325	6	79	36	204	2,310	281	1,966	63	4
Edna	5,813	15	0	0	5	10	92	18	69	5	1
El Campo	11,523	59	2	4	7	46	357	44	278	35	0
Electra	2,723	11	0	0	3	8	30	5	21	4	0
Elgin	10,567	10	0	1	2	7	19	4	13	2	0
El Paso[4]	685,288	2,167	28	261	289	1,589	8,507	847	7,245	415	14
Elsa	7,274	18	0	0	5	13	215	23	191	1	1
Emory	1,368	6	0	2	0	4	13	4	5	4	1
Ennis	20,557	40	3	9	7	21	384	48	301	35	1
Everman[4]	6,220	33	0	6	8	19	90	10	69	11	0
Fairfield	2,885	8	0	0	1	7	48	8	31	9	0
Fair Oaks Ranch[4]	10,497	4	0	2	1	1	111	25	79	7	0
Fairview[4]	9,375	2	0	0	1	1	43	7	35	1	0
Falfurrias	4,797	31	0	0	0	31	105	46	59	0	1
Farmers Branch[4]	51,078	77	0	16	15	46	1,011	146	675	190	3
Farmersville[4]	3,668	11	0	2	2	7	42	9	32	1	2
Farwell	1,283	0	0	0	0	0	12	6	4	2	0
Fate	16,917	8	0	5	0	3	100	13	80	7	0
Ferris	3,042	7	0	1	4	2	45	5	30	10	0
Flatonia[4]	1,436	1	0	0	0	1	17	4	9	4	0
Floresville	8,247	19	0	4	0	15	98	32	54	12	0
Flower Mound	80,907	45	1	15	8	21	552	59	463	30	0
Forest Hill[4]	13,058	48	1	5	12	30	328	46	209	73	1
Forney	29,366	23	0	1	10	12	456	37	379	40	0
Fort Stockton	8,429	17	0	1	1	15	106	19	80	7	1
Fort Worth	929,509	5,029	110	446	867	3,606	25,405	3,410	18,487	3,508	141
Frankston	1,164	3	0	1	0	2	17	0	16	1	0
Fredericksburg[4]	11,604	8	0	1	0	7	111	23	81	7	0
Freeport	12,144	48	1	3	2	42	224	49	174	1	1
Freer[4]	2,651	8	0	1	0	7	47	12	28	7	0
Friendswood[4]	40,795	36	0	6	4	26	234	40	169	25	1
Friona	3,775	4	0	1	0	3	23	5	15	3	0
Frisco	212,626	183	1	38	31	113	2,066	238	1,724	104	2
Fulshear	14,094	3	0	0	0	3	55	4	46	5	0
Gainesville[4]	16,986	75	1	13	12	49	550	85	420	45	4
Galveston[4]	50,751	327	6	80	65	176	1,694	225	1,217	252	1
Garden Ridge	4,235	3	1	0	0	2	14	2	10	2	0
Garland[4]	241,845	695	6	72	285	332	6,104	942	4,081	1,081	8
Garrison	871	0	0	0	0	0	4	1	3	0	1
Gatesville	12,394	19	1	4	1	13	132	30	89	13	2
Georgetown	84,210	123	4	50	16	53	1,077	148	836	93	3
Giddings[4]	5,126	24	1	7	2	14	87	0	80	7	1
Gilmer	5,171	34	0	5	4	25	179	10	155	14	0
Gladewater	6,333	20	0	2	1	17	166	36	109	21	0
Glenn Heights	13,662	36	0	7	7	22	192	37	137	18	1
Godley[4]	1,423	7	0	2	0	5	8	3	4	1	0
Graham	8,593	14	2	4	3	5	48	8	37	3	1
Granbury[4]	11,080	14	1	3	1	9	482	27	436	19	0
Grand Prairie	196,990	483	12	49	78	344	3,791	351	2,829	611	5
Grand Saline	3,178	10	1	1	1	7	31	11	9	11	0
Grapevine[4]	56,343	99	1	20	20	58	1,183	90	958	135	3
Greenville[4]	29,209	62	1	15	21	25	493	56	386	51	8
Gregory	1,886	1	0	1	0	0	12	6	6	0	0
Groesbeck	4,244	6	0	3	0	3	89	17	64	8	2
Groves[4]	15,412	88	1	6	11	70	317	52	229	36	1
Gun Barrel City	6,269	6	0	1	0	5	89	32	40	17	0
Gunter	1,696	0	0	0	0	0	5	0	4	1	0
Hallettsville	2,645	6	0	0	0	6	66	17	44	5	0
Hallsville[4]	4,382	1	0	0	0	1	14	5	8	1	0
Haltom City[4]	44,037	138	1	34	36	67	1,354	171	965	218	1
Hamilton	3,005	3	0	0	1	2	32	2	30	0	0
Hamlin	2,010	0	0	0	0	0	12	3	7	2	0
Harker Heights[4]	33,091	58	5	12	14	27	429	64	311	54	4
Harlingen	65,014	269	3	21	67	178	2,437	315	1,999	123	11
Haskell[4]	3,136	2	0	0	0	2	20	6	11	3	0
Hearne[4]	4,345	19	0	0	5	14	80	46	25	9	0
Heath	9,584	8	0	1	0	7	46	4	41	1	0
Hedwig Village	2,643	5	0	0	2	3	162	3	149	10	0
Helotes	10,301	3	0	1	1	1	125	45	75	5	0
Henderson	13,093	73	1	5	5	62	545	93	420	32	2
Hereford	14,534	117	0	0	11	106	280	57	187	36	4
Hewitt	15,092	14	0	6	1	7	138	25	102	11	1
Hickory Creek[4]	4,979	3	0	0	1	2	70	6	54	10	0
Hidalgo	14,370	30	0	5	2	23	145	30	102	13	0
Highland Park	9,160	4	0	1	3	0	199	41	143	15	0
Highland Village	16,848	9	0	5	2	2	79	8	68	3	0
Hill Country Village	1,127	1	0	0	0	1	46	10	30	6	0
Hillsboro	8,480	11	1	4	2	4	167	14	140	13	0
Hitchcock	8,023	18	0	2	2	14	103	38	53	12	2
Hollywood Park	3,370	2	0	0	1	1	51	7	37	7	0
Hondo	9,506	21	0	5	2	14	161	36	119	6	3
Honey Grove	1,745	1	0	1	0	0	22	6	15	1	0
Hooks[4]	2,706	8	0	2	0	6	37	11	19	7	0

Table 8. Offenses Known to Law Enforcement, by Selected State and City, 2020—Continued

(Number.)

State/city	Population	Violent crime	Murder and nonnegligent manslaughter	Rape[1]	Robbery	Aggravated assault	Property crime	Burglary	Larceny-theft	Motor vehicle theft	Arson[2]
Horizon City	19,973	16	0	0	2	14	108	13	83	12	0
Horseshoe Bay	4,085	5	0	0	0	5	5	2	3	0	0
Houston	2,346,155	29,474	400	1,137	8,757	19,180	98,043	15,788	67,474	14,781	532
Howe[4]	3,442	4	0	1	0	3	5	0	5	0	0
Hudson	5,035	5	0	0	0	5	85	32	48	5	0
Hudson Oaks	2,587	0	0	0	0	0	95	4	80	11	0
Humble[4]	15,901	163	3	37	46	77	1,328	88	1,039	201	2
Huntington	2,110	0	0	0	0	0	13	6	7	0	0
Huntsville	42,648	157	1	23	20	113	674	95	509	70	4
Hurst[4]	38,796	97	2	18	23	54	1,018	94	821	103	1
Hutto[4]	29,590	25	0	7	4	14	199	46	132	21	0
Idalou	2,308	3	0	0	0	3	31	4	24	3	1
Ingleside[4]	10,296	32	0	8	2	22	126	38	74	14	2
Ingram	1,859	4	0	0	0	4	15	4	11	0	0
Iowa Colony	3,686	6	0	2	1	3	41	15	21	5	0
Iowa Park	6,334	6	0	0	0	6	40	6	28	6	0
Irving[4]	242,976	780	9	130	222	419	6,223	673	4,581	969	11
Jacinto City	10,455	15	0	1	10	4	317	23	246	48	0
Jacksboro	4,372	6	0	1	0	5	39	6	29	4	0
Jacksonville	14,843	40	0	8	3	29	243	71	150	22	1
Jamaica Beach[4]	1,089	4	0	0	0	4	8	5	1	2	0
Jarrell	1,953	0	0	0	0	0	23	3	18	2	0
Jasper	7,543	31	1	0	1	29	254	46	194	14	1
Jersey Village[4]	7,921	17	0	2	7	8	264	60	152	52	0
Jones Creek	2,079	2	0	0	0	2	20	2	16	2	0
Jonestown	2,139	12	0	0	0	12	43	10	29	4	0
Josephine[4]	2,182	2	0	0	0	2	14	1	10	3	0
Joshua[4]	8,319	23	0	1	1	21	61	13	44	4	0
Jourdanton	4,467	4	0	0	0	4	2	0	1	1	0
Junction[4]	2,387	1	1	0	0	0	5	2	3	0	0
Karnes City[4]	3,419	11	0	0	0	11	39	3	35	1	1
Katy	22,797	48	0	11	12	25	719	50	607	62	0
Kaufman	7,930	30	0	3	3	24	167	26	123	18	0
Keene	6,619	15	0	3	0	12	39	10	25	4	0
Keller[4]	48,117	39	1	10	1	27	333	38	273	22	0
Kemah[4]	2,046	8	0	3	0	5	93	11	76	6	0
Kemp	1,259	2	0	0	0	2	21	4	14	3	0
Kenedy[4]	3,357	10	0	2	2	6	109	32	65	12	1
Kennedale[4]	8,881	10	0	2	2	6	137	38	81	18	1
Kerens	1,519	0	0	0	0	0	34	18	8	8	0
Kermit	6,583	11	0	0	1	10	126	50	67	9	0
Kerrville	23,912	65	0	14	1	50	244	23	203	18	0
Kilgore	15,016	54	1	7	8	38	317	38	241	38	0
Killeen[4,5]	154,417	1,033	26	87	159	761			1,851	436	5
Kingsville	25,195	118	1	23	11	83	581	130	432	19	0
Knox City	1,118	5	0	2	0	3	17	8	8	1	0
Kountze	2,104	6	0	0	2	4	39	13	21	5	0
Kyle	51,306	81	1	30	7	43	544	48	449	47	1
Lacy-Lakeview	6,748	31	0	5	6	20	194	48	133	13	3
La Feria	7,232	29	0	0	2	27	94	20	71	3	0
La Grange	4,680	15	0	4	0	11	95	7	79	9	0
La Grulla	1,710	2	0	0	0	2	2	0	1	1	0
Laguna Vista	3,183	4	0	0	0	4	19	5	13	1	0
La Joya	4,326	17	0	1	0	16	25	4	21	0	0
Lake Dallas[4]	8,174	15	0	2	3	10	103	18	73	12	0
Lake Jackson[4]	27,265	46	2	8	2	34	600	46	501	53	0
Lakeport	998	0	0	0	0	0	3	0	1	2	0
Lakeview, Harrison County[4]	6,231	6	0	0	1	5	66	11	50	5	2
Lakeway	16,537	15	0	5	4	6	220	35	170	15	0
Lake Worth[4]	4,921	20	0	3	8	9	270	17	229	24	0
La Marque[4]	17,656	94	2	11	20	61	747	101	576	70	1
Lamesa	9,119	56	0	13	2	41	367	92	242	33	2
Lampasas	8,132	23	0	3	0	20	197	27	159	11	0
Lancaster	39,587	204	1	17	53	133	948	117	666	165	2
La Porte[4]	35,102	81	0	14	12	55	441	64	322	55	0
Laredo	265,515	859	12	90	156	601	3,836	626	2,994	216	60
Lavon[4,5]	3,944	4	0	0	0	4		9		0	0
League City[4]	110,518	127	1	37	25	64	1,493	166	1,201	126	0
Leander[4]	68,571	62	0	24	4	34	600	78	465	57	2
Leon Valley	12,453	23	0	2	5	16	532	59	389	84	0
Lewisville	110,800	324	3	76	73	172	1,949	275	1,428	246	16
Liberty	9,418	29	0	3	0	26	164	14	137	13	2
Liberty Hill[4]	3,345	4	0	1	2	1	48	14	31	3	0
Linden[4]	1,908	4	0	1	0	3	24	8	15	1	1
Little Elm[4]	57,482	85	2	28	5	50	219	26	165	28	1
Littlefield	5,786	20	2	0	1	17	123	46	65	12	0
Live Oak[4]	16,910	27	2	6	9	10	556	51	436	69	1
Livingston	5,240	22	0	1	5	16	252	10	227	15	0
Llano	3,525	7	0	1	1	5	44	13	26	5	0
Lockhart	14,297	17	0	2	1	14	178	34	130	14	0
Lone Star	1,472	3	0	0	0	3	2	1	0	1	0
Longview	81,751	276	10	62	47	157	2,362	461	1,729	172	3
Lorena	1,762	2	0	1	0	1	24	2	16	6	0

Table 8. Offenses Known to Law Enforcement, by Selected State and City, 2020—Continued

(Number.)

State/city	Population	Violent crime	Murder and nonnegligent manslaughter	Rape[1]	Robbery	Aggravated assault	Property crime	Burglary	Larceny-theft	Motor vehicle theft	Arson[2]
Los Fresnos	7,929	19	0	2	1	16	110	9	96	5	0
Lubbock	262,146	2,852	28	225	431	2,168	10,770	2,296	7,316	1,158	102
Lufkin4,[5]	35,007	284	2	32	46	204			1,103	119	0
Luling	5,923	50	1	9	4	36	67	14	43	10	1
Lumberton	13,195	16	0	5	0	11	155	9	121	25	0
Lytle	3,135	2	0	0	1	1	109	8	88	13	0
Madisonville	4,715	12	0	0	1	11	60	19	35	6	0
Magnolia[4]	2,193	8	0	0	3	5	31	7	20	4	0
Manor	15,569	32	1	6	6	19	211	22	166	23	1
Mansfield[4]	74,360	68	3	8	17	40	863	90	698	75	2
Manvel	13,971	15	0	3	2	10	91	20	64	7	0
Marble Falls	7,157	33	0	8	2	23	145	29	112	4	0
Marfa	1,589	12	0	0	0	12	6	0	3	3	0
Marlin[4]	5,539	38	0	0	4	34	74	31	33	10	0
Marshall[4]	22,755	115	3	9	15	88	500	121	345	34	4
Mathis	4,694	24	1	2	3	18	91	24	57	10	2
McAllen	144,569	123	3	43	23	54	2,791	139	2,603	49	2
McGregor	5,368	17	0	9	0	8	46	8	38	0	0
McKinney	208,335	280	1	59	44	176	1,950	218	1,519	213	4
Meadows Place	4,587	6	0	0	4	2	139	10	128	1	0
Melissa	13,424	9	0	1	0	8	101	22	77	2	0
Memorial Villages	12,375	3	0	0	2	1	79	7	66	6	0
Mercedes[4]	16,699	85	2	12	9	62	497	52	404	41	7
Mesquite	141,325	619	11	69	149	390	4,997	735	3,408	854	11
Mexia	7,329	30	0	4	2	24	143	18	106	19	2
Midland	150,529	549	10	81	50	408	3,119	404	2,249	466	16
Midlothian[4]	34,962	32	0	5	7	20	308	30	265	13	0
Mineola	4,797	4	0	0	0	4	115	18	94	3	0
Mineral Wells	15,057	48	1	12	4	31	509	165	301	43	4
Mission	85,052	132	1	27	14	90	1,304	133	1,096	75	14
Missouri City[4]	76,476	130	2	15	41	72	689	88	547	54	3
Monahans	7,924	35	0	5	3	27	137	31	84	22	1
Mont Belvieu	6,954	13	0	3	1	9	136	13	91	32	0
Montgomery[4]	1,488	7	0	1	2	4	21	5	13	3	0
Morgans Point Resort[4]	4,738	3	0	0	1	2	18	5	8	5	0
Moulton	901	0	0	0	0	0	2	1	1	0	0
Mount Pleasant[4]	15,974	90	0	14	11	65	353	68	248	37	4
Muleshoe	5,005	3	0	2	0	1	16	3	8	5	0
Murphy	20,798	8	0	3	1	4	168	14	150	4	0
Mustang Ridge[4]	999	16	0	0	0	16	28	1	16	11	0
Nacogdoches	32,873	120	2	26	16	76	943	141	744	50	4
Naples[4]	1,307	3	0	0	1	2	7	1	4	2	0
Nash	3,938	49	0	11	1	37	59	14	45	0	0
Nassau Bay[4]	3,968	17	1	2	3	11	98	32	55	11	1
Natalia	1,610	4	0	3	0	1	12	5	6	1	0
Navasota	8,104	51	0	9	11	31	203	62	110	31	1
Nederland	17,413	50	1	8	4	37	278	48	194	36	1
Needville[4]	3,121	2	0	0	0	2	4	0	4	0	0
New Boston[4]	4,588	47	1	3	4	39	108	10	90	8	2
New Braunfels	94,751	219	6	10	25	178	1,230	206	866	158	3
Newton	2,359	3	0	0	0	3	22	14	6	2	0
Nixon	2,560	8	0	0	0	8	16	9	5	2	0
Nocona	2,999	6	0	1	0	5	8	4	2	2	0
Northeast[4]	3,485	1	0	1	0	0	84	2	76	6	0
Northlake	3,582	5	0	1	2	2	62	7	51	4	0
Oak Ridge North	3,171	5	0	0	2	3	51	7	40	4	0
Odessa[4]	126,288	1,020	13	107	106	794	3,163	586	2,113	464	22
Olmos Park	2,492	1	0	0	0	1	42	4	34	4	0
Olney	3,080	12	0	1	0	11	86	61	21	4	2
Olton	2,043	11	0	2	0	9	47	16	27	4	4
Onalaska	3,006	14	0	4	1	9	39	9	22	8	2
Orange	18,064	81	2	9	12	58	321	92	182	47	0
Ore City	1,238	3	0	1	0	2	13	7	5	1	0
Overton	2,498	7	0	1	0	6	14	3	11	0	0
Ovilla[4]	4,247	1	0	0	0	1	12	1	11	0	0
Oyster Creek	1,203	9	0	3	0	6	15	1	10	4	0
Palacios	4,516	17	0	2	2	13	64	11	51	2	1
Palestine	17,625	100	2	14	4	80	357	78	236	43	1
Palmer[4]	2,136	2	0	0	2	0	23	3	19	1	0
Palmhurst[4]	2,753	1	0	0	0	1	96	3	93	0	0
Palmview	5,806	108	1	8	6	93	276	58	207	11	3
Pampa	16,975	78	0	15	3	60	509	97	383	29	3
Panhandle	2,298	2	0	0	0	2	14	4	7	3	0
Pantego	2,533	7	0	1	0	6	92	18	58	16	0
Paris[4]	24,801	246	3	38	16	189	709	147	482	80	2
Parker	5,364	3	0	0	0	3	23	2	19	2	0
Pasadena	151,421	866	8	77	163	618	3,533	420	2,494	619	23
Patton Village[4]	2,228	9	0	3	1	5	13	5	7	1	0
Pearland	126,111	125	3	30	34	58	1,799	180	1,498	121	1
Pearsall	10,783	21	0	2	2	17	169	123	35	11	0
Pecos	10,667	41	0	2	1	38	144	33	89	22	0
Pelican Bay	2,064	5	0	1	0	4	36	10	22	4	0
Penitas	4,756	16	0	1	1	14	65	13	50	2	0

Table 8. Offenses Known to Law Enforcement, by Selected State and City, 2020—Continued

(Number.)

State/city	Population	Violent crime	Murder and nonnegligent manslaughter	Rape[1]	Robbery	Aggravated assault	Property crime	Burglary	Larceny-theft	Motor vehicle theft	Arson[2]
Perryton	8,486	23	0	4	0	19	109	17	82	10	0
Pflugerville	67,559	81	6	0	14	61	926	149	664	113	2
Pharr	80,098	364	0	58	26	280	1,255	200	983	72	3
Pilot Point	4,582	6	0	1	1	4	9	3	3	3	1
Pinehurst	1,963	22	0	0	1	21	57	18	30	9	0
Pineland	795	5	0	1	0	4	7	5	2	0	0
Pittsburg	4,717	28	0	2	3	23	57	18	30	9	0
Plano	290,786	452	3	101	114	234	4,784	616	3,728	440	11
Pleasanton[4]	11,006	19	1	3	5	10	229	33	181	15	0
Ponder	2,521	2	0	2	0	0	14	1	12	1	0
Port Aransas	4,362	19	0	4	1	14	194	24	153	17	0
Port Arthur[4]	54,257	422	7	42	76	297	1,253	346	775	132	4
Port Isabel	6,244	8	1	1	0	6	82	10	71	1	0
Portland	17,468	38	1	4	5	28	319	20	272	27	0
Port Lavaca	11,817	28	1	4	2	21	113	34	65	14	0
Port Neches	12,616	28	1	4	2	21	136	28	96	12	0
Poteet	3,535	5	0	2	0	2	69	22	41	6	3
Prairie View	7,126	23	1	2	5	15	56	26	23	7	0
Premont	2,531	17	0	0	0	17	42	39	0	3	3
Primera	5,250	3	0	2	1	0	28	5	17	6	0
Princeton	15,031	22	0	7	3	12	169	19	141	9	1
Prosper	27,250	33	0	5	2	26	231	34	187	10	1
Queen City	1,432	4	0	0	0	4	28	11	12	5	0
Quitman4,[5]	1,854	0	0	0	0	0			12	1	0
Rancho Viejo[4]	2,462	3	0	0	0	3	9	1	8	0	0
Raymondville[4]	10,833	86	3	6	2	75	179	55	113	11	2
Red Oak[4]	13,801	22	0	2	7	13	248	62	166	20	2
Refugio	2,718	4	0	0	2	2	17	2	13	2	0
Reno, Lamar County	3,364	11	0	0	0	11	26	5	20	1	0
Reno, Parker County	3,294	20	0	1	0	19	32	14	9	9	0
Richardson[4]	124,190	158	6	21	52	79	2,424	374	1,747	303	4
Richland Hills	7,971	24	0	6	6	12	247	30	199	18	0
Richmond[4]	12,630	50	0	7	14	29	198	28	145	25	0
Richwood[4]	4,044	7	1	5	0	1	56	6	49	1	0
Rio Grande City[4]	14,587	21	0	0	1	20	311	82	201	28	1
Rio Hondo	2,744	2	0	1	0	1	22	8	13	1	0
River Oaks[4]	7,653	12	1	1	3	7	93	35	43	15	0
Roanoke[4]	9,862	10	0	5	1	4	147	12	126	9	0
Robinson[4]	12,087	20	0	6	2	12	169	35	123	11	1
Robstown	11,238	40	1	3	4	32	287	50	218	19	1
Rockdale	5,503	20	0	3	0	17	131	35	82	14	0
Rockport[4]	10,672	17	0	0	2	15	446	134	293	19	2
Rockwall	46,867	59	0	11	17	31	805	55	681	69	0
Rollingwood	1,607	1	0	0	0	1	24	4	16	4	0
Roma	11,559	30	1	2	1	26	103	15	71	17	1
Roman Forest[4]	2,058	3	0	0	1	2	19	0	18	1	0
Rosenberg	39,162	161	4	32	26	99	629	146	418	65	0
Round Rock[4]	137,593	185	3	25	55	102	2,282	235	1,954	93	3
Rowlett	68,810	100	0	17	13	70	1,057	142	816	99	3
Royse City	15,388	26	0	7	5	14	205	25	167	13	0
Runaway Bay	1,612	2	0	0	0	2	2	2	0	0	0
Rusk	5,606	17	0	1	0	16	77	25	46	6	0
Sabinal	1,670	1	0	0	0	1	12	1	10	1	0
Sachse	26,799	16	0	9	3	4	167	23	133	11	3
Saginaw[4]	24,822	51	2	17	11	21	465	24	382	59	0
Salado	2,393	0	0	0	0	0	28	10	13	5	0
San Angelo	101,860	357	7	65	41	244	3,039	475	2,242	322	16
San Antonio[4]	1,573,189	11,569	130	1,187	2,163	8,089	57,057	7,919	42,158	6,980	236
San Augustine[4]	1,865	0	0	0	0	0	2	0	2	0	0
San Benito[4]	24,237	197	0	9	7	181	674	124	497	53	2
San Elizario	9,070	12	0	1	0	11	25	9	13	3	1
Sanger[4]	8,953	7	0	1	0	6	107	15	73	19	0
San Juan	37,337	139	1	12	15	111	738	84	615	39	3
San Marcos	67,432	283	2	99	32	150	1,419	260	1,017	142	4
San Saba	3,164	13	4	1	1	7	39	8	25	6	2
Sansom Park Village[4]	5,890	23	1	6	2	14	71	14	50	7	0
Santa Fe[4]	13,577	34	0	22	4	8	171	40	107	24	0
Santa Rosa	2,707	0	0	0	0	0	11	2	9	0	0
Schertz	43,315	61	0	11	7	43	460	75	347	38	0
Schulenburg	2,920	15	0	0	1	14	46	4	38	4	0
Seabrook[4]	14,415	48	0	21	3	24	208	33	145	30	0
Seagoville[4]	17,120	27	0	5	7	15	376	45	222	109	2
Sealy	6,484	7	0	1	1	5	94	34	54	6	0
Seguin	30,513	69	0	14	10	45	672	105	508	59	0
Selma[4]	12,013	12	0	1	0	11	260	24	213	23	0
Seminole	7,978	18	0	1	1	16	79	18	50	11	1
Seven Points[4]	1,532	3	0	1	0	2	40	4	30	6	0
Seymour	2,532	9	0	2	0	7	28	4	15	9	0
Shavano Park[4]	4,098	3	0	0	2	1	42	4	35	3	0
Shenandoah	3,098	13	1	4	3	5	201	11	169	21	0
Sherman[4]	44,611	197	6	34	24	133	1,095	222	769	104	2
Shiner	2,172	2	0	1	0	1	7	3	2	2	0
Silsbee	6,613	10	1	2	1	6	102	13	73	16	0

Table 8. Offenses Known to Law Enforcement, by Selected State and City, 2020—Continued

(Number.)

State/city	Population	Violent crime	Murder and nonnegligent manslaughter	Rape[1]	Robbery	Aggravated assault	Property crime	Burglary	Larceny-theft	Motor vehicle theft	Arson[2]
Sinton	5,324	37	0	4	3	30	168	30	125	13	2
Slaton	5,864	35	0	7	1	27	186	49	120	17	0
Smithville[4]	4,600	9	0	1	1	7	31	3	27	1	0
Snyder	11,004	82	1	5	1	75	116	32	76	8	4
Socorro	34,626	48	0	4	5	39	217	22	174	21	2
Somerset[4]	2,000	2	1	0	0	1	16	6	9	1	0
Somerville[4]	1,475	17	0	2	0	15	58	22	32	4	0
Sonora	2,765	3	0	1	0	2	15	9	3	3	0
Sour Lake	1,937	9	0	0	0	9	22	6	12	4	0
South Houston	17,485	94	4	2	38	50	500	73	306	121	0
Southlake[4]	33,083	14	0	2	6	6	236	27	182	27	0
South Padre Island	2,772	43	0	12	3	28	374	25	337	12	0
Southside Place	1,902	3	0	0	0	3	11	0	11	0	0
Spearman	3,245	10	0	1	0	9	11	4	5	2	0
Splendora[4]	2,337	6	0	0	0	6	29	7	17	5	0
Spring Valley	4,389	1	0	0	0	1	81	2	65	14	0
Stafford	17,423	57	1	9	18	29	545	51	442	52	0
Stamford	2,921	8	1	0	1	6	45	15	23	7	0
Stanton[4]	3,061	6	0	0	0	6	35	6	22	7	0
Stephenville[4]	21,777	35	0	15	1	19	328	50	251	27	0
Sugar Land[4]	119,671	68	4	8	20	36	1,277	111	1,077	89	0
Sulphur Springs[4]	16,322	39	3	9	6	21	172	22	114	36	0
Sunrise Beach Village	806	0	0	0	0	0	4	0	4	0	0
Surfside Beach	591	6	0	1	1	4	28	2	18	8	0
Sweeny	3,716	9	0	2	2	5	66	17	47	2	3
Sweetwater	10,419	20	0	1	0	19	133	51	77	5	2
Tatum	1,384	3	0	0	1	2	10	2	7	1	0
Taylor[4]	17,622	32	1	6	4	21	415	92	301	22	2
Teague	3,511	9	0	0	1	8	73	30	34	9	0
Temple	79,878	297	8	64	29	196	2,098	302	1,460	336	1
Tenaha	1,145	5	0	0	0	5	1	1	0	0	0
Terrell	19,204	61	3	13	9	36	503	71	367	65	2
Terrell Hills	5,512	9	1	1	4	3	97	54	36	7	0
Texas City[4]	50,660	178	11	35	29	103	1,396	186	1,043	167	1
Tioga	1,081	1	0	1	0	0	0	0	0	0	0
Tomball	11,901	44	0	3	9	32	326	25	245	56	1
Tool	2,310	2	0	0	0	2	10	2	3	5	0
Trophy Club[4]	13,053	0	0	0	0	0	52	9	36	7	0
Troup	2,063	5	0	2	1	2	37	8	24	5	0
Troy	2,060	4	0	2	0	2	50	3	43	4	0
Tulia	4,618	37	0	0	2	35	113	12	94	7	3
Tye	1,345	2	0	1	0	1	10	4	5	1	0
Tyler	108,139	472	6	53	69	344	3,296	523	2,563	210	2
Universal City[4]	21,162	65	1	11	10	43	523	80	384	59	1
University Park	25,253	4	0	1	1	2	239	46	161	32	0
Uvalde[4]	16,027	64	0	8	4	52	617	79	507	31	0
Valley Mills	1,177	0	0	0	0	0	2	1	0	1	0
Van	2,753	5	0	3	1	1	17	6	10	1	0
Van Alstyne	4,557	13	0	0	1	12	28	1	26	1	0
Venus[4]	4,570	13	0	1	1	11	36	5	29	2	0
Vernon	10,253	39	0	8	5	26	149	29	100	20	0
Victoria	67,407	311	2	34	42	233	1,823	354	1,345	124	4
Vidor	10,370	17	0	0	6	11	181	56	112	13	0
Waco	140,870	905	14	80	142	669	4,854	870	3,568	416	25
Wake Village[4]	5,309	9	0	1	0	8	54	16	30	8	0
Waller	3,654	18	0	3	5	10	52	14	28	10	1
Wallis	1,309	7	1	2	0	4	14	7	4	3	0
Watauga	24,588	35	2	8	8	17	310	38	245	27	2
Waxahachie[4]	39,039	71	0	20	15	36	701	83	539	79	0
Weatherford[4]	34,522	85	0	27	8	50	561	62	441	58	0
Webster[4]	11,545	71	0	7	26	38	786	89	609	88	0
Weimar[4]	2,235	3	0	0	0	3	16	0	10	6	1
Weslaco	42,184	136	1	28	28	79	1,350	142	1,170	38	1
West	3,008	3	0	0	0	3	16	8	5	3	0
West Columbia	3,823	4	0	1	0	3	20	1	17	2	0
West Lake Hills	3,310	4	0	1	0	3	80	5	72	3	0
West Orange[4]	3,199	18	0	0	2	16	79	8	66	5	0
Westover Hills	688	0	0	0	0	0	10	3	7	0	1
West University Place	15,700	5	0	0	5	0	146	22	115	9	0
Westworth[4]	2,790	4	0	0	1	3	136	11	114	11	0
Whitehouse	9,047	15	1	1	0	13	65	12	46	7	1
White Oak[4]	6,303	11	0	2	2	7	83	13	64	6	0
Whitesboro	4,158	9	0	0	1	8	24	2	19	3	0
Whitewright[4]	1,734	1	0	0	1	0	19	8	7	4	0
Whitney[4]	2,170	6	0	0	1	5	47	17	26	4	0
Wichita Falls[4]	104,673	405	9	83	76	237	3,222	626	2,318	278	1
Willis[4]	7,166	35	0	5	4	26	149	17	114	18	0
Willow Park	6,096	7	0	1	1	5	60	5	50	5	0
Wills Point	3,667	15	0	0	0	15	43	19	19	5	0
Wilmer[4]	4,919	12	0	0	6	6	113	25	73	15	0
Windcrest[4]	5,930	15	0	0	2	13	218	20	185	13	0
Winnsboro	3,302	7	1	2	1	3	46	17	25	4	0
Wolfforth	5,735	5	0	1	0	4	38	4	30	4	0

Table 8. Offenses Known to Law Enforcement, by Selected State and City, 2020—Continued

(Number.)

State/city	Population	Violent crime	Murder and nonnegligent manslaughter	Rape[1]	Robbery	Aggravated assault	Property crime	Burglary	Larceny-theft	Motor vehicle theft	Arson[2]
Woodsboro	1,399	0	0	0	0	0	2	0	2	0	0
Woodway	9,089	12	0	3	1	8	85	4	77	4	0
Wortham	988	1	0	0	0	1	38	30	7	1	0
Wylie	54,460	41	0	17	6	18	374	20	324	30	1
Yoakum	5,956	12	0	1	1	10	57	35	21	1	0
UTAH											
Bluffdale	17,826	35	0	9	2	24	248	46	184	18	0
Bountiful	44,129	35	0	10	0	25	363	44	290	29	2
Brian Head[4]	94	2	0	0	0	2	12	1	10	1	0
Brigham City[4]	19,792	33	0	8	1	24	274	41	201	32	2
Cedar City[4]	35,486	63	3	22	2	36	533	76	411	46	0
Centerville	17,855	20	0	17	0	3	396	66	300	30	1
Clearfield	32,358	69	1	13	10	45	525	60	413	52	2
Clinton	22,725	14	0	0	2	12	256	20	225	11	0
Cottonwood Heights[4]	33,871	48	0	11	11	26	924	96	742	86	3
Draper	49,326	71	0	30	10	31	1,138	142	903	93	13
Enoch[4]	7,340	11	0	2	0	9	32	6	20	6	0
Ephraim	7,450	11	0	7	0	4	42	4	38	0	0
Farmington	26,256	13	0	9	3	1	243	35	193	15	0
Grantsville	12,468	27	4	14	0	9	129	14	100	15	7
Harrisville	7,029	12	0	0	2	10	357	28	310	19	0
Heber	17,849	22	0	4	2	16	172	15	141	16	0
Helper	2,094	3	0	2	0	1	28	3	23	2	1
Herriman[4]	56,312	37	0	9	3	25	492	58	376	58	3
Hurricane	19,776	38	1	7	1	29	180	20	139	21	1
La Verkin	4,491	12	0	4	0	8	85	5	77	3	0
Layton	79,240	142	3	68	22	49	1,409	173	1,126	110	7
Lindon	11,218	1	0	1	0	0	329	26	284	19	0
Logan	51,899	100	0	41	6	53	592	82	472	38	2
Lone Peak	30,191	5	0	1	0	4	274	29	220	25	2
Mapleton[4]	11,068	4	0	1	1	2	54	8	43	3	0
Moab	5,362	47	2	22	1	22	149	12	128	9	3
Mount Pleasant	3,561	4	0	4	0	0	20	2	15	3	0
Murray	49,169	237	2	35	50	150	3,271	343	2,339	589	4
Naples	2,126	4	0	1	0	3	11	1	8	2	0
Nephi[4]	6,498	4	0	1	0	3	91	20	66	5	0
North Ogden	20,960	11	1	2	2	6	257	79	163	15	3
North Park	16,529	10	0	8	0	2	94	7	70	17	0
North Salt Lake	21,540	14	0	7	0	7	465	68	350	47	1
Ogden	88,309	446	4	79	75	288	2,915	375	2,151	389	18
Orem[4]	98,902	106	0	27	15	64	2,033	194	1,666	173	2
Park City	8,632	26	0	1	2	23	246	27	198	21	0
Payson[4]	20,498	18	0	2	4	12	378	34	317	27	0
Perry[4]	5,335	13	0	5	1	7	74	9	62	3	2
Pleasant Grove	38,803	31	0	5	0	26	336	53	258	25	0
Pleasant View	11,212	6	0	2	0	4	103	35	62	6	0
Price	8,291	25	0	4	2	19	136	24	110	2	0
Riverdale	8,876	24	2	6	1	15	389	12	351	26	1
Riverton	45,095	31	0	15	2	14	580	86	434	60	3
Roosevelt	7,359	49	0	27	4	18	323	30	225	68	3
Roy	39,849	52	0	20	4	28	505	62	385	58	3
Salem	8,902	1	0	0	0	1	50	4	41	5	0
Salt Lake City	202,187	1,865	17	277	487	1,084	14,865	1,545	11,128	2,192	67
Sandy	97,091	175	2	33	28	112	2,979	412	2,211	356	13
Santa Clara/Ivins	18,229	20	0	6	1	13	136	29	99	8	1
Santaquin/Genola[4]	14,933	6	0	3	0	3	75	12	58	5	0
Saratoga Springs	35,623	39	0	16	3	20	272	39	221	12	0
South Jordan	80,090	105	2	32	12	59	1,441	181	1,144	116	5
South Ogden	17,266	24	0	8	1	15	266	44	191	31	0
South Salt Lake	25,816	249	4	39	73	133	2,376	235	1,679	462	12
Spanish Fork	41,605	31	0	13	4	14	469	30	421	18	5
Springdale	641	4	0	0	0	4	19	2	17	0	0
Springville[4]	33,728	26	1	7	3	15	440	30	383	27	1
St. George	91,673	148	3	42	10	93	1,025	148	772	105	1
Sunset	5,387	12	0	4	0	8	91	13	68	10	0
Syracuse	32,343	24	0	15	3	6	232	24	193	15	0
Tooele[4]	36,527	107	1	31	10	65	815	130	597	88	7
Washington	30,622	32	1	8	1	22	434	40	362	32	1
West Bountiful	5,861	7	0	6	0	1	140	6	112	22	0
West Jordan	117,955	291	4	43	44	200	2,979	308	2,353	318	6
West Valley	135,887	718	6	97	96	519	4,525	722	2,833	970	16
Woods Cross	11,625	33	0	7	1	25	235	23	158	54	0
VERMONT											
Barre	8,471	47	0	4	0	43	197	21	174	2	2
Barre Town	7,698	9	1	2	0	6	60	3	57	0	0
Bellows Falls	2,946	3	0	1	0	2	30	3	27	0	1
Bennington	14,879	30	0	1	6	23	311	50	253	8	2
Berlin	2,770	9	0	2	1	6	109	6	103	0	0
Bradford	2,691	0	0	0	0	0	18	0	18	0	0
Brandon	3,710	1	0	0	0	1	43	4	38	1	0
Brattleboro	11,256	44	1	6	4	33	458	40	403	15	0

Table 8. Offenses Known to Law Enforcement, by Selected State and City, 2020—Continued

(Number.)

State/city	Population	Violent crime	Murder and nonnegligent manslaughter	Rape[1]	Robbery	Aggravated assault	Property crime	Burglary	Larceny-theft	Motor vehicle theft	Arson[2]
Brighton	1,161	0	0	0	0	0	1	0	1	0	0
Bristol	3,835	1	0	0	0	1	7	2	5	0	0
Burlington	42,862	151	1	36	16	98	1,032	109	906	17	3
Canaan	916	0	0	0	0	0	2	1	1	0	0
Castleton	4,490	3	0	0	0	3	25	2	19	4	0
Chester	3,011	3	0	0	0	3	18	5	13	0	0
Colchester	17,129	15	0	4	1	10	250	21	226	3	0
Dover	1,052	1	0	0	0	1	36	4	30	2	0
Essex	22,156	32	0	2	2	28	329	36	287	6	2
Fair Haven	2,536	2	0	0	0	2	35	1	32	2	0
Hardwick	2,846	0	0	0	0	0	21	1	20	0	0
Hartford	9,515	39	0	7	1	31	129	20	96	13	0
Hinesburg	4,540	1	0	0	0	1	17	5	11	1	0
Killington	750	0	0	0	0	0	2	0	2	0	0
Ludlow	1,854	4	0	0	0	4	9	1	8	0	0
Lyndonville	1,160	4	0	0	0	4	16	0	16	0	0
Manchester	4,206	6	0	0	0	6	28	1	25	2	0
Middlebury	8,813	5	0	1	1	3	79	5	72	2	0
Milton	10,882	13	0	3	1	9	106	18	85	3	0
Montpelier	7,321	16	0	10	0	6	170	9	155	6	2
Morristown	5,532	9	0	1	1	7	83	5	76	2	0
Newport	4,222	29	1	4	1	23	57	6	50	1	1
Northfield	6,560	4	0	0	0	4	17	2	14	1	1
Norwich	3,409	3	0	1	0	2	19	7	11	1	0
Richmond	4,123	3	0	0	0	3	12	2	9	1	0
Royalton	2,881	0	0	0	0	0	13	2	11	0	0
Rutland	14,930	44	0	8	5	31	322	40	263	19	5
Rutland Town	4,117	5	0	4	0	1	47	0	45	2	0
Shelburne	7,706	3	0	0	0	3	129	7	117	5	0
South Burlington	19,690	33	0	5	6	22	608	33	557	18	0
Springfield	8,859	17	0	3	0	14	121	20	99	2	0
St. Albans	6,788	29	0	6	1	22	217	20	196	1	2
St. Johnsbury	7,112	22	0	4	3	15	154	23	128	3	0
Stowe	4,444	6	0	2	0	4	66	3	63	0	3
Swanton	6,569	8	1	1	1	5	66	5	59	2	0
Thetford	2,525	5	0	0	0	5	6	2	4	0	0
Vergennes	2,577	2	0	1	1	0	72	41	30	1	0
Weathersfield	2,727	1	0	0	0	1	9	3	5	1	0
Williston	10,247	7	0	0	0	7	213	7	198	8	0
Wilmington	1,787	4	0	0	0	4	12	2	5	5	0
Windsor	3,272	4	0	0	0	4	10	1	9	0	0
Winhall	726	0	0	0	0	0	11	3	8	0	0
Winooski	7,341	31	0	3	3	25	209	27	177	5	2
Woodstock	2,907	1	0	1	0	0	10	2	7	1	0
VIRGINIA											
Abingdon	7,828	8	0	3	0	5	104	6	88	10	0
Alexandria	161,525	295	3	12	83	197	2,793	128	2,322	343	3
Altavista	3,401	11	0	1	2	8	176	4	165	7	0
Amherst	2,174	1	0	0	0	1	13	2	10	1	0
Ashland	7,947	17	0	3	3	11	133	9	117	7	0
Bedford	6,601	5	1	1	0	3	69	4	65	0	1
Berryville	4,393	2	0	2	0	0	40	4	35	1	0
Big Stone Gap	5,080	7	1	3	0	3	73	4	61	8	8
Blacksburg	44,422	29	0	13	2	14	310	29	266	15	0
Blackstone	3,299	10	0	0	1	9	102	3	84	15	3
Bowling Green	1,182	0	0	0	0	0	8	0	8	0	0
Bridgewater	6,204	1	0	0	1	0	20	4	15	1	0
Broadway	4,010	3	0	0	1	2	16	5	10	1	0
Buena Vista	6,459	3	0	0	0	3	16	3	13	0	0
Cape Charles	1,020	1	0	0	0	1	10	0	7	3	0
Cedar Bluff	989	0	0	0	0	0	8	0	6	2	0
Charlottesville	47,671	189	5	25	28	131	916	79	765	72	2
Chase City	2,201	6	0	0	1	5	27	8	17	2	0
Chatham	1,422	2	0	0	1	1	6	1	5	0	0
Chesapeake	247,118	1,020	15	80	112	813	4,413	388	3,697	328	19
Chilhowie	1,690	3	0	0	1	2	16	2	12	2	0
Chincoteague	2,868	4	1	1	0	2	37	2	34	1	0
Christiansburg	22,643	37	0	13	2	22	479	44	424	11	2
Clifton Forge	3,455	7	1	2	0	4	37	4	30	3	2
Clintwood	1,267	0	0	0	0	0	15	1	13	1	0
Coeburn	1,824	10	4	1	0	5	23	4	18	1	0
Colonial Beach	3,628	17	2	3	0	12	56	6	32	18	0
Colonial Heights	17,360	63	0	8	12	43	638	14	611	13	1
Covington	5,490	9	1	2	0	6	94	9	80	5	0
Crewe	2,109	9	0	0	0	9	31	16	12	3	0
Culpeper	19,131	38	2	5	10	21	318	6	302	10	4
Damascus	772	2	0	1	0	1	42	8	33	1	1
Danville	39,704	109	5	17	12	75	1,129	114	957	58	13
Dublin	2,590	8	0	5	1	2	27	0	22	5	0
Dumfries	6,038	2	0	1	1	0	52	1	29	22	0
Elkton	2,923	2	0	1	0	1	17	0	14	3	0
Emporia	5,282	20	2	2	4	12	179	31	138	10	3

Table 8. Offenses Known to Law Enforcement, by Selected State and City, 2020—Continued

(Number.)

State/city	Population	Violent crime	Murder and nonnegligent manslaughter	Rape[1]	Robbery	Aggravated assault	Property crime	Burglary	Larceny-theft	Motor vehicle theft	Arson[2]
Exmore	1,362	7	0	0	0	7	34	5	28	1	1
Fairfax City	24,161	20	0	3	12	5	407	34	332	41	0
Falls Church	14,877	20	1	2	5	12	220	17	177	26	2
Farmville	7,806	21	0	3	0	18	163	3	158	2	1
Franklin	7,896	24	2	3	7	12	276	35	230	11	0
Fredericksburg	29,592	117	3	18	16	80	809	29	743	37	7
Front Royal	15,387	39	0	21	2	16	307	12	274	21	3
Galax	6,275	16	0	7	1	8	226	22	186	18	1
Gate City	1,850	1	0	0	0	1	29	8	14	7	1
Gordonsville	1,641	2	0	2	0	0	31	5	26	0	0
Gretna	1,181	1	0	0	1	0	7	1	6	0	0
Grundy	887	1	0	0	0	1	59	0	58	1	0
Halifax	1,203	0	0	0	0	0	9	4	4	1	0
Hampton	134,082	357	24	33	95	205	3,338	301	2,765	272	18
Harrisonburg	53,442	117	1	15	14	87	811	74	688	49	2
Herndon	24,739	42	1	4	23	14	245	14	202	29	0
Hillsville	2,654	1	0	0	0	1	48	7	41	0	0
Honaker	1,306	1	0	0	0	1	4	1	3	0	0
Hopewell	22,498	83	6	4	12	61	454	74	338	42	1
Jonesville	919	2	0	1	0	1	8	0	8	0	0
Kenbridge	1,190	2	0	0	0	2	4	0	4	0	0
Lebanon	3,118	3	2	1	0	0	89	11	76	2	0
Leesburg	55,070	122	1	17	21	83	535	35	480	20	4
Lexington	7,487	9	0	2	0	7	46	3	42	1	0
Louisa	1,753	0	0	0	0	0	31	0	27	4	0
Luray	4,842	12	0	2	1	9	91	10	78	3	0
Lynchburg	82,871	367	3	36	51	277	1,350	177	1,047	126	4
Manassas	41,386	128	1	18	30	79	662	46	562	54	3
Manassas Park	17,839	26	0	7	6	13	128	7	102	19	1
Marion	5,515	25	0	5	0	20	156	15	131	10	0
Martinsville	12,417	48	1	6	7	34	335	53	256	26	0
Middletown	1,411	1	0	1	0	0	6	1	5	0	0
Mount Jackson	2,126	1	0	1	0	0	33	8	25	0	0
New Market	2,261	2	0	0	0	2	30	2	28	0	0
Newport News	178,896	1,119	25	67	104	923	3,648	416	2,896	336	23
Norfolk	242,516	1,543	49	103	259	1,132	6,591	519	5,282	790	7
Norton	3,975	8	0	1	0	7	223	5	206	12	2
Occoquan	1,104	0	0	0	0	0	1	1	0	0	0
Onancock	1,206	5	0	4	1	0	28	10	16	2	0
Onley	498	2	0	0	0	2	20	0	19	1	0
Orange	5,140	15	0	1	0	14	84	1	77	6	0
Pearisburg	2,619	10	1	2	1	6	102	41	60	1	0
Pennington Gap	1,705	4	0	0	0	4	59	13	43	3	0
Petersburg	31,195	197	24	14	20	139	807	92	605	110	1
Poquoson	12,275	28	0	6	1	21	93	6	86	1	2
Portsmouth	94,205	867	34	26	222	585	4,277	465	3,314	498	7
Pulaski	8,674	34	0	13	4	17	273	37	226	10	2
Purcellville	10,485	4	0	1	0	3	45	4	41	0	0
Radford	18,450	45	1	17	2	25	196	26	158	12	1
Rich Creek	738	0	0	0	0	0	11	1	10	0	0
Richlands	5,172	7	0	1	1	5	104	38	63	3	0
Richmond	233,350	814	66	20	274	454	6,816	771	5,434	611	51
Roanoke	99,335	448	15	38	90	305	3,809	412	3,048	349	25
Rocky Mount	4,718	8	0	5	0	3	219	7	201	11	3
Rural Retreat	1,444	0	0	0	0	0	10	0	10	0	0
Salem	25,326	13	1	1	4	7	480	25	411	44	5
Saltville	1,885	1	0	0	0	1	17	1	13	3	0
Shenandoah	2,327	4	0	1	1	2	16	3	12	1	0
Smithfield	8,518	14	0	0	2	12	100	10	84	6	0
South Boston	7,528	29	1	5	5	18	241	37	192	12	0
South Hill	4,322	21	0	1	3	17	187	14	164	9	1
Stanley	1,672	0	0	0	0	0	22	4	17	1	1
Staunton	25,048	45	2	10	6	27	549	54	469	26	4
Stephens City	2,091	0	0	0	0	0	11	0	11	0	0
Strasburg	6,703	13	0	1	0	12	64	8	52	4	0
Suffolk	92,881	366	3	18	49	296	1,715	157	1,398	160	9
Tappahannock	2,397	9	0	0	0	9	60	4	54	2	0
Tazewell	4,088	6	1	3	0	2	97	26	67	4	0
Timberville	2,710	2	0	0	0	2	20	3	16	1	0
Victoria	1,615	1	0	0	0	1	7	1	4	2	0
Vienna	16,570	10	0	3	3	4	214	7	178	29	0
Vinton	8,117	35	0	2	3	30	223	20	192	11	2
Virginia Beach	450,858	445	17	60	124	244	6,816	499	5,693	624	27
Warrenton	10,073	11	2	2	1	6	135	9	118	8	0
Warsaw	1,485	0	0	0	0	0	43	22	20	1	0
Waverly	1,932	3	0	0	0	3	16	0	16	0	0
Waynesboro	22,801	56	2	17	6	31	479	31	415	33	6
West Point	3,250	8	0	1	2	5	32	11	18	3	0
Williamsburg	15,086	21	0	7	0	14	183	13	161	9	1
Winchester	28,279	72	2	21	10	39	586	56	495	35	7
Windsor	2,774	6	0	1	1	4	33	2	28	3	0
Wise	4,381	6	0	0	0	6	41	2	36	3	0
Woodstock	5,279	10	0	0	1	9	126	5	119	2	0

Table 8. Offenses Known to Law Enforcement, by Selected State and City, 2020—Continued

(Number.)

State/city	Population	Violent crime	Murder and nonnegligent manslaughter	Rape[1]	Robbery	Aggravated assault	Property crime	Burglary	Larceny-theft	Motor vehicle theft	Arson[2]
Wytheville	7,890	9	0	7	1	1	183	10	158	15	0
WASHINGTON											
Aberdeen	16,744	56	0	11	8	37	659	122	479	58	6
Algona	3,228	4	0	1	0	3	71	10	47	14	0
Anacortes	17,735	15	0	2	7	6	398	43	327	28	0
Arlington	20,825	59	3	9	10	37	662	91	511	60	4
Auburn	82,779	362	10	40	121	191	3,394	584	2,150	660	19
Bainbridge Island	25,561	16	0	4	1	11	244	30	202	12	0
Battle Ground	21,669	22	0	7	3	12	332	44	265	23	1
Beaux Arts	327	0	0	0	0	0	2	1	0	1	0
Bellevue	150,548	175	4	19	68	84	4,526	597	3,641	288	13
Bellingham	93,629	240	0	29	80	131	4,306	610	3,320	376	18
Bingen	745	1	0	0	0	1	28	4	23	1	0
Black Diamond	4,858	1	0	0	0	1	19	7	11	1	0
Blaine	5,717	10	0	2	0	8	124	54	66	4	0
Bonney Lake	21,584	32	1	3	3	25	441	56	353	32	8
Bothell	48,323	39	1	7	13	18	1,187	163	925	99	5
Bremerton	41,817	143	1	16	23	103	1,342	224	945	173	5
Brewster	2,355	0	0	0	0	0	14	2	8	4	0
Brier	7,055	3	0	0	1	2	69	15	53	1	0
Buckley	5,663	20	0	2	1	17	67	16	45	6	2
Burien	51,879	231	4	26	64	137	2,183	455	1,244	484	15
Burlington	9,321	11	0	1	6	4	522	41	454	27	1
Camas	24,979	8	0	4	1	3	283	38	213	32	3
Carnation	2,345	1	0	0	0	1	30	8	20	2	0
Castle Rock	2,319	9	0	2	0	7	40	2	32	6	0
Centralia	17,867	55	1	10	11	33	537	104	396	37	3
Chehalis	7,700	20	0	2	6	12	440	45	376	19	1
Cheney	12,741	18	0	6	0	12	240	48	157	35	0
Chewelah	2,685	3	1	1	1	0	17	3	11	3	0
Cle Elum	3,023	7	0	1	1	5	115	29	74	12	0
Clyde Hill	3,432	1	0	0	0	1	35	15	19	1	0
College Place	9,374	9	0	2	1	6	204	19	178	7	0
Colville	4,845	3	0	0	0	3	0	0	0	0	0
Connell	5,725	6	0	3	0	3	21	5	14	2	0
Coulee Dam	1,078	1	0	0	0	1	21	7	12	2	0
Covington	21,613	34	0	2	13	19	553	93	415	45	2
Darrington	1,429	7	0	0	0	7	31	14	15	2	1
Des Moines	32,652	109	2	10	56	41	1,152	126	770	256	7
Dupont	9,668	22	0	1	2	19	116	16	94	6	1
Duvall	8,275	3	0	2	0	1	69	4	54	11	3
East Wenatchee	14,336	12	0	3	3	6	228	16	192	20	1
Eatonville	3,058	10	0	2	0	8	26	4	16	6	0
Edgewood	13,553	26	0	6	5	15	300	73	188	39	1
Edmonds	42,934	90	2	14	33	41	1,201	202	918	81	4
Ellensburg	21,448	53	2	10	7	34	583	88	472	23	1
Elma	3,357	6	0	3	0	3	75	12	57	6	0
Enumclaw	12,315	9	0	3	1	5	222	30	170	22	1
Ephrata	8,184	35	0	7	5	23	375	89	249	37	0
Everett	112,439	379	4	37	98	240	3,654	515	2,436	703	13
Federal Way	97,071	344	6	30	121	187	2,542	465	1,745	332	24
Ferndale	15,337	13	0	1	2	10	205	35	161	9	1
Fife	10,301	142	4	10	35	93	901	78	539	284	5
Fircrest	6,869	8	0	0	1	7	119	19	90	10	0
Gig Harbor	11,216	18	0	0	5	13	450	71	350	29	0
Gold Bar	2,374	1	0	0	0	1	32	15	16	1	0
Goldendale	3,516	7	0	2	0	5	99	22	65	12	0
Grand Coulee	2,054	5	0	3	0	2	61	26	26	9	0
Grandview	11,099	15	0	5	3	7	241	56	138	47	0
Granite Falls	4,341	9	0	1	4	4	51	15	35	1	0
Hoquiam	8,647	8	0	1	1	6	180	20	147	13	1
Ilwaco	997	1	0	0	0	1	6	1	2	3	0
Index	215	0	0	0	0	0	1	0	1	0	0
Issaquah	40,659	22	1	8	6	7	1,159	125	974	60	2
Kalama	2,852	2	0	0	0	2	43	9	28	6	0
Kelso	12,476	43	2	19	5	17	419	55	318	46	5
Kenmore	23,397	8	0	3	1	4	298	43	223	32	6
Kennewick	85,526	215	1	38	46	130	2,836	521	2,097	218	19
Kent	133,883	470	8	78	184	200	5,393	1,054	3,378	961	15
Kettle Falls	1,641	4	0	2	0	2	28	6	20	2	0
Kirkland	94,470	109	1	25	18	65	2,010	215	1,629	166	8
La Center	3,459	6	0	3	0	3	63	9	48	6	0
Lacey	53,826	83	0	13	21	49	1,386	160	1,099	127	7
Lake Forest Park	13,604	0	0	0	0	0	375	40	310	25	0
Lake Stevens	34,600	56	0	11	12	33	328	60	232	36	2
Lakewood	61,432	381	4	32	72	273	2,620	445	1,721	454	8
Liberty Lake	11,410	14	0	3	1	10	114	8	105	1	0
Long Beach	1,508	5	0	0	0	5	14	6	8	0	0
Longview	38,629	99	0	25	20	54	1,196	214	846	136	8
Lynden	15,625	20	0	10	1	9	241	36	194	11	0
Lynnwood	39,517	92	0	17	39	36	1,637	210	1,230	197	5
Maple Valley	27,736	15	1	4	2	8	358	85	240	33	4

Table 8. Offenses Known to Law Enforcement, by Selected State and City, 2020—Continued

(Number.)

State/city	Population	Violent crime	Murder and nonnegligent manslaughter	Rape[1]	Robbery	Aggravated assault	Property crime	Burglary	Larceny-theft	Motor vehicle theft	Arson[2]
Marysville	71,522	96	2	24	25	45	1,006	187	677	142	9
Mattawa	4,790	1	0	0	0	1	27	2	11	14	0
Medina	3,324	1	0	1	1	0	52	15	36	1	0
Mercer Island	26,268	4	0	1	2	1	400	74	314	12	0
Mill Creek	21,214	35	0	6	8	21	328	40	250	38	1
Milton	8,413	23	0	2	4	17	246	39	161	46	3
Monroe	20,065	34	0	4	5	25	435	42	367	26	3
Montesano	4,059	7	0	2	0	5	44	4	39	1	0
Moses Lake	24,524	87	1	2	17	67	872	118	676	78	5
Mountlake Terrace	21,504	35	0	5	10	20	518	91	361	66	4
Mount Vernon	36,513	70	1	9	13	47	1,109	142	857	110	3
Moxee	4,177	6	0	2	1	3	26	5	14	7	0
Mukilteo	21,573	30	0	3	6	21	398	57	308	33	1
Newcastle	12,523	8	0	1	3	4	211	28	164	19	0
Newport	2,205	1	0	0	0	1	32	3	24	5	0
Normandy Park	6,633	3	0	0	2	1	116	20	83	13	0
North Bend	7,620	5	0	1	3	1	205	25	167	13	1
Oak Harbor	23,721	25	0	2	1	22	96	16	70	10	0
Oakville	692	1	0	1	0	0	15	6	8	1	0
Ocean Shores	6,604	5	0	1	1	3	90	33	50	7	0
Olympia	53,571	268	1	24	69	174	1,753	271	1,284	198	12
Oroville	1,671	4	0	1	0	3	98	15	80	3	0
Orting	8,848	9	0	1	1	7	141	18	107	16	2
Othello	8,509	16	0	1	2	13	141	26	91	24	0
Pacific	7,243	10	1	4	1	4	169	14	112	43	0
Palouse	1,084	0	0	0	0	0	0	0	0	0	0
Pasco	76,970	183	3	26	60	94	1,351	230	960	161	21
Port Angeles	20,364	140	1	28	10	101	579	95	441	43	9
Port Orchard	14,886	61	0	9	8	44	550	100	380	70	2
Port Townsend	9,914	19	0	2	4	13	206	41	151	14	1
Poulsbo	11,401	10	0	3	1	6	222	34	168	20	2
Prosser	6,451	8	0	1	3	4	119	19	94	6	1
Puyallup	42,974	94	2	13	38	41	2,548	388	1,857	303	21
Quincy	8,183	17	0	3	0	14	163	45	88	30	0
Raymond	3,009	3	0	1	0	2	17	4	13	0	0
Redmond	74,154	74	0	12	19	43	1,742	207	1,443	92	2
Renton	102,856	348	6	37	108	197	4,342	498	3,063	781	11
Richland	59,370	164	3	33	18	110	1,553	267	1,216	70	5
Ridgefield	9,835	7	0	1	0	6	192	32	148	12	1
Ritzville	1,651	1	1	0	0	0	68	18	48	2	0
Roy	827	4	0	0	0	4	18	3	12	3	0
Royal City	2,247	3	0	0	1	2	31	8	17	6	0
Ruston	856	2	0	0	0	2	34	4	26	4	1
Sammamish	66,878	17	1	6	0	10	442	68	341	33	4
SeaTac	29,282	141	4	17	52	68	1,394	194	838	362	2
Seattle	771,517	4,832	52	301	1,471	3,008	37,593	10,427	22,255	4,911	208
Sedro Woolley	12,189	16	1	1	2	12	247	41	189	17	1
Selah	8,170	6	1	1	4	0	148	14	120	14	0
Sequim	7,768	10	0	2	0	8	228	33	188	7	1
Shelton	10,749	49	1	13	11	24	517	54	434	29	3
Shoreline	57,472	116	2	17	38	59	1,515	228	1,063	224	14
Skykomish	223	0	0	0	0	0	0	0	0	0	0
Snohomish	10,269	25	0	3	11	11	344	70	243	31	4
Snoqualmie	13,987	5	0	1	0	4	165	14	143	8	0
Soap Lake	1,609	5	0	0	0	5	58	18	32	8	0
South Bend	1,706	3	0	2	0	1	9	1	5	3	0
Spokane	223,524	1,341	19	187	280	855	11,514	1,745	8,666	1,103	105
Spokane Valley	102,366	342	3	28	77	234	4,370	691	3,339	340	11
Stanwood	7,410	8	0	4	0	4	126	23	89	14	2
Steilacoom	6,436	13	0	2	1	10	81	14	53	14	0
Sultan	5,476	7	0	0	0	7	88	28	50	10	1
Sumner	10,544	32	0	3	6	23	427	85	270	72	2
Sunnyside	16,888	30	0	4	7	19	721	100	532	89	0
Tacoma	220,123	1,856	28	127	435	1,266	12,123	1,987	7,967	2,169	134
Tenino	1,886	10	0	1	1	8	22	3	14	5	0
Toledo	777	0	0	0	0	0	6	3	3	0	0
Toppenish	8,792	57	2	2	10	43	485	134	283	68	3
Tukwila	20,483	151	3	27	61	60	2,953	222	2,201	530	13
Tumwater	24,493	63	0	10	13	40	613	94	453	66	2
Twisp	970	0	0	0	0	0	10	3	7	0	0
Union Gap	6,206	23	0	0	8	15	382	52	289	41	0
University Place	34,339	117	1	10	28	78	904	210	622	72	4
Vancouver	186,440	884	5	137	167	575	6,709	1,065	4,448	1,196	61
Walla Walla	32,944	83	0	21	11	51	749	126	573	50	7
Warden	2,825	4	0	0	0	4	34	8	21	5	1
Washougal	16,334	35	1	17	3	14	283	36	222	25	0
Wenatchee	34,525	67	0	16	6	45	570	72	448	50	3
Westport	2,102	4	0	3	1	0	85	9	70	6	2
West Richland	15,464	18	0	3	0	15	205	59	137	9	1
White Salmon	2,732	2	0	1	1	0	67	11	52	4	0
Winlock	1,436	0	0	0	0	0	10	1	9	0	0
Woodinville	13,547	14	0	5	4	5	383	47	313	23	1
Woodway	1,400	1	0	0	1	0	8	5	3	0	0

Table 8. Offenses Known to Law Enforcement, by Selected State and City, 2020—Continued

(Number.)

State/city	Population	Violent crime	Murder and nonnegligent manslaughter	Rape[1]	Robbery	Aggravated assault	Property crime	Burglary	Larceny-theft	Motor vehicle theft	Arson[2]
Yakima	93,862	639	9	22	100	508	3,220	599	2,115	506	29
Yarrow Point	1,166	0	0	0	0	0	11	3	8	0	0
Yelm	9,799	24	0	5	4	15	354	60	277	17	1
WEST VIRGINIA											
Alderson	1,119	11	0	0	0	11	22	1	17	4	0
Barboursville	4,291	3	0	1	0	2	101	0	101	0	0
Beckley	15,762	137	2	8	11	116	905	149	708	48	4
Bluefield	9,543	112	0	12	0	100	10	0	10	0	1
Bridgeport	8,924	20	0	4	0	16	73	8	59	6	0
Buckhannon	5,373	5	0	2	0	3	91	0	91	0	2
Chapmanville	1,080	0	0	0	0	0	14	3	11	0	0
Charleston	46,038	424	11	37	51	325	2,122	506	1,423	193	33
Charles Town	6,123	9	0	1	2	6	54	23	29	2	0
Clarksburg	15,092	66	0	11	4	51	580	50	498	32	5
Dunbar	7,010	56	0	3	11	42	195	45	131	19	4
Fairmont	18,352	85	3	11	9	62	272	86	172	14	5
Fayetteville	2,695	4	0	0	0	4	132	2	129	1	0
Follansbee	2,682	1	0	0	0	1	12	2	10	0	1
Glen Dale	1,355	2	0	0	0	2	9	5	3	1	0
Grafton	4,963	1	0	0	0	1	77	13	48	16	0
Huntington	44,684	368	7	35	69	257	1,642	378	1,083	181	22
Kenova	2,931	0	0	0	0	0	25	5	18	2	2
Keyser	4,863	0	0	0	0	0	48	15	33	0	1
Lewisburg	3,803	0	0	0	0	0	62	0	58	4	0
Madison	2,631	7	1	1	1	4	39	16	17	6	0
Milton	2,547	5	0	2	0	3	45	6	38	1	0
Moorefield	2,403	33	0	1	0	32	95	10	82	3	0
Morgantown	30,775	48	0	14	7	27	636	87	517	32	1
Moundsville	8,175	21	0	3	0	18	90	0	90	0	1
Nitro	6,314	6	0	0	0	6	178	9	163	6	0
Oak Hill	8,017	4	0	0	0	4	7	0	7	0	0
Parkersburg	29,096	106	2	29	23	52	1,269	265	911	93	34
Point Pleasant	4,032	2	0	1	0	1	57	12	44	1	0
Princeton	5,627	15	0	1	0	14	24	0	24	0	0
Romney	1,680	22	0	0	0	22	6	2	3	1	0
South Charleston	11,898	52	0	2	4	46	688	61	590	37	2
St. Albans	9,802	33	1	3	4	25	224	37	169	18	0
Summersville	3,243	5	0	0	0	5	79	1	75	3	0
Vienna	10,049	9	0	1	1	7	348	10	331	7	0
Weirton	18,111	12	2	3	0	7	24	0	24	0	0
Wheeling	26,222	330	1	31	28	270	582	180	361	41	3
WISCONSIN											
Adams	1,884	7	0	4	0	3	35	2	33	0	0
Algoma	3,035	2	0	0	0	2	18	1	17	0	0
Altoona	8,009	19	0	2	2	15	191	36	143	12	0
Appleton	74,255	198	1	36	19	142	1,155	128	964	63	5
Arcadia	3,051	0	0	0	0	0	14	1	11	2	0
Ashwaubenon	17,183	34	1	13	3	17	277	15	235	27	0
Athens	1,075	1	0	1	0	0	6	1	5	0	0
Avoca	621	0	0	0	0	0	0	0	0	0	0
Barneveld	1,253	0	0	0	0	0	1	0	0	1	0
Barron	3,308	7	1	1	0	5	21	1	17	3	0
Bayfield	470	2	0	0	0	2	15	2	13	0	0
Bayside	4,322	3	0	1	1	1	27	2	22	3	0
Beaver Dam	16,426	19	0	3	3	13	206	7	188	11	0
Belleville	2,473	2	0	0	0	2	29	2	27	0	0
Beloit	36,921	179	2	23	34	120	1,069	117	878	74	12
Beloit Town	7,741	13	0	1	1	11	110	20	79	11	0
Berlin	5,369	4	0	0	0	4	80	10	64	6	0
Big Bend	1,487	3	0	0	0	3	18	2	13	3	0
Birchwood	426	0	0	0	0	0	0	0	0	0	0
Black River Falls	3,449	7	0	4	0	3	92	4	84	4	1
Bloomer[4]	3,500	10	0	0	0	10	62	8	52	2	2
Bloomfield	6,363	6	0	2	0	4	44	4	35	5	1
Boscobel	3,118	8	0	2	0	6	29	3	25	1	0
Boyceville[4]	1,131	1	0	0	0	1	12	2	9	1	0
Brandon-Fairwater	1,205	0	0	0	0	0	0	0	0	0	0
Brillion	3,067	4	0	0	0	4	24	4	20	0	1
Brodhead	3,242	1	0	0	0	1	22	4	18	0	0
Brookfield	39,252	32	0	6	10	16	652	38	602	12	0
Brookfield Township	6,564	13	0	2	3	8	101	9	91	1	0
Brooklyn	1,472	1	0	0	0	1	24	3	21	0	0
Brown Deer	11,808	47	1	4	16	26	444	19	391	34	3
Brownsville	584	0	0	0	0	0	3	0	3	0	0
Burlington	11,025	17	0	1	1	15	123	8	113	2	1
Butler[4]	1,793	5	0	1	2	2	57	2	50	5	0
Caledonia	25,323	20	0	1	0	19	167	34	121	12	0
Campbellsport	1,807	0	0	0	0	0	9	0	9	0	0
Campbell Township	4,296	3	0	0	0	3	75	6	66	3	0
Cashton[4]	1,113	0	0	0	0	0	3	0	3	0	0
Cedarburg	11,621	7	0	1	0	6	79	5	74	0	0

Table 8. Offenses Known to Law Enforcement, by Selected State and City, 2020—Continued

(Number.)

State/city	Population	Violent crime	Murder and nonnegligent manslaughter	Rape[1]	Robbery	Aggravated assault	Property crime	Burglary	Larceny- theft	Motor vehicle theft	Arson[2]
Chetek	2,083	4	0	0	0	4	5	1	4	0	1
Chilton	3,851	6	0	0	0	6	48	3	45	0	0
Chippewa Falls	14,437	22	0	2	0	20	126	19	92	15	2
Cleveland	1,450	0	0	0	0	0	2	0	2	0	0
Clinton	2,139	0	0	0	0	0	36	2	31	3	0
Clintonville	4,372	10	0	6	0	4	81	7	74	0	0
Colby-Abbotsford	4,185	5	0	0	0	5	37	1	35	1	0
Columbus	5,134	4	0	0	2	2	110	3	102	5	0
Cornell[4]	1,401	2	0	0	0	2	14	3	10	1	0
Cottage Grove	7,233	1	0	0	0	1	27	2	24	1	0
Crandon	1,787	6	0	0	0	6	7	0	6	1	1
Cross Plains	4,362	1	0	0	0	1	45	4	37	4	0
Cudahy	18,064	34	1	6	3	24	200	26	130	44	0
Cumberland	2,096	1	0	0	0	1	1	0	0	1	0
Darlington	2,325	1	0	0	0	1	11	0	9	2	0
Deforest	10,901	11	0	3	0	8	148	7	137	4	0
Delafield	7,586	1	0	0	0	1	137	7	129	1	0
Delavan	9,836	14	1	4	0	9	188	13	170	5	0
Delavan Town[4]	5,337	3	0	0	1	2	24	1	20	3	0
De Pere	25,090	27	0	7	1	19	164	21	138	5	0
Dodgeville	4,679	5	0	2	0	3	83	12	69	2	0
Durand	1,786	2	0	2	0	0	3	0	3	0	0
Eagle Village	2,177	0	0	0	0	0	11	0	11	0	0
East Troy[4]	4,313	8	0	0	0	8	16	1	14	2	0
Eau Claire	69,086	191	2	41	38	110	1,927	334	1,494	99	8
Edgar	1,438	1	0	0	0	1	7	0	6	1	0
Edgerton	5,655	2	0	1	1	0	41	2	38	1	0
Elkhart Lake[4]	1,022	1	0	0	0	1	2	0	1	1	0
Elkhorn	10,014	17	0	6	3	8	100	8	82	10	1
Elk Mound[4]	882	0	0	0	0	0	12	2	10	0	0
Ellsworth	3,320	4	0	1	0	3	21	1	17	3	0
Elm Grove	6,160	2	0	2	0	0	118	5	111	2	1
Evansville	5,489	0	0	0	0	0	12	2	10	0	0
Everest Metropolitan	17,361	56	0	15	2	39	179	30	138	11	0
Fall Creek[4]	1,286	0	0	0	0	0	7	0	6	1	0
Fall River	1,744	2	0	0	0	2	0	0	0	0	0
Fennimore	2,449	4	0	0	0	4	5	1	3	1	0
Fitchburg	31,483	83	0	11	21	51	541	107	372	62	3
Fond du Lac	43,295	134	1	25	9	99	878	66	776	36	5
Fontana[4]	1,747	1	0	1	0	0	12	0	7	5	0
Fort Atkinson[4]	12,425	21	0	9	0	12	170	17	145	8	0
Fox Crossing	19,099	13	0	2	1	10	127	21	99	7	0
Fox Point	6,522	1	0	0	0	1	87	3	72	12	0
Fox Valley Metro	22,737	16	0	6	0	10	58	11	37	10	0
Franklin	35,814	30	0	8	6	16	649	40	586	23	2
Frederic	1,084	2	0	1	0	1	21	2	19	0	0
Fulton	3,457	0	0	0	0	0	2	0	2	0	0
Galesville	1,606	0	0	0	0	0	10	4	5	1	0
Geneva Town	5,045	1	0	0	0	1	10	1	8	1	0
Germantown	20,133	13	0	0	6	7	554	12	535	7	0
Gillett	1,285	1	0	0	0	1	19	4	15	0	0
Glendale	12,714	24	1	2	12	9	529	17	449	63	4
Grafton	11,738	3	0	0	2	1	168	3	161	4	0
Grand Chute	23,579	53	0	10	6	37	818	20	763	35	3
Grand Rapids	7,393	0	0	0	0	0	18	5	13	0	0
Grantsburg	1,275	11	0	0	1	10	18	0	18	0	0
Green Bay	104,649	552	6	71	45	430	1,600	206	1,279	115	12
Greendale	14,141	20	0	2	0	18	161	10	145	6	1
Greenfield	37,237	55	0	3	13	39	956	53	837	66	3
Green Lake	968	0	0	0	0	0	6	0	5	1	0
Hales Corners	7,548	6	0	2	1	3	117	5	111	1	0
Hancock	404	0	0	0	0	0	0	0	0	0	0
Hartford	15,573	17	0	13	3	1	189	6	175	8	2
Hartford Township	3,561	0	0	0	0	0	0	0	0	0	0
Hartland[4]	9,343	2	0	1	0	1	35	1	34	0	0
Hayward	2,307	14	0	2	1	11	43	3	38	2	0
Hazel Green	1,216	0	0	0	0	0	7	2	5	0	0
Highland	825	0	0	0	0	0	2	1	1	0	0
Hobart-Lawrence	16,178	6	0	2	0	4	103	63	39	1	0
Holmen	10,135	7	0	3	0	4	82	6	71	5	0
Horicon	3,644	7	0	1	0	6	32	0	30	2	0
Hortonville	2,936	2	0	1	0	1	21	1	20	0	0
Hudson	14,255	38	1	1	3	33	329	7	302	20	0
Hurley	1,425	0	0	0	0	0	20	0	18	2	0
Independence	1,299	0	0	0	0	0	19	3	14	2	0
Iron Ridge	887	0	0	0	0	0	0	0	0	0	0
Iron River	1,135	2	0	0	0	2	12	5	7	0	0
Janesville	64,682	145	4	31	36	74	1,392	136	1,200	56	7
Jefferson	7,986	12	0	1	3	8	130	3	121	6	1
Juneau	2,653	0	0	0	0	0	19	3	16	0	0
Kaukauna	16,357	23	2	7	2	12	94	7	80	7	1
Kenosha	100,005	391	7	37	83	264	1,443	214	1,004	225	35
Kewaskum	4,290	2	0	2	0	0	23	1	21	1	0

Table 8. Offenses Known to Law Enforcement, by Selected State and City, 2020—Continued

(Number.)

State/city	Population	Violent crime	Murder and nonnegligent manslaughter	Rape[1]	Robbery	Aggravated assault	Property crime	Burglary	Larceny-theft	Motor vehicle theft	Arson[2]
Kewaunee	2,838	1	0	0	0	1	28	0	28	0	0
Kiel	3,805	8	0	0	0	8	25	2	23	0	0
Kohler[4]	2,053	0	0	0	0	0	74	2	71	1	0
Kronenwetter	8,181	5	0	2	0	3	30	9	19	2	0
La Crosse	51,211	131	1	34	26	70	2,236	170	1,958	108	3
Ladysmith	3,097	3	0	0	0	3	22	1	21	0	0
La Farge	761	0	0	0	0	0	1	0	1	0	0
Lake Delton	2,994	20	0	4	2	14	266	6	248	12	0
Lake Geneva	8,157	10	2	2	0	6	125	3	120	2	1
Lake Hallie[4]	6,777	14	1	4	0	9	73	2	66	5	0
Lake Mills	6,013	16	0	2	2	12	11	0	11	0	0
Lancaster	3,682	13	0	2	0	11	19	1	17	1	0
Linden	526	0	0	0	0	0	0	0	0	0	0
Linn Township	2,405	3	0	0	0	3	24	6	17	1	0
Lodi	3,096	2	0	0	1	1	53	2	49	2	0
Lomira	2,453	1	0	0	0	1	18	2	15	1	0
Madison	262,736	842	10	74	165	593	7,301	1,307	5,346	648	15
Manawa	1,262	3	0	1	0	2	7	2	3	2	0
Marathon City	1,505	1	0	0	0	1	6	1	4	1	0
Marinette[4]	10,497	26	0	5	0	21	197	21	169	7	0
Marion	1,170	2	0	0	0	2	6	0	5	1	0
Markesan	1,394	2	0	1	1	0	12	0	12	0	0
Marshall Village	3,998	13	0	1	1	11	37	2	32	3	0
Marshfield	18,403	33	0	24	0	9	375	31	331	13	0
Mauston	4,348	11	0	2	0	9	90	9	78	3	1
Mayville	4,862	7	0	1	0	6	34	2	31	1	0
McFarland	9,161	6	0	0	0	6	50	9	36	5	0
Medford[4]	4,274	12	0	4	1	7	55	0	54	1	0
Menasha	17,910	41	0	8	3	30	212	34	171	7	2
Menomonie	16,582	74	1	12	0	61	300	21	257	22	0
Mequon[4]	24,527	12	0	1	1	10	205	18	180	7	0
Merrill	8,984	12	0	1	0	11	143	17	121	5	0
Middleton	20,322	12	0	2	2	8	220	22	176	22	0
Milton	5,636	3	0	0	0	3	37	3	28	6	0
Milton Town	3,168	0	0	0	0	0	1	0	1	0	0
Milwaukee	589,105	9,407	191	431	1,925	6,860	16,074	3,408	8,178	4,488	287
Mineral Point	2,461	0	0	0	0	0	31	3	24	4	0
Minocqua	4,422	6	0	2	0	4	34	3	29	2	0
Mishicot	1,383	0	0	0	0	0	9	0	9	0	0
Monona	8,245	10	0	1	5	4	429	15	388	26	0
Monroe[4]	10,538	2	0	1	0	1	173	7	159	7	0
Montello	1,464	0	0	0	0	0	12	0	12	0	0
Mosinee	4,080	3	0	0	0	3	35	5	26	4	0
Mount Horeb	7,579	10	0	3	2	5	30	5	25	0	0
Mount Pleasant	27,125	48	0	2	11	35	490	38	431	21	1
Mukwonago	8,137	8	0	2	0	6	80	0	80	0	1
Mukwonago Town	8,168	4	0	1	0	3	11	1	10	0	0
Muscoda	1,234	2	0	0	0	2	7	1	5	1	0
Muskego	25,237	8	0	0	2	6	210	90	107	13	0
Neenah	26,390	57	1	12	5	39	315	21	282	12	2
Neillsville	2,403	2	0	1	0	1	22	1	13	8	0
Nekoosa	2,405	2	1	0	0	1	17	5	12	0	0
New Berlin	39,703	28	0	10	3	15	457	21	427	9	0
New Glarus[4]	2,148	0	0	0	0	0	32	1	30	1	0
New Holstein	3,088	3	0	0	0	3	15	1	13	1	0
New London	7,070	9	0	6	0	3	67	2	64	1	1
New Richmond	9,535	14	1	0	1	12	133	10	116	7	2
Niagara[4]	1,535	0	0	0	0	0	6	0	6	0	0
North Fond du Lac	5,089	5	0	0	0	5	52	4	40	8	3
North Hudson	3,815	2	0	0	0	2	43	0	42	1	0
North Prairie	2,240	0	0	0	0	0	4	0	4	0	0
Norwalk	630	0	0	0	0	0	0	0	0	0	0
Oak Creek	36,502	49	0	9	12	28	749	69	629	51	2
Oconomowoc	17,116	12	0	2	0	10	135	3	126	6	0
Oconomowoc Lake	604	0	0	0	0	0	2	0	2	0	0
Oconomowoc Town	8,743	1	0	0	0	1	11	3	4	4	0
Oconto	4,548	25	0	1	1	23	57	5	50	2	1
Oconto Falls	2,785	3	0	1	0	2	23	4	18	1	0
Omro	3,590	5	0	0	0	5	30	3	25	2	0
Onalaska	19,072	19	0	1	5	13	715	44	655	16	0
Oregon	10,718	7	0	3	1	3	47	9	38	0	0
Osceola	2,556	5	0	0	1	4	39	6	31	2	0
Oshkosh	67,080	187	4	48	12	123	1,239	138	1,036	65	3
Osseo	1,673	2	0	0	1	1	21	1	16	4	0
Palmyra	1,753	3	0	1	0	2	13	0	13	0	0
Park Falls	2,207	0	0	0	0	0	0	0	0	0	0
Peshtigo[4]	3,329	2	0	2	0	0	19	2	17	0	0
Pewaukee Village	8,102	4	0	2	0	2	143	3	134	6	1
Phillips	1,322	3	0	1	0	2	22	3	17	2	0
Pittsville	819	0	0	0	0	0	65	2	62	1	0
Plainfield	833	0	0	0	0	0	0	0	0	0	0
Platteville	12,184	27	0	3	0	24	353	19	321	13	1
Pleasant Prairie	21,181	33	0	0	11	22	307	21	262	24	0

Table 8. Offenses Known to Law Enforcement, by Selected State and City, 2020—Continued

(Number.)

State/city	Population	Violent crime	Murder and nonnegligent manslaughter	Rape[1]	Robbery	Aggravated assault	Property crime	Burglary	Larceny-theft	Motor vehicle theft	Arson[2]
Plover	13,201	28	1	6	0	21	236	28	202	6	3
Plymouth[4]	8,762	4	0	2	0	2	71	3	68	0	0
Port Edwards	1,757	1	0	0	0	1	8	0	5	3	0
Port Washington	11,982	9	0	3	0	6	86	3	78	5	0
Poynette	2,507	4	0	1	0	3	2	0	2	0	0
Prairie du Chien	5,539	5	0	4	0	1	124	4	111	9	0
Prescott	4,299	4	0	1	0	3	27	5	19	3	2
Princeton	1,165	0	0	0	0	0	9	0	9	0	0
Pulaski	3,742	7	0	1	0	6	23	0	22	1	0
Racine	76,573	414	2	36	86	290	1,381	321	916	144	15
Reedsburg	9,549	9	0	4	0	5	120	9	105	6	0
Rhinelander	7,629	15	0	4	0	11	109	5	100	4	1
Rice Lake	8,526	41	0	8	1	32	210	5	195	10	0
Richland Center	4,918	6	0	3	0	3	33	0	31	2	0
Rio	1,038	0	0	0	0	0	6	2	4	0	0
Ripon	7,854	15	0	6	0	9	73	3	69	1	0
Ripon Town	1,380	0	0	0	0	0	0	0	0	0	0
River Falls	16,141	13	0	2	0	11	238	22	200	16	1
Rome Town	2,755	3	0	2	0	1	22	7	15	0	0
Rosendale	1,028	0	0	0	0	0	0	0	0	0	0
Rothschild	5,268	4	0	1	1	2	49	7	42	0	0
Sauk Prairie	4,650	4	0	0	1	3	48	2	36	10	0
Saukville	4,431	1	0	0	0	1	63	2	59	2	0
Seymour	3,454	6	0	1	0	5	18	1	16	1	0
Sharon	1,552	0	0	0	0	0	0	0	0	0	0
Shawano[4]	8,896	19	0	3	0	16	225	19	196	10	1
Sheboygan	47,814	157	1	33	15	108	832	97	702	33	10
Sheboygan Falls[4]	7,938	3	0	1	0	2	38	4	32	2	0
Shorewood[4]	13,133	16	0	1	7	8	258	24	207	27	0
Shorewood Hills	2,058	2	0	0	0	2	30	2	27	1	0
Siren	771	6	0	3	1	2	5	0	5	0	1
Slinger	5,621	2	0	2	0	0	47	4	42	1	0
South Milwaukee	20,626	23	1	5	4	13	287	13	260	14	0
Sparta[4]	9,865	40	0	6	1	33	81	11	70	0	0
Spooner	2,557	11	0	2	0	9	41	9	30	2	0
Spring Green	1,643	0	0	0	0	0	5	1	4	0	0
Spring Valley	1,348	2	0	2	0	0	4	0	4	0	0
Stanley	3,722	8	0	0	0	8	36	0	36	0	0
St. Croix Falls[4]	2,037	9	0	1	1	7	59	1	42	16	0
Stevens Point	25,790	34	0	9	0	25	252	26	215	11	2
St. Francis[4]	9,733	8	0	3	1	4	137	40	86	11	0
Stoughton	13,164	17	0	2	1	14	172	29	135	8	0
Strum	1,087	0	0	0	0	0	0	0	0	0	0
Sturgeon Bay	8,913	6	1	1	0	4	65	6	51	8	0
Sturtevant	6,659	5	0	4	0	1	24	2	20	2	0
Summit	5,087	8	0	5	0	3	26	8	17	1	1
Sun Prairie	35,272	25	0	4	6	15	539	58	416	65	0
Superior[4]	25,845	48	1	6	10	31	1,011	166	750	95	3
Theresa	1,199	0	0	0	0	0	10	1	9	0	0
Thiensville[4]	3,116	0	0	0	0	0	11	1	7	3	0
Thorp	1,610	0	0	0	0	0	0	0	0	0	0
Tomah	9,418	19	0	4	0	15	192	18	172	2	0
Tomahawk	3,111	4	0	1	0	3	42	2	39	1	0
Town of East Troy[4]	4,060	0	0	0	0	0	13	0	13	0	0
Town of Madison	6,920	27	2	4	7	14	129	23	89	17	0
Twin Lakes	6,230	22	0	2	0	20	28	5	22	1	1
Two Rivers	10,970	25	0	2	0	23	99	10	84	5	1
Verona	13,548	12	0	4	2	6	125	13	104	8	0
Viroqua	4,407	2	0	1	0	1	92	2	88	2	0
Walworth	2,828	3	0	0	0	3	33	3	25	5	0
Washburn	2,028	7	0	2	0	5	9	2	7	0	0
Waterford Town	6,526	1	0	0	0	1	84	11	70	3	0
Waterloo	3,332	12	0	1	0	11	32	3	26	3	0
Watertown	23,437	52	0	6	7	39	181	14	162	5	1
Waukesha	72,421	123	1	17	21	84	595	62	477	56	0
Waunakee[4]	14,280	10	0	1	0	9	76	13	61	2	0
Waupaca[4]	5,953	15	1	2	1	11	120	13	104	3	0
Waupun	11,184	13	0	6	0	7	43	4	36	3	0
Wausau	38,492	174	0	26	14	134	560	66	435	59	4
Wautoma	2,135	2	0	1	0	1	244	3	239	2	0
Wauwatosa	48,265	67	0	2	32	33	1,092	72	924	96	1
Webster[4]	616	3	0	1	0	2	15	1	11	3	0
West Allis	59,778	191	0	28	70	93	1,715	237	1,303	175	10
West Bend	31,603	80	0	17	4	59	513	18	480	15	1
Westby	2,259	1	1	0	0	0	32	2	29	1	0
Westfield	1,268	0	0	0	0	0	11	0	9	2	0
West Milwaukee	4,081	43	0	2	17	24	898	40	821	37	0
West Salem	5,037	10	0	2	0	8	31	1	29	1	0
Whitefish Bay	13,734	5	0	0	2	3	159	6	134	19	0
Whitehall	1,570	1	0	0	0	1	18	1	16	1	0
Whitewater	14,952	37	0	5	1	31	146	25	115	6	0
Wild Rose	680	0	0	0	0	0	1	0	0	1	0
Wilton	498	0	0	0	0	0	2	0	1	1	0

Table 8. Offenses Known to Law Enforcement, by Selected State and City, 2020—Continued

(Number.)

State/city	Population	Violent crime	Murder and nonnegligent manslaughter	Rape[1]	Robbery	Aggravated assault	Property crime	Burglary	Larceny-theft	Motor vehicle theft	Arson[2]
Wisconsin Dells[4]	3,025	19	0	7	2	10	100	7	86	7	0
Wisconsin Rapids	17,524	29	0	13	1	15	503	43	438	22	1
Woodruff	1,975	0	0	0	0	0	7	1	6	0	0
WYOMING											
Afton	2,055	0	0	0	0	0	3	0	3	0	0
Buffalo	4,573	6	0	1	0	5	51	5	42	4	0
Casper	58,244	124	2	59	14	49	1,659	222	1,270	167	10
Cheyenne	64,751	244	2	35	27	180	2,186	172	1,768	246	9
Cody	9,816	21	0	5	0	16	118	26	87	5	0
Diamondville[4]	759	2	0	1	0	1	0	0	0	0	0
Douglas[4]	6,394	8	0	0	0	8	65	11	49	5	1
Evanston[4]	11,563	48	0	33	2	13	218	26	181	11	0
Evansville[4]	3,005	9	0	0	0	9	78	3	67	8	0
Gillette[4]	32,093	62	2	11	1	48	617	58	525	34	3
Glenrock[4]	2,568	4	0	1	0	3	12	0	12	0	0
Green River	11,691	31	0	0	0	31	77	15	61	1	0
Greybull	1,837	2	0	0	0	2	8	3	3	2	0
Hanna	762	1	0	0	0	1	0	0	0	0	0
Kemmerer	2,760	1	0	0	0	1	11	0	11	0	0
Lander	7,441	2	2	0	0	0	184	8	164	12	0
Lusk	1,521	1	0	1	0	0	17	3	12	2	0
Mills	4,040	3	0	0	0	3	71	16	47	8	0
Moorcroft	1,092	3	0	0	0	3	12	0	8	4	0
Newcastle[4]	3,383	9	0	5	0	4	42	7	34	1	1
Pine Bluffs	1,158	3	0	3	0	0	7	3	0	4	0
Powell	6,165	15	0	5	1	9	128	28	94	6	5
Rawlins	8,434	18	0	4	0	14	113	15	87	11	4
Riverton[4]	10,772	59	1	21	5	32	456	46	343	67	2
Rock Springs	22,615	58	0	20	1	37	307	39	245	23	6
Saratoga	1,607	6	0	1	0	5	6	1	4	1	0
Sheridan[4]	17,991	16	0	2	0	14	264	32	217	15	2
Thermopolis[4]	2,738	3	0	1	0	2	40	5	34	1	0
Torrington	6,623	32	0	7	0	25	77	7	69	1	0
Wheatland	3,445	6	0	0	0	6	80	22	50	8	0
Worland[4]	4,975	6	0	1	0	5	29	4	23	2	0

1 The figures shown in this column for the offense of rape were reported using only the revised Uniform Crime Reporting (UCR) definition of rape. See the chapter notes for further explanation.   2 The FBI does not publish arson data unless it receives data from either the agency or the state for all 12 months of the calendar year.   3 Limited data for 2020 were available for Alabama, Maryland and Pennsylvania.   4 Because of changes in the state/local agency's reporting practices, figures are not comparable to previous years' data.   5 The FBI determined that the agency's data were overreported. Consequently, those data are not included in this table.   6 The FBI determined that the state did not follow national UCR Program guidelines for reporting an offense. Consequently, those figures are not included in this table. The agency of Rockford submits independently and therefore includes all offenses.   7 The FBI determined that the agency's data were underreported. Consequently, those data are not included in this table.   8 This agency submits rape data classified according to the legacy UCR definition; therefore the rape offense and violent crime total, which rape is a part of, is not included in this table.   9 Arson offenses are reported by the Toledo Fire Department; therefore, those figures are not included in this report.

Table 9. Offenses Known to Law Enforcement, by Selected State and University and College, 2020

(Number.)

State and university/college	Student enrollment[1]	Violent crime	Murder and nonnegligent manslaughter	Rape[2]	Robbery	Aggravated assault	Property crime	Burglary	Larceny-theft	Motor vehicle theft	Arson[3]
ALABAMA[4]											
ALASKA											
University of Alaska											
Anchorage	23,371	2	0	1	1	0	42	6	33	3	1
Fairbanks	12,297	1	0	1	0	0	25	1	22	2	0
ARIZONA											
Arizona State University, Main Campus	139,085	16	0	10	0	6	462	42	406	14	1
Arizona Western College[5]	11,521	0	0	0	0	0	6	0	6	0	0
Central Arizona College[5]	8,518	0	0	0	0	0	7	0	6	1	1
Northern Arizona University	34,934	17	0	12	1	4	162	6	156	0	1
Pima Community College	33,708	1	0	0	0	1	29	7	21	1	0
ARKANSAS											
Beebe	4,716	0	0	0	0	0	3	0	2	1	0
Jonesboro	18,977	9	0	1	1	7	26	4	22	0	0
Newport	4,869	0	0	0	0	0	1	0	1	0	0
Arkansas Tech University	13,722	3	0	3	0	0	38	5	33	0	0
Henderson State University	4,565	0	0	0	0	0	15	4	9	2	0
Southern Arkansas University	5,182	3	2	1	0	0	20	3	17	0	0
Southern Arkansas University Tech	1,968	2	0	2	0	0	1	0	1	0	0
University of Arkansas											
Fayetteville	30,459	5	0	2	1	2	139	13	94	32	0
Medical Sciences	2,996	5	0	1	0	4	90	1	86	3	0
Monticello	3,716	0	0	0	0	0	12	0	12	0	0
University of Arkansas Community College at											
Morrilton	2,475	0	0	0	0	0	0	0	0	0	0
University of Central Arkansas	12,741	1	0	0	0	1	45	5	40	0	2
CALIFORNIA											
Allan Hancock College	15,587	0	0	0	0	0	1	0	1	0	0
California State Polytechnic University											
Pomona	28,547	2	0	1	0	1	77	18	54	5	0
San Luis Obispo	23,278	6	0	3	0	3	101	12	83	6	1
California State University											
Bakersfield	12,944	1	0	1	0	0	28	3	24	1	0
Channel Islands	8,348	2	0	1	0	1	28	1	27	0	0
Chico	19,323	3	0	0	0	3	66	6	58	2	4
Dominguez Hills	18,196	4	0	3	0	1	25	13	12	0	1
East Bay	18,549	4	0	3	1	0	26	8	17	1	0
Fresno	26,765	3	0	2	1	0	107	22	78	7	0
Fullerton	46,588	4	0	2	0	2	65	11	50	4	0
Long Beach	41,344	4	0	1	3	0	70	14	50	6	0
Los Angeles	29,963	3	0	2	1	0	45	2	40	3	0
Monterey Bay	8,476	6	0	3	0	3	39	16	21	2	0
Northridge	43,348	5	0	3	0	2	69	5	58	6	1
Sacramento	35,644	5	0	1	1	3	77	14	62	1	0
San Bernardino	21,967	3	0	1	0	2	34	4	26	4	0
San Jose	38,805	19	0	8	5	6	161	50	105	6	2
San Marcos	17,136	0	0	0	0	0	17	4	12	1	0
Stanislaus	11,821	3	0	2	0	1	21	3	18	0	2
Chaffey College	30,177	0	0	0	0	0	15	8	1	6	0
College of the Sequoias	16,022	0	0	0	0	0	12	2	10	0	0
Contra Costa Community College	54,940	2	0	2	0	0	62	15	42	5	0
Cuesta College	15,640	0	0	0	0	0	6	5	1	0	0
El Camino College	34,373	1	0	0	1	0	14	0	12	2	0
Foothill-De Anza College	58,890	0	0	0	0	0	10	4	5	1	1
Humboldt State University	8,622	0	0	0	0	0	56	14	39	3	2
Irvine Valley College	19,299	0	0	0	0	0	1	1	0	0	0
Marin Community College	7,327	0	0	0	0	0	9	1	8	0	1
Mt. San Jacinto College	21,317	0	0	0	0	0	8	2	6	0	0
Pasadena Community College	36,788	1	0	0	0	1	14	1	11	2	0
Riverside Community College	62,345	0	0	0	0	0	27	16	11	0	2
San Bernardino Community College	29,194	0	0	0	0	0	23	2	19	2	0
San Diego State University	37,838	10	0	3	3	4	222	70	140	12	2
San Francisco State University	33,236	2	0	1	1	0	87	25	58	4	0
San Jose/Evergreen Community College	29,405	1	0	0	0	1	17	0	16	1	0
Sonoma County Junior College	29,046	0	0	0	0	0	24	7	17	0	0
Sonoma State University	10,360	4	0	1	0	3	27	6	21	0	0
State Center Community College District	68,277	0	0	0	0	0	57	10	46	1	1
University of California											
Berkeley	45,183	71	0	11	8	52	366	50	278	38	3
Davis	40,623	5	0	3	0	2	686	100	565	21	2
Irvine	38,105	31	0	6	3	22	442	27	404	11	1
Los Angeles	47,103	31	0	9	4	18	548	142	383	23	10
Medical Center, Sacramento[6]		3	0	0	0	3	99	2	93	4	0
Merced	8,939	2	0	2	0	0	12	5	5	2	0
Riverside	25,816	3	0	1	0	2	220	46	159	15	1
San Diego	39,811	12	0	3	2	7	436	35	365	36	0
San Francisco	3,185	9	1	2	0	6	384	35	336	13	3
Santa Barbara	27,685	23	0	17	0	6	311	33	274	4	1

Table 9. Offenses Known to Law Enforcement, by Selected State and University and College, 2020—Continued

(Number.)

State and university/college	Student enrollment[1]	Violent crime	Murder and nonnegligent manslaughter	Rape[2]	Robbery	Aggravated assault	Property crime	Burglary	Larceny-theft	Motor vehicle theft	Arson[3]
Santa Cruz	20,839	8	0	3	1	4	104	23	76	5	4
Ventura County Community College District	50,235	3	0	0	1	2	31	15	15	1	1
West Valley-Mission College	24,630	1	0	1	0	0	11	3	7	1	0
COLORADO											
Adams State University	3,696	0	0	0	0	0	5	0	5	0	0
Aims Community College	8,895	0	0	0	0	0	1	0	0	1	0
Arapahoe Community College	15,565	0	0	0	0	0	0	0	0	0	0
Auraria Higher Education Center[6]		5	1	1	2	1	73	9	58	6	0
Colorado School of Mines	6,639	1	0	1	0	0	45	2	41	2	2
Fort Lewis College	3,743	1	0	1	0	0	11	1	10	0	0
Pikes Peak Community College	18,701	0	0	0	0	0	8	0	8	0	0
Red Rocks Community College	11,967	0	0	0	0	0	3	0	3	0	0
University of Colorado											
Boulder	40,353	18	0	4	2	12	404	19	374	11	8
Colorado Springs	17,001	3	0	3	0	0	34	0	30	4	0
Denver	32,857	2	0	0	0	2	115	5	65	45	1
University of Northern Colorado	15,950	1	0	1	0	0	102	10	86	6	0
CONNECTICUT											
Central Connecticut State University	13,866	1	0	1	0	0	6	0	6	0	0
Eastern Connecticut State University	5,714	2	0	1	0	1	8	0	8	0	0
Southern Connecticut State University	11,492	1	0	1	0	0	9	0	9	0	0
University of Connecticut, Storrs, Avery Point, and Hartford[6]		2	0	2	0	0	53	10	39	4	2
Western Connecticut State University	6,535	0	0	0	0	0	4	0	4	0	0
Yale University[5]	14,389	3	0	1	2	0	228	27	199	2	0
DELAWARE											
Delaware State University	5,003	6	0	5	0	1	57	15	42	0	0
University of Delaware	25,885	4	0	4	0	0	67	4	62	1	0
FLORIDA											
Florida A&M University	11,100	0	0	0	0	0	71	35	35	1	0
Florida Atlantic University	36,970	6	0	4	0	2	34	8	22	4	0
Florida Gulf Coast University	16,940	5	0	3	0	2	20	1	19	0	0
Florida International University	72,780	4	0	2	1	1	74	3	70	1	0
Florida Polytechnic University	1,487	0	0	0	0	0	0	0	0	0	0
Florida Southwestern State College	21,995	0	0	0	0	0	3	1	2	0	0
Florida State University											
Panama City[6]		0	0	0	0	0	2	1	1	0	1
Tallahassee	46,825	5	0	3	0	2	171	8	133	30	0
New College of Florida	865	1	0	1	0	0	18	1	17	0	0
Northwest Florida State College	7,691	0	0	0	0	0	1	0	1	0	0
Pensacola State College	13,758	0	0	0	0	0	9	2	7	0	0
Santa Fe College	19,711	0	0	0	0	0	5	0	5	0	0
Tallahassee Community College	16,760	2	0	1	0	1	13	0	12	1	0
University of Central Florida	80,378	7	0	4	1	2	146	13	128	5	0
University of Florida	58,749	9	0	4	3	2	237	17	202	18	0
University of North Florida	20,094	3	0	1	1	1	67	10	57	0	0
University of South Florida											
St. Petersburg	5,694	1	0	1	0	0	13	0	12	1	0
Tampa	51,808	8	0	3	3	2	172	10	153	9	1
University of West Florida	16,122	1	0	1	0	0	19	0	16	3	0
GEORGIA											
Agnes Scott College[5]	1,076	0	0	0	0	0	10	4	6	0	0
Albany Technical College[5]	4,583	0	0	0	0	0	0	0	0	0	0
Athens Technical College	6,365	0	0	0	0	0	0	0	0	0	0
Atlanta Metropolitan State College	3,277	0	0	0	0	0	0	0	0	0	0
Atlanta Technical College[5]	5,725	0	0	0	0	0	3	0	3	0	0
Augusta University[5]	9,575	2	0	0	0	2	100	3	97	0	0
Bainbridge State College5, [6]		0	0	0	0	0	0	0	0	0	0
Chattahoochee Technical College[5]	15,030	0	0	0	0	0	0	0	0	0	0
Emory University[5]	16,024	14	0	6	1	7	208	11	193	4	0
Fort Valley State University[5]	3,049	4	0	2	0	2	9	1	8	0	0
Georgia College and State University[5]	8,066	1	0	1	0	0	31	1	22	8	0
Georgia Gwinnett College[5]	15,382	0	0	0	0	0	11	1	10	0	0
Georgia Institute of Technology[5]	38,951	7	0	1	2	4	200	30	148	22	0
Georgia Southern University[5]	30,628	0	0	0	0	0	35	2	31	2	0
Georgia Southwestern State University	3,646	4	0	4	0	0	5	0	5	0	0
Georgia State University[5]	40,505	6	0	0	2	4	99	2	94	3	2
Gwinnett Technical College[5]	12,364	0	0	0	0	0	0	0	0	0	0
Kennesaw State University[5]	41,654	8	0	4	1	3	43	5	36	2	0
Mercer University	9,767	1	0	0	1	0	34	2	26	6	1
Middle Georgia State University	9,654	2	0	1	0	1	19	0	17	2	0
Piedmont College[5]	3,357	0	0	0	0	0	0	0	0	0	0
Southern Crescent Technical College[5]	7,088	0	0	0	0	0	4	4	0	0	0
Spelman College[5]	2,206	0	0	0	0	0	3	0	2	1	0
University of North Georgia[5]	23,032	2	0	2	0	0	10	2	8	0	0
University of West Georgia[5]	16,353	4	0	1	1	2	18	1	17	0	1
West Georgia Technical College[5]	10,043	0	0	0	0	0	2	0	2	0	0

Table 9. Offenses Known to Law Enforcement, by Selected State and University and College, 2020—Continued

(Number.)

State and university/college	Student enrollment[1]	Violent crime	Murder and nonnegligent manslaughter	Rape[2]	Robbery	Aggravated assault	Property crime	Burglary	Larceny-theft	Motor vehicle theft	Arson[3]
ILLINOIS[7]											
College of DuPage	41,901	0	0	0	0	0		0		0	0
College of Lake County	22,809	0	0	0	0	0		0		0	0
Eastern Illinois University	9,526	6	0	3	0	3		1		0	0
Elgin Community College	14,547	0	0	0	0	0		0		0	0
Governors State University	5,954	0	0	0	0	0		0		0	0
Illinois State University	22,907	8	0	6	0	2		3		0	0
Joliet Junior College	23,030	3	0	0	0	3		0		0	0
Lake Land College	17,396	0	0	0	0	0		0		0	0
Lewis University	7,875	0	0	0	0	0		1		0	0
McHenry County College	10,941	0	0	0	0	0		0		0	0
Morton College	6,951	0	0	0	0	0		0		0	0
Northeastern Illinois University	9,993	0	0	0	0	0		0		0	0
Northern Illinois University	19,437	6	0	2	1	3		3		1	1
Oakton Community College	17,553	0	0	0	0	0		0		0	0
Rend Lake College	4,370	0	0	0	0	0		0		0	0
Rock Valley College	9,920	0	0	0	0	0		0		0	0
Southern Illinois University, School of Medicine[6]		0	0	0	0	0		0		0	0
South Suburban College	8,839	0	0	0	0	0		0		0	0
Southwestern Illinois College	15,299	0	0	0	0	0		2		0	0
Triton College	17,385	0	0	0	0	0		0		0	0
University of Chicago,Cook County	19,659	20	0	0	17	3		12		3	1
University of Illinois											
Chicago	34,529	17	0	2	4	11		19		2	0
Urbana	54,985	10	0	3	5	2		7		4	3
Waubonsee Community College	16,110	0	0	0	0	0		0		0	0
INDIANA											
Indiana State University	15,388	14	0	0	0	14	68	1	65	2	
Indiana University											
Kokomo	3,786	0	0	0	0	0	1	0	1	0	0
South Bend	6,168	1	0	0	0	1	15	2	13	0	1
Purdue University	47,412	3	0	3	0	0	231	20	205	6	
University of Indianapolis	6,850	3	0	1	0	2	76	2	67	7	0
IOWA											
Iowa State University	37,944	3	0	2	0	1	104	11	87	6	0
University of Iowa	35,339	43	0	13	1	29	145	13	130	2	0
University of Northern Iowa	13,040	5	0	3	0	2	26	1	25	0	0
KANSAS											
Butler Community College	12,005	1	0	0	0	1	0	0	0	0	0
Garden City Community College	2,470	0	0	0	0	0	4	1	3	0	0
Kansas City Kansas Community College	8,463	0	0	0	0	0	12	0	10	2	0
Kansas State University	24,546	1	0	0	0	1	95	5	89	1	0
Pittsburg State University	8,009	0	0	0	0	0	39	0	39	0	0
University of Kansas											
Main Campus	31,088	2	0	1	0	1	81	5	70	6	0
Medical Center[6]		26	0	1	1	24	175	0	168	7	0
KENTUCKY											
Eastern Kentucky University	18,481	2	0	2	0	0	83	11	69	3	0
Morehead State University	11,462	0	0	0	0	0	17	1	16	0	0
Murray State University	10,714	2	0	2	0	0	26	3	22	1	0
Northern Kentucky University	17,151	0	0	0	0	0	19	3	15	1	1
University of Kentucky	30,981	7	0	4	2	1	411	15	383	13	2
University of Louisville	24,770	13	0	1	8	4	191	17	157	17	4
Western Kentucky University	23,228	4	0	3	1	0	76	5	69	2	0
LOUISIANA											
Delgado Community College	20,166	0	0	0	0	0	3	1	2	0	0
Grambling State University	5,979	6	0	0	0	6	28	5	23	0	0
Louisiana State University											
Baton Rouge	33,758	9	0	4	3	2	179	38	133	8	0
Health Sciences Center, New Orleans	3,204	0	0	0	0	0	0	0	0	0	0
Shreveport	9,963	0	0	0	0	0	12	5	7	0	0
Louisiana Tech University	13,345	1	0	1	0	0	54	1	53	0	1
McNeese State University[5]	8,553	1	0	0	0	1	21	3	17	1	0
Nicholls State University	7,520	1	0	0	0	1	19	1	18	0	0
Southeastern Louisiana University	17,352	7	0	4	1	2	47	3	43	1	0
Southern University and A&M College, Baton Rouge	7,747	1	0	0	0	1	60	8	49	3	0
Tulane University	14,768	0	0	0	0	0	126	27	96	3	2
University of Louisiana											
Lafayette	19,221	6	0	1	1	4	82	12	69	1	1
Monroe	10,030	4	0	2	0	2	24	0	23	1	0
University of New Orleans	10,089	6	0	2	0	4	93	17	76	0	0
MAINE											
University of Maine											
Farmington[5]	2,461	1	0	1	0	0	3	0	3	0	0
Orono	13,091	0	0	0	0	0	32	5	27	0	0
University of Southern Maine	10,606	2	0	2	0	0	17	0	16	1	0

Table 9. Offenses Known to Law Enforcement, by Selected State and University and College, 2020—Continued

(Number.)

State and university/college	Student enrollment[1]	Violent crime	Murder and nonnegligent manslaughter	Rape[2]	Robbery	Aggravated assault	Property crime	Burglary	Larceny-theft	Motor vehicle theft	Arson[3]
MARYLAND[4]											
Bowie State University	7,069	0	0	0	0	0	9	3	6	0	0
University of Maryland, Baltimore County	15,726	0	0	0	0	0	36	10	23	3	0
MASSACHUSETTS											
Assumption College	2,659	2	0	2	0	0	4	0	4	0	0
Babson College	4,095	2	0	0	0	2	14	1	13	0	0
Becker College	2,160	0	0	0	0	0	6	2	4	0	0
Bentley University	5,735	2	0	1	0	1	13	2	11	0	0
Boston College	15,981	1	0	1	0	0	41	9	31	1	1
Boston University	42,779	10	0	6	1	3	232	15	213	4	0
Bridgewater State University	13,583	1	0	1	0	0	9	0	9	0	0
Bristol Community College[5]	9,979	0	0	0	0	0	1	0	1	0	0
Bunker Hill Community College	18,239	0	0	0	0	0	6	0	6	0	
Clark University[5]	3,473	0	0	0	0	0	21	7	14	0	0
College of the Holy Cross	3,005	0	0	0	0	0	11	6	4	1	
Dean College	1,632	0	0	0	0	0	4	0	4	0	0
Emerson College	5,028	2	0	0	1	1	23	1	22	0	
Endicott College[5]	6,885	0	0	0	0	0	2	0	2	0	
Fitchburg State University	11,130	2	0	2	0	0	9	1	8	0	0
Gordon College[5]	2,397	1	0	1	0	0	24	0	24	0	
Greenfield Community College[5]	2,517	0	0	0	0	0	0	0	0	0	0
Harvard University	41,987	4	0	2	0	2	281	57	220	4	
Holyoke Community College	6,832	0	0	0	0	0	5	0	5	0	0
Lasell College	2,353	1	0	1	0	0	6	1	5	0	0
Massachusetts Bay Community College[5]	6,946	0	0	0	0	0	0	0	0	0	0
Massachusetts College of Liberal Arts	1,929	1	0	1	0	0	4	0	4	0	0
Massachusetts Institute of Technology	12,321	1	0	1	0	0	115	23	92	0	0
Massasoit Community College	10,162	1	0	0	0	1	2	0	2	0	0
Merrimack College	5,426	3	0	3	0	0	14	2	12	0	0
Mount Holyoke College	2,610	0	0	0	0	0	10	2	8	0	
Mount Wachusett Community College	5,152	0	0	0	0	0	5	1	4	0	
Northeastern University[5]	28,374	11	0	3	2	6	179	8	163	8	1
Quinsigamond Community College	9,527	0	0	0	0	0	2	1	1	0	0
Salem State University	10,069	2	0	2	0	0	12	3	9	0	0
Springfield Technical Community College	6,799	0	0	0	0	0	3	1	2	0	0
Tufts University											
Medford	12,781	0	0	0	0	0	25	6	19	0	0
Suffolk[6]		0	0	0	0	0	14	0	14	0	0
Worcester[6]		0	0	0	0	0	1	0	1	0	0
University of Massachusetts											
Amherst	35,116	1	0	0	0	1	68	9	59	0	0
Harbor Campus, Boston	19,356	0	0	0	0	0	9	0	9	0	0
Medical Center, Worcester	1,227	13	0	3	1	9	24	1	21	2	0
Wentworth Institute of Technology[5]	5,437	1	0	0	0	1	16	0	16	0	
Western New England University[5]	4,048	4	0	0	0	4	15	1	14	0	
Westfield State University	7,421	1	0	0	0	1	4	1	3	0	0
Wheaton College	1,785	2	0	1	0	1	14	7	7	0	0
Worcester Polytechnic Institute	7,505	1	0	1	0	0	21	2	19	0	0
Worcester State University	9,691	1	0	1	0	0	6	0	6	0	0
MICHIGAN											
Central Michigan University	24,917	3	0	0	0	3	37	1	36	0	0
Delta College	10,809	0	0	0	0	0	1	0	1	0	0
Eastern Michigan University	22,327	2	0	1	1	0	36	3	32	1	0
Ferris State University	15,739	5	0	3	1	1	16	3	11	2	0
Grand Rapids Community College	19,391	0	0	0	0	0	12	1	10	1	0
Grand Valley State University	27,752	5	0	5	0	0	30	3	26	1	0
Kalamazoo Valley Community College	11,591	0	0	0	0	0	4	0	4	0	0
Kellogg Community College	7,182	0	0	0	0	0	6	0	6	0	0
Kirtland Community College	1,914	0	0	0	0	0	0	0	0	0	0
Lansing Community College	16,382	0	0	0	0	0	17	1	16	0	0
Macomb Community College	28,017	0	0	0	0	0	12	0	11	1	0
Michigan State University	55,332	20	0	14	0	6	212	18	172	22	0
Michigan Technological University	7,657	0	0	0	0	0	27	0	27	0	0
Mott Community College	10,176	0	0	0	0	0	1	0	1	0	0
Northern Michigan University	9,092	1	0	0	0	1	17	0	17	0	0
Oakland Community College	25,217	0	0	0	0	0	10	0	10	0	0
Oakland University	22,351	1	0	1	0	0	19	0	19	0	0
Saginaw Valley State University	9,491	3	0	1	0	2	18	1	17	0	0
Schoolcraft College	16,388	0	0	0	0	0	3	0	3	0	0
University of Michigan											
Ann Arbor	48,218	39	0	23	2	14	335	11	316	8	0
Dearborn	10,906	0	0	0	0	0	4	0	4	0	0
Flint	8,806	3	0	0	0	3	7	0	7	0	0
Washtenaw Community College	21,182	0	0	0	0	0	6	0	6	0	0
Western Michigan University	25,010	3	0	1	1	1	61	8	51	2	5
MINNESOTA											
University of Minnesota											
Morris[5]	1,658	2	0	2	0	0	3	1	2	0	0
Twin Cities	61,787	22	0	2	13	7	322	26	270	26	3

Table 9. Offenses Known to Law Enforcement, by Selected State and University and College, 2020—Continued

(Number.)

State and university/college	Student enrollment[1]	Violent crime	Murder and nonnegligent manslaughter	Rape[2]	Robbery	Aggravated assault	Property crime	Burglary	Larceny-theft	Motor vehicle theft	Arson[3]
MISSISSIPPI											
Coahoma Community College	2,529	1	0	1	0	0	5	5	0	0	0
Holmes Community College, Goodman[5]	8,352	0	0	0	0	0	8	5	3	0	0
Mississippi State University[5]	24,251	2	0	0	1	1	36	3	30	3	0
University of Mississippi, Oxford[5]	25,133	4	0	4	0	0	22	2	19	1	0
MISSOURI											
Lincoln University	3,114	0	0	0	0	0	21	6	15	0	0
Metropolitan Community College	22,969	0	0	0	0	0	28	4	21	3	0
Mineral Area College	3,606	0	0	0	0	0	0	0	0	0	0
Missouri University of Science and Technology[5]	9,265	2	0	0	0	2	92	6	86	0	0
Southeast Missouri State University[5]	12,645	1	0	1	0	0	23	2	21	0	0
St. Louis Community College, Meramec[5]	27,771	0	0	0	0	0	22	1	20	1	0
University of Central Missouri	15,993	0	0	0	0	0	65	9	52	4	0
University of Missouri											
Columbia[5]	33,333	15	0	7	2	6	164	12	143	9	1
Kansas City	19,166	4	0	0	0	4	33	7	23	3	0
Washington University[5]	17,794	1	0	1	0	0	56	3	53	0	0
						1					
MONTANA											
Montana State University	18,898	3	0	2	0	1	86	5	80	1	0
University of Montana	13,140	9	0	3	1	5	55	3	50	2	1
NEBRASKA											
University of Nebraska, Kearney	7,859	2	0	2	0	0	12	2	10	0	0
NEVADA											
University of Nevada, Reno[5]	24,246	11	0	6	0	5	101	15	80	6	1
NEW HAMPSHIRE											
Plymouth State University	5,868	1	0	1	0	0	17	0	16	1	0
University of New Hampshire	16,673	10	0	7	2	1	60	7	53	0	0
NEW JERSEY											
Brookdale Community College	17,100	0	0	0	0	0	9	0	9	0	0
Essex County College	10,496	0	0	0	0	0	0	0	0	0	0
Kean University	16,738	1	0	1	0	0	17	2	15	0	0
Middlesex County College	16,328	1	0	1	0	0	1	0	1	0	0
Monmouth University	6,704	0	0	0	0	0	4	0	4	0	0
Montclair State University	24,235	1	0	0	0	1	16	1	15	0	0
New Jersey Institute of Technology	13,236	1	0	0	1	0	23	1	21	1	0
Princeton University	8,720	4	0	3	1	0	90	11	69	10	0
Rowan University	23,011	5	0	1	3	1	47	5	41	1	1
Rutgers University											
Camden	8,154	4	0	0	3	1	35	1	34	0	0
Newark	15,897	9	0	2	5	2	138	5	132	1	0
New Brunswick	57,162	8	0	1	2	5	133	14	116	3	0
Stevens Institute of Technology	7,990	0	0	0	0	0	9	1	8	0	0
Stockton University	11,457	3	0	1	0	2	16	0	16	0	0
The College of New Jersey	8,825	1	0	1	0	0	16	0	16	0	0
William Paterson University	12,113	3	0	2	0	1	26	2	24	0	0
NEW MEXICO											
Eastern New Mexico University[5]	7,520	1	0	0	0	1	9	0	8	1	0
New Mexico State University[5]	16,143	5	0	4	0	1	112	25	79	8	0
NEW YORK											
Cornell University[5]	24,189	1	0	0	0	1	142	20	121	1	0
Ithaca College	7,003	7	0	6	1	0	27	3	24	0	
State University of New York Police											
Albany	20,325	0	0	0	0	0	62	11	51	0	0
Alfred	4,166	3	0	2	0	1	14	1	11	2	0
Binghamton	19,454	0	0	0	0	0	87	5	82	0	0
Brockport	9,603	0	0	0	0	0	19	1	18	0	1
Buffalo	35,111	6	0	2	1	3	92	12	79	1	0
Buffalo State College	10,467	6	0	4	0	2	38	5	30	3	0
Canton	4,985	0	0	0	0	0	7	0	7	0	0
Cobleskill	3,065	1	0	1	0	0	6	0	6	0	0
Cortland	7,737	2	0	2	0	0	11	2	9	0	1
Delhi	3,638	0	0	0	0	0	11	1	10	0	0
Downstate Medical	2,092	0	0	0	0	0	17	0	17	0	0
Environmental Science	2,370	0	0	0	0	0	18	1	17	0	0
Maritime	1,947	0	0	0	0	0	11	1	10	0	0
Morrisville	3,345	3	0	0	1	2	27	11	16	0	1
New Paltz	8,895	1	0	1	0	0	20	0	20	0	0
Old Westbury	6,442	2	0	1	1	0	6	1	5	0	0
Oneonta	7,131	0	0	0	0	0	18	0	18	0	0
Optometry	408	0	0	0	0	0	1	0	1	0	0
Oswego	9,381	2	0	2	0	0	36	5	31	0	2
Plattsburgh	6,475	1	0	1	0	0	28	1	27	0	0
Potsdam	3,918	1	0	1	0	0	25	3	22	0	0
Purchase	4,753	0	0	0	0	0	11	3	8	0	0
Stony Brook	30,458	11	0	4	1	6	81	4	76	1	0
Upstate Medical	1,661	6	0	1	0	5	74	4	68	2	0

Table 9. Offenses Known to Law Enforcement, by Selected State and University and College, 2020—Continued

(Number.)

State and university/college	Student enrollment[1]	Violent crime	Murder and nonnegligent manslaughter	Rape[2]	Robbery	Aggravated assault	Property crime	Burglary	Larceny-theft	Motor vehicle theft	Arson[3]
NORTH CAROLINA											
Duke University	18,159	3	0	1	0	2	330	11	298	21	0
East Carolina University	32,028	0	0	0	0	0	54	2	52	0	0
Elon University	7,277	1	0	1	0	0	37	5	31	1	0
Methodist University	2,295	2	0	1	0	1	6	1	5	0	0
North Carolina Central University[5]	9,201	4	0	1	1	2	60	14	43	3	1
North Carolina State University, Raleigh	39,822	19	1	1	2	15	181	44	134	3	1
University of North Carolina											
Asheville	4,358	0	0	0	0	0	17	2	14	1	2
Chapel Hill	32,346	4	0	1	0	3	75	17	53	5	0
Charlotte	34,024	1	0	0	0	1	83	0	80	3	0
Greensboro	22,610	9	0	3	3	3	50	5	43	2	0
Wilmington	19,400	3	0	2	0	1	156	7	146	3	3
Wake Forest University	9,032	1	0	0	1	0	68	5	61	2	0
Western Carolina University	13,342	4	0	3	0	1	39	5	31	3	0
NORTH DAKOTA											
Bismarck State College	4,848	0	0	0	0	0	0	0	0	0	0
North Dakota State College of Science	3,625	0	0	0	0	0	11	0	9	2	0
North Dakota State University	14,503	2	0	1	0	1	58	3	54	1	0
University of North Dakota	17,050	1	0	0	1	0	77	11	64	2	1
OHIO											
Bowling Green State University	20,534	3	0	3	0	0	52	8	44	0	0
Cuyahoga Community College	33,892	1	0	0	0	1	14	2	12	0	0
Kent State University	33,013	3	0	3	0	0	60	2	55	3	0
Miami University	22,010	16	0	14	2	0	75	3	72	0	1
Ohio State University, Columbus	66,178	28	0	11	5	12	337	15	311	11	0
Ohio University[5]	33,920	2	0	2	0	0	56	9	47	0	0
Shawnee State University	3,994	2	0	1	1	0	12	0	12	0	0
University of Akron	21,260	4	1	3	0	0	61	4	54	3	0
University of Cincinnati[5]	43,692	9	0	4	2	3	102	9	88	5	1
University of Toledo	22,439	2	0	1	0	1	46	9	33	4	0
OKLAHOMA											
Bacone College	322	1	0	0	1	0	3	1	2	0	0
Cameron University[5]	5,370	0	0	0	0	0	16	3	13	0	0
East Central University	4,289	2	0	1	1	0	14	2	12	0	0
Eastern Oklahoma State College	1,950	0	0	0	0	0	0	0	0	0	0
Langston University	2,607	1	0	0	0	1	35	7	28	0	1
Mid-America Christian University	2,362	0	0	0	0	0	6	2	4	0	0
Northeastern Oklahoma A&M College[5]	2,456	3	0	3	0	0	25	16	8	1	0
Northeastern State University, Tahlequah	9,277	2	0	1	0	1	16	10	6	0	0
Northwestern Oklahoma State University	2,363	0	0	0	0	0	0	0	0	0	0
Oklahoma City Community College	17,861	1	0	0	0	1	8	0	8	0	0
Oklahoma City University	3,163	1	0	1	0	0	19	3	11	5	0
Oklahoma State University											
Main Campus	27,200	6	0	4	0	2	145	13	129	3	0
Okmulgee	3,167	3	0	0	0	3	6	0	6	0	0
Tulsa	1,133	0	0	0	0	0	4	0	4	0	0
Rogers State University[5]	4,383	0	0	0	0	0	4	0	4	0	0
Seminole State College	2,053	0	0	0	0	0	1	0	1	0	0
Southeastern Oklahoma State University	5,698	0	0	0	0	0	5	2	3	0	0
Southwestern Oklahoma State University	5,989	0	0	0	0	0	6	0	6	0	0
Tulsa Community College	22,918	0	0	0	0	0	13	2	10	1	0
University of Central Oklahoma	17,985	2	0	1	0	1	32	7	24	1	0
University of Oklahoma											
Health Sciences Center	3,697	5	0	3	0	2	66	4	55	7	0
Norman	32,189	16	0	15	0	1	251	19	225	7	0
OREGON											
Portland State University	32,445	6	0	0	1	5	328	71	249	8	14
PENNSYLVANIA[4]											
RHODE ISLAND											
Brown University	10,760	0	0	0	0	0	47	8	39	0	0
University of Rhode Island	20,628	3	0	2	0	1	20	3	17	0	0
SOUTH CAROLINA											
Bob Jones University	3,455	0	0	0	0	0	0	0	0	0	0
Clemson University	28,310	1	0	1	0	0	75	6	61	8	0
Coastal Carolina University	11,982	4	0	1	1	2	44	6	37	1	0
College of Charleston	12,907	0	0	0	0	0	26	0	26	0	0
Francis Marion University	4,395	1	0	0	0	1	9	1	8	0	0
Medical University of South Carolina	3,402	11	0	2	1	8	98	2	87	9	0
Orangeburg-Calhoun Technical College	3,385	0	0	0	0	0	0	0	0	0	0
The Citadel	4,458	1	0	1	0	0	27	1	23	3	0
University of South Carolina											
Beaufort	2,375	3	0	3	0	0	6	0	6	0	0
Columbia	37,510	4	0	3	0	1	160	11	136	13	0
Upstate	7,249	0	0	0	0	0	3	0	3	0	5
Winthrop University	6,801	1	0	1	0	0	18	8	9	1	0

Table 9. Offenses Known to Law Enforcement, by Selected State and University and College, 2020—Continued

(Number.)

State and university/college	Student enrollment[1]	Violent crime	Murder and nonnegligent manslaughter	Rape[2]	Robbery	Aggravated assault	Property crime	Burglary	Larceny-theft	Motor vehicle theft	Arson[3]
SOUTH DAKOTA										
South Dakota School of Mines and Technology	3,076	0	0	0	0	0	5	0	5	0	0
South Dakota State University	14,785	0	0	0	0	0	7	0	7	0	0
TENNESSEE										
Austin Peay State University	12,707	3	0	0	1	2	19	4	14	1	0
Chattanooga State Community College	10,630	0	0	0	0	0	2	0	2	0	0
Christian Brothers University	2,330	0	0	0	0	0	7	0	7	0	0
Cleveland State Community College	4,284	0	0	0	0	0	3	2	1	0	0
Columbia State Community College	8,199	0	0	0	0	0	0	0	0	0	0
East Tennessee State University	16,350	6	0	2	0	4	35	4	30	1	1
Jackson State Community College	6,590	0	0	0	0	0	0	0	0	0	0
Lincoln Memorial University	5,587	0	0	0	0	0	3	0	3	0	0
Middle Tennessee State University	25,239	3	0	2	0	1	51	9	41	1	0
Motlow State Community College	8,577	0	0	0	0	0	1	0	1	0	0
Nashville State Community College	11,161	0	0	0	0	0	0	0	0	0	0
Northeast State Community College	7,465	0	0	0	0	0	2	0	2	0	0
Pellissippi State Community College	15,089	0	0	0	0	0	6	0	6	0	0
Roane State Community College	7,178	0	0	0	0	0	3	1	2	0	0
Southwest Tennessee Community College	13,176	0	0	0	0	0	7	2	4	1	0
Tennessee State University	8,723	2	0	2	0	0	20	3	15	2	0
Tennessee Technological University	11,154	0	0	0	0	0	74	3	69	2	0
University of Memphis	24,603	5	0	0	2	3	76	15	56	5	0
University of Tennessee											
Chattanooga	12,718	3	0	1	1	1	121	16	102	3	1
Health Science Center	3,412	1	0	0	0	1	22	2	20	0	1
Knoxville	31,477	4	0	2	1	1	120	16	93	11	0
Martin	8,264	4	0	4	0	0	16	0	16	0	0
University of the South	2,004	6	0	3	0	3	57	18	37	2	0
Vanderbilt University	13,634	12	0	4	3	5	323	9	308	6	1
Volunteer State Community College	11,772	0	0	0	0	0	3	0	3	0	0
Walters State Community College	7,739	0	0	0	0	0	4	1	3	0	0
TEXAS										
Alamo Colleges District	101,122	2	0	0	1	1	89	20	61	8	0
Amarillo College[5]	12,510	0	0	0	0	0	10	5	5	0	0
Angelo State University	11,737	2	0	2	0	0	10	0	10	0	0
Austin Community College District	58,856	2	0	0	0	2	15	2	13	0	1
Baylor Health Care System5, [6]		11	0	2	2	7	298	4	280	14	0
Baylor University, Waco	18,956	1	0	1	0	0	112	6	101	5	1
Brazosport College[5]	6,278	0	0	0	0	0	0	0	0	0	0
Dallas County Community College District	167,464	1	0	1	0	0	21	3	17	1	1
El Paso Community College	38,292	0	0	0	0	0	10	0	10	0	0
Hardin-Simmons University	2,555	0	0	0	0	0	21	3	18	0	0
Houston Community College[5]	81,570	1	0	0	0	1	54	4	46	4	0
Kilgore College	7,108	0	0	0	0	0	7	2	5	0	0
Lamar University, Beaumont	19,727	0	0	0	0	0	41	5	33	3	0
Lone Star College System District	109,742	0	0	0	0	0	14	4	7	3	0
Prairie View A&M University	10,565	7	0	4	1	2	77	24	51	2	0
Rice University	7,542	1	0	0	1	0	101	14	80	7	0
Southern Methodist University	12,825	6	0	3	1	2	109	13	92	4	0
Stephen F. Austin State University	14,948	2	0	1	0	1	22	0	22	0	0
St. Mary's University	3,899	1	0	1	0	0	16	0	13	3	0
Sul Ross State University	2,755	0	0	0	0	0	2	0	2	0	0
Tarleton State University[5]	15,191	6	0	6	0	0	37	5	31	1	0
Texas A&M University											
College Station[5]	73,267	12	0	4	1	7	231	16	188	27	0
Commerce	14,618	2	0	1	0	1	32	3	29	0	0
Texas Southern University	10,979	6	0	2	1	3	91	11	72	8	0
Texas State Technical College, Waco[5]	14,746	5	0	2	1	2	35	6	28	1	0
Texas State University, San Marcos[5]	42,780	3	0	1	0	2	51	15	32	4	0
Texas Tech University, Lubbock	41,153	4	0	3	0	1	232	10	214	8	1
Texas Woman's University	19,075	0	0	0	0	0	18	3	14	1	0
Tyler Junior College	16,477	3	0	2	0	1	16	1	15	0	0
University of Houston											
Central Campus[5]	51,999	12	0	5	4	3	272	26	208	38	0
Downtown Campus[5]	17,682	0	0	0	0	0	3	0	3	0	0
University of North Texas, Denton	43,963	6	0	5	0	1	120	8	107	5	0
University of Texas											
Arlington[5]	60,035	5	0	2	2	1	88	8	75	5	0
Austin[5]	55,128	5	0	3	0	2	216	21	185	10	0
Dallas[5]	31,419	0	0	0	0	0	63	4	51	8	0
El Paso[5]	29,881	1	0	0	0	1	32	6	24	2	0
Health Science Center, San Antonio	3,881	1	0	0	0	1	18	0	16	2	0
Health Science Center, Tyler[5]	98	0	0	0	0	0	8	0	7	1	0
Houston	7,104	6	0	2	1	3	263	7	243	13	0
Permian Basin[5]	8,165	2	0	1	0	1	17	1	16	0	0
Rio Grande Valley[5]	33,766	1	0	1	0	0	27	1	25	1	0
San Antonio[5]	35,755	3	0	2	1	0	64	5	57	2	0
Southwestern Medical School[5]	2,514	2	0	1	1	0	170	6	147	17	0
Tyler[5]	12,289	0	0	0	0	0	16	4	12	0	0
West Texas A&M University	11,875	1	0	1	0	0	22	0	22	0	0

Table 9. Offenses Known to Law Enforcement, by Selected State and University and College, 2020—Continued

(Number.)

State and university/college	Student enrollment[1]	Violent crime	Murder and nonnegligent manslaughter	Rape[2]	Robbery	Aggravated assault	Property crime	Burglary	Larceny-theft	Motor vehicle theft	Arson[3]
UTAH										
Brigham Young University	39,233	4	0	1	0	3	119	1	117	1	0
Dixie State University	12,263	1	0	1	0	0	27	0	25	2	0
Southern Utah University	14,369	1	0	1	0	0	15	0	13	2	0
Utah State University											
Eastern[6]		0	0	0	0	0	5	0	5	0	0
Logan	32,963	1	0	1	0	0	35	4	29	2	0
VERMONT										
University of Vermont	15,698	2	0	2	0	0	77	4	72	1	1
VIRGINIA										
Christopher Newport University	5,117	0	0	0	0	0	43	2	38	3	1
College of William and Mary	9,765	0	0	0	0	0	48	3	45	0	0
Emory and Henry College	1,340	0	0	0	0	0	0	0	0	0	0
George Mason University	48,678	0	0	0	0	0	42	1	41	0	0
James Madison University	24,152	5	0	4	0	1	59	4	54	1	0
Norfolk State University	5,806	8	0	3	2	3	32	0	30	2	0
Old Dominion University	28,046	13	0	1	7	5	126	4	94	28	0
Radford University	11,085	8	0	5	3	0	33	1	32	0	3
University of Virginia	28,593	18	0	8	2	8	119	7	108	4	0
University of Virginia's College at Wise	3,376	0	0	0	0	0	5	0	4	1	0
Virginia Commonwealth University	33,462	17	0	3	2	12	290	10	273	7	4
Virginia Military Institute	1,738	2	0	1	1	0	13	2	11	0	0
Virginia Polytechnic Institute and State University	36,882	3	0	1	0	2	130	7	123	0	0
WASHINGTON										
Central Washington University	17,678	2	0	1	0	1	50	2	48	0	0
Eastern Washington University	15,961	1	0	0	0	1	14	2	10	2	1
Evergreen State College	4,036	0	0	0	0	0	4	0	4	0	0
University of Washington	56,315	16	0	5	2	9	456	101	337	18	1
Washington State University											
Pullman	35,149	4	0	3	0	1	28	4	24	0	0
Vancouver[6]		1	0	0	1	0	3	3	0	0	0
Western Washington University	17,966	1	0	1	0	0	46	9	36	1	1
WEST VIRGINIA										
West Virginia University, Morgantown	29,323	6	1	3	1	1	83	8	75	0	0
WISCONSIN										
Marquette University	12,285	34	0	1	16	17	423	35	346	42	0
University of Wisconsin											
Eau Claire	12,637	0	0	0	0	0	30	0	30	0	0
Green Bay	10,185	0	0	0	0	0	12	0	12	0	0
La Crosse	11,500	1	0	1	0	0	16	0	16	0	0
Madison	47,392	9	2	1	0	6	159	19	136	4	1
Oshkosh	19,257	0	0	0	0	0	25	1	24	0	0
Parkside	5,031	0	0	0	0	0	4	0	4	0	0
River Falls	6,847	1	0	0	0	1	26	2	24	0	0
Stevens Point	10,201	2	0	2	0	0	25	0	25	0	0
Stout	10,113	2	0	0	0	2	59	2	57	0	0
Superior	3,181	0	0	0	0	0	18	0	18	0	0
Whitewater	15,155	0	0	0	0	0	12	0	12	0	0
WYOMING										
University of Wyoming	13,926	0	0	0	0	0	40	1	38	1	0

NOTE: Caution should be exercised in making any intercampus comparisons or ranking schools because university/college crime statistics are affected by a variety of factors. These include demographic characteristics of the surrounding community, ratio of male to female students, number of on-campus residents, accessibility of the campus to outside visitors, size of enrollment, etc.
1 The student enrollment figures provided by the United States Department of Education are for the 2019 school year, the most recent available. The enrollment figures include full-time and part-time students.   2 The figures shown in this column for the offense of rape were reported using only the revised Uniform Crime Reporting definition of rape. See chapter notes for more detail.   3 The FBI does not publish arson data unless it receives data from either the agency or the state for all 12 months of the calendar year.   4 Limited data for 2019 were available for Alabama, Maryland, and Pennsylvania.   5 Because of changes in the state/local agency's reporting practices, figures are not comparable to previous years' data.   6 Student enrollment figures were not available.   7 The FBI determined that the agency's data were underreported. Consequently, those data are not included in this table.

Table 10. Offenses Known to Law Enforcement, by Selected State Metropolitan and Nonmetropolitan Counties, 2020

(Number.)

State/county	Violent crime	Murder and nonnegligent manslaughter	Rape[1]	Robbery	Aggravated assault	Property crime	Burglary	Larceny-theft	Motor vehicle theft	Arson[2]
ALABAMA[3]										
Metropolitan Counties										
Autauga	59	3	14	3	39	267	53	178	36	
Nonmetropolitan Counties	67	1	12	2	52	313	80	179	54	
Clarke	42	2	6	2	32	53	27	17	9	
Marengo	26	6	2	1	17	88	27	42	19	
ARIZONA										
Metropolitan Counties										
Mohave	153	11	10	7	125	1,637	445	1,018	174	
Pima[4]	922	23	59	145	695	7,020	1,036	5,494	490	64
Pinal	269	7	2	18	242	1,438	328	921	189	12
Yavapai	193	1	15	2	175	837	158	578	101	
Yuma	155	8	25	6	116	830	243	480	107	11
Nonmetropolitan Counties										
Gila	186	6	4	2	174	370	52	236	82	
Graham	9	0	0	0	9	98	17	70	11	
Greenlee	4	1	2	0	1	27	13	11	3	0
Navajo	46	3	0	1	42	261	101	116	44	
Santa Cruz	3	0	0	0	3	104	16	67	21	
ARKANSAS										
Metropolitan Counties										
Benton	149	1	21	4	123	494	191	238	65	3
Cleveland	40	0	2	1	37	111	40	58	13	0
Craighead	55	0	9	3	43	305	125	143	37	7
Crawford	46	0	3	0	43	214	32	161	21	1
Crittenden	158	6	24	9	119	236	63	145	28	9
Faulkner	155	1	25	2	127	791	172	496	123	8
Franklin	63	4	6	0	53	144	57	68	19	0
Garland	295	0	38	10	247	1,299	544	621	134	0
Grant	19	0	5	2	12	212	37	164	11	0
Jefferson	121	1	16	6	98	359	81	211	67	4
Lincoln	3	0	2	0	1	28	4	18	6	0
Little River	24	0	5	0	19	67	11	41	15	2
Lonoke	108	4	18	2	84	471	71	284	116	4
Madison	63	0	13	2	48	111	35	60	16	4
Miller	54	0	12	1	41	198	69	105	24	0
Perry	39	0	4	0	35	93	19	74	0	0
Poinsett	50	0	10	2	38	118	38	67	13	4
Pulaski	641	7	33	29	572	1,595	318	1,050	227	18
Saline	185	0	25	7	153	649	256	293	100	5
Sebastian	51	0	7	1	43	141	40	86	15	3
Washington	190	3	20	1	166	571	137	364	70	3
Nonmetropolitan Counties										
Arkansas	22	0	2	0	20	78	6	46	26	1
Ashley	23	1	2	1	19	113	16	79	18	1
Baxter	66	4	17	0	45	493	94	351	48	2
Boone	195	4	45	2	144	205	45	127	33	2
Bradley	14	0	2	0	12	49	25	21	3	1
Calhoun	13	0	2	0	11	50	19	25	6	0
Carroll	41	2	1	0	38	149	27	78	44	5
Chicot	4	0	2	0	2	78	12	66	0	1
Clark	12	0	4	0	8	56	21	29	6	1
Cleburne	153	1	16	2	134	311	104	175	32	13
Columbia	41	3	2	0	36	81	16	56	9	1
Conway	56	0	6	0	50	217	38	160	19	7
Drew	21	2	3	2	14	117	42	60	15	2
Fulton	25	1	5	0	19	59	0	52	7	2
Hempstead	41	0	7	3	31	138	25	92	21	0
Howard	18	1	2	1	14	29	16	12	1	2
Independence	196	2	40	6	148	421	119	248	54	13
Izard	60	0	10	1	49	192	68	112	12	1
Jackson	37	1	8	2	26	133	9	86	38	0
Johnson	81	0	19	2	60	94	42	45	7	1
Lee	11	1	2	0	8	110	27	67	16	11
Logan	53	0	4	1	48	171	48	103	20	1
Mississippi	37	0	4	1	32	319	114	148	57	3
Monroe	7	0	2	0	5	22	4	16	2	0
Nevada	12	0	2	3	7	23	11	10	2	0
Pike	26	0	7	0	19	133	30	99	4	3
Polk	61	0	5	0	56	59	12	45	2	0
Pope	84	0	14	1	69	259	82	143	34	5
Prairie	4	0	2	1	1	55	13	37	5	0
Randolph	30	1	9	0	20	107	22	73	12	2
Scott	25	2	1	1	21	49	18	25	6	3
Searcy	16	0	2	0	14	15	11	4	0	0
Sevier	20	0	7	0	13	61	23	29	9	1

Table 10. Offenses Known to Law Enforcement, by Selected State Metropolitan and Nonmetropolitan Counties, 2020—Continued

(Number.)

State/county	Violent crime	Murder and nonnegligent manslaughter	Rape[1]	Robbery	Aggravated assault	Property crime	Burglary	Larceny-theft	Motor vehicle theft	Arson[2]
St. Francis	35	1	8	4	22	164	64	88	12	2
Union	61	0	3	3	55	238	71	140	27	0
Van Buren	43	0	1	0	42	151	36	88	27	6
White	207	4	39	8	156	672	166	422	84	10
Yell	52	2	9	2	39	148	48	85	15	7
CALIFORNIA										
Metropolitan Counties										
Alameda	700	5	27	162	506	2,286	369	1,165	752	22
Butte	341	5	44	27	265	1,120	422	674	24	5
Contra Costa	298	4	14	82	198	1,178	304	827	47	5
El Dorado	219	0	45	30	144	1,735	361	1,353	21	5
Fresno	1,137	10	56	135	936	3,035	1,067	1,374	594	248
Imperial	200	1	16	9	174	711	239	372	100	35
Kern	3,369	59	143	454	2,713	8,708	2,445	3,599	2,664	279
Kings	103	2	15	18	68	377	119	242	16	2
Los Angeles	5,605	96	270	1,256	3,983	15,554	2,381	8,323	4,850	285
Madera	231	4	22	30	175	673	118	528	27	4
Marin	90	1	7	13	69	812	151	656	5	1
Merced	467	3	19	30	415	1,357	360	797	200	10
Monterey	221	3	30	25	163	1,084	242	803	39	5
Napa	57	0	11	4	42	336	147	175	14	4
Orange	254	1	24	27	202	909	106	682	121	4
Placer	220	2	19	24	175	952	247	674	31	5
Riverside	964	43	32	149	740	6,901	1,242	3,969	1,690	25
Sacramento	2,579	48	186	560	1,785	7,753	2,228	5,349	176	90
San Benito	33	1	5	2	25	158	41	100	17	0
San Bernardino	1,859	23	104	133	1,599	3,251	902	1,421	928	72
San Diego	1,435	19	100	182	1,134	3,894	742	2,318	834	38
San Joaquin	822	16	18	150	638	2,652	600	1,880	172	44
San Luis Obispo	260	1	28	12	219	1,065	314	718	33	6
San Mateo	319	2	85	74	158	2,896	334	2,172	390	13
Santa Barbara	225	0	34	32	159	1,616	277	1,279	60	15
Santa Clara	323	1	46	26	250	1,296	188	854	254	0
Santa Cruz	315	6	29	39	241	1,566	348	1,172	46	9
Shasta	393	7	22	23	341	666	303	319	44	5
Solano	115	4	15	12	84	419	126	204	89	14
Sonoma	586	1	56	39	490	986	357	621	8	26
Stanislaus	436	/	20	117	292	1,171	365	764	42	8
Sutter	69	1	4	12	52	530	145	318	67	2
Tulare[5]	344	9	29	65	241	1,884	603	1,260	21	0
Ventura	98	1	20	13	64	730	129	517	84	13
Yolo	64	2	5	4	53	266	87	157	22	2
Yuba	256	2	17	40	197	880	247	608	25	24
Nonmetropolitan Counties										
Alpine	19	0	0	0	19	13	4	9	0	0
Amador	90	2	5	7	76	312	92	218	2	3
Calaveras	146	0	18	5	123	557	209	335	13	0
Colusa	24	0	3	3	18	165	55	108	2	3
Del Norte	121	2	44	15	60	313	95	212	6	13
Glenn	128	2	14	5	107	288	85	170	33	1
Humboldt	288	5	23	33	227	967	364	577	26	18
Inyo	101	1	7	8	85	165	67	97	1	3
Lake	193	1	10	11	171	465	237	224	4	11
Lassen	70	0	3	7	60	106	55	48	3	2
Mariposa	61	0	12	1	48	183	54	125	4	0
Mendocino	187	6	22	12	147	664	187	474	3	19
Modoc	23	1	0	1	21	31	10	19	2	1
Mono	21	2	3	2	14	58	26	31	1	1
Nevada	116	4	13	10	89	342	146	189	7	1
Plumas	159	1	18	0	140	282	92	186	4	2
Sierra	4	0	0	0	4	17	7	10	0	0
Siskiyou	98	2	13	4	79	154	69	77	8	2
Tehama	161	5	14	12	130	384	131	238	15	1
Trinity	82	2	3	7	70	147	56	86	5	4
Tuolumne	205	0	75	12	118	603	268	328	7	11
COLORADO										
Metropolitan Counties										
Adams	620	3	96	67	454	3,151	397	1,664	1,090	47
Arapahoe	221	0	21	15	185	2,352	402	1,378	572	13
Boulder	80	0	8	8	64	760	175	511	74	8
Clear Creek	9	0	0	0	9	50	5	36	9	1
Douglas	326	3	82	13	228	2,426	370	1,738	318	47
Elbert	12	1	6	1	4	11	1	5	5	1
El Paso	545	9	131	45	360	2,334	389	1,618	327	33
Gilpin	11	0	3	0	8	84	16	61	7	0
Mesa	193	0	41	10	142	1,370	342	848	180	16
Park	38	0	6	0	32	45	15	23	7	1
Pueblo[6]	35	2	0	10	23		216		140	3

Table 10. Offenses Known to Law Enforcement, by Selected State Metropolitan and Nonmetropolitan Counties, 2020—Continued

(Number.)

State/county	Violent crime	Murder and nonnegligent manslaughter	Rape[1]	Robbery	Aggravated assault	Property crime	Burglary	Larceny-theft	Motor vehicle theft	Arson[2]
Teller	31	0	7	1	23	80	21	47	12	0
Weld	204	2	39	0	163	809	143	486	180	13
Nonmetropolitan Counties										
Bent	17	0	4	1	12	112	34	66	12	0
Chaffee	5	0	1	0	4	97	15	61	21	0
Cheyenne	1	0	0	0	1	5	1	3	1	0
Conejos	6	0	3	0	3	38	33	1	4	1
Crowley	5	0	3	0	2	60	20	34	6	1
Custer	12	0	1	3	8	79	24	50	5	2
Delta	12	1	6	1	4	222	80	122	20	7
Dolores	4	0	1	0	3	11	5	3	3	0
Eagle	30	1	10	0	19	110	13	86	11	3
Fremont	39	1	15	0	23	174	49	89	36	2
Garfield	58	0	15	0	43	244	71	132	41	12
Gunnison	3	0	0	0	3	25	3	19	3	0
Hinsdale	0	0	0	0	0	4	0	3	1	0
Huerfano	22	0	2	4	16	158	55	78	25	4
Jackson	6	0	1	0	5	24	10	10	4	0
Kiowa	0	0	0	0	0	4	0	3	1	0
La Plata	32	0	12	1	19	285	110	139	36	4
Las Animas	5	0	1	0	4	72	21	38	13	4
Logan	21	1	5	1	14	101	35	50	16	5
Mineral	0	0	0	0	0	0	0	0	0	0
Moffat	8	1	0	0	7	39	16	20	3	0
Montezuma	24	0	2	1	21	149	49	83	17	2
Montrose	36	1	2	1	32	196	27	141	28	3
Morgan	27	0	3	0	24	126	45	63	18	3
Otero	17	0	4	2	11	52	16	24	12	0
Ouray	6	0	1	0	5	26	6	18	2	0
Phillips	1	0	0	0	1	8	0	2	6	0
Pitkin	3	0	1	0	2	26	3	21	2	0
Prowers	9	0	0	0	9	14	3	9	2	1
Rio Blanco	4	0	1	0	3	14	1	13	0	0
Rio Grande	4	0	1	0	3	57	15	40	2	0
Routt	8	1	2	0	5	64	18	40	6	1
San Juan	0	0	0	0	0	4	0	4	0	0
San Miguel	8	0	8	0	0	3	0	1	2	0
Sedgwick	1	0	0	0	1	1	1	0	0	0
Summit	39	0	7	1	31	225	40	162	23	2
Washington	7	0	1	0	6	57	10	32	15	2
Yuma	3	0	1	0	2	62	16	35	11	1
DELAWARE										
Metropolitan Counties										
New Castle County Police Department	934	11	62	128	733	4,466	629	3,247	590	3
FLORIDA										
Metropolitan Counties										
Alachua	911	6	98	133	674	1,838	379	1,280	179	23
Baker	131	2	11	3	115	274	33	212	29	0
Bay	319	4	30	22	263	1,873	378	1,310	185	3
Brevard	518	7	52	52	407	2,925	526	2,138	261	15
Broward	333	8	19	49	257	507	66	396	45	1
Charlotte	278	1	32	19	226	1,376	207	1,060	109	6
Citrus	403	7	25	38	333	1,926	334	1,402	190	6
Clay	491	5	81	70	335	2,420	314	1,928	178	19
Collier	837	5	61	120	651	3,416	377	2,732	307	15
Escambia	1,604	27	198	324	1,055	6,782	1,395	4,743	644	27
Flagler	216	0	27	6	183	758	83	628	47	2
Gadsden	75	3	10	6	56	227	110	96	21	0
Gilchrist	24	0	2	0	22	84	28	47	9	1
Hernando	440	7	51	49	333	2,058	342	1,560	156	23
Highlands	207	5	21	24	157	1,432	259	1,043	130	7
Hillsborough	1,878	37	248	262	1,331	8,728	1,191	6,610	927	39
Indian River	156	3	9	18	126	1,404	129	1,135	140	3
Jefferson	93	0	5	0	88	136	47	75	14	2
Lake	472	12	72	50	338	1,933	401	1,282	250	13
Lee	1,367	22	179	217	949	4,195	677	3,029	489	27
Leon	271	5	27	29	210	1,283	247	923	113	2
Levy	454	1	33	5	415	429	174	205	50	2
Manatee	1,474	8	187	178	1,101	4,342	611	3,331	400	16
Marion	1,094	16	125	73	880	3,781	890	2,436	455	4
Martin	305	5	70	39	191	1,409	170	1,166	73	3
Miami-Dade	6,096	113	410	967	4,606	26,907	2,400	21,458	3,049	113
Nassau	152	1	30	7	114	900	310	490	100	1
Okaloosa	471	3	62	26	380	1,902	236	1,496	170	2
Orange	4,564	69	394	817	3,284	15,877	2,353	11,698	1,826	0
Osceola	732	11	76	110	535	3,974	797	2,893	284	3
Palm Beach	1,438	22	196	230	990	8,539	892	6,745	902	33
Pasco	1,457	14	173	193	1,077	5,516	832	4,154	530	52

Table 10. Offenses Known to Law Enforcement, by Selected State Metropolitan and Nonmetropolitan Counties, 2020—Continued

(Number.)

State/county	Violent crime	Murder and nonnegligent manslaughter	Rape[1]	Robbery	Aggravated assault	Property crime	Burglary	Larceny-theft	Motor vehicle theft	Arson[2]
Pinellas	512	6	100	73	333	3,082	439	2,410	233	19
Polk	1,327	22	78	89	1,138	4,500	792	3,168	540	5
Santa Rosa	221	5	43	15	158	1,276	267	904	105	4
Sarasota	489	3	40	63	383	3,844	553	3,077	214	3
Seminole	438	8	77	51	302	1,852	258	1,463	131	5
St. Johns	293	4	11	23	255	1,654	225	1,300	129	4
St. Lucie	297	6	41	40	210	1,072	186	788	98	8
Sumter	210	2	20	14	174	783	128	571	84	4
Volusia	645	8	91	120	426	1,798	329	1,276	193	11
Wakulla	82	2	7	4	69	421	112	282	27	0
Walton	87	1	16	3	67	680	149	472	59	2
Nonmetropolitan Counties										
Bradford	34	0	3	4	27	76	29	40	7	1
Calhoun	33	3	1	2	27	78	22	44	12	0
Columbia	170	2	18	22	128	802	334	425	43	1
DeSoto	137	2	20	11	104	453	134	284	35	3
Dixie	80	1	8	4	67	139	76	44	19	4
Franklin	32	0	3	0	29	211	44	160	7	0
Glades	33	0	2	2	29	93	17	62	14	0
Gulf	60	0	8	0	52	159	47	103	9	4
Hamilton	46	1	3	5	37	195	69	115	11	0
Hardee	74	1	6	5	62	283	66	181	36	3
Hendry	117	4	6	20	87	550	233	256	61	4
Holmes	57	1	4	0	52	156	47	92	17	1
Lafayette	26	0	0	2	24	21	9	10	2	0
Liberty	6	0	0	0	6	54	6	48	0	0
Madison	127	1	5	3	118	162	46	114	2	0
Monroe	190	3	17	16	154	520	58	437	25	1
Okeechobee	194	4	20	21	149	832	168	582	82	1
Putnam	89	3	14	19	53	745	174	526	45	2
Suwannee	157	1	13	7	136	444	151	260	33	1
Taylor	65	1	6	0	58	208	91	87	30	1
Union	37	1	3	2	31	97	41	45	11	1
Washington	27	1	1	0	25	110	37	52	21	1
GEORGIA										
Metropolitan Counties										
Barrow	98	0	16	10	72	968	144	727	97	7
Bartow[4]	101	4	18	10	69	1,373	171	1,063	139	23
Bibb[4]	1,438	40	56	207	1,135	5,199	886	3,616	697	50
Brantle[4]	36	0	4	3	29	349	90	232	27	5
Brooks[4]	43	2	3	0	38	164	41	100	23	1
Bryan[4]	60	2	16	2	40	191	28	143	20	1
Burke[4]	36	1	2	8	25	221	59	138	24	5
Butts[4]	34	1	6	5	22	185	14	128	43	1
Carroll	172	3	14	16	139	1,094	298	656	140	7
Catoosa[4]	98	0	12	3	83	549	105	372	72	3
Cherokee[4]	144	1	22	12	109	728	123	543	62	2
Clayton County Police Department[4]	1,504	34	128	320	1,022	5,565	791	3,877	897	25
Cobb[4]	26	0	9	1	16	302	1	294	7	1
Cobb County Police Department[4]	1,353	26	138	266	923	7,980	1,007	6,097	876	17
Coweta	647	5	56	17	569	841	145	619	77	4
Crawford[4]	23	2	6	0	15	148	48	89	11	0
Dougherty[4]	1	0	0	0	1	10	0	9	1	0
Dougherty County Police Department[4]	56	1	3	3	49	259	66	143	50	0
Douglas[4]	244	4	16	19	205	1,045	163	749	133	2
Echols	3	0	1	0	2	13	2	8	3	0
Effingham[4]	37	3	6	3	25	277	85	153	39	4
Fayette[4]	38	1	4	3	30	323	53	242	28	2
Floyd[4]	14	0	4	0	10	1	0	1	0	0
Floyd County Police Department[4]	183	3	44	5	131	556	105	380	71	3
Forsyth[4]	132	0	29	13	90	1,103	159	865	79	2
Hall	274	7	41	21	205	1,308	210	938	160	3
Haralson[4]	86	2	9	4	71	340	89	183	68	3
Harris[4]	5	1	0	1	3	94	17	68	9	0
Heard	21	0	1	1	19	118	29	76	13	1
Jasper[4]	38	0	4	1	33	162	30	104	28	5
Jones[4]	45	0	6	3	36	296	47	210	39	3
Lanier[4]	13	0	4	0	9	106	26	68	12	1
Lee[4]	66	2	14	8	42	385	76	259	50	2
Liberty	17	1	4	5	7	165	33	114	18	6
Long[4]	15	3	7	3	2	85	22	45	18	1
Lowndes[4]	141	0	35	18	88	970	150	718	102	8
Madison[4]	74	0	5	1	68	312	81	184	47	9
Marion[4]	6	1	3	0	2	31	7	18	6	1
McDuffie[4]	40	1	7	0	32	149	47	80	22	0
Meriwether	45	1	5	1	38	158	50	84	24	0
Murray[4]	97	2	24	3	68	422	68	316	38	1
Muscogee[4]	4	0	0	0	4	3	0	3	0	0
Newton	279	4	25	29	221	1,214	197	848	169	6

Table 10. Offenses Known to Law Enforcement, by Selected State Metropolitan and Nonmetropolitan Counties, 2020—Continued

(Number.)

State/county	Violent crime	Murder and nonnegligent manslaughter	Rape[1]	Robbery	Aggravated assault	Property crime	Burglary	Larceny-theft	Motor vehicle theft	Arson[2]
Oglethorpe[4]	39	0	2	2	35	125	29	85	11	2
Paulding	375	1	43	17	314	1,279	201	966	112	12
Peach	38	0	8	2	28	177	44	110	23	0
Pickens[4]	61	0	15	1	45	227	41	161	25	0
Pike[4]	31	0	8	5	18	170	27	123	20	1
Spalding[4]	142	2	14	7	119	596	124	382	90	2
Twiggs[4]	15	0	1	0	14	107	21	71	15	4
Walton[4]	40	1	5	4	30	279	24	219	36	0
Whitfield[4]	284	1	28	7	248	1,051	201	738	112	2
Worth[4]	52	1	9	2	40	170	55	82	33	2
Nonmetropolitan Counties										
Atkinson[4]	23	0	1	1	21	76	17	48	11	0
Baldwin[4]	119	3	14	5	97	527	64	405	58	1
Banks[4]	37	0	5	2	30	320	31	273	16	2
Ben Hill[4]	44	1	6	1	36	166	43	108	15	0
Berrien[4]	28	1	10	0	17	151	48	90	13	1
Bleckley[4]	21	1	4	2	14	94	16	62	16	0
Charlton	17	1	3	2	11	55	17	27	11	
Chattooga[4]	23	1	6	1	15	255	42	191	22	1
Clay[4]	8	0	0	1	7	31	9	21	1	0
Cook[4]	17	0	2	0	15	148	39	95	14	0
Crisp	14	0	1	2	11	265	58	196	11	2
Decatur[4]	32	1	9	2	20	263	73	160	30	3
Dodge[4]	22	0	5	2	15	192	88	91	13	0
Early[4]	15	0	0	0	15	77	28	42	7	0
Elbert	21	1	4	1	15	157	46	104	7	2
Franklin[4]	24	0	2	0	22	207	65	115	27	2
Gilmer[4]	91	1	20	2	68	210	52	135	23	2
Gordon	61	0	9	5	47	437	95	296	46	0
Grady[4]	35	1	6	0	28	300	97	161	42	0
Greene[4]	35	2	3	1	29	131	24	89	18	0
Habersham[4]	16	0	5	1	10	259	53	176	30	1
Hancock[4]	16	0	4	2	10	48	5	38	5	0
Irwin[4]	8	1	0	2	5	76	14	50	12	3
Jackson[4]	81	1	9	4	67	643	120	455	68	8
Jeff Davis[4]	23	0	3	1	19	63	12	38	13	0
Jenkins[4]	7	0	1	0	6	37	11	22	4	1
Laurens	74	3	9	4	58	418	100	271	47	3
Lumpkin[4]	55	0	6	1	48	235	29	192	14	2
Mitchell[4]	21	0	7	0	14	251	58	153	40	2
Pierce	48	0	4	6	38	277	69	180	28	2
Polk	5	0	0	0	5	1	1	0	0	0
Polk County Police Department[4]	44	0	3	4	37	459	99	296	64	7
Pulaski[4]	35	1	5	4	25	192	44	129	19	2
Rabun[4]	9	0	3	1	5	170	29	125	16	0
Seminole[4]	13	0	1	2	10	75	21	49	5	2
Sumter	19	1	2	3	13	104	43	55	6	1
Tattnall[4]	26	0	9	2	15	201	58	111	32	2
Thomas[4]	63	1	14	2	46	409	99	269	41	2
Tift	178	0	8	14	156	592	119	405	68	0
Towns[4]	14	0	1	0	13	60	15	41	4	0
Treutlen[4]	2	0	0	1	1	47	12	28	7	2
Turner[4]	10	0	0	0	10	60	21	34	5	0
Union[4]	12	0	3	0	9	217	41	160	16	5
Ware[4]	42	2	4	1	35	137	31	79	27	1
Webster[4]	0	0	0	0	0	0	0	0	0	0
White	24	0	4	0	20	91	24	54	13	1
Wilcox[4]	9	0	5	0	4	57	25	25	7	0
Wilkes[4]	94	0	1	5	88	199	55	125	19	0
Wilkinson[4]	10	0	1	1	8	31	10	18	3	2
HAWAII										
Nonmetropolitan Counties										
Hawaii Police Department	613	13	109	59	432	4,030	655	2,710	665	71
Kauai Police Department	194	1	59	10	124	1,083	184	806	93	12
IDAHO										
Metropolitan Counties										
Ada	243	0	41	7	195	685	152	498	35	4
Boise	29	0	4	0	25	48	5	34	9	2
Bonneville	130	1	17	6	106	654	171	419	64	4
Butte	4	0	1	0	3	5	2	1	2	0
Canyon	152	0	33	2	117	397	143	173	81	6
Gem	14	0	1	0	13	44	21	21	2	0
Jefferson	13	1	4	1	7	143	30	84	29	1
Jerome	34	0	5	2	27	77	16	46	15	2
Kootenai	101	1	12	3	85	750	156	551	43	12
Nez Perce	12	2	2	0	8	49	11	32	6	0
Owyhee	17	1	5	0	11	49	13	29	7	0
Power	16	0	2	0	14	55	11	30	14	1
Twin Falls[7]	51	0	11	0	40			30	13	1

Table 10. Offenses Known to Law Enforcement, by Selected State Metropolitan and Nonmetropolitan Counties, 2020—Continued

(Number.)

State/county	Violent crime	Murder and nonnegligent manslaughter	Rape[1]	Robbery	Aggravated assault	Property crime	Burglary	Larceny-theft	Motor vehicle theft	Arson[2]
Nonmetropolitan Counties										
Adams	9	2	0	0	7	48	9	37	2	0
Bear Lake	0	0	0	0	0	0	0	0	0	0
Benewah	30	0	0	0	30	53	13	38	2	2
Bingham	29	0	10	1	18	161	37	110	14	0
Blaine	12	0	2	0	10	9	6	3	0	1
Bonner	46	1	8	0	37	252	83	146	23	2
Boundary	12	0	6	0	6	38	13	21	4	0
Camas	2	0	0	0	2	2	0	2	0	0
Caribou	6	0	0	0	6	16	3	10	3	0
Cassia	36	0	5	0	31	228	29	173	26	1
Clearwater	11	0	0	0	11	6	2	4	0	0
Custer	7	0	3	0	4	20	4	15	1	0
Elmore	32	0	4	3	25	13	3	10	0	0
Fremont	18	0	1	0	17	39	4	32	3	0
Gooding	19	0	1	0	18	45	17	19	9	0
Latah	17	0	3	0	14	101	34	62	5	1
Lemhi	7	0	0	0	7	3	2	1	0	0
Lewis	2	0	0	0	2	40	5	28	7	0
Lincoln	5	0	3	0	2	21	7	12	2	0
Madison	11	0	2	0	9	11	2	6	3	0
Minidoka	9	0	3	0	6	106	35	62	9	1
Oneida	2	0	0	0	2	37	11	22	4	0
Payette	27	0	3	0	24	60	11	43	6	0
Shoshone	29	0	5	0	24	99	23	66	10	0
Teton	13	0	6	1	6	23	0	21	2	0
Valley	19	0	11	0	8	59	21	33	5	1
Washington	10	0	0	0	10	15	1	9	5	0
ILLINOIS[8]										
Metropolitan Counties										
Alexander	6	0	0	0	6		6		0	0
Champaign	22	1	13	6	2		97		58	5
Clinton	6	0	0	0	6		7		1	0
Cook	222	2	55	35	130		117		116	6
DeKalb	24	0	1	2	21		37		3	0
Fulton	13	1	6	0	6		53		10	4
Grundy	12	1	4	1	6		22		3	3
Henry	11	0	0	0	11		17		2	0
Jackson	34	1	8	1	24		90		26	4
Jersey	24	0	7	0	17		96		5	3
Johnson	13	0	0	0	13		17		9	1
Kane	92	0	18	12	62		73		30	4
Kankakee	40	1	8	3	28		72		32	5
Kendall	18	1	8	2	7		31		18	1
Lake	92	2	18	16	56		140		80	5
Macon	30	0	4	1	25		39		6	1
Macoupin	10	0	0	0	10		57		36	4
Madison	162	1	39	14	108		242		98	13
Marshall	4	0	1	0	3		25		7	1
McHenry	66	1	21	0	44		58		19	1
McLean	36	0	10	0	26		41		15	1
Mercer	10	1	7	0	2		48		8	1
Monroe	15	0	1	0	14		18		9	0
Peoria	85	0	17	8	60		216		70	3
Piatt	20	0	5	0	15		18		7	1
Rock Island	40	0	8	1	31		86		15	0
Sangamon	182	1	20	12	149		205		77	1
Stark	7	0	0	0	7		8		6	0
Tazewell	24	0	5	2	17		41		21	0
Vermilion	54	0	0	4	50		116		24	1
Will[7]	158	5	45	17	91				78	5
Winnebago	102	3	34	6	59		125		41	2
Nonmetropolitan Counties										
Bureau	18	0	6	0	12		35		11	5
Carroll	6	0	0	0	6		5		1	0
Christian	10	0	1	1	8		12		12	1
Clark	11	1	2	1	7		3		2	0
Clay	5	0	0	0	5		22		7	0
Coles	19	0	8	1	10		10		3	1
Crawford	9	0	1	1	7		22		8	1
Cumberland	1	0	0	0	1		3			0
Effingham	20	0	1	0	19		17		15	1
Fayette	2	0	0	2	0		30		13	0
Ford	11	0	5	0	6		25		0	0
Franklin	17	0	2	2	13		44		1	0
Gallatin	3	0	1	0	2		7		1	0
Hancock	6	2	2	0	2		29		7	1
Iroquois	12	0	2	1	9		42		12	0
Jasper[7]	16	0	3	0	13		17			1
Jefferson	39	0	4	2	33		67		19	0

Table 10. Offenses Known to Law Enforcement, by Selected State Metropolitan and Nonmetropolitan Counties, 2020—Continued

(Number.)

State/county	Violent crime	Murder and nonnegligent manslaughter	Rape[1]	Robbery	Aggravated assault	Property crime	Burglary	Larceny-theft	Motor vehicle theft	Arson[2]
Jo Daviess	6	0	2	0	4		29		2	0
Knox	62	0	11	0	51		62		23	2
La Salle	65	0	24	2	39		40		14	1
Lee	25	0	0	1	24		24		6	5
Livingston	40	0	16	4	20		53		15	1
Logan	18	0	4	1	13		27		6	1
Marion	17	0	8	1	8		83		22	0
McDonough	5	0	3	0	2		10		2	0
Montgomery	34	1	0	1	32		38		2	0
Morgan	10	0	5	0	5		22		0	0
Ogle	23	1	0	1	21		34		13	1
Perry	10	0	0	0	10		26		9	1
Putnam	6	0	1	0	5		4		2	0
Randolph	6	0	1	0	5		1		0	0
Schuyler	0	0	0	0	0		0		0	0
Scott	1	0	0	0	1		6		2	0
Stephenson	13	0	8	2	3		16		4	0
Union	15	0	7	0	8		29		8	0
Wabash	1	0	0	0	1		1		0	0
Warren	14	0	2	2	10		26		6	0
Washington	7	0	0	0	7		16		5	0
Wayne	7	0	0	0	7		37		17	3
Whiteside	17	0	5	1	11		38		8	1
INDIANA										
Metropolitan Counties										
Clark	59	0	1	5	53	356	90	197	69	1
Franklin	8	0	0	0	8	116	40	58	18	0
Hancock	55	0	5	2	48	190	42	105	43	0
Hendricks	46	1	13	6	26	469	49	355	65	0
Howard[4]	53	0	3	2	48	138	42	82	14	0
Johnson	18	4	6	1	7	205	17	165	23	3
Lake	45	3	4	4	34	314	57	226	31	0
La Porte[7]	45	1	8	1	35			205	58	0
Monroe[4]	35	1	9	9	16	555	52	446	57	2
St. Joseph	78	1	19	16	42	1,254	287	806	161	5
Tippecanoe	48	0	16	1	31	430	98	290	42	4
Vigo	91	0	17	8	66	914	254	528	132	10
Nonmetropolitan Counties										
Greene	30	0	16	4	10	179	24	120	35	1
Jackson[4]	17	0	1	0	16	32	6	17	9	
Jennings	8	0	3	1	4	99	51	32	16	1
Kosciusko	107	1	25	1	80	410	79	276	55	0
Miami[4]	16	0	1	3	12	77	21	50	6	2
Montgomery	15	0	4	1	10	197	60	106	31	1
Noble	20	0	8	1	11	155	49	73	33	1
Starke[4]	45	1	7	0	37	223	68	114	41	2
Steuben[4]	13	0	7	0	6	251	62	139	50	0
Wells	5	0	4	0	1	38	13	16	9	0
IOWA										
Metropolitan Counties										
Black Hawk	42	0	15	0	27	130	69	40	21	2
Boone[7]	14	0	2	0	12			9	4	0
Bremer	2	0	1	0	1	37	13	19	5	0
Dallas	48	2	8	1	37	83	19	59	5	0
Dubuque	22	0	8	0	14	148	48	84	16	0
Grundy	5	0	0	0	5	54	28	22	4	0
Guthrie	1	0	0	0	1	41	20	18	3	0
Harrison	9	1	2	1	5	56	10	40	6	1
Jasper	11	0	3	0	8	30	12	11	7	0
Linn	28	1	10	0	17	263	109	117	37	0
Madison	9	1	3	0	5	43	17	20	6	1
Mills	13	0	1	0	12	70	12	49	9	0
Polk	120	3	1	11	105	711	188	417	106	9
Pottawattamie	55	0	15	0	40	241	65	139	37	1
Scott	28	0	3	1	24	163	64	81	18	1
Story	18	1	1	0	16	96	33	48	15	1
Warren	36	0	5	0	31	136	45	75	16	1
Washington	39	0	3	1	35	85	31	45	9	0
Woodbury	32	0	4	1	27	93	27	49	17	2
Nonmetropolitan Counties										
Adair	8	0	0	0	8	26	3	16	7	0
Adams	9	0	2	0	7	23	12	8	3	0
Allamakee	2	0	2	0	0	32	6	19	7	0
Appanoose	16	0	1	0	15	93	36	47	10	1
Buchanan	24	0	9	0	15	78	27	34	17	6
Buena Vista	10	0	0	0	10	44	25	19	0	1
Butler	4	0	1	0	3	37	25	11	1	0

Table 10. Offenses Known to Law Enforcement, by Selected State Metropolitan and Nonmetropolitan Counties, 2020—Continued

(Number.)

State/county	Violent crime	Murder and nonnegligent manslaughter	Rape[1]	Robbery	Aggravated assault	Property crime	Burglary	Larceny-theft	Motor vehicle theft	Arson[2]
Calhoun	2	0	0	0	2	13	1	10	2	1
Carroll	3	0	0	0	3	10	4	3	3	0
Cass	12	0	2	0	10	44	9	27	8	0
Cedar	8	1	5	0	2	36	9	22	5	0
Cerro Gordo	15	0	1	0	14	120	42	56	22	0
Cherokee	5	0	0	0	5	18	8	6	4	0
Chickasaw	8	0	2	0	6	23	12	10	1	0
Clarke	4	0	2	0	2	26	6	13	7	1
Clay	5	0	0	0	5	15	6	6	3	0
Clayton	11	0	1	0	10	27	8	17	2	0
Clinton	28	0	7	0	21	139	45	73	21	0
Crawford	3	0	1	0	2	2	1	0	1	1
Davis	0	0	0	0	0	9	5	3	1	0
Delaware	27	0	5	0	22	41	16	15	10	0
Des Moines[7]	11	0	0	0	11			53	12	0
Dickinson	9	0	4	0	5	24	9	11	4	0
Emmet	13	0	1	0	12	16	5	10	1	0
Fayette	20	0	3	1	16	52	16	22	14	1
Floyd	3	0	1	0	2	14	8	5	1	0
Fremont	40	0	14	0	26	75	21	38	16	1
Hamilton	3	0	1	0	2	44	22	18	4	2
Hancock	3	0	0	0	3	34	20	11	3	0
Hardin	11	0	3	0	8	74	35	37	2	1
Henry	33	0	3	0	30	66	15	40	11	0
Howard	2	0	1	0	1	27	10	13	4	1
Humboldt	0	0	0	0	0	59	13	37	9	0
Ida	8	0	1	0	7	57	12	41	4	1
Iowa	15	0	0	0	15	19	5	8	6	0
Jackson	10	0	0	1	9	52	17	34	1	0
Jefferson	4	0	0	0	4	30	16	11	3	1
Keokuk	9	0	0	0	9	37	5	25	7	1
Kossuth	13	0	0	0	13	20	8	10	2	0
Lee	12	0	0	1	11	86	33	40	13	0
Louisa	15	0	0	0	15	56	17	31	8	1
Lucas	12	0	3	0	9	60	22	30	8	0
Lyon	15	0	8	0	7	44	19	17	8	1
Mahaska	10	1	1	0	8	56	15	29	12	1
Marion	36	1	22	0	13	48	10	33	5	0
Marshall	44	0	4	0	40	89	34	41	14	0
Mitchell	3	0	1	0	2	13	2	10	1	0
Monona	11	0	1	0	10	30	6	21	3	0
Monroe	3	0	2	0	1	14	8	4	2	0
Muscatine	19	0	4	1	14	58	22	23	13	0
O'Brien	33	0	9	1	23	103	41	46	16	1
Osceola	10	0	2	0	8	54	8	41	5	0
Page	4	0	0	0	4	13	4	6	3	0
Palo Alto	12	1	1	0	10	52	23	27	2	0
Plymouth	6	1	1	0	4	28	13	10	5	0
Pocahontas	11	0	3	0	8	30	12	13	5	0
Poweshiek	13	0	4	1	8	56	13	36	7	1
Ringgold	3	0	0	0	3	25	6	17	2	0
Sac	6	0	1	0	5	36	16	20	0	1
Shelby	3	0	0	0	3	20	11	9	0	0
Sioux	11	1	9	0	1	56	16	34	6	0
Tama	18	0	2	0	16	46	21	18	7	0
Taylor	7	1	0	0	6	11	3	6	2	0
Union	8	0	0	0	8	40	9	28	3	0
Van Buren	9	0	0	1	8	31	11	15	5	0
Wapello	24	0	1	0	23	96	51	38	7	1
Wayne	14	0	6	1	7	23	10	9	4	0
Webster	33	0	2	0	31	127	42	67	18	0
Worth	8	0	0	0	8	27	7	13	7	0
KANSAS										
Metropolitan Counties										
Butler	48	1	8	2	37	329	105	201	23	9
Geary	8	0	1	0	7	34	12	16	6	1
Harvey	22	0	1	0	21	48	17	19	12	2
Jackson	9	0	0	0	9	100	11	78	11	1
Jefferson[7]	48	0	6	2	40			144	37	0
Johnson	73	1	11	1	60	319	39	241	39	6
Leavenworth	57	2	8	2	45	150	43	80	27	8
Miami	43	0	2	2	39	131	42	68	21	5
Osage	22	0	0	0	22	54	24	20	10	3
Pottawatomie[7]	37	0	3	0	34			98	12	1
Riley County Police Department	212	3	26	13	170	1,266	202	967	97	16
Sedgwick	97	2	4	4	87	365	99	216	50	3
Shawnee[7]	85	0	6	8	71			579	77	5
Sumner[7]	22	1	1	6	14			89	14	0
Wabaunsee	16	0	0	1	15	94	37	49	8	1
Wyandotte	30	1	6	3	20	51	3	42	6	0

Table 10. Offenses Known to Law Enforcement, by Selected State Metropolitan and Nonmetropolitan Counties, 2020—Continued

(Number.)

State/county	Violent crime	Murder and nonnegligent manslaughter	Rape[1]	Robbery	Aggravated assault	Property crime	Burglary	Larceny-theft	Motor vehicle theft	Arson[2]
Nonmetropolitan Counties										
Allen	25	1	2	1	21	54	17	30	7	1
Anderson	14	0	4	0	10	32	12	15	5	0
Atchison	3	0	2	0	1	2	0	2	0	0
Barber	8	0	0	0	8	16	5	10	1	0
Barton[7]	8	0	1	0	7			44	9	6
Bourbon	18	0	2	0	16	48	21	19	8	2
Brown	5	0	2	0	3	12	3	5	4	1
Cherokee	30	1	3	2	24	175	54	84	37	6
Clark	3	0	0	0	3	11	1	7	3	0
Clay	8	0	2	0	6	12	3	3	6	2
Cloud	14	0	0	0	14	48	18	25	5	2
Comanche	2	0	1	0	1	6	2	4	0	0
Cowley	21	0	4	0	17	103	37	56	10	1
Ellis	9	0	2	1	6	35	12	17	6	2
Ellsworth	4	0	0	0	4	42	22	17	3	0
Finney	39	1	3	2	33	158	66	64	28	4
Ford	14	0	1	3	10	54	10	37	7	0
Franklin	32	0	2	0	30	97	31	51	15	2
Grant	3	0	1	0	2	9	6	3	0	0
Gray	9	0	0	0	9	45	11	31	3	3
Greeley	1	0	0	0	1	3	2	1	0	0
Greenwood	12	1	2	1	8	68	18	40	10	3
Hamilton	6	1	0	0	5	24	3	20	1	0
Harper	4	0	0	0	4	51	23	25	3	0
Haskell	7	0	0	0	7	17	2	9	6	0
Hodgeman	2	0	0	0	2	5	2	3	0	0
Kearny	18	0	2	1	15	57	14	35	8	2
Kingman	1	0	0	0	1	78	35	39	4	0
Kiowa	6	0	0	0	6	19	10	7	2	0
Labette[7]	9	0	1	0	8			30	7	0
Lane	4	0	0	0	4	24	16	8	0	2
Logan	7	0	0	0	7	6	2	4	0	0
Marion[7]	9	0	0	1	8			19	16	0
Marshall	1	0	0	0	1	16	4	11	1	3
McPherson	13	0	1	1	11	54	29	19	6	0
Montgomery[7]	15	0	3	1	11			68	15	0
Morris	8	0	0	0	8	18	5	12	1	0
Morton	0	0	0	0	0	14	8	6	0	0
Nemaha	7	0	2	0	5	38	12	21	5	1
Neosho[7]	8	0	2	0	6			32	2	0
Ness	13	0	0	0	13	21	8	12	1	0
Norton	5	0	1	0	4	12	5	2	5	0
Republic	3	0	2	0	1	22	6	16	0	0
Rice	5	0	0	0	5	11	1	9	1	0
Rooks	1	0	0	0	1	31	5	21	5	2
Rush[7]	8	0	2	1	5			52	5	0
Russell	8	0	0	0	8	37	13	19	5	0
Saline	22	0	0	2	20	98	29	57	12	6
Scott	4	0	0	0	4	1	0	1	0	0
Seward	4	0	1	0	3	6	1	5	0	0
Sherman	0	0	0	0	0	0	0	0	0	0
Smith	1	0	0	0	1	8	3	4	1	0
Stafford	2	0	1	0	1	11	2	5	4	0
Thomas	8	0	0	0	8	19	4	12	3	0
Trego	0	0	0	0	0	6	2	3	1	0
Washington	3	0	1	0	2	13	3	9	1	0
Wilson	3	0	1	0	2	30	11	14	5	1
Woodson	2	0	0	1	1	44	24	18	2	1
KENTUCKY										
Metropolitan Counties										
Allen	9	0	3	0	6	102	35	48	19	0
Boone	73	0	28	6	39	747	124	527	96	4
Bourbon	1	0	0	0	1	67	23	34	10	2
Boyd	13	0	0	2	11	192	65	104	23	1
Bracken	0	0	0	0	0	41	11	20	10	0
Bullitt	41	3	8	6	24	380	90	198	92	1
Butler	2	0	0	1	1	30	5	13	12	0
Campbell	0	0	0	0	0	0	0	0	0	0
Campbell County Police Department	17	0	5	2	10	116	28	72	16	1
Carter	4	0	1	0	3	42	10	20	12	1
Christian	23	1	7	4	11	254	82	128	44	1
Clark	10	0	4	1	5	132	32	81	19	1
Daviess	29	1	9	6	13	377	101	228	48	2
Edmonson	4	0	0	1	3	19	4	11	4	0
Fayette	1	0	0	0	1	0	0	0	0	0
Gallatin	0	0	0	0	0	18	5	10	3	1
Grant	5	0	2	0	3	149	33	91	25	0
Greenup	3	0	1	0	2	32	3	19	10	0
Hancock	1	0	1	0	0	24	10	8	6	0

Table 10. Offenses Known to Law Enforcement, by Selected State Metropolitan and Nonmetropolitan Counties, 2020—Continued

(Number.)

State/county	Violent crime	Murder and nonnegligent manslaughter	Rape[1]	Robbery	Aggravated assault	Property crime	Burglary	Larceny-theft	Motor vehicle theft	Arson[2]
Hardin	30	1	1	4	24	148	39	91	18	1
Henderson	9	0	3	3	3	174	46	96	32	0
Henry	1	0	0	0	1	20	9	9	2	0
Jefferson	1	0	0	1	0	2	0	2	0	0
Jessamine	14	1	5	2	6	190	42	123	25	6
Kenton	0	0	0	0	0	2	0	2	0	0
Kenton County Police Department	28	3	9	2	14	96	40	47	9	0
Larue	3	0	0	0	3	33	8	15	10	0
McLean	6	0	2	0	4	58	23	22	13	0
Meade	24	0	6	0	18	120	29	65	26	0
Oldham	1	0	0	1	0	3	0	3	0	0
Oldham County Police Department	25	0	5	6	14	471	76	351	44	4
Pendleton	1	0	0	0	1	85	26	48	11	2
Scott	5	0	0	1	4	155	33	91	31	0
Shelby	21	0	5	5	11	195	41	126	28	2
Spencer	3	0	0	1	2	55	12	36	7	1
Trigg	6	0	0	1	5	91	40	45	6	1
Warren	55	2	13	8	32	583	124	363	96	3
Woodford	1	0	0	0	1	19	1	17	1	0
Nonmetropolitan Counties										
Anderson	4	0	0	0	4	27	7	12	8	0
Ballard	15	0	0	0	15	52	22	20	10	0
Barren	16	0	3	0	13	129	44	57	28	1
Bath	6	0	0	0	6	42	14	21	7	0
Bell	11	1	2	0	8	88	32	42	14	1
Boyle	0	0	0	0	0	29	9	16	4	0
Breathitt	3	1	0	0	2	21	2	11	8	0
Breckinridge	10	0	1	1	8	56	9	30	17	2
Caldwell	2	0	0	0	2	23	2	9	12	0
Calloway	9	0	4	0	5	172	70	88	14	3
Carlisle	1	0	0	0	1	18	8	7	3	0
Carroll	6	0	1	0	5	57	11	31	15	1
Casey	4	0	0	0	4	40	18	13	9	0
Clay	17	3	0	2	12	78	15	34	29	0
Clinton	5	0	0	0	5	13	5	6	2	1
Crittenden	3	0	1	0	2	26	9	16	1	0
Cumberland	2	0	0	0	2	25	20	3	2	0
Elliott	0	0	0	0	0	2	1	0	1	0
Estill	5	0	0	1	4	35	9	17	9	0
Fleming	2	0	0	0	2	8	3	2	3	0
Floyd	7	0	1	0	6	56	19	24	13	0
Franklin	8	1	3	1	3	178	65	91	22	0
Fulton	0	0	0	0	0	5	1	3	1	0
Garrard County Police Department	5	0	0	0	5	54	13	30	11	0
Graves	19	0	10	1	8	198	87	90	21	2
Grayson	14	0	0	1	13	82	26	46	10	0
Green	1	0	0	0	1	7	2	2	3	0
Harlan	1	0	0	0	1	22	11	8	3	0
Harrison	3	0	0	1	2	72	32	33	7	0
Hart	3	0	0	0	3	35	12	21	2	0
Hickman	2	0	1	0	1	22	4	12	6	0
Hopkins	11	0	3	3	5	153	33	86	34	0
Jackson	4	0	0	0	4	77	21	29	27	2
Johnson	5	0	1	1	3	43	13	13	17	0
Knott	1	0	0	0	1	30	8	14	8	0
Knox	5	0	1	0	4	62	15	20	27	0
Laurel	52	8	8	8	28	447	108	244	95	0
Lawrence	9	0	1	0	8	44	13	17	14	1
Lee	0	0	0	0	0	14	4	6	4	1
Leslie	4	0	0	0	4	27	3	15	9	1
Letcher	0	0	0	0	0	10	4	5	1	0
Lewis	0	0	0	0	0	17	5	4	8	0
Lincoln	8	1	1	0	6	69	31	23	15	0
Livingston	5	0	3	0	2	50	20	26	4	0
Logan	18	0	6	2	10	86	32	35	19	1
Lyon	5	0	0	2	3	54	20	29	5	1
Madison	22	0	6	5	11	242	49	166	27	0
Magoffin	2	0	0	0	2	19	3	10	6	1
Marion	6	1	2	0	3	32	8	11	13	1
Marshall	33	0	11	4	18	244	84	134	26	1
Martin	6	0	0	0	6	22	1	16	5	0
Mason	5	0	0	0	5	76	20	39	17	0
McCracken	43	2	18	5	18	422	110	260	52	6
McCreary	5	0	0	0	5	55	19	20	16	0
Menifee	0	0	0	0	0	10	2	5	3	1
Mercer	2	0	0	1	1	20	9	9	2	0
Metcalfe	4	0	0	0	4	25	14	9	2	0
Monroe	0	0	0	0	0	9	2	4	3	0
Montgomery	12	1	3	2	6	244	66	132	46	1
Morgan	6	0	0	0	6	52	15	31	6	2

Table 10. Offenses Known to Law Enforcement, by Selected State Metropolitan and Nonmetropolitan Counties, 2020—Continued

(Number.)

State/county	Violent crime	Murder and nonnegligent manslaughter	Rape[1]	Robbery	Aggravated assault	Property crime	Burglary	Larceny-theft	Motor vehicle theft	Arson[2]
Muhlenberg	7	0	3	2	2	62	29	24	9	0
Nelson	15	2	4	3	6	225	41	143	41	0
Nicholas	1	0	0	0	1	6	6	0	0	0
Ohio	18	0	6	2	10	123	48	44	31	1
Owen	0	0	0	0	0	42	13	24	5	0
Owsley	0	0	0	0	0	2	1	0	1	0
Perry	16	0	1	5	10	56	11	17	28	0
Pike	0	0	0	0	0	56	11	38	7	0
Powell	0	0	0	0	0	18	3	9	6	0
Pulaski	46	1	8	4	33	324	129	137	58	1
Rockcastle	9	0	2	1	6	78	29	19	30	0
Rowan	8	0	0	0	8	77	17	47	13	0
Russell	3	0	1	0	2	31	5	19	7	0
Simpson	4	0	1	0	3	40	8	19	13	1
Taylor	9	0	3	0	6	185	89	83	13	0
Todd	3	0	1	0	2	55	29	17	9	0
Trimble	3	0	0	0	3	21	10	7	4	1
Union	6	0	0	0	6	51	23	23	5	2
Washington	2	0	0	0	2	39	18	14	7	1
Wayne	8	0	1	1	6	34	15	11	8	0
Webster	3	0	0	0	3	32	7	17	8	0
Whitley	13	0	0	1	12	116	41	52	23	1
Wolfe	2	0	0	0	2	26	9	10	7	0
LOUISIANA										
Metropolitan Counties										
Ascension	400	3	24	28	345	1,990	402	1,402	186	12
Assumption	66	1	3	1	61	202	23	157	22	0
Bossier	114	4	10	6	94	571	131	398	42	3
Caddo	44	0	0	7	37	651	111	486	54	3
Calcasieu	1,060	8	76	29	947	4,264	1,096	2,810	358	7
De Soto	107	3	6	10	88	381	115	225	41	1
Iberville[4]	123	1	1	2	119	236	47	166	23	2
Lafayette	206	3	14	17	172	935	205	566	164	6
Lafourche	234	9	22	0	203	1,988	340	1,558	90	3
Livingston	457	1	46	12	398	2,488	473	1,850	165	0
Morehouse	42	0	5	3	34	162	35	115	12	0
Ouachita	788	2	56	42	688	2,512	643	1,623	246	3
Plaquemines	60	0	2	1	57	152	23	113	16	0
Pointe Coupee	147	0	5	4	138	233	62	153	18	0
Rapides	380	1	24	17	338	1,514	560	796	158	7
St. Charles[4]	182	3	9	6	164	949	143	756	50	2
St. Helena	95	4	1	3	87	158	20	126	12	1
St. James	57	4	4	0	49	279	33	221	25	0
St. John the Baptist	155	14	2	0	139	865	135	667	63	2
St. Martin	168	0	14	11	143	558	138	367	53	0
St. Tammany	333	11	37	18	267	1,332	224	989	119	6
Tangipahoa	1,242	8	40	68	1,126	1,847	449	1,162	236	9
Terrebonne[4]	218	1	12	8	197	1,783	267	1,409	107	1
Nonmetropolitan Counties										
Allen	28	0	13	0	15	387	36	326	25	0
Beauregard	39	2	2	1	34	240	48	153	39	5
Bienville[4]	35	1	8	0	26	132	51	67	14	0
Claiborne	14	0	0	1	13	58	17	39	2	0
Concordia	98	0	5	7	86	222	66	142	14	2
East Carroll	24	3	2	0	19	23	13	8	2	1
Evangeline	63	0	1	2	60	193	46	103	44	0
Franklin	51	3	3	0	45	105	26	68	11	0
Jackson[4]	15	0	4	0	11	69	14	53	2	1
La Salle	37	0	0	1	36	30	16	13	1	0
Lincoln[4]	63	4	2	0	57	204	70	121	13	0
Madison	30	2	0	0	28	28	10	15	3	0
Natchitoches	59	1	1	2	55	417	90	261	66	0
Red River	27	0	1	0	26	141	36	95	10	0
Richland[4]	47	3	2	3	39	74	28	31	15	1
Sabine	69	4	6	0	59	217	8	191	18	0
St. Landry	148	7	8	8	125	742	312	372	58	0
St. Mary	204	0	17	17	170	474	113	346	15	2
Vernon	90	1	5	3	81	363	69	262	32	2
Washington	357	5	70	9	273	494	123	305	66	4
Winn	25	1	2	0	22	57	15	15	27	0
MAINE										
Metropolitan Counties										
Androscoggin[4]	23	0	10	1	12	115	17	93	5	1
Cumberland[4]	41	0	15	2	24	318	59	243	16	0
Penobscot	10	0	0	1	9	304	53	223	28	0
Sagadahoc[4]	5	0	0	0	5	55	12	39	4	1
Nonmetropolitan Counties										
York[4]	18	0	10	1	7	277	56	201	20	0

Table 10. Offenses Known to Law Enforcement, by Selected State Metropolitan and Nonmetropolitan Counties, 2020—Continued

(Number.)

State/county	Violent crime	Murder and nonnegligent manslaughter	Rape[1]	Robbery	Aggravated assault	Property crime	Burglary	Larceny-theft	Motor vehicle theft	Arson[2]
Aroostook	10	0	0	1	9	69	25	38	6	1
Franklin	3	0	2	0	1	81	20	51	10	0
Hancock	14	0	5	2	7	105	16	84	5	0
Kennebec	33	0	11	1	21	204	40	146	18	1
Knox	4	0	1	1	2	155	24	119	12	1
Lincoln[4]	27	0	16	1	10	151	22	119	10	1
Oxford	26	0	11	0	15	269	42	212	15	0
Piscataquis	7	0	2	0	5	71	12	54	5	0
Somerset	40	0	20	2	18	277	45	217	15	0
Waldo[4]	9	0	3	0	6	80	13	59	8	0
Washington	23	0	7	0	16	119	34	77	8	0
MARYLAND[3]										
Metropolitan Counties										
Montgomery County Police Department	1,432	17	265	418	732	13,916	1,245	11,588	1,083	9
MICHIGAN										
Metropolitan Counties										
Bay	40	1	17	5	17	395	57	297	41	0
Berrien	116	0	26	4	86	647	137	443	67	5
Calhoun	143	2	28	3	110	506	110	353	43	4
Clinton	24	0	5	1	18	113	24	84	5	0
Eaton	151	1	31	11	108	913	89	753	71	2
Genesee	105	0	21	1	83	311	43	241	27	2
Ingham	203	3	48	5	147	565	108	393	64	3
Ionia	78	1	26	3	48	166	22	129	15	2
Kalamazoo	384	2	52	42	288	2,774	483	1,915	376	14
Kent	438	2	113	42	281	2,587	326	1,960	301	19
Lapeer	57	0	21	0	36	166	57	91	18	0
Livingston	62	0	15	6	41	423	62	338	23	3
Macomb	287	0	55	16	216	848	112	641	95	9
Midland	37	1	11	0	25	208	40	152	16	3
Montcalm	17	0	4	1	12	104	24	73	7	5
Oakland	25	0	13	0	12	23	3	19	1	0
Ottawa	586	3	194	20	369	1,921	323	1,468	130	22
Saginaw	79	0	14	4	61	370	51	291	28	2
Shiawassee	19	0	5	0	14	128	35	89	4	2
St. Clair	138	1	27	4	106	580	111	419	50	10
Washtenaw	703	5	55	54	589	1,276	199	890	107	10
Wayne	12	0	1	0	11	0	0	0	0	0
Nonmetropolitan Counties										
Alcona	16	0	6	0	10	86	16	66	4	0
Alger	2	0	0	0	2	7	1	4	2	0
Allegan	94	1	7	3	83	660	171	422	67	4
Alpena	14	0	7	0	7	47	4	39	4	0
Antrim	36	0	12	0	24	161	41	107	13	0
Arenac	46	0	5	0	41	97	30	59	8	1
Baraga	2	0	0	0	2	14	3	11	0	0
Barry	46	0	15	0	31	292	63	213	16	3
Benzie	28	4	4	0	20	64	10	52	2	2
Branch	13	0	5	0	8	106	37	63	6	1
Charlevoix	33	0	7	0	26	77	24	48	5	0
Cheboygan	24	0	4	0	20	24	5	16	3	0
Chippewa	14	0	1	0	13	23	1	21	1	0
Clare	66	0	14	1	51	301	91	164	46	5
Crawford	31	0	9	1	21	55	18	33	4	2
Delta	4	0	4	0	0	48	10	35	3	0
Dickinson	0	0	0	0	0	0	0	0	0	0
Emmet	25	0	8	0	17	74	16	56	2	0
Gladwin	35	0	3	1	31	152	56	84	12	4
Gogebic	12	0	2	0	10	38	5	29	4	0
Grand Traverse	132	0	32	3	97	446	76	349	21	8
Gratiot	53	0	14	3	36	228	17	202	9	2
Hillsdale	90	0	17	0	73	180	46	113	21	3
Houghton	0	0	0	0	0	10	2	6	2	0
Huron	29	2	7	0	20	103	26	66	11	1
Iosco	0	0	0	0	0	7	3	4	0	0
Iron	0	0	0	0	0	0	0	0	0	0
Isabella	57	0	15	3	39	287	47	204	36	2
Kalkaska	56	0	4	0	52	87	15	63	9	1
Keweenaw	2	0	0	0	2	18	3	14	1	0
Lake	56	0	5	2	49	262	83	166	13	3
Leelanau	0	0	0	0	0	0	0	0	0	0
Lenawee	36	1	14	1	20	196	51	125	20	1
Luce	7	0	0	0	7	53	6	43	4	0
Mackinac	5	0	2	0	3	90	26	58	6	0
Manistee	26	1	9	1	15	98	28	63	7	0
Marquette	18	0	5	0	13	125	7	110	8	1
Mason	43	0	8	0	35	114	14	95	5	1
Mecosta	72	0	16	0	56	245	40	190	15	3
Menominee	3	0	0	0	3	14	4	8	2	0

Table 10. Offenses Known to Law Enforcement, by Selected State Metropolitan and Nonmetropolitan Counties, 2020—Continued

(Number.)

State/county	Violent crime	Murder and nonnegligent manslaughter	Rape[1]	Robbery	Aggravated assault	Property crime	Burglary	Larceny-theft	Motor vehicle theft	Arson[2]
Missaukee	15	0	4	0	11	117	25	83	9	0
Montmorency	4	0	1	0	3	11	2	7	2	0
Newaygo	64	0	17	0	47	176	44	114	18	5
Oceana	58	0	11	0	47	192	30	154	8	3
Ogemaw	9	0	2	0	7	110	24	81	5	0
Ontonagon	3	0	0	0	3	11	2	9	0	0
Osceola	9	0	1	0	8	20	7	10	3	0
Oscoda	22	0	1	0	21	53	17	32	4	0
Otsego	4	0	1	0	3	24	5	16	3	0
Presque Isle	11	0	1	0	10	22	5	17	0	0
Sanilac	37	0	13	1	23	73	23	41	9	2
Schoolcraft	0	0	0	0	0	2	0	2	0	0
St. Joseph	82	0	14	3	65	242	72	128	42	2
Tuscola	57	0	17	0	40	135	41	70	24	1
Van Buren	69	0	9	1	59	252	76	152	24	3
MINNESOTA										
Metropolitan Counties										
Anoka[4]	71	3	18	4	46	838	119	637	82	4
Benton[4]	17	0	1	0	16	127	30	76	21	3
Blue Earth	33	0	4	2	27	93	25	57	11	0
Carlton[4]	13	0	2	0	11	139	33	95	11	1
Carver	42	0	14	5	23	616	74	510	32	2
Chisago[4]	27	0	11	0	16	145	16	99	30	2
Clay	13	1	2	0	10	83	42	29	12	2
Dakota	17	0	2	0	15	39	26	9	4	0
Dodge[4]	13	0	5	0	8	113	41	63	9	0
Fillmore[4]	4	0	1	0	3	46	6	40	0	0
Hennepin	40	0	2	1	37	45	0	43	2	0
Houston[4]	3	0	0	0	3	27	8	14	5	0
Isanti[4]	33	0	3	2	28	281	56	194	31	0
Lake[4]	2	0	0	0	2	48	18	25	5	0
Le Sueur	16	0	2	0	14	83	6	73	4	0
Mille Lacs	30	1	3	3	23	278	72	169	37	1
Nicollet[4]	2	0	0	0	2	59	17	35	7	1
Olmsted	65	1	17	3	44	321	120	168	33	1
Polk[4]	14	0	1	0	13	103	34	58	11	0
Ramsey	128	1	10	20	97	1,493	169	1,113	211	5
Scott[4]	17	1	1	1	14	136	20	107	9	0
Sherburne	43	1	14	1	27	284	39	221	24	1
Stearns	21	0	13	0	8	221	36	175	10	2
St. Louis	105	2	26	2	75	514	158	316	40	4
Wabasha	4	0	1	0	3	18	1	13	4	1
Washington[4]	51	0	16	3	32	785	120	597	68	0
Wright[4]	91	0	25	7	59	1,098	155	877	66	4
Nonmetropolitan Counties										
Aitkin[4]	23	1	8	0	14	247	94	138	15	2
Becker	24	0	9	0	15	120	49	50	21	1
Beltrami	52	3	3	4	42	312	103	174	35	2
Big Stone[4]	3	0	1	0	2	49	12	30	7	0
Brown[4]	4	0	2	0	2	33	12	19	2	1
Cass[4]	36	0	0	1	35	511	148	327	36	1
Chippewa[4]	0	0	0	0	0	4	2	2	0	0
Clearwater	13	0	2	0	11	42	11	22	9	0
Cook[4]	18	0	7	0	11	68	3	63	2	1
Crow Wing[4]	44	0	15	2	27	273	78	172	23	2
Douglas	16	0	3	0	13	184	34	138	12	2
Faribault	5	0	1	0	4	27	4	16	7	1
Freeborn	10	0	1	0	9	117	39	68	10	1
Goodhue	12	1	4	0	7	223	28	156	39	0
Grant[4]	2	0	0	0	2	4	1	3	0	0
Hubbard	24	0	9	2	13	174	53	108	13	1
Itasca[4]	32	0	9	1	22	157	40	100	17	3
Jackson[4]	4	0	1	0	3	30	5	18	7	0
Kanabec	6	0	0	0	6	96	10	82	4	0
Kandiyohi	17	0	3	0	14	202	15	166	21	3
Kittson[4]	1	0	0	0	1	0	0	0	0	0
Koochiching[4]	2	0	0	0	2	34	16	13	5	0
Lake of the Woods	1	0	0	0	1	2	0	2	0	0
Lincoln	4	0	0	0	4	4	0	3	1	0
Lyon	14	0	3	0	11	34	12	16	6	0
Marshall	0	0	0	0	0	4	0	4	0	0
Martin	6	0	1	0	5	11	3	7	1	0
McLeod[4]	9	0	3	0	6	78	15	58	5	0
Meeker[4]	20	0	3	0	17	109	24	63	22	1
Morrison[4]	20	0	2	0	18	207	36	146	25	0
Murray[4]	1	0	0	0	1	19	6	11	2	0
Nobles	11	0	4	0	7	26	14	9	3	0
Norman[4]	3	0	0	0	3	48	14	27	7	0
Otter Tail	26	0	8	0	18	217	63	134	20	2

Table 10. Offenses Known to Law Enforcement, by Selected State Metropolitan and Nonmetropolitan Counties, 2020—Continued

(Number.)

State/county	Violent crime	Murder and nonnegligent manslaughter	Rape[1]	Robbery	Aggravated assault	Property crime	Burglary	Larceny-theft	Motor vehicle theft	Arson[2]
Pennington[4]	2	0	0	1	1	26	8	17	1	0
Pine[4]	95	1	12	6	76	775	226	456	93	5
Pipestone[4]	8	0	4	0	4	69	5	61	3	0
Pope[4]	4	0	1	0	3	51	10	32	9	0
Red Lake[4]	4	0	1	0	3	3	1	0	2	0
Redwood	7	0	2	0	5	53	14	35	4	0
Renville[4]	6	0	0	0	6	82	17	61	4	0
Rice[4]	23	0	4	0	19	137	34	88	15	4
Rock	7	0	2	0	5	47	13	22	12	0
Roseau[4]	7	1	1	0	5	59	12	45	2	0
Sibley[4]	2	0	1	0	1	2	1	1	0	0
Steele	8	0	3	2	3	103	21	71	11	0
Stevens[4]	5	0	0	0	5	18	5	12	1	0
Swift	0	0	0	0	0	2	1	1	0	0
Todd[4]	19	1	4	0	14	144	37	98	9	1
Traverse[4]	1	0	0	0	1	17	1	14	2	0
Wadena	12	0	0	0	12	7	2	3	2	0
Waseca	8	0	0	0	8	72	22	46	4	1
Watonwan[4]	7	0	3	0	4	44	16	25	3	1
Wilkin[4]	0	0	0	0	0	24	3	20	1	0
Winona[4]	22	1	6	0	15	80	13	61	6	1
Yellow Medicine[4]	1	0	0	0	1	35	8	23	4	0
MISSISSIPPI										
Metropolitan Counties										
DeSoto	55	1	15	7	32	368	62	239	67	3
Harrison	44	0	16	4	24	789	144	528	117	7
Hinds	78	4	1	4	69	330	125	145	60	2
Lamar	51	3	10	2	36	627	149	429	49	1
Madison	56	3	9	10	34	208	69	114	25	3
Rankin	64	1	7	4	52	432	46	332	54	4
Stone[4]	38	0	21	1	16	160	26	102	32	4
Tunica[4]	56	2	3	9	42	446	70	309	67	0
Nonmetropolitan Counties										
Alcorn	17	0	4	3	10	304	98	167	39	0
Claiborne	32	3	0	0	29	12	10	1	1	0
Clay[4]	21	0	1	1	19	45	18	24	3	2
George	36	0	15	1	20	327	86	172	69	2
Jasper	14	0	3	2	9	99	25	60	14	1
Lafayette	34	1	11	3	19	153	46	102	5	0
Leake	53	0	7	1	45	142	53	75	14	3
Lee	55	1	10	5	39	631	162	407	62	8
Leflore	129	7	3	13	106	269	85	166	18	5
Lincoln	31	2	2	17	10	264	80	156	28	0
Marion	42	5	7	2	28	131	55	65	11	0
Monroe[4]	65	0	13	2	50	177	56	94	27	3
Pontotoc	68	1	22	10	35	235	90	98	47	0
Tishomingo	22	0	7	0	15	146	62	72	12	5
Union	24	1	3	2	18	176	50	102	24	1
Warren	18	2	2	1	13	201	24	147	30	0
Washington	12	1	0	4	7	241	83	116	42	
MISSOURI										
Metropolitan Counties										
Bates	3	0	1	2	0	90	45	42	3	0
Boone[4]	107	1	27	9	70	636	101	431	104	8
Buchanan	45	0	18	1	26	204	38	102	64	5
Caldwell	20	0	0	1	19	73	29	32	12	2
Callaway[4]	47	2	13	0	32	437	122	272	43	
Cape Girardeau[4]	68	1	9	3	55	195	85	98	12	1
Cass	91	1	3	1	86	222	74	121	27	0
Christian	44	0	2	2	40	243	84	133	26	0
Clay[4]	33	0	6	4	23	184	49	85	50	1
Clinton	19	0	4	0	15	69	20	36	13	
Cole[4]	41	0	4	1	36	354	60	253	41	1
Dallas	1	0	0	0	1	40	14	25	1	0
DeKalb	23	1	0	0	22	64	23	32	9	0
Franklin	42	0	2	2	38	382	78	212	92	0
Howard[4]	17	1	3	0	13	40	8	32	0	1
Jackson	104	1	11	10	82	484	63	287	134	15
Jasper	96	0	12	4	80	596	116	372	108	0
Jefferson[4]	532	3	32	17	480	2,497	557	1,461	479	12
Lafayette[4]	0	0	0	0	0	54	0	43	11	0
Lincoln[4]	115	0	13	0	102	183	57	112	14	0
Newton[4]	74	2	11	7	54	619	125	391	103	2
Osage	3	0	2	0	1	140	47	75	18	0
Platte[4]	44	0	10	2	32	288	47	185	56	1
Ray	91	0	0	1	90	80	34	38	8	
St. Charles[4]	0	0	0	0	0	0	0	0	0	0
St. Charles County Police Department[4]	178	0	14	8	156	838	127	569	142	4

Table 10. Offenses Known to Law Enforcement, by Selected State Metropolitan and Nonmetropolitan Counties, 2020—Continued

(Number.)

State/county	Violent crime	Murder and nonnegligent manslaughter	Rape[1]	Robbery	Aggravated assault	Property crime	Burglary	Larceny-theft	Motor vehicle theft	Arson[2]
St. Louis County Police Department[4]	2,001	43	101	317	1,540	7,772	1,120	5,030	1,622	66
Warren[4]	63	0	16	1	46	207	52	112	43	0
Nonmetropolitan Counties										
Adair[4]	8	0	0	0	8	91	28	56	7	0
Atchison	2	0	2	0	0	5	1	3	1	0
Audrain[4]	29	0	6	0	23	122	35	68	19	4
Benton	36	2	2	0	32	191	69	68	54	1
Butler[4]	68	0	14	6	48	608	133	356	119	4
Camden[4]	98	0	13	0	85	393	101	232	60	1
Carter[4]	36	0	1	1	34	36	10	21	5	2
Cedar	44	0	9	0	35	97	41	55	1	0
Clark[4]	13	0	1	0	12	82	32	45	5	2
Crawford	16	0	0	0	16	220	66	108	46	0
Dent[4]	13	1	5	0	7	65	30	28	7	1
Douglas[4]	14	0	3	0	11	35	12	15	8	1
Gasconade	36	0	2	2	32	124	41	58	25	0
Gentry	2	0	0	0	2	26	5	11	10	0
Grundy[4]	3	0	0	0	3	19	4	7	8	0
Henry	48	0	3	1	44	206	74	101	31	6
Hickory	3	0	0	0	3	67	21	38	8	0
Holt	3	0	1	0	2	44	21	18	5	0
Howell	91	1	2	1	87	380	102	215	63	0
Iron	12	0	2	0	10	63	18	36	9	1
Johnson[4]	25	2	1	0	22	263	57	165	41	0
Lawrence[4]	29	2	9	2	16	235	54	160	21	1
Lewis	8	0	1	1	6	55	16	32	7	2
Livingston[4]	3	0	0	0	3	17	3	11	3	1
Madison[4]	1	0	1	0	0	19	5	13	1	0
McDonald[4]	63	2	7	2	52	170	56	114	0	2
Mississippi[4]	5	0	3	0	2	30	7	22	1	0
Monroe	13	1	2	0	10	27	5	13	9	0
Montgomery	0	0	0	0	0	47	11	34	2	0
New Madrid[4]	24	2	2	1	19	84	19	56	9	2
Nodaway[4]	1	0	0	0	1	54	16	33	5	0
Oregon[4]	22	0	4	1	17	59	22	26	11	2
Pemiscot[4]	27	1	1	2	23	90	12	56	22	1
Perry[4]	28	0	1	0	27	29	10	16	3	0
Pettis[4]	18	0	2	1	15	34	14	16	4	1
Phelps[4]	41	1	10	0	30	238	62	131	45	1
Pike[4]	19	0	2	1	16	91	37	47	7	1
Pulaski[4]	51	0	11	2	38	177	34	121	22	1
Ralls[4]	16	0	0	0	16	65	11	50	4	0
Randolph[4]	22	0	3	0	19	79	24	49	6	0
Ripley[4]	3	1	0	0	2	100	27	54	19	0
Saline[4]	58	1	0	0	57	57	19	30	8	2
Schuyler[4]	4	0	0	0	4	67	11	50	6	1
Shannon	17	3	1	0	13	26	4	12	10	2
Shelby	0	0	0	0	0	17	2	12	3	0
St. Clair[4]	24	0	3	0	21	133	70	38	25	1
Ste. Genevieve	54	0	7	0	47	133	20	75	38	0
Stoddard[4]	26	0	5	0	21	217	61	135	21	4
Stone[4]	181	1	16	44	120	302	84	180	38	2
Taney[4]	75	1	8	3	63	219	29	150	40	0
Washington	91	2	16	0	73	457	128	219	110	3
Wayne[4]	17	1	0	0	16	157	59	83	15	1
Worth	4	1	0	0	3	12	3	4	5	1
Wright	19	0	2	0	17	50	18	19	13	1
MONTANA										
Metropolitan Counties										
Carbon	14	0	1	0	13	61	12	43	6	0
Cascade	93	0	12	0	81	262	62	184	16	3
Missoula	104	2	14	0	88	280	98	157	25	2
Stillwater	25	0	3	0	22	50	12	31	7	0
Yellowstone	147	1	10	6	130	809	110	556	143	7
Nonmetropolitan Counties										
Beaverhead	0	0	0	0	0	1	0	1	0	0
Big Horn	72	0	8	5	59	213	33	128	52	2
Blaine	7	0	2	1	4	9	2	6	1	0
Broadwater	22	0	0	0	22	40	11	26	3	1
Butte-Silver Bow[7]	142	0	10	11	121			1,108	197	5
Carter	0	0	0	0	0	0	0	0	0	0
Chouteau	4	0	0	0	4	4	1	3	0	0
Custer	4	0	2	0	2	6	2	4	0	0
Dawson	5	0	2	0	3	41	4	35	2	1
Deer Lodge	17	0	0	0	17	189	49	121	19	3
Fergus	11	0	1	0	10	19	4	14	1	1
Flathead	191	6	26	6	153	800	134	521	145	5
Gallatin	127	1	38	0	88	400	23	330	47	2

Table 10. Offenses Known to Law Enforcement, by Selected State Metropolitan and Nonmetropolitan Counties, 2020—Continued

(Number.)

State/county	Violent crime	Murder and nonnegligent manslaughter	Rape[1]	Robbery	Aggravated assault	Property crime	Burglary	Larceny-theft	Motor vehicle theft	Arson[2]
Garfield	1	0	0	0	1	3	0	3	0	0
Glacier	12	1	1	0	10	37	7	18	12	0
Golden Valley	2	0	1	0	1	0	0	0	0	0
Granite	2	0	0	0	2	17	3	11	3	0
Hill	30	1	4	1	24	106	7	90	9	1
Jefferson	25	0	2	1	22	89	15	63	11	2
Lake	135	2	16	6	111	335	62	185	88	8
Lewis and Clark	90	1	15	3	71	317	66	204	47	1
Liberty	0	0	0	0	0	0	0	0	0	0
Lincoln	17	0	3	0	14	44	2	38	4	1
Madison	8	1	0	0	7	39	11	23	5	0
McCone	0	0	0	0	0	1	0	0	1	0
Meagher	1	0	1	0	0	5	0	4	1	0
Mineral	18	0	0	0	18	36	5	22	9	1
Musselshell	27	0	0	0	27	38	1	28	9	0
Park	11	0	3	1	7	43	2	35	6	3
Phillips	21	0	5	0	16	37	10	21	6	0
Pondera	6	0	0	0	6	9	0	7	2	1
Powder River	0	0			0	0	0	0	0	0
Powell[7]			2	0	19	15	9	5	1	0
Prairie	11	0	0	0	11	2	0	2	0	0
Ravalli	101	5	7	1	88	350	75	245	30	7
Richland	14	0	1	0	13	28	4	16	8	0
Roosevelt	53	2	1	1	49	61	18	23	20	2
Rosebud	4	0	0	0	4	12	2	9	1	0
Sanders	7	0	1	0	6	52	5	43	4	0
Sheridan	10	0	2	0	8	39	6	32	1	1
Sweet Grass	20	0	4	0	16	36	3	28	5	1
Teton	13	0	1	0	12	31	0	25	6	0
Toole	41	0	8	1	32	45	5	39	1	1
Valley	14	0	2	0	12	38	4	32	2	0
Wheatland	2	0	0	0	2	1	0	1	0	0
Wibaux	1	0	0	0	1	0	0	0	0	0
NEBRASKA										
Metropolitan Counties										
Cass	22	0	10	0	12	182	41	114	27	1
Dixon	5	0	1	0	4	26	9	13	4	0
Douglas	78	1	20	8	49	507	88	338	81	8
Hall	31	0	6	0	25	101	24	62	15	1
Saunders	12	0	1	1	10	49	18	25	6	0
Washington	4	0	0	0	4	50	13	34	3	0
Nonmetropolitan Counties										
Adams	11	0	7	0	4	82	23	51	8	0
Boone	3	0	0	0	3	19	5	12	2	1
Box Butte	1	0	0	0	1	9	3	6	0	
Buffalo	19	0	5	1	13	110	10	79	21	0
Cheyenne	9	0	2	0	7	11	4	3	4	0
Custer	0	0	0	0	0	20	1	16	3	1
Dawes	0	0	0	0	0	5	0	5	0	
Fillmore	8	0	0	0	8	12	4	7	1	0
Franklin	0	0	0	0	0	18	5	9	4	
Frontier	5	1	3	0	1	28	3	23	2	0
Gage	20	0	2	0	18	37	9	28	0	1
Gosper	2	0	1	0	1	11	3	8	0	1
Johnson	11	0	1	0	10	17	5	11	1	0
Kearney	9	0	4	0	5	29	11	17	1	0
Keith	5	0	0	0	5	20	5	13	2	0
Keya Paha	0	0	0	0	0	0	0	0	0	
Knox[4]	0	0	0	0	0	29	7	16	6	0
Lincoln	11	0	2	1	8	82	25	45	12	0
Madison	11	0	2	1	8	15	4	8	3	1
Nemaha	7	0	2	0	5	29	13	11	5	0
Pawnee	3	0	0	1	2	21	7	7	7	0
Perkins	4	0	1	0	3	20	7	9	4	0
Phelps	7	0	4	0	3	22	5	15	2	0
Saline	12	0	2	0	10	23	7	16	0	1
Thayer	9	0	0	0	9	19	2	16	1	0
Valley	3	0	0	0	3	4	0	4	0	0
Wayne	3	0	1	0	2	16	2	13	1	1
NEVADA										
Metropolitan Counties										
Carson City[4]	216	1	62	13	140	617	155	384	78	9
Storey	36	3	2	2	29	86	19	60	7	0
Washoe[4]	241	2	41	8	190	722	182	460	80	19
Nonmetropolitan Counties										
Churchill	26	2	4	3	17	175	66	81	28	4
Douglas[4]	54	3	9	5	37	531	57	440	34	7

Table 10. Offenses Known to Law Enforcement, by Selected State Metropolitan and Nonmetropolitan Counties, 2020—Continued

(Number.)

State/county	Violent crime	Murder and nonnegligent manslaughter	Rape[1]	Robbery	Aggravated assault	Property crime	Burglary	Larceny-theft	Motor vehicle theft	Arson[2]
Elko[4]	86	2	14	3	67	192	42	119	31	1
Humboldt	28	0	2	0	26	68	36	17	15	
Lander	50	0	6	0	44	88	36	36	16	4
Lincoln	1	0	0	0	1	36	13	17	6	0
Lyon[4]	153	1	16	11	125	521	142	307	72	10
Nye[4]	168	3	21	22	122	677	218	338	121	21
Pershing	49	2	2	0	45	27	10	15	2	1
White Pine	26	1	6	2	17	81	33	35	13	1
NEW HAMPSHIRE										
Metropolitan Counties										
Strafford	1	0	0	0	1	0	0	0	0	1
Nonmetropolitan Counties										
Carroll	3	0	1	0	2	51	3	42	6	0
Cheshire	2	0	1	0	1	8	2	6	0	0
Grafton	8	0	7	0	1	1	0	1	0	0
Merrimack	0	0	0	0	0	0	0	0	0	0
NEW JERSEY										
Metropolitan Counties										
Atlantic	0	0	0	0	0	0	0	0	0	0
Bergen	0	0	0	0	0	0	0	0	0	0
Burlington	0	0	0	0	0	0	0	0	0	0
Camden	2	0	0	1	1	11	0	11	0	0
Cape May	0	0	0	0	0	0	0	0	0	0
Cumberland	0	0	0	0	0	0	0	0	0	0
Essex	90	0	7	28	55	108	14	88	6	0
Gloucester	0	0	0	0	0	0	0	0	0	0
Hudson	0	0	0	0	0	0	0	0	0	0
Hunterdon	0	0	0	0	0	0	0	0	0	0
Mercer	4	0	0	0	4	4	0	3	1	0
Middlesex	0	0	0	0	0	0	0	0	0	0
Monmouth	3	0	0	0	3	0	0	0	0	0
Morris	0	0	0	0	0	0	0	0	0	0
Ocean	2	0	0	0	2	2	1	1	0	0
Passaic	0	0	0	0	0	0	0	0	0	0
Salem	0	0	0	0	0	0	0	0	0	0
Somerset	2	0	0	0	2	0	0	0	0	0
Sussex	0	0	0	0	0	0	0	0	0	0
Union	0	0	0	0	0	0	0	0	0	0
Warren	0	0	0	0	0	0	0	0	0	0
NEW MEXICO										
Metropolitan Counties										
Dona Ana	305	5	31	19	250	978	289	542	147	9
San Juan	186	2	27	5	152	358	103	207	48	8
Valencia	178	1	25	7	145	601	228	255	118	
Nonmetropolitan Counties										
Curry	16	0	1	2	13	104	65	31	8	
Eddy	73	3	13	2	55	544	124	302	118	
NEW YORK										
Metropolitan Counties										
Albany	12	0	4	0	8	111	11	92	8	0
Broome[4]	34	1	15	5	13	460	71	356	33	1
Chemung	9	0	1	0	8	172	13	152	7	0
Dutchess	34	0	11	4	19	376	42	308	26	
Erie	52	2	0	6	44	570	57	488	25	5
Herkimer	0	0	0	0	0	0	0	0	0	0
Jefferson[4]	10	0	3	0	7	190	12	173	5	
Madison	20	1	4	3	12	98	20	70	8	2
Monroe[4]	134	0	23	30	81	2,014	251	1,629	134	4
Nassau	1,304	14	45	358	887	8,572	752	7,365	455	
Niagara[4]	28	0	10	8	10	536	81	400	55	6
Oneida	47	1	27	3	16	245	33	196	16	7
Onondaga	219	1	39	33	146	1,686	212	1,254	220	3
Ontario	58	1	27	2	28	705	95	595	15	3
Orange	2	0	0	0	2	15	0	15	0	0
Oswego	35	0	8	6	21	256	51	165	40	4
Putnam	12	0	3	0	9	117	20	87	10	0
Rensselaer	20	0	6	3	11	147	23	117	7	0
Schenectady	4	0	0	1	3	10	1	8	1	0
Schoharie	4	0	1	0	3	37	5	28	4	0
Suffolk	18	0	0	0	18	0	0	0	0	0
Suffolk County Police Department	1,118	30	98	291	699	14,907	973	12,769	1,165	59
Tioga	14	0	2	1	11	118	16	96	6	0
Tompkins	27	0	7	0	20	242	21	211	10	0
Ulster	5	0	1	1	3	115	18	92	5	2
Warren	32	0	23	1	8	304	40	260	4	2

Table 10. Offenses Known to Law Enforcement, by Selected State Metropolitan and Nonmetropolitan Counties, 2020—Continued

(Number.)

State/county	Violent crime	Murder and nonnegligent manslaughter	Rape[1]	Robbery	Aggravated assault	Property crime	Burglary	Larceny-theft	Motor vehicle theft	Arson[2]
Westchester Public Safety	15	0	0	5	10	150	15	134	1	4
Yates	10	1	4	0	5	123	15	106	2	0
Nonmetropolitan Counties										
Allegany	0	0	0	0	0	1	1	0	0	0
Columbia	26	0	7	5	14	253	53	193	7	1
Delaware	30	1	12	0	17	159	51	102	6	1
Essex	1	0	0	0	1	1	0	1	0	0
Fulton	13	0	2	0	11	243	47	181	15	1
Genesee	26	0	13	1	12	231	33	176	22	3
Greene	11	0	2	1	8	23	4	18	1	3
Hamilton	0	0	0	0	0	10	0	10	0	0
Montgomery	6	0	0	0	6	238	14	218	6	0
Schuyler	6	0	1	2	3	9	3	6	0	1
Seneca[4]	7	0	2	1	4	81	8	67	6	0
Steuben	10	0	5	1	4	73	21	45	7	3
St. Lawrence[4]	8	0	0	0	8	19	4	15	0	1
Sullivan	23	3	3	2	15	222	24	191	7	0
Wyoming	20	0	8	1	11	128	17	108	3	0
NORTH CAROLINA										
Metropolitan Counties										
Alamance	147	5	7	9	126	576	164	338	74	5
Alexander	60	1	10	2	47	429	135	251	43	4
Anson	35	1	1	1	32	209	99	90	20	6
Buncombe	216	3	9	32	172	1,808	475	1,043	290	17
Cabarrus	52	0	5	5	42	675	168	453	54	4
Caldwell	60	1	5	5	49	950	294	537	119	6
Camden	13	2	2	1	8	53	15	35	3	2
Catawba	150	1	39	18	92	1,050	261	654	135	15
Craven	142	6	5	9	122	767	251	438	78	2
Currituck	70	0	6	2	62	283	67	197	19	5
Davidson	83	1	3	11	68	1,305	368	757	180	12
Durham	101	1	1	25	74	622	186	368	68	5
Edgecombe	140	1	3	10	126	346	123	198	25	3
Forsyth	254	1	22	20	211	1,568	381	1,057	130	12
Franklin	106	3	9	7	87	531	142	345	44	3
Gaston	18	0	0	0	18	4	0	4	0	0
Gaston County Police Department	229	3	38	27	161	1,075	302	604	169	17
Gates[4]	16	0	3	0	13	89	21	59	9	1
Granville	41	1	7	3	30	287	95	177	15	4
Guilford	227	5	11	40	171	988	274	578	136	11
Harnett[4]	229	5	18	18	188	1,552	462	905	185	31
Haywood	77	3	14	5	55	831	346	407	78	4
Iredell	140	2	8	9	121	793	271	454	68	9
Johnston	136	4	27	20	85	1,471	356	1,001	114	7
Lincoln	143	2	10	7	124	1,003	243	693	67	6
Madison	16	0	5	0	11	164	58	83	23	2
New Hanover	143	2	19	25	97	1,304	207	1,042	55	6
Onslow	162	1	14	16	131	1,427	403	906	118	7
Orange	65	2	5	3	55	414	108	267	39	2
Pamlico	26	1	6	0	19	196	40	135	21	1
Person	54	2	4	5	43	303	110	165	28	3
Pitt	177	5	3	30	139	765	204	517	44	7
Rockingham	81	3	20	8	50	639	204	367	68	2
Rowan	185	3	24	21	137	1,100	272	690	138	9
Union	206	2	34	22	148	1,850	362	1,339	149	11
Wake	254	8	13	29	204	1,258	341	785	132	13
Wayne	176	5	7	17	147	1,145	359	601	185	10
Yadkin	46	0	7	3	36	456	131	276	49	0
Nonmetropolitan Counties										
Ashe	36	0	11	0	25	200	85	98	17	1
Avery	25	0	3	0	22	124	34	82	8	1
Bertie	7	0	1	4	2	43	12	26	5	0
Bladen	137	5	11	7	114	498	172	259	67	6
Carteret	85	1	16	4	64	604	197	370	37	3
Caswell	18	3	4	3	8	121	35	75	11	1
Cherokee	72	0	8	2	62	949	299	588	62	10
Chowan	19	1	3	2	13	87	43	40	4	0
Cleveland	138	3	24	17	94	690	232	362	96	3
Dare	23	2	6	0	15	261	64	190	7	2
Duplin	77	4	6	10	57	851	413	344	94	5
Greene	49	9	11	2	27	234	76	138	20	3
Hertford	22	7	2	1	12	146	59	77	10	1
Jackson	95	0	18	1	76	886	405	413	68	19
McDowell	65	2	18	5	40	666	235	349	82	14
Mitchell	7	0	4	1	2	33	4	24	5	1
Montgomery	49	1	6	2	40	247	60	149	38	1
Moore	58	2	8	5	43	595	150	420	25	6
Pasquotank	88	1	8	3	76	266	115	130	21	3

Table 10. Offenses Known to Law Enforcement, by Selected State Metropolitan and Nonmetropolitan Counties, 2020—Continued

(Number.)

State/county	Violent crime	Murder and nonnegligent manslaughter	Rape[1]	Robbery	Aggravated assault	Property crime	Burglary	Larceny-theft	Motor vehicle theft	Arson[2]
Polk[4]	15	1	2	1	11	218	87	111	20	1
Richmond	188	6	15	25	142	1,059	407	569	83	20
Robeson	1,035	35	17	81	902	2,412	990	1,200	222	45
Sampson	140	3	24	13	100	767	316	353	98	17
Scotland	42	3	2	4	33	190	105	72	13	2
Stanly	47	0	7	2	38	389	142	205	42	1
Surry	97	3	25	11	58	778	149	481	148	15
Swain	36	2	4	2	28	310	197	99	14	3
Transylvania	37	1	6	0	30	214	63	130	21	1
Vance	199	3	18	23	155	465	173	240	52	12
Watauga	20	1	4	1	14	185	57	121	7	3
Wilkes	134	2	19	4	109	659	213	356	90	13
Wilson	44	1	1	4	38	291	61	197	33	2
Yancey	12	0	4	4	4	187	74	102	11	0
NORTH DAKOTA										
Metropolitan Counties										
Burleigh	28	2	1	0	25	121	33	67	21	3
Cass	17	2	2	0	13	152	57	69	26	1
Grand Forks	16	1	3	0	12	91	26	53	12	0
Morton	5	0	2	0	3	84	16	59	9	1
Oliver	0	0	0	0	0	3	0	3	0	0
Nonmetropolitan Counties										
Adams	1	0	1	0	0	19	4	14	1	0
Barnes	6	0	2	0	4	25	7	15	3	0
Benson	1	1	0	0	0	11	2	4	5	0
Billings	1	0	0	0	1	3	0	2	1	0
Bottineau	3	0	0	0	3	56	11	33	12	1
Bowman	0	0	0	0	0	4	3	1	0	0
Burke	1	0	0	0	1	0	0	0	0	0
Cavalier	4	0	0	0	4	17	5	11	1	0
Dickey	0	0	0	0	0	6	2	2	2	0
Divide	2	0	0	0	2	19	3	15	1	0
Dunn	0	0	0	0	0	8	1	4	3	0
Eddy	0	0	0	0	0	17	2	10	5	1
Emmons	2	0	0	0	2	44	16	21	7	1
Foster	0	0	0	0	0	6	3	3	0	0
Golden Valley	3	0	2	0	1	3	1	2	0	0
Grant	0	0	0	0	0	8	3	5	0	0
Griggs	0	0	0	0	0	12	7	5	0	0
Hettinger	4	0	2	0	2	17	5	9	3	0
Kidder	0	0	0	0	0	6	2	4	0	0
Lamoure	1	0	1	0	0	8	1	5	2	0
Logan	0	0	0	0	0	11	7	4	0	0
McHenry	24	0	7	0	17	40	9	20	11	0
McIntosh	0	0	0	0	0	4	3	1	0	0
McKenzie	25	0	6	2	17	116	25	71	20	1
McLean	5	0	1	0	4	91	25	55	11	0
Mercer	2	0	0	0	2	30	7	20	3	1
Mountrail	3	0	0	2	1	72	10	44	18	0
Nelson	0	0	0	0	0	25	10	13	2	1
Pembina	6	0	2	0	4	42	8	29	5	2
Pierce	3	0	1	0	2	22	3	12	7	1
Ramsey	3	0	2	0	1	23	2	14	7	0
Ransom	2	0	1	0	1	30	7	18	5	0
Renville	3	0	1	0	2	11	1	10	0	0
Richland	7	0	1	0	6	91	20	57	14	0
Rolette	5	0	1	0	4	9	2	2	5	0
Sargent	2	0	0	0	2	11	2	6	3	1
Sheridan	0	0	0	0	0	4	0	4	0	0
Sioux	0	0	0	0	0	0	0	0	0	0
Slope	0	0	0	0	0	0	0	0	0	0
Stark	3	0	1	0	2	76	14	51	11	0
Steele	0	0	0	0	0	4	2	1	1	0
Stutsman	4	0	2	0	2	53	17	28	8	0
Towner	2	0	2	0	0	23	8	10	5	0
Traill	1	0	0	0	1	24	8	9	7	0
Walsh	6	0	2	1	3	78	11	54	13	1
Ward	45	0	7	2	36	123	41	63	19	2
Williams	9	0	1	2	6	138	20	85	33	0
OHIO										
Metropolitan Counties										
Allen[4, 9]		0		13	14	523	123	353	47	1
Belmont	51	1	20	2	28	152	31	115	6	0
Carroll	6	0	1	0	5	63	26	34	3	0
Clark	53	1	5	3	44	713	148	537	28	3
Clermont	82	1	17	3	61	838	193	579	66	4
Delaware	45	0	15	12	18	874	115	730	29	2
Fairfield	56	2	8	5	41	930	89	804	37	0

Table 10. Offenses Known to Law Enforcement, by Selected State Metropolitan and Nonmetropolitan Counties, 2020—Continued

(Number.)

State/county	Violent crime	Murder and nonnegligent manslaughter	Rape[1]	Robbery	Aggravated assault	Property crime	Burglary	Larceny-theft	Motor vehicle theft	Arson[2]
Fulton	10	0	2	1	7	176	44	126	6	0
Greene	40	0	14	2	24	349	70	244	35	1
Hocking	29	0	8	3	18	321	88	205	28	2
Jefferson	18	0	4	0	14	56	14	34	8	2
Lake	275	3	16	4	252	282	65	207	10	0
Lawrence	66	0	22	2	42	377	72	272	33	1
Licking	67	0	16	2	49	692	126	511	55	2
Lorain	68	1	16	9	42	448	159	270	19	6
Lucas	83	0	16	7	60	609	107	448	54	2
Madison	23	0	7	2	14	225	38	154	33	0
Mahoning[4]	5	0	2	1	2	56	6	49	1	0
Medina	12	0	5	1	6	277	84	165	28	1
Miami	28	0	6	1	21	325	98	212	15	5
Montgomery	305	5	37	52	211	968	208	581	179	17
Morrow	25	0	6	1	18	67	24	35	8	2
Perry	4	0	1	0	3	49	10	32	7	0
Pickaway	28	0	6	2	20	579	160	395	24	1
Richland	67	1	29	6	31	607	132	449	26	3
Stark	131	0	31	18	82	1,634	349	1,135	150	9
Summit	86	1	28	12	45	988	127	780	81	2
Trumbull	21	1	0	1	19	181	61	112	8	2
Union	31	0	9	0	22	179	40	131	8	4
Wood	29	1	5	3	20	234	29	192	13	2
Nonmetropolitan Counties										
Adams	6	0	1	1	4	156	46	84	26	1
Ashland	28	1	15	0	12	105	39	59	7	1
Ashtabula	43	1	8	4	30	417	66	320	31	2
Athens	14	0	2	1	11	342	69	254	19	1
Auglaize	6	0	2	0	4	57	6	46	5	0
Champaign	20	0	2	1	17	173	31	126	16	1
Clinton	16	0	5	1	10	79	21	45	13	0
Columbiana	32	1	8	0	23	306	94	191	21	6
Coshocton	72	2	18	1	51	472	103	342	27	7
Crawford	6	0	2	0	4	79	32	41	6	1
Defiance	10	1	2	0	7	96	25	67	4	2
Erie	8	0	0	0	8	139	20	114	5	0
Fayette	25	1	6	3	15	277	67	188	22	1
Gallia	20	1	3	2	14	264	75	164	25	1
Hancock	31	0	16	3	12	190	30	143	17	1
Hardin	13	0	1	0	12	60	9	48	3	0
Harrison	8	2	2	1	3	33	8	23	2	0
Henry	17	1	2	0	14	142	38	100	4	1
Highland	43	0	20	1	22	330	93	193	44	2
Jackson	41	4	17	1	19	183	39	130	14	2
Logan	27	0	2	1	24	135	31	96	8	0
Meigs	22	0	2	1	19	245	84	132	29	2
Mercer	6	0	4	0	2	49	5	44	0	0
Monroe	10	0	2	0	8	27	7	13	7	3
Morgan	34	1	2	2	29	107	34	54	19	1
Muskingum	110	0	28	6	76	607	155	416	36	9
Paulding	11	0	2	2	7	159	53	101	5	0
Pike	55	1	18	5	31	536	125	304	107	12
Preble	13	0	4	2	7	173	29	128	16	1
Putnam	21	0	9	0	12	79	15	53	11	0
Ross	106	2	28	12	64	1,183	306	752	125	15
Scioto	36	0	13	4	19	531	121	350	60	10
Shelby	4	0	3	0	1	126	22	97	7	1
Tuscarawas	40	1	15	0	24	260	86	140	34	2
Van Wert	20	1	4	2	13	81	26	49	6	0
Vinton	9	0	2	0	7	85	32	36	17	1
Washington	16	1	8	0	7	213	60	136	17	3
OKLAHOMA										
Metropolitan Counties										
Canadian	21	0	5	0	16	138	34	69	35	3
Cleveland	43	1	12	1	29	213	87	105	21	2
Comanche	13	1	4	2	6	130	57	52	21	4
Cotton	9	0	0	1	8	23	3	12	8	1
Creek	52	5	4	1	42	360	124	166	70	3
Garfield	14	0	2	0	12	116	45	62	9	2
Grady	37	1	8	0	28	277	79	163	35	3
Lincoln	55	1	8	1	45	325	118	142	65	6
Logan	45	0	12	3	30	410	139	201	70	3
McClain	32	0	9	3	20	235	87	114	34	1
Oklahoma	45	4	1	1	39	189	41	96	52	1
Okmulgee	41	1	5	1	34	158	49	80	29	1
Osage	42	2	6	5	29	321	118	146	57	6
Pawnee	30	0	5	0	25	125	22	66	37	0
Rogers[4]	128	0	20	2	106	410	138	203	69	3
Sequoyah	61	0	16	2	43	230	97	103	30	6

Table 10. Offenses Known to Law Enforcement, by Selected State Metropolitan and Nonmetropolitan Counties, 2020—Continued

(Number.)

State/county	Violent crime	Murder and nonnegligent manslaughter	Rape[1]	Robbery	Aggravated assault	Property crime	Burglary	Larceny-theft	Motor vehicle theft	Arson[2]
Tulsa	203	0	21	22	160	954	305	465	184	10
Wagoner	78	0	6	5	67	317	96	184	37	11
Nonmetropolitan Counties										
Adair	31	2	4	0	25	132	43	52	37	7
Alfalfa	2	0	0	0	2	39	7	26	6	0
Atoka	7	0	0	0	7	45	10	30	5	1
Beaver	4	0	0	0	4	27	8	16	3	0
Beckham	9	0	2	0	7	80	30	42	8	1
Blaine	14	0	0	0	14	86	25	51	10	0
Bryan	39	1	9	5	24	235	77	120	38	2
Caddo	16	0	4	1	11	129	45	63	21	4
Carter	23	0	7	1	15	179	57	97	25	9
Cherokee	77	1	9	2	65	454	127	232	95	11
Choctaw[4]	47	3	2	1	41	72	23	29	20	0
Cimarron	1	0	1	0	0	9	3	4	2	0
Coal	6	0	1	0	5	15	4	7	4	0
Craig	15	0	5	0	10	108	52	51	5	3
Custer	6	0	0	0	6	97	41	49	7	1
Delaware	54	3	9	1	41	336	108	168	60	9
Dewey	14	1	3	0	10	41	11	22	8	0
Ellis	8	0	0	2	6	70	29	36	5	1
Garvin	33	0	4	0	29	242	85	122	35	4
Grant	5	0	2	0	3	42	9	31	2	0
Harmon	1	0	0	0	1	15	4	11	0	0
Harper	2	0	1	0	1	7	1	6	0	0
Haskell	7	0	2	1	4	73	23	40	10	4
Hughes	12	0	1	1	10	108	27	62	19	1
Jackson	9	0	2	0	7	32	6	22	4	0
Jefferson	2	0	0	0	2	18	2	12	4	0
Johnston	25	0	2	1	22	45	16	20	9	1
Kay[4]	19	0	3	1	15	135	50	65	20	7
Kingfisher	8	0	1	0	7	60	9	45	6	2
Kiowa	4	0	0	0	4	16	4	9	3	0
Latimer	12	0	0	0	12	87	26	32	29	3
Le Flore	51	1	3	0	47	237	77	121	39	4
Love	12	0	3	0	9	119	21	83	15	2
Major	7	0	1	0	6	45	7	31	7	0
Marshall	7	0	0	1	6	192	72	82	38	0
Mayes	74	0	18	2	54	347	104	158	85	9
McCurtain	58	1	3	0	54	319	116	159	44	11
McIntosh	37	0	6	3	28	212	88	78	46	4
Murray	4	0	2	0	2	23	3	17	3	0
Muskogee	58	3	9	2	44	235	91	105	39	6
Noble	10	2	0	0	8	61	13	37	11	0
Nowata	5	0	0	0	5	37	11	21	5	0
Okfuskee	14	5	1	1	7	93	34	47	12	0
Ottawa	26	1	1	2	22	174	42	102	30	6
Payne	38	0	6	2	30	251	68	135	48	7
Pittsburg	73	0	11	1	61	376	156	171	49	7
Pontotoc	22	0	0	0	22	168	55	89	24	5
Pottawatomie	43	4	9	2	28	393	125	203	65	4
Pushmataha	16	0	0	0	16	114	72	31	11	4
Roger Mills	10	0	1	0	9	21	8	13	0	0
Seminole	29	1	3	0	25	323	112	167	44	8
Stephens	28	0	4	0	24	117	45	60	12	1
Texas	1	0	1	0	0	59	13	38	8	1
Tillman	2	0	0	0	2	26	10	11	5	0
Washita	11	0	2	0	9	31	10	18	3	1
Woods	5	0	1	0	4	22	7	13	2	0
Woodward	17	1	3	0	13	63	16	40	7	0
OREGON										
Metropolitan Counties										
Clackamas	443	1	56	84	302	4,384	636	3,139	609	29
Deschutes	85	0	14	9	62	585	78	437	70	12
Josephine	96	5	9	8	74	322	38	132	152	11
Linn	66	2	15	5	44	827	198	526	103	24
Multnomah[7]			19	22	123	1,432	132	994	306	18
Polk	42	0	2	5	35	343	108	209	26	5
Washington	438	1	106	44	287	2,789	345	2,041	403	35
Yamhill	51	1	12	4	34	440	100	280	60	8
Nonmetropolitan Counties										
Baker	7	0	0	1	6	124	21	89	14	2
Clatsop	44	1	4	2	37	187	40	128	19	0
Crook	33	0	2	0	31	87	19	62	6	1
Douglas	218	1	21	7	189	952	217	518	217	16
Gilliam	3	0	1	0	2	32	11	17	4	0
Jefferson	9	2	4	0	3	123	19	78	26	2
Lincoln	49	0	9	2	38	319	92	211	16	3
Morrow	29	0	4	1	24	124	22	85	17	5

Table 10. Offenses Known to Law Enforcement, by Selected State Metropolitan and Nonmetropolitan Counties, 2020—Continued

(Number.)

State/county	Violent crime	Murder and nonnegligent manslaughter	Rape[1]	Robbery	Aggravated assault	Property crime	Burglary	Larceny-theft	Motor vehicle theft	Arson[2]
Sherman	6	0	1	1	4	46	2	35	9	0
Tillamook	38	0	7	1	30	327	76	208	43	0
Umatilla	45	5	4	3	33	387	124	205	58	8
Union	10	2	1	0	7	202	41	144	17	3
Wallowa[4]	0	0	0	0	0	48	8	36	4	1
Wasco	30	0	7	0	23	178	34	128	16	1
PENNSYLVANIA[3]										
Metropolitan Counties										
Allegheny County Police Department	206	0	41	6	159	110	14	88	8	1
Washington	2	0	0	0	2	3	0	3	0	
Nonmetropolitan Counties										
Warren	0	0	0	0	0	0	0	0	0	0
SOUTH CAROLINA										
Metropolitan Counties										
Anderson	820	15	73	55	677	4,679	781	3,289	609	20
Beaufort	455	10	39	34	372	1,879	295	1,428	156	16
Berkeley	459	13	40	63	343	2,443	481	1,663	299	20
Calhoun	54	7	4	3	40	235	49	153	33	1
Chester	125	10	8	8	99	430	94	301	35	2
Clarendon	113	3	11	9	90	628	159	420	49	5
Dorchester	321	4	25	43	249	1,724	306	1,208	210	6
Edgefield	8	0	1	0	7	137	31	79	27	0
Fairfield	133	6	1	7	119	432	114	268	50	11
Florence	597	17	58	59	463	2,153	433	1,433	287	18
Greenville	1,865	29	169	254	1,413	8,471	1,467	5,947	1,057	57
Horry	1	0	0	0	1	1	0	1	0	0
Horry County Police Department	920	24	115	71	710	4,905	672	3,755	478	31
Kershaw	180	4	27	9	140	1,242	255	861	126	7
Lancaster	320	3	37	27	253	1,686	331	1,244	111	7
Laurens	239	2	24	12	201	1,121	275	724	122	14
Lexington	638	10	71	85	472	5,828	1,249	3,748	831	24
Pickens	247	1	18	11	217	1,346	337	817	192	8
Richland	2,115	19	110	248	1,738	8,728	1,262	6,384	1,082	45
Saluda	38	0	7	3	28	186	45	112	29	1
Spartanburg	997	5	47	64	881	4,808	1,167	3,043	598	39
Sumter	464	11	27	28	398	1,343	316	874	153	19
York	372	9	40	52	271	2,283	432	1,642	209	10
Nonmetropolitan Counties										
Abbeville	63	0	6	2	55	285	85	177	23	6
Allendale	5	0	1	0	4	44	6	28	10	1
Bamberg	21	1	0	4	16	133	34	70	29	0
Barnwell	115	4	1	1	109	246	69	146	31	2
Colleton	200	6	16	10	168	773	181	503	89	11
Georgetown	172	1	11	14	146	800	154	581	65	8
Lee	64	4	0	6	54	335	89	194	52	2
Marion	103	6	7	7	83	430	120	271	39	3
Marlboro	90	4	10	7	69	236	58	159	19	3
McCormick	5	0	0	0	5	71	11	54	6	1
Newberry	114	1	10	3	100	261	48	191	22	1
Oconee	199	3	29	12	155	1,743	362	1,201	180	13
Orangeburg	874	15	14	59	786	2,517	658	1,555	304	10
Union	16	1	2	2	11	196	38	146	12	1
SOUTH DAKOTA										
Metropolitan Counties										
Lincoln	49	0	11	0	38	350	136	176	38	1
McCook	6	0	2	0	4	31	18	12	1	0
Meade	31	0	7	1	23	157	23	118	16	0
Minnehaha	57	2	7	5	43	391	181	161	49	1
Pennington	177	1	80	6	90	441	112	281	48	3
Turner	23	0	4	0	19	57	18	33	6	0
Union	10	0	0	0	10	46	6	37	3	0
Nonmetropolitan Counties										
Aurora	1	0	0	0	1	1	0	1	0	0
Beadle	3	0	2	0	1	6	0	6	0	0
Bennett	3	0	1	0	2	9	5	0	4	0
Bon Homme	4	0	0	0	4	1	0	0	1	0
Brookings	10	0	2	0	8	32	9	23	0	0
Brown	8	1	2	0	5	42	17	19	6	0
Brule	1	0	0	0	1	5	0	4	1	0
Butte	5	0	1	0	4	26	4	21	1	1
Campbell	3	0	0	0	3	0	0	0	0	0
Charles Mix	17	0	2	0	15	37	13	17	7	0
Clay	2	0	1	0	1	47	12	28	7	1
Codington	8	0	1	0	7	44	8	27	9	2
Corson	6	0	0	0	6	21	9	11	1	1
Custer	11	0	5	0	6	131	19	96	16	0

Table 10. Offenses Known to Law Enforcement, by Selected State Metropolitan and Nonmetropolitan Counties, 2020—Continued

(Number.)

State/county	Violent crime	Murder and nonnegligent manslaughter	Rape[1]	Robbery	Aggravated assault	Property crime	Burglary	Larceny-theft	Motor vehicle theft	Arson[2]
Davison	6	0	3	0	3	14	9	2	3	0
Day	6	0	0	0	6	43	22	14	7	2
Deuel	3	0	0	0	3	8	2	5	1	0
Edmunds	1	0	0	0	1	1	1	0	0	0
Faulk	2	0	0	0	2	7	0	7	0	0
Gregory	1	0	0	0	1	0	0	0	0	0
Hamlin	9	1	3	0	5	35	4	26	5	1
Hanson	1	0	0	0	1	10	1	6	3	0
Harding	2	0	0	0	2	2	0	2	0	0
Hughes	9	0	1	0	8	18	3	7	8	0
Hutchinson	1	0	0	0	1	6	3	2	1	0
Jerauld	1	0	0	1	0	7	0	7	0	0
Jones	0	0	0	0	0	1	1	0	0	0
Kingsbury	4	0	3	0	1	5	1	2	2	0
Lake	4	0	4	0	0	20	6	14	0	0
Lawrence	7	0	1	0	6	52	28	24	0	0
Lyman	5	0	2	0	3	14	4	7	3	0
Marshall	7	0	1	0	6	38	8	30	0	0
McPherson	0	0	0	0	0	14	9	5	0	0
Mellette	7	0	0	0	7	8	2	3	3	0
Miner	1	0	0	0	1	5	1	1	3	0
Moody	0	0	0	0	0	2	1	1	0	0
Perkins	2	0	1	0	1	15	8	6	1	0
Potter	0	0	0	0	0	3	1	2	0	0
Roberts	23	0	0	0	23	9	2	6	1	1
Sanborn	3	0	2	0	1	5	0	2	3	0
Spink	18	0	2	0	16	45	16	25	4	3
Stanley	5	0	0	0	5	12	1	8	3	0
Sully	1	0	1	0	0	2	0	2	0	0
Todd	0	0	0	0	0	4	3	0	1	0
Tripp	1	0	1	0	0	4	0	4	0	0
Walworth	0	0	0	0	0	2	1	1	0	0
Yankton	10	0	1	0	9	88	23	55	10	0
Ziebach	0	0	0	0	0	0	0	0	0	0
TENNESSEE										
Metropolitan Counties										
Anderson	121	1	8	3	109	458	139	245	74	14
Blount	287	2	49	10	226	866	240	515	111	0
Bradley	209	3	16	7	183	797	183	506	108	2
Campbell	34	1	8	0	25	109	36	53	20	0
Cannon	9	0	0	0	9	49	20	18	11	1
Cheatham	96	0	8	1	87	270	49	175	46	4
Chester	18	1	1	0	16	37	12	17	8	0
Crockett	9	0	0	0	9	77	13	51	13	0
Dickson	115	0	15	3	97	313	83	180	50	8
Fayette	64	0	1	4	59	144	29	81	34	0
Gibson	62	2	4	6	50	177	67	85	25	1
Grainger	63	0	0	1	62	183	32	119	32	2
Hamblen	106	0	11	3	92	406	97	234	75	6
Hartsville/Trousdale	55	0	5	7	43	142	25	104	13	0
Hawkins	76	1	12	1	62	551	103	339	109	0
Jefferson	60	1	13	3	43	390	113	228	49	7
Knox	532	8	55	31	438	3,394	533	2,280	581	23
Loudon	112	1	8	3	100	394	77	248	69	3
Macon	62	0	2	0	60	79	22	41	16	1
Madison	70	0	5	3	62	302	69	198	35	1
Marion	83	0	2	2	79	220	38	113	69	0
Maury	154	1	29	4	120	520	85	324	111	2
Montgomery	123	1	9	1	112	473	80	335	58	3
Morgan	64	1	1	0	62	210	62	105	43	1
Polk	45	0	2	2	41	267	51	165	51	1
Roane	66	2	3	1	60	200	55	114	31	1
Robertson	100	1	7	2	90	264	76	146	42	0
Rutherford	219	3	22	8	186	648	122	452	74	7
Sequatchie	34	0	5	1	28	155	39	69	47	2
Shelby	784	9	32	49	694	2,565	416	1,877	272	11
Smith	38	1	0	0	37	120	27	77	16	1
Stewart	45	0	2	1	42	74	19	39	16	0
Sullivan	310	3	40	5	262	936	195	571	170	15
Sumner	121	2	9	5	105	375	80	242	53	3
Tipton	135	0	15	5	115	400	92	261	47	0
Unicoi	25	0	2	0	23	59	16	33	10	0
Union	42	1	4	3	34	181	51	98	32	2
Washington	150	3	14	5	128	700	128	386	186	6
Williamson	110	1	13	4	92	307	68	215	24	1
Wilson	105	0	3	4	98	526	119	350	57	1
Nonmetropolitan Counties										
Bedford	70	0	6	2	62	234	60	141	33	2
Benton	30	2	7	2	19	136	43	72	21	2

Table 10. Offenses Known to Law Enforcement, by Selected State Metropolitan and Nonmetropolitan Counties, 2020—Continued

(Number.)

State/county	Violent crime	Murder and nonnegligent manslaughter	Rape[1]	Robbery	Aggravated assault	Property crime	Burglary	Larceny-theft	Motor vehicle theft	Arson[2]
Bledsoe	15	0	0	0	15	50	8	25	17	1
Carroll	30	2	5	1	22	138	51	74	13	0
Claiborne	46	0	5	3	38	220	48	132	40	3
Clay	4	0	0	0	4	49	18	25	6	1
Cocke	133	2	7	2	122	366	86	192	88	8
Coffee	105	1	9	2	93	405	94	249	62	1
Cumberland	65	3	3	0	59	606	188	344	74	0
Decatur	45	0	7	2	36	136	50	67	19	5
DeKalb	13	0	2	0	11	100	24	53	23	2
Dyer	49	0	4	1	44	196	50	121	25	0
Fentress	47	0	10	0	37	226	68	133	25	1
Franklin	110	3	8	4	95	232	45	154	33	2
Giles	57	0	5	0	52	144	35	84	25	0
Greene	205	2	16	2	185	777	196	437	144	7
Grundy	81	0	3	1	77	222	31	144	47	2
Hancock	7	0	0	0	7	15	2	11	2	0
Hardeman	87	0	9	0	78	140	55	66	19	2
Hardin	63	1	5	4	53	441	149	242	50	1
Haywood	27	1	1	3	22	124	37	64	23	0
Henderson	65	1	10	0	54	221	82	103	36	1
Henry	47	3	6	0	38	263	84	148	31	5
Hickman	106	1	12	0	93	415	107	235	73	3
Houston	42	1	0	0	41	75	13	54	8	2
Humphreys	43	1	2	2	38	101	31	49	21	0
Jackson	24	0	2	1	21	61	10	37	14	1
Johnson	38	1	10	0	27	128	32	68	28	1
Lake	6	1	1	0	4	37	10	26	1	0
Lauderdale	73	2	6	1	64	176	53	106	17	1
Lawrence	77	0	12	1	64	296	96	147	53	1
Lewis	26	0	1	0	25	83	24	46	13	2
Lincoln	54	0	5	2	47	333	99	194	40	2
Marshall	28	0	1	1	26	80	17	47	16	0
McMinn	92	0	8	10	74	422	111	223	88	8
McNairy	41	0	1	1	39	201	56	110	35	2
Meigs	55	0	5	2	48	214	45	122	47	4
Monroe	193	2	19	4	168	813	221	453	139	11
Moore	13	0	4	0	9	43	11	28	4	0
Obion	52	0	3	0	49	217	76	126	15	2
Overton	24	0	5	0	19	159	11	109	39	3
Perry	9	0	0	0	9	35	7	24	4	1
Pickett	12	0	1	0	11	44	16	22	6	2
Rhea	74	1	7	0	66	251	29	168	54	1
Scott	45	0	3	1	41	167	90	55	22	1
Sevier	159	0	13	7	139	686	124	426	136	5
Van Buren	1	0	1	0	0	31	2	25	4	2
Warren	90	2	9	2	77	320	63	188	69	7
Wayne	18	0	0	0	18	90	21	45	24	1
Weakley	27	1	2	1	23	101	40	51	10	0
White	47	0	6	1	40	226	43	145	38	4
TEXAS										
Metropolitan Counties										
Atascosa	64	3	0	5	56	532	121	333	78	1
Austin	14	1	3	1	9	79	18	44	17	0
Bandera	13	0	1	0	12	205	60	122	23	0
Bastrop	198	1	27	21	149	636	152	387	97	4
Bell[4]	74	2	17	3	52	724	155	494	75	0
Bexar[4]	785	16	155	78	536	5,296	1,171	3,539	586	46
Brazoria	234	5	13	35	181	1,186	212	792	182	4
Brazos[4]	29	0	9	2	18	289	53	212	24	0
Burleson[4]	15	0	4	0	11	112	31	73	8	0
Caldwell[4]	17	0	6	2	9	96	20	59	17	3
Callahan	12	0	0	0	12	40	11	21	8	0
Cameron	182	2	43	13	124	804	224	525	55	2
Carson	12	0	0	0	12	15	6	7	2	0
Chambers	120	· 4	12	7	97	576	101	407	68	1
Collin	72	2	36	1	33	302	57	199	46	0
Comal	138	1	34	8	95	609	172	367	70	0
Coryell[4]	21	0	1	2	18	111	39	62	10	1
Crosby	3	0	0	0	3	27	14	8	5	1
Dallas[4]	44	0	19	4	21	213	43	134	36	0
Denton[4]	82	0	32	3	47	450	60	326	64	0
Ector	149	6	2	56	85	1,874	279	1,177	418	3
El Paso[4]	350	5	49	22	274	590	114	412	64	3
Fort Bend	1,003	11	151	113	728	4,689	674	3,652	363	0
Goliad	22	0	1	1	20	98	46	42	10	1
Grayson[4]	47	2	13	4	28	334	80	202	52	6
Gregg	82	3	19	4	56	407	88	245	74	2
Guadalupe	86	0	40	6	40	442	106	289	47	4
Hardin[4]	29	1	8	3	17	249	91	96	62	5
Harris[6]	8,813	133	1,010	2,082	5,588	43,757	6,585	30,334	6,838	

Table 10. Offenses Known to Law Enforcement, by Selected State Metropolitan and Nonmetropolitan Counties, 2020—Continued

(Number.)

State/county	Violent crime	Murder and nonnegligent manslaughter	Rape[1]	Robbery	Aggravated assault	Property crime	Burglary	Larceny-theft	Motor vehicle theft	Arson[2]
Harrison	94	2	0	3	89	464	124	262	78	0
Hays[4]	120	6	19	9	86	772	155	556	61	1
Hidalgo[4]	482	15	107	70	290	2,952	671	1,939	342	8
Hudspeth	2	0	1	0	1	15	5	6	4	0
Hunt[4]	336	1	26	6	303	494	104	275	115	1
Irion	1	0	0	0	1	13	1	8	4	0
Johnson[4]	188	1	34	9	144	643	151	407	85	4
Jones	6	1	1	0	4	41	14	23	4	0
Kaufman	106	2	35	10	59	665	176	382	107	2
Kendall	25	0	5	1	19	116	26	65	25	0
Lampasas[4]	12	0	1	0	11	114	42	63	9	1
Liberty	248	11	50	14	173	712	204	323	185	2
Lubbock	63	3	15	10	35	491	152	264	75	1
Lynn[4]	3	0	0	0	3	14	3	10	1	0
Martin	6	0	1	0	5	67	6	61	0	0
McLennan	81	0	20	3	58	612	171	379	62	8
Medina[4]	69	2	11	6	50	335	99	176	60	0
Midland	107	3	8	3	93	768	100	462	206	2
Nueces	66	2	15	1	48	135	36	98	1	4
Oldham[4]	2	0	0	0	2	14	5	6	3	0
Orange[4]	77	0	9	8	60	503	172	238	93	1
Potter	24	0	3	0	21	216	35	126	55	4
Randall	56	3	16	6	31	285	97	156	32	0
Robertson	6	0	2	0	4	114	33	70	11	1
Rockwall	14	0	2	1	11	64	14	42	8	0
Rusk	65	0	17	4	44	541	138	314	89	5
San Patricio	34	0	0	0	34	143	38	91	14	1
Smith	366	11	46	22	287	1,462	381	862	219	12
Sterling	4	0	0	0	4	16	5	8	3	0
Tarrant[4]	147	5	37	13	92	800	208	427	165	2
Taylor	48	1	13	0	34	95	36	49	10	0
Tom Green[4]	33	1	13	0	19	181	61	97	23	1
Travis[4]	761	3	93	79	586	3,474	695	2,332	447	23
Upshur[4]	53	3	12	3	35	286	114	139	33	6
Victoria	116	4	23	11	78	284	91	165	28	0
Waller	60	1	27	12	20	286	86	179	21	0
Webb[4]	64	0	4	2	58	239	78	135	26	1
Wichita	52	0	0	0	52	118	43	55	20	0
Williamson	170	0	43	21	106	1,850	319	1,409	122	2
Wilson[4]	16	1	9	0	6	174	54	95	25	1
Wise	92	0	21	4	67	342	94	201	47	0
Nonmetropolitan Counties										
Anderson	32	2	0	3	27	359	130	203	26	0
Andrews	11	2	1	1	7	150	15	124	11	0
Angelina	109	1	22	8	78	517	157	291	69	4
Aransas	60	1	10	1	48	224	73	136	15	0
Bailey[4]	0	0	0	0	0	25	5	15	5	0
Blanco[4]	25	1	0	0	24	57	19	37	1	5
Borden[4]	0	0	0	0	0	10	6	3	1	0
Bosque[4]	6	0	0	0	6	67	28	35	4	1
Brewster	4	0	1	0	3	18	9	6	3	0
Briscoe	1	0	0	0	1	5	0	2	3	0
Brooks[4]	1	0	0	0	1	3	1	0	2	0
Brown[4]	37	0	10	1	26	229	90	112	27	1
Burnet	52	1	9	3	39	237	59	143	35	9
Calhoun	20	0	8	0	12	87	23	53	11	1
Camp	18	0	5	0	13	66	16	41	9	0
Cass	19	1	3	1	14	192	75	90	27	4
Castro	3	0	0	0	3	24	4	13	7	0
Cherokee	49	1	5	0	43	441	120	253	68	1
Coke	3	0	0	0	3	18	9	7	2	0
Colorado	11	2	1	3	5	131	40	72	19	0
Comanche	10	4	0	0	6	55	17	35	3	1
Cooke[4]	25	3	5	0	17	124	44	55	25	1
Crane	3	0	1	0	2	10	1	7	2	0
Crockett	3	1	0	0	2	9	6	1	2	0
Dallam[4]	3	0	0	0	3	13	4	3	6	0
Dawson[4]	5	0	0	0	5	61	24	33	4	0
Deaf Smith	3	0	0	0	3	55	22	25	8	2
Delta	2	0	1	0	1	13	9	3	1	2
Dimmit	9	0	4	0	5	114	36	72	6	1
Donley[4]	4	0	1	0	3	23	10	10	3	
Duval	18	0	2	0	16	99	10	55	34	0
Eastland	6	1	4	0	1	40	14	18	8	4
Erath[4]	29	0	7	1	21	62	24	36	2	0
Fayette	23	0	12	1	10	107	48	40	19	0
Fisher	11	0	0	0	11	9	3	4	2	0
Floyd[4]	3	0	1	0	2	32	8	22	2	0
Franklin	19	0	4	1	14	49	19	25	5	0
Freestone[4]	23	0	1	0	22	82	30	40	12	1

Table 10. Offenses Known to Law Enforcement, by Selected State Metropolitan and Nonmetropolitan Counties, 2020—Continued

(Number.)

State/county	Violent crime	Murder and nonnegligent manslaughter	Rape[1]	Robbery	Aggravated assault	Property crime	Burglary	Larceny-theft	Motor vehicle theft	Arson[2]
Frio	10	0	0	0	10	63	23	33	7	0
Gaines	9	0	0	0	9	91	22	45	24	2
Garza	22	0	10	0	12	18	9	7	2	0
Gillespie[4]	9	0	3	1	5	30	8	20	2	0
Glasscock	2	0	0	0	2	20	6	9	5	0
Gonzales	24	0	8	0	16	99	26	62	11	0
Gray[4]	8	0	0	1	7	47	11	26	10	0
Grimes[4]	27	0	7	0	20	131	45	60	26	0
Hale	12	0	2	1	9	50	21	28	1	0
Hall	0	0	0	0	0	7	3	3	1	0
Hamilton[4]	3	0	0	0	3	21	4	16	1	0
Hardeman	2	0	0	0	2	23	6	17	0	0
Hemphill	7	0	6	0	1	10	2	8	0	0
Henderson	130	2	58	1	69	436	221	158	57	0
Hill	31	0	9	1	21	265	75	166	24	2
Hockley[4]	13	0	1	1	11	103	38	51	14	0
Hood	75	2	14	0	59	357	81	246	30	5
Hopkins[4]	30	2	8	1	19	73	15	38	20	1
Houston	7	0	1	0	6	82	40	40	2	0
Hutchinson	12	0	5	0	7	75	22	48	5	0
Jack[4]	10	0	2	0	8	36	12	19	5	0
Jackson	10	0	4	0	6	78	29	35	14	0
Jasper	76	1	18	3	54	390	138	170	82	3
Jim Hogg	12	0	2	0	10	33	17	12	4	0
Jim Wells	84	2	5	1	76	250	118	91	41	2
Karnes[4]	4	0	1	1	2	84	39	33	12	0
Kenedy	2	0	0	0	2	10	0	3	7	0
Kerr	40	2	15	0	23	173	55	109	9	1
Kinney	0	0	0	0	0	0	0	0	0	0
Kleberg[4]	20	0	7	1	12	37	13	20	4	1
Lamar	22	0	1	0	21	158	48	99	11	0
Lamb	4	0	1	0	3	72	27	38	7	0
Lavaca[7]	6	0	1	0	5			25	3	0
Lee[4]	14	0	5	0	9	85	35	38	12	0
Leon	4	0	1	0	3	111	41	66	4	0
Llano[4]	24	0	4	0	20	214	42	148	24	4
Loving[4]	2	0	0	0	2	16	1	14	1	0
Madison[4]	11	0	1	1	9	47	18	23	6	1
Marion[4]	16	0	2	1	13	100	35	55	10	0
Mason[4]	3	0	0	0	3	9	5	4	0	1
Matagorda[4]	70	2	11	3	54	272	56	176	40	0
Maverick	46	2	2	3	39	324	108	183	33	3
McCulloch	4	0	1	1	2	24	7	13	4	0
Menard	1	0	0	0	1	0	0	0	0	0
Milam[4]	9	0	1	1	7	59	12	44	3	0
Mills	9	0	0	0	9	13	4	9	0	0
Mitchell	1	0	0	0	1	20	9	9	2	1
Montague[4]	18	0	4	1	13	100	38	56	6	2
Moore[4]	4	0	1	0	3	34	17	15	2	0
Morris	10	0	4	0	6	59	18	34	7	0
Nacogdoches	65	1	12	0	52	312	73	206	33	2
Navarro	58	1	8	3	46	325	152	153	20	4
Newton[4]	20	3	3	1	13	79	33	37	9	3
Nolan	4	0	1	0	3	27	4	23	0	0
Palo Pinto[4]	13	0	1	1	11	133	32	80	21	0
Panola	42	0	4	1	37	251	68	167	16	0
Parmer	1	0	0	0	1	18	2	14	2	0
Pecos	0	0	0	0	0	100	19	69	12	0
Polk[6]	80	5	24	8	43		170		64	2
Presidio	0	0	0	0	0	0	0	0	0	0
Rains[4]	12	0	2	0	10	38	9	28	1	0
Reagan	8	0	0	0	8	24	5	12	7	0
Real	6	0	2	0	4	49	20	24	5	0
Red River[4]	30	1	3	1	25	66	33	28	5	3
Reeves	20	1	0	0	19	90	13	51	26	0
Refugio[4]	2	0	0	0	2	30	12	12	6	0
Roberts	0	0	0	0	0	1	0	1	0	0
Runnels	7	0	1	0	6	14	12	2	0	0
Sabine[4]	15	2	1	2	10	58	25	21	12	3
San Augustine	13	0	2	0	11	53	27	17	9	1
San Jacinto	38	0	31	1	6	711	325	318	68	0
San Saba	10	0	0	0	10	23	5	14	4	3
Schleicher[4]	2	0	0	0	2	18	14	4	0	0
Shelby	33	1	7	0	25	183	64	98	21	3
Somervell[4]	15	0	10	1	4	70	34	36	0	0
Starr	74	2	5	5	62	242	67	140	35	5
Sutton[4]	3	0	0	0	3	2	0	2	0	0
Terry	4	0	0	1	3	44	17	18	9	0
Titus[4]	41	0	8	2	31	176	51	104	21	2
Trinity[4]	12	1	2	2	7	59	15	35	9	3
Tyler[4]	34	0	3	3	28	171	80	66	25	5

Table 10. Offenses Known to Law Enforcement, by Selected State Metropolitan and Nonmetropolitan Counties, 2020—Continued

(Number.)

State/county	Violent crime	Murder and nonnegligent manslaughter	Rape[1]	Robbery	Aggravated assault	Property crime	Burglary	Larceny-theft	Motor vehicle theft	Arson[2]
Upton[4]	4	0	0	0	4	16	3	10	3	0
Uvalde	28	0	0	2	26	70	23	40	7	0
Val Verde[4]	41	0	6	3	32	107	45	48	14	2
Walker[4]	58	0	6	4	48	183	58	101	24	1
Ward	13	0	2	0	11	146	29	115	2	0
Washington	43	1	8	3	31	101	26	65	10	4
Wharton	57	0	1	3	53	283	76	173	34	0
Wheeler[4]	3	0	1	1	1	12	3	9	0	0
Wilbarger[4]	0	0	0	0	0	16	5	6	5	0
Willacy[4]	13	0	2	2	9	60	29	30	1	2
Winkler[4]	4	0	1	0	3	74	16	46	12	0
Yoakum	5	0	0	0	5	30	3	24	3	0
Zapata[4]	16	0	0	3	13	108	36	72	0	0
Zavala	11	1	1	0	9	44	12	24	8	0
UTAH										
Metropolitan Counties										
Box Elder[4]	12	0	2	0	10	111	17	80	14	0
Cache[4]	38	1	21	0	16	206	26	134	46	0
Davis	21	1	5	1	14	280	37	224	19	1
Juab[4]	2	1	0	0	1	54	9	36	9	0
Salt Lake County Unified Police Department	719	16	141	120	442	8,901	991	6,623	1,287	25
Tooele[4]	33	2	12	2	17	252	23	202	27	0
Utah	50	0	10	5	35	379	43	302	34	3
Washington	35	0	5	0	30	132	24	92	16	4
Weber	111	2	38	7	64	1,004	211	656	137	2
Nonmetropolitan Counties										
Beaver[4]	10	0	5	0	5	87	19	61	7	0
Carbon	11	0	2	0	9	91	22	62	7	1
Duchesne	50	3	19	0	28	265	46	173	46	8
Grand	13	0	2	1	10	88	14	60	14	0
Iron[4]	20	1	9	0	10	110	38	55	17	0
Kane	18	0	4	0	14	20	3	16	1	0
Millard	40	0	6	0	34	184	34	134	16	0
San Juan	5	0	1	0	4	51	9	38	4	1
Sevier[4]	11	0	3	0	8	65	12	51	2	1
Summit	27	0	1	2	24	454	42	362	50	1
Uintah	51	1	12	0	38	201	68	97	36	4
Wasatch	18	0	4	0	14	94	13	65	16	1
VERMONT										
Metropolitan Counties										
Franklin	13	0	6	0	7	14	2	12	0	0
Grand Isle	12	0	0	0	12	38	12	24	2	0
Nonmetropolitan Counties										
Addison	0	0	0	0	0	1	0	0	1	0
Bennington	1	0	0	0	1	5	2	3	0	0
Essex	2	0	0	0	2	13	4	8	1	0
Lamoille	4	0	0	0	4	34	1	33	0	0
Orange	9	0	4	0	5	21	2	18	1	0
Orleans	3	0	0	0	3	43	9	33	1	0
Rutland	0	0	0	0	0	17	2	15	0	0
Washington	0	0	0	0	0	0	0	0	0	0
Windham	0	0	0	0	0	15	0	15	0	0
Windsor	1	0	0	0	1	5	2	3	0	0
VIRGINIA										
Metropolitan Counties										
Albemarle County Police Department	119	7	27	12	73	1,296	116	1,107	73	7
Amelia	18	1	3	1	13	122	27	81	14	0
Amherst	60	0	14	2	44	336	21	276	39	0
Appomattox	10	1	2	1	6	66	11	55	0	0
Arlington County Police Department	371	3	46	117	205	3,160	150	2,704	306	4
Augusta	122	0	33	3	86	774	171	544	59	4
Bedford	86	1	10	3	72	444	83	306	55	2
Botetourt	31	0	3	6	22	210	13	174	23	1
Campbell	101	3	20	5	73	620	68	501	51	2
Charles City	11	0	2	0	8	34	13	20	1	1
Chesterfield County Police Department	477	11	109	132	225	5,008	559	4,110	339	24
Clarke	7	0	1	1	5	54	9	40	5	1
Craig	1	0	0	0	1	40	9	29	2	0
Culpeper	12	0	2	1	9	125	14	95	16	0
Dinwiddie	70	1	7	4	58	258	48	197	13	2
Fairfax County Police Department	925	16	154	312	443	13,575	620	11,698	1,257	15
Fauquier	47	3	18	7	19	288	34	232	22	0
Fluvanna	24	0	7	2	15	107	21	73	13	1
Franklin	66	7	11	3	45	496	62	366	68	5
Frederick	73	3	16	6	48	880	97	700	83	1
Giles	12	2	4	0	6	77	19	47	11	0

Table 10. Offenses Known to Law Enforcement, by Selected State Metropolitan and Nonmetropolitan Counties, 2020—Continued

(Number.)

State/county	Violent crime	Murder and nonnegligent manslaughter	Rape[1]	Robbery	Aggravated assault	Property crime	Burglary	Larceny-theft	Motor vehicle theft	Arson[2]
Gloucester	27	3	9	1	14	479	45	407	27	1
Goochland	12	0	4	3	5	188	12	152	24	1
Greene	20	1	1	3	15	190	11	170	9	1
Hanover	174	0	30	5	139	778	21	711	46	5
Henrico County Police Department	514	16	32	109	357	6,947	414	6,023	510	27
Isle of Wight	42	1	6	5	30	192	13	168	11	0
James City County Police Department	71	2	12	10	47	632	48	567	17	3
King and Queen	7	0	0	0	7	40	5	33	2	0
King William	17	0	1	1	15	71	5	62	4	0
Loudoun	308	1	127	32	148	2,122	152	1,826	144	20
Madison	9	1	5	0	3	65	6	56	3	1
Mathews	6	0	1	1	4	69	8	59	2	0
Montgomery	77	1	13	1	62	273	50	185	38	9
Nelson	36	0	13	0	23	205	41	142	22	0
New Kent	32	0	3	2	27	243	32	198	13	3
Powhatan	38	0	4	0	34	220	16	195	9	2
Prince George County Police Department	119	1	12	9	97	412	60	313	39	2
Prince William County Police Department	942	7	82	145	708	4,636	417	3,805	414	33
Pulaski	36	0	11	4	21	516	72	430	14	2
Rappahannock	7	0	1	0	6	30	6	22	2	0
Roanoke County Police Department	194	1	17	22	154	1,105	108	917	80	6
Rockingham	69	4	21	0	44	326	84	224	18	0
Scott	37	2	9	4	22	233	70	140	23	5
Southampton	18	0	3	2	13	178	28	126	24	2
Spotsylvania	150	5	30	11	104	780	43	664	73	2
Stafford	307	2	65	37	203	1,172	71	1,034	67	6
Sussex	18	1	4	1	12	76	21	43	12	0
Warren	19	0	16	0	3	263	17	236	10	5
Washington	52	5	6	0	41	589	82	451	56	3
York	65	5	11	6	43	725	46	648	31	2
Nonmetropolitan Counties										
Accomack	105	11	10	11	73	303	50	244	9	1
Alleghany	19	0	8	0	11	54	14	35	5	2
Bath	1	0	0	0	1	18	0	16	2	0
Bland	6	1	4	0	1	42	16	24	2	0
Brunswick	9	0	0	0	9	101	21	72	8	0
Buchanan	37	1	12	1	23	260	34	189	37	4
Buckingham	20	1	2	2	15	153	31	103	19	2
Caroline	51	1	14	1	35	214	23	186	5	0
Carroll	34	0	9	2	23	227	48	153	26	0
Charlotte	13	0	4	3	6	136	33	93	10	0
Cumberland	22	0	4	0	18	42	7	33	2	0
Dickenson	21	1	3	1	16	76	27	39	10	0
Essex	13	0	4	1	8	21	8	8	5	0
Floyd	18	1	8	0	9	61	13	44	4	1
Grayson	11	0	3	1	7	131	16	92	23	1
Greensville	13	1	1	1	10	62	15	36	11	0
Halifax	21	1	9	2	9	217	59	120	38	3
Henry	134	7	22	16	89	889	178	640	71	6
Highland	1	0	0	0	1	12	3	9	0	0
King George	60	1	9	7	43	214	26	166	22	3
Lancaster	40	1	2	2	35	47	10	35	2	0
Lee	27	0	5	2	20	224	45	166	13	2
Louisa	39	1	13	1	24	328	30	266	32	5
Lunenburg	13	0	2	0	11	33	17	16	0	0
Mecklenburg	25	4	3	1	17	142	32	98	12	2
Middlesex	18	0	6	0	12	94	14	74	6	1
Northampton	23	1	2	2	18	60	13	42	5	0
Northumberland	11	0	4	1	6	53	9	38	6	1
Nottoway	22	2	2	1	17	85	22	58	5	3
Orange	27	0	6	1	20	163	20	126	17	0
Page	6	0	1	0	5	140	27	105	8	2
Patrick	43	1	8	4	30	252	50	186	16	4
Pittsylvania	77	3	25	4	45	339	83	242	14	6
Prince Edward	21	0	4	1	16	81	11	62	8	2
Richmond	0	0	0	0	0	14	3	10	1	0
Rockbridge	43	0	6	3	34	210	26	175	9	3
Russell	23	1	6	2	14	140	40	90	10	3
Shenandoah	46	0	9	2	35	224	26	191	7	0
Smyth	19	5	3	1	10	153	16	119	18	3
Surry	4	0	1	1	2	27	5	16	6	0
Tazewell	37	3	9	2	23	302	59	210	33	4
Westmoreland	20	2	5	1	12	89	19	66	4	1
Wise	44	0	10	0	34	271	41	177	53	0
Wythe	23	3	9	1	10	189	14	150	25	2
WASHINGTON										
Metropolitan Counties										
Asotin	22	0	5	1	16	157	57	90	10	0
Benton	99	1	8	5	85	646	187	405	54	4

Table 10. Offenses Known to Law Enforcement, by Selected State Metropolitan and Nonmetropolitan Counties, 2020—Continued

(Number.)

State/county	Violent crime	Murder and nonnegligent manslaughter	Rape[1]	Robbery	Aggravated assault	Property crime	Burglary	Larceny-theft	Motor vehicle theft	Arson[2]
Chelan	42	1	3	3	35	315	86	202	27	1
Clark	354	3	82	39	230	2,861	460	1,850	551	22
Cowlitz	53	0	14	1	38	355	126	174	55	5
Douglas	20	0	8	4	8	276	64	185	27	2
Franklin	25	1	4	1	19	138	35	87	16	8
King	563	10	53	151	349	3,645	718	2,307	620	73
Kitsap	356	4	99	23	230	2,448	477	1,731	240	16
Pierce	1,096	12	87	164	833	7,093	1,618	4,330	1,145	55
Skagit	71	0	6	8	57	817	196	560	61	2
Skamania	8	0	0	0	8	138	43	85	10	1
Snohomish	504	1	64	84	355	4,339	792	2,764	783	27
Spokane	202	3	41	23	135	2,786	578	1,979	229	13
Stevens	31	2	2	2	25	350	114	188	48	2
Thurston	209	2	20	19	168	1,484	402	878	204	8
Walla Walla	37	1	3	2	31	314	110	169	35	2
Whatcom	142	5	29	7	101	474	129	302	43	2
Yakima	168	9	33	28	98	1,345	404	667	274	8
Nonmetropolitan Counties										
Adams	18	0	7	1	10	107	41	45	21	3
Clallam	80	1	16	6	57	546	135	374	37	3
Columbia	3	0	0	0	3	65	31	30	4	0
Ferry	1	0	0	0	1	43	5	32	6	1
Garfield	17	0	1	0	16	20	4	13	3	0
Grant	101	4	15	8	74	876	226	479	171	5
Grays Harbor	30	2	7	1	20	229	77	134	18	5
Island	44	0	9	1	34	503	158	310	35	1
Jefferson	22	1	2	1	18	284	169	107	8	1
Kittitas	25	3	6	1	15	237	67	142	28	5
Klickitat	3	0	1	0	2	41	33	7	1	0
Lewis	67	2	11	5	49	387	133	223	31	2
Lincoln	8	0	4	0	4	125	35	74	16	7
Mason	74	2	15	5	52	836	328	419	89	2
Pacific	18	0	1	1	16	136	61	60	15	0
Pend Oreille	21	2	6	0	13	136	38	76	22	0
San Juan	5	0	1	1	3	92	9	76	7	0
Wahkiakum	6	0	1	0	5	34	7	25	2	2
Whitman	15	0	3	0	12	64	17	33	14	1
WEST VIRGINIA										
Metropolitan Counties										
Berkeley	77	2	13	0	62	49	0	49	0	3
Brooke	6	0	2	0	4	2	0	2	0	0
Cabell	40	1	5	3	31	447	53	377	17	4
Fayette	62	0	10	1	51	235	70	132	33	3
Hampshire	30	0	0	0	30	89	24	58	7	0
Hancock	8	0	4	0	4	2	0	2	0	0
Jackson	35	1	4	0	30	16	6	7	3	0
Jefferson	28	1	8	2	17	202	29	156	17	2
Kanawha	441	13	35	12	381	1,228	397	649	182	21
Marshall	16	0	7	0	9	71	18	38	15	2
Mineral	14	0	1	0	13	54	4	48	2	1
Morgan	37	0	2	1	34	31	10	19	2	0
Preston	9	0	3	1	5	119	0	107	12	0
Raleigh	126	5	17	6	98	645	192	417	36	10
Wirt	12	0	0	0	12	35	18	16	1	3
Wood	105	0	11	1	93	323	81	194	48	4
Nonmetropolitan Counties										
Calhoun	2	0	0	0	2	11	2	8	1	0
Doddridge	12	1	3	0	8	41	13	23	5	1
Greenbrier	8	0	0	1	7	88	27	50	11	1
Hardy	24	1	0	0	23	9	2	6	1	0
Harrison	39	1	7	3	28	104	16	70	18	2
Lewis	11	1	0	0	10	6	3	2	1	0
Logan	91	2	0	0	89	2	0	2	0	2
McDowell	14	3	1	0	10	1	0	1	0	0
Mingo	5	3	0	1	1	6	2	3	1	0
Nicholas	173	2	2	0	169	10	0	10	0	1
Randolph	92	0	4	3	85	148	60	84	4	0
Upshur	8	0	3	0	5	5	0	5	0	1
Wetzel	20	0	0	0	20	23	9	10	4	0
Wyoming	90	0	0	0	90	80	25	43	12	0
WISCONSIN										
Metropolitan Counties										
Brown	48	0	16	1	31	580	28	529	23	4
Calumet	21	0	5	0	16	85	13	66	6	0
Chippewa	40	0	17	1	22	268	97	156	15	0
Columbia	26	0	9	1	16	235	73	145	17	1
Dane	120	2	19	8	91	768	139	570	59	6

Table 10. Offenses Known to Law Enforcement, by Selected State Metropolitan and Nonmetropolitan Counties, 2020—Continued

(Number.)

State/county	Violent crime	Murder and nonnegligent manslaughter	Rape[1]	Robbery	Aggravated assault	Property crime	Burglary	Larceny-theft	Motor vehicle theft	Arson[2]
Douglas[4]	11	0	0	2	9	228	79	128	21	1
Eau Claire	20	0	6	1	13	217	59	142	16	0
Fond du Lac	23	1	11	1	10	162	56	98	8	3
Green	3	0	1	0	2	68	3	61	4	0
Iowa	16	0	4	1	11	34	5	26	3	0
Kenosha	59	1	14	5	39	331	51	254	26	3
Kewaunee	16	1	5	1	9	37	7	29	1	0
La Crosse	34	0	4	0	30	134	49	75	10	0
Lincoln	68	0	16	0	52	115	20	82	13	1
Marathon	68	3	10	3	52	284	68	198	18	1
Milwaukee	118	3	6	11	98	147	7	72	68	1
Oconto	8	0	4	0	4	249	119	119	11	0
Outagamie	42	0	11	1	30	314	109	183	22	0
Ozaukee	12	1	2	0	9	81	5	70	6	0
Pierce	12	1	0	0	11	113	37	69	7	0
Racine[4]	35	1	10	3	21	153	27	105	21	1
Rock	39	0	7	3	29	212	41	157	14	1
Sheboygan[4]	44	0	19	0	25	343	28	291	24	2
St. Croix	34	0	1	4	29	294	53	213	28	1
Washington	17	1	3	2	11	192	29	148	15	0
Waukesha[4]	47	5	15	3	24	279	25	225	29	3
Winnebago	20	1	5	0	14	288	143	137	8	0
Nonmetropolitan Counties										
Ashland	20	0	0	0	20	54	21	25	8	0
Barron	23	1	5	0	17	127	40	72	15	1
Bayfield	15	1	1	0	13	93	18	65	10	2
Buffalo[4]	5	0	1	1	3	19	2	12	5	0
Burnett	45	2	6	2	35	297	106	165	26	1
Clark	23	0	0	0	23	110	27	65	18	0
Crawford	20	1	3	1	15	160	11	145	4	1
Dodge	39	1	5	0	33	135	19	101	15	0
Door	9	0	2	0	7	97	17	78	2	0
Florence	12	0	0	0	12	5	1	4	0	0
Forest	12	0	3	0	9	42	11	27	4	0
Grant	29	2	10	0	17	115	15	84	16	0
Green Lake	4	0	0	0	4	50	7	40	3	0
Iron	4	0	0	0	4	46	4	39	3	0
Jackson	8	0	0	0	8	139	40	80	19	0
Jefferson	23	2	1	4	16	221	27	179	15	2
Juneau	27	0	15	2	10	186	75	96	15	0
Lafayette[4]	8	0	3	0	5	52	14	33	5	1
Manitowoc	24	0	0	1	23	136	32	88	16	0
Marinette[4]	24	1	4	0	19	182	44	129	9	0
Marquette	7	0	3	0	4	70	17	49	4	0
Menominee	1	0	1	0	0	11	1	10	0	0
Monroe	50	0	7	0	43	249	195	46	8	1
Oneida	24	0	6	0	18	82	18	60	4	2
Pepin	3	0	1	0	2	27	9	17	1	0
Polk	30	0	5	1	24	202	56	124	22	0
Portage	30	1	8	0	21	121	43	68	10	0
Price	5	0	1	1	3	84	16	64	4	1
Rusk	34	3	6	1	24	35	7	23	5	1
Sauk	22	1	4	1	16	247	52	174	21	0
Sawyer	35	1	9	0	25	138	23	103	12	3
Shawano[4]	31	0	6	3	22	231	54	153	24	2
Taylor[4]	15	0	5	0	10	62	13	44	5	1
Trempealeau[4]	13	0	4	0	9	58	16	35	7	0
Vernon	4	0	0	0	4	94	9	80	5	3
Vilas	4	0	0	1	3	93	20	67	6	0
Walworth	17	0	1	1	15	94	19	65	10	2
Washburn	15	0	1	0	14	90	21	63	6	0
Waushara	21	0	8	0	13	113	31	80	2	0
Wood	17	0	16	1	0	127	31	82	14	0
WYOMING										
Metropolitan Counties										
Laramie	83	1	5	2	75	424	98	277	49	1
Natrona[4]	47	2	12	2	31	146	33	83	30	0
Nonmetropolitan Counties										
Big Horn	5	0	3	0	2	22	6	14	2	0
Campbell	41	0	8	0	33	116	28	73	15	0
Carbon	9	0	2	0	7	25	2	22	1	1
Converse[4]	9	0	3	0	6	35	6	23	6	1
Crook[4]	5	0	3	0	2	17	5	12	0	0
Fremont	16	1	2	0	13	199	28	147	24	1
Goshen	16	1	3	0	12	60	26	31	3	1
Hot Springs[4]	0	0	0	0	0	19	2	17	0	0
Johnson	9	0	4	0	5	42	7	30	5	0
Lincoln	19	0	2	0	17	84	24	56	4	0

Table 10. Offenses Known to Law Enforcement, by Selected State Metropolitan and Nonmetropolitan Counties, 2020—Continued

(Number.)

State/county	Violent crime	Murder and nonnegligent manslaughter	Rape[1]	Robbery	Aggravated assault	Property crime	Burglary	Larceny-theft	Motor vehicle theft	Arson[2]
Niobrara	3	0	1	0	2	13	0	11	2	0
Park	17	0	7	0	10	74	29	40	5	1
Platte	2	0	1	0	1	48	2	39	7	0
Sheridan[4]	10	3	0	1	6	45	18	21	6	0
Sublette	1	0	0	0	1	43	5	35	3	0
Sweetwater	16	0	7	1	8	76	10	54	12	1
Uinta[4]	8	0	2	0	6	37	2	31	4	0
Washakie[4]	3	0	1	1	1	6	1	4	1	0
Weston	3	0	0	0	3	0	0	0	0	0

1 The figures shown in this column for the offense of rape were reported using only the revised Uniform Crime Reporting (UCR) definition of rape. See chapter notes for more detail.   2 The FBI does not publish arson data unless it receives data from either the agency or the state for all 12 months of the calendar year.   3 Limited data for 2020 were available for Alabama, Maryland, and Pennsylvania.   4 Because of changes in the state/local agency's reporting practices, figures are not comparable to previous years' data.   5 The Tulare County Highway Patrol collects the motor vehicle thefts for this county. These data can be found in Table 11.   6 The FBI determined that the agency's data were underreported. Consequently, those data are not included in this table.   7 The FBI determined that the agency's data were overreported. Consequently, those data are not included in this table.   8 The FBI determined that the state did not follow national UCR Program guidelines for reporting an offense. Consequently, this figure is not included in this table.   9 This agency submits rape data classified according to the legacy UCR definition; therefore, the rape offense and violent crime total, which rape is a part of, is not included in this table. See the chapter notes for more detail.

Table 11. Offenses Known to Law Enforcement, by Selected State, Tribal, and Other Agencies, 2020

(Number.)

State/other agency unit/office	Violent crime	Murder and nonnegligent manslaughter	Rape[1]	Robbery	Aggravated assault	Property crime	Burglary	Larceny-theft	Motor vehicle theft	Arson[2]
ALABAMA[3]										
ALASKA										
State Agencies										
Alaska State Troopers	1,327	19	267	40	1,001	2,377	752	1,246	379	25
Tribal Agencies										
Metlakatla Tribal	0	0	0	0	0	0	0	0	0	0
Other Agencies										
Fairbanks International Airport	2	0	0	0	2	10	0	7	3	0
Ted Stevens Anchorage International Airport	6	0	0	0	6	54	1	40	13	1
ARIZONA										
Tribal Agencies										
Ak-Chin Tribal	4	0	2	0	2	2	0	2	0	0
Cocopah Tribal	1	0	0	0	1	11	2	9	0	0
Colorado River Tribal	19	0	1	5	13	70	5	59	6	
Fort McDowell Tribal	9	0	0	0	9	52	2	45	5	
Fort Mojave Tribal	11	0	1	0	10	18	6	9	3	0
Hopi Resource Enforcement Agency	56	1	5	2	48	32	24	0	8	0
Hualapai Tribal	15	0	0	2	13	38	8	30	0	0
Kaibab Paiute Tribal	0	0	0	0	0	0	0	0	0	0
Salt River Tribal	475	0	3	10	462	624	110	468	46	3
San Carlos Apache	1,159	4	16	12	1,127	230	130	82	18	67
Tonto Apache Tribal	4	0	0	0	4	10	1	9	0	0
Truxton Canon Agency	6	0	0	1	5	0	0	0	0	0
White Mountain Apache Tribal	430	3	21	3	403	285	122	153	10	31
Yavapai-Apache Nation	2	0	0	0	2	3	0	2	1	0
Yavapai-Prescott Tribal	3	0	0	0	3	94	5	87	2	0
Other Agencies										
Tucson Airport Authority[4]	1	0	0	0	1	35	3	26	6	0
ARKANSAS										
State Agencies										
State Capitol Police	0	0	0	0	0	27	1	26	0	0
Other Agencies										
Fort Smith Public Schools	0	0	0	0	0	44	6	38	0	0
Northwest Arkansas Regional Airport	0	0	0	0	0	15	4	11	0	0
	0	0	0	0	0	23	2	12	9	0
CALIFORNIA										
State Agencies										
Atascadero State Hospital	53	0	0	0	53	0	0	0	0	0
California State Fair	1	0	0	0	1	24	6	15	3	2
Coalinga State Hospital	227	0	5	0	222	2	0	2	0	1
Department of Parks and Recreation										
Angeles	0	0	0	0	0	29	4	24	1	0
Bay Area	0	0	0	0	0	6	3	3	0	0
Calaveras County	0	0	0	0	0	10	7	1	2	0
Capital	0	0	0	0	0	10	7	3	0	0
Channel Coast	5	1	1	1	2	67	2	65	0	0
Colorado	0	0	0	0	0	2	1	1	0	0
Diablo Range	0	0	0	0	0	2	0	2	0	0
Four Rivers District	2	0	0	1	1	2	0	2	0	0
Gold Fields District	3	0	1	1	1	54	0	54	0	0
Hungry Valley	0	0	0	0	0	0	0	0	0	0
Inland Empire	2	0	1	0	1	0	0	0	0	0
Monterey County	0	0	0	0	0	52	13	37	2	0
North Coast Redwoods	3	0	0	0	3	60	1	58	1	2
Northern Buttes	0	0	0	0	0	4	0	4	0	0
Oceano Dunes	1	0	0	0	1	41	0	40	1	0
Ocotillo Wells	0	0	0	0	0	0	0	0	0	0
Orange Coast	0	0	0	0	0	78	41	36	1	0
San Diego Coast	8	0	0	0	8	96	7	89	0	2
San Joaquin	4	0	0	0	4	0	0	0	0	0
San Luis Obispo Coast	0	0	0	0	0	18	0	17	1	0
Santa Cruz Mountains	1	0	0	1	0	74	0	74	0	1
Sierra	0	0	0	0	0	0	0	0	0	0
Sonoma-Mendocino Coast	1	0	0	0	1	17	3	14	0	0
Tehachapi District	0	0	0	0	0	2	2	0	0	0
Fairview Developmental Center	0	0	0	0	0	1	0	0	1	0
Highway Patrol										
Alameda County	0	0	0	0	0	271	1	40	230	0
Alpine County	0	0	0	0	0	1	0	1	0	0
Amador County	0	0	0	0	0	38	0	13	25	0
Butte County	1	0	0	0	1	168	0	70	98	0
Calaveras County	0	0	0	0	0	74	0	35	39	0
Colusa County	0	0	0	0	0	20	0	7	13	0
Contra Costa County	0	0	0	0	0	528	0	53	475	0
Del Norte County	1	0	0	0	1	45	0	23	22	0
El Dorado County	1	0	0	0	1	139	2	100	37	0
Fresno County	0	0	0	0	0	187	0	30	157	0
Glenn County	2	0	0	1	1	39	0	11	28	0
Humboldt County	5	0	0	0	5	251	3	88	160	0

Table 11. Offenses Known to Law Enforcement, by Selected State, Tribal, and Other Agencies, 2020—Continued

(Number.)

State/other agency unit/office	Violent crime	Murder and nonnegligent manslaughter	Rape[1]	Robbery	Aggravated assault	Property crime	Burglary	Larceny-theft	Motor vehicle theft	Arson[2]
Imperial County	1	0	0	0	1	62	0	9	53	0
Inyo County	0	0	0	0	0	23	0	4	19	0
Kern County	1	1	0	0	0	345	0	41	304	0
Kings County	0	0	0	0	0	152	0	0	152	0
Lake County	2	0	0	0	2	198	1	51	146	0
Lassen County	0	0	0	0	0	38	0	6	32	0
Los Angeles County	59	1	0	1	57	602	5	137	460	0
Madera County	0	0	0	0	0	158	0	30	128	0
Marin County	0	0	0	0	0	143	0	108	35	0
Mariposa County	0	0	0	0	0	17	0	7	10	0
Mendocino County	0	0	0	0	0	106	0	25	81	0
Merced County	0	0	0	0	0	343	0	71	272	0
Modoc County	0	0	0	0	0	3	0	3	0	0
Mono County	0	0	0	0	0	7	1	5	1	0
Monterey County	1	0	0	0	1	307	2	85	220	0
Napa County	0	0	0	0	0	45	0	17	28	0
Nevada County	0	0	0	0	0	111	0	28	83	0
Orange County	7	0	0	1	6	57	3	29	25	0
Placer County	1	0	0	0	1	161	1	32	128	0
Plumas County	0	0	0	0	0	12	0	3	9	0
Riverside County	16	4	0	0	12	45	0	11	34	1
Sacramento County	13	0	0	0	13	2,721	1	1,082	1,638	2
San Benito County	0	0	0	0	0	22	0	3	19	0
San Bernardino County	37	0	0	0	37	133	3	44	86	0
San Diego County	26	0	0	0	26	153	1	31	121	0
San Francisco County	0	0	0	0	0	10	0	4	6	0
San Joaquin County	0	0	0	0	0	587	0	137	450	0
San Luis Obispo County	0	0	0	0	0	101	0	27	74	0
San Mateo County	0	0	0	0	0	37	1	20	16	0
Santa Barbara County	0	0	0	0	0	217	0	55	162	0
Santa Clara County	4	0	0	0	4	84	1	20	63	0
Santa Cruz County	0	0	0	0	0	470	0	119	351	0
Shasta County	1	0	0	0	1	237	0	72	165	0
Sierra County	0	0	0	0	0	0	0	0	0	0
Siskiyou County	1	0	0	0	1	43	2	22	19	0
Solano County	0	0	0	0	0	64	0	0	64	0
Sonoma County	7	0	0	0	7	142	0	91	51	0
Stanislaus County	0	0	0	0	0	226	1	94	131	0
Sutter County	0	0	0	0	0	45	0	7	38	0
Tehama County	0	0	0	0	0	115	0	28	87	0
Trinity County	0	0	0	0	0	51	0	24	27	0
Tulare County	0	0	0	0	0	803	0	179	624	30
Tuolumne County	0	0	0	0	0	111	1	51	59	0
Ventura County	0	0	0	0	0	26	0	6	20	0
Yolo County	0	0	0	0	0	55	0	11	44	0
Yuba County	0	0	0	0	0	441	0	45	396	0
Metropolitan State Hospital	845	0	23	0	822	3	2	1	0	1
Napa State Hospital	113	0	0	0	113	2	1	1	0	0
Patton State Hospital	263	0	0	0	263	0	0	0	0	0
Porterville Developmental Center	31	0	1	0	30	6	2	4	0	0
Tribal Agencies										
Hoopa Valley Tribal	4	0	0	0	4	5	2	3	0	0
Sycuan Tribal	17	0	2	4	11	79	21	38	20	0
Table Mountain Rancheria	8	0	0	3	5	117	8	93	16	0
Yurok Tribal	15	0	0	2	13	28	10	14	4	
Other Agencies										
Baldwin Park Unified School District	0	0	0	0	0	26	11	13	2	0
Clovis Unified School District	1	0	0	0	1	5	0	5	0	0
East Bay Regional Park District	43	1	7	12	23	310	60	235	15	33
Fontana Unified School District	4	0	0	2	2	52	25	26	1	2
Kern High School District	15	0	0	4	11	102	34	58	10	0
Los Angeles County Metropolitan Transportation Authority	6	0	0	2	4	11	2	9	0	1
Los Angeles Transportation Services Bureau	192	0	3	89	100	131	6	110	15	5
Monterey Peninsula Airport	0	0	0	0	0	1	0	1	0	0
Port of San Diego Harbor	80	0	8	15	57	449	78	368	3	5
San Bernardino Unified School District	12	0	0	10	2	137	68	67	2	7
San Francisco Bay Area Rapid Transit										
Alameda County	184	0	4	126	54	642	9	577	56	2
Contra Costa County	40	0	0	23	17	243	1	202	40	0
San Francisco County	115	0	1	101	13	185	1	184	0	1
San Mateo County	11	0	1	6	4	80	1	75	4	1
Santa Clara Transit District	77	0	3	30	44	85	4	59	22	0
Shasta County Marshal	0	0	0	0	0	0	0	0	0	0
Stockton Unified School District	24	0	1	9	14	82	25	55	2	0
Twin Rivers Unified School District	6	0	0	3	3	109	86	18	5	0
Union Pacific Railroad										
Alameda County	0	0	0	0	0	48	16	32	0	1
Amador County	0	0	0	0	0	0	0	0	0	0
Butte County	0	0	0	0	0	5	1	4	0	0
Calaveras County	0	0	0	0	0	0	0	0	0	0
Colusa County	0	0	0	0	0	0	0	0	0	0

Table 11. Offenses Known to Law Enforcement, by Selected State, Tribal, and Other Agencies, 2020—Continued

(Number.)

State/other agency unit/office	Violent crime	Murder and nonnegligent manslaughter	Rape[1]	Robbery	Aggravated assault	Property crime	Burglary	Larceny-theft	Motor vehicle theft	Arson[2]
Contra Costa County	0	0	0	0	0	0	0	0	0	0
El Dorado County	0	0	0	0	0	0	0	0	0	0
Fresno County	0	0	0	0	0	10	0	10	0	0
Glenn County	0	0	0	0	0	0	0	0	0	0
Humboldt County	1	0	0	0	1	19	6	13	0	0
Imperial County	0	0	0	0	0	1	1	0	0	0
Inyo County	0	0	0	0	0	0	0	0	0	0
Kern County	1	0	0	0	1	57	23	34	0	0
Kings County	0	0	0	0	0	0	0	0	0	0
Lassen County	0	0	0	0	0	1	0	1	0	0
Los Angeles County	3	0	0	0	3	2,276	1,670	606	0	0
Madera County	0	0	0	0	0	1	0	1	0	0
Marin County	0	0	0	0	0	0	0	0	0	0
Mendocino County	0	0	0	0	0	0	0	0	0	0
Merced County	0	0	0	0	0	0	0	0	0	0
Modoc County	0	0	0	0	0	0	0	0	0	0
Monterey County	0	0	0	0	0	0	0	0	0	0
Napa County	0	0	0	0	0	0	0	0	0	0
Nevada County	0	0	0	0	0	0	0	0	0	0
Orange County	0	0	0	0	0	3	0	3	0	0
Placer County	0	0	0	0	0	6	0	6	0	0
Plumas County	0	0	0	0	0	0	0	0	0	0
Riverside County	1	0	0	0	1	30	20	10	0	0
Sacramento County	0	0	0	0	0	16	4	12	0	0
San Benito County	0	0	0	0	0	0	0	0	0	0
San Bernardino County	2	0	0	0	2	83	51	32	0	0
San Francisco County	0	0	0	0	0	0	0	0	0	0
San Joaquin County	0	0	0	0	0	420	17	403	0	0
San Luis Obispo County	0	0	0	0	0	0	0	0	0	2
San Mateo County	0	0	0	0	0	1	0	1	0	0
Santa Barbara County	0	0	0	0	0	0	0	0	0	1
Santa Clara County	0	0	0	0	0	2	0	2	0	0
Santa Cruz County	0	0	0	0	0	0	0	0	0	0
Shasta County	0	0	0	0	0	7	3	4	0	0
Sierra County	0	0	0	0	0	0	0	0	0	0
Siskiyou County	0	0	0	0	0	12	8	4	0	0
Solano County	0	0	0	0	0	1	0	1	0	0
Sonoma County	0	0	0	0	0	0	0	0	0	0
Stanislaus County	0	0	0	0	0	6	1	5	0	0
Sutter County	0	0	0	0	0	0	0	0	0	0
Tehama County	0	0	0	0	0	1	0	1	0	0
Trinity County	0	0	0	0	0	0	0	0	0	0
Tulare County	0	0	0	0	0	4	0	4	0	0
Ventura County	0	0	0	0	0	1	0	1	0	0
Yolo County	0	0	0	0	0	2	2	0	0	0
Yuba County	0	0	0	0	0	3	0	3	0	0
COLORADO										
State Agencies										
Colorado Bureau of Investigation	0	0	0	0	0	0	0	0	0	0
Colorado Mental Health Institute	0	0	0	0	0	7	0	7	0	0
Division of Gaming Criminal Enforcement and Investigations Section, Golden	0	0	0	0	0	0	0	0	0	0
State Patrol	17	0	0	0	17	43	5	7	31	0
Other Agencies										
Delta Montrose Drug Task Force	0	0	0	0	0	1	0	1	0	0
Southwest Drug Task Force	0	0	0	0	0	0	0	0	0	0
CONNECTICUT										
State Agencies										
Connecticut State Police	213	9	51	27	126	1,874	374	1,009	491	9
Department of Energy and Environmental Protection	5	0	0	0	5	31	2	28	1	1
Department of Motor Vehicles	0	0	0	0	0	0	0	0	0	0
State Capitol Police	1	0	0	1	0	1	0	1	0	0
Tribal Agencies										
Mashantucket Pequot Tribal	17	0	1	2	14	105	5	100	0	0
Mohegan Tribal	14	0	2	2	10	131	1	123	7	1
Other Agencies										
Metropolitan Transportation Authority[4]	0	0	0	0	0	33	4	29	0	0
DELAWARE										
State Agencies										
Alcohol and Tobacco Enforcement	0	0	0	0	0	0	0	0	0	0
Animal Welfare										
Kent County	0	0	0	0	0	0	0	0	0	0
New Castle County	0	0	0	0	0	0	0	0	0	0
Sussex County	0	0	0	0	0	0	0	0	0	0
Attorney General										
New Castle County	0	0	0	0	0	1	0	1	0	0
Sussex County	0	0	0	0	0	0	0	0	0	0
Environmental Control	0	0	0	0	0	5	0	5	0	0
Fish and Wildlife	1	0	0	0	1	13	0	13	0	0

Table 11. Offenses Known to Law Enforcement, by Selected State, Tribal, and Other Agencies, 2020—Continued

(Number.)

State/other agency unit/office	Violent crime	Murder and nonnegligent manslaughter	Rape[1]	Robbery	Aggravated assault	Property crime	Burglary	Larceny-theft	Motor vehicle theft	Arson[2]
Park Rangers	4	0	1	0	3	81	23	57	1	0
River and Bay Authority	1	0	0	0	1	0	0	0	0	0
State Capitol Police	1	0	1	0	0	17	2	15	0	0
State Fire Marshal	12	0	0	0	12	6	6	0	0	111
State Police										
Headquarters	3	0	2	0	1	0	0	0	0	0
Kent County	319	4	36	18	261	846	184	572	90	1
New Castle County	466	7	30	124	305	3,643	331	3,105	207	2
Sussex County	422	5	28	23	366	1,915	281	1,542	92	3
Other Agencies										
Amtrak Police	0	0	0	0	0	2	0	2	0	0
DISTRICT OF COLUMBIA										
Other Agencies										
District of Columbia Fire and Emergency Medical Services, Arson Investigation Unit	0	0	0	0	0	0	0	0	0	205
Metro Transit Police	299	3	4	165	127	440	1	410	29	2
FLORIDA										
State Agencies										
Capitol Police	0	0	0	0	0	17	2	14	1	0
Department of Corrections, Office of the Inspector General										
Alachua County	0	0	0	0	0	0	0	0	0	0
Baker County	0	0	0	0	0	0	0	0	0	0
Bay County	0	0	0	0	0	0	0	0	0	0
Bradford County	0	0	0	0	0	0	0	0	0	0
Brevard County	0	0	0	0	0	0	0	0	0	0
Broward County	0	0	0	0	0	0	0	0	0	0
Calhoun County	0	0	0	0	0	0	0	0	0	0
Charlotte County	0	0	0	0	0	0	0	0	0	0
Citrus County	0	0	0	0	0	0	0	0	0	0
Clay County	0	0	0	0	0	0	0	0	0	0
Collier County	0	0	0	0	0	0	0	0	0	0
Columbia County	0	0	0	0	0	0	0	0	0	0
DeSoto County	0	0	0	0	0	0	0	0	0	0
Dixie County	0	0	0	0	0	0	0	0	0	0
Duval County	0	0	0	0	0	0	0	0	0	0
Escambia County	0	0	0	0	0	0	0	0	0	0
Flagler County	0	0	0	0	0	0	0	0	0	0
Franklin County	0	0	0	0	0	0	0	0	0	0
Gadsden County	0	0	0	0	0	0	0	0	0	0
Gilchrist County	0	0	0	0	0	0	0	0	0	0
Glades County	0	0	0	0	0	0	0	0	0	0
Gulf County	0	0	0	0	0	0	0	0	0	0
Hamilton County	0	0	0	0	0	0	0	0	0	0
Hardee County	0	0	0	0	0	0	0	0	0	0
Hendry County	0	0	0	0	0	0	0	0	0	0
Hernando County	0	0	0	0	0	0	0	0	0	0
Highlands County	0	0	0	0	0	0	0	0	0	0
Hillsborough County	0	0	0	0	0	0	0	0	0	0
Holmes County	0	0	0	0	0	0	0	0	0	0
Indian River County	0	0	0	0	0	0	0	0	0	0
Jackson County	0	0	0	0	0	0	0	0	0	0
Jefferson County	0	0	0	0	0	0	0	0	0	0
Lafayette County	0	0	0	0	0	0	0	0	0	0
Lake County	0	0	0	0	0	0	0	0	0	0
Lee County	0	0	0	0	0	0	0	0	0	0
Leon County	0	0	0	0	0	0	0	0	0	0
Levy County	0	0	0	0	0	0	0	0	0	0
Liberty County	0	0	0	0	0	0	0	0	0	0
Madison County	0	0	0	0	0	0	0	0	0	0
Manatee County	0	0	0	0	0	0	0	0	0	0
Marion County	0	0	0	0	0	0	0	0	0	0
Martin County	0	0	0	0	0	0	0	0	0	0
Miami-Dade County	0	0	0	0	0	0	0	0	0	0
Monroe County	0	0	0	0	0	0	0	0	0	0
Nassau County	0	0	0	0	0	0	0	0	0	0
Okaloosa County	0	0	0	0	0	0	0	0	0	0
Okeechobee County	0	0	0	0	0	0	0	0	0	0
Orange County	0	0	0	0	0	0	0	0	0	0
Osceola County	0	0	0	0	0	0	0	0	0	0
Palm Beach County	0	0	0	0	0	0	0	0	0	0
Pasco County	0	0	0	0	0	0	0	0	0	0
Pinellas County	0	0	0	0	0	0	0	0	0	0
Polk County	0	0	0	0	0	0	0	0	0	0
Putnam County	0	0	0	0	0	0	0	0	0	0
Santa Rosa County	0	0	0	0	0	0	0	0	0	0
Sarasota County	0	0	0	0	0	0	0	0	0	0
Seminole County	0	0	0	0	0	0	0	0	0	0
St. Johns County	0	0	0	0	0	0	0	0	0	0
St. Lucie County	0	0	0	0	0	0	0	0	0	0

Table 11. Offenses Known to Law Enforcement, by Selected State, Tribal, and Other Agencies, 2020—Continued

(Number.)

State/other agency unit/office	Violent crime	Murder and nonnegligent manslaughter	Rape[1]	Robbery	Aggravated assault	Property crime	Burglary	Larceny-theft	Motor vehicle theft	Arson[2]
Sumter County	0	0	0	0	0	0	0	0	0	0
Suwannee County	0	0	0	0	0	0	0	0	0	0
Taylor County	0	0	0	0	0	0	0	0	0	0
Union County	0	0	0	0	0	0	0	0	0	0
Volusia County	0	0	0	0	0	0	0	0	0	0
Wakulla County	0	0	0	0	0	0	0	0	0	0
Walton County	0	0	0	0	0	0	0	0	0	0
Washington County	0	0	0	0	0	0	0	0	0	0
Department of Law Enforcement										
Duval County, Jacksonville	0	0	0	0	0	1	0	1	0	0
Escambia County, Pensacola	0	0	0	0	0	0	0	0	0	0
Hillsborough County, Tampa	0	0	0	0	0	1	0	1	0	0
Lee County, Fort Myers	0	0	0	0	0	0	0	0	0	0
Leon County, Tallahassee	2	0	2	0	0	1	0	1	0	0
Miami-Dade County, Miami	1	0	1	0	0	0	0	0	0	0
Orange County, Orlando	1	0	1	0	0	0	0	0	0	0
Division of Alcoholic Beverages and Tobacco										
Alachua County	0	0	0	0	0	0	0	0	0	0
Baker County	0	0	0	0	0	0	0	0	0	0
Bay County	0	0	0	0	0	0	0	0	0	0
Bradford County	0	0	0	0	0	0	0	0	0	0
Brevard County	0	0	0	0	0	0	0	0	0	0
Broward County	0	0	0	0	0	0	0	0	0	0
Calhoun County	0	0	0	0	0	0	0	0	0	0
Charlotte County	0	0	0	0	0	0	0	0	0	0
Citrus County	0	0	0	0	0	0	0	0	0	0
Clay County	0	0	0	0	0	0	0	0	0	0
Collier County	0	0	0	0	0	0	0	0	0	0
Columbia County	0	0	0	0	0	0	0	0	0	0
DeSoto County	0	0	0	0	0	0	0	0	0	0
Dixie County	0	0	0	0	0	0	0	0	0	0
Duval County	0	0	0	0	0	0	0	0	0	0
Escambia County	0	0	0	0	0	0	0	0	0	0
Flagler County	0	0	0	0	0	0	0	0	0	0
Franklin County	0	0	0	0	0	0	0	0	0	0
Gadsden County	0	0	0	0	0	0	0	0	0	0
Gilchrist County	0	0	0	0	0	0	0	0	0	0
Glades County	0	0	0	0	0	0	0	0	0	0
Gulf County	0	0	0	0	0	0	0	0	0	0
Hamilton County	0	0	U	0	0	0	0	0	0	0
Hardee County	0	0	0	0	0	0	0	0	0	0
Hendry County	0	0	0	0	0	0	0	0	0	0
Hernando County	0	0	0	0	0	0	0	0	0	0
Highlands County	0	0	0	0	0	0	0	0	0	0
Hillsborough County	0	0	0	0	0	0	0	0	0	0
Holmes County	0	0	0	0	0	0	0	0	0	0
Indian River County	0	0	0	0	0	0	0	0	0	0
Jackson County	0	0	0	0	0	0	0	0	0	0
Jefferson County	0	0	0	0	0	0	0	0	0	0
Lafayette County	0	0	0	0	0	0	0	0	0	0
Lake County	0	0	0	0	0	0	0	0	0	0
Lee County	0	0	0	0	0	0	0	0	0	0
Leon County	0	0	0	0	0	0	0	0	0	0
Levy County	0	0	0	0	0	0	0	0	0	0
Liberty County	0	0	0	0	0	0	0	0	0	0
Madison County	0	0	0	0	0	0	0	0	0	0
Manatee County	0	0	0	0	0	0	0	0	0	0
Marion County	0	0	0	0	0	0	0	0	0	0
Martin County	0	0	0	0	0	0	0	0	0	0
Miami-Dade County	0	0	0	0	0	0	0	0	0	0
Monroe County	0	0	0	0	0	0	0	0	0	0
Nassau County	0	0	0	0	0	0	0	0	0	0
Okaloosa County	0	0	0	0	0	0	0	0	0	0
Okeechobee County	0	0	0	0	0	0	0	0	0	0
Orange County	0	0	0	0	0	0	0	0	0	0
Osceola County	0	0	0	0	0	0	0	0	0	0
Palm Beach County	0	0	0	0	0	0	0	0	0	0
Pasco County	0	0	0	0	0	0	0	0	0	0
Pinellas County	0	0	0	0	0	0	0	0	0	0
Polk County	0	0	0	0	0	0	0	0	0	0
Putnam County	0	0	0	0	0	0	0	0	0	0
Santa Rosa County	0	0	0	0	0	0	0	0	0	0
Sarasota County	0	0	0	0	0	0	0	0	0	0
Seminole County	0	0	0	0	0	0	0	0	0	0
St. Johns County	0	0	0	0	0	0	0	0	0	0
St. Lucie County	0	0	0	0	0	0	0	0	0	0
Sumter County	0	0	0	0	0	0	0	0	0	0
Suwannee County	0	0	0	0	0	0	0	0	0	0
Taylor County	0	0	0	0	0	0	0	0	0	0
Union County	0	0	0	0	0	0	0	0	0	0
Volusia County	0	0	0	0	0	0	0	0	0	0
Wakulla County	0	0	0	0	0	0	0	0	0	0

Table 11. Offenses Known to Law Enforcement, by Selected State, Tribal, and Other Agencies, 2020—Continued

(Number.)

State/other agency unit/office	Violent crime	Murder and nonnegligent manslaughter	Rape[1]	Robbery	Aggravated assault	Property crime	Burglary	Larceny-theft	Motor vehicle theft	Arson[2]
Walton County	0	0	0	0	0	0	0	0	0	0
Washington County	0	0	0	0	0	0	0	0	0	0
Division of Investigative and Forensic Services										
Broward County	0	0	0	0	0	0	0	0	0	0
Duval County	0	0	0	0	0	0	0	0	0	0
Escambia County	0	0	0	0	0	0	0	0	0	0
Hillsborough County	0	0	0	0	0	0	0	0	0	0
Lee County	0	0	0	0	0	0	0	0	0	0
Leon County	0	0	0	0	0	0	0	0	0	0
Miami-Dade County	0	0	0	0	0	0	0	0	0	0
Orange County	0	0	0	0	0	0	0	0	0	0
Palm Beach County	0	0	0	0	0	0	0	0	0	0
Pinellas County	0	0	0	0	0	0	0	0	0	0
Fish and Wildlife Conservation Commission										
Alachua County	0	0	0	0	0	0	0	0	0	0
Baker County	0	0	0	0	0	0	0	0	0	0
Bay County	0	0	0	0	0	0	0	0	0	0
Bradford County	0	0	0	0	0	0	0	0	0	0
Brevard County	0	0	0	0	0	0	0	0	0	0
Broward County	0	0	0	0	0	0	0	0	0	0
Calhoun County	0	0	0	0	0	0	0	0	0	0
Charlotte County	0	0	0	0	0	0	0	0	0	0
Citrus County	0	0	0	0	0	0	0	0	0	0
Clay County	0	0	0	0	0	0	0	0	0	0
Collier County	0	0	0	0	0	0	0	0	0	0
Columbia County	0	0	0	0	0	0	0	0	0	0
DeSoto County	0	0	0	0	0	0	0	0	0	0
Dixie County	0	0	0	0	0	0	0	0	0	0
Duval County	0	0	0	0	0	0	0	0	0	0
Escambia County	0	0	0	0	0	0	0	0	0	0
Flagler County	0	0	0	0	0	0	0	0	0	0
Franklin County	0	0	0	0	0	0	0	0	0	0
Gadsden County	0	0	0	0	0	0	0	0	0	0
Gilchrist County	0	0	0	0	0	0	0	0	0	0
Glades County	0	0	0	0	0	0	0	0	0	0
Gulf County	0	0	0	0	0	0	0	0	0	0
Hamilton County	0	0	0	0	0	0	0	0	0	0
Hardee County	0	0	0	0	0	0	0	0	0	0
Hendry County	0	0	0	0	0	0	0	0	0	0
Hernando County	0	0	0	0	0	0	0	0	0	0
Highlands County	0	0	0	0	0	0	0	0	0	0
Hillsborough County	0	0	0	0	0	0	0	0	0	0
Holmes County	0	0	0	0	0	0	0	0	0	0
Indian River County	0	0	0	0	0	0	0	0	0	0
Jackson County	0	0	0	0	0	0	0	0	0	0
Jefferson County	0	0	0	0	0	0	0	0	0	0
Lafayette County	0	0	0	0	0	0	0	0	0	0
Lake County	0	0	0	0	0	0	0	0	0	0
Lee County	0	0	0	0	0	0	0	0	0	0
Leon County	0	0	0	0	0	0	0	0	0	0
Levy County	0	0	0	0	0	0	0	0	0	0
Liberty County	0	0	0	0	0	0	0	0	0	0
Madison County	0	0	0	0	0	0	0	0	0	0
Manatee County	0	0	0	0	0	0	0	0	0	0
Marion County	0	0	0	0	0	0	0	0	0	0
Martin County	0	0	0	0	0	0	0	0	0	0
Miami-Dade County	0	0	0	0	0	0	0	0	0	0
Monroe County	0	0	0	0	0	0	0	0	0	0
Nassau County	0	0	0	0	0	0	0	0	0	0
Okaloosa County	0	0	0	0	0	0	0	0	0	0
Okeechobee County	0	0	0	0	0	0	0	0	0	0
Orange County	0	0	0	0	0	0	0	0	0	0
Osceola County	0	0	0	0	0	0	0	0	0	0
Palm Beach County	0	0	0	0	0	0	0	0	0	0
Pasco County	0	0	0	0	0	0	0	0	0	0
Pinellas County	0	0	0	0	0	0	0	0	0	0
Polk County	0	0	0	0	0	0	0	0	0	0
Putnam County	0	0	0	0	0	0	0	0	0	0
Santa Rosa County	0	0	0	0	0	0	0	0	0	0
Sarasota County	0	0	0	0	0	0	0	0	0	0
Seminole County	0	0	0	0	0	0	0	0	0	0
St. Johns County	0	0	0	0	0	0	0	0	0	0
St. Lucie County	0	0	0	0	0	0	0	0	0	0
Sumter County	0	0	0	0	0	0	0	0	0	0
Suwannee County	0	0	0	0	0	0	0	0	0	0
Taylor County	0	0	0	0	0	0	0	0	0	0
Union County	0	0	0	0	0	0	0	0	0	0
Volusia County	0	0	0	0	0	0	0	0	0	0
Wakulla County	0	0	0	0	0	0	0	0	0	0
Walton County	0	0	0	0	0	0	0	0	0	0
Washington County	0	0	0	0	0	0	0	0	0	0

Table 11. Offenses Known to Law Enforcement, by Selected State, Tribal, and Other Agencies, 2020—Continued

(Number.)

State/other agency unit/office	Violent crime	Murder and nonnegligent manslaughter	Rape[1]	Robbery	Aggravated assault	Property crime	Burglary	Larceny-theft	Motor vehicle theft	Arson[2]
Highway Patrol										
Alachua County	1	0	0	0	1	2	0	1	1	0
Baker County	1	0	0	0	1	0	0	0	0	0
Bay County	2	0	0	0	2	5	0	4	1	0
Bradford County	0	0	0	0	0	2	0	1	1	0
Brevard County	1	0	0	0	1	2	0	1	1	0
Broward County	6	0	0	0	6	14	0	10	4	0
Calhoun County	1	0	0	0	1	0	0	0	0	0
Charlotte County	0	0	0	0	0	3	0	1	2	0
Citrus County	2	0	0	0	2	2	0	1	1	0
Clay County	1	0	0	0	1	0	0	0	0	0
Collier County	3	0	0	0	3	11	0	9	2	0
Columbia County	6	0	0	0	6	9	0	4	5	0
DeSoto County	0	0	0	0	0	0	0	0	0	0
Dixie County	0	0	0	0	0	0	0	0	0	0
Duval County	7	0	0	0	7	29	0	20	9	0
Escambia County	7	0	0	0	7	6	0	1	5	0
Flagler County	0	0	0	0	0	2	0	0	2	0
Franklin County	0	0	0	0	0	0	0	0	0	0
Gadsden County	3	0	0	0	3	6	0	1	5	0
Gilchrist County	1	0	0	0	1	0	0	0	0	0
Glades County	0	0	0	0	0	2	0	2	0	0
Gulf County	0	0	0	0	0	0	0	0	0	0
Hamilton County	0	0	0	0	0	4	0	3	1	0
Hardee County	0	0	0	0	0	0	0	0	0	0
Hendry County	0	0	0	0	0	2	0	1	1	0
Hernando County	6	0	0	0	6	4	0	3	1	0
Highlands County	0	0	0	0	0	0	0	0	0	0
Hillsborough County	16	0	0	0	16	19	0	15	4	0
Holmes County	0	0	0	0	0	0	0	0	0	0
Indian River County	0	0	0	0	0	2	0	1	1	0
Jackson County	0	0	0	0	0	3	0	2	1	0
Jefferson County	4	0	0	0	4	6	0	3	3	0
Lafayette County	0	0	0	0	0	0	0	0	0	0
Lake County	1	0	0	0	1	1	0	1	0	0
Lee County	4	0	0	0	4	11	0	11	0	0
Leon County	9	0	0	1	8	16	0	11	5	0
Levy County	0	0	0	0	0	3	0	1	2	0
Liberty County	0	0	0	0	0	0	0	0	0	0
Madison County	1	0	0	0	1	4	0	3	1	0
Manatee County	3	0	0	0	3	3	U	1	2	0
Marion County	1	0	0	0	1	1	0	0	1	0
Martin County	3	0	0	0	3	0	0	0	0	0
Miami-Dade County	33	0	0	0	33	43	0	30	13	0
Monroe County	1	0	0	0	1	0	0	0	0	0
Nassau County	0	0	0	0	0	2	0	1	1	0
Okaloosa County	2	0	0	0	2	3	0	2	1	0
Okeechobee County	0	0	0	0	0	0	0	0	0	0
Orange County	15	0	0	0	15	15	0	9	6	0
Osceola County	3	0	0	0	3	1	0	1	0	0
Palm Beach County	31	0	0	0	31	21	0	10	11	0
Pasco County	15	0	0	0	15	14	0	4	10	0
Pinellas County	13	0	0	0	13	13	0	8	5	0
Polk County	8	0	0	0	8	9	0	3	6	0
Putnam County	1	0	0	0	1	1	0	1	0	0
Santa Rosa County	2	0	0	0	2	2	0	0	2	0
Sarasota County	1	0	0	0	1	1	0	0	1	0
Seminole County	0	0	0	0	0	2	0	0	2	0
St. Johns County	0	0	0	0	0	5	0	1	4	0
St. Lucie County	3	0	0	0	3	6	0	3	3	0
Sumter County	1	0	0	0	1	10	0	5	5	0
Suwannee County	1	0	0	0	1	4	0	2	2	0
Taylor County	3	0	0	0	3	0	0	0	0	0
Union County	0	0	0	0	0	0	0	0	0	0
Volusia County	1	0	0	0	1	3	0	1	2	0
Wakulla County	0	0	0	0	0	0	0	0	0	0
Walton County	1	0	0	0	1	2	0	1	1	0
Washington County	1	0	0	0	1	0	0	0	0	0
Other Agencies										
Clay County School Board	6	0	2	0	4	24	0	24	0	0
Duval County Schools	23	0	0	3	20	138	51	83	4	1
Florida School for the Deaf and Blind	0	0	0	0	0	1	0	1	0	0
Fort Lauderdale Airport	3	0	0	2	1	235	7	184	44	0
Jackson County School District	4	0	2	0	2	4	1	3	0	0
Jacksonville Aviation Authority	0	0	0	0	0	42	1	9	32	0
Lee County Port Authority	0	0	0	0	0	22	0	21	1	0
Melbourne International Airport	0	0	0	0	0	5	0	1	4	0
Miami-Dade County Public Schools	27	0	5	8	14	218	80	133	5	1
Northwest Florida Beaches International Airport	0	0	0	0	0	4	0	4	0	0
Palm Beach County School District	40	0	15	8	17	134	11	121	2	2
Port Everglades	5	0	2	0	3	21	3	15	3	0
Sarasota County Schools	5	0	0	1	4	43	7	36	0	0

Table 11. Offenses Known to Law Enforcement, by Selected State, Tribal, and Other Agencies, 2020—Continued

(Number.)

State/other agency unit/office	Violent crime	Murder and nonnegligent manslaughter	Rape[1]	Robbery	Aggravated assault	Property crime	Burglary	Larceny-theft	Motor vehicle theft	Arson[2]
Sarasota-Manatee Airport Authority	0	0	0	0	0	26	0	1	25	0
St. Petersburg-Clearwater International Airport	0	0	0	0	0	8	0	7	1	0
Tampa International Airport	3	0	1	1	1	540	3	513	24	0
Volusia County Beach Safety	12	0	2	2	8	111	51	59	1	0
GEORGIA										
State Agencies										
Georgia Department of Transportation, Office of Investigations	0	0	0	0	0	0	0	0	0	0
Georgia Forestry Commission	0	0	0	0	0	3	1	2	0	11
Georgia Public Safety Training Center	0	0	0	0	0	0	0	0	0	0
Georgia World Congress	1	0	0	1	0	31	3	27	1	0
Ports Authority, Savannah	0	0	0	0	0	6	2	4	0	0
Other Agencies										
Atlanta Public Schools[5]	14	0	12	2	0	75	21	52	2	0
Cobb County Board of Education	10	0	8	0	2	66	12	54	0	0
Decatur County Schools	0	0	0	0	0	0	0	0	0	0
Fayette County Marshal	0	0	0	0	0	0	0	0	0	0
Forsyth County Fire Investigation Unit	0	0	0	0	0	0	0	0	0	5
Fulton County Marshal	0	0	0	0	0	4	0	1	3	0
Fulton County School System	6	0	1	1	4	79	5	72	2	1
Gwinnett County Public Schools	15	0	8	3	4	84	3	80	1	0
Hall County Marshal	0	0	0	0	0	0	0	0	0	0
Metropolitan Atlanta Rapid Transit Authority[5]	128	2	0	38	88	160	3	145	12	5
Muscogee County Schools	1	0	0	0	1	69	6	63	0	0
IDAHO										
State Agencies										
Attorney General	0	0	0	0	0	0	0	0	0	0
Idaho State Lottery Security Division	0	0	0	0	0	18	0	18	0	0
Idaho State Police	49	9	12	0	28	8	1	7	0	0
Tribal Agencies										
Coeur d'Alene Tribal	7	0	1	0	6	40	12	26	2	0
Fort Hall Tribal	51	0	2	0	49	118	14	80	24	0
Kootenai Tribal	0	0	0	0	0	4	4	0	0	0
Nez Perce Tribal	18	0	0	1	17	17	4	9	4	0
ILLINOIS[5]										
State Agencies										
Illinois Department of Natural Resources	0	0	0	0	0		1		0	0
Illinois State Police	575	28	81	43	423		23		2	2
Secretary of State Police	1	0	0	1	0		1		3	1
Other Agencies										
Alton & Southern Railway	0	0	0	0	0	0	0	0	0	340
Cook County Forest Preserve	13	0	5	3	5		3		3	0
Crystal Lake Park District	3	0	0	0	3		3		0	0
Decatur Park District	3	0	1	0	2		4		0	0
Fox Valley Park District	1	0	0	0	1		1		0	0
Kane County Forest Preserve	0	0	0	0	0		5		0	2
Lake County Forest Preserve	0	0	0	0	0		1		0	0
McHenry County Conservation District	0	0	0	0	0		0		0	0
Springfield Park District	24	0	0	5	19		19		6	3
Terminal Railroad Association	0	0	0	0	0		0		0	0
Tri-County Drug Enforcement Narcotics Team	0	0	0	0	0		1		0	0
INDIANA										
State Agencies										
Indiana Gaming Commission	14	1	0	0	13	259	0	259	0	0
Indiana State Excise Police	0	0	0	0	0	0	0	0	0	
Indiana State Police	565	19	104	14	428	827	68	576	183	4
Other Agencies										
Indiana Harbor Belt Railroad	0	0	0	0	0	0	0	0	0	0
Indianapolis International Airport	2	0	0	0	2	110	3	67	40	0
Indianapolis Public Schools	12	0	5	2	5	15	5	8	2	0
IOWA										
State Agencies										
State Patrol										
District 1	2	0	0	0	2	4	0	2	2	0
District 2	0	0	0	0	0	1	0	1	0	0
District 3	2	0	0	0	2	0	0	0	0	0
District 4	0	0	0	0	0	1	0	1	0	0
District 5	0	0	0	0	0	0	0	0	0	0
District 6	0	0	0	0	0	0	0	0	0	0
District 7	0	0	0	0	0	0	0	0	0	0
District 8	1	0	0	0	1	1	0	0	1	0
District 9	0	0	0	0	0	0	0	0	0	0
District 10	0	0	0	0	0	0	0	0	0	0
District 11	4	0	0	0	4	1	0	1	0	0

Table 11. Offenses Known to Law Enforcement, by Selected State, Tribal, and Other Agencies, 2020—Continued

(Number.)

State/other agency unit/office	Violent crime	Murder and nonnegligent manslaughter	Rape[1]	Robbery	Aggravated assault	Property crime	Burglary	Larceny-theft	Motor vehicle theft	Arson[2]
District 12	3	0	0	0	3	1	0	0	1	0
District 13	0	0	0	0	0	0	0	0	0	0
Other Agencies										
Southeast Iowa Interagency Drug Task Force	0	0	0	0	0	0	0	0	0	0
KANSAS										
State Agencies										
Highway Patrol										
Capitol	2	0	0	1	1	10	0	6	4	0
Troop A	23	0	0	1	22	0	0	0	0	0
Troop B	11	0	0	0	11	7	0	3	4	0
Troop C	2	0	0	0	2	5	0	2	3	0
Troop D	4	0	0	0	4	4	0	0	4	0
Troop E	3	0	0	0	3	0	0	0	0	0
Troop F	10	0	0	0	10	4	0	3	1	0
Troop G	13	0	0	0	13	23	6	13	4	0
Troop H	12	1	0	0	11	6	1	4	1	0
Troop N	0	0	0	0	0	0	0	0	0	0
Troop S	0	0	0	0	0	1	0	1	0	0
Kansas Department of Wildlife and Parks	7	0	1	0	6	18	2	14	2	0
Kansas Lottery Security Division	0	0	0	0	0	0	0	0	0	0
Securities Office, Investigation Section	0	0	0	0	0	0	0	0	0	0
Tribal Agencies										
Iowa Tribal	0	0	0	0	0	0	0	0	0	0
Kickapoo Tribal	7	0	0	0	7	10	7	0	3	0
Potawatomi Tribal	2	0	0	0	2	19	3	15	1	0
Sac and Fox Tribal	1	0	0	0	1	14	0	10	4	0
Johnson County Park	1	0	0	0	1	73	6	67	0	1
Other Agencies										
Johnson County Park	1	0	0	0	1	73	6	67	0	1
Kansas City Fire Department, Fire Investigation Division	1	0	0	0	1	2	0	1	1	31
Unified School District, Goddard	0	0	0	0	0	3	1	2	0	1
KENTUCKY										
State Agencies										
Fish and Wildlife Enforcement	2	0	0	0	2	9	0	9	0	0
Kentucky Horse Park	0	0	0	0	0	5	2	3	0	0
Motor Vehicle Enforcement	0	0	0	0	0	2	0	2	0	0
Park Security	0	0	0	0	0	31	2	26	3	0
State Police										
Ashland	31	1	16	2	12	157	50	82	25	3
Bowling Green	28	1	12	1	14	85	18	44	23	1
Campbellsburg	42	1	21	2	18	136	43	65	28	0
Columbia	50	5	18	1	26	87	29	44	14	3
Drug Enforcement Area[2]	1	0	0	0	1	6	0	6	0	0
Dry Ridge	23	1	12	1	9	85	39	32	14	0
Electronic Crimes	2	0	2	0	0	0	0	0	0	0
Elizabethtown	40	3	20	1	16	120	28	59	33	1
Frankfort	21	4	10	1	6	71	10	45	16	2
Harlan	44	2	19	1	22	230	89	84	57	5
Hazard	51	6	12	4	29	128	50	37	41	3
Henderson	16	0	6	1	9	86	20	58	8	2
London	60	1	31	0	28	174	52	74	48	11
Madisonville	22	2	11	1	8	60	22	31	7	0
Mayfield	58	7	23	2	26	109	30	65	14	2
Morehead	58	5	18	2	33	148	52	72	24	5
Pikeville	74	0	16	7	51	339	103	120	116	4
Richmond	51	6	13	6	26	124	54	50	20	3
Vehicle Investigations	0	0	0	0	0	2	0	2	0	0
West Drug Enforcement Branch	0	0	0	0	0	3	0	3	0	1
Other Agencies										
Barren County Drug Task Force	0	0	0	0	0	2	0	2	0	0
Bluegrass Narcotics Task Force	0	0	0	0	0	0	0	0	0	0
Cincinnati-Northern Kentucky International Airport	0	0	0	0	0	39	0	29	10	0
Fayette County Schools	7	0	1	0	6	35	3	32	0	1
Garrard County Constable District[3]	0	0	0	0	0	0	0	0	0	0
Gateway Area Drug Task Force	0	0	0	0	0	0	0	0	0	0
Greater Hardin County Narcotics Task Force	1	0	0	0	1	0	0	0	0	0
Jefferson County School District	10	0	0	1	9	79	54	22	3	1
Lake Cumberland Area Drug Enforcement Task Force	0	0	0	0	0	0	0	0	0	0
Lexington Bluegrass Airport	0	0	0	0	0	16	0	3	13	0
Louisville Regional Airport Authority	0	0	0	0	0	108	1	42	65	0
McCreary County Constable District[4]	0	0	0	0	0	0	0	0	0	0
Northern Kentucky Drug Strike Force	0	0	0	0	0	0	0	0	0	0
South Central Kentucky Drug Task Force	0	0	0	0	0	2	0	2	0	0
MAINE										
State Agencies										
Bureau of Capitol Police[4]	0	0	0	0	0	2	1	0	1	0
Drug Enforcement Agency	0	0	0	0	0	1	1	0	0	0

Table 11. Offenses Known to Law Enforcement, by Selected State, Tribal, and Other Agencies, 2020—Continued

(Number.)

State/other agency unit/office	Violent crime	Murder and nonnegligent manslaughter	Rape[1]	Robbery	Aggravated assault	Property crime	Burglary	Larceny-theft	Motor vehicle theft	Arson[2]
State Fire Marshal[4]	1	0	0	0	1	3	2	1	0	107
State Police	120	7	61	1	51	800	204	526	70	2
MARYLAND[3]										
MASSACHUSETTS										
State Agencies										
Division of Law Enforcement, Environmental Police	8	0	0	0	8	8	2	3	3	6
State Police										
Berkshire County	3	0	1	1	1	42	14	22	6	
Bristol County	26	0	0	2	24	2	0	0	2	
Essex County	0	0	0	0	0	0	0	0	0	
Franklin County	11	0	1	2	8	0	0	0	0	
Hampden County	18	0	0	1	17	10	2	1	7	
Hampshire County	7	0	0	0	7	1	0	1	0	
Middlesex County	0	0	0	0	0	0	0	0	0	
Suffolk County	0	0	0	0	0	0	0	0	0	
Worcester County	9	0	0	0	9	6	0	2	4	
MICHIGAN										
State Agencies										
Department of Natural Resources Law Enforcement Division	6	0	0	0	6	12	1	8	3	1
State Police										
Alcona County	4	0	3	0	1	7	2	3	2	1
Alger County	22	0	6	0	16	28	8	16	4	1
Allegan County	69	1	39	0	29	299	130	144	25	5
Alpena County	30	2	11	0	17	83	22	57	4	0
Antrim County	15	0	9	0	6	37	15	18	4	1
Arenac County	8	0	7	0	1	4	0	2	2	0
Baraga County	15	0	0	0	15	12	2	8	2	1
Barry County	31	0	9	2	20	127	45	71	11	0
Bay County	46	2	18	1	25	90	31	52	7	0
Benzie County	9	0	5	0	4	9	5	3	1	0
Berrien County	45	1	19	5	20	132	45	79	8	2
Branch County	69	1	25	1	42	130	52	60	18	4
Calhoun County	48	1	20	0	27	92	30	43	19	0
Cass County	13	0	5	3	5	95	70	19	6	1
Charlevoix County	6	1	1	0	4	5	3	2	0	0
Cheboygan County	20	1	8	0	11	34	25	6	3	0
Chippewa County	62	2	10	0	50	26	12	12	2	0
Clare County	16	0	5	0	11	25	9	11	5	0
Clinton County	6	0	5	0	1	22	5	13	4	0
Crawford County	14	0	8	0	6	19	5	13	1	1
Delta County	19	0	9	0	10	48	13	32	3	0
Dickinson County	13	0	7	0	6	46	10	28	8	1
Eaton County	31	0	14	0	17	114	40	58	16	0
Emmet County	14	0	9	0	5	68	43	23	2	0
Genesee County	211	15	79	6	111	144	75	43	26	4
Gladwin County	16	0	12	1	3	9	3	5	1	0
Gogebic County	12	0	1	0	11	14	6	8	0	1
Grand Traverse County	33	0	22	1	10	49	14	30	5	2
Gratiot County	15	0	13	0	2	10	0	9	1	0
Hillsdale County	72	0	20	1	51	98	32	50	16	3
Houghton County	22	0	6	0	16	71	16	48	7	1
Huron County	6	0	3	0	3	18	3	13	2	0
Ingham County	35	1	20	0	14	45	17	23	5	2
Ionia County	51	1	20	0	30	74	10	56	8	1
Iosco County	38	0	14	1	23	60	24	32	4	3
Iron County	11	0	5	0	6	27	11	14	2	2
Isabella County	44	1	17	2	24	65	19	33	13	4
Jackson County	114	2	44	3	65	121	26	70	25	2
Kalamazoo County	29	0	12	0	17	78	9	51	18	1
Kalkaska County	13	0	8	0	5	16	7	7	2	1
Kent County	37	0	20	0	17	21	0	17	4	0
Keweenaw County	1	0	0	0	1	0	0	0	0	0
Lake County	28	0	9	0	19	14	4	7	3	1
Lapeer County	30	0	4	0	26	38	10	23	5	0
Leelanau County	0	0	0	0	0	7	2	5	0	0
Lenawee County	33	0	24	0	9	55	17	30	8	1
Livingston County	72	0	29	1	42	132	26	97	9	1
Luce County	14	0	3	0	11	30	17	9	4	0
Mackinac County	10	0	3	0	7	24	6	18	0	0
Macomb County	40	2	10	0	28	21	5	10	6	1
Manistee County	13	1	3	0	9	63	17	45	1	0
Marquette County	86	0	8	1	77	108	19	77	12	1
Mason County	16	0	10	0	6	40	10	30	0	0
Mecosta County	16	0	12	0	4	51	29	19	3	0
Menominee County	9	0	1	0	8	33	15	16	2	0
Midland County	20	0	13	0	7	34	12	19	3	0
Missaukee County	15	0	11	0	4	25	7	15	3	0
Monroe County	44	0	13	3	28	83	28	40	15	0
Montcalm County	147	2	45	3	97	233	66	129	38	3

Table 11. Offenses Known to Law Enforcement, by Selected State, Tribal, and Other Agencies, 2020—Continued

(Number.)

State/other agency unit/office	Violent crime	Murder and nonnegligent manslaughter	Rape[1]	Robbery	Aggravated assault	Property crime	Burglary	Larceny-theft	Motor vehicle theft	Arson[2]
Montmorency County	3	0	3	0	0	7	1	4	2	0
Muskegon County	53	0	18	0	35	127	32	84	11	2
Newaygo County	65	0	24	0	41	144	60	72	12	2
Oakland County	90	1	15	6	68	153	33	91	29	1
Oceana County	45	0	22	1	22	86	17	62	7	1
Ogemaw County	39	0	16	0	23	36	18	16	2	2
Ontonagon County	13	0	6	0	7	7	2	4	1	0
Osceola County	33	0	21	1	11	32	17	14	1	2
Oscoda County	4	0	3	0	1	8	3	5	0	0
Otsego County	40	2	18	0	20	38	13	19	6	1
Ottawa County	2	0	2	0	0	0	0	0	0	0
Presque Isle County	7	1	0	0	6	4	1	2	1	0
Roscommon County	28	0	17	0	11	38	15	20	3	0
Saginaw County	94	5	35	2	52	91	39	43	9	4
Sanilac County	23	0	14	0	9	20	11	8	1	1
Schoolcraft County	8	1	3	0	4	54	21	30	3	0
Shiawassee County	61	0	16	2	43	208	83	106	19	2
St. Clair County	27	0	9	0	18	29	10	18	1	1
St. Joseph County	41	0	7	1	33	210	64	108	38	3
Tuscola County	54	0	29	1	24	60	30	24	6	0
Van Buren County	56	2	14	2	38	141	36	82	23	5
Washtenaw County	83	1	30	1	51	105	28	65	12	0
Wayne County	147	7	23	5	112	84	2	57	25	1
Wexford County	38	0	21	0	17	68	16	45	7	0
Tribal Agencies										
Little River Band of Ottawa Indians	1	0	0	0	1	21	0	18	3	0
Nottawaseppi Huron Band of Potawatomi	6	0	1	1	4	85	2	79	4	0
Other Agencies										
Bishop International Airport	0	0	0	0	0	15	0	3	12	0
Capitol Region Airport Authority	0	0	0	0	0	4	0	1	3	0
Genesee County Parks and Recreation	2	0	0	1	1	16	2	12	2	0
Gerald R. Ford International Airport	0	0	0	0	0	13	0	2	11	0
Huron-Clinton Metropolitan Authority										
Hudson Mills Metropark	1	0	0	0	1	1	0	1	0	0
Kensington Metropark	1	0	1	0	0	4	0	4	0	0
Lower Huron Metropark	0	0	0	0	0	7	0	7	0	0
Stony Creek Metropark	5	0	0	0	5	14	1	13	0	1
Wayne County Airport	8	0	0	0	8	140	0	65	75	0
MINNESOTA										
State Agencies										
Bureau of Criminal Apprehension	0	0	0	0	0	0	0	0	0	0
Capitol Security, St. Paul	0	0	0	0	0	0	0	0	0	0
Department of Natural Resources										
Enforcement Division[4]	0	0	0	0	0	2	0	0	2	0
Minnesota State Patrol	0	0	0	0	0	0	0	0	0	0
State Patrol										
Brainerd	0	0	0	0	0	2	0	1	1	0
Detroit Lakes	0	0	0	0	0	0	0	0	0	0
Duluth	0	0	0	0	0	1	0	1	0	0
Golden Valley	0	0	0	0	0	3	0	1	2	0
Mankato	0	0	0	0	0	0	0	0	0	0
Marshall	0	0	0	0	0	0	0	0	0	0
Oakdale	0	0	0	0	0	0	0	0	0	0
Rochester	0	0	0	0	0	0	0	0	0	0
St. Cloud	0	0	0	0	0	0	0	0	0	0
Thief River Falls	0	0	0	0	0	0	0	0	0	0
Virginia	0	0	0	0	0	0	0	0	0	0
Tribal Agencies										
Fond du Lac Tribal[4]	15	0	1	0	14	80	13	55	12	2
Mille Lacs Tribal[4]	38	0	1	4	33	140	18	107	15	0
Other Agencies										
Metropolitan Transit Commission	252	2	2	147	101	344	4	331	9	9
Minneapolis-St. Paul International Airport	4	0	0	0	4	149	1	114	34	0
Three Rivers Park District[4]	1	0	0	0	1	147	2	145	0	0
MISSISSIPPI										
State Agencies										
State Capitol Police	1	0	0	0	1	32	11	20	1	0
MISSOURI										
State Agencies										
Division of Alcohol and Tobacco Control[4]	0	0	0	0	0	0	0	0	0	0
Missouri State Highway Patrol	77	1	3	0	73	198	6	131	61	0
Other Agencies										
Clay County Park Authority	11	0	0	0	11	18	1	14	3	0
Jackson County Park Rangers	0	0	0	0	0	0	0	0	0	0
Kansas City International Airport	0	0	0	0	0	163	2	36	125	
Logan-Rogersville School District[4]	2	0	0	0	2	1	0	1	0	0
Terminal Railroad[4]	0	0	0	0	0	1	0	1	0	0

Table 11. Offenses Known to Law Enforcement, by Selected State, Tribal, and Other Agencies, 2020—Continued

(Number.)

State/other agency unit/office	Violent crime	Murder and nonnegligent manslaughter	Rape[1]	Robbery	Aggravated assault	Property crime	Burglary	Larceny-theft	Motor vehicle theft	Arson[2]
MONTANA										
Tribal Agencies										
Blackfeet Agency	447	3	12	1	431	51	12	25	14	0
Crow Agency	71	3	6	0	62	194	45	87	62	4
Fort Belknap Tribal	22	0	2	0	20	25	5	12	8	1
Fort Peck Assiniboine and Sioux Tribes	103	0	0	4	99	30	10	0	20	3
Northern Cheyenne Agency	119	0	7	1	111	61	14	33	14	1
Rocky Boy's Tribal	49	1	3	3	42	70	9	35	26	0
NEBRASKA										
Tribal Agencies										
Omaha Tribal	26	0	3	0	23	13	0	0	13	1
Santee Tribal	5	0	1	0	4	5	0	1	4	0
Winnebago Tribal	47	1	0	0	46	10	4	2	4	1
NEVADA										
State Agencies										
Attorney General Investigations Division	0	0	0	0	0	15	0	15	0	0
Capitol Police[4]	9	0	0	0	9	26	10	12	4	1
Department of Public Safety, Investigative Division[4]	8	5	2	0	1	17	15	1	1	0
Highway Patrol										
Northeastern Division	0	0	0	0	0	3	1	2	0	0
Southern Division	34	0	0	1	33	14	2	3	9	0
Secretary of State Securities Division, Enforcement Section	0	0	0	0	0	0	0	0	0	0
State Fire Marshal	0	0	0	0	0	0	0	0	0	8
Tribal Agencies										
Eastern Nevada Agency	2	0	0	0	2	3	1	1	1	0
Ely Shoshone Tribal	0	0	0	0	0	0	0	0	0	0
Fallon Tribal	4	0	0	0	4	12	1	7	4	0
Las Vegas Paiute Tribal	1	0	0	0	1	2	0	2	0	0
Lovelock Paiute Tribal	1	0	0	0	1	0	0	0	0	0
Moapa Tribal	0	0	0	0	0	110	0	110	0	2
Pyramid Lake Tribal	12	1	1	1	9	41	11	13	17	0
Reno-Sparks Indian Colony	7	0	1	1	5	133	3	129	1	3
South Fork Band Tribal	0	0	0	0	0	0	0	0	0	0
Western Nevada Agency	4	0	0	0	4	11	8	2	1	0
Western Shoshone Tribal	1	0	0	0	1	2	2	0	0	0
Yomba Shoshone Tribal	0	0	0	0	0	2	1	1	0	0
Other Agencies										
Clark County School District	62	0	0	28	34	391	106	272	13	0
Las Vegas Fire and Rescue, Arson Bomb Unit	0	0	0	0	0	0	0	0	0	61
Reno Municipal Court Marshal[4]	0	0	0	0	0	0	0	0	0	0
Reno Tahoe Airport Authority[4]	0	0	0	0	0	37	0	28	9	0
Washoe County School District[4]	25	0	0	1	24	71	25	44	2	5
NEW HAMPSHIRE										
State Agencies										
Liquor Commission	0	0	0	0	0	47	1	46	0	0
State Police										
Carroll County	2	0	0	0	2	3	0	2	1	0
Cheshire County	8	1	2	0	5	17	3	10	4	0
Coos County	8	0	3	0	5	27	4	22	1	1
Grafton County	3	0	2	0	1	41	15	19	7	0
Hillsborough County	1	0	1	0	0	4	0	2	2	0
Merrimack County	3	0	0	0	3	15	4	8	3	0
Rockingham County	1	0	1	0	0	3	0	1	2	0
Strafford County	0	0	0	0	0	1	0	1	0	0
Sullivan County	4	0	1	0	3	27	11	14	2	0
NEW JERSEY										
State Agencies										
Department of Corrections	79	0	0	0	79	0	0	0	0	0
Department of Human Services	33	0	0	1	32	16	0	16	0	2
Division of Fish and Wildlife	0	0	0	0	0	4	0	4	0	0
New Jersey Transit Police	18	0	0	0	18	182	1	174	7	1
Palisades Interstate Parkway	0	0	0	0	0	0	0	0	0	0
Port Authority of New York and New Jersey	45	0	0	6	39	275	13	257	5	0
State Park Police	3	0	2	0	1	48	17	30	1	1
State Police	105	0	0	0	105	0	0	0	0	0
State Police										
Atlantic County	29	0	5	5	19	379	30	342	7	
Bergen County	9	3	1	0	5	42	0	40	2	0
Burlington County	29	0	7	1	21	203	55	131	17	0
Camden County	9	0	1	1	7	14	0	10	4	0
Cape May County	10	0	2	2	6	97	24	67	6	0
Cumberland County	35	1	3	3	28	288	117	148	23	0
Essex County	5	0	0	3	2	17	1	11	5	0
Gloucester County	3	0	0	0	3	4	0	3	1	0
Hudson County	1	0	1	0	0	2	1	1	0	0

Table 11. Offenses Known to Law Enforcement, by Selected State, Tribal, and Other Agencies, 2020—Continued

(Number.)

State/other agency unit/office	Violent crime	Murder and nonnegligent manslaughter	Rape[1]	Robbery	Aggravated assault	Property crime	Burglary	Larceny-theft	Motor vehicle theft	Arson[2]
Hunterdon County	6	0	0	1	5	73	18	51	4	0
Mercer County	8	0	1	0	7	22	4	12	6	0
Middlesex County	6	0	1	1	4	20	2	17	1	0
Monmouth County	6	0	1	2	3	128	34	85	9	0
Morris County	6	0	1	0	5	11	2	6	3	0
Ocean County	4	0	0	0	4	22	7	13	2	0
Passaic County	2	0	0	0	2	5	0	2	3	0
Salem County	18	0	4	7	7	165	54	99	12	0
Somerset County	1	0	0	0	1	5	1	2	2	0
Sussex County	18	0	9	0	9	197	53	130	14	0
Union County	5	0	1	1	3	0	0	0	0	0
Warren County	11	0	1	2	8	79	14	59	6	0
Other Agencies										
Park Police										
Morris County	0	0	0	0	0	17	1	16	0	0
Union County	14	0	2	2	10	31	0	31	0	0
Prosecutor										
Atlantic County	0	0	0	0	0	0	0	0	0	0
Bergen County	0	0	0	0	0	0	0	0	0	0
Burlington County	0	0	0	0	0	0	0	0	0	0
Camden County	0	0	0	0	0	0	0	0	0	0
Cape May County	0	0	0	0	0	0	0	0	0	0
Cumberland County	0	0	0	0	0	0	0	0	0	0
Essex County	0	0	0	0	0	0	0	0	0	0
Gloucester County	0	0	0	0	0	0	0	0	0	0
Hudson County	0	0	0	0	0	0	0	0	0	0
Hunterdon County	0	0	0	0	0	0	0	0	0	0
Mercer County	0	0	0	0	0	0	0	0	0	0
Middlesex County	0	0	0	0	0	0	0	0	0	0
Monmouth County	0	0	0	0	0	0	0	0	0	0
Morris County	1	0	0	0	1	0	0	0	0	1
Ocean County	0	0	0	0	0	0	0	0	0	0
Passaic County	0	0	0	0	0	0	0	0	0	0
Salem County	0	0	0	0	0	0	0	0	0	0
Somerset County	0	0	0	0	0	0	0	0	0	0
Sussex County	0	0	0	0	0	0	0	0	0	0
Union County	0	0	0	0	0	0	0	0	0	0
Warren County	0	0	0	0	0	0	0	0	0	0
NEW MEXICO										
Tribal Agencies										
Taos Pueblo	5	0	0	1	4	11	0	7	4	3
NEW YORK										
State Agencies										
State Police										
Albany County	26	0	18	2	6	77	4	71	2	2
Allegany County	56	2	32	3	19	213	68	129	16	2
Broome County	74	1	32	1	40	384	72	288	24	5
Cattaraugus County	39	0	18	1	20	199	48	135	16	1
Cayuga County	55	0	26	0	29	191	50	126	15	2
Chautauqua County	32	0	13	2	17	126	30	92	4	0
Chemung County	89	1	29	1	58	164	16	139	9	1
Chenango County	56	0	34	2	20	153	43	98	12	1
Clinton County	94	1	55	2	36	719	96	603	20	21
Columbia County	37	0	16	3	18	155	23	118	14	6
Cortland County	23	0	12	0	11	81	12	68	1	2
Delaware County	28	0	15	1	12	135	28	99	8	0
Dutchess County	155	1	39	5	110	448	31	400	17	3
Erie County	38	0	16	0	22	287	21	241	25	1
Essex County	44	0	27	4	13	206	43	153	10	0
Franklin County	42	0	25	3	14	321	76	226	19	9
Fulton County	11	0	11	0	0	70	24	44	2	0
Genesee County	8	0	6	1	1	91	12	70	9	0
Greene County	172	0	22	1	149	197	41	148	8	1
Hamilton County	6	0	4	0	2	25	5	17	3	0
Herkimer County	44	0	27	1	16	172	52	111	9	2
Jefferson County	75	0	28	1	46	510	71	427	12	7
Lewis County	16	0	11	0	5	75	25	44	6	0
Livingston County	16	0	15	0	1	32	6	25	1	0
Madison County	32	0	23	1	8	133	24	102	7	0
Monroe County	45	0	37	1	7	49	1	37	11	0
Montgomery County	14	1	6	0	7	92	10	75	7	0
Nassau County	9	0	1	2	6	10	0	6	4	0
New York County	9	0	7	0	2	16	0	6	10	0
Niagara County	38	1	21	0	16	214	21	179	14	0
Oneida County	88	1	34	3	50	356	63	269	24	
Onondaga County	76	0	35	3	38	573	55	462	56	6
Ontario County	34	0	21	1	12	245	34	195	16	2
Orange County	105	0	80	4	21	390	32	335	23	0
Orleans County	12	0	9	0	3	63	15	40	8	1
Oswego County	88	0	56	3	29	439	93	310	36	3

Table 11. Offenses Known to Law Enforcement, by Selected State, Tribal, and Other Agencies, 2020—Continued

(Number.)

State/other agency unit/office	Violent crime	Murder and nonnegligent manslaughter	Rape[1]	Robbery	Aggravated assault	Property crime	Burglary	Larceny-theft	Motor vehicle theft	Arson[2]
Otsego County	44	0	22	4	18	329	49	260	20	0
Putnam County	17	0	6	1	10	71	7	55	9	0
Rensselaer County	44	0	27	6	11	268	32	218	18	4
Rockland County	3	0	2	0	1	4	0	4	0	0
Saratoga County	79	2	42	2	33	456	48	385	23	3
Schenectady County	10	0	8	0	2	38	5	30	3	0
Schoharie County	19	0	10	0	9	99	15	78	6	1
Schuyler County	4	0	3	0	1	23	6	17	0	0
Seneca County	19	0	14	0	5	88	3	83	2	0
Steuben County	63	2	41	2	18	312	61	222	29	4
St. Lawrence County	60	1	34	3	22	313	78	227	8	5
Suffolk County	19	0	12	1	6	16	3	10	3	2
Sullivan County	71	0	33	6	32	204	46	139	19	2
Tioga County	29	0	15	0	14	67	20	38	9	0
Tompkins County	25	0	17	1	7	223	26	187	10	3
Ulster County	65	1	36	1	27	367	38	311	18	3
Warren County	33	0	24	1	8	230	25	198	7	1
Washington County	33	0	24	0	9	88	19	55	14	4
Wayne County	67	1	28	7	31	362	60	281	21	7
Westchester County	111	1	22	4	84	329	27	275	27	3
Wyoming County	13	0	6	0	7	25	6	18	1	0
Yates County	3	0	2	0	1	23	3	20	0	0
Other Agencies										
New York City Department of Environmental Protection Police										
Ashokan Precinct	1	0	0	0	1	0	0	0	0	0
Beerston Precinct	0	0	0	0	0	2	0	2	0	0
Eastview Precinct	0	0	0	0	0	17	0	17	0	0
Gilboa Precinct	0	0	0	0	0	0	0	0	0	0
Grahamsville Precinct	0	0	0	0	0	0	0	0	0	0
Hillview Precinct	0	0	0	0	0	0	0	0	0	0
New York City Metropolitan Transportation Authority	0	0	0	0	0	0	0	0	0	0
Niagara Frontier Transportation Authority	31	0	0	15	16	67	1	39	27	0
NORTH CAROLINA										
State Agencies										
State Capitol Police	25	0	11	0	14	15	2	13	0	0
State Park Rangers										
Chimney Rock	0	0	0	0	0	2	0	2	0	0
Jockey's Ridge	0	0	0	0	0	0	0	0	0	0
Merchants Millpond	0	0	0	0	0	0	0	0	0	0
Pettigrew	0	0	0	0	0	0	0	0	0	0
Other Agencies										
Raleigh-Durham International Airport	1	0	0	0	1	84	0	46	38	0
University of North Carolina Hospitals	3	0	2	0	1	39	0	38	1	0
WakeMed Campus Police	14	0	0	1	13	97	6	89	2	0
NORTH DAKOTA										
State Agencies										
North Dakota Highway Patrol	9	0	0	0	9	21	1	1	19	0
Tribal Agencies										
Fort Totten Agency	180	0	4	7	169	205	52	98	55	8
Standing Rock Agency	51	1	4	0	46	15	3	5	7	0
Turtle Mountain Agency	310	0	10	0	300	474	114	213	147	3
OHIO										
State Agencies										
Ohio Department of Natural Resources	30	0	5	0	25	255	4	247	4	6
Ohio Investigative Unit	0	0	0	0	0	0	0	0	0	0
Ohio State Highway Patrol	243	5	22	2	214	155	11	91	53	6
Other Agencies										
Hamilton County Park District	0	0	0	0	0	69	1	68	0	1
Lake Metroparks	0	0	0	0	0	0	0	0	0	0
Toledo Fire Department Fire Investigation Unit	0	0	0	0	0	0	0	0	0	117
OKLAHOMA										
State Agencies										
Capitol Park Police	0	0	0	0	0	0	0	0	0	0
Oklahoma Highway Patrol	15	3	0	0	12	18	0	1	17	1
State Bureau of Investigation	0	0	0	0	0	0	0	0	0	0
State Park Rangers	8	0	4	0	4	62	11	46	5	1
Tribal Agencies										
Absentee Shawnee Tribal	2	0	0	0	2	13	4	7	2	0
Anadarko Agency	2	0	0	0	2	48	4	37	7	0
Cherokee Nation	11	0	1	1	9	36	7	21	8	0
Citizen Potawatomi Nation	4	0	1	0	3	121	3	104	14	1
Concho Agency[4]	10	0	1	0	9	31	5	17	9	0
Eastern Shawnee Tribal	2	0	0	0	2	57	2	50	5	0
Iowa Tribal[4]	1	0	0	0	1	4	0	4	0	0
Kaw Tribal	0	0	0	0	0	7	3	4	0	0
Kickapoo Tribal	7	0	0	2	5	35	5	21	9	1

Table 11. Offenses Known to Law Enforcement, by Selected State, Tribal, and Other Agencies, 2020—Continued

(Number.)

State/other agency unit/office	Violent crime	Murder and nonnegligent manslaughter	Rape[1]	Robbery	Aggravated assault	Property crime	Burglary	Larceny-theft	Motor vehicle theft	Arson[2]
Miami Agency	7	0	0	1	6	55	4	47	4	1
Miami Tribal	0	0	0	0	0	3	2	1	0	0
Otoe-Missouria Tribal	3	0	1	0	2	10	4	6	0	0
Pawnee Tribal	1	0	0	0	1	5	1	4	0	0
Ponca Tribal	8	0	0	3	5	18	3	9	6	2
Quapaw Tribal[4]	6	0	0	0	6	140	12	118	10	3
Sac and Fox Tribal[4]	6	0	0	0	6	26	9	13	4	0
Seminole Nation Lighthorse	2	0	0	0	2	22	3	16	3	0
Tonkawa Tribal	2	0	1	0	1	13	0	13	0	0
Wyandotte Nation	1	0	0	1	0	18	3	12	3	0
Other Agencies										
Beggs Public Schools	0	0	0	0	0	0	0	0	0	0
District 1 Narcotics Task Force	0	0	0	0	0	0	0	0	0	0
Jenks Public Schools	0	0	0	0	0	0	0	0	0	0
Lawton Public Schools	3	1	2	0	0	14	0	13	1	0
Muskogee City Schools	4	0	2	0	2	0	0	0	0	0
Putnam City Campus	2	0	0	0	2	1	1	0	0	0
Victory Life	0	0	0	0	0	0	0	0	0	0
OREGON										
State Agencies										
Liquor Commission										
Baker County	0	0	0	0	0	0	0	0	0	0
Benton County	0	0	0	0	0	0	0	0	0	0
Clackamas County	0	0	0	0	0	0	0	0	0	0
Clatsop County	0	0	0	0	0	0	0	0	0	0
Columbia County	0	0	0	0	0	0	0	0	0	0
Coos County	0	0	0	0	0	0	0	0	0	0
Crook County	0	0	0	0	0	0	0	0	0	0
Deschutes County	0	0	0	0	0	0	0	0	0	0
Douglas County	0	0	0	0	0	0	0	0	0	0
Gilliam County	0	0	0	0	0	0	0	0	0	0
Grant County	0	0	0	0	0	0	0	0	0	0
Hood River County	0	0	0	0	0	0	0	0	0	0
Jackson County	0	0	0	0	0	0	0	0	0	0
Klamath County	0	0	0	0	0	0	0	0	0	0
Lane County	0	0	0	0	0	0	0	0	0	0
Lincoln County	0	0	0	0	0	0	0	0	0	0
Marion County	0	0	0	0	0	0	0	0	0	0
Multnomah County	0	0	0	0	0	0	0	0	0	0
Polk County	0	0	0	0	0	0	0	0	0	0
Sherman County	0	0	0	0	0	0	0	0	0	0
Umatilla County	0	0	0	0	0	0	0	0	0	0
Washington County	0	0	0	0	0	0	0	0	0	0
Wheeler County	0	0	0	0	0	0	0	0	0	0
Yamhill County	0	0	0	0	0	0	0	0	0	0
State Police										
Baker County	1	0	0	0	1	9	2	7	0	2
Benton County	8	0	0	0	8	173	4	168	1	0
Clackamas County	17	0	0	1	16	30	0	18	12	0
Clatsop County	4	0	0	0	4	10	1	9	0	0
Columbia County	9	0	0	0	9	12	0	10	2	0
Coos County	5	0	0	0	5	24	2	17	5	1
Curry County	6	0	0	0	6	22	0	21	1	0
Deschutes County	10	0	1	0	9	6	2	3	1	2
Douglas County	25	0	1	0	24	39	6	25	8	1
Grant County	3	0	0	0	3	1	0	0	1	0
Harney County	2	0	0	0	2	3	1	2	0	0
Hood River County	3	0	0	0	3	8	0	6	2	0
Jackson County	16	0	0	1	15	34	2	25	7	1
Jefferson County	1	0	0	0	1	3	0	2	1	0
Josephine County	23	4	4	1	14	18	2	12	4	3
Klamath County	6	0	0	0	6	23	4	15	4	0
Lake County	8	1	2	0	5	2	0	1	1	0
Lane County	26	0	1	0	25	48	6	33	9	2
Lincoln County	8	0	0	0	8	43	1	42	0	0
Linn County	10	0	1	1	8	41	2	32	7	0
Malheur County	10	0	0	0	10	6	1	3	2	1
Marion County	59	0	2	1	56	116	10	88	18	5
Multnomah County	3	0	0	0	3	12	0	9	3	0
Polk County	6	0	0	0	6	9	1	8	0	0
Tillamook County	2	0	0	0	2	43	1	39	3	0
Umatilla County	24	0	3	0	21	12	4	5	3	1
Union County	1	0	0	0	1	6	1	5	0	0
Wasco County	2	0	0	0	2	8	0	7	1	0
Washington County	3	0	1	0	2	2	0	1	1	0
Yamhill County	5	0	1	0	4	3	0	2	1	0
Tribal Agencies										
Columbia River Inter-Tribal Fisheries Enforcement	6	0	0	0	6	2	2	0	0	0
Coos, Lower Umpqua, and Siuslaw Tribal	0	0	0	0	0	9	0	9	0	
Coquille Tribal	0	0	0	0	0	1	0	1	0	0
Siletz Tribal	4	0	1	0	3	8	2	3	3	0

Table 11. Offenses Known to Law Enforcement, by Selected State, Tribal, and Other Agencies, 2020—Continued

(Number.)

State/other agency unit/office	Violent crime	Murder and nonnegligent manslaughter	Rape[1]	Robbery	Aggravated assault	Property crime	Burglary	Larceny-theft	Motor vehicle theft	Arson[2]
Other Agencies										
Hillsboro School District	0	0	0	0	0	0	0	0	0	0
Port of Portland	8	0	0	1	7	380	6	314	60	3
PENNSYLVANIA[3]										
State Agencies										
Bureau of Forestry										
Adams County	0	0	0	0	0	0	0	0	0	0
Allegheny County	0	0	0	0	0	0	0	0	0	0
Armstrong County	0	0	0	0	0	0	0	0	0	1
Beaver County	0	0	0	0	0	0	0	0	0	0
Bedford County	0	0	0	0	0	0	0	0	0	1
Berks County	0	0	0	0	0	0	0	0	0	3
Blair County	0	0	0	0	0	0	0	0	0	20
Bradford County	0	0	0	0	0	0	0	0	0	1
Bucks County	0	0	0	0	0	0	0	0	0	0
Butler County	0	0	0	0	0	0	0	0	0	0
Cambria County	0	0	0	0	0	0	0	0	0	0
Cameron County	0	0	0	0	0	0	0	0	0	4
Carbon County	0	0	0	0	0	0	0	0	0	7
Centre County	0	0	0	0	0	0	0	0	0	1
Chester County	0	0	0	0	0	0	0	0	0	2
Clarion County	0	0	0	0	0	0	0	0	0	0
Clearfield County	0	0	0	0	0	0	0	0	0	3
Clinton County	0	0	0	0	0	0	0	0	0	0
Columbia County	0	0	0	0	0	0	0	0	0	0
Crawford County	0	0	0	0	0	0	0	0	0	0
Cumberland County	0	0	0	0	0	0	0	0	0	7
Dauphin County	0	0	0	0	0	0	0	0	0	12
Delaware County	0	0	0	0	0	0	0	0	0	0
Elk County	0	0	0	0	0	0	0	0	0	0
Erie County	0	0	0	0	0	0	0	0	0	0
Fayette County	0	0	0	0	0	0	0	0	0	11
Forest County	0	0	0	0	0	0	0	0	0	0
Franklin County	0	0	0	0	0	0	0	0	0	6
Fulton County	0	0	0	0	0	0	0	0	0	0
Greene County	0	0	0	0	0	0	0	0	0	1
Huntingdon County	0	0	0	0	0	0	0	0	0	1
Indiana County	0	0	0	0	0	0	0	0	0	8
Jefferson County	0	0	0	0	0	0	0	0	0	0
Juniata County	0	0	0	0	0	0	0	0	0	0
Lackawanna County	0	0	0	0	0	0	0	0	0	4
Lancaster County	0	0	0	0	0	0	0	0	0	3
Lawrence County	0	0	0	0	0	0	0	0	0	1
Lebanon County	0	0	0	0	0	0	0	0	0	0
Lehigh County	0	0	0	0	0	0	0	0	0	0
Luzerne County	0	0	0	0	0	0	0	0	0	12
Lycoming County	0	0	0	0	0	0	0	0	0	0
McKean County	0	0	0	0	0	0	0	0	0	0
Mercer County	0	0	0	0	0	0	0	0	0	0
Mifflin County	0	0	0	0	0	0	0	0	0	3
Monroe County	0	0	0	0	0	0	0	0	0	2
Montgomery County	0	0	0	0	0	0	0	0	0	1
Montour County	0	0	0	0	0	0	0	0	0	1
Northampton County	0	0	0	0	0	0	0	0	0	0
Northumberland County	0	0	0	0	0	0	0	0	0	1
Perry County	0	0	0	0	0	0	0	0	0	1
Philadelphia County	0	0	0	0	0	0	0	0	0	0
Pike County	0	0	0	0	0	0	0	0	0	0
Potter County	0	0	0	0	0	0	0	0	0	1
Schuylkill County	0	0	0	0	0	0	0	0	0	23
Snyder County	0	0	0	0	0	0	0	0	0	1
Somerset County	0	0	0	0	0	0	0	0	0	0
Sullivan County	0	0	0	0	0	0	0	0	0	0
Susquehanna County	0	0	0	0	0	0	0	0	0	0
Tioga County	0	0	0	0	0	0	0	0	0	0
Union County	0	0	0	0	0	0	0	0	0	0
Venango County	0	0	0	0	0	0	0	0	0	0
Warren County	0	0	0	0	0	0	0	0	0	0
Washington County	0	0	0	0	0	0	0	0	0	0
Wayne County	0	0	0	0	0	0	0	0	0	0
Westmoreland County	0	0	0	0	0	0	0	0	0	8
Wyoming County	0	0	0	0	0	0	0	0	0	0
York County	0	0	0	0	0	0	0	0	0	1
Bureau of Narcotics										
Adams County	0	0	0	0	0	0	0	0	0	0
Chester County	0	0	0	0	0	0	0	0	0	0
Cumberland County	0	0	0	0	0	0	0	0	0	0
Dauphin County	0	0	0	0	0	0	0	0	0	0
Delaware County	0	0	0	0	0	0	0	0	0	0
Franklin County	0	0	0	0	0	0	0	0	0	0
Fulton County	0	0	0	0	0	0	0	0	0	0
Lancaster County	0	0	0	0	0	0	0	0	0	0

Table 11. Offenses Known to Law Enforcement, by Selected State, Tribal, and Other Agencies, 2020—Continued

(Number.)

State/other agency unit/office	Violent crime	Murder and nonnegligent manslaughter	Rape[1]	Robbery	Aggravated assault	Property crime	Burglary	Larceny-theft	Motor vehicle theft	Arson[2]
Lebanon County	0	0	0	0	0	0	0	0	0	0
Perry County	0	0	0	0	0	0	0	0	0	0
York County	0	0	0	0	0	0	0	0	0	0
State Park Rangers										
Ben Rush	0	0	0	0	0	1	0	1	0	0
Little Pine	0	0	0	0	0	1	0	1	0	0
Memorial Lake	0	0	0	0	0	2	0	2	0	0
State Police	0	0	0	0	0	0	0	0	0	0
Other Agencies										
County Detective										
Berks County	62	2	0	0	60	5	1	3	1	0
Lawrence County	1	0	1	0	0	1	0	1	0	0
RHODE ISLAND										
State Agencies										
Department of Environmental Management	1	0	0	0	1	11	0	11	0	1
Rhode Island State Police Headquarters	40	0	21	1	18	53	0	36	17	1
State Police										
Chepachet/Scituate	17	1	2	0	14	17	0	15	2	1
Hope Valley	8	0	2	0	6	19	0	11	8	0
Lincoln	23	0	3	1	19	37	0	26	11	2
Wickford	8	0	1	0	7	20	0	14	6	0
T.F. Green Airport	0	0	0	0	0	29	0	18	11	1
SOUTH CAROLINA										
State Agencies										
Department of Mental Health	3	0	0	0	3	8	0	8	0	0
Department of Natural Resources										
Allendale County	0	0	0	0	0	0	0	0	0	0
Anderson County	0	0	0	0	0	0	0	0	0	0
Barnwell County	0	0	0	0	0	0	0	0	0	0
Beaufort County	0	0	0	0	0	0	0	0	0	0
Berkeley County	0	0	0	0	0	0	0	0	0	0
Calhoun County	0	0	0	0	0	0	0	0	0	0
Charleston County	0	0	0	0	0	0	0	0	0	0
Cherokee County	0	0	0	0	0	0	0	0	0	0
Chester County	0	0	0	0	0	0	0	0	0	0
Darlington County	0	0	0	0	0	0	0	0	0	0
Dillon County	0	0	0	0	0	0	0	0	0	0
Dorchester County	0	0	0	0	0	0	0	0	0	0
Fairfield County	0	0	0	0	0	0	0	0	0	0
Florence County	0	0	0	0	0	0	0	0	0	0
Georgetown County	0	0	0	0	0	0	0	0	0	0
Greenville County	0	0	0	0	0	0	0	0	0	0
Greenwood County	0	0	0	0	0	0	0	0	0	0
Hampton County	0	0	0	0	0	0	0	0	0	0
Horry County	0	0	0	0	0	0	0	0	0	0
Jasper County	0	0	0	0	0	0	0	0	0	0
Kershaw County	0	0	0	0	0	0	0	0	0	0
Lancaster County	0	0	0	0	0	0	0	0	0	0
Laurens County	0	0	0	0	0	0	0	0	0	0
Lee County	0	0	0	0	0	0	0	0	0	0
Lexington County	0	0	0	0	0	0	0	0	0	0
Marion County	0	0	0	0	0	0	0	0	0	0
McCormick County	0	0	0	0	0	0	0	0	0	0
Newberry County	0	0	0	0	0	0	0	0	0	0
Oconee County	0	0	0	0	0	0	0	0	0	0
Orangeburg County	0	0	0	0	0	0	0	0	0	0
Pickens County	0	0	0	0	0	0	0	0	0	0
Richland County	0	0	0	0	0	0	0	0	0	0
Saluda County	0	0	0	0	0	0	0	0	0	0
Spartanburg County	0	0	0	0	0	0	0	0	0	0
Sumter County	0	0	0	0	0	0	0	0	0	0
Union County	0	0	0	0	0	0	0	0	0	0
Williamsburg County	0	0	0	0	0	0	0	0	0	0
York County	0	0	0	0	0	0	0	0	0	0
Highway Patrol										
Abbeville County	0	0	0	0	0	0	0	0	0	0
Aiken County	0	0	0	0	0	3	0	0	3	0
Anderson County	0	0	0	0	0	0	0	0	0	0
Bamberg County	0	0	0	0	0	0	0	0	0	0
Barnwell County	0	0	0	0	0	0	0	0	0	0
Beaufort County	0	0	0	0	0	0	0	0	0	0
Berkeley County	0	0	0	0	0	0	0	0	0	0
Charleston County	0	0	0	0	0	0	0	0	0	0
Cherokee County	0	0	0	0	0	0	0	0	0	0
Chesterfield County	0	0	0	0	0	0	0	0	0	0
Clarendon County	0	0	0	0	0	0	0	0	0	0
Colleton County	0	0	0	0	0	0	0	0	0	0
Darlington County	0	0	0	0	0	0	0	0	0	0
Dillon County	0	0	0	0	0	0	0	0	0	0
Dorchester County	0	0	0	0	0	0	0	0	0	0

Table 11. Offenses Known to Law Enforcement, by Selected State, Tribal, and Other Agencies, 2020—Continued

(Number.)

State/other agency unit/office	Violent crime	Murder and nonnegligent manslaughter	Rape[1]	Robbery	Aggravated assault	Property crime	Burglary	Larceny-theft	Motor vehicle theft	Arson[2]
Edgefield County	0	0	0	0	0	0	0	0	0	0
Florence County	0	0	0	0	0	0	0	0	0	0
Georgetown County	0	0	0	0	0	0	0	0	0	0
Greenville County	0	0	0	0	0	1	0	0	1	0
Greenwood County	0	0	0	0	0	0	0	0	0	0
Hampton County	0	0	0	0	0	0	0	0	0	0
Horry County	0	0	0	0	0	0	0	0	0	0
Jasper County	0	0	0	0	0	0	0	0	0	0
Kershaw County	0	0	0	0	0	0	0	0	0	0
Lancaster County	0	0	0	0	0	0	0	0	0	0
Laurens County	0	0	0	0	0	0	0	0	0	0
Lee County	0	0	0	0	0	0	0	0	0	0
Lexington County	0	0	0	0	0	1	0	0	1	0
Marion County	0	0	0	0	0	0	0	0	0	0
Marlboro County	0	0	0	0	0	0	0	0	0	0
Newberry County	0	0	0	0	0	0	0	0	0	0
Oconee County	0	0	0	0	0	0	0	0	0	0
Orangeburg County	0	0	0	0	0	0	0	0	0	0
Pickens County	0	0	0	0	0	1	0	0	1	0
Richland County	0	0	0	0	0	0	0	0	0	0
Saluda County	0	0	0	0	0	0	0	0	0	0
Spartanburg County	0	0	0	0	0	1	0	0	1	0
Sumter County	0	0	0	0	0	0	0	0	0	0
Williamsburg County	0	0	0	0	0	0	0	0	0	0
York County	0	0	0	0	0	0	0	0	0	0
South Carolina School for the Deaf and Blind	0	0	0	0	0	0	0	0	0	0
State Museum	0	0	0	0	0	0	0	0	0	0
State Ports Authority	0	0	0	0	0	0	0	0	0	0
Other Agencies										
Charleston County Aviation Authority	0	0	0	0	0	19	0	8	11	0
Columbia Metropolitan Airport	0	0	0	0	0	22	0	6	16	0
Greenville Hospital										
Greenville	8	0	2	0	6	57	0	53	4	0
Laurens	1	0	0	0	1	1	0	1	0	0
Oconee	2	0	0	0	2	10	1	9	0	0
Greenville-Spartanburg International Airport	1	0	0	0	1	31	1	10	20	0
Lexington County Medical Center	0	0	0	0	0	40	1	36	3	0
SOUTH DAKOTA										
State Agencies										
Division of Criminal Investigation	0	0	0	0	0	0	0	0	0	0
Highway Patrol	14	0	0	0	14	15	1	10	4	0
Tribal Agencies										
Cheyenne River Tribal	403	1	4	1	397	32	20	4	8	0
Crow Creek Tribal	85	0	6	1	78	71	2	32	37	3
Flandreau Santee Sioux Tribal[4]	5	0	0	0	5	7	3	3	1	0
Lower Brule Tribal	58	0	7	0	51	44	5	15	24	1
Pine Ridge Sioux Tribal	238	0	4	0	234	19	3	8	8	4
TENNESSEE										
State Agencies										
Alcoholic Beverage Commission	0	0	0	0	0	0	0	0	0	0
Department of Agriculture, Agricultural Crime Unit	0	0	0	0	0	0	0	0	0	1
Department of Correction, Internal Affairs	11	1	0	0	10	0	0	0	0	0
Department of Safety	121	2	0	0	119	125	1	24	100	0
State Park Rangers										
Bicentennial Capitol Mall	0	0	0	0	0	0	0	0	0	0
Big Hill Pond	0	0	0	0	0	0	0	0	0	0
Big Ridge	0	0	0	0	0	1	0	1	0	0
Bledsoe Creek	0	0	0	0	0	0	0	0	0	0
Booker T. Washington	0	0	0	0	0	1	0	1	0	0
Burgess Falls Natural Area	0	0	0	0	0	0	0	0	0	0
Cedars of Lebanon	0	0	0	0	0	4	0	4	0	0
Chickasaw	0	0	0	0	0	0	0	0	0	0
Cordell Hull Birthplace	0	0	0	0	0	0	0	0	0	0
Cove Lake	0	0	0	0	0	5	0	5	0	0
Cumberland Mountain	0	0	0	0	0	0	0	0	0	0
Cumberland Trail	0	0	0	0	0	2	0	1	1	0
Cummins Falls	0	0	0	0	0	0	0	0	0	0
David Crockett	0	0	0	0	0	0	0	0	0	0
Davy Crockett Birthplace	0	0	0	0	0	0	0	0	0	0
Dunbar Cave Natural Area	0	0	0	0	0	0	0	0	0	0
Edgar Evins	0	0	0	0	0	5	0	5	0	0
Fall Creek Falls	0	0	0	0	0	8	0	8	0	0
Fort Loudon State Historic Park	0	0	0	0	0	1	0	1	0	0
Fort Pillow State Historic Park	0	0	0	0	0	0	0	0	0	0
Frozen Head Natural Area	0	0	0	0	0	0	0	0	0	0
Harpeth Scenic Rivers	0	0	0	0	0	8	0	8	0	1
Harrison Bay	0	0	0	0	0	6	1	5	0	0
Henry Horton	0	0	0	0	0	2	0	2	0	0

Table 11. Offenses Known to Law Enforcement, by Selected State, Tribal, and Other Agencies, 2020—Continued

(Number.)

State/other agency unit/office	Violent crime	Murder and nonnegligent manslaughter	Rape[1]	Robbery	Aggravated assault	Property crime	Burglary	Larceny-theft	Motor vehicle theft	Arson[2]
Hiwassee/Ocoee State Scenic Rivers	0	0	0	0	0	0	0	0	0	0
Indian Mountain	0	0	0	0	0	0	0	0	0	0
Johnsonville State Historic Park	0	0	0	0	0	0	0	0	0	0
Long Hunter	1	0	0	1	0	18	0	18	0	1
Meeman-Shelby Forest	0	0	0	0	0	1	0	1	0	0
Montgomery Bell	0	0	0	0	0	0	0	0	0	0
Mousetail Landing	0	0	0	0	0	0	0	0	0	0
Natchez Trace	0	0	0	0	0	4	0	4	0	0
Nathan Bedford Forrest	0	0	0	0	0	1	0	1	0	0
Norris Dam	0	0	0	0	0	2	0	2	0	0
Old Stone Fort State Archaeological Park	0	0	0	0	0	0	0	0	0	0
Panther Creek	0	0	0	0	0	0	0	0	0	0
Paris Landing	0	0	0	0	0	1	0	1	0	0
Pickett	0	0	0	0	0	1	0	1	0	0
Pickwick Landing	0	0	0	0	0	3	0	3	0	0
Pinson Mounds State Archaeological Park	0	0	0	0	0	0	0	0	0	0
Radnor Lake Natural Area	0	0	0	0	0	2	0	2	0	0
Red Clay State Historic Park	0	0	0	0	0	0	0	0	0	0
Reelfoot Lake	0	0	0	0	0	3	0	3	0	0
Roan Mountain	0	0	0	0	0	0	0	0	0	0
Rock Island	1	0	1	0	0	6	0	6	0	0
Rocky Fork	0	0	0	0	0	0	0	0	0	0
Seven Islands Birding Park	0	0	0	0	0	0	0	0	0	0
Sgt. Alvin C. York	0	0	0	0	0	0	0	0	0	0
South Cumberland Recreation Area	0	0	0	0	0	5	0	5	0	0
Standing Stone	0	0	0	0	0	1	0	1	0	0
Sycamore Shoals State Historic Park	0	0	0	0	0	0	0	0	0	0
Tim's Ford	0	0	0	0	0	0	0	0	0	0
T.O. Fuller	1	0	0	0	1	0	0	0	0	2
Warrior's Path	0	0	0	0	0	1	0	1	0	0
TennCare Office of Inspector General	0	0	0	0	0	0	0	0	0	0
Tennessee Bureau of Investigation	9	0	2	0	7	3	0	3	0	4
Tennessee Department of Revenue, Special Investigations Unit	0	0	0	0	0	0	0	0	0	0
Wildlife Resources Agency										
Region 1	0	0	0	0	0	0	0	0	0	0
Region 2	1	0	0	0	1	0	0	0	0	0
Region 3	0	0	0	0	0	0	0	0	0	0
Region 4	0	0	0	0	0	0	0	0	0	0
Other Agencies										
7th Judicial District Crime Task Force	1	0	0	0	1	0	0	0	0	0
Chattanooga Housing Authority	0	0	0	0	0	0	0	0	0	0
Chattanooga Metropolitan Airport	0	0	0	0	0	0	0	0	0	0
Dickson City Park Ranger Division	0	0	0	0	0	3	0	3	0	0
Drug Task Force										
1st Judicial District	0	0	0	0	0	0	0	0	0	0
2nd Judicial District	0	0	0	0	0	0	0	0	0	0
3rd Judicial District	0	0	0	0	0	0	0	0	0	0
4th Judicial District	0	0	0	0	0	1	0	1	0	0
5th Judicial District	0	0	0	0	0	0	0	0	0	0
8th Judicial District	0	0	0	0	0	0	0	0	0	0
9th Judicial District	0	0	0	0	0	5	0	5	0	0
10th Judicial District	0	0	0	0	0	0	0	0	0	0
12th Judicial District	0	0	0	0	0	3	0	0	3	0
14th Judicial District	0	0	0	0	0	0	0	0	0	0
15th Judicial District	0	0	0	0	0	0	0	0	0	0
17th Judicial District	0	0	0	0	0	0	0	0	0	0
18th Judicial District	0	0	0	0	0	0	0	0	0	0
19th Judicial District	1	0	0	0	1	0	0	0	0	0
21st Judicial District	0	0	0	0	0	0	0	0	0	0
22nd Judicial District	0	0	0	0	0	0	0	0	0	0
23rd Judicial District	0	0	0	0	0	1	0	0	1	0
24th Judicial District	0	0	0	0	0	1	0	1	0	1
25th Judicial District	0	0	0	0	0	0	0	0	0	0
27th Judicial District	0	0	0	0	0	0	0	0	0	0
31st Judicial District	0	0	0	0	0	0	0	0	0	0
Knoxville Metropolitan Airport	0	0	0	0	0	7	0	4	3	0
Memphis-Shelby County Airport Authority	2	0	0	1	1	253	7	108	138	0
Metropolitan Nashville Park Police	4	0	0	0	4	87	3	83	1	0
Nashville International Airport	0	0	0	0	0	24	0	18	6	0
Tri-Cities Regional Airport	0	0	0	0	0	2	0	0	2	0
West Tennessee Violent Crime Task Force	0	0	0	0	0	0	0	0	0	0
TEXAS										
Other Agencies										
Dallas-Fort Worth International Airport	15	0	0	3	12	356	9	322	25	0
Denton County Water District	12	0	4	2	6	88	16	68	4	0
Hospital District										
Dallas County	8	0	0	1	7	131	4	121	6	0
Tarrant County	2	0	2	0	0	80	1	75	4	0
Houston Metropolitan Transit Authority	6	0	0	3	3	50	0	48	2	1

Table 11. Offenses Known to Law Enforcement, by Selected State, Tribal, and Other Agencies, 2020—Continued

(Number.)

State/other agency unit/office	Violent crime	Murder and nonnegligent manslaughter	Rape[1]	Robbery	Aggravated assault	Property crime	Burglary	Larceny-theft	Motor vehicle theft	Arson[2]
Independent School District										
Aldine	3	0	0	2	1	47	8	37	2	0
Alief	10	0	0	1	9	44	7	35	2	0
Angleton[4]	3	0	0	0	3	4	1	3	0	0
Austin[4,6]	14	0	10	0	4		30		3	6
Barbers Hill	0	0	0	0	0	3	2	1	0	0
Bay City	2	0	0	0	2	9	0	9	0	0
Brazosport[4]	3	0	1	0	2	7	2	5	0	0
Brownsboro	1	0	0	1	0	0	0	0	0	0
Calhoun County	0	0	0	0	0	1	0	1	0	0
Conroe	9	0	6	1	2	50	6	40	4	1
Corpus Christi	52	0	0	5	47	43	12	26	5	0
Duncanville	1	0	0	1	0	17	1	14	2	0
Ector County	29	0	1	0	28	14	5	6	3	0
El Paso	8	0	2	2	4	90	16	74	0	1
Floresville[4]	2	0	0	0	2	8	1	7	0	0
Fort Bend	43	0	0	4	39	89	8	79	2	1
Houston	15	0	2	4	9	217	93	116	8	3
Humble[4]	2	1	0	0	1	43	5	38	0	0
Hutto	0	0	0	0	0	6	2	4	0	0
Judson	2	0	2	0	0	24	3	21	0	0
Katy	11	0	6	2	3	120	1	119	0	0
Killeen[4]	2	0	1	0	1	13	1	12	0	0
Klein	6	0	3	0	3	68	3	64	1	0
Mansfield	2	0	0	0	2	51	1	50	0	0
Northside	8	0	1	3	4	0	0	0	0	0
Pasadena[4]	1	0	0	1	0	34	10	20	4	1
Pflugerville	3	0	0	1	2	33	4	29	0	1
Pleasanton	0	0	0	0	0	0	0	0	0	0
Roma	0	0	0	0	0	2	0	2	0	0
Spring	5	0	2	0	3	27	5	20	2	0
Spring Branch[4]	3	0	1	1	1	32	4	27	1	0
Terrell	2	0	1	0	1	0	0	0	0	0
Trinity	0	0	0	0	0	3	2	1	0	0
Van Vleck	0	0	0	0	0	4	0	4	0	0
Vensus	0	0	0	0	0	5	1	4	0	0
Wharton	0	0	0	0	0	0	0	0	0	0
Port of Brownsville[4]	0	0	0	0	0	5	0	5	0	0
Port of Houston Authority[4]	1	0	0	0	1	8	0	7	1	0
UTAH										
State Agencies										
Parks and Recreation	8	0	1	0	7	40	4	26	10	2
Utah Highway Patrol	59	1	6	6	46	87	1	64	22	0
Wildlife Resources	2	0	0	0	2	11	0	9	2	0
Tribal Agencies										
Goshute Tribal	0	0	0	0	0	0	0	0	0	0
Uintah and Ouray Tribal	11	0	4	0	7	17	4	5	8	1
Other Agencies										
Cache-Rich Drug Task Force	0	0	0	0	0	1	0	1	0	0
Davis Metropolitan Narcotics Strike Force	0	0	0	0	0	0	0	0	0	0
Granite School District	5	0	0	0	5	54	1	50	3	2
Utah County Major Crimes Task Force	0	0	0	0	0	2	0	1	1	0
Utah Transit Authority	25	0	1	11	13	1,399	0	1,358	41	2
Weber Morgan Narcotics Strike Force	5	0	0	1	4	0	0	0	0	0
VERMONT										
State Agencies										
Attorney General	1	0	1	0	0	0	0	0	0	0
Department of Liquor Control, Division of Enforcement and Licensing	0	0	0	0	0	0	0	0	0	0
Fish and Wildlife Department, Law Enforcement Division	0	0	0	0	0	1	0	1	0	0
Secretary of State, Investigations Unit	0	0	0	0	0	1	0	1	0	0
State Police										
Derby	31	0	2	2	27	147	44	96	7	1
Middlesex	39	0	8	1	30	169	27	132	10	1
New Haven	17	0	3	0	14	121	33	83	5	1
Royalton	27	1	1	0	25	74	19	40	15	0
Rutland	39	0	6	2	31	75	26	37	12	3
Shaftsbury	28	0	2	0	26	66	19	44	3	1
St. Albans	49	0	25	1	23	145	31	109	5	1
St. Johnsbury	32	0	4	3	25	214	50	154	10	1
Westminster	16	1	4	0	11	158	18	122	18	1
Williston	18	3	3	0	12	97	23	70	4	5
Vermont State Police	7	4	0	0	3	1	0	0	1	0
Vermont State Police Headquarters, Bureau of Criminal Investigations	0	0	0	0	0	0	0	0	0	0
Other Agencies										
Chittenden Unit for Special Investigations	19	0	19	0	0	0	0	0	0	0
VIRGINIA										
State Agencies										

Table 11. Offenses Known to Law Enforcement, by Selected State, Tribal, and Other Agencies, 2020—Continued

(Number.)

State/other agency unit/office	Violent crime	Murder and nonnegligent manslaughter	Rape[1]	Robbery	Aggravated assault	Property crime	Burglary	Larceny-theft	Motor vehicle theft	Arson[2]
Department of Conservation and Recreation	0	0	0	0	0	80	1	79	0	1
Department of Game and Inland Fisheries, Enforcement Division	1	0	0	0	1	30	0	30	0	0
Department of Motor Vehicles	0	0	0	0	0	56	0	15	41	0
State Police										
Accomack County	7	0	0	0	7	9	0	6	3	3
Albemarle County	0	0	0	0	0	2	0	2	0	0
Alexandria	9	2	0	0	7	3	0	2	1	0
Appomattox County	0	0	0	0	0	1	0	1	0	0
Arlington County	5	0	0	0	5	3	0	1	2	0
Augusta County	4	0	1	0	3	8	0	8	0	2
Bedford County	2	0	0	0	2	6	0	6	0	0
Bland County	3	2	0	1	0	5	0	4	1	0
Botetourt County	10	0	0	1	9	6	0	5	1	0
Buchanan County	2	0	0	0	2	6	0	5	1	2
Buckingham County	1	0	0	0	1	1	0	1	0	0
Campbell County	2	0	0	0	2	1	0	1	0	0
Caroline County	7	0	0	0	7	26	0	3	23	0
Carroll County	1	0	0	0	1	4	1	1	2	0
Charlotte County	1	0	1	0	0	0	0	0	0	0
Charlottesville	0	0	0	0	0	0	0	0	0	0
Chesapeake	10	0	0	0	10	14	0	6	8	0
Chesterfield County	5	0	0	0	5	5	0	5	0	0
Colonial Heights	1	0	0	0	1	1	0	0	1	0
Covington	0	0	0	0	0	3	0	3	0	0
Culpeper County	2	0	0	0	2	0	0	0	0	0
Danville	0	0	0	0	0	0	0	0	0	0
Dickenson County	3	0	0	0	3	2	0	1	1	0
Fairfax County	22	0	1	0	21	40	0	17	23	0
Fauquier County	1	0	0	0	1	0	0	0	0	0
Franklin County	6	0	0	0	6	5	0	2	3	0
Frederick County	3	0	0	0	3	2	1	1	0	0
Fredericksburg	2	0	0	0	2	0	0	0	0	0
Giles County	0	0	0	0	0	6	0	5	1	0
Gloucester County	4	0	1	0	3	0	0	0	0	0
Greensville County	6	0	0	0	6	1	0	0	1	0
Halifax County	4	0	0	0	4	5	1	2	2	1
Hampton	13	0	0	0	13	7	0	1	6	0
Hanover County	5	0	0	0	5	4	0	1	3	0
Harrisonburg	1	0	0	0	1	2	0	2	0	0
Henrico County	14	0	0	0	14	5	0	4	1	0
Henry County	13	2	0	1	10	8	0	5	3	0
James City County	3	0	3	0	0	1	0	1	0	0
Lancaster County	5	2	0	0	3	0	0	0	0	0
Lee County	4	0	0	0	4	18	0	5	13	0
Loudoun County	3	0	0	0	3	3	0	0	3	0
Lunenburg County	2	1	0	1	0	1	0	0	1	0
Lynchburg	0	0	0	0	0	0	0	0	0	0
Mecklenburg County	2	0	0	0	2	4	1	2	1	0
Montgomery County	3	0	0	0	3	1	0	1	0	0
Nelson County	2	0	0	0	2	2	2	0	0	0
New Kent County	9	0	0	0	9	2	0	2	0	0
Newport News	7	0	0	0	7	5	0	2	3	0
Norfolk	14	1	0	0	13	3	0	1	2	0
Northampton County	7	0	0	0	7	3	0	2	1	0
Nottoway County	0	0	0	0	0	1	0	1	0	1
Orange County	4	0	1	0	3	0	0	0	0	2
Page County	1	0	1	0	0	1	0	1	0	1
Patrick County	2	0	0	0	2	0	0	0	0	0
Pittsylvania County	9	1	0	0	8	23	0	2	21	0
Portsmouth	9	0	0	0	9	4	0	1	3	0
Prince Edward County	2	0	1	1	0	1	1	0	0	3
Prince William County	9	0	0	0	9	15	0	8	7	1
Pulaski County	7	0	2	0	5	9	1	5	3	0
Richmond	12	0	1	0	11	3	0	2	1	0
Roanoke	3	0	0	0	3	4	0	4	0	1
Roanoke County	5	0	2	1	2	8	0	6	2	0
Rockbridge County	4	0	0	0	4	3	0	3	0	0
Rockingham County	5	0	0	0	5	28	0	12	16	0
Russell County	9	0	1	0	8	4	0	2	2	1
Scott County	2	0	0	0	2	5	0	1	4	2
Shenandoah County	7	0	0	0	7	5	0	3	2	0
Smyth County	6	0	2	0	4	5	0	2	3	0
Southampton County	0	0	0	0	0	4	1	3	0	0
Spotsylvania County	4	0	0	0	4	8	0	5	3	0
Stafford County	4	0	1	0	3	5	0	2	3	1
Staunton	2	0	1	0	1	2	0	2	0	0
Suffolk	0	0	0	0	0	3	0	1	2	0
Tazewell County	9	2	1	0	6	12	1	11	0	1
Virginia Beach	8	0	0	0	8	13	0	4	9	0
Warren County	5	0	0	0	5	2	0	2	0	0
Washington County	3	0	1	0	2	8	0	7	1	4

Table 11. Offenses Known to Law Enforcement, by Selected State, Tribal, and Other Agencies, 2020—Continued

(Number.)

State/other agency unit/office	Violent crime	Murder and nonnegligent manslaughter	Rape[1]	Robbery	Aggravated assault	Property crime	Burglary	Larceny-theft	Motor vehicle theft	Arson[2]
Waynesboro	2	0	1	0	1	0	0	0	0	0
Winchester	1	0	0	0	1	0	0	0	0	0
Wise County	1	0	0	0	1	6	1	5	0	1
Wythe County	16	0	1	2	13	12	0	9	3	1
York County	7	0	0	0	7	0	0	0	0	0
Virginia State Capitol	3	0	0	0	3	10	1	9	0	0
Other Agencies										
Norfolk Airport Authority	0	0	0	0	0	36	0	30	6	0
Port Authority, Norfolk	0	0	0	0	0	3	0	3	0	0
Reagan National Airport	7	0	0	0	7	194	0	167	27	0
Richmond International Airport	1	0	0	0	1	33	0	13	20	0
WASHINGTON										
State Agencies										
State Insurance Commissioner, Special Investigations Unit	0	0	0	0	0	1	0	1	0	0
Washington State Patrol	0	0	0	0	0	0	0	0	0	0
Tribal Agencies										
Chehalis Tribal	34	0	0	1	33	69	8	53	8	1
Colville Tribal	29	1	2	2	24	194	48	120	26	14
Elwha Klallam Tribal	0	0	0	0	0	0	0	0	0	0
Jamestown S'Klallam Tribal	0	0	0	0	0	12	0	11	1	0
Kalispel Tribal	8	0	2	2	4	224	20	187	17	1
Makah Tribal	5	0	0	0	5	5	2	2	1	0
Muckleshoot Tribal	8	0	0	0	8	30	9	19	2	0
Nooksack Tribal	2	0	0	0	2	24	7	17	0	0
Puyallup Tribal	27	0	4	18	5	637	130	330	177	1
Quinault Indian Nation	6	0	0	0	6	6	1	3	2	0
Shoalwater Bay Tribal	0	0	0	0	0	0	0	0	0	
Skokomish Tribal	6	0	0	0	6	26	6	14	6	0
Snoqualmie Tribal	0	0	0	0	0	0	0	0	0	0
Spokane Agency	4	0	0	1	3	92	12	62	18	2
Squaxin Island Tribal	14	0	0	0	14	60	1	51	8	0
Stillaguamish Tribal	5	0	0	2	3	56	3	47	6	0
Suquamish Tribal	10	0	1	1	8	65	8	54	3	
Swinomish Tribal	2	0	0	0	2	32	4	23	5	0
Tulalip Tribal	20	0	0	7	13	596	16	524	56	0
Upper Skagit Tribal	7	0	1	0	6	28	0	26	2	0
Yakama Nation	50	3	25	5	17	606	163	284	159	26
Other Agencies	0	0	0	0	0	0	0	0	0	0
Port of Seattle	11	0	0	6	5	631	52	523	56	3
WEST VIRGINIA										
State Agencies										
Department of Natural Resources										
Hampshire County	0	0	0	0	0	0	0	0	0	0
Pendleton County	0	0	0	0	0	0	0	0	0	0
State Police, Bureau of Criminal Investigations										
Beckley	0	0	0	0	0	0	0	0	0	0
Charleston	0	0	0	0	0	0	0	0	0	0
Martinsburg	0	0	0	0	0	0	0	0	0	0
State Police	0	0	0	0	0	0	0	0	0	0
Beckley	14	0	4	0	10	217	35	160	22	0
Berkeley Springs	7	0	6	0	1	58	6	35	17	0
Bridgeport	17	1	8	1	7	134	19	101	14	1
Buckhannon	6	0	5	0	1	76	27	40	9	1
Clay	9	2	1	0	6	123	73	35	15	5
Elkins	17	0	6	0	11	80	31	42	7	1
Fairmont	4	0	2	0	2	59	16	36	7	1
Franklin	5	3	0	0	2	37	21	15	1	1
Gauley Bridge	3	0	0	0	3	13	1	10	2	0
Glenville	9	0	3	0	6	45	23	15	7	1
Grafton	5	0	2	0	3	22	6	13	3	0
Grantsville	6	0	2	0	4	26	4	21	1	0
Hamlin	25	0	15	2	8	187	52	86	49	5
Harrisville	2	0	1	0	1	28	5	18	5	0
Hinton	6	2	1	0	3	37	9	25	3	1
Huntington	49	0	33	1	15	196	26	143	27	1
Internet Crimes Against Children Unit	2	0	2	0	0	0	0	0	0	0
Jesse	11	0	4	0	7	14	6	8	0	1
Keyser	12	4	5	0	3	105	9	89	7	0
Kingwood	21	1	3	1	16	95	21	50	24	4
Lewisburg	8	0	3	0	5	121	26	83	12	0
Logan	19	0	7	2	10	61	14	32	15	2
Madison	13	1	6	1	5	81	8	52	21	2
Marlinton	9	1	3	0	5	36	14	17	5	1
Martinsburg	64	0	46	3	15	302	32	227	43	1
Moorefield	21	0	10	0	11	80	22	41	17	0
Morgantown	14	0	7	1	6	166	31	119	16	0
Moundsville	17	0	5	0	12	14	5	6	3	0
Oak Hill	1	0	1	0	0	63	16	45	2	2
Paden City	18	0	13	2	3	29	14	13	2	0

Table 11. Offenses Known to Law Enforcement, by Selected State, Tribal, and Other Agencies, 2020—Continued

(Number.)

State/other agency unit/office	Violent crime	Murder and nonnegligent manslaughter	Rape[1]	Robbery	Aggravated assault	Property crime	Burglary	Larceny-theft	Motor vehicle theft	Arson[2]
Parkersburg	20	0	15	0	5	35	6	24	5	0
Parsons	4	0	0	0	4	16	1	14	1	0
Philippi	15	0	4	1	10	42	11	25	6	0
Point Pleasant	11	0	8	0	3	45	14	26	5	0
Princeton	25	1	1	0	23	228	32	156	40	0
Quincy	3	0	2	0	1	124	17	93	14	3
Rainelle	6	0	2	0	4	52	23	24	5	0
Ripley	2	0	1	0	1	43	4	31	8	0
Romney	7	0	6	0	1	48	4	43	1	0
South Charleston	36	0	27	0	9	413	45	328	40	0
Spencer	19	1	2	1	15	34	11	20	3	0
St. Marys	4	0	4	0	0	12	5	6	1	0
Summersville	6	1	1	1	3	51	14	30	7	1
Sutton	12	0	5	2	5	83	18	52	13	1
Union	9	3	3	0	3	39	18	18	3	1
Upperglade	6	0	0	0	6	52	21	18	13	2
Wayne	24	2	8	1	13	191	53	94	44	5
Welch	16	0	4	3	9	32	15	7	10	0
Weston	9	0	5	1	3	101	31	62	8	0
West Union	6	0	4	0	2	44	8	19	17	0
Wheeling	2	0	1	1	0	7	1	6	0	0
Whitesville	3	0	0	1	2	30	9	16	5	0
Williamson	9	2	4	2	1	78	10	36	32	3
Winfield	6	0	5	0	1	118	21	80	17	0
State Police, Parkway Authority, Raleigh County	0	0	0	0	0	5	0	3	2	0
Marshall County Drug Task Force	0	0	0	0	0	0	0	0	0	0
Other Agencies										
Metropolitan Drug Enforcement Network Team	0	0	0	0	0	0	0	0	0	0
Mon Metro Drug Task Force	0	0	0	0	0	0	0	0	0	0
WISCONSIN										
State Agencies										
Capitol Police	6	0	0	0	6	8	0	8	0	0
Department of Natural Resources	0	0	0	0	0	0	0	0	0	0
State Fair Park Police	0	0	0	0	0	1	0	1	0	0
Wisconsin State Patrol	8	0	0	1	7	0	0	0	0	0
Tribal Agencies										
Lac Courte Oreilles Tribal	28	0	2	2	24	51	6	34	11	1
Lac du Flambeau Tribal	43	0	5	0	38	172	14	143	15	0
Menominee Tribal	92	0	0	0	92	26	1	13	12	0
Oneida Tribal	24	0	10	1	13	132	6	116	10	1
St. Croix Tribal	0	0	0	0	0	24	2	15	7	0
WYOMING										
Tribal Agencies										
Wind River Agency	95	0	21	0	74	173	18	90	65	0
PUERTO RICO AND OTHER OUTLYING AREAS										
Puerto Rico	5,196	529	148	1,177	3,342	13,241	2,952	8,311	1,978	

1 The figures shown in this column for the offense of rape were reported using the revised Uniform Crime Reporting (UCR) definition of rape. See notes for further explanation.   2 The FBI does not publish arson data unless it receives data from either the agency or the state for all 12 months of the calendar year.   3 Limited data for 2020 were available for Alabama, Maryland, and Pennsylvania.   4 Because of changes in the state/local agency's reporting practices, figures are not comparable to previous years' data.   5 The FBI determined that the agency's data were overreported. Consequently, those data are not included in this table.   6 The FBI determined that the agency's data were underreported. Consequently, those data are not included in this table.

Table 12. Crime Trends, by Population Group, 2019–2020

(Number, percent change.)

Population group	Violent crime	Murder and nonnegligent manslaughter	Rape[1]	Robbery	Aggravated assault	Property crime	Burglary	Larceny-theft	Motor vehicle theft	Arson	Number of agencies	Estimated population, 2020
Total, All Agencies												
2019	1,099,647	14,440	127,821	238,036	719,350	5,977,531	968,856	4,327,744	650,351	30,580	13,827	294,203,623
2020	1,147,914	18,623	111,947	215,106	802,238	5,563,304	893,344	3,906,065	726,283	37,612		
Percent change	4.4	29.0	-12.4	-9.6	11.5	-6.9	-7.8	-9.7	11.7	23.0		
Total, Cities												
2019	882,969	11,195	95,780	209,835	566,159	4,799,777	727,290	3,528,095	520,810	23,582	9,985	200,688,039
2020	922,257	14,794	82,808	189,624	635,031	4,457,179	679,313	3,162,763	585,754	29,349		
Percent change	4.4	32.1	-13.5	-9.6	12.2	-7.1	-6.6	-10.4	12.5	24.5		
Group I (250,000 and over)												
2019	431,053	5,837	36,083	119,853	269,280	1,794,877	280,025	1,263,441	242,884	8,527	84	60,095,451
2020	454,913	7,833	30,592	109,133	307,355	1,672,010	268,045	1,122,909	270,136	10,920		
Percent change	5.5	34.2	-15.2	-8.9	14.1	-6.8	-4.3	-11.1	11.2	28.1		
1,000,000 and over (Group I subset)												
2019	185,593	1,987	14,984	55,642	112,980	646,333	100,111	453,510	90,773	1,939	11	27,146,381
2020	192,910	2,779	12,140	51,754	126,237	611,719	96,553	409,536	102,979	2,651		
Percent change	3.9	39.9	-19.0	-7.0	11.7	-5.4	-3.6	-9.7	13.4	36.7		
500,000 to 999,999 (Group I subset)												
2019	134,189	2,136	10,004	36,403	85,646	601,095	94,854	424,586	78,525	3,130	23	16,076,918
2020	143,079	2,764	8,408	31,758	100,149	552,774	91,945	373,324	83,597	3,908		
Percent change	6.6	29.4	-16.0	-12.8	16.9	-8.0	-3.1	-12.1	6.5	24.9		
250,000 to 499,999 (Group I subset)												
2019	111,271	1,714	11,095	27,808	70,654	547,449	85,060	385,345	73,586	3,458	50	16,872,152
2020	118,924	2,290	10,044	25,621	80,969	507,517	79,547	340,049	83,560	4,361		
Percent change	6.9	33.6	-9.5	-7.9	14.6	-7.3	-6.5	-11.8	13.6	26.1		
Group II (100,000 to 249,999)												
2019	140,351	1,857	15,917	33,730	88,847	844,224	125,334	616,880	97,847	4,163	223	32,301,225
2020	148,026	2,502	14,018	30,139	101,367	793,009	117,723	559,645	110,199	5,442		
Percent change	5.5	34.7	-11.9	-10.6	14.1	-6.1	-6.1	-9.3	12.6	30.7		
Group III (50,000 to 99,999)												
2019	107,242	1,226	12,891	24,427	68,698	705,455	102,260	530,921	68,854	3,420	475	33,149,178
2020	111,601	1,551	11,562	21,473	77,015	662,747	93,319	485,558	79,762	4,108		
Percent change	4.1	26.5	-10.3	-12.1	12.1	-6.1	-8.7	-8.5	15.8	20.1		
Group IV (25,000 to 49,999)												
2019	76,663	906	10,933	14,756	50,068	549,474	80,610	420,821	45,423	2,620	831	28,909,214
2020	80,251	1,150	9,841	13,670	55,590	510,310	73,590	381,353	52,087	3,280		
Percent change	4.7	26.9	-10.0	-7.4	11.0	-7.1	-8.7	-9.4	14.7	25.2		
Group V (10,000 to 24,999)												
2019	66,763	782	10,273	10,292	45,416	491,918	75,598	376,751	37,260	2,309	1,645	26,337,532
2020	68,750	1,039	9,001	9,539	49,171	458,635	68,695	344,088	43,119	2,733		
Percent change	3.0	32.9	-12.4	-7.3	8.3	-6.8	-9.1	-8.7	15.7	18.4		
Group VI (under 10,000)												
2019	60,897	587	9,683	6,777	43,850	413,829	63,463	319,281	28,542	2,543	6,727	19,895,439
2020	58,716	719	7,794	5,670	44,533	360,468	57,941	269,210	30,451	2,866		
Percent change	-3.6	22.5	-19.5	-16.3	1.6	-12.9	-8.7	-15.7	6.7	12.7		
Metropolitan Counties												
2019	170,794	2,391	23,214	26,110	119,079	955,842	177,543	668,556	104,641	5,102	1,697	71,020,687
2020	177,270	2,807	21,133	23,373	129,957	894,680	156,865	617,695	114,150	5,970		
Percent change	3.8	17.4	-9.0	-10.5	9.1	-6.4	-11.6	-7.6	9.1	17.0		
Nonmetropolitan Counties[2]												
2019	45,884	854	8,827	2,091	34,112	221,912	64,023	131,093	24,900	1,896	2,145	22,494,897
2020	48,387	1,022	8,006	2,109	37,250	211,445	57,166	125,607	26,379	2,293		
Percent change	5.5	19.7	-9.3	0.9	9.2	-4.7	-10.7	-4.2	5.9	20.9		
Suburban Areas[3]												
2019	294,113	3,691	41,756	49,027	199,639	1,908,002	309,769	1,406,493	182,277	9,463	7,430	125,892,017
2020	300,262	4,429	37,220	43,886	214,727	1,765,243	277,444	1,273,709	202,906	11,184		
Percent change	2.1	20.0	-10.9	-10.5	7.6	-7.5	-10.4	-9.4	11.3	18.2		

1 The figures shown in this column for the offense of rape were reported using only the revised Uniform Crime Reporting definition of rape. See chapter notes for more detail.   2 Includes state police agencies that report aggregately for the entire state.   3 Suburban areas include law enforcement agencies in cities with less than 50,000 inhabitants and county law enforcement agencies that are within a Metropolitan Statistical Area. Suburban areas exclude all metropolitan agencies associated with a principal city. The agencies associated with suburban areas also appear in other groups within this table.

Table 13. Crime Trends, by Suburban and Nonsuburban Cities,[1] by Population Group, 2019–2020

(Number, percent change.)

Population group	Violent crime	Murder and nonnegligent manslaughter	Rape[2]	Robbery	Aggravated assault	Property crime	Burglary	Larceny-theft	Motor vehicle theft	Arson	Number of agencies	Estimated population, 20120
Suburban Cities												
2019	123,319	1,300	18,542	22,917	80,560	952,160	132,226	737,937	77,636	4,361		
2020	122,992	1,622	16,087	20,513	84,770	870,563	120,579	656,014	88,756	5,214	5,733	54,871,330
Percent change	-0.3	24.8	-13.2	-10.5	5.2	-8.6	-8.8	-11.1	14.3	19.6		
Group IV (25,000 to 49,999)												
2019	47,813	526	7,085	10,232	29,970	376,273	51,409	290,403	32,919	1,542		
2020	49,111	644	6,363	9,507	32,597	353,078	46,976	265,325	38,737	2,040	658	22,704,238
Percent change	2.7	22.4	-10.2	-7.1	8.8	-6.2	-8.6	-8.6	17.7	32.3		
Group V (10,000 to 24,999)												
2019	42,603	470	6,306	7,579	28,248	322,339	46,279	247,732	26,927	1,401		
2020	43,654	617	5,658	6,944	30,435	301,971	41,951	227,016	31,390	1,614	1,243	20,074,390
Percent change	2.5	31.3	-10.3	-8.4	7.7	-6.3	-9.4	-8.4	16.6	15.2		
Group VI (under 10,000)												
2019	32,903	304	5,151	5,106	22,342	253,548	34,538	199,802	17,790	1,418		
2020	30,227	361	4,066	4,062	21,738	215,514	31,652	163,673	18,629	1,560	3,832	12,092,702
Percent change	-8.1	18.8	-21.1	-20.4	-2.7	-15.0	-8.4	-18.1	4.7	10.0		
Nonsuburban Cities												
2019	56,800	645	9,339	4,813	42,003	359,759	63,291	270,479	23,759	2,230		
2020	58,454	839	7,902	4,648	45,065	330,379	58,617	242,957	26,140	2,665	3,315	15,290,958
Percent change	2.9	30.1	-15.4	-3.4	7.3	-8.2	-7.4	-10.2	10.0	19.5		
Group IV (25,000 to 49,999)												
2019	7,244	86	1,237	858	5,063	49,422	8,351	37,051	3,759	261		
2020	7,582	95	1,158	830	5,499	46,841	8,450	34,169	3,914	308	62	2,006,781
Percent change	4.7	10.5	-6.4	-3.3	8.6	-5.2	1.2	-7.8	4.1	18.0		
Group V (10,000 to 24,999)												
2019	21,600	276	3,571	2,286	15,467	150,094	26,016	113,985	9,248	845		
2020	22,392	386	3,017	2,212	16,777	138,613	23,880	103,277	10,404	1,052	360	5,489,178
Percent change	3.7	39.9	-15.5	-3.2	8.5	-7.6	-8.2	-9.4	12.5	24.5		
Group VI (under 10,000)												
2019	27,956	283	4,531	1,669	21,473	160,243	28,924	119,443	10,752	1,124		
2020	28,480	358	3,727	1,606	22,789	144,925	26,287	105,511	11,822	1,305	2,893	7,794,999
Percent change	1.9	26.5	-17.7	-3.8	6.1	-9.6	-9.1	-11.7	10.0	16.1		

1 Suburban cities include law enforcement agencies in cities with less than 50,000 inhabitants that are within a Metropolitan Statistical Area. Suburban cities exclude all metropolitan agencies associated with a principal city. Nonsuburban cities include law enforcement agencies in cities with less than 50,000 inhabitants that are not associated with a Metropolitan Statistical Area.   2 The figures shown in this column for the offense of rape were reported using only the revised Uniform Crime Reporting definition of rape. See chapter notes for more detail.

Table 14. Crime Trends, by Metropolitan and Nonmetropolitan Counties,[1] by Population Group, 2019–2020

(Number, percent change.)

Population group and range	Violent crime	Murder and nonnegligent manslaughter	Rape[2]	Robbery	Aggravated assault	Property crime	Burglary	Larceny-theft	Motor vehicle theft	Arson	Number of agencies	Estimated population, 2020
Metropolitan Counties												
100,000 and over												
2019	114,972	1,596	13,900	22,020	77,456	653,838	107,266	475,199	68,214	3,159		
2020	119,994	1,889	12,217	19,687	86,201	605,084	93,419	433,699	74,288	3,678	167	45,379,252
Percent change	4.4	18.4	-12.1	-10.6	11.3	-7.5	-12.9	-8.7	8.9	16.4		
25,000 to 99,999												
2019	37,615	591	6,039	3,021	27,964	219,896	52,630	143,266	22,789	1,211		
2020	39,541	641	5,748	2,763	30,389	212,676	47,285	138,751	25,234	1,406	401	20,874,056
Percent change	5.1	8.5	-4.8	-8.5	8.7	-3.3	-10.2	-3.2	10.7	16.1		
Under 25,000												
2019	18,207	204	3,275	1,069	13,659	82,108	17,647	50,091	13,638	732		
2020	17,735	277	3,168	923	13,367	76,920	16,161	45,245	14,628	886	1,129	4,767,379
Percent change	-2.6	35.8	-3.3	-13.7	-2.1	-6.3	-8.4	-9.7	7.3	21.0		
Nonmetropolitan Counties												
25,000 and over												
2019	19,531	323	3,405	1,197	14,606	101,496	28,715	61,381	10,645	755		
2020	20,335	409	3,050	1,158	15,718	96,100	25,067	58,884	11,217	932	239	9,876,646
Percent change	4.1	26.6	-10.4	-3.3	7.6	-5.3	-12.7	-4.1	5.4	23.4		
10,000 to 24,999												
2019	14,396	274	2,491	623	11,008	74,060	22,500	43,102	7,802	656		
2020	15,439	326	2,251	593	12,269	70,096	19,834	40,946	8,597	719	534	8,573,146
Percent change	7.2	19.0	-9.6	-4.8	11.5	-5.4	-11.8	-5.0	10.2	9.6		
Under 10,000												
2019	11,957	257	2,931	271	8,498	46,356	12,808	26,610	6,453	485		
2020	12,613	287	2,705	358	9,263	45,249	12,265	25,777	6,565	642	1,372	4,045,105
Percent change	5.5	11.7	-7.7	32.1	9.0	-2.4	-4.2	-3.1	1.7	32.4		

1 Metropolitan counties include sheriffs and county law enforcement agencies associated with a Metropolitan Statistical Area. Nonmetropolitan counties include sheriffs and county law enforcement agencies that are not associated with a Metropolitan Statistical Area.   2 The figures shown in this column for the offense of rape were reported using only the revised Uniform Crime Reporting definition of rape. See notes for further detail.

Table 15. Crime Trends, Additional Information About Selected Offenses, by Population Group, 2019–2020

(Number, percent change.)

Population group	Rape[1]		Robbery				Aggravated assault			
	Rape	Assault to rape-attempts	Firearm	Knife or cutting instrument	Other weapon	Strong-arm	Firearm	Knife or cutting instrument	Other weapon	Hands, fists, feet, etc.
Total, All Agencies										
2019	117,345	4,936	83,657	19,207	23,515	99,753	190,338	120,133	207,621	171,965
2020	103,199	4,133	77,179	18,590	22,414	85,340	266,983	126,421	220,157	157,466
Percent change	-12.1	-16.3	-7.7	-3.2	-4.7	-14.4	40.3	5.2	6.0	-8.4
Total, Cities										
2019	87,085	3,771	71,542	17,081	20,626	88,897	152,908	98,256	160,304	127,259
2020	75,736	3,065	66,437	16,577	19,589	75,659	215,325	103,323	170,280	116,940
Percent change	-13.0	-18.7	-7.1	-3.0	-5.0	-14.9	40.8	5.2	6.2	-8.1
Group I (250,000 and over)										
2019	32,628	1,670	42,251	9,771	11,168	48,673	85,295	47,860	75,140	45,702
2020	27,947	1,299	39,092	9,634	10,472	42,066	119,576	49,977	79,824	41,381
Percent change	-14.3	-22.2	-7.5	-1.4	-6.2	-13.6	40.2	4.4	6.2	-9.5
1,000,000 and over (Group I subset)										
2019	12,466	733	15,378	4,802	5,188	22,284	24,692	21,287	28,480	23,238
2020	10,313	481	14,649	5,005	5,035	19,196	34,892	22,639	30,390	21,719
Percent change	-17.3	-34.4	-4.7	4.2	-2.9	-13.9	41.3	6.4	6.7	-6.5
500,000 to 999,999 (Group I subset)										
2019	9,535	469	15,390	2,836	3,712	14,465	33,825	14,534	26,746	10,541
2020	8,001	407	14,025	2,622	3,176	11,935	47,726	15,066	27,669	9,688
Percent change	-16.1	-13.2	-8.9	-7.5	-14.4	-17.5	41.1	3.7	3.5	-8.1
250,000 to 499,999 (Group I subset)										
2019	10,627	468	11,483	2,133	2,268	11,924	26,778	12,039	19,914	11,923
2020	9,633	411	10,418	2,007	2,261	10,935	36,958	12,272	21,765	9,974
Percent change	-9.4	-12.2	-9.3	-5.9	-0.3	-8.3	38.0	1.9	9.3	-16.3
Group II (100,000 to 249,999)										
2019	14,992	584	11,794	2,914	3,437	14,864	24,908	16,390	25,778	19,478
2020	13,145	533	10,944	2,673	3,447	12,472	35,472	17,497	27,803	17,879
Percent change	-12.3	-8.7	-7.2	-8.3	0.3	-16.1	42.4	6.8	7.9	-8.2
Group III (50,000 to 99,999)										
2019	11,902	483	7,475	2,057	2,629	11,462	16,211	12,021	21,048	17,320
2020	10,788	346	6,766	1,911	2,407	9,572	22,930	12,751	21,566	17,530
Percent change	-9.4	-28.4	-9.5	-7.1	-8.4	-16.5	41.4	6.1	2.5	1.2
Group IV (25,000 to 49,999)										
2019	9,838	300	4,695	1,078	1,548	6,522	11,127	8,540	14,250	13,336
2020	8,817	300	4,653	1,168	1,513	5,540	16,016	9,181	15,297	12,078
Percent change	-10.4	0.0	-0.9	8.3	-2.3	-15.1	43.9	7.5	7.3	-9.4
Group V (10,000 to 24,999)										
2019	9,074	289	3,341	803	1,139	4,097	8,675	7,189	12,776	13,565
2020	8,013	248	3,169	790	1,075	3,566	12,557	7,651	13,749	12,205
Percent change	-11.7	-14.2	-5.1	-1.6	-5.6	-13.0	44.7	6.4	7.6	-10.0
Group VI (under 10,000)										
2019	8,651	445	1,986	458	705	3,279	6,692	6,256	11,312	17,858
2020	7,026	339	1,813	401	675	2,443	8,774	6,266	12,041	15,867
Percent change	-18.8	-23.8	-8.7	-12.4	-4.3	-25.5	31.1	0.2	6.4	-11.1
Metropolitan Counties										
2019	21,984	846	11,183	1,970	2,602	10,165	29,991	17,718	37,203	32,973
2020	19,953	805	9,857	1,856	2,509	9,003	41,567	18,732	38,765	29,754
Percent change	-9.2	-4.8	-11.9	-5.8	-3.6	-11.4	38.6	5.7	4.2	-9.8
Nonmetropolitan Counties										
2019	8,276	319	932	156	287	691	7,439	4,159	10,114	11,733
2020	7,510	263	885	157	316	678	10,091	4,366	11,112	10,772
Percent change	-9.3	-17.6	-5.0	0.6	10.1	-1.9	35.6	5.0	9.9	-8.2
Suburban Areas[2]										
2019	38,302	1,450	18,128	3,567	5,061	20,315	44,578	30,269	60,235	58,209
2020	34,142	1,322	16,541	3,470	4,805	17,240	62,294	31,905	62,791	51,657
Percent change	-10.9	-8.8	-8.8	-2.7	-5.1	-15.1	39.7	5.4	4.2	-11.3

Table 15. Crime Trends, Additional Information About Selected Offenses, by Population Group, 2019–2020 —Continued

(Number, percent change.)

Population group	Burglary			Motor vehicle theft			Arson			Number of agencies	Estimated population, 2020
	Forcible entry	Unlawful entry	Attempted forcible entry	Autos	Trucks and buses	Other vehicles	Structure	Mobile	Other		
Total, All Agencies											
2019	523,839	354,613	60,161	472,576	102,281	58,038	12,586	6,832	10,018		
2020	483,712	323,985	58,398	522,620	118,947	64,999	13,902	8,756	13,440	13,159	282,835,011
Percent change	-7.7	-8.6	-2.9	10.6	16.3	12.0	10.5	28.2	34.2		
Total, Cities											
2019	391,133	262,104	47,729	382,527	82,196	39,826	9,727	4,991	7,801		
2020	368,504	241,299	45,866	425,349	95,985	45,951	10,845	6,519	10,583	9,405	190,858,629
Percent change	-5.8	-7.9	-3.9	11.2	16.8	15.4	11.5	30.6	35.7		
Group I (250,000 and over)											
2019	163,230	88,237	18,949	171,359	47,320	15,113	3,374	2,127	2,606		
2020	157,068	83,221	19,113	186,940	55,128	18,015	3,796	2,985	3,503	83	57,401,853
Percent change	-3.8	-5.7	0.9	9.1	16.5	19.2	12.5	40.3	34.4		
1,000,000 and over (Group I subset)											
2019	57,824	26,256	6,422	49,105	26,901	5,675	610	431	478		
2020	56,840	24,614	6,456	54,021	31,425	7,480	768	593	654	10	24,452,783
Percent change	-1.7	-6.3	0.5	10.0	16.8	31.8	25.9	37.6	36.8		
500,000 to 999,999 (Group I subset)											
2019	55,881	32,324	6,649	62,613	10,608	5,304	1,262	820	1,048		
2020	52,875	31,958	7,112	66,024	11,855	5,718	1,373	1,175	1,360	23	16,076,918
Percent change	-5.4	-1.1	7.0	5.4	11.8	7.8	8.8	43.3	29.8		
250,000 to 499,999 (Group I subset)											
2019	49,525	29,657	5,878	59,641	9,811	4,134	1,502	876	1,080		
2020	47,353	26,649	5,545	66,895	11,848	4,817	1,655	1,217	1,489	50	16,872,152
Percent change	-4.4	-10.1	-5.7	12.2	20.8	16.5	10.2	38.9	37.9		
Group II (100,000 to 249,999)											
2019	67,307	46,368	9,153	75,215	14,092	7,465	1,667	946	1,427		
2020	64,463	42,600	8,377	83,800	16,182	9,070	1,862	1,176	2,204	217	31,472,092
Percent change	-4.2	-8.1	-8.5	11.4	14.8	21.5	11.7	24.3	54.4		
Group III (50,000 to 99,999)											
2019	53,589	38,934	6,667	52,233	9,341	6,079	1,320	688	1,287		
2020	48,804	35,790	6,031	59,881	11,449	7,010	1,502	835	1,666	454	31,774,613
Percent change	-8.9	-8.1	-9.5	14.6	22.6	15.3	13.8	21.4	29.4		
Group IV (25,000 to 49,999)											
2019	39,437	31,685	5,170	34,583	4,769	4,286	1,114	443	926		
2020	36,325	28,400	5,142	39,552	5,451	4,742	1,307	555	1,199	773	26,961,554
Percent change	-7.9	-10.4	-0.5	14.4	14.3	10.6	17.3	25.3	29.5		
Group V (10,000 to 24,999)											
2019	37,177	30,206	4,141	27,707	3,959	3,476	969	359	835		
2020	33,837	27,547	3,709	32,414	4,617	3,683	1,094	456	1,035	1,533	24,492,869
Percent change	-9.0	-8.8	-10.4	17.0	16.6	6.0	12.9	27.0	24.0		
Group VI (under 10,000)											
2019	30,393	26,674	3,649	21,430	2,715	3,407	1,283	428	720		
2020	28,007	23,741	3,494	22,762	3,158	3,431	1,284	512	976	6,345	18,755,648
Percent change	-7.9	-11.0	-4.2	6.2	16.3	0.7	0.1	19.6	35.6		
Metropolitan Counties											
2019	97,064	67,726	10,107	73,491	16,071	14,184	1,980	1,425	1,643		
2020	83,929	59,948	10,520	79,594	18,528	15,084	2,098	1,672	2,118	1,657	70,005,809
Percent change	-13.5	-11.5	4.1	8.3	15.3	6.3	6.0	17.3	28.9		
Nonmetropolitan Counties											
2019	35,642	24,783	2,325	16,558	4,014	4,028	879	416	574		
2020	31,279	22,738	2,012	17,677	4,434	3,964	959	565	739	2,097	21,970,573
Percent change	-12.2	-8.3	-13.5	6.8	10.5	-1.6	9.1	35.8	28.7		
Suburban Areas[2]											
2019	161,795	118,719	18,958	131,657	24,007	21,664	3,845	2,210	3,106		
2020	143,243	105,982	18,990	146,306	27,949	22,901	4,180	2,627	4,017	6,983	120,808,272
Percent change	-11.5	-10.7	0.2	11.1	16.4	5.7	8.7	18.9	29.3		

1 The figures shown in the rape column include only those reported by law enforcement agencies that used the revised Uniform Crime Reporting (UCR) definition of rape. See notes for more detail.   2 Suburban areas include law enforcement agencies in cities with less than 50,000 inhabitants and county law enforcement agencies that are within a Metropolitan Statistical Area. Suburban areas exclude all metropolitan agencies associated with a principal city. The agencies associated with suburban areas also appear in other groups within this table.

Table 16. Rate: Number of Crimes Per 100,000 Population, by Population Group, 2020

(Number, rate.)

Population group	Violent crime		Murder and nonnegligent manslaughter		Rape[1]		Robbery		Aggravated assault	
	Number of offenses known	Rate	Number of offenses known	Rate	Number of offenses known	Rate	Number of offenses known	Rate	Number of offenses known	Rate
Total, All Agencies	1,106,727	404.5	17,597	6.4	107,907	39.4	207,636	75.9	773,587	282.9
Total, Cities	894,132	469.4	14,108	7.4	80,176	42.1	185,379	97.4	614,469	322.7
Group I (250,000 and over)	444,979	753.7	7,575	12.8	30,208	51.2	108,259	183.4	298,937	506.3
1,000,000 and over (Group I subset)	192,910	710.6	2,779	10.2	12,140	44.7	51,754	190.6	126,237	465.0
500,000 to 999,999 (Group I subset)	41.571 pt	874.7	2,556	16.3	8,593	54.7	29,848	190.1	96,379	613.7
250,000 to 499,999 (Group I subset)	114,693	708.5	2,240	13.8	9,475	58.5	26,657	164.7	76,321	471.4
Group II (100,000 to 249,999)	146,782	471.6	2,384	7.7	13,803	44.3	29,435	94.6	101,160	325.0
Group III (50,000 to 99,999)	109,725	347.2	1,469	4.6	11,324	35.8	20,896	66.2	76,036	240.6
Group IV (25,000 to 49,999)	74,413	279.0	1,050	3.9	9,100	34.1	12,706	47.6	51,557	193.6
Group V (10,000 to 24,999)	65,196	266.8	993	4.1	8,597	35.2	8,998	36.9	46,608	191.1
Group VI (under 10,000)	53,037	301.4	637	3.6	7,144	40.6	5,085	28.9	40,171	228.3
Metropolitan Counties	166,369	265.0	2,516	4.0	19,838	31.6	20,189	32.2	123,826	197.2
Nonmetropolitan Counties[2]	46,226	227.5	973	4.8	7,893	38.9	2,068	10.2	35,292	173.7
Suburban Areas[3]	271,751	250.4	3,888	3.6	33,299	30.7	37,638	34.7	196,926	181.5

Table 16. Rate: Number of Crimes Per 100,000 Population, by Population Group, 2020—Continued

(Number, rate.)

Population group	Property crime		Burglary		Larceny-theft		Motor vehicle theft	
	Number of offenses known	Rate	Number of offenses known	Rate	Number of offenses known	Rate	Number of offenses known	Rate
Total, All Agencies	5,304,354	1,938.9	858,592	315.0	3,740,519	1,422.6	705,243	257.8
Total, Cities	4,293,456	2,254.0	658,718	347.1	3,059,998	1,686.7	574,740	301.8
Group I (250,000 and over)	1,635,354	2,769.9	264,458	447.9	1,103,756	1,958.9	267,140	452.5
1,000,000 and over (Group I subset)	609,068	2,243.6	96,553	355.7	409,536	1,674.8	102,979	379.3
500,000 to 999,999 (Group I subset)	547,124	3,483.7	91,506	582.6	372,525	2,372.0	83,093	529.1
250,000 to 499,999 (Group I subset)	479,162	2,959.8	76,399	471.9	321,695	1,987.1	81,068	500.8
Group II (100,000 to 249,999)	772,260	2,481.1	114,538	371.4	547,196	1,797.4	110,526	355.1
Group III (50,000 to 99,999)	640,987	2,028.1	92,111	291.9	470,968	1,551.6	77,908	246.5
Group IV (25,000 to 49,999)	475,556	1,782.8	68,387	258.2	357,646	1,435.0	49,523	185.7
Group V (10,000 to 24,999)	435,899	1,784.1	65,472	269.2	329,152	1,448.8	41,275	169.0
Group VI (under 10,000)	333,400	1,894.4	53,752	306.3	251,280	1,510.9	28,368	161.2
Metropolitan Counties	809,432	1,289.1	144,818	231.6	559,531	906.9	105,083	167.4
Nonmetropolitan Counties[2]	201,466	991.7	55,056	272.2	120,990	610.5	25,420	125.2
Suburban Areas[3]	1,616,701	1,489.8	251,026	231.3	1,181,850	1,089.1	183,825	169.4

NOTE: Due to a system upgrade, the rates in this table are now caculated using aggregate popualtion for each individual offense. The agency counts and population are provided for each individual offense.
1 The figures shown in this column for the offense of rape were reported using only the revised Uniform Crime Reporting definition of rape. See the chapter notes for further explanation.   2 Includes state police agencies that report aggregately for the entire state.   3 Suburban areas include law enforcement agencies in cities with less than 50,000 inhabitants and county law enforcement agencies that are within a Metropolitan Statistical Area. Suburban areas exclude all metropolitan agencies associated with a principal city. The agencies associated with suburban areas also appear in other groups within this table.

Table 17. Rate: Number of Crimes Per 100,000 Inhabitants, by Suburban and Nonsuburban Cities,[1] by Population Group, 2020

(Number, rate.)

Population group	Violent crime		Murder and nonnegligent manslaughter		Rape[2]		Robbery		Aggravated assault	
	Number of offenses known	Rate	Number of offenses known	Rate	Number of offenses known	Rate	Number of offenses known	Rate	Number of offenses known	Rate
Total, Suburban Cities	107,531	228.6	1,398	3.0	13,885	29.5	17,645	37.5	74,603	158.6
Group IV (25,000 to 49,999)	43,159	218.8	560	2.8	5,469	27.7	8,400	42.6	28,730	145.6
Group V (10,000 to 24,999)	38,571	222.8	522	3.0	4,947	28.6	5,879	34.0	27,223	157.2
Group VI (under 10,000)	25,801	258.3	316	3.2	3,469	34.8	3,366	33.7	18,650	186.7
Total, Nonsuburban Cities	50,659	399.5	744	5.9	6,770	53.5	3,994	31.5	39,151	308.8
Group IV (25,000 to 49,999)	5,465	378.1	73	5.1	863	59.7	601	41.6	3,928	271.8
Group V (10,000 to 24,999)	20,324	436.4	366	7.9	2,643	56.9	2,004	43.0	15,311	328.8
Group VI (under 10,000)	24,870	378.1	305	4.6	3,264	49.6	1,389	21.1	19,912	302.7

Population group	Property crime		Burglary		Larceny-theft		Motor vehicle theft	
	Number of offenses known	Rate	Number of offenses known	Rate	Number of offenses known	Rate	Number of offenses known	Rate
Total, Suburban Cities	813,590	1,729.8	108,784	231.3	624,467	1,327.7	80,339	170.8
Group IV (25,000 to 49,999)	330,574	1,675.5	43,107	218.5	252,082	1,277.7	35,385	179.4
Group V (10,000 to 24,999)	284,878	1,645.3	37,886	218.8	218,700	1,263.1	28,292	163.4
Group VI (under 10,000)	198,138	1,983.5	27,791	278.2	153,685	1,538.5	16,662	166.8
Total, Nonsuburban Cities	293,678	2,316.2	51,223	404.0	219,449	1,730.8	23,006	181.4
Group IV (25,000 to 49,999)	36,263	2,509.2	5,736	396.9	27,533	1,905.1	2,994	207.2
Group V (10,000 to 24,999)	126,954	2,726.1	21,999	472.4	95,592	2,052.7	9,363	201.1
Group VI (under 10,000)	130,461	1,983.5	23,488	357.1	96,324	1,464.5	10,649	161.9

NOTE: Due to a system upgrade, the rates in this table are now caculated using aggregate popualtion for each individual offense. The agency counts and population are provided for each individual offense.
1 Suburban cities include law enforcement agencies in cities with less than 50,000 inhabitants that are within a Metropolitan Statistical Area. Suburban cities exclude all metropolitan agencies associated with a principal city. Nonsuburban cities include law enforcement agencies in cities with less than 50,000 inhabitants that are not associated with a Metropolitan Statistical Area. 2 The figures shown in this column for the offense of rape were reported using only the revised Uniform Crime Reporting definition of rape. See chapter notes for more detail.

Table 18. Rate: Number of Crimes Per 100,000 Inhabitants, by Metropolitan and Nonmetropolitan Counties,[1] by Population Group, 2020

(Number, rate.)

Population group	Violent crime		Murder and nonnegligent manslaughter		Rape[2]		Robbery		Aggravated assault	
	Number of offenses known	Rate	Number of offenses known	Rate	Number of offenses known	Rate	Number of offenses known	Rate	Number of offenses known	Rate
Metropolitan Counties										
100,000 and over	109,089	275.9	1,641	4.1	11,153	28.2	16,736	42.3	79,559	201.2
25,000 to 99,999	38,661	217.3	583	3.3	5,251	29.5	2,403	13.5	30,424	171.0
Under 25,000	16,470	397.5	266	6.4	3,010	73.1	854	20.6	12,340	297.9
Nonmetropolitan Counties										
25,000 and over	19,438	220.0	381	4.3	2,968	33.6	1,140	12.9	14,949	169.2
10,000 to 24,999	14,345	189.7	304	4.0	2,130	28.2	530	7.0	11,381	150.5
Under 10,000	10,944	329.1	250	7.5	2,533	76.2	306	9.2	7,855	236.2

Table 18. Rate: Number of Crimes Per 100,000 Inhabitants, by Metropolitan and Nonmetropolitan Counties,[1] by Population Group, 2020—Continued

(Number, rate.)

Population group	Property crime		Burglary		Larceny-theft		Motor vehicle theft	
	Number of offenses known	Rate	Number of offenses known	Rate	Number of offenses known	Rate	Number of offenses known	Rate
Metropolitan Counties								
100,000 and over	536,853	1,357.6	84,086	212.6	386,022	976.2	66,745	168.8
25,000 to 99,999	193,972	1,090.0	43,489	244.4	128,069	719.7	22,414	126.0
Under 25,000	72,286	1,744.8	14,667	354.0	43,292	1,045.0	14,327	345.8
Nonmetropolitan Counties								
25,000 and over	90,805	1,027.8	24,347	275.6	55,809	631.7	10,649	120.5
10,000 to 24,999	65,995	872.8	18,540	245.2	39,440	521.6	8,015	106.0
Under 10,000	41,403	1,244.9	10,955	329.4	24,305	730.8	6,143	184.7

NOTE: Due to a system upgrade, the rates in this table are now caculated using aggregate popualtion for each individual offense. The agency counts and population are provided for each individual offense.

1 Metropolitan counties include sheriffs and county law enforcement agencies associated with a Metropolitan Statistical Area. Nonmetropolitan counties include sheriffs and county law enforcement agencies that are not associated with a Metropolitan Statistical Area.   2 The figures shown in this column for the offense of rape were reported using only the revised Uniform Crime Reporting definition of rape. See the chapter notes for further explanation.

Table 19. Rate: Number of Crimes Per 100,000 Inhabitants, Additional Information About Selected Offenses, by Population Group, 2020

(Number, rate.)

Population group	Rape[1]		Robbery				Aggravated assault		
	Rape	Assault to rape-attempts	Firearm	Knife or cutting instrument	Other weapon	Strong-arm	Firearm	Knife or cutting instrument	Other weapon
Total, All Agencies									
Number of offenses known	99,247	3,967	73,084	17,796	21,778	83,485	259,215	121,624	211,483
Rate	37.9	1.5	27.9	6.8	8.3	31.8	98.8	46.4	80.6
Total, Cities									
Number of offenses known	73,194	2,976	63,948	16,078	19,228	74,920	209,633	100,206	163,747
Rate	40.4	1.6	35.3	8.9	10.6	41.4	115.8	55.3	90.4
Group I (250,000 and over)									
Number of offenses known	27,556	1,306	38,145	9,407	10,342	42,496	116,495	48,880	76,948
Rate	48.9	2.3	67.7	16.7	18.4	75.4	206.7	86.7	136.6
1,000,000 and over (Group I subset)									
Number of offenses known	10,313	481	14,649	5,005	5,035	19,196	34,892	22,639	30,390
Rate	42.2	2.0	59.9	20.5	20.6	78.5	142.7	92.6	124.3
500,000 to 999,999 (Group I subset)									
Number of offenses known	8,172	421	13,310	2,453	3,095	10,990	46,652	14,610	25,877
Rate	52.0	2.7	84.7	15.6	19.7	70.0	297.0	93.0	164.8
250,000 to 499,999 (Group I subset)									
Number of offenses known	9,071	404	10,186	1,949	2,212	12,310	34,951	11,631	20,681
Rate	56.0	2.5	62.9	12.0	13.7	76.0	215.9	71.8	127.7
Group II (100,000 to 249,999)									
Number of offenses known	12,953	538	10,547	2,642	3,409	12,289	35,783	17,367	27,435
Rate	42.5	1.8	34.6	8.7	11.2	40.4	117.5	57.0	90.1
Group III (50,000 to 99,999)									
Number of offenses known	10,572	338	6,448	1,863	2,434	9,415	22,365	12,562	21,578
Rate	34.8	1.1	21.2	6.1	8.0	31.0	73.7	41.4	71.1
Group IV (25,000 to 49,999)									
Number of offenses known	8,076	261	4,248	1,067	1,409	5,109	14,662	8,426	14,113
Rate	32.6	1.1	17.1	4.3	5.7	20.6	59.2	34.0	57.0
Group V (10,000 to 24,999)									
Number of offenses known	7,600	236	2,994	745	1,008	3,402	12,388	7,293	12,718
Rate	33.7	1.0	13.3	3.3	4.5	15.1	54.9	32.3	56.4
Group VI (under 10,000)									
Number of offenses known	6,437	297	1,566	354	626	2,209	7,940	5,678	10,955
Rate	38.9	1.8	9.5	2.1	3.8	13.3	47.9	34.3	66.1
Metropolitan Counties									
Number of offenses known	18,672	742	8,292	1,566	2,216	7,919	39,950	17,312	37,079
Rate	30.4	1.2	13.5	2.5	3.6	12.9	65.0	28.2	60.3
Nonmetropolitan Counties									
Number of offenses known	7,381	249	844	152	334	646	9,632	4,106	10,657
Rate	37.4	1.3	4.3	0.8	1.7	3.3	48.8	20.8	54.0
Suburban Areas[2]									
Number of offenses known	32,080	1,219	14,500	3,068	4,395	15,675	59,564	29,569	59,571
Rate	29.6	1.1	13.4	2.8	4.1	14.4	54.9	27.2	54.9

Table 19. Rate: Number of Crimes Per 100,000 Inhabitants, Additional Information About Selected Offenses, by Population Group, 2020—Continued

(Number, rate.)

Population group	Hands, fists, feet, etc.	Burglary			Motor vehicle theft		
		Forcible entry	Unlawful entry	Attempted forcible entry	Autos	Trucks and buses	Other vehicles
Total, All Agencies							
Number of offenses known	149,984	465,177	312,018	55,066	506,408	115,406	62,578
Rate	57.2	177.6	119.1	21.0	193.1	44.0	23.9
Total, Cities							
Number of offenses known	112,212	357,389	233,877	44,911	417,068	94,155	44,876
Rate	62.0	197.7	129.4	24.8	230.4	52.0	24.8
Group I (250,000 and over)							
Number of offenses known	40,017	154,830	81,911	19,074	185,120	54,252	17,715
Rate	71.0	274.8	145.4	33.9	328.5	96.3	31.4
1,000,000 and over (Group I subset)							
Number of offenses known	21,719	56,840	24,614	6,456	54,021	31,425	7,480
Rate	88.8	232.4	100.7	26.4	220.9	128.5	30.6
500,000 to 999,999 (Group I subset)							
Number of offenses known	9,240	52,818	31,537	7,151	65,990	11,510	5,593
Rate	58.8	336.3	200.8	45.5	420.2	73.3	35.6
250,000 to 499,999 (Group I subset)							
Number of offenses known	9,058	45,172	25,760	5,467	65,109	11,317	4,642
Rate	56.0	279.0	159.1	33.8	402.2	69.9	28.7
Group II (100,000 to 249,999)							
Number of offenses known	18,293	62,205	42,045	8,168	84,359	16,047	9,079
Rate	60.1	206.3	139.4	27.1	277.1	52.7	29.8
Group III (50,000 to 99,999)							
Number of offenses known	17,399	48,447	35,352	5,951	58,475	11,202	6,890
Rate	57.3	159.6	116.5	19.6	192.6	36.9	22.7
Group IV (25,000 to 49,999)							
Number of offenses known	11,128	33,482	26,667	4,864	37,111	5,216	4,587
Rate	44.9	135.1	107.6	19.6	149.8	21.1	18.5
Group V (10,000 to 24,999)							
Number of offenses known	11,383	32,273	26,001	3,619	30,851	4,466	3,418
Rate	50.5	143.0	115.2	16.0	136.7	19.8	15.1
Group VI (under 10,000)							
Number of offenses known	13,992	26,152	21,901	3,235	21,152	2,972	3,187
Rate	84.5	157.9	132.2	19.5	127.7	17.9	19.2
Metropolitan Counties							
Number of offenses known	27,982	77,833	56,265	8,144	72,702	16,966	13,818
Rate	45.5	126.6	91.5	13.2	118.2	27.6	22.5
Nonmetropolitan Counties							
Number of offenses known	9,790	29,955	21,876	2,011	16,638	4,285	3,884
Rate	49.6	151.9	110.9	10.2	84.4	21.7	19.7
Suburban Areas[2]							
Number of offenses known	48,224	134,722	100,033	16,271	136,390	26,163	21,272
Rate	44.4	124.2	92.2	15.0	125.7	24.1	19.6

NOTE: Due to a system upgrade, the rates in this table are now caculated using aggregate popualtion for each individual offense. The agency counts and population are provided for each individual offense.
1 The figures shown in this column for the offense of rape were reported using only the revised Uniform Crime Reporting definition of rape. See the chapter notes for further explanation. 2 Suburban areas include law enforcement agencies in cities with less than 50,000 inhabitants and county law enforcement agencies that are within a Metropolitan Statistical Area. Suburban areas exclude all metropolitan agencies associated with a principal city. The agencies associated with suburban areas also appear in other groups within this table.

Table 20. Murder, by Selected State and Type of Weapon, 2020

(Number.)

State	Total murders[1]	Total firearms	Handguns	Rifles	Shotguns	Firearms (type unknown)	Knives or cutting instruments	Other weapons	Hands, fists, feet, etc.[2]
Alabama[3]	24	18	10	0	3	5	1	5	0
Alaska	48	22	16	0	4	2	10	10	6
Arizona	425	292	219	14	3	56	49	74	10
Arkansas	308	235	104	14	3	114	31	30	12
California	2,202	1,606	1,032	41	31	502	297	198	101
Colorado	293	202	141	8	1	52	40	37	14
Connecticut	140	98	23	0	0	75	27	14	1
Delaware	74	66	32	3	1	30	3	1	4
District of Columbia	201	174	163	1	0	10	14	8	5
Florida[4]	1	1	1	0	0	0	0	0	0
Georgia	558	442	228	28	4	182	36	61	19
Hawaii	17	6	2	0	2	2	2	8	1
Idaho	39	25	18	2	0	5	4	5	5
Illinois	1,035	896	762	9	0	125	69	48	22
Indiana	465	366	246	8	2	110	33	47	19
Iowa	111	84	33	3	5	43	10	14	3
Kansas	88	62	31	6	3	22	10	12	4
Kentucky	309	261	155	18	2	86	20	19	9
Louisiana	697	593	242	26	6	319	51	39	14
Maine	22	15	10	0	0	5	4	1	2
Maryland[3]	490	400	354	10	2	34	50	21	19
Massachusetts	160	117	64	0	1	52	26	14	3
Michigan	751	595	237	30	3	325	52	85	19
Minnesota	189	142	79	5	6	52	17	21	9
Mississippi	212	193	108	15	5	65	5	12	2
Missouri	567	470	265	17	3	185	35	54	8
Montana	57	28	16	1	0	11	11	12	6
Nebraska	62	41	31	3	6	1	7	12	2
Nevada	172	107	77	2	2	26	19	30	16
New Hampshire	12	6	3	0	0	3	3	1	2
New Jersey	329	229	156	2	0	71	55	32	13
New Mexico	137	87	28	4	2	53	23	21	6
New York	799	517	415	5	6	91	150	79	53
North Carolina	742	580	325	25	8	222	50	81	31
North Dakota	31	14	5	2	1	6	7	4	6
Ohio	781	600	269	4	6	321	59	91	31
Oklahoma	292	197	140	4	7	46	29	55	11
Oregon	119	84	43	5	1	35	15	16	4
Pennsylvania[3]	254	223	201	8	2	12	12	11	8
Rhode Island	32	24	4	0	0	20	2	4	2
South Carolina	524	441	235	13	5	188	34	43	6
South Dakota	49	20	13	2	0	5	7	17	5
Tennessee	663	566	234	24	12	296	36	38	23
Texas	1,926	1,491	751	63	34	643	176	185	74
Utah	92	67	43	2	3	19	9	15	1
Vermont	14	9	6	0	0	3	2	1	2
Virginia	524	423	212	11	3	197	47	44	10
Washington	298	177	102	6	5	64	46	54	21
West Virginia	102	69	38	7	3	21	7	22	4
Wisconsin	303	227	85	2	7	133	29	38	9
Wyoming	14	12	10	1	0	1	1	1	0

1 Total number of murders for which supplemental homicide data were received.   2 Pushed is included in hands, fists, feet, etc.   3 Limited data for 2020 were available for Alabama, Maryland and Pennsylvania.   4 Data submitted through the Bureau of Indian Affairs.

Table 21. Robbery, by State and Type of Weapon, 2020

(Number.)

State	Total robberies[1]	Firearms	Knives or cutting instruments	Other weapons	Strong-arm	Agency count	Population
Alabama[2]	38	18	5	5	10	22	173,869
Alaska	703	160	73	98	372	32	719,120
Arizona	6,042	2,127	698	775	2,442	93	6,630,193
Arkansas	1,418	691	95	157	475	249	2,730,633
California	44,634	11,154	4,352	5,824	23,304	730	39,299,122
Colorado	3,831	1,450	378	563	1,440	198	5,039,047
Connecticut	2,033	756	213	220	844	107	3,557,006
Delaware	700	271	58	67	304	54	984,527
District of Columbia	2,373	1,092	214	149	918	3	712,816
Florida	13,452	4,996	1,001	1,359	6,096	675	21,640,034
Georgia	2,695	1,387	106	227	975	290	6,076,607
Hawaii	69	5	1	50	13	2	273,390
Idaho	157	40	16	22	79	97	1,634,314
Illinois[3]	238	109	11	22	96	1	144,795
Indiana	3,354	1,910	202	351	891	109	3,662,556
Iowa	895	361	82	103	349	214	2,768,788
Kansas	244	91	21	24	108	198	1,457,584
Kentucky	1,133	531	78	131	393	336	3,713,933
Louisiana	3,000	1,579	146	239	1,036	120	3,412,735
Maine	170	43	23	31	73	130	1,350,141
Maryland[2]	457	157	75	45	180	6	1,124,569
Massachusetts	2,984	776	560	386	1,262	344	6,713,971
Michigan	4,362	1,939	243	394	1,786	620	9,503,274
Minnesota	3,712	1,341	255	534	1,582	354	5,269,267
Mississippi	389	232	14	57	86	82	1,286,107
Missouri	4,426	2,412	249	433	1,332	378	5,284,619
Montana	268	53	25	66	124	98	1,030,357
Nebraska	539	257	46	42	194	73	1,095,293
Nevada	2,778	1,022	277	325	1,154	51	3,128,568
New Hampshire	235	55	41	23	116	180	1,279,545
New Jersey	4,384	1,342	397	368	2,277	577	8,882,371
New Mexico	1,628	721	232	235	440	20	932,857
New York	17,109	3,176	2,580	1,875	9,478	457	17,703,567
North Carolina	6,296	3,327	470	515	1,984	288	8,731,507
North Dakota	149	41	19	15	74	103	759,161
Ohio	6,949	2,256	301	474	3,918	394	8,804,775
Oklahoma	2,312	1,008	213	231	860	414	3,927,308
Oregon	2,024	446	234	403	941	172	3,570,671
Pennsylvania[2]	127	51	10	9	57	106	170,825
Rhode Island	336	107	66	38	125	45	1,041,521
South Carolina	2,792	1,614	193	214	771	241	4,499,154
South Dakota	245	75	37	44	89	118	838,825
Tennessee	5,520	3,424	318	430	1,348	456	6,618,548
Texas	26,267	13,655	1,995	2,628	7,989	848	27,275,732
Utah	1,174	347	144	156	527	103	2,856,632
Vermont	64	15	12	5	32	82	619,602
Virginia	2,922	1,471	252	260	939	319	8,541,146
Washington	5,156	1,398	558	791	2,409	235	7,554,132
West Virginia	289	115	36	44	94	131	1,177,351
Wisconsin	3,013	1,467	162	307	1,077	379	5,543,214
Wyoming	58	13	9	14	22	54	510,568

1 The number of robberies from agencies that submitted 12 months of data in 2020 for which breakdowns by type of weapon were included.   2 Limited data for 2020 were available for Alabama, Maryland and Pennsylvania.   3 Limited data were received.

Table 22. Aggravated Assault, by State and Type of Weapon, 2020

(Number.)

State	Total aggravated assaults[1]	Firearms	Knives or cutting instruments	Other weapons	Personal weapons	Agency count	Population
Alabama[2]	484	103	70	268	43	22	173,869
Alaska	4,200	926	734	1,452	1,088	32	719,120
Arizona	22,248	7,499	3,404	5,035	6,310	93	6,630,193
Arkansas	15,468	6,197	1,605	3,250	4,416	249	2,730,633
California	113,464	24,688	17,537	38,108	33,131	730	39,299,122
Colorado	15,571	5,694	3,139	4,251	2,487	198	5,039,047
Connecticut	3,692	932	917	1,131	712	107	3,557,006
Delaware	3,224	1,476	549	948	251	54	984,527
District of Columbia	4,242	1,285	1,148	1,543	266	3	712,816
Florida	60,581	23,034	10,494	18,741	8,312	675	21,640,034
Georgia	15,921	7,430	1,872	3,445	3,174	290	6,076,607
Hawaii	556	18	54	93	391	2	273,390
Idaho	3,094	699	449	992	954	97	1,634,314
Illinois[3]	1,731	957	151	237	386	1	144,795
Indiana	12,156	4,449	1,259	2,996	3,452	109	3,662,556
Iowa	6,674	1,136	919	1,648	2,971	214	2,768,788
Kansas	3,311	900	454	1,089	868	198	1,457,584
Kentucky	2,854	620	469	1,384	381	336	3,713,933
Louisiana	18,992	7,428	2,306	5,948	3,310	120	3,412,735
Maine	788	76	127	298	287	130	1,350,141
Maryland[2]	801	174	292	164	171	6	1,124,569
Massachusetts	15,974	2,253	3,805	7,105	2,811	344	6,713,971
Michigan	35,309	13,790	5,717	9,806	5,996	620	9,503,274
Minnesota	8,966	2,853	1,743	2,319	2,051	354	5,269,267
Mississippi	2,015	989	247	459	320	82	1,286,107
Missouri	23,737	10,933	2,464	7,061	3,279	378	5,284,619
Montana	3,979	664	409	1,221	1,685	98	1,030,357
Nebraska	3,075	1,113	502	878	582	73	1,095,293
Nevada	9,600	3,159	2,290	2,082	2,069	51	3,128,568
New Hampshire	1,032	259	221	252	300	180	1,279,545
New Jersey	11,365	2,273	2,139	3,470	3,483	577	8,882,371
New Mexico	7,307	2,699	1,336	2,284	988	20	932,857
New York	45,160	6,893	12,125	12,931	13,211	457	17,703,567
North Carolina	27,878	16,504	3,225	4,579	3,570	288	8,731,507
North Dakota	1,876	88	262	704	822	103	759,161
Ohio	19,457	9,763	3,093	5,006	1,595	394	8,804,775
Oklahoma	13,183	4,299	1,976	3,892	3,016	414	3,927,308
Oregon	7,564	1,345	1,298	2,674	2,247	172	3,570,671
Pennsylvania[2]	603	171	63	57	312	106	170,825
Rhode Island	1,638	325	381	483	449	45	1,041,521
South Carolina	18,543	9,995	2,476	3,841	2,231	241	4,499,154
South Dakota	3,213	394	666	781	1,372	118	838,825
Tennessee	36,689	19,984	5,018	9,890	1,797	456	6,618,548
Texas	85,339	37,300	15,611	22,850	9,578	848	27,275,732
Utah	4,485	908	902	1,442	1,233	103	2,856,632
Vermont	788	104	126	142	416	82	619,602
Virginia	12,047	4,996	1,644	3,078	2,329	319	8,541,146
Washington	14,314	3,710	2,162	4,758	3,684	235	7,554,132
West Virginia	3,269	1,100	351	648	1,170	131	1,177,351
Wisconsin	13,008	4,502	1,276	3,515	3,715	379	5,543,214
Wyoming	841	128	147	254	312	54	510,568

1 The number of aggravated assaults from agencies that submitted 12 months of data in 2020 for which breakdowns by type of weapon were included.   2 Limited data for 2020 were available for Alabama, Maryland and Pennsylvania.   3 Limited data were received.

Table 23. Offense Analysis, Number and Percent Change, 2019–2020

(Number, percent, dollars; 12,751 agencies; 2020 estimated population 277,124,125.)

Classification	Number of offenses, 2020	Percent change from 2019	Percent distribution[1]	Average value (dollars)
Murder	16,896	+28.4	NA	X
Rape[2]	105,273	-12.1	NA	X
Robbery	198,877	-9.9	100.0%	1,834
By location				
Street/highway	63,667	-15.2	32.0%	1,719
Commercial house	33,586	-9.1	16.9%	1,497
Gas or service station	7,188	8.3	3.6%	1,469
Convenience store	14,727	0.8	7.4%	1,005
Residence	34,809	-1.6	17.5%	2,236
Bank	2,179	-29.9	1.1%	4,339
Miscellaneous	42,721	-12.8	21.5%	2,161
Burglary	859,572	-7.5	100.0%	2,692
By location				
Residence (dwelling)	477,436	-58.8	55.5%	7,937
Residence, night	183,098	-7.7	21.3%	2,140
Residence, day	232,623	-21.4	27.1%	2,321
Residence, unknown	61,715	-29.7	7.2%	3,477
Nonresidence (store, office, etc.)	382,136	19.7	44.5%	9,779
Nonresidence, night	183,590	14.9	21.4%	2,974
Nonresidence, day	145,599	12.1	16.9%	2,822
Nonresidence, unknown	52,947	-7.3	6.2%	3,982
Larceny-theft (except motor vehicle theft)	3,800,545	-9.6	100.0%	1,482
By type				
Pocket-picking	15,602	-40.2	0.4%	1,233
Purse-snatching	11,634	-21.5	0.3%	634
Shoplifting	795,530	-14.8	20.9%	306
From motor vehicles (except accessories)	1,046,216	-7.0	27.5%	1,053
Motor vehicle accessories	324,328	19.4	8.5%	873
Bicycles	130,491	1.7	3.4%	724
From buildings	322,014	-22.6	8.5%	1,616
From coin-operated machines	7,268	-19.4	0.2%	816
All others	1,147,462	-10.4	30.2%	2,926
By value				
Over $200	1,831,657	-7.8	48.2%	3,026
$50 to $200	768,675	-12.7	20.2%	101
Under $50	1,200,213	-10.2	31.6%	10
Motor Vehicle Theft	692,517	11.7	NA	9,166

NA = Not available.
X = Not applicable.
1 Because of rounding, the percentages may not add to 100.0.   2 The figures shown in this column for the offense of rape were reported using only the revised Uniform Crime Reporting definition of rape. See the chapter notes for further explanation.

Table 24. Property Stolen and Recovered, by Type and Value, 2020

(Dollars, percent; 12,903 agencies; 2020 estimated population 275,056,054.)

Type of property	Value of property (dollars)		Percent recovered
	Stolen	Recovered	
Total	$13,808,565,134	$4,298,423,601	31.1
Currency, notes, etc.	1,245,350,575	31,941,249	2.6
Jewelry and precious metals	837,911,482	25,033,119	3.0
Clothing and furs	340,253,807	19,232,176	5.7
Locally stolen motor vehicles	6,452,048,172	3,640,955,256	56.4
Office equipment	303,766,541	17,763,680	5.8
Televisions, radios, stereos, etc.	207,809,902	9,497,929	4.6
Firearms	135,177,366	14,248,649	10.5
Household goods	275,789,411	107,637,809	39.0
Consumable goods	152,385,338	11,958,702	7.8
Livestock	11,743,047	1,162,991	9.9
Miscellaneous	3,846,329,493	418,992,041	10.9

SECTION III

OFFENSES CLEARED

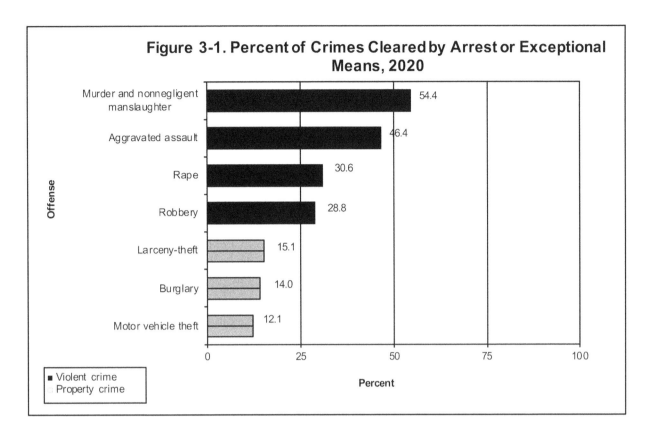

Figure 3-1. Percent of Crimes Cleared by Arrest or Exceptional Means, 2020

Law enforcement agencies that report crime to the Federal Bureau of Investigation (FBI) can clear, or "close," offenses in one of two ways: by arrest or by exceptional means. However, the administrative closing of a case by a local law enforcement agency does not necessarily mean that the agency can clear an offense for Uniform Crime Reporting (UCR) purposes. To clear an offense within the program's guidelines, the reporting agency must adhere to certain criteria, which are outlined in this section. (The UCR program does not distinguish between offenses cleared by arrest and those cleared by exceptional means in its data presentations. The distinction is made solely for the purpose of a definition and not for data collection and publication.) See Appendix I for information on the UCR program's statistical methodology.

Important Note: Rape Data

In 2013, the FBI UCR Program initiated the collection of rape data within the Summary Reporting System under a revised definition. The changes bring uniformity to the offense in both the Summary Reporting System (SRS) and the National Incident-Based Reporting System (NIBRS) by capturing data (1) without regard to gender, (2) including penetration of any bodily orifice by any object or body part, and (3) including offenses where physical force is not involved. The term "forcible" was removed, and the definition changed to the revised UCR definition below.

- Legacy UCR definition of rape: The carnal knowledge of a female forcibly and against her will. This definition has ceased to be used by the FBI.

- Revised UCR definition of rape: Penetration, no matter how slight, of the vagina or anus with any body part or object, or oral penetration by a sex organ of another person, without the consent of the victim. This is the definition currently in use; unless specified otherwise, "rape" refers to this definition.

Cleared by Arrest

In the UCR program, a law enforcement agency reports that an offense is cleared by arrest, or solved for crime reporting purposes, when at least one person is arrested, charged with the commission of the offense, and turned over to the court for prosecution (whether following

273

arrest, court summons, or police notice). To qualify as a clearance, *all* of these conditions must be met.

In its calculations, the UCR program counts the number of offenses that are cleared, not the number of arrestees. Therefore, the arrest of one person may clear several crimes, and the arrest of many persons may clear only one offense. In addition, some clearances recorded by an agency during a particular calendar year, such as 2020, may pertain to offenses that occurred in previous years.

Cleared by Exceptional Means

In certain situations, elements beyond law enforcement's control prevent the agency from arresting and formally charging the offender. When this occurs, the agency can clear the offense *exceptionally*. There are four UCR program requirements that law enforcement must meet in order to clear an offense by exceptional means. The agency must have:

- Identified the offender

- Gathered enough evidence to support an arrest, make a charge, and turn over the offender to the court for prosecution

- Identified the offender's exact location so that the suspect could be taken into custody immediately

- Encountered a circumstance outside the control of law enforcement that prohibits the agency from arresting, charging, and prosecuting the offender

Examples of exceptional clearances include, but are not limited to, the death of the offender (e.g., suicide or justifiably killed by a law enforcement officer or a citizen), the victim's refusal to cooperate with the prosecution after the offender has been identified, or the denial of extradition because the offender committed a crime in another jurisdiction and is being prosecuted for that offense. In the UCR program, the recovery of property does not clear an offense.

National Clearances

A review of the data for 2020 revealed law enforcement agencies in the United States cleared 41.7 percent of violent crimes (murder, rape, robbery, and aggravated assault) and 14.6 percent of property crimes (burglary, larceny-theft, and motor vehicle theft) brought to their attention. In addition, law enforcement cleared 21.5 percent of arson offenses, which are reported in a slightly different manner than the other property crimes. (Table 25)

As in most years, law enforcement agencies cleared a higher percentage of violent crimes than property crimes in 2020. As a rule, clearance rates generally rise due to the more vigorous investigative efforts put forth for violent

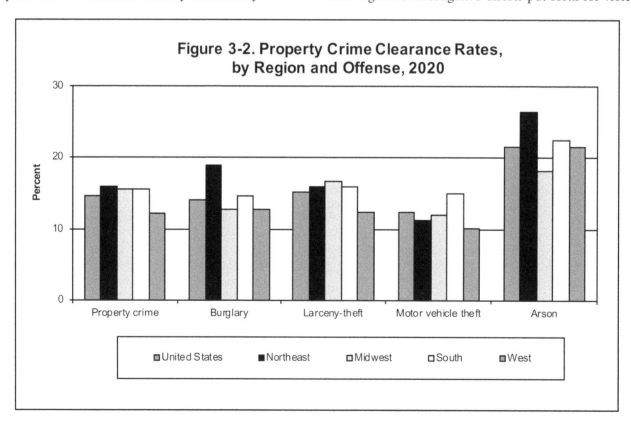

Figure 3-2. Property Crime Clearance Rates, by Region and Offense, 2020

crimes. In addition, violent crimes more often involve victims and/or witnesses who are able to identify the perpetrators.

A breakdown of the clearances for violent crimes for 2020 revealed that the nation's law enforcement agencies cleared 54.4 percent of murder offenses, 46.4 percent of aggravated assault offenses, 30.6 percent of rape offenses, and 28.8 percent of robbery offenses. These numbers were generally lower than the 2019 values; this could be due to issues arising from the COVID-19 pandemic. (Table 25)

For property crime offenses in 2020, law enforcement agencies throughout the nation collectively 14.0 percent of burglary offenses, 15.1 percent of larceny-theft offenses, and 12.3 percent of motor vehicle theft offenses. These clearances were also lower than 2018, and also perhaps due to the global pandemic. (Table 25)

Regional Clearances

The UCR program divides the nation into four regions: the Northeast, the Midwest, the South, and the West. (See Appendix III for further details.) A review of clearance data for 2020 by region showed that agencies in the West cleared the greatest proportion of their violent crime offenses (45.8 percent). Law enforcement agencies in the Midwest and South cleared 40.5 percent and 40.2 percent of their violent crimes, respectively. The Northeast, which usually clears the greatest percentage of violent crimes, cleared the least in 2020, at 39.2 percent. This could perhaps be due to the fallout from the pandemic. (Table 26)

For murder and nonnegligent manslaughter in 2020, the West cleared 59.8 percent of offenses, followed by the South (55.9 percent). The Midwest cleared 49.3 percent and the Northeast cleared 43.6 percent of these offenses. Rape offenses were cleared 26.6 percent of the time in the Northeast, 29.9 percent of the time in the Midwest, 32.4 percent of the time in the South, and 30.4 percent of the time in the West. For robbery, the West had the highest clearance rate, at 32.6 percent, while the Midwest had the lowest clearance rate, at 24.0 percent. The West also had the highest proportion of clearances for aggravated assault (52.0 percent). The South had the lowest proportion of aggravated assault clearances (43.6 percent). (Table 26)

Clearance data for 2020 showed that, among the regions, law enforcement agencies in the Northeast cleared the highest percentage of their property crimes (16.0 percent). Agencies in the Midwest and South cleared 15.5 percent and 15.6 percent, respectively. Agencies in the West cleared 12.2 percent of their property crimes. (Table 26)

Agencies in the Northeast cleared the highest percentage of burglary offenses at 19.0 percent, followed by the South at 14.6 percent, and the Midwest and the West at 12.8 percent each. For larceny-theft, the Midwest (16.7 percent) was followed by the Northeast at 16.0 percent, the South at 15.9 percent, and the West at 12.43 percent. The South cleared the highest proportion of motor vehicle thefts at 15.0 percent, followed by the Midwest at 11.9 percent, the Northeast at 11.0 percent, and the West at 10.1 percent. The Northeast cleared the greatest percentage of arson offenses (26.4 percent), followed by the South (22.4 percent), the West (21.6 percent), and the Midwest (18.2 percent.). (Table 26)

Clearances by Population Groups

The UCR program uses the following population group designations in its data presentations: cities (grouped according to population size) and counties (classified as either metropolitan or nonmetropolitan counties). A breakdown of these classifications is furnished in Appendix III.

CITIES

In 2020, the clearance data collected showed that law enforcement agencies in the nation's cities cleared 39.5 percent of their violent crime offenses. Among the city population groups and subsets, agencies in the smallest cities, those with fewer than 10,000 inhabitants, cleared the greatest proportion of their violent crime offenses (52.8 percent), and law enforcement in cities with 1,000,000 or more inhabitants cleared the smallest proportion of their violent crime offenses (30.9 percent). (Table 25)

The clearance data for murder showed that among the city population groups and subsets, cities with populations of 10,000 to 24,999 inhabitants cleared the greatest percentage of their murders (62.3 percent). Law enforcement agencies in cities with 500,000 to 999,999 inhabitants cleared the lowest percentage of their murders (44.9 percent). For rape, cities with 50,000 to 99,999 inhabitants cleared the largest percentage of offenses at 32.9 percent, while cities with 250,000 to 499,999 inhabitants cleared the lowest percentage of offenses at 23.9 percent. Cities with under 10,000 inhabitants cleared the greatest percentage of their robbery offenses at 39.7 percent, and cities with 1,000,000 or more inhabitants cleared the lowest proportion of their robbery offenses at 23.0 percent. For aggravated assault, cities with fewer than 10,000 inhabitants cleared the highest proportion of offenses (58.0 percent); cities with 1,000,000 or more inhabitants cleared the lowest percentage of offenses (34.3 percent). (Table 25)

In 2020, agencies in the nation's cities collectively cleared 14.4 percent of their property crime offenses. Law enforcement in cities with 10,000 to 24,999 inhabitants cleared the highest proportion of the property crimes (21.8 percent) brought to their attention; cities with 1,000,000 or more inhabitants cleared the smallest proportion of their property crimes (7.5 percent). (Table 25)

Law enforcement agencies in cities cleared 13.5 percent of burglaries, 15.1 percent of larceny-thefts, 11.2 percent of motor vehicle thefts, and 20.7 percent of arsons in 2020. For burglaries, cities with fewer than 10,000 inhabitants cleared the largest percentage of their offenses at 18.3 percent, while cities with 1,000,000 or more inhabitants cleared the smallest percentage of their offenses at 9.7 percent. Cities with 10,000 to 24,999 inhabitants cleared the greatest percentage of their larceny-theft offenses (23.4 percent), and cities with 1,000,000 or more inhabitants cleared the lowest proportion of larceny-theft offenses (7.0 percent). For motor vehicle theft, cities with fewer than 10,000 inhabitants cleared the highest percentages of their offenses at 20.7 percent, while cities with 1,000,000 or more inhabitants cleared the lowest percentage (7.6 percent). Cities with 50,000 to 99,999 inhabitants cleared the greatest percentage of their arson offenses, at 27.3 percent, and cities with 1,000,000 or more inhabitants cleared the lowest percentage (9.7 percent). (Table 25)

METROPOLITAN AND NONMETROPOLITAN COUNTIES

In 2020, law enforcement agencies in metropolitan counties cleared 50.3 percent of their violent crime offenses. Of the violent crimes made known to law enforcement agencies in metropolitan counties, murder offenses had the highest proportion of clearance (61.8 percent), followed by aggravated assaults (54.6 percent), rapes (37.2 percent), and robberies (35.4 percent). Law enforcement agencies in metropolitan counties cleared 15.5 percent of their total property crimes, 15.6 percent of burglaries, 15.3 percent of larceny-thefts, 15.7 percent of motor vehicle thefts, and 23.7 percent of their arsons. (Table 25)

Like their counterparts in metropolitan counties, nonmetropolitan counties collectively cleared a greater proportion of their violent crimes than did the nation as a whole in 2020. Nonmetropolitan counties cleared 50.8 percent of their violent crime offenses and 15.1 percent of property crimes. Of the violent crimes known to them, law enforcement in nonmetropolitan counties had the highest number of clearances for murder (62.1 percent), with 34.3 percent of rapes, 37.8 percent of robberies, and 54.8 percent of aggravated assaults being cleared. Agencies in nonmetropolitan counties reported clearing 15.1 percent of property crimes, including 15.2 percent of their burglaries, 13.6 percent of their larceny-thefts, 20.7

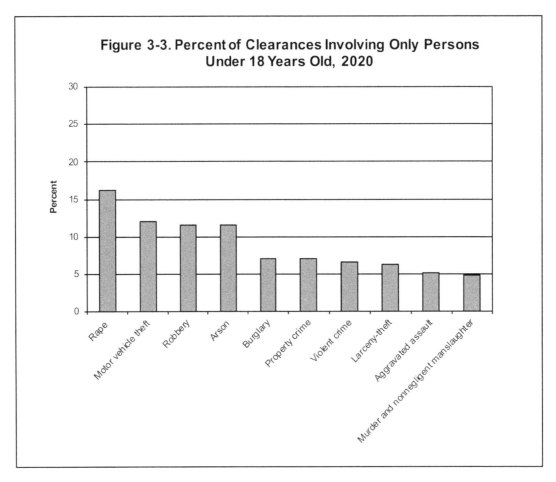

Figure 3-3. Percent of Clearances Involving Only Persons Under 18 Years Old, 2020

percent of their motor vehicle thefts, and 26.2 percent of their arsons. In suburban areas, 50.1 percent of violent crimes (60.7 percent of murders, 34.4 percent of rapes, 35.7 percent of robberies, and 55.3 percent of aggravated assaults) and 17.5 percent of property crimes (15.9 percent of burglaries, 18.2 percent of larceny-thefts, 15.1 percent of motor vehicle thefts, and 24.2 percent of arsons) were cleared in 2020. (Table 25)

Clearances by Classification Group and Type

For rape, by classification group and type, law enforcement agencies cleared 34.9 percent of assault-to-rape attempts and 30.5 percent of rapes in 2020. Cleared robbery offenses included 31.5 percent of offenses involving knives or other cutting instruments, 28.4 percent of offenses involving strong-arm tactics, 27.6 percent of offenses involving other weapons, and 21.6 percent of offenses involving firearms. For aggravated assaults, agencies cleared 55.1 percent of offenses involving hands, feet, fists, etc.; 51.9 percent of offenses involving knives or other cutting instruments; 46.0 percent of offenses involving other weapons; and 27.4 percent of offenses involving firearms. (Table 27)

For property crime clearances grouped by classification and type, data showed that the highest percentage of burglary clearances in the nation in 2020 (15.8 percent) were for offenses that involved unlawful entry. Law enforcement agencies cleared 12.9 percent of burglaries involving forcible entry and 13.9 percent of burglaries involving attempted forcible entry. For motor vehicle theft, agencies cleared 13.1 percent of motor vehicle theft offenses involving automobiles, 10.3 percent of motor vehicle theft offenses involving trucks and buses, and 9.4 percent of motor vehicle offenses involving other vehicles. (Table 27)

In 2020, 25.6 percent of structural arson offenses were cleared by arrest or exceptional means, while 10.6 percent of mobile arson offenses and 24.0 percent of other arson crimes were cleared. (Table 27)

CLEARANCES AND JUVENILES

When an offender under 18 years of age is cited to appear in juvenile court or before other juvenile authorities, the UCR program considers the incident for which the juvenile is being held responsible to be cleared by arrest, although a physical arrest may not have occurred. In addition, according to program definitions, clearances that include both adult and juvenile offenders are classified as clearances for crimes committed by adults. Therefore, the juvenile clearance data are limited to those clearances involving juveniles only, and the figures in this publication should not be used to present a definitive picture of juvenile involvement in crime.

Of the clearances for violent crimes that were reported in the nation in 2020, 6.6 percent involved only juveniles. In the nation's cities, collectively, 6.6 percent of violent crime clearances also involved only juveniles, with juveniles in cities exclusively involved in 5.0 percent of murder clearances, 13.5 percent of rape clearances, 11.7 percent of robbery clearances, and 5.2 percent of aggravated assault clearances. Of the nation's city population groups and subsets, cities with under 10,000 inhabitants had the highest percentage of overall clearances for violent crime only involving juveniles (7.5 percent); cities with 500,000 to 999,999 inhabitants and cities with 1,000,000 or more inhabitants had the lowest percentages, 5.9 percent each. (Table 28)

Law enforcement agencies in metropolitan counties reported that 6.9 percent of their violent crime clearances—including 4.7 percent of their murder clearances, 16.5 percent of their rape clearances, 12.1 percent of their robbery clearances, and 5.3 percent of their aggravated assault clearances—involved only juveniles. Agencies in nonmetropolitan counties reported that 5.6 percent of their clearances for violent crime involved only juveniles, including 3.3 percent of their murder clearances, 17.0 percent of their rape clearances, 4.5 percent of their robbery clearances, and 4.2 percent of their aggravated assault clearances. In suburban areas, 7.1 percent of violent crimes, 4.8 percent of murders, 16.3 percent of rapes, 12.3 percent of robberies, and 5.6 percent of aggravated assaults involved only juveniles. (Table 28)

In 2020, 7.0 percent of clearances for property crime involved only juveniles. In cities collectively, 6.7 percent of the clearances for property crime, 6.8 percent of clearances for burglary, 5.9 percent of clearances for larceny-theft, 12.3 percent of clearances for motor vehicle theft, and 11.0 percent of clearances for arson involved juveniles only. Among the population groups and subsets labeled *city*, the percentages of clearances involving only juveniles for overall property crime ranged from a low of 5.6 percent in cities with 500,000 to 999,999 inhabitants to a high of 8.5 percent in cities with populations of 250,000 to 499,999 inhabitants. (Table 28)

Metropolitan counties reported that 8.6 percent of all property crime clearances, 8.3 percent of burglary clearances, 7.8 percent of larceny-theft clearances, 12.4 percent of motor vehicle theft clearances, and 14.4 percent of arson clearances in 2020 involved persons under 18 years of age. In nonmetropolitan counties, 6.3 percent of property crime clearances, 6.0 percent of burglary clearances, 5.6 percent of larceny-theft clearances, 8.5 percent of motor vehicle theft clearances, and 9.5 percent of arson clearances involved juveniles exclusively. In suburban areas, 15.0 percent of arson clearances involved only juveniles, as did 7.5 percent of property crimes, 8.3 percent of burglaries, 6.6 percent of larceny-thefts, and 12.3 percent of motor vehicle thefts. (Table 28)

Table 25. Number and Percent of Offenses Cleared by Arrest or Exceptional Means, by Population Group, 2020

(Number, percent.)

Population group	Violent crime	Murder and nonnegligent manslaughter	Rape[1]	Robbery	Aggravated assault	Property crime	Burglary	Larceny-theft	Motor vehicle theft	Arson[2]	Number of agencies	Estimated population, 2020
Total, All Agencies												
Offenses known	1,137,525	18,109	110,095	209,643	799,678	5,670,244	898,176	4,004,124	727,045	40,899	13,804	288,224,102
Percent cleared by arrest	41.7	54.4	30.6	28.8	46.4	14.6	14.0	15.1	12.3	21.5		
Total Cities												
Offenses known	902,091	14,168	80,482	183,590	623,851	4,528,049	677,169	3,236,517	582,325	32,038	9,871	193,856,641
Percent cleared by arrest	39.5	52.3	28.5	27.8	44.0	14.4	13.5	15.1	11.2	20.7		
Group I (250,000 and over)												
Offenses known	438,385	7,303	29,775	105,215	296,092	1,693,877	267,123	1,146,402	266,470	13,882	84	58,292,525
Percent cleared by arrest	32.3	47.3	25.6	23.8	35.7	9.2	10.8	8.9	8.7	14.0		
1,000,000 and over (Group I subset)												
Offenses known	166,327	2,008	10,794	43,885	109,640	595,381	87,910	409,536	92,926	5,009	10	24,452,783
Percent cleared by arrest	30.9	48.9	25.0	23.0	34.3	7.5	9.7	7.0	7.6	9.7		
500,000 to 999,999 (Group I subset)												
Offenses known	151,635	3,005	9,031	34,116	105,483	590,900	99,666	396,817	89,984	4,433	24	16,967,590
Percent cleared by arrest	33.2	44.9	28.2	24.1	36.3	9.3	10.9	8.7	9.4	16.7		
250,000 to 499,999 (Group I subset)												
Offenses known	120,423	2,290	9,950	27,214	80,969	507,596	79,547	340,049	83,560	4,440	50	16,872,152
Percent cleared by arrest	33.1	49.0	23.9	24.8	36.6	11.0	11.9	11.2	9.3	16.1		
Group II (100,000 to 249,999)												
Offenses known	147,671	2,482	13,834	29,726	101,629	799,322	117,152	564,511	112,380	5,279	218	31,572,750
Percent cleared by arrest	41.1	55.5	28.6	29.9	45.7	13.0	13.2	13.4	10.8	24.9		
Group III (50,000 to 99,999)												
Offenses known	111,246	1,534	11,399	21,076	77,237	674,088	93,809	496,226	79,971	4,082	459	32,114,069
Percent cleared by arrest	47.4	57.8	32.9	33.9	52.9	16.5	15.1	17.3	12.2	27.3		
Group IV (25,000 to 49,999)												
Offenses known	77,198	1,103	9,268	13,026	53,801	515,758	71,974	390,166	50,481	3,137	786	27,406,287
Percent cleared by arrest	46.3	58.0	29.8	34.2	51.9	18.9	15.3	20.2	13.7	24.2		
Group V (10,000 to 24,999)												
Offenses known	67,169	996	8,511	8,956	48,706	470,604	68,457	357,439	42,035	2,673	1,572	25,072,927
Percent cleared by arrest	49.4	62.3	29.6	35.9	55.1	21.8	16.8	23.4	16.3	26.4		
Group VI (under 10,000)												
Offenses known	60,422	750	7,695	5,591	46,386	374,400	58,654	281,773	30,988	2,985	6,752	19,398,083
Percent cleared by arrest	52.8	58.5	30.5	39.7	58.0	21.4	18.3	22.1	20.7	26.8		
Metropolitan Counties												
Offenses known	185,468	2,907	21,380	23,863	137,318	920,546	161,052	635,640	117,370	6,484	1,731	71,573,154
Percent cleared by arrest	50.3	61.8	37.2	35.4	54.6	15.5	15.6	15.3	15.7	23.7		
Nonmetropolitan Counties												
Offenses known	49,966	1,034	8,233	2,190	38,509	221,649	59,955	131,967	27,350	2,377	2,202	22,794,307
Percent cleared by arrest	50.8	62.1	34.3	37.8	54.8	15.1	15.2	13.6	20.7	26.2		
Suburban Areas[3]												
Offenses known	303,760	4,450	36,426	43,096	219,788	1,803,833	278,407	1,310,538	203,377	11,511	7,275	123,406,306
Percent cleared by arrest	50.1	60.7	34.4	35.7	55.3	17.5	15.9	18.2	15.1	24.2		

1 The figures shown in this column for the offense of rape were reported using only the revised Uniform Crime Reporting definition of rape.   2 Not all agencies submit reports for arson to the FBI. As a result, the number of reports the FBI uses to compute the percent of offenses cleared for arson is less than the number it uses to compute the percent of offenses cleared for all other offenses.   3 Suburban area includes law enforcement agencies in cities with less than 50,000 inhabitants and county law enforcement agencies that are within a Metropolitan Statistical Area. Suburban area excludes all metropolitan agencies associated with a principal city. The agencies associated with suburban areas also appear in other groups within this table.

Table 26. Number and Percent of Offenses Cleared by Arrest or Exceptional Means, by Region and Geographic Division, 2020

(Number, percent.)

Geographic region/division	Violent crime	Murder and nonnegligent manslaughter	Rape[1]	Robbery	Aggravated assault	Property crime	Burglary	Larceny-theft	Motor vehicle theft	Arson[2]	Number of agencies	Estimated population, 2020
Total, All Agencies												
Offenses known	1,137,525	18,109	110,095	209,643	799,678	5,670,244	898,176	4,004,124	727,045	40,899	13,804	288,224,102
Percent cleared by arrest	41.7	54.4	30.6	28.8	46.4	14.6	14.0	15.1	12.3	21.5		
Northeast												
Offenses known	123,273	1,565	10,848	27,926	82,934	558,820	68,059	439,212	48,870	2,679	2,292	43,704,953
Percent cleared by arrest	39.2	43.6	26.6	26.3	45.1	16.0	19.0	16.0	11.2	26.4		
New England												
Offenses known	34,377	379	4,043	5,857	24,098	179,469	22,908	136,619	18,811	1,131	931	14,743,475
Percent cleared by arrest	48.3	52.2	28.1	26.4	56.9	15.0	16.8	15.1	10.8	28.2		
Middle Atlantic												
Offenses known	88,896	1,186	6,805	22,069	58,836	379,351	45,151	302,593	30,059	1,548	1,361	28,961,478
Percent cleared by arrest	35.7	40.8	25.7	26.3	40.3	16.4	20.1	16.4	11.4	25.1		
Midwest												
Offenses known	201,425	3,576	23,421	29,893	144,535	952,938	152,605	675,934	116,919	7,480	3,690	51,461,147
Percent cleared by arrest	40.5	49.3	29.9	24.0	45.4	15.5	12.8	16.7	11.9	18.2		
East North Central												
Offenses known	121,108	2,330	14,355	18,701	85,722	509,744	83,724	363,241	58,443	4,336	1,755	30,943,029
Percent cleared by arrest	38.3	43.7	29.5	23.1	42.9	14.8	12.7	15.9	10.7	17.1		
West North Central												
Offenses known	80,317	1,246	9,066	11,192	58,813	443,194	68,881	312,693	58,476	3,144	1,935	20,518,118
Percent cleared by arrest	43.7	59.9	30.6	25.4	48.9	16.3	12.8	17.7	13.1	19.7		
South												
Offenses known	492,662	8,996	44,050	82,599	357,017	2,406,498	391,041	1,736,309	267,093	12,055	5,708	116,917,467
Percent cleared by arrest	40.2	55.9	32.4	28.1	43.6	15.6	14.6	15.9	15.0	22.4		
South Atlantic												
Offenses known	227,332	4,422	19,315	39,103	164,492	1,122,215	167,026	838,984	110,541	5,664	2,587	60,677,083
Percent cleared by arrest	45.0	59.3	40.7	35.0	47.5	17.9	18.7	17.8	17.4	27.2		
East South Central												
Offenses known	69,960	1,342	5,223	9,534	53,861	323,432	55,579	226,848	39,449	1,556	1,225	16,004,814
Percent cleared by arrest	41.0	48.4	38.0	26.1	43.7	18.7	16.2	19.0	20.6	23.4		
West South Central												
Offenses known	195,370	3,232	19,512	33,962	138,664	960,851	168,436	670,477	117,103	4,835	1,896	40,235,570
Percent cleared by arrest	34.5	54.5	22.6	20.6	39.0	11.9	9.9	12.5	10.9	16.4		
West												
Offenses known	320,165	3,972	31,776	69,225	215,192	1,751,988	286,471	1,152,669	294,163	18,685	2,114	76,140,535
Percent cleared by arrest	45.8	59.8	30.1	32.6	52.0	12.2	12.8	12.4	10.1	21.6		
Mountain												
Offenses known	104,878	1,289	12,872	16,426	74,291	555,272	83,777	387,633	79,898	3,964	891	23,944,023
Percent cleared by arrest	45.0	63.9	26.4	29.7	51.2	16.0	13.9	17.1	12.1	27.6		
Pacific												
Offenses known	215,287	2,683	18,904	52,799	140,901	1,196,716	202,694	765,036	214,265	14,721	1,223	52,196,512
Percent cleared by arrest	46.1	57.8	32.7	33.5	52.5	10.5	12.4	10.1	9.4	19.9		

1 The figures shown in this column for the offense of rape were reported using only the revised Uniform Crime Reporting definition of rape.   2 Not all agencies submit reports for arson to the FBI. As a result, the number of reports the FBI uses to compute the percent of offenses cleared for arson is less than the number it uses to compute the percent of offenses cleared for all other offenses.

Table 27. Number and Percent of Offenses Cleared by Arrest or Exceptional Means, Additional Information About Selected Offenses, by Population Group, 2020

(Number, percent.)

Population group	Rape[1] Rape by force	Rape[1] Assault to rape-attempts	Robbery Firearm	Robbery Knife or cutting instrument	Robbery Other weapon	Robbery Strong-arm	Aggravated assault Firearm	Aggravated assault Knife or cutting instrument	Aggravated assault Other weapon	Aggravated assault Hands, fists, feet, etc.
Total, All Agencies										
Offenses known	105,827	4,267	79,628	18,871	23,024	88,120	277,820	129,643	228,271	163,946
Percent cleared by arrest	30.5	34.9	21.6	31.5	27.6	28.4	27.4	51.9	46.0	55.1
Total Cities										
Offenses known	77,326	3,156	68,433	16,819	20,078	78,260	222,235	105,575	174,826	121,217
Percent cleared by arrest	28.3	34.6	21.6	31.4	27.3	28.4	25.8	51.6	45.5	55.0
Group I (250,000 and over)										
Offenses known	28,450	1,325	40,525	9,770	10,722	44,198	122,444	50,748	81,056	41,844
Percent cleared by arrest	25.2	33.7	19.6	27.5	24.1	24.6	22.1	46.3	38.8	45.0
1,000,000 and over (Group I subset)										
Offenses known	10,313	481	14,649	5,005	5,035	19,196	34,892	22,639	30,390	21,719
Percent cleared by arrest	24.5	35.8	18.6	27.7	24.8	24.8	21.7	44.1	36.6	41.3
500,000 to 999,999 (Group I subset)										
Offenses known	8,584	447	15,458	2,758	3,426	12,474	50,594	15,837	28,901	10,151
Percent cleared by arrest	27.7	37.4	19.5	27.2	23.1	27.1	22.9	49.7	41.8	48.7
250,000 to 499,999 (Group I subset)										
Offenses known	9,553	397	10,418	2,007	2,261	12,528	36,958	12,272	21,765	9,974
Percent cleared by arrest	23.8	27.2	21.2	27.8	23.9	21.9	21.3	45.9	37.8	49.3
Group II (100,000 to 249,999)										
Offenses known	13,286	548	11,049	2,688	3,472	12,517	36,981	17,794	28,299	18,555
Percent cleared by arrest	28.3	35.2	22.0	33.5	27.8	30.5	25.7	53.2	48.1	56.6
Group III (50,000 to 99,999)										
Offenses known	11,045	354	6,884	1,938	2,537	9,717	23,402	12,983	22,454	18,398
Percent cleared by arrest	32.7	40.4	24.9	36.5	32.8	33.1	30.0	55.7	52.2	62.4
Group IV (25,000 to 49,999)										
Offenses known	8,967	301	4,713	1,185	1,533	5,595	16,471	9,366	15,666	12,298
Percent cleared by arrest	29.7	32.6	25.6	38.2	29.0	34.9	31.4	56.3	51.6	57.1
Group V (10,000 to 24,999)										
Offenses known	8,253	258	3,352	820	1,102	3,682	13,577	7,994	14,455	12,680
Percent cleared by arrest	29.3	38.0	28.1	40.6	33.9	35.5	36.0	59.8	54.0	62.1
Group VI (under 10,000)										
Offenses known	7,325	370	1,910	418	712	2,551	9,360	6,690	12,896	17,442
Percent cleared by arrest	30.5	30.8	28.7	46.2	41.2	41.9	40.7	62.5	54.1	62.9
Metropolitan Counties										
Offenses known	20,549	831	10,243	1,888	2,583	9,149	44,797	19,529	41,627	31,365
Percent cleared by arrest	37.2	37.7	20.9	32.2	29.9	28.0	31.0	52.1	46.0	55.3
Nonmetropolitan Counties										
Offenses known	7,952	280	952	164	363	711	10,788	4,539	11,818	11,364
Percent cleared by arrest	34.4	30.4	30.3	40.9	27.5	36.8	44.3	59.2	52.9	55.5
Suburban Areas[3]										
Offenses known	35,069	1,357	17,100	3,540	4,921	17,535	66,324	33,105	66,516	53,845
Percent cleared by arrest	34.3	35.7	22.8	35.8	31.8	32.4	32.5	55.5	48.7	57.7

Table 27. Number and Percent of Offenses Cleared by Arrest or Exceptional Means, Additional Information About Selected Offenses, by Population Group, 2020—Continued

(Number, percent.)

Population group	Burglary			Motor vehicle theft			Arson[2]			Number of agencies	Estimated population, 2020
	Forcible entry	Unlawful entry	Attempted forcible entry	Autos	Trucks and buses	Other vehicles	Structure	Mobile	Other		
Total, All Agencies											
Offenses known	502,319	335,526	60,331	538,769	121,243	67,033	15,060	9,515	16,346	13,804	288,224,102
Percent cleared by arrest	12.9	15.8	13.9	13.1	10.3	9.4	25.6	10.6	24.0		
Total Cities											
Offenses known	381,252	248,627	47,290	437,444	97,640	47,241	11,753	7,038	13,269	9,871	193,856,641
Percent cleared by arrest	12.4	15.3	13.7	12.0	8.9	8.4	24.2	9.9	23.3		
Group I (250,000 and over)											
Offenses known	162,264	85,002	19,857	192,199	55,924	18,347	4,444	3,419	6,041	84	58,292,525
Percent cleared by arrest	10.1	12.0	11.7	9.5	7.0	6.2	17.6	6.8	15.4		
1,000,000 and over (Group I subset)											
Offenses known	56,840	24,614	6,456	54,021	31,425	7,480	1,138	834	3,037	10	24,452,783
Percent cleared by arrest	8.6	11.5	12.1	9.0	5.7	5.6	17.7	5.8	7.8		
500,000 to 999,999 (Group I subset)											
Offenses known	58,071	33,739	7,856	71,283	12,651	6,050	1,621	1,349	1,485	24	16,967,590
Percent cleared by arrest	10.4	11.7	11.1	9.7	9.3	6.2	17.4	7.9	23.9		
250,000 to 499,999 (Group I subset)											
Offenses known	47,353	26,649	5,545	66,895	11,848	4,817	1,685	1,236	1,519	50	16,872,152
Percent cleared by arrest	11.4	12.6	12.2	9.7	7.9	7.2	17.7	6.4	22.3		
Group II (100,000 to 249,999)											
Offenses known	65,213	43,493	8,446	86,569	16,449	9,362	1,877	1,184	2,218	218	31,572,750
Percent cleared by arrest	12.1	14.5	14.6	11.4	9.4	7.5	26.3	10.4	31.4		
Group III (50,000 to 99,999)											
Offenses known	50,788	36,841	6,180	61,181	11,614	7,176	1,531	844	1,707	459	32,114,069
Percent cleared by arrest	13.9	16.8	14.9	12.9	10.3	8.6	31.0	12.1	31.5		
Group IV (25,000 to 49,999)											
Offenses known	37,330	29,428	5,216	40,007	5,537	4,937	1,343	565	1,229	786	27,406,287
Percent cleared by arrest	14.4	16.7	14.9	14.2	13.0	10.0	27.0	13.6	26.0		
Group V (10,000 to 24,999)											
Offenses known	35,529	29,015	3,913	33,505	4,733	3,797	1,138	474	1,061	1,572	25,072,927
Percent cleared by arrest	15.4	18.6	15.9	17.1	13.8	12.1	30.2	15.2	27.4		
Group VI (under 10,000)											
Offenses known	30,128	24,848	3,678	23,983	3,383	3,622	1,420	552	1,013	6,752	19,398,083
Percent cleared by arrest	16.6	20.6	16.4	21.7	19.2	15.3	27.7	16.5	31.2		
Metropolitan Counties											
Offenses known	87,788	62,423	10,841	82,866	18,979	15,525	2,303	1,874	2,307	1,731	71,573,154
Percent cleared by arrest	14.3	17.6	14.9	16.5	15.7	11.2	30.1	11.4	27.4		
Nonmetropolitan Counties											
Offenses known	33,279	24,476	2,200	18,459	4,624	4,267	1,004	603	770	2,202	22,794,307
Percent cleared by arrest	14.8	16.0	13.7	22.9	17.7	14.5	31.5	16.7	26.8		
Suburban Areas[3]											
Offenses known	148,994	109,902	19,511	151,165	28,638	23,574	4,417	2,849	4,245	7,275	123,406,306
Percent cleared by arrest	14.6	17.9	14.8	15.7	14.8	11.1	29.5	12.1	26.8		

1 The figures shown in the rape column include only those reported by law enforcement agencies that used the revised Uniform Crime Reporting definition of rape.   2 Not all agencies submit reports for arson to the FBI. As a result, the number of reports the FBI uses to compute the percent of offenses cleared for arson is less than the number it uses to compute the percent of offenses cleared for all other offenses. Agencies must report arson clearances by detailed property classification as specified on the *Monthly Return of Arson Offenses Known to Law Enforcement* to be included in this table; therefore, clearances in this table may differ from other clearance tables.   3 Suburban area includes law enforcement agencies in cities with less than 50,000 inhabitants and county law enforcement agencies that are within a Metropolitan Statistical Area. Suburban area excludes all metropolitan agencies associated with a principal city. The agencies associated with suburban areas also appear in other groups within this table.

Table 28. Number of Offenses Cleared by Arrest or Exceptional Means and Percent Involving Persons Under 18 Years of Age, by Population Group, 2020

(Number, percent.)

Population group	Violent crime	Murder and nonnegligent manslaughter	Rape[1]	Robbery	Aggravated assault	Property crime	Burglary	Larceny-theft	Motor vehicle theft	Arson[2]	Number of agencies	Estimated population, 2020
Total, All Agencies												
Total clearances	474,611	9,855	33,738	60,287	370,731	826,856	126,029	602,711	89,322	8,794	13,804	288,224,102
Percent under 18 years	6.6	4.8	14.5	11.6	5.1	7.0	7.1	6.2	12.1	11.5		
Total Cities												
Total clearances	355,996	7,416	22,964	51,008	274,608	651,019	91,718	487,385	65,284	6,632	9,871	193,856,641
Percent under 18 years	6.6	5.0	13.5	11.7	5.2	6.7	6.8	5.9	12.3	11.0		
Group I (250,000 and over)												
Total clearances	141,721	3,453	7,622	25,075	105,571	155,565	28,830	101,489	23,305	1,941	84	58,292,525
Percent under 18 years	6.3	5.0	11.7	12.4	4.5	6.8	5.5	5.9	12.2	5.3		
1,000,000 and over (Group I subset)												
Total clearances	51,435	981	2,695	10,115	37,644	44,864	8,488	28,837	7,052	487	10	24,452,783
Percent under 18 years	5.9	4.6	10.0	12.4	3.9	5.9	4.0	5.8	8.7	3.3		
500,000 to 999,999 (Group I subset)												
Total clearances	50,379	1,350	2,546	8,222	38,261	54,732	10,890	34,614	8,489	739	24	16,967,590
Percent under 18 years	5.9	5.7	12.7	10.9	4.4	5.6	4.6	4.4	12.0	5.0		
250,000 to 499,999 (Group I subset)												
Total clearances	39,907	1,122	2,381	6,738	29,666	55,969	9,452	38,038	7,764	715	50	16,872,152
Percent under 18 years	7.4	4.6	12.6	14.1	5.5	8.5	7.9	7.3	15.7	7.0		
Group II (100,000 to 249,999)												
Total clearances	60,720	1,377	3,951	8,898	46,494	104,296	15,444	75,453	12,087	1,312	218	31,572,750
Percent under 18 years	6.3	5.2	13.4	10.2	5.0	7.0	6.4	6.2	12.6	8.8		
Group III (50,000 to 99,999)												
Total clearances	52,677	886	3,755	7,141	40,895	110,985	14,178	85,959	9,735	1,113	459	32,114,069
Percent under 18 years	7.0	4.2	13.8	11.3	5.7	7.1	6.8	6.4	12.6	14.2		
Group IV (25,000 to 49,999)												
Total clearances	35,780	640	2,765	4,459	27,916	97,475	11,044	78,768	6,904	759	786	27,406,287
Percent under 18 years	7.1	6.1	15.8	11.1	5.7	6.5	7.5	5.7	13.4	11.9		
Group V (10,000 to 24,999)												
Total clearances	33,177	621	2,521	3,214	26,821	102,596	11,490	83,547	6,852	707	1,572	25,072,927
Percent under 18 years	6.8	5.0	15.6	10.3	5.5	6.5	8.3	5.6	12.7	17.4		
Group VI (under 10,000)												
Total clearances	31,921	439	2,350	2,221	26,911	80,102	10,732	62,169	6,401	800	6,752	19,398,083
Percent under 18 years	7.5	3.6	14.3	14.5	6.3	6.5	8.7	5.7	10.3	17.3		
Metropolitan Counties												
Total clearances	93,218	1,797	7,953	8,452	75,016	142,444	25,178	97,355	18,372	1,539	1,731	71,573,154
Percent under 18 years	6.9	4.7	16.5	12.1	5.3	8.6	8.3	7.8	12.4	14.4		
Nonmetropolitan Counties												
Total clearances	25,397	642	2,821	827	21,107	33,393	9,133	17,971	5,666	623	2,202	22,794,307
Percent under 18 years	5.6	3.3	17.0	4.5	4.2	6.3	6.0	5.6	8.5	9.5		
Suburban Areas[3]												
Total clearances	152,082	2,703	12,513	15,402	121,464	316,055	44,358	238,281	30,629	2,787	7,275	123,406,306
Percent under 18 years	7.1	4.8	16.3	12.3	5.6	7.5	8.3	6.6	12.3	15.0		

1 The figures shown in this column for the offense of rape were reported using only the revised Uniform Crime Reporting definition of rape.   2 Not all agencies submit reports for arson to the FBI. As a result, the number of reports the FBI uses to compute the percent of offenses cleared for arson is less than the number it uses to compute the percent of offenses cleared for all other offenses.   3 Suburban area includes law enforcement agencies in cities with less than 50,000 inhabitants and county law enforcement agencies that are within a Metropolitan Statistical Area. Suburban area excludes all metropolitan agencies associated with a principal city. The agencies associated with suburban areas also appear in other groups within this table.

SECTION IV

PERSONS ARRESTED

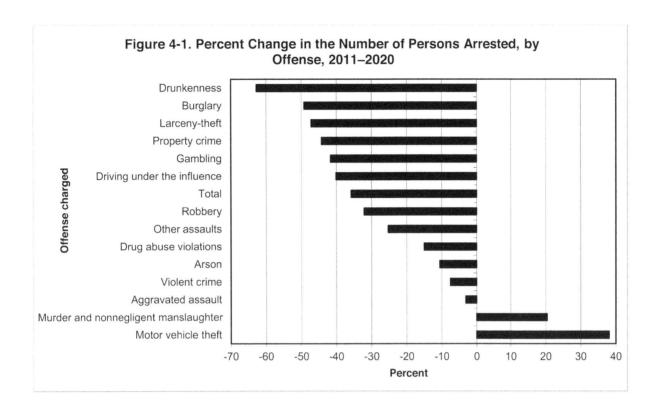

Figure 4-1. Percent Change in the Number of Persons Arrested, by Offense, 2011–2020

In the Uniform Crime Reporting (UCR) program, one arrest is counted for each separate instance in which an individual is arrested, cited, or summoned for criminal acts in Part I and Part II crimes. (See Appendix I for additional information concerning Part I and Part II crimes.) One person may be arrested multiple times during the year; as a result, the arrest figures in this section should not be taken as the total number of individuals arrested. Instead, it provides the number of *arrest occurrences* reported by law enforcement. Information regarding the UCR program's statistical methodology and table construction can be found in Appendix I.

Important Note: Rape Data

In 2013, the UCR Program initiated the collection of rape data under a revised definition and removed the term "forcible" from the offense name. The UCR Program now defines rape as follows:

Rape (revised definition): Penetration, no matter how slight, of the vagina or anus with any body part or object, or oral penetration by a sex organ of another person,

without the consent of the victim. (This includes the offenses of rape, sodomy, and sexual assault with an object as converted from data submitted via the National Incident-Based Reporting System.)

Rape (legacy definition): The carnal knowledge of a female forcibly and against her will. For tables within this publication that present data for 2019 only or provide a 2-year trend, the rape figures are an aggregate total of the data submitted based on both the legacy and revised UCR definitions. For 5- and 10-year trend tables, the rape figures for the previous year (2014 or 2009) are based on the legacy definition and the 2019 rape figures are an aggregate total based on both the legacy and revised definitions. For this reason, a percent change is not provided.

Data Collection: Juveniles

The UCR Program considers a juvenile to be an individual under 18 years of age regardless of state definition. The program does not collect data regarding police contact with a juvenile who has not committed an offense, nor does it collect data on situations in which police take a juvenile into custody for his or her protection, e.g., neglect cases.

National Volume, Trends, and Rates

VOLUME

The FBI estimated that an estimated 7,632,473 arrests occurred in 2020 for all offenses (except traffic violations). Of these arrests, 482,408 were for violent crimes, and 871,370 were for property crimes UCR does not collect data for traffic violations. Of the total violent crimes in 2020, aggravated assaults accounted for approximately 79.0 percent of the violent crime total, or 381,189 incidents. Robbery had the next highest proportion with 14.1 percent, or 67,903 incidents; followed by rape at 4.3 percent (20,872 incidents) and murder and non-negligent manslaughter, at 2.6 percent (12,444 incidents). Of the estimated arrests for property crimes in 2020, 629,024 (72.2 percent) were for larceny-theft, 149,352 (17.1 percent) were for burglary, 83,219 (9.6 percent) were for motor vehicle theft, and 9,775 (1.1 percent) were for arson. Outside of these categories, the most frequent identifiable arrests made in 2020 were for drug abuse violations (estimated at 1,155,610 arrests). These arrests comprised 15.1 percent of the total number of all arrests. (Table 29)

A comparison of arrest figures from 2019 to 2020 revealed a 22.3 percent decrease. This number, as well as any of the data involving the year 2020, should be interpreted with caution, given the effects of the COVID-19 pandemic on the United States. Arrests for violent crimes decreased 4.1 percent and arrests for property crimes decreased 21.0 percent over this time period. An examination of the 5-year and 10-year arrest trends showed that the total number of arrests in 2020 fell 26.4 percent from the 2016 total. Arrests for violent crimes showed a 4.8 percent decrease from 2016 to 2020 and property crimes showed a 33.5 percent decrease. In the 10-year trend data (2011 to 2020), the number of arrests decreased 35.8 percent. For violent crimes, the number of arrests fell 7.5 percent, while arrests for property crimes decreased 44.2 percent. (Tables 32, 34, and 36)

TRENDS

The number of adults arrested for violent crime (arrestees age 18 years and over) decreased 21.2 percent from 2019 to 2020, decreased 24.6 percent from 2016 to 2020, and decreased 31.3 percent from 2011 to 2020. The number of juveniles arrested for violent crime (arrestees under 18 years of age) decreased 26.2 percent from 2019 to 2020, decreased 47.8 percent from 2016 to 2020, and decreased 68.8 percent from 2011 to 2020. (Tables 32, 34, and 36)

The trend data for murder and nonnegligent manslaughter showed that the number of arrests for this offense increased 16.9 percent from 2019 to 2020, increased 10.1 percent from 2016 to 2020, and increased 20.4 percent from 2011 to 2020. The number of adults arrested for murder increased 17.3 percent from 2019 to 2020, increased 9.6 percent from 2016 to 2020, and rose 20.3 percent from 2011 to 2020. The number of juveniles arrested for murder increased 11.8 percent from 2019 to 2020, increased 16.3 percent from 2016 to 2020, and rose 21.3 percent from 2011 to 2020. (Tables 32, 34, and 36)

For rape, the trend data showed that arrests decreased 12.7 percent from 2019 to 2020, with adult arrests decreasing 9.7 percent and juvenile arrests falling 27.4 percent. The five-year data (2016 to 2020) shows arrests decreasing 8.9 percent overall, with adult arrests falling 7.6 percent and juvenile arrests decreasing 15.8 percent. The 10-year trend data percentages were not calculated due to the program changes in the classification of rape data. (Tables 32, 34, and 36)

For robbery, the data showed that arrests decreased 11.7 percent from 2019 to 2020, with adult arrests decreasing 8.6 percent and juvenile arrests falling 23.8 percent. The 5-year trend data showed that total robbery arrests fell 24.6 percent from 2016 to 2020; adult arrests decreased 23.7 percent and juvenile arrests dropped 28.7 percent during this period. The 10-year trend data showed that arrests fell 32.1 percent from 2011 to 2020, with adult arrests dropping 29.0 percent and juvenile arrests falling by 43.9 percent. (Tables 32, 34, and 36)

The aggravated assault trend data showed that the number of arrests for this offense fell 2.7 percent from 2019 to 2020, decreased 0.4 percent from 2016 to 2020, and fell 3.1 percent from 2011 to 2020. The number of adults arrested for aggravated assault fell 0.7 percent from 2019 to 2020, rose 1.7 percent from 2016 to 2020, and increased 1.5 percent from 2011 to 2020. The number of juveniles arrested for aggravated assault decreased 0.6 percent from 2019 to 2020, fell 28.7 percent from 2016 to 2020, and dropped 47.8 percent from 2011 to 2020. (Tables 32, 34, and 36)

The 2-year, 5-year, and 10-year trend data showed that the number of arrests for property crime decreased 21.0 percent from 2019 to 2020, decreased 33.5 percent from 2016 to 2020, and decreased 44.2 percent from 2011 to 2020. The number of adults arrested for property crime offenses (arrestees age 18 years and over) decreased 19.0 percent from 2019 to 2020, decreased 29.6 percent from 2016 to 2020, and decreased 35.6 percent from 2011 to 2020. The number of juveniles arrested for property crime (arrestees under 18 years of age) decreased 37.1 percent from 2019 to 2020, decreased 58.1 percent from

2016 to 2020, and decreased 76.6 percent from 2011 to 2020. (Tables 32, 34, and 36)

The trend data for burglary showed that the number of arrests for this offense decreased 11.7 percent from 2019 to 2020, decreased 27.7 percent from 2016 to 2020, and decreased 49.2 percent from 2011 to 2020. The number of adults arrested for burglary fell 9.8 percent from 2019 to 2020, fell 23.2 percent from 2016 to 2020, and decreased 42.4 percent from 2011 to 2020. The number of juveniles arrested for burglary decreased 25.3 percent from 2019 to 2020, decreased 52.3 percent from 2016 to 2020, and fell 75.1 percent from 2011 to 2020. (Tables 32, 34, and 36)

For larceny-theft, the 2-year trend data showed that arrests fell 25.2 percent from 2019 to 2020, with adult arrests decreasing 23.1 percent and juvenile arrests decreasing 44.4 percent. The 5-year trend data showed that total larceny-theft arrests decreased 37.7 percent from 2016 to 2020; adult arrests fell 33.7 percent, while juvenile arrests dropped by 64.3 percent during this period. The 10-year trend data showed that larceny-theft arrests fell 47.2 percent from 2011 to 2020, with adult arrests decreasing by

38.5 percent and juvenile arrests falling by 80.5 percent. (Tables 32, 34, and 36)

For motor vehicle theft, the 2-year trend data showed that arrests rose 1.0 percent from 2019 to 2020, with adult arrests increasing 3.2 percent and juvenile arrests decreasing 10.3 percent. The 5-year trend data showed that total motor vehicle theft arrests dropped 0.5 percent from 2016 to 2020; juvenile arrests fell 11.5 percent and adult arrests increased 1.7 percent during this period. The 10-year trend data showed that arrests rose 38.1 percent from 2011 to 2020, with adult arrests rising 48.0 percent and juvenile arrests dropping 1.0 percent. (Tables 32, 34, and 36)

The arson trend data showed that the number of arrests for this offense increased 14.3 percent from 2019 to 2020, rose 13.8 percent from 2016 to 2020, and fell 10.6 percent from 2011 to 2020. The number of adults arrested for arson rose 23.7 percent from 2019 to 2020, increased 36.6 percent from 2016 to 2020, and increased 40.9 percent from 2011 to 2020. The number of juveniles arrested for arson dropped 24.4 percent from 2019 to 2020, dropped

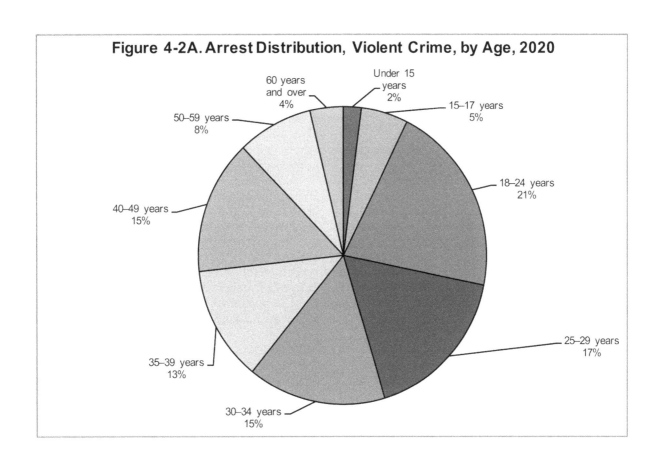

Figure 4-2A. Arrest Distribution, Violent Crime, by Age, 2020

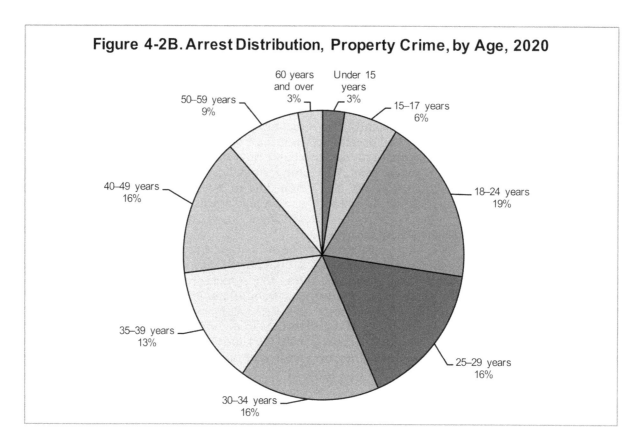

Figure 4-2B. Arrest Distribution, Property Crime, by Age, 2020

60 years and over 3%
Under 15 years 3%
15–17 years 6%
18–24 years 19%
25–29 years 16%
30–34 years 16%
35–39 years 13%
40–49 years 16%
50–59 years 9%

47.4 percent from 2016 to 2020, and dropped 73.8 percent from 2011 to 2020. (Tables 32, 34, and 36)

RATES

The rate of arrests was estimated at 2,312.2 arrests per 100,000 inhabitants in 2020. The arrest rate for violent crime was 147.9 arrests per 100,000 inhabitants, and the arrest rate for property crime was 267.3 arrests per 100,000 inhabitants. Law enforcement agencies throughout the nation reported arrest rates of 3.8 for murder, 6.3 for rape, 21.0 for robbery, and 116.8 for aggravated assault per 100,000 inhabitants in 2020. Law enforcement agencies throughout the nation reported arrest rates of 45.7 for burglary, 193.1 for larceny-theft, 25.5 for motor vehicle theft, and 3.0 for arson per 100,000 inhabitants in 2020. (Table 30)

By Age, Sex, and Race

Law enforcement agencies that contributed arrest data to the UCR program reported information on the age, sex, and race of the persons they arrested. According to the data for 2020, adults accounted for 94.4 percent of arrestees nationally. (Table 38)

A review of arrest data by age from 2019 to 2020 showed that arrests of adults decreased 21.2 percent during this period, with a 1.8 percent decrease in arrests for violent crime and a 19.0 percent drop in arrests for property crimes. The arrest total for juveniles (those under 18 years of age) decreased 36.7 percent from 2019 to 2020. Over the 2-year period, arrests of juveniles for violent crimes fell 26.2 percent; juvenile arrests for property crimes decreased 37.1 percent. (Table 36)

By sex, males accounted for 73.5 percent of all persons arrested in 2020. Males represented 79.2 percent of arrestees for violent crime, 87.5 percent of arrestees for murder, 97.2 percent of arrestees for rape, 84.8 percent for robbery, and 76.9 percent for aggravated assault. Females accounted for 20.8 percent of violent crime arrestees, 12.5 percent of murder arrestees, 2.8 percent of rape arrestees, 15.2 percent of robbery arrestees, and 23.1 percent of aggravated assault arrestees. (Table 42)

Most arrestees for property crime in 2020 (94.4 percent) were over 18 years of age. By sex, males accounted for 65.8 percent of arrestees for property crime, 80.8 percent of arrestees for burglary, 60.5 percent of arrestees for larceny-theft, 77.8 percent of arrestees for motor vehicle theft, and 79.0 percent of arrestees for arson. Females accounted for 34.2 percent of property crime arrestees. Of the four property crimes, larceny-theft had the highest proportion of female arrestees at 39.5 percent. (Tables 38 and 42)

In 2020, 70.0 percent of all persons arrested were White, 26.0 percent were Black, and the remaining 4.0 percent were of other races (American Indian or Alaskan Native, Asian, and Native Hawaiian or Pacific Islander). Of all arrestees for violent crimes, 60.1 percent were White, 35.5 percent were Black, and 4.4 percent were of other races. For murder, 46.0 percent of arrestees were White, 51.0 percent were Black, and 3.0 percent were of other races. For rape, 70.6 percent of arrestees were White, 25.4 percent were Black, and 4.0 percent of arrestees were of other races. For robbery, 47.6 percent of arrestees were White, 49.3 percent of arrestees were Black, and 3.1 percent of arrestees were of other races. For aggravated assault, 62.3 percent of arrestees were White, 33.1 percent of arrestees were Black, and 4.6 percent were of other races. (Table 43)

Of all arrestees for property crimes in 2020, 68.4 percent were White, 28.2 percent were Black, and 3.4 percent were of other races. For burglary, 69.4 percent of arrestees were White, 27.6 percent were Black, and 3.0 percent were of other races. For larceny-theft, 67.9 percent of arrestees were White, 28.7 percent were Black, and 3.5 percent were of other races. For motor vehicle theft, 69.9 percent of arrestees were White, 26.4 percent of arrestees were Black, and 3.9 percent were of other races. For arson, 72.8 percent of arrestees were White, 22.2 percent were Black, and 4.9 percent were of other races. (Table 43)

Outside of the scope of violent and property crimes, White adults were most commonly arrested for drug abuse violations (572,858 arrests) and driving under the influence (417,593 arrests). Black adults were most frequently arrested for drug abuse violations (195,695 arrests) and other assaults (190,453 arrests). (Table 43)

Regional Arrest Rates

The UCR program divides the United States into four regions: the Northeast, the Midwest, the South, and the West. (Appendix III provides more information about the regions.) Law enforcement agencies in the Northeast had an overall arrest rate of 2,476.8 arrests per 100,000 inhabitants, below the national rate (3,011.0 arrests per 100,000 inhabitants). In this region, the arrest rate for violent crimes was 104.3 arrests per 100,000 inhabitants, and for property crime, the arrest rate was 296.2 arrests per 100,000 inhabitants. In the Midwest, law enforcement agencies reported an arrest rate of 2,973.1 arrests per 100,000 inhabitants. The arrest rate for violent crimes was 128.0 and the arrest rate for property crime was 355.3. Law enforcement agencies in the South, the nation's most populous region, reported an arrest rate of 3,217.8 per 100,000 inhabitants. Arrests for violent crime occurred at a rate of 140.3 arrests per 100,000 residents, and for property crime, the arrest rate was 375.2 arrests per 100,000 inhabitants. In the West, law enforcement agencies reported an overall arrest rate of 3,075.1 arrests

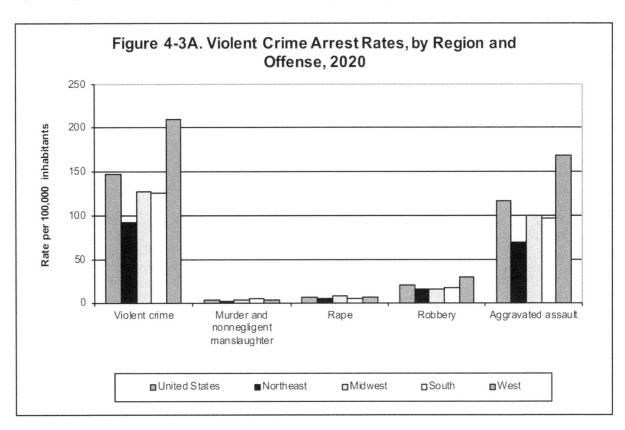

Figure 4-3A. Violent Crime Arrest Rates, by Region and Offense, 2020

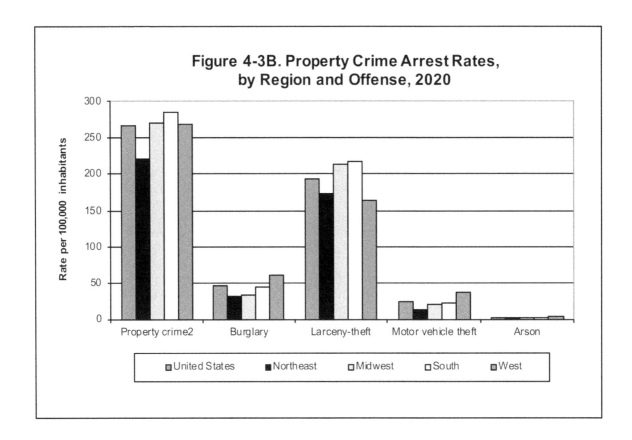

Figure 4-3B. Property Crime Arrest Rates, by Region and Offense, 2020

per 100,000 inhabitants. The region's violent crime arrest rate was 217.2, the highest of the regions, while its property crime arrest rate was 324.5. (Table 30)

The regional murder arrest rates (per 100,000 inhabitants) were 1.9 in the Northeast, 3.7 in the Midwest, 4.6 in the South, and 3.8 in the West. For rape, the regional arrest rates were 5.4 in the Northeast, 7.7 in the Midwest, 5.8 in the South, and 6.4 in the West. Regional arrest rates for robbery were 15.5 in the Northeast, 15.2 in the Midwest, 18.1 in the South, and 30.1 in the West. For aggravated assault, the regional arrest rates were 70.0 in the Northeast, 100.3 in the Midwest, 97.1 in the South, and 169.0 in the West. (Table 30)

The regional burglary arrest rates (per 100,000 inhabitants) were 32.3 in the Northeast, 33.7 in the Midwest, 44.3 in the South, and 60.5 in the West. For larceny-theft, the regional arrest rates were 173.2 in the Northeast, 213.2 in the Midwest, 216.2 in the South, and 164.7 in the West. Regional arrest rates for motor vehicle theft were 12.9 in the Northeast, 20.2 in the Midwest, 22.8 in the South, and 37.3 in the West. For arson, the regional arrest rates were 2.0 in the Northeast, 2.2 in the Midwest, 2.1 in the South, and 4.9 in the West. (Table 30)

Population Groups: Trends and Rates

The national UCR program aggregates data by various population groups, which include cities, metropolitan counties, and nonmetropolitan counties. Definitions of these groups can be found in Appendix III. The total number of arrests in U.S. cities fell 22.2 percent from 2019 to 2020. The number of arrests for violent crimes fell 4.5 percent and arrests for property crimes decreased 21.5 percent during the 2-year time frame. (Table 44)

In 2020, law enforcement agencies in cities collectively recorded an arrest rate of 2,409.4 arrests per 100,000 inhabitants. The nation's smallest cities, those with fewer than 10,000 inhabitants, had the highest arrest rate among the city population groups with 3,538.0 arrests per 100,000 inhabitants. Law enforcement agencies in cities with 250,000 or more inhabitants recorded the lowest rate, 2,683.8. In the nation's metropolitan counties, law enforcement agencies reported an arrest rate of 1,963.5 per 100,000 inhabitants. Agencies in nonmetropolitan counties reported an arrest rate of 2,414.1, and agencies in suburban areas reported an arrest rate of 2,086.9. (Table 31)

By population group, law enforcement agencies in the nation's cities collectively reported 167.1 violent crime arrests per 100,000 inhabitants in 2020. In the city population groups, cities with 250,000 or more inhabitants reported the highest violent crime arrest rate (224.8) and cities with 25,000 to 49,999 inhabitants reported the lowest violent crime arrest rate (113.9). Cities reported an overall murder arrest rate of 4.1 per 100,000 inhabitants; cities with 250,000 or more inhabitants had the highest murder arrest rate (6.5) and cities with 25,000 to 49,999 inhabitants had the lowest murder arrest rate (2.3). The collective city rape arrest rate was 6.5 per 100,000 inhabitants, with the highest rate in cities with 250,000 or more inhabitants (7.3) and the lowest rate in cities with 25,000 to 49,999 inhabitants (5.4). The overall robbery arrest rate for cities was 26.0 per 100,000 inhabitants; cities with 250,000 or more inhabitants had the highest robbery arrest rate (41.9) and cities with fewer than 10,000 inhabitants had the lowest robbery arrest rate (12.7). For aggravated assault, the collective city arrest rate was 130.5 per 100,000 inhabitants, with the greatest arrest rate in cities with 250,000 or more inhabitants (169.2) and the lowest arrest rate in cities with 25,000 to 49,999 inhabitants (89.1). (Table 31)

Agencies in metropolitan counties reported a violent crime arrest rate of 108.1 per 100,000 inhabitants, with arrest rates of 3.1 for murder, 5.5 for rape, 10.8 for robbery, and 88.8 for aggravated assault. Agencies in nonmetropolitan counties reported arrest rates of 91.1 for violent crime, 3.4 for murder, 5.2 for rape, 12.4 for robbery, and 84.0 for aggravated assault. Agencies in suburban areas reported arrest rates of 104.1 for violent crime, 2.4 for murder, 5.2 for rape, 12.4 for robbery, and 84.0 for aggravated assault. (Table 31)

By population group, law enforcement agencies in the nation's cities collectively reported 316.7 property crime arrests per 100,000 inhabitants in 2020. In the city population groups, cities with less than 10,000 inhabitants reported the highest property crime arrest rate (379.2) and cities with 250,000 or more inhabitants reported the lowest property crime arrest rate (257.6). Cities reported an overall burglary arrest rate of 50.5 per 100,000 inhabitants; cities with 100,000 to 249,999 inhabitants had the highest burglary arrest rate (55.1) and cities with 25,000 to 49,999 inhabitants had the lowest burglary arrest rate (44.2). The collective city larceny-theft arrest rate was 234.7 per 100,000 inhabitants, with the highest rate in cities with 10,000 to 24,999 inhabitants (316.5) and the lowest rate in cities with 250,000 or more inhabitants (163.9). The overall motor vehicle theft arrest rate for cities was 28.2 per 100,000 inhabitants; cities with 250,000 or more inhabitants had the highest motor vehicle theft arrest rate (35.3), and cities with 25,000 to 49,999 inhabitants had the lowest motor vehicle theft arrest rate (19.9). For arson, the collective city arrest rate was 3.4 per 100,000 inhabitants, with the greatest arrest rate in cities with 100,000 to 249,999 inhabitants (3.9) and the lowest arrest rate in cities with 25,000 to 49,999 inhabitants (2.7). (Table 31)

Agencies in metropolitan counties reported a property crime arrest rate of 162.4 per 100,000 inhabitants, with arrest rates of 33.3 for burglary, 107.6 for larceny-theft, 19.4 for motor vehicle theft, and 2.1 for arson. Agencies in nonmetropolitan counties reported arrest rates of 127.8 for property crime, 37.8 for burglary, 68.6 for larceny-theft, 19.0 for motor vehicle theft, and 2.4 for arson. Agencies in suburban areas reported arrest rates of 232.6 for property crime, 35.9 for burglary, 175.3 for larceny-theft, 19.2 for motor vehicle theft, and 2.2 for arson. (Table 31)

In suburban areas, the rates per 100,000 inhabitants for violent crime and property crime were 113.4 and 305.6, respectively. The rate for murder was 2.3 for rape, 6.3; for robbery, 16.0; and for aggravated assault, 88.7. Specific property crime rates included 41.9 for burglary, 241.5 for larceny-theft, 20.0 for motor vehicle theft, and 2.3 for arson. (Table 31)

Community Types

In 2020, law enforcement agencies in the nation's cities reported that 93.8 percent of arrests in their jurisdictions were of adults and 6.2 percent of arrests were of juveniles. Adults accounted for 92.3 percent of arrestees for violent crimes, while juveniles accounted for 7.7 percent of these arrests. Adults made up 91.3 percent of the arrestees for property crimes, and juveniles accounted for the remaining 8.7 percent. Of all arrests in the nation's cities in 2020, 25.9 percent were of individuals under 25 years of age. In metropolitan counties, 23.4 percent of arrests were of individuals under 25 years of age. In nonmetropolitan counties, 21.7 percent of persons arrested were of individuals under 25 years of age, and in suburban areas, 25.4 percent of arrestees were under 25 years old. (Tables 46, 47, 53, 59, and 65)

Males accounted for 73.3 percent and females accounted for 26.7 percent of arrestees in the nation's cities in 2020. In metropolitan counties, males comprised 74.3 percent of arrestees; in nonmetropolitan counties, males represented 73.8 percent of all arrestees; and in suburban areas, males comprised 73.3 percent of arrestees. (Tables 48, 54, 60, and 66)

By race, 67.6 percent of arrestees in the nation's cities in 2020 were White, 28.1 percent were Black, and 4.3 percent were of other races (American Indian or Alaska Native and Asian or Pacific Islander). Whites accounted for 73.9 percent of arrestees in metropolitan counties in 2020, Blacks made up 24.0 percent of arrestees, and persons of other races made up 2.1 percent of the total. In nonmetropolitan counties, Whites made up 82.2 percent of arrestees, Blacks accounted for 12.4 percent of arrestees, and other races made up 5.4 percent of the total. In suburban areas, Whites made up 73.4 percent of arrestees, Blacks accounted for 24.2 percent of arrestees, and other races made up 2.3 percent of the total. (Tables 49, 55, 61, and 67)

Table 29. Estimated Number of Arrests, 2020

(Number.)

Offense	Arrests
Total[1]	7,632,473
Violent crime[2]	482,408
Murder and nonnegligent manslaughter	12,444
Rape[3]	20,872
Robbery	67,903
Aggravated assault	381,189
Property crime[2]	871,370
Burglary	149,352
Larceny-theft	629,024
Motor vehicle theft	83,219
Arson	9,775
Other assaults	906,980
Forgery and counterfeiting	32,499
Fraud	79,518
Embezzlement	9,393
Stolen property; buying, receiving, possessing	88,316
Vandalism	173,774
Weapons; carrying, possessing, etc.	166,197
Prostitution and commercialized vice	16,770
Sex offenses (except forcible rape and prostitution)	31,793
Drug abuse violations	1,155,610
Gambling	1,625
Offenses against the family and children	59,396
Driving under the influence	778,906
Liquor laws	104,201
Drunkenness	194,249
Disorderly conduct	225,804
Vagrancy	13,653
All other offenses (except traffic)	2,228,332
Suspicion	363
Curfew and loitering law violations	11,679

1Does not include suspicion. 2Violent crimes are offenses of murder and nonnegligent manslaughter, rape, robbery, and aggravated assault. Property crimes are offenses of burglary, larceny-theft, motor vehicle theft, and arson. 3 The rape figures in this table are an aggregate total of the data submitted using both the revised and legacy Uniform Crime Reporting definitions.

Table 30. Number and Rate of Arrests, by Geographic Region, 2020

(Number, rate per 100,000 inhabitants.)

Offense charged	United States total (10,466 agencies; population 228,864,358)		Northeast (2,015 agencies; population 32,300,146)		Midwest (2,844 agencies; population 44,977,955)		South (3,791 agencies; population 78,729,908)		West (1,816 agencies; population 72,856,349)	
	Total	Rate	Total	Rate	Total	Rate	Total	Rate	Total	Rate
Total[1]	5,291,886	2,312.2	565,777	1,751.6	1,052,926	2,341.0	1,895,649	2,407.8	1,777,534	2,439.8
Violent crime[2]	338,443	147.9	29,952	92.7	57,087	126.9	98,867	125.6	152,537	209.4
Murder and nonnegligent manslaughter	8,701	3.8	609	1.9	1,684	3.7	3,606	4.6	2,802	3.8
Rape[3]	14,462	6.3	1,739	5.4	3,452	7.7	4,574	5.8	4,697	6.4
Robbery	48,035	21.0	5,008	15.5	6,850	15.2	14,277	18.1	21,900	30.1
Aggravated assault	267,245	116.8	22,596	70.0	45,101	100.3	76,410	97.1	123,138	169.0
Property crime[2]	611,731	267.3	71,184	220.4	121,082	269.2	224,668	285.4	194,797	267.4
Burglary	104,535	45.7	10,424	32.3	15,139	33.7	34,876	44.3	44,096	60.5
Larceny-theft	442,016	193.1	55,952	173.2	95,879	213.2	170,187	216.2	119,998	164.7
Motor vehicle theft	58,326	25.5	4,156	12.9	9,078	20.2	17,945	22.8	27,147	37.3
Arson	6,854	3.0	652	2.0	986	2.2	1,660	2.1	3,556	4.9
Other assaults	633,704	276.9	81,111	251.1	134,078	298.1	230,240	292.4	188,275	258.4
Forgery and counterfeiting	22,559	9.9	2,903	9.0	4,406	9.8	9,278	11.8	5,972	8.2
Fraud	54,756	23.9	5,680	17.6	12,259	27.3	23,234	29.5	13,583	18.6
Embezzlement	6,592	2.9	411	1.3	1,411	3.1	3,192	4.1	1,578	2.2
Stolen property; buying, receiving, possessing	61,868	27.0	6,679	20.7	12,453	27.7	18,839	23.9	23,897	32.8
Vandalism	121,403	53.0	19,369	60.0	22,704	50.5	29,776	37.8	49,554	68.0
Weapons; carrying, possessing, etc.	115,832	50.6	8,927	27.6	27,124	60.3	36,955	46.9	42,826	58.8
Prostitution and commercialized vice	11,754	5.1	688	2.1	791	1.8	2,849	3.6	7,426	10.2
Sex offenses (except forcible rape and prostitution)	22,065	9.6	2,748	8.5	3,495	7.8	4,483	5.7	11,339	15.6
Drug abuse violations	801,546	350.2	91,969	284.7	131,965	293.4	302,931	384.8	274,681	377.0
Gambling	1,191	0.5	121	0.4	39	0.1	316	0.4	715	1.0
Offenses against the family and children	40,498	17.7	6,342	19.6	7,891	17.5	15,779	20.0	10,486	14.4
Driving under the influence	531,846	232.4	55,264	171.1	118,960	264.5	162,960	207.0	194,662	267.2
Liquor laws	70,875	31.0	4,657	14.4	28,061	62.4	16,554	21.0	21,603	29.7
Drunkenness	135,744	59.3	3,287	10.2	13,518	30.1	77,483	98.4	41,456	56.9
Disorderly conduct	156,502	68.4	24,078	74.5	55,086	122.5	41,543	52.8	35,795	49.1
Vagrancy	9,795	4.3	453	1.4	1,626	3.6	2,744	3.5	4,972	6.8
All other offenses (except traffic)	1,534,972	670.7	149,693	463.4	296,119	658.4	590,122	749.6	499,038	685.0
Suspicion	238	0.1	57	0.2	18	*	17	*	146	0.2
Curfew and loitering law violations	8,210	3.6	261	0.8	2,771	6.2	2,836	3.6	2,342	3.2

* = Less than one-tenth of 1 percent.
1 Does not include suspicion.   2 Violent crimes are offenses of murder and nonnegligent manslaughter, rape, robbery, and aggravated assault. Property crimes are offenses of burglary, larceny-theft, motor vehicle theft, and arson.   3 The rape figures in this table are aggregate totals of the data submitted based on both the legacy and revised Uniform Crime Reporting definitions.

Table 31. Number and Rate of Arrests, by Population Group, 2020

(Number, rate per 100,000 inhabitants.)

Offense charged	Total (10,466 agencies; population 228,864,358)		Total cities (7,634 cities; population 159,832,632)		Group I (72 cities, 250,000 and over; population 44,271,326)		Group II (189 cities, 100,000 to 249,999; population 27,356,047)		Group III (398 cities, 50,000 to 99,999; population 27,901,884)	
	Total	Rate	Total	Rate	Total	Rate	Total	Rate	Total	Rate
Total[2]	5,291,886	2,312.2	3,851,077	2,409.4	924,243	2,087.7	653,477	2,388.8	638,180	2,287.2
Violent crime[3]	338,443	147.9	267,047	167.1	99,537	224.8	52,274	191.1	43,245	155.0
Murder and nonnegligent manslaughter	8,701	3.8	6,510	4.1	2,877	6.5	1,354	4.9	828	3.0
Rape[4]	14,462	6.3	10,360	6.5	3,214	7.3	1,767	6.5	1,699	6.1
Robbery	48,035	21.0	41,569	26.0	18,541	41.9	7,707	28.2	6,468	23.2
Aggravated assault	267,245	116.8	208,608	130.5	74,905	169.2	41,446	151.5	34,250	122.8
Property crime[3]	611,731	267.3	506,199	316.7	114,060	257.6	85,923	314.1	87,236	312.7
Burglary	104,535	45.7	80,714	50.5	24,305	54.9	15,073	55.1	13,191	47.3
Larceny-theft	442,016	193.1	375,128	234.7	72,545	163.9	60,638	221.7	66,049	236.7
Motor vehicle theft	58,326	25.5	44,997	28.2	15,633	35.3	9,138	33.4	7,094	25.4
Arson	6,854	3.0	5,360	3.4	1,577	3.6	1,074	3.9	902	3.2
Other assaults	633,704	276.9	490,395	306.8	140,917	318.3	86,010	314.4	82,501	295.7
Forgery and counterfeiting	22,559	9.9	17,093	10.7	2,872	6.5	2,933	10.7	3,137	11.2
Fraud	54,756	23.9	40,644	25.4	7,754	17.5	5,888	21.5	6,964	25.0
Embezzlement	6,592	2.9	5,322	3.3	1,515	3.4	794	2.9	981	3.5
Stolen property; buying, receiving, possessing	61,868	27.0	46,638	29.2	14,083	31.8	8,560	31.3	8,596	30.8
Vandalism	121,403	53.0	96,164	60.2	27,373	61.8	16,463	60.2	16,242	58.2
Weapons; carrying, possessing, etc.	115,832	50.6	88,908	55.6	35,855	81.0	15,984	58.4	12,559	45.0
Prostitution and commercialized vice	11,754	5.1	10,617	6.6	7,381	16.7	1,651	6.0	712	2.6
Sex offenses (except forcible rape and prostitution)	22,065	9.6	16,162	10.1	5,040	11.4	2,780	10.2	2,818	10.1
Drug abuse violations	801,546	350.2	561,935	351.6	112,526	254.2	103,839	379.6	101,925	365.3
Gambling	1,191	0.5	861	0.5	322	0.7	236	0.9	177	0.6
Offenses against the family and children	40,498	17.7	26,519	16.6	6,291	14.2	3,527	12.9	3,386	12.1
Driving under the influence	531,846	232.4	311,168	194.7	66,656	150.6	46,421	169.7	48,732	174.7
Liquor laws	70,875	31.0	53,701	33.6	6,728	15.2	6,517	23.8	6,470	23.2
Drunkenness	135,744	59.3	115,065	72.0	16,215	36.6	23,564	86.1	19,891	71.3
Disorderly conduct	156,502	68.4	128,297	80.3	22,438	50.7	19,143	70.0	19,679	70.5
Vagrancy	9,795	4.3	8,813	5.5	2,742	6.2	2,705	9.9	1,188	4.3
All other offenses (except traffic)	1,534,972	670.7	1,052,267	658.4	232,421	525.0	167,283	611.5	170,432	610.8
Suspicion	238	0.1	200	0.1	3	*	0	0.0	12	*
Curfew and loitering law violations	8,210	3.6	7,262	4.5	1,517	3.4	982	3.6	1,309	4.7

Table 31. Number and Rate of Arrests, by Population Group, 2020—Continued

(Number, rate per 100,000 inhabitants.)

Offense charged	Group IV (664 cities, 25,000 to 49,999; population 23,023,304)		Group V (1,351 cities, 10,000 to 24,999; population 21,468,840)		Group VI (4,960 cities, under 10,000; population 15,811,231)		Metropolitan counties (1,195 agencies; population 50,082,964)		Nonmetropolitan counties (1,637 agencies; population 18,948,762)		Suburban areas[1] (5,475 agencies; population 94,124,752)	
	Total	Rate	Total	Rate	Total	Rate	Total	Rate	Total	Rate	Total	Rate
Total[2]	517,766	2,248.9	558,011	2,599.2	559,400	3,538.0	983,370	1,963.5	457,439	2,414.1	1,964,322	2,086.9
Violent crime[3]	26,233	113.9	24,695	115.0	21,063	133.2	54,143	108.1	17,253	91.1	97,976	104.1
Murder and nonnegligent manslaughter	537	2.3	532	2.5	382	2.4	1,554	3.1	637	3.4	2,282	2.4
Rape[4]	1,251	5.4	1,305	6.1	1,124	7.1	2,733	5.5	1,369	7.2	4,929	5.2
Robbery	3,936	17.1	2,902	13.5	2,015	12.7	5,390	10.8	1,076	5.7	11,687	12.4
Aggravated assault	20,509	89.1	19,956	93.0	17,542	110.9	44,466	88.8	14,171	74.8	79,078	84.0
Property crime[3]	76,071	330.4	82,959	386.4	59,950	379.2	81,314	162.4	24,218	127.8	218,927	232.6
Burglary	10,173	44.2	9,834	45.8	8,138	51.5	16,654	33.3	7,167	37.8	33,777	35.9
Larceny-theft	60,701	263.7	67,948	316.5	47,247	298.8	53,892	107.6	12,996	68.6	164,967	175.3
Motor vehicle theft	4,575	19.9	4,553	21.2	4,004	25.3	9,729	19.4	3,600	19.0	18,095	19.2
Arson	622	2.7	624	2.9	561	3.5	1,039	2.1	455	2.4	2,088	2.2
Other assaults	63,697	276.7	62,775	292.4	54,495	344.7	102,954	205.6	40,355	213.0	212,497	225.8
Forgery and counterfeiting	2,562	11.1	2,627	12.2	2,962	18.7	4,244	8.5	1,222	6.4	9,273	9.9
Fraud	6,085	26.4	6,056	28.2	7,897	49.9	10,675	21.3	3,437	18.1	23,240	24.7
Embezzlement	850	3.7	696	3.2	486	3.1	979	2.0	291	1.5	2,275	2.4
Stolen property; buying, receiving, possessing	6,018	26.1	5,412	25.2	3,969	25.1	11,739	23.4	3,491	18.4	22,898	24.3
Vandalism	12,267	53.3	12,616	58.8	11,203	70.9	19,020	38.0	6,219	32.8	39,983	42.5
Weapons; carrying, possessing, etc.	8,707	37.8	8,244	38.4	7,559	47.8	20,177	40.3	6,747	35.6	36,425	38.7
Prostitution and commercialized vice	468	2.0	284	1.3	121	0.8	1,054	2.1	83	0.4	1,689	1.8
Sex offenses (except forcible rape and prostitution)	1,974	8.6	1,840	8.6	1,710	10.8	4,333	8.7	1,570	8.3	7,889	8.4
Drug abuse violations	77,694	337.5	81,110	377.8	84,841	536.6	162,238	323.9	77,373	408.3	317,731	337.6
Gambling	32	0.1	59	0.3	35	0.2	273	0.5	57	0.3	359	0.4
Offenses against the family and children	3,781	16.4	4,064	18.9	5,470	34.6	8,915	17.8	5,064	26.7	15,426	16.4
Driving under the influence	44,414	192.9	51,461	239.7	53,484	338.3	140,244	280.0	80,434	424.5	235,930	250.7
Liquor laws	7,642	33.2	10,203	47.5	16,141	102.1	9,189	18.3	7,985	42.1	27,056	28.7
Drunkenness	14,789	64.2	15,990	74.5	24,616	155.7	14,141	28.2	6,538	34.5	39,762	42.2
Disorderly conduct	19,059	82.8	22,277	103.8	25,701	162.5	18,076	36.1	10,129	53.5	55,216	58.7
Vagrancy	892	3.9	659	3.1	627	4.0	803	1.6	179	0.9	2,126	2.3
All other offenses (except traffic)	143,434	623.0	162,716	757.9	175,981	1,113.0	318,146	635.2	164,559	868.4	594,985	632.1
Suspicion	16	0.1	54	0.3	115	0.7	3	*	35	0.2	122	0.1
Curfew and loitering law violations	1,097	4.8	1,268	5.9	1,089	6.9	713	1.4	235	1.2	2,659	2.8

* = Less than one-tenth of one percent.
1 Suburban areas include law enforcement agencies in cities with less than 50,000 inhabitants and county law enforcement agencies that are within a Metropolitan Statistical Area. Suburban areas exclude all metropolitan agencies associated with a principal city. The agencies associated with suburban areas also appear in other groups within this table.   2 Does not include suspicion.   3 Violent crimes are offenses of murder and nonnegligent manslaughter, forcible rape, robbery, and aggravated assault. Property crimes are offenses of burglary, larceny-theft, motor vehicle theft, and arson.   4 The rape figures in this table are aggregate totals of the data submitted based on both the legacy and revised Uniform Crime Reporting definitions.

Table 32. Ten-Year Arrest Trends, 2011 and 2020

(Number, percent change; 8,708 agencies; 2020 estimated population 180,606,800; 2011 estimated population 170,682,854.)

Offense charged	Number of persons arrested								
	Total, all ages			Under 18 years of age			18 years of age and over		
	2011	2020	Percent change	2011	2020	Percent change	2011	2020	Percent change
Total[1]	6,440,166	4,136,575	-35.8	768,471	240,121	-68.8	5,671,695	3,896,454	-31.3
Violent crime[2]	267,941	247,966	-7.5	31,103	17,730	-43.0	236,838	230,236	-2.8
Murder and nonnegligent manslaughter	5,095	6,135	+20.4	376	456	+21.3	4,719	5,679	+20.3
Rape[3]	10,230	11,006	NA	1,557	1,661		8,673	9,345	NA
Robbery	48,155	32,700	-32.1	9,965	5,595	-43.9	38,190	27,105	-29.0
Aggravated assault	204,461	198,125	-3.1	19,205	10,018	-47.8	185,256	188,107	+1.5
Property crime[2]	878,975	490,655	-44.2	183,084	42,776	-76.6	695,891	447,879	-35.6
Burglary	160,004	81,350	-49.2	33,098	8,251	-75.1	126,906	73,099	-42.4
Larceny-theft	680,688	359,412	-47.2	140,780	27,417	-80.5	539,908	331,995	-38.5
Motor vehicle theft	32,157	44,419	+38.1	6,454	6,387	-1.0	25,703	38,032	+48.0
Arson	6,126	5,474	-10.6	2,752	721	-73.8	3,374	4,753	+40.9
Other assaults	650,128	484,992	-25.4	98,892	39,639	-59.9	551,236	445,353	-19.2
Forgery and counterfeiting	36,910	18,761	-49.2	848	285	-66.4	36,062	18,476	-48.8
Fraud	92,521	44,734	-51.6	2,973	1,517	-49.0	89,548	43,217	-51.7
Embezzlement	9,016	5,358	-40.6	224	270	+20.5	8,792	5,088	-42.1
Stolen property; buying, receiving, possessing	53,257	48,649	-8.7	7,828	4,304	-45.0	45,429	44,345	-2.4
Vandalism	125,018	92,761	-25.8	36,960	13,680	-63.0	88,058	79,081	-10.2
Weapons; carrying, possessing, etc.	75,788	82,728	+9.2	14,392	5,666	-60.6	61,396	77,062	+25.5
Prostitution and commercialized vice	16,099	5,081	-68.4	310	39	-87.4	15,789	5,042	-68.1
Sex offenses (except forcible rape and prostitution)	35,350	17,104	-51.6	6,840	2,229	-67.4	28,510	14,875	-47.8
Drug abuse violations	759,311	645,454	-15.0	77,623	24,723	-68.1	681,688	620,731	-8.9
Gambling	1,523	888	-41.7	91	31	-65.9	1,432	857	-40.2
Offenses against the family and children	67,172	31,872	-52.6	1,923	1,368	-28.9	65,249	30,504	-53.2
Driving under the influence	626,737	375,190	-40.1	5,690	3,090	-45.7	621,047	372,100	-40.1
Liquor laws	257,232	58,057	-77.4	52,527	10,732	-79.6	204,705	47,325	-76.9
Drunkenness	297,165	110,581	-62.8	7,033	1,262	-82.1	290,132	109,319	-62.3
Disorderly conduct	277,249	127,096	-54.2	67,460	14,470	-78.6	209,789	112,626	-46.3
Vagrancy	10,490	6,631	-36.8	536	145	-72.9	9,954	6,486	-34.8
All other offenses (except traffic)	1,873,768	1,235,290	-34.1	143,618	49,438	-65.6	1,730,150	1,185,852	-31.5
Suspicion	225	156	-30.7	22	21	-4.5	203	135	-33.5
Curfew and loitering law violations	28,516	6,727	-76.4	28,516	6,727	-76.4	NA	NA	NA

NA = Not available.

1 Does not include suspicion.   2 Violent crimes are offenses of murder and nonnegligent manslaughter, rape, robbery, and aggravated assault. Property crimes are offenses of burglary, larceny-theft, motor vehicle theft, and arson.   3 The 2011 rape figures are based on the legacy definition, and the 2020 rape figures are aggregate totals based on both the legacy and revised Uniform Crime Reporting definitions. For this reason, a percent change is not provided.

Table 33. Ten-Year Arrest Trends, by Age and Sex, 2011 and 2020

(Number, percent change; 8,708 agencies; 2020 estimated population 180,606,800; 2011 estimated population 170,682,854.)

Offense charged	Male						Female					
	Total			Under 18			Total			Under 18		
	2011	2020	Percent change	2011	2020	Percent change	2011	2020	Percent change	2011	2020	Percent change
Total[1]	4,739,491	3,025,473	-36.2	538,477	169,388	-68.5	1,700,675	1,111,102	-34.7	229,994	70,733	-69.2
Violent crime[2]	215,616	196,651	-8.8	25,625	14,343	-44.0	52,325	51,315	-1.9	5,478	3,387	-38.2
Murder and nonnegligent manslaughter	4,474	5,364	+19.9	347	418	+20.5	621	771	+24.2	29	38	+31.0
Rape[3]	10,087	10,729		1,518	1,593	NA	143	277		39	68	NA
Robbery	42,033	27,658	-34.2	9,047	4,911	-45.7	6,122	5,042	-17.6	918	684	-25.5
Aggravated assault	159,022	152,900	-3.8	14,713	7,421	-49.6	45,439	45,225	-0.5	4,492	2,597	-42.2
Property crime[2]	544,261	318,610	-41.5	115,101	30,237	-73.7	334,714	172,045	-48.6	67,983	12,539	-81.6
Burglary	132,876	65,334	-50.8	28,721	7,097	-75.3	27,128	16,016	-41.0	4,377	1,154	-73.6
Larceny-theft	380,270	214,514	-43.6	78,707	17,452	-77.8	300,418	144,898	-51.8	62,073	9,965	-83.9
Motor vehicle theft	26,042	34,434	+32.2	5,324	5,083	-4.5	6,115	9,985	+63.3	1,130	1,304	+15.4
Arson	5,073	4,328	-14.7	2,349	605	-74.2	1,053	1,146	+8.8	403	116	-71.2
Other assaults	471,484	346,595	-26.5	63,970	24,694	-61.4	178,644	138,397	-22.5	34,922	14,945	-57.2
Forgery and counterfeiting	22,700	12,617	-44.4	588	226	-61.6	14,210	6,144	-56.8	260	59	-77.3
Fraud	53,577	28,563	-46.7	1,959	997	-49.1	38,944	16,171	-58.5	1,014	520	-48.7
Embezzlement	4,428	2,673	-39.6	138	143	+3.6	4,588	2,685	-41.5	86	127	+47.7
Stolen property; buying, receiving, possessing	42,232	38,329	-9.2	6,444	3,625	-43.7	11,025	10,320	-6.4	1,384	679	-50.9
Vandalism	101,433	71,362	-29.6	31,320	10,860	-65.3	23,585	21,399	-9.3	5,640	2,820	-50.0
Weapons; carrying, possessing, etc.	69,583	74,689	+7.3	12,986	5,197	-60.0	6,205	8,039	+29.6	1,406	469	-66.6
Prostitution and commercialized vice	5,296	2,526	-52.3	71	21	-70.4	10,803	2,555	-76.3	239	18	-92.5
Sex offenses (except forcible rape and prostitution)	32,847	16,174	-50.8	6,052	2,011	-66.8	2,503	930	-62.8	788	218	-72.3
Drug abuse violations	599,260	481,073	-19.7	63,672	18,413	-71.1	160,051	164,381	+2.7	13,951	6,310	-54.8
Gambling	1,163	587	-49.5	79	25	-68.4	360	301	-16.4	12	6	-50.0
Offenses against the family and children	51,527	21,806	-57.7	1,174	777	-33.8	15,645	10,066	-35.7	749	591	-21.1
Driving under the influence	469,662	277,711	-40.9	4,207	2,273	-46.0	157,075	97,479	-37.9	1,483	817	-44.9
Liquor laws	178,929	40,560	-77.3	31,330	6,282	-79.9	78,303	17,497	-77.7	21,197	4,450	-79.0
Drunkenness	241,900	85,992	-64.5	5,175	845	-83.7	55,265	24,589	-55.5	1,858	417	-77.6
Disorderly conduct	199,498	89,536	-55.1	44,100	9,167	-79.2	77,751	37,560	-51.7	23,360	5,303	-77.3
Vagrancy	8,413	5,180	-38.4	445	113	-74.6	2,077	1,451	-30.1	91	32	-64.8
All other offenses (except traffic)	1,406,293	909,860	-35.3	104,652	34,760	-66.8	467,475	325,430	-30.4	38,966	14,678	-62.3
Suspicion	175	91	-48.0	19	12	-36.8	50	65	+30.0	3	9	+200.0
Curfew and loitering law violations	19,389	4,379	-77.4	19,389	4,379	-77.4	9,127	2,348	-74.3	9,127	2,348	-74.3

NA = Not available.

1 Does not include suspicion.   2 Violent crimes are offenses of murder and nonnegligent manslaughter, rape, robbery, and aggravated assault. Property crimes are offenses of burglary, larceny-theft, motor vehicle theft, and arson.   3 The 2011 rape figures are based on the legacy definition, and the 2020 rape figures are aggregate totals based on both the legacy and revised Uniform Crime Reporting definitions. For this reason, a percent change is not provided.

Table 34. Five-Year Arrest Trends, by Age, 2016 and 2020

(Number, percent change; 9,329 agencies; 2020 estimated population 200,962,238; 2016 estimated population 196,853,348.)

| | Number of persons arrested | | | | | | | | |
| | Total, all ages | | | Under 18 years of age | | | 18 years of age and over | | |
Offense charged	2016	2020	Percent change	2016	2020	Percent change	2016	2020	Percent change
Total[1]	6,479,915	4,768,317	-26.4	512,375	267,338	-47.8	5,967,540	4,500,979	-24.6
Violent crime[2]	306,674	292,029	-4.8	28,750	20,918	-27.2	277,924	271,111	-2.5
Murder and nonnegligent manslaughter	6,585	7,250	+10.1	460	535	+16.3	6,125	6,715	+9.6
Rape[3]	13,839	12,609	-8.9	2,152	1,812	-15.8	11,687	10,797	-7.6
Robbery	53,164	40,083	-24.6	9,759	6,957	-28.7	43,405	33,126	-23.7
Aggravated assault	233,086	232,087	-0.4	16,379	11,614	-29.1	216,707	220,473	+1.7
Property crime[2]	829,059	551,243	-33.5	112,981	47,291	-58.1	716,078	503,952	-29.6
Burglary	128,847	93,195	-27.7	19,778	9,433	-52.3	109,069	83,762	-23.2
Larceny-theft	644,576	401,887	-37.7	83,553	29,845	-64.3	561,023	372,042	-33.7
Motor vehicle theft	50,192	49,965	-0.5	8,174	7,237	-11.5	42,018	42,728	+1.7
Arson	5,444	6,196	+13.8	1,476	776	-47.4	3,968	5,420	+36.6
Other assaults	654,284	563,102	-13.9	76,185	44,961	-41.0	578,099	518,141	-10.4
Forgery and counterfeiting	34,923	20,762	-40.5	737	304	-58.8	34,186	20,458	-40.2
Fraud	78,230	49,721	-36.4	2,498	1,658	-33.6	75,732	48,063	-36.5
Embezzlement	10,236	6,166	-39.8	333	285	-14.4	9,903	5,881	-40.6
Stolen property; buying, receiving, possessing	60,363	57,208	-5.2	6,556	5,220	-20.4	53,807	51,988	-3.4
Vandalism	121,150	109,530	-9.6	24,312	15,005	-38.3	96,838	94,525	-2.4
Weapons; carrying, possessing, etc.	91,760	99,827	+8.8	11,092	6,630	-40.2	80,668	93,197	+15.5
Prostitution and commercialized vice	18,795	8,492	-54.8	294	74	-74.8	18,501	8,418	-54.5
Sex offenses (except forcible rape and prostitution)	29,938	20,310	-32.2	5,085	2,542	-50.0	24,853	17,768	-28.5
Drug abuse violations	956,732	726,791	-24.0	60,401	26,608	-55.9	896,331	700,183	-21.9
Gambling	1,197	997	-16.7	77	38	-50.6	1,120	959	-14.4
Offenses against the family and children	56,169	36,340	-35.3	2,341	1,436	-38.7	53,828	34,904	-35.2
Driving under the influence	614,726	474,472	-22.8	3,962	3,598	-9.2	610,764	470,874	-22.9
Liquor laws	142,435	65,069	-54.3	23,444	11,435	-51.2	118,991	53,634	-54.9
Drunkenness	219,596	125,293	-42.9	3,055	1,408	-53.9	216,541	123,885	-42.8
Disorderly conduct	207,631	143,595	-30.8	36,665	15,961	-56.5	170,966	127,634	-25.3
Vagrancy	14,185	9,189	-35.2	502	184	-63.3	13,683	9,005	-34.2
All other offenses (except traffic)	2,015,881	1,400,889	-30.5	97,154	54,490	-43.9	1,918,727	1,346,399	-29.8
Suspicion	313	189	-39.6	25	23	-8.0	288	166	-42.4
Curfew and loitering law violations	15,951	7,292	-54.3	15,951	7,292	-54.3	NA	NA	NA

NA = Not available.
1 Does not include suspicion.   2 Violent crimes are offenses of murder and nonnegligent manslaughter, rape, robbery, and aggravated assault. Property crimes are offenses of burglary, larceny-theft, motor vehicle theft, and arson.   3 The rape figures in this table are aggregate totals of the data submitted based on both the legacy and revised Uniform Crime Reporting definitions.

Table 35. Five-Year Arrest Trends, by Age and Sex, 2016 and 2020

(Number, percent change; 9,329 agencies; 2020 estimated population 200,962,238; 2016 estimated population 196,853,348.)

Offense charged	Male						Female					
	Total			Under 18			Total			Under 18		
	2016	2020	Percent change	2016	2020	Percent change	2016	2020	Percent change	2016	2020	Percent change
Total[1]	4,711,002	3,499,671	-25.7	358,548	189,199	-47.2	1,768,913	1,268,646	-28.3	153,827	78,139	-49.2
Violent crime[2]	243,347	231,354	-4.9	23,328	16,993	-27.2	63,327	60,675	-4.2	5,422	3,925	-27.6
Murder and nonnegligent manslaughter	5,766	6,316	+9.5	407	490	+20.4	819	934	+14.0	53	45	-15.1
Rape[3]	13,433	12,248	-8.8	2,054	1,738	-15.4	406	361	-11.1	98	74	-24.5
Robbery	45,253	33,984	-24.9	8,651	6,130	-29.1	7,911	6,099	-22.9	1,108	827	-25.4
Aggravated assault	178,895	178,806	+0.0	12,216	8,635	-29.3	54,191	53,281	-1.7	4,163	2,979	-28.4
Property crime[2]	517,879	361,275	-30.2	74,286	33,716	-54.6	311,180	189,968	-39.0	38,695	13,575	-64.9
Burglary	104,047	75,184	-27.7	17,407	8,157	-53.1	24,800	18,011	-27.4	2,371	1,276	-46.2
Larceny-theft	370,695	242,442	-34.6	49,118	19,122	-61.1	273,881	159,445	-41.8	34,435	10,723	-68.9
Motor vehicle theft	38,828	38,733	-0.2	6,495	5,784	-10.9	11,364	11,232	-1.2	1,679	1,453	-13.5
Arson	4,309	4,916	+14.1	1,266	653	-48.4	1,135	1,280	+12.8	210	123	-41.4
Other assaults	467,988	401,421	-14.2	48,273	27,889	-42.2	186,296	161,681	-13.2	27,912	17,072	-38.8
Forgery and counterfeiting	22,625	14,104	-37.7	537	242	-54.9	12,298	6,658	-45.9	200	62	-69.0
Fraud	48,435	32,154	-33.6	1,676	1,087	-35.1	29,795	17,567	-41.0	822	571	-30.5
Embezzlement	5,056	3,158	-37.5	179	152	-15.1	5,180	3,008	-41.9	154	133	-13.6
Stolen property; buying, receiving, possessing	47,255	45,254	-4.2	5,483	4,433	-19.2	13,108	11,954	-8.8	1,073	787	-26.7
Vandalism	95,001	84,079	-11.5	20,205	11,890	-41.2	26,149	25,451	-2.7	4,107	3,115	-24.2
Weapons; carrying, possessing, etc.	83,042	90,256	+8.7	9,906	6,074	-38.7	8,718	9,571	+9.8	1,186	556	-53.1
Prostitution and commercialized vice	7,101	3,613	-49.1	71	28	-60.6	11,694	4,879	-58.3	223	46	-79.4
Sex offenses (except forcible rape and prostitution)	27,698	19,113	-31.0	4,451	2,295	-48.4	2,240	1,197	-46.6	634	247	-61.0
Drug abuse violations	726,930	544,788	-25.1	46,068	19,839	-56.9	229,802	182,003	-20.8	14,333	6,769	-52.8
Gambling	958	679	-29.1	70	32	-54.3	239	318	+33.1	7	6	-14.3
Offenses against the family and children	40,138	24,698	-38.5	1,417	825	-41.8	16,031	11,642	-27.4	924	611	-33.9
Driving under the influence	456,806	352,972	-22.7	2,930	2,657	-9.3	157,920	121,500	-23.1	1,032	941	-8.8
Liquor laws	99,619	45,671	-54.2	14,053	6,688	-52.4	42,816	19,398	-54.7	9,391	4,747	-49.5
Drunkenness	175,006	97,346	-44.4	2,144	939	-56.2	44,590	27,947	-37.3	911	469	-48.5
Disorderly conduct	147,496	100,841	-31.6	23,488	10,085	-57.1	60,135	42,754	-28.9	13,177	5,876	-55.4
Vagrancy	10,843	7,036	-35.1	370	135	-63.5	3,342	2,153	-35.6	132	49	-62.9
All other offenses (except traffic)	1,477,228	1,035,073	-29.9	69,062	38,414	-44.4	538,653	365,816	-32.1	28,092	16,076	-42.8
Suspicion	246	122	-50.4	18	13	-27.8	67	67	+0.0	7	10	+42.9
Curfew and loitering law violations	10,551	4,786	-54.6	10,551	4,786	-54.6	5,400	2,506	-53.6	5,400	2,506	-53.6

1 Does not include suspicion.   2 Violent crimes are offenses of murder and nonnegligent manslaughter, rape, robbery, and aggravated assault. Property crimes are offenses of burglary, larceny-theft, motor vehicle theft, and arson.   3 The rape figures in this table are aggregate totals of the data submitted based on both the legacy and revised Uniform Crime Reporting definitions.

Table 36. Current Year Over Previous Year Arrest Trends, 2019–2020

(Number, percent change; 9,245 agencies; 2020 estimated population 199,329,726; 2019 estimated population 198,464,294.)

Offense charged	Total, all ages			Under 15 years of age			Under 18 years of age			18 years of age and over		
	2019	2020	Percent change	2019	2020	Percent change	2019	2020	Percent change	2019	2020	Percent change
Total[1]	5,945,932	4,620,603	-22.3	133,506	76,275	-42.9	415,981	263,317	-36.7	5,529,951	4,357,286	-21.2
Violent crime[2]	303,843	291,290	-4.1	8,882	5,761	-35.1	28,961	21,370	-26.2	274,882	269,920	-1.8
Murder and nonnegligent manslaughter	6,424	7,509	+16.9	50	59	+18.0	510	570	+11.8	5,914	6,939	+17.3
Rape[3]	14,601	12,742	-12.7	1,122	784	-30.1	2,524	1,832	-27.4	12,077	10,910	-9.7
Robbery	46,622	41,145	-11.7	2,038	1,543	-24.3	9,664	7,368	-23.8	36,958	33,777	-8.6
Aggravated assault	236,196	229,894	-2.7	5,672	3,375	-40.5	16,263	11,600	-28.7	219,933	218,294	-0.7
Property crime[2]	686,252	542,450	-21.0	22,677	13,623	-39.9	75,353	47,383	-37.1	610,899	495,067	-19.0
Burglary	103,980	91,817	-11.7	4,119	3,041	-26.2	12,807	9,561	-25.3	91,173	82,256	-9.8
Larceny-theft	527,116	394,234	-25.2	15,731	8,007	-49.1	53,216	29,599	-44.4	473,900	364,635	-23.1
Motor vehicle theft	49,783	50,257	+1.0	2,240	2,146	-4.2	8,281	7,430	-10.3	41,502	42,827	+3.2
Arson	5,373	6,142	+14.3	587	429	-26.9	1,049	793	-24.4	4,324	5,349	+23.7
Other assaults	613,181	553,284	-9.8	31,927	17,000	-46.8	73,463	43,819	-40.4	539,718	509,465	-5.6
Forgery and counterfeiting	28,784	20,156	-30.0	89	47	-47.2	557	305	-45.2	28,227	19,851	-29.7
Fraud	70,458	48,575	-31.1	553	433	-21.7	2,323	1,672	-28.0	68,135	46,903	-31.2
Embezzlement	9,056	5,928	-34.5	17	9	-47.1	365	287	-21.4	8,691	5,641	-35.1
Stolen property; buying, receiving, possessing	57,805	55,940	-3.2	1,254	1,138	-9.3	5,914	5,388	-8.9	51,891	50,552	-2.6
Vandalism	110,704	106,599	-3.7	8,454	5,826	-31.1	19,353	14,652	-24.3	91,351	91,947	+0.7
Weapons; carrying, possessing, etc.	94,199	99,430	+5.6	2,844	1,298	-54.4	9,830	6,774	-31.1	84,369	92,656	+9.8
Prostitution and commercialized vice	12,360	6,864	-44.5	22	6	-72.7	102	36	-64.7	12,258	6,828	-44.3
Sex offenses (except forcible rape and prostitution)	24,572	19,085	-22.3	1,999	1,206	-39.7	4,141	2,473	-40.3	20,431	16,612	-18.7
Drug abuse violations	927,890	709,607	-23.5	9,337	3,978	-57.4	47,811	25,971	-45.7	880,079	683,636	-22.3
Gambling	1,286	945	-26.5	9	7	-22.2	71	37	-47.9	1,215	908	-25.3
Offenses against the family and children	49,486	35,667	-27.9	632	429	-32.1	1,730	1,346	-22.2	47,756	34,321	-28.1
Driving under the influence	576,138	465,982	-19.1	79	50	-36.7	3,208	3,500	+9.1	572,930	462,482	-19.3
Liquor laws	95,438	62,473	-34.5	2,296	1,355	-41.0	14,824	10,998	-25.8	80,614	51,475	-36.1
Drunkenness	182,242	114,892	-37.0	295	228	-22.7	2,022	1,292	-36.1	180,220	113,600	-37.0
Disorderly conduct	180,812	138,200	-23.6	13,856	6,076	-56.1	31,733	15,310	-51.8	149,079	122,890	-17.6
Vagrancy	11,593	8,531	-26.4	62	44	-29.0	229	186	-18.8	11,364	8,345	-26.6
All other offenses (except traffic)	1,900,410	1,327,322	-30.2	25,073	15,231	-39.3	84,568	53,135	-37.2	1,815,842	1,274,187	-29.8
Suspicion	182	179	-1.6	2	7	+250.0	6	25	+316.7	176	154	-12.5
Curfew and loitering law violations	9,423	7,383	-21.6	3,149	2,530	-19.7	9,423	7,383	-21.6	NA	NA	NA

NA = Not available.

1 Does not include suspicion.   2 Violent crimes are offenses of murder and nonnegligent manslaughter, rape, robbery, and aggravated assault. Property crimes are offenses of burglary, larceny-theft, motor vehicle theft, and arson.   3 The rape figures in this table are aggregate totals of the data submitted based on both the legacy and revised Uniform Crime Reporting definitions.

Table 37. Current Year Over Previous Year Arrest Trends, by Age and Sex, 2019–2020

(Number, percent change; 9,245 agencies; 2020 estimated population 199,329,726; 2019 estimated population 198,464,294.)

Offense charged	Male Total			Male Under 18			Female Total			Female Under 18		
	2019	2020	Percent change	2019	2020	Percent change	2019	2020	Percent change	2019	2020	Percent change
Total[1]	4,303,444	3,395,439	-21.1	289,458	186,781	-35.5	1,642,488	1,225,164	-25.4	126,523	76,536	-39.5
Violent crime[2]	239,598	230,675	-3.7	23,423	17,318	-26.1	64,245	60,615	-5.7	5,538	4,052	-26.8
Murder and nonnegligent manslaughter	5,672	6,583	+16.1	469	522	+11.3	752	926	+23.1	41	48	+17.1
Rape[3]	14,082	12,371	-12.2	2,381	1,755	-26.3	519	371	-28.5	143	77	-46.2
Robbery	39,183	34,870	-11.0	8,550	6,470	-24.3	7,439	6,275	-15.6	1,114	898	-19.4
Aggravated assault	180,661	176,851	-2.1	12,023	8,571	-28.7	55,535	53,043	-4.5	4,240	3,029	-28.6
Property crime[2]	427,303	356,342	-16.6	50,309	33,831	-32.8	258,949	186,108	-28.1	25,044	13,552	-45.9
Burglary	82,470	74,329	-9.9	11,036	8,279	-25.0	21,510	17,488	-18.7	1,771	1,282	-27.6
Larceny-theft	302,522	238,106	-21.3	31,777	18,915	-40.5	224,594	156,128	-30.5	21,439	10,684	-50.2
Motor vehicle theft	38,102	39,042	+2.5	6,600	5,968	-9.6	11,681	11,215	-4.0	1,681	1,462	-13.0
Arson	4,209	4,865	+15.6	896	669	-25.3	1,164	1,277	+9.7	153	124	-19.0
Other assaults	434,691	395,816	-8.9	46,030	27,227	-40.8	178,490	157,468	-11.8	27,433	16,592	-39.5
Forgery and counterfeiting	19,186	13,662	-28.8	428	245	-42.8	9,598	6,494	-32.3	129	60	-53.5
Fraud	45,083	31,410	-30.3	1,577	1,106	-29.9	25,375	17,165	-32.4	746	566	-24.1
Embezzlement	4,468	3,021	-32.4	199	152	-23.6	4,588	2,907	-36.6	166	135	-18.7
Stolen property; buying, receiving, possessing	44,860	44,288	-1.3	4,874	4,554	-6.6	12,945	11,652	-10.0	1,040	834	-19.8
Vandalism	85,067	81,859	-3.8	15,614	11,609	-25.7	25,637	24,740	-3.5	3,739	3,043	-18.6
Weapons; carrying, possessing, etc.	85,093	89,988	+5.8	8,836	6,231	-29.5	9,106	9,442	+3.7	994	543	-45.4
Prostitution and commercialized vice	5,175	3,322	-35.8	59	19	-67.8	7,185	3,542	-50.7	43	17	-60.5
Sex offenses (except forcible rape and prostitution)	22,936	18,015	-21.5	3,685	2,233	-39.4	1,636	1,070	-34.6	456	240	-47.4
Drug abuse violations	690,924	531,435	-23.1	35,252	19,378	-45.0	236,966	178,172	-24.8	12,559	6,593	-47.5
Gambling	944	646	-31.6	62	31	-50.0	342	299	-12.6	9	6	-33.3
Offenses against the family and children	34,711	24,351	-29.8	1,023	778	-23.9	14,775	11,316	-23.4	707	568	-19.7
Driving under the influence	425,867	347,070	-18.5	2,418	2,586	+6.9	150,271	118,912	-20.9	790	914	+15.7
Liquor laws	66,077	43,782	-33.7	8,520	6,453	-24.3	29,361	18,691	-36.3	6,304	4,545	-27.9
Drunkenness	142,728	89,503	-37.3	1,371	857	-37.5	39,514	25,389	-35.7	651	435	-33.2
Disorderly conduct	127,463	97,138	-23.8	19,993	9,691	-51.5	53,349	41,062	-23.0	11,740	5,619	-52.1
Vagrancy	8,927	6,532	-26.8	167	135	-19.2	2,666	1,999	-25.0	62	51	-17.7
All other offenses (except traffic)	1,386,107	981,786	-29.2	59,382	37,549	-36.8	514,303	345,536	-32.8	25,186	15,586	-38.1
Suspicion	121	111	-8.3	6	15	+150.0	61	68	+11.5	0	10	
Curfew and loitering law violations	6,236	4,798	-23.1	6,236	4,798	-23.1	3,187	2,585	-18.9	3,187	2,585	-18.9

1 Does not include suspicion.   2 Violent crimes are offenses of murder and nonnegligent manslaughter, rape, robbery, and aggravated assault. Property crimes are offenses of burglary, larceny-theft, motor vehicle theft, and arson.   3 The rape figures in this table are aggregate totals of the data submitted based on both the legacy and revised Uniform Crime Reporting definitions.

Table 38. Arrests, Distribution by Age, 2020

(Number, percent; 10,466 agencies; 2020 estimated population 228,864,358.)

Offense charged	Total, all ages	Ages under 15	Ages under 18	Ages 18 and over	Under 10	10–12	13–14	15	16	17	18	19	20
Total	5,292,124	85,931	297,074	4,995,050	1,173	18,341	66,417	56,289	70,035	84,819	124,170	139,693	147,239
Total percent distribution[1]	100.0	1.6	5.6	94.4	*	0.3	1.3	1.1	1.3	1.6	2.3	2.6	2.8
Violent crime[2]	338,443	6,664	24,671	313,772	73	1,436	5,155	4,697	6,051	7,259	9,254	9,581	9,974
Violent crime percent distribution[1]	100.0	2.0	7.3	92.7	*	0.4	1.5	1.4	1.8	2.1	2.7	2.8	2.9
Murder and nonnegligent manslaughter	8,701	64	654	8,047	1	8	55	95	197	298	417	436	416
Rape[3]	14,462	885	2,065	12,397	7	284	594	384	379	417	543	517	488
Robbery	48,035	1,780	8,517	39,518	2	192	1,586	1,740	2,297	2,700	2,948	2,391	2,111
Aggravated assault	267,245	3,935	13,435	253,810	63	952	2,920	2,478	3,178	3,844	5,346	6,237	6,959
Property crime[2]	611,731	15,140	52,640	559,091	165	2,845	12,130	10,853	12,762	13,885	17,019	16,405	15,854
Property crime percent distribution[1]	100.0	2.5	8.6	91.4	*	0.5	2.0	1.8	2.1	2.3	2.8	2.7	2.6
Burglary	104,535	3,362	10,563	93,972	63	682	2,617	2,222	2,399	2,580	2,963	2,830	2,791
Larceny-theft	442,016	8,918	32,948	409,068	73	1,725	7,120	6,521	8,181	9,328	12,129	11,804	11,391
Motor vehicle theft	58,326	2,387	8,273	50,053	6	267	2,114	1,945	2,060	1,881	1,837	1,655	1,559
Arson	6,854	473	856	5,998	23	171	279	165	122	96	90	116	113
Other assaults	633,704	19,459	50,129	583,575	235	5,105	14,119	9,695	10,401	10,574	12,094	13,582	15,898
Forgery and counterfeiting	22,559	47	333	22,226	0	6	41	51	81	154	606	826	844
Fraud	54,756	470	1,816	52,940	1	59	410	359	415	572	1,093	1,350	1,500
Embezzlement	6,592	9	302	6,290	0	2	7	6	96	191	360	351	282
Stolen property; buying, receiving, possessing	61,868	1,232	5,814	56,054	2	120	1,110	1,260	1,581	1,741	2,115	2,033	1,885
Vandalism	121,403	6,493	16,392	105,011	161	1,686	4,646	3,203	3,404	3,292	3,675	3,712	3,539
Weapons; carrying, possessing, etc.	115,832	1,478	7,809	108,023	19	309	1,150	1,327	1,995	3,009	4,342	4,702	4,874
Prostitution and commercialized vice	11,754	11	77	11,677	0	1	10	12	22	32	327	469	577
Sex offenses (except forcible rape and prostitution)	22,065	1,329	2,751	19,314	39	379	911	448	490	484	585	604	544
Drug abuse violations	801,546	4,539	29,368	772,178	25	560	3,954	4,589	7,676	12,564	23,399	26,677	27,410
Gambling	1,191	11	58	1,133	0	5	6	10	20	17	15	14	35
Offenses against the family and children	40,498	508	1,579	38,919	22	111	375	331	392	348	500	539	741
Driving under the influence	531,846	64	4,003	527,843	1	3	60	216	1,030	2,693	7,145	10,270	12,678
Liquor laws	70,875	1,525	12,372	58,503	4	157	1,364	2,023	3,485	5,339	9,762	9,691	7,687
Drunkenness	135,744	273	1,696	134,048	1	32	240	298	418	707	1,869	2,218	2,491
Disorderly conduct	156,502	6,767	17,041	139,461	92	1,749	4,926	3,332	3,471	3,471	3,860	4,121	4,142
Vagrancy	9,795	46	192	9,603	2	5	39	37	55	54	257	252	224
All other offenses (except traffic)	1,534,972	17,056	59,790	1,475,182	315	3,331	13,410	11,650	14,099	16,985	25,887	32,289	36,058
Suspicion	238	11	31	207	2	5	4	5	5	10	6	7	2
Curfew and loitering law violations	8,210	2,799	8,210	NA	14	435	2,350	1,887	2,086	1,438	NA	NA	NA

Table 38. Arrests, Distribution by Age, 2020—Continued

(Number, percent; 10,466 agencies; 2020 estimated population 228,864,358.)

Offense charged	21	22	23	24	25–29	30–34	35–39	40–44	45–49	50–54	55–59	60–64	65 and over
Total	150,875	153,388	155,109	160,772	891,452	843,664	699,253	503,816	345,710	276,095	211,052	115,466	77,296
Total percent distribution[1]	2.9	2.9	2.9	3.0	16.8	15.9	13.2	9.5	6.5	5.2	4.0	2.2	1.5
Violent crime[2]	10,299	10,678	10,467	10,784	58,297	52,213	42,340	29,338	20,091	15,840	12,355	6,995	5,266
Violent crime percent distribution[1]	3.0	3.2	3.1	3.2	17.2	15.4	12.5	8.7	5.9	4.7	3.7	2.1	1.6
Murder and nonnegligent manslaughter	411	365	377	327	1,662	1,097	837	590	353	257	218	144	140
Rape[3]	485	415	373	409	1,786	1,759	1,648	1,193	883	676	547	331	344
Robbery	1,841	1,725	1,506	1,562	7,781	6,222	4,411	2,781	1,657	1,269	811	329	173
Aggravated assault	7,562	8,173	8,211	8,486	47,068	43,135	35,444	24,774	17,198	13,638	10,779	6,191	4,609
Property crime[2]	15,698	15,782	15,978	16,841	99,140	99,599	81,263	56,996	38,006	30,941	22,072	11,054	6,443
Property crime percent distribution[1]	2.6	2.6	2.6	2.8	16.2	16.3	13.3	9.3	6.2	5.1	3.6	1.8	1.1
Burglary	2,621	2,754	2,857	3,073	17,900	17,791	13,906	9,454	5,816	4,363	2,966	1,285	602
Larceny-theft	11,318	11,226	11,350	11,845	69,606	70,726	59,093	42,191	29,228	24,526	17,868	9,204	5,563
Motor vehicle theft	1,624	1,678	1,641	1,752	10,626	10,014	7,311	4,665	2,494	1,683	977	380	157
Arson	135	124	130	171	1,008	1,068	953	686	468	369	261	185	121
Other assaults	17,326	17,919	18,316	18,829	104,699	98,056	81,332	59,863	41,827	33,654	25,417	14,115	10,648
Forgery and counterfeiting	551	639	593	659	4,060	3,910	3,443	2,257	1,522	1,079	700	346	191
Fraud	1,420	1,505	1,515	1,659	9,606	9,575	8,082	5,662	3,667	2,724	2,011	949	622
Embezzlement	268	237	220	221	1,006	898	747	564	408	322	244	107	55
Stolen property; buying, receiving, possessing	1,836	1,863	1,772	2,027	11,124	10,722	8,219	5,280	3,117	2,032	1,244	545	240
Vandalism	3,637	3,652	3,804	3,865	20,453	18,108	14,185	9,600	5,844	4,627	3,290	1,691	1,329
Weapons; carrying, possessing, etc.	5,388	5,179	5,021	4,730	22,660	17,246	12,538	8,176	4,929	3,387	2,504	1,391	956
Prostitution and commercialized vice	661	550	492	496	2,298	1,671	1,195	916	686	535	380	216	208
Sex offenses (except forcible rape and prostitution)	522	441	432	451	2,558	2,636	2,577	2,052	1,493	1,302	1,219	873	1,025
Drug abuse violations	26,213	26,133	26,075	26,746	146,637	134,106	109,123	75,320	47,701	35,338	24,722	11,643	4,935
Gambling	20	24	28	20	148	158	173	145	124	92	69	27	41
Offenses against the family and children	788	858	978	1,044	6,866	7,832	6,782	4,808	2,962	1,931	1,215	646	429
Driving under the influence	17,333	18,174	18,700	19,206	95,345	81,406	65,880	50,403	38,812	32,798	28,092	17,706	13,895
Liquor laws	1,565	1,190	1,029	934	4,630	4,247	3,874	3,186	2,839	2,537	1,592	980	
Drunkenness	3,404	3,464	3,505	3,755	20,303	20,313	19,003	14,408	11,528	10,722	9,293	5,028	2,744
Disorderly conduct	4,790	4,581	4,372	4,449	22,692	21,425	18,313	13,856	9,949	8,586	7,065	4,141	3,119
Vagrancy	212	227	227	208	1,370	1,383	1,213	1,057	822	798	693	407	253
All other offenses (except traffic)	38,940	40,286	41,583	43,839	257,542	258,117	218,938	159,900	109,366	86,616	65,920	35,989	23,912
Suspicion	4	6	2	9	18	43	33	29	17	11	10	5	5
Curfew and loitering law violations	NA	NA	NA	NA	NA	NA	NA	NA	NA	NA	NA	NA	NA

NA = Not available.
* = Less than one-tenth of one percent.
1 Because of rounding, the percentages may not sum to 100 percent.   2 Violent crimes are offenses of murder and nonnegligent manslaughter, rape, robbery, and aggravated assault. Property crimes are offenses of burglary, larceny-theft, motor vehicle theft, and arson.   3 The rape figures in this table are aggregate totals of the data submitted based on both the legacy and revised Uniform Crime Reporting definitions.

Table 39. Male Arrests, Distribution by Age, 2020

(Number, percent; 10,466 agencies; 2020 estimated population 228,864,358.)

Offense charged	Total, all ages	Ages under 15	Ages under 18	Ages 18 and over	Under 10	10–12	13–14	15	16	17	18	19	20
Total	3,891,282	58,315	210,535	3,680,747	952	12,613	44,750	39,686	50,387	62,147	91,222	101,735	106,702
Total percent distribution[1]	100.0	1.5	5.4	94.6	*	0.3	1.2	1.0	1.3	1.6	2.3	2.6	2.7
Violent crime[2]	267,935	5,167	19,979	247,956	63	1,128	3,976	3,796	4,952	6,064	7,684	7,765	7,883
Violent crime percent distribution[1]	100.0	1.9	7.5	92.5	*	0.4	1.5	1.4	1.8	2.3	2.9	2.9	2.9
Murder and nonnegligent manslaughter	7,611	57	601	7,010	1	7	49	90	179	275	385	391	373
Rape[3]	14,050	843	1,982	12,068	7	270	566	368	365	406	532	506	478
Robbery	40,725	1,523	7,471	33,254	2	163	1,358	1,518	2,036	2,394	2,600	2,090	1,820
Aggravated assault	205,549	2,744	9,925	195,624	53	688	2,003	1,820	2,372	2,989	4,167	4,778	5,212
Property crime[2]	402,790	10,905	37,509	365,281	128	2,091	8,686	7,965	9,032	9,607	11,134	10,424	9,983
Property crime percent distribution[1]	100.0	2.7	9.3	90.7	*	0.5	2.2	2.0	2.2	2.4	2.8	2.6	2.5
Burglary	84,454	2,867	9,143	75,311	54	585	2,228	1,924	2,094	2,258	2,520	2,347	2,273
Larceny-theft	267,564	5,834	21,025	246,539	49	1,158	4,627	4,332	5,143	5,716	7,033	6,669	6,401
Motor vehicle theft	45,359	1,806	6,627	38,732	2	206	1,598	1,572	1,693	1,556	1,512	1,314	1,224
Arson	5,413	398	714	4,699	23	142	233	137	102	77	69	94	85
Other assaults	452,374	11,778	31,044	421,330	191	3,255	8,332	5,932	6,600	6,734	7,878	8,874	10,435
Forgery and counterfeiting	15,318	39	267	15,051	0	6	33	41	70	117	425	566	580
Fraud	35,624	316	1,199	34,425	1	44	271	231	281	371	747	881	987
Embezzlement	3,387	6	163	3,224	0	2	4	3	54	100	176	184	151
Stolen property; buying, receiving, possessing	48,944	1,015	4,904	44,040	2	94	919	1,034	1,350	1,505	1,778	1,649	1,507
Vandalism	93,181	5,194	12,931	80,250	145	1,363	3,686	2,538	2,679	2,520	2,855	2,794	2,651
Weapons; carrying, possessing, etc.	104,992	1,298	7,185	97,807	17	253	1,028	1,226	1,844	2,817	4,067	4,362	4,502
Prostitution and commercialized vice	4,942	7	30	4,912	0	1	6	6	7	10	34	83	91
Sex offenses (except forcible rape and prostitution)	20,780	1,189	2,489	18,291	32	331	826	403	443	454	551	574	520
Drug abuse violations	600,966	3,064	21,951	579,015	17	357	2,690	3,411	5,811	9,665	17,841	20,115	20,589
Gambling	825	6	40	785	0	2	4	8	15	11	12	9	26
Offenses against the family and children	27,429	281	910	26,519	17	69	195	188	221	220	342	348	467
Driving under the influence	396,682	46	2,972	393,710	0	2	44	154	751	2,021	5,491	7,780	9,499
Liquor laws	49,833	729	7,286	42,547	2	73	654	1,123	2,044	3,390	6,386	6,522	5,226
Drunkenness	105,399	157	1,096	104,303	1	20	136	172	276	491	1,366	1,653	1,832
Disorderly conduct	109,929	4,119	10,717	99,212	77	1,120	2,922	2,040	2,214	2,344	2,588	2,747	2,759
Vagrancy	7,479	36	138	7,341	2	4	30	30	32	40	193	192	162
All other offenses (except traffic)	1,136,942	11,228	42,327	1,094,615	243	2,155	8,830	8,140	10,285	12,674	19,670	24,207	26,850
Suspicion	153	6	20	133	2	2	2	5	3	6	4	6	2
Curfew and loitering law violations	5,378	1,729	5,378	NA	12	241	1,476	1,240	1,423	986	NA	NA	NA

Table 39. Male Arrests, Distribution by Age, 2020—Continued

(Number, percent; 10,466 agencies; 2020 estimated population 228,864,358.)

Offense charged	21	22	23	24	25–29	30–34	35–39	40–44	45–49	50–54	55–59	60–64	65 and over
Total	109,746	111,537	112,998	117,438	652,842	613,094	507,489	371,070	256,954	209,214	164,812	92,184	61,710
Total percent distribution[1]	2.8	2.9	2.9	3.0	16.8	15.8	13.0	9.5	6.6	5.4	4.2	2.4	1.6
Violent crime[2]	8,053	8,376	8,077	8,348	45,741	40,782	33,283	23,229	15,963	12,564	9,970	5,793	4,445
Violent crime percent distribution[1]	3.0	3.1	3.0	3.1	17.1	15.2	12.4	8.7	6.0	4.7	3.7	2.2	1.7
Murder and nonnegligent manslaughter	368	322	341	269	1,461	931	702	518	296	212	194	123	124
Rape[3]	468	405	363	398	1,734	1,697	1,594	1,161	861	663	538	326	344
Robbery	1,544	1,456	1,270	1,292	6,517	5,132	3,638	2,273	1,396	1,072	707	295	152
Aggravated assault	5,673	6,193	6,103	6,389	36,029	33,022	27,349	19,277	13,410	10,617	8,531	5,049	3,825
Property crime[2]	9,955	9,966	10,382	10,984	65,228	64,951	52,170	37,303	24,812	20,826	15,323	7,612	4,228
Property crime percent distribution[1]	2.5	2.5	2.6	2.7	16.2	16.1	13.0	9.3	6.2	5.2	3.8	1.9	1.0
Burglary	2,134	2,240	2,313	2,448	14,279	13,956	10,929	7,546	4,704	3,561	2,472	1,089	500
Larceny-theft	6,473	6,353	6,696	7,036	42,081	42,580	34,999	25,549	17,770	15,566	11,810	6,038	3,485
Motor vehicle theft	1,245	1,280	1,264	1,357	8,085	7,595	5,512	3,648	1,983	1,411	831	329	142
Arson	103	93	109	143	783	820	730	560	355	288	210	156	101
Other assaults	11,549	12,133	12,623	13,121	75,032	70,952	59,540	44,447	31,110	25,033	19,324	11,006	8,273
Forgery and counterfeiting	384	444	422	448	2,764	2,550	2,200	1,506	1,028	788	530	271	145
Fraud	907	1,010	1,000	1,116	6,253	6,059	5,101	3,625	2,352	1,833	1,426	685	443
Embezzlement	138	121	130	126	558	454	365	258	183	157	133	59	31
Stolen property; buying, receiving, possessing	1,458	1,477	1,404	1,539	8,526	8,232	6,318	4,170	2,547	1,693	1,053	479	210
Vandalism	2,690	2,756	2,853	2,899	15,560	13,811	10,940	7,435	4,524	3,542	2,589	1,332	1,019
Weapons; carrying, possessing, etc.	4,982	4,733	4,585	4,320	20,398	15,396	11,159	7,289	4,465	3,063	2,291	1,300	895
Prostitution and commercialized vice	134	117	126	149	803	802	661	560	425	326	251	165	185
Sex offenses (except forcible rape and prostitution)	498	421	410	425	2,396	2,476	2,404	1,949	1,407	1,248	1,158	846	1,008
Drug abuse violations	19,506	19,724	19,357	19,930	109,727	98,678	79,849	55,781	36,142	27,684	20,067	9,767	4,258
Gambling	14	19	24	13	104	93	118	101	92	64	40	25	31
Offenses against the family and children	475	502	587	631	4,223	5,118	4,690	3,581	2,296	1,511	918	499	331
Driving under the influence	12,847	13,327	13,688	14,170	70,887	60,592	48,768	37,580	28,726	24,395	21,276	13,655	11,029
Liquor laws	1,127	872	747	680	3,461	3,245	2,999	2,419	2,224	2,240	2,163	1,392	844
Drunkenness	2,606	2,671	2,670	2,908	15,536	15,531	14,398	11,069	9,011	8,605	7,850	4,204	2,393
Disorderly conduct	3,307	3,060	3,014	3,059	15,906	15,055	13,005	9,940	7,267	6,305	5,405	3,296	2,499
Vagrancy	166	172	162	158	1,075	1,040	904	791	621	605	560	338	202
All other offenses (except traffic)	28,947	29,631	30,736	32,410	188,649	187,255	158,595	118,020	81,745	66,729	52,478	29,456	19,237
Suspicion	3	5	1	4	15	22	22	17	14	3	7	4	4
Curfew and loitering law violations	NA	NA	NA	NA	NA	NA	NA	NA	NA	NA	NA	NA	NA

NA = Not available.
* = Less than one-tenth of one percent.
1 Because of rounding, the percentages may not sum to 100 percent.
2 Violent crimes are offenses of murder and nonnegligent manslaughter, rape, robbery, and aggravated assault. Property crimes are offenses of burglary, larceny-theft, motor vehicle theft, and arson.
3 The rape figures in this table are aggregate totals of the data submitted based on both the legacy and revised Uniform Crime Reporting definitions.

Table 40. Female Arrests, Distribution by Age, 2020

(Number, percent; 10,466 agencies; 2020 estimated population 228,864,358.)

Offense charged	Total, all ages	Ages under 15	Ages under 18	Ages 18 and over	Under 10	10–12	13–14	15	16	17	18	19	20
Total	1,400,842	27,616	86,539	1,314,303	221	5,728	21,667	16,603	19,648	22,672	32,948	37,958	40,537
Total percent distribution[1]	100.0	2.0	6.2	93.8	*	0.4	1.5	1.2	1.4	1.6	2.4	2.7	2.9
Violent crime[2]	70,508	1,497	4,692	65,816	10	308	1,179	901	1,099	1,195	1,570	1,816	2,091
Violent crime percent distribution[1]	100.0	2.1	6.7	93.3	*	0.4	1.7	1.3	1.6	1.7	2.2	2.6	3.0
Murder and nonnegligent manslaughter	1,090	7	53	1,037	0	1	6	5	18	23	32	45	43
Rape[3]	412	42	83	329	0	14	28	16	14	11	11	11	10
Robbery	7,310	257	1,046	6,264	0	29	228	222	261	306	348	301	291
Aggravated assault	61,696	1,191	3,510	58,186	10	264	917	658	806	855	1,179	1,459	1,747
Property crime[2]	208,941	4,235	15,131	193,810	37	754	3,444	2,888	3,730	4,278	5,885	5,981	5,871
Property crime percent distribution[1]	100.0	2.0	7.2	92.8	*	0.4	1.6	1.4	1.8	2.0	2.8	2.9	2.8
Burglary	20,081	495	1,420	18,661	9	97	389	298	305	322	443	483	518
Larceny-theft	174,452	3,084	11,923	162,529	24	567	2,493	2,189	3,038	3,612	5,096	5,135	4,990
Motor vehicle theft	12,967	581	1,646	11,321	4	61	516	373	367	325	325	341	335
Arson	1,441	75	142	1,299	0	29	46	28	20	19	21	22	28
Other assaults	181,330	7,681	19,085	162,245	44	1,850	5,787	3,763	3,801	3,840	4,216	4,708	5,463
Forgery and counterfeiting	7,241	8	66	7,175	0	0	8	10	11	37	181	260	264
Fraud	19,132	154	617	18,515	0	15	139	128	134	201	346	469	513
Embezzlement	3,205	3	139	3,066	0	0	3	3	42	91	184	167	131
Stolen property; buying, receiving, possessing	12,924	217	910	12,014	0	26	191	226	231	236	337	384	378
Vandalism	28,222	1,299	3,461	24,761	16	323	960	665	725	772	820	918	888
Weapons; carrying, possessing, etc.	10,840	180	624	10,216	2	56	122	101	151	192	275	340	372
Prostitution and commercialized vice	6,812	4	47	6,765	0	0	4	6	15	22	293	386	486
Sex offenses (except forcible rape and prostitution)	1,285	140	262	1,023	7	48	85	45	47	30	34	30	24
Drug abuse violations	200,580	1,475	7,417	193,163	8	203	1,264	1,178	1,865	2,899	5,558	6,562	6,821
Gambling	366	5	18	348	0	3	2	2	5	6	3	5	9
Offenses against the family and children	13,069	227	669	12,400	5	42	180	143	171	128	158	191	274
Driving under the influence	135,164	18	1,031	134,133	1	1	16	62	279	672	1,654	2,490	3,179
Liquor laws	21,042	796	5,086	15,956	2	84	710	900	1,441	1,949	3,376	3,169	2,461
Drunkenness	30,345	116	600	29,745	0	12	104	126	142	216	503	565	659
Disorderly conduct	46,573	2,648	6,324	40,249	15	629	2,004	1,292	1,257	1,127	1,272	1,374	1,383
Vagrancy	2,316	10	54	2,262	0	1	9	7	23	14	64	60	62
All other offenses (except traffic)	398,030	5,828	17,463	380,567	72	1,176	4,580	3,510	3,814	4,311	6,217	8,082	9,208
Suspicion	85	5	11	74	0	3	2	0	2	4	2	1	0
Curfew and loitering law violations	2,832	1,070	2,832	NA	2	194	874	647	663	452	NA	NA	NA

Table 40. Female Arrests, Distribution by Age, 2020—Continued

Offense charged	21	22	23	24	25–29	30–34	35–39	40–44	45–49	50–54	55–59	60–64	65 and over
Total	41,129	41,851	42,111	43,334	238,610	230,570	191,764	132,746	88,756	66,881	46,240	23,282	15,586
Total percent distribution[1]	2.9	3.0	3.0	3.1	17.0	16.5	13.7	9.5	6.3	4.8	3.3	1.7	1.1
Violent crime[2]	2,246	2,302	2,390	2,436	12,556	11,431	9,057	6,109	4,128	3,276	2,385	1,202	821
Violent crime percent distribution[1]	3.2	3.3	3.4	3.5	17.8	16.2	12.8	8.7	5.9	4.6	3.4	1.7	1.2
Murder and nonnegligent manslaughter	43	43	36	58	201	166	135	72	57	45	24	21	16
Rape[3]	17	10	10	11	52	62	54	32	22	13	9	5	0
Robbery	297	269	236	270	1,264	1,090	773	508	261	197	104	34	21
Aggravated assault	1,889	1,980	2,108	2,097	11,039	10,113	8,095	5,497	3,788	3,021	2,248	1,142	784
Property crime[2]	5,743	5,816	5,596	5,857	33,912	34,648	29,093	19,693	13,194	10,115	6,749	3,442	2,215
Property crime percent distribution[1]	2.7	2.8	2.7	2.8	16.2	16.6	13.9	9.4	6.3	4.8	3.2	1.6	1.1
Burglary	487	514	544	625	3,621	3,835	2,977	1,908	1,112	802	494	196	102
Larceny-theft	4,845	4,873	4,654	4,809	27,525	28,146	24,094	16,642	11,458	8,960	6,058	3,166	2,078
Motor vehicle theft	379	398	377	395	2,541	2,419	1,799	1,017	511	272	146	51	15
Arson	32	31	21	28	225	248	223	126	113	81	51	29	20
Other assaults	5,777	5,786	5,693	5,708	29,667	27,104	21,792	15,416	10,717	8,621	6,093	3,109	2,375
Forgery and counterfeiting	167	195	171	211	1,296	1,360	1,243	751	494	291	170	75	46
Fraud	513	495	515	543	3,353	3,516	2,981	2,037	1,315	891	585	264	179
Embezzlement	130	116	90	95	448	444	382	306	225	165	111	48	24
Stolen property; buying, receiving, possessing	378	386	368	488	2,598	2,490	1,901	1,110	570	339	191	66	30
Vandalism	947	896	951	966	4,893	4,297	3,245	2,165	1,320	1,085	701	359	310
Weapons; carrying, possessing, etc.	406	446	436	410	2,262	1,850	1,379	887	464	324	213	91	61
Prostitution and commercialized vice	527	433	366	347	1,495	869	534	356	261	209	129	51	23
Sex offenses (except forcible rape and prostitution)	24	20	22	26	162	160	173	103	86	54	61	27	17
Drug abuse violations	6,707	6,409	6,718	6,816	36,910	35,428	29,274	19,539	11,559	7,654	4,655	1,876	677
Gambling	6	5	4	7	44	65	55	44	32	28	29	2	10
Offenses against the family and children	313	356	391	413	2,643	2,714	2,092	1,227	666	420	297	147	98
Driving under the influence	4,486	4,847	5,012	5,036	24,458	20,814	17,112	12,823	10,086	8,403	6,816	4,051	2,866
Liquor laws	438	318	282	254	1,169	1,002	875	767	615	520	374	200	136
Drunkenness	798	793	835	847	4,767	4,782	4,605	3,339	2,517	2,117	1,443	824	351
Disorderly conduct	1,483	1,521	1,358	1,390	6,786	6,370	5,308	3,916	2,682	2,281	1,660	845	620
Vagrancy	46	55	65	50	295	343	309	266	201	193	133	69	51
All other offenses (except traffic)	9,993	10,655	10,847	11,429	68,893	70,862	60,343	41,880	27,621	19,887	13,442	6,533	4,675
Suspicion	1	1	1	5	3	21	11	12	3	8	3	1	1
Curfew and loitering law violations	NA	NA	NA	NA	NA	NA	NA	NA	NA	NA	NA	NA	NA

NA = Not available.
* = Less than one-tenth of one percent.
1 Because of rounding, the percentages may not sum to 100 percent. 2 Violent crimes are offenses of murder and nonnegligent manslaughter, rape, robbery, and aggravated assault. Property crimes are offenses of burglary, larceny-theft, motor vehicle theft, and arson. 3 The rape figures in this table are aggregate totals of the data submitted based on both the legacy and revised Uniform Crime Reporting definitions.

Table 41. Arrests of Persons Under 15, 18, 21, and 25 Years of Age, 2020

(Number, percent; 10,466 agencies; 2020 estimated population 228,864,358.)

Offense charged	Total, all ages	Number of persons arrested				Percent of total all ages			
		Under 15	Under 18	Under 21	Under 25	Under 15	Under 18	Under 21	Under 25
Total	5,292,124	85,931	297,074	708,176	1,328,320	1.6	5.6	13.4	25.1
Violent crime[1]	338,443	6,664	24,671	53,480	95,708	2.0	7.3	15.8	28.3
Murder and nonnegligent manslaughter	8,701	64	654	1,923	3,403	0.7	7.5	22.1	39.1
Rape[2]	14,462	885	2,065	3,613	5,295	6.1	14.3	25.0	36.6
Robbery	48,035	1,780	8,517	15,967	22,601	3.7	17.7	33.2	47.1
Aggravated assault	267,245	3,935	13,435	31,977	64,409	1.5	5.0	12.0	24.1
Property crime[1]	611,731	15,140	52,640	101,918	166,217	2.5	8.6	16.7	27.2
Burglary	104,535	3,362	10,563	19,147	30,452	3.2	10.1	18.3	29.1
Larceny-theft	442,016	8,918	32,948	68,272	114,011	2.0	7.5	15.4	25.8
Motor vehicle theft	58,326	2,387	8,273	13,324	20,019	4.1	14.2	22.8	34.3
Arson	6,854	473	856	1,175	1,735	6.9	12.5	17.1	25.3
Other assaults	633,704	19,459	50,129	91,703	164,093	3.1	7.9	14.5	25.9
Forgery and counterfeiting	22,559	47	333	2,609	5,051	0.2	1.5	11.6	22.4
Fraud	54,756	470	1,816	5,759	11,858	0.9	3.3	10.5	21.7
Embezzlement	6,592	9	302	1,295	2,241	0.1	4.6	19.6	34.0
Stolen property; buying, receiving, possessing	61,868	1,232	5,814	11,847	19,345	2.0	9.4	19.1	31.3
Vandalism	121,403	6,493	16,392	27,318	42,276	5.3	13.5	22.5	34.8
Weapons; carrying, possessing, etc.	115,832	1,478	7,809	21,727	42,045	1.3	6.7	18.8	36.3
Prostitution and commercialized vice	11,754	11	77	1,450	3,649	0.1	0.7	12.3	31.0
Sex offenses (except forcible rape and prostitution)	22,065	1,329	2,751	4,484	6,330	6.0	12.5	20.3	28.7
Drug abuse violations	801,546	4,539	29,368	106,854	212,021	0.6	3.7	13.3	26.5
Gambling	1,191	11	58	122	214	0.9	4.9	10.2	18.0
Offenses against the family and children	40,498	508	1,579	3,359	7,027	1.3	3.9	8.3	17.4
Driving under the influence	531,846	64	4,003	34,096	107,509	*	0.8	6.4	20.2
Liquor laws	70,875	1,525	12,372	39,512	44,230	2.2	17.5	55.7	62.4
Drunkenness	135,744	273	1,696	8,274	22,402	0.2	1.2	6.1	16.5
Disorderly conduct	156,502	6,767	17,041	29,164	47,356	4.3	10.9	18.6	30.3
Vagrancy	9,795	46	192	925	1,799	0.5	2.0	9.4	18.4
All other offenses (except traffic)	1,534,972	17,056	59,790	154,024	318,672	1.1	3.9	10.0	20.8
Suspicion	238	11	31	46	67	4.6	13.0	19.3	28.2
Curfew and loitering law violations	8,210	2,799	8,210	8,210	8,210	34.1	100.0	100.0	100.0

* = Less than one-tenth of one percent.
1 Violent crimes in this table are offenses of murder and nonnegligent manslaughter, rape, robbery, and aggravated assault. Property crimes are offenses of burglary, larceny-theft, motor vehicle theft, and arson.   2 The rape figures in this table are aggregate totals of the data submitted based on both the legacy and revised Uniform Crime Reporting definitions.

Table 42. Arrests, Distribution by Sex, 2020

(Number, percent; 10,466 agencies; 2020 estimated population 228,864,358.)

Offense charged	Number of persons arrested			Percent male	Percent female	Percent distribution[1]		
	Total	Male	Female			Total	Male	Female
Total	5,292,124	3,891,282	1,400,842	73.5	26.5	100.0	100.0	100.0
Violent crime[2]	338,443	267,935	70,508	79.2	20.8	6.4	6.9	5.0
Murder and nonnegligent manslaughter	8,701	7,611	1,090	87.5	12.5	0.2	0.2	0.1
Rape[3]	14,462	14,050	412	97.2	2.8	0.3	0.4	*
Robbery	48,035	40,725	7,310	84.8	15.2	0.9	1.0	0.5
Aggravated assault	267,245	205,549	61,696	76.9	23.1	5.0	5.3	4.4
Property crime[2]	611,731	402,790	208,941	65.8	34.2	11.6	10.4	14.9
Burglary	104,535	84,454	20,081	80.8	19.2	2.0	2.2	1.4
Larceny-theft	442,016	267,564	174,452	60.5	39.5	8.4	6.9	12.5
Motor vehicle theft	58,326	45,359	12,967	77.8	22.2	1.1	1.2	0.9
Arson	6,854	5,413	1,441	79.0	21.0	0.1	0.1	0.1
Other assaults	633,704	452,374	181,330	71.4	28.6	12.0	11.6	12.9
Forgery and counterfeiting	22,559	15,318	7,241	67.9	32.1	0.4	0.4	0.5
Fraud	54,756	35,624	19,132	65.1	34.9	1.0	0.9	1.4
Embezzlement	6,592	3,387	3,205	51.4	48.6	0.1	0.1	0.2
Stolen property; buying, receiving, possessing	61,868	48,944	12,924	79.1	20.9	1.2	1.3	0.9
Vandalism	121,403	93,181	28,222	76.8	23.2	2.3	2.4	2.0
Weapons; carrying, possessing, etc.	115,832	104,992	10,840	90.6	9.4	2.2	2.7	0.8
Prostitution and commercialized vice	11,754	4,942	6,812	42.0	58.0	0.2	0.1	0.5
Sex offenses (except forcible rape and prostitution)	22,065	20,780	1,285	94.2	5.8	0.4	0.5	0.1
Drug abuse violations	801,546	600,966	200,580	75.0	25.0	15.1	15.4	14.3
Gambling	1,191	825	366	69.3	30.7	*	*	*
Offenses against the family and children	40,498	27,429	13,069	67.7	32.3	0.8	0.7	0.9
Driving under the influence	531,846	396,682	135,164	74.6	25.4	10.0	10.2	9.6
Liquor laws	70,875	49,833	21,042	70.3	29.7	1.3	1.3	1.5
Drunkenness	135,744	105,399	30,345	77.6	22.4	2.6	2.7	2.2
Disorderly conduct	156,502	109,929	46,573	70.2	29.8	3.0	2.8	3.3
Vagrancy	9,795	7,479	2,316	76.4	23.6	0.2	0.2	0.2
All other offenses (except traffic)	1,534,972	1,136,942	398,030	74.1	25.9	29.0	29.2	28.4
Suspicion	238	153	85	64.3	35.7	*	*	*
Curfew and loitering law violations	8,210	5,378	2,832	65.5	34.5	0.2	0.1	0.2

* = Less than one-tenth of 1 percent.

1 Because of rounding, the percentages may not sum to 100.   2 Violent crimes in this table are offenses of murder and nonnegligent manslaughter, rape, robbery, and aggravated assault. Property crimes are offenses of burglary, larceny-theft, motor vehicle theft, and arson.   3 The rape figures in this table are aggregate totals of the data submitted based on both the legacy and revised Uniform Crime Reporting definitions.

Table 43. Arrests, Distribution by Race, 2020

(Number, percent; 10,466 agencies; 2020 estimated population 228,864,358.)

Offense charged	Total arrests						Percent distribution[1]						Arrests under 18					
	Total	White	Black	American Indian or Alaskan Native	Asian	Native Hawaiian or Other Pacific Islander	Total	White	Black	American Indian or Alaskan Native	Asian	Native Hawaiian or Other Pacific Islander	Total	White	Black	American Indian or Alaskan Native	Asian	Native Hawaiian or Other Pacific Islander
Total	5,213,213	3,648,470	1,356,208	129,815	64,863	13,857	100.0	70.0	26.0	2.5	1.2	0.3	290,848	185,324	93,954	7,912	3,009	649
Violent crime[2]	334,923	201,322	118,971	8,068	5,289	1,273	100.0	60.1	35.5	2.4	1.6	0.4	24,287	12,464	10,959	565	235	64
Murder and nonnegligent manslaughter	8,618	3,968	4,394	123	110	23	100.0	46.0	51.0	1.4	1.3	0.3	646	250	376	10	7	3
Rape[3]	14,181	10,011	3,606	286	227	51	100.0	70.6	25.4	2.0	1.6	0.4	2,009	1,449	494	41	22	3
Robbery	47,674	22,688	23,519	712	501	254	100.0	47.6	49.3	1.5	1.1	0.5	8,437	3,176	5,097	65	67	32
Aggravated assault	264,450	164,655	87,452	6,947	4,451	945	100.0	62.3	33.1	2.6	1.7	0.4	13,195	7,589	4,992	449	139	26
Property crime[2]	603,810	413,096	170,218	12,463	6,705	1,328	100.0	68.4	28.2	2.1	1.1	0.2	51,659	28,911	20,861	1,107	640	140
Burglary	103,568	71,826	28,603	1,659	1,251	229	100.0	69.4	27.6	1.6	1.2	0.2	10,392	5,953	4,099	201	102	37
Larceny-theft	435,625	295,929	124,867	9,396	4,578	855	100.0	67.9	28.7	2.2	1.1	0.2	32,254	18,567	12,501	654	448	84
Motor vehicle theft	57,823	40,394	15,237	1,244	727	221	100.0	69.9	26.4	2.2	1.3	0.4	8,173	3,789	4,065	223	79	17
Arson	6,794	4,947	1,511	164	149	23	100.0	72.8	22.2	2.4	2.2	0.3	840	602	196	29	11	2
Other assaults	625,158	409,055	190,453	15,330	8,771	1,549	100.0	65.4	30.5	2.5	1.4	0.2	49,159	30,792	16,682	1,133	467	85
Forgery and counterfeiting	22,289	15,304	6,350	229	374	32	100.0	68.7	28.5	1.0	1.7	0.1	324	192	121	4	7	0
Fraud	53,968	35,568	16,385	1,111	816	88	100.0	65.9	30.4	2.1	1.5	0.2	1,791	986	718	52	32	3
Embezzlement	6,490	3,942	2,351	71	115	11	100.0	60.7	36.2	1.1	1.8	0.2	294	136	137	2	19	0
Stolen property; buying, receiving, possessing	61,086	38,267	20,856	988	825	150	100.0	62.6	34.1	1.6	1.4	0.2	5,714	1,825	3,722	108	39	20
Vandalism	119,655	81,656	33,131	3,020	1,573	275	100.0	68.2	27.7	2.5	1.3	0.2	16,015	11,584	3,847	430	135	19
Weapons; carrying, possessing, etc.	114,690	59,798	52,094	1,226	1,243	329	100.0	52.1	45.4	1.1	1.1	0.3	7,725	3,750	3,791	78	96	10
Prostitution and commercialized vice	11,692	6,209	4,792	52	582	57	100.0	53.1	41.0	0.4	5.0	0.5	76	37	35	2	1	1
Sex offenses (except forcible rape and prostitution)	21,774	16,090	4,664	457	504	59	100.0	73.9	21.4	2.1	2.3	0.3	2,674	2,047	541	45	38	3
Drug abuse violations	791,450	572,858	195,695	12,010	9,051	1,836	100.0	72.4	24.7	1.5	1.1	0.2	28,742	21,193	6,479	702	307	61
Gambling	1,174	777	258	6	123	10	100.0	66.2	22.0	0.5	10.5	0.9	56	35	18	1	2	0
Offenses against the family and children	39,583	27,000	9,318	2,870	342	53	100.0	68.2	23.5	7.3	0.9	0.1	1,519	1,058	242	210	6	3
Driving under the influence	516,965	417,593	77,366	11,419	8,898	1,689	100.0	80.8	15.0	2.2	1.7	0.3	3,822	3,350	253	155	57	7
Liquor laws	68,586	53,638	9,290	4,642	892	124	100.0	78.2	13.5	6.8	1.3	0.2	11,904	10,179	678	886	136	25
Drunkenness	134,508	102,205	18,957	11,706	1,371	269	100.0	76.0	14.1	8.7	1.0	0.2	1,545	1,079	245	200	18	3
Disorderly conduct	153,881	100,607	44,284	7,267	1,353	370	100.0	65.4	28.8	4.7	0.9	0.2	16,708	9,726	6,164	648	137	33
Vagrancy	9,710	6,394	2,775	396	129	16	100.0	65.8	28.6	4.1	1.3	0.2	191	138	45	3	5	0
All other offenses (except traffic)	1,513,490	1,081,163	375,977	36,219	15,830	4,301	100.0	71.4	24.8	2.4	1.0	0.3	58,542	40,060	16,430	1,360	557	135
Suspicion	264	166	42	53	2	1	100.0	62.9	15.9	20.1	0.8	0.4	34	20	5	9	0	0
Curfew and loitering law violations	8,067	5,762	1,981	212	75	37	100.0	71.4	24.6	2.6	0.9	0.5	8,067	5,762	1,981	212	75	37

Table 43. Arrests, Distribution by Race, 2020—Continued

(Number, percent; 10,466 agencies; 2020 estimated population 228,864,358.)

Offense charged	Percent distribution[1]						Arrests 18 and over						Percent distribution[1]					
	Total	White	Black	American Indian or Alaskan Native	Asian	Native Hawaiian or Other Pacific Islander	Total	White	Black	American Indian or Alaskan Native	Asian	Native Hawaiian or Other Pacific Islander	Total	White	Black	American Indian or Alaskan Native	Asian	Native Hawaiian or Other Pacific Islander
Total	100.0	63.7	32.3	2.7	1.0	0.2	4,922,365	3,463,146	1,262,254	121,903	61,854	13,208	100.0	70.4	25.6	2.5	1.3	0.3
Violent crime[2]	100.0	51.3	45.1	2.3	1.0	0.3	310,636	188,858	108,012	7,503	5,054	1,209	100.0	60.8	34.8	2.4	1.6	0.4
Murder and nonnegligent manslaughter	100.0	38.7	58.2	1.5	1.1	0.5	7,972	3,718	4,018	113	103	20	100.0	46.6	50.4	1.4	1.3	0.3
Rape[3]	100.0	72.1	24.6	2.0	1.1	0.1	12,172	8,562	3,112	245	205	48	100.0	70.3	25.6	2.0	1.7	0.4
Robbery	100.0	37.6	60.4	0.8	0.8	0.4	39,237	19,512	18,422	647	434	222	100.0	49.7	47.0	1.6	1.1	0.6
Aggravated assault	100.0	57.5	37.8	3.4	1.1	0.2	251,255	157,066	82,460	6,498	4,312	919	100.0	62.5	32.8	2.6	1.7	0.4
Property crime[2]	100.0	56.0	40.4	2.1	1.2	0.3	552,151	384,185	149,357	11,356	6,065	1,188	100.0	69.6	27.1	2.1	1.1	0.2
Burglary	100.0	57.3	39.4	1.9	1.0	0.4	93,176	65,873	24,504	1,458	1,149	192	100.0	70.7	26.3	1.6	1.2	0.2
Larceny-theft	100.0	57.6	38.8	2.0	1.4	0.3	403,371	277,362	112,366	8,742	4,130	771	100.0	68.8	27.9	2.2	1.0	0.2
Motor vehicle theft	100.0	46.4	49.7	2.7	1.0	0.2	49,650	36,605	11,172	1,021	648	204	100.0	73.7	22.5	2.1	1.3	0.4
Arson	100.0	71.7	23.3	3.5	1.3	0.2	5,954	4,345	1,315	135	138	21	100.0	73.0	22.1	2.3	2.3	0.4
Other assaults	100.0	62.6	33.9	2.3	0.9	0.2	575,999	378,263	173,771	14,197	8,304	1,464	100.0	65.7	30.2	2.5	1.4	0.3
Forgery and counterfeiting	100.0	59.3	37.3	1.2	2.2	0.0	21,965	15,112	6,229	225	367	32	100.0	68.8	28.4	1.0	1.7	0.1
Fraud	100.0	55.1	40.1	2.9	1.8	0.2	52,177	34,582	15,667	1,059	784	85	100.0	66.3	30.0	2.0	1.5	0.2
Embezzlement	100.0	46.3	46.6	0.7	6.5	0.0	6,196	3,806	2,214	69	96	11	100.0	61.4	35.7	1.1	1.5	0.2
Stolen property; buying, receiving, possessing	100.0	31.9	65.1	1.9	0.7	0.4	55,372	36,442	17,134	880	786	130	100.0	65.8	30.9	1.6	1.4	0.2
Vandalism	100.0	72.3	24.0	2.7	0.8	0.1	103,640	70,072	29,284	2,590	1,438	256	100.0	67.6	28.3	2.5	1.4	0.2
Weapons; carrying, possessing, etc.	100.0	48.5	49.1	1.0	1.2	0.1	106,965	56,048	48,303	1,148	1,147	319	100.0	52.4	45.2	1.1	1.1	0.3
Prostitution and commercialized vice	100.0	48.7	46.1	2.6	1.3	1.3	11,616	6,172	4,757	50	581	56	100.0	53.1	41.0	0.4	5.0	0.5
Sex offenses (except forcible rape and prostitution)	100.0	76.6	20.2	1.7	1.4	0.1	19,100	14,043	4,123	412	466	56	100.0	73.5	21.6	2.2	2.4	0.3
Drug abuse violations	100.0	73.7	22.5	2.4	1.1	0.2	762,708	551,665	189,216	11,308	8,744	1,775	100.0	72.3	24.8	1.5	1.1	0.2
Gambling	100.0	62.5	32.1	1.8	3.6	0.0	1,118	742	240	5	121	10	100.0	66.4	21.5	0.4	10.8	0.9
Offenses against the family and children	100.0	69.7	15.9	13.8	0.4	0.2	38,064	25,942	9,076	2,660	336	50	100.0	68.2	23.8	7.0	0.9	0.1
Driving under the influence	100.0	87.7	6.6	4.1	1.5	0.2	513,143	414,243	77,113	11,264	8,841	1,682	100.0	80.7	15.0	2.2	1.7	0.3
Liquor laws	100.0	85.5	5.7	7.4	1.1	0.2	56,682	43,459	8,612	3,756	756	99	100.0	76.7	15.2	6.6	1.3	0.2
Drunkenness	100.0	69.8	15.9	12.9	1.2	0.2	132,963	101,126	18,712	11,506	1,353	266	100.0	76.1	14.1	8.7	1.0	0.2
Disorderly conduct	100.0	58.2	36.9	3.9	0.8	0.2	137,173	90,881	38,120	6,619	1,216	337	100.0	66.3	27.8	4.8	0.9	0.2
Vagrancy	100.0	72.3	23.6	1.6	2.6	0.0	9,519	6,256	2,730	393	124	16	100.0	65.7	28.7	4.1	1.3	0.2
All other offenses (except traffic)	100.0	68.4	28.1	2.3	1.0	0.2	1,454,948	1,041,103	359,547	34,859	15,273	4,166	100.0	71.6	24.7	2.4	1.0	0.3
Suspicion	100.0	58.8	14.7	26.5	0.0	0.0	230	146	37	44	2	1	100.0	63.5	16.1	19.1	0.9	0.4
Curfew and loitering law violations	100.0	71.4	24.6	2.6	0.9	0.5	NA	NA	NA	NA	NA	NA	NA	NA	NA	NA	NA	NA

NA = Not available.
1 Because of rounding, the percentages may not sum to 100.   2 Violent crimes are offenses of murder and nonnegligent manslaughter, rape, robbery, and aggravated assault. Property crimes are offenses of burglary, larceny-theft, motor vehicle theft, and arson.   3 The rape figures in this table are aggregate totals of the data submitted based on both the legacy and revised Uniform Crime Reporting definitions.

Table 43A. Arrests, Distribution by Ethnicity, 2020

(Number, percent; 10,466 agencies; 2020 estimated population 228,864,358.)

Offense charged	Total arrests			Percent distribution[1]			Arrests under 18		
	Total[2]	Hispanic or Latino	Not Hispanic or Latino	Total[2]	Hispanic or Latino	Not Hispanic or Latino	Total[2]	Hispanic or Latino	Not Hispanic or Latino
Total	4,477,428	928,437	3,548,991	100.0	20.7	79.3	241,426	57,668	183,758
Violent crime[3]	294,088	78,577	215,511	100.0	26.7	73.3	20,987	5,792	15,195
Murder and nonnegligent manslaughter	7,269	1,633	5,636	100.0	22.5	77.5	543	154	389
Rape[4]	11,857	3,509	8,348	100.0	29.6	70.4	1,613	386	1,227
Robbery	41,970	10,887	31,083	100.0	25.9	74.1	7,514	2,049	5,465
Aggravated assault	232,992	62,548	170,444	100.0	26.8	73.2	11,317	3,203	8,114
Property crime[3]	515,672	91,320	424,352	100.0	17.7	82.3	42,868	9,314	33,554
Burglary	89,960	19,591	70,369	100.0	21.8	78.2	8,371	2,100	6,271
Larceny-theft	368,820	55,986	312,834	100.0	15.2	84.8	26,760	5,366	21,394
Motor vehicle theft	51,063	14,473	36,590	100.0	28.3	71.7	7,023	1,710	5,313
Arson	5,829	1,270	4,559	100.0	21.8	78.2	714	138	576
Other assaults	532,225	107,191	425,034	100.0	20.1	79.9	41,249	9,526	31,723
Forgery and counterfeiting	19,625	3,332	16,293	100.0	17.0	83.0	281	74	207
Fraud	46,491	6,896	39,595	100.0	14.8	85.2	1,430	307	1,123
Embezzlement	5,562	828	4,734	100.0	14.9	85.1	246	33	213
Stolen property; buying, receiving, possessing	52,652	10,875	41,777	100.0	20.7	79.3	4,745	989	3,756
Vandalism	102,777	21,209	81,568	100.0	20.6	79.4	13,422	2,971	10,451
Weapons; carrying, possessing, etc.	94,295	23,456	70,839	100.0	24.9	75.1	6,582	2,190	4,392
Prostitution and commercialized vice	10,949	2,725	8,224	100.0	24.9	75.1	63	12	51
Sex offenses (except forcible rape and prostitution)	18,924	5,754	13,170	100.0	30.4	69.6	2,201	588	1,613
Drug abuse violations	711,136	155,970	555,166	100.0	21.9	78.1	25,056	7,311	17,745
Gambling	1,111	468	643	100.0	42.1	57.9	49	29	20
Offenses against the family and children	34,157	5,542	28,615	100.0	16.2	83.8	1,271	272	999
Driving under the influence	435,235	123,406	311,829	100.0	28.4	71.6	3,124	999	2,125
Liquor laws	54,050	9,496	44,554	100.0	17.6	82.4	9,435	1,705	7,730
Drunkenness	128,105	31,408	96,697	100.0	24.5	75.5	1,433	467	966
Disorderly conduct	119,408	16,711	102,697	100.0	14.0	86.0	12,758	2,383	10,375
Vagrancy	8,832	1,608	7,224	100.0	18.2	81.8	124	32	92
All other offenses (except traffic)	1,285,377	229,968	1,055,409	100.0	17.9	82.1	47,522	10,998	36,524
Suspicion	205	22	183	100.0	10.7	89.3	28	1	27
Curfew and loitering law violations	6,552	1,675	4,877	100.0	25.6	74.4	6,552	1,675	4,877

Table 43A. Arrests, Distribution by Ethnicity, 2020—Continued

(Number, percent; 10,466 agencies; 2020 estimated population 228,864,358.)

Offense charged	Percent distribution[1]				Arrests 18 and over			Percent distribution[1]	
	Total[2]	Hispanic or Latino	Not Hispanic or Latino	Total[2]	Hispanic or Latino	Not Hispanic or Latino	Total[2]	Hispanic or Latino	Not Hispanic or Latino
Total	100.0	23.9	76.1	4,236,002	870,769	3,365,233	100.0	20.6	79.4
Violent crime[3]	100.0	27.6	72.4	273,101	72,785	200,316	100.0	26.7	73.3
Murder and nonnegligent manslaughter	100.0	28.4	71.6	6,726	1,479	5,247	100.0	22.0	78.0
Rape[4]	100.0	23.9	76.1	10,244	3,123	7,121	100.0	30.5	69.5
Robbery	100.0	27.3	72.7	34,456	8,838	25,618	100.0	25.7	74.3
Aggravated assault	100.0	28.3	71.7	221,675	59,345	162,330	100.0	26.8	73.2
Property crime[3]	100.0	21.7	78.3	472,804	82,006	390,798	100.0	17.3	82.7
Burglary	100.0	25.1	74.9	81,589	17,491	64,098	100.0	21.4	78.6
Larceny-theft	100.0	20.1	79.9	342,060	50,620	291,440	100.0	14.8	85.2
Motor vehicle theft	100.0	24.3	75.7	44,040	12,763	31,277	100.0	29.0	71.0
Arson	100.0	19.3	80.7	5,115	1,132	3,983	100.0	22.1	77.9
Other assaults	100.0	23.1	76.9	490,976	97,665	393,311	100.0	19.9	80.1
Forgery and counterfeiting	100.0	26.3	73.7	19,344	3,258	16,086	100.0	16.8	83.2
Fraud	100.0	21.5	78.5	45,061	6,589	38,472	100.0	14.6	85.4
Embezzlement	100.0	13.4	86.6	5,316	795	4,521	100.0	15.0	85.0
Stolen property; buying, receiving, possessing	100.0	20.8	79.2	47,907	9,886	38,021	100.0	20.6	79.4
Vandalism	100.0	22.1	77.9	89,355	18,238	71,117	100.0	20.4	79.6
Weapons; carrying, possessing, etc.	100.0	33.3	66.7	87,713	21,266	66,447	100.0	24.2	75.8
Prostitution and commercialized vice	100.0	19.0	81.0	10,886	2,713	8,173	100.0	24.9	75.1
Sex offenses (except forcible rape and prostitution)	100.0	26.7	73.3	16,723	5,166	11,557	100.0	30.9	69.1
Drug abuse violations	100.0	29.2	70.8	686,080	148,659	537,421	100.0	21.7	78.3
Gambling	100.0	59.2	40.8	1,062	439	623	100.0	41.3	58.7
Offenses against the family and children	100.0	21.4	78.6	32,886	5,270	27,616	100.0	16.0	84.0
Driving under the influence	100.0	32.0	68.0	432,111	122,407	309,704	100.0	28.3	71.7
Liquor laws	100.0	18.1	81.9	44,615	7,791	36,824	100.0	17.5	82.5
Drunkenness	100.0	32.6	67.4	126,672	30,941	95,731	100.0	24.4	75.6
Disorderly conduct	100.0	18.7	81.3	106,650	14,328	92,322	100.0	13.4	86.6
Vagrancy	100.0	25.8	74.2	8,708	1,576	7,132	100.0	18.1	81.9
All other offenses (except traffic)	100.0	23.1	76.9	1,237,855	218,970	1,018,885	100.0	17.7	82.3
Suspicion	100.0	3.6	96.4	177	21	156	100.0	11.9	88.1
Curfew and loitering law violations	100.0	25.6	74.4	NA	NA	NA	NA	NA	NA

NA = Not available.
1 Because of rounding, the percentages may not sum to 100.   2 The ethnicity totals are representative of those agencies that provided ethnicity breakdowns. Not all agencies provide ethnicity data; therefore, the race and ethnicity totals will not be equal.
3 Violent crimes are offenses of murder and nonnegligent manslaughter, rape, robbery, and aggravated assault. Property crimes are offenses of burglary, larceny-theft, motor vehicle theft, and arson.   4 The rape figures in this table are aggregate totals of the data submitted based on both the legacy and revised Uniform Crime Reporting definitions.

Table 44. Arrest Trends, Cities, 2019–2020

(Number, percent change; 6,841 agencies; 2020 estimated population 140,331,250; 2019 estimated population 139,813,132.)

| Offense charged | Number of persons arrested | | | | | | | | |
| | Total, all ages | | | Under 18 years of age | | | 18 years of age and over | | |
	2019	2020	Percent change	2019	2020	Percent change	2019	2020	Percent change
Total[1]	4,348,178	3,384,987	-22.2	339,874	213,227	-37.3	4,008,304	3,171,760	-20.9
Violent crime[2]	241,690	230,819	-4.5	24,029	17,729	-26.2	217,661	213,090	-2.1
Murder and nonnegligent manslaughter	4,795	5,724	+19.4	419	467	+11.5	4,376	5,257	+20.1
Rape[3]	10,513	9,134	-13.1	1,736	1,257	-27.6	8,777	7,877	-10.3
Robbery	40,712	35,687	-12.3	8,625	6,642	-23.0	32,087	29,045	-9.5
Aggravated assault	185,670	180,274	-2.9	13,249	9,363	-29.3	172,421	170,911	-0.9
Property crime[2]	577,013	452,731	-21.5	65,473	40,261	-38.5	511,540	412,470	-19.4
Burglary	80,581	71,371	-11.4	10,420	7,633	-26.7	70,161	63,738	-9.2
Larceny-theft	453,761	337,188	-25.7	47,242	25,809	-45.4	406,519	311,379	-23.4
Motor vehicle theft	38,465	39,317	+2.2	6,959	6,194	-11.0	31,506	33,123	+5.1
Arson	4,206	4,855	+15.4	852	625	-26.6	3,354	4,230	+26.1
Other assaults	478448	429714	-10.2	57323	34111	-40.5	421125	395603	-6.1
Forgery and counterfeiting	22,303	15,404	-30.9	471	251	-46.7	21,832	15,153	-30.6
Fraud	52,793	36,345	-31.2	1,905	1,345	-29.4	50,888	35,000	-31.2
Embezzlement	7,445	4,838	-35.0	320	253	-20.9	7,125	4,585	-35.6
Stolen property; buying, receiving, possessing	43,871	42,619	-2.9	5,082	4,453	-12.4	38,789	38,166	-1.6
Vandalism	87,973	85,288	-3.1	15,757	11,756	-25.4	72,216	73,532	+1.8
Weapons; carrying, possessing, etc.	72,333	76,850	+6.2	8,295	5,789	-30.2	64,038	71,061	+11.0
Prostitution and commercialized vice	10,664	5,806	-45.6	75	23	-69.3	10,589	5,783	-45.4
Sex offenses (except forcible rape and prostitution)	18,375	14,150	-23.0	3,080	1,778	-42.3	15,295	12,372	-19.1
Drug abuse violations	670,131	507,824	-24.2	38,034	20,414	-46.3	632,097	487,410	-22.9
Gambling	909	695	-23.5	51	30	-41.2	858	665	-22.5
Offenses against the family and children	26,602	23,349	-12.2	1,416	1,150	-18.8	25,186	22,199	-11.9
Driving under the influence	343,589	272,121	-20.8	2,071	2,243	+8.3	341,518	269,878	-21.0
Liquor laws	75,137	47,184	-37.2	10,728	7,772	-27.6	64,409	39,412	-38.8
Drunkenness	155,386	97,370	-37.3	1,680	1,116	-33.6	153,706	96,254	-37.4
Disorderly conduct	150,583	114,127	-24.2	26,724	12,842	-51.9	123,859	101,285	-18.2
Vagrancy	10,029	7,777	-22.5	219	174	-20.5	9,810	7,603	-22.5
All other offenses (except traffic)	1,294,402	913,443	-29.4	68,639	43,204	-37.1	1,225,763	870,239	-29.0
Suspicion	142	141	-0.7	5	17	+240.0	137	124	-9.5
Curfew and loitering law violations	8,502	6,533	-23.2	8,502	6,533	-23.2	NA	NA	NA

NA = Not available.

1 Does not include suspicion.   2 Violent crimes are offenses of murder and nonnegligent manslaughter, rape, robbery, and aggravated assault. Property crimes are offenses of burglary, larceny-theft, motor vehicle theft, and arson.   3 The rape figures in this table are aggregate totals of the data submitted based on both the legacy and revised Uniform Crime Reporting definitions.

Table 45. Arrest Trends, Cities, by Age and Sex, 2019–2020

(Number, percent change; 6,841 agencies; 2020 estimated population 140,331,250; 2019 estimated population 139,813,132.)

Offense charged	Male						Female					
	Total			Under 18			Total			Under 18		
	2019	2020	Percent change	2019	2020	Percent change	2019	2020	Percent change	2019	2020	Percent change
Total[1]	3,135,642	2,481,028	-20.9	235,198	150,844	-35.9	1,212,536	903,959	-25.4	104,676	62,383	-40.4
Violent crime[2]	189,770	181,941	-4.1	19,453	14,392	-26.0	51,920	48,878	-5.9	4,576	3,337	-27.1
Murder and nonnegligent manslaughter	4,232	5,051	+19.4	388	428	+10.3	563	673	+19.5	31	39	+25.8
Rape[3]	10,181	8,864	-12.9	1,652	1,208	-26.9	332	270	-18.7	84	49	-41.7
Robbery	34,232	30,294	-11.5	7,641	5,839	-23.6	6,480	5,393	-16.8	984	803	-18.4
Aggravated assault	141,125	137,732	-2.4	9,772	6,917	-29.2	44,545	42,542	-4.5	3,477	2,446	-29.7
Property crime[2]	354,725	294,307	-17.0	43,024	28,334	-34.1	222,288	158,424	-28.7	22,449	11,927	-46.9
Burglary	63,786	57,900	-9.2	8,968	6,569	-26.8	16,795	13,471	-19.8	1,452	1,064	-26.7
Larceny-theft	258,149	202,076	-21.7	27,751	16,252	-41.4	195,612	135,112	-30.9	19,491	9,557	-51.0
Motor vehicle theft	29,523	30,498	+3.3	5,582	4,979	-10.8	8,942	8,819	-1.4	1,377	1,215	-11.8
Arson	3,267	3,833	+17.3	723	534	-26.1	939	1,022	+8.8	129	91	-29.5
Other assaults	337,622	306,007	-9.4	35,579	21,041	-40.9	140,826	123,707	-12.2	21,744	13,070	-39.9
Forgery and counterfeiting	14,814	10,387	-29.9	358	203	-43.3	7,489	5,017	-33.0	113	48	-57.5
Fraud	34,026	23,374	-31.3	1,293	882	-31.8	18,767	12,971	-30.9	612	463	-24.3
Embezzlement	3,641	2,478	-31.9	177	129	-27.1	3,804	2,360	-38.0	143	124	-13.3
Stolen property; buying, receiving, possessing	33,954	33,759	-0.6	4,200	3,784	-9.9	9,917	8,860	-10.7	882	669	-24.1
Vandalism	67,298	65,166	-3.2	12,684	9,313	-26.6	20,675	20,122	-2.7	3,073	2,443	-20.5
Weapons; carrying, possessing, etc.	65,554	69,689	+6.3	7,486	5,347	-28.6	6,779	7,161	+5.6	809	442	-45.4
Prostitution and commercialized vice	4,333	2,691	-37.9	41	11	-73.2	6,331	3,115	-50.8	34	12	-64.7
Sex offenses (except forcible rape and prostitution)	17,143	13,325	-22.3	2,725	1,592	-41.6	1,232	825	-33.0	355	186	-47.6
Drug abuse violations	504,455	384,947	-23.7	27,998	15,288	-45.4	165,676	122,877	-25.8	10,036	5,126	-48.9
Gambling	666	473	-29.0	47	24	-48.9	243	222	-8.6	4	6	+50.0
Offenses against the family and children	16,890	15,138	-10.4	808	652	-19.3	9,712	8,211	-15.5	608	498	-18.1
Driving under the influence	252,919	201,665	-20.3	1,538	1,642	+6.8	90,670	70,456	-22.3	533	601	+12.8
Liquor laws	52,149	33,247	-36.2	6,173	4,546	-26.4	22,988	13,937	-39.4	4,555	3,226	-29.2
Drunkenness	122,465	76,351	-37.7	1,123	735	-34.6	32,921	21,019	-36.2	557	381	-31.6
Disorderly conduct	106,038	80,056	-24.5	16,645	8,083	-51.4	44,545	34,071	-23.5	10,079	4,759	-52.8
Vagrancy	7,729	5,938	-23.2	160	126	-21.3	2,300	1,839	-20.0	59	48	-18.6
All other offenses (except traffic)	943,813	675,820	-28.4	48,048	30,451	-36.6	350,589	237,623	-32.2	20,591	12,753	-38.1
Suspicion	91	83	-8.8	5	12	+140.0	51	58	+13.7	0	5	
Curfew and loitering law violations	5,638	4,269	-24.3	5,638	4,269	-24.3	2,864	2,264	-20.9	2,864	2,264	-20.9

1 Does not include suspicion.   2 Violent crimes are offenses of murder and nonnegligent manslaughter, rape, robbery, and aggravated assault. Property crimes are offenses of burglary, larceny-theft, motor vehicle theft, and arson.   3 The rape figures in this table are aggregate totals of the data submitted based on both the legacy and revised Uniform Crime Reporting definitions.

Table 46. Arrests, Cities, Distribution by Age, 2020

(Number, percent; 7,634 agencies; 2020 estimated population 159,832,632.)

Offense charged	Total, all ages	Ages under 15	Ages under 18	Ages 18 and over	Under 10	10–12	13–14	15	16	17	18	19	20
Total	3,851,277	70,529	238,424	3,612,853	922	14,926	54,681	45,465	55,840	66,590	93,813	104,216	109,401
Total percent distribution[1]	100.0	1.8	6.2	93.8	*	0.4	1.4	1.2	1.4	1.7	2.4	2.7	2.8
Violent crime[2]	267,047	5,486	20,454	246,593	60	1,139	4,287	3,928	5,028	6,012	7,443	7,674	8,088
Violent crime percent distribution[1]	100.0	2.1	7.7	92.3	*	0.4	1.6	1.5	1.9	2.3	2.8	2.9	3.0
Murder and nonnegligent manslaughter	6,510	48	520	5,990	1	3	44	78	161	233	340	338	319
Rape[3]	10,360	609	1,419	8,941	7	190	412	265	254	291	353	345	333
Robbery	41,569	1,631	7,679	33,890	2	185	1,444	1,575	2,092	2,381	2,560	2,067	1,842
Aggravated assault	208,608	3,198	10,836	197,772	50	761	2,387	2,010	2,521	3,107	4,190	4,924	5,594
Property crime[2]	506,199	12,825	44,275	461,924	147	2,385	10,293	9,058	10,662	11,730	13,959	13,633	13,124
Property crime percent distribution[1]	100.0	2.5	8.7	91.3	*	0.5	2.0	1.8	2.1	2.3	2.8	2.7	2.6
Burglary	80,714	2,721	8,383	72,331	58	550	2,113	1,721	1,870	2,071	2,304	2,241	2,163
Larceny-theft	375,128	7,715	28,382	346,746	63	1,483	6,169	5,589	7,002	8,076	10,161	10,013	9,677
Motor vehicle theft	44,997	2,014	6,839	38,158	5	221	1,788	1,626	1,694	1,505	1,430	1,292	1,197
Arson	5,360	375	671	4,689	21	131	223	122	96	78	64	87	87
Other assaults	490,395	15,347	38,945	451,450	184	4,026	11,137	7,427	7,917	8,254	9,520	10,711	12,769
Forgery and counterfeiting	17,093	43	269	16,824	0	6	37	44	66	116	489	699	669
Fraud	40,644	386	1,443	39,201	1	53	332	280	331	446	856	1,070	1,180
Embezzlement	5,322	6	265	5,057	0	1	5	5	83	171	297	290	245
Stolen property; buying, receiving, possessing	46,638	1,037	4,782	41,856	2	101	934	1,022	1,289	1,434	1,652	1,572	1,494
Vandalism	96,164	5,267	13,019	83,145	132	1,365	3,770	2,573	2,635	2,544	2,821	2,918	2,832
Weapons; carrying, possessing, etc.	88,908	1,239	6,619	82,289	15	242	982	1,145	1,703	2,532	3,573	3,804	3,915
Prostitution and commercialized vice	10,617	5	57	10,560	0	0	5	7	19	26	308	445	547
Sex offenses (except forcible rape and prostitution)	16,162	962	1,959	14,203	24	277	661	309	356	332	405	443	368
Drug abuse violations	561,935	3,736	22,808	539,127	14	467	3,255	3,659	5,975	9,438	16,820	18,800	19,325
Gambling	861	6	31	830	0	2	4	5	12	8	13	8	29
Offenses against the family and children	26,519	431	1,357	25,162	20	103	308	280	347	299	407	428	577
Driving under the influence	311,168	51	2,591	308,577	0	1	50	143	670	1,727	4,252	6,030	7,615
Liquor laws	53,701	1,178	8,746	44,955	4	132	1,042	1,501	2,451	3,616	7,117	7,236	5,716
Drunkenness	115,065	244	1,488	113,577	1	29	214	255	359	630	1,558	1,886	2,098
Disorderly conduct	128,297	5,640	13,995	114,302	57	1,454	4,129	2,718	2,826	2,811	3,300	3,570	3,556
Vagrancy	8,813	42	179	8,634	2	5	35	33	51	53	238	233	202
All other offenses (except traffic)	1,052,267	14,046	47,857	1,004,410	246	2,738	11,062	9,436	11,224	13,151	18,779	22,760	25,051
Suspicion	200	9	23	177	2	3	4	2	5	7	6	6	1
Curfew and loitering law violations	7,262	2,543	7,262	NA	11	397	2,135	1,635	1,831	1,253	NA	NA	NA

Table 46. Arrests, Cities, Distribution by Age, 2020—Continued

(Number, percent; 7,634 agencies; 2020 estimated population 159,832,632.)

Offense charged	21	22	23	24	25–29	30–34	35–39	40–44	45–49	50–54	55–59	60–64	65 and over
Total	110,690	112,363	113,333	117,043	648,064	609,848	499,479	358,009	245,376	198,840	153,008	84,099	55,271
Total percent distribution[1]	2.9	2.9	2.9	3.0	16.8	15.8	13.0	9.3	6.4	5.2	4.0	2.2	1.4
Violent crime[2]	8,313	8,589	8,508	8,681	46,848	41,377	32,833	22,551	15,351	12,023	9,257	5,273	3,784
Violent crime percent distribution[1]	3.1	3.2	3.2	3.3	17.5	15.5	12.3	8.4	5.7	4.5	3.5	2.0	1.4
Murder and nonnegligent manslaughter	324	280	284	276	1,246	812	615	418	252	170	141	87	88
Rape[3]	334	296	277	303	1,336	1,354	1,192	861	642	478	383	233	221
Robbery	1,595	1,489	1,314	1,338	6,752	5,327	3,775	2,310	1,386	1,055	680	275	125
Aggravated assault	6,060	6,524	6,633	6,764	37,514	33,884	27,251	18,962	13,071	10,320	8,053	4,678	3,350
Property crime[2]	12,863	13,059	13,342	13,979	82,039	82,163	66,783	46,980	31,278	25,725	18,340	9,235	5,422
Property crime percent distribution[1]	2.5	2.6	2.6	2.8	16.2	16.2	13.2	9.3	6.2	5.1	3.6	1.8	1.1
Burglary	2,005	2,154	2,221	2,440	13,868	13,546	10,545	7,101	4,405	3,460	2,343	1,051	484
Larceny-theft	9,502	9,495	9,740	10,068	59,204	60,136	50,052	35,827	24,645	20,685	15,041	7,758	4,742
Motor vehicle theft	1,254	1,312	1,283	1,341	8,133	7,659	5,450	3,514	1,863	1,286	752	289	103
Arson	102	98	98	130	834	822	736	538	365	294	204	137	93
Other assaults	13,779	14,414	14,792	15,004	82,751	76,205	62,181	45,402	31,246	25,192	19,168	10,580	7,736
Forgery and counterfeiting	398	471	421	485	3,057	2,944	2,648	1,691	1,135	799	518	255	145
Fraud	1,075	1,152	1,182	1,268	7,123	7,209	5,928	4,089	2,606	1,920	1,409	709	425
Embezzlement	223	208	177	186	829	722	579	419	316	256	182	82	46
Stolen property; buying, receiving, possessing	1,379	1,407	1,322	1,518	8,358	8,025	6,033	3,881	2,263	1,467	922	399	164
Vandalism	2,871	2,966	3,036	3,105	16,364	14,380	11,181	7,605	4,621	3,586	2,572	1,327	960
Weapons; carrying, possessing, etc.	4,310	4,134	3,930	3,658	17,555	13,141	9,228	5,929	3,458	2,383	1,718	933	620
Prostitution and commercialized vice	624	523	460	460	2,106	1,490	1,045	796	586	470	323	197	180
Sex offenses (except forcible rape and prostitution)	372	325	310	327	1,932	1,979	1,945	1,490	1,101	954	904	652	696
Drug abuse violations	18,108	18,011	18,004	18,671	103,384	94,234	75,934	51,966	32,821	24,515	17,156	8,029	3,349
Gambling	14	21	21	16	109	120	124	98	89	71	47	20	30
Offenses against the family and children	628	626	721	775	4,720	4,987	4,071	2,811	1,753	1,174	759	429	296
Driving under the influence	10,448	10,822	11,043	11,191	55,648	47,694	38,321	29,271	22,509	18,893	16,230	10,396	8,214
Liquor laws	1,215	887	781	706	3,544	3,257	3,048	2,541	2,306	2,285	2,173	1,336	807
Drunkenness	2,925	2,962	2,971	3,153	17,113	17,039	15,997	12,131	9,794	9,180	8,040	4,375	2,355
Disorderly conduct	4,109	3,918	3,675	3,723	18,838	17,490	14,800	11,180	7,948	6,801	5,637	3,313	2,444
Vagrancy	184	202	206	190	1,217	1,231	1,099	943	739	724	637	360	229
All other offenses (except traffic)	26,850	27,660	28,429	29,941	174,513	174,127	145,674	106,208	73,441	60,411	47,007	26,194	17,365
Suspicion	2	6	2	6	16	34	27	27	15	11	9	5	4
Curfew and loitering law violations	NA	NA	NA	NA	NA	NA	NA	NA	NA	NA	NA	NA	NA

NA = Not available.

* = Less than one-tenth of one percent.

1 Because of rounding, the percentages may not sum to 100.   2 Violent crimes are offenses of murder and nonnegligent manslaughter, rape, robbery, and aggravated assault. Property crimes are offenses of burglary, larceny-theft, motor vehicle theft, and arson.   3 The rape figures in this table are aggregate totals of the data submitted based on both the legacy and revised Uniform Crime Reporting definitions.

Table 47. Arrests, Cities, Persons Under 15, 18, 21, and 25 Years of Age, 2020

(Number; percent; 7,634 agencies; 2020 estimated population 159,832,632.)

Offense charged	Total, all ages	Number of persons arrested				Percent of total of all ages			
		Under 15	Under 18	Under 21	Under 25	Under 15	Under 18	Under 21	Under 25
Total	3,851,277	70,529	238,424	545,854	999,283	1.8	6.2	14.2	25.9
Violent crime[1]	267,047	5,486	20,454	43,659	77,750	2.1	7.7	16.3	29.1
Murder and nonnegligent manslaughter	6,510	48	520	1,517	2,681	0.7	8.0	23.3	41.2
Rape[2]	10,360	609	1,419	2,450	3,660	5.9	13.7	23.6	35.3
Robbery	41,569	1,631	7,679	14,148	19,884	3.9	18.5	34.0	47.8
Aggravated assault	208,608	3,198	10,836	25,544	51,525	1.5	5.2	12.2	24.7
Property crime[1]	506,199	12,825	44,275	84,991	138,234	2.5	8.7	16.8	27.3
Burglary	80,714	2,721	8,383	15,091	23,911	3.4	10.4	18.7	29.6
Larceny-theft	375,128	7,715	28,382	58,233	97,038	2.1	7.6	15.5	25.9
Motor vehicle theft	44,997	2,014	6,839	10,758	15,948	4.5	15.2	23.9	35.4
Arson	5,360	375	671	909	1,337	7.0	12.5	17.0	24.9
Other assaults	490,395	15,347	38,945	71,945	129,934	3.1	7.9	14.7	26.5
Forgery and counterfeiting	17,093	43	269	2,126	3,901	0.3	1.6	12.4	22.8
Fraud	40,644	386	1,443	4,549	9,226	0.9	3.6	11.2	22.7
Embezzlement	5,322	6	265	1,097	1,891	0.1	5.0	20.6	35.5
Stolen property; buying, receiving, possessing	46,638	1,037	4,782	9,500	15,126	2.2	10.3	20.4	32.4
Vandalism	96,164	5,267	13,019	21,590	33,568	5.5	13.5	22.5	34.9
Weapons; carrying, possessing, etc.	88,908	1,239	6,619	17,911	33,943	1.4	7.4	20.1	38.2
Prostitution and commercialized vice	10,617	5	57	1,357	3,424	*	0.5	12.8	32.3
Sex offenses (except forcible rape and prostitution)	16,162	962	1,959	3,175	4,509	6.0	12.1	19.6	27.9
Drug abuse violations	561,935	3,736	22,808	77,753	150,547	0.7	4.1	13.8	26.8
Gambling	861	6	31	81	153	0.7	3.6	9.4	17.8
Offenses against the family and children	26,519	431	1,357	2,769	5,519	1.6	5.1	10.4	20.8
Driving under the influence	311,168	51	2,591	20,488	63,992	*	0.8	6.6	20.6
Liquor laws	53,701	1,178	8,746	28,815	32,404	2.2	16.3	53.7	60.3
Drunkenness	115,065	244	1,488	7,030	19,041	0.2	1.3	6.1	16.5
Disorderly conduct	128,297	5,640	13,995	24,421	39,846	4.4	10.9	19.0	31.1
Vagrancy	8,813	42	179	852	1,634	0.5	2.0	9.7	18.5
All other offenses (except traffic)	1,052,267	14,046	47,857	114,447	227,327	1.3	4.5	10.9	21.6
Suspicion	200	9	23	36	52	4.5	11.5	18.0	26.0
Curfew and loitering law violations	7,262	2,543	7,262	7,262	7,262	35.0	100.0	100.0	100.0

* = Less than one-tenth of one percent.
1 Violent crimes are offenses of murder and nonnegligent manslaughter, rape, robbery, and aggravated assault. Property crimes are offenses of burglary, larceny-theft, motor vehicle theft, and arson. 2 The rape figures in this table are aggregate totals of the data submitted based on both the legacy and revised Uniform Crime Reporting definitions.

Table 48. Arrests, Cities, Distribution by Sex, 2020

(Number, percent;7,634 agencies; 2020 estimated population 159,832,632.)

Offense charged	Number of persons arrested			Percent male	Percent female	Percent distribution[1]		
	Total	Male	Female			Total	Male	Female
Total	3,851,277	2,822,740	1,028,537	73.3	26.7	100.0	100.0	100.0
Violent crime[2]	267,047	210,289	56,758	78.7	21.3	6.9	7.4	5.5
Murder and nonnegligent manslaughter	6,510	5,741	769	88.2	11.8	0.2	0.2	0.1
Rape[3]	10,360	10,062	298	97.1	2.9	0.3	0.4	*
Robbery	41,569	35,282	6,287	84.9	15.1	1.1	1.2	0.6
Aggravated assault	208,608	159,204	49,404	76.3	23.7	5.4	5.6	4.8
Property crime[2]	506,199	329,593	176,606	65.1	34.9	13.1	11.7	17.2
Burglary	80,714	65,245	15,469	80.8	19.2	2.1	2.3	1.5
Larceny-theft	375,128	225,192	149,936	60.0	40.0	9.7	8.0	14.6
Motor vehicle theft	44,997	34,942	10,055	77.7	22.3	1.2	1.2	1.0
Arson	5,360	4,214	1,146	78.6	21.4	0.1	0.1	0.1
Other assaults	490,395	348,226	142,169	71.0	29.0	12.7	12.3	13.8
Forgery and counterfeiting	17,093	11,526	5,567	67.4	32.6	0.4	0.4	0.5
Fraud	40,644	26,271	14,373	64.6	35.4	1.1	0.9	1.4
Embezzlement	5,322	2,740	2,582	51.5	48.5	0.1	0.1	0.3
Stolen property; buying, receiving, possessing	46,638	36,886	9,752	79.1	20.9	1.2	1.3	0.9
Vandalism	96,164	73,469	22,695	76.4	23.6	2.5	2.6	2.2
Weapons; carrying, possessing, etc.	88,908	80,740	8,168	90.8	9.2	2.3	2.9	0.8
Prostitution and commercialized vice	10,617	4,267	6,350	40.2	59.8	0.3	0.2	0.6
Sex offenses (except forcible rape and prostitution)	16,162	15,193	969	94.0	6.0	0.4	0.5	0.1
Drug abuse violations	561,935	426,272	135,663	75.9	24.1	14.6	15.1	13.2
Gambling	861	608	253	70.6	29.4	*	*	*
Offenses against the family and children	26,519	17,020	9,499	64.2	35.8	0.7	0.6	0.9
Driving under the influence	311,168	230,897	80,271	74.2	25.8	8.1	8.2	7.8
Liquor laws	53,701	37,960	15,741	70.7	29.3	1.4	1.3	1.5
Drunkenness	115,065	89,661	25,404	77.9	22.1	3.0	3.2	2.5
Disorderly conduct	128,297	89,935	38,362	70.1	29.9	3.3	3.2	3.7
Vagrancy	8,813	6,707	2,106	76.1	23.9	0.2	0.2	0.2
All other offenses (except traffic)	1,052,267	779,571	272,696	74.1	25.9	27.3	27.6	26.5
Suspicion	200	125	75	62.5	37.5	*	*	*
Curfew and loitering law violations	7,262	4,784	2,478	65.9	34.1	0.2	0.2	0.2

* = Less than one-tenth of 1 percent.
1 Because of rounding, the percentages may not sum to 100.   2 Violent crimes are offenses of murder and nonnegligent manslaughter, rape, robbery, and aggravated assault. Property crimes are offenses of burglary, larceny-theft, motor vehicle theft, and arson.   3 The rape figures in this table are aggregate totals of the data submitted based on both the legacy and revised Uniform Crime Reporting definitions.

Table 49. Arrests, Cities, Distribution by Race, 2020

(Number, percent; 7,634 agencies; 2020 estimated population 159,832,632.)

Offense charged	Total arrests						Percent distribution[1]						Arrests under 18					
	Total	White	Black	American Indian or Alaskan Native	Asian	Native Hawaiian or Other Pacific Islander	Total	White	Black	American Indian or Alaskan Native	Asian	Native Hawaiian or Other Pacific Islander	Total	White	Black	American Indian or Alaskan Native	Asian	Native Hawaiian or Other Pacific Islander
Total	3,801,295	2,568,795	1,068,582	106,077	49,702	8,139	100.0	67.6	28.1	2.8	1.3	0.2	233,664	145,138	78,932	6,703	2,470	421
Violent crime[2]	264,244	150,319	101,962	6,664	4,423	876	100.0	56.9	38.6	2.5	1.7	0.3	20,133	9,867	9,533	489	193	51
Murder and nonnegligent manslaughter	6,447	2,680	3,595	73	85	14	100.0	41.6	55.8	1.1	1.3	0.2	513	196	301	7	6	3
Rape[3]	10,164	6,777	2,964	215	182	26	100.0	66.7	29.2	2.1	1.8	0.3	1,377	936	392	32	16	1
Robbery	41,265	19,146	20,970	629	399	121	100.0	46.4	50.8	1.5	1.0	0.3	7,614	2,803	4,671	57	55	28
Aggravated assault	206,368	121,716	74,433	5,747	3,757	715	100.0	59.0	36.1	2.8	1.8	0.3	10,629	5,932	4,169	393	116	19
Property crime[2]	499,491	336,712	145,099	11,208	5,623	849	100.0	67.4	29.0	2.2	1.1	0.2	43,440	23,809	18,011	969	544	107
Burglary	79,984	52,984	24,457	1,310	1,074	159	100.0	66.2	30.6	1.6	1.3	0.2	8,244	4,524	3,466	142	82	30
Larceny-theft	369,594	249,968	106,514	8,739	3,825	548	100.0	67.6	28.8	2.4	1.0	0.1	27,780	15,878	10,845	615	378	64
Motor vehicle theft	44,604	30,006	12,844	1,028	596	130	100.0	67.3	28.8	2.3	1.3	0.3	6,756	2,939	3,542	188	74	13
Arson	5,309	3,754	1,284	131	128	12	100.0	70.7	24.2	2.5	2.4	0.2	660	468	158	24	10	0
Other assaults	483,922	301,722	161,366	12,461	7,270	1,103	100.0	62.3	33.3	2.6	1.5	0.2	38,181	23,499	13,369	896	362	55
Forgery and counterfeiting	16,900	11,620	4,772	193	295	20	100.0	68.8	28.2	1.1	1.7	0.1	263	154	100	3	6	0
Fraud	40,104	25,781	12,770	887	613	53	100.0	64.3	31.8	2.2	1.5	0.1	1,425	763	593	42	24	3
Embezzlement	5,239	3,111	1,955	64	99	10	100.0	59.4	37.3	1.2	1.9	0.2	258	116	121	2	19	0
Stolen property; buying, receiving, possessing	46,053	27,588	16,861	796	691	117	100.0	59.9	36.6	1.7	1.5	0.3	4,700	1,406	3,159	84	36	15
Vandalism	94,762	63,073	27,608	2,596	1,276	209	100.0	66.6	29.1	2.7	1.3	0.2	12,718	9,100	3,131	364	109	14
Weapons; carrying, possessing, etc.	88,057	43,247	42,648	931	1,003	228	100.0	49.1	48.4	1.1	1.1	0.3	6,552	3,133	3,254	71	86	8
Prostitution and commercialized vice	10,560	5,529	4,442	47	491	51	100.0	52.4	42.1	0.4	4.6	0.5	56	22	30	2	1	1
Sex offenses (except forcible rape and prostitution)	15,959	11,259	3,830	406	424	40	100.0	70.5	24.0	2.5	2.7	0.3	1,905	1,423	410	38	32	2
Drug abuse violations	556,826	396,584	143,071	9,120	6,835	1,216	100.0	71.2	25.7	1.6	1.2	0.2	22,402	16,345	5,158	593	264	42
Gambling	852	535	196	2	110	9	100.0	62.8	23.0	0.2	12.9	1.1	29	14	13	1	1	0
Offenses against the family and children	25,711	17,038	5,856	2,495	282	40	100.0	66.3	22.8	9.7	1.1	0.2	1,298	880	212	201	5	0
Driving under the influence	306,030	242,551	48,889	8,356	5,152	1,082	100.0	79.3	16.0	2.7	1.7	0.4	2,483	2,144	175	120	39	5
Liquor laws	52,275	39,803	7,614	4,057	715	86	100.0	76.1	14.6	7.8	1.4	0.2	8,490	7,077	549	746	104	14
Drunkenness	114,038	84,776	16,531	11,336	1,162	233	100.0	74.3	14.5	9.9	1.0	0.2	1,340	913	209	198	18	2
Disorderly conduct	126,138	79,998	38,363	6,425	1,157	195	100.0	63.4	30.4	5.1	0.9	0.2	13,730	7,887	5,134	560	120	29
Vagrancy	8,743	5,682	2,550	375	121	15	100.0	65.0	29.2	4.3	1.4	0.2	178	127	43	3	5	0
All other offenses (except traffic)	1,038,048	716,685	280,353	27,412	11,900	1,698	100.0	69.0	27.0	2.6	1.1	0.2	46,931	31,387	13,918	1,117	444	65
Suspicion	216	121	41	51	2	1	100.0	56.0	19.0	23.6	0.9	0.5	25	11	5	9	0	0
Curfew and loitering law violations	7,127	5,061	1,805	195	58	8	100.0	71.0	25.3	2.7	0.8	0.1	7,127	5,061	1,805	195	58	8

Table 49. Arrests, Cities, Distribution by Race, 2020—Continued

(Number, percent; 7,634 agencies; 2020 estimated population 159,832,632.)

Offense charged	Percent distribution[1]						Arrests 18 and over						Percent distribution[1]					
	Total	White	Black	American Indian or Alaskan Native	Asian	Native Hawaiian or Other Pacific Islander	Total	White	Black	American Indian or Alaskan Native	Asian	Native Hawaiian or Other Pacific Islander	Total	White	Black	American Indian or Alaskan Native	Asian	Native Hawaiian or Other Pacific Islander
Total	100.0	62.1	33.8	2.9	1.1	0.2	3,567,631	2,423,657	989,650	99,374	47,232	7,718	100.0	67.9	27.7	2.8	1.3	0.2
Violent crime[2]	100.0	49.0	47.4	2.4	1.0	0.3	244,111	140,452	92,429	6,175	4,230	825	100.0	57.5	37.9	2.5	1.7	0.3
Murder and nonnegligent manslaughter	100.0	38.2	58.7	1.4	1.2	0.6	5,934	2,484	3,294	66	79	11	100.0	41.9	55.5	1.1	1.3	0.2
Rape[3]	100.0	68.0	28.5	2.3	1.2	0.1	8,787	5,841	2,572	183	166	25	100.0	66.5	29.3	2.1	1.9	0.3
Robbery	100.0	36.8	61.3	0.7	0.7	0.4	33,651	16,343	16,299	572	344	93	100.0	48.6	48.4	1.7	1.0	0.3
Aggravated assault	100.0	55.8	39.2	3.7	1.1	0.2	195,739	115,784	70,264	5,354	3,641	696	100.0	59.2	35.9	2.7	1.9	0.4
Property crime[2]	100.0	54.8	41.5	2.2	1.3	0.2	456,051	312,903	127,088	10,239	5,079	742	100.0	68.6	27.9	2.2	1.1	0.2
Burglary	100.0	54.9	42.0	1.7	1.0	0.4	71,740	48,460	20,991	1,168	992	129	100.0	67.5	29.3	1.6	1.4	0.2
Larceny-theft	100.0	57.2	39.0	2.2	1.4	0.2	341,814	234,090	95,669	8,124	3,447	484	100.0	68.5	28.0	2.4	1.0	0.1
Motor vehicle theft	100.0	43.5	52.4	2.8	1.1	0.2	37,848	27,067	9,302	840	522	117	100.0	71.5	24.6	2.2	1.4	0.3
Arson	100.0	70.9	23.9	3.6	1.5	0.0	4,649	3,286	1,126	107	118	12	100.0	70.7	24.2	2.3	2.5	0.3
Other assaults	100.0	61.5	35.0	2.3	0.9	0.1	445,741	278,223	147,997	11,565	6,908	1,048	100.0	62.4	33.2	2.6	1.5	0.2
Forgery and counterfeiting	100.0	58.6	38.0	1.1	2.3	0.0	16,637	11,466	4,672	190	289	20	100.0	68.9	28.1	1.1	1.7	0.1
Fraud	100.0	53.5	41.6	2.9	1.7	0.2	38,679	25,018	12,177	845	589	50	100.0	64.7	31.5	2.2	1.5	0.1
Embezzlement	100.0	45.0	46.9	0.8	7.4	0.0	4,981	2,995	1,834	62	80	10	100.0	60.1	36.8	1.2	1.6	0.2
Stolen property; buying, receiving, possessing	100.0	29.9	67.2	1.8	0.8	0.3	41,353	26,182	13,702	712	655	102	100.0	63.3	33.1	1.7	1.6	0.2
Vandalism	100.0	71.6	24.6	2.9	0.9	0.1	82,044	53,973	24,477	2,232	1,167	195	100.0	65.8	29.8	2.7	1.4	0.2
Weapons; carrying, possessing, etc.	100.0	47.8	49.7	1.1	1.3	0.1	81,505	40,114	39,394	860	917	220	100.0	49.2	48.3	1.1	1.1	0.3
Prostitution and commercialized vice	100.0	39.3	53.6	3.6	1.8	1.8	10,504	5,507	4,412	45	490	50	100.0	52.4	42.0	0.4	4.7	0.5
Sex offenses (except forcible rape and prostitution)	100.0	74.7	21.5	2.0	1.7	0.1	14,054	9,836	3,420	368	392	38	100.0	70.0	24.3	2.6	2.8	0.3
Drug abuse violations	100.0	73.0	23.0	2.6	1.2	0.2	534,424	380,239	137,913	8,527	6,571	1,174	100.0	71.1	25.8	1.6	1.2	0.2
Gambling	100.0	48.3	44.8	3.4	3.4	0.0	823	521	183	1	109	9	100.0	63.3	22.2	0.1	13.2	1.1
Offenses against the family and children	100.0	67.8	16.3	15.5	0.4	0.0	24,413	16,158	5,644	2,294	277	40	100.0	66.2	23.1	9.4	1.1	0.2
Driving under the influence	100.0	86.3	7.0	4.8	1.6	0.2	303,547	240,407	48,714	8,236	5,113	1,077	100.0	79.2	16.0	2.7	1.7	0.4
Liquor laws	100.0	83.4	6.5	8.8	1.2	0.2	43,785	32,726	7,065	3,311	611	72	100.0	74.7	16.1	7.6	1.4	0.2
Drunkenness	100.0	68.1	15.6	14.8	1.3	0.1	112,698	83,863	16,322	11,138	1,144	231	100.0	74.4	14.5	9.9	1.0	0.2
Disorderly conduct	100.0	57.4	37.4	4.1	0.9	0.2	112,408	72,111	33,229	5,865	1,037	166	100.0	64.2	29.6	5.2	0.9	0.1
Vagrancy	100.0	71.3	24.2	1.7	2.8	0.0	8,565	5,555	2,507	372	116	15	100.0	64.9	29.3	4.3	1.4	0.2
All other offenses (except traffic)	100.0	66.9	29.7	2.4	0.9	0.1	991,117	685,298	266,435	26,295	11,456	1,633	100.0	69.1	26.9	2.7	1.2	0.2
Suspicion	100.0	44.0	20.0	36.0	0.0	0.0	191	110	36	42	2	1	100.0	57.6	18.8	22.0	1.0	0.5
Curfew and loitering law violations	100.0	71.0	25.3	2.7	0.8	0.1	NA	NA	NA	NA	NA	NA	NA	NA	NA	NA	NA	NA

NA = Not available.

1 Because of rounding, the percentages may not sum to 100.   2 Violent crimes are offenses of murder and nonnegligent manslaughter, rape, robbery, and aggravated assault. Property crimes are offenses of burglary, larceny-theft, motor vehicle theft, and arson.   3 The rape figures in this table are aggregate totals of the data submitted based on both the legacy and revised Uniform Crime Reporting definitions.

Table 49A. Arrests, Cities, Distribution by Ethnicity, 2020

(Number, percent; 7,634 agencies; 2020 estimated population 159,832,632.)

Offense charged	Total arrests			Percent distribution[1]			Arrests under 18		
	Total[2]	Hispanic or Latino	Not Hispanic or Latino	Total[2]	Hispanic or Latino	Not Hispanic or Latino	Total[2]	Hispanic or Latino	Not Hispanic or Latino
Total	3,299,854	726,732	2,573,122	100.0	22.0	78.0	195,901	49,310	146,591
Violent crime[3]	233,818	65,793	168,025	100.0	28.1	71.9	17,595	5,046	12,549
Murder and nonnegligent manslaughter	5,447	1,286	4,161	100.0	23.6	76.4	444	137	307
Rape[4]	8,701	2,787	5,914	100.0	32.0	68.0	1,143	318	825
Robbery	36,611	9,676	26,935	100.0	26.4	73.6	6,782	1,857	4,925
Aggravated assault	183,059	52,044	131,015	100.0	28.4	71.6	9,226	2,734	6,492
Property crime[3]	427,403	79,467	347,936	100.0	18.6	81.4	36,222	8,122	28,100
Burglary	70,068	16,750	53,318	100.0	23.9	76.1	6,737	1,778	4,959
Larceny-theft	312,981	49,800	263,181	100.0	15.9	84.1	23,068	4,771	18,297
Motor vehicle theft	39,778	11,854	27,924	100.0	29.8	70.2	5,848	1,454	4,394
Arson	4,576	1,063	3,513	100.0	23.2	76.8	569	119	450
Other assaults	415,068	89,737	325,331	100.0	21.6	78.4	32,549	8,079	24,470
Forgery and counterfeiting	14,989	2,537	12,452	100.0	16.9	83.1	226	62	164
Fraud	34,644	5,266	29,378	100.0	15.2	84.8	1,114	237	877
Embezzlement	4,537	714	3,823	100.0	15.7	84.3	213	31	182
Stolen property; buying, receiving, possessing	39,664	8,862	30,802	100.0	22.3	77.7	3,883	844	3,039
Vandalism	81,879	18,017	63,862	100.0	22.0	78.0	10,759	2,588	8,171
Weapons; carrying, possessing, etc.	73,107	19,137	53,970	100.0	26.2	73.8	5,635	1,952	3,683
Prostitution and commercialized vice	9,968	2,535	7,433	100.0	25.4	74.6	53	12	41
Sex offenses (except forcible rape and prostitution)	13,976	4,442	9,534	100.0	31.8	68.2	1,623	502	1,121
Drug abuse violations	505,054	122,309	382,745	100.0	24.2	75.8	19,719	6,081	13,638
Gambling	820	360	460	100.0	43.9	56.1	23	13	10
Offenses against the family and children	21,993	4,422	17,571	100.0	20.1	79.9	1,103	240	863
Driving under the influence	264,457	77,007	187,450	100.0	29.1	70.9	2,064	710	1,354
Liquor laws	42,006	7,657	34,349	100.0	18.2	81.8	6,838	1,387	5,451
Drunkenness	108,742	26,696	82,046	100.0	24.5	75.5	1,265	423	842
Disorderly conduct	98,475	14,815	83,660	100.0	15.0	85.0	10,653	2,147	8,506
Vagrancy	7,993	1,454	6,539	100.0	18.2	81.8	114	29	85
All other offenses (except traffic)	895,248	173,904	721,344	100.0	19.4	80.6	38,382	9,215	29,167
Suspicion	163	11	152	100.0	6.7	93.3	18	0	18
Curfew and loitering law violations	5,850	1,590	4,260	100.0	27.2	72.8	5,850	1,590	4,260

Table 49A. Arrests, Cities, Distribution by Ethnicity, 2020—Continued

(Number, percent; 7,634 agencies; 2020 estimated population 159,832,632.)

| Offense charged | Percent distribution[1] | | | | Arrests 18 and over | | | Percent distribution[1] | |
	Total[2]	Hispanic or Latino	Not Hispanic or Latino	Total[2]	Hispanic or Latino	Not Hispanic or Latino	Total[2]	Hispanic or Latino	Not Hispanic or Latino
Total	100.0	25.2	74.8	3,103,953	677,422	2,426,531	100.0	21.8	78.2
Violent crime[3]	100.0	28.7	71.3	216,223	60,747	155,476	100.0	28.1	71.9
Murder and nonnegligent manslaughter	100.0	30.9	69.1	5,003	1,149	3,854	100.0	23.0	77.0
Rape[4]	100.0	27.8	72.2	7,558	2,469	5,089	100.0	32.7	67.3
Robbery	100.0	27.4	72.6	29,829	7,819	22,010	100.0	26.2	73.8
Aggravated assault	100.0	29.6	70.4	173,833	49,310	124,523	100.0	28.4	71.6
Property crime[3]	100.0	22.4	77.6	391,181	71,345	319,836	100.0	18.2	81.8
Burglary	100.0	26.4	73.6	63,331	14,972	48,359	100.0	23.6	76.4
Larceny-theft	100.0	20.7	79.3	289,913	45,029	244,884	100.0	15.5	84.5
Motor vehicle theft	100.0	24.9	75.1	33,930	10,400	23,530	100.0	30.7	69.3
Arson	100.0	20.9	79.1	4,007	944	3,063	100.0	23.6	76.4
Other assaults	100.0	24.8	75.2	382,519	81,658	300,861	100.0	21.3	78.7
Forgery and counterfeiting	100.0	27.4	72.6	14,763	2,475	12,288	100.0	16.8	83.2
Fraud	100.0	21.3	78.7	33,530	5,029	28,501	100.0	15.0	85.0
Embezzlement	100.0	14.6	85.4	4,324	683	3,641	100.0	15.8	84.2
Stolen property; buying, receiving, possessing	100.0	21.7	78.3	35,781	8,018	27,763	100.0	22.4	77.6
Vandalism	100.0	24.1	75.9	71,120	15,429	55,691	100.0	21.7	78.3
Weapons; carrying, possessing, etc.	100.0	34.6	65.4	67,472	17,185	50,287	100.0	25.5	74.5
Prostitution and commercialized vice	100.0	22.6	77.4	9,915	2,523	7,392	100.0	25.4	74.6
Sex offenses (except forcible rape and prostitution)	100.0	30.9	69.1	12,353	3,940	8,413	100.0	31.9	68.1
Drug abuse violations	100.0	30.8	69.2	485,335	116,228	369,107	100.0	23.9	76.1
Gambling	100.0	56.5	43.5	797	347	450	100.0	43.5	56.5
Offenses against the family and children	100.0	21.8	78.2	20,890	4,182	16,708	100.0	20.0	80.0
Driving under the influence	100.0	34.4	65.6	262,393	76,297	186,096	100.0	29.1	70.9
Liquor laws	100.0	20.3	79.7	35,168	6,270	28,898	100.0	17.8	82.2
Drunkenness	100.0	33.4	66.6	107,477	26,273	81,204	100.0	24.4	75.6
Disorderly conduct	100.0	20.2	79.8	87,822	12,668	75,154	100.0	14.4	85.6
Vagrancy	100.0	25.4	74.6	7,879	1,425	6,454	100.0	18.1	81.9
All other offenses (except traffic)	100.0	24.0	76.0	856,866	164,689	692,177	100.0	19.2	80.8
Suspicion	100.0	0.0	100.0	145	11	134	100.0	7.6	92.4
Curfew and loitering law violations	100.0	27.2	72.8	NA	NA	NA	NA	NA	NA

NA = Not available.

1 Because of rounding, the percentages may not sum to 100.   2 The ethnicity totals are representative of those agencies that provided ethnicity breakdowns. Not all agencies provide ethnicity data; therefore, the race and ethnicity totals will not equal.
3 Violent crimes are offenses of murder and nonnegligent manslaughter, rape, robbery, and aggravated assault. Property crimes are offenses of burglary, larceny-theft, motor vehicle theft, and arson.   4 The rape figures in this table are aggregate totals of the data submitted based on both the legacy and revised Uniform Crime Reporting definitions.

Table 50. Arrest Trends, Metropolitan Counties, 2019–2020

(Number, percent change; 1,008 agencies; 2020 estimated population 42,367,070; 2019 estimated population 42,067,490.)

Offense charged	Number of persons arrested								
	Total, all ages			Under 18 years of age			18 years of age and over		
	2019	2020	Percent change	2019	2020	Percent change	2019	2020	Percent change
Total[1]	1,089,827	838,935	-23.0	57,377	36,871	-35.7	1,032,450	802,064	-22.3
Violent crime[2]	46,681	44,950	-3.7	3,961	2,868	-27.6	42,720	42,082	-1.5
Murder and nonnegligent manslaughter	1,142	1,223	+7.1	62	68	+9.7	1,080	1,155	+6.9
Rape[3]	2,753	2,375	-13.7	541	385	-28.8	2,212	1,990	-10.0
Robbery	5,158	4,456	-13.6	984	676	-31.3	4,174	3,780	-9.4
Aggravated assault	37,628	36,896	-1.9	2,374	1,739	-26.7	35,254	35,157	-0.3
Property crime[2]	84,350	68,280	-19.1	7,946	5,555	-30.1	76,404	62,725	-17.9
Burglary	16,290	14,127	-13.3	1,782	1,391	-21.9	14,508	12,736	-12.2
Larceny-theft	59,163	45,514	-23.1	5,034	3,099	-38.4	54,129	42,415	-21.6
Motor vehicle theft	8,090	7,782	-3.8	981	947	-3.5	7,109	6,835	-3.9
Arson	807	857	+6.2	149	118	-20.8	658	739	+12.3
Other assaults	95,315	87,802	-7.9	12,749	7,633	-40.1	82,566	80,169	-2.9
Forgery and counterfeiting	4,858	3,671	-24.4	76	45	-40.8	4,782	3,626	-24.2
Fraud	13,207	9,224	-30.2	333	263	-21.0	12,874	8,961	-30.4
Embezzlement	1,257	832	-33.8	42	31	-26.2	1,215	801	-34.1
Stolen property; buying, receiving, possessing	10,668	10,251	-3.9	698	746	+6.9	9,970	9,505	-4.7
Vandalism	16,687	15,741	-5.7	2,693	2,134	-20.8	13,994	13,607	-2.8
Weapons; carrying, possessing, etc.	16,128	16,756	+3.9	1,301	822	-36.8	14,827	15,934	+7.5
Prostitution and commercialized vice	1,578	987	-37.5	21	9	-57.1	1,557	978	-37.2
Sex offenses (except forcible rape and prostitution)	4,460	3,567	-20.0	747	492	-34.1	3,713	3,075	-17.2
Drug abuse violations	176,117	135,876	-22.8	7,456	4,018	-46.1	168,661	131,858	-21.8
Gambling	292	212	-27.4	19	7	-63.2	273	205	-24.9
Offenses against the family and children	16,357	7,904	-51.7	217	108	-50.2	16,140	7,796	-51.7
Driving under the influence	150,715	123,940	-17.8	665	702	+5.6	150,050	123,238	-17.9
Liquor laws	12,065	7,957	-34.0	2,412	1,627	-32.5	9,653	6,330	-34.4
Drunkenness	17,808	11,834	-33.5	238	126	-47.1	17,570	11,708	-33.4
Disorderly conduct	19,673	15,311	-22.2	3,642	1,766	-51.5	16,031	13,545	-15.5
Vagrancy	1,394	628	-54.9	8	11	+37.5	1,386	617	-55.5
All other offenses (except traffic)	399,469	272,557	-31.8	11,405	7,253	-36.4	388,064	265,304	-31.6
Suspicion	33	3	-90.9	0	0		33	3	-90.9
Curfew and loitering law violations	748	655	-12.4	748	655	-12.4	NA	NA	NA

NA = Not available.
1 Does not include suspicion.   2 Violent crimes in this table are offenses of murder and nonnegligent manslaughter, rape, robbery, and aggravated assault. Property crimes are offenses of burglary, larceny-theft, motor vehicle theft, and arson.   3 The rape figures in this table are aggregate totals of the data submitted based on both the legacy and revised Uniform Crime Reporting definitions.

Table 51. Arrest Trends, Metropolitan Counties, by Age and Sex, 2019–2020

(Number, percent change; 1,008 agencies; 2020 estimated population 42,367,070; 2019 estimated population 42,067,490.)

Offense charged	Male						Female					
	Total			Under 18			Total			Under 18		
	2019	2020	Percent change	2019	2020	Percent change	2019	2020	Percent change	2019	2020	Percent change
Total[1]	797,943	621,599	-22.1	40,906	26,507	-35.2	291,884	217,336	-25.5	16,471	10,364	-37.1
Violent crime[2]	37,204	35,879	-3.6	3,178	2,278	-28.3	9,477	9,071	-4.3	783	590	-24.6
Murder and nonnegligent manslaughter	1,022	1,070	+4.7	55	62	+12.7	120	153	+27.5	7	6	-14.3
Rape[3]	2,637	2,320	-12.0	505	367	-27.3	116	55	-52.6	36	18	-50.0
Robbery	4,315	3,774	-12.5	862	589	-31.7	843	682	-19.1	122	87	-28.7
Aggravated assault	29,230	28,715	-1.8	1,756	1,260	-28.2	8,398	8,181	-2.6	618	479	-22.5
Property crime[2]	55,081	46,573	-15.4	5,742	4,233	-26.3	29,269	21,707	-25.8	2,204	1,322	-40.0
Burglary	12,975	11,355	-12.5	1,528	1,223	-20.0	3,315	2,772	-16.4	254	168	-33.9
Larceny-theft	35,303	28,403	-19.5	3,317	2,143	-35.4	23,860	17,111	-28.3	1,717	956	-44.3
Motor vehicle theft	6,154	6,133	-0.3	764	771	+0.9	1,936	1,649	-14.8	217	176	-18.9
Arson	649	682	+5.1	133	96	-27.8	158	175	+10.8	16	22	+37.5
Other assaults	67,972	63,394	-6.7	8,169	4,830	-40.9	27,343	24,408	-10.7	4,580	2,803	-38.8
Forgery and counterfeiting	3,311	2,568	-22.4	64	34	-46.9	1,547	1,103	-28.7	12	11	-8.3
Fraud	8,400	6,141	-26.9	229	181	-21.0	4,807	3,083	-35.9	104	82	-21.2
Embezzlement	650	432	-33.5	20	21	+5.0	607	400	-34.1	22	10	-54.5
Stolen property; buying, receiving, possessing	8,386	8,091	-3.5	568	620	+9.2	2,282	2,160	-5.3	130	126	-3.1
Vandalism	12,963	12,318	-5.0	2,173	1,714	-21.1	3,724	3,423	-8.1	520	420	-19.2
Weapons; carrying, possessing, etc.	14,436	15,087	+4.5	1,134	731	-35.5	1,692	1,669	-1.4	167	91	-45.5
Prostitution and commercialized vice	757	576	-23.9	15	5	-66.7	821	411	-49.9	6	4	-33.3
Sex offenses (except forcible rape and prostitution)	4,171	3,397	-18.6	669	455	-32.0	289	170	-41.2	78	37	-52.6
Drug abuse violations	128,927	99,913	-22.5	5,572	2,991	-46.3	47,190	35,963	-23.8	1,884	1,027	-45.5
Gambling	205	145	-29.3	14	7	-50.0	87	67	-23.0	5	0	-100.0
Offenses against the family and children	12,959	5,880	-54.6	142	74	-47.9	3,398	2,024	-40.4	75	34	-54.7
Driving under the influence	111,384	92,581	-16.9	521	529	+1.5	39,331	31,359	-20.3	144	173	+20.1
Liquor laws	8,337	5,497	-34.1	1,386	954	-31.2	3,728	2,460	-34.0	1,026	673	-34.4
Drunkenness	13,771	9,074	-34.1	176	86	-51.1	4,037	2,760	-31.6	62	40	-35.5
Disorderly conduct	13,924	10,909	-21.7	2,421	1,133	-53.2	5,749	4,402	-23.4	1,221	633	-48.2
Vagrancy	1,075	498	-53.7	6	8	+33.3	319	130	-59.2	2	3	+50.0
All other offenses (except traffic)	293,525	202,211	-31.1	8,202	5,188	-36.7	105,944	70,346	-33.6	3,203	2,065	-35.5
Suspicion	25	3	-88.0	0	0		8	0	-100.0	0	0	
Curfew and loitering law violations	505	435	-13.9	505	435	-13.9	243	220	-9.5	243	220	-9.5

1 Does not include suspicion.   2 Violent crimes are offenses of murder and nonnegligent manslaughter, rape, robbery, and aggravated assault. Property crimes are offenses of burglary, larceny-theft, motor vehicle theft, and arson.   3 The rape figures in this table are aggregate totals of the data submitted based on both the legacy and revised Uniform Crime Reporting definitions.

Table 52. Arrests, Metropolitan Counties, Distribution by Age, 2020

(Number, percent; 1,195 agencies; 2020 estimated population 50,082,964.)

Offense charged	Total, all ages	Ages under 15	Ages under 18	Ages 18 and over	Under 10	10–12	13–14	15	16	17	18	19	20
Total	983,373	11,711	43,670	939,703	167	2,504	9,040	8,261	10,689	13,009	20,806	24,079	25,980
Total percent distribution[1]	100.0	1.2	4.4	95.6	*	0.3	0.9	0.8	1.1	1.3	2.1	2.4	2.6
Violent crime[2]	54,143	908	3,372	50,771	7	201	700	631	847	986	1,433	1,514	1,468
Violent crime percent distribution[1]	100.0	1.7	6.2	93.8	*	0.4	1.3	1.2	1.6	1.8	2.6	2.8	2.7
Murder and nonnegligent manslaughter	1,554	7	95	1,459	0	2	5	12	28	48	57	84	75
Rape[3]	2,733	189	437	2,296	0	60	129	82	92	74	126	114	109
Robbery	5,390	142	784	4,606	0	7	135	155	193	294	357	281	236
Aggravated assault	44,466	570	2,056	42,410	7	132	431	382	534	570	893	1,035	1,048
Property crime[2]	81,314	1,769	6,644	74,670	8	331	1,430	1,433	1,722	1,720	2,420	2,144	2,131
Property crime percent distribution[1]	100.0	2.2	8.2	91.8	*	0.4	1.8	1.8	2.1	2.1	3.0	2.6	2.6
Burglary	16,654	439	1,604	15,050	1	77	361	379	405	381	454	406	433
Larceny-theft	53,892	992	3,799	50,093	4	200	788	769	1,006	1,032	1,664	1,475	1,412
Motor vehicle theft	9,729	270	1,108	8,621	1	29	240	253	292	293	283	242	269
Arson	1,039	68	133	906	2	25	41	32	19	14	19	21	17
Other assaults	102,954	3,295	8,847	94,107	40	846	2,409	1,804	1,955	1,793	1,886	2,124	2,320
Forgery and counterfeiting	4,244	4	53	4,191	0	0	4	7	14	28	93	103	153
Fraud	10,675	70	305	10,370	0	4	66	68	72	95	194	221	257
Embezzlement	979	1	34	945	0	0	1	1	13	19	55	53	31
Stolen property; buying, receiving, possessing	11,739	162	821	10,918	0	13	149	186	237	236	371	345	311
Vandalism	19,020	928	2,554	16,466	17	230	681	477	594	555	662	592	534
Weapons; carrying, possessing, etc.	20,177	193	1,000	19,177	3	53	137	155	254	398	650	758	804
Prostitution and commercialized vice	1,054	6	13	1,041	0	1	5	1	2	4	19	21	29
Sex offenses (except forcible rape and prostitution)	4,333	251	552	3,781	11	67	173	103	89	109	118	115	136
Drug abuse violations	162,238	615	4,808	157,430	4	69	542	717	1,271	2,205	4,483	5,383	5,445
Gambling	273	5	26	247	0	3	2	4	8	9	2	6	5
Offenses against the family and children	8,915	36	128	8,787	2	6	28	25	30	37	44	68	99
Driving under the influence	140,244	6	776	139,468	1	0	5	32	189	549	1,651	2,530	3,139
Liquor laws	9,189	185	1,902	7,287	0	12	173	288	533	896	1,345	1,253	1,021
Drunkenness	14,141	21	146	13,995	0	1	20	38	40	47	211	220	277
Disorderly conduct	18,076	845	2,229	15,847	25	224	596	450	471	463	381	378	380
Vagrancy	803	3	12	791	0	0	3	4	4	1	16	14	16
All other offenses (except traffic)	318,146	2,229	8,735	309,411	48	424	1,757	1,640	2,141	2,725	4,772	6,236	7,424
Suspicion	3	0	0	3	0	0	0	0	0	0	0	1	0
Curfew and loitering law violations	713	179	713	NA	1	19	159	197	203	134	NA	NA	NA

Table 52. Arrests, Metropolitan Counties, Distribution by Age, 2020—Continued

(Number, percent; 1,195 agencies; 2020 estimated population 50,082,964.)

Offense charged	21	22	23	24	25–29	30–34	35–39	40–44	45–49	50–54	55–59	60–64	65 and over
Total	27,610	28,298	28,878	30,583	169,211	160,391	134,849	97,332	66,780	51,910	38,604	20,555	13,837
Total percent distribution[1]	2.8	2.9	2.9	3.1	17.2	16.3	13.7	9.9	6.8	5.3	3.9	2.1	1.4
Violent crime[2]	1,495	1,628	1,507	1,685	8,910	8,261	7,141	5,040	3,437	2,796	2,223	1,203	1,030
Violent crime percent distribution[1]	2.8	3.0	2.8	3.1	16.5	15.3	13.2	9.3	6.3	5.2	4.1	2.2	1.9
Murder and nonnegligent manslaughter	58	68	70	39	326	202	149	121	62	47	46	29	26
Rape[3]	96	71	58	73	304	285	291	228	160	124	108	66	83
Robbery	214	212	173	195	856	734	502	346	183	160	101	37	19
Aggravated assault	1,127	1,277	1,206	1,378	7,424	7,040	6,199	4,345	3,032	2,465	1,968	1,071	902
Property crime[2]	2,184	2,109	2,033	2,238	13,160	13,273	10,979	7,587	5,129	4,103	2,980	1,436	764
Property crime percent distribution[1]	2.7	2.6	2.5	2.8	16.2	16.3	13.5	9.3	6.3	5.0	3.7	1.8	0.9
Burglary	409	417	455	441	2,813	2,975	2,326	1,626	987	634	445	152	77
Larceny-theft	1,487	1,410	1,295	1,468	8,366	8,385	7,178	5,042	3,628	3,107	2,339	1,196	641
Motor vehicle theft	266	263	260	302	1,855	1,741	1,328	809	447	302	158	63	33
Arson	22	19	23	27	126	172	147	110	67	60	38	25	13
Other assaults	2,612	2,619	2,572	2,837	16,007	15,476	13,572	10,140	7,367	5,941	4,300	2,413	1,921
Forgery and counterfeiting	122	134	134	146	801	761	595	431	263	217	136	70	32
Fraud	265	278	262	310	1,892	1,789	1,582	1,161	777	620	445	177	140
Embezzlement	40	24	38	29	140	130	122	101	74	45	43	16	4
Stolen property; buying, receiving, possessing	336	354	355	395	2,150	2,071	1,682	1,056	637	447	248	107	53
Vandalism	596	525	616	586	3,154	2,795	2,220	1,484	875	764	533	281	249
Weapons; carrying, possessing, etc.	861	834	876	830	3,958	3,041	2,353	1,554	998	688	505	268	199
Prostitution and commercialized vice	35	25	32	35	182	173	135	110	95	61	51	15	23
Sex offenses (except forcible rape and prostitution)	104	81	72	92	466	474	469	433	298	265	246	170	242
Drug abuse violations	5,441	5,448	5,386	5,557	29,505	27,186	22,360	15,502	10,008	7,323	4,978	2,390	1,035
Gambling	4	2	6	3	32	30	46	37	30	15	16	6	7
Offenses against the family and children	106	147	169	152	1,378	1,877	1,726	1,281	747	492	292	135	74
Driving under the influence	4,344	4,764	4,995	5,344	26,486	22,099	17,602	13,339	10,106	8,500	7,091	4,296	3,182
Liquor laws	174	153	134	127	610	572	490	378	295	294	211	134	96
Drunkenness	330	360	376	419	2,239	2,275	2,039	1,504	1,114	1,048	858	471	254
Disorderly conduct	434	403	428	476	2,505	2,475	2,192	1,606	1,258	1,098	901	537	395
Vagrancy	22	21	14	13	117	123	99	95	73	64	47	41	16
All other offenses (except traffic)	8,105	8,389	8,873	9,309	55,519	55,509	47,444	34,493	23,199	17,129	12,500	6,389	4,121
Suspicion	0	0	0	0	0	1	1	0	0	0	0	0	0
Curfew and loitering law violations	NA	NA	NA	NA	NA	NA	NA	NA	NA	NA	NA	NA	NA

NA = Not available.
* = Less than one-tenth of one percent.
1 Because of rounding, the percentages may not sum to 100.   2 Violent crimes are offenses of murder and nonnegligent manslaughter, rape, robbery, and aggravated assault. Property crimes are offenses of burglary, larceny-theft, motor vehicle theft, and arson.   3 The rape figures in this table are aggregate totals of the data submitted based on both the legacy and revised Uniform Crime Reporting definitions.

Table 53. Arrests, Metropolitan Counties, Persons Under 15, 18, 21, and 25 Years of Age, 2020

(Number, percent; 1,195 agencies; 2020 estimated population 50,082,964.)

Offense charged	Total, all ages	Number of persons arrested				Percent of total all ages			
		Under 15	Under 18	Under 21	Under 25	Under 15	Under 18	Under 21	Under 25
Total	983,373	11,711	43,670	114,535	229,904	1.2	4.4	11.6	23.4
Violent crime[1]	54,143	908	3,372	7,787	14,102	1.7	6.2	14.4	26.0
Murder and nonnegligent manslaughter	1,554	7	95	311	546	0.5	6.1	20.0	35.1
Rape[2]	2,733	189	437	786	1,084	6.9	16.0	28.8	39.7
Robbery	5,390	142	784	1,658	2,452	2.6	14.5	30.8	45.5
Aggravated assault	44,466	570	2,056	5,032	10,020	1.3	4.6	11.3	22.5
Property crime[1]	81,314	1,769	6,644	13,339	21,903	2.2	8.2	16.4	26.9
Burglary	16,654	439	1,604	2,897	4,619	2.6	9.6	17.4	27.7
Larceny-theft	53,892	992	3,799	8,350	14,010	1.8	7.0	15.5	26.0
Motor vehicle theft	9,729	270	1,108	1,902	2,993	2.8	11.4	19.5	30.8
Arson	1,039	68	133	190	281	6.5	12.8	18.3	27.0
Other assaults	102,954	3,295	8,847	15,177	25,817	3.2	8.6	14.7	25.1
Forgery and counterfeiting	4,244	4	53	402	938	0.1	1.2	9.5	22.1
Fraud	10,675	70	305	977	2,092	0.7	2.9	9.2	19.6
Embezzlement	979	1	34	173	304	0.1	3.5	17.7	31.1
Stolen property; buying, receiving, possessing	11,739	162	821	1,848	3,288	1.4	7.0	15.7	28.0
Vandalism	19,020	928	2,554	4,342	6,665	4.9	13.4	22.8	35.0
Weapons; carrying, possessing, etc.	20,177	193	1,000	3,212	6,613	1.0	5.0	15.9	32.8
Prostitution and commercialized vice	1,054	6	13	82	209	0.6	1.2	7.8	19.8
Sex offenses (except forcible rape and prostitution)	4,333	251	552	921	1,270	5.8	12.7	21.3	29.3
Drug abuse violations	162,238	615	4,808	20,119	41,951	0.4	3.0	12.4	25.9
Gambling	273	5	26	39	54	1.8	9.5	14.3	19.8
Offenses against the family and children	8,915	36	128	339	913	0.4	1.4	3.8	10.2
Driving under the influence	140,244	6	776	8,096	27,543	*	0.6	5.8	19.6
Liquor laws	9,189	185	1,902	5,521	6,109	2.0	20.7	60.1	66.5
Drunkenness	14,141	21	146	854	2,339	0.1	1.0	6.0	16.5
Disorderly conduct	18,076	845	2,229	3,368	5,109	4.7	12.3	18.6	28.3
Vagrancy	803	3	12	58	128	0.4	1.5	7.2	15.9
All other offenses (except traffic)	318,146	2,229	8,735	27,167	61,843	0.7	2.7	8.5	19.4
Suspicion	3	0	0	1	1	0.0	0.0	33.3	33.3
Curfew and loitering law violations	713	179	713	713	713	25.1	100.0	100.0	100.0

* = Less than one-tenth of one percent.
1 Violent crimes are offenses of murder and nonnegligent manslaughter, rape, robbery, and aggravated assault. Property crimes are offenses of burglary, larceny-theft, motor vehicle theft, and arson.   2 The rape figures in this table are aggregate totals of the data submitted based on both the legacy and revised Uniform Crime Reporting definitions.

Table 54. Arrests, Metropolitan Counties, Distribution by Sex, 2020

(Number, percent; 1,195 agencies; 2020 estimated population 50,082,964.)

Offense charged	Number of persons arrested			Percent male	Percent female	Percent distribution[1]		
	Total	Male	Female			Total	Male	Female
Total	983,373	730,968	252,405	74.3	25.7	100.0	100.0	100.0
Violent crime[2]	54,143	43,344	10,799	80.1	19.9	5.5	5.9	4.3
Murder and nonnegligent manslaughter	1,554	1,342	212	86.4	13.6	0.2	0.2	0.1
Rape[3]	2,733	2,669	64	97.7	2.3	0.3	0.4	*
Robbery	5,390	4,579	811	85.0	15.0	0.5	0.6	0.3
Aggravated assault	44,466	34,754	9,712	78.2	21.8	4.5	4.8	3.8
Property crime[2]	81,314	55,706	25,608	68.5	31.5	8.3	7.6	10.1
Burglary	16,654	13,466	3,188	80.9	19.1	1.7	1.8	1.3
Larceny-theft	53,892	33,750	20,142	62.6	37.4	5.5	4.6	8.0
Motor vehicle theft	9,729	7,659	2,070	78.7	21.3	1.0	1.0	0.8
Arson	1,039	831	208	80.0	20.0	0.1	0.1	0.1
Other assaults	102,954	74,341	28,613	72.2	27.8	10.5	10.2	11.3
Forgery and counterfeiting	4,244	2,980	1,264	70.2	29.8	0.4	0.4	0.5
Fraud	10,675	7,167	3,508	67.1	32.9	1.1	1.0	1.4
Embezzlement	979	513	466	52.4	47.6	0.1	0.1	0.2
Stolen property; buying, receiving, possessing	11,739	9,292	2,447	79.2	20.8	1.2	1.3	1.0
Vandalism	19,020	14,817	4,203	77.9	22.1	1.9	2.0	1.7
Weapons; carrying, possessing, etc.	20,177	18,217	1,960	90.3	9.7	2.1	2.5	0.8
Prostitution and commercialized vice	1,054	613	441	58.2	41.8	0.1	0.1	0.2
Sex offenses (except forcible rape and prostitution)	4,333	4,103	230	94.7	5.3	0.4	0.6	0.1
Drug abuse violations	162,238	120,117	42,121	74.0	26.0	16.5	16.4	16.7
Gambling	273	177	96	64.8	35.2	*	*	*
Offenses against the family and children	8,915	6,604	2,311	74.1	25.9	0.9	0.9	0.9
Driving under the influence	140,244	104,994	35,250	74.9	25.1	14.3	14.4	14.0
Liquor laws	9,189	6,379	2,810	69.4	30.6	0.9	0.9	1.1
Drunkenness	14,141	11,030	3,111	78.0	22.0	1.4	1.5	1.2
Disorderly conduct	18,076	12,849	5,227	71.1	28.9	1.8	1.8	2.1
Vagrancy	803	633	170	78.8	21.2	0.1	0.1	0.1
All other offenses (except traffic)	318,146	236,614	81,532	74.4	25.6	32.4	32.4	32.3
Suspicion	3	3	0	100.0	0.0	*	*	0
Curfew and loitering law violations	713	475	238	66.6	33.4	0.1	0.1	0.1

* = Less than one-tenth of one percent.
1 Because of rounding, the percentages may not sum to 100.   2 Violent crimes are offenses of murder and nonnegligent manslaughter, rape, robbery, and aggravated assault. Property crimes are offenses of burglary, larceny-theft, motor vehicle theft, and arson.   3 The rape figures in this table are aggregate totals of the data submitted based on both the legacy and revised Uniform Crime Reporting definitions.

Table 55. Arrests, Metropolitan Counties, Distribution by Race, 2020

(Number, percent; 1,195 agencies; 2020 estimated population 50,082,964.)

Offense charged	Total arrests						Percent distribution[1]						Arrests under 18					
	Total	White	Black	American Indian or Alaskan Native	Asian	Native Hawaiian or Other Pacific Islander	Total	White	Black	American Indian or Alaskan Native	Asian	Native Hawaiian or Other Pacific Islander	Total	White	Black	American Indian or Alaskan Native	Asian	Native Hawaiian or Other Pacific Islander
Total	969,062	715,694	232,718	8,591	10,863	1,196	100.0	73.9	24.0	0.9	1.1	0.1	42,877	28,661	13,214	516	433	53
Violent crime[2]	53,727	37,599	14,842	431	734	121	100.0	70.0	27.6	0.8	1.4	0.2	3,323	1,959	1,284	35	40	5
Murder and nonnegligent manslaughter	1,543	863	647	16	14	3	100.0	55.9	41.9	1.0	0.9	0.2	95	36	58	1	0	0
Rape[3]	2,684	2,123	509	13	36	3	100.0	79.1	19.0	0.5	1.3	0.1	427	334	86	1	6	0
Robbery	5,341	2,880	2,342	43	59	17	100.0	53.9	43.8	0.8	1.1	0.3	769	337	410	6	12	4
Aggravated assault	44,159	31,733	11,344	359	625	98	100.0	71.9	25.7	0.8	1.4	0.2	2,032	1,252	730	27	22	1
Property crime[2]	80,552	56,491	22,640	509	844	68	100.0	70.1	28.1	0.6	1.0	0.1	6,556	3,819	2,597	41	88	11
Burglary	16,521	12,835	3,449	98	126	13	100.0	77.7	20.9	0.6	0.8	0.1	1,585	1,001	550	15	17	2
Larceny-theft	53,335	35,381	16,971	326	616	41	100.0	66.3	31.8	0.6	1.2	0.1	3,740	2,110	1,538	18	65	9
Motor vehicle theft	9,665	7,464	2,027	75	86	13	100.0	77.2	21.0	0.8	0.9	0.1	1,101	612	476	8	5	0
Arson	1,031	811	193	10	16	1	100.0	78.7	18.7	1.0	1.6	0.1	130	96	33	0	1	0
Other assaults	101,788	74,374	25,059	968	1,267	120	100.0	73.1	24.6	1.0	1.2	0.1	8,701	5,499	2,979	121	94	8
Forgery and counterfeiting	4,205	2,707	1,399	19	76	4	100.0	64.4	33.3	0.5	1.8	0.1	52	31	19	1	1	0
Fraud	10,560	7,119	3,167	86	179	9	100.0	67.4	30.0	0.8	1.7	0.1	303	178	115	5	5	0
Embezzlement	965	575	368	5	16	1	100.0	59.6	38.1	0.5	1.7	0.1	33	18	15	0	0	0
Stolen property; buying, receiving, possessing	11,633	8,030	3,346	104	120	33	100.0	69.0	28.8	0.9	1.0	0.3	812	293	493	18	3	5
Vandalism	18,783	13,530	4,807	191	241	14	100.0	72.0	25.6	1.0	1.3	0.1	2,504	1,821	628	32	22	1
Weapons; carrying, possessing, etc.	20,032	11,748	7,984	106	168	26	100.0	58.6	39.9	0.5	0.8	0.1	987	505	467	5	8	2
Prostitution and commercialized vice	1,047	611	345	4	85	2	100.0	58.4	33.0	0.4	8.1	0.2	13	8	5	0	0	0
Sex offenses (except forcible rape and prostitution)	4,276	3,479	705	13	67	12	100.0	81.4	16.5	0.3	1.6	0.3	537	411	116	4	6	0
Drug abuse violations	160,647	117,080	40,784	970	1,628	185	100.0	72.9	25.4	0.6	1.0	0.1	4,707	3,514	1,116	41	32	4
Gambling	269	198	57	3	11	0	100.0	73.6	21.2	1.1	4.1	0.0	26	20	5	0	1	0
Offenses against the family and children	8,858	6,030	2,737	34	50	7	100.0	68.1	30.9	0.4	0.6	0.1	127	97	27	3	0	0
Driving under the influence	134,556	109,838	21,182	878	2,481	177	100.0	81.6	15.7	0.7	1.8	0.1	741	667	53	5	15	1
Liquor laws	8,949	7,413	1,247	159	121	9	100.0	82.8	13.9	1.8	1.4	0.1	1,847	1,692	104	30	19	2
Drunkenness	14,020	11,670	2,023	119	180	28	100.0	83.2	14.4	0.8	1.3	0.2	144	111	32	0	0	1
Disorderly conduct	17,886	12,739	4,765	263	107	12	100.0	71.2	26.6	1.5	0.6	0.1	2,194	1,268	874	34	15	3
Vagrancy	797	572	214	2	8	1	100.0	71.8	26.9	0.3	1.0	0.1	12	11	1	0	0	0
All other offenses (except traffic)	314,804	233,362	74,873	3,726	2,476	367	100.0	74.1	23.8	1.2	0.8	0.1	8,551	6,210	2,111	140	80	10
Suspicion	1	0	1	0	0	0	100.0	0.0	100.0	0.0	0.0	0.0	0	0	0	0	0	0
Curfew and loitering law violations	707	529	173	1	4	0	100.0	74.8	24.5	0.1	0.6	0.0	707	529	173	1	4	0

Table 55. Arrests, Metropolitan Counties, Distribution by Race, 2020—Continued

(Number, percent; 1,195 agencies; 2020 estimated population 50,082,964.)

Offense charged	Percent distribution[1]						Arrests 18 and over						Percent distribution[1]					
	Total	White	Black	American Indian or Alaskan Native	Asian	Native Hawaiian or Other Pacific Islander	Total	White	Black	American Indian or Alaskan Native	Asian	Native Hawaiian or Other Pacific Islander	Total	White	Black	American Indian or Alaskan Native	Asian	Native Hawaiian or Other Pacific Islander
Total	100.0	66.8	30.8	1.2	1.0	0.1	926,185	687,033	219,504	8,075	10,430	1,143	100.0	74.2	23.7	0.9	1.1	0.1
Violent crime[2]	100.0	59.0	38.6	1.1	1.2	0.2	50,404	35,640	13,558	396	694	116	100.0	70.7	26.9	0.8	1.4	0.2
Murder and nonnegligent manslaughter	100.0	37.9	61.1	1.1	0.0	0.0	1,448	827	589	15	14	3	100.0	57.1	40.7	1.0	1.0	0.2
Rape[3]	100.0	78.2	20.1	0.2	1.4	0.0	2,257	1,789	423	12	30	3	100.0	79.3	18.7	0.5	1.3	0.1
Robbery	100.0	43.8	53.3	0.8	1.6	0.5	4,572	2,543	1,932	37	47	13	100.0	55.6	42.3	0.8	1.0	0.3
Aggravated assault	100.0	61.6	35.9	1.3	1.1	*	42,127	30,481	10,614	332	603	97	100.0	72.4	25.2	0.8	1.4	0.2
Property crime[2]	100.0	58.3	39.6	0.6	1.3	0.2	73,996	52,672	20,043	468	756	57	100.0	71.2	27.1	0.6	1.0	0.1
Burglary	100.0	63.2	34.7	0.9	1.1	0.1	14,936	11,834	2,899	83	109	11	100.0	79.2	19.4	0.6	0.7	0.1
Larceny-theft	100.0	56.4	41.1	0.5	1.7	0.2	49,595	33,271	15,433	308	551	32	100.0	67.1	31.1	0.6	1.1	0.1
Motor vehicle theft	100.0	55.6	43.2	0.7	0.5	0.0	8,564	6,852	1,551	67	81	13	100.0	80.0	18.1	0.8	0.9	0.2
Arson	100.0	73.8	25.4	0.0	0.8	0.0	901	715	160	10	15	1	100.0	79.4	17.8	1.1	1.7	0.1
Other assaults	100.0	63.2	34.2	1.4	1.1	0.1	93,087	68,875	22,080	847	1,173	112	100.0	74.0	23.7	0.9	1.3	0.1
Forgery and counterfeiting	100.0	59.6	36.5	1.9	1.9	0.0	4,153	2,676	1,380	18	75	4	100.0	64.4	33.2	0.4	1.8	0.1
Fraud	100.0	58.7	38.0	1.7	1.7	0.0	10,257	6,941	3,052	81	174	9	100.0	67.7	29.8	0.8	1.7	0.1
Embezzlement	100.0	54.5	45.5	0.0	0.0	0.0	932	557	353	5	16	1	100.0	59.8	37.9	0.5	1.7	0.1
Stolen property; buying, receiving, possessing	100.0	36.1	60.7	2.2	0.4	0.6	10,821	7,737	2,853	86	117	28	100.0	71.5	26.4	0.8	1.1	0.3
Vandalism	100.0	72.7	25.1	1.3	0.9	*	16,279	11,709	4,179	159	219	13	100.0	71.9	25.7	1.0	1.3	0.1
Weapons; carrying, possessing, etc.	100.0	51.2	47.3	0.5	0.8	0.2	19,045	11,243	7,517	101	160	24	100.0	59.0	39.5	0.5	0.8	0.1
Prostitution and commercialized vice	100.0	61.5	38.5	0.0	0.0	0.0	1,034	603	340	4	85	2	100.0	58.3	32.9	0.4	8.2	0.2
Sex offenses (except forcible rape and prostitution)	100.0	76.5	21.6	0.7	1.1	0.0	3,739	3,068	589	9	61	12	100.0	82.1	15.8	0.2	1.6	0.3
Drug abuse violations	100.0	74.7	23.7	0.9	0.7	0.1	155,940	113,566	39,668	929	1,596	181	100.0	72.8	25.4	0.6	1.0	0.1
Gambling	100.0	76.9	19.2	0.0	3.8	0.0	243	178	52	3	10	0	100.0	73.3	21.4	1.2	4.1	0.0
Offenses against the family and children	100.0	76.4	21.3	2.4	0.0	0.0	8,731	5,933	2,710	31	50	7	100.0	68.0	31.0	0.4	0.6	0.1
Driving under the influence	100.0	90.0	7.2	0.7	2.0	0.1	133,815	109,171	21,129	873	2,466	176	100.0	81.6	15.8	0.7	1.8	0.1
Liquor laws	100.0	91.6	5.6	1.6	1.0	0.1	7,102	5,721	1,143	129	102	7	100.0	80.6	16.1	1.8	1.4	0.1
Drunkenness	100.0	77.1	22.2	0.0	0.0	0.7	13,876	11,559	1,991	119	180	27	100.0	83.3	14.3	0.9	1.3	0.2
Disorderly conduct	100.0	57.8	39.8	1.5	0.7	0.1	15,692	11,471	3,891	229	92	9	100.0	73.1	24.8	1.5	0.6	0.1
Vagrancy	100.0	91.7	8.3	0.0	0.0	0.0	785	561	213	2	8	1	100.0	71.5	27.1	0.3	1.0	0.1
All other offenses (except traffic)	100.0	72.6	24.7	1.6	0.9	0.1	306,253	227,152	72,762	3,586	2,396	357	100.0	74.2	23.8	1.2	0.8	0.1
Suspicion							1	0	1	0	0	0	100.0	0.0	100.0	0.0	0.0	0.0
Curfew and loitering law violations	100.0	74.8	24.5	0.1	0.6	0.0	NA	NA	NA	NA	NA	NA	NA	NA	NA	NA	NA	NA

NA = Not available.
* = Less than one-tenth of one percent.
1 Because of rounding, the percentages may not sum to 100.   2 Violent crimes are offenses of murder and nonnegligent manslaughter, rape, robbery, and aggravated assault. Property crimes are offenses of burglary, larceny-theft, motor vehicle theft, and arson.   3 The rape figures in this table are an aggregate total of the data submitted using both the revised and legacy Uniform Crime Reporting definitions.

Table 55A. Arrests, Metropolitan Counties, Distribution by Ethnicity, 2020

(Number, percent; 1,195 agencies; 2020 estimated population 50,082,964.)

Offense charged	Total arrests			Percent distribution[1]			Arrests under 18		
	Total[2]	Hispanic or Latino	Not Hispanic or Latino	Total[2]	Hispanic or Latino	Not Hispanic or Latino	Total[2]	Hispanic or Latino	Not Hispanic or Latino
Total	838,460	172,566	665,894	100.0	20.6	79.4	35,085	7,183	27,902
Violent crime[3]	47,819	11,721	36,098	100.0	24.5	75.5	2,807	671	2,136
Murder and nonnegligent manslaughter	1,322	313	1,009	100.0	23.7	76.3	71	16	55
Rape[4]	2,231	613	1,618	100.0	27.5	72.5	332	55	277
Robbery	4,827	1,171	3,656	100.0	24.3	75.7	691	186	505
Aggravated assault	39,439	9,624	29,815	100.0	24.4	75.6	1,713	414	1,299
Property crime[3]	70,282	10,729	59,553	100.0	15.3	84.7	5,466	1,096	4,370
Burglary	14,402	2,509	11,893	100.0	17.4	82.6	1,257	287	970
Larceny-theft	46,424	5,649	40,775	100.0	12.2	87.8	3,161	565	2,596
Motor vehicle theft	8,554	2,392	6,162	100.0	28.0	72.0	940	230	710
Arson	902	179	723	100.0	19.8	80.2	108	14	94
Other assaults	87,239	15,130	72,109	100.0	17.3	82.7	7,139	1,310	5,829
Forgery and counterfeiting	3,735	719	3,016	100.0	19.3	80.7	47	10	37
Fraud	9,310	1,424	7,886	100.0	15.3	84.7	268	66	202
Embezzlement	848	110	738	100.0	13.0	87.0	30	2	28
Stolen property; buying, receiving, possessing	10,204	1,845	8,359	100.0	18.1	81.9	691	125	566
Vandalism	16,151	2,859	13,292	100.0	17.7	82.3	2,053	330	1,723
Weapons; carrying, possessing, etc.	16,533	3,915	12,618	100.0	23.7	76.3	803	226	577
Prostitution and commercialized vice	938	183	755	100.0	19.5	80.5	9	0	9
Sex offenses (except forcible rape and prostitution)	3,791	1,206	2,585	100.0	31.8	68.2	418	79	339
Drug abuse violations	145,106	28,484	116,622	100.0	19.6	80.4	4,029	1,024	3,005
Gambling	259	94	165	100.0	36.3	63.7	25	15	10
Offenses against the family and children	7,794	827	6,967	100.0	10.6	89.4	87	22	65
Driving under the influence	119,809	39,670	80,139	100.0	33.1	66.9	622	207	415
Liquor laws	6,768	1,278	5,490	100.0	18.9	81.1	1,447	217	1,230
Drunkenness	13,516	4,084	9,432	100.0	30.2	69.8	115	37	78
Disorderly conduct	14,197	1,417	12,780	100.0	10.0	90.0	1,589	198	1,391
Vagrancy	692	131	561	100.0	18.9	81.1	9	3	6
All other offenses (except traffic)	262,901	46,664	216,237	100.0	17.7	82.3	6,863	1,469	5,394
Suspicion	0	0	0				0	0	0
Curfew and loitering law violations	568	76	492	100.0	13.4	86.6	568	76	492

Table 55A. Arrests, Metropolitan Counties, Distribution by Ethnicity, 2020—Continued

(Number, percent; 1,195 agencies; 2020 estimated population 50,082,964.)

| Offense charged | Percent distribution[1] | | | | Arrests 18 and over | | | Percent distribution[1] | |
	Total[2]	Hispanic or Latino	Not Hispanic or Latino	Total[2]	Hispanic or Latino	Not Hispanic or Latino	Total[2]	Hispanic or Latino	Not Hispanic or Latino
Total	100.0	20.5	79.5	803,375	165,383	637,992	100.0	20.6	79.4
Violent crime[3]	100.0	23.9	76.1	45,012	11,050	33,962	100.0	24.5	75.5
Murder and nonnegligent manslaughter	100.0	22.5	77.5	1,251	297	954	100.0	23.7	76.3
Rape[4]	100.0	16.6	83.4	1,899	558	1,341	100.0	29.4	70.6
Robbery	100.0	26.9	73.1	4,136	985	3,151	100.0	23.8	76.2
Aggravated assault	100.0	24.2	75.8	37,726	9,210	28,516	100.0	24.4	75.6
Property crime[3]	100.0	20.1	79.9	64,816	9,633	55,183	100.0	14.9	85.1
Burglary	100.0	22.8	77.2	13,145	2,222	10,923	100.0	16.9	83.1
Larceny-theft	100.0	17.9	82.1	43,263	5,084	38,179	100.0	11.8	88.2
Motor vehicle theft	100.0	24.5	75.5	7,614	2,162	5,452	100.0	28.4	71.6
Arson	100.0	13.0	87.0	794	165	629	100.0	20.8	79.2
Other assaults	100.0	18.3	81.7	80,100	13,820	66,280	100.0	17.3	82.7
Forgery and counterfeiting	100.0	21.3	78.7	3,688	709	2,979	100.0	19.2	80.8
Fraud	100.0	24.6	75.4	9,042	1,358	7,684	100.0	15.0	85.0
Embezzlement	100.0	6.7	93.3	818	108	710	100.0	13.2	86.8
Stolen property; buying, receiving, possessing	100.0	18.1	81.9	9,513	1,720	7,793	100.0	18.1	81.9
Vandalism	100.0	16.1	83.9	14,098	2,529	11,569	100.0	17.9	82.1
Weapons; carrying, possessing, etc.	100.0	28.1	71.9	15,730	3,689	12,041	100.0	23.5	76.5
Prostitution and commercialized vice	100.0	0.0	100.0	929	183	746	100.0	19.7	80.3
Sex offenses (except forcible rape and prostitution)	100.0	18.9	81.1	3,373	1,127	2,246	100.0	33.4	66.6
Drug abuse violations	100.0	25.4	74.6	141,077	27,460	113,617	100.0	19.5	80.5
Gambling	100.0	60.0	40.0	234	79	155	100.0	33.8	66.2
Offenses against the family and children	100.0	25.3	74.7	7,707	805	6,902	100.0	10.4	89.6
Driving under the influence	100.0	33.3	66.7	119,187	39,463	79,724	100.0	33.1	66.9
Liquor laws	100.0	15.0	85.0	5,321	1,061	4,260	100.0	19.9	80.1
Drunkenness	100.0	32.2	67.8	13,401	4,047	9,354	100.0	30.2	69.8
Disorderly conduct	100.0	12.5	87.5	12,608	1,219	11,389	100.0	9.7	90.3
Vagrancy	100.0	33.3	66.7	683	128	555	100.0	18.7	81.3
All other offenses (except traffic)	100.0	21.4	78.6	256,038	45,195	210,843	100.0	17.7	82.3
Suspicion				0	0	0			
Curfew and loitering law violations	100.0	13.4	86.6	NA	NA	NA	NA	NA	NA

NA = Not available.
1 Because of rounding, the percentages may not sum to 100.   2 The ethnicity totals are representative of those agencies that provided ethnicity breakdowns. Not all agencies provide ethnicity data; therefore, the race and ethnicity totals will not equal.
3 Violent crimes are offenses of murder and nonnegligent manslaughter, rape, robbery, and aggravated assault. Property crimes are offenses of burglary, larceny-theft, motor vehicle theft, and arson.   4 The rape figures in this table are an aggregate total of the data submitted using both the revised and legacy Uniform Crime Reporting definitions.

Table 56. Arrest Trends, Nonmetropolitan Counties, 2019–2020

(Number, percent change; 1,396 agencies; 2020 estimated population 16,631,406; 2019 estimated population 16,583,672.)

Offense charged	Number of persons arrested								
	Total, all ages			Under 18 years of age			18 years of age and over		
	2019	2020	Percent change	2019	2020	Percent change	2019	2020	Percent change
Total[1]	507,927	396,681	-21.9	18,730	13,219	-29.4	489,197	383,462	-21.6
Violent crime[2]	15,472	15,521	+0.3	971	773	-20.4	14,501	14,748	+1.7
Murder and nonnegligent manslaughter	487	562	+15.4	29	35	+20.7	458	527	+15.1
Rape[3]	1,335	1,233	-7.6	247	190	(23.1)	1,088	1,043	-4.1
Robbery	752	1,002	+33.2	55	50	-9.1	697	952	+36.6
Aggravated assault	12,898	12,724	-1.3	640	498	-22.2	12,258	12,226	-0.3
Property crime[2]	24,889	21,439	-13.9	1,934	1,567	-19.0	22,955	19,872	-13.4
Burglary	7,109	6,319	-11.1	605	537	-11.2	6,504	5,782	-11.1
Larceny-theft	14,192	11,532	-18.7	940	691	-26.5	13,252	10,841	-18.2
Motor vehicle theft	3,228	3,158	-2.2	341	289	-15.2	2,887	2,869	-0.6
Arson	360	430	+19.4	48	50	+4.2	312	380	+21.8
Other assaults	39,418	35,768	-9.3	3,391	2,075	-38.8	36,027	33,693	-6.5
Forgery and counterfeiting	1,623	1,081	-33.4	10	9	-10.0	1,613	1,072	-33.5
Fraud	4,458	3,006	-32.6	85	64	-24.7	4,373	2,942	-32.7
Embezzlement	354	258	-27.1	3	3	+0.0	351	255	-27.4
Stolen property; buying, receiving, possessing	3,266	3,070	-6.0	134	189	+41.0	3,132	2,881	-8.0
Vandalism	6,044	5,570	-7.8	903	762	-15.6	5,141	4,808	-6.5
Weapons; carrying, possessing, etc.	5,738	5,824	+1.5	234	163	-30.3	5,504	5,661	+2.9
Prostitution and commercialized vice	118	71	-39.8	6	4	(33.3)	112	67	-40.2
Sex offenses (except forcible rape and prostitution)	1,737	1,368	-21.2	314	203	-35.4	1,423	1,165	-18.1
Drug abuse violations	81,642	65,907	-19.3	2,321	1,539	-33.7	79,321	64,368	-18.9
Gambling	85	38	-55.3	1	0	-100.0	84	38	-54.8
Offenses against the family and children	6,527	4,414	-32.4	97	88	-9.3	6,430	4,326	-32.7
Driving under the influence	81,834	69,921	-14.6	472	555	+17.6	81,362	69,366	-14.7
Liquor laws	8,236	7,332	-11.0	1,684	1,599	-5.0	6,552	5,733	-12.5
Drunkenness	9,048	5,688	-37.1	104	50	-51.9	8,944	5,638	-37.0
Disorderly conduct	10,556	8,762	-17.0	1,367	702	-48.6	9,189	8,060	-12.3
Vagrancy	170	126	-25.9	2	1	-50.0	168	125	-25.6
All other offenses (except traffic)	206,539	141,322	-31.6	4,524	2,678	-40.8	202,015	138,644	-31.4
Suspicion	7	35	+400.0	1	8	+700.0	6	27	+350.0
Curfew and loitering law violations	173	195	+12.7	173	195	+12.7	NA	NA	NA

NA = Not available.
1 Does not include suspicion.   2 Violent crimes are offenses of murder and nonnegligent manslaughter, rape, robbery, and aggravated assault. Property crimes are offenses of burglary, larceny-theft, motor vehicle theft, and arson.   3 The rape figures in this table are aggregate totals of the data submitted based on both the legacy and revised Uniform Crime Reporting definitions.

Table 57. Arrest Trends, Nonmetropolitan Counties, by Age and Sex, 2019–2020

(Number, percent; 1,396 agencies; 2020 estimated population 16,631,406; 2019 estimated population 16,583,672.)

Offense charged	Male						Female					
	Total			Under 18			Total			Under 18		
	2019	2020	Percent change	2019	2020	Percent change	2019	2020	Percent change	2019	2020	Percent change
Total[1]	369,859	292,812	-20.8	13,354	9,430	-29.4	138,068	103,869	-24.8	5,376	3,789	-29.5
Violent crime[2]	12,624	12,855	+1.8	792	648	-18.2	2,848	2,666	-6.4	179	125	-30.2
Murder and nonnegligent manslaughter	418	462	+10.5	26	32	+23.1	69	100	+44.9	3	3	+0.0
Rape[3]	1,264	1,187	-6.1	224	180	-19.6	71	46	-35.2	23	10	-56.5
Robbery	636	802	+26.1	47	42	-10.6	116	200	+72.4	8	8	+0.0
Aggravated assault	10,306	10,404	+1.0	495	394	-20.4	2,592	2,320	-10.5	145	104	(28.3)
Property crime[2]	17,497	15,462	-11.6	1,543	1,264	-18.1	7,392	5,977	-19.1	391	303	-22.5
Burglary	5,709	5,074	-11.1	540	487	-9.8	1,400	1,245	-11.1	65	50	-23.1
Larceny-theft	9,070	7,627	-15.9	709	520	-26.7	5,122	3,905	-23.8	231	171	-26.0
Motor vehicle theft	2,425	2,411	-0.6	254	218	-14.2	803	747	-7.0	87	71	-18.4
Arson	293	350	+19.5	40	39	-2.5	67	80	+19.4	8	11	+37.5
Other assaults	29,097	26,415	-9.2	2,282	1,356	-40.6	10,321	9,353	-9.4	1,109	719	-35.2
Forgery and counterfeiting	1,061	707	-33.4	6	8	+33.3	562	374	-33.5	4	1	-75.0
Fraud	2,657	1,895	-28.7	55	43	-21.8	1,801	1,111	-38.3	30	21	-30.0
Embezzlement	177	111	-37.3	2	2	+0.0	177	147	-16.9	1	1	0.0
Stolen property; buying, receiving, possessing	2,520	2,438	-3.3	106	150	+41.5	746	632	-15.3	28	39	+39.3
Vandalism	4,806	4,375	-9.0	757	582	-23.1	1,238	1,195	-3.5	146	180	+23.3
Weapons; carrying, possessing, etc.	5,103	5,212	+2.1	216	153	-29.2	635	612	-3.6	18	10	-44.4
Prostitution and commercialized vice	85	55	-35.3	3	3	+0.0	33	16	-51.5	3	1	-66.7
Sex offenses (except forcible rape and prostitution)	1,622	1,293	-20.3	291	186	-36.1	115	75	-34.8	23	17	-26.1
Drug abuse violations	57,542	46,575	-19.1	1,682	1,099	-34.7	24,100	19,332	-19.8	639	440	-31.1
Gambling	73	28	-61.6	1	0	-100	12	10	-16.7	0	0	
Offenses against the family and children	4,862	3,333	-31.4	73	52	-28.8	1,665	1,081	-35.1	24	36	+50.0
Driving under the influence	61,564	52,824	-14.2	359	415	15.6	20,270	17,097	-15.7	113	140	+23.9
Liquor laws	5,591	5,038	-9.9	961	953	-0.8	2,645	2,294	-13.3	723	646	-10.7
Drunkenness	6,492	4,078	-37.2	72	36	-50.0	2,556	1,610	-37.0	32	14	-56.3
Disorderly conduct	7,501	6,173	-17.7	927	475	-48.8	3,055	2,589	-15.3	440	227	-48.4
Vagrancy	123	96	-22.0	1	1	+0.0	47	30	-36.2	1	0	-100.0
All other offenses (except traffic)	148,769	103,755	-30.3	3,132	1,910	-39.0	57,770	37,567	-35.0	1,392	768	-44.8
Suspicion	5	25	+400.0	1	3	+200.0	2	10	+400.0	0	5	
Curfew and loitering law violations	93	94	+1.1	93	94	+1.1	80	101	+26.3	80	101	+26.3

1 Does not include suspicion.   2 Violent crimes are offenses of murder and nonnegligent manslaughter, rape, robbery, and aggravated assault. Property crimes are offenses of burglary, larceny-theft, motor vehicle theft, and arson.   3 The rape figures in this table are aggregate totals of the data submitted based on both the legacy and revised Uniform Crime Reporting definitions.

Table 58. Arrests, Nonmetropolitan Counties, Distribution by Age, 2020

(Number, percent; 1,637 agencies; 2020 estimated population 18,948,762.)

Offense charged	Total, all ages	Ages under 15	Ages under 18	Ages 18 and over	Under 10	10–12	13–14	15	16	17	18	19	20
Total	457,474	3,691	14,980	442,494	84	911	2,696	2,563	3,506	5,220	9,551	11,398	11,858
Total percent distribution[1]	100.0	0.8	3.3	96.7	*	0.2	0.6	0.6	0.8	1.1	2.1	2.5	2.6
Violent crime[2]	17,253	270	845	16,408	6	96	168	138	176	261	378	393	418
Violent crime percent distribution[1]	100.0	1.6	4.9	95.1	*	0.6	1.0	0.8	1.0	1.5	2.2	2.3	2.4
Murder and nonnegligent manslaughter	637	9	39	598	0	3	6	5	8	17	20	14	22
Rape[3]	1,369	87	209	1,160	0	34	53	37	33	52	64	58	46
Robbery	1,076	7	54	1,022	0	0	7	10	12	25	31	43	33
Aggravated assault	14,171	167	543	13,628	6	59	102	86	123	167	263	278	317
Property crime[2]	24,218	546	1,721	22,497	10	129	407	362	378	435	640	628	599
Property crime percent distribution[1]	100.0	2.3	7.1	92.9	*	0.5	1.7	1.5	1.6	1.8	2.6	2.6	2.5
Burglary	7,167	202	576	6,591	4	55	143	122	124	128	205	183	195
Larceny-theft	12,996	211	767	12,229	6	42	163	163	173	220	304	316	302
Motor vehicle theft	3,600	103	326	3,274	0	17	86	66	74	83	124	121	93
Arson	455	30	52	403	0	15	15	11	7	4	7	8	9
Other assaults	40,355	817	2,337	38,018	11	233	573	464	529	527	688	747	809
Forgery and counterfeiting	1,222	0	11	1,211	0	0	0	0	1	10	24	24	22
Fraud	3,437	14	68	3,369	0	2	12	11	12	31	43	59	63
Embezzlement	291	2	3	288	0	1	1	0	0	1	8	8	6
Stolen property; buying, receiving, possessing	3,491	33	211	3,280	0	6	27	52	55	71	92	116	80
Vandalism	6,219	298	819	5,400	12	91	195	153	175	193	192	202	173
Weapons; carrying, possessing, etc.	6,747	46	190	6,557	1	14	31	27	38	79	119	140	155
Prostitution and commercialized vice	83	0	7	76	0	0	0	4	1	2	0	3	1
Sex offenses (except forcible rape and prostitution)	1,570	116	240	1,330	4	35	77	36	45	43	62	46	40
Drug abuse violations	77,373	188	1,752	75,621	7	24	157	213	430	921	2,096	2,494	2,640
Gambling	57	0	1	56	0	0	0	1	0	0	0	0	1
Offenses against the family and children	5,064	41	94	4,970	0	2	39	26	15	12	49	43	65
Driving under the influence	80,434	7	636	79,798	0	2	5	41	171	417	1,242	1,710	1,924
Liquor laws	7,985	162	1,724	6,261	0	13	149	234	501	827	1,300	1,202	950
Drunkenness	6,538	8	62	6,476	0	2	6	5	19	30	100	112	116
Disorderly conduct	10,129	282	817	9,312	10	71	201	164	174	197	179	173	206
Vagrancy	179	1	1	178	0	0	1	0	0	0	3	5	6
All other offenses (except traffic)	164,559	781	3,198	161,361	21	169	591	574	734	1,109	2,336	3,293	3,583
Suspicion	35	2	8	27	0	2	0	3	0	3	0	0	1
Curfew and loitering law violations	235	77	235	NA	2	19	56	55	52	51	NA	NA	NA

Table 58. Arrests, Nonmetropolitan Counties, Distribution by Age, 2020—Continued

(Number, percent; 1,637 agencies; 2020 estimated population 18,948,762.)

Offense charged	21	22	23	24	25–29	30–34	35–39	40–44	45–49	50–54	55–59	60–64	65 and over
Total	12,575	12,727	12,898	13,146	74,177	73,425	64,925	48,475	33,554	25,345	19,440	10,812	8,188
Total percent distribution[1]	2.7	2.8	2.8	2.9	16.2	16.1	14.2	10.6	7.3	5.5	4.2	2.4	1.8
Violent crime[2]	491	461	452	418	2,539	2,575	2,366	1,747	1,303	1,021	875	519	452
Violent crime percent distribution[1]	2.8	2.7	2.6	2.4	14.7	14.9	13.7	10.1	7.6	5.9	5.1	3.0	2.6
Murder and nonnegligent manslaughter	29	17	23	12	90	83	73	51	39	40	31	28	26
Rape[3]	55	48	38	33	146	120	165	104	81	74	56	32	40
Robbery	32	24	19	29	173	161	134	125	88	54	30	17	29
Aggravated assault	375	372	372	344	2,130	2,211	1,994	1,467	1,095	853	758	442	357
Property crime[2]	651	614	603	624	3,941	4,163	3,501	2,429	1,599	1,113	752	383	257
Property crime percent distribution[1]	2.7	2.5	2.5	2.6	16.3	17.2	14.5	10.0	6.6	4.6	3.1	1.6	1.1
Burglary	207	183	181	192	1,219	1,270	1,035	727	424	269	178	82	41
Larceny-theft	329	321	315	309	2,036	2,205	1,863	1,322	955	734	488	250	180
Motor vehicle theft	104	103	98	109	638	614	533	342	184	95	67	28	21
Arson	11	7	9	14	48	74	70	38	36	15	19	23	15
Other assaults	935	886	952	988	5,941	6,375	5,579	4,321	3,214	2,521	1,949	1,122	991
Forgery and counterfeiting	31	34	38	28	202	205	200	135	124	63	46	21	14
Fraud	80	75	71	81	591	577	572	412	284	184	157	63	57
Embezzlement	5	5	5	6	37	46	46	44	18	21	19	9	5
Stolen property; buying, receiving, possessing	121	102	95	114	616	626	504	343	217	118	74	39	23
Vandalism	170	161	152	174	935	933	784	511	348	277	185	83	120
Weapons; carrying, possessing, etc.	217	211	215	242	1,147	1,064	957	693	473	316	281	190	137
Prostitution and commercialized vice	2	2	0	1	10	8	15	10	5	4	6	4	5
Sex offenses (except forcible rape and prostitution)	46	35	50	32	160	183	163	129	94	83	69	51	87
Drug abuse violations	2,664	2,674	2,685	2,518	13,748	12,686	10,829	7,852	4,872	3,500	2,588	1,224	551
Gambling	2	1	1	1	7	8	3	10	5	6	6	1	4
Offenses against the family and children	54	85	88	117	768	968	985	716	462	265	164	82	59
Driving under the influence	2,541	2,588	2,662	2,671	13,211	11,613	9,957	7,793	6,197	5,405	4,771	3,014	2,499
Liquor laws	176	150	114	101	476	418	336	267	238	181	153	122	77
Drunkenness	149	142	158	183	951	999	967	773	620	494	395	182	135
Disorderly conduct	247	260	269	250	1,349	1,460	1,321	1,070	743	687	527	291	280
Vagrancy	6	4	7	5	36	29	15	19	10	10	9	6	8
All other offenses (except traffic)	3,985	4,237	4,281	4,589	27,510	28,481	25,820	19,199	12,726	9,076	6,413	3,406	2,426
Suspicion	2	0	0	3	2	8	5	2	2	0	1	0	1
Curfew and loitering law violations	NA	NA	NA	NA	NA	NA	NA	NA	NA	NA	NA	NA	NA

NA = Not available.
* = Less than one-tenth of one percent.
1 Because of rounding, the percentages may not sum to 100.   2 Violent crimes are offenses of murder and nonnegligent manslaughter, rape, robbery, and aggravated assault. Property crimes are offenses of burglary, larceny-theft, motor vehicle theft, and arson.   3 The rape figures in this table are aggregate totals of the data submitted based on both the legacy and revised Uniform Crime Reporting definitions.

Table 59. Arrests, Nonmetropolitan Counties, Persons Under 15, 18, 21, and 25 Years of Age, 2020

(Number, percent; 1,637 agencies; 2020 estimated population 18,948,762.)

Offense charged	Total, all ages	Number of persons arrested				Percent of total all ages			
		Under 15	Under 18	Under 21	Under 25	Under 15	Under 18	Under 21	Under 25
Total	457,474	3,691	14,980	47,787	99,133	0.8	3.3	10.4	21.7
Violent crime[1]	17,253	270	845	2,034	3,856	1.6	4.9	11.8	22.3
Murder and nonnegligent manslaughter	637	9	39	95	176	1.4	6.1	14.9	27.6
Rape[2]	1,369	87	209	377	551	6.4	15.3	27.5	40.2
Robbery	1,076	7	54	161	265	0.7	5.0	15.0	24.6
Aggravated assault	14,171	167	543	1,401	2,864	1.2	3.8	9.9	20.2
Property crime[1]	24,218	546	1,721	3,588	6,080	2.3	7.1	14.8	25.1
Burglary	7,167	202	576	1,159	1,922	2.8	8.0	16.2	26.8
Larceny-theft	12,996	211	767	1,689	2,963	1.6	5.9	13.0	22.8
Motor vehicle theft	3,600	103	326	664	1,078	2.9	9.1	18.4	29.9
Arson	455	30	52	76	117	6.6	11.4	16.7	25.7
Other assaults	40,355	817	2,337	4,581	8,342	2.0	5.8	11.4	20.7
Forgery and counterfeiting	1,222	0	11	81	212	0.0	0.9	6.6	17.3
Fraud	3,437	14	68	233	540	0.4	2.0	6.8	15.7
Embezzlement	291	2	3	25	46	0.7	1.0	8.6	15.8
Stolen property; buying, receiving, possessing	3,491	33	211	499	931	0.9	6.0	14.3	26.7
Vandalism	6,219	298	819	1,386	2,043	4.8	13.2	22.3	32.9
Weapons; carrying, possessing, etc.	6,747	46	190	604	1,489	0.7	2.8	9.0	22.1
Prostitution and commercialized vice	83	0	7	11	16	0.0	8.4	13.3	19.3
Sex offenses (except forcible rape and prostitution)	1,570	116	240	388	551	7.4	15.3	24.7	35.1
Drug abuse violations	77,373	188	1,752	8,982	19,523	0.2	2.3	11.6	25.2
Gambling	57	0	1	2	7	0.0	1.8	3.5	12.3
Offenses against the family and children	5,064	41	94	251	595	0.8	1.9	5.0	11.7
Driving under the influence	80,434	7	636	5,512	15,974	*	0.8	6.9	19.9
Liquor laws	7,985	162	1,724	5,176	5,717	2.0	21.6	64.8	71.6
Drunkenness	6,538	8	62	390	1,022	0.1	0.9	6.0	15.6
Disorderly conduct	10,129	282	817	1,375	2,401	2.8	8.1	13.6	23.7
Vagrancy	179	1	1	15	37	0.6	0.6	8.4	20.7
All other offenses (except traffic)	164,559	781	3,198	12,410	29,502	0.5	1.9	7.5	17.9
Suspicion	35	2	8	9	14	5.7	22.9	25.7	40.0
Curfew and loitering law violations	235	77	235	235	235	32.8	100.0	100.0	100.0

* = Less than one-tenth of one percent.
1 Violent crimes are offenses of murder and nonnegligent manslaughter, rape, robbery, and aggravated assault. Property crimes are offenses of burglary, larceny-theft, motor vehicle theft, and arson.   2 The rape figures in this table are aggregate totals of the data submitted based on both the legacy and revised Uniform Crime Reporting definitions.

Table 60. Arrests, Nonmetropolitan Counties, Distribution by Sex, 2020

(Number, percent; 1,637 agencies; 2020 estimated population 18,948,762.)

Offense charged	Number of persons arrested			Percent male	Percent female	Percent distribution[1]		
	Total	Male	Female			Total	Male	Female
Total	457,474	337,574	119,900	73.8	26.2	100.0	100.0	100.0
Violent crime[2]	17,253	14,302	2,951	82.9	17.1	3.8	4.2	2.5
Murder and nonnegligent manslaughter	637	528	109	82.9	17.1	0.1	0.2	0.1
Rape[3]	1,369	1,319	50	96.3	3.7	0.3	0.4	*
Robbery	1,076	864	212	80.3	19.7	0.2	0.3	0.2
Aggravated assault	14,171	11,591	2,580	81.8	18.2	3.1	3.4	2.2
Property crime[2]	24,218	17,491	6,727	72.2	27.8	5.3	5.2	5.6
Burglary	7,167	5,743	1,424	80.1	19.9	1.6	1.7	1.2
Larceny-theft	12,996	8,622	4,374	66.3	33.7	2.8	2.6	3.6
Motor vehicle theft	3,600	2,758	842	76.6	23.4	0.8	0.8	0.7
Arson	455	368	87	80.9	19.1	0.1	0.1	0.1
Other assaults	40,355	29,807	10,548	73.9	26.1	8.8	8.8	8.8
Forgery and counterfeiting	1,222	812	410	66.4	33.6	0.3	0.2	0.3
Fraud	3,437	2,186	1,251	63.6	36.4	0.8	0.6	1.0
Embezzlement	291	134	157	46.0	54.0	0.1	*	0.1
Stolen property; buying, receiving, possessing	3,491	2,766	725	79.2	20.8	0.8	0.8	0.6
Vandalism	6,219	4,895	1,324	78.7	21.3	1.4	1.5	1.1
Weapons; carrying, possessing, etc.	6,747	6,035	712	89.4	10.6	1.5	1.8	0.6
Prostitution and commercialized vice	83	62	21	74.7	25.3	*	*	*
Sex offenses (except forcible rape and prostitution)	1,570	1,484	86	94.5	5.5	0.3	0.4	0.1
Drug abuse violations	77,373	54,577	22,796	70.5	29.5	16.9	16.2	19.0
Gambling	57	40	17	70.2	29.8	*	*	*
Offenses against the family and children	5,064	3,805	1,259	75.1	24.9	1.1	1.1	1.1
Driving under the influence	80,434	60,791	19,643	75.6	24.4	17.6	18.0	16.4
Liquor laws	7,985	5,494	2,491	68.8	31.2	1.7	1.6	2.1
Drunkenness	6,538	4,708	1,830	72.0	28.0	1.4	1.4	1.5
Disorderly conduct	10,129	7,145	2,984	70.5	29.5	2.2	2.1	2.5
Vagrancy	179	139	40	77.7	22.3	*	*	*
All other offenses (except traffic)	164,559	120,757	43,802	73.4	26.6	36.0	35.8	36.5
Suspicion	35	25	10	71.4	28.6	*	*	*
Curfew and loitering law violations	235	119	116	50.6	49.4	0.1	*	0.1

* = Less than one-tenth of 1 percent.
1 Because of rounding, the percentages may not sum to 100.   2 Violent crimes are offenses of murder and nonnegligent manslaughter, rape, robbery, and aggravated assault. Property crimes are offenses of burglary, larceny-theft, motor vehicle theft, and arson.   3 The rape figures in this table are aggregate totals of the data submitted based on both the legacy and revised Uniform Crime Reporting definitions.

Table 61. Arrests, Nonmetropolitan Counties, Distribution by Race, 2020

(Number, percent; 1,637 agencies; 2020 estimated population 18,948,762.)

Offense charged	Total arrests						Percent distribution[1]						Arrests under 18					
	Total	White	Black	American Indian or Alaskan Native	Asian	Native Hawaiian or Other Pacific Islander	Total	White	Black	American Indian or Alaskan Native	Asian	Native Hawaiian or Other Pacific Islander	Total	White	Black	American Indian or Alaskan Native	Asian	Native Hawaiian or Other Pacific Islander
Total	442,856	363,981	54,908	15,147	4,298	4,522	100.0	82.2	12.4	3.4	1.0	1.0	14,307	11,525	1,808	693	106	175
Violent crime[2]	16,952	13,404	2,167	973	132	276	100.0	79.1	12.8	5.7	0.8	1.6	831	638	142	41	2	8
Murder and nonnegligent manslaughter	628	425	152	34	11	6	100.0	67.7	24.2	5.4	1.8	1.0	38	18	17	2	1	0
Rape[3]	1,333	1,111	133	58	9	22	100.0	83.3	10.0	4.4	0.7	1.7	205	179	16	8	0	2
Robbery	1,068	662	207	40	43	116	100.0	62.0	19.4	3.7	4.0	10.9	54	36	16	2	0	0
Aggravated assault	13,923	11,206	1,675	841	69	132	100.0	80.5	12.0	6.0	0.5	0.9	534	405	93	29	1	6
Property crime[2]	23,767	19,893	2,479	746	238	411	100.0	83.7	10.4	3.1	1.0	1.7	1,663	1,283	253	97	8	22
Burglary	7,063	6,007	697	251	51	57	100.0	85.0	9.9	3.6	0.7	0.8	563	428	83	44	3	5
Larceny-theft	12,696	10,580	1,382	331	137	266	100.0	83.3	10.9	2.6	1.1	2.1	734	579	118	21	5	11
Motor vehicle theft	3,554	2,924	366	141	45	78	100.0	82.3	10.3	4.0	1.3	2.2	316	238	47	27	0	4
Arson	454	382	34	23	5	10	100.0	84.1	7.5	5.1	1.1	2.2	50	38	5	5	0	2
Other assaults	39,448	32,959	4,028	1,901	234	326	100.0	83.6	10.2	4.8	0.6	0.8	2,277	1,794	334	116	11	22
Forgery and counterfeiting	1,184	977	179	17	3	8	100.0	82.5	15.1	1.4	0.3	0.7	9	7	2	0	0	0
Fraud	3,304	2,668	448	138	24	26	100.0	80.8	13.6	4.2	0.7	0.8	63	45	10	5	3	0
Embezzlement	286	256	28	2	0	0	100.0	89.5	9.8	0.7	0.0	0.0	3	2	1	0	0	0
Stolen property; buying, receiving, possessing	3,400	2,649	649	88	14	0	100.0	77.9	19.1	2.6	0.4	0.0	202	126	70	6	0	0
Vandalism	6,110	5,053	716	233	56	52	100.0	82.7	11.7	3.8	0.9	0.9	793	663	88	34	4	4
Weapons; carrying, possessing, etc.	6,601	4,803	1,462	189	72	75	100.0	72.8	22.1	2.9	1.1	1.1	186	112	70	2	2	0
Prostitution and commercialized vice	85	69	5	1	6	4	100.0	81.2	5.9	1.2	7.1	4.7	7	7	0	0	0	0
Sex offenses (except forcible rape and prostitution)	1,539	1,352	129	38	13	7	100.0	87.8	8.4	2.5	0.8	0.5	232	213	15	3	0	1
Drug abuse violations	73,977	59,194	11,840	1,920	588	435	100.0	80.0	16.0	2.6	0.8	0.6	1,633	1,334	205	68	11	15
Gambling	53	44	5	1	2	1	100.0	83.0	9.4	1.9	3.8	1.9	1	1	0	0	0	0
Offenses against the family and children	5,014	3,932	725	341	10	6	100.0	78.4	14.5	6.8	0.2	0.1	94	81	3	6	1	3
Driving under the influence	76,379	65,204	7,295	2,185	1,265	430	100.0	85.4	9.6	2.9	1.7	0.6	598	539	25	30	3	1
Liquor laws	7,362	6,422	429	426	56	29	100.0	87.2	5.8	5.8	0.8	0.4	1,567	1,410	25	110	13	9
Drunkenness	6,450	5,759	403	251	29	8	100.0	89.3	6.2	3.9	0.4	0.1	61	55	4	2	0	0
Disorderly conduct	9,857	7,870	1,156	579	89	163	100.0	79.8	11.7	5.9	0.9	1.7	784	571	156	54	2	1
Vagrancy	170	140	11	19	0	0	100.0	82.4	6.5	11.2	0.0	0.0	1	0	1	0	0	0
All other offenses (except traffic)	160,638	131,116	20,751	5,081	1,454	2,236	100.0	81.6	12.9	3.2	0.9	1.4	3,060	2,463	401	103	33	60
Suspicion	47	45	0	2	0	0	100.0	95.7	0.0	4.3	0.0	0.0	9	9	0	0	0	0
Curfew and loitering law violations	233	172	3	16	13	29	100.0	73.8	1.3	6.9	5.6	12.4	233	172	3	16	13	29

Table 61. Arrests, Nonmetropolitan Counties, Distribution by Race, 2020—Continued

(Number, percent; 1,637 agencies; 2020 estimated population 18,948,762.)

Offense charged	Percent distribution[1]						Arrests 18 and over						Percent distribution[1]					
	Total	White	Black	American Indian or Alaskan Native	Asian	Native Hawaiian or Other Pacific Islander	Total	White	Black	American Indian or Alaskan Native	Asian	Native Hawaiian or Other Pacific Islander	Total	White	Black	American Indian or Alaskan Native	Asian	Native Hawaiian or Other Pacific Islander
Total	100.0	80.6	12.6	4.8	0.7	1.2	428,549	352,456	53,100	14,454	4,192	4,347	100.0	82.2	12.4	3.4	1.0	1.0
Violent crime[2]	100.0	76.8	17.1	4.9	0.2	1.0	16,121	12,766	2,025	932	130	268	100.0	79.2	12.6	5.8	0.8	1.7
Murder and nonnegligent manslaughter	100.0	47.4	44.7	5.3	2.6	0.0	590	407	135	32	10	6	100.0	69.0	22.9	5.4	1.7	1.0
Rape[3]	100.0	87.3	7.8	3.9	0.0	1.0	1,128	932	117	50	9	20	100.0	82.6	10.4	4.4	0.8	1.8
Robbery	100.0	66.7	29.6	3.7	0.0	0.0	1,014	626	191	38	43	116	100.0	61.7	18.8	3.7	4.2	11.4
Aggravated assault	100.0	75.8	17.4	5.4	0.2	1.1	13,389	10,801	1,582	812	68	126	100.0	80.7	11.8	6.1	0.5	0.9
Property crime[2]	100.0	77.1	15.2	5.8	0.5	1.3	22,104	18,610	2,226	649	230	389	100.0	84.2	10.1	2.9	1.0	1.8
Burglary	100.0	76.0	14.7	7.8	0.5	0.9	6,500	5,579	614	207	48	52	100.0	85.8	9.4	3.2	0.7	0.8
Larceny-theft	100.0	78.9	16.1	2.9	0.7	1.5	11,962	10,001	1,264	310	132	255	100.0	83.6	10.6	2.6	1.1	2.1
Motor vehicle theft	100.0	75.3	14.9	8.5	0.0	1.3	3,238	2,686	319	114	45	74	100.0	83.0	9.9	3.5	1.4	2.3
Arson	100.0	76.0	10.0	10.0	0.0	4.0	404	344	29	18	5	8	100.0	85.1	7.2	4.5	1.2	2.0
Other assaults	100.0	78.8	14.7	5.1	0.5	1	37,171	31,165	3,694	1,785	223	304	100.0	83.8	9.9	4.8	0.6	0.8
Forgery and counterfeiting	100.0	77.8	22.2	0.0	0.0	0.0	1,175	970	177	17	3	8	100.0	82.6	15.1	1.4	0.3	0.7
Fraud	100.0	71.4	15.9	7.9	4.8	0.0	3,241	2,623	438	133	21	26	100.0	80.9	13.5	4.1	0.6	0.8
Embezzlement	100.0	66.7	33.3	0.0	0.0	0.0	283	254	27	2	0	0	100.0	89.8	9.5	0.7	0.0	0.0
Stolen property; buying, receiving, possessing	100.0	62.4	34.7	3.0	0.0	0.0	3,198	2,523	579	82	14	0	100.0	78.9	18.1	2.6	0.4	0.0
Vandalism	100.0	83.6	11.1	4.3	0.5	0.5	5,317	4,390	628	199	52	48	100.0	82.6	11.8	3.7	1.0	0.9
Weapons; carrying, possessing, etc.	100.0	60.2	37.6	1.1	1.1	0.0	6,415	4,691	1,392	187	70	75	100.0	73.1	21.7	2.9	1.1	1.2
Prostitution and commercialized vice	100.0	100.0	0.0	0.0	0.0	0.0	78	62	5	1	6	4	100.0	79.5	6.4	1.3	7.7	5.1
Sex offenses (except forcible rape and prostitution)	100.0	91.8	6.5	1.3	0.0	0.4	1,307	1,139	114	35	13	6	100.0	87.1	8.7	2.7	1.0	0.5
Drug abuse violations	100.0	81.7	12.6	4.2	0.7	0.9	72,344	57,860	11,635	1,852	577	420	100.0	80.0	16.1	2.6	0.8	0.6
Gambling	100.0	100.0	0.0	0.0	0.0	0.0	52	43	5	1	2	1	100.0	82.7	9.6	1.9	3.8	1.9
Offenses against the family and children	100.0	86.2	3.2	6.4	1.1	3.2	4,920	3,851	722	335	9	3	100.0	78.3	14.7	6.8	0.2	0.1
Driving under the influence	100.0	90.1	4.2	5.0	0.5	0.2	75,781	64,665	7,270	2,155	1,262	429	100.0	85.3	9.6	2.8	1.7	0.6
Liquor laws	100.0	90.0	1.6	7.0	0.8	0.6	5,795	5,012	404	316	43	20	100.0	86.5	7.0	5.5	0.7	0.3
Drunkenness	100.0	90.2	6.6	3.3	0.0	0.0	6,389	5,704	399	249	29	8	100.0	89.3	6.2	3.9	0.5	0.1
Disorderly conduct	100.0	72.8	19.9	6.9	0.3	0.1	9,073	7,299	1,000	525	87	162	100.0	80.4	11.0	5.8	1.0	1.8
Vagrancy	100.0	0.0	100.0	0.0	0.0	0.0	169	140	10	19	0	0	100.0	82.8	5.9	11.2	0.0	0.0
All other offenses (except traffic)	100.0	80.5	13.1	3.4	1.1	2	157,578	128,653	20,350	4,978	1,421	2,176	100.0	81.6	12.9	3.2	0.9	1.4
Suspicion	100.0	100.0	0.0	0.0	0.0	0.0	38	36	0	2	0	0	100.0	94.7	0.0	5.3	0.0	0.0
Curfew and loitering law violations	100.0	73.8	1.3	6.9	5.6	12.4	NA	NA	NA	NA	NA	NA	NA	NA	NA	NA	NA	NA

NA = Not available.

1 Because of rounding, the percentages may not sum to 100. 2 Violent crimes are offenses of murder and nonnegligent manslaughter, rape, robbery, and aggravated assault. Property crimes are offenses of burglary, larceny-theft, motor vehicle theft, and arson. 3 The rape figures in this table are aggregate totals of the data submitted based on both the legacy and revised Uniform Crime Reporting definitions.

Table 61A. Arrests, Nonmetropolitan Counties, Distribution by Ethnicity, 2020

(Number, percent; 1,637 agencies; 2020 estimated population 18,948,762.)

Offense charged	Total arrests			Percent distribution[1]			Arrests under 18		
	Total[2]	Hispanic or Latino	Not Hispanic or Latino	Total[2]	Hispanic or Latino	Not Hispanic or Latino	Total2	Hispanic or Latino	Not Hispanic or Latino
Total	339,114	29,139	309,975	100.0	8.6	91.4	10,440	1,175	9,265
Violent crime[3]	12,451	1,063	11,388	100.0	8.5	91.5	585	75	510
Murder and nonnegligent manslaughter	500	34	466	100.0	6.8	93.2	28	1	27
Rape[4]	925	109	816	100.0	11.8	88.2	138	13	125
Robbery	532	40	492	100.0	7.5	92.5	41	6	35
Aggravated assault	10,494	880	9,614	100.0	8.4	91.6	378	55	323
Property crime[3]	17,987	1,124	16,863	100.0	6.2	93.8	1,180	96	1,084
Burglary	5,490	332	5,158	100.0	6.0	94.0	377	35	342
Larceny-theft	9,415	537	8,878	100.0	5.7	94.3	531	30	501
Motor vehicle theft	2,731	227	2,504	100.0	8.3	91.7	235	26	209
Arson	351	28	323	100.0	8.0	92.0	37	5	32
Other assaults	29,918	2,324	27,594	100.0	7.8	92.2	1,561	137	1,424
Forgery and counterfeiting	901	76	825	100.0	8.4	91.6	8	2	6
Fraud	2,537	206	2,331	100.0	8.1	91.9	48	4	44
Embezzlement	177	4	173	100.0	2.3	97.7	3	0	3
Stolen property; buying, receiving, possessing	2,784	168	2,616	100.0	6.0	94.0	171	20	151
Vandalism	4,747	333	4,414	100.0	7.0	93.0	610	53	557
Weapons; carrying, possessing, etc.	4,655	404	4,251	100.0	8.7	91.3	144	12	132
Prostitution and commercialized vice	43	7	36	100.0	16.3	83.7	1	0	1
Sex offenses (except forcible rape and prostitution)	1,157	106	1,051	100.0	9.2	90.8	160	7	153
Drug abuse violations	60,976	5,177	55,799	100.0	8.5	91.5	1,308	206	1,102
Gambling	32	14	18	100.0	43.8	56.3	1	1	0
Offenses against the family and children	4,370	293	4,077	100.0	6.7	93.3	81	10	71
Driving under the influence	50,969	6,729	44,240	100.0	13.2	86.8	438	82	356
Liquor laws	5,276	561	4,715	100.0	10.6	89.4	1,150	101	1,049
Drunkenness	5,847	628	5,219	100.0	10.7	89.3	53	7	46
Disorderly conduct	6,736	479	6,257	100.0	7.1	92.9	516	38	478
Vagrancy	147	23	124	100.0	15.6	84.4	1	0	1
All other offenses (except traffic)	127,228	9,400	117,828	100.0	7.4	92.6	2,277	314	1,963
Suspicion	42	11	31	100.0	26.2	73.8	10	1	9
Curfew and loitering law violations	134	9	125	100.0	6.7	93.3	134	9	125

Table 61A. Arrests, Nonmetropolitan Counties, Distribution by Ethnicity, 2020—Continued

(Number, percent; 1,637 agencies; 2020 estimated population 18,948,762.)

Offense charged	Percent distribution[1]			Arrests 18 and over			Percent distribution[1]		
	Total[2]	Hispanic or Latino	Not Hispanic or Latino	Total[2]	Hispanic or Latino	Not Hispanic or Latino	Total[2]	Hispanic or Latino	Not Hispanic or Latino
Total	100.0	11.3	88.7	328,674	27,964	300,710	100.0	8.5	91.5
Violent crime[3]	100.0	12.8	87.2	11,866	988	10,878	100.0	8.3	91.7
Murder and nonnegligent manslaughter	100.0	3.6	96.4	472	33	439	100.0	7.0	93.0
Rape[4]	100.0	9.4	90.6	787	96	691	100.0	12.2	87.8
Robbery	100.0	14.6	85.4	491	34	457	100.0	6.9	93.1
Aggravated assault	100.0	14.6	85.4	10,116	825	9,291	100.0	8.2	91.8
Property crime[3]	100.0	8.1	91.9	16,807	1,028	15,779	100.0	6.1	93.9
Burglary	100.0	9.3	90.7	5,113	297	4,816	100.0	5.8	94.2
Larceny-theft	100.0	5.6	94.4	8,884	507	8,377	100.0	5.7	94.3
Motor vehicle theft	100.0	11.1	88.9	2,496	201	2,295	100.0	8.1	91.9
Arson	100.0	13.5	86.5	314	23	291	100.0	7.3	92.7
Other assaults	100.0	8.8	91.2	28,357	2,187	26,170	100.0	7.7	92.3
Forgery and counterfeiting	100.0	25.0	75.0	893	74	819	100.0	8.3	91.7
Fraud	100.0	8.3	91.7	2,489	202	2,287	100.0	8.1	91.9
Embezzlement	100.0	0.0	100.0	174	4	170	100.0	2.3	97.7
Stolen property; buying, receiving, possessing	100.0	11.7	88.3	2,613	148	2,465	100.0	5.7	94.3
Vandalism	100.0	8.7	91.3	4,137	280	3,857	100.0	6.8	93.2
Weapons; carrying, possessing, etc.	100.0	8.3	91.7	4,511	392	4,119	100.0	8.7	91.3
Prostitution and commercialized vice	100.0	0.0	100.0	42	7	35	100.0	16.7	83.3
Sex offenses (except forcible rape and prostitution)	100.0	4.4	95.6	997	99	898	100.0	9.9	90.1
Drug abuse violations	100.0	15.7	84.3	59,668	4,971	54,697	100.0	8.3	91.7
Gambling	100.0	100.0	0.0	31	13	18	100.0	41.9	58.1
Offenses against the family and children	100.0	12.3	87.7	4,289	283	4,006	100.0	6.6	93.4
Driving under the influence	100.0	18.7	81.3	50,531	6,647	43,884	100.0	13.2	86.8
Liquor laws	100.0	8.8	91.2	4,126	460	3,666	100.0	11.1	88.9
Drunkenness	100.0	13.2	86.8	5,794	621	5,173	100.0	10.7	89.3
Disorderly conduct	100.0	7.4	92.6	6,220	441	5,779	100.0	7.1	92.9
Vagrancy	100.0	0.0	100.0	146	23	123	100.0	15.8	84.2
All other offenses (except traffic)	100.0	13.8	86.2	124,951	9,086	115,865	100.0	7.3	92.7
Suspicion	100	10	90	32	10	22	100.0	31.3	68.8
Curfew and loitering law violations	100.0	6.7	93.3	NA	NA	NA	NA	NA	NA

NA = Not available.
1 Because of rounding, the percentages may not sum to 100.   2 The ethnicity totals are representative of those agencies that provided ethnicity breakdowns. Not all agencies provide ethnicity data; therefore, the race and ethnicity totals will not be equal.
3 Violent crimes are offenses of murder and nonnegligent manslaughter, rape, robbery, and aggravated assault. Property crimes are offenses of burglary, larceny-theft, motor vehicle theft, and arson.   4 The rape figures in this table are aggregate totals of the data submitted based on both the legacy and revised Uniform Crime Reporting definitions.

Table 62. Arrest Trends, Suburban Areas,[1] 2019–2020

(Number, percent change; 4,908 agencies; 2020 estimated population 83,553,706; 2019 estimated population 83,105,781.)

Offense charged	Number of persons arrested								
	Total, all ages			Under 18 years of age			18 years of age and over		
	2019	2020	Percent change	2019	2020	Percent change	2019	2020	Percent change
Total[2]	2,281,612	1,751,123	-23.3	159,753	97,970	-38.7	2,121,859	1,653,153	-22.1
Violent crime[3]	90,368	85,991	-4.8	9,264	6,366	-31.3	81,104	79,625	-1.8
Murder and nonnegligent manslaughter	1,806	1,897	+5.0	127	127	+0.0	1,679	1,770	+5.4
Rape[4]	5,257	4,458	-15.2	1,007	692	-31.3	4,250	3,766	-11.4
Robbery	11,740	10,303	-12.2	2,449	1,835	-25.1	9,291	8,468	-8.9
Aggravated assault	71,565	69,333	-3.1	5,681	3,712	-34.7	65,884	65,621	-0.4
Property crime[3]	246,826	196,499	-20.4	26,041	16,515	-36.6	220,785	179,984	-18.5
Burglary	34,703	30,277	-12.8	4,336	3,432	-20.8	30,367	26,845	-11.6
Larceny-theft	194,546	148,766	-23.5	18,903	10,611	-43.9	175,643	138,155	-21.3
Motor vehicle theft	15,820	15,602	-1.4	2,392	2,166	-9.4	13,428	13,436	+0.1
Arson	1,757	1,854	+5.5	410	306	-25.4	1,347	1,548	+14.9
Other assaults	212,962	190,704	-10.5	29,625	17,002	-42.6	183,337	173,702	-5.3
Forgery and counterfeiting	11,700	8,410	-28.1	232	149	-35.8	11,468	8,261	-28.0
Fraud	29,502	21,154	-28.3	1,020	720	-29.4	28,482	20,434	-28.3
Embezzlement	3,227	2,057	-36.3	126	106	-15.9	3,101	1,951	-37.1
Stolen property; buying, receiving, possessing	21,242	20,795	-2.1	1,927	1,746	-9.4	19,315	19,049	-1.4
Vandalism	37,592	35,484	-5.6	7,368	5,719	-22.4	30,224	29,765	-1.5
Weapons; carrying, possessing, etc.	31,443	31,851	+1.3	3,463	2,002	-42.2	27,980	29,849	+6.7
Prostitution and commercialized vice	2,667	1,572	-41.1	36	14	-61.1	2,631	1,558	-40.8
Sex offenses (except forcible rape and prostitution)	9,032	6,935	-23.2	1,675	1,007	-39.9	7,357	5,928	-19.4
Drug abuse violations	369,570	280,946	-24.0	21,739	11,248	-48.3	347,831	269,698	-22.5
Gambling	464	291	-37.3	50	16	-68.0	414	275	-33.6
Offenses against the family and children	23,203	13,864	-40.2	514	446	-13.2	22,689	13,418	-40.9
Driving under the influence	265,340	211,629	-20.2	1,312	1,351	+3.0	264,028	210,278	-20.4
Liquor laws	36,567	24,201	-33.8	6,171	4,304	-30.3	30,396	19,897	-34.5
Drunkenness	56,533	35,422	-37.3	908	621	-31.6	55,625	34,801	-37.4
Disorderly conduct	65,757	49,609	-24.6	12,698	5,840	-54.0	53,059	43,769	-17.5
Vagrancy	2,765	1,790	-35.3	42	70	+66.7	2,723	1,720	-36.8
All other offenses (except traffic)	761,688	529,439	-30.5	32,378	20,248	-37.5	729,310	509,191	-30.2
Suspicion	136	98	-27.9	3	7	+133.3	133	91	-31.6
Curfew and loitering law violations	3,164	2,480	-21.6	3,164	2,480	-21.6	NA	NA	NA

NA = Not available.

1 Suburban areas include law enforcement agencies in cities with less than 50,000 inhabitants and county law enforcement agencies that are within a Metropolitan Statistical Area. Suburban areas exclude all metropolitan agencies associated with a principal city.   2 Does not include suspicion.   3 Violent crimes are offenses of murder and nonnegligent manslaughter, rape, robbery, and aggravated assault. Property crimes are offenses of burglary, larceny-theft, motor vehicle theft, and arson.
4 The rape figures in this table are aggregate totals of the data submitted based on both the legacy and revised Uniform Crime Reporting definitions.

Table 63. Arrest Trends, Suburban Areas[1], by Age and Sex, 2019–2020

(Number, percent change; 4,908 agencies; 2020 estimated population 83,553,706; 2019 estimated population 83,105,781.)

Offense charged	Male Total 2019	Male Total 2020	Male Total Percent change	Male Under 18 2019	Male Under 18 2020	Male Under 18 Percent change	Female Total 2019	Female Total 2020	Female Total Percent change	Female Under 18 2019	Female Under 18 2020	Female Under 18 Percent change
Total[2]	1,645,958	1,280,649	-22.2	111,893	69,945	-37.5	635,654	470,474	-26.0	47,860	28,025	-41.4
Violent crime[3]	71,816	68,547	-4.6	7,352	5,128	-30.3	18,552	17,444	-6.0	1,912	1,238	-35.3
Murder and nonnegligent manslaughter	1,607	1,668	+3.8	115	115	+0.0	199	229	+15.1	12	12	+0.0
Rape[4]	5,065	4,358	-14.0	939	666	-29.1	192	100	-47.9	68	26	-61.8
Robbery	9,847	8,772	-10.9	2,120	1,596	-24.7	1,893	1,531	-19.1	329	239	-27.4
Aggravated assault	55,297	53,749	-2.8	4,178	2,751	-34.2	16,268	15,584	-4.2	1,503	961	-36.1
Property crime[3]	152,267	126,842	-16.7	17,610	11,950	-32.1	94,559	69,657	-26.3	8,431	4,565	-45.9
Burglary	27,643	24,450	-11.6	3,745	2,985	-20.3	7,060	5,827	-17.5	591	447	-24.4
Larceny-theft	111,110	88,746	-20.1	11,614	6,968	-40.0	83,436	60,020	-28.1	7,289	3,643	-50.0
Motor vehicle theft	12,102	12,159	+0.5	1,894	1,738	-8.2	3,718	3,443	-7.4	498	428	-14.1
Arson	1,412	1,487	+5.3	357	259	-27.5	345	367	+6.4	53	47	-11.3
Other assaults	150,855	136,545	-9.5	18,929	10,748	-43.2	62,107	54,159	-12.8	10,696	6,254	-41.5
Forgery and counterfeiting	7,950	5,750	-27.7	184	120	-34.8	3,750	2,660	-29.1	48	29	-39.6
Fraud	18,977	14,002	-26.2	708	496	-29.9	10,525	7,152	-32.0	312	224	-28.2
Embezzlement	1,560	1,037	-33.5	64	55	-14.1	1,667	1,020	-38.8	62	51	-17.7
Stolen property; buying, receiving, possessing	16,521	16,287	-1.4	1,570	1,464	-6.8	4,721	4,508	-4.5	357	282	-21.0
Vandalism	29,417	27,737	-5.7	6,060	4,625	-23.7	8,175	7,747	-5.2	1,308	1,094	-16.4
Weapons; carrying, possessing, etc.	28,122	28,559	+1.6	3,039	1,789	-41.1	3,321	3,292	-0.9	424	213	-49.8
Prostitution and commercialized vice	1,216	867	-28.7	28	8	-71.4	1,451	705	-51.4	8	6	-25.0
Sex offenses (except forcible rape and prostitution)	8,443	6,583	-22.0	1,463	919	-37.2	589	352	-40.2	212	88	-58.5
Drug abuse violations	271,506	207,388	-23.6	15,943	8,345	-47.7	98,064	73,558	-25.0	5,796	2,903	-49.9
Gambling	334	197	-41.0	43	14	-67.4	130	94	-27.7	7	2	-71.4
Offenses against the family and children	17,394	9,909	-43.0	307	292	-4.9	5,809	3,955	-31.9	207	154	-25.6
Driving under the influence	194,731	157,025	-19.4	1,009	1,016	+0.7	70,609	54,604	-22.7	303	335	+10.6
Liquor laws	24,947	16,654	-33.2	3,560	2,588	-27.3	11,620	7,547	-35.1	2,611	1,716	-34.3
Drunkenness	43,606	27,306	-37.4	605	388	-35.9	12,927	8,116	-37.2	303	233	-23.1
Disorderly conduct	46,637	35,213	-24.5	8,210	3,814	-53.5	19,120	14,396	-24.7	4,488	2,026	-54.9
Vagrancy	2,144	1,434	-33.1	32	47	+46.9	621	356	-42.7	10	23	+130.0
All other offenses (except traffic)	555,345	391,130	-29.6	23,007	14,502	-37.0	206,343	138,309	-33.0	9,371	5,746	-38.7
Suspicion	90	54	-40.0	3	6	+100.0	46	44	-4.3	0	1	
Curfew and loitering law violations	2,170	1,637	-24.6	2,170	1,637	-24.6	994	843	-15.2	994	843	-15.2

1 Suburban areas include law enforcement agencies in cities with less than 50,000 inhabitants and county law enforcement agencies that are within a Metropolitan Statistical Area. Suburban areas exclude all metropolitan agencies associated with a principal city.   2 Does not include suspicion.   3 Violent crimes are offenses of murder and nonnegligent manslaughter, rape, robbery, and aggravated assault. Property crimes are offenses of burglary, larceny-theft, motor vehicle theft, and arson.
4 The rape figures in this table are aggregate totals of the data submitted based on both the legacy and revised Uniform Crime Reporting definitions.

Table 64. Arrests, Suburban Areas,[1] Distribution by Age, 2020

(Number, percent; 5,475 agencies; 2020 estimated population 94,124,752.)

Offense charged	Total, all ages	Ages under 15	Ages under 18	Ages 18 and over	Under 10	10–12	13–14	15	16	17	18	19	20
Total	1,964,444	30,377	109,588	1,854,856	420	6,413	23,544	20,634	26,403	32,174	49,393	53,957	54,826
Total percent distribution[2]	100.0	1.5	5.6	94.4	*	0.3	1.2	1.1	1.3	1.6	2.5	2.7	2.8
Violent crime[3]	97,976	1,963	7,179	90,797	18	434	1,511	1,353	1,756	2,107	2,764	2,807	2,770
Violent crime percent distribution[2]	100.0	2.0	7.3	92.7	*	0.4	1.5	1.4	1.8	2.2	2.8	2.9	2.8
Murder and nonnegligent manslaughter	2,282	9	156	2,126	0	2	7	26	48	73	102	117	118
Rape[4]	4,929	314	762	4,167	2	83	229	138	161	149	227	208	179
Robbery	11,687	430	2,083	9,604	0	46	384	402	554	697	766	601	532
Aggravated assault	79,078	1,210	4,178	74,900	16	303	891	787	993	1,188	1,669	1,881	1,941
Property crime[3]	218,927	4,920	18,356	200,571	40	932	3,948	3,734	4,670	5,032	6,375	5,833	5,709
Property crime percent distribution[2]	100.0	2.2	8.4	91.6	*	0.4	1.8	1.7	2.1	2.3	2.9	2.7	2.6
Burglary	33,777	1,104	3,768	30,009	8	219	877	803	938	923	1,023	876	889
Larceny-theft	164,967	3,017	11,840	153,127	19	591	2,407	2,309	3,037	3,477	4,717	4,390	4,297
Motor vehicle theft	18,095	625	2,416	15,679	3	67	555	546	645	600	600	526	492
Arson	2,088	174	332	1,756	10	55	109	76	50	32	35	41	31
Other assaults	212,497	7,293	18,988	193,509	91	1,898	5,304	3,777	4,038	3,880	4,203	4,637	4,940
Forgery and counterfeiting	9,273	15	161	9,112	0	1	14	22	46	78	291	342	359
Fraud	23,240	171	784	22,456	1	21	149	170	184	259	481	558	617
Embezzlement	2,275	1	113	2,162	0	0	1	2	41	69	137	128	87
Stolen property; buying, receiving, possessing	22,898	407	1,898	21,000	0	33	374	408	537	546	791	733	686
Vandalism	39,983	2,450	6,340	33,643	53	598	1,799	1,217	1,359	1,314	1,466	1,356	1,179
Weapons; carrying, possessing, etc.	36,425	551	2,267	34,158	6	136	409	376	535	805	1,254	1,377	1,443
Prostitution and commercialized vice	1,689	7	23	1,666	0	1	6	5	6	5	29	31	42
Sex offenses (except forcible rape and prostitution)	7,889	504	1,102	6,787	22	136	346	203	188	207	232	239	217
Drug abuse violations	317,731	1,864	12,741	304,990	10	219	1,635	1,948	3,319	5,610	10,750	12,042	11,458
Gambling	359	6	35	324	0	3	3	5	13	11	5	8	13
Offenses against the family and children	15,426	127	480	14,946	7	27	93	103	121	129	159	162	219
Driving under the influence	235,930	18	1,487	234,443	1	0	17	58	374	1,037	2,885	4,226	5,164
Liquor laws	27,056	527	4,846	22,210	0	57	470	742	1,349	2,228	4,589	4,135	3,126
Drunkenness	39,762	141	665	39,097	1	18	122	124	168	232	674	706	809
Disorderly conduct	55,216	2,391	6,564	48,652	47	584	1,760	1,329	1,427	1,417	1,472	1,480	1,407
Vagrancy	2,126	12	71	2,055	0	0	12	13	24	22	69	60	42
All other offenses (except traffic)	594,985	6,148	22,822	572,163	118	1,202	4,828	4,427	5,527	6,720	10,762	13,092	14,538
Suspicion	122	0	7	115	0	0	0	0	2	5	5	5	1
Curfew and loitering law violations	2,659	861	2,659	NA	5	113	743	618	719	461	NA	NA	NA

Table 64. Arrests, Suburban Areas,[1] Distribution by Age, 2020—Continued

(Number, percent; 5,475 agencies; 2020 estimated population 94,124,752.)

Offense charged	21	22	23	24	25–29	30–34	35–39	40–44	45–49	50–54	55–59	60–64	65 and over
Total	56,503	57,121	57,325	59,732	327,941	311,205	259,392	187,384	129,349	102,544	77,502	42,122	28,560
Total percent distribution[2]	2.9	2.9	2.9	3.0	16.7	15.8	13.2	9.5	6.6	5.2	3.9	2.1	1.5
Violent crime[3]	2,870	3,008	2,808	2,978	16,202	14,827	12,489	8,744	6,095	4,819	3,783	2,099	1,734
Violent crime percent distribution[2]	2.9	3.1	2.9	3.0	16.5	15.1	12.7	8.9	6.2	4.9	3.9	2.1	1.8
Murder and nonnegligent manslaughter	93	89	103	57	466	286	221	160	96	69	59	44	46
Rape[4]	179	137	116	142	567	559	532	395	266	217	193	116	134
Robbery	459	446	366	382	1,803	1,542	1,029	670	378	298	206	84	42
Aggravated assault	2,139	2,336	2,223	2,397	13,366	12,440	10,707	7,519	5,355	4,235	3,325	1,855	1,512
Property crime[3]	5,618	5,474	5,512	5,814	34,533	35,506	29,208	20,461	14,061	11,591	8,289	4,236	2,351
Property crime percent distribution[2]	2.6	2.5	2.5	2.7	15.8	16.2	13.3	9.3	6.4	5.3	3.8	1.9	1.1
Burglary	833	844	920	902	5,593	5,746	4,535	3,024	1,931	1,360	949	399	185
Larceny-theft	4,264	4,107	4,055	4,325	25,334	26,326	22,021	15,770	11,243	9,587	6,968	3,657	2,066
Motor vehicle theft	478	493	493	541	3,329	3,103	2,362	1,463	765	538	305	127	64
Arson	43	30	44	46	277	331	290	204	122	106	67	53	36
Other assaults	5,569	5,563	5,697	6,030	33,308	31,591	27,436	20,389	14,676	11,962	8,690	4,920	3,898
Forgery and counterfeiting	233	271	242	276	1,671	1,563	1,373	923	588	441	308	154	77
Fraud	606	672	625	709	4,112	3,910	3,372	2,323	1,611	1,246	914	406	294
Embezzlement	108	74	82	77	325	282	243	216	142	112	97	38	14
Stolen property; buying, receiving, possessing	658	685	661	716	4,069	3,942	3,164	2,027	1,210	851	488	221	98
Vandalism	1,249	1,180	1,252	1,218	6,216	5,579	4,439	2,991	1,835	1,531	1,078	587	487
Weapons; carrying, possessing, etc.	1,588	1,563	1,539	1,497	6,932	5,330	4,102	2,737	1,717	1,261	941	490	387
Prostitution and commercialized vice	57	48	46	56	289	263	228	167	146	106	81	33	44
Sex offenses (except forcible rape and prostitution)	197	150	144	167	840	886	857	728	531	459	454	298	388
Drug abuse violations	11,164	10,980	10,780	10,890	57,266	51,885	42,030	29,024	18,315	13,318	9,068	4,188	1,832
Gambling	5	3	8	4	47	34	59	48	36	20	17	8	9
Offenses against the family and children	251	284	336	322	2,465	3,120	2,756	1,982	1,191	811	480	244	164
Driving under the influence	7,296	7,899	8,112	8,564	42,717	36,591	29,467	22,560	17,527	14,868	12,751	7,886	5,930
Liquor laws	531	440	357	339	1,654	1,457	1,271	1,028	846	892	757	481	307
Drunkenness	1,015	1,023	1,038	1,090	5,942	6,027	5,490	4,141	3,211	3,040	2,647	1,469	775
Disorderly conduct	1,684	1,544	1,473	1,540	7,620	7,265	6,319	4,753	3,625	3,128	2,600	1,586	1,156
Vagrancy	42	47	41	43	314	316	257	232	169	177	109	95	42
All other offenses (except traffic)	15,761	16,209	16,571	17,397	101,410	100,808	84,815	61,892	41,805	31,907	23,944	12,680	8,572
Suspicion	1	4	1	5	9	23	17	18	12	4	6	3	1
Curfew and loitering law violations	NA	NA	NA	NA	NA	NA	NA	NA	NA	NA	NA	NA	NA

NA = Not available.
* = Less than one-tenth of one percent.
1 Suburban areas include law enforcement agencies in cities with less than 50,000 inhabitants and county law enforcement agencies that are within a Metropolitan Statistical Area. Suburban areas exclude all metropolitan agencies associated with a principal city.   2 Because of rounding, the percentages may not sum to 100.   3 Violent crimes are offenses of murder and nonnegligent manslaughter, rape, robbery, and aggravated assault. Property crimes are offenses of burglary, larceny-theft, motor vehicle theft, and arson.   4 The rape figures in this table are aggregate totals of the data submitted based on both the legacy and revised Uniform Crime Reporting definitions.

Table 65. Arrests, Suburban Areas,[1] Persons Under 15, 18, 21, and 25 Years of Age, 2020

(Number, percent; 5,475 agencies; 2020 estimated population 94,124,752.)

Offense charged	Total, all ages	Number of persons arrested				Percent of total all ages			
		Under 15	Under 18	Under 21	Under 25	Under 15	Under 18	Under 21	Under 25
Total	1,964,444	30,377	109,588	267,764	498,445	1.5	5.6	13.6	25.4
Violent crime[2]	97,976	1,963	7,179	15,520	27,184	2.0	7.3	15.8	27.7
Murder and nonnegligent manslaughter	2,282	9	156	493	835	0.4	6.8	21.6	36.6
Rape[3]	4,929	314	762	1,376	1,950	6.4	15.5	27.9	39.6
Robbery	11,687	430	2,083	3,982	5,635	3.7	17.8	34.1	48.2
Aggravated assault	79,078	1,210	4,178	9,669	18,764	1.5	5.3	12.2	23.7
Property crime[2]	218,927	4,920	18,356	36,273	58,691	2.2	8.4	16.6	26.8
Burglary	33,777	1,104	3,768	6,556	10,055	3.3	11.2	19.4	29.8
Larceny-theft	164,967	3,017	11,840	25,244	41,995	1.8	7.2	15.3	25.5
Motor vehicle theft	18,095	625	2,416	4,034	6,039	3.5	13.4	22.3	33.4
Arson	2,088	174	332	439	602	8.3	15.9	21.0	28.8
Other assaults	212,497	7,293	18,988	32,768	55,627	3.4	8.9	15.4	26.2
Forgery and counterfeiting	9,273	15	161	1,153	2,175	0.2	1.7	12.4	23.5
Fraud	23,240	171	784	2,440	5,052	0.7	3.4	10.5	21.7
Embezzlement	2,275	1	113	465	806	*	5.0	20.4	35.4
Stolen property; buying, receiving, possessing	22,898	407	1,898	4,108	6,828	1.8	8.3	17.9	29.8
Vandalism	39,983	2,450	6,340	10,341	15,240	6.1	15.9	25.9	38.1
Weapons; carrying, possessing, etc.	36,425	551	2,267	6,341	12,528	1.5	6.2	17.4	34.4
Prostitution and commercialized vice	1,689	7	23	125	332	0.4	1.4	7.4	19.7
Sex offenses (except forcible rape and prostitution)	7,889	504	1,102	1,790	2,448	6.4	14.0	22.7	31.0
Drug abuse violations	317,731	1,864	12,741	46,991	90,805	0.6	4.0	14.8	28.6
Gambling	359	6	35	61	81	1.7	9.7	17.0	22.6
Offenses against the family and children	15,426	127	480	1,020	2,213	0.8	3.1	6.6	14.3
Driving under the influence	235,930	18	1,487	13,762	45,633	*	0.6	5.8	19.3
Liquor laws	27,056	527	4,846	16,696	18,363	1.9	17.9	61.7	67.9
Drunkenness	39,762	141	665	2,854	7,020	0.4	1.7	7.2	17.7
Disorderly conduct	55,216	2,391	6,564	10,923	17,164	4.3	11.9	19.8	31.1
Vagrancy	2,126	12	71	242	415	0.6	3.3	11.4	19.5
All other offenses (except traffic)	594,985	6,148	22,822	61,214	127,152	1.0	3.8	10.3	21.4
Suspicion	122	0	7	18	29	0.0	5.7	14.8	23.8
Curfew and loitering law violations	2,659	861	2,659	2,659	2,659	32.4	100.0	100.0	100.0

* = Less than one-tenth of one percent.
1 Suburban areas include law enforcement agencies in cities with less than 50,000 inhabitants and county law enforcement agencies that are within a Metropolitan Statistical Area. Suburban areas exclude all metropolitan agencies associated with a principal city.   2 Violent crimes are offenses of murder and nonnegligent manslaughter, rape, robbery, and aggravated assault. Property crimes are offenses of burglary, larceny-theft, motor vehicle theft, and arson.   3 The rape figures in this table are aggregate totals of the data submitted based on both the legacy and revised Uniform Crime Reporting definitions.

Table 66. Arrests, Suburban Areas,[1] Distribution by Sex, 2020

(Number, percent; 5,475 agencies; 2020 estimated population 94,124,752.)

Offense charged	Number of persons arrested			Percent male	Percent female	Percent distribution[2]		
	Total	Male	Female			Total	Male	Female
Total	1,964,444	1,439,254	525,190	73.3	26.7	100.0	100.0	100.0
Violent crime[3]	97,976	78,220	19,756	79.8	20.2	5.0	5.4	3.8
Murder and nonnegligent manslaughter	2,282	1,990	292	87.2	12.8	0.1	0.1	0.1
Rape[4]	4,929	4,817	112	97.7	2.3	0.3	0.3	*
Robbery	11,687	9,980	1,707	85.4	14.6	0.6	0.7	0.3
Aggravated assault	79,078	61,433	17,645	77.7	22.3	4.0	4.3	3.4
Property crime[3]	218,927	141,557	77,370	64.7	35.3	11.1	9.8	14.7
Burglary	33,777	27,317	6,460	80.9	19.1	1.7	1.9	1.2
Larceny-theft	164,967	98,438	66,529	59.7	40.3	8.4	6.8	12.7
Motor vehicle theft	18,095	14,129	3,966	78.1	21.9	0.9	1.0	0.8
Arson	2,088	1,673	415	80.1	19.9	0.1	0.1	0.1
Other assaults	212,497	152,171	60,326	71.6	28.4	10.8	10.6	11.5
Forgery and counterfeiting	9,273	6,351	2,922	68.5	31.5	0.5	0.4	0.6
Fraud	23,240	15,437	7,803	66.4	33.6	1.2	1.1	1.5
Embezzlement	2,275	1,159	1,116	50.9	49.1	0.1	0.1	0.2
Stolen property; buying, receiving, possessing	22,898	17,973	4,925	78.5	21.5	1.2	1.2	0.9
Vandalism	39,983	31,162	8,821	77.9	22.1	2.0	2.2	1.7
Weapons; carrying, possessing, etc.	36,425	32,714	3,711	89.8	10.2	1.9	2.3	0.7
Prostitution and commercialized vice	1,689	941	748	55.7	44.3	0.1	0.1	0.1
Sex offenses (except forcible rape and prostitution)	7,889	7,468	421	94.7	5.3	0.4	0.5	0.1
Drug abuse violations	317,731	235,268	82,463	74.0	26.0	16.2	16.3	15.7
Gambling	359	233	126	64.9	35.1	*	*	*
Offenses against the family and children	15,426	10,969	4,457	71.1	28.9	0.8	0.8	0.8
Driving under the influence	235,930	175,264	60,666	74.3	25.7	12.0	12.2	11.6
Liquor laws	27,056	18,774	8,282	69.4	30.6	1.4	1.3	1.6
Drunkenness	39,762	30,783	8,979	77.4	22.6	2.0	2.1	1.7
Disorderly conduct	55,216	39,108	16,108	70.8	29.2	2.8	2.7	3.1
Vagrancy	2,126	1,693	433	79.6	20.4	0.1	0.1	0.1
All other offenses (except traffic)	594,985	440,172	154,813	74.0	26.0	30.3	30.6	29.5
Suspicion	122	76	46	62.3	37.7	*	*	*
Curfew and loitering law violations	2,659	1,761	898	66.2	33.8	0.1	0.1	0.2

* = Less than one-tenth of one percent.
1 Suburban areas include law enforcement agencies in cities with less than 50,000 inhabitants and county law enforcement agencies that are within a Metropolitan Statistical Area. Suburban areas exclude all metropolitan agencies associated with a principal city.   2 Because of rounding, the percentages may not sum to 100.   3 Violent crimes are offenses of murder and nonnegligent manslaughter, rape, robbery, and aggravated assault. Property crimes are offenses of burglary, larceny-theft, motor vehicle theft, and arson.   4 The rape figures in this table are aggregate totals of the data submitted based on both the legacy and revised Uniform Crime Reporting definitions.

Table 67. Arrests, Suburban Areas,[1] Distribution by Race, 2020

(Number, percent; 5,475 agencies; 2020 estimated population 94,124,752.)

Offense charged	Total arrests						Percent distribution[2]						Arrests under 18					
	Total	White	Black	American Indian or Alaskan Native	Asian	Native Hawaiian or Other Pacific Islander	Total	White	Black	American Indian or Alaskan Native	Asian	Native Hawaiian or Other Pacific Islander	Total	White	Black	American Indian or Alaskan Native	Asian	Native Hawaiian or Other Pacific Islander
Total	1,935,105	1,421,302	469,053	20,638	21,307	2,805	100.0	73.4	24.2	1.1	1.1	0.1	107,357	73,222	31,646	1,231	1,101	157
Violent crime[3]	97,096	66,145	28,506	918	1,328	199	100.0	68.1	29.4	0.9	1.4	0.2	7,079	4,100	2,823	73	69	14
Murder and nonnegligent manslaughter	2,266	1,237	982	21	23	3	100.0	54.6	43.3	0.9	1.0	0.1	155	66	87	1	1	0
Rape[4]	4,827	3,716	1,001	37	69	4	100.0	77.0	20.7	0.8	1.4	0.1	745	582	149	6	8	0
Robbery	11,574	5,973	5,372	98	101	30	100.0	51.6	46.4	0.8	0.9	0.3	2,052	824	1,190	9	19	10
Aggravated assault	78,429	55,219	21,151	762	1,135	162	100.0	70.4	27.0	1.0	1.4	0.2	4,127	2,628	1,397	57	41	4
Property crime[3]	215,722	148,919	62,353	2,082	2,139	229	100.0	69.0	28.9	1.0	1.0	0.1	18,008	10,371	7,199	165	236	37
Burglary	33,452	25,025	7,845	230	304	48	100.0	74.8	23.5	0.7	0.9	0.1	3,722	2,298	1,333	33	41	17
Larceny-theft	162,260	108,901	49,892	1,677	1,643	147	100.0	67.1	30.7	1.0	1.0	0.1	11,569	6,601	4,669	100	181	18
Motor vehicle theft	17,945	13,366	4,234	155	158	32	100.0	74.5	23.6	0.9	0.9	0.2	2,391	1,221	1,127	30	11	2
Arson	2,065	1,627	382	20	34	2	100.0	78.8	18.5	1.0	1.6	0.1	326	251	70	2	3	0
Other assaults	209,629	150,864	53,379	2,397	2,643	346	100.0	72.0	25.5	1.1	1.3	0.2	18,591	12,138	6,030	221	175	27
Forgery and counterfeiting	9,165	6,116	2,841	48	152	8	100.0	66.7	31.0	0.5	1.7	0.1	157	93	62	1	1	0
Fraud	22,913	14,643	7,673	235	335	27	100.0	63.9	33.5	1.0	1.5	0.1	774	428	325	6	13	2
Embezzlement	2,233	1,383	810	7	31	2	100.0	61.9	36.3	0.3	1.4	0.1	109	55	52	0	2	0
Stolen property; buying, receiving, possessing	22,647	15,120	6,989	214	274	50	100.0	66.8	30.9	0.9	1.2	0.2	1,868	658	1,166	20	17	7
Vandalism	39,398	29,003	9,425	437	488	45	100.0	73.6	23.9	1.1	1.2	0.1	6,191	4,727	1,332	75	55	2
Weapons; carrying, possessing, etc.	36,080	21,448	14,012	223	340	57	100.0	59.4	38.8	0.6	0.9	0.2	2,237	1,243	953	14	24	3
Prostitution and commercialized vice	1,668	1,020	504	5	133	6	100.0	61.2	30.2	0.3	8.0	0.4	22	11	10	0	0	1
Sex offenses (except forcible rape and prostitution)	7,779	6,101	1,454	54	147	23	100.0	78.4	18.7	0.7	1.9	0.3	1,070	817	227	13	12	1
Drug abuse violations	314,259	231,813	76,477	2,401	3,095	473	100.0	73.8	24.3	0.8	1.0	0.2	12,474	9,593	2,628	112	120	21
Gambling	351	251	84	3	12	1	100.0	71.5	23.9	0.9	3.4	0.3	33	23	9	0	1	0
Offenses against the family and children	15,220	10,843	3,916	324	125	12	100.0	71.2	25.7	2.1	0.8	0.1	471	351	96	23	1	0
Driving under the Influence	228,504	187,358	35,071	1,894	3,810	371	100.0	82.0	15.3	0.8	1.7	0.2	1,430	1,289	99	19	21	2
Liquor laws	26,390	21,411	4,076	481	383	39	100.0	81.1	15.4	1.8	1.5	0.1	4,719	4,264	301	80	69	5
Drunkenness	39,446	33,131	5,422	433	386	74	100.0	84.0	13.7	1.1	1.0	0.2	657	450	189	9	7	2
Disorderly conduct	54,506	37,652	14,917	1,461	425	51	100.0	69.1	27.4	2.7	0.8	0.1	6,450	3,913	2,376	101	54	6
Vagrancy	2,103	1,345	710	27	18	3	100.0	64.0	33.8	1.3	0.9	0.1	71	60	8	1	2	0
All other offenses (except traffic)	587,290	434,700	139,810	6,971	5,024	785	100.0	74.0	23.8	1.2	0.9	0.1	22,352	16,684	5,164	276	204	24
Suspicion	121	86	32	1	1	1	100.0	71.1	26.4	0.8	0.8	0.8	9	4	5	0	0	0
Curfew and loitering law violations	2,585	1,950	592	22	18	3	100.0	75.4	22.9	0.9	0.7	0.1	2,585	1,950	592	22	18	3

Table 67. Arrests, Suburban Areas,[1] Distribution by Race, 2020—Continued

(Number, percent; 5,475 agencies; 2020 estimated population 94,124,752.)

Offense charged	Percent distribution[2]						Arrests 18 and over						Percent distribution[2]					
	Total	White	Black	American Indian or Alaskan Native	Asian	Native Hawaiian or Other Pacific Islander	Total	White	Black	American Indian or Alaskan Native	Asian	Native Hawaiian or Other Pacific Islander	Total	White	Black	American Indian or Alaskan Native	Asian	Native Hawaiian or Other Pacific Islander
Total	100.0	68.2	29.5	1.1	1.0	0.1	1,827,748	1,348,080	437,407	19,407	20,206	2,648	100.0	73.8	23.9	1.1	1.1	0.1
Violent crime[3]	100.0	57.9	39.9	1.0	1.0	0.2	90,017	62,045	25,683	845	1,259	185	100.0	68.9	28.5	0.9	1.4	0.2
Murder and nonnegligent manslaughter	100.0	42.6	56.1	0.6	0.6	0.0	2,111	1,171	895	20	22	3	100.0	55.5	42.4	0.9	1.0	0.1
Rape[4]	100.0	78.1	20.0	0.8	1.1	0.0	4,082	3,134	852	31	61	4	100.0	76.8	20.9	0.8	1.5	0.1
Robbery	100.0	40.2	58.0	0.4	0.9	0.5	9,522	5,149	4,182	89	82	20	100.0	54.1	43.9	0.9	0.9	0.2
Aggravated assault	100.0	63.7	33.9	1.4	1.0	0.1	74,302	52,591	19,754	705	1,094	158	100.0	70.8	26.6	0.9	1.5	0.2
Property crime[3]	100.0	57.6	40.0	0.9	1.3	0.2	197,714	138,548	55,154	1,917	1,903	192	100.0	70.1	27.9	1.0	1.0	0.1
Burglary	100.0	61.7	35.8	0.9	1.1	0.5	29,730	22,727	6,512	197	263	31	100.0	76.4	21.9	0.7	0.9	0.1
Larceny-theft	100.0	57.1	40.4	0.9	1.6	0.2	150,691	102,300	45,223	1,577	1,462	129	100.0	67.9	30.0	1.0	1.0	0.1
Motor vehicle theft	100.0	51.1	47.1	1.3	0.5	0.1	15,554	12,145	3,107	125	147	30	100.0	78.1	20.0	0.8	0.9	0.2
Arson	100.0	77.0	21.5	0.6	0.9	0.0	1,739	1,376	312	18	31	2	100.0	79.1	17.9	1.0	1.8	0.1
Other assaults	100.0	65.3	32.4	1.2	0.9	0.1	191,038	138,726	47,349	2,176	2,468	319	100.0	72.6	24.8	1.1	1.3	0.2
Forgery and counterfeiting	100.0	59.2	39.5	0.6	0.6	0.0	9,008	6,023	2,779	47	151	8	100.0	66.9	30.9	0.5	1.7	0.1
Fraud	100.0	55.3	42.0	0.8	1.7	0.3	22,139	14,215	7,348	229	322	25	100.0	64.2	33.2	1.0	1.5	0.1
Embezzlement	100.0	50.5	47.7	0.0	1.8	0.0	2,124	1,328	758	7	29	2	100.0	62.5	35.7	0.3	1.4	0.1
Stolen property; buying, receiving, possessing	100.0	35.2	62.4	1.1	0.9	0.4	20,779	14,462	5,823	194	257	43	100.0	69.6	28.0	0.9	1.2	0.2
Vandalism	100.0	76.4	21.5	1.2	0.9	*	33,207	24,276	8,093	362	433	43	100.0	73.1	24.4	1.1	1.3	0.1
Weapons; carrying, possessing, etc.	100.0	55.6	42.6	0.6	1.1	0.1	33,843	20,205	13,059	209	316	54	100.0	59.7	38.6	0.6	0.9	0.2
Prostitution and commercialized vice	100.0	50.0	45.5	0.0	0.0	4.5	1,646	1,009	494	5	133	5	100.0	61.3	30.0	0.3	8.1	0.3
Sex offenses (except forcible rape and prostitution)	100.0	76.4	21.2	1.2	1.1	0.1	6,709	5,284	1,227	41	135	22	100.0	78.8	18.3	0.6	2.0	0.3
Drug abuse violations	100.0	76.9	21.1	0.9	1.0	0.2	301,785	222,220	73,849	2,289	2,975	452	100.0	73.6	24.5	0.8	1.0	0.1
Gambling	100.0	69.7	27.3	0.0	3.0	0.0	318	228	75	3	11	1	100.0	71.7	23.6	0.9	3.5	0.3
Offenses against the family and children	100.0	74.5	20.4	4.9	0.2	0.0	14,749	10,492	3,820	301	124	12	100.0	71.1	25.9	2.0	0.8	0.1
Driving under the influence	100.0	90.1	6.9	1.3	1.5	0.1	227,074	186,069	34,972	1,875	3,789	369	100.0	81.9	15.4	0.8	1.7	0.2
Liquor laws	100.0	90.4	6.4	1.7	1.5	0.1	21,671	17,147	3,775	401	314	34	100.0	79.1	17.4	1.9	1.4	0.2
Drunkenness	100.0	68.5	28.8	1.4	1.1	0.3	38,789	32,681	5,233	424	379	72	100.0	84.3	13.5	1.1	1.0	0.2
Disorderly conduct	100.0	60.7	36.8	1.6	0.8	0.1	48,056	33,739	12,541	1,360	371	45	100.0	70.2	26.1	2.8	0.8	0.1
Vagrancy	100.0	84.5	11.3	1.4	2.8	0.0	2,032	1,285	702	26	16	3	100.0	63.2	34.5	1.3	0.8	0.1
All other offenses (except traffic)	100.0	74.6	23.1	1.2	0.9	0.1	564,938	418,016	134,646	6,695	4,820	761	100.0	74.0	23.8	1.2	0.9	0.1
Suspicion	100.0	44.4	55.6	0.0	0.0	0.0	112	82	27	1	1	1	100.0	73.2	24.1	0.9	0.9	0.9
Curfew and loitering law violations	100.0	75.4	22.9	0.9	0.7	0.1	NA	NA	NA	NA	NA	NA	NA	NA	NA	NA	NA	NA

NA = Not available.
* = Less than one-tenth of one percent.
1 Suburban areas include law enforcement agencies in cities with less than 50,000 inhabitants and county law enforcement agencies that are within a Metropolitan Statistical Area. Suburban areas exclude all metropolitan agencies associated with a principal city.   2 Because of rounding, the percentages may not sum to 100.   3 Violent crimes are offenses of murder and nonnegligent manslaughter, rape, robbery, and aggravated assault. Property crimes are offenses of burglary, larceny-theft, motor vehicle theft, and arson.   4 The rape figures in this table are aggregate totals of the data submitted based on both the legacy and revised Uniform Crime Reporting definitions.

Table 67A. Arrests, Suburban Areas,[1] Distribution by Ethnicity, 2020

(Number, percent; 5,475 agencies; 2020 estimated population 94,124,752.)

Offense charged	Total arrests			Percent distribution[2]			Arrests under 18		
	Total[3]	Hispanic or Latino	Not Hispanic or Latino	Total[3]	Hispanic or Latino	Not Hispanic or Latino	Total[3]	Hispanic or Latino	Not Hispanic or Latino
Total	1,665,752	323,978	1,341,774	100.0	19.4	80.6	87,945	18,693	69,252
Violent crime[4]	85,756	21,312	64,444	100.0	24.9	75.1	6,036	1,508	4,528
Murder and nonnegligent manslaughter	1,947	457	1,490	100.0	23.5	76.5	121	32	89
Rape[5]	4,026	1,077	2,949	100.0	26.8	73.2	577	118	459
Robbery	10,292	2,420	7,872	100.0	23.5	76.5	1,811	438	1,373
Aggravated assault	69,491	17,358	52,133	100.0	25.0	75.0	3,527	920	2,607
Property crime[4]	183,992	27,345	156,647	100.0	14.9	85.1	14,839	2,798	12,041
Burglary	29,307	5,714	23,593	100.0	19.5	80.5	3,000	694	2,306
Larceny-theft	137,046	16,945	120,101	100.0	12.4	87.6	9,544	1,596	7,948
Motor vehicle theft	15,838	4,319	11,519	100.0	27.3	72.7	2,010	466	1,544
Arson	1,801	367	1,434	100.0	20.4	79.6	285	42	243
Other assaults	178,141	31,177	146,964	100.0	17.5	82.5	15,377	3,223	12,154
Forgery and counterfeiting	8,105	1,354	6,751	100.0	16.7	83.3	136	28	108
Fraud	19,987	2,699	17,288	100.0	13.5	86.5	614	150	464
Embezzlement	1,912	253	1,659	100.0	13.2	86.8	96	11	85
Stolen property; buying, receiving, possessing	19,785	3,568	16,217	100.0	18.0	82.0	1,559	315	1,244
Vandalism	33,913	5,992	27,921	100.0	17.7	82.3	5,122	920	4,202
Weapons; carrying, possessing, etc.	30,125	7,086	23,039	100.0	23.5	76.5	1,890	576	1,314
Prostitution and commercialized vice	1,474	292	1,182	100.0	19.8	80.2	17	0	17
Sex offenses (except forcible rape and prostitution)	6,866	2,101	4,765	100.0	30.6	69.4	865	179	686
Drug abuse violations	282,288	57,039	225,249	100.0	20.2	79.8	10,868	2,905	7,963
Gambling	335	126	209	100.0	37.6	62.4	31	18	13
Offenses against the family and children	13,320	1,534	11,786	100.0	11.5	88.5	364	48	316
Driving under the influence	197,728	57,123	140,605	100.0	28.9	71.1	1,194	356	838
Liquor laws	20,376	3,116	17,260	100.0	15.3	84.7	3,666	571	3,095
Drunkenness	37,330	9,842	27,488	100.0	26.4	73.6	613	177	436
Disorderly conduct	43,149	5,040	38,109	100.0	11.7	88.3	4,880	789	4,091
Vagrancy	1,761	291	1,470	100.0	16.5	83.5	37	15	22
All other offenses (except traffic)	497,464	86,371	411,093	100.0	17.4	82.6	17,869	3,797	14,072
Suspicion	77	8	69	100.0	10.4	89.6	4	0	4
Curfew and loitering law violations	1,868	309	1,559	100.0	16.5	83.5	1,868	309	1,559

Table 67A. Arrests, Suburban Areas,[1] Distribution by Ethnicity, 2020—Continued

(Number, percent; 5,475 agencies; 2020 estimated population 94,124,752.)

Offense charged	Percent distribution[2]			Arrests 18 and over			Percent distribution[2]		
	Total[3]	Hispanic or Latino	Not Hispanic or Latino	Total[3]	Hispanic or Latino	Not Hispanic or Latino	Total[3]	Hispanic or Latino	Not Hispanic or Latino
Total	100.0	21.3	78.7	1,577,807	305,285	1,272,522	100.0	19.3	80.7
Violent crime[4]	100.0	25.0	75.0	79,720	19,804	59,916	100.0	24.8	75.2
Murder and nonnegligent manslaughter	100.0	26.4	73.6	1,826	425	1,401	100.0	23.3	76.7
Rape[5]	100.0	20.5	79.5	3,449	959	2,490	100.0	27.8	72.2
Robbery	100.0	24.2	75.8	8,481	1,982	6,499	100.0	23.4	76.6
Aggravated assault	100.0	26.1	73.9	65,964	16,438	49,526	100.0	24.9	75.1
Property crime[4]	100.0	18.9	81.1	169,153	24,547	144,606	100.0	14.5	85.5
Burglary	100.0	23.1	76.9	26,307	5,020	21,287	100.0	19.1	80.9
Larceny-theft	100.0	16.7	83.3	127,502	15,349	112,153	100.0	12.0	88.0
Motor vehicle theft	100.0	23.2	76.8	13,828	3,853	9,975	100.0	27.9	72.1
Arson	100.0	14.7	85.3	1,516	325	1,191	100.0	21.4	78.6
Other assaults	100.0	21.0	79.0	162,764	27,954	134,810	100.0	17.2	82.8
Forgery and counterfeiting	100.0	20.6	79.4	7,969	1,326	6,643	100.0	16.6	83.4
Fraud	100.0	24.4	75.6	19,373	2,549	16,824	100.0	13.2	86.8
Embezzlement	100.0	11.5	88.5	1,816	242	1,574	100.0	13.3	86.7
Stolen property; buying, receiving, possessing	100.0	20.2	79.8	18,226	3,253	14,973	100.0	17.8	82.2
Vandalism	100.0	18.0	82.0	28,791	5,072	23,719	100.0	17.6	82.4
Weapons; carrying, possessing, etc.	100.0	30.5	69.5	28,235	6,510	21,725	100.0	23.1	76.9
Prostitution and commercialized vice	100.0	0.0	100.0	1,457	292	1,165	100.0	20.0	80.0
Sex offenses (except forcible rape and prostitution)	100.0	20.7	79.3	6,001	1,922	4,079	100.0	32.0	68.0
Drug abuse violations	100.0	26.7	73.3	271,420	54,134	217,286	100.0	19.9	80.1
Gambling	100.0	58.1	41.9	304	108	196	100.0	35.5	64.5
Offenses against the family and children	100.0	13.2	86.8	12,956	1,486	11,470	100.0	11.5	88.5
Driving under the influence	100.0	29.8	70.2	196,534	56,767	139,767	100.0	28.9	71.1
Liquor laws	100.0	15.6	84.4	16,710	2,545	14,165	100.0	15.2	84.8
Drunkenness	100.0	28.9	71.1	36,717	9,665	27,052	100.0	26.3	73.7
Disorderly conduct	100.0	16.2	83.8	38,269	4,251	34,018	100.0	11.1	88.9
Vagrancy	100.0	40.5	59.5	1,724	276	1,448	100.0	16.0	84.0
All other offenses (except traffic)	100.0	21.2	78.8	479,595	82,574	397,021	100.0	17.2	82.8
Suspicion	100.0	0.0	100.0	73	8	65	100.0	11.0	89.0
Curfew and loitering law violations	100.0	16.5	83.5	NA	NA	NA	NA	NA	NA

NA = Not available.

1 Suburban areas include law enforcement agencies in cities with less than 50,000 inhabitants and county law enforcement agencies that are within a Metropolitan Statistical Area. Suburban areas exclude all metropolitan agencies associated with a principal city.   2 Because of rounding, the percentages may not sum to 100.   3 The ethnicity totals are representative of those agencies that provided ethnicity breakdowns. Not all agencies provide ethnicity data; therefore, the race and ethnicity totals will not equal.   4 Violent crimes are offenses of murder and nonnegligent manslaughter, rape, robbery, and aggravated assault.   Property crimes are offenses of burglary, larceny-theft, motor vehicle theft, and arson.   5 The rape figures in this table are aggregate totals of the data submitted based on both the legacy and revised Uniform Crime Reporting definitions.

Table 68. Police Disposition of Juvenile Offenders Taken into Custody, 2020

(Number, percent.)

Population group	Total[1]	Handled within department and released	Referred to juvenile court jurisdiction	Referred to welfare agency	Referred to other police agency	Referred to criminal or adult court	Referred to other authorities not specified	Number of agencies	Estimated population, 2020
Total Agencies									
Number	315,048	58,393	141,313	1,643	4,965	2,953	105,781	10,466	228,864,358
Percent[2]	100.0	18.5	44.9	0.5	1.6	0.9	33.6		
Total Cities									
Number	274,674	45,842	135,669	1,514	4,839	2,803	84,007	7,634	159,832,632
Percent[2]	100.0	16.7	49.4	0.6	1.8	1.0	30.6		
Group I (250,000 and over)									
Number	35,953	9,280	8,685	33	352	261	17,342	72	44,271,326
Percent[2]	100.0	25.8	24.2	0.1	1.0	0.7	48.2		
Group II (100,000 to 249,999)									
Number	27,917	6,842	6,780	0	75	50	14,170	189	27,356,047
Percent[2]	100.0	24.5	24.3	0.0	0.3	0.2	50.8		
Group III (50,000 to 99,999)									
Number	32,679	7,154	8,488	117	191	99	16,630	398	27,901,884
Percent[2]	100.0	21.9	26.0	0.4	0.6	0.3	50.9		
Group IV (25,000 to 49,999)									
Number	23,002	6,419	4,609	38	59	27	11,850	664	23,023,304
Percent[2]	100.0	27.9	20.0	0.2	0.3	0.1	51.5		
Group V (10,000 to 24,999)									
Number	25,311	5,927	5,180	17	49	214	13,924	1,351	21,468,840
Percent[2]	100.0	23.4	20.5	0.1	0.2	0.8	55.0		
Group VI (under 10,000)									
Number	129,812	10,220	101,927	1,309	4,113	2,152	10,091	4,960	15,811,231
Percent[2]	100.0	7.9	78.5	1.0	3.2	1.7	7.8		
Metropolitan Counties									
Number	31,439	9,568	4,388	74	87	116	17,206	1,195	50,082,964
Percent[2]	100.0	30.4	14.0	0.2	0.3	0.4	54.7		
Nonmetropolitan Counties									
Number	8,935	2,983	1,256	55	39	34	4,568	1,637	18,948,762
Percent[2]	100.0	33.4	14.1	0.6	0.4	0.4	51.1		
Suburban Areas[3]									
Number	162,027	20,998	97,276	478	2,811	1,154	39,310	5,475	94,124,752
Percent[2]	100.0	13.0	60.0	0.3	1.7	0.7	24.3		

1 Includes all offenses except traffic and neglect cases.   2 Because of rounding, the percentages may not sum to 100.   3 Suburban areas include law enforcement agencies in cities with less than 50,000 inhabitants and county law enforcement agencies that are within a Metropolitan Statistical Area. Suburban areas exclude all metropolitan agencies associated with a principal city. The agencies associated with suburban areas also appear in other groups within this table.

Table 69. Arrests, by State, 2020

(Number.)

State	Total, all classes[1]	Violent crime[2]	Property crime[2]	Murder and nonnegligent manslaughter	Rape[3]	Robbery	Aggravated assault	Burglary	Larceny-theft	Motor vehicle theft	Arson	Other assaults	Forgery and counterfeiting	Fraud	Embez-zlement	Stolen property; buying, receiving, possessing	Vandalism
Alabama[5]																	
Under 18	40	6	9	0	0	1	5	4	5	0	0	7	0	1	0	0	3
Total, all ages	2,050	104	189	8	7	11	78	47	127	14	1	158	24	43	2	19	19
Alaska																	
Under 18	1,052	146	198	3	21	17	105	69	68	53	8	300	0	9	1	0	131
Total, all ages	26,353	2,598	2,396	33	160	287	2,118	471	1,545	338	42	4,591	53	199	35	66	1,063
Arizona																	
Under 18	13,454	1,049	1,865	22	40	320	667	343	1,219	273	30	2,707	6	34	6	88	1,165
Total, all ages	187,255	11,663	26,624	340	322	1,872	9,129	3,521	21,221	1,670	212	23,451	610	1,462	345	1,022	8,781
Arkansas																	
Under 18	5,173	415	920	25	49	80	261	205	647	62	6	1,060	6	27	1	166	189
Total, all ages	96,862	5,534	10,925	195	281	437	4,621	1,702	8,608	553	62	10,858	618	625	29	1,672	1,518
California																	
Under 18	23,588	4,643	3,820	79	150	1,953	2,461	1,563	1,259	920	78	3,910	23	113	9	590	1,470
Total, all ages	847,606	100,579	72,990	1,594	2,060	13,636	83,289	26,220	28,350	16,369	2,051	68,962	2,753	5,042	680	14,631	17,493
Colorado																	
Under 18	9,095	706	1,632	32	76	215	383	199	1,081	301	51	1,015	6	43	6	16	597
Total, all ages	145,095	8,659	21,458	236	441	1,199	6,783	2,649	15,064	3,452	293	15,449	488	1,820	39	654	5,215
Connecticut																	
Under 18	3,791	232	956	10	23	103	96	132	569	244	11	761	8	14	4	152	189
Total, all ages	68,484	2,664	8,799	105	188	589	1,782	1,146	6,919	667	67	14,921	294	563	75	332	1,529
Delaware																	
Under 18	1,862	215	382	1	11	90	113	132	184	59	7	459	1	27	2	89	124
Total, all ages	24,636	1,796	4,147	17	74	315	1,390	643	3,327	159	18	5,392	122	827	92	346	850
District of Columbia[6]																	
Under 18	263	64	28	0	0	57	7	0	25	3	0	59	0	0	0	6	1
Total, all ages	4,093	205	85	2	3	121	79	1	73	11	0	373	0	2	0	19	48
Florida[7,8]																	
Under 18	31,471	2,702	8,802	73	216	1,012	1,401	2,313	4,584	1,866	39	5,816	24	263	15	160	648
Total, all ages	506,402	34,186	66,397	840	1,815	5,464	26,067	12,554	46,430	7,156	257	75,236	1,207	8,216	647	1,301	5,791
Georgia																	
Under 18	6,383	538	1,190	15	55	120	348	222	839	121	8	1,259	18	56	0	133	335
Total, all ages	110,543	6,002	11,561	202	282	505	5,013	1,387	9,355	717	102	11,906	695	1,653	8	1,322	2,642
Hawaii																	
Under 18	340	19	35	1	4	3	11	7	22	5	1	39	0	1	0	0	13
Total, all ages	10,996	773	1,089	26	54	405	288	176	709	186	18	709	13	45	1	0	146
Idaho																	
Under 18	3,912	141	591	5	37	5	94	104	437	32	18	439	0	33	2	15	185
Total, all ages	45,397	1,738	3,371	68	145	58	1,467	593	2,584	149	45	3,330	58	403	34	176	725
Illinois[7]																	
Under 18	456	37	37	1	1	23	12	7	23	2	5	65	0	0	0	24	32
Total, all ages	5,615	407	434	13	15	53	326	49	355	13	17	1,013	5	27	0	57	341
Indiana																	
Under 18	4,298	404	684	10	25	137	232	98	447	133	6	778	6	13	7	46	126
Total, all ages	75,450	3,978	7,915	130	142	648	3,058	1,004	5,975	884	52	8,426	515	626	79	376	479
Iowa																	
Under 18	7,019	490	1,550	6	57	84	343	254	1,029	237	30	1,263	11	33	6	53	550
Total, all ages	78,092	5,129	9,056	56	258	279	4,536	1,446	6,862	642	106	7,260	393	455	40	285	2,049
Kansas																	
Under 18	3,248	125	366	8	12	15	90	37	287	37	5	555	3	11	0	43	213
Total, all ages	46,140	1,619	3,542	46	83	88	1,402	380	2,853	272	37	6,137	147	350	22	515	1,364
Kentucky																	
Under 18	1,920	158	495	4	31	63	60	143	250	96	6	485	3	5	8	104	62
Total, all ages	141,158	2,105	9,318	109	226	426	1,344	2,006	6,535	712	65	9,965	477	779	273	1,558	963
Louisiana																	
Under 18	8,590	754	1,804	46	52	189	467	714	872	208	10	1,493	2	44	3	328	343
Total, all ages	116,373	8,721	18,062	329	313	910	7,169	3,653	13,334	996	79	15,397	357	884	82	2,101	2,976
Maine																	
Under 18	1,689	37	388	0	6	13	18	93	219	55	21	349	0	9	1	3	174
Total, all ages	32,189	704	4,136	12	62	110	520	454	3,366	257	59	4,431	118	301	20	105	961
Maryland[5]																	
Under 18	709	81	279	0	7	58	16	102	126	51	0	79	0	0	0	1	31
Total, all ages	8,248	589	1,851	16	83	170	320	305	1,372	173	1	622	28	54	3	9	162
Massachusetts																	
Under 18	3,159	388	490	1	13	81	293	175	218	79	18	757	10	23	0	100	262
Total, all ages	76,381	5,948	6,310	39	254	534	5,121	1,102	4,646	493	69	14,781	247	565	44	787	1,901
Michigan																	
Under 18	7,354	806	1,487	20	130	152	504	326	881	257	23	1,786	18	71	34	234	300
Total, all ages	158,199	12,774	14,782	347	753	1,047	10,627	2,322	11,088	1,185	187	26,410	498	2,166	651	2,121	2,636
Minnesota																	
Under 18	10,504	747	2,033	14	70	355	308	199	1,457	349	28	1,364	15	127	4	264	461
Total, all ages	112,814	5,424	17,889	142	465	1,014	3,803	1,857	14,715	1,201	116	12,532	846	2,904	44	2,219	2,337
Mississippi																	
Under 18	1,367	92	339	6	2	41	43	61	248	28	2	212	0	7	1	21	30
Total, all ages	35,473	918	3,541	95	60	182	581	625	2,660	238	18	3,095	99	320	124	338	318
Missouri																	
Under 18	8,644	714	1,413	19	49	191	455	229	932	236	16	1,414	16	33	24	356	381
Total, all ages	139,175	8,528	18,691	375	397	1,085	6,671	2,605	14,066	1,898	122	15,739	735	1,243	200	3,006	3,437
Montana																	
Under 18	3,258	199	486	3	10	13	173	35	393	50	8	415	1	6	3	14	194
Total, all ages	30,254	2,147	4,028	29	62	110	1,946	304	3,383	307	34	4,395	114	125	32	190	1,025

Table 69. Arrests, by State, 2020—Continued

(Number.)

State	Weapons; carrying, possessing, etc.	Prostitution and commercialized vice	Sex offenses (except rape and prostitution)	Drug abuse violations	Gambling	Offenses against the family and children	Driving under the influence	Liquor laws	Drunkenness[4]	Disorderly conduct	Vagrancy	All other offenses (except traffic)	Suspicion	Curfew and loitering law violations	Number of agencies	Estimated population, 2020
Alabama[5]																
Under 18	0	0	0	2	0	0	0	2	0	2	0	8	0	0	7	66,582
Total, all ages	14	0	11	131	0	20	76	16	44	23	0	1,157	0	0		
Alaska																
Under 18	11	0	11	56	0	0	32	47	0	10	0	100	0	0	31	719,120
Total, all ages	332	1	242	808	0	101	3,008	275	19	655	44	9,865	2	0		
Arizona																
Under 18	281	5	216	1,432	9	85	124	615	32	1,040	38	2,101	1	555	86	6,456,926
Total, all ages	3,600	368	1,051	21,945	9	1,595	14,909	3,567	1,291	11,128	572	52,697	10	555		
Arkansas																
Under 18	96	1	13	562	0	5	43	88	30	351	0	1,034	0	166	249	2,730,633
Total, all ages	1,008	17	77	15,294	8	253	4,938	872	3,123	2,027	300	37,000	0	166		
California																
Under 18	1,734	5	434	1,184	1	3	437	443	267	359	33	3,715	0	395	673	38,994,766
Total, all ages	28,407	4,453	7,258	185,985	675	308	95,778	2,728	35,841	2,636	3,289	196,723	0	395		
Colorado																
Under 18	176	0	63	812	0	21	232	609	2	635	0	2,221	0	303	197	5,074,548
Total, all ages	2,341	113	300	9,231	0	1,764	14,421	3,396	34	4,221	89	55,100	0	303		
Connecticut																
Under 18	73	0	29	203	1	21	16	9	0	607	0	515	0	1	107	3,557,006
Total, all ages	1,022	42	291	4,422	7	1,706	5,151	59	0	8,711	41	17,854	0	1		
Delaware																
Under 18	56	0	16	96	0	0	2	22	6	84	0	257	0	24	54	984,527
Total, all ages	343	31	99	3,308	9	147	294	198	238	782	142	5,449	0	24		
District of Columbia[6]																
Under 18	6	0	0	1	0	0	0	0	0	14	0	84	0	0	2	0
Total, all ages	43	0	30	274	0	1	1	608	14	216	1	2,173	0	0		
Florida[7,8]																
Under 18	717	1	248	1,537	0	0	134	282	0	0	0	10,122	0	0	572	21,634,872
Total, all ages	7,470	940	2,921	68,471	109	0	29,073	5,993	0	0	0	198,444	0	0		
Georgia																
Under 18	170	3	74	604	1	16	75	29	2	400	0	1,374	0	106	289	6,073,704
Total, all ages	1,235	107	362	17,294	9	686	12,808	569	561	5,171	823	35,023	0	106		
Hawaii																
Under 18	0	0	0	32	0	3	5	16	0	2	0	104	0	71	2	273,390
Total, all ages	161	13	23	847	1	3	1,067	76	0	496	0	5,462	0	71		
Idaho																
Under 18	37	0	47	566	0	14	99	167	20	165	1	1,300	7	83	98	1,660,406
Total, all ages	273	11	197	9,153	0	529	6,713	984	420	1,425	26	15,730	18	83		
Illinois[7]																
Under 18	22	0	0	56	0	0	1	5	0	79	0	82	0	16	1	144,795
Total, all ages	160	1	14	280	0	140	231	28	0	445	3	2,013	0	16		
Indiana																
Under 18	139	0	44	418	0	11	49	180	19	149	0	1,175	0	50	109	3,535,979
Total, all ages	2,274	36	253	11,978	2	299	8,874	903	819	1,880	34	25,651	3	50		
Iowa																
Under 18	89	0	20	721	0	4	93	481	65	419	0	1,085	0	86	216	2,850,739
Total, all ages	914	11	93	8,166	2	906	9,190	2,071	2,483	1,922	6	27,575	0	86		
Kansas																
Under 18	18	1	21	549	0	10	103	474	0	86	0	670	0	0	220	1,700,866
Total, all ages	384	30	108	7,837	0	221	6,192	1,568	87	929	0	15,087	1	0		
Kentucky																
Under 18	37	0	13	190	0	0	28	1	23	28	0	280	0	0	336	3,713,933
Total, all ages	407	15	177	17,118	0	3,403	12,122	31	9,101	2,900	2	70,444	0	0		
Louisiana																
Under 18	322	1	62	588	6	55	18	45	33	958	30	1,544	1	156	114	3,362,830
Total, all ages	3,508	207	711	20,052	46	838	3,778	1,014	1,115	4,742	145	31,465	16	156		
Maine																
Under 18	1	0	26	121	0	2	22	226	1	56	0	263	0	10	129	1,349,630
Total, all ages	130	37	112	3,188	1	81	4,095	910	3	860	2	11,984	0	10		
Maryland[5]																
Under 18	30	0	8	110	0	0	3	19	0	10	0	58	0	0	6	1,124,569
Total, all ages	172	14	26	1,386	0	23	1,621	508	3	335	3	839	0	0		
Massachusetts																
Under 18	62	0	36	92	0	15	31	69	7	95	0	722	0	0	339	5,984,273
Total, all ages	974	107	272	5,708	10	1,140	6,597	598	1,381	2,085	12	26,913	1	0		
Michigan																
Under 18	303	9	95	229	0	2	139	172	1	230	0	1,323	0	115	621	9,517,637
Total, all ages	9,312	211	482	10,963	12	875	20,416	2,890	124	3,678	42	47,041	0	115		
Minnesota																
Under 18	224	0	76	789	2	5	177	1,034	0	834	0	1,921	0	427	354	5,269,267
Total, all ages	2,359	25	491	13,875	6	300	16,981	4,106	23	5,166	151	24,709	0	427		
Mississippi																
Under 18	62	1	5	106	1	16	35	14	8	188	1	180	0	48	75	1,135,598
Total, all ages	667	9	80	5,283	4	379	4,727	248	1,157	2,280	12	11,826	0	48		
Missouri																
Under 18	131	0	69	893	0	32	135	293	6	572	1	1,715	0	446	259	4,935,179
Total, all ages	2,910	39	358	24,691	6	913	13,687	1,811	181	5,530	389	36,635	0	446		
Montana																
Under 18	5	1	22	193	0	80	69	486	135	244	0	521	0	184	97	1,069,494
Total, all ages	72	5	118	2,364	1	863	3,914	1,315	447	2,329	3	6,583	0	184		

Table 69. Arrests, by State, 2020—Continued

(Number.)

State	Total, all classes[1]	Violent crime[2]	Property crime[2]	Murder and nonnegligent manslaughter	Rape[3]	Robbery	Aggravated assault	Burglary	Larceny-theft	Motor vehicle theft	Arson	Other assaults	Forgery and counterfeiting	Fraud	Embezzlement	Stolen property; buying, receiving, possessing	Vandalism
Nebraska																	
Under 18	4,634	170	918	2	26	77	65	53	740	108	17	806	4	53	5	95	344
Total, all ages	35,682	1,675	4,765	35	194	256	1,190	294	4,097	315	59	5,765	141	572	25	522	1,372
Nevada																	
Under 18	6,339	472	653	6	57	194	215	133	449	59	12	1,606	3	98	5	135	218
Total, all ages	110,516	5,816	8,106	134	360	1,189	4,133	2,148	5,284	574	100	19,503	409	1,399	242	1,822	2,026
New Hampshire																	
Under 18	2,313	42	163	0	5	6	31	10	126	22	5	405	4	8	3	11	148
Total, all ages	35,548	655	2,724	2	71	107	475	234	2,325	143	22	4,920	165	456	62	370	1,010
New Jersey																	
Under 18	8,448	717	1,442	18	42	324	333	336	932	134	40	554	20	40	6	444	362
Total, all ages	168,018	8,937	16,124	164	327	1,781	6,665	2,783	12,595	587	159	18,869	580	1,885	107	2,448	2,828
New Mexico																	
Under 18	601	82	69	1	3	19	59	25	32	11	1	132	1	1	0	16	32
Total, all ages	28,483	2,264	3,115	20	42	178	2,024	372	2,529	191	23	4,677	19	99	52	496	1,146
New York[7]																	
Under 18	6,317	809	1,816	26	116	317	350	394	1,008	383	31	777	19	29	2	308	898
Total, all ages	152,107	9,218	29,730	259	694	1,744	6,521	4,088	23,644	1,786	212	18,313	1,343	1,486	20	2,277	9,942
North Carolina																	
Under 18	6,962	648	1,936	29	19	326	274	491	1,136	276	33	1,067	3	67	15	370	240
Total, all ages	197,222	10,029	25,582	469	199	2,157	7,204	5,724	18,340	1,274	244	21,359	644	2,606	629	3,429	2,562
North Dakota																	
Under 18	3,595	90	365	0	12	7	71	53	241	67	4	449	8	31	3	36	153
Total, all ages	32,614	1,010	2,931	25	51	64	870	363	2,244	305	19	3,138	164	542	36	343	477
Ohio																	
Under 18	13,308	720	1,829	20	63	306	331	373	1,197	232	27	3,141	5	81	1	331	587
Total, all ages	140,837	7,159	19,714	293	333	1,314	5,219	2,844	15,996	763	111	28,780	244	1,201	2	1,734	2,924
Oklahoma																	
Under 18	5,110	385	1,079	11	13	129	232	220	662	172	25	571	1	28	21	174	202
Total, all ages	83,796	4,882	13,294	161	144	600	3,977	2,287	9,328	1,497	182	7,992	390	1,032	306	2,101	1,666
Oregon																	
Under 18	4,687	302	902	5	30	87	180	182	589	93	38	732	9	35	2	16	381
Total, all ages	98,495	4,753	16,264	68	198	889	3,598	2,103	11,815	1,934	412	9,750	476	1,273	58	587	3,750
Pennsylvania[5]																	
Under 18	176	12	30	1	1	1	9	5	23	2	0	10	0	0	0	4	4
Total, all ages	2,224	110	333	3	6	14	87	31	289	12	1	146	24	32	1	23	34
Rhode Island																	
Under 18	1,300	69	221	1	11	13	44	33	134	42	12	197	2	8	1	51	92
Total, all ages	19,266	967	1,741	15	71	95	786	384	1,173	150	34	3,247	93	213	46	259	816
South Carolina																	
Under 18	5,416	485	1,181	39	64	147	235	268	795	103	15	974	4	42	14	123	294
Total, all ages	122,532	6,630	18,917	359	385	912	4,974	2,556	15,208	1,033	120	13,720	798	2,332	203	2,336	2,594
South Dakota																	
Under 18	3,842	141	442	1	4	11	125	47	294	96	5	554	2	40	4	62	119
Total, all ages	48,621	1,974	2,364	24	35	68	1,847	299	1,656	383	26	4,974	124	576	18	256	489
Tennessee																	
Under 18	12,090	885	2,463	19	49	267	550	347	1,436	659	21	2,412	12	76	16	109	578
Total, all ages	235,233	12,729	30,012	340	307	1,342	10,740	3,988	22,193	3,687	144	25,563	1,311	3,533	437	1,705	3,769
Texas																	
Under 18	32,451	3,117	6,177	82	253	1,158	1,624	1,063	4,053	996	65	6,435	55	180	12	97	1,033
Total, all ages	489,316	30,678	53,286	923	1,656	5,087	23,012	7,655	39,550	5,637	444	73,456	2,553	4,706	210	804	6,062
Utah																	
Under 18	7,869	252	1,423	5	59	58	130	102	1,214	88	19	863	2	34	1	89	588
Total, all ages	82,809	2,631	11,356	60	291	345	1,935	788	10,058	438	72	7,849	493	706	35	1,152	2,778
Vermont																	
Under 18	498	37	73	0	11	3	23	24	44	5	0	125	0	1	1	2	56
Total, all ages	11,617	749	1,287	10	66	34	639	202	995	61	29	1,483	39	179	36	78	348
Virginia																	
Under 18	9,118	488	1,575	25	65	175	223	210	1,166	171	28	1,642	14	75	23	101	373
Total, all ages	201,479	6,651	20,407	336	463	1,020	4,832	1,734	17,481	1,043	149	26,895	1,002	3,629	776	781	3,195
Washington																	
Under 18	6,741	703	1,381	10	60	299	334	366	835	153	27	1,803	4	22	0	88	659
Total, all ages	143,840	8,445	21,982	186	521	1,716	6,022	4,540	15,816	1,390	236	23,689	467	913	23	3,051	4,904
West Virginia																	
Under 18	384	26	41	1	8	1	16	13	20	8	0	126	0	1	0	4	28
Total, all ages	26,652	1,294	3,491	45	91	82	1,076	563	2,696	201	31	3,489	160	209	18	299	432
Wisconsin																	
Under 18	21,163	774	2,677	21	157	211	385	321	1,871	457	28	1,336	8	120	45	292	1,294
Total, all ages	179,705	7,410	18,999	198	726	934	5,552	1,676	15,972	1,217	134	13,904	594	1,597	294	1,019	4,799
Wyoming																	
Under 18	2,544	39	307	0	6	2	31	41	214	45	7	382	0	6	0	10	148
Total, all ages	20,581	471	2,018	8	41	16	406	211	1,640	149	18	1,920	19	97	2	50	502

Table 69. Arrests, by State, 2020—Continued

(Number.)

State	Weapons; carrying, possessing, etc.	Prostitution and commercialized vice	Sex offenses (except rape and prostitution)	Drug abuse violations	Gambling	Offenses against the family and children	Driving under the influence	Liquor laws	Drunkenness4	Disorderly conduct	Vagrancy	All other offenses (except traffic)	Suspicion	Curfew and loitering law violations	Number of agencies	Estimated population, 2020
Nebraska																
Under 18	78	0	33	548	0	176	43	256	6	153	0	857	1	88	72	1,092,666
Total, all ages	669	24	200	4,431	1	694	3,152	1,130	331	1,753	9	8,354	9	88		
Nevada																
Under 18	149	29	55	806	8	19	62	341	149	259	1	1,010	12	249	52	3,130,836
Total, all ages	2,624	2,099	765	10,130	26	724	9,530	1,906	224	2,032	573	40,221	90	249		
New Hampshire																
Under 18	1	0	27	196	0	7	36	250	96	44	0	858	0	14	181	1,311,307
Total, all ages	126	23	100	4,382	1	140	3,919	1,406	1,749	799	118	12,409	0	14		
New Jersey																
Under 18	407	1	94	1,771	19	35	60	202	3	594	10	1,448	2	217	577	8,882,371
Total, all ages	3,636	300	778	37,799	65	2,658	14,316	927	69	7,577	143	47,699	56	217		
New Mexico																
Under 18	21	0	2	27	0	18	20	33	0	14	0	133	0	0	17	930,644
Total, all ages	327	34	14	1,317	0	2,032	2,291	618	6	665	77	9,232	2	0		
New York[7]																
Under 18	171	0	136	542	0	8	58	21	0	95	0	628	0	0	453	9,397,374
Total, all ages	2,629	167	1,092	33,690	35	295	17,047	214	0	1,607	137	22,865	0	0		
North Carolina																
Under 18	203	2	25	627	0	5	109	52	8	245	0	1,307	0	33	288	8,731,507
Total, all ages	3,295	150	365	33,156	17	2,925	11,646	834	836	2,525	89	74,511	0	33		
North Dakota																
Under 18	13	0	26	336	0	231	55	450	5	456	0	718	0	170	103	759,161
Total, all ages	284	14	81	4,593	0	408	4,454	2,655	290	1,755	8	9,260	1	170		
Ohio																
Under 18	267	0	63	621	0	31	43	389	12	820	0	4,039	1	327	393	8,804,775
Total, all ages	4,133	246	378	16,005	5	481	9,668	2,826	2,375	6,946	8	35,679	2	327		
Oklahoma																
Under 18	149	0	26	580	0	20	90	66	144	307	0	892	0	375	414	3,927,308
Total, all ages	2,916	67	318	11,428	4	411	8,516	579	6,706	1,921	52	18,839	1	375		
Oregon																
Under 18	60	1	34	554	0	0	87	307	0	285	0	795	0	185	173	3,624,887
Total, all ages	2,068	47	321	8,844	1	263	9,790	1,617	2	5,707	13	32,726	0	185		
Pennsylvania[5]																
Under 18	4	0	8	33	0	1	2	48	2	4	0	13	0	1	102	157,062
Total, all ages	60	3	14	639	0	57	205	63	64	207	0	208	0	1		
Rhode Island																
Under 18	51	0	5	66	0	17	5	48	0	214	0	235	0	18	45	1,041,521
Total, all ages	329	8	55	1,392	2	56	1,977	428	21	1,583	0	6,015	0	18		
South Carolina																
Under 18	268	1	29	826	0	8	42	95	30	287	0	687	0	26	240	4,367,377
Total, all ages	2,914	167	224	25,577	23	753	10,521	3,077	3,121	7,031	432	21,136	0	26		
South Dakota																
Under 18	42	0	9	574	0	189	80	467	100	298	0	651	0	68	117	823,677
Total, all ages	272	5	51	7,298	1	1,038	5,980	2,210	6,805	2,379	559	11,178	2	68		
Tennessee																
Under 18	294	0	65	1,415	2	17	103	210	79	576	0	2,336	0	442	443	6,075,815
Total, all ages	2,526	297	412	37,188	31	1,703	17,040	1,633	8,884	3,962	9	82,047	0	442		
Texas																
Under 18	821	12	148	4,297	4	165	405	622	318	538	5	6,938	0	1,072	827	26,746,620
Total, all ages	12,916	1,474	1,049	82,337	155	3,124	55,964	4,647	29,367	5,245	660	119,551	0	1,072		
Utah																
Under 18	91	1	124	1,325	0	16	208	546	40	228	4	1,832	0	202	103	2,856,632
Total, all ages	868	69	498	12,474	1	1,762	8,372	2,634	1,795	1,828	36	25,269	1	202		
Vermont																
Under 18	1	0	10	22	0	0	11	25	0	46	0	88	0	0	82	619,602
Total, all ages	21	1	34	749	0	209	1,957	52	0	649	0	3,746	0	0		
Virginia																
Under 18	199	0	58	960	2	41	81	170	36	206	0	2,687	0	387	316	8,511,554
Total, all ages	4,584	277	493	27,090	10	1,018	16,483	1,512	12,912	1,931	67	71,379	0	387		
Washington																
Under 18	128	0	64	342	0	2	176	329	9	118	1	903	1	8	234	7,554,132
Total, all ages	1,697	210	476	8,173	1	242	22,125	994	68	1,867	167	44,320	18	8		
West Virginia																
Under 18	6	0	7	51	0	0	4	9	0	12	0	68	0	1	131	1,177,351
Total, all ages	407	17	49	6,015	0	95	2,425	208	301	452	7	7,283	0	1		
Wisconsin																
Under 18	289	3	295	1,844	2	166	222	1,474	0	3,533	37	5,774	0	978	379	5,543,214
Total, all ages	3,453	149	986	21,848	4	1,616	20,135	5,863	0	22,703	417	52,937	0	978		
Wyoming																
Under 18	11	0	8	400	0	7	33	416	2	92	30	541	5	107	53	510,568
Total, all ages	56	3	76	3,410	0	300	2,744	1,493	1,309	806	83	5,110	5	107		

NOTE: Because the number of agencies submitting arrest data varies from year to year, users are cautioned about making direct comparisons between 2020 arrest totals and those published in previous years' editions of Crime in the United States. Further, arrest figures may vary widely from state to state because some Part II crimes are not considered crimes in some states.
1 Does not include traffic arrests.   2 Violent crimes are offenses of murder and nonnegligent manslaughter, rape, robbery, and aggravated assault. Property crimes are offenses of burglary, larceny-theft, motor vehicle theft, and arson.   3 The rape figures in this table are aggregate totals of the data submitted based on both the legacy and revised Uniform Crime Reporting definitions.   4 Drunkenness is not considered a crime in some states; therefore, the figures vary widely from state to state.   5 Limited data for 2020 were available for Alabama, Maryland, and Pennsylvania.   6 Includes arrests reported by the District of Columbia Fire and Emergency Medical Services: Arson Investigation Unit and the Metro Transit Police. These agencies have no population associated with them.   7 See 2020 arrest data information.   8 The Florida arrest counts for offenses against the family and children, drunkenness, disorderly conduct, vagrancy, suspicion, and curfew and loitering law violations are included under the category All other offenses.

SECTION V

LAW ENFORCEMENT PERSONNEL

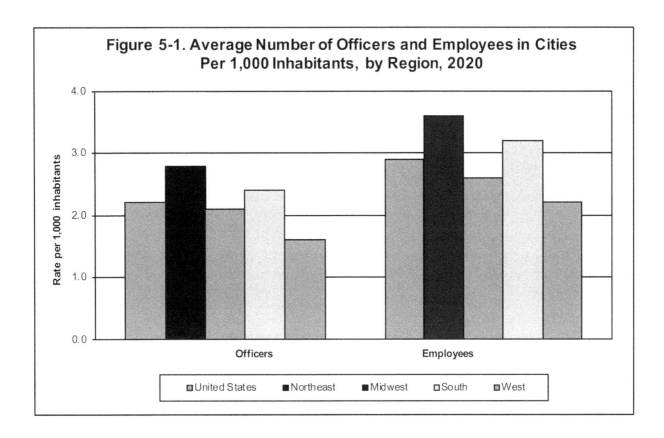

Figure 5-1. Average Number of Officers and Employees in Cities Per 1,000 Inhabitants, by Region, 2020

The Uniform Crime Reporting (UCR) program defines law enforcement officers as individuals who ordinarily carry a firearm and a badge, have full arrest powers, and are paid from government funds set aside specifically for sworn law enforcement representatives. Because of law enforcement's varied service requirements and functions, as well as the distinct demographic traits and characteristics of jurisdictions, readers should use caution when comparing staffing levels between agencies based on police employment data from the UCR program. In addition, the data presented here reflect existing staff levels and should not be interpreted as preferred officer strengths recommended by the Federal Bureau of Investigation (FBI). Also, readers should note that the totals given for sworn officers for any particular agency reflect both patrol officers on the street and officers assigned to various other duties, such as administrative and investigative positions and assignments to special teams.

Each year, law enforcement agencies across the United States report the total number of sworn law enforcement officers and civilians in their agencies as of October 31 to the UCR program. Civilian employees include personnel such as clerks, radio dispatchers, meter attendants, stenographers, jailers, correctional officers, and mechanics, (provided that they are full-time employees of the agency).

Due to the varied service requirements and functions of law enforcement and the distinctive demographic traits and characteristics of each jurisdiction, caution should be exercised when comparing agencies' staffing levels based on the UCR Program's police employment data. The data presented here reflect existing staffing levels and should not be interpreted as FBI-preferred or FBI-recommended officer strengths. The total number of sworn officers for any particular agency reflects patrol officers on the street and officers assigned to other duties, such as those in administrative, investigative, and special-teams roles.

This section of *Crime in the United States* presents those data as the number and rate of law enforcement officers and civilian employees throughout the United States. In 2020, 696,644 sworn officers and 309,135 civilians provided law enforcement services to more than 292 million people nationwide. These law enforcement personnel were employed by 13,377 state, city, university/college, metropolitan/nonmetropolitan county, and other designated law enforcement agencies. Of the slightly more than 1 million law enforcement employees, 72.4 percent were male. (Table 74)

The data in this section are broken down by geographic region and division, population group, state, city, university/college, metropolitan/nonmetropolitan county, and other law enforcement agency groups. (Information about geographic regions and divisions and population groups can be found in Appendix III.) UCR program staff compute the rate of sworn officers and law enforcement employees by taking the number of employees (sworn officers only or in combination with civilians), dividing by the population for which the agency provides law enforcement service, and multiplying by 1,000.

- Tables 70 and 71 present the number and rate of law enforcement personnel per 1,000 inhabitants collectively employed by agencies, broken down by geographic region and division by population group

- Tables 72 and 73 provide a count of law enforcement agencies by population group, based on the employment rate ranges for sworn officer and civilian employees per 1,000 inhabitants

- Table 74 provides the number of total officers, the percentage of male and female sworn officers, and the civilian employees by population group

- Table 75 lists the percentage of full-time civilian law enforcement employees by population group

- Table 76 breaks down by state the number of sworn law enforcement officers and civilians employed by state law enforcement agencies

- Table 77 provides the number of total officers, the percentage of male and female sworn officers, and the civilian employees by state

- Tables 78 to 80 list the number of law enforcement employees for cities, universities and colleges, and metropolitan and nonmetropolitan counties

- Table 81 supplies employee data for those law enforcement agencies that serve selected transit systems, parks and forests, schools and school districts, hospitals, etc., in the nation

The demographic traits and characteristics of a jurisdiction affect its requirements for law enforcement service. For instance, a village between two large cities may require more law enforcement than a community of the same size with no urban center nearby. A town with legal gambling may have different law enforcement needs than a town near a military base. A city largely made up of college students may have different law enforcement needs than a city whose residents are mainly retirees.

Similarly, the functions of law enforcement agencies are diverse. Employees of these agencies patrol local streets and major highways, protect citizens in the nation's smallest towns and largest cities, and conduct investigations on offenses at the local and state levels. State police in one area may enforce traffic laws on state highways and interstates; in another area, they may be responsible for investigating violent crimes. Sheriff's departments may collect tax monies, serve as the enforcement authority for local and state courts, administer jail facilities, or carry out some combination of these duties. This has an impact on an agency's staffing levels.

Because of the differing service requirements and functions, care should be taken when drawing comparisons between and among the staffing levels of law enforcement agencies. The data in this section are not intended as recommended or preferred officer strength; they should be used merely as guides. Adequate staffing levels can be determined only after careful study of the conditions that affect the service requirements in a particular jurisdiction.

RATE

The UCR program computes these rates by taking the number of employees, dividing by the population of the agency's jurisdiction, and multiplying by 1,000.

An examination of the 2020 law enforcement employee data by population group showed that the nation's cities had a collective rate of 2.9 law enforcement employees per 1,000 inhabitants. Cities with fewer than 10,000 inhabitants had the highest rate of law enforcement employees, with a rate of 5.6 per 1,000 inhabitants. Cities with 25,000 to 49,999 inhabitants, 50,000 to 99,999 inhabitants, and 100,000 to 249,999 inhabitants had the lowest rate of law enforcement employees (2.1 per 1,000 in population for each). The nation's largest cities, those with 250,000 or more inhabitants, averaged 3.3 law enforcement employees for every 1,000 inhabitants. (Table 70)

SWORN PERSONNEL

An analysis of the 2020 data showed that law enforcement agencies in the cities in the Northeast had the highest rate of sworn officers—2.8 per 1,000 inhabitants, followed by the South (2.4), the Midwest (2.1), and the West (1.6). (Table 71)

By population group in 2020, there were 2.2 sworn officers for each 1,000 resident population. Cities with fewer than

10,000 inhabitants had the highest rate at 4.3 sworn officers per 1,000 inhabitants. The nation's largest cities, those with 250,000 or more inhabitants, averaged 2.5 officers per 1,000 inhabitants. The lowest rates were in cities with 50,000 to 99,999 inhabitants and 100,000 to 249,999 inhabitants (1.6 per 1,000 resident population for each). (Table 71)

Males accounted for 86.9 percent of all full-time sworn law enforcement officers in 2020. Cities with populations of 1 million and over employed the highest percentage (18.5 percent) of full-time female officers. Of the city population groups and subsets, cities with populations of 10,000 to 24,999 inhabitants employed the highest percentage (90.4 percent) of male officers. In metropolitan counties, 85.7 percent of officers were male; in nonmetropolitan counties, 91.2 percent of officers were male; and in suburban areas, 87.2 percent of officers were male. (Table 74)

CIVILIAN EMPLOYEES

Civilian employees provide a myriad of services to the nation's law enforcement and criminal justice agencies. Among other duties, they dispatch officers, provide administrative and record keeping support, and query local, state, and national databases.

In 2020, 30.7 percent of all law enforcement employees in the nation were civilians. Male employees accounted for 40.0 percent of all full-time civilian law enforcement employees in 2020. In cities, civilians made up 22.3 percent of law enforcement agency employees. Civilians made up 41.9 percent of law enforcement employees in metropolitan counties, 41.3 percent of law enforcement employees in nonmetropolitan counties, and 34.9 percent of law enforcement employees in suburban areas. (Table 74)

Table 70. Full-Time Law Enforcement Employees,[1] by Region and Geographic Division and Population Group, 2020

(Number, rate per 1,000 inhabitants.)

Region/geographic division	Total (10,293 cities; population 198,498,223)	Group I (86 cities, 250,000 and over; population 63,000,994)	Group II (212 cities, 100,000 to 249,999; population 30,779,686)	Group III (430 cities, 50,000 to 99,999; population 29,997,046)	Group IV (789 cities, 25,000 to 49,999; population 27,195,395)	Group V (1,681 cities, 10,000 to 24,999; population 26,678,434)	Group VI (7,095 cities, under 10,000; population 20,846,668)	Total city agencies	2020 estimated city population	County[2] (3,084 agencies; population 93,625,066)	Total city and county agencies	2020 estimated total agency population	Suburban areas[3] (7,147 agencies; population 124,916,229)
Total, United States													
Number of employees	569,097	206,548	64,935	61,530	57,759	62,007	116,318	10,293	198,498,223	436,682	13,377	292,123,289	469,639
Average number of employees per 1,000 inhabitants	2.9	3.3	2.1	2.1	2.1	2.3	5.6			4.7			3.8
Northeast													
Number of employees	156,175	64,592	8,085	15,054	17,682	19,244	31,518	2,530	43,951,402				
Average number of employees per 1,000 inhabitants	3.6	5.5	2.9	2.4	2.2	2.2	5.1						
New England													
Number of employees	34,492	2,715	4,388	6,069	7,399	7,365	6,556	807	13,067,841				
Average number of employees per 1,000 inhabitants	2.6	3.9	2.9	2.3	2.2	2.3	3.7						
Middle Atlantic													
Number of employees	121,683	61,877	3,697	8,985	10,283	11,879	24,962	1,723	30,883,561				
Average number of employees per 1,000 inhabitants	3.9	5.6	2.9	2.5	2.1	2.1	5.6						
Midwest													
Number of employees	97,840	34,713	7,983	10,636	12,445	13,740	18,323	2,439	38,130,123				
Average number of employees per 1,000 inhabitants	2.6	3.6	1.9	1.8	1.9	2.1	3.5						
East North Central													
Number of employees	67,105	28,583	4,413	6,883	9,312	8,477	9,437	1,336	25,111,109				
Average number of employees per 1,000 inhabitants	2.7	4.0	1.9	1.9	1.9	2.0	3.3						
West North Central													
Number of employees	30,735	6,130	3,570	3,753	3,133	5,263	8,886	1,103	13,019,014				
Average number of employees per 1,000 inhabitants	2.4	2.6	1.9	1.6	1.8	2.1	3.8						
South													
Number of employees	197,564	54,447	28,857	20,952	18,948	22,117	52,243	3,963	62,648,093				
Average number of employees per 1,000 inhabitants	3.2	2.8	2.4	2.4	2.6	2.9	7.2						
South Atlantic													
Number of employees	90,405	23,428	13,555	11,509	9,179	9,829	22,905	1,646	26,109,579				
Average number of employees per 1,000 inhabitants	3.5	3.4	2.6	2.6	2.7	3.1	8.0						
East South Central													
Number of employees	36,272	6,538	5,126	2,747	4,442	4,999	12,420	958	10,192,793				
Average number of employees per 1,000 inhabitants	3.6	2.8	3.1	2.5	2.7	3.0	6.8						
West South Central													
Number of employees	70,887	24,481	10,176	6,696	5,327	7,289	16,918	1,359	26,345,721				
Average number of employees per 1,000 inhabitants	2.7	2.3	2.1	2.1	2.3	2.6	6.5						
West													
Number of employees	117,518	52,796	20,010	14,888	8,684	6,906	14,234	1,361	53,768,605				
Average number of employees per 1,000 inhabitants	2.2	2.4	1.7	1.6	1.7	2.0	6.6						
Mountain													
Number of employees	42,385	18,894	5,783	4,585	3,422	2,460	7,241	600	17,194,281				
Average number of employees per 1,000 inhabitants	2.5	2.4	2.0	1.9	1.8	2.3	6.7						
Pacific													
Number of employees	75,133	33,902	14,227	10,303	5,262	4,446	6,993	761	36,574,324				
Average number of employees per 1,000 inhabitants	2.1	2.4	1.6	1.5	1.7	1.9	6.6						

1 Full-time law enforcement employees include civilians.   2 The designation county is a combination of both metropolitan and nonmetropolitan counties.   3 Suburban areas include law enforcement agencies in cities with less than 50,000 inhabitants and county law enforcement agencies that are within a Metropolitan Statistical Area. Suburban areas exclude all metropolitan agencies associated with a principal city. The agencies associated with suburban areas also appear in other groups within this table.

Table 71. Full-Time Law Enforcement Officers, by Region, Geographic Division, and Population Group, 2019

(Number, rate per 1,000 inhabitants.)

Region/geographic division	Total (10,293 cities; population 198,498,223)	Group I (86 cities, 250,000 and over; population 63,000,994)	Group II (212 cities, 100,000 to 249,999; population 30,779,686)	Group III (430 cities, 50,000 to 99,999; population 29,997,046)	Group IV (789 cities, 25,000 to 49,999; population 27,195,395)	Group V (1,681 cities, 10,000 to 24,999; population 26,678,434)	Group VI (7,095 cities, under 10,000; population 20,846,668)	Total city agencies	2020 estimated city population	County[1] (3,084 agencies; population 93,625,066)	Total city and county agencies	2020 estimated total agency population	Suburban areas[2] (7,147 agencies; population 124,916,229)
Total													
Number of officers	442,266	158,544	49,681	47,902	46,218	50,478	89,443	10,293	198,498,223	254,378	13,377	292,123,289	305,724
Average number of officers per 1,000 inhabitants	2.2	2.5	1.6	1.6	1.7	1.9	4.3			2.7			2.4
Northeast													
Number of officers	122,737	46,326	6,908	12,525	14,916	16,438	25,624	2,530	43,951,402				
Average number of officers per 1,000 inhabitants	2.8	4.0	2.5	2.0	1.8	1.8	4.1						
New England													
Number of officers	28,138	2,132	3,733	5,125	6,149	5,929	5,070	807	13,067,841				
Average number of officers per 1,000 inhabitants	2.2	3.1	2.5	2.0	1.9	1.9	2.9						
Middle Atlantic													
Number of officers	94,599	44,194	3,175	7,400	8,767	10,509	20,554	1,723	30,883,561				
Average number of officers per 1,000 inhabitants	3.1	4.0	2.5	2.0	1.8	1.8	4.6						
Midwest													
Number of officers	81,692	30,043	6,570	8,686	9,951	11,470	14,972	2,439	38,130,123				
Average number of officers per 1,000 inhabitants	2.1	3.1	1.6	1.5	1.5	1.7	2.9						
East North Central													
Number of officers	56,966	25,129	3,689	5,607	7,431	7,131	7,979	1,336	25,111,109				
Average number of officers per 1,000 inhabitants	2.3	3.5	1.6	1.5	1.5	1.7	2.8						
West North Central													
Number of officers	24,726	4,914	2,881	3,079	2,520	4,339	6,993	1,103	13,019,014				
Average number of officers per 1,000 inhabitants	1.9	2.1	1.5	1.3	1.5	1.7	3.0						
South													
Number of officers	152,739	42,941	21,847	16,212	15,013	17,416	39,310	3,963	62,648,093				
Average number of officers per 1,000 inhabitants	2.4	2.2	1.8	1.9	2.0	2.3	5.4						
South Atlantic													
Number of officers	70,345	18,010	10,385	8,946	7,380	7,838	17,786	1,646	26,109,579				
Average number of officers per 1,000 inhabitants	2.7	2.6	2.0	2.0	2.1	2.5	6.2						
East South Central													
Number of officers	28,351	5,187	3,951	2,196	3,570	4,034	9,413	958	10,192,793				
Average number of officers per 1,000 inhabitants	2.8	2.2	2.4	2.0	2.2	2.4	5.1						
West South Central													
Number of officers	54,043	19,744	7,511	5,070	4,063	5,544	12,111	1,359	26,345,721				
Average number of officers per 1,000 inhabitants	2.1	1.9	1.5	1.6	1.7	2.0	4.7						
West													
Number of officers	85,098	39,234	14,356	10,479	6,338	5,154	9,537	1,361	53,768,605				
Average number of officers per 1,000 inhabitants	1.6	1.8	1.2	1.1	1.2	1.5	4.4						
Mountain													
Number of officers	30,858	13,972	4,359	3,264	2,607	1,840	4,816	600	17,194,281				
Average number of officers per 1,000 inhabitants	1.8	1.8	1.5	1.3	1.4	1.7	4.4						
Pacific													
Number of officers	54,240	25,262	9,997	7,215	3,731	3,314	4,721	761	36,574,324				
Average number of officers per 1,000 inhabitants	1.5	1.8	1.1	1.1	1.2	1.4	4.4						

1 The designation county is a combination of both metropolitan and nonmetropolitan counties.   2 Suburban areas include law enforcement agencies in cities with less than 50,000 inhabitants and county law enforcement agencies that are within a Metropolitan Statistical Area. Suburban areas exclude all metropolitan agencies associated with a principal city. The agencies associated with suburban areas also appear in other groups within this table.

Table 72. Full-Time Law Enforcement Employees,[1] Range in Rate, by Population Group, 2020

(Number, rate per 1,000 inhabitants.)

Rate range	Total cities[2] (10,293 cities; population 198,498,223)	Group I (86 cities, 250,000 and over; population 63,000,994)	Group II (212 cities, 100,000 to 249,999; population 30,779,686)	Group III (430 cities, 50,000 to 99,999; population 29,997,046)	Group IV (789 cities, 25,000 to 49,999; population 27,195,395)	Group V (1,681 cities, 10,000 to 24,999; population 26,678,434)	Group VI (7,095 cities, under 10,000; population 20,846,668)
Total Cities							
Number	8,997	86	212	430	789	1,681	5,799
Percent[3]	100.0%	100.0%	100.0%	100.0%	100.0%	100.0%	100.0%
0.1–0.5							
Number	79	0	0	0	2	4	73
Percent	0.9%	0.0%	0.0%	0.0%	0.3%	0.2%	1.3%
0.6–1.0							
Number	397	0	1	10	24	44	318
Percent	4.4%	0.0%	0.5%	2.3%	3.0%	2.6%	5.5%
1.1–1.5							
Number	1,118	3	53	99	143	207	613
Percent	12.4%	3.5%	25.0%	23.0%	18.1%	12.3%	10.6%
1.6–2.0							
Number	1,808	19	65	128	227	443	926
Percent	20.1%	22.1%	30.7%	29.8%	28.8%	26.4%	16.0%
2.1–2.5							
Number	1,683	32	45	105	204	394	903
Percent	18.7%	37.2%	21.2%	24.4%	25.9%	23.4%	15.6%
2.6–3.0							
Number	1,251	9	23	53	106	315	745
Percent	13.9%	10.5%	10.8%	12.3%	13.4%	18.7%	12.8%
3.1–3.5							
Number	762	5	17	19	56	127	538
Percent	8.5%	5.8%	8.0%	4.4%	7.1%	7.6%	9.3%
3.6–4.0							
Number	533	8	5	9	16	70	425
Percent	5.9%	9.3%	2.4%	2.1%	2.0%	4.2%	7.3%
4.1–4.5							
Number	374	1	2	2	3	44	322
Percent	4.2%	1.2%	0.9%	0.5%	0 4%	2.6%	5.6%
4.6–5.0							
Number	211	6	1	2	2	12	188
Percent	2.3%	7.0%	0.5%	0.5%	0.3%	0.7%	3.2%
5.1 and over							
Number	781	3	0	3	6	21	748
Percent	8.7%	3.5%	0.0%	0.7%	0.8%	1.2%	12.9%

1 Full-time law enforcement employees include civilians.   2 The number of agencies used to compile these figures differs from other tables that include data about law enforcement employees because agencies with no resident population are excluded from this table. Agencies not included in this table are associated with universities and colleges (see Table 79) and other agencies (see Table 81), as well as some state agencies that have concurrent jurisdiction with other local law enforcement.   3 Because of rounding, the percentages may not sum to 100.

Table 73. Full-Time Law Enforcement Officers, Range in Rate, by Population Group, 2020

(Number, rate per 1,000 inhabitants.)

Rate range	Total cities[1] (10,293 cities; population 198,498,223)	Group I (86 cities, 250,000 and over; population 63,000,994)	Group II (212 cities, 100,000 to 249,999; population 30,779,686)	Group III (430 cities, 50,000 to 99,999; population 29,997,046)	Group IV (789 cities, 25,000 to 49,999; population 27,195,395)	Group V (1,681 cities, 10,000 to 24,999; population 26,678,434)	Group VI (7,095 cities, under 10,000; population 20,846,668)
Total Cities							
Number	8,997	86	212	430	789	1,681	5,799
Percent[2]	100.0%	100.0%	100.0%	100.0%	100.0%	100.0%	100.0%
0.1–0.5							
Number	87	0	0	1	3	4	79
Percent	1.0%	0.0%	0.0%	0.2%	0.4%	0.2%	1.4%
0.6–1.0							
Number	655	3	39	81	86	75	371
Percent	7.3%	3.5%	18.4%	18.8%	10.9%	4.5%	6.4%
1.1–1.5							
Number	1,716	21	83	135	252	439	786
Percent	19.1%	24.4%	39.2%	31.4%	31.9%	26.1%	13.6%
1.6–2.0							
Number	2,202	29	52	133	254	574	1,160
Percent	24.5%	33.7%	24.5%	30.9%	32.2%	34.1%	20.0%
2.1–2.5							
Number	1,584	14	19	57	130	353	1,011
Percent	17.6%	16.3%	9.0%	13.3%	16.5%	21.0%	17.4%
2.6–3.0							
Number	936	5	14	13	51	136	717
Percent	10.4%	5.8%	6.6%	3.0%	6.5%	8.1%	12.4%
3.1–3.5							
Number	597	4	3	6	6	59	519
Percent	6.6%	4.7%	1.4%	1.4%	0.8%	3.5%	8.9%
3.6–4.0							
Number	354	4	2	1	3	29	315
Percent	3.9%	4.7%	0.9%	0.2%	0.4%	1.7%	5.4%
4.1–4.5							
Number	223	4	0	1	2	5	211
Percent	2.5%	4.7%	0.0%	0.2%	0.3%	0.3%	3.6%
4.6–5.0							
Number	146	1	0	1	0	3	141
Percent	1.6%	1.2%	0.0%	0.2%	0.0%	0.2%	2.4%
5.1 and over							
Number	497	1	0	1	2	4	489
Percent	5.5%	1.2%	0.0%	0.2%	0.3%	0.2%	8.4%

1 The number of agencies used to compile these figures differs from other tables that include data about law enforcement officers because agencies with no resident population are excluded from this table. Agencies not included in this table are associated with universities and colleges (see Table 79) and other agencies (see Table 81), as well as some state agencies that have concurrent jurisdiction with other local law enforcement.   2 Because of rounding, the percentages may not sum to 100.

Table 74. Full-Time Law Enforcement Employees, by Population Group, Percent Male and Female, 2020

(Number, percent.)

Population group	Total law enforcement employees (number)	Law enforcement employees (percent)		Total officers (number)	Officers (percent)		Civilians (number) Total civilians	Civilians (percent)		Agencies (number)	Population, 2020, estimated
		Male	Female		Male	Female		Male	Female		
Total Agencies	1,005,779	72.4	27.6	696,644	86.9	13.1	309,135	40.0	60.0	13,377	292,123,289
Total Cities	569,097	74.7	25.3	442,266	86.6	13.4	126,831	33.0	67.0	10,293	198,498,223
Group I (250,000 and over)	206,548	71.6	28.4	158,544	82.8	17.2	48,004	34.7	65.3	86	63,000,994
1,000,000 and over (Group I subset)	112,568	70.3	29.7	85,503	81.5	18.5	27,065	34.8	65.2	12	28,733,047
500,000 to 999,999 (Group I subset)	53,408	73.9	26.1	41,501	84.2	15.8	11,907	38.0	62.0	25	17,887,908
250,000 to 499,999 (Group I subset)	40,572	72.3	27.7	31,540	84.3	15.7	9,032	30.2	69.8	49	16,380,039
Group II (100,000 to 249,999)	64,935	73.1	26.9	49,681	87.1	12.9	15,254	27.5	72.5	212	30,779,686
Group III (50,000 to 99,999)	61,530	74.9	25.1	47,902	88.1	11.9	13,628	28.6	71.4	430	29,997,046
Group IV (25,000 to 49,999)	57,759	77.3	22.7	46,218	89.6	10.4	11,541	28.2	71.8	789	27,195,395
Group V (10,000 to 24,999)	62,007	78.5	21.5	50,478	90.4	9.6	11,529	26.7	73.3	1,681	26,678,434
Group VI (under 10,000)	116,318	77.4	22.6	89,443	88.6	11.4	26,875	40.1	59.9	7,095	20,846,668
Metropolitan Counties	310,351	68.9	31.1	180,168	85.7	14.3	130,183	45.7	54.3	1,245	70,981,908
Nonmetropolitan Counties	126,331	71.1	28.9	74,210	91.2	8.8	52,121	42.5	57.5	1,839	22,643,158
Suburban Areas[1]	469,639	72.0	28.0	305,724	87.2	12.8	163,915	43.7	56.3	7,147	124,916,229

1 Suburban areas include law enforcement agencies in cities with less than 50,000 inhabitants and county law enforcement agencies that are within a Metropolitan Statistical Area. Suburban areas exclude all metropolitan agencies associated with a principal city. The agencies associated with suburban areas also appear in other groups within this table.

Table 75. Full-Time Civilian Law Enforcement Employees, by Population Group, 2020

(Number, percent.)

Population group	Civilian employees (percent)	Agencies (number)	Population, 2020, estimated
Total Agencies	30.7	13,377	292,123,289
Total Cities	22.3	10,293	198,498,223
Group I (250,000 and over)	23.2	86	63,000,994
1,000,000 and over (Group I subset)	24.0	12	28,733,047
500,000 to 999,999 (Group I subset)	22.3	25	17,887,908
250,000 to 499,999 (Group I subset)	22.3	49	16,380,039
Group II (100,000 to 249,999)	23.5	212	30,779,686
Group III (50,000 to 99,999)	22.1	430	29,997,046
Group IV (25,000 to 49,999)	20.0	789	27,195,395
Group V (10,000 to 24,999)	18.6	1,681	26,678,434
Group VI (under 10,000)	23.1	7,095	20,846,668
Metropolitan Counties	41.9	1,245	70,981,908
Nonmetropolitan Counties	41.3	1,839	22,643,158
Suburban Areas[1]	34.9	7,147	124,916,229

1 Suburban areas include law enforcement agencies in cities with less than 50,000 inhabitants and county law enforcement agencies that are within a Metropolitan Statistical Area. Suburban areas exclude all metropolitan agencies associated with a principal city. The agencies associated with suburban areas also appear in other groups within this table.

Table 76. Full-Time State Law Enforcement Employees, by Selected State, 2020

(Number.)

State/agency	Law enforcement employees	Officers		Civilians	
		Male	Female	Male	Female
Alabama					
Other state agencies	1,639	974	43	143	479
Alaska					
State Troopers	598	337	22	111	128
Arizona					
Department of Public Safety	1,946	1,062	43	377	464
Arkansas					
State Patrol	921	515	22	116	268
Other state agencies	38	26	3	1	8
California					
Highway Patrol	10,204	6,574	427	1,328	1,875
Other state agencies	1,406	1,084	195	52	75
Colorado					
State Patrol	1,094	686	52	140	216
Other state agencies	461	77	13	132	239
Connecticut					
State Police	1,071	799	75	85	112
Other state agencies	143	102	18	14	9
Delaware					
State Police	977	646	95	89	147
Other state agencies	807	254	33	158	362
Florida					
Highway Patrol	2,236	1,642	174	119	301
Other state agencies	3,320	1,468	235	571	1,046
Georgia					
Department of Public Safety	1,505	1,022	30	169	284
Other state agencies	1,302	392	105	206	599
Idaho					
State Police	538	278	16	71	173
Other state agencies	2	1	1	0	0
Illinois					
State Police	3,002	1,652	177	510	663
Indiana					
State Police	1,682	1,154	57	187	284
Other state agencies	82	64	12	0	6
Iowa					
Department of Public Safety	858	512	33	141	172
Kansas[1]					
Other state agencies	609	313	27	92	177
Kentucky					
State Police	1,811	980	24	355	452
Other state agencies	178	167	8	0	3
Louisiana[2]					
State Police					
Maine					
State Police	414	268	28	47	71
Other state agencies	59	29	1	20	9
Maryland					
State Police	2,124	1,294	99	371	360
Other state agencies	1,484	925	116	190	253
Massachusetts					
State Police	2,831	2,144	118	206	363
Other state agencies	234	205	20	2	7
Michigan					
State Police	3,006	1,762	176	435	633
Other state agencies	262	217	18	8	19
Minnesota					
State Police	640	475	52	41	72
Other state agencies	514	82	19	177	236
Mississippi[2]					
Other state agencies	113	83	15	3	12

Table 76. Full-Time State Law Enforcement Employees, by Selected State, 2020—Continued

(Number.)

State/agency	Law enforcement employees	Officers		Civilians	
		Male	Female	Male	Female
Missouri					
State Highway Patrol	2,313	1,154	58	514	587
Other state agencies	416	249	28	102	37
Montana					
Highway Patrol	308	218	15	30	45
Other state agencies	45	17	2	13	13
Nebraska					
State Patrol	706	402	29	102	173
Nevada					
Highway Patrol	847	645	62	54	86
Other state agencies	406	88	20	113	185
New Hampshire					
State Police	494	315	26	46	107
Other state agencies	34	15	6	4	9
New Jersey					
State Police	4,570	2,740	679	541	610
Other state agencies	8,502	5,344	1,071	1,027	1,060
Port Authority of New York and New Jersey[3]	2,382	1,949	256	80	97
New Mexico[2]					
State Police					
New York					
State Police	5,637	4,330	536	286	485
Other state agencies	270	209	30	13	18
North Carolina					
Highway Patrol	2,163	1,577	49	295	242
Other state agencies	1,150	714	147	111	178
North Dakota					
Highway Patrol	198	145	7	17	29
Ohio					
State Highway Patrol	2,518	1,465	144	435	474
Other state agencies	333	276	25	10	22
Oklahoma					
Highway Patrol	1,383	750	15	276	342
Other state agencies	419	118	27	102	172
Oregon					
State Police	1,280	635	55	204	386
Other state agencies	97	60	25	0	12
Pennsylvania					
State Police	6,389	4,245	314	823	1,007
Other state agencies	348	267	30	30	21
Rhode Island					
State Police	300	222	27	25	26
Other state agencies	75	52	6	11	6
South Carolina					
Highway Patrol	1,257	890	59	98	210
Other State Agency	679	474	42	78	85
South Dakota					
Highway Patrol	259	161	17	46	35
Other state agencies	174	46	3	48	77
Tennessee					
Department of Safety	1,712	814	52	245	601
Other state agencies	1,275	724	223	110	218
Texas					
Department of Public Safety	9,964	3,769	305	1,809	4,081
Utah					
Highway Patrol	721	538	32	30	121
Other state agencies	176	143	9	10	14
Vermont					
State Police	412	275	45	26	66
Other state agencies	183	76	8	43	56
Virginia					
State Police	2,675	1,799	130	259	487
Other state agencies	726	492	55	60	119

Table 76. Full-Time State Law Enforcement Employees, by Selected State, 2020—Continued

(Number.)

State/agency	Law enforcement employees	Officers		Civilians	
		Male	Female	Male	Female
Washington					
State Patrol	2,207	981	107	536	583
Other state agencies	290	140	25	62	63
West Virginia					
State Police	1,016	607	26	138	245
Other state agencies	221	173	1	19	28
Wisconsin[2]					
Other state agencies	48	29	8	6	5
Wyoming					
Highway Patrol	353	189	8	74	82
Other state agencies	83	35	2	12	34

Note: Caution should be used when comparing data from one state to that of another. The responsibilities of the various state police, highway patrol, and department of public safety agencies range from full law enforcement duties to only traffic patrol, which can impact both the level of employment for agencies as well as the ratio of sworn officers to civilians employed. Any valid comparison must take these factors and the other identified variables affecting crime into consideration.
1 The FBI determined that the Kansas Highway Patrol's data were not comparable to previous year's data. Consequently, those data are not included in this table.   2 Police employee data were not received from the State Police/Highway Patrol for the state.   3 Data reported are the number of law enforcement employees for the state of New Jersey.

Table 77. Full-Time Law Enforcement Employees, by State, 2020

(Number.)

State	Total law enforcement employees	Total officers		Total civilians		Total agencies	Population, 2020, estimated
		Male	Female	Male	Female		
Alabama	17,985	11,203	1,014	2,003	3,765	387	4,851,203
Alaska	2,002	1,170	120	265	447	37	730,400
Arizona	22,526	11,308	1,450	4,485	5,283	110	7,359,580
Arkansas	10,442	6,087	724	1,375	2,256	288	3,011,972
California	120,756	68,774	10,862	15,350	25,770	460	33,781,093
Colorado	18,853	10,801	1,885	2,260	3,907	237	5,753,378
Connecticut	9,163	6,814	892	595	862	107	3,557,006
Delaware	3,810	2,407	320	387	696	55	985,364
District of Columbia	4,975	3,267	919	309	480	3	712,816
Florida	74,207	38,522	7,330	10,838	17,517	335	20,251,225
Georgia	34,491	20,679	4,421	2,966	6,425	451	9,552,544
Hawaii	3,698	2,561	335	257	545	4	1,407,006
Idaho	5,839	2,775	228	1,258	1,578	109	1,822,223
Illinois	36,422	21,791	4,614	5,289	4,728	323	8,657,369
Indiana	11,620	7,474	729	1,604	1,813	106	3,873,793
Iowa	8,316	4,911	502	1,202	1,701	243	3,073,517
Kansas	8,107	4,978	683	896	1,550	287	2,126,574
Kentucky	9,697	6,939	519	868	1,371	274	3,825,181
Louisiana	8,254	4,774	1,282	804	1,394	88	1,644,970
Maine	2,937	2,152	206	213	366	133	1,350,141
Maryland	20,114	13,308	2,073	1,778	2,955	123	5,876,631
Massachusetts	20,521	15,157	1,562	1,572	2,230	314	6,446,417
Michigan	24,985	15,603	2,395	3,295	3,692	614	9,584,727
Minnesota	15,530	8,757	1,224	2,443	3,106	397	5,643,318
Mississippi	7,630	4,439	540	997	1,654	180	2,420,875
Missouri	16,375	10,397	1,297	1,926	2,755	347	4,631,677
Montana	3,411	1,860	153	654	744	111	1,077,405
Nebraska	5,252	3,287	409	511	1,045	154	1,877,623
Nevada	10,471	6,483	941	718	2,329	48	2,852,910
New Hampshire	3,718	2,583	280	253	602	178	1,304,483
New Jersey	49,586	33,711	4,917	4,485	6,473	528	8,542,489
New Mexico	1,428	871	117	169	271	47	434,293
New York	79,011	48,743	9,002	7,816	13,450	375	17,057,766
North Carolina	34,612	21,269	3,074	4,498	5,771	519	10,593,215
North Dakota	2,556	1,601	229	302	424	106	763,847
Ohio	18,928	12,415	1,667	1,875	2,971	258	6,262,555
Oklahoma	13,055	8,017	779	1,835	2,424	429	3,975,951
Oregon	10,937	5,761	720	1,931	2,525	195	4,218,085
Pennsylvania	30,251	23,043	2,776	1,619	2,813	975	9,658,390
Rhode Island	3,122	2,301	214	247	360	48	1,057,125
South Carolina	16,451	10,196	1,712	1,717	2,826	343	5,079,159
South Dakota	3,082	1,648	175	573	686	133	877,647
Tennessee	27,972	15,718	1,933	4,702	5,619	448	6,812,631
Texas	97,865	50,894	7,829	16,501	22,641	961	28,635,940
Utah	7,699	4,901	425	1,082	1,291	137	3,175,411
Vermont	1,641	1,058	145	155	283	85	622,368
Virginia	24,598	16,650	2,730	1,416	3,802	283	8,588,686
Washington	15,947	9,820	1,153	2,005	2,969	255	7,663,848
West Virginia	4,580	3,478	142	359	601	284	1,774,872
Wisconsin	17,617	10,316	1,790	2,351	3,160	406	5,725,072
Wyoming	2,734	1,390	144	505	695	59	560,518

Table 78. Full-Time Law Enforcement Employees, by Selected State and City, 2020

(Number.)

State/city	Population	Total law enforcement employees	Total officers	Total civilians
ALABAMA				
Abbeville	2,545	10	9	1
Adamsville	4,257	25	14	11
Addison	714	3	3	0
Alabaster	33,750	79	63	16
Albertville	21,769	67	45	22
Alexander City	14,251	68	53	15
Aliceville	2,230	6	5	1
Altoona	910	5	5	0
Andalusia	8,643	35	28	7
Anniston	21,112	89	82	7
Arab	8,416	35	26	9
Ardmore	1,495	9	5	4
Argo	4,377	7	7	0
Arley	344	2	2	0
Ashford	2,184	4	4	0
Ashland	1,880	9	8	1
Ashville	2,380	4	4	0
Athens	28,039	57	46	11
Atmore	8,997	34	25	9
Attalla	5,742	28	22	6
Auburn	67,814	139	130	9
Baker Hill	249	4	3	1
Bay Minette	9,482	30	22	8
Bayou La Batre	2,466	18	13	5
Bear Creek	1,068	2	2	0
Berry	1,090	4	4	0
Bessemer	26,347	157	112	45
Birmingham	209,081	1,034	828	206
Blountsville	1,668	5	5	0
Boaz	9,730	33	22	11
Brantley	764	5	4	1
Brent	4,725	7	7	0
Brewton	5,189	33	24	9
Bridgeport	2,282	10	6	4
Brighton	2,757	14	8	6
Brilliant	870	1	1	0
Brookside	1,325	16	12	4
Brookwood	1,851	6	6	0
Brundidge	1,884	10	6	4
Calera	15,093	43	34	9
Camden	1,739	11	9	2
Camp Hill	944	5	5	0
Carrollton	935	3	3	0
Cedar Bluff	1,823	6	6	0
Centre	3,547	14	13	1
Centreville	2,591	6	6	0
Chatom	1,171	3	3	0
Cherokee	1,004	1	1	0
Chickasaw	5,661	20	20	0
Childersburg	4,804	20	18	2
Citronelle	3,856	20	11	9
Clanton	8,812	26	25	1
Clayton	2,831	4	4	0
Clio	1,263	4	4	0
Coaling	1,663	4	4	0
Coffeeville	319	3	3	0
Collinsville	2,012	8	4	4
Columbia	737	2	2	0
Columbiana	4,596	15	11	4
Coosada	1,307	7	6	1
Cordova	1,825	6	4	2
Cottonwood	1,252	3	3	0
Courtland	585	2	2	0
Creola	2,049	9	4	5
Crossville	1,856	5	5	0
Cullman	16,134	58	51	7
Dadeville	3,035	16	15	1
Daleville	5,080	22	16	6
Daphne	27,496	89	59	30
Dauphin Island	1,347	16	8	8
Decatur	54,295	152	133	19
Demopolis	6,525	26	22	4
Dora	1,890	12	8	4
Dothan	69,265	235	164	71
Double Springs	1,056	7	7	0
Douglas	782	5	5	0
East Brewton	2,343	21	10	11
Eclectic	1,016	9	8	1
Elba	3,796	17	12	5
Elberta	1,775	11	10	1
Enterprise	28,569	74	58	16
Eufaula	11,568	55	34	21
Eutaw	2,570	8	7	1
Evergreen	3,482	25	19	6

Table 78. Full-Time Law Enforcement Employees, by Selected State and City, 2020—Continued

(Number.)

State/city	Population	Total law enforcement employees	Total officers	Total civilians
Excel	623	2	2	0
Fairfield	10,512	5	4	1
Fairhope	23,517	64	41	23
Falkville	1,254	8	6	2
Fayette	4,239	12	12	0
Flomaton	1,388	12	7	5
Florala	1,898	8	8	0
Florence	40,936	137	110	27
Foley	21,036	93	65	28
Fort Deposit	1,136	3	3	0
Fort Payne	14,071	35	35	0
Frisco City	1,137	2	2	0
Fultondale	9,391	35	28	7
Fyffe	1,048	5	5	0
Gadsden	34,791	126	97	29
Gantt	215	6	4	2
Gardendale	14,198	41	31	10
Geneva	4,273	13	12	1
Georgiana	1,594	8	5	3
Geraldine	897	6	6	0
Gilbertown	191	3	2	1
Glencoe	5,063	10	9	1
Goodwater	1,298	8	4	4
Gordo	1,600	4	4	0
Gordon	325	1	1	0
Grant	918	2	2	0
Greensboro	2,245	9	9	0
Greenville	7,318	29	26	3
Grove Hill	1,717	7	6	1
Guin	2,264	7	7	0
Gulf Shores	12,985	71	50	21
Guntersville	8,606	46	35	11
Gurley	809	6	6	0
Hackleburg	1,234	4	4	0
Haleyville	4,115	16	11	5
Hamilton	6,575	16	14	2
Hanceville	3,494	11	9	2
Harpersville	1,734	9	8	1
Hartford	2,574	15	11	4
Hartselle	14,486	29	28	1
Hayneville	769	5	4	1
Headland	4,733	31	16	15
Heflin	3,400	12	11	1
Helena	20,279	35	30	5
Henagar	2,364	13	9	4
Highland Lake	410	6	6	0
Hillsboro	518	2	2	0
Hokes Bluff	4,254	9	9	0
Hollywood	982	5	5	0
Homewood	25,407	118	81	37
Hoover	86,321	219	182	37
Hueytown	15,235	44	35	9
Huntsville	202,884	662	450	212
Ider	717	7	3	4
Irondale	12,949	39	32	7
Jackson	4,583	24	20	4
Jacksons Gap	827	2	2	0
Jacksonville	12,475	34	27	7
Jasper	13,327	70	46	24
Jemison	2,678	13	12	1
Killen	951	4	4	0
Kimberly	3,660	6	6	0
Kinsey	2,274	1	1	0
Kinston	548	2	1	1
LaFayette	2,901	14	13	1
Lake View	2,756	3	3	0
Lanett	6,117	31	29	2
Leeds	12,068	31	30	1
Leesburg	1,014	3	3	0
Leighton	754	4	3	1
Level Plains	1,994	5	5	0
Lexington	706	4	4	0
Lincoln	6,843	20	18	2
Linden	1,856	7	7	0
Lineville	2,231	11	7	4
Lipscomb	2,132	9	4	5
Littleville	990	7	5	2
Livingston	3,240	10	7	3
Louisville	456	2	2	0
Loxley	3,235	25	16	9
Luverne	2,737	13	11	2
Lynn	633	1	1	0
Madison	52,573	109	78	31
Maplesville	699	7	7	0
Margaret	5,222	7	7	0

Table 78. Full-Time Law Enforcement Employees, by Selected State and City, 2020—Continued

(Number.)

State/city	Population	Total law enforcement employees	Total officers	Total civilians
Marion	3,067	5	5	0
McIntosh	213	8	8	0
McKenzie	488	3	3	0
Mentone	369	2	2	0
Midfield	4,967	18	14	4
Midland City	2,377	4	4	0
Millbrook	15,993	56	40	16
Millport	973	1	1	0
Millry	492	1	1	0
Mobile	243,900	747	495	252
Monroeville	5,638	29	23	6
Montevallo	6,784	20	16	4
Montgomery	197,755	569	485	84
Moody	13,220	28	27	1
Morris	2,176	5	5	0
Moulton	3,217	11	11	0
Moundville	2,463	11	10	1
Mountain Brook	20,281	69	56	13
Mount Vernon	1,487	5	4	1
Munford	1,344	1	1	0
Muscle Shoals	14,737	28	26	2
Napier Field	343	3	2	1
New Brockton	1,275	6	5	1
New Hope	2,927	6	6	0
New Site	759	2	2	0
Newton	1,450	10	8	2
Newville	509	1	1	0
North Courtland	619	1	1	0
Northport	26,372	75	57	18
Notasulga	808	8	3	5
Oakman	718	1	1	0
Odenville	3,915	10	10	0
Ohatchee	1,153	6	6	0
Oneonta	6,576	27	26	1
Opelika	31,437	111	89	22
Opp	6,361	29	21	8
Orange Beach	6,329	75	49	26
Owens Crossroads	2,206	4	4	0
Oxford	21,191	71	69	2
Ozark	14,215	39	32	7
Parrish	932	2	2	0
Pelham	24,188	82	66	16
Pell City	14,195	42	40	2
Phenix City	36,883	104	80	24
Pickensville	575	1	1	0
Piedmont	4,501	22	16	6
Pine Hill	840	5	5	0
Pleasant Grove	9,551	20	15	5
Powell	968	4	4	0
Prattville	36,162	87	80	7
Priceville	3,940	7	7	0
Prichard	21,305	56	35	21
Ragland	1,731	4	4	0
Rainbow City	9,610	37	23	14
Rainsville	5,138	14	10	4
Ranburne	397	3	2	1
Red Bay	3,077	13	9	4
Red Level	477	2	2	0
Reform	1,537	6	6	0
River Falls	536	3	3	0
Riverside	2,395	5	5	0
Roanoke	5,894	28	23	5
Robertsdale	6,961	28	16	12
Rogersville	1,250	6	6	0
Russellville	9,723	31	27	4
Samson	1,844	7	7	0
Saraland	14,751	58	46	12
Sardis City	1,783	5	5	0
Satsuma	6,195	18	14	4
Scottsboro	14,398	69	42	27
Selma	16,876	58	42	16
Sheffield	8,886	31	29	2
Shorter	388	6	5	1
Silverhill	1,238	7	6	1
Skyline	837	1	1	0
Slocomb	1,890	11	11	0
Snead	838	13	13	0
Somerville	774	4	4	0
Southside	8,957	19	13	6
Spanish Fort	9,511	28	24	4
Springville	4,325	11	11	0
Steele	1,094	3	3	0
Stevenson	1,941	7	5	2
St. Florian	708	4	4	0
Sulligent	1,825	6	6	0

Table 78. Full-Time Law Enforcement Employees, by Selected State and City, 2020—Continued

(Number.)

State/city	Population	Total law enforcement employees	Total officers	Total civilians
Summerdale	1,804	12	11	1
Sylacauga	11,955	40	39	1
Sylvania	1,897	3	3	0
Talladega	15,398	47	43	4
Tallassee	4,482	27	20	7
Tarrant	6,080	26	20	6
Taylor	2,437	5	4	1
Thomasville	3,799	21	21	0
Thorsby	2,063	6	6	0
Town Creek	1,032	2	2	0
Trafford	615	1	1	0
Triana	1,026	3	3	0
Trinity	2,490	7	7	0
Troy	19,041	80	62	18
Trussville	22,961	78	65	13
Tuscaloosa	102,391	354	283	71
Tuscumbia	8,446	28	21	7
Tuskegee	7,973	29	18	11
Union Springs	3,365	21	12	9
Uniontown	2,181	6	5	1
Valley	9,101	29	27	2
Valley Head	548	2	2	0
Vance	1,672	5	5	0
Vernon	1,835	9	9	0
Vestavia Hills	34,489	102	99	3
Wadley	710	5	5	0
Warrior	3,214	17	10	7
Weaver	3,060	11	8	3
Wedowee	791	10	9	1
West Blocton	1,248	1	1	0
Wetumpka	8,562	33	30	3
Winfield	4,497	14	13	1
Woodstock	1,663	5	5	0
York	2,208	4	4	0
ALASKA				
Anchorage	286,388	592	425	167
Bethel	6,642	24	11	13
Bristol Bay Borough	817	9	4	5
Cordova	2,161	10	4	6
Craig	1,268	10	5	5
Dillingham	2,364	20	8	12
Fairbanks	30,832	38	33	5
Haines	2,524	10	5	5
Homer	6,028	22	12	10
Hoonah	794	9	5	4
Juneau	31,925	83	48	35
Kenai	7,885	27	17	10
Ketchikan	8,307	38	25	13
Klawock	790	2	2	0
Kodiak	5,778	39	16	23
Kotzebue	3,249	18	10	8
Nome	3,900	17	10	7
North Pole	2,090	13	11	2
North Slope Borough	9,836	76	45	31
Palmer	7,641	24	14	10
Petersburg	3,259	14	8	6
Sand Point	1,073	6	5	1
Seward	2,806	22	9	13
Sitka	8,420	26	14	12
Skagway	1,206	9	3	6
Soldotna	4,782	17	14	3
Unalaska	4,439	23	12	11
Valdez	3,841	12	12	0
Wasilla	11,228	30	26	4
Whittier	203	5	5	0
Wrangell	2,508	11	5	6
ARIZONA				
Apache Junction	43,385	101	65	36
Avondale	89,338	198	133	65
Benson	4,854	22	15	7
Bisbee	5,184	20	14	6
Buckeye	83,608	130	96	34
Bullhead City	41,035	101	67	34
Camp Verde	11,223	35	22	13
Casa Grande	59,822	99	80	19
Chandler	264,071	472	318	154
Chino Valley	12,564	31	26	5
Clarkdale	4,433	9	8	1
Clifton	3,761	10	4	6
Colorado City	4,838	13	9	4
Coolidge	13,277	40	27	13
Cottonwood	12,380	52	29	23
Douglas	16,044	42	28	14

Table 78. Full-Time Law Enforcement Employees, by Selected State and City, 2020—Continued

(Number.)

State/city	Population	Total law enforcement employees	Total officers	Total civilians
Eagar	4,944	8	6	2
El Mirage	36,221	69	51	18
Eloy	19,981	36	26	10
Flagstaff	76,107	149	104	45
Florence	27,571	34	25	9
Fredonia	1,275	3	3	0
Gilbert	259,629	422	289	133
Glendale	255,468	548	400	148
Globe	7,328	27	23	4
Goodyear	89,607	154	115	39
Hayden	976	5	5	0
Holbrook	5,088	13	11	2
Huachuca City	1,723	7	5	2
Jerome	456	5	5	0
Kearny	2,193	12	8	4
Kingman	31,351	64	47	17
Lake Havasu City	56,243	109	71	38
Mammoth	1,709	4	4	0
Marana	50,942	124	96	28
Maricopa	53,165	84	67	17
Mesa	527,361	1,268	828	440
Miami	1,774	12	7	5
Nogales	20,026	63	46	17
Oro Valley	46,634	122	96	26
Page	7,546	30	19	11
Paradise Valley	14,859	45	34	11
Parker	3,224	12	10	2
Patagonia	870	3	3	0
Payson	15,869	44	25	19
Peoria	178,486	297	197	100
Phoenix	1,708,960	3,903	2,939	964
Pima	2,580	5	5	0
Pinetop-Lakeside	4,490	18	14	4
Prescott	44,835	90	75	15
Prescott Valley	47,459	95	72	23
Quartzsite	3,772	12	11	1
Safford	10,033	24	21	3
Sahuarita	32,053	59	49	10
San Luis	35,574	59	37	22
Scottsdale	263,006	613	379	234
Sedona	10,373	43	24	19
Show Low	11,527	51	30	21
Sierra Vista	42,800	84	66	18
Snowflake-Taylor	10,384	16	14	2
Somerton	16,811	27	19	8
South Tucson	5,723	17	16	1
Springerville	1,979	8	6	2
St. Johns	3,514	10	7	3
Superior	3,212	10	9	1
Surprise	144,620	199	140	59
Tempe	199,935	487	346	141
Thatcher	5,242	12	11	1
Tolleson	7,470	46	30	16
Tombstone	1,294	9	7	2
Tucson	550,448	1,087	855	232
Wellton	3,062	7	6	1
Wickenburg	7,041	25	20	5
Willcox	3,509	18	11	7
Williams	3,271	21	11	10
Winslow	9,298	43	23	20
Yuma	99,096	227	137	90
ARKANSAS				
Alexander	3,524	10	10	0
Alma	5,904	19	15	4
Altus	726	1	1	0
Amity	681	3	1	2
Arkadelphia	10,732	29	23	6
Ashdown	4,367	14	12	2
Ash Flat	1,099	6	6	0
Atkins	3,040	9	8	1
Augusta	1,917	5	5	0
Austin	4,401	4	4	0
Bald Knob	2,864	14	8	6
Barling	5,076	10	10	0
Batesville	10,938	26	25	1
Bay	1,823	4	4	0
Beebe	8,268	23	17	6
Bella Vista	29,138	52	36	16
Benton	37,542	77	68	9
Bentonville	57,575	115	83	32
Berryville	5,577	16	14	2
Blytheville	13,239	53	36	17
Booneville	3,765	13	9	4
Bradford	734	2	2	0

Table 78. Full-Time Law Enforcement Employees, by Selected State and City, 2020—Continued

(Number.)

State/city	Population	Total law enforcement employees	Total officers	Total civilians
Brinkley	2,531	15	9	6
Bryant	21,497	57	46	11
Bull Shoals	1,945	7	4	3
Cabot	26,593	54	43	11
Caddo Valley	637	5	4	1
Camden	10,605	36	18	18
Cammack Village	713	4	4	0
Caraway	1,283	3	3	0
Carlisle	2,149	9	5	4
Cave Springs	5,888	9	9	0
Centerton	17,220	24	22	2
Charleston	2,462	5	5	0
Cherokee Village	4,657	8	7	1
Cherry Valley	576	1	1	0
Clarendon	1,330	3	3	0
Clarksville	9,829	23	19	4
Clinton	2,505	8	7	1
Conway	68,599	162	118	44
Corning	3,018	10	6	4
Cotter	949	3	3	0
Crossett	4,723	26	17	9
Damascus	382	1	1	0
Danville	2,391	6	5	1
Dardanelle	4,520	17	11	6
Decatur	1,801	5	5	0
De Queen	6,526	17	14	3
Des Arc	1,568	6	6	0
DeWitt	2,976	13	8	5
Diamond City	802	1	1	0
Diaz	1,196	3	3	0
Dover	1,446	5	5	0
Dumas	3,984	16	12	4
Dyer	901	1	1	0
Earle	2,156	3	3	0
El Dorado	17,523	67	51	16
Elkins	3,588	10	10	0
England	2,673	12	8	4
Etowah	313	1	1	0
Eudora	1,866	6	4	2
Eureka Springs	2,110	18	13	5
Fairfield Bay	2,173	17	7	10
Farmington	7,575	18	18	0
Fayetteville	89,252	171	125	46
Flippin	1,319	7	7	0
Fordyce	3,646	11	7	4
Forrest City	13,656	38	29	9
Fort Smith	88,071	193	148	45
Gassville	2,168	4	4	0
Gentry	4,086	12	10	2
Gillett	680	2	1	1
Glenwood	2,117	4	4	0
Gosnell	3,066	6	6	0
Gravette	3,558	12	11	1
Greenbrier	5,779	14	9	5
Green Forest	2,760	14	12	2
Greenland	1,416	4	4	0
Greenwood	9,449	20	18	2
Greers Ferry	853	5	4	1
Gurdon	2,069	5	4	1
Guy	792	2	2	0
Hamburg	2,574	7	6	1
Hampton	1,251	4	4	0
Hardy	765	5	5	0
Harrisburg	2,309	7	5	2
Harrison	13,096	45	34	11
Haskell	4,667	8	8	0
Hazen	1,331	7	6	1
Heber Springs	6,880	17	16	1
Helena-West Helena	10,086	28	15	13
Higginson	737	1	1	0
Highfill	641	4	4	0
Highland	1,113	3	3	0
Hope	9,543	35	25	10
Hot Springs	38,893	137	100	37
Hughes	1,193	4	3	1
Huntsville	2,585	10	8	2
Jacksonville	28,217	67	56	11
Johnson	3,781	9	8	1
Jonesboro	79,702	178	163	15
Judsonia	1,991	4	3	1
Kensett	1,613	3	3	0
Lake City	2,720	4	4	0
Lakeview	718	2	2	0
Lake Village	2,155	13	7	6
Lamar	1,734	3	3	0

Table 78. Full-Time Law Enforcement Employees, by Selected State and City, 2020—Continued

(Number.)

State/city	Population	Total law enforcement employees	Total officers	Total civilians
Lavaca	2,441	3	3	0
Leachville	1,835	5	4	1
Lead Hill	265	1	1	0
Lewisville	1,097	2	2	0
Lincoln	2,503	6	6	0
Little Flock	2,816	7	7	0
Little Rock	197,688	736	560	176
Lonoke	4,178	16	12	4
Lowell	9,825	27	21	6
Luxora	1,011	1	1	0
Magnolia	11,434	24	22	2
Malvern	10,966	23	21	2
Mammoth Spring	959	2	2	0
Mansfield	1,090	4	4	0
Marianna	3,325	23	13	10
Marion	12,285	34	29	5
Marked Tree	2,405	14	8	6
Marmaduke	1,265	4	4	0
Marshall	1,330	4	4	0
Marvell	892	7	4	3
Maumelle	18,307	49	37	12
Mayflower	2,418	9	8	1
McCrory	1,464	6	5	1
McGehee	3,631	25	13	12
McRae	667	1	1	0
Mena	5,461	14	13	1
Menifee	319	2	1	1
Mineral Springs	1,142	4	3	1
Monette	1,602	3	3	0
Monticello	9,348	29	21	8
Morrilton	6,631	27	24	3
Mountainburg	612	1	1	0
Mountain Home	12,582	38	31	7
Mountain View	2,875	11	10	1
Mulberry	1,697	4	4	0
Murfreesboro	1,576	3	3	0
Nashville	4,360	17	16	1
Newport	7,423	24	18	6
North Little Rock	66,303	218	185	33
Ola	1,203	4	3	1
Osceola	6,527	34	24	10
Ozark	3,583	13	11	2
Paragould	29,288	57	51	6
Paris	3,345	13	8	5
Patterson	385	1	1	0
Pea Ridge	6,398	16	15	1
Perryville	1,457	5	5	0
Piggott	3,494	7	7	0
Pine Bluff	40,718	134	111	23
Plumerville	768	2	2	0
Pocahontas	6,647	18	17	1
Pottsville	3,390	9	7	2
Prairie Grove	7,058	16	16	0
Prescott	2,957	12	6	6
Quitman	714	4	4	0
Ravenden	448	1	1	0
Redfield	1,540	7	6	1
Rogers	70,194	154	116	38
Rose Bud	488	4	3	1
Russellville	29,266	61	55	6
Salem	1,679	4	4	0
Searcy	23,742	72	53	19
Shannon Hills	4,098	5	5	0
Sheridan	4,963	30	16	14
Sherwood	31,636	100	76	24
Siloam Springs	17,332	54	39	15
Springdale	85,146	205	146	59
Stamps	1,442	1	1	0
Star City	2,005	6	5	1
St. Charles	210	1	1	0
Stuttgart	8,402	30	22	8
Sulphur Springs	530	3	3	0
Swifton	726	2	2	0
Texarkana	29,622	86	75	11
Trumann	6,934	26	19	7
Tuckerman	1,663	4	4	0
Turrell	549	1	1	0
Tyronza	717	2	2	0
Van Buren	23,779	64	50	14
Vilonia	4,719	8	8	0
Waldron	3,344	10	9	1
Walnut Ridge	5,023	8	8	0
Ward	5,517	12	11	1
Warren	5,546	23	14	9
Weiner	669	1	1	0

Table 78. Full-Time Law Enforcement Employees, by Selected State and City, 2020—Continued

(Number.)

State/city	Population	Total law enforcement employees	Total officers	Total civilians
West Fork	2,688	7	6	1
West Memphis	24,205	95	75	20
White Hall	4,904	19	17	2
Wilson	805	1	1	0
Wynne	7,682	22	20	2
CALIFORNIA				
Alameda	78,047	105	72	33
Albany	19,830	31	22	9
Alhambra	83,817	124	81	43
Alturas	2,535	8	8	0
Anaheim	351,913	556	402	154
Anderson	10,705	27	19	8
Angels Camp	3,974	7	6	1
Antioch	112,481	166	120	46
Arcadia	58,122	89	63	26
Arcata	18,516	38	25	13
Arroyo Grande	18,054	25	22	3
Arvin	22,149	24	16	8
Atascadero	30,266	38	28	10
Atherton	7,162	28	20	8
Atwater	29,704	33	23	10
Auburn	14,293	27	20	7
Avenal	13,321	19	17	2
Azusa	50,373	80	53	27
Bakersfield	388,265	588	403	185
Baldwin Park	75,233	84	63	21
Banning	31,392	42	26	16
Barstow	24,041	58	41	17
Bear Valley	121	6	5	1
Beaumont	52,884	56	41	15
Bell	35,526	41	30	11
Bell Gardens	42,008	67	45	22
Belmont	27,063	44	32	12
Belvedere	2,107	6	6	0
Benicia	28,374	49	31	18
Berkeley	122,346	254	163	91
Beverly Hills	33,776	226	134	92
Bishop	3,733	19	11	8
Blythe	19,590	30	20	10
Brawley	26,363	40	26	14
Brea	43,705	100	57	43
Brentwood	66,061	95	64	31
Brisbane	4,716	17	14	3
Broadmoor	4,176	8	7	1
Buena Park	81,901	130	87	43
Burbank	102,419	230	147	83
Burlingame	31,126	59	39	20
Calexico	39,957	39	24	15
California City	14,286	25	14	11
Calistoga	5,255	16	11	5
Campbell	41,921	73	42	31
Capitola	10,020	27	21	6
Carlsbad	116,516	180	128	52
Carmel	3,825	21	14	7
Cathedral City	55,417	67	47	20
Central Marin	34,593	44	40	4
Ceres	49,028	63	47	16
Chico	105,355	144	94	50
Chino	96,309	165	114	51
Chowchilla	18,278	30	20	10
Chula Vista	278,027	342	243	99
Citrus Heights	88,314	130	83	47
Claremont	36,422	62	38	24
Clayton	12,420	13	11	2
Clearlake	15,268	39	21	18
Cloverdale	8,660	21	13	8
Clovis	116,809	165	98	67
Coalinga	17,061	24	17	7
Colma	1,495	24	18	6
Colton	55,117	76	52	24
Colusa	6,042	10	9	1
Concord	130,074	178	135	43
Corcoran	21,700	31	17	14
Corning	7,714	21	13	8
Corona	171,848	209	142	67
Coronado	23,750	70	47	23
Costa Mesa	113,317	190	129	61
Cotati	7,426	17	12	5
Covina	47,413	80	58	22
Crescent City	6,706	13	12	1
Culver City	39,218	144	110	34
Cypress	49,124	60	45	15
Daly City	106,855	127	98	29
Davis	69,853	88	56	32

Table 78. Full-Time Law Enforcement Employees, by Selected State and City, 2020—Continued

(Number.)

State/city	Population	Total law enforcement employees	Total officers	Total civilians
Delano	53,625	68	50	18
Del Rey Oaks	1,657	10	10	0
Desert Hot Springs	29,074	33	26	7
Dinuba	24,807	46	33	13
Dixon	20,967	31	26	5
Dos Palos	5,594	16	11	5
Downey	111,054	160	116	44
East Palo Alto	29,439	45	37	8
El Cajon	103,035	176	120	56
El Centro	44,238	63	43	20
El Cerrito	25,725	46	38	8
Elk Grove	177,331	242	135	107
El Monte	115,690	157	118	39
El Segundo	16,605	73	53	20
Emeryville	12,328	54	37	17
Escalon	7,625	13	12	1
Escondido	152,446	208	151	57
Etna	716	4	4	0
Eureka	26,656	71	46	25
Exeter	10,501	18	17	1
Fairfax	7,530	16	11	5
Fairfield	118,491	179	117	62
Farmersville	10,716	17	16	1
Ferndale	1,350	8	8	0
Firebaugh	8,377	17	12	5
Folsom	82,427	102	75	27
Fontana	216,553	297	186	111
Fort Bragg	7,289	19	14	5
Fortuna	12,283	24	18	6
Foster City	34,291	52	37	15
Fountain Valley	55,345	77	58	19
Fowler	6,929	12	12	0
Fremont	244,259	301	195	106
Fresno	535,472	1,026	788	238
Fullerton	139,011	181	121	60
Galt	26,867	44	31	13
Gardena	59,385	104	82	22
Garden Grove	171,698	236	171	65
Gilroy	60,269	90	60	30
Glendale	200,168	354	225	129
Glendora	51,676	78	48	30
Gonzales	8,321	13	10	3
Grass Valley	12,811	32	26	6
Greenfield	17,643	30	24	6
Gridley	7,320	17	11	6
Grover Beach	13,491	26	19	7
Guadalupe	7,865	15	13	2
Gustine	5,922	9	7	2
Hanford	58,075	86	60	26
Hawthorne	86,269	137	92	45
Hayward	160,891	287	174	113
Healdsburg	11,907	23	16	7
Hemet	86,058	104	70	34
Hercules	26,524	26	22	4
Hermosa Beach	19,300	64	35	29
Hillsborough	11,447	35	26	9
Hollister	41,438	39	31	8
Huntington Beach	200,128	321	199	122
Huntington Park	57,442	82	54	28
Huron	7,343	8	6	2
Imperial	18,528	24	21	3
Indio	93,219	112	70	42
Inglewood	107,986	249	191	58
Ione	8,674	9	9	0
Irvine	297,069	319	218	101
Irwindale	1,449	34	27	7
Jackson	4,861	10	9	1
Kensington	5,077	10	10	0
Kerman	15,478	27	23	4
King City	14,214	18	16	2
Kingsburg	12,182	21	18	3
Laguna Beach	22,834	98	54	44
La Habra	60,672	98	68	30
Lakeport	5,035	12	11	1
Lake Shastina	2,561	3	3	0
La Mesa	59,488	92	66	26
La Palma	15,415	26	19	7
La Verne	32,073	52	37	15
Lemoore	26,980	40	32	8
Lincoln	48,887	32	24	8
Lindsay	13,668	18	17	1
Livermore	91,200	125	88	37
Livingston	15,115	25	16	9
Lodi	68,207	100	71	29
Lompoc	42,915	60	35	25

Table 78. Full-Time Law Enforcement Employees, by Selected State and City, 2020—Continued

(Number.)

State/city	Population	Total law enforcement employees	Total officers	Total civilians
Long Beach	462,654	1,174	809	365
Los Alamitos	11,400	23	19	4
Los Altos	30,203	45	32	13
Los Angeles	4,000,587	12,863	9,863	3,000
Los Banos	41,631	71	43	28
Los Gatos	30,271	59	39	20
Madera	66,351	97	69	28
Mammoth Lakes	8,236	19	15	4
Manhattan Beach	35,190	99	60	39
Manteca	84,929	101	73	28
Marina	23,147	36	28	8
Martinez	38,543	46	33	13
Marysville	12,519	27	17	10
McFarland	15,858	14	11	3
Mendota	11,531	16	14	2
Menifee	96,837	80	58	22
Menlo Park	35,002	57	42	15
Merced	84,197	132	94	38
Mill Valley	14,297	26	20	6
Milpitas	86,416	121	82	39
Modesto	216,560	302	203	99
Monrovia	36,302	71	44	27
Montclair	40,473	61	36	25
Montebello	61,895	93	70	23
Monterey	28,209	65	48	17
Monterey Park	59,609	106	75	31
Moraga	17,986	13	11	2
Morgan Hill	46,925	58	38	20
Morro Bay	10,577	19	17	2
Mountain View	83,745	132	88	44
Mount Shasta	3,261	12	8	4
Murrieta	117,639	151	100	51
Napa	78,237	112	69	43
National City	61,710	114	82	32
Nevada City	3,156	10	8	2
Newark	49,934	75	51	24
Newman	11,965	14	12	2
Newport Beach	84,448	217	137	80
Novato	55,926	75	54	21
Oakdale	23,926	31	22	9
Oakland	437,923	1,056	740	316
Oceanside	176,616	299	208	91
Ontario	187,464	337	258	79
Orange	138,846	218	150	68
Orange Cove	10,334	11	10	1
Orland	7,878	14	11	3
Oroville	20,983	37	21	16
Oxnard	210,064	325	227	98
Pacifica	38,677	34	31	3
Pacific Grove	15,451	32	21	11
Palm Springs	48,952	147	97	50
Palo Alto	65,459	123	80	43
Palos Verdes Estates	13,255	26	17	9
Paradise	4,072	24	16	8
Parlier	15,734	22	18	4
Pasadena	141,473	358	233	125
Paso Robles	32,428	50	35	15
Petaluma	60,806	96	57	39
Piedmont	11,184	30	20	10
Pinole	19,350	43	26	17
Pismo Beach	8,226	31	19	12
Pittsburg	73,673	103	85	18
Placentia	51,260	68	48	20
Placerville	11,255	26	18	8
Pleasant Hill	35,032	56	43	13
Pleasanton	83,164	109	78	31
Pomona	151,982	244	152	92
Porterville	59,757	100	68	32
Port Hueneme	21,949	30	20	10
Red Bluff	14,590	36	23	13
Redding	92,895	142	101	41
Redlands	71,820	117	84	33
Redondo Beach	66,729	143	85	58
Redwood City	86,983	116	84	32
Reedley	25,800	45	30	15
Rialto	104,004	141	106	35
Richmond	111,367	200	145	55
Ridgecrest	29,120	49	31	18
Rio Dell	3,347	5	5	0
Rio Vista	10,020	14	12	2
Ripon	16,616	32	22	10
Riverside	334,370	522	379	143
Rocklin	70,219	84	60	24
Rohnert Park	43,572	97	71	26
Roseville	144,128	196	136	60

Table 78. Full-Time Law Enforcement Employees, by Selected State and City, 2020—Continued

(Number.)

State/city	Population	Total law enforcement employees	Total officers	Total civilians
Ross	2,454	8	8	0
Sacramento	519,050	1,012	684	328
Salinas	155,984	200	150	50
San Bernardino	216,365	334	239	95
San Bruno	42,997	57	42	15
Sand City	407	11	10	1
San Diego	1,437,608	2,424	1,846	578
San Fernando	24,399	40	27	13
San Francisco	881,514	2,992	2,239	753
San Gabriel	39,927	64	51	13
Sanger	25,457	40	35	5
San Jose	1,029,542	1,631	1,170	461
San Leandro	89,239	130	89	41
San Luis Obispo	47,722	84	59	25
San Marino	13,042	34	26	8
San Mateo	105,246	151	108	43
San Pablo	31,164	83	56	27
San Rafael	58,512	89	64	25
San Ramon	76,502	83	67	16
Santa Ana	333,107	594	366	228
Santa Barbara	91,692	199	131	68
Santa Clara	131,976	216	145	71
Santa Cruz	65,073	115	83	32
Santa Maria	108,140	181	133	48
Santa Monica	90,474	373	212	161
Santa Paula	29,861	42	31	11
Santa Rosa	176,932	252	174	78
Sausalito	7,080	25	19	6
Scotts Valley	11,777	24	17	7
Seal Beach	23,873	52	37	15
Seaside	33,822	44	32	12
Sebastopol	7,697	21	15	6
Selma	24,982	44	32	12
Shafter	20,799	41	28	13
Sierra Madre	10,779	21	16	5
Signal Hill	11,467	44	32	12
Simi Valley	125,742	165	124	41
Soledad	26,000	21	17	4
Sonora	4,860	17	10	7
South Gate	93,336	123	77	46
South Lake Tahoe	22,286	53	37	16
South Pasadena	25,299	50	34	16
South San Francisco	68,260	109	79	30
Stallion Springs	2,488	4	4	0
St. Helena	6,134	17	11	6
Stockton	314,981	663	468	195
Suisun City	29,842	33	21	12
Sunnyvale	154,133	289	217	72
Susanville	14,740	19	16	3
Sutter Creek	2,634	5	5	0
Taft	9,274	22	12	10
Tehachapi	12,873	27	17	10
Tiburon	9,098	17	13	4
Torrance	143,421	298	194	104
Tracy	96,067	142	92	50
Truckee	16,800	40	25	15
Tulare	66,207	113	67	46
Tulelake	975	2	2	0
Turlock	74,183	111	76	35
Tustin	79,795	141	90	51
Ukiah	15,992	43	27	16
Union City	74,625	86	69	17
Upland	77,511	102	71	31
Vacaville	101,616	171	116	55
Vallejo	122,326	163	111	52
Ventura	109,295	186	131	55
Vernon	110	55	44	11
Visalia	135,733	216	150	66
Walnut Creek	70,849	117	80	37
Watsonville	54,151	87	69	18
Weed	2,699	14	8	6
West Covina	104,989	133	90	43
Westminster	90,741	123	89	34
Westmorland	2,256	3	3	0
West Sacramento	54,068	95	71	24
Wheatland	3,916	8	8	0
Whittier	85,074	169	120	49
Williams	5,443	12	10	2
Willits	4,887	12	8	4
Winters	7,397	11	9	2
Woodlake	7,697	12	11	1
Woodland	61,123	81	66	15
Yreka	7,489	21	13	8
Yuba City	67,165	88	64	24

Table 78. Full-Time Law Enforcement Employees, by Selected State and City, 2020—Continued

(Number.)

State/city	Population	Total law enforcement employees	Total officers	Total civilians
COLORADO				
Alamosa	9,669	29	25	4
Arvada	122,983	242	185	57
Aspen	7,478	36	25	11
Ault	1,913	6	5	1
Aurora	385,720	906	770	136
Avon	6,526	21	19	2
Basalt	4,195	11	10	1
Bayfield	2,731	9	8	1
Black Hawk	129	34	23	11
Blue River	929	4	4	0
Boulder	106,598	264	176	88
Breckenridge	4,991	25	21	4
Brighton	42,536	110	79	31
Broomfield	71,795	222	115	107
Brush	5,413	15	10	5
Buena Vista	2,902	8	7	1
Burlington	3,043	7	3	4
Calhan	840	4	4	0
Canon City	16,761	45	37	8
Carbondale	6,955	15	12	3
Castle Rock	71,150	113	82	31
Cedaredge	2,301	5	4	1
Centennial	112,104	173	143	30
Center	2,266	18	6	12
Cherry Hills Village	6,722	28	23	5
Collbran	699	3	3	0
Colorado Springs	485,083	1,018	725	293
Columbine Valley	1,528	6	6	0
Commerce City	62,164	135	105	30
Cortez	8,764	51	28	23
Craig	8,975	25	20	5
Crested Butte	1,751	9	8	1
Cripple Creek	1,261	20	11	9
Dacono	6,285	17	13	4
De Beque	520	5	5	0
Del Norte	1,556	4	3	1
Delta	9,011	24	18	6
Denver	737,709	1,818	1,552	266
Dillon	974	9	8	1
Dinosaur	331	3	3	0
Durango	19,220	63	50	13
Eagle	7,043	13	12	1
Eaton	5,911	12	10	2
Edgewater	5,353	18	18	0
Elizabeth	1,591	10	9	1
Empire	307	3	2	1
Englewood	35,464	106	76	30
Erie	28,198	44	37	7
Estes Park	6,480	36	22	14
Evans	21,515	38	35	3
Fairplay	797	3	3	0
Federal Heights	12,983	40	25	15
Firestone	17,013	37	30	7
Florence	3,952	13	11	2
Fort Collins	173,274	323	222	101
Fort Lupton	8,421	24	19	5
Fort Morgan	11,471	32	25	7
Fountain	31,297	59	51	8
Fowler	1,136	5	4	1
Fraser/Winter Park	2,438	11	10	1
Frederick	14,712	29	24	5
Frisco	3,231	12	9	3
Fruita	13,574	19	16	3
Garden City	269	4	4	0
Georgetown	1,121	3	3	0
Glendale	5,243	40	27	13
Glenwood Springs	9,976	26	19	7
Golden	20,981	61	45	16
Granby	2,174	10	8	2
Grand Junction	64,149	214	111	103
Greeley	110,505	212	155	57
Green Mountain Falls	730	1	1	0
Greenwood Village	15,945	84	63	21
Gunnison	6,736	20	15	5
Gypsum	7,479	4	4	0
Haxtun	899	2	2	0
Hayden	1,999	6	4	2
Holyoke	2,195	4	4	0
Hotchkiss	929	4	4	0
Hudson	2,817	8	6	2
Hugo	782	2	2	0
Idaho Springs	1,793	12	9	3
Ignacio	914	8	8	0
Johnstown	15,932	27	24	3

Table 78. Full-Time Law Enforcement Employees, by Selected State and City, 2020—Continued

(Number.)

State/city	Population	Total law enforcement employees	Total officers	Total civilians
Kersey	1,704	5	4	1
Lafayette	31,457	47	36	11
La Junta	6,859	19	10	9
Lakeside	8	5	4	1
Lakewood	159,719	408	295	113
Lamar	7,625	20	14	6
La Salle	2,389	6	6	0
La Veta	813	1	1	0
Leadville	2,900	9	6	3
Limon	1,960	6	5	1
Littleton	48,805	99	74	25
Lochbuie	7,653	13	10	3
Log Lane Village	852	2	2	0
Lone Tree	13,423	58	49	9
Longmont	98,545	227	156	71
Louisville	21,101	37	31	6
Loveland	80,302	159	108	51
Mancos	1,440	4	4	0
Manitou Springs	5,435	18	15	3
Manzanola	415	3	2	1
Mead	4,897	11	9	2
Meeker	2,231	6	5	1
Milliken	8,509	15	11	4
Monte Vista	4,104	15	13	2
Montrose	19,864	61	41	20
Monument	8,361	22	19	3
Morrison	425	9	8	1
Mountain View	540	10	9	1
Mountain Village	1,439	10	7	3
Mount Crested Butte	883	9	8	1
Nederland	1,543	4	4	0
New Castle	5,289	10	9	1
Northglenn	39,161	78	62	16
Oak Creek	966	3	3	0
Olathe	1,834	5	5	0
Ouray	1,037	5	5	0
Pagosa Springs	2,127	7	6	1
Palisade	2,745	10	9	1
Palmer Lake	3,048	2	2	0
Paonia	1,470	6	5	1
Parachute	1,121	5	4	1
Parker	59,245	105	67	38
Platteville	3,905	9	8	1
Pueblo	113,002	265	208	57
Rangely	2,254	12	6	6
Ridgway	1,057	3	3	0
Rifle	9,747	24	19	5
Rocky Ford	3,798	10	5	5
Salida	6,183	21	18	3
Severance	7,040	9	8	1
Sheridan	6,246	35	34	1
Silt	3,222	7	5	2
Silverthorne	5,021	19	16	3
Simla	643	1	1	0
Snowmass Village	2,723	12	9	3
South Fork	422	3	3	0
Springfield	1,366	4	3	1
Steamboat Springs	13,345	39	26	13
Sterling	14,459	27	21	6
Telluride	2,508	14	10	4
Thornton	144,156	311	236	75
Timnath	6,289	11	9	2
Trinidad	8,114	36	23	13
Vail	5,450	61	28	33
Westminster	113,941	267	193	74
Wheat Ridge	31,451	106	86	20
Wiggins	1,201	2	2	0
Windsor	32,169	50	43	7
Woodland Park	7,969	34	25	9
Wray	2,345	7	6	1
Yuma	3,475	9	8	1
CONNECTICUT				
Ansonia	18,586	52	42	10
Avon	18,289	41	31	10
Berlin	20,497	53	41	12
Bethel	19,932	52	39	13
Bloomfield	21,294	56	43	13
Branford	27,886	60	48	12
Bridgeport	144,350	409	364	45
Bristol	59,886	142	117	25
Brookfield	17,031	44	34	10
Canton	10,249	20	15	5
Cheshire	28,897	60	47	13
Clinton	12,890	36	27	9

Table 78. Full-Time Law Enforcement Employees, by Selected State and City, 2020—Continued

(Number.)

State/city	Population	Total law enforcement employees	Total officers	Total civilians
Coventry	12,404	21	16	5
Cromwell	13,822	37	27	10
Danbury	85,080	154	149	5
Darien	21,840	63	51	12
Derby	12,281	35	33	2
East Hampton	12,783	20	18	2
East Hartford	49,720	155	118	37
East Haven	28,498	58	54	4
East Lyme	18,391	34	26	8
Easton	7,522	20	15	5
East Windsor	11,723	35	25	10
Enfield	43,551	117	95	22
Fairfield	62,311	107	100	7
Farmington	25,512	58	44	14
Glastonbury	34,487	76	59	17
Granby	11,531	21	16	5
Greenwich	63,012	177	150	27
Groton	8,861	33	26	7
Groton Long Point	506	5	5	0
Groton Town	28,890	82	65	17
Guilford	22,106	42	35	7
Hamden	60,440	122	96	26
Hartford	121,749	458	430	28
Ledyard	14,575	31	22	9
Madison	18,004	41	30	11
Manchester	57,510	145	113	32
Meriden	59,238	127	116	11
Middlebury	7,819	14	12	2
Middletown	46,106	136	112	24
Milford	54,968	130	108	22
Monroe	19,427	53	44	9
Naugatuck	31,024	69	58	11
New Britain	72,412	163	155	8
New Canaan	20,281	53	47	6
New Haven	130,299	375	325	50
Newington	29,957	63	50	13
New London	26,776	84	68	16
New Milford	26,668	59	46	13
Newtown	27,924	47	44	3
North Branford	14,115	28	22	6
North Haven	23,639	61	49	12
Norwalk	89,140	202	175	27
Norwich	38,576	101	87	14
Old Saybrook	10,042	30	22	8
Orange	13,922	53	43	10
Plainfield	15,095	26	17	9
Plainville	17,519	49	40	9
Plymouth	11,529	22	20	2
Portland	9,242	13	12	1
Putnam	9,370	20	15	5
Redding	9,112	23	16	7
Ridgefield	24,990	46	41	5
Rocky Hill	20,160	47	35	12
Seymour	16,426	43	40	3
Shelton	41,302	50	44	6
Simsbury	25,614	46	36	10
Southington	43,906	88	69	19
South Windsor	26,213	58	44	14
Stamford	130,425	288	263	25
Stonington	18,563	48	37	11
Stratford	51,895	108	103	5
Suffield	15,820	25	19	6
Thomaston	7,497	27	16	11
Torrington	33,796	82	73	9
Trumbull	35,632	88	77	11
Vernon	29,379	64	50	14
Wallingford	44,236	95	74	21
Waterbury	107,263	333	287	46
Waterford	18,664	54	49	5
Watertown	21,475	49	40	9
West Hartford	62,911	146	124	22
West Haven	54,516	135	127	8
Weston	10,258	18	17	1
Westport	28,728	77	63	14
Wethersfield	25,936	61	47	14
Willimantic	17,737	49	44	5
Wilton	18,375	46	43	3
Winchester	10,536	25	22	3
Windsor	28,692	58	45	13
Windsor Locks	12,894	35	27	8
Wolcott	16,573	33	25	8
Woodbridge	8,725	31	23	8
DELAWARE				
Bethany Beach	1,268	11	10	1

Table 78. Full-Time Law Enforcement Employees, by Selected State and City, 2020—Continued

(Number.)

State/city	Population	Total law enforcement employees	Total officers	Total civilians
Blades	1,479	3	3	0
Bridgeville	2,409	7	7	0
Camden	3,562	10	9	1
Cheswold	1,718	4	4	0
Clayton	3,577	10	9	1
Dagsboro	943	3	3	0
Delaware City	1,844	4	3	1
Delmar	1,850	13	12	1
Dewey Beach	407	11	9	2
Dover	38,428	123	92	31
Ellendale	442	1	1	0
Elsmere	5,851	12	11	1
Felton	1,429	3	3	0
Fenwick Island	453	7	7	0
Frederica	859	2	2	0
Georgetown	7,698	23	21	2
Greenwood	1,159	4	3	1
Harrington	3,646	11	10	1
Laurel	4,431	19	18	1
Lewes	3,378	12	11	1
Middletown	23,385	45	38	7
Milford	11,994	48	35	13
Millsboro	4,613	18	16	2
Milton	3,066	9	8	1
Newark	33,752	90	73	17
New Castle	5,420	18	17	1
Newport	1,035	6	6	0
Ocean View	2,231	12	11	1
Rehoboth Beach	1,573	29	18	11
Seaford	8,145	35	28	7
Selbyville	2,585	9	8	1
Smyrna	12,011	33	25	8
South Bethany	540	6	6	0
Wilmington	70,100	349	293	56
Wyoming	1,577	3	3	0
DISTRICT OF COLUMBIA				
Washington	712,816	4,466	3,766	700
FLORIDA				
Alachua	9,998	37	28	9
Altamonte Springs	44,440	112	95	17
Apopka	54,842	139	104	35
Arcadia	8,392	22	18	4
Atlantic Beach	14,012	39	26	13
Atlantis	2,144	16	11	5
Auburndale	17,046	45	37	8
Aventura	37,114	124	88	36
Bal Harbour Village	2,992	36	24	12
Bartow	20,507	55	35	20
Bay Harbor Islands	5,821	25	21	4
Belleair	4,297	17	15	2
Belle Isle	7,392	20	18	2
Belleview	5,168	17	15	2
Biscayne Park	3,063	10	10	0
Blountstown	2,435	20	14	6
Boca Raton	101,583	314	214	100
Bonifay	2,698	6	5	1
Bowling Green	2,882	6	6	0
Boynton Beach	79,913	194	134	60
Bradenton	60,688	152	119	33
Bradenton Beach	1,292	10	10	0
Cape Coral	199,503	337	255	82
Casselberry	29,080	63	53	10
Cedar Key	719	3	3	0
Chiefland	2,181	14	12	2
Clearwater	117,859	336	237	99
Clermont	39,932	87	80	7
Clewiston	8,125	22	16	6
Cocoa	18,769	93	62	31
Cocoa Beach	11,763	58	39	19
Coconut Creek	62,220	140	105	35
Coral Gables	50,017	268	178	90
Coral Springs	135,027	307	216	91
Crestview	25,787	43	38	5
Cross City	1,711	5	5	0
Dade City	7,444	31	23	8
Davenport	6,516	15	14	1
Davie	107,988	262	186	76
Daytona Beach	70,084	287	231	56
Daytona Beach Shores	4,656	38	29	9
DeFuniak Springs	7,200	27	20	7
DeLand	35,874	75	58	17
Delray Beach	70,487	235	162	73
Doral	68,425	196	145	51

Table 78. Full-Time Law Enforcement Employees, by Selected State and City, 2020—Continued

(Number.)

State/city	Population	Total law enforcement employees	Total officers	Total civilians
Dunnellon	1,852	10	9	1
Eatonville	2,223	14	12	2
Edgewater	24,166	37	31	6
El Portal	2,397	9	9	0
Eustis	21,642	51	37	14
Fernandina Beach	13,383	40	35	5
Flagler Beach	5,195	18	15	3
Florida City	11,826	44	34	10
Fort Lauderdale	184,347	674	517	157
Fort Myers	90,380	310	233	77
Fort Pierce	46,574	143	114	29
Fort Walton Beach	22,871	61	50	11
Fruitland Park	12,021	21	20	1
Gainesville	135,076	367	268	99
Golden Beach	934	27	19	8
Graceville	2,109	9	9	0
Green Cove Springs	8,783	28	21	7
Groveland	17,622	52	37	15
Gulf Breeze	7,037	29	20	9
Gulfport	12,378	34	30	4
Gulf Stream	995	13	13	0
Haines City	26,719	68	54	14
Havana	1,703	14	10	4
Hialeah	234,235	350	277	73
Hialeah Gardens	23,667	61	43	18
Hillsboro Beach	2,027	19	15	4
Holly Hill	12,440	25	21	4
Hollywood	156,434	407	319	88
Holmes Beach	4,360	23	17	6
Homestead	70,538	146	113	33
Howey-in-the-Hills	1,191	6	6	0
Indialantic	2,929	18	12	6
Indian Creek Village	89	13	9	4
Indian Harbour Beach	8,602	28	20	8
Indian River Shores	4,363	26	22	4
Indian Shores	3,787	13	12	1
Interlachen	1,471	3	3	0
Jacksonville	920,508	3,078	1,789	1,289
Jacksonville Beach	23,894	86	67	19
Jasper	4,127	6	6	0
Jay	646	8	7	1
Juno Beach	3,710	15	13	2
Jupiter	67,054	140	111	29
Jupiter Inlet Colony	459	4	4	0
Jupiter Island	942	23	18	5
Kenneth City	5,131	15	14	1
Key Biscayne	12,898	47	36	11
Key Colony Beach	804	4	4	0
Kissimmee	74,337	226	148	78
Lady Lake	16,255	33	28	5
Lake Alfred	6,425	18	13	5
Lake City	12,403	53	38	15
Lake Clarke Shores	3,653	11	10	1
Lake Hamilton	1,530	9	7	2
Lake Helen	2,822	7	6	1
Lakeland	113,876	351	239	112
Lake Mary	17,947	54	46	8
Lake Placid	2,498	10	8	2
Lake Wales	17,075	52	45	7
Lantana	12,825	37	30	7
Largo	85,594	164	133	31
Lauderhill	72,421	145	114	31
Lawtey	725	3	3	0
Leesburg	24,063	88	64	24
Lighthouse Point	11,373	40	32	8
Live Oak	6,985	22	19	3
Longboat Key	7,342	21	18	3
Longwood	15,793	48	43	5
Lynn Haven	20,733	50	37	13
Madison	2,735	16	15	1
Maitland	17,863	61	53	8
Manalapan	473	16	14	2
Marco Island	18,121	36	32	4
Margate	59,449	147	113	34
Marianna	5,644	21	16	5
Mascotte	6,468	14	12	2
Medley	888	54	40	14
Melbourne	83,806	221	145	76
Melbourne Beach	3,321	11	10	1
Melbourne Village	698	4	4	0
Miami	476,102	1,737	1,317	420
Miami Beach	89,017	500	416	84
Miami Gardens	110,284	261	212	49
Miami Shores	10,358	46	39	7
Miami Springs	13,925	57	46	11

Table 78. Full-Time Law Enforcement Employees, by Selected State and City, 2020—Continued

(Number.)

State/city	Population	Total law enforcement employees	Total officers	Total civilians
Midway	2,995	5	4	1
Milton	10,728	27	20	7
Miramar	143,470	283	203	80
Monticello	2,397	14	8	6
Mount Dora	14,801	63	47	16
Naples	22,388	101	68	33
Neptune Beach	7,285	30	22	8
New Port Richey	16,954	58	42	16
New Smyrna Beach	28,380	60	45	15
Niceville	16,345	37	29	8
North Bay Village	8,165	35	26	9
North Miami	63,109	149	118	31
North Miami Beach	43,273	137	104	33
North Palm Beach	13,255	37	32	5
North Port	72,389	158	121	37
Oakland	3,193	13	12	1
Ocala	61,275	290	187	103
Ocean Ridge	1,976	23	18	5
Ocoee	49,877	110	87	23
Okeechobee	5,833	30	22	8
Opa Locka	15,962	52	44	8
Orange City	12,454	30	26	4
Orange Park	8,864	35	26	9
Orlando	293,363	1,074	806	268
Ormond Beach	44,271	85	65	20
Oviedo	42,903	77	71	6
Palatka	10,436	35	32	3
Palm Bay	116,897	212	151	61
Palm Beach	8,891	94	65	29
Palm Beach Gardens	58,629	178	122	56
Palmetto	13,873	48	34	14
Palm Springs	25,451	61	43	18
Panama City	34,672	120	85	35
Panama City Beach	12,703	87	67	20
Parker	4,241	11	10	1
Pembroke Pines	175,757	331	235	96
Pensacola	53,083	180	134	46
Perry	6,865	22	20	2
Pinellas Park	54,114	125	108	17
Plantation	95,669	253	164	89
Plant City	40,330	83	66	17
Ponce Inlet	3,340	14	12	2
Port Orange	65,828	109	83	26
Port Richey	2,963	22	15	7
Port St. Lucie	206,450	310	242	68
Punta Gorda	20,766	55	37	18
Quincy	6,707	36	25	11
Riviera Beach	35,798	151	110	41
Rockledge	28,614	66	50	16
Sanford	62,342	155	139	16
Sanibel	7,511	36	23	13
Sarasota	59,002	224	175	49
Satellite Beach	11,252	34	24	10
Sea Ranch Lakes	626	11	7	4
Sebastian	26,626	57	41	16
Sebring	10,664	39	33	6
Sewall's Point	2,252	10	9	1
Shalimar	850	5	4	1
Sneads	1,771	7	6	1
South Daytona	13,176	33	27	6
South Miami	11,933	57	50	7
Springfield	8,542	28	24	4
Starke	5,415	18	16	2
St. Augustine Beach	7,101	22	20	2
St. Cloud	56,828	137	93	44
St. Petersburg	267,690	776	557	219
Stuart	16,347	61	45	16
Sunny Isles Beach	21,907	65	52	13
Sunrise	96,428	236	181	55
Surfside	5,659	37	31	6
Sweetwater	21,109	57	51	6
Tallahassee	196,012	459	366	93
Tampa	407,350	1,181	926	255
Tavares	18,221	32	29	3
Temple Terrace	26,890	68	51	17
Tequesta	6,193	20	19	1
Titusville	46,919	129	86	43
Treasure Island	6,946	23	19	4
Trenton	2,179	3	2	1
Umatilla	3,910	9	8	1
Valparaiso	5,449	17	12	5
Venice	24,366	68	50	18
Vero Beach	17,776	76	57	19
Village of Pinecrest	19,255	69	47	22
Virginia Gardens	2,380	8	7	1

Table 78. Full-Time Law Enforcement Employees, by Selected State and City, 2020—Continued

(Number.)

State/city	Population	Total law enforcement employees	Total officers	Total civilians
Wauchula	4,773	18	15	3
Welaka	718	1	1	0
West Melbourne	25,020	57	51	6
West Miami	9,154	26	21	5
West Palm Beach	113,268	390	292	98
White Springs	765	2	2	0
Wildwood	7,568	40	36	4
Wilton Manors	12,885	47	33	14
Winter Garden	47,484	104	77	27
Winter Haven	46,275	113	81	32
Winter Park	31,183	103	74	29
Winter Springs	37,788	64	50	14
Zephyrhills	16,772	51	36	15
GEORGIA				
Abbeville	2,654	7	6	1
Acworth	23,085	67	48	19
Adairsville	4,998	18	16	2
Alamo	3,340	4	4	0
Alapaha	676	2	1	1
Albany	71,567	196	162	34
Alma	3,370	17	15	2
Alpharetta	68,326	120	108	12
Alto	1,200	5	2	3
Americus	14,910	41	32	9
Aragon	1,344	9	4	5
Arcade	1,991	3	3	0
Athens-Clarke County	128,152	273	215	58
Atlanta	515,945	2,015	1,548	467
Attapulgus	423	2	1	1
Auburn	7,730	20	16	4
Austell	7,245	33	23	10
Avondale Estates	3,149	15	15	0
Bainbridge	12,006	50	37	13
Ball Ground	2,290	5	5	0
Barnesville	6,653	18	18	0
Bartow	246	1	1	0
Baxley	4,655	12	11	1
Blackshear	3,535	20	17	3
Blairsville	646	8	7	1
Blakely	4,521	16	14	2
Bloomingdale	2,691	17	15	2
Blue Ridge	1,474	8	8	0
Blythe	709	3	3	0
Boston	1,317	5	5	0
Bowdon	2,107	8	7	1
Braselton	13,758	19	18	1
Braswell	384	2	1	1
Bremen	6,685	21	19	2
Brookhaven	56,248	86	72	14
Brooklet	1,870	5	4	1
Brunswick	16,365	61	56	5
Buchanan	1,184	9	8	1
Buena Vista	2,037	4	4	0
Butler	1,739	7	7	0
Byron	5,304	28	25	3
Cairo	9,340	26	23	3
Calhoun	17,387	52	44	8
Camilla	4,981	21	18	3
Canon	790	1	1	0
Canton	31,416	61	53	8
Carrollton	27,609	85	70	15
Cartersville	21,995	57	47	10
Cave Spring	1,061	3	3	0
Cecil	283	3	2	1
Cedartown	10,020	36	32	4
Centerville	7,960	20	17	3
Chamblee	30,716	77	63	14
Chatsworth	4,290	18	17	1
Chickamauga	3,258	7	7	0
Clarkston	12,697	15	15	0
Claxton	2,185	15	10	5
Cleveland	4,251	17	16	1
Cochran	4,984	12	11	1
Cohutta	637	4	4	0
College Park	15,204	109	82	27
Columbus	195,998	487	386	101
Conyers	16,368	83	61	22
Coolidge	529	3	3	0
Cordele	10,451	27	18	9
Cornelia	4,741	20	18	2
Covington	14,330	61	48	13
Cumming	6,669	22	20	2
Dallas	14,280	34	24	10
Dalton	33,723	99	86	13

Table 78. Full-Time Law Enforcement Employees, by Selected State and City, 2020—Continued

(Number.)

State/city	Population	Total law enforcement employees	Total officers	Total civilians
Darien	1,920	10	10	0
Dawson	4,073	14	8	6
Decatur	26,473	59	47	12
Demorest	2,157	11	7	4
Dillard	378	4	3	1
Doerun	732	5	4	1
Donalsonville	2,445	10	9	1
Doraville	10,329	57	40	17
Douglas	11,696	39	34	5
Douglasville	34,409	110	95	15
Dublin	15,849	71	59	12
Duluth	29,946	74	57	17
Dunwoody	49,687	74	61	13
East Ellijay	571	7	7	0
Eastman	5,018	16	14	2
Eatonton	6,753	23	16	7
Edison	1,380	5	4	1
Elberton	4,303	25	23	2
Ellaville	1,872	4	4	0
Ellijay	1,725	12	11	1
Emerson	1,610	9	8	1
Enigma	1,352	6	4	2
Eton	903	4	4	0
Euharlee	4,393	12	11	1
Fairburn	17,220	54	43	11
Fayetteville	18,202	62	54	8
Fitzgerald	8,611	32	24	8
Flowery Branch	8,671	18	16	2
Folkston	5,072	7	7	0
Forest Park	20,202	85	64	21
Forsyth	4,160	20	18	2
Fort Oglethorpe	10,072	29	26	3
Fort Valley	8,877	35	23	12
Franklin	968	8	8	0
Franklin Springs	1,222	2	2	0
Gainesville	44,398	117	101	16
Garden City	8,716	42	35	7
Glennville	5,004	11	9	2
Gordon	1,841	11	6	5
Grantville	3,322	14	13	1
Gray	3,273	14	13	1
Greensboro	3,299	20	16	4
Greenville	842	8	6	2
Griffin	22,773	81	72	9
Grovetown	15,650	31	22	9
Guyton	2,297	5	5	0
Hagan	962	4	3	1
Hahira	3,060	11	9	2
Hampton	8,201	20	18	2
Hartwell	4,445	27	22	5
Hazlehurst	4,126	13	11	2
Helen	565	12	11	1
Hephzibah	3,933	7	7	0
Hiawassee	916	5	5	0
Hinesville	33,316	95	82	13
Hiram	4,301	20	17	3
Hogansville	3,138	20	15	5
Holly Springs	16,345	39	38	1
Homeland	943	7	7	0
Homerville	2,340	10	8	2
Irwinton	552	2	2	0
Jackson	5,259	15	13	2
Jacksonville	132	1	1	0
Jasper	4,009	19	17	2
Jefferson	12,349	26	24	2
Jesup	9,807	33	31	2
Johns Creek	85,408	86	77	9
Jonesboro	4,994	32	20	12
Kennesaw	34,481	69	59	10
Kingston	684	2	1	1
LaGrange	30,406	105	86	19
Lake City	2,855	17	15	2
Lakeland	3,273	11	9	2
Lavonia	2,204	14	14	0
Lawrenceville	31,256	92	68	24
Leesburg	3,073	13	13	0
Leslie	367	4	3	1
Lilburn	12,941	34	29	5
Lithonia	2,374	7	6	1
Locust Grove	8,575	29	26	3
Loganville	13,187	34	32	2
Lookout Mountain	1,571	7	7	0
Louisville	2,187	6	6	0
Ludowici	2,355	10	6	4
Lyons	4,218	20	16	4

Table 78. Full-Time Law Enforcement Employees, by Selected State and City, 2020—Continued

(Number.)

State/city	Population	Total law enforcement employees	Total officers	Total civilians
Madison	4,236	12	11	1
Manchester	3,942	19	14	5
Marietta	61,348	178	132	46
Marshallville	1,206	2	2	0
Maysville	2,135	3	3	0
McDonough	27,338	54	48	6
McIntyre	601	5	5	0
McRae-Helena	8,246	12	11	1
Metter	3,927	13	12	1
Midville	252	1	1	0
Midway	2,059	6	4	2
Milledgeville	18,751	58	41	17
Millen	2,730	11	11	0
Milton	40,368	44	38	6
Monroe	13,761	50	47	3
Montezuma	2,903	12	10	2
Morrow	7,327	24	22	2
Moultrie	14,199	41	37	4
Mount Airy	1,268	5	1	4
Mount Zion	1,825	7	6	1
Nahunta	1,152	4	4	0
Nashville	4,839	17	12	5
Newington	261	1	1	0
Newnan	42,658	101	86	15
Norcross	16,778	60	36	24
Norman Park	961	2	2	0
Oakwood	4,180	21	20	1
Ocilla	3,759	13	13	0
Oglethorpe	1,138	6	5	1
Omega	1,231	6	5	1
Oxford	2,372	4	4	0
Palmetto	4,890	17	14	3
Peachtree City	36,421	69	64	5
Pearson	2,035	6	5	1
Pelham	3,420	13	11	2
Pembroke	2,685	10	9	1
Pendergrass	576	2	2	0
Perry	18,417	49	41	8
Pine Lake	757	4	4	0
Pine Mountain	1,430	11	10	1
Pooler	26,634	65	57	8
Port Wentworth	10,281	39	28	11
Powder Springs	15,971	31	29	2
Remerton	1,074	9	8	1
Richmond Hill	14,437	39	33	6
Rincon	10,525	19	17	2
Ringgold	3,646	9	8	1
Rochelle	1,096	7	5	2
Rockmart	4,458	22	20	2
Rome	36,747	91	81	10
Roswell	95,396	185	138	47
Sandersville	5,346	21	15	6
Sandy Springs	111,219	160	141	19
Smyrna	57,317	140	93	47
Snellville	20,282	57	45	12
Social Circle	4,583	16	15	1
South Fulton	100,658	156	138	18
Sparks	2,010	3	3	0
Sparta	1,213	12	7	5
Springfield	4,281	10	9	1
Stapleton	388	2	2	0
Statesboro	33,498	91	77	14
Stone Mountain	6,332	19	18	1
Summerville	4,215	16	14	2
Suwanee	21,633	51	39	12
Swainsboro	7,577	25	23	2
Sylvania	2,449	11	8	3
Sylvester	5,732	30	25	5
Tallapoosa	3,186	12	10	2
Temple	4,832	16	13	3
Thomaston	8,711	29	25	4
Thunderbolt	2,634	9	7	2
Toccoa	8,312	32	31	1
Tunnel Hill	911	3	3	0
Twin City	1,696	2	2	0
Tybee Island	3,072	38	25	13
Tyrone	7,575	16	16	0
Union City	22,744	65	59	6
Valdosta	56,628	162	138	24
Vidalia	10,398	39	28	11
Villa Rica	16,296	52	43	9
Warner Robins	78,508	156	113	43
Warwick	383	5	3	2
Waycross	13,363	64	51	13
Waynesboro	5,308	30	23	7

Table 78. Full-Time Law Enforcement Employees, by Selected State and City, 2020—Continued

(Number.)

State/city	Population	Total law enforcement employees	Total officers	Total civilians
Winder	18,376	42	34	8
Woodstock	34,252	64	55	9
HAWAII				
Honolulu	966,438	2,516	2,005	511
IDAHO				
Aberdeen	1,975	5	5	0
American Falls	4,298	10	8	2
Ashton	1,042	2	2	0
Bellevue	2,471	2	2	0
Blackfoot	12,036	30	27	3
Boise	231,223	373	288	85
Bonners Ferry	2,652	7	7	0
Buhl	4,544	9	8	1
Caldwell	59,987	89	75	14
Chubbuck	15,773	35	22	13
Coeur d'Alene	53,405	114	92	22
Cottonwood	944	1	1	0
Emmett	7,114	15	14	1
Filer	2,980	5	5	0
Fruitland	5,505	16	12	4
Garden City	12,084	36	28	8
Gooding	3,429	9	7	2
Grangeville	3,246	6	6	0
Hailey	8,778	13	12	1
Heyburn	3,489	8	7	1
Homedale	2,730	6	5	1
Idaho City	470	1	1	0
Idaho Falls	63,457	134	89	45
Jerome	12,120	23	20	3
Kellogg	2,136	8	8	0
Ketchum	2,872	11	10	1
Kimberly	4,146	9	8	1
Lewiston	32,886	68	46	22
McCall	3,677	13	11	2
Meridian	119,203	154	124	30
Middleton	8,877	10	9	1
Montpelier	2,533	4	3	1
Moscow	25,918	41	34	7
Mountain Home	14,597	33	29	4
Nampa	101,411	185	128	57
Orofino	3,088	6	5	1
Osburn	1,557	2	2	0
Parma	2,167	5	5	0
Payette	7,753	16	14	2
Pinehurst	1,627	2	2	0
Pocatello	56,900	128	91	37
Ponderay	1,170	8	7	1
Post Falls	37,317	70	47	23
Preston	5,592	9	8	1
Priest River	1,911	6	5	1
Rathdrum	9,449	18	15	3
Rexburg	29,865	41	32	9
Rigby	4,332	8	7	1
Rupert	5,927	13	12	1
Salmon	3,171	9	9	0
Sandpoint	9,111	24	20	4
Shelley	4,470	8	8	0
Shoshone	1,504	6	6	0
Soda Springs	3,020	7	7	0
Spirit Lake	2,610	7	6	1
St. Anthony	3,552	6	6	0
Sun Valley	1,495	12	11	1
Twin Falls	50,872	94	75	19
Weiser	5,364	13	10	3
Wilder	1,858	4	4	0
ILLINOIS				
Abingdon	3,026	6	6	0
Addison	36,411	127	63	64
Albers	1,130	2	1	1
Algonquin	30,990	51	44	7
Alsip	18,646	44	41	3
Alton	26,027	81	58	23
Amboy	2,301	2	2	0
Antioch	14,141	29	26	3
Arlington Heights	74,706	128	101	27
Ashland	1,176	1	1	0
Assumption	1,055	2	2	0
Aurora	197,709	352	291	61
Aviston	2,153	1	1	0
Bannockburn	1,508	7	7	0
Barrington	10,205	27	23	4
Barrington Hills	4,185	20	16	4

Table 78. Full-Time Law Enforcement Employees, by Selected State and City, 2020—Continued

(Number.)

State/city	Population	Total law enforcement employees	Total officers	Total civilians
Belleville	40,537	93	72	21
Bellwood	18,629	43	39	4
Bensenville	18,009	36	32	4
Bethany	1,227	2	2	0
Bloomingdale	21,746	55	43	12
Bolingbrook	74,665	128	112	16
Bourbonnais	19,551	27	26	1
Bradley	15,251	37	34	3
Bridgeview	16,056	32	32	0
Buffalo Grove	40,380	74	58	16
Burr Ridge	10,782	31	27	4
Cambridge	2,069	1	1	0
Campton Hills	11,092	7	7	0
Carbondale	24,933	73	57	16
Carlinville	5,434	18	13	5
Carlyle	3,174	8	7	1
Carpentersville	37,201	61	57	4
Cary	18,036	26	25	1
Centralia	12,123	32	24	8
Champaign	89,785	134	113	21
Channahon	13,312	29	27	2
Chatham	13,152	21	15	6
Chenoa	3,110	4	4	0
Chicago	2,693,598	13,562	12,727	835
Chicago Heights	29,207	86	74	12
Chicago Ridge	13,885	37	32	5
Chillicothe	6,004	12	12	0
Cicero	80,420	179	154	25
Clarendon Hills	8,787	14	13	1
Collinsville	24,261	61	43	18
Cortland	4,421	6	6	0
Crest Hill	20,328	31	29	2
Crete	7,996	20	18	2
Crystal Lake	39,726	76	67	9
Danville	30,208	74	62	12
Deerfield	18,692	55	41	14
DeKalb	42,710	71	57	14
Des Plaines	58,950	102	89	13
Downers Grove	49,070	84	67	17
Dupo	3,845	8	8	0
Du Quoin	5,624	14	10	4
Dwight	3,955	10	9	1
Earlville	1,575	4	3	1
East Dundee	3,260	13	12	1
East Moline	20,573	38	35	3
Edwardsville	25,327	59	44	15
Effingham	12,531	40	25	15
Elburn	6,043	9	8	1
Elgin	111,127	238	184	54
Elk Grove Village	32,290	97	83	14
Elmhurst	47,034	87	66	21
Elmwood Park	24,011	41	35	6
Elwood	2,220	11	10	1
Evanston	73,352	168	119	49
Evergreen Park	19,070	74	56	18
Fairfield	4,914	13	9	4
Fairview Heights	16,217	49	45	4
Farmer City	1,927	5	5	0
Farmington	2,200	6	6	0
Flora	4,829	18	12	6
Flossmoor	9,123	25	20	5
Fox Lake	10,426	33	28	5
Frankfort	19,551	36	33	3
Freeport	23,583	56	39	17
Galena	3,131	11	10	1
Geneva	21,831	44	35	9
Genoa	5,244	7	6	1
Gibson City	3,214	8	7	1
Glencoe	8,837	42	36	6
Glendale Heights	33,539	68	50	18
Glen Ellyn	27,704	47	39	8
Glenwood	8,685	26	23	3
Golf	493	1	1	0
Granite City	27,982	70	57	13
Greenfield	979	2	2	0
Gurnee	30,281	96	62	34
Hanover Park	37,350	81	58	23
Havana	2,954	14	9	5
Henning	232	1	1	0
Herscher	1,494	3	3	0
Hickory Hills	13,672	38	27	11
Highland	9,819	26	19	7
Hillside	7,902	33	24	9
Hinckley	2,048	3	3	0
Hodgkins	1,979	23	21	2

Table 78. Full-Time Law Enforcement Employees, by Selected State and City, 2020—Continued

(Number.)

State/city	Population	Total law enforcement employees	Total officers	Total civilians
Homewood	18,636	43	38	5
Hoopeston	4,972	19	10	9
Hopedale	820	1	1	0
Huntley	27,566	41	36	5
Island Lake	8,014	14	13	1
Itasca	9,944	23	20	3
Jacksonville	18,515	37	33	4
Joliet	147,324	317	254	63
Kankakee	25,863	66	62	4
Kenilworth	2,471	9	8	1
Kingston	1,170	2	2	0
Kirkland	1,727	2	2	0
La Grange	15,295	29	25	4
Lake Bluff	5,548	16	14	2
Lake Forest	19,452	43	37	6
Lake in the Hills	28,598	47	39	8
Lake Zurich	19,895	47	30	17
Lansing	27,297	73	56	17
Lemont	17,432	27	22	5
Lincoln	13,417	29	27	2
Lincolnshire	7,962	27	25	2
Lindenhurst	14,174	14	12	2
Lisle	23,351	48	37	11
Litchfield	6,668	16	15	1
Lombard	44,392	74	62	12
Loves Park	23,303	39	37	2
Lovington	1,016	2	2	0
Lyons	10,332	19	16	3
Mackinaw	1,878	3	3	0
Manteno	8,980	20	19	1
Maple Park	1,371	1	1	0
Marissa	1,788	4	3	1
Markham	12,289	33	31	2
Marseilles	4,804	10	9	1
Matteson	19,494	54	36	18
McHenry	27,061	78	46	32
Metropolis	5,881	18	13	5
Midlothian	14,294	32	29	3
Milan	4,969	16	15	1
Milledgeville	943	2	2	0
Minier	1,183	2	2	0
Moline	41,128	87	81	6
Monee	5,054	16	15	1
Montgomery	19,783	36	32	4
Monticello	5,532	9	7	2
Morris	15,216	31	27	4
Morrison	3,966	8	8	0
Morton	16,267	22	18	4
Mount Carmel	6,971	17	12	5
Mount Pulaski	1,454	2	2	0
Mount Zion	5,788	12	10	2
Mundelein	31,053	79	51	28
Murphysboro	7,345	23	15	8
Naperville	149,137	264	174	90
Neoga	1,598	3	3	0
New Athens	1,865	4	4	0
New Lenox	27,230	43	37	6
Niles	28,839	69	55	14
Normal	54,677	89	81	8
North Pekin	1,540	6	6	0
North Riverside	6,402	25	23	2
Oak Brook	8,029	49	41	8
Oakbrook Terrace	2,097	25	21	4
Oak Park	52,435	134	109	25
Oakwood Hills	2,023	4	3	1
O'Fallon	29,672	63	47	16
Orion	1,791	2	2	0
Orland Park	57,993	128	98	30
Oswego	36,934	60	49	11
Ottawa	17,983	52	36	16
Palatine	67,358	139	106	33
Palestine	1,263	2	2	0
Palos Heights	12,520	30	27	3
Palos Hills	17,013	33	30	3
Palos Park	4,723	11	10	1
Pana	5,327	13	8	5
Park Ridge	36,888	68	54	14
Pawnee	2,628	3	3	0
Pekin	31,834	61	53	8
Peoria	109,924	224	203	21
Peoria Heights	5,748	16	14	2
Petersburg	2,202	5	5	0
Plano	11,755	25	23	2
Polo	2,153	5	5	0
Pontiac	11,184	21	19	2

Table 78. Full-Time Law Enforcement Employees, by Selected State and City, 2020—Continued

(Number.)

State/city	Population	Total law enforcement employees	Total officers	Total civilians
Princeton	7,420	18	16	2
Prophetstown	1,924	4	4	0
Prospect Heights	15,845	26	22	4
Richmond	1,908	5	5	0
River Forest	10,776	29	27	2
River Grove	9,843	30	26	4
Riverton	3,430	10	10	0
Riverwoods	3,550	7	7	0
Rochelle	8,998	30	21	9
Rochester	3,709	9	9	0
Rockdale	1,901	6	6	0
Rockford	144,795	332	289	43
Rock Island	36,981	99	75	24
Round Lake	18,069	29	26	3
Roxana	1,423	5	4	1
Salem	6,921	24	17	7
San Jose	589	2	2	0
Savanna	2,769	7	7	0
Shiloh	13,701	21	20	1
Silvis	7,470	20	17	3
Skokie	62,462	151	109	42
South Barrington	5,044	22	19	3
South Beloit	7,594	14	13	1
South Elgin	25,084	39	35	4
South Holland	21,218	49	46	3
Springfield	113,912	257	229	28
Spring Grove	5,698	8	7	1
Spring Valley	5,081	12	11	1
St. Charles	32,949	67	57	10
St. Elmo	1,397	3	3	0
Sterling	14,361	34	27	7
Streator	13,019	26	22	4
Sumner	2,959	2	2	0
Sycamore	18,413	30	28	2
Taylorville	10,264	20	20	0
Thayer	651	1	1	0
Trenton	2,576	5	5	0
University Park	6,861	18	16	2
Urbana	42,211	70	58	12
Vandalia	6,647	12	12	0
Vernon Hills	26,693	65	40	25
Villa Park	21,421	45	36	9
Waterloo	10,645	19	18	1
Watseka	4,713	12	11	1
Wauconda	13,488	27	25	2
Waukegan	85,739	188	146	42
West Chicago	26,768	46	41	5
West Dundee	8,215	20	18	2
Westmont	24,416	40	35	5
Wheaton	52,706	83	68	15
Wheeling	38,753	84	55	29
White Hall	2,309	10	6	4
Willow Springs	5,606	10	9	1
Winfield	9,693	19	16	3
Winnetka	12,328	32	26	6
Wood Dale	13,588	43	34	9
Woodstock	25,283	42	39	3
Worth	10,430	27	25	2
Yorkville	21,052	33	30	3
INDIANA				
Anderson	54,623	113	95	18
Angola	8,748	23	19	4
Auburn	13,560	26	23	3
Austin	4,100	9	9	0
Bargersville	8,342	13	12	1
Bedford	13,192	39	31	8
Bluffton	10,173	32	20	12
Brownsburg	27,621	57	51	6
Carmel	103,100	153	128	25
Cedar Lake	13,372	20	18	2
Chesterton	14,203	26	22	4
Columbus	48,505	22	21	1
Crawfordsville	16,137	45	40	5
Cumberland	6,097	18	16	2
Danville	10,247	20	18	2
Dyer	15,932	35	32	3
Edinburgh	4,603	13	12	1
Ellettsville	6,804	12	11	1
Elwood	8,372	18	17	1
Evansville	117,747	310	283	27
Fairmount	2,749	7	6	1
Fort Wayne	272,270	538	474	64
Franklin	25,825	60	54	6
Gas City	5,732	11	11	0

Table 78. Full-Time Law Enforcement Employees, by Selected State and City, 2020—Continued

(Number.)

State/city	Population	Total law enforcement employees	Total officers	Total civilians
Goshen	34,409	72	64	8
Greenfield	23,273	45	41	4
Greenwood	60,460	71	63	8
Hammond	74,966	241	204	37
Hartford City	5,606	11	10	1
Highland	22,165	43	37	6
Hobart	27,791	78	67	11
Huntingburg	6,182	15	14	1
Huntington	17,096	36	33	3
Indianapolis	890,672	2,656	2,086	570
Jasper	15,790	31	23	8
Kendallville	9,897	28	19	9
Lafayette	72,040	184	132	52
La Porte	21,515	46	42	4
Lawrence	49,865	81	61	20
Lebanon	16,097	42	40	2
Linton	5,179	15	9	6
Mount Vernon	6,471	15	15	0
Muncie	67,760	109	95	14
Munster	22,357	46	41	5
Nappanee	6,864	21	18	3
New Haven	16,044	31	23	8
New Palestine	2,615	7	7	0
New Whiteland	6,332	8	7	1
Noblesville	66,127	99	89	10
North Webster	1,170	5	5	0
Pittsboro	3,698	9	8	1
Plainfield	36,239	65	59	6
Porter	4,832	14	11	3
Richmond	35,192	82	72	10
Roseland	636	4	3	1
Schererville	28,454	67	52	15
Shelbyville	19,451	58	45	13
Shirley	892	2	2	0
South Bend	102,119	272	224	48
Speedway	12,235	50	35	15
St. John	19,289	25	23	2
Terre Haute	60,604	141	132	9
Valparaiso	34,139	63	57	6
Walkerton	2,269	10	6	4
Washington	12,612	28	21	7
West Lafayette	52,104	65	46	19
Winchester	4,634	13	13	0
Zionsville	28,824	37	35	2
IOWA				
Ackley	1,488	2	2	0
Adel	5,696	12	11	1
Albia	3,670	7	6	1
Algona	5,380	14	10	4
Altoona	19,804	37	35	2
Ames	67,109	79	55	24
Anamosa	5,536	9	8	1
Ankeny	70,301	72	62	10
Asbury	5,909	5	5	0
Atlantic	6,465	13	12	1
Audubon	1,871	4	4	0
Belle Plaine	2,430	5	5	0
Belmond	2,252	5	5	0
Bettendorf	36,926	51	45	6
Bloomfield	2,683	6	5	1
Blue Grass	1,686	4	3	1
Boone	12,355	18	17	1
Burlington	24,622	50	44	6
Camanche	4,356	9	9	0
Carlisle	4,341	9	8	1
Carroll	9,800	16	15	1
Carter Lake	3,784	11	10	1
Cedar Falls	40,675	67	66	1
Cedar Rapids	134,330	282	219	63
Centerville	5,425	17	10	7
Charles City	7,269	21	14	7
Cherokee	4,826	7	6	1
Clarinda	5,343	9	8	1
Clarion	2,695	6	6	0
Clear Lake	7,526	22	15	7
Clinton	24,905	53	47	6
Clive	17,447	33	29	4
Colfax	2,061	4	4	0
Coralville	22,699	37	33	4
Council Bluffs	62,144	134	115	19
Creston	7,701	16	12	4
Davenport	101,806	189	167	22
Dayton	769	1	1	0
Decorah	7,516	14	13	1

Table 78. Full-Time Law Enforcement Employees, by Selected State and City, 2020—Continued

(Number.)

State/city	Population	Total law enforcement employees	Total officers	Total civilians
Denison	8,234	20	13	7
Des Moines	215,290	464	367	97
DeWitt	5,178	11	10	1
Dubuque	57,904	110	102	8
Durant	1,864	4	4	0
Dyersville	4,357	7	7	0
Dysart	1,307	2	2	0
Eagle Grove	3,388	5	5	0
Eldora	2,599	5	5	0
Eldridge	6,991	10	9	1
Emmetsburg	3,661	7	6	1
Estherville	5,595	11	11	0
Evansdale	4,742	8	7	1
Fairfield	10,538	20	13	7
Forest City	4,013	9	8	1
Fort Dodge	23,755	44	40	4
Fort Madison	10,239	19	17	2
Glenwood	5,402	11	10	1
Gowrie	944	1	1	0
Grinnell	9,104	13	11	2
Grundy Center	2,666	5	5	0
Hampton	4,176	8	7	1
Harlan	4,732	9	8	1
Hawarden	2,434	4	4	0
Hiawatha	7,465	16	16	0
Humboldt	4,577	6	6	0
Huxley	4,124	6	6	0
Independence	6,141	11	9	2
Indianola	16,154	24	21	3
Iowa City	75,964	103	81	22
Iowa Falls	5,034	14	10	4
Jefferson	4,075	7	7	0
Johnston	23,252	35	30	5
Keokuk	10,091	27	23	4
Knoxville	7,155	15	13	2
Lake City	1,633	3	3	0
Lansing	928	3	3	0
Le Claire	3,990	8	7	1
Le Mars	10,110	17	15	2
Leon	1,808	3	3	0
Lisbon	2,259	2	2	0
Manchester	4,965	16	10	6
Maquoketa	5,966	18	11	7
Marengo	2,460	3	3	0
Marion	40,968	60	46	14
Marshalltown	26,564	42	37	5
Mason City	26,811	45	39	6
Mechanicsville	1,127	1	1	0
Monticello	3,891	8	7	1
Mount Pleasant	8,670	16	14	2
Mount Vernon	4,463	7	6	1
Muscatine	23,616	43	39	4
Nevada	6,662	11	9	2
New Hampton	3,389	6	6	0
Newton	15,176	32	27	5
North Liberty	20,294	24	22	2
Norwalk	12,313	20	19	1
Oelwein	5,846	14	10	4
Ogden	1,972	2	2	0
Onawa	2,739	5	5	0
Orange City	6,195	7	7	0
Osage	3,548	7	6	1
Osceola	5,275	12	11	1
Oskaloosa	11,505	16	14	2
Ottumwa	24,293	50	38	12
Pella	10,225	24	18	6
Perry	7,669	19	12	7
Pleasant Hill	10,158	22	20	2
Polk City	5,165	7	7	0
Postville	2,034	4	4	0
Prairie City	1,723	2	2	0
Princeton	953	1	1	0
Red Oak	5,230	12	10	2
Rock Valley	3,899	6	6	0
Sac City	2,051	4	4	0
Sergeant Bluff	5,226	9	8	1
Sheldon	5,069	6	6	0
Shenandoah	4,786	10	9	1
Sigourney	2,013	2	1	1
Sioux Center	7,669	8	8	0
Sioux City	82,628	150	125	25
Spencer	10,922	30	20	10
Spirit Lake	5,189	11	10	1
State Center	1,432	2	2	0
Storm Lake	10,282	24	20	4

Table 78. Full-Time Law Enforcement Employees, by Selected State and City, 2020—Continued

(Number.)

State/city	Population	Total law enforcement employees	Total officers	Total civilians
Story City	3,307	5	5	0
Tama	2,717	6	6	0
Tipton	3,224	7	6	1
Toledo	2,123	6	6	0
University Heights	1,025	5	5	0
Urbandale	44,959	60	51	9
Van Meter	1,324	2	2	0
Vinton	5,056	10	9	1
Walcott	1,636	3	3	0
Washington	7,227	12	11	1
Waterloo	67,200	128	119	9
Waukee	25,590	30	26	4
Waukon	3,594	5	4	1
Waverly	10,234	15	14	1
Webster City	7,630	19	12	7
West Branch	2,510	4	4	0
West Burlington	2,878	10	10	0
West Des Moines	69,252	102	89	13
West Liberty	3,768	6	6	0
Williamsburg	3,175	7	7	0
Wilton	2,828	4	4	0
Windsor Heights	4,798	13	12	1
Winterset	5,403	8	8	0
KANSAS				
Abilene	6,133	17	14	3
Altamont	1,012	3	3	0
Andover	13,592	34	26	8
Anthony	2,051	4	3	1
Arkansas City	11,589	31	27	4
Arma	1,413	5	5	0
Atchison	10,421	25	24	1
Attica	550	1	1	0
Augusta	9,339	32	25	7
Baldwin City	4,720	13	11	2
Basehor	6,742	17	15	2
Baxter Springs	3,915	9	8	1
Bel Aire	8,490	11	10	1
Belle Plaine	1,543	5	5	0
Beloit	3,604	8	7	1
Benton	869	2	2	0
Blue Rapids	955	2	2	0
Bonner Springs	7,955	26	23	3
Buhler	1,272	3	3	0
Burden	525	2	2	0
Burlingame	898	2	2	0
Burlington	2,530	9	7	2
Burrton	855	2	2	0
Caldwell	978	3	3	0
Caney	1,943	11	6	5
Canton	689	1	1	0
Carbondale	1,362	3	3	0
Cedar Vale	501	1	1	0
Chanute	9,034	20	18	2
Chapman	1,332	3	3	0
Chase	434	1	1	0
Cheney	2,174	6	6	0
Cherokee	708	1	1	0
Cherryvale	2,114	6	5	1
Chetopa	1,007	4	4	0
Claflin	596	1	1	0
Clay Center	3,944	8	7	1
Clearwater	2,559	7	6	1
Coffeyville	9,171	32	24	8
Colby	5,365	19	13	6
Coldwater	727	1	1	0
Columbus	3,025	9	8	1
Colwich	1,483	3	3	0
Conway Springs	1,212	4	4	0
Council Grove	2,112	8	7	1
Derby	25,229	57	48	9
Dodge City	27,066	54	42	12
Eastborough	729	6	6	0
Edwardsville	4,503	18	17	1
El Dorado	12,924	23	20	3
Elkhart	1,714	3	3	0
Ellinwood	1,923	5	5	0
Ellis	2,004	4	4	0
Ellsworth	2,943	7	6	1
Elwood	1,188	3	3	0
Emporia	24,564	48	41	7
Eudora	6,440	12	12	0
Fairway	3,970	9	9	0
Fredonia	2,199	7	6	1
Frontenac	3,382	10	7	3

Table 78. Full-Time Law Enforcement Employees, by Selected State and City, 2020—Continued

(Number.)

State/city	Population	Total law enforcement employees	Total officers	Total civilians
Galena	2,832	10	8	2
Galva	876	1	1	0
Garden City	26,360	86	60	26
Gardner	22,370	39	34	5
Garnett	3,216	7	7	0
Girard	2,659	7	6	1
Goddard	4,840	13	12	1
Goodland	4,397	9	8	1
Grandview Plaza	1,503	8	7	1
Great Bend	14,864	34	30	4
Hays	20,769	8	7	1
Haysville	11,395	29	23	6
Herington	2,241	8	7	1
Hesston	3,744	8	7	1
Hiawatha	3,103	11	10	1
Highland	992	1	1	0
Hill City	1,403	4	4	0
Hillsboro	2,796	5	5	0
Hoisington	2,446	7	6	1
Holcomb	2,070	2	1	1
Holton	3,196	6	6	0
Holyrood	411	1	1	0
Hoxie	1,193	2	2	0
Hugoton	3,724	8	6	2
Hutchinson	40,186	96	65	31
Independence	8,405	26	19	7
Inman	1,328	4	4	0
Iola	5,220	18	17	1
Junction City	21,242	69	45	24
Kanopolis	448	1	1	0
Kechi	2,015	5	4	1
Kingman	2,807	7	7	0
Kiowa	921	1	1	0
La Cygne	1,116	2	2	0
Lake Quivira	936	1	1	0
Lansing	12,023	17	16	1
Larned	3,632	6	6	0
Lawrence	99,368	169	143	26
Leavenworth	36,023	72	55	17
Leawood	35,054	81	60	21
Lebo	882	1	1	0
Lenexa	56,508	135	87	48
Liberal	19,028	48	38	10
Lindsborg	3,273	8	7	1
Little River	519	1	1	0
Louisburg	4,590	12	11	1
Lyndon	1,017	1	1	0
Lyons	3,478	7	6	1
Macksville	528	1	1	0
Marion	1,759	5	5	0
Marquette	594	1	1	0
Marysville	3,265	9	8	1
McLouth	845	1	1	0
McPherson	13,053	40	32	8
Meade	1,502	4	3	1
Medicine Lodge	1,816	4	4	0
Merriam	11,087	36	31	5
Minneapolis	1,885	5	5	0
Mission	9,979	30	27	3
Mission Hills	3,555	3	3	0
Moran	505	1	1	0
Mound City	676	1	1	0
Moundridge	1,869	4	4	0
Mount Hope	800	2	2	0
Mulberry	521	1	1	0
Mulvane	6,528	21	14	7
Neodesha	2,239	8	7	1
Newton	18,830	42	38	4
North Newton	1,761	4	4	0
Oakley	2,077	9	5	4
Oberlin	1,691	5	5	0
Olathe	142,228	211	184	27
Osage City	2,795	7	7	0
Oswego	1,663	5	5	0
Ottawa	12,212	28	23	5
Overland Park	198,036	325	257	68
Oxford	994	3	3	0
Paola	5,730	21	15	6
Parsons	9,373	29	21	8
Peabody	1,090	2	2	0
Pleasanton	1,157	3	3	0
Prairie Village	22,390	61	47	14
Pratt	6,460	20	15	5
Roeland Park	6,683	17	15	2
Rose Hill	3,972	9	8	1

Table 78. Full-Time Law Enforcement Employees, by Selected State and City, 2020—Continued

(Number.)

State/city	Population	Total law enforcement employees	Total officers	Total civilians
Russell	4,412	9	8	1
Salina	46,400	108	81	27
Scott City	3,738	13	8	5
Sedgwick	1,654	2	2	0
Seneca	2,083	4	4	0
Shawnee	66,208	109	89	20
Smith Center	1,559	2	2	0
Spearville	785	1	1	0
Spring Hill	7,572	13	12	1
Sterling	2,195	5	5	0
St. George	1,049	2	2	0
St. Marys	2,656	6	6	0
Topeka	125,024	330	285	45
Troy	954	1	1	0
Ulysses	5,546	11	10	1
Valley Center	7,383	18	16	2
WaKeeney	1,751	5	5	0
Wamego	4,769	13	8	5
Wathena	1,287	2	2	0
Wellington	7,608	19	16	3
Wellsville	1,773	6	5	1
Westwood	1,657	8	7	1
Winfield	11,900	27	22	5
Yates Center	1,311	4	4	0
KENTUCKY				
Adairville	883	1	1	0
Alexandria	9,861	21	17	4
Anchorage	2,431	14	10	4
Ashland	19,979	51	48	3
Auburn	1,384	2	2	0
Augusta	1,143	2	2	0
Bancroft	514	1	1	0
Bardstown	13,330	34	31	3
Beattyville	1,212	6	6	0
Beaver Dam	3,578	6	6	0
Bellefonte	816	5	5	0
Bellevue	5,695	12	11	1
Berea	16,311	38	33	5
Bloomfield	1,071	1	1	0
Bowling Green	71,861	159	120	39
Brandenburg	2,898	5	5	0
Burkesville	1,456	10	6	4
Burnside	844	5	5	0
Calvert City	2,497	8	7	1
Carrollton	3,763	15	14	1
Catlettsburg	1,734	7	7	0
Cave City	2,439	9	9	0
Central City	5,703	12	12	0
Clay	1,087	2	2	0
Clay City	1,090	3	3	0
Cloverport	1,152	1	1	0
Coal Run Village	1,501	4	3	1
Cold Spring	6,641	14	14	0
Columbia	4,609	16	15	1
Corbin	7,190	30	24	6
Covington	40,324	121	110	11
Danville	16,826	31	29	2
Dayton	5,639	12	11	1
Eddyville	2,544	3	3	0
Edgewood	8,776	17	17	0
Edmonton	1,593	7	7	0
Elizabethtown	30,505	80	60	20
Elkton	2,127	8	7	1
Elsmere	8,618	15	15	0
Eminence	2,591	6	6	0
Erlanger	23,441	46	44	2
Eubank	331	1	1	0
Falmouth	2,091	8	7	1
Flatwoods	7,041	12	12	0
Florence	33,397	68	66	2
Fort Mitchell	8,249	13	13	0
Fort Thomas	16,273	31	23	8
Fort Wright	5,752	14	14	0
Frankfort	27,803	59	57	2
Franklin	9,072	24	23	1
Georgetown	35,702	82	57	25
Glasgow	14,537	45	37	8
Grayson	3,870	11	10	1
Greenville	4,174	12	11	1
Guthrie	1,408	3	3	0
Hardinsburg	2,338	5	5	0
Harlan	1,480	15	10	5
Harrodsburg	8,553	25	18	7
Hawesville	991	1	1	0

Table 78. Full-Time Law Enforcement Employees, by Selected State and City, 2020—Continued

(Number.)

State/city	Population	Total law enforcement employees	Total officers	Total civilians
Heritage Creek	1,139	11	11	0
Highland Heights	7,069	12	11	1
Hillview	9,311	20	20	0
Hodgenville	3,251	8	8	0
Hopkinsville	30,532	103	69	34
Hustonville	368	1	1	0
Hyden	328	1	1	0
Independence	28,957	36	34	2
Indian Hills	2,978	8	8	0
Irvine	2,279	5	5	0
Jackson	1,913	12	8	4
Jamestown	1,791	4	4	0
Jeffersontown	27,700	67	54	13
Jenkins	1,899	4	4	0
Junction City	2,312	3	3	0
La Grange	9,142	17	15	2
Lakeside Park-Crestview Hills	6,134	13	12	1
Lancaster	3,873	12	12	0
Lawrenceburg	11,565	21	14	7
Lebanon	5,726	25	17	8
Leitchfield	6,880	21	20	1
Lewisburg	803	1	1	0
Lexington	325,851	670	580	90
Louisa	2,313	6	6	0
Louisville Metro	673,730	1,388	1,124	264
Loyall	592	2	2	0
Ludlow	4,499	12	11	1
Madisonville	18,494	59	46	13
Manchester	1,274	11	11	0
Marion	2,821	9	6	3
Martin	547	2	2	0
Mayfield	9,791	26	25	1
Maysville	8,695	36	26	10
Middlesboro	8,968	26	21	5
Middletown	7,910	17	16	1
Millersburg	779	2	2	0
Monticello	5,966	9	9	0
Morehead	7,644	28	19	9
Morganfield	3,350	5	5	0
Mount Sterling	7,268	23	21	2
Mount Washington	14,964	27	25	2
Muldraugh	991	3	3	0
Murray	19,499	48	40	8
Newport	14,874	44	40	4
Nicholasville	31,191	74	67	7
Oak Grove	7,299	16	16	0
Olive Hill	1,548	8	7	1
Owensboro	60,430	125	93	32
Owingsville	1,580	5	5	0
Paducah	24,850	97	69	28
Paintsville	3,964	9	8	1
Park Hills	2,983	8	8	0
Pewee Valley	1,585	1	1	0
Pikeville	6,501	32	23	9
Pineville	1,709	7	7	0
Pioneer Village	2,967	5	5	0
Pippa Passes	671	7	1	6
Powderly	735	3	2	1
Prestonsburg	3,500	18	13	5
Prospect	4,929	8	7	1
Providence	2,979	5	5	0
Radcliff	22,950	45	34	11
Ravenna	554	1	1	0
Richmond	36,691	70	61	9
Russell	3,208	12	12	0
Russell Springs	2,661	10	9	1
Russellville	7,125	25	24	1
Science Hill	696	3	3	0
Scottsville	4,576	26	16	10
Sebree	1,523	1	1	0
Shelbyville	16,863	31	30	1
Shepherdsville	12,567	38	36	2
Shively	15,735	36	30	6
Simpsonville	2,974	10	10	0
Smiths Grove	807	1	1	0
Somerset	11,622	52	47	5
Southgate	4,039	8	8	0
South Shore	1,050	1	1	0
Springfield	2,980	15	8	7
Stamping Ground	819	2	2	0
Stanton	2,701	8	8	0
St. Matthews	18,162	43	37	6
Tompkinsville	2,242	10	7	3
Trenton	374	1	1	0
Vanceburg	1,393	5	5	0

Table 78. Full-Time Law Enforcement Employees, by Selected State and City, 2020—Continued

(Number.)

State/city	Population	Total law enforcement employees	Total officers	Total civilians
Versailles	26,899	35	34	1
Villa Hills	7,478	14	14	0
Vine Grove	6,596	11	11	0
Warsaw	1,705	4	4	0
West Buechel	1,277	11	11	0
West Point	870	3	3	0
Whitesburg	1,813	6	5	1
Wilder	3,058	10	10	0
Williamstown	3,907	7	6	1
Wilmore	6,496	9	8	1
Winchester	18,570	47	31	16
LOUISIANA				
Abbeville	12,018	37	34	3
Alexandria	45,986	159	127	32
Baker	13,122	36	34	2
Basile	1,779	9	8	1
Bastrop	9,889	22	22	0
Bernice	1,583	3	3	0
Berwick	4,365	14	13	1
Bossier City	68,869	200	161	39
Breaux Bridge	8,149	29	26	3
Broussard	13,299	37	33	4
Carencro	9,668	30	28	2
Church Point	4,336	16	16	0
Crowley	12,515	38	32	6
De Ridder	10,583	27	26	1
Dixie Inn	261	2	2	0
Erath	2,031	11	7	4
Eunice	9,751	40	29	11
Gonzales	11,092	48	43	5
Haughton	3,278	14	13	1
Iowa	3,184	18	14	4
Jennings	9,737	27	21	6
Kaplan	4,402	20	14	6
Kinder	2,357	15	11	4
Lafayette	126,679	327	275	52
Lake Charles	79,077	174	140	34
Mansfield	4,587	22	16	6
Marksville	5,299	24	17	7
Minden	11,711	29	28	1
Monroe	47,119	158	123	35
Opelousas	15,820	58	45	13
Patterson	5,758	25	25	0
Pineville	14,079	77	69	8
Plaquemine	6,479	29	20	9
Port Allen	4,695	21	20	1
Rayne	7,997	24	23	1
Rayville	3,450	10	10	0
Ruston	21,846	49	37	12
Scott	8,696	30	28	2
Springhill	4,720	19	14	5
Sterlington	3,135	3	3	0
Sulphur	20,029	65	52	13
Tallulah	6,596	13	7	6
Thibodaux	14,418	62	42	20
Tickfaw	772	5	5	0
Vidalia	3,765	33	25	8
Ville Platte	6,991	24	17	7
Welsh	3,227	14	14	0
Westlake	4,997	17	14	3
West Monroe	12,134	64	49	15
Winnfield	4,201	22	14	8
Youngsville	15,654	34	30	4
MAINE				
Ashland	1,208	3	3	0
Auburn	23,455	59	52	7
Augusta	18,653	56	45	11
Baileyville	1,439	5	5	0
Bangor	32,179	97	81	16
Bar Harbor	7,716	28	20	8
Bath	8,322	24	19	5
Belfast	6,681	17	16	1
Berwick	7,944	13	12	1
Biddeford	21,530	84	57	27
Boothbay Harbor	2,219	9	8	1
Brewer	8,988	23	21	2
Bridgton	5,459	10	9	1
Brunswick	20,566	47	32	15
Bucksport	4,927	13	10	3
Buxton	8,360	14	8	6
Calais	2,993	7	7	0
Camden	4,776	12	11	1
Cape Elizabeth	9,340	15	14	1

Table 78. Full-Time Law Enforcement Employees, by Selected State and City, 2020—Continued

(Number.)

State/city	Population	Total law enforcement employees	Total officers	Total civilians
Caribou	7,532	15	14	1
Carrabassett Valley	788	1	1	0
Clinton	3,340	4	4	0
Cumberland	8,327	14	12	2
Damariscotta	2,144	6	5	1
Dexter	3,687	6	6	0
Dover-Foxcroft	4,018	5	5	0
East Millinocket	2,922	5	5	0
Eastport	1,258	1	1	0
Eliot	6,990	8	7	1
Ellsworth	8,231	22	19	3
Fairfield	6,531	12	12	0
Falmouth	12,444	28	19	9
Farmington	7,764	12	11	1
Fort Fairfield	3,263	2	2	0
Fort Kent	3,831	9	4	5
Freeport	8,637	18	16	2
Fryeburg	3,452	5	5	0
Gardiner	5,639	14	13	1
Gorham	18,167	25	22	3
Gouldsboro	1,742	2	2	0
Greenville	1,599	3	3	0
Hallowell	2,382	5	5	0
Hampden	7,428	11	11	0
Holden	3,106	4	4	0
Houlton	5,713	15	10	5
Islesboro	560	1	1	0
Jay	4,600	8	7	1
Kennebunk	11,719	26	23	3
Kennebunkport	3,671	18	13	5
Kittery	9,855	29	22	7
Lewiston	36,186	93	80	13
Limestone	2,159	3	3	0
Lincoln	4,838	6	5	1
Lisbon	9,004	18	13	5
Livermore Falls	3,154	6	6	0
Machias	2,007	3	3	0
Madawaska	3,704	7	6	1
Mechanic Falls	2,974	6	6	0
Mexico	2,624	5	5	0
Milbridge	1,288	1	1	0
Millinocket	4,226	7	6	1
Milo	2,279	3	3	0
Monmouth	4,139	4	4	0
Newport	3,272	6	6	0
North Berwick	4,744	9	8	1
Norway	4,989	10	9	1
Oakland	6,317	11	10	1
Ogunquit	932	12	11	1
Old Orchard Beach	9,061	25	22	3
Old Town	7,388	16	15	1
Orono	10,851	15	14	1
Oxford	4,095	8	7	1
Paris	5,149	9	8	1
Phippsburg	2,274	1	1	0
Pittsfield	3,971	7	6	1
Portland	66,229	203	148	55
Presque Isle	8,937	19	14	5
Rangeley	1,153	3	3	0
Richmond	3,477	4	4	0
Rockland	7,151	19	17	2
Rockport	3,367	6	6	0
Rumford	5,735	13	12	1
Sabattus	5,054	9	8	1
Saco	20,133	47	31	16
Sanford	21,272	43	39	4
Scarborough	21,237	59	39	20
Searsport	2,635	3	3	0
Skowhegan	8,202	17	16	1
South Berwick	7,605	11	10	1
South Portland	25,593	62	53	9
Southwest Harbor	1,795	8	4	4
Thomaston	2,741	5	5	0
Topsham	8,891	15	14	1
Veazie	1,823	4	4	0
Waldoboro	5,070	7	7	0
Washburn	1,526	2	2	0
Waterville	16,654	41	30	11
Wells	10,803	33	24	9
Westbrook	19,256	43	39	4
Wilton	3,944	4	4	0
Windham	18,720	30	27	3
Winslow	7,599	11	10	1
Winter Harbor	511	1	1	0
Winthrop	5,983	14	9	5

Table 78. Full-Time Law Enforcement Employees, by Selected State and City, 2020—Continued

(Number.)

State/city	Population	Total law enforcement employees	Total officers	Total civilians
Wiscasset	3,767	4	3	1
Yarmouth	8,617	15	14	1
York	13,377	37	26	11
MARYLAND				
Aberdeen	16,140	54	41	13
Annapolis	39,315	146	115	31
Baltimore	588,594	2,940	2,465	475
Baltimore City Sheriff		183	122	61
Bel Air	10,116	41	31	10
Berlin	4,914	19	14	5
Berwyn Heights	3,269	11	10	1
Bladensburg	9,455	34	23	11
Boonsboro	3,677	5	4	1
Bowie	59,008	80	63	17
Brentwood	3,485	4	3	1
Brunswick	6,562	16	16	0
Cambridge	12,239	42	39	3
Capitol Heights	4,537	13	11	2
Centreville	5,026	11	11	0
Chestertown	5,027	12	11	1
Cheverly	6,456	16	13	3
Chevy Chase Village	2,067	17	11	6
Colmar Manor	1,459	5	4	1
Cottage City	1,361	5	4	1
Crisfield	2,548	14	10	4
Cumberland	19,122	63	48	15
Delmar	3,384	13	12	1
Denton	4,525	13	12	1
District Heights	6,010	10	9	1
Edmonston	1,497	6	5	1
Elkton	15,639	45	39	6
Fairmount Heights	1,530	1	1	0
Federalsburg	2,653	10	9	1
Forest Heights	2,574	8	7	1
Frederick	73,042	192	146	46
Frostburg	8,451	21	17	4
Fruitland	5,362	23	20	3
Glenarden	6,177	18	16	2
Greenbelt	23,342	62	47	15
Greensboro	1,874	5	5	0
Hagerstown	40,136	108	91	17
Hampstead	6,410	10	9	1
Havre de Grace	14,132	42	31	11
Hurlock	2,015	11	10	1
Hyattsville	18,305	61	44	17
Landover Hills	1,642	6	5	1
La Plata	9,728	21	20	1
Laurel	25,704	82	64	18
Luke	59	1	1	0
Manchester	4,855	7	6	1
Morningside	1,286	9	8	1
Mount Airy	9,476	10	8	2
Mount Rainier	8,126	19	14	5
New Carrollton	12,990	31	19	12
North East	3,648	11	10	1
Oakland	1,806	2	2	0
Ocean City	6,926	130	104	26
Ocean Pines	11,710	19	15	4
Perryville	4,428	12	11	1
Pocomoke City	4,078	24	17	7
Princess Anne	3,535	12	11	1
Ridgely	1,659	5	5	0
Rising Sun	2,780	5	5	0
Riverdale Park	7,229	30	23	7
Rock Hall	1,270	3	3	0
Salisbury	33,233	111	82	29
Seat Pleasant	4,761	29	24	5
Smithsburg	2,972	4	3	1
Snow Hill	2,043	7	7	0
St. Michaels	1,041	10	9	1
Sykesville	3,960	8	7	1
Takoma Park	17,831	61	40	21
Taneytown	6,824	16	14	2
Thurmont	6,977	15	12	3
University Park	2,639	8	7	1
Upper Marlboro	675	4	3	1
Westminster	18,654	55	45	10
MASSACHUSETTS				
Abington	17,306	33	30	3
Acton	23,728	54	43	11
Acushnet	10,604	24	20	4
Adams	7,959	18	17	1
Agawam	28,533	66	53	13

Table 78. Full-Time Law Enforcement Employees, by Selected State and City, 2020—Continued

(Number.)

State/city	Population	Total law enforcement employees	Total officers	Total civilians
Amesbury	17,578	39	33	6
Amherst	40,061	55	37	18
Andover	36,534	69	50	19
Aquinnah	322	4	4	0
Arlington	45,582	82	68	14
Ashburnham	6,344	16	12	4
Ashby	3,217	8	7	1
Ashfield	1,715	2	2	0
Ashland	17,842	31	25	6
Athol	11,682	26	19	7
Attleboro	45,181	97	82	15
Auburn	16,736	50	38	12
Avon	4,561	20	15	5
Ayer	8,237	30	20	10
Barnstable	44,169	138	111	27
Barre	5,568	10	9	1
Becket	1,709	4	4	0
Bedford	14,135	35	28	7
Belchertown	15,148	26	20	6
Bellingham	17,331	34	26	8
Belmont	26,136	60	47	13
Berkley	6,864	13	13	0
Berlin	3,266	11	10	1
Bernardston	2,086	3	3	0
Beverly	42,229	73	69	4
Billerica	43,473	81	63	18
Blackstone	9,269	22	18	4
Bolton	5,455	13	12	1
Boston	697,323	2,715	2,132	583
Bourne	19,657	51	43	8
Boxborough	5,856	19	13	6
Boxford	8,328	9	9	0
Boylston	4,728	14	10	4
Braintree	37,278	98	82	16
Brewster	9,714	29	24	5
Bridgewater	8,107	45	43	2
Brockton	99,171	211	187	24
Brookfield	3,442	5	5	0
Brookline	59,057	187	137	50
Buckland	1,845	2	2	0
Burlington	28,960	68	61	7
Cambridge	119,938	312	271	41
Canton	24,015	45	45	0
Carlisle	5,267	15	10	5
Carver	12,197	22	17	5
Charlton	13,720	24	18	6
Chatham	5,935	27	21	6
Chelmsford	35,369	62	57	5
Chelsea	39,995	115	107	8
Cheshire	3,118	1	1	0
Chicopee	54,918	125	121	4
Clinton	13,967	36	26	10
Cohasset	8,653	20	19	1
Concord	18,952	42	33	9
Dalton	6,500	9	8	1
Danvers	27,517	57	45	12
Dartmouth	33,986	86	71	15
Dedham	25,217	58	54	4
Deerfield	4,976	10	9	1
Dennis	13,760	51	44	7
Dighton	8,026	15	14	1
Douglas	9,054	18	14	4
Dover	6,176	17	16	1
Dracut	31,708	44	41	3
Dudley	11,745	16	15	1
Dunstable	3,410	9	8	1
Duxbury	16,561	33	31	2
East Bridgewater	15,103	31	22	9
East Brookfield	2,200	4	4	0
Eastham	4,874	23	17	6
Easthampton	15,804	35	29	6
East Longmeadow	16,181	28	25	3
Easton	25,176	46	36	10
Edgartown	4,374	20	19	1
Essex	3,812	11	10	1
Everett	46,765	125	117	8
Fairhaven	16,014	37	31	6
Fall River	89,136	272	221	51
Falmouth	30,769	60	56	4
Fitchburg	40,443	92	77	15
Foxborough	18,539	41	39	2
Framingham	74,680	147	129	18
Franklin	34,281	55	53	2
Freetown	9,401	19	19	0
Gardner	20,629	51	32	19

Table 78. Full-Time Law Enforcement Employees, by Selected State and City, 2020—Continued

(Number.)

State/city	Population	Total law enforcement employees	Total officers	Total civilians
Georgetown	8,783	18	13	5
Gill	1,464	2	2	0
Gloucester	30,445	67	60	7
Goshen	1,059	2	2	0
Grafton	18,908	24	20	4
Granby	6,297	15	11	4
Great Barrington	6,928	18	17	1
Greenfield	17,239	47	34	13
Groton	11,337	26	19	7
Groveland	6,856	13	11	2
Hadley	5,352	22	16	6
Halifax	8,207	11	10	1
Hamilton	8,038	18	13	5
Hanson	11,367	24	23	1
Hardwick	3,047	5	5	0
Harwich	12,068	34	28	6
Haverhill	64,015	117	100	17
Hingham	25,816	49	47	2
Hinsdale	1,899	5	4	1
Holbrook	11,035	23	22	1
Holden	19,412	39	24	15
Holland	2,473	2	2	0
Holliston	14,986	30	25	5
Holyoke	40,002	128	113	15
Hopedale	5,924	17	13	4
Hopkinton	18,806	36	26	10
Hudson	19,839	44	33	11
Hull	10,850	27	24	3
Ipswich	14,097	29	25	4
Kingston	14,481	32	24	8
Lakeville	12,053	24	19	5
Lancaster	8,040	12	11	1
Lanesboro	2,924	6	6	0
Lawrence	79,997	181	158	23
Leicester	11,329	21	20	1
Lenox	4,930	10	10	0
Leominster	41,598	92	76	16
Leverett	1,836	3	3	0
Lexington	33,138	61	45	16
Lincoln	7,092	18	13	5
Littleton	10,326	28	20	8
Longmeadow	15,640	27	25	2
Lowell	110,876	310	232	78
Ludlow	21,171	52	40	12
Lunenburg	11,874	17	16	1
Lynn	94,223	195	177	18
Lynnfield	13,093	27	21	6
Malden	60,231	110	101	9
Mansfield	24,484	46	37	9
Marblehead	20,525	39	30	9
Marion	5,396	15	15	0
Marlborough	39,498	81	67	14
Mashpee	14,180	44	35	9
Mattapoisett	6,659	20	20	0
Maynard	11,420	27	21	6
Medfield	13,034	25	19	6
Medway	13,534	26	25	1
Melrose	27,975	44	43	1
Mendon	6,232	17	14	3
Methuen	50,810	101	84	17
Middleboro	26,606	48	44	4
Middleton	10,189	17	16	1
Millbury	13,949	59	49	10
Millis	8,339	23	18	5
Millville	3,247	6	5	1
Milton	27,600	60	52	8
Montague	8,185	22	17	5
Nahant	3,505	13	12	1
Nantucket	11,484	56	38	18
Natick	36,200	70	54	16
Needham	31,586	59	50	9
New Bedford	94,886	291	248	43
Newburyport	18,288	37	32	5
Newton	88,281	194	149	45
Norfolk	12,068	23	21	2
North Adams	12,620	36	24	12
Northampton	28,428	66	59	7
North Andover	31,341	52	38	14
North Attleboro	29,280	62	45	17
Northborough	15,105	28	20	8
Northbridge	16,699	26	18	8
Northfield	2,950	3	3	0
North Reading	15,886	35	32	3
Norton	19,932	35	34	1
Norwell	11,605	26	23	3

Table 78. Full-Time Law Enforcement Employees, by Selected State and City, 2020—Continued

(Number.)

State/city	Population	Total law enforcement employees	Total officers	Total civilians
Norwood	29,791	72	61	11
Oak Bluffs	4,677	19	17	2
Oakham	1,953	1	1	0
Orleans	5,745	28	22	6
Oxford	13,967	29	22	7
Palmer	12,200	29	22	7
Paxton	4,953	17	16	1
Peabody	52,975	102	85	17
Pelham	1,312	2	2	0
Pembroke	19,211	32	31	1
Pepperell	12,114	17	16	1
Petersham	1,244	2	2	0
Pittsfield	41,865	107	86	21
Plymouth	64,199	144	128	16
Plympton	3,105	9	8	1
Princeton	3,477	7	6	1
Provincetown	2,947	24	18	6
Quincy	94,519	258	224	34
Randolph	32,052	64	59	5
Raynham	14,512	38	30	8
Reading	25,417	59	44	15
Rehoboth	12,406	32	26	6
Revere	52,930	106	100	6
Rockland	18,652	34	31	3
Rockport	7,279	17	16	1
Rowley	6,509	17	12	5
Salem	43,154	103	92	11
Salisbury	9,630	26	15	11
Sandwich	20,008	44	34	10
Saugus	28,397	82	67	15
Scituate	19,655	34	33	1
Seekonk	15,927	40	38	2
Sharon	19,011	34	30	4
Sheffield	3,115	5	5	0
Shelburne	1,830	3	3	0
Sherborn	4,335	15	14	1
Shirley	7,632	13	11	2
Shrewsbury	38,656	59	45	14
Somerset	18,024	38	33	5
Somerville	81,552	155	122	33
Southampton	6,213	13	9	4
Southborough	10,202	25	20	5
Southbridge	16,805	49	38	11
South Hadley	17,613	33	28	5
Southwick	9,732	24	18	6
Spencer	11,896	23	18	5
Springfield	153,084	622	474	148
Stockbridge	1,884	7	6	1
Stoneham	24,329	45	37	8
Stoughton	29,067	69	58	11
Stow	7,266	12	10	2
Sturbridge	9,585	27	20	7
Sudbury	19,778	41	30	11
Sunderland	3,622	6	5	1
Sutton	9,600	19	15	4
Swampscott	15,391	29	28	1
Swansea	16,854	39	34	5
Templeton	8,110	14	9	5
Tewksbury	31,237	71	62	9
Tisbury	4,108	15	13	2
Topsfield	6,668	12	11	1
Townsend	9,515	14	13	1
Truro	1,997	17	12	5
Uxbridge	14,202	26	19	7
Wakefield	27,114	48	47	1
Walpole	25,273	55	44	11
Waltham	62,339	212	148	64
Wareham	23,619	52	43	9
Warren	5,203	7	6	1
Watertown	36,201	79	67	12
Webster	16,876	32	30	2
Wellesley	28,687	57	42	15
Wellfleet	2,707	20	15	5
Wenham	5,296	11	10	1
Westborough	19,138	37	35	2
West Brookfield	3,715	6	6	0
Westfield	41,072	84	80	4
Westford	25,011	52	48	4
Westminster	8,038	18	14	4
Weston	12,146	36	26	10
Westport	16,003	32	29	3
West Tisbury	2,919	10	9	1
Westwood	16,578	37	29	8
Weymouth	58,090	117	98	19
Wilbraham	14,690	28	27	1

Table 78. Full-Time Law Enforcement Employees, by Selected State and City, 2020—Continued

(Number.)

State/city	Population	Total law enforcement employees	Total officers	Total civilians
Williamsburg	2,464	1	1	0
Williamstown	7,397	14	12	2
Wilmington	23,437	54	50	4
Winchendon	10,908	21	15	6
Winchester	22,827	49	40	9
Winthrop	18,561	31	30	1
Woburn	40,142	84	79	5
Worcester	184,850	492	442	50
Wrentham	12,112	23	22	1
Yarmouth	23,015	75	61	14
MICHIGAN				
Adrian	20,540	32	30	2
Adrian Township	6,237	2	2	0
Akron	372	1	1	0
Albion	8,381	20	19	1
Allegan	5,023	9	8	1
Allen Park	26,809	42	38	4
Alma	8,839	17	14	3
Almont	2,809	7	7	0
Alpena	9,900	18	16	2
Ann Arbor	120,647	145	118	27
Argentine Township	6,473	5	5	0
Armada	1,714	2	2	0
Auburn Hills	25,149	55	50	5
Augusta	900	9	6	3
Bad Axe	2,893	7	7	0
Bangor	1,827	6	6	0
Baraga	1,935	2	2	0
Baroda-Lake Township	3,890	6	5	1
Barryton	353	1	1	0
Barry Township	3,531	4	4	0
Bath Township	13,167	13	12	1
Battle Creek	60,479	123	103	20
Bay City	32,485	58	52	6
Beaverton	1,177	4	4	0
Belding	5,741	7	7	0
Bellaire	1,064	2	2	0
Belleville	3,887	8	7	1
Bellevue	1,305	2	2	0
Benton Harbor	9,710	30	29	1
Benton Township	14,251	27	21	6
Berkley	15,410	37	29	8
Berrien Springs-Oronoko Township	8,894	9	8	1
Beverly Hills	10,363	27	23	4
Big Rapids	10,355	20	18	2
Birch Run	1,468	6	5	1
Birmingham	21,536	44	33	11
Blackman Township	37,034	41	40	1
Blissfield	3,259	7	6	1
Bloomfield Hills	4,012	25	22	3
Bloomfield Township	42,059	81	65	16
Boyne City	3,729	7	6	1
Breckenridge	1,267	1	1	0
Bridgeport Township	9,736	9	8	1
Bridgman	2,204	5	5	0
Brighton	7,679	18	16	2
Bronson	2,298	4	4	0
Brown City	1,242	1	1	0
Brownstown Township	32,255	37	30	7
Buchanan	4,242	9	8	1
Buena Vista Township	8,047	13	12	1
Burton	28,427	38	36	2
Cadillac	10,513	17	16	1
Cambridge Township	5,679	4	4	0
Canton Township	94,128	102	93	9
Capac	1,832	2	2	0
Carleton	2,354	4	3	1
Caro	3,959	7	7	0
Carrollton Township	5,599	6	6	0
Carson City	1,111	1	1	0
Caseville	730	2	2	0
Caspian-Gaastra	1,162	1	1	0
Cass City	2,260	4	4	0
Cassopolis	1,692	5	5	0
Center Line	8,162	25	20	5
Central Lake	938	1	1	0
Charlevoix	2,486	8	7	1
Charlotte	9,091	16	15	1
Cheboygan	4,668	9	9	0
Chelsea	5,471	14	10	4
Chesaning	2,221	2	1	1
Chesterfield Township	47,059	59	45	14
Chikaming Township	3,078	7	6	1
Chocolay Township	5,918	5	4	1

Table 78. Full-Time Law Enforcement Employees, by Selected State and City, 2020—Continued

(Number.)

State/city	Population	Total law enforcement employees	Total officers	Total civilians
Clare	3,071	7	7	0
Clawson	11,846	19	18	1
Clayton Township	7,057	7	6	1
Clay Township	8,886	23	18	5
Clinton	2,285	4	4	0
Clinton Township	100,884	103	94	9
Clio	2,482	4	4	0
Coldwater	12,076	20	18	2
Coleman	1,199	2	2	0
Coloma Township	6,319	10	7	3
Colon	1,155	3	3	0
Columbia Township	7,350	7	7	0
Constantine	2,110	6	5	1
Corunna	3,327	3	3	0
Covert Township	2,891	9	9	0
Croswell	2,269	5	5	0
Crystal Falls	1,354	1	1	0
Davison	4,848	6	5	1
Davison Township	19,197	22	20	2
Dearborn	93,507	230	186	44
Dearborn Heights	55,105	105	81	24
Decatur	1,724	5	5	0
Denton Township	5,421	4	4	0
Detroit	659,616	3,149	2,528	621
DeWitt	4,844	7	6	1
DeWitt Township	15,756	16	15	1
Dowagiac	5,648	14	13	1
Dryden Township	4,724	4	4	0
Dundee	4,681	5	5	0
Durand	3,818	5	5	0
East Grand Rapids	12,105	30	28	2
East Jordan	2,348	5	5	0
East Lansing	48,098	60	51	9
Eastpointe	32,046	47	42	5
Eaton Rapids	5,248	10	9	1
Eau Claire	594	1	1	0
Ecorse	9,576	19	19	0
Elk Rapids	1,613	5	5	0
Elkton	743	1	1	0
Emmett Township	11,611	16	14	2
Erie Township	4,308	4	3	1
Escanaba	12,111	44	32	12
Essexville	3,257	8	8	0
Evart	1,879	3	3	0
Fair Haven Township	1,038	1	1	0
Farmington	10,503	24	23	1
Farmington Hills	80,708	135	99	36
Fennville	1,433	5	5	0
Fenton	11,369	18	15	3
Ferndale	20,048	49	39	10
Flat Rock	10,019	20	18	2
Flint	94,842	117	95	22
Flint Township	30,178	48	41	7
Flushing	7,827	10	10	0
Flushing Township	10,133	9	8	1
Forsyth Township	6,182	10	8	2
Fowlerville	2,895	6	5	1
Frankenmuth	5,595	9	7	2
Frankfort	1,291	3	3	0
Franklin	3,256	11	11	0
Fraser	14,480	30	29	1
Fremont	4,077	9	8	1
Fruitport Township	14,476	10	10	0
Gagetown	360	1	1	0
Gaines Township	6,103	1	1	0
Galien	527	2	1	1
Garden City	26,282	38	35	3
Garfield Township	850	1	1	0
Gaylord	3,692	12	11	1
Genesee Township	20,325	21	18	3
Gerrish Township	2,946	6	6	0
Gibraltar	4,505	10	9	1
Gladstone	4,670	11	10	1
Gladwin	2,887	5	5	0
Grand Beach/Michiana	463	5	5	0
Grand Blanc	7,831	18	16	2
Grand Blanc Township	36,498	48	41	7
Grand Haven	11,126	33	30	3
Grand Ledge	7,908	16	16	0
Grand Rapids	202,513	360	291	69
Grandville	15,913	27	25	2
Grant	883	2	2	0
Grayling	1,848	6	5	1
Green Oak Township	19,154	19	17	2
Greenville	8,415	17	15	2

Table 78. Full-Time Law Enforcement Employees, by Selected State and City, 2020—Continued

(Number.)

State/city	Population	Total law enforcement employees	Total officers	Total civilians
Grosse Ile Township	10,114	23	17	6
Grosse Pointe	5,127	21	21	0
Grosse Pointe Farms	9,077	37	32	5
Grosse Pointe Park	10,998	38	33	5
Grosse Pointe Shores	2,786	18	18	0
Grosse Pointe Woods	15,269	37	31	6
Hamburg Township	21,867	19	18	1
Hampton Township	9,354	10	10	0
Hamtramck	21,514	38	33	5
Hancock	4,487	10	10	0
Harbor Beach	1,575	4	4	0
Harbor Springs	1,207	7	6	1
Harper Woods	13,679	31	27	4
Hart	2,064	5	5	0
Hartford	2,582	5	5	0
Hastings	7,307	17	15	2
Hazel Park	16,340	43	37	6
Hesperia	927	3	3	0
Highland Park	10,680	12	11	1
Hillsdale	7,972	14	12	2
Holland	33,228	67	58	9
Holly	6,157	10	10	0
Home Township	1,370	1	1	0
Houghton	7,760	14	13	1
Howell	9,620	20	18	2
Hudson	2,200	3	3	0
Huntington Woods	6,268	17	16	1
Huron Township	16,288	29	22	7
Imlay City	3,567	10	9	1
Inkster	24,173	39	29	10
Ionia	11,153	17	15	2
Iron Mountain	7,274	15	14	1
Iron River	2,807	4	4	0
Ironwood	4,816	11	11	0
Ishpeming	6,410	12	11	1
Ishpeming Township	3,513	1	1	0
Jackson	32,332	52	43	9
Jonesville	2,210	3	3	0
Kalamazoo	76,411	258	235	23
Kalamazoo Township	24,562	36	32	4
Kalkaska	2,103	5	5	0
Keego Harbor	3,431	5	5	0
Kentwood	52,263	90	70	20
Kingsford	4,931	19	19	0
Kingston	406	1	1	0
Kinross Township	7,439	2	2	0
Laingsburg	1,285	1	1	0
Lake Angelus	308	1	1	0
Lake Linden	942	1	1	0
Lake Odessa	2,043	4	4	0
Lake Orion	3,206	4	4	0
Lakeview	1,002	3	3	0
L'Anse	1,824	4	4	0
Lansing	118,651	250	199	51
Lansing Township	8,254	16	15	1
Lapeer	8,505	22	19	3
Lathrup Village	4,090	11	10	1
Laurium	1,889	4	4	0
Lawton	1,800	4	4	0
Leslie	1,903	4	4	0
Lexington	1,114	3	3	0
Lincoln Park	36,140	53	46	7
Lincoln Township	14,587	13	12	1
Linden	3,934	5	5	0
Litchfield	1,327	2	2	0
Livonia	93,342	157	118	39
Lowell	4,216	6	5	1
Ludington	8,111	16	14	2
Luna Pier	1,392	1	1	0
Mackinac Island	469	8	8	0
Mackinaw City	794	6	6	0
Madison Heights	29,906	62	48	14
Madison Township	8,229	5	5	0
Mancelona	1,364	1	1	0
Manistee	6,103	12	12	0
Manistique	2,923	8	8	0
Manton	1,588	1	1	0
Marine City	4,038	5	4	1
Marlette	1,755	4	4	0
Marquette	20,957	38	33	5
Marshall	6,954	15	15	0
Marysville	9,643	16	14	2
Mason	8,480	13	12	1
Mattawan	1,981	6	6	0
Mayville	878	3	3	0
Melvindale	10,199	23	23	0

Table 78. Full-Time Law Enforcement Employees, by Selected State and City, 2020—Continued

(Number.)

State/city	Population	Total law enforcement employees	Total officers	Total civilians
Memphis	1,174	1	1	0
Mendon	848	1	1	0
Menominee	7,971	16	15	1
Meridian Township	43,598	37	34	3
Metamora Township	4,283	5	5	0
Metro Police Authority of Genesee County	19,883	29	26	3
Midland	41,682	52	50	2
Milan	6,065	17	12	5
Milford	17,038	21	19	2
Millington	989	2	2	0
Monroe	19,433	42	36	6
Montague	2,361	4	4	0
Montrose Township	7,431	9	8	1
Morenci	2,139	7	7	0
Morrice	908	2	2	0
Mount Morris	2,822	5	5	0
Mount Morris Township	20,207	29	25	4
Mount Pleasant	24,668	34	28	6
Munising	2,188	4	4	0
Muskegon	36,391	83	74	9
Muskegon Heights	10,724	25	22	3
Muskegon Township	18,022	15	14	1
Napoleon Township	6,767	5	5	0
Nashville	1,691	1	1	0
Negaunee	4,520	9	9	0
Newaygo	2,076	7	7	0
New Baltimore	12,377	25	15	10
New Buffalo	1,866	7	7	0
New Era	439	1	1	0
Niles	11,102	28	17	11
Northfield Township	8,720	11	10	1
North Muskegon	3,793	8	8	0
Northville	5,956	14	13	1
Northville Township	29,434	47	34	13
Norton Shores	24,742	35	33	2
Norway	2,736	6	6	0
Novi	61,554	93	70	23
Oak Park	29,432	61	48	13
Olivet	1,782	2	2	0
Ontwa Township-Edwardsburg	6,602	9	8	1
Orchard Lake	2,483	9	8	1
Oscoda Township	6,741	13	12	1
Otsego	3,997	6	5	1
Ovid	1,616	2	2	0
Owosso	14,363	17	17	0
Oxford	3,570	13	9	4
Paw Paw	3,351	9	8	1
Pentwater	847	2	2	0
Perry	2,084	4	4	0
Petoskey	5,767	19	18	1
Pigeon	1,111	2	2	0
Pinckney	2,419	6	6	0
Pittsfield Township	39,400	40	39	1
Plainwell	3,774	9	8	1
Pleasant Ridge	2,423	5	5	0
Plymouth	9,159	17	16	1
Plymouth Township	26,988	43	28	15
Portage	49,798	78	59	19
Port Austin	618	2	2	0
Port Huron	28,602	62	54	8
Portland	3,955	6	6	0
Potterville	2,765	2	2	0
Prairieville Township	3,534	2	2	0
Quincy	1,614	3	3	0
Raisin Township	7,784	4	4	0
Reading	1,040	2	2	0
Redford Township	46,510	67	59	8
Reed City	2,388	4	4	0
Reese	1,355	2	2	0
Richfield Township, Genesee County	8,292	11	9	2
Richfield Township, Roscommon County	3,653	4	4	0
Richland	841	4	4	0
Richland Township, Saginaw County	3,904	4	4	0
Richmond	5,856	13	10	3
River Rouge	7,369	27	19	8
Riverview	11,986	22	21	1
Rochester	13,362	30	22	8
Rockford	6,472	11	10	1
Rockwood	3,145	9	8	1
Rogers City	2,636	6	6	0
Romeo	3,607	10	7	3
Romulus	23,533	55	42	13
Roosevelt Park	3,793	5	5	0
Roseville	46,983	70	67	3
Rothbury	448	1	1	0

Table 78. Full-Time Law Enforcement Employees, by Selected State and City, 2020—Continued

(Number.)

State/city	Population	Total law enforcement employees	Total officers	Total civilians
Royal Oak	59,506	112	78	34
Saginaw	47,767	63	55	8
Saginaw Township	38,971	48	43	5
Saline	9,400	17	13	4
Sandusky	2,503	6	5	1
Saugatuck-Douglas	2,322	5	4	1
Sault Ste. Marie	13,340	25	23	2
Schoolcraft	1,554	3	3	0
Scottville	1,211	2	2	0
Sebewaing	1,618	2	2	0
Shelby	2,008	2	2	0
Shelby Township	81,416	101	76	25
Shepherd	1,484	2	2	0
Somerset Township	4,520	3	3	0
Southfield	72,794	149	124	25
Southgate	28,848	42	37	5
South Haven	4,341	23	18	5
South Lyon	11,877	17	16	1
South Rockwood	1,655	2	2	0
Sparta	4,429	5	5	0
Spring Arbor Township	7,838	2	2	0
Springport Township	2,156	2	2	0
Stanton	1,423	1	1	0
St. Charles	1,880	1	1	0
St. Clair	5,259	8	8	0
St. Clair Shores	58,898	88	84	4
Sterling Heights	132,745	171	150	21
St. Ignace	2,311	5	5	0
St. Johns	7,954	12	11	1
St. Joseph	8,313	24	22	2
St. Joseph Township	9,638	12	11	1
St. Louis	7,244	8	7	1
Stockbridge	1,253	2	2	0
Sturgis	10,831	24	19	5
Sumpter Township	9,348	18	16	2
Sylvan Lake	1,869	5	5	0
Tawas	4,492	5	4	1
Taylor	60,698	93	79	14
Tecumseh	8,392	15	14	1
Thetford Township	6,605	1	1	0
Thomas Township	11,411	9	8	1
Three Oaks	1,537	3	3	0
Three Rivers	7,604	17	15	2
Tittabawassee Township	10,009	7	6	1
Traverse City	15,855	33	30	3
Trenton	18,085	34	33	1
Troy	84,441	149	103	46
Tuscarora Township	2,904	9	8	1
Ubly	779	1	1	0
Unadilla Township	3,468	3	3	0
Union City	1,561	5	5	0
Utica	5,149	19	15	4
Van Buren Township	28,355	56	40	16
Vassar	2,525	5	5	0
Vernon	767	1	1	0
Vicksburg	3,554	6	6	0
Walker	25,020	41	37	4
Walled Lake	7,142	6	6	0
Warren	133,928	234	198	36
Waterford Township	72,735	79	61	18
Watersmeet Township	1,350	1	1	0
Watervliet	1,639	3	3	0
Wayland	4,241	7	6	1
Wayne	16,734	26	23	3
West Bloomfield Township	65,711	110	80	30
West Branch	2,042	5	5	0
Westland	81,244	95	77	18
White Cloud	1,385	2	2	0
Whitehall	2,846	8	8	0
White Lake Township	31,505	38	29	9
White Pigeon	1,526	4	4	0
Williamston	3,976	7	6	1
Wixom	14,110	23	20	3
Wolverine Lake	4,835	7	7	0
Woodhaven	12,427	31	29	2
Wyandotte	24,757	46	35	11
Wyoming	76,071	100	86	14
Yale	1,861	4	4	0
Ypsilanti	20,240	35	31	4
Zeeland	5,540	11	10	1
Zilwaukee	1,516	1	1	0
MINNESOTA				
Aitkin	1,969	7	6	1
Akeley	444	1	1	0

Table 78. Full-Time Law Enforcement Employees, by Selected State and City, 2020—Continued

(Number.)

State/city	Population	Total law enforcement employees	Total officers	Total civilians
Albany	2,787	4	3	1
Albert Lea	17,599	29	26	3
Alexandria	13,978	27	24	3
Annandale	3,549	6	5	1
Anoka	17,593	39	29	10
Appleton	1,316	3	3	0
Apple Valley	55,846	59	51	8
Arlington	2,136	5	4	1
Atwater	1,117	1	1	0
Audubon	520	1	1	0
Austin	25,267	37	34	3
Avon	1,613	4	3	1
Babbitt	1,485	5	5	0
Bagley	1,409	3	3	0
Barnesville	2,606	5	5	0
Battle Lake	935	3	3	0
Baxter	8,447	16	15	1
Bayport	3,799	6	6	0
Becker	4,997	8	7	1
Belgrade/Brooten	1,535	3	3	0
Belle Plaine	7,243	12	10	2
Bemidji	15,567	37	34	3
Benson	3,022	7	6	1
Big Lake	11,355	16	13	3
Blackduck	839	2	2	0
Blaine	66,588	81	66	15
Blooming Prairie	1,930	3	3	0
Bloomington	85,159	145	119	26
Blue Earth	3,087	5	5	0
Bovey	782	2	2	0
Braham	1,819	5	5	0
Brainerd	13,417	27	22	5
Breckenridge	3,148	8	8	0
Breezy Point	2,424	7	6	1
Breitung Township	611	2	2	0
Brooklyn Center	30,744	58	47	11
Brooklyn Park	80,897	134	99	35
Brownton	716	1	1	0
Buffalo	16,550	21	17	4
Buffalo Lake	680	2	2	0
Burnsville	61,445	85	75	10
Caledonia	2,741	6	5	1
Callaway	230	1	1	0
Cambridge	9,302	15	14	1
Canby	1,658	3	3	0
Cannon Falls	4,046	8	6	2
Centennial Lakes	11,704	18	16	2
Champlin	25,517	31	26	5
Chaska	27,353	32	26	6
Chatfield	2,834	5	5	0
Chisholm	4,835	12	11	1
Clara City	1,267	2	2	0
Clearbrook	521	1	1	0
Cloquet	11,995	23	21	2
Cold Spring/Richmond	5,791	11	10	1
Coleraine	1,972	2	2	0
Columbia Heights	21,291	32	25	7
Coon Rapids	63,162	74	63	11
Corcoran	6,352	10	9	1
Cottage Grove	37,940	47	41	6
Crookston	7,749	17	15	2
Crosby	2,316	9	8	1
Crosslake	2,378	6	6	0
Crystal	22,987	40	34	6
Danube	453	1	1	0
Dawson/Boyd	1,540	3	3	0
Dayton	6,958	10	8	2
Deephaven	3,963	8	7	1
Deer River	929	4	4	0
Deerwood	532	3	3	0
Detroit Lakes	9,352	19	17	2
Dilworth	4,469	8	7	1
Duluth	85,555	177	152	25
Dundas	1,679	3	3	0
Eagan	66,618	86	73	13
Eagle Lake	3,172	3	3	0
East Grand Forks	8,526	25	23	2
East Range	3,558	8	8	0
Eden Prairie	65,353	93	70	23
Eden Valley	1,039	1	1	0
Edina	53,422	77	56	21
Elko New Market	4,855	5	5	0
Elk River	25,467	42	33	9
Ely	3,344	8	7	1
Emily	843	2	2	0

Table 78. Full-Time Law Enforcement Employees, by Selected State and City, 2020—Continued

(Number.)

State/city	Population	Total law enforcement employees	Total officers	Total civilians
Eveleth	3,553	11	10	1
Fairfax	1,120	2	2	0
Fairmont	9,964	20	18	2
Faribault	23,958	43	35	8
Farmington	23,318	28	25	3
Fergus Falls	13,834	28	23	5
Floodwood	521	3	2	1
Foley	2,678	4	4	0
Forest Lake	21,230	28	25	3
Frazee	1,395	3	3	0
Fridley	27,892	51	43	8
Fulda	1,197	2	2	0
Gaylord	2,196	4	4	0
Gilbert	1,779	7	6	1
Glencoe	5,532	9	8	1
Glenwood	2,617	6	5	1
Glyndon	1,370	4	4	0
Golden Valley	22,060	43	31	12
Goodhue	1,177	2	2	0
Goodview	4,119	5	4	1
Grand Rapids	11,253	23	20	3
Granite Falls	2,677	7	6	1
Hallock	914	1	1	0
Hastings	22,959	34	30	4
Hawley	2,213	5	5	0
Hector	1,039	3	3	0
Henderson	934	2	2	0
Henning	809	2	2	0
Hermantown	9,661	18	15	3
Hibbing	15,802	29	26	3
Hill City	580	1	1	0
Hokah	543	1	1	0
Hopkins	18,568	38	30	8
Houston	963	2	2	0
Howard Lake	2,155	3	3	0
Hutchinson	13,966	34	22	12
International Falls	5,747	12	12	0
Inver Grove Heights	35,861	45	40	5
Isanti	6,219	11	10	1
Isle	801	4	4	0
Janesville	2,251	4	4	0
Jordan	6,514	12	10	2
Kasson	6,549	9	8	1
Keewatin	1,008	3	3	0
La Crescent	5,016	9	8	1
Lake City	5,129	11	10	1
Lake Crystal	2,482	3	3	0
Lakefield	1,605	3	3	0
Lake Park	794	2	2	0
Lakes Area	10,000	15	13	2
Lake Shore	1,064	2	2	0
Lakeville	68,688	69	60	9
Le Center	2,517	3	3	0
Lester Prairie	1,724	3	3	0
Le Sueur	4,058	8	7	1
Lewiston	1,539	2	2	0
Lino Lakes	22,337	28	25	3
Litchfield	6,641	11	10	1
Little Falls	8,682	17	15	2
Long Prairie	3,284	6	6	0
Lonsdale	4,269	8	7	1
Madelia	2,247	4	4	0
Madison Lake	1,192	1	1	0
Mankato	43,276	64	56	8
Maple Grove	73,939	79	66	13
Mapleton	2,189	3	3	0
Maplewood	41,096	60	55	5
Marshall	13,466	25	22	3
Medina	6,952	12	11	1
Melrose	3,663	6	5	1
Menahga	1,302	3	3	0
Mendota Heights	11,373	21	20	1
Milaca	2,927	7	6	1
Minneapolis	435,116	974	833	141
Minneota	1,352	1	1	0
Minnesota Lake	634	1	1	0
Minnetonka	54,561	63	55	8
Minnetrista	10,738	17	13	4
Montevideo	5,009	12	11	1
Montgomery	3,061	8	7	1
Moorhead	44,132	67	53	14
Moose Lake	2,815	5	5	0
Morgan	834	1	1	0
Morris	5,339	10	8	2
Motley	658	2	2	0

Table 78. Full-Time Law Enforcement Employees, by Selected State and City, 2020—Continued

(Number.)

State/city	Population	Total law enforcement employees	Total officers	Total civilians
Mounds View	13,421	23	21	2
Mountain Lake	2,029	4	4	0
Nashwauk	948	4	4	0
New Brighton	22,843	35	29	6
New Hope	20,970	39	29	10
New Prague	8,374	12	10	2
New Richland	1,179	2	2	0
New Ulm	13,181	22	22	0
New York Mills	1,226	3	3	0
Nisswa	2,112	6	6	0
North Branch	10,841	14	12	2
Northfield	20,820	29	24	5
North Mankato	14,008	16	15	1
North St. Paul	12,591	19	17	2
Oakdale	27,990	39	31	8
Oak Park Heights	5,071	10	9	1
Olivia	2,316	5	5	0
Onamia	862	3	3	0
Orono	20,387	31	27	4
Ortonville	1,767	4	4	0
Osakis	1,745	3	3	0
Osseo	2,775	8	7	1
Owatonna	25,720	40	36	4
Parkers Prairie	996	2	2	0
Park Rapids	4,280	12	11	1
Paynesville	2,530	5	5	0
Pelican Rapids	2,563	5	5	0
Pequot Lakes	2,315	7	6	1
Perham	3,724	7	6	1
Pierz	1,362	2	2	0
Pike Bay	1,706	1	1	0
Pine River	925	3	3	0
Plainview	3,293	8	7	1
Plymouth	80,843	96	79	17
Preston	1,285	3	3	0
Princeton	4,728	14	12	2
Prior Lake	27,748	34	30	4
Proctor	3,025	8	7	1
Ramsey	28,205	30	27	3
Red Wing	16,304	32	27	5
Redwood Falls	4,930	14	12	2
Renville	1,178	3	3	0
Rice	1,404	2	2	0
Richfield	36,493	55	46	9
Robbinsdale	14,437	29	23	6
Rochester	120,336	209	145	64
Rogers	13,769	23	20	3
Roseau	2,677	6	5	1
Rosemount	25,597	28	25	3
Roseville	36,675	58	49	9
Rushford	1,692	3	3	0
Sartell	19,262	23	20	3
Sauk Centre	4,528	8	7	1
Sauk Rapids	14,300	18	17	1
Savage	33,020	45	35	10
Sebeka	661	2	2	0
Shakopee	42,076	58	46	12
Sherburn	1,082	4	4	0
Silver Bay	1,750	5	5	0
Slayton	1,956	5	4	1
Sleepy Eye	3,331	7	7	0
South Lake Minnetonka	12,867	19	16	3
South St. Paul	20,053	35	30	5
Springfield	1,989	5	5	0
Spring Grove	1,258	3	3	0
Spring Lake Park	6,978	14	11	3
St. Anthony	9,095	23	20	3
Staples	2,999	8	7	1
Starbuck	1,267	4	4	0
St. Charles	3,760	7	7	0
St. Cloud	68,751	135	109	26
St. Francis	7,997	15	12	3
Stillwater	19,736	27	22	5
St. James	4,380	9	8	1
St. Joseph	7,448	11	10	1
St. Louis Park	49,058	69	56	13
St. Paul	309,859	763	621	142
St. Paul Park	5,374	8	8	0
St. Peter	12,041	20	14	6
Thief River Falls	8,849	17	15	2
Tracy	2,068	3	3	0
Trimont	695	1	1	0
Truman	1,034	2	2	0
Twin Valley	748	2	2	0
Two Harbors	3,506	9	8	1

Table 78. Full-Time Law Enforcement Employees, by Selected State and City, 2020—Continued

(Number.)

State/city	Population	Total law enforcement employees	Total officers	Total civilians
Tyler	1,062	2	2	0
Verndale	567	2	2	0
Virginia	8,337	24	24	0
Wabasha	2,468	9	8	1
Wadena	4,108	10	9	1
Waite Park	7,812	21	18	3
Walker	932	3	3	0
Walnut Grove	799	1	1	0
Warroad	1,795	6	5	1
Waseca	8,805	20	18	2
Waterville	1,894	4	4	0
Wayzata	6,602	16	14	2
Wells	2,152	5	5	0
Westbrook	700	1	1	0
West Concord	766	1	1	0
West Hennepin	5,995	12	10	2
West St. Paul	20,007	35	31	4
Wheaton	1,275	3	3	0
White Bear Lake	26,036	35	31	4
Willmar	19,901	39	35	4
Windom	4,358	10	9	1
Winnebago	1,330	3	3	0
Winona	26,487	43	39	4
Winsted	2,230	4	4	0
Winthrop	1,340	3	3	0
Woodbury	74,110	79	68	11
Worthington	13,131	35	24	11
Wyoming	8,095	10	9	1
Zumbrota	3,526	6	6	0
MISSISSIPPI				
Aberdeen	5,163	19	14	5
Ackerman	1,438	5	5	0
Amory	6,740	28	21	7
Batesville	7,193	53	41	12
Bay Springs	1,645	8	7	1
Biloxi	46,433	179	126	53
Booneville	8,472	28	21	7
Brandon	24,545	47	34	13
Brookhaven	11,886	45	35	10
Bruce	1,805	6	6	0
Byram	11,418	41	28	13
Canton	12,103	31	19	12
Carthage	4,753	22	16	6
Charleston	1,836	10	10	0
Clarksdale	14,591	39	31	8
Cleveland	10,944	55	46	9
Clinton	24,349	75	56	19
Coldwater	1,518	5	5	0
Collins	2,409	28	20	8
Crenshaw	841	2	2	0
Decatur	1,692	5	5	0
D'Iberville	14,298	37	34	3
Drew	1,576	1	1	0
Durant	2,220	8	4	4
Edwards	1,000	3	3	0
Ellisville	4,573	10	8	2
Eupora	1,985	8	7	1
Fayette	1,420	7	5	2
Flora	1,859	10	9	1
Florence	4,536	19	16	3
Flowood	9,564	62	48	14
Forest	5,517	20	16	4
Fulton	3,984	11	11	0
Gautier	18,479	40	28	12
Gloster	860	7	4	3
Grenada	12,131	38	32	6
Gulfport	72,142	211	158	53
Hattiesburg	45,870	166	103	63
Hazlehurst	3,699	21	13	8
Hernando	16,675	53	42	11
Hollandale	2,264	12	6	6
Holly Springs	7,799	22	18	4
Horn Lake	27,404	60	43	17
Houston	3,405	4	2	2
Indianola	8,877	28	20	8
Inverness	851	3	3	0
Iuka	2,926	12	9	3
Kosciusko	6,652	21	21	0
Laurel	18,317	65	46	19
Leland	3,694	20	14	6
Lexington	1,425	11	11	0
Long Beach	16,161	46	31	15
Louisville	5,917	21	20	1
Lucedale	3,179	21	15	6

Table 78. Full-Time Law Enforcement Employees, by Selected State and City, 2020—Continued

(Number.)

State/city	Population	Total law enforcement employees	Total officers	Total civilians
Madison	25,831	92	71	21
Magee	4,062	42	32	10
Mendenhall	2,374	8	5	3
Meridian	35,855	89	69	20
Morton	3,509	11	11	0
Moss Point	13,315	34	25	9
Natchez	14,497	46	38	8
New Augusta	597	1	1	0
Newton	3,133	16	14	2
Ocean Springs	17,917	48	34	14
Okolona	2,577	9	9	0
Olive Branch	39,566	103	84	19
Oxford	28,866	91	79	12
Pascagoula	21,633	69	49	20
Pass Christian	6,527	27	20	7
Pearl	26,596	80	60	20
Petal	10,652	30	26	4
Philadelphia	7,036	32	23	9
Picayune	10,826	39	26	13
Pickens	979	4	4	0
Poplarville	2,901	8	8	0
Purvis	2,416	14	11	3
Quitman	2,089	8	8	0
Raymond	2,142	11	10	1
Richland	7,276	48	35	13
Ridgeland	24,080	84	58	26
Rolling Fork	1,908	11	10	1
Ruleville	2,512	16	16	0
Sandersville	728	15	15	0
Shelby	1,920	7	2	5
Southaven	56,573	156	123	33
Starkville	25,854	66	57	9
Stonewall	963	8	8	0
Summit	1,555	7	6	1
Sunflower	960	2	2	0
Terry	1,246	2	2	0
Tupelo	38,383	124	110	14
Union	1,888	8	7	1
Utica	890	2	2	0
Vicksburg	21,420	63	49	14
Water Valley	3,242	10	9	1
Waveland	6,287	20	19	1
Waynesboro	4,779	10	10	0
West Point	10,314	34	30	4
Wiggins	4,555	21	15	6
Winona	3,861	8	8	0
Yazoo City	10,806	19	14	5
MISSOURI				
Adrian	1,588	4	4	0
Advance	1,335	3	3	0
Annapolis	341	1	1	0
Arbyrd	457	1	1	0
Arcadia	555	3	3	0
Arnold	21,115	62	54	8
Ashland	3,996	8	7	1
Aurora	7,441	24	17	7
Auxvasse	977	6	6	0
Ava	2,852	12	7	5
Ballwin	30,044	56	45	11
Bel-Nor	1,391	8	8	0
Belton	23,698	61	39	22
Berkeley	8,809	34	27	7
Birch Tree	646	1	1	0
Bonne Terre	7,135	10	10	0
Boonville	8,450	28	21	7
Bourbon	1,579	5	5	0
Bowling Green	5,617	12	10	2
Branson	11,745	68	48	20
Branson West	443	14	14	0
Breckenridge Hills	4,548	18	16	2
Brentwood	7,957	29	28	1
Bridgeton	11,521	65	57	8
Brookfield	4,179	12	10	2
Buckner	3,016	8	7	1
Buffalo	3,092	8	7	1
California	4,429	8	7	1
Calverton Park	1,266	12	9	3
Cameron	9,618	24	16	8
Campbell	1,788	8	8	0
Canalou	297	1	1	0
Carl Junction	8,366	16	11	5
Caruthersville	5,268	14	13	1
Cassville	3,293	10	10	0
Centralia	4,298	13	9	4

Table 78. Full-Time Law Enforcement Employees, by Selected State and City, 2020—Continued

(Number.)

State/city	Population	Total law enforcement employees	Total officers	Total civilians
Charleston	5,422	18	12	6
Chesterfield	47,544	112	98	14
Chillicothe	9,735	27	18	9
Clarkton	1,138	2	2	0
Clayton	16,837	54	45	9
Clever	2,842	7	6	1
Columbia	124,829	195	158	37
Country Club Hills	1,244	7	7	0
Country Club Village	2,501	1	1	0
Crestwood	11,829	30	24	6
Creve Coeur	18,716	52	47	5
Crocker	1,030	3	3	0
Crystal City	4,685	22	16	6
Cuba	3,286	16	15	1
Delta	423	1	1	0
De Soto	6,341	28	19	9
Dexter	7,807	26	18	8
Diamond	912	2	2	0
Doniphan	1,907	10	6	4
East Prairie	2,922	9	4	5
Edgar Springs	193	1	1	0
Edmundson	828	11	10	1
Eldon	4,721	13	12	1
El Dorado Springs	3,617	12	8	4
Ellisville	9,927	25	24	1
Ellsinore	427	2	2	0
Excelsior Springs	11,802	32	23	9
Farmington	19,446	32	30	2
Fayette	2,689	7	7	0
Ferguson	20,454	39	34	5
Flordell Hills	799	8	8	0
Florissant	50,812	118	92	26
Fordland	852	1	1	0
Forsyth	2,570	7	6	1
Fredericktown	3,984	15	14	1
Frontenac	3,839	22	21	1
Fulton	12,578	30	24	6
Galena	437	1	1	0
Gideon	960	2	2	0
Grain Valley	14,722	28	23	5
Granby	2,080	4	4	0
Grandview	24,890	66	52	14
Hamllton	1,671	5	5	0
Hannibal	17,299	45	34	11
Hardin	533	1	1	0
Harrisonville	10,083	29	23	6
Hartville	605	2	2	0
Hayti	2,458	5	5	0
Hazelwood	25,051	78	59	19
Herculaneum	4,216	9	8	1
Hermann	2,332	12	6	6
Higginsville	4,589	22	10	12
Highlandville	1,066	1	1	0
Hillsdale	1,549	12	11	1
Holden	2,234	7	7	0
Holts Summit	5,157	12	10	2
Houston	2,081	8	8	0
Howardville	333	2	1	1
Independence	116,648	257	176	81
Ironton	1,381	8	8	0
Jackson	14,955	30	29	1
Jasper	976	2	2	0
Jefferson City	42,653	124	88	36
Kansas City	499,335	1,241	989	252
Kearney	11,164	17	16	1
Kennett	10,005	40	30	10
Kirkwood	27,834	88	60	28
Knob Noster	2,792	8	7	1
Ladue	8,627	34	29	5
La Grange	888	5	5	0
Lake Lafayette	337	1	1	0
Lake Lotawana	2,129	7	6	1
Lake Ozark	1,856	16	11	5
Lakeshire	1,384	10	10	0
Lake St. Louis	17,136	42	34	8
Lake Tapawingo	718	4	3	1
Lake Winnebago	1,285	7	7	0
La Plata	1,302	4	4	0
Laurie	969	4	4	0
Leadington	622	1	1	0
Lee's Summit	100,268	192	140	52
Lexington	4,513	10	8	2
Licking	3,070	5	5	0
Lincoln	1,194	4	4	0
Linn	1,610	5	5	0

Table 78. Full-Time Law Enforcement Employees, by Selected State and City, 2020—Continued

(Number.)

State/city	Population	Total law enforcement employees	Total officers	Total civilians
Lone Jack	1,357	9	8	1
Louisiana	3,191	6	5	1
Malden	3,851	15	13	2
Manchester	18,072	39	35	4
Mansfield	1,240	5	5	0
Maplewood	8,096	35	33	2
Marble Hill	1,461	5	4	1
Marionville	2,175	2	2	0
Marshall	12,817	31	24	7
Marshfield	7,667	12	11	1
Maryland Heights	26,901	112	77	35
Memphis	1,835	3	3	0
Merriam Woods	1,858	5	5	0
Mexico	11,517	29	28	1
Milan	1,755	4	4	0
Miner	930	10	10	0
Moline Acres	2,338	18	17	1
Monett	9,150	23	21	2
Morehouse	854	1	1	0
Moscow Mills	3,620	8	8	0
Mound City	1,026	2	2	0
Mountain View	2,641	8	7	1
Mount Vernon	4,502	11	11	0
Neosho	12,077	29	27	2
New Franklin	1,054	3	3	0
New London	987	2	2	0
Nixa	22,924	39	33	6
Normandy	7,405	26	25	1
Northwoods	4,350	16	15	1
Oakland	1,366	88	60	28
Odessa	5,238	11	10	1
Old Monroe	290	2	1	1
Olivette	7,829	23	22	1
Oregon	756	1	1	0
Oronogo	2,700	4	4	0
Orrick	800	2	2	0
Osage Beach	4,696	25	23	2
Overland	15,497	51	45	6
Ozark	20,788	39	36	3
Palmyra	3,597	9	8	1
Peculiar	5,582	9	8	1
Perry	696	1	1	0
Pevely	6,020	21	15	6
Piedmont	1,879	6	6	0
Pierce City	1,311	2	2	0
Pilot Grove	760	1	1	0
Pineville	808	4	4	0
Platte City	4,987	12	12	0
Platte Woods	407	4	4	0
Pleasant Hill	8,744	20	13	7
Pleasant Valley	3,042	27	14	13
Poplar Bluff	16,927	54	42	12
Puxico	842	1	1	0
Queen City	628	1	1	0
Qulin	456	1	1	0
Raymore	22,545	39	26	13
Raytown	28,922	48	34	14
Reeds Spring	863	3	3	0
Republic	17,174	25	21	4
Rich Hill	1,309	2	2	0
Richland	1,785	5	5	0
Richmond	5,638	12	10	2
Richmond Heights	8,831	37	36	1
Riverside	3,574	36	27	9
Riverview	2,820	13	12	1
Rogersville	3,960	10	10	0
Rolla	20,522	58	35	23
Salem	4,915	18	13	5
Salisbury	1,513	4	3	1
Sarcoxie	1,548	3	3	0
Savannah	5,240	6	5	1
Scott City	4,458	18	13	5
Sedalia	21,639	60	43	17
Seligman	841	4	4	0
Senath	1,595	3	3	0
Seneca	2,392	6	6	0
Seymour	2,021	7	7	0
Shrewsbury	6,074	23	21	2
Sikeston	15,987	66	48	18
Smithville	11,097	20	19	1
Southwest City	954	3	3	0
Springfield	168,856	404	329	75
St. Ann	12,586	67	46	21
Steele	1,861	4	4	0
St. John	6,318	23	22	1

Table 78. Full-Time Law Enforcement Employees, by Selected State and City, 2020—Continued

(Number.)

State/city	Population	Total law enforcement employees	Total officers	Total civilians
St. Joseph	74,680	169	128	41
St. Louis	298,422	1,659	1,262	397
Stover	1,094	3	3	0
Strasburg	142	2	2	0
St. Robert	6,485	27	19	8
Sullivan	7,128	26	19	7
Summersville	489	3	3	0
Sunset Hills	8,445	32	25	7
Thayer	2,121	13	8	5
Town and Country	11,142	30	29	1
Troy	13,089	25	23	2
Truesdale	905	1	1	0
Union	12,195	26	24	2
University City	34,045	91	70	21
Van Buren	795	5	5	0
Velda City	1,355	7	4	3
Verona	599	2	2	0
Versailles	2,477	17	16	1
Viburnum	648	3	3	0
Vienna	591	2	2	0
Vinita Park	10,951	42	40	2
Walnut Grove	794	2	2	0
Warrensburg	20,591	31	26	5
Warrenton	8,450	27	23	4
Warson Woods	1,892	6	6	0
Washington	14,092	32	29	3
Waynesville	5,338	27	25	2
Weatherby Lake	2,115	15	15	0
Webb City	12,264	27	23	4
Webster Groves	22,798	48	46	2
Wellington	804	3	3	0
Wellsville	1,153	3	3	0
Weston	1,834	4	4	0
Willow Springs	2,090	12	10	2
Winona	1,289	1	1	0
Woodson Terrace	4,032	20	18	2
Wright City	4,458	15	14	1
MONTANA				
Baker	1,907	4	4	0
Belgrade	9,762	23	19	4
Billings	110,157	184	156	28
Boulder	1,287	3	3	0
Bozeman	51,460	69	60	9
Bridger	760	3	3	0
Chinook	1,260	4	4	0
Colstrip	2,249	11	7	4
Columbia Falls	6,023	11	10	1
Columbus	2,100	4	4	0
Conrad	2,458	5	5	0
Cut Bank	3,075	9	7	2
Deer Lodge	2,822	6	6	0
Dillon	4,318	11	10	1
East Helena	2,113	4	4	0
Ennis	1,012	1	1	0
Eureka	1,407	4	4	0
Fairview	867	3	3	0
Fort Benton	1,429	4	4	0
Glasgow	3,326	10	6	4
Glendive	4,908	15	10	5
Great Falls	58,345	127	87	40
Hamilton	4,970	15	14	1
Havre	9,820	26	20	6
Helena	33,629	69	47	22
Hot Springs	587	2	2	0
Kalispell	25,125	51	41	10
Laurel	6,732	20	14	6
Lewistown	5,772	24	13	11
Libby	2,797	6	6	0
Livingston	7,892	14	14	0
Manhattan	1,955	4	4	0
Miles City	8,250	17	16	1
Missoula	76,468	144	116	28
Plains	1,149	2	2	0
Polson	5,115	16	15	1
Red Lodge	2,324	7	7	0
Ronan City	2,141	6	6	0
Sidney	6,279	12	11	1
Stevensville	2,100	4	3	1
Thompson Falls	1,439	4	4	0
Troy	966	4	4	0
West Yellowstone	1,388	11	5	6
Whitefish	8,523	20	17	3
Wolf Point	2,744	8	6	2

Table 78. Full-Time Law Enforcement Employees, by Selected State and City, 2020—Continued

(Number.)

State/city	Population	Total law enforcement employees	Total officers	Total civilians
NEBRASKA				
Albion	1,576	6	3	3
Alliance	8,051	23	15	8
Aurora	4,554	11	10	1
Bayard	1,071	4	4	0
Beatrice	12,238	36	22	14
Bellevue	53,761	106	93	13
Bennington	1,527	3	3	0
Blair	7,919	18	16	2
Boys Town	545	14	14	0
Broken Bow	3,492	8	7	1
Burwell	1,157	2	2	0
Central City	2,867	7	6	1
Chadron	5,366	18	11	7
Columbus	23,597	43	36	7
Crete	7,009	13	13	0
Emerson	787	1	1	0
Falls City	4,094	13	9	4
Fremont	26,381	41	35	6
Gering	8,086	19	17	2
Gordon	1,512	8	6	2
Gothenburg	3,432	7	6	1
Grand Island	51,547	101	84	17
Harvard	959	2	2	0
Hastings	24,638	53	39	14
Holdrege	5,399	17	10	7
Imperial	2,053	4	4	0
Kearney	34,201	73	57	16
Kimball	2,359	4	4	0
Laurel	911	1	1	0
La Vista	17,228	45	39	6
Lexington	10,103	21	19	2
Lincoln	292,600	481	342	139
Madison	2,390	3	3	0
McCook	7,543	23	16	7
Milford	2,090	3	3	0
Minden	2,954	6	6	0
Mitchell	1,614	4	4	0
Morrill	885	2	2	0
Nebraska City	7,292	15	14	1
Neligh	1,488	3	3	0
Norfolk	24,467	58	40	18
North Platte	23,523	62	40	22
Ogallala	4,472	10	9	1
Omaha	480,297	1,012	867	145
O'Neill	3,565	8	7	1
Ord	2,069	4	4	0
Papillion	20,512	50	46	4
Pierce	1,724	3	3	0
Plattsmouth	6,435	17	14	3
Ralston	7,422	15	14	1
Ravenna	1,357	2	2	0
Schuyler	6,312	11	9	2
Scottsbluff	15,665	35	31	4
Scribner	793	1	1	0
Seward	7,242	13	11	2
Sidney	6,049	13	11	2
South Sioux City	12,746	28	27	1
St. Paul	2,336	4	4	0
Superior	1,791	2	2	0
Sutton	1,427	2	2	0
Tekamah	1,696	5	5	0
Tilden	927	1	1	0
Valentine	2,704	6	5	1
Valley	2,948	5	5	0
Wahoo	4,550	7	7	0
Waterloo	922	4	4	0
Wayne	5,658	11	6	5
West Point	3,273	7	5	2
Wymore	1,324	2	2	0
York	7,854	17	15	2
NEVADA				
Boulder City	16,346	48	35	13
Carlin	2,268	7	5	2
Elko	20,697	45	38	7
Fallon	8,648	40	27	13
Henderson	328,056	654	463	191
Las Vegas Metropolitan Police Department	1,693,061	5,716	4,115	1,601
Lovelock	1,822	5	2	3
Mesquite	20,290	49	36	13
Reno	259,168	469	339	130
Sparks	106,664	159	108	51
West Wendover	4,258	21	12	9

Table 78. Full-Time Law Enforcement Employees, by Selected State and City, 2020—Continued

(Number.)

State/city	Population	Total law enforcement employees	Total officers	Total civilians
Winnemucca	7,786	28	23	5
Yerington	3,256	7	6	1
NEW HAMPSHIRE				
Alexandria	1,618	1	1	0
Allenstown	4,462	11	10	1
Alstead	1,938	2	2	0
Alton	5,343	14	12	2
Amherst	11,414	20	19	1
Antrim	2,697	7	6	1
Ashland	2,053	5	5	0
Atkinson	7,196	9	8	1
Auburn	5,662	12	10	2
Barnstead	4,762	4	4	0
Barrington	9,358	14	13	1
Bartlett	2,807	4	4	0
Bedford	22,788	53	40	13
Belmont	7,342	17	14	3
Bennington	1,518	2	2	0
Berlin	10,140	31	23	8
Bethlehem	2,579	6	6	0
Boscawen	4,032	8	7	1
Bow	8,032	13	12	1
Bradford	1,714	3	3	0
Brentwood	4,525	4	3	1
Bristol	3,102	10	9	1
Brookline	5,506	9	8	1
Campton	3,297	9	7	2
Canaan	3,894	6	5	1
Candia	3,970	8	7	1
Canterbury	2,475	3	3	0
Carroll	745	4	4	0
Center Harbor	1,099	5	4	1
Charlestown	5,010	11	7	4
Chester	5,334	9	8	1
Chesterfield	3,630	5	4	1
Chichester	2,726	5	5	0
Claremont	12,887	27	21	6
Colebrook	2,121	5	5	0
Concord	43,737	93	81	12
Conway	10,269	30	22	8
Danville	4,581	5	5	0
Deerfield	4,576	9	8	1
Deering	1,978	2	2	0
Derry	33,555	69	56	13
Dover	32,480	76	49	27
Dublin	1,538	4	3	1
Dunbarton	2,894	5	5	0
Durham	16,510	20	17	3
East Kingston	2,428	6	5	1
Effingham	1,479	1	1	0
Enfield	4,526	8	7	1
Epping	7,115	16	15	1
Epsom	4,787	7	6	1
Exeter	15,448	32	24	8
Farmington	7,003	15	14	1
Fitzwilliam	2,367	4	3	1
Franconia	1,105	4	4	0
Franklin	8,711	25	17	8
Freedom	1,593	2	2	0
Fremont	4,764	6	5	1
Gilford	7,258	26	20	6
Gilmanton	3,779	6	5	1
Goffstown	18,098	45	30	15
Gorham	2,587	10	6	4
Grantham	2,942	6	5	1
Greenland	4,194	10	9	1
Hampstead	8,654	9	9	0
Hampton	15,570	42	35	7
Hampton Falls	2,437	4	4	0
Hancock	1,657	3	3	0
Hanover	11,498	28	17	11
Haverhill	4,551	7	6	1
Henniker	5,039	9	8	1
Hillsborough	6,001	23	15	8
Hinsdale	3,893	9	6	3
Holderness	2,106	7	6	1
Hollis	8,040	18	15	3
Hooksett	14,668	40	29	11
Hopkinton	5,781	6	5	1
Hudson	25,748	67	51	16
Jackson	863	4	4	0
Jaffrey	5,258	12	11	1
Keene	22,707	51	40	11
Kensington	2,107	6	5	1

Table 78. Full-Time Law Enforcement Employees, by Selected State and City, 2020—Continued

(Number.)

State/city	Population	Total law enforcement employees	Total officers	Total civilians
Kingston	6,500	7	6	1
Laconia	16,669	54	45	9
Lancaster	3,229	9	7	2
Lebanon	13,709	46	33	13
Lee	4,601	9	8	1
Lincoln	1,771	16	10	6
Lisbon	1,577	3	3	0
Litchfield	8,682	14	12	2
Littleton	5,862	15	13	2
Londonderry	26,812	69	56	13
Loudon	5,675	6	5	1
Lyme	1,671	2	2	0
Madison	2,618	4	4	0
Manchester	113,018	279	225	54
Marlborough	2,078	2	2	0
Mason	1,438	3	3	0
Meredith	6,484	17	13	4
Merrimack	26,602	52	39	13
Middleton	1,845	4	4	0
Milford	16,561	32	27	5
Milton	4,633	7	6	1
Mont Vernon	2,686	4	4	0
Moultonborough	4,198	9	8	1
Nashua	89,671	233	174	59
New Boston	5,966	10	9	1
Newbury	2,246	5	5	0
New Castle	981	4	4	0
New Durham	2,715	5	5	0
Newfields	1,744	5	4	1
New Hampton	2,231	5	4	1
Newington	821	12	11	1
New Ipswich	5,425	6	5	1
New London	4,300	14	9	5
Newmarket	9,192	20	13	7
Newport	6,342	16	11	5
Newton	4,969	7	6	1
Northfield	4,956	9	8	1
North Hampton	4,513	13	12	1
Northumberland	2,123	3	3	0
Northwood	4,321	9	8	1
Nottingham	5,182	9	8	1
Orford	1,308	1	1	0
Ossipee	4,389	10	9	1
Pelham	14,373	30	23	7
Pembroke	7,212	14	12	2
Peterborough	6,736	14	12	2
Pittsburg	815	2	2	0
Pittsfield	4,126	6	6	0
Plainfield	2,404	2	2	0
Plaistow	7,738	22	15	7
Plymouth	6,850	18	11	7
Portsmouth	22,032	84	65	19
Raymond	10,583	24	16	8
Rindge	6,100	9	8	1
Rochester	31,762	72	57	15
Rollinsford	2,596	4	4	0
Rye	5,495	11	10	1
Salem	29,943	79	63	16
Sanbornton	3,000	7	6	1
Sandown	6,620	8	7	1
Sandwich	1,362	2	2	0
Seabrook	8,871	30	25	5
Somersworth	12,005	34	27	7
South Hampton	829	2	2	0
Springfield	1,344	2	2	0
Strafford	4,242	6	6	0
Stratham	7,521	12	11	1
Sugar Hill	579	2	2	0
Sunapee	3,501	6	5	1
Swanzey	7,219	12	11	1
Tamworth	3,101	3	3	0
Thornton	2,541	7	6	1
Tilton	3,546	20	16	4
Troy	2,100	2	2	0
Tuftonboro	2,425	4	4	0
Wakefield	5,799	14	12	2
Warner	2,931	5	4	1
Washington	1,101	1	1	0
Waterville Valley	240	6	6	0
Weare	9,124	12	11	1
Webster	1,962	2	2	0
Whitefield	2,200	7	6	1
Wilton	3,801	7	7	0
Winchester	4,213	9	8	1
Windham	15,017	28	21	7

Table 78. Full-Time Law Enforcement Employees, by Selected State and City, 2020—Continued

(Number.)

State/city	Population	Total law enforcement employees	Total officers	Total civilians
Wolfeboro	6,433	19	13	6
Woodstock	1,364	6	6	0
NEW JERSEY				
Aberdeen Township	19,471	49	42	7
Absecon	8,856	30	24	6
Allendale	6,751	20	15	5
Allenhurst	482	13	9	4
Allentown	1,770	7	6	1
Alpine	1,845	12	12	0
Andover Township	5,826	17	12	5
Asbury Park	15,331	93	89	4
Atlantic City	37,550	224	190	34
Atlantic Highlands	4,348	19	14	5
Audubon	8,608	18	17	1
Avalon	1,225	28	21	7
Avon-by-the-Sea	1,771	12	12	0
Barnegat Township	23,998	55	53	2
Barrington	6,601	17	15	2
Bay Head	979	10	9	1
Bayonne	65,013	247	184	63
Beach Haven	1,210	13	12	1
Beachwood	11,357	22	20	2
Bedminster Township	7,963	18	16	2
Belleville	36,533	101	96	5
Bellmawr	11,318	22	21	1
Belmar	5,518	30	24	6
Belvidere	2,548	7	6	1
Bergenfield	27,347	51	43	8
Berkeley Heights Township	13,371	30	27	3
Berkeley Township	42,168	92	70	22
Berlin	7,517	19	18	1
Berlin Township	5,721	19	18	1
Bernards Township	27,130	41	38	3
Bernardsville	7,593	26	20	6
Beverly	2,472	8	8	0
Blairstown Township	5,665	9	8	1
Bloomfield	50,221	150	126	24
Bloomingdale	8,098	20	19	1
Bogota	8,342	20	15	5
Boonton	8,977	25	23	2
Boonton Township	4,228	13	13	0
Bordentown City	3,778	14	14	0
Bordentown Township	11,974	25	23	2
Bound Brook	10,174	31	25	6
Bradley Beach	4,131	22	18	4
Branchburg Township	14,526	29	27	2
Brick Township	76,326	211	141	70
Bridgeton	24,032	74	61	13
Bridgewater Township	44,006	81	73	8
Brielle	4,656	17	16	1
Brigantine	8,566	45	35	10
Brooklawn	1,892	8	8	0
Burlington City	9,849	37	33	4
Burlington Township	22,595	56	47	9
Butler	7,643	17	16	1
Byram Township	7,880	14	14	0
Caldwell	7,938	18	18	0
Camden County Police Department	73,127	423	386	37
Cape May	3,401	27	22	5
Carlstadt	6,126	28	26	2
Carney's Point Township	7,632	20	19	1
Carteret	23,444	74	64	10
Cedar Grove Township	12,483	31	30	1
Chatham	8,586	25	21	4
Chatham Township	10,071	24	22	2
Cherry Hill Township	71,220	164	135	29
Chesilhurst	1,615	10	9	1
Chesterfield Township	7,557	12	11	1
Chester Township	7,640	24	23	1
Cinnaminson Township	16,429	28	28	0
Clark Township	16,026	47	36	11
Clayton	8,790	16	15	1
Clementon	4,950	12	12	0
Cliffside Park	26,400	44	43	1
Clifton	85,058	194	158	36
Clinton	2,684	10	10	0
Clinton Township	12,465	24	23	1
Closter	8,511	21	20	1
Collingswood	13,864	31	27	4
Colts Neck Township	9,786	27	26	1
Cranbury Township	4,086	22	21	1
Cranford Township	24,186	66	52	14
Cresskill	8,672	29	24	5
Deal	715	22	18	4

Table 78. Full-Time Law Enforcement Employees, by Selected State and City, 2020—Continued

(Number.)

State/city	Population	Total law enforcement employees	Total officers	Total civilians
Delanco Township	4,448	13	12	1
Delaware Township	4,410	8	7	1
Delran Township	16,444	32	28	4
Demarest	4,884	16	16	0
Denville Township	16,400	42	33	9
Deptford Township	30,275	73	67	6
Dover	17,654	43	39	4
Dumont	17,507	40	32	8
Dunellen	7,192	19	19	0
Eastampton Township	6,156	20	19	1
East Brunswick Township	47,573	106	83	23
East Greenwich Township	10,834	22	21	1
East Hanover Township	10,881	38	34	4
East Newark	2,614	7	7	0
East Orange	64,320	243	192	51
East Rutherford	9,767	39	38	1
East Windsor Township	27,265	48	43	5
Eatontown	12,124	49	37	12
Edgewater	13,573	31	29	2
Edgewater Park Township	8,618	17	15	2
Edison Township	99,584	231	184	47
Egg Harbor City	4,031	15	14	1
Egg Harbor Township	42,110	133	86	47
Elizabeth	129,518	407	312	95
Elk Township	4,168	12	11	1
Elmer	1,299	2	2	0
Elmwood Park	19,994	54	49	5
Emerson	7,610	25	22	3
Englewood	28,514	101	77	24
Englewood Cliffs	5,351	22	21	1
Englishtown	1,921	7	7	0
Essex Fells	2,083	13	13	0
Evesham Township	45,148	88	79	9
Ewing Township	36,325	97	77	20
Fairfield Township, Essex County	7,468	43	39	4
Fair Haven	5,696	13	13	0
Fair Lawn	32,910	69	60	9
Fairview	14,209	36	33	3
Fanwood	7,732	17	16	1
Far Hills	903	6	6	0
Flemington	4,577	15	15	0
Florence Township	12,527	31	29	2
Florham Park	11,455	38	32	6
Fort Lee	38,921	112	93	19
Franklin	4,684	17	16	1
Franklin Lakes	11,166	33	26	7
Franklin Township, Gloucester County	16,226	41	37	4
Franklin Township, Hunterdon County	3,557	6	6	0
Franklin Township, Somerset County	66,138	124	103	21
Freehold Borough	11,643	34	30	4
Freehold Township	34,456	72	68	4
Frenchtown	1,347	3	2	1
Galloway Township	35,444	83	63	20
Garfield	31,908	68	59	9
Garwood	4,360	20	16	4
Gibbsboro	2,210	9	9	0
Glassboro	20,461	55	50	5
Glen Ridge	7,574	29	23	6
Glen Rock	11,705	25	23	2
Gloucester City	11,182	38	36	2
Gloucester Township	63,755	150	128	22
Green Brook Township	7,004	23	22	1
Greenwich Township, Gloucester County	4,777	17	16	1
Greenwich Township, Warren County	5,415	12	12	0
Guttenberg	11,100	29	26	3
Hackettstown	9,316	20	19	1
Haddonfield	11,274	25	22	3
Haddon Heights	7,527	16	15	1
Haddon Township	14,510	27	25	2
Haledon	8,280	20	20	0
Hamburg	3,110	9	8	1
Hamilton Township, Atlantic County	25,654	82	56	26
Hamilton Township, Mercer County	86,805	202	168	34
Hammonton	13,845	36	30	6
Hanover Township	14,290	39	32	7
Harding Township	3,750	15	14	1
Hardyston Township	7,744	23	17	6
Harrington Park	4,730	11	11	0
Harrison	20,937	50	41	9
Harrison Township	13,178	24	23	1
Harvey Cedars	345	9	9	0
Hasbrouck Heights	11,988	31	29	2
Haworth	3,391	13	12	1
Hawthorne	18,728	39	33	6
Hazlet Township	19,593	45	42	3

Table 78. Full-Time Law Enforcement Employees, by Selected State and City, 2020—Continued

(Number.)

State/city	Population	Total law enforcement employees	Total officers	Total civilians
High Bridge	3,385	7	7	0
Highland Park	13,666	35	28	7
Highlands	4,682	16	15	1
Hightstown	5,273	14	13	1
Hillsborough Township	40,210	63	54	9
Hillsdale	10,308	25	20	5
Hillside Township	21,995	74	64	10
Hi-Nella	856	12	12	0
Hoboken	52,902	148	133	15
Ho-Ho-Kus	4,058	20	16	4
Holland Township	5,074	8	7	1
Holmdel Township	16,726	51	43	8
Hopatcong	14,086	35	29	6
Hopewell Township	17,641	38	29	9
Howell Township	52,048	129	114	15
Independence Township	5,386	10	9	1
Irvington	54,306	201	144	57
Island Heights	1,685	7	7	0
Jackson Township	58,120	110	90	20
Jamesburg	5,878	21	16	5
Jefferson Township	20,626	42	34	8
Jersey City	263,273	1,284	1,005	279
Keansburg	9,582	42	33	9
Kearny	41,037	114	108	6
Kenilworth	8,211	32	27	5
Keyport	6,951	22	20	2
Kinnelon	9,859	17	16	1
Lacey Township	29,524	56	42	14
Lakehurst	2,718	12	10	2
Lakewood Township	108,023	189	148	41
Lambertville	3,788	12	10	2
Laurel Springs	1,860	7	7	0
Lavallette	1,868	14	12	2
Lawnside	2,872	10	9	1
Lawrence Township, Mercer County	32,282	67	60	7
Lebanon Township	6,055	11	10	1
Leonia	9,033	22	19	3
Lincoln Park	10,051	30	24	6
Linden	42,515	184	140	44
Lindenwold	17,206	47	44	3
Linwood	6,612	18	17	1
Little Egg Harbor Township	21,928	55	43	12
Little Falls Township	14,463	34	28	6
Little Ferry	10,736	30	25	5
Little Silver	5,761	20	15	5
Livingston Township	30,372	87	70	17
Lodi	24,343	50	47	3
Logan Township	5,847	23	22	1
Long Beach Township	3,075	47	35	12
Long Branch	30,175	118	94	24
Long Hill Township	8,389	25	23	2
Longport	846	12	12	0
Lopatcong Township	8,419	17	16	1
Lower Alloways Creek Township	1,660	12	12	0
Lower Township	21,177	57	51	6
Lumberton Township	12,153	26	24	2
Lyndhurst Township	23,169	55	52	3
Madison	17,850	35	27	8
Magnolia	4,259	12	12	0
Mahwah Township	26,201	60	51	9
Manalapan Township	39,353	62	58	4
Manasquan	5,796	22	17	5
Manchester Township	43,856	123	74	49
Mansfield Township, Burlington County	8,527	16	15	1
Mansfield Township, Warren County	7,325	16	15	1
Mantoloking	245	11	10	1
Mantua Township	14,769	29	27	2
Manville	10,116	26	23	3
Maple Shade Township	18,402	38	34	4
Maplewood Township	25,531	75	63	12
Margate City	5,813	37	28	9
Marlboro Township	39,593	115	89	26
Matawan	8,613	25	24	1
Maywood	9,610	26	22	4
Medford Lakes	3,888	11	10	1
Medford Township	23,433	39	35	4
Mendham	4,825	15	14	1
Mendham Township	5,632	16	15	1
Merchantville	3,688	16	14	2
Metuchen	14,639	34	29	5
Middlesex Borough	13,669	32	29	3
Middle Township	18,093	66	55	11
Middletown Township	65,170	118	108	10
Midland Park	7,214	18	17	1
Millburn Township	20,053	64	58	6

Table 78. Full-Time Law Enforcement Employees, by Selected State and City, 2020—Continued

(Number.)

State/city	Population	Total law enforcement employees	Total officers	Total civilians
Milltown	6,967	19	16	3
Millville	27,272	87	76	11
Monmouth Beach	3,235	10	9	1
Monroe Township, Gloucester County	36,893	68	64	4
Monroe Township, Middlesex County	45,653	87	66	21
Montclair	38,621	130	107	23
Montgomery Township	23,268	40	34	6
Montvale	8,643	26	24	2
Montville Township	20,982	42	37	5
Moonachie	2,700	22	19	3
Moorestown Township	20,491	36	31	5
Morris Plains	6,335	19	17	2
Morristown	19,337	61	57	4
Morris Township	22,100	54	49	5
Mountain Lakes	4,224	14	13	1
Mountainside	6,902	26	21	5
Mount Arlington	5,944	16	15	1
Mount Ephraim	4,573	14	13	1
Mount Holly Township	9,546	27	24	3
Mount Laurel Township	41,179	82	75	7
Mount Olive Township	28,973	60	50	10
Mullica Township	5,825	15	14	1
Neptune City	4,573	19	18	1
Neptune Township	27,320	88	76	12
Netcong	3,116	13	12	1
Newark	282,242	1,407	1,062	345
New Brunswick	55,701	164	146	18
New Hanover Township	7,859	3	3	0
New Milford	16,417	43	41	2
New Providence	13,741	27	25	2
Newton	8,008	27	22	5
North Arlington	15,695	39	31	8
North Bergen Township	60,567	136	116	20
North Brunswick Township	41,383	98	81	17
North Caldwell	6,666	21	16	5
Northfield	7,979	23	22	1
North Haledon	8,382	28	22	6
North Hanover Township	7,443	11	10	1
North Plainfield	21,279	53	45	8
Northvale	4,955	14	14	0
North Wildwood	3,731	37	29	8
Norwood	5,792	17	16	1
Nutley Township	28,408	83	70	13
Oakland	12,929	34	28	6
Oaklyn	3,942	17	16	1
Ocean City	10,893	82	66	16
Ocean Gate	2,042	12	11	1
Oceanport	5,708	16	15	1
Ocean Township, Monmouth County	26,462	74	61	13
Ocean Township, Ocean County	9,184	31	21	10
Ogdensburg	2,237	6	6	0
Old Bridge Township	65,537	122	101	21
Old Tappan	5,904	14	13	1
Oradell	8,137	24	23	1
Orange City	30,541	163	134	29
Palisades Park	20,818	42	39	3
Palmyra	7,114	17	16	1
Paramus	26,222	125	101	24
Park Ridge	8,688	21	20	1
Parsippany-Troy Hills Township	51,317	128	99	29
Passaic	69,610	194	159	35
Paterson	144,947	430	403	27
Paulsboro	5,820	21	19	2
Peapack-Gladstone	2,606	9	8	1
Pemberton Borough	1,315	6	6	0
Pemberton Township	26,875	43	38	5
Pennington	2,575	6	6	0
Pennsauken Township	35,698	96	89	7
Penns Grove	4,721	15	14	1
Pennsville Township	12,315	23	21	2
Pequannock Township	14,887	36	31	5
Perth Amboy	51,384	141	122	19
Phillipsburg	14,136	38	37	1
Pine Beach	2,192	7	6	1
Pine Hill	10,427	24	21	3
Pine Valley	11	6	6	0
Piscataway Township	56,870	95	77	18
Pitman	8,701	19	18	1
Plainfield	50,333	142	121	21
Plainsboro Township	22,847	48	36	12
Pleasantville	20,135	71	65	6
Plumsted Township	8,598	15	14	1
Pohatcong Township	3,158	16	15	1
Point Pleasant	18,842	40	31	9
Point Pleasant Beach	4,543	31	25	6

Table 78. Full-Time Law Enforcement Employees, by Selected State and City, 2020—Continued

(Number.)

State/city	Population	Total law enforcement employees	Total officers	Total civilians
Pompton Lakes	10,961	29	24	5
Princeton	31,458	55	51	4
Prospect Park	5,834	19	18	1
Rahway	30,157	87	76	11
Ramsey	14,904	41	34	7
Randolph Township	25,311	41	35	6
Raritan	7,888	22	21	1
Raritan Township	22,402	41	38	3
Readington Township	15,813	25	23	2
Red Bank	11,929	45	39	6
Ridgefield	11,171	30	28	2
Ridgefield Park	12,904	44	37	7
Ridgewood	25,036	50	45	5
Ringwood	12,177	26	21	5
Riverdale	4,198	22	17	5
River Edge	11,431	27	24	3
Riverside Township	7,788	18	18	0
Riverton	2,676	6	6	0
River Vale Township	10,007	24	23	1
Robbinsville Township	14,628	37	29	8
Rochelle Park Township	5,566	26	22	4
Rockaway	6,250	16	15	1
Rockaway Township	26,046	61	50	11
Roseland	5,829	25	24	1
Roselle	21,867	66	53	13
Roselle Park	13,604	36	34	2
Roxbury Township	22,439	45	42	3
Rumson	6,675	21	16	5
Runnemede	8,273	19	18	1
Rutherford	18,307	43	41	2
Saddle Brook Township	13,533	35	33	2
Saddle River	3,170	23	18	5
Salem	4,661	19	17	2
Sayreville	44,282	103	88	15
Scotch Plains Township	24,313	52	49	3
Sea Bright	1,325	17	11	6
Sea Girt	1,758	13	12	1
Sea Isle City	2,019	28	22	6
Seaside Heights	2,917	28	25	3
Seaside Park	1,541	13	12	1
Secaucus	22,535	89	74	15
Ship Bottom	1,156	12	10	2
Shrewsbury	4,082	20	16	4
Somerdale	5,511	16	15	1
Somers Point	10,108	38	30	8
Somerville	12,084	33	31	2
South Amboy	9,235	34	28	6
South Bound Brook	4,526	14	13	1
South Brunswick Township	45,877	106	82	24
South Hackensack Township	2,438	24	21	3
South Orange Village	16,732	52	46	6
South Plainfield	24,100	72	58	14
South River	15,731	40	31	9
South Toms River	3,701	13	12	1
Sparta Township	18,467	44	32	12
Spotswood	8,216	29	25	4
Springfield Township, Burlington County	3,241	11	10	1
Springfield Township, Union County	17,639	49	45	4
Spring Lake	2,894	14	14	0
Spring Lake Heights	4,502	15	15	0
Stafford Township	28,029	72	55	17
Stanhope	3,275	9	8	1
Stone Harbor	804	19	17	2
Stratford	6,937	14	14	0
Summit	21,917	51	47	4
Surf City	1,203	10	10	0
Teaneck Township	40,290	108	93	15
Tenafly	14,427	40	34	6
Tewksbury Township	5,754	13	12	1
Tinton Falls	17,388	44	42	2
Toms River Township	94,561	207	162	45
Totowa	10,777	32	28	4
Trenton	82,909	323	255	68
Tuckerton	3,396	14	13	1
Union Beach	5,210	21	17	4
Union City	68,055	199	162	37
Union Township	58,613	187	135	52
Upper Saddle River	8,199	21	17	4
Ventnor City	9,815	50	37	13
Vernon Township	21,819	41	33	8
Verona	13,368	35	29	6
Vineland	59,288	153	120	33
Voorhees Township	29,130	62	52	10
Waldwick	10,156	26	21	5
Wallington	11,499	24	23	1

Table 78. Full-Time Law Enforcement Employees, by Selected State and City, 2020—Continued

(Number.)

State/city	Population	Total law enforcement employees	Total officers	Total civilians
Wall Township	25,489	87	71	16
Wanaque	11,828	28	23	5
Warren Township	15,689	37	30	7
Washington Township, Bergen County	9,171	26	21	5
Washington Township, Gloucester County	47,551	92	84	8
Washington Township, Morris County	18,086	30	29	1
Washington Township, Warren County	6,323	30	28	2
Watchung	6,018	36	30	6
Waterford Township	10,675	26	25	1
Wayne Township	53,162	146	118	28
Weehawken Township	14,874	66	55	11
Westampton Township	8,632	26	23	3
West Amwell Township	2,728	6	6	0
West Caldwell Township	10,841	31	26	5
West Deptford Township	20,878	45	42	3
Westfield	29,389	74	61	13
West Long Branch	7,860	22	21	1
West Milford Township	26,310	52	45	7
West New York	52,977	133	120	13
West Orange	47,666	112	98	14
Westville	4,123	14	13	1
West Wildwood	545	6	6	0
West Windsor Township	27,944	61	49	12
Westwood	11,079	31	26	5
Wharton	6,343	23	21	2
Wildwood	4,908	51	41	10
Wildwood Crest	3,024	28	25	3
Willingboro Township	32,048	71	63	8
Winfield Township	1,504	9	9	0
Winslow Township	38,460	80	74	6
Woodbridge Township	100,119	263	203	60
Woodbury	9,744	30	27	3
Woodbury Heights	2,949	8	7	1
Woodcliff Lake	5,845	20	19	1
Woodland Park	12,653	32	27	5
Woodlynne	2,906	8	6	2
Wood-Ridge	9,489	28	24	4
Woodstown	3,429	10	9	1
Woolwich Township	13,278	29	28	1
Wyckoff Township	16,950	27	27	0
NEW MEXICO				
Artesia	12,451	45	25	20
Capitan	1,425	4	3	1
Clovis	38,326	75	50	25
Cuba	760	5	4	1
Dexter	1,241	6	5	1
Farmington	44,191	164	124	40
Hobbs	39,751	131	89	42
Las Vegas	12,799	54	43	11
Los Alamos	19,581	72	34	38
Los Lunas	16,170	69	34	35
Magdalena	872	3	3	0
Moriarty	1,846	10	9	1
Mountainair	866	6	5	1
Peralta	3,576	14	13	1
Roswell	47,451	94	72	22
Santa Clara	1,746	4	3	1
San Ysidro	202	3	2	1
Springer	892	1	1	0
Sunland Park	18,437	25	20	5
Tatum	833	9	4	5
Texico	1,061	2	2	0
NEW YORK				
Addison Town and Village	2,458	3	3	0
Akron Village	2,852	1	1	0
Albany	96,318	371	295	76
Albion Village	5,698	13	12	1
Alfred Village	3,970	5	5	0
Altamont Village	1,664	1	1	0
Amherst Town	121,304	183	155	28
Amityville Village	9,387	22	21	1
Amsterdam	17,675	42	38	4
Arcade Village	1,919	6	6	0
Ardsley Village	4,515	19	19	0
Asharoken Village	644	3	3	0
Attica Village	2,389	5	5	0
Avon Village	3,272	5	5	0
Baldwinsville Village	7,895	13	12	1
Ballston Spa Village	5,204	4	4	0
Batavia	14,278	36	33	3
Bath Village	5,438	11	10	1
Beacon	13,984	36	33	3

Table 78. Full-Time Law Enforcement Employees, by Selected State and City, 2020—Continued

(Number.)

State/city	Population	Total law enforcement employees	Total officers	Total civilians
Bedford Town	17,672	43	38	5
Bethlehem Town	35,039	53	38	15
Blooming Grove Town	11,822	17	15	2
Bolivar Village	968	1	1	0
Brant Town	2,056	1	1	0
Briarcliff Manor Village	8,126	20	20	0
Bronxville Village	6,422	23	21	2
Buffalo	254,627	927	752	175
Cairo Town	6,390	2	2	0
Cambridge Village	1,803	3	3	0
Camden Village	2,151	2	2	0
Camillus Town and Village	24,098	28	24	4
Canajoharie Village	2,122	5	5	0
Canandaigua	10,112	27	25	2
Canastota Village	4,518	6	6	0
Canisteo Village	2,120	3	3	0
Canton Village	6,516	11	10	1
Carmel Town	34,093	39	32	7
Carthage Village	3,250	4	4	0
Catskill Village	3,787	16	14	2
Cayuga Heights Village	3,589	7	6	1
Cazenovia Village	2,851	6	5	1
Central Square Village	1,740	4	4	0
Centre Island Village	409	6	6	0
Cheektowaga Town	76,536	156	119	37
Chester Town	8,095	15	15	0
Chester Village	4,108	15	14	1
Chittenango Village	4,826	2	1	1
Clayton Village	1,816	2	2	0
Cobleskill Village	4,323	11	11	0
Coeymans Town	7,247	3	2	1
Cohoes	16,746	34	31	3
Colchester Town	1,947	2	2	0
Colonie Town	79,082	144	109	35
Corning	10,469	25	21	4
Cornwall-on-Hudson Village	2,911	3	3	0
Cornwall Town	9,538	11	9	2
Cortland	18,615	46	44	2
Cuba Town	3,059	5	5	0
Deerpark Town	7,732	4	4	0
Delhi Village	2,935	5	5	0
Depew Village	14,965	33	27	6
DeWitt Town	24,947	46	43	3
Dobbs Ferry Village	11,037	29	27	2
Dolgeville Village	2,055	4	4	0
Dryden Village	2,066	4	4	0
Dunkirk	11,673	38	37	1
East Aurora-Aurora Town	13,748	21	16	5
Eastchester Town	19,991	50	48	2
East Fishkill Town	29,578	33	26	7
East Greenbush Town	16,186	33	24	9
East Hampton Town	19,927	92	65	27
East Hampton Village	1,140	29	24	5
Eden Town	7,602	2	1	1
Ellicott Town	4,981	13	13	0
Ellicottville	1,563	4	4	0
Elmira	26,820	79	70	9
Elmira Heights Village	3,774	9	9	0
Elmira Town	5,529	4	4	0
Elmsford Village	5,279	24	21	3
Evans Town	16,061	25	19	6
Fallsburg Town	12,264	21	21	0
Florida Village	2,931	1	1	0
Fort Edward Village	3,256	5	5	0
Fort Plain Village	2,212	3	3	0
Frankfort Town	4,752	3	3	0
Fredonia Village	10,205	18	14	4
Freeport Village	42,962	112	100	12
Fulton City	11,017	36	35	1
Garden City Village	22,465	65	51	14
Geddes Town	10,002	18	16	2
Geneseo Village	8,130	9	9	0
Geneva	12,569	35	33	2
Glen Cove	27,186	58	53	5
Glens Falls	14,215	32	30	2
Glenville Town	21,609	25	24	1
Gloversville	14,656	37	34	3
Goshen Town	8,938	6	6	0
Goshen Village	5,361	21	18	3
Gouverneur Village	3,637	8	5	3
Granville Village	2,428	6	6	0
Great Neck Estates Village	2,892	17	14	3
Greene Village	1,400	1	1	0
Greenwich Village	1,708	1	1	0
Greenwood Lake Village	3,080	4	4	0

Table 78. Full-Time Law Enforcement Employees, by Selected State and City, 2020—Continued

(Number.)

State/city	Population	Total law enforcement employees	Total officers	Total civilians
Groton Village	2,211	1	1	0
Guilderland Town	34,103	53	37	16
Hamburg Town	46,513	64	62	2
Hamburg Village	9,744	14	13	1
Hamilton Village	4,077	5	5	0
Harriman Village	2,455	7	7	0
Harrison Town	29,110	79	68	11
Hastings-on-Hudson Village	7,853	21	21	0
Hempstead Village	55,230	142	113	29
Herkimer Village	7,212	19	19	0
Holley Village	1,669	1	1	0
Homer Village	3,081	5	4	1
Horseheads Village	6,325	10	10	0
Hudson Falls Village	7,029	12	12	0
Hunter Town	2,620	3	3	0
Huntington Bay Village	1,436	4	4	0
Hyde Park Town	20,766	20	16	4
Ilion Village	7,613	18	17	1
Irondequoit Town	49,889	58	48	10
Irvington Village	6,478	23	23	0
Ithaca	30,927	69	61	8
Jamestown	28,842	70	60	10
Johnstown	8,183	24	23	1
Kenmore Village	14,968	29	25	4
Kensington Village	1,193	6	6	0
Kent Town	13,123	23	18	5
Kings Point Village	5,315	21	19	2
Kingston	22,682	74	69	5
Lackawanna	17,674	51	44	7
Lake Placid Village	2,339	16	14	2
Lake Success Village	3,161	27	24	3
Lakewood-Busti	7,125	11	10	1
Lancaster Town	37,633	65	50	15
Larchmont Village	6,112	25	23	2
Le Roy Village	4,246	7	7	0
Lewisboro Town	12,533	3	3	0
Liberty Village	4,182	19	17	2
Little Falls	4,604	12	11	1
Liverpool Village	2,191	4	4	0
Lloyd Town	10,484	12	10	2
Lockport	20,212	49	47	2
Lowville Village	3,297	6	6	0
Lynbrook Village	19,441	58	50	8
Macedon Town and Village	8,856	7	6	1
Malone Village	5,566	13	13	0
Malverne Village	8,482	22	22	0
Mamaroneck Town	12,017	37	36	1
Mamaroneck Village	19,154	58	50	8
Manlius Town	24,139	38	34	4
Marlborough Town	8,579	11	8	3
Massena Village	10,123	24	19	5
Maybrook Village	3,773	3	3	0
Mechanicville	5,018	10	10	0
Medina Village	5,613	13	12	1
Menands Village	3,850	14	11	3
Middleport Village	1,733	3	3	0
Middletown	28,194	79	68	11
Mohawk Village	2,507	4	4	0
Monroe Village	8,609	22	18	4
Montgomery Town	9,222	14	11	3
Montgomery Village	4,617	4	4	0
Monticello Village	6,338	22	20	2
Moriah Town	4,437	2	2	0
Mount Morris Village	2,765	3	3	0
Mount Pleasant Town	26,966	55	47	8
Mount Vernon	67,339	225	164	61
Newark Village	8,784	14	14	0
New Berlin Town	1,507	1	1	0
Newburgh	28,095	74	62	12
Newburgh Town	31,691	56	45	11
New Castle Town	17,824	41	38	3
New Paltz Town and Village	14,040	24	21	3
New Windsor Town	27,980	62	50	12
New York	8,300,377	50,083	34,018	16,065
New York Mills Village	3,200	4	4	0
Niagara Falls	47,474	154	137	17
Niskayuna Town	22,428	31	29	2
North Castle Town	12,266	34	32	2
North Greenbush Town	12,264	20	18	2
Northport Village	7,258	21	17	4
Norwich	6,474	20	20	0
Ocean Beach Village	83	4	4	0
Ogdensburg	10,364	26	22	4
Old Brookville Village	2,196	34	26	8
Old Westbury Village	4,603	30	25	5

Table 78. Full-Time Law Enforcement Employees, by Selected State and City, 2020—Continued

(Number.)

State/city	Population	Total law enforcement employees	Total officers	Total civilians
Olean	13,334	41	34	7
Oneida	10,849	28	24	4
Oneonta City	13,904	28	22	6
Orchard Park Town	29,653	47	36	11
Ossining Village	24,786	65	57	8
Oswego City	17,138	54	47	7
Owego Village	3,846	4	3	1
Oxford Village	1,372	2	2	0
Oyster Bay Cove Village	4,300	14	14	0
Peekskill	24,371	61	51	10
Pelham Manor Village	5,535	24	23	1
Pelham Village	6,956	29	26	3
Penn Yan Village	4,900	13	12	1
Perry Village	3,471	3	3	0
Plattsburgh City	19,460	48	42	6
Pleasantville Village	7,280	23	21	2
Port Chester Village	29,181	60	58	2
Port Dickinson Village	1,513	5	4	1
Port Jervis	8,526	31	30	1
Portville Village	941	1	1	0
Port Washington	19,391	68	60	8
Poughkeepsie	30,480	115	89	26
Poughkeepsie Town	38,934	95	80	15
Pound Ridge Town	5,133	2	1	1
Quogue Village	1,019	15	14	1
Rensselaer City	9,149	35	28	7
Riverhead Town	33,461	94	79	15
Rochester	205,199	810	711	99
Rockville Centre Village	24,604	65	56	9
Rome	31,978	69	67	2
Rosendale Town	5,755	2	2	0
Rotterdam Town	30,071	44	40	4
Rye	15,692	41	37	4
Rye Brook Village	9,542	28	27	1
Sag Harbor Village	2,296	13	12	1
Salamanca	5,360	18	18	0
Sands Point Village	2,919	20	20	0
Saranac Lake Village	5,177	12	12	0
Saugerties Town	18,956	28	24	4
Scarsdale Village	17,953	44	39	5
Schenectady	65,176	174	150	24
Schodack Town	11,617	9	8	1
Scotia Village	7,631	14	13	1
Shandaken Town	2,921	4	4	0
Shawangunk Town	13,782	3	3	0
Shelter Island Town	2,419	11	10	1
Sherrill	2,964	3	3	0
Sidney Village	3,553	8	8	0
Skaneateles Village	2,466	2	2	0
Sleepy Hollow Village	10,064	27	27	0
Solvay Village	6,196	14	13	1
Southampton Town	51,162	144	99	45
Southampton Village	3,330	48	33	15
South Glens Falls Village	3,647	5	5	0
Southold Town	19,957	65	48	17
Suffern Village	11,037	25	21	4
Syracuse	142,011	493	422	71
Tarrytown Village	11,383	37	33	4
Tonawanda	14,700	34	28	6
Tonawanda Town	56,503	147	100	47
Troy	49,052	137	127	10
Trumansburg Village	1,709	1	1	0
Tuckahoe Village	6,554	26	23	3
Tupper Lake Village	3,420	8	8	0
Tuxedo Park Village	598	4	3	1
Tuxedo Town	2,969	6	6	0
Ulster Town	12,626	28	24	4
Walden Village	6,666	15	12	3
Wappingers Falls Village	5,540	4	2	2
Warsaw Village	3,225	5	5	0
Warwick Town	18,459	35	30	5
Washingtonville Village	5,755	16	15	1
Waterford Town and Village	8,466	11	9	2
Waterloo Village	4,842	9	8	1
Watertown	24,624	65	62	3
Watervliet	9,863	23	22	1
Watkins Glen Village	1,874	5	5	0
Waverly Village	4,083	11	10	1
Webb Town	1,779	6	6	0
Weedsport Village	1,695	1	1	0
Wellsville Village	4,343	12	11	1
Westfield Village	2,941	6	6	0
Westhampton Beach Village	1,806	16	14	2
West Seneca Town	45,278	73	60	13
White Plains	58,240	211	201	10

Table 78. Full-Time Law Enforcement Employees, by Selected State and City, 2020—Continued

(Number.)

State/city	Population	Total law enforcement employees	Total officers	Total civilians
Whitesboro Village	3,595	5	5	0
Whitestown Town	8,948	7	7	0
Windham Town	1,672	1	1	0
Woodbury Town	11,133	25	20	5
Woodstock Town	5,754	10	10	0
Yonkers	200,816	688	607	81
Yorktown Town	36,284	67	58	9
Yorkville Village	2,556	3	3	0
NORTH CAROLINA				
Aberdeen	8,189	29	27	2
Ahoskie	4,733	14	12	2
Albemarle	16,287	48	41	7
Andrews	1,854	5	5	0
Angier	5,533	15	15	0
Apex	62,320	114	95	19
Archdale	11,521	31	25	6
Asheboro	25,994	84	76	8
Asheville	93,980	252	202	50
Atlantic Beach	1,513	17	16	1
Ayden	5,155	23	19	4
Badin	1,973	5	5	0
Bailey	561	2	2	0
Bakersville	443	1	1	0
Bald Head Island	185	26	25	1
Banner Elk	1,160	9	8	1
Beaufort	4,481	19	18	1
Beech Mountain	325	14	10	4
Belhaven	1,567	6	5	1
Belmont	12,848	45	39	6
Benson	3,995	17	16	1
Bessemer City	5,605	15	14	1
Bethel	1,614	4	4	0
Beulaville	1,292	6	6	0
Biltmore Forest	1,424	16	12	4
Biscoe	1,713	9	8	1
Black Creek	770	3	3	0
Black Mountain	8,197	23	19	4
Bladenboro	1,599	6	6	0
Blowing Rock	1,334	15	13	2
Boiling Spring Lakes	6,396	14	14	0
Boiling Springs	4,523	10	10	0
Boone	19,975	47	36	11
Boonville	1,139	3	3	0
Brevard	7,954	27	23	4
Bridgeton	438	1	1	0
Broadway	1,295	4	4	0
Bryson City	1,455	7	6	1
Bunn	390	3	2	1
Burgaw	4,182	15	15	0
Burlington	55,003	176	133	43
Burnsville	1,642	8	8	0
Butner	7,887	38	32	6
Candor	815	4	4	0
Canton	4,364	20	15	5
Cape Carteret	2,069	7	7	0
Carolina Beach	6,479	27	26	1
Carrboro	21,377	38	35	3
Carthage	2,582	11	10	1
Cary	174,441	212	174	38
Caswell Beach	435	4	4	0
Chadbourn	1,698	7	6	1
Chapel Hill	64,853	120	95	25
Charlotte-Mecklenburg[1]	958,358	2,320	1,749	571
Cherryville	6,110	19	14	5
China Grove	4,227	13	13	0
Chocowinity	789	3	3	0
Claremont	1,414	8	8	0
Clayton	26,087	49	46	3
Cleveland	874	4	4	0
Clinton	8,431	28	24	4
Coats	2,545	7	7	0
Columbus	998	9	8	1
Concord	98,411	205	184	21
Conover	8,567	28	25	3
Conway	718	2	2	0
Cooleemee	984	1	1	0
Cornelius	30,904	75	57	18
Cramerton	4,491	13	13	0
Creedmoor	4,669	19	15	4
Dallas	4,835	15	13	2
Davidson	13,313	23	21	2
Dobson	1,534	8	8	0
Drexel	1,851	5	5	0
Duck	398	12	11	1

Table 78. Full-Time Law Enforcement Employees, by Selected State and City, 2020—Continued

(Number.)

State/city	Population	Total law enforcement employees	Total officers	Total civilians
Dunn	9,763	47	42	5
Durham	284,925	679	507	172
East Bend	599	2	2	0
East Spencer	1,552	8	8	0
Eden	14,799	45	42	3
Edenton	4,575	19	17	2
Elizabeth City	17,652	71	61	10
Elizabethtown	3,349	17	16	1
Elkin	4,009	22	18	4
Elon	12,609	21	20	1
Emerald Isle	3,698	20	18	2
Enfield	2,247	7	6	1
Erwin	5,227	11	10	1
Fair Bluff	874	4	4	0
Fairmont	2,585	9	9	0
Farmville	4,775	24	19	5
Fayetteville	212,033	528	372	156
Fletcher	8,508	17	16	1
Forest City	7,130	33	31	2
Four Oaks	2,291	8	8	0
Foxfire Village	1,057	3	3	0
Franklin	4,130	19	18	1
Franklinton	2,267	9	6	3
Fremont	1,260	4	4	0
Fuquay-Varina	32,091	55	48	7
Garner	32,093	72	63	9
Garysburg	904	2	2	0
Gaston	1,007	4	4	0
Gastonia	77,918	189	166	23
Gibsonville	7,437	19	18	1
Glen Alpine	1,482	4	4	0
Goldsboro	34,051	101	89	12
Graham	15,801	42	39	3
Granite Falls	4,654	18	14	4
Granite Quarry	3,018	9	9	0
Greensboro	299,887	746	643	103
Greenville	94,372	243	195	48
Grifton	2,689	7	7	0
Hamlet	6,302	17	15	2
Havelock	19,722	36	28	8
Haw River	2,563	8	8	0
Henderson	14,861	47	39	8
Hendersonville	14,275	56	42	14
Hertford	2,109	8	7	1
Hickory	41,300	143	112	31
Highlands	988	14	13	1
High Point	113,727	288	243	45
Hillsborough	7,226	27	25	2
Holden Beach	674	8	8	0
Holly Ridge	3,077	11	10	1
Holly Springs	39,600	78	63	15
Hope Mills	15,924	36	31	5
Hot Springs	579	1	1	0
Hudson	3,703	15	14	1
Huntersville	59,470	100	92	8
Indian Beach	119	5	5	0
Jackson	448	1	1	0
Jacksonville	71,842	149	120	29
Jefferson	1,526	6	6	0
Jonesville	2,207	9	8	1
Kannapolis	51,837	104	78	26
Kenansville	839	3	3	0
Kenly	1,612	7	7	0
Kernersville	24,835	83	64	19
Kill Devil Hills	7,407	35	29	6
King	6,860	26	23	3
Kings Mountain	11,015	42	33	9
Kinston	19,862	82	70	12
Kitty Hawk	3,606	18	16	2
Knightdale	18,735	33	30	3
Kure Beach	2,107	14	13	1
Lake Lure	1,152	10	9	1
Lake Royale	2,506	12	8	4
Lake Waccamaw	1,393	5	5	0
Landis	3,144	10	10	0
Laurel Park	2,350	8	8	0
Laurinburg	14,905	42	40	2
Leland	24,967	41	38	3
Lenoir	17,880	67	51	16
Lexington	18,933	63	53	10
Liberty	2,658	10	9	1
Lilesville	479	1	1	0
Lillington	3,710	15	14	1
Lincolnton	11,300	35	31	4
Littleton	582	3	3	0

Table 78. Full-Time Law Enforcement Employees, by Selected State and City, 2020—Continued

(Number.)

State/city	Population	Total law enforcement employees	Total officers	Total civilians
Locust	3,275	15	15	0
Long View	4,936	16	16	0
Louisburg	3,641	17	16	1
Lowell	3,738	8	8	0
Lumberton	20,370	92	83	9
Madison	2,103	15	15	0
Maggie Valley	1,247	12	11	1
Magnolia	953	2	2	0
Maiden	3,456	20	19	1
Manteo	1,471	9	8	1
Marion	7,861	25	23	2
Marshall	912	4	4	0
Mars Hill	1,949	6	6	0
Marshville	2,825	9	9	0
Matthews	33,860	74	58	16
Maxton	2,335	10	6	4
Mayodan	2,372	15	15	0
Maysville	925	2	2	0
Mebane	16,894	38	34	4
Micro	548	2	2	0
Middlesex	826	5	5	0
Mint Hill	28,209	39	36	3
Misenheimer	760	5	5	0
Mocksville	5,274	18	17	1
Monroe	35,836	100	87	13
Montreat	889	5	5	0
Mooresville	39,692	110	82	28
Morehead City	9,729	44	41	3
Morganton	16,550	90	56	34
Morrisville	30,264	41	39	2
Mount Airy	10,186	44	33	11
Mount Gilead	1,138	7	7	0
Mount Holly	16,575	41	32	9
Mount Olive	4,573	16	15	1
Murfreesboro	2,978	8	7	1
Murphy	1,661	11	10	1
Nags Head	2,999	25	23	2
Nashville	5,549	18	17	1
Navassa	2,423	1	1	0
New Bern	30,047	111	85	26
Newland	684	5	5	0
Newport	4,646	10	10	0
Newton	13,204	41	32	9
Newton Grove	564	3	3	0
Norlina	1,039	3	3	0
North Topsail Beach	743	14	12	2
Northwest	791	3	3	0
North Wilkesboro	4,192	25	24	1
Norwood	2,457	9	9	0
Oakboro	1,918	8	8	0
Oak Island	8,581	26	24	2
Ocean Isle Beach	680	14	13	1
Old Fort	926	4	4	0
Oriental	857	2	2	0
Oxford	8,934	31	23	8
Parkton	437	2	2	0
Pembroke	2,940	17	14	3
Pikeville	674	4	4	0
Pilot Mountain	1,406	9	8	1
Pinebluff	1,658	3	3	0
Pinehurst	16,837	28	23	5
Pine Knoll Shores	1,325	9	9	0
Pine Level	2,059	5	5	0
Pinetops	1,220	12	7	5
Pineville	9,214	50	39	11
Pink Hill	503	1	1	0
Pittsboro	4,440	13	12	1
Plymouth	3,311	14	13	1
Polkton	2,491	2	2	0
Princeton	1,423	5	5	0
Raeford	4,990	18	16	2
Raleigh	482,264	822	695	127
Ramseur	1,689	5	5	0
Randleman	4,114	15	15	0
Ranlo	3,694	12	11	1
Red Springs	3,282	16	15	1
Reidsville	13,936	52	45	7
Richlands	1,726	7	7	0
River Bend	3,016	6	6	0
Roanoke Rapids	14,178	40	36	4
Robbins	1,233	6	6	0
Robersonville	1,328	6	6	0
Rockingham	8,567	38	36	2
Rockwell	2,164	8	8	0
Rocky Mount	53,520	183	145	38

Table 78. Full-Time Law Enforcement Employees, by Selected State and City, 2020—Continued

(Number.)

State/city	Population	Total law enforcement employees	Total officers	Total civilians
Rolesville	9,304	21	20	1
Rose Hill	1,617	6	6	0
Rowland	987	6	5	1
Roxboro	8,304	38	33	5
Rutherfordton	4,077	14	14	0
Salisbury	34,045	84	76	8
Saluda	695	4	4	0
Sanford	30,299	95	72	23
Scotland Neck	1,819	9	8	1
Seagrove	229	1	1	0
Selma	7,218	21	20	1
Seven Devils	217	6	6	0
Shallotte	4,457	16	15	1
Sharpsburg	2,012	9	8	1
Shelby	19,994	86	73	13
Siler City	8,267	22	16	6
Smithfield	13,215	40	36	4
Snow Hill	1,503	7	7	0
Southern Pines	14,924	46	38	8
Southern Shores	2,986	13	12	1
Southport	4,102	12	12	0
Sparta	1,721	6	6	0
Spencer	3,256	12	12	0
Spindale	4,192	9	9	0
Spring Hope	1,309	7	7	0
Spring Lake	12,062	31	28	3
Spruce Pine	2,133	11	11	0
Stallings	16,426	23	21	2
Stanfield	1,555	5	5	0
Stanley	3,788	12	11	1
Stantonsburg	778	4	4	0
Star	846	4	4	0
Statesville	27,879	100	76	24
Stoneville	1,252	5	5	0
St. Pauls	2,285	19	14	5
Sugar Mountain	197	5	5	0
Sunset Beach	4,092	15	15	0
Surf City	2,537	23	22	1
Swansboro	3,425	13	12	1
Sylva	2,757	14	14	0
Tabor City	4,181	11	10	1
Tarboro	10,629	33	27	6
Taylorsville	2,167	12	12	0
Taylortown	867	2	2	0
Thomasville	26,631	71	65	6
Topsail Beach	434	9	8	1
Trent Woods	4,005	6	6	0
Troutman	2,806	15	15	0
Troy	3,194	11	10	1
Tryon	1,613	9	7	2
Valdese	4,416	12	11	1
Vanceboro	961	4	4	0
Vass	799	4	4	0
Wadesboro	5,221	29	24	5
Wagram	771	1	1	0
Wake Forest	47,738	100	82	18
Wallace	3,859	20	16	4
Walnut Creek	862	4	3	1
Warrenton	826	5	4	1
Warsaw	3,086	14	12	2
Washington	9,459	43	32	11
Waxhaw	18,222	31	27	4
Waynesville	10,174	46	35	11
Weaverville	4,065	17	16	1
Weldon	1,452	8	8	0
Wendell	8,951	18	16	2
West Jefferson	1,313	9	9	0
Whispering Pines	3,451	8	7	1
Whitakers	698	2	2	0
White Lake	764	6	6	0
Whiteville	5,293	29	26	3
Wilkesboro	3,440	24	22	2
Williamston	5,145	23	20	3
Wilmington	125,794	327	253	74
Wilson	49,486	130	114	16
Wilson's Mills	2,815	7	7	0
Windsor	3,353	9	9	0
Wingate	4,741	5	5	0
Winston-Salem	250,021	669	498	171
Winterville	10,010	20	19	1
Woodfin	6,767	15	14	1
Woodland	693	1	1	0
Wrightsville Beach	2,563	22	20	2
Yadkinville	2,865	14	13	1
Youngsville	1,402	11	10	1
Zebulon	6,104	21	20	1

Table 78. Full-Time Law Enforcement Employees, by Selected State and City, 2020—Continued

(Number.)

State/city	Population	Total law enforcement employees	Total officers	Total civilians
NORTH DAKOTA				
Belfield	1,039	1	1	0
Berthold	483	1	1	0
Beulah	3,141	6	5	1
Bismarck	74,997	159	129	30
Bowman	1,594	4	3	1
Burlington	1,218	2	2	0
Carrington	1,971	4	4	0
Cavalier	1,226	3	3	0
Devils Lake	7,339	21	19	2
Dickinson	23,801	61	41	20
Ellendale	1,232	2	2	0
Emerado	451	1	1	0
Fargo	126,927	204	181	23
Grafton	4,143	10	9	1
Grand Forks	56,163	106	91	15
Harvey	1,630	4	4	0
Hazen	2,298	5	5	0
Jamestown	15,044	33	29	4
Kenmare	1,013	2	2	0
Killdeer	1,202	5	5	0
Lamoure	883	1	1	0
Lincoln	4,006	6	6	0
Lisbon	2,041	4	4	0
Mandan	23,221	45	38	7
Medora	131	2	2	0
Minot	48,108	110	83	27
Napoleon	747	1	1	0
New Town	2,677	5	5	0
Northwood	890	2	2	0
Oakes	1,685	3	3	0
Powers Lake	285	2	2	0
Ray	945	1	1	0
Rolette	592	1	1	0
Rolla	1,249	4	4	0
Rugby	2,561	3	3	0
Stanley	2,868	4	4	0
Steele	711	1	1	0
Surrey	1,452	2	2	0
Thompson	1,025	1	1	0
Tioga	1,348	7	5	2
Valley City	6,288	17	14	3
Wahpeton	7,731	18	16	2
Watford City	9,309	27	21	6
West Fargo	38,561	78	65	13
Williston	31,046	87	74	13
Wishek	880	2	2	0
OHIO				
Ada	5,500	8	8	0
Amherst	12,244	31	23	8
Andover	1,090	3	3	0
Archbold	4,319	11	11	0
Ashland	20,247	37	30	7
Aurora	16,430	37	29	8
Bainbridge Township	11,442	26	22	4
Barberton	25,890	42	41	1
Bath Township, Summit County	9,635	30	23	7
Bay Village	15,135	26	22	4
Beavercreek	48,029	66	50	16
Beaver Township	6,358	14	10	4
Bedford	12,383	39	34	5
Bellefontaine	13,240	37	30	7
Bellville	1,933	6	6	0
Belpre	6,381	16	11	5
Bethel	2,823	6	5	1
Bluffton	4,054	9	9	0
Boardman	38,625	79	59	20
Bowling Green	31,621	52	39	13
Brunswick	34,948	50	38	12
Butler Township	7,816	19	18	1
Cambridge	10,243	29	23	6
Canal Fulton	5,406	11	10	1
Canton	70,124	208	167	41
Carey	3,541	15	12	3
Catawba Island Township	3,522	5	5	0
Celina	10,427	21	16	5
Centerville	23,670	56	41	15
Chagrin Falls	3,921	14	13	1
Cincinnati	304,724	1,124	1,005	119
Circleville	14,113	29	20	9
Clayton	13,219	19	18	1
Clearcreek Township	16,312	17	16	1
Cleveland	379,121	1,788	1,546	242
Clyde	6,141	20	16	4

Table 78. Full-Time Law Enforcement Employees, by Selected State and City, 2020—Continued

(Number.)

State/city	Population	Total law enforcement employees	Total officers	Total civilians
Colerain Township	59,307	64	54	10
Columbiana	6,233	17	14	3
Columbus	911,383	2,277	1,897	380
Columbus Grove	2,071	3	3	0
Covington	2,720	7	6	1
Danville	1,012	4	4	0
Defiance	16,576	32	28	4
Delaware	42,064	63	55	8
Dublin	49,954	113	70	43
East Cleveland	16,859	44	42	2
East Liverpool	10,539	22	17	5
Eaton	8,118	16	15	1
Elida	1,795	3	2	1
Elmore	1,391	4	4	0
Englewood	13,435	26	19	7
Evendale	2,725	22	20	2
Fairborn	33,951	72	49	23
Fairfax	1,701	11	10	1
Fairfield	42,558	80	61	19
Fairfield Township	22,978	24	22	2
Fayette	1,237	5	5	0
Findlay	41,237	82	64	18
Forest Park	18,571	43	36	7
Fort Loramie	1,527	2	2	0
Fort Recovery	1,458	3	3	0
Genoa Township	28,758	28	26	2
Germantown	5,517	12	11	1
German Township, Montgomery County	2,894	6	6	0
Greenhills	3,563	11	10	1
Green Springs	1,300	2	2	0
Greenville	12,549	30	23	7
Groveport	5,649	25	24	1
Harrison	12,133	24	21	3
Heath	11,015	27	19	8
Hilliard	37,585	75	63	12
Hinckley Township	8,117	14	13	1
Hiram	1,135	3	3	0
Holland	1,650	9	9	0
Howland Township	16,318	19	19	0
Hubbard	7,370	13	13	0
Huber Heights	38,158	72	52	20
Hudson	22,234	35	29	6
Hunting Valley	716	11	11	0
Ironton	10,469	16	15	1
Jackson Township, Mahoning County	1,999	7	7	0
Jamestown	2,148	5	5	0
Kent	29,732	59	42	17
Kirtland Hills	644	8	7	1
Lancaster	40,700	78	62	16
Lockland	3,440	14	14	0
Lordstown	3,241	13	9	4
Loudonville	2,614	7	7	0
Louisville	9,370	13	13	0
Lyndhurst	13,291	35	28	7
Macedonia	12,098	33	24	9
Madeira	9,303	15	14	1
Madison Township, Franklin County	19,828	17	16	1
Mansfield	46,476	115	79	36
Mariemont	3,524	10	10	0
Maumee	13,605	50	38	12
Medina	25,882	50	39	11
Medina Township	9,105	10	10	0
Mentor-on-the-Lake	7,385	14	9	5
Miamisburg	20,140	37	35	2
Miami Township, Clermont County	42,931	45	42	3
Middletown	48,814	127	88	39
Mifflin Township	2,609	6	6	0
Milan	1,330	3	3	0
Milford	6,872	21	19	2
Milton Township	2,415	5	5	0
Minerva Park	1,326	10	9	1
Minster	2,818	8	7	1
Mogadore	3,816	8	8	0
Monroeville	1,345	5	5	0
Montgomery	10,929	25	22	3
Napoleon	8,148	22	17	5
Navarre	1,804	6	6	0
Newark	50,625	86	76	10
New Boston	2,080	12	8	4
New Bremen	2,959	7	7	0
Newcomerstown	3,728	9	6	3
New London	2,347	5	5	0
Newtown	2,671	9	8	1
Niles	18,070	40	35	5
North Olmsted	31,176	59	46	13

Table 78. Full-Time Law Enforcement Employees, by Selected State and City, 2020—Continued

(Number.)

State/city	Population	Total law enforcement employees	Total officers	Total civilians
North Randall	983	10	10	0
North Ridgeville	34,972	46	40	6
Northwood	5,458	23	18	5
Norton	11,951	17	16	1
Norwalk	16,843	32	25	7
Oberlin	8,178	23	17	6
Orrville	8,427	17	16	1
Ottawa	4,346	8	8	0
Ottoville	962	2	2	0
Oxford Township	2,210	3	3	0
Peninsula	554	3	3	0
Perkins Township	11,636	21	20	1
Perrysburg Township	13,011	31	24	7
Perry Township, Columbiana County	4,259	4	4	0
Perry Township, Franklin County	3,761	12	11	1
Perry Township, Stark County	28,005	27	24	3
Pierce Township	11,789	19	18	1
Plain City	4,628	12	11	1
Poland Township	11,772	12	12	0
Port Clinton	6,159	21	16	5
Portsmouth	20,151	52	41	11
Powell	13,593	22	20	2
Reynoldsburg	38,600	84	67	17
Rockford	1,102	2	2	0
Rocky River	19,951	38	34	4
Rossford	6,587	17	16	1
Russell Township	5,199	11	10	1
Salem	11,538	23	23	0
Salineville	1,209	2	2	0
Seaman	891	2	2	0
Sebring	4,163	12	7	5
Seven Hills	11,561	18	17	1
Shaker Heights	26,859	79	64	15
Sharonville	13,712	51	40	11
Shawnee Hills	837	4	4	0
Shawnee Township	12,044	18	13	5
Sidney	20,372	47	36	11
Silver Lake	2,491	9	8	1
South Russell	3,736	9	9	0
Spencerville	2,154	4	4	0
Springboro	19,109	35	31	4
Springfield	58,696	134	124	10
Springfield Township, Hamilton County	35,947	51	45	6
Springfield Township, Mahoning County	6,352	10	10	0
St. Henry	2,568	3	3	0
St. Marys	8,142	21	16	5
Stow	34,781	51	42	9
Strasburg	2,697	5	5	0
Strongsville	44,623	87	68	19
Sugarcreek	2,236	9	9	0
Sugarcreek Township	8,484	19	17	2
Sylvania	19,337	38	31	7
Sylvania Township	29,711	62	44	18
Tallmadge	17,517	30	26	4
Tiffin	17,543	38	28	10
Toledo	271,237	682	609	73
Trenton	13,281	22	17	5
Troy	26,407	45	42	3
Uhrichsville	5,304	9	9	0
Union Township, Clermont County	48,733	63	49	14
University Heights	12,711	32	29	3
Upper Sandusky	6,423	17	13	4
Urbana	11,351	18	18	0
Valley View, Cuyahoga County	1,992	20	18	2
Vandalia	14,968	39	30	9
Van Wert	10,659	28	20	8
Wadsworth	24,324	40	31	9
Warren	38,462	72	67	5
Wells Township	2,624	5	5	0
West Carrollton	12,833	22	20	2
West Salem	1,513	1	1	0
West Union	3,152	5	4	1
Whitehall	19,014	63	49	14
Whitehouse	4,932	11	11	0
Wickliffe	12,743	39	29	10
Williamsburg	2,579	6	6	0
Willoughby	23,058	56	42	14
Wooster	26,424	47	43	4
Worthington	14,822	37	33	4
Xenia	27,095	69	44	25
Zanesville	25,136	96	57	39
OKLAHOMA				
Achille	545	3	2	1
Ada	17,278	37	34	3

Table 78. Full-Time Law Enforcement Employees, by Selected State and City, 2020—Continued

(Number.)

State/city	Population	Total law enforcement employees	Total officers	Total civilians
Adair	809	4	4	0
Allen	925	4	3	1
Altus	18,184	51	39	12
Alva	4,944	10	10	0
Amber	487	2	2	0
Anadarko	6,473	19	18	1
Antlers	2,308	16	6	10
Apache	1,387	3	3	0
Arcadia	273	1	1	0
Ardmore	24,718	63	44	19
Arkoma	1,889	4	2	2
Atoka	3,019	17	16	1
Barnsdall	1,140	4	4	0
Bartlesville	36,183	82	62	20
Beaver	1,387	1	1	0
Beggs	1,233	5	3	2
Bennington	370	2	2	0
Bernice	581	1	1	0
Bethany	19,239	35	26	9
Big Cabin	248	1	1	0
Binger	628	1	1	0
Bixby	28,840	43	32	11
Blackwell	6,508	22	14	8
Blanchard	9,090	15	10	5
Boise City	1,067	2	2	0
Bokchito	694	6	5	1
Bokoshe	496	3	2	1
Boley	1,173	2	2	0
Boswell	679	3	3	0
Bristow	4,196	15	11	4
Broken Arrow	111,488	201	148	53
Broken Bow	4,081	18	12	6
Burns Flat	1,885	4	4	0
Cache	2,810	4	3	1
Caddo	1,115	4	4	0
Calera	2,393	11	10	1
Calvin	273	2	1	1
Caney	197	4	3	1
Canton	585	3	3	0
Carnegie	1,636	8	4	4
Carney	620	2	2	0
Cashion	879	2	2	0
Catoosa	6,930	18	16	2
Cement	472	1	1	0
Chandler	3,084	11	8	3
Chattanooga	451	2	1	1
Checotah	3,069	13	10	3
Chelsea	1,899	4	4	0
Cherokee	1,489	3	3	0
Chickasha	16,478	37	28	9
Choctaw	12,850	21	17	4
Chouteau	2,090	10	9	1
Claremore	18,757	45	38	7
Clayton	782	8	4	4
Cleveland	3,112	8	8	0
Clinton	9,094	26	17	9
Coalgate	1,774	6	6	0
Colbert	1,264	3	2	1
Colcord	852	6	5	1
Collinsville	7,441	20	11	9
Comanche	1,547	6	6	0
Commerce	2,502	5	5	0
Cordell	2,715	5	4	1
Covington	534	1	1	0
Coweta	10,109	23	15	8
Crescent	1,577	7	5	2
Cushing	7,592	24	16	8
Cyril	1,006	2	2	0
Davenport	806	2	2	0
Davis	2,921	10	8	2
Del City	21,750	51	38	13
Depew	479	2	2	0
Dewar	848	3	3	0
Dewey	3,381	12	10	2
Dibble	868	4	3	1
Dickson	1,252	4	3	1
Disney	302	1	1	0
Drumright	2,827	6	6	0
Duncan	22,226	67	48	19
Durant	19,007	41	36	5
Earlsboro	623	3	2	1
Edmond	95,571	154	117	37
Eldorado	402	1	1	0
Elgin	3,313	5	5	0
Elk City	11,571	35	26	9

Table 78. Full-Time Law Enforcement Employees, by Selected State and City, 2020—Continued

(Number.)

State/city	Population	Total law enforcement employees	Total officers	Total civilians
Elmore City	712	5	4	1
El Reno	20,348	49	34	15
Enid	49,708	113	85	28
Erick	993	1	1	0
Eufaula	2,849	11	10	1
Fairfax	1,253	3	1	2
Fairland	1,028	3	2	1
Fairview	2,596	9	5	4
Fletcher	1,138	2	2	0
Forest Park	1,077	4	2	2
Fort Gibson	3,936	15	14	1
Fort Towson	487	2	2	0
Frederick	3,504	8	6	2
Gans	299	1	1	0
Garber	805	1	1	0
Geary	1,263	12	6	6
Geronimo	1,208	1	1	0
Glenpool	14,319	32	24	8
Goodwell	1,267	4	4	0
Gore	948	5	4	1
Grandfield	922	1	1	0
Granite	1,946	4	4	0
Grove	7,210	30	21	9
Guthrie	11,829	38	26	12
Guymon	10,939	22	17	5
Haileyville	745	3	3	0
Harrah	6,681	11	10	1
Hartshorne	1,944	4	3	1
Haskell	1,922	8	8	0
Healdton	2,671	4	4	0
Heavener	3,286	9	8	1
Hennessey	2,233	9	5	4
Henryetta	5,527	15	11	4
Hinton	3,221	6	6	0
Hobart	3,393	12	7	5
Holdenville	5,470	11	10	1
Hollis	1,853	9	5	4
Hominy	3,370	8	4	4
Hooker	1,835	2	2	0
Howe	787	2	2	0
Hugo	5,067	25	16	9
Hulbert	581	4	3	1
Hydro	933	3	3	0
Idabel	6,827	25	20	5
Inola	1,804	6	5	1
Jay	2,546	14	9	5
Jenks	24,639	35	24	11
Jennings	353	1	1	0
Jones	3,225	6	6	0
Kansas	801	5	5	0
Kellyville	1,146	2	2	0
Keota	547	2	2	0
Kiefer	2,053	5	5	0
Kingfisher	4,939	14	14	0
Kingston	1,683	7	7	0
Kiowa	670	8	6	2
Konawa	1,186	5	5	0
Krebs	1,933	9	7	2
Lahoma	617	1	1	0
Langley	821	4	4	0
Langston	1,872	3	2	1
Laverne	1,327	1	1	0
Lawton	92,507	208	170	38
Lexington	2,188	9	5	4
Lindsay	2,770	16	9	7
Locust Grove	1,392	9	8	1
Lone Grove	5,153	11	7	4
Luther	1,829	7	6	1
Madill	4,063	12	11	1
Mangum	2,667	11	6	5
Mannford	3,207	11	7	4
Marietta	2,785	8	8	0
Marlow	4,393	14	9	5
Maud	1,061	3	3	0
Maysville	1,202	6	5	1
McAlester	17,752	41	39	2
McCurtain	500	4	3	1
McLoud	4,767	11	10	1
Medford	932	3	3	0
Medicine Park	460	2	2	0
Meeker	1,140	5	5	0
Miami	13,032	33	32	1
Midwest City	57,730	125	99	26
Minco	1,650	5	5	0
Moore	62,840	95	90	5

Table 78. Full-Time Law Enforcement Employees, by Selected State and City, 2020—Continued

(Number.)

State/city	Population	Total law enforcement employees	Total officers	Total civilians
Mooreland	1,165	4	3	1
Morris	1,414	3	3	0
Mounds	1,273	1	1	0
Mountain View	729	2	2	0
Muldrow	3,228	13	8	5
Muskogee	36,884	92	84	8
Mustang	23,658	37	26	11
Newcastle	11,038	30	22	8
Newkirk	2,155	6	6	0
Nichols Hills	3,966	24	16	8
Nicoma Park	2,473	6	5	1
Ninnekah	1,052	4	3	1
Noble	7,117	18	13	5
Norman	126,480	230	164	66
North Enid	928	3	3	0
Nowata	3,533	8	6	2
Oilton	1,014	3	3	0
Okarche	1,344	6	5	1
Okeene	1,131	2	2	0
Okemah	3,120	14	9	5
Oklahoma City	663,661	1,443	1,161	282
Okmulgee	11,627	21	18	3
Olustee	549	1	1	0
Oologah	1,179	5	5	0
Owasso	37,815	84	62	22
Paoli	613	2	2	0
Pauls Valley	6,111	18	14	4
Pawhuska	3,386	17	9	8
Pawnee	2,096	5	5	0
Perkins	2,815	8	8	0
Perry	4,807	18	12	6
Piedmont	8,931	12	10	2
Pocola	4,128	12	8	4
Ponca City	23,484	65	46	19
Pond Creek	831	2	2	0
Porum	698	4	4	0
Poteau	8,899	35	27	8
Prague	2,365	14	9	5
Pryor Creek	9,361	38	29	9
Purcell	6,445	23	20	3
Quinton	978	4	4	0
Ramona	546	5	4	1
Rattan	295	2	2	0
Ringling	946	1	1	0
Roland	3,998	11	8	3
Rush Springs	1,259	5	5	0
Salina	1,393	7	6	1
Sallisaw	8,448	30	22	8
Sand Springs	20,026	44	31	13
Sapulpa	21,394	53	43	10
Savanna	641	8	6	2
Sawyer	312	3	2	1
Sayre	4,500	12	6	6
Seiling	855	1	1	0
Seminole	6,994	12	11	1
Shady Point	996	1	1	0
Shattuck	1,247	1	1	0
Shawnee	31,606	89	72	17
Skiatook	8,135	23	19	4
Snyder	1,265	3	3	0
South Coffeyville	729	5	5	0
Spavinaw	428	1	1	0
Spencer	3,973	5	3	2
Sperry	1,354	4	4	0
Spiro	2,157	4	4	0
Sportsmen Acres	307	1	1	0
Stigler	2,680	14	9	5
Stillwater	50,831	118	74	44
Stilwell	4,070	18	12	6
Stratford	1,525	4	4	0
Stringtown	401	5	5	0
Stroud	2,701	11	7	4
Sulphur	5,055	12	10	2
Tahlequah	16,936	46	40	6
Talala	279	1	1	0
Talihina	1,078	8	5	3
Tecumseh	6,652	13	10	3
Texhoma	898	2	2	0
Thackerville	520	2	1	1
The Village	9,632	29	23	6
Thomas	1,200	1	1	0
Tipton	750	1	1	0
Tishomingo	3,085	9	7	2
Tonkawa	2,956	13	8	5
Tryon	502	2	1	1

Table 78. Full-Time Law Enforcement Employees, by Selected State and City, 2020—Continued

(Number.)

State/city	Population	Total law enforcement employees	Total officers	Total civilians
Tulsa	402,166	1,034	819	215
Tupelo	300	3	3	0
Tushka	388	3	3	0
Tuttle	7,768	19	13	6
Tyrone	738	2	1	1
Union City	2,221	8	7	1
Valley Brook	770	7	7	0
Valliant	736	4	4	0
Velma	592	2	2	0
Verden	538	4	2	2
Verdigris	4,669	7	6	1
Vian	1,356	6	6	0
Vici	705	1	1	0
Vinita	5,264	21	15	6
Wagoner	9,283	21	16	5
Walters	2,334	5	5	0
Warner	1,584	4	4	0
Warr Acres	10,140	30	25	5
Washington	605	4	2	2
Watonga	2,820	10	7	3
Watts	312	3	2	1
Waukomis	1,297	2	2	0
Waynoka	912	4	4	0
Weatherford	12,155	40	25	15
Webbers Falls	590	4	4	0
Weleetka	949	9	6	3
Wellston	772	3	3	0
West Siloam Springs	862	12	11	1
Westville	1,542	9	5	4
Wetumka	1,193	12	6	6
Wewoka	3,202	5	5	0
Wilburton	2,512	7	6	1
Wilson	1,692	4	4	0
Wister	1,058	3	3	0
Woodward	12,143	23	19	4
Wright City	732	3	2	1
Wyandotte	323	11	9	2
Wynnewood	2,201	6	5	1
Yale	1,222	7	4	3
Yukon	28,735	69	52	17
OREGON				
Albany	55,926	89	56	33
Ashland	21,419	36	29	7
Astoria	10,076	27	16	11
Aumsville	4,249	8	7	1
Baker City	9,808	16	15	1
Bandon	3,161	9	6	3
Beaverton	100,085	176	131	45
Bend	103,485	131	97	34
Black Butte	8	8	7	1
Boardman	3,811	13	12	1
Brookings	6,495	23	15	8
Burns	2,794	4	4	0
Canby	18,074	30	26	4
Cannon Beach	1,777	10	7	3
Carlton	2,202	4	4	0
Central Point	19,032	33	27	6
Coburg	1,187	5	4	1
Columbia City	2,030	2	2	0
Coos Bay	16,403	36	24	12
Coquille	3,944	7	6	1
Corvallis	59,375	109	73	36
Cottage Grove	10,556	32	17	15
Dallas	17,265	15	10	5
Eagle Point	9,681	12	11	1
Enterprise	2,002	4	4	0
Eugene	174,513	317	197	120
Florence	9,228	23	16	7
Forest Grove	26,065	35	30	5
Gearhart	1,662	3	3	0
Gervais	2,795	6	5	1
Gladstone	12,418	18	15	3
Gold Beach	2,310	8	6	2
Grants Pass	38,420	92	57	35
Gresham	109,767	155	127	28
Hermiston	17,896	33	28	5
Hillsboro	111,146	185	135	50
Hines	1,543	4	4	0
Hood River	7,863	14	13	1
Hubbard	3,615	7	6	1
Independence	10,477	20	15	5
Jacksonville	2,912	6	5	1
John Day	1,663	5	4	1
Junction City	6,333	16	10	6

Table 78. Full-Time Law Enforcement Employees, by Selected State and City, 2020—Continued

(Number.)

State/city	Population	Total law enforcement employees	Total officers	Total civilians
Keizer	40,087	47	40	7
King City	4,512	7	6	1
Klamath Falls	22,693	38	34	4
La Grande	13,674	30	18	12
Lake Oswego	40,171	67	41	26
Lebanon	17,635	40	27	13
Lincoln City	9,275	38	24	14
Madras	7,140	11	10	1
Malin	835	7	7	0
Manzanita	668	4	4	0
McMinnville	35,040	48	42	6
Medford	84,016	165	114	51
Milton-Freewater	7,075	16	11	5
Milwaukie	21,040	42	37	5
Molalla	9,351	18	16	2
Monmouth	10,708	15	14	1
Mount Angel	3,647	8	6	2
Myrtle Creek	3,493	9	7	2
Myrtle Point	2,564	6	5	1
Newberg-Dundee	24,081	47	33	14
Newport	10,950	28	21	7
North Bend	9,778	24	17	7
Nyssa	3,176	7	7	0
Oakridge	3,389	6	5	1
Ontario	10,952	29	24	5
Oregon City	37,892	52	44	8
Pendleton	16,804	27	23	4
Philomath	5,805	10	9	1
Phoenix	4,680	11	9	2
Pilot Rock	1,510	2	2	0
Portland	662,941	1,132	873	259
Port Orford	1,155	5	5	0
Prineville	10,919	31	21	10
Rainier	2,021	6	5	1
Redmond	33,198	54	43	11
Reedsport	4,111	15	10	5
Rockaway Beach	1,429	3	3	0
Rogue River	2,355	8	6	2
Roseburg	23,551	43	38	5
Salem	176,632	336	189	147
Sandy	11,598	19	15	4
Scappoose	7,666	11	10	1
Seaside	6,938	27	19	8
Sherwood	20,052	28	24	4
Silverton	10,782	19	16	3
Springfield	63,666	93	60	33
Stanfield	2,119	4	4	0
Stayton	8,364	13	12	1
St. Helens	13,818	22	19	3
Sunriver	1,393	13	12	1
Sutherlin	8,223	18	14	4
Sweet Home	10,099	21	14	7
Talent	6,671	9	7	2
The Dalles	15,849	28	25	3
Tigard	56,377	83	67	16
Tillamook	5,392	11	8	3
Toledo	3,665	13	7	6
Tualatin	28,030	47	40	7
Turner	2,153	2	2	0
Umatilla	7,366	15	13	2
Vernonia	2,294	6	5	1
Warrenton	5,823	14	12	2
West Linn	26,916	34	30	4
Winston	5,528	12	10	2
Woodburn	26,521	41	32	9
Yamhill	1,187	6	3	3
PENNSYLVANIA				
Abington Township, Montgomery County	55,310	108	90	18
Adams Township, Butler County	14,255	17	17	0
Adams Township, Cambria County	5,474	5	5	0
Akron	4,029	3	3	0
Alburtis	2,669	4	4	0
Aldan	4,160	7	5	2
Aliquippa	8,780	15	14	1
Allegheny Township, Blair County	6,490	10	9	1
Allegheny Township, Westmoreland County	7,993	11	10	1
Allegheny Valley Regional	3,241	2	2	0
Allentown	121,818	234	214	20
Altoona	43,090	71	63	8
Ambler	6,498	14	13	1
Ambridge	6,553	10	10	0
Amity Township	13,237	15	14	1
Annville Township	5,087	6	5	1

Table 78. Full-Time Law Enforcement Employees, by Selected State and City, 2020—Continued

(Number.)

State/city	Population	Total law enforcement employees	Total officers	Total civilians
Apollo	1,510	1	1	0
Archbald	7,033	7	7	0
Ashland	2,664	2	2	0
Ashley	2,715	3	3	0
Aspinwall	2,682	5	5	0
Aston Township	16,753	22	20	2
Athens	3,170	4	4	0
Athens Township	5,053	11	10	1
Avalon	4,518	5	5	0
Avoca	2,625	3	3	0
Avonmore Boro	945	2	1	1
Baden	3,853	3	3	0
Baldwin Borough	19,508	25	24	1
Baldwin Township	1,931	5	5	0
Bally	1,267	2	2	0
Bangor	5,224	7	7	0
Beaver	4,238	11	10	1
Beaver Falls	9,418	17	16	1
Beaver Meadows	831	2	1	1
Bedford	2,660	5	5	0
Bedminster Township	7,300	8	7	1
Bell Acres	1,365	5	5	0
Bellefonte	6,247	11	10	1
Bellevue	8,002	14	13	1
Bellwood	1,741	3	3	0
Bensalem Township	60,517	129	102	27
Bentleyville	2,469	1	1	0
Berlin	1,925	2	2	0
Bern Township	6,984	12	12	0
Bernville	945	1	1	0
Berwick	9,839	17	16	1
Bethel Park	32,350	45	37	8
Bethel Township, Berks County	4,176	6	5	1
Bethlehem	75,909	167	153	14
Bethlehem Township	24,403	36	35	1
Bigler Township Regional	1,224	1	1	0
Biglerville	1,221	2	2	0
Birdsboro	5,145	8	7	1
Birmingham Township	4,200	3	3	0
Blairsville	3,196	5	5	0
Blair Township	4,475	5	5	0
Blakely	6,173	9	9	0
Blawnox	1,382	3	3	0
Bloomsburg Town	13,700	22	17	5
Bonneauville	1,841	1	1	0
Brackenridge	3,122	4	4	0
Bradford	8,150	19	19	0
Bradford Township	4,560	5	5	0
Branch Township	1,730	2	2	0
Brecknock Township, Berks County	4,701	5	5	0
Brentwood	9,228	16	14	2
Briar Creek Township	2,926	5	5	0
Bridgeport	4,571	9	8	1
Bridgeville	4,883	9	8	1
Bridgewater	840	4	3	1
Brighton Township	8,270	12	12	0
Bristol	9,560	15	13	2
Bristol Township	53,355	61	54	7
Brookhaven	8,052	8	7	1
Brownsville	2,211	3	3	0
Bryn Athyn	1,408	4	4	0
Buckingham Township	20,255	22	20	2
Buffalo Township	7,407	8	8	0
Buffalo Valley Regional	12,699	16	15	1
Bushkill Township	8,655	16	15	1
Butler	12,792	25	24	1
Butler Township, Butler County	16,384	23	21	2
Butler Township, Luzerne County	10,023	11	10	1
Butler Township, Schuylkill County	5,539	5	5	0
Caernarvon Township, Berks County	4,191	8	7	1
California	6,653	9	8	1
Caln Township	14,323	19	18	1
Cambria Township	5,651	3	3	0
Cambridge Springs	2,677	3	3	0
Camp Hill	7,906	14	13	1
Canonsburg	8,734	18	17	1
Canton	1,850	3	3	0
Carbondale	8,329	9	9	0
Carlisle	19,249	34	32	2
Carmichaels	438	1	1	0
Carnegie	7,787	14	13	1
Carrolltown	777	2	2	0
Carroll Township, Washington County	5,420	3	3	0
Carroll Township, York County	6,583	13	13	0
Carroll Valley	3,949	3	2	1

Table 78. Full-Time Law Enforcement Employees, by Selected State and City, 2020—Continued

(Number.)

State/city	Population	Total law enforcement employees	Total officers	Total civilians
Castle Shannon	8,205	14	13	1
Catasauqua	6,617	10	9	1
Catawissa	1,457	5	5	0
Cecil Township	13,262	26	25	1
Center Township	11,423	19	18	1
Centerville	3,125	3	3	0
Central Berks Regional	13,624	21	20	1
Central Bucks Regional	15,526	30	26	4
Chambersburg	21,247	34	31	3
Charleroi Regional	6,418	11	11	0
Chartiers Township	8,134	14	14	0
Cheltenham Township	37,159	81	74	7
Chester	34,007	83	81	2
Chester Township	4,086	12	12	0
Chippewa Township	7,901	9	8	1
Churchill	2,909	7	7	0
Clairton	6,513	14	14	0
Clarion	5,766	9	8	1
Clarks Summit	6,218	5	5	0
Clearfield	5,801	7	7	0
Cleona	2,235	4	4	0
Clifton Heights	6,702	12	11	1
Clymer	1,256	2	2	0
Coaldale	2,125	4	4	0
Coal Township	10,192	12	11	1
Coatesville	13,068	31	27	4
Cochranton	1,070	2	2	0
Collegeville	5,183	8	8	0
Collier Township	8,348	19	18	1
Collingdale	8,795	11	10	1
Colonial Regional	18,309	27	25	2
Columbia	10,351	22	19	3
Conemaugh Township, Cambria County	1,806	1	1	0
Conemaugh Township, Somerset County	6,799	6	6	0
Conewago Township, Adams County	7,243	11	10	1
Conewango Township	3,312	4	4	0
Conneaut Lake Regional	4,745	4	4	0
Connellsville	7,247	15	15	0
Conshohocken	8,069	21	19	2
Conway	2,055	5	5	0
Conyngham	1,862	3	3	0
Coopersburg	2,588	7	7	0
Coplay	3,222	6	5	1
Coraopolis	5,400	14	10	4
Cornwall	4,406	7	6	1
Corry	6,165	10	9	1
Coudersport	2,389	3	3	0
Courtdale	715	9	9	0
Covington Township	2,271	3	3	0
Crafton	6,157	10	9	1
Cranberry Township	32,051	34	31	3
Crescent Township	2,539	6	6	0
Cresson	1,537	2	2	0
Cresson Township	2,487	1	1	0
Croyle Township	2,202	1	1	0
Cumberland Township, Adams County	6,267	12	12	0
Cumberland Township, Greene County	6,108	6	6	0
Cumru Township	15,512	27	26	1
Curwensville	2,369	4	3	1
Dallas	2,787	6	6	0
Dallas Township	9,304	13	12	1
Dalton	1,183	3	3	0
Danville	4,642	9	8	1
Darby	10,703	14	13	1
Darby Township	9,281	14	13	1
Darlington Township	1,863	1	1	0
Delmont	2,510	5	5	0
Derry	2,494	3	3	0
Derry Township, Dauphin County	25,313	41	39	2
Donegal Township	3,252	2	2	0
Donora	4,539	5	5	0
Dormont	8,247	14	13	1
Douglass Township, Berks County	3,622	6	6	0
Douglass Township, Montgomery County	10,588	14	12	2
Downingtown	7,898	22	18	4
Doylestown Township	17,368	22	20	2
Dublin Borough	2,130	2	2	0
DuBois	7,319	14	13	1
Duncansville	1,155	2	2	0
Dunmore	12,837	21	20	1
Dupont	2,679	2	2	0
Duquesne	5,556	16	16	0
Duryea	4,845	2	2	0
East Berlin	1,548	3	1	2
East Brandywine Township	9,346	17	15	2

Table 78. Full-Time Law Enforcement Employees, by Selected State and City, 2020—Continued

(Number.)

State/city	Population	Total law enforcement employees	Total officers	Total civilians
East Cocalico Township	10,713	16	15	1
East Coventry Township	6,760	8	7	1
East Deer Township	1,430	1	1	0
East Earl Township	6,934	6	6	0
Eastern Adams Regional	7,425	5	5	0
Eastern Pike Regional	4,614	11	10	1
East Fallowfield Township	7,568	7	7	0
East Franklin Township	3,817	1	1	0
East Greenville	2,942	3	3	0
East Hempfield Township	24,831	37	33	4
East Lampeter Township	17,103	41	38	3
East Lansdowne	2,671	5	4	1
East Marlborough Township	7,608	2	2	0
East Norriton Township	14,010	29	28	1
Easton	27,232	65	60	5
East Pennsboro Township	21,556	23	22	1
East Pikeland Township	7,574	11	11	0
Easttown Township	10,652	14	13	1
East Vincent Township	7,402	7	7	0
East Whiteland Township	13,106	22	21	1
Ebensburg	3,023	5	5	0
Economy	9,108	14	13	1
Eddystone	2,412	10	9	1
Edgewood	2,991	8	8	0
Edgeworth	1,643	5	4	1
Edinboro	5,422	8	8	0
Edwardsville	4,709	6	6	0
Elizabeth	1,965	1	1	0
Elizabethtown	11,436	18	16	2
Elizabeth Township	12,916	12	12	0
Ellwood City	7,227	11	10	1
Emmaus	11,498	20	18	2
Emporium	1,790	2	2	0
Ephrata	13,920	34	31	3
Erie	94,842	194	173	21
Etna	3,294	7	6	1
Evans City-Seven Fields Regional	4,417	5	5	0
Everett	1,707	3	3	0
Exeter	5,532	3	3	0
Exeter Township, Berks County	25,815	35	33	2
Exeter Township, Luzerne County	2,352	5	5	0
Fairview Township, Luzerne County	4,514	7	7	0
Fairview Township, York County	17,709	20	18	2
Falls Township, Bucks County	33,465	62	55	7
Farrell	4,541	16	15	1
Fawn Township	2,288	1	1	0
Ferguson Township	19,646	24	22	2
Ferndale	1,479	2	2	0
Findlay Township	6,140	25	18	7
Fleetwood	4,105	9	8	1
Folcroft	6,633	13	12	1
Ford City	2,741	3	3	0
Forest City	1,725	2	2	0
Forest Hills	6,272	9	9	0
Forks Township	15,879	23	22	1
Forty Fort	4,028	5	5	0
Forward Township	3,260	1	1	0
Fountain Hill	4,708	11	10	1
Fox Chapel	5,062	11	11	0
Frackville	3,590	5	5	0
Franconia Township	13,400	11	10	1
Franklin	5,956	25	15	10
Franklin Park	15,042	19	17	2
Franklin Township, Beaver County	3,811	4	4	0
Franklin Township, Carbon County	4,169	4	4	0
Frazer Township	1,116	2	2	0
Freedom Township	3,318	3	3	0
Freemansburg	2,627	3	3	0
Freeport	1,663	2	2	0
Galeton	1,070	1	1	0
Gallitzin	1,738	2	2	0
Geistown	2,250	3	3	0
German Township	4,747	3	3	0
Gettysburg	7,738	11	10	1
Gilpin Township	2,379	2	2	0
Girard	2,892	4	4	0
Glassport	4,296	9	9	0
Glenolden	7,165	9	8	1
Granville Township	4,974	10	8	2
Greenfield Township	2,008	1	1	0
Greenfield Township, Blair County	3,943	3	3	0
Greensburg	14,030	32	26	6
Green Tree	4,882	10	10	0
Greenville	5,202	10	9	1
Grove City	7,702	11	10	1

Table 78. Full-Time Law Enforcement Employees, by Selected State and City, 2020—Continued

(Number.)

State/city	Population	Total law enforcement employees	Total officers	Total civilians
Hamburg	4,369	7	6	1
Hampden Township	31,034	26	25	1
Hampton Township	18,161	20	19	1
Hanover	15,767	26	24	2
Hanover Township, Luzerne County	10,797	18	18	0
Harmar Township	3,006	8	8	0
Harmony Township	2,974	11	11	0
Harrisburg	49,244	159	129	30
Harrison Township	10,211	14	13	1
Harveys Lake	2,773	5	5	0
Hastings	1,142	2	2	0
Hatboro	7,516	18	15	3
Hatfield Township	21,246	30	28	2
Haverford Township	49,638	76	70	6
Hazleton	24,726	41	39	2
Hegins Township	3,346	2	2	0
Heidelberg	1,203	4	4	0
Hellam Township	8,626	12	12	0
Hellertown	5,825	10	10	0
Hemlock Township	2,261	9	9	0
Hempfield Township, Mercer County	3,535	8	7	1
Hermitage	15,368	34	31	3
Highspire	2,370	5	5	0
Hilltown Township	15,911	19	17	2
Hollidaysburg	5,664	11	9	2
Homer City	1,576	1	1	0
Homestead	3,144	11	10	1
Honesdale	4,257	5	5	0
Honey Brook	1,763	1	1	0
Hopewell Township	12,583	17	16	1
Horsham Township	26,522	47	40	7
Hughestown	1,348	1	1	0
Hughesville	2,019	3	3	0
Hummelstown	4,857	7	6	1
Huntingdon	6,920	12	12	0
Independence Township, Beaver County	2,323	2	2	0
Indiana	13,084	20	19	1
Indiana Township	7,109	10	10	0
Indian Lake	376	2	2	0
Ingram	3,185	4	4	0
Irwin	3,718	3	3	0
Jackson Township, Butler County	4,325	11	10	1
Jackson Township, Cambria County	3,967	3	3	0
Jackson Township, Luzerne County	4,662	7	7	0
Jeannette	9,011	14	13	1
Jefferson Hills Borough	11,152	20	19	1
Jefferson Township, Mercer County	1,794	2	2	0
Jenkins Township	4,569	5	5	0
Jenkintown	4,419	16	14	2
Jim Thorpe	4,644	9	8	1
Johnsonburg	2,271	3	3	0
Johnstown	20,390	42	38	4
Kane	3,419	4	4	0
Kennedy Township	8,159	12	10	2
Kennett Square	6,219	14	11	3
Kennett Township	8,387	10	9	1
Kidder Township	1,938	7	7	0
Kingston	12,774	21	19	2
Kingston Township	6,887	13	13	0
Kiskiminetas Township	4,440	2	2	0
Kline Township	1,353	1	1	0
Knox	1,061	2	2	0
Kulpmont	2,736	3	3	0
Kutztown	5,090	14	12	2
Lake City	2,835	3	3	0
Lancaster	59,264	161	143	18
Lancaster Township, Butler County	2,802	4	4	0
Langhorne Borough	1,576	1	1	0
Lansdale	17,173	32	25	7
Lansdowne	10,650	18	16	2
Lansford	3,789	6	6	0
Latimore Township	2,711	1	1	0
Latrobe	7,777	15	14	1
Laureldale	3,911	5	5	0
Lawrence Park Township	3,718	8	8	0
Lawrence Township, Clearfield County	7,507	11	10	1
Lebanon	25,925	41	38	3
Leechburg	1,972	3	3	0
Leetsdale	1,152	5	5	0
Leet Township	1,579	4	4	0
Lehighton	5,293	11	10	1
Lehigh Township, Northampton County	10,425	13	12	1
Lehman Township	3,491	6	6	0
Lewistown	8,102	14	13	1
Liberty	2,443	1	1	0

Table 78. Full-Time Law Enforcement Employees, by Selected State and City, 2020—Continued

(Number.)

State/city	Population	Total law enforcement employees	Total officers	Total civilians
Liberty Township, Adams County	1,270	1	1	0
Limerick Township	19,441	31	29	2
Lincoln	1,017	3	2	1
Linesville	970	1	1	0
Lititz	9,499	15	14	1
Littlestown	4,518	9	9	0
Lock Haven	9,011	16	14	2
Locust Township	1,375	5	5	0
Logan Township	12,185	18	16	2
Lower Allen Township	20,535	25	22	3
Lower Burrell	11,006	18	17	1
Lower Chichester Township	3,474	5	5	0
Lower Frederick Township	4,936	4	4	0
Lower Gwynedd Township	11,506	19	18	1
Lower Heidelberg Township	6,259	11	10	1
Lower Makefield Township	32,830	42	39	3
Lower Merion Township	60,353	146	130	16
Lower Moreland Township	13,125	31	26	5
Lower Paxton Township	50,230	65	58	7
Lower Pottsgrove Township	12,156	22	20	2
Lower Providence Township	27,030	33	31	2
Lower Salford Township	15,593	21	19	2
Lower Saucon Township	10,845	16	15	1
Lower Southampton Township	19,205	34	32	2
Lower Swatara Township	9,001	18	16	2
Lower Windsor Township	7,597	11	10	1
Luzerne	2,808	3	3	0
Luzerne Township	5,898	1	1	0
Lykens	1,768	1	1	0
Macungie	3,190	4	4	0
Mahanoy Township	3,174	7	6	1
Mahoning Township, Carbon County	4,232	6	5	1
Mahoning Township, Lawrence County	2,835	2	2	0
Mahoning Township, Montour County	4,137	8	7	1
Malvern	3,510	8	7	1
Manheim	4,848	18	17	1
Manheim Township	40,811	77	65	12
Manor	3,360	4	4	0
Manor Township, Armstrong County	4,019	3	3	0
Manor Township, Lancaster County	21,177	21	19	2
Mansfield	2,847	5	5	0
Marcus Hook	2,403	6	5	1
Marion Township, Beaver County	864	2	2	0
Marlborough Township	3,404	4	4	0
Marple Township	24,015	34	31	3
Martinsburg	1,824	3	3	0
Marysville	2,562	2	2	0
Masontown	3,257	4	4	0
Mayfield	1,683	2	2	0
McAdoo	2,141	3	3	0
McCandless	28,151	31	29	2
McDonald Borough	2,040	6	5	1
McKeesport	20,647	43	40	3
McKees Rocks	5,830	10	9	1
McSherrystown	3,096	5	5	0
Meadville	12,579	27	22	5
Mechanicsburg	8,992	18	16	2
Media	5,724	16	15	1
Mercer	1,865	4	4	0
Mercersburg	1,530	2	2	0
Meshoppen	1,411	2	2	0
Meyersdale	2,002	5	5	0
Middleburg	1,267	4	3	1
Middlesex Township, Butler County	5,839	4	4	0
Middlesex Township, Cumberland County	7,455	13	12	1
Middletown	9,669	11	11	0
Middletown Township	44,918	63	58	5
Midland	2,451	4	4	0
Mifflinburg	3,470	8	7	1
Mifflin County Regional	16,897	14	14	0
Milford	978	2	2	0
Millbourne	1,160	1	1	0
Millcreek Township, Erie County	52,329	78	61	17
Millcreek Township, Lebanon County	5,842	2	2	0
Millersburg	2,515	3	2	1
Millersville	8,385	15	13	2
Millvale	3,646	7	7	0
Milton	6,563	9	8	1
Minersville	4,131	6	6	0
Mohnton	3,021	3	3	0
Monaca	5,387	11	11	0
Monessen	7,186	13	12	1
Monongahela	9,749	8	7	1
Monroeville	27,275	56	46	10

Table 78. Full-Time Law Enforcement Employees, by Selected State and City, 2020—Continued

(Number.)

State/city	Population	Total law enforcement employees	Total officers	Total civilians
Montgomery Township	26,315	45	36	9
Montoursville	4,375	7	6	1
Montrose	1,462	5	5	0
Moon Township	25,575	38	30	8
Moore Township	9,456	12	11	1
Moosic	5,845	9	9	0
Morrisville	8,499	11	11	0
Morton	2,672	5	5	0
Moscow	2,037	2	2	0
Mount Carmel	5,709	9	9	0
Mount Carmel Township	2,959	7	7	0
Mount Holly Springs	2,055	4	4	0
Mount Joy	8,378	12	11	1
Mount Lebanon	31,799	54	43	11
Mount Oliver	3,267	10	10	0
Mount Pleasant	4,199	3	3	0
Mount Pleasant Township	3,517	5	5	0
Mount Union	2,327	4	4	0
Muhlenberg Township	20,417	30	28	2
Muncy	2,404	3	3	0
Muncy Township	1,202	2	2	0
Munhall	10,965	26	24	2
Murrysville	19,537	23	21	2
Nanticoke	10,296	12	11	1
Nanty Glo	2,445	2	2	0
Narberth	4,342	10	6	4
Nazareth	5,698	6	5	1
Neshannock Township	9,163	8	8	0
Nesquehoning	3,240	5	5	0
Nether Providence Township	13,788	15	14	1
Newberry Township	15,989	19	17	2
New Bethlehem	2,686	3	3	0
New Brighton	8,627	9	9	0
New Britain Township	11,568	14	13	1
New Castle	21,445	40	37	3
New Cumberland	7,289	10	9	1
New Hanover Township	13,483	12	11	1
New Holland	5,472	15	15	0
New Hope	2,530	10	9	1
New Kensington	12,205	26	22	4
Newport Township	5,340	5	5	0
New Sewickley Township	7,136	11	10	1
Newtown	2,238	6	6	0
Newtown Township, Bucks County	22,723	33	29	4
Newtown Township, Delaware County	14,150	22	20	2
Newville	1,349	4	4	0
New Wilmington	2,170	5	5	0
Norristown	34,339	81	68	13
Northampton	9,867	15	13	2
Northampton Township	39,103	49	43	6
North Belle Vernon	1,844	2	2	0
North Braddock	4,648	1	1	0
North Catasauqua	2,829	4	4	0
North Cornwall Township	7,972	10	9	1
North Coventry Township	7,969	13	12	1
North East, Erie County	4,006	7	7	0
Northeastern Regional	11,992	13	12	1
Northern Berks Regional	13,537	14	13	1
Northern Cambria Borough	3,471	3	3	0
Northern Lancaster County Regional	41,322	35	31	4
Northern Regional	36,504	42	40	2
Northern York County Regional	86,465	64	60	4
North Fayette Township	14,913	25	21	4
North Hopewell Township	2,768	2	2	0
North Huntingdon Township	30,350	34	28	6
North Lebanon Township	12,272	14	12	2
North Londonderry Township	8,658	10	9	1
North Middleton Township	11,886	11	10	1
North Sewickley Township	5,357	1	1	0
North Strabane Township	14,596	26	25	1
Northumberland	3,587	6	6	0
North Versailles Township	11,992	24	19	5
North Wales	3,268	5	5	0
North Woodbury	2,589	2	2	0
Norwood	5,898	7	6	1
Oakmont	6,568	7	7	0
O'Hara Township	8,788	17	16	1
Ohio Township	7,209	20	18	2
Ohioville	3,264	2	2	0
Oil City	9,521	17	16	1
Old Forge	7,849	7	7	0
Old Lycoming Township	4,907	10	9	1
Olyphant	5,008	7	7	0
Orangeville Area	3,568	1	1	0
Orwigsburg	2,936	6	6	0

Table 78. Full-Time Law Enforcement Employees, by Selected State and City, 2020—Continued

(Number.)

State/city	Population	Total law enforcement employees	Total officers	Total civilians
Oxford	5,640	10	9	1
Palmerton	5,326	10	9	1
Palmer Township	21,506	37	35	2
Palmyra	7,616	12	11	1
Parkesburg	4,040	8	7	1
Parkside	2,330	1	1	0
Parks Township	2,545	2	2	0
Patterson Township	4,125	4	4	0
Patton	1,581	2	2	0
Patton Township	15,874	22	20	2
Penbrook	2,982	7	7	0
Penndel	2,140	1	1	0
Penn Hills	40,636	52	49	3
Pennridge Regional	10,946	12	11	1
Penn Township, Butler County	4,858	5	4	1
Penn Township, Westmoreland County	19,275	24	22	2
Penn Township, York County	16,737	25	22	3
Perkasie	8,765	19	17	2
Perryopolis	1,653	2	2	0
Peters Township	22,137	26	25	1
Philadelphia	1,586,666	7,140	6,359	781
Phoenixville	17,024	32	31	1
Pine Creek Township	3,222	2	2	0
Pine Grove	2,056	2	2	0
Pitcairn	3,144	2	2	0
Pittsburgh	298,608	1,036	998	38
Pittston Township	3,359	6	6	0
Plains Township	9,636	20	20	0
Pleasant Hills	8,001	20	18	2
Plum	27,082	29	27	2
Plumstead Township	14,730	18	16	2
Plymouth Township, Montgomery County	17,645	52	45	7
Pocono Mountain Regional	43,250	48	43	5
Pocono Township	11,091	20	19	1
Point Township	3,582	6	6	0
Polk	763	2	2	0
Portage	2,357	2	2	0
Port Allegany	1,982	3	3	0
Port Vue	3,635	2	2	0
Pottstown	22,626	58	44	14
Pottsville	13,384	24	23	1
Prospect Park	6,496	9	8	1
Pulaski Township, Lawrence County	3,207	2	2	0
Punxsutawney	5,678	10	9	1
Pymatuning Township	3,004	10	7	3
Quakertown	8,762	24	21	3
Quarryville	2,774	5	5	0
Raccoon Township	2,884	4	4	0
Radnor Township	31,910	46	42	4
Ralpho Township	4,184	6	6	0
Rankin	2,018	1	1	0
Reading	88,412	186	162	24
Reading Township	5,902	2	2	0
Redstone Township	4,136	2	2	0
Renovo	1,202	1	1	0
Reserve Township	3,212	6	6	0
Reynoldsville	2,635	2	2	0
Rice Township	3,570	6	6	0
Richland Township, Bucks County	13,357	18	16	2
Richland Township, Cambria County	11,715	21	20	1
Ridgway	3,717	8	7	1
Ridley Park	7,070	10	10	0
Ridley Township	31,242	35	32	3
Riverside	1,845	3	3	0
Roaring Brook Township	1,989	2	2	0
Roaring Spring	2,421	3	3	0
Robeson Township	7,457	5	5	0
Robinson Township, Allegheny County	13,904	29	28	1
Rochester	3,416	8	7	1
Rochester Township	2,617	3	3	0
Rockledge	2,529	5	5	0
Ross Township	30,403	44	43	1
Rostraver Township	10,970	18	17	1
Royalton	1,036	1	1	0
Royersford	4,753	9	8	1
Rural Valley	807	1	1	0
Rush Township	3,241	1	1	0
Sadsbury Township, Chester County	4,174	4	4	0
Salem Township, Luzerne County	4,189	7	7	0
Salisbury Township	13,985	21	19	2
Sandy Lake	621	1	1	0
Sandy Township	10,422	13	12	1
Saxonburg	1,429	2	2	0
Saxton	676	3	3	0

Table 78. Full-Time Law Enforcement Employees, by Selected State and City, 2020—Continued

(Number.)

State/city	Population	Total law enforcement employees	Total officers	Total civilians
Sayre	6,334	13	11	2
Schuylkill Haven	5,069	8	8	0
Schuylkill Township, Chester County	8,626	13	11	2
Scottdale	4,066	6	6	0
Scott Township, Allegheny County	16,362	22	21	1
Scott Township, Columbia County	5,048	8	8	0
Scott Township, Lackawanna County	4,729	4	4	0
Scranton	76,719	153	140	13
Selinsgrove	5,931	6	5	1
Sewickley Heights	806	3	3	0
Shaler Township	27,612	28	26	2
Shamokin	6,908	10	10	0
Shamokin Dam	1,709	3	3	0
Sharon	12,820	31	30	1
Sharon Hill	5,690	12	11	1
Sharpsburg	3,304	6	6	0
Sharpsville	4,038	6	6	0
Shenandoah	4,727	6	6	0
Shenango Township, Lawrence County	7,080	8	8	0
Shenango Township, Mercer County	3,648	11	11	0
Shillington	5,322	7	6	1
Shinglehouse	1,046	1	1	0
Shippensburg	5,570	11	10	1
Shippingport	187	2	2	0
Shiremanstown	1,629	2	2	0
Silver Spring Township	18,910	24	23	1
Sinking Spring	4,119	7	6	1
Slate Belt Regional	12,530	21	20	1
Slatington	4,316	6	6	0
Slippery Rock	3,518	4	4	0
Smethport	1,517	2	2	0
Smith Township	4,341	5	5	0
Solebury Township	8,537	18	16	2
Somerset	5,810	8	7	1
Souderton	7,134	7	6	1
South Abington Township	8,872	11	10	1
South Beaver Township	2,637	4	4	0
South Buffalo Township	2,506	2	2	0
South Coatesville	1,472	2	2	0
South Connellsville Borough	1,853	1	1	0
Southern Chester County Regional	16,477	20	18	2
Southern Regional York County	12,864	16	15	1
South Fayette Township	16,123	21	20	1
South Fork	833	1	1	0
South Greensburg	1,983	2	2	0
South Heidelberg Township	12,368	14	14	0
South Park Township	13,650	16	15	1
South Pymatuning Township	2,494	4	4	0
South Strabane Township	9,439	21	20	1
Southwest Greensburg	2,004	11	11	0
Southwest Regional, Fayette County	2,620	1	1	0
Southwest Regional, Washington County	130	1	1	0
South Whitehall Township	20,042	41	39	2
Spring City	3,301	3	3	0
Springdale	3,275	4	4	0
Springettsbury Township	26,884	32	29	3
Springfield Township, Bucks County	5,032	4	4	0
Springfield Township, Delaware County	24,276	39	34	5
Springfield Township, Montgomery County	19,901	31	29	2
Spring Garden Township	13,293	24	20	4
Spring Township, Berks County	27,717	29	28	1
Spring Township, Centre County	8,120	9	8	1
State College	58,471	65	55	10
St. Clair Boro	2,811	5	5	0
Steelton	5,959	15	14	1
St. Marys City	12,177	16	15	1
Stockertown	926	1	1	0
Stoneboro	973	1	1	0
Stonycreek Township	2,558	4	4	0
Stowe Township	6,095	11	10	1
Strasburg	3,053	5	5	0
Stroud Area Regional	35,441	56	47	9
Sugarcreek	4,861	2	2	0
Summerhill Township	2,236	2	2	0
Summit Hill	2,946	5	5	0
Summit Township	2,101	1	1	0
Sunbury	9,306	10	8	2
Susquehanna Regional	8,433	16	14	2
Susquehanna Township, Dauphin County	25,233	44	40	4
Swarthmore	6,364	8	8	0
Swatara Township	26,820	53	50	3
Sweden Township	812	1	1	0
Swissvale	8,609	15	15	0
Swoyersville	4,997	5	5	0

Table 78. Full-Time Law Enforcement Employees, by Selected State and City, 2020—Continued

(Number.)

State/city	Population	Total law enforcement employees	Total officers	Total civilians
Sykesville	1,110	1	1	0
Tamaqua	6,617	10	9	1
Tarentum	4,347	10	10	0
Tatamy	1,173	2	2	0
Taylor	5,876	8	8	0
Throop	3,875	8	8	0
Tiadaghton Valley Regional	7,512	11	11	0
Tilden Township	3,622	4	4	0
Tinicum Township, Bucks County	3,948	3	3	0
Tinicum Township, Delaware County	4,113	18	16	2
Tioga	645	2	1	1
Titusville	5,112	11	11	0
Towamencin Township	18,536	25	23	2
Towanda	2,797	6	6	0
Trafford	3,019	5	5	0
Tredyffrin Township	29,401	47	42	5
Troy	1,224	2	2	0
Tullytown	2,176	5	4	1
Tulpehocken Township	3,477	3	3	0
Tunkhannock	1,683	3	3	0
Tunkhannock Township, Wyoming County	5,998	8	8	0
Turtle Creek	5,116	5	5	0
Tyrone	5,105	9	7	2
Union City	3,096	4	3	1
Uniontown	9,653	21	20	1
Union Township, Lawrence County	4,817	11	11	0
Upland	3,327	8	7	1
Upper Allen Township	20,655	24	23	1
Upper Burrell Township	2,201	2	2	0
Upper Chichester Township	16,987	24	23	1
Upper Darby Township	82,947	128	116	12
Upper Dublin Township	26,658	42	37	5
Upper Gwynedd Township	15,850	24	21	3
Upper Macungie Township	25,811	32	29	3
Upper Makefield Township	8,646	17	16	1
Upper Merion Township	33,595	86	70	16
Upper Moreland Township	24,031	43	37	6
Upper Nazareth Township	7,161	10	9	1
Upper Perkiomen	3,856	4	4	0
Upper Pottsgrove Township	5,799	9	9	0
Upper Providence Township, Delaware County	10,479	16	15	1
Upper Providence Township, Montgomery County	24,725	29	27	2
Upper Saucon Township	17,603	25	23	2
Upper Southampton Township	14,934	25	22	3
Upper St. Clair Township	19,791	35	28	7
Upper Uwchlan Township	11,887	12	12	0
Upper Yoder Township	4,989	6	6	0
Uwchlan Township	18,924	24	23	1
Valley Township	7,884	7	7	0
Vernon Township	5,341	4	4	0
Verona	2,401	4	3	1
Versailles	1,455	2	2	0
Walnutport	2,089	4	4	0
Warminster Township	32,300	47	43	4
Warren	8,979	18	16	2
Warrington Township	24,689	37	36	1
Warwick Township, Bucks County	14,725	18	17	1
Washington Township, Fayette County	3,575	4	4	0
Washington Township, Franklin County	14,853	12	10	2
Washington Township, Westmoreland County	7,023	9	9	0
Washington, Washington County	13,371	33	31	2
Watsontown	2,241	6	6	0
Waverly Township	1,676	3	3	0
Waynesboro	10,921	21	19	2
Waynesburg	3,941	8	8	0
Weatherly	2,451	4	4	0
Wellsboro	3,223	7	7	0
Wesleyville	3,093	8	7	1
West Brandywine Township	7,474	10	9	1
West Caln Township	9,120	4	4	0
West Chester	20,211	57	44	13
West Conshohocken	1,445	13	12	1
West Deer Township	12,009	15	14	1
West Earl Township	8,457	8	7	1
West Fallowfield Township	2,592	2	2	0
West Goshen Township	23,100	36	32	4
West Hazleton	4,342	5	5	0
West Hempfield Township	16,808	22	21	1
West Hills Regional	9,793	12	11	1
West Homestead	1,857	13	12	1
West Lampeter Township	16,036	19	17	2

Table 78. Full-Time Law Enforcement Employees, by Selected State and City, 2020—Continued

(Number.)

State/city	Population	Total law enforcement employees	Total officers	Total civilians
West Mahanoy Township	2,693	3	3	0
West Manchester Township	18,808	32	28	4
West Manheim Township	8,765	11	11	0
West Mead Township	4,994	2	2	0
West Mifflin	19,632	40	33	7
West Newton	2,462	2	2	0
West Norriton Township	15,608	30	27	3
West Penn Township	4,278	2	2	0
West Pikeland Township	4,071	4	4	0
West Pike Run	1,525	1	1	0
West Pittston	4,746	3	3	0
West Pottsgrove Township	3,836	6	6	0
West Reading	4,298	17	15	2
West Sadsbury Township	2,504	5	5	0
West Shore Regional	7,696	13	12	1
Westtown-East Goshen Regional	32,317	32	29	3
West View	6,489	11	10	1
West Vincent Township	6,081	7	6	1
West Whiteland Township	19,923	29	27	2
Whitehall	13,352	24	19	5
Whitehall Township	27,953	52	47	5
White Haven Borough	1,100	1	1	0
Whitemarsh Township	18,453	42	36	6
White Oak	7,398	14	13	1
Whitpain Township	19,279	37	29	8
Wiconisco Township	1,204	1	1	0
Wilkes-Barre	40,683	83	79	4
Wilkes-Barre Township	2,875	15	14	1
Wilkinsburg	15,230	26	24	2
Wilkins Township	6,109	12	12	0
Williamsburg	1,169	2	2	0
Williamsport	28,055	50	46	4
Willistown Township	11,071	18	16	2
Wilson	7,797	15	14	1
Windber	3,780	3	2	1
Womelsdorf	2,912	3	3	0
Woodward Township	2,361	2	2	0
Wright Township	5,625	7	6	1
Wyoming	3,004	4	4	0
Wyomissing	10,658	21	20	1
Yardley	2,522	5	5	0
Yeadon	11,502	18	17	1
York	43,940	109	92	17
York Area Regional	56,505	51	46	5
Youngsville	1,600	2	2	0
Zelienople	3,580	9	8	1
Zerbe Township	1,743	1	1	0
RHODE ISLAND				
Barrington	15,986	32	25	7
Bristol	21,748	49	40	9
Burrillville	16,904	32	25	7
Central Falls	19,530	46	38	8
Charlestown	7,803	25	20	5
Coventry	34,740	81	57	24
Cranston	81,313	178	148	30
Cumberland	35,357	51	42	9
East Greenwich	13,084	38	31	7
East Providence	47,542	110	92	18
Foster	4,747	13	9	4
Glocester	10,358	21	16	5
Hopkinton	8,025	19	14	5
Jamestown	5,493	19	14	5
Johnston	29,458	78	65	13
Lincoln	22,029	43	35	8
Little Compton	3,463	14	10	4
Middletown	15,817	40	36	4
Narragansett	15,248	51	38	13
Newport	24,202	100	83	17
New Shoreham	1,025	11	5	6
North Kingstown	26,221	60	52	8
North Providence	32,652	68	61	7
North Smithfield	12,616	33	26	7
Pawtucket	72,017	171	140	31
Portsmouth	17,162	39	36	3
Providence	179,603	510	420	90
Richmond	7,724	16	14	2
Scituate	10,739	24	15	9
Smithfield	21,893	54	40	14
South Kingstown	30,238	67	52	15
Tiverton	15,604	40	27	13
Warren	10,469	30	25	5
Warwick	80,605	201	165	36
Westerly	22,277	66	51	15
West Greenwich	6,399	19	13	6

Table 78. Full-Time Law Enforcement Employees, by Selected State and City, 2020—Continued

(Number.)

State/city	Population	Total law enforcement employees	Total officers	Total civilians
West Warwick	28,831	58	48	10
Woonsocket	41,693	113	100	13
SOUTH CAROLINA				
Abbeville	4,990	20	19	1
Aiken	31,007	117	87	30
Allendale	2,870	6	6	0
Anderson	27,815	144	106	38
Atlantic Beach	459	5	4	1
Aynor	1,025	6	6	0
Bamberg	3,147	10	8	2
Barnwell	4,241	17	15	2
Batesburg-Leesville	5,419	31	26	5
Beaufort	13,561	50	45	5
Belton	4,488	14	13	1
Bennettsville	7,591	29	27	2
Bethune	352	1	1	0
Blacksburg	1,885	11	11	0
Blackville	2,166	8	7	1
Bluffton	27,549	63	57	6
Bonneau	490	4	2	2
Bowman	880	4	2	2
Branchville	946	3	2	1
Burnettown	2,762	2	2	0
Calhoun Falls	1,892	4	4	0
Camden	7,264	33	29	4
Cameron	396	1	1	0
Campobello	601	11	10	1
Cayce	14,117	83	56	27
Central	5,407	12	11	1
Chapin	1,657	6	6	0
Charleston	139,582	505	409	96
Cheraw	5,529	29	23	6
Chesnee	969	6	5	1
Chester	5,354	21	19	2
Chesterfield	1,409	5	5	0
Clemson	17,951	42	31	11
Clover	6,693	22	17	5
Columbia	131,777	431	343	88
Conway	27,120	59	52	7
Coward	773	1	1	0
Cowpens	2,450	9	7	2
Darlington	5,895	35	32	3
Denmark	2,876	10	9	1
Dillon	6,261	25	23	2
Due West	1,200	5	5	0
Duncan	3,679	23	22	1
Easley	21,512	58	48	10
Edgefield	4,816	10	10	0
Edisto Beach	405	7	7	0
Ehrhardt	476	2	1	1
Elgin	1,616	7	5	2
Elloree	635	3	3	0
Estill	1,838	7	6	1
Eutawville	288	2	2	0
Florence	38,597	91	78	13
Folly Beach	2,676	23	17	6
Forest Acres	10,283	33	26	7
Fort Lawn	885	3	2	1
Fort Mill	23,966	65	56	9
Fountain Inn	10,820	33	25	8
Gaffney	12,631	38	34	4
Gaston	1,706	3	3	0
Georgetown	8,697	34	29	5
Gifford	260	5	2	3
Goose Creek	44,522	88	65	23
Great Falls	1,866	5	5	0
Greeleyville	375	1	1	0
Greenville	72,014	249	206	43
Greenwood	23,422	54	49	5
Greer	34,320	79	59	20
Hampton	2,474	14	13	1
Hanahan	28,143	32	30	2
Hardeeville	7,970	27	25	2
Harleyville	702	2	2	0
Hartsville	7,519	40	38	2
Holly Hill	1,168	6	6	0
Honea Path	3,857	15	13	2
Irmo	12,639	26	23	3
Isle of Palms	4,385	27	18	9
Iva	1,335	9	9	0
Jackson	1,812	4	3	1
Johnsonville	1,484	7	6	1
Johnston	2,382	9	9	0
Jonesville	831	3	3	0

Table 78. Full-Time Law Enforcement Employees, by Selected State and City, 2020—Continued

(Number.)

State/city	Population	Total law enforcement employees	Total officers	Total civilians
Kingstree	3,035	9	6	3
Lake City	6,477	22	22	0
Lake View	752	3	3	0
Landrum	2,713	13	11	2
Lane	446	4	1	3
Latta	1,275	9	8	1
Laurens	8,830	32	26	6
Lexington	22,592	64	61	3
Liberty	3,143	15	10	5
Loris	2,804	14	11	3
Lyman	3,768	13	13	0
Manning	3,869	20	19	1
Marion	6,268	19	16	3
Mauldin	25,662	59	47	12
McColl	1,949	7	6	1
McCormick	2,310	6	6	0
Moncks Corner	12,580	33	29	4
Mount Pleasant	94,704	175	158	17
Mullins	4,196	21	16	5
Myrtle Beach	35,658	304	203	101
Newberry	10,181	27	25	2
New Ellenton	2,164	2	2	0
Nichols	332	1	1	0
Ninety Six	2,042	8	8	0
North	702	5	5	0
North Augusta	24,139	92	65	27
North Charleston	117,503	396	321	75
North Myrtle Beach	17,183	147	80	67
Orangeburg	12,529	68	38	30
Pageland	2,629	14	10	4
Pamplico	1,219	3	3	0
Pawleys Island	109	5	4	1
Pelion	714	2	2	0
Port Royal	13,553	26	25	1
Prosperity	1,295	4	4	0
Quinby	922	1	1	0
Ridgeland	3,788	14	13	1
Ridge Spring	749	2	2	0
Ridgeville	1,678	1	1	0
Rock Hill	76,016	201	152	49
Salley	417	1	1	0
Saluda	3,610	9	8	1
Scranton	863	2	1	1
Seneca	8,581	44	30	14
Simpsonville	24,960	55	44	11
South Congaree	2,504	7	6	1
Spartanburg	37,469	143	120	23
Springdale	2,745	12	11	1
Springfield	479	3	3	0
St. George	2,217	12	10	2
St. Matthews	1,901	7	6	1
Sullivans Island	1,939	12	10	2
Summerton	921	5	5	0
Summerville	53,711	140	116	24
Sumter	39,542	155	111	44
Surfside Beach	4,608	22	17	5
Swansea	974	3	3	0
Tega Cay	11,813	34	26	8
Travelers Rest	5,435	22	16	6
Trenton	199	1	1	0
Union	7,565	28	25	3
Wagener	841	2	2	0
Walhalla	4,498	14	13	1
Walterboro	5,387	33	31	2
Ware Shoals	2,152	7	7	0
Wellford	2,754	10	8	2
West Columbia	18,143	63	53	10
West Pelzer	954	4	3	1
West Union	337	3	3	0
Whitmire	1,455	4	3	1
Williamston	4,294	19	18	1
Winnsboro	3,144	18	17	1
Woodruff	4,457	11	10	1
York	8,486	40	34	6
SOUTH DAKOTA				
Aberdeen	28,494	58	49	9
Alcester	749	2	2	0
Avon	590	1	1	0
Belle Fourche	5,712	13	11	2
Beresford	2,028	5	5	0
Box Elder	10,402	19	18	1
Brandon	10,205	14	13	1
Brookings	24,682	47	35	12
Burke	584	1	1	0

Table 78. Full-Time Law Enforcement Employees, by Selected State and City, 2020—Continued

(Number.)

State/city	Population	Total law enforcement employees	Total officers	Total civilians
Canton	3,615	6	6	0
Centerville	870	2	2	0
Chamberlain	2,364	6	6	0
Clark	1,053	2	2	0
Deadwood	1,293	18	15	3
Eagle Butte	1,349	1	1	0
Elk Point	1,860	5	5	0
Faith	410	1	1	0
Flandreau	2,314	8	7	1
Freeman	1,272	2	2	0
Gettysburg	1,070	2	2	0
Groton	1,477	4	4	0
Hot Springs	3,477	9	7	2
Huron	13,469	25	25	0
Jefferson	507	2	2	0
Kadoka	724	1	1	0
Kimball	670	1	1	0
Lead	2,923	7	6	1
Lennox	2,520	5	5	0
Madison	7,357	14	13	1
Martin	1,042	3	3	0
Menno	615	1	1	0
Milbank	3,077	7	7	0
Miller	1,318	4	4	0
Mitchell	15,726	23	21	2
Mobridge	3,442	16	8	8
Murdo	432	2	2	0
North Sioux City	2,975	9	8	1
Parkston	1,473	2	2	0
Philip	764	2	2	0
Pierre	13,888	40	25	15
Platte	1,261	2	2	0
Rapid City	78,492	171	134	37
Scotland	800	2	2	0
Sioux Falls	187,370	308	273	35
Sisseton	2,392	7	7	0
Spearfish	11,902	32	21	11
Springfield	1,915	2	2	0
Sturgis	6,955	18	15	3
Summerset	2,769	4	4	0
Tea	6,340	8	8	0
Tripp	621	1	1	0
Tyndall	1,017	2	2	0
Vermillion	10,969	20	19	1
Wagner	1,544	6	6	0
Watertown	22,248	54	36	18
Webster	1,709	5	5	0
Whitewood	984	5	4	1
Winner	2,813	12	12	0
Yankton	14,712	31	30	1
TENNESSEE				
Adamsville	2,161	8	7	1
Alamo	2,268	4	4	0
Alcoa	10,174	54	46	8
Alexandria	1,017	4	3	1
Algood	4,584	15	15	0
Ardmore	1,221	9	5	4
Ashland City	4,785	18	16	2
Athens	14,059	33	31	2
Atoka	9,632	23	22	1
Baileyton	454	3	3	0
Bartlett	59,714	158	121	37
Baxter	1,551	7	7	0
Bean Station	3,098	7	6	1
Belle Meade	2,854	21	15	6
Bells	2,439	3	3	0
Benton	1,268	7	6	1
Berry Hill	505	18	14	4
Big Sandy	519	1	1	0
Blaine	1,861	4	4	0
Bluff City	1,667	8	8	0
Bolivar	4,892	27	24	3
Bradford	970	4	4	0
Brentwood	43,454	80	63	17
Brighton	2,911	7	7	0
Bristol	27,013	88	69	19
Brownsville	9,340	39	35	4
Bruceton	1,387	2	2	0
Burns	1,467	1	1	0
Calhoun	501	3	3	0
Camden	3,637	18	13	5
Carthage	2,343	12	8	4
Caryville	2,130	6	6	0
Celina	1,412	8	6	2

Table 78. Full-Time Law Enforcement Employees, by Selected State and City, 2020—Continued

(Number.)

State/city	Population	Total law enforcement employees	Total officers	Total civilians
Centerville	3,533	18	15	3
Chapel Hill	1,548	7	6	1
Charleston	703	2	2	0
Chattanooga	184,211	573	470	103
Church Hill	6,655	10	9	1
Clarksville	161,167	368	304	64
Cleveland	45,994	124	105	19
Clifton	2,651	5	5	0
Clinton	10,111	43	33	10
Collegedale	11,750	25	24	1
Collierville	51,677	140	107	33
Collinwood	940	4	4	0
Columbia	41,013	94	83	11
Cookeville	35,119	93	72	21
Coopertown	4,621	5	4	1
Cornersville	1,307	2	2	0
Covington	8,818	33	32	1
Cowan	1,650	3	3	0
Cross Plains	1,841	1	1	0
Crossville	11,885	45	42	3
Cumberland City	306	2	2	0
Dandridge	3,229	12	11	1
Dayton	7,367	18	18	0
Decatur	1,668	6	6	0
Decaturville	862	1	1	0
Decherd	2,374	13	12	1
Dickson	15,680	66	59	7
Dover	1,562	5	5	0
Dresden	2,921	9	8	1
Dunlap	5,214	13	12	1
Dyer	2,195	7	6	1
Dyersburg	16,226	68	60	8
Eagleville	779	4	4	0
East Ridge	21,202	48	44	4
Elizabethton	13,432	46	42	4
Elkton	522	2	2	0
Englewood	1,535	6	5	1
Erin	1,274	5	4	1
Erwin	5,901	17	16	1
Estill Springs	2,035	6	6	0
Ethridge	488	5	4	1
Etowah	3,495	13	12	1
Falrvlew	9,300	22	22	0
Fayetteville	7,077	29	27	2
Franklin	85,722	135	123	12
Friendship	662	1	1	0
Gainesboro	960	6	3	3
Gallatin	44,584	97	86	11
Gallaway	644	2	1	1
Gatlinburg	3,846	47	45	2
Germantown	39,264	130	107	23
Gibson	383	3	2	1
Gleason	1,368	5	5	0
Goodlettsville	16,896	55	41	14
Gordonsville	1,249	7	6	1
Grand Junction	267	3	3	0
Graysville	1,587	4	4	0
Greenbrier	6,896	16	15	1
Greeneville	14,875	56	54	2
Greenfield	2,074	7	6	1
Halls	2,047	8	8	0
Harriman	6,110	20	19	1
Henderson	6,361	16	16	0
Hendersonville	58,901	141	125	16
Henry	448	1	1	0
Hohenwald	3,822	17	16	1
Hollow Rock	677	2	1	1
Hornbeak	467	1	1	0
Humboldt	8,116	31	26	5
Huntingdon	3,818	17	13	4
Huntland	841	4	4	0
Jacksboro	2,060	6	5	1
Jackson	67,234	239	202	37
Jamestown	2,123	9	9	0
Jasper	3,459	8	8	0
Jefferson City	8,188	31	29	2
Jellico	2,148	4	3	1
Johnson City	67,293	168	139	29
Jonesborough	5,675	23	18	5
Kenton	1,185	2	2	0
Kimball	1,452	9	9	0
Kingsport	54,260	152	112	40
Kingston	5,998	13	12	1
Kingston Springs	2,726	8	7	1
Knoxville	188,672	495	371	124

Table 78. Full-Time Law Enforcement Employees, by Selected State and City, 2020—Continued

(Number.)

State/city	Population	Total law enforcement employees	Total officers	Total civilians
Lafayette	5,428	23	16	7
La Follette	6,606	27	21	6
La Vergne	36,067	73	58	15
Lawrenceburg	11,093	39	34	5
Lebanon	37,832	128	100	28
Lenoir City	9,404	29	27	2
Lewisburg	12,515	31	30	1
Lexington	7,915	34	28	6
Livingston	4,046	23	18	5
Lookout Mountain	1,892	21	16	5
Loretto	1,780	5	5	0
Loudon	5,953	16	15	1
Madisonville	5,031	21	18	3
Manchester	11,145	38	34	4
Martin	10,380	37	27	10
Maryville	30,006	63	57	6
Mason	1,525	4	4	0
Maynardville	2,435	4	4	0
McEwen	1,731	5	5	0
McKenzie	5,323	21	16	5
McMinnville	13,783	40	36	4
Medina	4,365	10	9	1
Memphis	650,937	2,563	2,064	499
Metropolitan Nashville Police Department	688,013	1,917	1,419	498
Middleton	627	3	3	0
Milan	7,585	33	26	7
Millersville	6,811	13	11	2
Millington	10,626	39	31	8
Minor Hill	532	2	2	0
Monteagle	1,231	7	6	1
Monterey	2,906	10	9	1
Morristown	30,330	86	81	5
Moscow	553	4	4	0
Mountain City	2,429	9	9	0
Mount Carmel	5,284	9	8	1
Mount Juliet	38,685	79	63	16
Mount Pleasant	4,934	20	14	6
Munford	6,134	18	18	0
Murfreesboro	151,769	324	265	59
Newbern	3,289	11	11	0
New Johnsonville	1,868	6	5	1
New Market	1,379	5	4	1
Newport	6,880	32	28	4
New Tazewell	2,707	10	10	0
Niota	735	3	2	1
Nolensville	10,665	15	14	1
Norris	1,603	5	5	0
Oakland	8,558	21	19	2
Oak Ridge	29,139	82	64	18
Obion	1,032	2	2	0
Oliver Springs	3,416	14	10	4
Oneida	3,696	15	10	5
Paris	10,047	39	27	12
Parsons	2,283	8	8	0
Petersburg	571	1	1	0
Pigeon Forge	6,311	76	58	18
Pikeville	1,756	3	3	0
Piperton	2,057	8	8	0
Pittman Center	578	4	4	0
Plainview	2,160	2	2	0
Pleasant View	4,874	8	8	0
Portland	13,208	36	32	4
Pulaski	7,571	26	23	3
Puryear	662	1	1	0
Red Bank	11,861	25	23	2
Red Boiling Springs	1,135	4	4	0
Ridgely	1,605	5	3	2
Ripley	7,686	32	26	6
Rockwood	5,410	15	14	1
Rocky Top	1,774	9	6	3
Rogersville	4,368	18	13	5
Rossville	1,003	7	7	0
Rutherford	1,058	5	4	1
Rutledge	1,362	3	3	0
Savannah	6,928	23	21	2
Scotts Hill	978	3	3	0
Selmer	4,289	19	17	2
Sevierville	17,395	76	60	16
Sharon	911	2	1	1
Shelbyville	22,306	55	45	10
Signal Mountain	8,644	17	15	2
Smithville	4,929	15	14	1
Smyrna	52,984	109	86	23
Soddy-Daisy	13,697	35	28	7
Somerville	3,282	12	11	1

Table 78. Full-Time Law Enforcement Employees, by Selected State and City, 2020—Continued

(Number.)

State/city	Population	Total law enforcement employees	Total officers	Total civilians
South Carthage	1,408	4	4	0
South Fulton	2,195	9	8	1
South Pittsburg	3,022	8	8	0
Sparta	4,960	15	13	2
Spencer	1,700	2	2	0
Spring City	1,850	8	7	1
Springfield	17,372	41	37	4
Spring Hill	45,765	64	60	4
St. Joseph	833	1	1	0
Surgoinsville	1,755	1	1	0
Sweetwater	5,904	20	19	1
Tazewell	2,281	7	7	0
Tellico Plains	915	5	5	0
Tiptonville	3,920	7	7	0
Townsend	467	4	4	0
Tracy City	1,391	4	4	0
Trenton	4,168	20	14	6
Trimble	609	1	1	0
Troy	1,313	5	5	0
Tullahoma	19,664	34	29	5
Tusculum	2,692	2	2	0
Unicoi	3,592	4	4	0
Union City	10,263	40	30	10
Vonore	1,559	9	9	0
Wartburg	924	6	6	0
Wartrace	700	2	1	1
Watertown	1,528	6	6	0
Waverly	4,154	14	13	1
Waynesboro	2,417	7	7	0
Westmoreland	2,421	10	8	2
White Bluff	3,706	5	5	0
White House	12,936	26	23	3
White Pine	2,353	11	10	1
Whiteville	4,436	8	7	1
Whitwell	1,731	5	5	0
Winchester	9,029	25	23	2
Woodbury	2,919	10	10	0
TEXAS				
Abernathy	2,694	5	5	0
Abilene	124,061	275	211	64
Addison	16,778	71	60	11
Alamo	20,078	46	34	12
Alamo Heights	8,807	34	21	13
Alba	550	2	2	0
Alice	18,634	36	27	9
Allen	108,218	207	144	63
Alpine	5,978	20	12	8
Alton	18,632	28	22	6
Alvarado	4,626	19	17	2
Alvin	27,015	78	50	28
Amarillo	200,296	416	354	62
Andrews	14,487	19	18	1
Angleton	19,500	51	35	16
Anna	16,036	20	19	1
Anthony	5,389	17	16	1
Aransas Pass	8,414	42	28	14
Archer City	1,687	2	2	0
Arcola	2,811	8	8	0
Argyle	4,527	14	12	2
Arlington	402,700	876	682	194
Arp	1,037	8	7	1
Athens	12,757	32	24	8
Atlanta	5,451	16	11	5
Aubrey	5,274	15	15	0
Austin	1,000,276	2,290	1,738	552
Azle	13,660	41	30	11
Baird	1,485	2	2	0
Balch Springs	25,189	53	36	17
Balcones Heights	3,362	25	17	8
Ballinger	3,629	9	7	2
Bangs	1,518	3	3	0
Bartonville	1,810	5	5	0
Bastrop	9,479	25	21	4
Bay City	17,505	57	35	22
Bayou Vista	1,644	6	6	0
Baytown	77,823	217	164	53
Beaumont	116,766	320	261	59
Bedford	49,274	125	76	49
Bee Cave	7,255	20	19	1
Beeville	12,788	31	23	8
Bellaire	19,210	57	41	16
Bellmead	10,835	28	18	10
Bells	1,528	4	4	0
Bellville	4,233	12	11	1

Table 78. Full-Time Law Enforcement Employees, by Selected State and City, 2020—Continued

(Number.)

State/city	Population	Total law enforcement employees	Total officers	Total civilians
Belton	23,435	48	35	13
Benbrook	23,766	51	40	11
Bertram	1,491	6	6	0
Beverly Hills	1,984	13	7	6
Big Sandy	1,418	4	4	0
Big Spring	28,294	49	38	11
Bishop	3,048	10	6	4
Blanco	2,103	10	9	1
Blue Mound	2,450	13	8	5
Boerne	19,342	62	42	20
Bogata	1,053	5	5	0
Bonham	10,416	29	20	9
Borger	12,318	29	27	2
Bovina	1,768	3	3	0
Bowie	5,103	21	15	6
Boyd	1,557	6	6	0
Brady	5,280	12	11	1
Brazoria	3,059	12	8	4
Breckenridge	5,386	18	12	6
Bremond	971	3	3	0
Brenham	18,106	42	37	5
Bridge City	7,864	22	16	6
Bridgeport	6,732	24	15	9
Brookshire	5,948	23	18	5
Brookside Village	1,583	4	4	0
Brownfield	9,324	29	24	5
Brownsboro	1,309	4	4	0
Brownsville	183,627	312	225	87
Brownwood	18,367	61	38	23
Bryan	87,435	183	153	30
Buda	18,531	25	22	3
Bullard	3,900	12	11	1
Bulverde	5,370	17	16	1
Burkburnett	11,321	23	17	6
Burleson	49,660	90	65	25
Burnet	6,455	21	19	2
Cactus	3,250	12	9	3
Caddo Mills	1,739	7	7	0
Caldwell	4,403	11	10	1
Cameron	5,458	14	10	4
Canton	3,895	20	15	5
Canyon	16,263	29	26	3
Carrollton	141,745	222	169	53
Carthage	6,395	21	15	6
Castroville	3,159	9	8	1
Cedar Hill	48,352	91	70	21
Cedar Park	82,653	130	94	36
Celina	18,165	33	30	3
Center	5,157	30	22	8
Chandler	3,233	8	8	0
Childress	6,039	11	10	1
Chillicothe	669	1	1	0
Cibolo	32,777	41	37	4
Cisco	3,774	10	8	2
Clarksville	3,042	5	5	0
Cleburne	31,486	68	52	16
Cleveland	8,285	30	20	10
Clifton	3,446	8	7	1
Clint	1,137	3	3	0
Clute	11,742	39	26	13
Clyde	3,838	10	9	1
Coleman	4,230	8	8	0
College Station	120,831	201	142	59
Colleyville	27,602	48	43	5
Collinsville	2,000	4	4	0
Colorado City	3,827	10	6	4
Comanche	4,183	12	11	1
Combes	3,002	7	7	0
Commerce	9,876	20	16	4
Conroe	94,451	186	142	44
Coppell	41,807	68	59	9
Copperas Cove	33,333	68	50	18
Corinth	22,367	37	32	5
Corpus Christi	329,050	626	425	201
Corsicana	23,914	53	39	14
Crandall	4,147	16	16	0
Crane	3,722	14	8	6
Crockett	6,327	17	15	2
Crosbyton	1,599	3	3	0
Crowley	16,909	38	24	14
Crystal City	7,158	17	10	7
Cuero	8,237	15	14	1
Cumby	800	5	5	0
Cuney	140	1	1	0
Daingerfield	2,362	7	6	1

Table 78. Full-Time Law Enforcement Employees, by Selected State and City, 2020—Continued

(Number.)

State/city	Population	Total law enforcement employees	Total officers	Total civilians
Dalhart	8,349	19	15	4
Dallas	1,363,028	3,646	3,137	509
Dalworthington Gardens	2,382	17	12	5
Danbury	1,765	1	1	0
Dawson	800	2	2	0
Dayton	8,510	28	19	9
Decatur	7,220	34	29	5
Deer Park	33,631	94	63	31
De Kalb	1,584	4	4	0
De Leon	2,193	4	4	0
Del Rio	35,733	77	54	23
Denison	25,858	68	52	16
Denton	144,569	229	185	44
Denver City	4,964	16	10	6
DeSoto	53,515	97	68	29
Devine	4,883	14	11	3
Diboll	5,182	17	12	5
Dickinson	21,364	46	30	16
Dilley	4,559	13	12	1
Dimmitt	4,065	7	5	2
Donna	16,400	48	35	13
Double Oak	3,089	8	8	0
Dublin	3,546	9	8	1
Dumas	13,729	30	23	7
Duncanville	38,847	71	61	10
Eagle Lake	3,793	9	8	1
Early	3,205	10	8	2
Eastland	3,836	13	11	2
Edinburg	103,491	215	156	59
Edna	5,813	10	8	2
El Campo	11,523	41	27	14
Electra	2,723	13	8	5
Elgin	10,567	26	22	4
El Paso	685,288	1,455	1,189	266
Elsa	7,274	24	18	6
Emory	1,368	5	4	1
Encinal	595	2	2	0
Ennis	20,557	44	34	10
Euless	57,881	137	89	48
Everman	6,220	20	16	4
Fairfield	2,885	14	10	4
Fair Oaks Ranch	10,497	25	22	3
Falfurrias	4,797	10	8	2
Farmers Branch	51,078	99	76	23
Farmersville	3,668	11	9	2
Fate	16,917	21	19	2
Ferris	3,042	15	10	5
Flatonia	1,436	8	8	0
Floresville	8,247	21	19	2
Flower Mound	80,907	145	96	49
Floydada	2,641	6	6	0
Forest Hill	13,058	29	21	8
Forney	29,366	46	31	15
Fort Stockton	8,429	31	20	11
Fort Worth	929,509	2,085	1,667	418
Franklin	1,649	5	5	0
Frankston	1,164	5	5	0
Fredericksburg	11,604	38	31	7
Freeport	12,144	47	32	15
Freer	2,651	9	6	3
Friendswood	40,795	80	58	22
Frisco	212,626	310	212	98
Fulshear	14,094	26	24	2
Fulton	1,502	1	1	0
Gainesville	16,986	55	41	14
Galena Park	10,740	25	19	6
Galveston	50,751	198	148	50
Ganado	2,062	3	3	0
Garden Ridge	4,235	12	11	1
Garland	241,845	477	354	123
Gatesville	12,394	33	21	12
Georgetown	84,210	120	88	32
George West	2,575	12	10	2
Giddings	5,126	17	12	5
Gilmer	5,171	19	15	4
Gladewater	6,333	20	15	5
Glenn Heights	13,662	22	15	7
Godley	1,423	6	6	0
Gonzales	7,568	26	18	8
Granbury	11,080	48	42	6
Grand Prairie	196,990	413	274	139
Grand Saline	3,178	11	10	1
Granger	1,514	2	2	0
Granite Shoals	5,096	14	11	3
Grapevine	56,343	147	93	54
Greenville	29,209	69	50	19

Table 78. Full-Time Law Enforcement Employees, by Selected State and City, 2020—Continued

(Number.)

State/city	Population	Total law enforcement employees	Total officers	Total civilians
Gregory	1,886	7	7	0
Groesbeck	4,244	9	9	0
Groves	15,412	22	20	2
Gun Barrel City	6,269	20	14	6
Gunter	1,696	5	5	0
Hallettsville	2,645	9	8	1
Hallsville	4,382	6	6	0
Haltom City	44,037	78	72	6
Hamilton	3,005	8	7	1
Hamlin	2,010	10	5	5
Harker Heights	33,091	67	53	14
Harlingen	65,014	169	125	44
Haskell	3,136	6	5	1
Hawkins	1,328	3	3	0
Hawley	622	2	2	0
Hearne	4,345	18	12	6
Heath	9,584	25	24	1
Hedwig Village	2,643	23	17	6
Helotes	10,301	31	30	1
Hemphill	1,243	4	4	0
Hempstead	8,699	21	17	4
Henderson	13,093	41	33	8
Hewitt	15,092	38	28	10
Hickory Creek	4,979	12	12	0
Highland Park	9,160	70	57	13
Highland Village	16,848	42	29	13
Hillsboro	8,480	34	25	9
Hitchcock	8,023	18	16	2
Hollywood Park	3,370	18	17	1
Hondo	9,506	27	23	4
Honey Grove	1,745	5	5	0
Hooks	2,706	7	7	0
Horizon City	19,973	41	23	18
Horseshoe Bay	4,085	25	21	4
Houston	2,346,155	6,223	5,212	1,011
Howe	3,442	8	7	1
Hudson	5,035	4	4	0
Hudson Oaks	2,587	12	11	1
Hughes Springs	1,704	4	4	0
Humble	15,901	75	60	15
Huntington	2,110	6	6	0
Huntsville	42,648	68	59	9
Hurst	38,796	119	71	48
Hutchins	5,941	26	18	8
Hutto	29,590	48	44	4
Idalou	2,308	4	4	0
Indian Lake	883	3	3	0
Ingleside	10,296	33	22	11
Ingram	1,859	8	7	1
Iowa Colony	3,686	9	9	0
Iowa Park	6,334	17	10	7
Irving	242,976	574	376	198
Italy	1,928	8	7	1
Itasca	1,743	6	6	0
Jacinto City	10,455	26	20	6
Jacksboro	4,372	11	10	1
Jacksonville	14,843	44	29	15
Jamaica Beach	1,089	6	6	0
Jarrell	1,953	6	6	0
Jasper	7,543	28	21	7
Jefferson	1,896	7	5	2
Jersey Village	7,921	26	24	2
Jones Creek	2,079	5	5	0
Jonestown	2,139	10	9	1
Josephine	2,182	5	5	0
Joshua	8,319	13	11	2
Jourdanton	4,467	10	9	1
Junction	2,387	9	7	2
Karnes City	3,419	9	8	1
Katy	22,797	82	66	16
Keller	48,117	82	50	32
Kemah	2,046	18	13	5
Kemp	1,259	6	6	0
Kempner	1,145	3	2	1
Kenedy	3,357	15	14	1
Kennedale	8,881	23	19	4
Kerens	1,519	5	5	0
Kermit	6,583	18	14	4
Kerrville	23,912	65	46	19
Kilgore	15,016	51	37	14
Killeen	154,417	285	235	50
Kingsville	25,195	71	45	26
Kirby	8,805	23	17	6
Knox City	1,118	2	2	0
Kountze	2,104	7	6	1
Kress	677	1	1	0

Table 78. Full-Time Law Enforcement Employees, by Selected State and City, 2020—Continued

(Number.)

State/city	Population	Total law enforcement employees	Total officers	Total civilians
Kyle	51,306	82	53	29
Lacy-Lakeview	6,748	20	12	8
La Feria	7,232	20	15	5
Lago Vista	7,740	25	18	7
La Grange	4,680	13	12	1
La Grulla	1,710	9	8	1
Laguna Vista	3,183	9	9	0
La Joya	4,326	17	12	5
Lake City	534	1	1	0
Lake Dallas	8,174	16	13	3
Lake Jackson	27,265	63	47	16
Lakeport	998	4	4	0
Lakeside	1,603	7	7	0
Lakeview, Harrison County	6,231	14	13	1
Lake Worth	4,921	33	26	7
La Marque	17,656	39	32	7
Lamesa	9,119	27	20	7
Lampasas	8,132	32	22	10
Lancaster	39,587	63	59	4
La Porte	35,102	103	79	24
Laredo	265,515	602	509	93
La Vernia	1,481	9	9	0
League City	110,518	163	116	47
Leander	68,571	84	64	20
Leon Valley	12,453	50	46	4
Levelland	13,502	35	24	11
Lewisville	110,800	219	165	54
Liberty	9,418	26	15	11
Liberty Hill	3,345	15	14	1
Lindale	6,675	25	17	8
Linden	1,908	6	5	1
Little Elm	57,482	81	73	8
Live Oak	16,910	45	34	11
Livingston	5,240	29	22	7
Log Cabin	779	4	4	0
Lone Star	1,472	6	5	1
Longview	81,751	214	170	44
Lorena	1,762	10	8	2
Los Indios	1,063	2	2	0
Lubbock	262,146	557	446	111
Lufkin	35,007	96	76	20
Lumberton	13,195	21	18	3
Lyford	2,531	3	3	0
Lytle	3,135	9	8	1
Madisonville	4,715	13	10	3
Magnolia	2,193	16	14	2
Manor	15,569	32	27	5
Mansfield	74,360	158	103	55
Manvel	13,971	28	22	6
Marble Falls	7,157	35	22	13
Marfa	1,589	5	5	0
Marion	1,262	3	3	0
Marlin	5,539	14	10	4
Marshall	22,755	65	49	16
Mathis	4,694	13	9	4
McAllen	144,569	428	286	142
McGregor	5,368	16	10	6
McKinney	208,335	287	218	69
Meadows Place	4,587	17	16	1
Melissa	13,424	14	14	0
Memorial Villages	12,375	46	33	13
Mercedes	16,699	41	33	8
Merkel	2,620	6	5	1
Mesquite	141,325	319	227	92
Mexia	7,329	18	16	2
Midland	150,529	243	152	91
Midlothian	34,962	95	66	29
Milford	749	3	3	0
Mineola	4,797	19	12	7
Mineral Wells	15,057	46	33	13
Mission	85,052	203	159	44
Missouri City	76,476	130	102	28
Monahans	7,924	20	15	5
Mont Belvieu	6,954	25	16	9
Montgomery	1,488	13	12	1
Morgans Point Resort	4,738	9	9	0
Moulton	901	4	4	0
Mount Pleasant	15,974	46	33	13
Muleshoe	5,005	13	7	6
Murphy	20,798	35	24	11
Mustang Ridge	999	5	5	0
Nacogdoches	32,873	86	57	29
Naples	1,307	3	3	0
Nash	3,938	9	9	0
Nassau Bay	3,968	15	14	1
Natalia	1,610	4	4	0

Table 78. Full-Time Law Enforcement Employees, by Selected State and City, 2020—Continued

(Number.)

State/city	Population	Total law enforcement employees	Total officers	Total civilians
Navasota	8,104	27	19	8
Nederland	17,413	41	27	14
New Boston	4,588	19	14	5
New Braunfels	94,751	172	137	35
Newton	2,359	4	4	0
Nixon	2,560	7	7	0
Nocona	2,999	6	5	1
Nolanville	6,048	11	10	1
Northeast	3,485	13	12	1
Northlake	3,582	18	16	2
North Richland Hills	71,520	187	113	74
Oak Ridge	256	3	1	2
Oak Ridge North	3,171	17	17	0
Odessa	126,288	198	137	61
Olmos Park	2,492	14	13	1
Olney	3,080	9	7	2
Omaha	975	3	3	0
Onalaska	3,006	8	8	0
Orange	18,064	58	42	16
Ore City	1,238	4	4	0
Overton	2,498	9	6	3
Ovilla	4,247	11	10	1
Oyster Creek	1,203	12	9	3
Palacios	4,516	13	9	4
Palestine	17,625	43	28	15
Palmer	2,136	11	10	1
Palmhurst	2,753	16	13	3
Palm Valley	1,232	5	5	0
Pampa	16,975	37	25	12
Panhandle	2,298	4	4	0
Pantego	2,533	16	11	5
Paris	24,801	69	46	23
Parker	5,364	12	11	1
Pasadena	151,421	373	282	91
Patton Village	2,228	8	8	0
Pearland	126,111	235	174	61
Pearsall	10,783	20	16	4
Pecos	10,667	53	23	30
Pelican Bay	2,064	9	8	1
Penitas	4,756	20	18	2
Perryton	8,486	22	13	9
Pflugerville	67,559	121	85	36
Pharr	80,098	162	125	37
Pilot Point	4,582	11	11	0
Pinehurst	1,963	8	6	2
Pineland	795	3	3	0
Pittsburg	4,717	12	10	2
Plainview	19,926	37	30	7
Plano	290,786	557	380	177
Pleasanton	11,006	30	23	7
Ponder	2,521	7	6	1
Port Aransas	4,362	28	19	9
Port Arthur	54,257	151	116	35
Port Isabel	6,244	21	16	5
Portland	17,468	49	34	15
Port Lavaca	11,817	23	17	6
Port Neches	12,616	25	22	3
Poteet	3,535	11	10	1
Pottsboro	2,528	10	8	2
Prairie View	7,126	13	12	1
Premont	2,531	6	6	0
Presidio	3,836	4	4	0
Primera	5,250	10	9	1
Princeton	15,031	27	25	2
Prosper	27,250	50	37	13
Queen City	1,432	5	5	0
Quitman	1,854	7	7	0
Rancho Viejo	2,462	8	8	0
Ranger	2,469	4	3	1
Raymondville	10,833	23	14	9
Red Oak	13,801	31	28	3
Refugio	2,718	9	7	2
Reno, Lamar County	3,364	6	5	1
Reno, Parker County	3,294	7	7	0
Richardson	124,190	255	165	90
Richland Hills	7,971	22	19	3
Richmond	12,630	40	28	12
Richwood	4,044	10	10	0
Riesel	1,040	3	3	0
Rio Grande City	14,587	45	33	12
Rio Hondo	2,744	7	7	0
River Oaks	7,653	22	16	6
Roanoke	9,862	39	29	10
Robinson	12,087	32	23	9
Robstown	11,238	31	22	9
Rockdale	5,503	15	10	5

Table 78. Full-Time Law Enforcement Employees, by Selected State and City, 2020—Continued

(Number.)

State/city	Population	Total law enforcement employees	Total officers	Total civilians
Rockport	10,672	34	27	7
Rockwall	46,867	100	79	21
Rollingwood	1,607	9	9	0
Roma	11,559	34	26	8
Roman Forest	2,058	11	10	1
Rosenberg	39,162	107	83	24
Round Rock	137,593	244	172	72
Rowlett	68,810	127	92	35
Royse City	15,388	25	21	4
Runaway Bay	1,612	5	5	0
Rusk	5,606	13	12	1
Sachse	26,799	46	32	14
Saginaw	24,822	51	39	12
Salado	2,393	5	5	0
San Angelo	101,860	198	165	33
San Antonio	1,573,189	3,087	2,379	708
San Benito	24,237	50	41	9
San Diego	4,196	6	5	1
San Elizario	9,070	3	3	0
Sanger	8,953	16	14	2
San Juan	37,337	59	43	16
San Marcos	67,432	150	109	41
Santa Fe	13,577	29	22	7
Schertz	43,315	97	61	36
Schulenburg	2,920	9	8	1
Seabrook	14,415	42	32	10
Seagoville	17,120	36	26	10
Sealy	6,484	26	23	3
Seguin	30,513	79	57	22
Selma	12,013	32	28	4
Seven Points	1,532	10	6	4
Seymour	2,532	7	4	3
Shallowater	2,586	5	5	0
Shavano Park	4,098	19	18	1
Shenandoah	3,098	26	25	1
Sherman	44,611	91	67	24
Silsbee	6,613	23	17	6
Sinton	5,324	12	11	1
Slaton	5,864	19	13	6
Socorro	34,626	58	36	22
Somerset	2,000	4	4	0
Somerville	1,475	3	2	1
Sonora	2,765	7	5	2
Sour Lake	1,937	7	5	2
South Houston	17,485	44	31	13
Southlake	33,083	78	70	8
South Padre Island	2,772	37	27	10
Southside Place	1,902	12	8	4
Splendora	2,337	15	13	2
Springtown	3,254	15	11	4
Spring Valley	4,389	24	18	6
Spur	1,186	3	2	1
Stafford	17,423	71	54	17
Stamford	2,921	7	6	1
Stanton	3,061	6	6	0
Stephenville	21,777	56	34	22
Stinnett	1,759	4	4	0
Stratford	2,062	3	2	1
Sugar Land	119,671	194	166	28
Sullivan City	4,186	16	10	6
Sulphur Springs	16,322	39	28	11
Sunrise Beach Village	806	5	5	0
Sunset Valley	675	14	13	1
Surfside Beach	591	21	18	3
Sweeny	3,716	8	8	0
Sweetwater	10,419	31	25	6
Tatum	1,384	6	6	0
Teague	3,511	7	6	1
Temple	79,878	185	146	39
Tenaha	1,145	3	3	0
Terrell	19,204	64	42	22
Terrell Hills	5,512	17	17	0
Texarkana	36,303	92	80	12
Texas City	50,660	114	88	26
The Colony	45,419	104	74	30
Thrall	993	2	2	0
Three Rivers	1,960	10	9	1
Tioga	1,081	4	4	0
Tomball	11,901	61	43	18
Tool	2,310	8	4	4
Trophy Club	13,053	24	20	4
Tulia	4,618	15	8	7
Tye	1,345	7	6	1
Tyler	108,139	230	185	45
Universal City	21,162	37	27	10
University Park	25,253	55	39	16

Table 78. Full-Time Law Enforcement Employees, by Selected State and City, 2020—Continued

(Number.)

State/city	Population	Total law enforcement employees	Total officers	Total civilians
Uvalde	16,027	55	39	16
Van	2,753	10	10	0
Van Alstyne	4,557	17	11	6
Venus	4,570	13	13	0
Vernon	10,253	28	21	7
Vidor	10,370	31	21	10
Waco	140,870	348	253	95
Waelder	1,141	3	3	0
Wake Village	5,309	10	9	1
Waller	3,654	15	13	2
Wallis	1,309	8	8	0
Watauga	24,588	47	36	11
Waxahachie	39,039	92	73	19
Weatherford	34,522	82	63	19
Webster	11,545	63	45	18
Weimar	2,235	8	7	1
Weslaco	42,184	100	76	24
West	3,008	9	9	0
West Columbia	3,823	20	13	7
West Lake Hills	3,310	15	14	1
West Orange	3,199	12	10	2
Westover Hills	688	16	11	5
West University Place	15,700	33	24	9
Westworth	2,790	18	13	5
Wharton	8,612	35	25	10
Whitehouse	9,047	16	15	1
White Oak	6,303	20	16	4
White Settlement	18,051	42	32	10
Whitewright	1,734	4	4	0
Wichita Falls	104,673	292	203	89
Willis	7,166	21	19	2
Willow Park	6,096	16	15	1
Wills Point	3,667	9	8	1
Wilmer	4,919	21	16	5
Windcrest	5,930	37	26	11
Wink	1,039	3	3	0
Winnsboro	3,302	18	12	6
Wolfforth	5,735	13	12	1
Woodsboro	1,399	2	2	0
Woodville	2,411	10	9	1
Woodway	9,089	42	32	10
Wortham	988	4	4	0
Wylie	54,460	77	64	13
Yoakum	5,956	19	12	7
UTAH				
Alta	378	8	4	4
American Fork/Cedar Hills	44,093	49	43	6
Aurora	1,056	1	1	0
Big Water	515	1	1	0
Blanding	3,663	6	5	1
Bluffdale	17,826	14	14	0
Bountiful	44,129	56	36	20
Brian Head	94	5	5	0
Brigham City	19,792	33	27	6
Cedar City	35,486	45	39	6
Centerville	17,855	24	19	5
Clearfield	32,358	43	31	12
Clinton	22,725	20	18	2
Cottonwood Heights	33,871	47	39	8
Draper	49,326	60	44	16
East Carbon	1,574	4	4	0
Enoch	7,340	12	7	5
Ephraim	7,450	8	7	1
Fairview	1,371	1	1	0
Farmington	26,256	26	23	3
Fountain Green	1,177	1	1	0
Grantsville	12,468	17	15	2
Harrisville	7,029	11	10	1
Heber	17,849	29	24	5
Helper	2,094	5	4	1
Herriman	56,312	42	37	5
Hildale	2,911	13	10	3
Hurricane	19,776	31	28	3
Kamas	2,328	2	2	0
Kanab	4,993	8	7	1
Kaysville	32,959	35	32	3
La Verkin	4,491	6	5	1
Layton	79,240	114	83	31
Lehi	72,654	61	56	5
Lindon	11,218	17	15	2
Logan	51,899	85	53	32
Lone Peak	30,191	27	22	5
Mantua	1,000	2	1	1
Mapleton	11,068	11	10	1
Moab	5,362	23	15	8

Table 78. Full-Time Law Enforcement Employees, by Selected State and City, 2020—Continued

(Number.)

State/city	Population	Total law enforcement employees	Total officers	Total civilians
Moroni	1,566	1	1	0
Mount Pleasant	3,561	4	4	0
Murray	49,169	90	76	14
Naples	2,126	5	4	1
Nephi	6,498	13	10	3
North Ogden	20,960	26	20	6
North Park	16,529	13	10	3
North Salt Lake	21,540	29	23	6
Ogden	88,309	166	129	37
Orem	98,902	123	91	32
Park City	8,632	37	32	5
Parowan	3,208	6	6	0
Payson	20,498	27	24	3
Perry	5,335	8	7	1
Pleasant Grove	38,803	32	28	4
Pleasant View	11,212	11	10	1
Price	8,291	18	15	3
Provo	117,041	228	198	30
Richfield	7,925	18	15	3
Riverdale	8,876	22	19	3
Riverton	45,095	39	35	4
Roosevelt	7,359	13	12	1
Roy	39,849	43	39	4
Salem	8,902	12	11	1
Salina	2,624	4	4	0
Salt Lake City	202,187	644	523	121
Sandy	97,091	142	110	32
Santa Clara/Ivins	18,229	16	13	3
Santaquin/Genola	14,933	14	12	2
Saratoga Springs	35,623	30	26	4
Smithfield	12,317	11	10	1
South Jordan	80,090	65	60	5
South Ogden	17,266	27	22	5
South Salt Lake	25,816	77	64	13
Spanish Fork	41,605	42	38	4
Spring City	1,090	1	1	0
Springdale	641	9	8	1
Springville	33,728	41	30	11
St. George	91,673	163	115	48
Stockton	688	4	3	1
Sunset	5,387	8	7	1
Syracuse	32,343	26	24	2
Tooele	36,527	44	37	7
Tremonton Garland	11,995	17	15	2
Vernal	10,606	22	20	2
Washington	30,622	39	28	11
Wellington	1,612	9	8	1
West Bountiful	5,861	11	10	1
West Jordan	117,955	146	121	25
West Valley	135,887	262	217	45
Willard	1,979	3	3	0
Woods Cross	11,625	18	17	1
VERMONT				
Barre	8,471	27	20	7
Barre Town	7,698	8	7	1
Bellows Falls	2,946	7	6	1
Bennington	14,879	33	25	8
Berlin	2,770	9	8	1
Bradford	2,691	2	2	0
Brandon	3,710	7	6	1
Brattleboro	11,256	33	21	12
Brighton	1,161	1	1	0
Bristol	3,835	3	3	0
Burlington	42,862	121	86	35
Canaan	916	1	1	0
Castleton	4,490	5	5	0
Chester	3,011	6	5	1
Colchester	17,129	37	29	8
Dover	1,052	7	6	1
Essex	22,156	32	26	6
Fair Haven	2,536	4	4	0
Hardwick	2,846	9	9	0
Hartford	9,515	28	19	9
Hinesburg	4,540	10	5	5
Killington	750	2	2	0
Ludlow	1,854	9	5	4
Lyndonville	1,160	3	3	0
Manchester	4,206	13	9	4
Middlebury	8,813	18	16	2
Milton	10,882	17	16	1
Montpelier	7,321	26	17	9
Morristown	5,532	10	10	0
Newport	4,222	16	12	4
Northfield	6,560	6	5	1
Norwich	3,409	5	4	1

Table 78. Full-Time Law Enforcement Employees, by Selected State and City, 2020—Continued

(Number.)

State/city	Population	Total law enforcement employees	Total officers	Total civilians
Pittsford	2,766	1	1	0
Richmond	4,123	3	3	0
Royalton	2,881	2	2	0
Rutland	14,930	47	34	13
Rutland Town	4,117	4	4	0
Shelburne	7,706	19	11	8
South Burlington	19,690	47	39	8
Springfield	8,859	20	14	6
St. Albans	6,788	34	24	10
St. Johnsbury	7,112	17	11	6
Stowe	4,444	12	12	0
Swanton	6,569	7	6	1
Thetford	2,525	3	3	0
Vergennes	2,577	8	8	0
Weathersfield	2,727	2	2	0
Williston	10,247	21	16	5
Wilmington	1,787	8	6	2
Windsor	3,272	8	7	1
Winhall	726	8	7	1
Winooski	7,341	18	14	4
Woodstock	2,907	7	6	1
VIRGINIA				
Abingdon	7,828	27	24	3
Alexandria	161,525	423	314	109
Altavista	3,401	14	13	1
Amherst	2,174	6	6	0
Ashland	7,947	27	25	2
Bedford	6,601	25	21	4
Berryville	4,393	10	9	1
Big Stone Gap	5,080	14	13	1
Blacksburg	44,422	75	65	10
Blackstone	3,299	15	12	3
Bluefield	4,780	23	20	3
Bowling Green	1,182	1	1	0
Bridgewater	6,204	9	9	0
Bristol	16,640	67	50	17
Broadway	4,010	5	5	0
Brookneal	1,096	1	1	0
Buena Vista	6,459	17	16	1
Burkeville	396	1	1	0
Cape Charles	1,020	10	10	0
Cedar Bluff	989	4	4	0
Charlottesville	47,671	126	101	25
Chase City	2,201	10	9	1
Chatham	1,422	2	2	0
Chesapeake	247,118	514	371	143
Chilhowie	1,690	6	6	0
Chincoteague	2,868	14	10	4
Christiansburg	22,643	69	62	7
Clarksville	1,159	6	5	1
Clifton Forge	3,455	10	9	1
Clintwood	1,267	3	3	0
Coeburn	1,824	9	8	1
Colonial Beach	3,628	11	10	1
Colonial Heights	17,360	58	54	4
Covington	5,490	23	14	9
Crewe	2,109	6	5	1
Culpeper	19,131	49	41	8
Damascus	772	4	4	0
Danville	39,704	131	116	15
Dayton	1,648	5	5	0
Dublin	2,590	8	7	1
Dumfries	6,038	11	10	1
Eastville	337	4	4	0
Elkton	2,923	5	4	1
Emporia	5,282	37	26	11
Exmore	1,362	7	7	0
Fairfax City	24,161	83	59	24
Falls Church	14,877	48	32	16
Farmville	7,806	28	26	2
Franklin	7,896	24	17	7
Fredericksburg	29,592	86	64	22
Front Royal	15,387	51	37	14
Galax	6,275	37	24	13
Gate City	1,850	5	5	0
Glade Spring	1,400	2	2	0
Glasgow	1,102	1	1	0
Glen Lyn	96	1	1	0
Gordonsville	1,641	7	7	0
Gretna	1,181	3	3	0
Grottoes	2,881	6	6	0
Grundy	887	5	5	0
Halifax	1,203	5	5	0
Hampton	134,082	426	325	101
Harrisonburg	53,442	123	101	22

Table 78. Full-Time Law Enforcement Employees, by Selected State and City, 2020—Continued

(Number.)

State/city	Population	Total law enforcement employees	Total officers	Total civilians
Haymarket	1,699	5	5	0
Haysi	463	1	1	0
Herndon	24,739	39	26	13
Hillsville	2,654	16	15	1
Honaker	1,306	2	2	0
Hopewell	22,498	80	62	18
Hurt	1,215	2	2	0
Independence	886	2	2	0
Jonesville	919	3	3	0
Kenbridge	1,190	3	3	0
Kilmarnock	1,384	6	6	0
La Crosse	572	1	1	0
Lawrenceville	983	6	6	0
Lebanon	3,118	13	12	1
Leesburg	55,070	99	82	17
Lexington	7,487	19	16	3
Louisa	1,753	6	6	0
Luray	4,842	14	13	1
Lynchburg	82,871	197	157	40
Manassas	41,386	124	92	32
Manassas Park	17,839	36	28	8
Marion	5,515	22	21	1
Martinsville	12,417	50	45	5
Middleburg	854	7	6	1
Middletown	1,411	5	4	1
Mount Jackson	2,126	6	6	0
Narrows	1,942	6	6	0
New Market	2,261	6	6	0
Newport News	178,896	623	449	174
Norfolk	242,516	807	656	151
Norton	3,975	23	16	7
Occoquan	1,104	2	2	0
Onancock	1,206	6	6	0
Onley	498	5	5	0
Orange	5,140	17	15	2
Parksley	804	1	1	0
Pearisburg	2,619	8	8	0
Pembroke	1,078	3	3	0
Pennington Gap	1,705	6	6	0
Petersburg	31,195	107	86	21
Pocahontas	348	1	1	0
Poquoson	12,275	28	24	4
Portsmouth	94,205	249	199	50
Pound	907	4	4	0
Pulaski	8,674	32	28	4
Purcellville	10,485	16	14	2
Radford	18,450	52	38	14
Remington	665	1	1	0
Rich Creek	738	1	1	0
Richlands	5,172	25	20	5
Richmond	233,350	1,048	846	202
Roanoke	99,335	274	228	46
Rocky Mount	4,718	22	20	2
Rural Retreat	1,444	1	1	0
Salem	25,326	86	62	24
Saltville	1,885	7	7	0
Shenandoah	2,327	7	6	1
Smithfield	8,518	24	20	4
South Boston	7,528	29	27	2
South Hill	4,322	22	20	2
Stanley	1,672	5	5	0
Staunton	25,048	63	48	15
Stephens City	2,091	1	1	0
St. Paul	840	6	6	0
Strasburg	6,703	19	18	1
Suffolk	92,881	233	178	55
Tappahannock	2,397	11	10	1
Tazewell	4,088	17	16	1
Timberville	2,710	6	6	0
Victoria	1,615	4	4	0
Vienna	16,570	49	39	10
Vinton	8,117	22	21	1
Virginia Beach	450,858	925	744	181
Warrenton	10,073	28	27	1
Warsaw	1,485	4	4	0
Waverly	1,932	12	7	5
Waynesboro	22,801	53	43	10
Weber City	1,200	5	4	1
West Point	3,250	10	9	1
Williamsburg	15,086	42	40	2
Winchester	28,279	98	73	25
Windsor	2,774	7	7	0
Wintergreen	165	16	12	4
Wise	4,381	12	11	1
Woodstock	5,279	20	18	2
Wytheville	7,890	25	22	3

Table 78. Full-Time Law Enforcement Employees, by Selected State and City, 2020—Continued

(Number.)

State/city	Population	Total law enforcement employees	Total officers	Total civilians
WASHINGTON				
Aberdeen	16,744	50	36	14
Airway Heights	10,010	22	20	2
Algona	3,228	9	7	2
Anacortes	17,735	30	24	6
Arlington	20,825	35	30	5
Asotin	1,293	1	1	0
Auburn	82,779	134	114	20
Bainbridge Island	25,561	27	23	4
Battle Ground	21,669	27	23	4
Bellevue	150,548	213	173	40
Bellingham	93,629	180	118	62
Black Diamond	4,858	12	10	2
Blaine	5,717	16	14	2
Bonney Lake	21,584	38	31	7
Bothell	48,323	95	67	28
Bremerton	41,817	68	55	13
Brewster	2,355	6	5	1
Brier	7,055	8	7	1
Buckley	5,663	12	10	2
Burien	51,879	70	48	22
Burlington	9,321	29	23	6
Camas	24,979	33	29	4
Carnation	2,345	2	2	0
Castle Rock	2,319	5	4	1
Centralia	17,867	38	27	11
Chehalis	7,700	22	17	5
Cheney	12,741	23	16	7
Chewelah	2,685	6	5	1
Clarkston	7,387	16	14	2
Cle Elum	3,023	9	8	1
Clyde Hill	3,432	10	9	1
Colfax	2,881	3	3	0
College Place	9,374	16	13	3
Colville	4,845	11	9	2
Connell	5,725	8	7	1
Cosmopolis	1,664	6	5	1
Coulee Dam	1,078	2	2	0
Covington	21,613	25	19	6
Des Moines	32,652	43	33	10
Dupont	9,668	14	12	2
Duvall	8,275	14	13	1
East Wenatchee	14,336	22	19	3
Eatonville	3,058	6	5	1
Edgewood	13,553	14	13	1
Edmonds	42,934	65	55	10
Ellensburg	21,448	34	26	8
Elma	3,357	10	8	2
Enumclaw	12,315	34	19	15
Ephrata	8,184	18	15	3
Everett	112,439	238	197	41
Everson	4,551	7	6	1
Federal Way	97,071	160	129	31
Ferndale	15,337	23	20	3
Fife	10,301	38	29	9
Fircrest	6,869	9	9	0
Forks	3,918	8	4	4
Garfield	610	1	1	0
Gig Harbor	11,216	20	18	2
Goldendale	3,516	11	9	2
Grand Coulee	2,054	8	8	0
Grandview	11,099	22	19	3
Granger	3,898	8	8	0
Hoquiam	8,647	25	23	2
Issaquah	40,659	56	34	22
Kalama	2,852	8	7	1
Kelso	12,476	31	27	4
Kenmore	23,397	20	15	5
Kennewick	85,526	114	99	15
Kent	133,883	207	151	56
Kettle Falls	1,641	5	4	1
Kirkland	94,470	150	109	41
Kittitas	1,513	3	3	0
La Center	3,459	8	7	1
Lacey	53,826	64	49	15
Lake Forest Park	13,604	23	20	3
Lake Stevens	34,600	41	33	8
Lakewood	61,432	108	95	13
Langley	1,155	3	3	0
Liberty Lake	11,410	14	13	1
Long Beach	1,508	7	6	1
Longview	38,629	69	57	12
Lynden	15,625	21	17	4
Lynnwood	39,517	97	66	31
Mabton	2,265	3	3	0

Table 78. Full-Time Law Enforcement Employees, by Selected State and City, 2020—Continued

(Number.)

State/city	Population	Total law enforcement employees	Total officers	Total civilians
Maple Valley	27,736	24	18	6
Marysville	71,522	103	74	29
Mattawa	4,790	6	5	1
McCleary	1,777	5	5	0
Medina	3,324	11	9	2
Mercer Island	26,268	35	30	5
Mill Creek	21,214	26	21	5
Milton	8,413	13	13	0
Monroe	20,065	41	31	10
Montesano	4,059	8	7	1
Morton	1,207	3	3	0
Moses Lake	24,524	46	38	8
Mountlake Terrace	21,504	35	27	8
Mount Vernon	36,513	53	39	14
Moxee	4,177	7	6	1
Mukilteo	21,573	33	26	7
Napavine	2,025	5	4	1
Newcastle	12,523	14	11	3
Newport	2,205	5	4	1
Normandy Park	6,633	11	10	1
Oak Harbor	23,721	39	28	11
Ocean Shores	6,604	12	10	2
Odessa	892	2	2	0
Olympia	53,571	105	72	33
Omak	4,776	10	8	2
Oroville	1,671	6	5	1
Orting	8,848	11	9	2
Othello	8,509	23	16	7
Pacific	7,243	12	11	1
Palouse	1,084	2	2	0
Pasco	76,970	92	82	10
Port Angeles	20,364	54	32	22
Port Orchard	14,886	25	20	5
Port Townsend	9,914	17	13	4
Poulsbo	11,401	22	20	2
Prosser	6,451	17	15	2
Pullman	35,071	44	29	15
Puyallup	42,974	86	65	21
Quincy	8,183	28	21	7
Raymond	3,009	7	6	1
Reardan	615	1	1	0
Redmond	74,154	122	85	37
Renton	102,856	153	120	33
Richland	59,370	77	60	17
Ridgefield	9,835	12	11	1
Ritzville	1,651	4	4	0
Roy	827	2	2	0
Royal City	2,247	3	3	0
Ruston	856	5	5	0
Sammamish	66,878	39	31	8
SeaTac	29,282	63	45	18
Seattle	771,517	1,900	1,341	559
Sedro Woolley	12,189	24	20	4
Selah	8,170	17	14	3
Sequim	7,768	24	20	4
Shelton	10,749	22	19	3
Shoreline	57,472	72	52	20
Snohomish	10,269	19	17	2
Snoqualmie	13,987	27	23	4
Soap Lake	1,609	7	6	1
South Bend	1,706	5	4	1
Spokane	223,524	422	342	80
Spokane Valley	102,366	130	106	24
Stanwood	7,410	13	11	2
Steilacoom	6,436	10	9	1
Sumas	1,561	7	6	1
Sumner	10,544	25	20	5
Sunnyside	16,888	43	25	18
Tacoma	220,123	383	341	42
Tenino	1,886	5	4	1
Tieton	1,323	2	2	0
Toledo	777	3	2	1
Toppenish	8,792	16	11	5
Tukwila	20,483	82	66	16
Tumwater	24,493	40	33	7
Twisp	970	3	3	0
Union Gap	6,206	19	16	3
University Place	34,339	17	16	1
Vancouver	186,440	264	218	46
Walla Walla	32,944	77	47	30
Wapato	5,003	9	7	2
Warden	2,825	5	4	1
Washougal	16,334	24	20	4
Wenatchee	34,525	54	43	11
Westport	2,102	8	7	1
West Richland	15,464	24	20	4

Table 78. Full-Time Law Enforcement Employees, by Selected State and City, 2020—Continued

(Number.)

State/city	Population	Total law enforcement employees	Total officers	Total civilians
White Salmon	2,732	7	6	1
Winlock	1,436	3	3	0
Winthrop	480	3	2	1
Woodinville	13,547	19	15	4
Woodland	6,612	12	10	2
Yakima	93,862	173	133	40
Yelm	9,799	17	15	2
Zillah	3,152	9	8	1
WEST VIRGINIA				
Alderson	1,119	4	4	0
Anmoore	729	2	2	0
Ansted	1,294	2	2	0
Athens	883	1	1	0
Barboursville	4,291	24	22	2
Barrackville	1,277	1	1	0
Beckley	15,762	62	46	16
Belington	1,900	3	3	0
Belle	1,112	3	3	0
Benwood	1,262	9	6	3
Berkeley Springs	593	2	2	0
Bethlehem	2,302	5	5	0
Bluefield	9,543	33	28	5
Bradshaw	265	1	1	0
Bramwell	334	2	2	0
Bridgeport	8,924	37	33	4
Buckhannon	5,373	12	11	1
Burnsville	473	1	1	0
Cameron	833	2	2	0
Cedar Grove	898	1	1	0
Ceredo	1,260	7	4	3
Chapmanville	1,080	4	4	0
Charleston	46,038	181	158	23
Charles Town	6,123	19	16	3
Chesapeake	1,399	2	2	0
Chester	2,347	6	5	1
Clarksburg	15,092	44	40	4
Clendenin	1,087	5	5	0
Danville	593	2	2	0
Davy	329	1	1	0
Delbarton	489	2	2	0
Dunbar	7,010	13	12	1
East Bank	860	1	1	0
Eleanor	1,594	1	1	0
Elkins	6,970	13	12	1
Fairmont	18,352	38	33	5
Fairview	403	1	1	0
Fayetteville	2,695	13	12	1
Follansbee	2,682	7	7	0
Fort Gay	684	3	3	0
Gary	770	1	1	0
Gassaway	839	1	1	0
Gauley Bridge	547	1	1	0
Gilbert	381	2	2	0
Glen Dale	1,355	6	6	0
Glenville	1,422	2	1	1
Grafton	4,963	9	8	1
Grant Town	592	1	1	0
Granville	3,767	14	14	0
Hamlin	1,038	3	2	1
Harpers Ferry/Bolivar	1,301	3	2	1
Harrisville	1,654	1	1	0
Hartford City	592	1	1	0
Hinton	2,324	6	5	1
Huntington	44,684	96	93	3
Hurricane	6,446	20	18	2
Iaeger	236	1	1	0
Kenova	2,931	14	10	4
Kermit	344	1	1	0
Keyser	4,863	12	8	4
Kimball	149	1	1	0
Kingwood	3,057	3	3	0
Lewisburg	3,803	15	13	2
Logan	1,439	11	8	3
Mabscott	1,248	2	2	0
Madison	2,631	8	7	1
Man	617	2	2	0
Mannington	2,018	4	4	0
Marlinton	952	1	1	0
Marmet	1,352	5	5	0
Martinsburg	17,479	54	43	11
Mason	932	5	4	1
Masontown	537	2	1	1
Matewan	416	2	1	1
McMechen	1,677	4	4	0
Milton	2,547	11	10	1

Table 78. Full-Time Law Enforcement Employees, by Selected State and City, 2020—Continued

(Number.)

State/city	Population	Total law enforcement employees	Total officers	Total civilians
Monongah	1,161	1	1	0
Montgomery	1,494	7	6	1
Moorefield	2,403	10	9	1
Morgantown	30,775	83	71	12
Moundsville	8,175	20	16	4
Mount Hope	1,260	4	3	1
Mullens	1,299	3	3	0
New Cumberland	997	2	1	1
New Haven	1,455	3	3	0
New Martinsville	5,092	14	10	4
Nitro	6,314	20	19	1
Nutter Fort	1,502	5	5	0
Oak Hill	8,017	20	16	4
Oceana	1,185	4	4	0
Paden City	2,306	5	4	1
Parkersburg	29,096	82	74	8
Parsons	1,383	1	1	0
Pennsboro	989	1	1	0
Petersburg	2,684	1	1	0
Philippi	3,293	6	6	0
Piedmont	794	1	1	0
Pineville	564	3	3	0
Point Pleasant	4,032	7	7	0
Pratt	551	3	2	1
Princeton	5,627	23	21	2
Rainelle	1,524	2	1	1
Ranson	5,341	19	17	2
Ravenswood	3,621	12	10	2
Reedsville	606	1	1	0
Rhodell	159	2	1	1
Richwood	1,834	3	3	0
Ripley	3,151	12	11	1
Rivesville	900	1	1	0
Romney	1,680	6	5	1
Ronceverte	1,660	6	6	0
Rupert	888	1	1	0
Salem	1,515	4	4	0
Shepherdstown	1,887	6	5	1
Shinnston	2,093	9	8	1
Sistersville	1,275	4	4	0
Sophia	1,220	5	5	0
South Charleston	11,898	49	46	3
Spencer	2,011	6	5	1
St. Albans	9,802	27	24	3
Star City	1,969	7	6	1
St. Marys	1,763	5	4	1
Stonewood	1,704	2	2	0
Summersville	3,243	17	16	1
Sutton	987	1	1	0
Sylvester	134	1	1	0
Terra Alta	1,501	2	2	0
Triadelphia	756	1	1	0
Vienna	10,049	24	20	4
War	668	3	3	0
Wayne	1,563	1	1	0
Webster Springs	652	5	4	1
Weirton	18,111	38	34	4
Welch	1,577	6	5	1
Wellsburg	2,502	6	5	1
West Liberty	1,418	1	1	0
West Logan	357	1	1	0
West Milford	604	2	2	0
Weston	3,831	8	6	2
Westover	4,192	13	12	1
West Union	796	1	1	0
Wheeling	26,222	79	68	11
White Hall	667	5	5	0
White Sulphur Springs	2,343	8	7	1
Whitesville	419	2	2	0
Williamson	2,625	6	5	1
Williamstown	2,864	8	7	1
Winfield	2,357	5	5	0
WISCONSIN				
Adams	1,884	3	3	0
Albany	990	3	3	0
Algoma	3,035	5	5	0
Altoona	8,009	15	14	1
Amery	2,799	6	6	0
Antigo	7,719	18	15	3
Appleton	74,255	139	112	27
Arcadia	3,051	4	4	0
Argyle	807	1	1	0
Ashland	7,804	40	19	21
Ashwaubenon	17,183	57	52	5
Athens	1,075	1	1	0

Table 78. Full-Time Law Enforcement Employees, by Selected State and City, 2020—Continued

(Number.)

State/city	Population	Total law enforcement employees	Total officers	Total civilians
Bangor	1,452	3	3	0
Baraboo	12,175	34	29	5
Barneveld	1,253	1	1	0
Barron	3,308	6	6	0
Bayfield	470	3	3	0
Bayside	4,322	13	13	0
Beaver Dam	16,426	36	32	4
Belleville	2,473	7	6	1
Beloit	36,921	79	69	10
Beloit Town	7,741	14	12	2
Berlin	5,369	11	10	1
Big Bend	1,487	3	3	0
Birchwood	426	1	1	0
Black River Falls	3,449	6	5	1
Blair	1,340	2	2	0
Blanchardville	787	1	1	0
Bloomer	3,500	8	7	1
Bloomfield	6,363	8	8	0
Blue Mounds	1,001	1	1	0
Boscobel	3,118	6	6	0
Boyceville	1,131	2	2	0
Brillion	3,067	8	8	0
Brodhead	3,242	12	8	4
Brookfield	39,252	101	85	16
Brookfield Township	6,564	15	14	1
Brown Deer	11,808	33	30	3
Brownsville	584	1	1	0
Burlington	11,025	23	22	1
Butler	1,793	9	8	1
Caledonia	25,323	37	35	2
Campbellsport	1,807	2	2	0
Campbell Township	4,296	5	5	0
Cashton	1,113	1	1	0
Cedarburg	11,621	28	20	8
Chenequa	606	10	8	2
Chetek	2,083	5	4	1
Chilton	3,851	16	8	8
Chippewa Falls	14,437	27	23	4
Cleveland	1,450	2	2	0
Clinton	2,139	10	5	5
Clintonville	4,372	15	11	4
Colby-Abbotsford	4,185	9	8	1
Colfax	1,157	2	2	0
Columbus	5,134	11	9	2
Cornell	1,401	3	3	0
Cottage Grove	7,233	15	13	2
Crandon	1,787	4	3	1
Cross Plains	4,362	7	6	1
Cuba City	2,023	4	4	0
Cudahy	18,064	42	32	10
Cumberland	2,096	7	7	0
Darlington	2,325	10	5	5
Deforest	10,901	21	18	3
Delavan	9,836	25	23	2
Delavan Town	5,337	13	12	1
Durand	1,786	4	4	0
Eagle River	1,615	7	6	1
Eagle Village	2,177	2	2	0
East Troy	4,313	8	8	0
Eau Claire	69,086	128	91	37
Edgar	1,438	1	1	0
Edgerton	5,655	11	10	1
Eleva	664	1	1	0
Elkhart Lake	1,022	3	3	0
Elkhorn	10,014	17	15	2
Elk Mound	882	2	1	1
Ellsworth	3,320	10	5	5
Elm Grove	6,160	23	16	7
Elroy	1,289	3	3	0
Evansville	5,489	11	10	1
Everest Metropolitan	17,361	33	29	4
Fall Creek	1,286	2	2	0
Fall River	1,744	2	2	0
Fennimore	2,449	12	6	6
Fitchburg	31,483	64	52	12
Fond du Lac	43,295	78	69	9
Fontana	1,747	8	7	1
Fort Atkinson	12,425	26	20	6
Fox Lake	1,442	4	3	1
Fox Point	6,522	18	17	1
Fox Valley Metro	22,737	28	26	2
Franklin	35,814	76	59	17
Frederic	1,084	2	2	0
Galesville	1,606	4	4	0
Geneva Town	5,045	8	7	1
Genoa City	2,978	7	6	1

Table 78. Full-Time Law Enforcement Employees, by Selected State and City, 2020—Continued

(Number.)

State/city	Population	Total law enforcement employees	Total officers	Total civilians
Germantown	20,133	40	32	8
Gillett	1,285	3	3	0
Gilman	390	1	1	0
Glendale	12,714	46	40	6
Grafton	11,738	27	21	6
Grand Chute	23,579	39	33	6
Grand Rapids	7,393	8	6	2
Grantsburg	1,275	3	3	0
Green Bay	104,649	219	181	38
Greendale	14,141	38	29	9
Greenfield	37,237	79	60	19
Green Lake	968	6	3	3
Hales Corners	7,548	17	16	1
Hammond	1,882	4	3	1
Hartford	15,573	31	27	4
Hartford Township	3,561	1	1	0
Hartland	9,343	19	17	2
Hazel Green	1,216	2	2	0
Highland	825	1	1	0
Hobart-Lawrence	16,178	13	12	1
Holmen	10,135	14	13	1
Horicon	3,644	8	7	1
Hortonville	2,936	7	6	1
Hudson	14,255	31	28	3
Hurley	1,425	7	6	1
Independence	1,299	3	3	0
Iron Ridge	887	1	1	0
Iron River	1,135	3	3	0
Jackson	7,247	12	11	1
Janesville	64,682	114	103	11
Jefferson	7,986	17	14	3
Juneau	2,653	5	4	1
Kaukauna	16,357	27	26	1
Kenosha	100,005	212	199	13
Kewaskum	4,290	8	8	0
Kewaunee	2,838	6	6	0
Kiel	3,805	8	7	1
Kohler	2,053	9	8	1
Kronenwetter	8,181	9	8	1
La Crosse	51,211	119	99	20
Ladysmith	3,097	8	8	0
La Farge	761	1	1	0
Lake Delton	2,994	46	21	25
Lake Geneva	8,157	34	25	9
Lake Hallie	6,777	11	10	1
Lake Mills	6,013	12	10	2
Lancaster	3,682	6	6	0
Lena	537	1	1	0
Linn Township	2,405	6	6	0
Lodi	3,096	13	6	7
Lomira	2,453	5	4	1
Luxemburg	2,576	1	1	0
Madison	262,736	617	505	112
Manawa	1,262	3	3	0
Manitowoc	32,458	73	63	10
Maple Bluff	1,310	5	5	0
Marathon City	1,505	3	3	0
Marinette	10,497	28	24	4
Marion	1,170	4	4	0
Markesan	1,394	4	4	0
Marshall Village	3,998	10	9	1
Marshfield	18,403	47	39	8
Mauston	4,348	10	9	1
Mayville	4,862	9	8	1
McFarland	9,161	19	17	2
Medford	4,274	10	9	1
Menasha	17,910	38	31	7
Menomonee Falls	38,290	131	59	72
Menomonie	16,582	31	26	5
Mequon	24,527	49	38	11
Merrill	8,984	25	22	3
Middleton	20,322	48	38	10
Milton	5,636	13	11	2
Milwaukee	589,105	2,190	1,752	438
Mineral Point	2,461	6	6	0
Minocqua	4,422	15	10	5
Mishicot	1,383	3	3	0
Mondovi	2,542	4	4	0
Monona	8,245	26	21	5
Monroe	10,538	32	25	7
Montello	1,464	3	2	1
Monticello	1,200	3	3	0
Mosinee	4,080	8	7	1
Mount Horeb	7,579	13	13	0
Mount Pleasant	27,125	61	55	6
Mukwonago	8,137	22	15	7

Table 78. Full-Time Law Enforcement Employees, by Selected State and City, 2020—Continued

(Number.)

State/city	Population	Total law enforcement employees	Total officers	Total civilians
Mukwonago Town	8,168	7	6	1
Muscoda	1,234	3	3	0
Muskego	25,237	44	34	10
Neenah	26,390	50	40	10
Neillsville	2,403	6	5	1
Nekoosa	2,405	7	7	0
New Berlin	39,703	80	66	14
New Glarus	2,148	4	4	0
New Holstein	3,088	7	6	1
New Lisbon	2,546	4	4	0
New London	7,070	19	17	2
New Richmond	9,535	19	18	1
Niagara	1,535	3	3	0
North Fond du Lac	5,089	11	9	2
North Hudson	3,815	6	5	1
Norwalk	630	1	1	0
Oak Creek	36,502	116	61	55
Oconomowoc	17,116	30	23	7
Oconomowoc Town	8,743	12	11	1
Oconto	4,548	9	9	0
Oconto Falls	2,785	6	6	0
Omro	3,590	8	7	1
Onalaska	19,072	30	28	2
Oregon	10,718	21	18	3
Osceola	2,556	6	5	1
Oshkosh	67,080	108	94	14
Osseo	1,673	4	4	0
Palmyra	1,753	6	6	0
Park Falls	2,207	6	6	0
Pepin	775	1	1	0
Peshtigo	3,329	6	6	0
Pewaukee Village	8,102	19	18	1
Phillips	1,322	5	5	0
Pittsville	819	2	2	0
Plainfield	833	1	1	0
Platteville	12,184	28	20	8
Pleasant Prairie	21,181	43	33	10
Plover	13,201	23	20	3
Plymouth	8,762	16	16	0
Portage	10,408	26	22	4
Port Edwards	1,757	3	3	0
Port Washington	11,982	24	19	5
Poynette	2,507	5	4	1
Prairie du Chien	5,539	13	12	1
Prescott	4,299	11	10	1
Pulaski	3,742	9	8	1
Racine	76,573	216	185	31
Reedsburg	9,549	28	22	6
Rhinelander	7,629	17	15	2
Rice Lake	8,526	18	18	0
Richland Center	4,918	13	11	2
Rio	1,038	4	2	2
Ripon	7,854	20	14	6
Ripon Town	1,380	1	1	0
River Falls	16,141	26	23	3
River Hills	1,571	11	11	0
Rome Town	2,755	7	7	0
Rosendale	1,028	1	1	0
Rothschild	5,268	14	12	2
Sauk Prairie	4,650	17	15	2
Saukville	4,431	14	12	2
Seymour	3,454	6	6	0
Sharon	1,552	5	4	1
Shawano	8,896	22	20	2
Sheboygan	47,814	101	82	19
Sheboygan Falls	7,938	17	15	2
Shiocton	912	3	2	1
Shorewood	13,133	28	24	4
Shorewood Hills	2,058	9	7	2
Shullsburg	1,188	1	1	0
Siren	771	4	3	1
Slinger	5,621	13	12	1
Somerset	2,951	6	5	1
South Milwaukee	20,626	39	33	6
Sparta	9,865	23	21	2
Spencer	1,874	4	4	0
Spooner	2,557	8	7	1
Spring Green	1,643	2	2	0
Spring Valley	1,348	2	2	0
Stanley	3,722	5	5	0
St. Croix Falls	2,037	7	6	1
Stevens Point	25,790	48	44	4
St. Francis	9,733	22	21	1
Stoughton	13,164	29	23	6
Strum	1,087	2	2	0
Sturgeon Bay	8,913	24	22	2

Table 78. Full-Time Law Enforcement Employees, by Selected State and City, 2020—Continued

(Number.)

State/city	Population	Total law enforcement employees	Total officers	Total civilians
Sturtevant	6,659	13	12	1
Summit	5,087	11	11	0
Sun Prairie	35,272	76	55	21
Superior	25,845	59	54	5
Theresa	1,199	4	2	2
Thiensville	3,116	8	7	1
Thorp	1,610	3	3	0
Three Lakes	2,112	5	5	0
Tomah	9,418	22	20	2
Tomahawk	3,111	9	8	1
Town of East Troy	4,060	7	6	1
Town of Madison	6,920	14	13	1
Trempealeau	1,680	3	3	0
Twin Lakes	6,230	18	13	5
Two Rivers	10,970	28	25	3
Verona	13,548	27	25	2
Viroqua	4,407	11	9	2
Walworth	2,828	19	18	1
Washburn	2,028	5	5	0
Waterford Town	6,526	14	7	7
Waterloo	3,332	7	6	1
Watertown	23,437	54	40	14
Waukesha	72,421	154	122	32
Waunakee	14,280	23	21	2
Waupaca	5,953	26	25	1
Waupun	11,184	18	16	2
Wausau	38,492	86	77	9
Wautoma	2,135	10	5	5
Wauwatosa	48,265	118	94	24
Webster	616	15	15	0
West Allis	59,778	153	121	32
West Bend	31,603	67	50	17
Westby	2,259	4	4	0
Westfield	1,268	2	2	0
West Milwaukee	4,081	25	20	5
West Salem	5,037	10	9	1
Whitefish Bay	13,734	23	22	1
Whitehall	1,570	4	4	0
Whitewater	14,952	34	24	10
Wild Rose	680	4	2	2
Williams Bay	2,646	8	7	1
Wind Point	1,692	1	1	0
Winneconne	2,497	6	5	1
Wisconsin Dells	3,025	20	15	5
Wisconsin Rapids	17,524	41	37	4
Woodruff	1,975	6	5	1
WYOMING				
Afton	2,055	4	4	0
Buffalo	4,573	19	10	9
Casper	58,244	154	99	55
Cheyenne	64,751	122	103	19
Cody	9,816	25	22	3
Diamondville	759	2	2	0
Douglas	6,394	17	14	3
Evanston	11,563	32	27	5
Evansville	3,005	11	9	2
Gillette	32,093	81	53	28
Glenrock	2,568	13	7	6
Green River	11,691	30	25	5
Greybull	1,837	6	5	1
Hanna	762	2	2	0
Jackson	10,668	32	26	6
Kemmerer	2,760	6	6	0
Lander	7,441	19	17	2
Laramie	32,913	69	44	25
Lusk	1,521	6	6	0
Mills	4,040	20	15	5
Moorcroft	1,092	4	3	1
Newcastle	3,383	17	8	9
Pine Bluffs	1,158	2	2	0
Powell	6,165	22	16	6
Rawlins	8,434	25	14	11
Riverton	10,772	42	30	12
Rock Springs	22,615	44	36	8
Saratoga	1,607	7	4	3
Sheridan	17,991	43	26	17
Thermopolis	2,738	12	7	5
Torrington	6,623	24	17	7
Wheatland	3,445	10	9	1
Worland	4,975	12	12	0

1 The employee data presented in this table for Charlotte-Mecklenburg represent only Charlotte-Mecklenburg Police Department and exclude Mecklenburg County Sheriff's Office.

Table 79. Full-Time Law Enforcement Employees, by Selected State and University or College, 2020

(Number.)

State and university/college	Student enrollment[1]	Law enforcement employees	Officers	Civilians
ALABAMA				
Alabama A&M University	6,686	40	18	22
Alabama State University	4,892	28	20	8
Auburn University, Montgomery	6,296	26	16	10
Bishop State Community College	4,563	7	6	1
Calhoun Community College	15,020	7	6	1
Coastal Alabama Community College	10,546	9	9	0
Enterprise State Community College	2,409	5	5	0
Jacksonville State University	9,766	29	19	10
Jefferson State Community College	13,617	13	11	2
Lawson State Community College	4,874	6	5	1
Samford University	6,041	16	13	3
Southern Union State Community College	7,060	5	5	0
Troy University	21,039	20	18	2
Tuskegee University	3,345	23	9	14
University of Alabama				
Birmingham	25,705	160	109	51
Huntsville	11,135	28	16	12
Tuscaloosa	42,432	153	88	65
University of Montevallo	2,841	20	10	10
University of North Alabama	8,901	13	12	1
University of South Alabama	16,889	28	21	7
University of West Alabama	7,908	13	8	5
Wallace Community College				
Dothan	6,283	2	2	0
Selma	2,448	5	2	3
ALASKA				
University of Alaska				
Anchorage	23,371	22	14	8
Fairbanks	12,297	13	7	6
ARIZONA				
Arizona State University	139,085	166	85	81
Arizona Western College	11,521	12	8	4
Central Arizona College	8,518	14	12	2
Northern Arizona University	34,934	34	23	11
Pima Community College	33,708	53	26	27
University of Arizona	48,653	107	62	45
Yavapai College	9,809	9	7	2
ARKANSAS				
Arkansas State University				
Beebe	4,716	6	5	1
Jonesboro	18,977	25	21	4
Arkansas Tech University	13,722	23	20	3
Henderson State University	4,565	9	8	1
Southern Arkansas University	5,182	11	10	1
Southern Arkansas University Tech	1,968	3	3	0
University of Arkansas				
Fayetteville	30,459	46	31	15
Little Rock	12,993	30	22	8
Medical Sciences	2,996	48	35	13
Monticello	3,716	10	8	2
Pine Bluff	2,818	15	11	4
University of Arkansas Community College at Morrilton	2,475	3	3	0
University of Central Arkansas	12,741	33	23	10
CALIFORNIA				
Allan Hancock College	15,587	12	6	6
California State Polytechnic University				
Pomona	28,547	54	21	33
San Luis Obispo	23,278	23	18	5
California State University				
Bakersfield	12,944	23	14	9
Channel Islands	8,348	26	13	13
Chico	19,323	27	18	9
Dominguez Hills	18,196	28	19	9
East Bay	18,549	21	12	9
Fresno	26,765	37	25	12
Fullerton	46,588	37	24	13
Long Beach	41,344	35	22	13
Los Angeles	29,963	32	17	15
Monterey Bay	8,476	25	15	10
Northridge	43,348	36	19	17
Sacramento	35,644	42	19	23
San Bernardino	21,967	30	19	11
San Jose	38,805	65	25	40
San Marcos	17,136	22	15	7
Stanislaus	11,821	19	12	7
Chaffey College	30,177	15	13	2
College of the Sequoias	16,022	7	6	1
Contra Costa Community College	54,940	34	21	13
Cuesta College	15,640	7	5	2

Table 79. Full-Time Law Enforcement Employees, by Selected State and University or College, 2020—Continued

(Number.)

State and university/college	Student enrollment[1]	Law enforcement employees	Officers	Civilians
El Camino College	34,373	18	11	7
Foothill-De Anza College	58,890	14	10	4
Humboldt State University	8,622	17	12	5
Irvine Valley College	19,299	14	9	5
Marin Community College	7,327	6	4	2
Pasadena Community College	36,788	14	9	5
Riverside Community College	62,345	24	18	6
San Bernardino Community College	29,194	17	10	7
San Diego State University	37,838	52	27	25
San Francisco State University	33,236	45	21	24
San Jose/Evergreen Community College	29,405	19	6	13
Sonoma County Junior College	29,046	20	9	11
Sonoma State University	10,360	14	13	1
State Center Community College District	68,277	26	20	6
University of California				
Berkeley	45,183	104	44	60
Davis	40,623	62	39	23
Irvine	38,105	107	47	60
Los Angeles	47,103	96	59	37
Merced	8,939	31	18	13
Riverside	25,816	40	31	9
San Diego	39,811	75	36	39
San Francisco	3,185	147	52	95
Santa Barbara	27,685	55	36	19
Santa Cruz	20,839	42	24	18
Ventura County Community College District	50,235	14	14	0
West Valley-Mission College	24,630	15	9	6
COLORADO				
Adams State University	3,696	6	5	1
Arapahoe Community College	15,565	10	9	1
Auraria Higher Education Center[2]		43	26	17
Colorado School of Mines	6,639	11	10	1
Colorado State University, Fort Collins	37,356	41	26	15
Fort Lewis College	3,743	8	7	1
Pikes Peak Community College	18,701	18	17	1
Red Rocks Community College	11,967	9	6	3
University of Colorado				
Boulder	40,353	83	39	44
Colorado Springs	17,001	28	17	11
Denver	32,857	59	25	34
University of Northern Colorado	15,950	23	16	7
CONNECTICUT				
Central Connecticut State University	13,866	26	18	8
Eastern Connecticut State University	5,714	22	13	9
Southern Connecticut State University	11,492	27	21	6
University of Connecticut, Storrs, Avery Point, and Hartford[2]		119	90	29
Western Connecticut State University	6,535	19	13	6
Yale University	14,389	106	91	15
DELAWARE				
Delaware State University	5,003	35	12	23
University of Delaware	25,885	78	49	29
FLORIDA				
Florida A&M University	11,100	29	23	6
Florida Atlantic University	36,970	76	44	32
Florida Gulf Coast University	16,940	25	18	7
Florida International University	72,780	99	68	31
Florida Polytechnic University	1,487	13	10	3
Florida SouthWestern State College	21,995	28	14	14
Florida State University				
Panama City[2]		4	3	1
Tallahassee	46,825	89	71	18
New College of Florida	865	18	14	4
Northwest Florida State College	7,691	6	6	0
Pensacola State College	13,758	14	9	5
Santa Fe College	19,711	22	17	5
Tallahassee Community College	16,760	21	11	10
University of Central Florida	80,378	135	82	53
University of Florida	58,749	121	85	36
University of North Florida	20,094	42	32	10
University of South Florida				
St. Petersburg	5,694	21	16	5
Tampa	51,808	74	48	26
University of West Florida	16,122	25	20	5
GEORGIA				
Abraham Baldwin Agricultural College	5,402	16	15	1
Agnes Scott College	1,076	14	7	7
Albany State University	7,576	34	21	13
Albany Technical College	4,583	2	2	0
Athens Technical College	6,365	3	2	1

Table 79. Full-Time Law Enforcement Employees, by Selected State and University or College, 2020—Continued

(Number.)

State and university/college	Student enrollment[1]	Law enforcement employees	Officers	Civilians
Atlanta Metropolitan State College	3,277	7	4	3
Atlanta Technical College	5,725	3	2	1
Augusta Technical College	6,341	6	6	0
Augusta University	9,575	57	42	15
Bainbridge State College[2]		7	5	2
Berry College	2,240	15	10	5
Chattahoochee Technical College	15,030	12	10	2
Clark Atlanta University	4,202	49	19	30
Clayton State University	8,550	25	14	11
College of Coastal Georgia	4,436	14	14	0
Columbus State University	9,926	29	22	7
Dalton State College	5,931	14	11	3
Emory University	16,024	78	58	20
Fort Valley State University	3,049	24	10	14
Georgia College and State University	8,066	19	13	6
Georgia Gwinnett College	15,382	29	24	5
Georgia Institute of Technology	38,951	105	77	28
Georgia Military College	16,848	6	4	2
Georgia Southern University	30,628	70	59	11
Georgia Southwestern State University	3,646	9	9	0
Georgia State University	40,505	274	137	137
Gordon State College	4,339	14	13	1
Gwinnett Technical College	12,364	4	3	1
Kennesaw State University	41,654	95	55	40
Mercer University	9,767	30	22	8
Middle Georgia State University	9,654	26	22	4
Morehouse College	2,441	29	9	20
Piedmont College	3,357	8	4	4
Southern Crescent Technical College	7,088	5	5	0
Spelman College	2,206	25	16	9
University of Georgia	42,708	91	69	22
University of North Georgia	23,032	47	38	9
University of West Georgia	16,353	33	24	9
West Georgia Technical College	10,043	11	11	0
Young Harris College	1,470	4	4	0
ILLINOIS				
Chicago State University	3,593	24	20	4
College of DuPage	41,901	20	16	4
Elgin Community College	14,547	18	16	2
John Wood Community College	2,935	5	4	1
Joliet Junior College	23,030	38	12	26
Lincoln Land Community College	10,222	14	12	2
McHenry County College	10,941	9	8	1
Millikin University	2,227	15	5	10
Morton College	6,951	5	4	1
Oakton Community College	17,553	14	12	2
Parkland College	11,367	16	13	3
Southern Illinois University, School of Medicine[2]		6	6	0
South Suburban College	8,839	13	7	6
University of Illinois, Urbana	54,985	95	61	34
Waubonsee Community College	16,110	8	7	1
INDIANA				
Ball State University	25,199	37	30	7
Indiana University				
Indianapolis	34,279	59	45	14
Kokomo	3,786	4	4	0
South Bend	6,168	14	12	2
Southeast	6,373	13	12	1
IOWA				
Iowa State University	37,944	52	35	17
University of Iowa	35,339	58	37	21
University of Northern Iowa	13,040	21	18	3
KANSAS				
Butler Community College	12,005	9	9	0
Emporia State University	7,177	9	9	0
Fort Hays State University	18,343	11	9	2
Kansas State University	24,546	33	23	10
Pittsburg State University	8,009	13	12	1
University of Kansas, Medical Center[2]		158	47	111
Washburn University	7,534	19	13	6
Wichita State University	17,371	43	29	14
KENTUCKY				
Kentucky State University	2,655	10	3	7
Morehead State University	11,462	19	12	7
Murray State University	10,714	22	15	7
Northern Kentucky University	17,151	20	14	6
University of Kentucky	30,981	173	51	122
University of Louisville	24,770	58	48	10
Western Kentucky University	23,228	30	20	10

Table 79. Full-Time Law Enforcement Employees, by Selected State and University or College, 2020—Continued

(Number.)

State and university/college	Student enrollment[1]	Law enforcement employees	Officers	Civilians
LOUISIANA				
Grambling State University	5,979	20	13	7
Louisiana State University, Eunice	3,677	2	2	0
Southeastern Louisiana University	17,352	28	23	5
University of Louisiana	19,221	42	39	3
MAINE				
University of Maine				
Farmington	2,461	5	4	1
Orono	13,091	22	14	8
University of Southern Maine	10,606	15	10	5
MARYLAND				
Bowie State University	7,069	25	12	13
Coppin State University	3,139	26	14	12
Frostburg State University	6,008	21	17	4
Hagerstown Community College	5,749	3	3	0
Morgan State University	8,443	52	33	19
Prince George's County Community College	16,981	22	15	7
Salisbury University	9,407	35	19	16
Towson University	25,754	57	41	16
University of Baltimore	6,045	25	14	11
University of Maryland				
Baltimore City	7,573	171	51	120
Baltimore County	15,726	39	25	14
College Park	44,486	120	79	41
Eastern Shore	3,517	38	12	26
MASSACHUSETTS				
Amherst College	1,946	17	12	5
Assumption College	2,659	18	12	6
Babson College	4,095	27	17	10
Becker College	2,160	16	11	5
Bentley University	5,735	28	20	8
Boston College	15,981	80	51	29
Boston University	42,779	58	46	12
Brandeis University	6,400	23	20	3
Bunker Hill Community College	18,239	19	16	3
Clark University	3,473	14	10	4
College of the Holy Cross	3,005	23	17	6
Emerson College	5,028	21	17	4
Endicott College	6,885	20	17	3
Fitchburg State University	11,130	26	21	5
Framingham State University	8,856	20	15	5
Gordon College	2,397	9	8	1
Harvard University	41,987	99	76	23
Holyoke Community College	6,832	13	10	3
Massachusetts College of Art	2,495	30	10	20
Massachusetts College of Liberal Arts	1,929	13	9	4
Massachusetts Institute of Technology	12,321	73	63	10
Massasoit Community College	10,162	17	16	1
Merrimack College	5,426	21	16	5
Mount Wachusett Community College	5,152	11	10	1
North Shore Community College	7,979	24	18	6
Quinsigamond Community College	9,527	13	11	2
Salem State University	10,069	24	21	3
Simmons College	7,780	26	16	10
Springfield College	3,297	31	20	11
Springfield Technical Community College	6,799	16	13	3
Tufts University, Medford	12,781	73	44	29
University of Massachusetts				
Amherst	35,116	76	58	18
Dartmouth	9,714	31	23	8
Medical Center, Worcester	1,227	36	30	6
Wellesley College	2,784	16	12	4
Wentworth Institute of Technology	5,437	22	16	6
Western New England University	4,048	27	17	10
Westfield State University	7,421	20	16	4
Worcester Polytechnic Institute	7,505	24	18	6
Worcester State University	9,691	21	16	5
MICHIGAN				
Central Michigan University	24,917	29	22	7
Delta College	10,809	9	6	3
Eastern Michigan University	22,327	44	34	10
Ferris State University	15,739	13	11	2
Grand Rapids Community College	19,391	17	13	4
Grand Valley State University	27,752	35	22	13
Kalamazoo Valley Community College	11,591	8	6	2
Kellogg Community College	7,182	3	3	0
Kirtland Community College	1,914	1	1	0
Lansing Community College	16,382	15	12	3
Macomb Community College	28,017	31	28	3

Table 79. Full-Time Law Enforcement Employees, by Selected State and University or College, 2020—Continued

(Number.)

State and university/college	Student enrollment[1]	Law enforcement employees	Officers	Civilians
Michigan State University	55,332	109	75	34
Michigan Technological University	7,657	15	11	4
Mott Community College	10,176	15	10	5
Northern Michigan University	9,092	21	19	2
Oakland Community College	25,217	23	22	1
Oakland University	22,351	31	22	9
Saginaw Valley State University	9,491	9	9	0
Schoolcraft College	16,388	14	9	5
University of Michigan				
Ann Arbor	48,218	77	63	14
Dearborn	10,906	28	14	14
Flint	8,806	28	18	10
Washtenaw Community College	21,182	12	5	7
Western Michigan University	25,010	36	33	3
MINNESOTA				
University of Minnesota				
Duluth	11,868	14	12	2
Morris	1,658	6	3	3
Twin Cities	61,787	90	56	34
MISSISSIPPI				
Coahoma Community College	2,529	7	6	1
East Mississippi Community College	6,066	3	3	0
Hinds Community College	16,579	16	15	1
Jackson State University	8,606	62	35	27
Mississippi State University	24,251	51	36	15
Northeast Mississippi Community College	4,337	9	8	1
University of Mississippi, Oxford	25,133	47	30	17
MISSOURI				
Lincoln University	3,114	20	9	11
Metropolitan Community College	22,969	36	29	7
Mineral Area College	3,606	6	6	0
Missouri Southern State University	6,699	8	7	1
Missouri University of Science and Technology	9,265	20	11	9
Missouri Western State University	6,163	9	8	1
Northwest Missouri State University	8,027	12	10	2
Southeast Missouri State University	12,645	21	14	7
Truman State University	6,344	9	8	1
University of Central Missouri	15,993	28	18	10
University of Missouri				
Columbia	33,333	70	48	22
Kansas City	19,166	35	25	10
St. Louis	20,378	24	20	4
Washington University	17,794	59	42	17
MONTANA				
Montana State University	18,898	26	19	7
Montana State University, Billings	5,749	11	8	3
University of Montana	13,140	24	15	9
NEBRASKA				
Metropolitan Community College, Douglas County	24,321	26	21	5
University of Nebraska				
Kearney	7,859	11	8	3
Lincoln	28,686	58	27	31
NEVADA				
University of Nevada, Reno	24,246	37	29	8
University Police Services	92,407	79	58	21
NEW HAMPSHIRE				
Plymouth State University	5,868	10	10	0
University of New Hampshire	16,673	36	20	16
NEW JERSEY				
Brookdale Community College	17,100	13	12	1
Essex County College	10,496	55	12	43
Kean University	16,738	47	23	24
Middlesex County College	16,328	19	11	8
Monmouth University	6,704	43	15	28
Montclair State University	24,235	44	38	6
Princeton University	8,720	103	35	68
Rowan University	23,011	83	33	50
Rutgers University				
Camden	8,154	67	18	49
Newark	15,897	153	59	94
New Brunswick	57,162	114	62	52
Stevens Institute of Technology	7,990	19	19	0
Stockton University	11,457	42	24	18
The College of New Jersey	8,825	28	18	10
William Paterson University	12,113	44	27	17

Table 79. Full-Time Law Enforcement Employees, by Selected State and University or College, 2020—Continued

(Number.)

State and university/college	Student enrollment[1]	Law enforcement employees	Officers	Civilians
NEW MEXICO				
Eastern New Mexico University	7,520	8	7	1
Western New Mexico University	4,138	7	6	1
NEW YORK				
Ithaca College	7,003	35	19	16
State University of New York Police				
Albany	20,325	56	37	19
Alfred	4,166	15	10	5
Binghamton	19,454	61	41	20
Brockport	9,603	18	14	4
Buffalo	35,111	75	62	13
Buffalo State College	10,467	34	30	4
Canton	4,985	10	9	1
Cobleskill	3,065	11	10	1
Cortland	7,737	27	19	8
Delhi	3,638	16	12	4
Downstate Medical	2,092	90	19	71
Environmental Science	2,370	16	11	5
Farmingdale	12,831	32	21	11
Fredonia	4,989	16	13	3
Geneseo	5,959	22	15	7
Maritime	1,947	15	10	5
Morrisville	3,345	16	13	3
Nanoscale Science and Engineering[2]		4	4	0
New Paltz	8,895	26	21	5
Old Westbury	6,442	23	19	4
Oneonta	7,131	23	14	9
Optometry	408	17	7	10
Oswego	9,381	23	18	5
Plattsburgh	6,475	19	15	4
Polytechnic Institute	3,402	17	12	5
Potsdam	3,918	14	11	3
Purchase	4,753	31	22	9
Stony Brook	30,458	156	58	98
Upstate Medical	1,661	101	19	82
NORTH CAROLINA				
Appalachian State University	20,714	47	27	20
Beaufort County Community College	2,049	4	4	0
Belmont Abbey College	1,677	8	8	0
Davidson College	2,006	8	7	1
Duke University	18,159	163	62	101
East Carolina University	32,028	69	55	14
Elizabeth City State University	1,922	23	13	10
Elon University	7,277	34	18	16
Fayetteville State University	7,880	32	13	19
Meredith College	2,048	14	3	11
Methodist University	2,295	22	9	13
North Carolina Agricultural and Technical State University	13,511	54	23	31
North Carolina Central University	9,201	37	19	18
North Carolina School of the Arts	1,057	22	14	8
North Carolina State University, Raleigh	39,822	69	52	17
Queens University	3,056	8	6	2
Saint Augustine's University	841	12	2	10
University of North Carolina				
Asheville	4,358	21	13	8
Chapel Hill	32,346	101	51	50
Charlotte	34,024	56	48	8
Greensboro	22,610	49	33	16
Pembroke	8,492	26	18	8
Wilmington	19,400	49	33	16
Wake Forest University	9,032	51	23	28
Western Carolina University	13,342	25	25	0
Winston-Salem State University	5,915	39	19	20
NORTH DAKOTA				
Bismarck State College	4,848	3	2	1
North Dakota State College of Science	3,625	4	3	1
North Dakota State University	14,503	23	15	8
University of North Dakota	17,050	20	19	1
OHIO				
Capital University	3,649	13	8	5
Columbus State Community College	46,559	45	24	21
Cuyahoga Community College	33,892	35	28	7
Lakeland Community College	9,309	15	11	4
Shawnee State University	3,994	11	8	3
Sinclair Community College	32,190	21	17	4
University of Cincinnati	43,692	138	63	75
University of Toledo	22,439	36	30	6
Wright State University	16,523	19	16	3

Table 79. Full-Time Law Enforcement Employees, by Selected State and University or College, 2020—Continued

(Number.)

State and university/college	Student enrollment[1]	Law enforcement employees	Officers	Civilians
OKLAHOMA				
Bacone College	322	3	3	0
Cameron University	5,370	13	13	0
East Central University	4,289	5	5	0
Eastern Oklahoma State College	1,950	5	5	0
Langston University	2,607	17	13	4
Mid-America Christian University	2,362	5	5	0
Northeastern Oklahoma A&M College	2,456	5	5	0
Northeastern State University, Tahlequah	9,277	15	11	4
Northwestern Oklahoma State University	2,363	3	3	0
Oklahoma City Community College	17,861	28	20	8
Oklahoma City University	3,163	10	6	4
Oklahoma State University				
Main Campus	27,200	44	33	11
Okmulgee	3,167	6	5	1
Tulsa	1,133	6	5	1
Rogers State University	4,383	6	6	0
Seminole State College	2,053	3	3	0
Southeastern Oklahoma State University	5,698	7	6	1
Southwestern Oklahoma State University	5,989	8	7	1
Tulsa Community College	22,918	43	32	11
University of Central Oklahoma	17,985	23	15	8
University of Oklahoma				
Health Sciences Center	3,697	66	41	25
Norman	32,189	63	32	31
OREGON				
Portland State University	32,445	27	12	15
University of Oregon	25,203	33	23	10
PENNSYLVANIA				
Bloomsburg University	9,843	20	15	5
California University	9,440	18	15	3
Cheyney University	517	10	9	1
Clarion University	5,677	15	10	5
Duquesne University	10,319	45	28	17
East Stroudsburg University	7,351	17	10	7
Edinboro University	5,949	14	13	1
Indiana University	13,070	27	21	6
Kutztown University	9,160	16	15	1
Lehigh University	7,330	36	26	10
Lock Haven University	3,803	14	10	4
Mansfield University	1,799	11	8	3
Millersville University	9,231	13	12	1
Pennsylvania State University				
Abington	4,379	10	7	3
Altoona	3,450	11	10	1
Beaver	693	6	6	0
Behrend	4,676	12	10	2
Berks	2,900	11	10	1
Brandywine	1,467	6	6	0
Dubois	638	2	2	0
Fayette	684	4	3	1
Greater Allegheny	519	5	3	2
Harrisburg	5,567	9	8	1
Hazleton	760	6	5	1
Lehigh Valley	1,054	3	3	0
Mont Alto	924	6	6	0
New Kensington	759	3	3	0
Schuylkill	698	6	6	0
University Park	49,935	103	53	50
Wilkes-Barre	541	2	2	0
Worthington Scranton	1,089	3	3	0
York	1,080	5	4	1
Shippensburg University	7,138	14	13	1
Slippery Rock University	10,366	13	12	1
University of Pittsburgh				
Bradford	1,393	5	4	1
Greensburg	1,640	11	10	1
Johnstown	2,732	12	9	3
Pittsburgh	31,667	141	79	62
Titusville	252	3	1	2
Wilkes University	6,978	27	15	12
RHODE ISLAND				
Brown University	10,760	80	52	28
University of Rhode Island	20,628	44	25	19
SOUTH CAROLINA				
Benedict College	2,312	12	3	9
Bob Jones University	3,455	3	3	0
Clemson University	28,310	57	37	20
Coastal Carolina University	11,982	46	32	14
College of Charleston	12,907	43	28	15

Table 79. Full-Time Law Enforcement Employees, by Selected State and University or College, 2020—Continued

(Number.)

State and university/college	Student enrollment[1]	Law enforcement employees	Officers	Civilians
Denmark Technical College	842	7	3	4
Erskine College	869	3	2	1
Francis Marion University	4,395	14	11	3
Furman University	3,143	22	15	7
Greenville Technical College	14,730	15	9	6
Lander University	3,284	22	12	10
Medical University of South Carolina	3,402	73	55	18
Midlands Technical College	13,163	6	5	1
Orangeburg-Calhoun Technical College	3,385	5	5	0
Presbyterian College	1,422	7	6	1
South Carolina State University	3,283	22	8	14
Spartanburg Methodist College	920	4	4	0
The Citadel	4,458	22	16	6
Tri-County Technical College	7,722	14	11	3
Trident Technical College	17,167	17	14	3
University of South Carolina				
Aiken	4,376	9	8	1
Beaufort	2,375	17	14	3
Columbia	37,510	103	68	35
Upstate	7,249	13	11	2
Winthrop University	6,801	15	9	6
SOUTH DAKOTA				
South Dakota School of Mines and Technology	3,076	4	1	3
South Dakota State University	14,785	18	14	4
University of South Dakota	12,904	15	12	3
TENNESSEE				
Austin Peay State University	12,707	27	16	11
Chattanooga State Community College	10,630	15	9	6
Christian Brothers University	2,330	23	9	14
Cleveland State Community College	4,284	4	3	1
Columbia State Community College	8,199	4	1	3
East Tennessee State University	16,350	25	18	7
Jackson State Community College	6,590	3	2	1
Lincoln Memorial University	5,587	26	6	20
Middle Tennessee State University	25,239	43	34	9
Motlow State Community College	8,577	3	3	0
Nashville State Community College	11,161	21	5	16
Northeast State Community College	7,465	8	7	1
Pellissippi State Community College	15,089	13	11	2
Roane State Community College	7,178	10	9	1
Southwest Tennessee Community College	13,176	25	22	3
Tennessee State University	8,723	55	19	36
Tennessee Technological University	11,154	18	13	5
University of Memphis	24,603	70	35	35
University of Tennessee				
Chattanooga	12,718	31	18	13
Health Science Center	3,412	64	32	32
Knoxville	31,477	89	55	34
Martin	8,264	13	9	4
University of the South	2,004	15	11	4
Vanderbilt University	13,634	234	80	154
Volunteer State Community College	11,772	14	11	3
Walters State Community College	7,739	11	10	1
TEXAS				
Abilene Christian University	5,864	15	14	1
Alvin Community College	8,115	14	12	2
Amarillo College	12,510	12	10	2
Angelo State University	11,737	20	15	5
Austin College	1,317	9	8	1
Austin Community College District	58,856	93	82	11
Baylor Health Care System[2]		149	53	96
Brazosport College	6,278	9	9	0
Central Texas College	28,248	9	8	1
Cisco College	4,763	1	1	0
College of the Mainland	5,932	8	7	1
Concordia University	3,038	5	4	1
Dallas County Community College District	167,464	154	129	25
El Paso Community College	38,292	43	35	8
Grayson College	5,522	8	7	1
Hardin-Simmons University	2,555	5	5	0
Houston Baptist University	4,374	11	10	1
Houston Community College	81,570	106	67	39
Kilgore College	7,108	7	7	0
Lamar University, Beaumont	19,727	63	18	45
Laredo Community College	13,381	21	19	2
Lone Star College System District	109,742	179	112	67
Lubbock Christian University	2,084	8	2	6
McLennan Community College	13,980	14	9	5
Midwestern State University	7,039	16	11	5
Paris Junior College	7,204	5	5	0
Prairie View A&M University	10,565	43	34	9

Table 79. Full-Time Law Enforcement Employees, by Selected State and University or College, 2020—Continued

(Number.)

State and university/college	Student enrollment[1]	Law enforcement employees	Officers	Civilians
Rice University	7,542	43	26	17
San Jacinto College, Central Campus	42,820	39	31	8
Southwestern University	1,480	9	6	3
Stephen F. Austin State University	14,948	43	27	16
St. Mary's University	3,899	19	16	3
St. Thomas University	3,890	6	6	0
Sul Ross State University	2,755	7	6	1
Tarleton State University	15,191	18	15	3
Texas A&M International University	9,511	27	20	7
Texas A&M University				
College Station	73,267	149	74	75
Commerce	14,618	32	23	9
Corpus Christi	14,249	26	16	10
Galveston[2]		12	11	1
San Antonio	7,961	22	14	8
Texas Christian University	11,499	47	24	23
Texas Southern University	10,979	76	34	42
Texas State Technical College				
Harlingen[2]		12	10	2
Waco	14,746	10	8	2
West Texas[2]		6	6	0
Texas State University, San Marcos	42,780	58	34	24
Texas Tech University, Lubbock	41,153	147	69	78
Texas Woman's University	19,075	45	20	25
Trinity Valley Community College	9,896	10	9	1
Tyler Junior College	16,477	27	16	11
University of Houston				
Central Campus	51,999	167	58	109
Clearlake	10,992	32	16	16
Downtown Campus	17,682	47	23	24
University of North Texas, Denton	43,963	64	42	22
University of Texas				
Arlington	60,035	101	45	56
Austin	55,128	146	93	53
Dallas	31,419	74	27	47
El Paso	29,881	53	28	25
Health Science Center, San Antonio	3,881	97	36	61
Health Science Center, Tyler	98	27	7	20
Houston	7,104	318	75	243
Medical Branch	4,054	130	68	62
Permian Basin	8,165	20	14	6
Rio Grande Valley	33,766	82	47	35
San Antonio	35,755	88	43	45
Southwestern Medical School	2,514	137	44	93
Tyler	12,289	32	12	20
West Texas A&M University	11,875	33	19	14
UTAH				
Brigham Young University	39,233	61	27	34
Dixie State University	12,263	8	7	1
Southern Utah University	14,369	6	5	1
Utah State University				
Eastern[2]		2	2	0
Logan	32,963	25	16	9
Utah Valley University	45,080	19	13	6
Weber State University	36,043	14	11	3
VERMONT				
University of Vermont	15,698	30	18	12
VIRGINIA				
Christopher Newport University	5,117	26	18	8
College of William and Mary	9,765	27	21	6
Eastern Virginia Medical School	1,436	51	19	32
Emory and Henry College	1,340	3	3	0
Ferrum College	1,155	8	8	0
George Mason University	48,678	53	45	8
Germanna Community College	9,583	9	2	7
Hampton University	4,802	33	15	18
James Madison University	24,152	43	33	10
J. Sargeant Reynolds Community College	13,001	18	13	5
Longwood University	5,864	20	17	3
Lord Fairfax Community College	9,054	5	5	0
Norfolk State University	5,806	35	15	20
Northern Virginia Community College	73,642	49	41	8
Old Dominion University	28,046	55	43	12
Radford University	11,085	27	19	8
Richard Bland College	2,746	5	4	1
Southwest Virginia Community College	3,056	3	3	0
Thomas Nelson Community College	11,588	11	7	4
University of Mary Washington	5,171	18	17	1
University of Richmond	4,602	33	22	11
University of Virginia	28,593	136	59	77
University of Virginia's College at Wise	3,376	10	9	1

Table 79. Full-Time Law Enforcement Employees, by Selected State and University or College, 2020—Continued

(Number.)

State and university/college	Student enrollment[1]	Law enforcement employees	Officers	Civilians
Virginia Commonwealth University	33,462	104	75	29
Virginia Military Institute	1,738	13	12	1
Virginia Polytechnic Institute and State University	36,882	57	43	14
Virginia State University	4,836	29	21	8
Virginia Western Community College	9,384	8	8	0
WASHINGTON				
Central Washington University	17,678	16	14	2
Eastern Washington University	15,961	13	12	1
Evergreen State College	4,036	13	7	6
University of Washington	56,315	66	37	29
Washington State University				
Pullman	35,149	26	22	4
Vancouver[2]		5	3	2
Western Washington University	17,966	20	13	7
WEST VIRGINIA				
Bluefield State College	1,456	3	3	0
Concord University	2,505	9	6	3
Fairmont State University	4,199	10	8	2
Glenville State College	1,833	5	3	2
Marshall University	16,452	29	27	2
Potomac State College	1,518	7	6	1
Shepherd University	4,523	9	7	2
West Liberty University	2,769	6	6	0
West Virginia State University	4,745	8	6	2
West Virginia University				
Institute of Technology	2,023	8	7	1
Morgantown	29,323	62	45	17
WISCONSIN				
University of Wisconsin				
Eau Claire	12,637	9	9	0
Green Bay	10,185	14	11	3
La Crosse	11,500	16	11	5
Madison	47,392	134	63	71
Milwaukee	31,363	43	33	10
Oshkosh	19,257	17	15	2
Parkside	5,031	12	8	4
Platteville	10,133	9	7	2
River Falls	6,847	7	7	0
Stevens Point	10,201	12	7	5
Stout	10,113	9	8	1
Superior	3,181	7	3	4
Whitewater	15,155	15	13	2
WYOMING				
University of Wyoming	13,926	25	15	10

1 The student enrollment figures provided by the United States Department of Education are for the 2019 school year, the most recent available. The enrollment figures include full-time and part-time students.   2 Student enrollment figures were not available.

Table 80. Full-Time Law Enforcement Employees, by Selected State Metropolitan and Nonmetropolitan Counties, 2020

(Number.)

State/county	Law enforcement employees	Officers	Civilians
ALABAMA			
Metropolitan Counties			
Autauga	45	31	14
Baldwin	328	143	185
Bibb	11	10	1
Blount	63	46	17
Calhoun	54	48	6
Chilton	22	19	3
Colbert	33	27	6
Elmore	121	56	65
Geneva	31	16	15
Greene	32	12	20
Hale	30	11	19
Henry	36	21	15
Houston	170	76	94
Jefferson	685	531	154
Lauderdale	73	53	20
Lawrence	46	22	24
Lee	171	84	87
Limestone	118	50	68
Lowndes	42	16	26
Madison	345	142	203
Mobile	547	185	362
Montgomery	160	114	46
Morgan	176	57	119
Pickens	32	10	22
Russell	119	42	77
Shelby	230	140	90
St. Clair	129	58	71
Tuscaloosa	199	102	97
Washington	23	11	12
Nonmetropolitan Counties			
Barbour	31	11	20
Bullock	8	7	1
Butler	14	12	2
Chambers	64	27	37
Cherokee	36	34	2
Choctaw	9	7	2
Clarke	47	16	31
Clay	23	13	10
Cleburne	28	8	20
Coffee	60	29	31
Conecuh	38	9	29
Coosa	16	9	7
Covington	32	24	8
Crenshaw	12	10	2
Cullman	140	76	64
Dallas	47	27	20
DeKalb	99	42	57
Escambia	63	27	36
Fayette	25	17	8
Franklin	52	21	31
Jackson	45	32	13
Lamar	21	10	11
Macon	38	19	19
Marengo	23	10	13
Marion	31	15	16
Marshall	94	50	44
Monroe	51	19	32
Perry	21	7	14
Pike	41	23	18
Randolph	49	18	31
Sumter	24	7	17
Talladega	94	41	53
Tallapoosa	54	23	31
Walker	85	42	43
Wilcox	23	7	16
Winston	29	10	19
ARIZONA			
Metropolitan Counties			
Cochise	175	85	90
Coconino	238	61	177
Maricopa	3,414	646	2,768
Mohave	261	86	175
Pima	1,405	505	900
Pinal	455	211	244
Yavapai	185	130	55
Yuma	331	77	254
Nonmetropolitan Counties			
Gila	121	42	79
Graham	69	23	46

Table 80. Full-Time Law Enforcement Employees, by Selected State Metropolitan and Nonmetropolitan Counties, 2020—Continued

(Number.)

State/county	Law enforcement employees	Officers	Civilians
Greenlee	47	17	30
La Paz	58	36	22
Navajo	127	49	78
Santa Cruz	78	36	42
ARKANSAS			
Metropolitan Counties			
Benton	257	179	78
Cleveland	15	10	5
Craighead	108	34	74
Crawford	79	35	44
Crittenden	140	38	102
Faulkner	159	52	107
Franklin	27	12	15
Garland	177	55	122
Grant	19	16	3
Jefferson	94	48	46
Lincoln	26	11	15
Little River	33	15	18
Lonoke	72	33	39
Madison	21	19	2
Miller	38	27	11
Perry	21	11	10
Poinsett	43	15	28
Pulaski	455	124	331
Saline	102	93	9
Sebastian	175	58	117
Washington	294	147	147
Nonmetropolitan Counties			
Arkansas	11	10	1
Ashley	41	19	22
Baxter	64	38	26
Boone	59	30	29
Bradley	7	5	2
Calhoun	12	6	6
Carroll	59	19	40
Chicot	8	7	1
Clark	32	15	17
Clay	10	9	1
Cleburne	49	25	24
Columbia	47	17	30
Conway	24	22	2
Cross	37	18	19
Dallas	29	5	24
Desha	8	7	1
Drew	14	13	1
Fulton	18	8	10
Greene	28	25	3
Hempstead	46	21	25
Hot Spring	31	29	2
Howard	23	11	12
Independence	59	35	24
Izard	19	17	2
Jackson	33	15	18
Johnson	17	15	2
Lafayette	25	20	5
Lawrence	33	14	19
Lee	11	6	5
Logan	48	14	34
Marion	15	13	2
Mississippi	97	40	57
Monroe	11	5	6
Montgomery	21	10	11
Nevada	28	6	22
Newton	21	8	13
Ouachita	30	20	10
Phillips	20	15	5
Pike	25	11	14
Polk	28	16	12
Pope	42	35	7
Prairie	8	8	0
Randolph	13	11	2
Scott	9	9	0
Searcy	5	5	0
Sevier	16	16	0
Sharp	34	14	20
St. Francis	43	20	23
Stone	19	10	9
Union	67	31	36
Van Buren	37	20	17
White	90	51	39
Woodruff	10	6	4
Yell	24	16	8

Table 80. Full-Time Law Enforcement Employees, by Selected State Metropolitan and Nonmetropolitan Counties, 2020—Continued

(Number.)

State/county	Law enforcement employees	Officers	Civilians
CALIFORNIA			
Metropolitan Counties			
Alameda	1,520	969	551
Butte	268	100	168
Contra Costa	933	634	299
El Dorado	362	167	195
Fresno	1,170	421	749
Imperial	276	192	84
Kern	1,122	762	360
Kings	292	89	203
Los Angeles	16,089	9,933	6,156
Madera	124	91	33
Marin	297	196	101
Merced	267	115	152
Monterey	448	312	136
Napa	141	108	33
Orange	3,644	1,879	1,765
Placer	543	251	292
Riverside	3,767	1,779	1,988
Sacramento	1,968	1,333	635
San Benito	58	25	33
San Bernardino	3,404	1,985	1,419
San Diego	4,180	2,582	1,598
San Francisco	1,039	847	192
San Joaquin	733	290	443
San Luis Obispo	421	303	118
San Mateo	724	319	405
Santa Barbara	689	489	200
Santa Clara	1,677	1,286	391
Santa Cruz	335	154	181
Shasta	200	141	59
Solano	505	135	370
Sonoma	595	225	370
Stanislaus	712	517	195
Sutter	126	100	26
Tulare	767	537	230
Ventura	1,234	743	491
Yolo	256	75	181
Yuba	174	132	42
Nonmetropolitan Counties			
Alpine	15	12	3
Amador	90	45	45
Calaveras	123	61	62
Colusa	61	40	21
Del Norte	53	21	32
Glenn	64	31	33
Humboldt	270	205	65
Inyo	80	37	43
Lake	120	92	28
Lassen	81	53	28
Mariposa	74	59	15
Mendocino	163	117	46
Modoc	31	23	8
Mono	44	23	21
Nevada	152	62	90
Plumas	60	33	27
Sierra	15	9	6
Siskiyou	94	65	29
Tehama	105	70	35
Trinity	49	39	10
Tuolumne	128	60	68
COLORADO			
Metropolitan Counties			
Adams	588	399	189
Arapahoe	605	437	168
Boulder	395	108	287
Clear Creek	73	27	46
Douglas	527	352	175
Elbert	50	40	10
El Paso	807	509	298
Gilpin	55	31	24
Jefferson	719	505	214
Larimer	423	285	138
Mesa	236	137	99
Park	48	26	22
Pueblo	351	152	199
Teller	85	48	37
Nonmetropolitan Counties			
Alamosa	61	26	35
Archuleta	39	18	21
Baca	13	5	8

Table 80. Full-Time Law Enforcement Employees, by Selected State Metropolitan and Nonmetropolitan Counties, 2020—Continued

(Number.)

State/county	Law enforcement employees	Officers	Civilians
Bent	30	13	17
Chaffee	53	22	31
Cheyenne	8	4	4
Conejos	27	11	16
Costilla	17	9	8
Crowley	15	8	7
Custer	17	10	7
Delta	68	33	35
Dolores	10	5	5
Eagle	82	48	34
Fremont	90	41	49
Garfield	139	50	89
Grand	50	21	29
Gunnison	26	12	14
Hinsdale	4	3	1
Huerfano	37	17	20
Jackson	8	3	5
Kiowa	7	4	3
Kit Carson	30	6	24
Lake	26	9	17
La Plata	124	91	33
Las Animas	30	10	20
Lincoln	24	10	14
Logan	49	21	28
Mineral	7	5	2
Moffat	36	19	17
Montezuma	72	25	47
Montrose	93	50	43
Morgan	53	20	33
Otero	22	13	9
Ouray	8	7	1
Phillips	4	4	0
Pitkin	57	24	33
Prowers	30	10	20
Rio Blanco	28	11	17
Rio Grande	44	17	27
Routt	49	25	24
Saguache	22	11	11
San Juan	4	4	0
San Miguel	32	11	21
Sedgwick	4	3	1
Summit	70	34	36
Washington	38	10	28
Yuma	23	9	14
DELAWARE			
Metropolitan Counties			
New Castle County Police Department	434	393	41
FLORIDA			
Metropolitan Counties			
Alachua	387	276	111
Baker	57	40	17
Bay	290	224	66
Brevard	1,331	553	778
Charlotte	449	310	139
Citrus	329	211	118
Clay	605	286	319
Collier	913	571	342
Escambia	677	426	251
Flagler	299	225	74
Gilchrist	49	33	16
Hernando	546	349	197
Highlands	350	159	191
Hillsborough	3,333	1,226	2,107
Indian River	474	189	285
Jefferson	57	27	30
Lake	705	289	416
Lee	1,533	690	843
Leon	702	274	428
Levy	148	113	35
Manatee	1,269	832	437
Marion	829	329	500
Martin	398	262	136
Miami-Dade	4,108	2,979	1,129
Nassau	259	148	111
Okaloosa	450	318	132
Orange	2,321	1,613	708
Osceola	660	410	250
Palm Beach	3,653	1,637	2,016
Pasco	1,030	660	370
Pinellas	2,376	795	1,581
Polk	1,193	680	513

Table 80. Full-Time Law Enforcement Employees, by Selected State Metropolitan and Nonmetropolitan Counties, 2020—Continued

(Number.)

State/county	Law enforcement employees	Officers	Civilians
Santa Rosa	422	217	205
Sarasota	967	425	542
Seminole	1,293	461	832
St. Johns	731	359	372
St. Lucie	741	316	425
Volusia	713	409	304
Wakulla	137	72	65
Walton	524	263	261
Nonmetropolitan Counties			
Bradford	89	42	47
Calhoun	23	19	4
Columbia	195	159	36
DeSoto	114	61	53
Franklin	58	33	25
Glades	127	31	96
Gulf	44	30	14
Hamilton	59	19	40
Hardee	110	79	31
Hendry	154	84	70
Jackson	73	48	25
Lafayette	34	14	20
Liberty	24	17	7
Madison	82	39	43
Monroe	503	199	304
Okeechobee	133	90	43
Putnam	216	117	99
Suwannee	115	80	35
Union	27	17	10
GEORGIA			
Metropolitan Counties			
Barrow	184	128	56
Bartow	224	186	38
Bibb	497	418	79
Brantley	43	39	4
Brooks	44	24	20
Bryan	70	37	33
Burke	112	95	17
Butts	104	63	41
Carroll	189	110	79
Catoosa	121	77	44
Chatham County Police Department	146	124	22
Cherokee	447	367	80
Clarke	145	114	31
Clayton	266	200	66
Clayton County Police Department	502	372	130
Cobb	698	422	276
Cobb County Police Department	705	638	67
Columbia	334	273	61
Coweta	264	176	88
Crawford	32	17	15
Dade	29	26	3
DeKalb	625	422	203
DeKalb County Police Department	974	735	239
Dougherty	224	210	14
Dougherty County Police Department	43	34	9
Douglas	360	235	125
Echols	9	9	0
Effingham	145	82	63
Fayette	212	135	77
Floyd	146	77	69
Floyd County Police Department	79	70	9
Forsyth	459	371	88
Fulton	930	699	231
Fulton County Police Department	76	36	40
Glynn County Police Department	125	114	11
Gwinnett County Police Department	1,053	795	258
Hall	406	278	128
Haralson	82	40	42
Harris	77	55	22
Heard	37	21	16
Henry	332	275	57
Henry County Police Department	273	228	45
Jasper	48	32	16
Jones	79	40	39
Lamar	58	35	23
Lanier	20	15	5
Lee	70	41	29
Liberty	124	69	55
Long	32	29	3
Lowndes	236	210	26
Madison	90	48	42

Table 80. Full-Time Law Enforcement Employees, by Selected State Metropolitan and Nonmetropolitan Counties, 2020—Continued

(Number.)

State/county	Law enforcement employees	Officers	Civilians
Marion	18	10	8
McDuffie	49	21	28
McIntosh	69	42	27
Meriwether	49	28	21
Monroe	125	78	47
Murray	83	44	39
Muscogee	372	307	65
Newton	277	161	116
Oconee	96	62	34
Oglethorpe	46	19	27
Paulding	301	250	51
Peach	61	33	28
Pickens	83	74	9
Pike	52	28	24
Spalding	176	105	71
Talbot	14	9	5
Terrell	29	12	17
Twiggs	49	35	14
Walton	211	190	21
Whitfield	216	186	30
Worth	44	32	12
Nonmetropolitan Counties			
Appling	65	29	36
Atkinson	21	8	13
Bacon	25	10	15
Baldwin	118	58	60
Banks	60	47	13
Ben Hill	47	25	22
Berrien	52	27	25
Bleckley	42	19	23
Bulloch	132	121	11
Calhoun	16	7	9
Candler	26	15	11
Charlton	29	18	11
Chattooga	47	28	19
Clay	8	7	1
Clinch	15	12	3
Coffee	129	57	72
Cook	50	30	20
Crisp	97	60	37
Decatur	62	30	32
Dodge	48	19	29
Early	42	23	19
Elbert	60	33	27
Fannin	55	39	16
Franklin	61	33	28
Gilmer	111	68	43
Glascock	6	5	1
Gordon	106	75	31
Grady	23	20	3
Greene	54	49	5
Habersham	83	55	28
Hart	47	28	19
Irwin	23	15	8
Jackson	170	98	72
Jeff Davis	39	18	21
Jefferson	52	49	3
Jenkins	21	11	10
Laurens	110	68	42
Lumpkin	73	50	23
Mitchell	55	26	29
Montgomery	27	12	15
Pierce	49	21	28
Polk	79	42	37
Polk County Police Department	39	36	3
Pulaski	35	19	16
Rabun	56	53	3
Schley	8	4	4
Screven	19	6	13
Seminole	36	25	11
Sumter	99	71	28
Tattnall	49	24	25
Taylor	20	11	9
Thomas	87	58	29
Tift	96	49	47
Towns	41	20	21
Treutlen	21	11	10
Troup	154	74	80
Turner	50	21	29
Union	48	43	5
Upson	73	37	36
Ware	117	50	67

Table 80. Full-Time Law Enforcement Employees, by Selected State Metropolitan and Nonmetropolitan Counties, 2020—Continued

(Number.)

State/county	Law enforcement employees	Officers	Civilians
Washington	73	36	37
Webster	4	4	0
White	78	49	29
Wilcox	19	13	6
Wilkes	55	27	28
Wilkinson	30	18	12
HAWAII			
Metropolitan Counties			
Maui Police Department	418	317	101
Nonmetropolitan Counties			
Hawaii Police Department	568	438	130
Kauai Police Department	196	136	60
IDAHO			
Metropolitan Counties			
Ada	782	170	612
Bannock	126	43	83
Boise	22	13	9
Bonneville	193	79	114
Butte	14	7	7
Canyon	280	69	211
Franklin	16	10	6
Gem	36	13	23
Jefferson	60	22	38
Jerome	56	22	34
Kootenai	311	99	212
Nez Perce	77	22	55
Owyhee	28	12	16
Power	27	10	17
Twin Falls	115	41	74
Nonmetropolitan Counties			
Adams	25	10	15
Bear Lake	14	8	6
Benewah	30	11	19
Bingham	87	35	52
Blaine	49	37	12
Bonner	101	40	61
Boundary	31	11	20
Camas	6	4	2
Caribou	26	8	18
Cassia	75	33	42
Clark	8	3	5
Clearwater	32	15	17
Custer	15	9	6
Elmore	66	22	44
Fremont	38	21	17
Gooding	36	16	20
Idaho	38	19	19
Latah	53	29	24
Lemhi	25	9	16
Lewis	12	8	4
Lincoln	11	8	3
Madison	70	20	50
Minidoka	64	21	43
Oneida	14	9	5
Payette	45	14	31
Shoshone	37	15	22
Teton	21	12	9
Valley	44	21	23
Washington	33	12	21
ILLINOIS			
Metropolitan Counties			
Alexander	10	7	3
Bond	22	12	10
Champaign	146	67	79
Clinton	35	16	19
Cook	5,198	1,558	3,640
DeKalb	107	40	67
Fulton	41	21	20
Grundy	52	30	22
Henry	67	22	45
Jackson	81	29	52
Kane	114	85	29
Kankakee	206	50	156
Kendall	126	57	69
Lake	467	147	320
Macon	148	48	100
Madison	167	84	83
Marshall	17	8	9

Table 80. Full-Time Law Enforcement Employees, by Selected State Metropolitan and Nonmetropolitan Counties, 2020—Continued

(Number.)

State/county	Law enforcement employees	Officers	Civilians
McHenry	361	104	257
McLean	128	49	79
Menard	19	9	10
Mercer	31	13	18
Piatt	33	13	20
Rock Island	176	62	114
Vermilion	88	41	47
Williamson	79	26	53
Winnebago	337	116	221
Woodford	51	25	26
Nonmetropolitan Counties			
Carroll	20	9	11
Cass	8	7	1
Christian	38	16	22
Cumberland	17	6	11
Edgar	8	7	1
Gallatin	4	4	0
Hancock	23	11	12
Hardin	14	5	9
Iroquois	27	15	12
Jefferson	58	21	37
Jo Daviess	38	19	19
La Salle	119	45	74
Lee	47	35	12
Livingston	64	29	35
Logan	46	19	27
Marion	41	33	8
Mason	20	9	11
McDonough	24	14	10
Montgomery	32	14	18
Pulaski	12	11	1
Putnam	12	7	5
Scott	6	3	3
Shelby	29	15	14
Stephenson	34	24	10
Wabash	11	5	6
Wayne	18	9	9
Whiteside	64	21	43
INDIANA			
Metropolitan Counties			
Bartholomew	106	44	62
Delaware	123	43	80
Hancock	84	40	44
Johnson	144	128	16
Lake	458	160	298
Monroe	63	46	17
Morgan	94	35	59
Ohio	9	8	1
Porter	164	68	96
Posey	30	16	14
St. Joseph	315	129	186
Vanderburgh	234	121	113
Vigo	133	42	91
Warrick	84	45	39
Nonmetropolitan Counties			
Daviess	104	24	80
Decatur	49	17	32
DeKalb	60	22	38
Fulton	31	14	17
Gibson	43	16	27
Grant	80	39	41
Greene	64	21	43
Jackson	73	19	54
Kosciusko	108	39	69
Miami	67	17	50
Montgomery	75	25	50
Noble	55	17	38
Pulaski	48	13	35
Starke	36	14	22
Steuben	52	23	29
Wells	42	17	25
IOWA			
Metropolitan Counties			
Black Hawk	138	78	60
Boone	28	13	15
Bremer	37	13	24
Dallas	80	31	49
Dubuque	91	78	13
Grundy	16	12	4

Table 80. Full-Time Law Enforcement Employees, by Selected State Metropolitan and Nonmetropolitan Counties, 2020—Continued

(Number.)

State/county	Law enforcement employees	Officers	Civilians
Guthrie	14	9	5
Harrison	2	2	0
Jasper	59	18	41
Johnson	96	83	13
Jones	28	11	17
Linn	195	126	69
Madison	20	10	10
Mills	26	11	15
Polk	508	155	353
Pottawattamie	207	54	153
Scott	166	49	117
Story	88	31	57
Warren	37	20	17
Washington	20	18	2
Woodbury	115	41	74
Nonmetropolitan Counties			
Adair	15	6	9
Adams	13	13	0
Allamakee	20	10	10
Appanoose	16	9	7
Audubon	12	6	6
Buchanan	30	13	17
Butler	18	12	6
Calhoun	12	7	5
Carroll	12	10	2
Cass	12	9	3
Cedar	38	13	25
Cerro Gordo	70	20	50
Cherokee	19	8	11
Chickasaw	18	10	8
Clarke	22	8	14
Clay	13	11	2
Clinton	47	25	22
Crawford	16	11	5
Davis	19	6	13
Decatur	16	6	10
Delaware	20	12	8
Des Moines	27	22	5
Dickinson	19	9	10
Emmet	15	8	7
Fayette	36	12	24
Floyd	20	12	8
Franklin	10	7	3
Fremont	27	10	17
Greene	19	9	10
Hamilton	31	11	20
Hancock	10	8	2
Hardin	29	11	18
Henry	37	12	25
Howard	18	9	9
Humboldt	22	9	13
Ida	18	10	8
Iowa	28	11	17
Jackson	12	10	2
Jefferson	31	11	20
Keokuk	10	5	5
Kossuth	25	10	15
Lee	43	18	25
Louisa	30	11	19
Lucas	11	5	6
Lyon	23	11	12
Mahaska	26	10	16
Marion	40	18	22
Marshall	52	18	34
Mitchell	16	7	9
Monona	16	7	9
Monroe	22	6	16
Montgomery	25	9	16
O'Brien	28	9	19
Osceola	14	9	5
Page	9	8	1
Palo Alto	17	8	9
Plymouth	33	12	21
Poweshiek	25	12	13
Ringgold	14	6	8
Sac	22	9	13
Shelby	12	10	2
Sioux	40	14	26
Tama	23	14	9
Union	13	6	7
Van Buren	12	6	6
Wapello	46	13	33

Table 80. Full-Time Law Enforcement Employees, by Selected State Metropolitan and Nonmetropolitan Counties, 2020—Continued

(Number.)

State/county	Law enforcement employees	Officers	Civilians
Webster	34	17	17
Winnebago	15	7	8
Winneshiek	14	12	2
Worth	26	13	13
Wright	11	10	1
KANSAS			
Metropolitan Counties			
Butler	109	63	46
Doniphan	17	6	11
Douglas	167	86	81
Geary	96	36	60
Harvey	25	23	2
Jackson	45	25	20
Jefferson	26	22	4
Johnson	652	490	162
Leavenworth	124	76	48
Linn	38	23	15
Osage	37	25	12
Pottawatomie	42	29	13
Riley County Police Department	208	108	100
Sedgwick	246	183	63
Sumner	25	19	6
Wabaunsee	24	12	12
Wyandotte	262	164	98
Nonmetropolitan Counties			
Allen	18	13	5
Anderson	31	9	22
Barton	42	20	22
Bourbon	15	12	3
Brown	19	9	10
Chase	8	4	4
Chautauqua	15	6	9
Cherokee	45	25	20
Cheyenne	8	7	1
Clark	10	5	5
Cloud	24	8	16
Coffey	40	14	26
Comanche	7	3	4
Cowley	46	24	22
Crawford	65	30	35
Decatur	3	3	0
Dickinson	24	19	5
Edwards	10	6	4
Elk	10	5	5
Ellis	40	19	21
Ellsworth	22	8	14
Ford	34	26	8
Franklin	34	30	4
Gove	5	4	1
Graham	8	3	5
Grant	15	6	9
Gray	15	9	6
Greeley	8	4	4
Greenwood	23	13	10
Hamilton	11	5	6
Haskell	14	9	5
Hodgeman	10	5	5
Kearny	61	10	51
Kingman	19	8	11
Lane	5	5	0
Lincoln	14	8	6
Logan	5	5	0
Marion	12	11	1
Marshall	26	11	15
McPherson	22	19	3
Mitchell	10	9	1
Morris	12	7	5
Morton	32	26	6
Nemaha	27	10	17
Neosho	30	16	14
Ness	12	7	5
Norton	11	5	6
Osborne	13	7	6
Ottawa	10	5	5
Pawnee	13	11	2
Phillips	11	8	3
Pratt	19	11	8
Rawlins	5	3	2
Reno	95	58	37
Rice	7	5	2
Rooks	10	10	0

Table 80. Full-Time Law Enforcement Employees, by Selected State Metropolitan and Nonmetropolitan Counties, 2020—Continued

(Number.)

State/county	Law enforcement employees	Officers	Civilians
Rush	12	7	5
Saline	49	38	11
Scott	9	4	5
Seward	24	16	8
Sherman	13	6	7
Smith	6	6	0
Stafford	9	4	5
Stanton	10	4	6
Stevens	17	6	11
Trego	5	3	2
Wallace	8	4	4
Washington	21	9	12
Wichita	10	5	5
Wilson	13	10	3
Woodson	12	7	5
KENTUCKY			
Metropolitan Counties			
Boone	165	160	5
Bourbon	11	10	1
Boyd	43	32	11
Butler	9	6	3
Carter	12	9	3
Christian	43	33	10
Clark	17	13	4
Daviess	43	37	6
Fayette	83	58	25
Grant	17	15	2
Greenup	18	17	1
Hardin	52	36	16
Henderson	22	16	6
Jefferson	258	202	56
Kenton	41	34	7
Kenton County Police Department	37	35	2
Larue	8	6	2
McLean	13	11	2
Meade	17	13	4
Oldham	16	13	3
Oldham County Police Department	46	43	3
Pendleton	9	8	1
Shelby	28	24	4
Spencer	9	7	2
Trigg	11	8	3
Warren	90	48	42
Woodford	11	9	2
Nonmetropolitan Counties			
Adair	10	8	2
Barren	24	19	5
Bath	6	4	2
Boyle	18	17	1
Breathitt	1	1	0
Calloway	28	25	3
Carroll	7	5	2
Casey	7	5	2
Clay	22	20	2
Crittenden	6	5	1
Elliott	2	1	1
Estill	7	5	2
Fleming	7	5	2
Franklin	34	31	3
Fulton	5	4	1
Garrard County Police Department	9	9	0
Graves	21	18	3
Grayson	17	12	5
Green	13	12	1
Hart	20	11	9
Hickman	2	1	1
Hopkins	39	31	8
Johnson	12	9	3
Knott	4	4	0
Knox	17	12	5
Laurel	44	29	15
Lawrence	10	8	2
Lee	4	2	2
Leslie	8	7	1
Letcher	8	4	4
Lewis	11	7	4
Lincoln	9	8	1
Logan	26	23	3
Lyon	10	7	3
Madison	33	30	3
Marion	11	8	3

Table 80. Full-Time Law Enforcement Employees, by Selected State Metropolitan and Nonmetropolitan Counties, 2020—Continued

(Number.)

State/county	Law enforcement employees	Officers	Civilians
Marshall	43	33	10
Martin	7	3	4
Mason	19	11	8
McCracken	48	42	6
McCreary	7	6	1
Menifee	4	4	0
Mercer	12	9	3
Metcalfe	6	5	1
Monroe	6	5	1
Montgomery	17	15	2
Morgan	5	5	0
Muhlenberg	17	15	2
Nelson	37	30	7
Nicholas	4	3	1
Ohio	24	20	4
Owen	7	6	1
Owsley	3	2	1
Perry	13	11	2
Pike	20	16	4
Powell	4	2	2
Robertson	2	1	1
Rockcastle	6	5	1
Russell	12	10	2
Simpson	20	16	4
Todd	8	6	2
Union	14	9	5
Washington	8	6	2
Wayne	14	13	1
Webster	9	7	2
LOUISIANA			
Metropolitan Counties			
Ascension	350	265	85
Bossier	403	321	82
Caddo	589	366	223
Calcasieu	864	516	348
Cameron	92	80	12
East Feliciana	49	49	0
Iberia	186	101	85
Iberville	147	83	64
Lafayette	712	493	219
Morehouse	122	122	0
Ouachita	376	376	0
Plaquemines	284	255	29
St. Helena	45	29	16
St. James	109	61	48
St. Martin	198	103	95
Nonmetropolitan Counties			
Allen	105	28	77
Beauregard	118	91	27
Caldwell	28	28	0
Claiborne	68	33	35
East Carroll	44	18	26
Evangeline	13	7	6
Lincoln	82	63	19
Madison	35	27	8
Red River	68	44	24
Richland	133	106	27
St. Landry	218	104	114
St. Mary	143	143	0
Tensas	34	19	15
Vernon	114	54	60
Washington	82	71	11
Winn	39	17	22
MAINE			
Metropolitan Counties			
Androscoggin	25	23	2
Cumberland	71	60	11
Penobscot	43	39	4
Sagadahoc	21	19	2
York	35	30	5
Nonmetropolitan Counties			
Aroostook	24	17	7
Franklin	15	14	1
Hancock	24	22	2
Kennebec	28	25	3
Knox	24	23	1
Lincoln	26	23	3
Oxford	26	24	2
Piscataquis	9	9	0

Table 80. Full-Time Law Enforcement Employees, by Selected State Metropolitan and Nonmetropolitan Counties, 2020—Continued

(Number.)

State/county	Law enforcement employees	Officers	Civilians
Somerset	26	23	3
Waldo	24	22	2
Washington	18	16	2
MARYLAND			
Metropolitan Counties			
Allegany	34	32	2
Anne Arundel	99	73	26
Anne Arundel County Police Department	1,000	773	227
Baltimore County Police Department	2,091	1,899	192
Calvert	173	145	28
Carroll	259	126	133
Cecil	114	94	20
Charles	467	299	168
Frederick	262	194	68
Harford	406	312	94
Howard	76	56	20
Howard County Police Department	671	469	202
Montgomery	195	158	37
Montgomery County Police Department	1,782	1,298	484
Prince George's County Police Department	1,776	1,535	241
Queen Anne's	72	63	9
Somerset	26	22	4
St. Mary's	317	226	91
Washington	247	105	142
Wicomico	112	91	21
Worcester	66	52	14
Nonmetropolitan Counties			
Caroline	40	36	4
Dorchester	44	40	4
Garrett	51	36	15
Kent	30	24	6
Talbot	41	37	4
MICHIGAN			
Metropolitan Counties			
Bay	89	43	46
Berrien	158	74	84
Calhoun	176	74	102
Cass	71	33	38
Clinton	61	26	35
Eaton	136	66	70
Genesee	269	116	153
Ingham	87	75	12
Ionia	52	23	29
Jackson	105	49	56
Kalamazoo	208	124	84
Kent	657	210	447
Lapeer	81	48	33
Livingston	133	58	75
Macomb	532	276	256
Midland	69	28	41
Monroe	154	77	77
Montcalm	44	18	26
Muskegon	108	48	60
Oakland	1,098	923	175
Ottawa	234	139	95
Saginaw	103	57	46
Shiawassee	51	20	31
St. Clair	188	83	105
Washtenaw	303	128	175
Wayne	920	629	291
Nonmetropolitan Counties			
Alcona	21	11	10
Alger	14	9	5
Allegan	103	57	46
Alpena	30	13	17
Antrim	50	19	31
Arenac	24	14	10
Baraga	14	6	8
Barry	55	30	25
Benzie	36	17	19
Branch	36	12	24
Charlevoix	40	22	18
Cheboygan	39	22	17
Chippewa	40	16	24
Clare	29	23	6
Crawford	30	15	15
Delta	18	17	1
Dickinson	29	12	17
Emmet	50	26	24

Table 80. Full-Time Law Enforcement Employees, by Selected State Metropolitan and Nonmetropolitan Counties, 2020—Continued

(Number.)

State/county	Law enforcement employees	Officers	Civilians
Gladwin	39	15	24
Gogebic	24	16	8
Grand Traverse	126	69	57
Gratiot	41	39	2
Hillsdale	35	21	14
Houghton	28	19	9
Huron	36	20	16
Iosco	23	5	18
Iron	19	9	10
Isabella	54	25	29
Kalkaska	56	36	20
Keweenaw	6	6	0
Lake	36	16	20
Leelanau	22	20	2
Lenawee	99	39	60
Luce	6	5	1
Mackinac	29	13	16
Manistee	39	17	22
Marquette	64	24	40
Mason	27	24	3
Mecosta	48	21	27
Menominee	16	15	1
Missaukee	28	14	14
Montmorency	27	14	13
Newaygo	66	26	40
Oceana	36	21	15
Ogemaw	32	15	17
Ontonagon	5	5	0
Osceola	40	22	18
Oscoda	18	12	6
Otsego	29	12	17
Presque Isle	15	15	0
Roscommon	41	28	13
Sanilac	58	27	31
Schoolcraft	11	4	7
St. Joseph	61	27	34
Tuscola	48	20	28
Van Buren	104	54	50
Wexford	53	25	28
MINNESOTA			
Metropolitan Counties			
Anoka	275	137	138
Benton	70	25	45
Blue Earth	78	35	43
Carlton	58	25	33
Carver	155	77	78
Chisago	99	44	55
Clay	91	34	57
Dakota	190	89	101
Dodge	40	24	16
Fillmore	31	20	11
Hennepin	860	326	534
Houston	33	13	20
Isanti	53	20	33
Lake	28	15	13
Le Sueur	48	21	27
Mille Lacs	80	36	44
Nicollet	43	16	27
Olmsted	181	164	17
Polk	51	32	19
Ramsey	465	211	254
Scott	144	53	91
Sherburne	290	78	212
Stearns	212	74	138
St. Louis	253	104	149
Wabasha	50	19	31
Washington	261	120	141
Wright	265	153	112
Nonmetropolitan Counties			
Aitkin	51	19	32
Becker	64	23	41
Beltrami	84	32	52
Big Stone	7	5	2
Brown	34	10	24
Cass	78	45	33
Chippewa	21	9	12
Clearwater	20	10	10
Cook	21	13	8
Cottonwood	22	10	12
Crow Wing	127	41	86
Douglas	84	35	49

Table 80. Full-Time Law Enforcement Employees, by Selected State Metropolitan and Nonmetropolitan Counties, 2020—Continued

(Number.)

State/county	Law enforcement employees	Officers	Civilians
Faribault	29	13	16
Freeborn	74	25	49
Goodhue	98	43	55
Grant	16	11	5
Hubbard	47	19	28
Itasca	75	32	43
Jackson	27	14	13
Kanabec	49	21	28
Kandiyohi	103	32	71
Kittson	11	6	5
Koochiching	20	10	10
Lac qui Parle	11	7	4
Lake of the Woods	14	7	7
Lincoln	13	7	6
Lyon	50	18	32
Mahnomen	19	12	7
Marshall	24	13	11
Martin	34	14	20
McLeod	65	28	37
Meeker	51	22	29
Morrison	53	21	32
Mower	81	27	54
Murray	18	12	6
Nobles	35	13	22
Norman	12	7	5
Otter Tail	83	38	45
Pennington	35	10	25
Pine	81	34	47
Pipestone	25	15	10
Pope	14	8	6
Red Lake	11	8	3
Redwood	29	13	16
Renville	38	15	23
Rice	59	32	27
Rock	17	12	5
Roseau	20	12	8
Sibley	28	14	14
Steele	28	22	6
Stevens	15	7	8
Swift	18	9	9
Todd	37	18	19
Traverse	14	6	8
Wadena	22	12	10
Waseca	31	14	17
Watonwan	18	8	10
Wilkin	18	7	11
Winona	63	21	42
Yellow Medicine	26	11	15
MISSISSIPPI			
Metropolitan Counties			
Copiah	21	15	6
Covington	32	18	14
DeSoto	305	154	151
Forrest	135	45	90
Harrison	289	121	168
Hinds	355	86	269
Jackson	193	152	41
Lamar	91	49	42
Marshall	78	49	29
Perry	22	12	10
Rankin	127	106	21
Stone	28	24	4
Tate	47	21	26
Tunica	95	50	45
Yazoo	15	13	2
Nonmetropolitan Counties			
Adams	73	38	35
Alcorn	25	18	7
Amite	15	5	10
Attala	13	11	2
Bolivar	1	1	0
Calhoun	15	6	9
Chickasaw	15	14	1
Choctaw	15	9	6
Claiborne	30	22	8
Clarke	24	15	9
Clay	37	13	24
Coahoma	50	24	26
Franklin	7	3	4
George	20	18	2
Greene	18	6	12

Table 80. Full-Time Law Enforcement Employees, by Selected State Metropolitan and Nonmetropolitan Counties, 2020—Continued

(Number.)

State/county	Law enforcement employees	Officers	Civilians
Grenada	30	28	2
Humphreys	23	10	13
Jasper	34	19	15
Jefferson Davis	21	10	11
Jones	40	35	5
Kemper	15	12	3
Lafayette	90	44	46
Lauderdale	127	54	73
Lawrence	25	9	16
Lee	162	52	110
Leflore	29	20	9
Lincoln	53	25	28
Lowndes	104	53	51
Marion	20	14	6
Monroe	65	38	27
Montgomery	8	7	1
Neshoba	17	15	2
Newton	25	13	12
Noxubee	11	5	6
Oktibbeha	34	32	2
Panola	73	38	35
Pearl River	73	35	38
Pike	35	33	2
Pontotoc	50	39	11
Prentiss	35	17	18
Scott	61	32	29
Sharkey	8	6	2
Smith	23	13	10
Sunflower	24	16	8
Tishomingo	16	12	4
Union	41	21	20
Walthall	27	14	13
Warren	37	34	3
Washington	53	40	13
Wayne	27	14	13
Webster	8	5	3
Wilkinson	18	6	12
Winston	10	9	1
Yalobusha	25	12	13
MISSOURI			
Metropolitan Counties			
Andrew	34	14	20
Bates	58	20	38
Bollinger	16	11	5
Callaway	37	34	3
Cape Girardeau	82	46	36
Cass	117	92	25
Christian	90	57	33
Clay	200	126	74
Clinton	23	14	9
Dallas	25	16	9
DeKalb	15	9	6
Franklin	160	130	30
Jasper	132	85	47
Jefferson	236	166	70
Lafayette	43	31	12
Lincoln	93	54	39
Osage	18	11	7
Platte	136	96	40
Polk	43	29	14
Ray	27	11	16
St. Charles	47	33	14
St. Charles County Police Department	177	139	38
St. Louis County Police Department	1,316	933	383
Warren	59	30	29
Webster	42	19	23
Nonmetropolitan Counties			
Atchison	10	5	5
Benton	25	15	10
Butler	47	29	18
Camden	112	57	55
Carroll	12	11	1
Cedar	21	14	7
Chariton	15	8	7
Clark	12	6	6
Crawford	37	23	14
Dade	14	9	5
Daviess	8	6	2
Dent	18	14	4
Gasconade	7	6	1
Gentry	6	6	0
Grundy	13	3	10

Table 80. Full-Time Law Enforcement Employees, by Selected State Metropolitan and Nonmetropolitan Counties, 2020—Continued

(Number.)

State/county	Law enforcement employees	Officers	Civilians
Harrison	6	5	1
Hickory	14	9	5
Howell	41	29	12
Iron	12	6	6
Johnson	71	40	31
Laclede	68	25	43
Lewis	13	7	6
Linn	9	8	1
Livingston	11	11	0
Macon	21	11	10
Madison	9	8	1
Maries	21	11	10
Mercer	6	2	4
Miller	22	19	3
Mississippi	21	11	10
Monroe	9	8	1
Montgomery	20	18	2
Nodaway	17	15	2
Ozark	17	10	7
Pemiscot	55	24	31
Pettis	37	31	6
Phelps	71	31	40
Pike	24	18	6
Pulaski	46	21	25
Ralls	14	14	0
Randolph	42	22	20
Ripley	12	11	1
Scotland	8	3	5
Shannon	8	3	5
Shelby	9	5	4
St. Clair	62	19	43
Ste. Genevieve	75	52	23
Stoddard	36	18	18
Taney	60	44	16
Worth	4	3	1
Wright	9	6	3
MONTANA			
Metropolitan Counties			
Carbon	20	12	8
Cascade	144	39	105
Missoula	179	54	125
Stillwater	21	12	9
Yellowstone	180	57	123
Nonmetropolitan Counties			
Beaverhead	16	6	10
Big Horn	30	14	16
Blaine	14	7	7
Broadwater	26	12	14
Butte-Silver Bow	101	51	50
Carter	5	4	1
Chouteau	23	9	14
Custer	9	7	2
Daniels	8	4	4
Dawson	63	8	55
Deer Lodge	21	21	0
Fallon	9	4	5
Fergus	22	10	12
Flathead	111	60	51
Gallatin	130	65	65
Garfield	4	3	1
Glacier	24	12	12
Golden Valley	3	3	0
Granite	11	5	6
Hill	25	11	14
Jefferson	22	13	9
Judith Basin	6	5	1
Lake	48	28	20
Lewis and Clark	121	48	73
Lincoln	42	21	21
Madison	22	14	8
McCone	6	4	2
Meagher	7	3	4
Mineral	20	8	12
Musselshell	8	6	2
Park	26	17	9
Petroleum	2	2	0
Phillips	14	7	7
Pondera	9	8	1
Powder River	8	4	4
Powell	10	5	5
Prairie	5	4	1
Ravalli	83	37	46

Table 80. Full-Time Law Enforcement Employees, by Selected State Metropolitan and Nonmetropolitan Counties, 2020—Continued

(Number.)

State/county	Law enforcement employees	Officers	Civilians
Richland	36	10	26
Roosevelt	44	15	29
Rosebud	25	13	12
Sanders	23	12	11
Sheridan	8	6	2
Sweet Grass	14	8	6
Teton	13	10	3
Toole	22	13	9
Treasure	2	2	0
Valley	25	9	16
Wheatland	9	5	4
Wibaux	3	3	0
NEBRASKA			
Metropolitan Counties			
Cass	40	22	18
Dakota	47	18	29
Dixon	18	8	10
Douglas	224	131	93
Hall	39	29	10
Howard	12	5	7
Lancaster	108	81	27
Sarpy	185	113	72
Saunders	24	13	11
Seward	20	18	2
Washington	58	30	28
Nonmetropolitan Counties			
Adams	21	18	3
Antelope	19	5	14
Boone	12	5	7
Box Butte	21	6	15
Boyd	4	4	0
Buffalo	49	28	21
Burt	11	6	5
Butler	12	11	1
Cedar	6	6	0
Chase	9	5	4
Cherry	6	5	1
Cheyenne	20	9	11
Clay	12	8	4
Cuming	6	5	1
Custer	8	8	0
Dawes	17	7	10
Dawson	67	26	41
Deuel	7	6	1
Dodge	28	24	4
Fillmore	13	6	7
Franklin	8	4	4
Frontier	7	4	3
Furnas	13	7	6
Gage	18	15	3
Garden	12	5	7
Garfield	2	2	0
Gosper	6	5	1
Grant	1	1	0
Hamilton	22	9	13
Harlan	8	4	4
Hayes	1	1	0
Hitchcock	8	5	3
Holt	8	6	2
Hooker	2	2	0
Jefferson	29	17	12
Johnson	13	7	6
Kearney	11	6	5
Keith	19	9	10
Keya Paha	1	1	0
Madison	62	32	30
McPherson	1	1	0
Morrill	14	9	5
Nance	7	6	1
Nemaha	11	11	0
Nuckolls	10	5	5
Otoe	32	16	16
Pawnee	5	4	1
Perkins	10	5	5
Phelps	26	7	19
Platte	65	22	43
Red Willow	21	5	16
Richardson	10	9	1
Rock	7	3	4
Saline	24	18	6
Scotts Bluff	25	19	6
Sheridan	18	7	11

Table 80. Full-Time Law Enforcement Employees, by Selected State Metropolitan and Nonmetropolitan Counties, 2020—Continued

(Number.)

State/county	Law enforcement employees	Officers	Civilians
Sherman	6	5	1
Sioux	3	3	0
Stanton	9	8	1
Thayer	14	8	6
Thomas	2	2	0
Thurston	14	8	6
Valley	10	5	5
Wayne	7	6	1
Webster	10	6	4
Wheeler	2	2	0
York	24	12	12
NEVADA			
Metropolitan Counties			
Carson City	143	101	42
Storey	29	27	2
Washoe	698	413	285
Nonmetropolitan Counties			
Churchill	48	40	8
Douglas	124	109	15
Humboldt	55	37	18
Lander	35	16	19
Lincoln	22	17	5
Lyon	115	79	36
Mineral	22	16	6
Nye	150	113	37
Pershing	18	11	7
White Pine	35	30	5
NEW HAMPSHIRE			
Metropolitan Counties			
Rockingham	48	25	23
Strafford	30	18	12
Nonmetropolitan Counties			
Carroll	24	12	12
Cheshire	20	10	10
Grafton	25	10	15
Merrimack	29	16	13
NEW JERSEY			
Metropolitan Counties			
Atlantic	136	109	27
Bergen	578	491	87
Burlington	88	71	17
Camden	228	198	30
Cape May	166	141	25
Cumberland	76	66	10
Essex	439	367	72
Gloucester	103	93	10
Hudson	394	258	136
Hunterdon	45	40	5
Mercer	189	150	39
Middlesex	240	196	44
Monmouth	633	415	218
Morris	117	90	27
Ocean	271	152	119
Passaic	696	562	134
Salem	245	200	45
Somerset	209	179	30
Sussex	88	69	19
Union	245	198	47
Warren	20	16	4
NEW MEXICO			
Metropolitan Counties			
San Juan	108	86	22
Valencia	59	46	13
Nonmetropolitan Counties			
Catron	10	6	4
Curry	25	15	10
San Miguel	11	7	4
Sierra	13	11	2
Taos	29	25	4
Union	9	7	2
NEW YORK			
Metropolitan Counties			
Albany	203	131	72
Chemung	48	43	5
Dutchess	127	105	22
Herkimer	20	10	10

Table 80. Full-Time Law Enforcement Employees, by Selected State Metropolitan and Nonmetropolitan Counties, 2020—Continued

(Number.)

State/county	Law enforcement employees	Officers	Civilians
Jefferson	58	43	15
Livingston	55	51	4
Madison	54	42	12
Nassau	3,177	2,276	901
Onondaga	232	191	41
Ontario	145	78	67
Orleans	39	26	13
Oswego	72	64	8
Putnam	107	86	21
Rensselaer	46	39	7
Saratoga	195	147	48
Schenectady	24	18	6
Schoharie	33	19	14
Suffolk	363	240	123
Suffolk County Police Department	2,937	2,410	527
Tompkins	44	40	4
Ulster	81	56	25
Warren	109	71	38
Washington	46	42	4
Wayne	81	74	7
Westchester Public Safety	352	285	67
Yates	30	26	4
Nonmetropolitan Counties			
Allegany	36	13	23
Cattaraugus	76	51	25
Cayuga	36	28	8
Chautauqua	113	68	45
Chenango	23	23	0
Clinton	25	25	0
Columbia	73	59	14
Delaware	24	18	6
Essex	20	19	1
Franklin	59	57	2
Fulton	54	29	25
Greene	35	33	2
Hamilton	7	6	1
Lewis	32	22	10
Montgomery	47	27	20
Otsego	19	16	3
Schuyler	21	18	3
Steuben	53	40	13
Wyoming	33	32	1
NORTH CAROLINA			
Metropolitan Counties			
Alamance	274	133	141
Alexander	82	39	43
Anson	58	31	27
Brunswick	309	173	136
Buncombe	366	221	145
Burke	139	88	51
Cabarrus	357	211	146
Caldwell	92	83	9
Camden	20	17	3
Catawba	229	154	75
Chatham	146	96	50
Craven	146	91	55
Cumberland	510	259	251
Currituck	96	62	34
Davidson	173	116	57
Davie	89	61	28
Durham	438	184	254
Edgecombe	124	54	70
Forsyth	548	239	309
Franklin	139	93	46
Gaston	225	115	110
Gaston County Police Department	232	130	102
Gates	16	14	2
Granville	114	63	51
Guilford	603	254	349
Harnett	218	144	74
Haywood	130	72	58
Henderson	221	145	76
Hoke	115	67	48
Iredell	275	189	86
Johnston	199	131	68
Jones	29	18	11
Lincoln	173	119	54
Madison	43	20	23
Mecklenburg[1]	1,108	298	810
Nash	133	89	44
New Hanover	561	385	176
Onslow	281	146	135

Table 80. Full-Time Law Enforcement Employees, by Selected State Metropolitan and Nonmetropolitan Counties, 2020—Continued

(Number.)

State/county	Law enforcement employees	Officers	Civilians
Orange	146	100	46
Pamlico	49	22	27
Pender	126	80	46
Person	89	51	38
Pitt	331	130	201
Randolph	253	179	74
Rockingham	147	93	54
Rowan	275	200	75
Stokes	81	53	28
Union	316	229	87
Wake	936	383	553
Wayne	133	126	7
Yadkin	79	41	38
Nonmetropolitan Counties			
Alleghany	44	25	19
Ashe	76	34	42
Avery	52	27	25
Beaufort	104	62	42
Bertie	41	26	15
Bladen	79	52	27
Carteret	102	65	37
Caswell	57	37	20
Cherokee	73	33	40
Chowan	36	16	20
Clay	32	18	14
Cleveland	193	112	81
Columbus	120	82	38
Dare	160	69	91
Duplin	92	70	22
Graham	23	21	2
Greene	49	24	25
Halifax	98	67	31
Hertford	56	23	33
Hyde	16	15	1
Jackson	80	57	23
Lee	126	88	38
Lenoir	103	57	46
Macon	72	51	21
Martin	44	39	5
McDowell	79	55	24
Mitchell	20	19	1
Montgomery	57	31	26
Moore	169	80	89
Northampton	62	38	24
Pasquotank	56	49	7
Perquimans	19	17	2
Polk	64	36	28
Richmond	64	59	5
Robeson	148	136	12
Rutherford	133	78	55
Sampson	137	92	45
Scotland	61	35	26
Stanly	95	57	38
Surry	139	84	55
Swain	52	30	22
Transylvania	84	56	28
Tyrrell	13	12	1
Vance	102	52	50
Warren	67	33	34
Washington	36	18	18
Watauga	80	49	31
Wilkes	138	80	58
Wilson	153	92	61
Yancey	44	23	21
NORTH DAKOTA			
Metropolitan Counties			
Burleigh	147	58	89
Cass	182	107	75
Grand Forks	39	33	6
Morton	43	36	7
Oliver	5	4	1
Nonmetropolitan Counties			
Adams	5	4	1
Barnes	11	10	1
Benson	2	2	0
Billings	6	6	0
Bottineau	21	11	10
Bowman	5	4	1
Burke	6	6	0
Cavalier	12	6	6
Dickey	5	4	1

Table 80. Full-Time Law Enforcement Employees, by Selected State Metropolitan and Nonmetropolitan Counties, 2020—Continued

(Number.)

State/county	Law enforcement employees	Officers	Civilians
Divide	6	5	1
Dunn	22	20	2
Eddy	6	5	1
Emmons	6	5	1
Foster	4	3	1
Golden Valley	5	3	2
Grant	5	5	0
Griggs	3	3	0
Hettinger	8	7	1
Kidder	3	2	1
Lamoure	6	5	1
Logan	3	3	0
McHenry	8	8	0
McIntosh	3	3	0
McKenzie	53	38	15
McLean	41	26	15
Mercer	25	14	11
Mountrail	23	11	12
Nelson	6	5	1
Pembina	16	9	7
Pierce	38	4	34
Ramsey	9	8	1
Ransom	6	5	1
Renville	7	6	1
Richland	38	18	20
Rolette	26	8	18
Sargent	6	5	1
Sheridan	5	4	1
Sioux	1	1	0
Slope	1	1	0
Stark	31	26	5
Steele	3	3	0
Stutsman	14	12	2
Towner	7	6	1
Traill	14	10	4
Walsh	18	11	7
Ward	104	42	62
Wells	5	4	1
Williams	90	44	46
OHIO			
Metropolitan Counties			
Allen	148	66	82
Brown	53	30	23
Clermont	215	87	128
Delaware	236	111	125
Fairfield	150	109	41
Fulton	24	22	2
Geauga	159	66	93
Greene	156	66	90
Madison	46	31	15
Medina	151	57	94
Miami	118	57	61
Morrow	48	26	22
Perry	26	17	9
Pickaway	86	38	48
Portage	158	79	79
Richland	143	54	89
Stark	250	121	129
Summit	391	319	72
Union	67	46	21
Warren	200	102	98
Wood	125	57	68
Nonmetropolitan Counties			
Ashland	83	54	29
Ashtabula	81	33	48
Athens	37	32	5
Auglaize	60	25	35
Champaign	29	25	4
Coshocton	59	39	20
Darke	64	29	35
Fayette	50	23	27
Hancock	97	39	58
Knox	68	46	22
Marion	61	33	28
Mercer	69	30	39
Morgan	15	8	7
Muskingum	124	77	47
Scioto	73	35	38
Washington	95	48	47
Wayne	76	51	25
Wyandot	33	16	17

Table 80. Full-Time Law Enforcement Employees, by Selected State Metropolitan and Nonmetropolitan Counties, 2020—Continued

(Number.)

State/county	Law enforcement employees	Officers	Civilians
OREGON			
Metropolitan Counties			
Canadian	110	64	46
Cleveland	185	73	112
Comanche	44	33	11
Cotton	9	4	5
Creek	89	38	51
Garfield	32	24	8
Grady	39	25	14
Lincoln	41	19	22
Logan	61	35	26
McClain	41	26	15
Oklahoma	203	143	60
Okmulgee	16	14	2
Osage	71	36	35
Pawnee	22	10	12
Rogers	49	44	5
Sequoyah	37	30	7
Tulsa	592	223	369
Wagoner	71	32	39
Nonmetropolitan Counties			
Adair	35	11	24
Alfalfa	12	7	5
Atoka	8	7	1
Beaver	14	7	7
Beckham	36	11	25
Blaine	23	11	12
Bryan	21	18	3
Caddo	33	14	19
Carter	59	20	39
Cherokee	30	23	7
Choctaw	13	5	8
Cimarron	6	2	4
Coal	14	10	4
Craig	27	14	13
Custer	38	13	25
Delaware	40	14	26
Dewey	16	7	9
Ellis	18	8	10
Garvin	30	16	14
Grant	10	6	4
Greer	9	2	7
Harmon	2	2	0
Harper	8	4	4
Haskell	27	10	17
Hughes	18	12	6
Jackson	37	11	26
Jefferson	13	3	10
Johnston	21	8	13
Kay	27	19	8
Kingfisher	26	9	17
Kiowa	11	6	5
Latimer	7	6	1
Le Flore	17	14	3
Love	24	24	0
Major	19	7	12
Marshall	30	6	24
Mayes	56	27	29
McCurtain	29	25	4
McIntosh	20	12	8
Murray	13	7	6
Muskogee	80	29	51
Noble	18	9	9
Nowata	19	4	15
Okfuskee	27	8	19
Ottawa	20	6	14
Payne	86	36	50
Pittsburg	57	24	33
Pontotoc	20	18	2
Pottawatomie	28	23	5
Pushmataha	16	14	2
Roger Mills	12	8	4
Seminole	19	13	6
Stephens	26	21	5
Texas	29	12	17
Tillman	3	3	0
Washington	60	30	30
Washita	29	6	23
Woods	8	7	1
Woodward	28	10	18

Table 80. Full-Time Law Enforcement Employees, by Selected State Metropolitan and Nonmetropolitan Counties, 2020—Continued

(Number.)

State/county	Law enforcement employees	Officers	Civilians
OREGON			
Metropolitan Counties			
Benton	84	69	15
Clackamas	431	195	236
Columbia	59	46	13
Deschutes	261	196	65
Jackson	172	130	42
Josephine	94	69	25
Lane	298	59	239
Linn	177	74	103
Marion	331	93	238
Multnomah	776	131	645
Polk	37	29	8
Washington	612	276	336
Yamhill	89	45	44
Nonmetropolitan Counties			
Baker	40	31	9
Clatsop	72	25	47
Coos	89	60	29
Crook	61	37	24
Curry	45	20	25
Douglas	136	65	71
Gilliam	9	8	1
Harney	24	17	7
Hood River	47	20	27
Jefferson	39	17	22
Klamath	99	34	65
Lake	21	20	1
Lincoln	89	29	60
Malheur	64	50	14
Morrow	39	27	12
Sherman	7	6	1
Tillamook	53	45	8
Umatilla	91	26	65
Union	34	16	18
Wallowa	13	5	8
Wasco	28	14	14
Wheeler	5	4	1
PENNSYLVANIA			
Metropolitan Counties			
Adams	17	13	4
Allegheny	188	155	33
Allegheny County Police Department	232	215	17
Beaver	23	18	5
Berks	108	93	15
Blair	27	24	3
Bucks	78	65	13
Butler	30	27	3
Centre	23	19	4
Chester	81	63	18
Cumberland	39	32	7
Erie	45	38	7
Franklin	34	23	11
Lancaster	64	55	9
Mercer	18	15	3
Monroe	38	26	12
Montgomery	136	113	23
Northampton	62	57	5
Pike	24	20	4
Washington	35	32	3
Wyoming	6	4	2
York	113	103	10
Nonmetropolitan Counties			
Bradford	12	10	2
Clarion	9	6	3
Elk	6	6	0
Greene	19	9	10
Indiana	25	22	3
Jefferson	10	8	2
Juniata	6	5	1
Lawrence	21	16	5
Northumberland	12	9	3
Schuylkill	21	17	4
Snyder	8	7	1
Tioga	10	8	2
Union	9	8	1
Warren	14	12	2
Wayne	17	14	3

Table 80. Full-Time Law Enforcement Employees, by Selected State Metropolitan and Nonmetropolitan Counties, 2020—Continued

(Number.)

State/county	Law enforcement employees	Officers	Civilians
SOUTH CAROLINA			
Metropolitan Counties			
Aiken	245	137	108
Anderson	313	169	144
Beaufort	308	221	87
Berkeley	213	180	33
Calhoun	25	22	3
Charleston	698	272	426
Chester	114	52	62
Clarendon	76	73	3
Darlington	111	68	43
Dorchester	273	147	126
Edgefield	62	34	28
Fairfield	56	48	8
Florence	256	216	40
Greenville	575	476	99
Horry	364	81	283
Horry County Police Department	286	260	26
Kershaw	80	69	11
Lancaster	188	130	58
Laurens	116	60	56
Lexington	434	287	147
Pickens	172	149	23
Richland	712	610	102
Saluda	56	23	33
Spartanburg	369	339	30
Sumter	194	106	88
York	256	161	95
Nonmetropolitan Counties			
Allendale	15	13	2
Bamberg	11	11	0
Barnwell	84	31	53
Cherokee	116	62	54
Chesterfield	70	50	20
Colleton	107	53	54
Dillon	47	37	10
Georgetown	168	99	69
Greenwood	138	67	71
Hampton	51	34	17
Lee	28	22	6
Marion	78	41	37
McCormick	38	19	19
Newberry	69	51	18
Oconee	188	106	82
Orangeburg	110	84	26
Union	30	28	2
SOUTH DAKOTA			
Metropolitan Counties			
Lincoln	29	25	4
McCook	9	8	1
Meade	50	18	32
Minnehaha	250	95	155
Pennington	431	99	332
Turner	11	9	2
Union	33	23	10
Nonmetropolitan Counties			
Aurora	4	3	1
Beadle	21	5	16
Bennett	6	3	3
Bon Homme	8	3	5
Brookings	49	17	32
Brown	70	15	55
Brule	5	4	1
Buffalo	1	1	0
Butte	16	6	10
Campbell	3	3	0
Charles Mix	23	8	15
Clark	3	3	0
Clay	16	8	8
Codington	13	10	3
Corson	5	5	0
Custer	13	12	1
Davison	8	6	2
Day	9	4	5
Deuel	6	5	1
Dewey	4	4	0
Douglas	4	4	0
Edmunds	9	4	5

Table 80. Full-Time Law Enforcement Employees, by Selected State Metropolitan and Nonmetropolitan Counties, 2020—Continued

(Number.)

State/county	Law enforcement employees	Officers	Civilians
Fall River	17	10	7
Faulk	17	4	13
Grant	11	5	6
Gregory	5	4	1
Haakon	2	2	0
Hamlin	6	6	0
Hand	4	3	1
Hanson	3	3	0
Harding	3	2	1
Hughes	48	6	42
Hutchinson	4	3	1
Hyde	2	2	0
Jackson	3	2	1
Jerauld	4	4	0
Jones	2	2	0
Kingsbury	6	5	1
Lake	8	8	0
Lawrence	42	19	23
Lyman	4	3	1
Marshall	11	6	5
McPherson	4	4	0
Mellette	5	4	1
Miner	4	3	1
Moody	10	6	4
Oglala Lakota	1	1	0
Perkins	8	7	1
Potter	2	1	1
Roberts	32	5	27
Sanborn	4	3	1
Spink	14	9	5
Stanley	7	6	1
Sully	3	3	0
Tripp	4	3	1
Walworth	10	3	7
Yankton	37	35	2
Ziebach	3	3	0
TENNESSEE			
Metropolitan Counties			
Anderson	186	71	115
Blount	307	183	124
Bradley	214	110	104
Campbell	75	33	42
Cannon	42	19	23
Carter	156	93	63
Cheatham	91	46	45
Chester	44	17	27
Crockett	36	14	22
Dickson	139	59	80
Fayette	84	45	39
Gibson	74	34	40
Grainger	46	25	21
Hamblen	103	42	61
Hamilton	412	171	241
Hartsville/Trousdale	29	22	7
Hawkins	116	69	47
Jefferson	102	60	42
Knox	991	400	591
Loudon	106	54	52
Macon	64	34	30
Madison	271	122	149
Marion	65	35	30
Maury	166	88	78
Montgomery	397	134	263
Morgan	51	26	25
Polk	64	27	37
Roane	85	45	40
Robertson	168	73	95
Rutherford	480	240	240
Sequatchie	47	20	27
Shelby	1,793	658	1,135
Smith	44	32	12
Stewart	61	24	37
Sullivan	322	145	177
Sumner	289	124	165
Tipton	106	60	46
Unicoi	61	27	34
Union	62	36	26
Washington	206	94	112
Williamson	294	191	103
Nonmetropolitan Counties			
Bedford	103	49	54
Benton	59	21	38

Table 80. Full-Time Law Enforcement Employees, by Selected State Metropolitan and Nonmetropolitan Counties, 2020—Continued

(Number.)

State/county	Law enforcement employees	Officers	Civilians
Bledsoe	39	13	26
Carroll	73	29	44
Claiborne	96	46	50
Clay	22	13	9
Cocke	88	46	42
Coffee	120	51	69
Cumberland	115	58	57
Decatur	34	15	19
DeKalb	51	28	23
Dyer	105	41	64
Fentress	44	19	25
Franklin	79	44	35
Giles	68	39	29
Greene	161	69	92
Grundy	41	18	23
Hancock	30	10	20
Hardeman	71	29	42
Hardin	55	27	28
Haywood	45	21	24
Henderson	71	31	40
Henry	68	32	36
Hickman	51	30	21
Houston	26	10	16
Humphreys	49	26	23
Jackson	35	15	20
Johnson	47	22	25
Lake	14	7	7
Lauderdale	56	18	38
Lawrence	93	54	39
Lewis	34	17	17
Lincoln	84	41	43
Marshall	53	27	26
McMinn	90	31	59
McNairy	41	19	22
Meigs	37	18	19
Monroe	59	49	10
Moore	30	17	13
Obion	66	35	31
Overton	61	27	34
Perry	32	14	18
Pickett	16	11	5
Putnam	164	79	85
Rhea	88	37	51
Scott	68	28	40
Sevier	212	106	106
Van Buren	21	7	14
Warren	113	55	58
Wayne	53	23	30
Weakley	47	26	21
White	79	33	46
TEXAS			
Metropolitan Counties			
Armstrong	6	2	4
Austin	72	35	37
Bandera	70	32	38
Bastrop	200	82	118
Bell	355	101	254
Bexar	1,699	580	1,119
Bowie	44	37	7
Brazoria	358	157	201
Brazos	252	103	149
Burleson	51	22	29
Caldwell	104	36	68
Callahan	15	6	9
Cameron	457	105	352
Carson	23	9	14
Chambers	123	62	61
Clay	27	14	13
Collin	535	164	371
Comal	370	177	193
Coryell	32	31	1
Crosby	15	6	9
Dallas	2,058	400	1,658
Denton	623	189	434
Ector	166	95	71
Ellis	229	87	142
El Paso	853	240	613
Falls	31	12	19
Fort Bend	791	567	224
Galveston	456	326	130
Goliad	29	15	14
Grayson	179	65	114
Gregg	251	104	147

Table 80. Full-Time Law Enforcement Employees, by Selected State Metropolitan and Nonmetropolitan Counties, 2020—Continued

(Number.)

State/county	Law enforcement employees	Officers	Civilians
Guadalupe	233	104	129
Hardin	77	36	41
Harris	5,114	2,295	2,819
Harrison	107	52	55
Hays	402	179	223
Hidalgo	806	276	530
Hudspeth	34	16	18
Hunt	143	49	94
Irion	11	6	5
Jefferson	397	136	261
Johnson	122	83	39
Jones	32	9	23
Kaufman	212	91	121
Kendall	99	51	48
Lampasas	32	14	18
Liberty	113	69	44
Lubbock	489	199	290
Lynn	21	7	14
Martin	18	8	10
McLennan	470	109	361
Medina	82	42	40
Midland	155	79	76
Montgomery	906	511	395
Nueces	267	44	223
Orange	133	60	73
Parker	134	97	37
Potter	208	95	113
Randall	217	92	125
Robertson	40	14	26
Rockwall	127	48	79
Rusk	70	36	34
San Patricio	98	55	43
Smith	352	164	188
Sterling	5	5	0
Tarrant	1,451	356	1,095
Taylor	243	70	173
Tom Green	196	74	122
Travis	1,645	348	1,297
Upshur	88	47	41
Victoria	202	115	87
Webb	324	143	181
Wichita	190	61	129
Williamson	535	251	284
Wilson	80	37	43
Wise	137	61	76
Nonmetropolitan Counties			
Anderson	69	33	36
Andrews	44	15	29
Angelina	112	49	63
Aransas	70	24	46
Bailey	23	8	15
Baylor	9	4	5
Bee	76	23	53
Blanco	36	17	19
Borden	4	3	1
Brewster	36	18	18
Briscoe	4	4	0
Brooks	42	18	24
Brown	71	32	39
Burnet	153	54	99
Calhoun	68	29	39
Camp	20	9	11
Cass	48	21	27
Castro	23	6	17
Cherokee	68	34	34
Childress	16	4	12
Cochran	14	7	7
Coke	6	5	1
Collingsworth	14	4	10
Colorado	52	23	29
Comanche	33	12	21
Concho	14	7	7
Cooke	87	33	54
Cottle	1	1	0
Crane	15	8	7
Crockett	16	7	9
Culberson	23	11	12
Dallam	7	6	1
Dawson	22	9	13
Deaf Smith	35	12	23
Delta	22	10	12
DeWitt	53	19	34

Table 80. Full-Time Law Enforcement Employees, by Selected State Metropolitan and Nonmetropolitan Counties, 2020—Continued

(Number.)

State/county	Law enforcement employees	Officers	Civilians
Dickens	7	3	4
Dimmit	67	32	35
Donley	10	5	5
Duval	33	15	18
Edwards	18	5	13
Erath	68	26	42
Fannin	27	15	12
Floyd	10	6	4
Franklin	29	28	1
Freestone	39	18	21
Frio	30	23	7
Gaines	40	18	22
Gillespie	55	33	22
Glasscock	5	4	1
Gonzales	56	20	36
Gray	41	14	27
Grimes	57	31	26
Hamilton	20	10	10
Hansford	13	7	6
Henderson	148	63	85
Hill	79	33	46
Hood	150	55	95
Hopkins	69	26	43
Houston	51	22	29
Howard	64	24	40
Hutchinson	36	14	22
Jack	36	20	16
Jackson	39	16	23
Jasper	48	21	27
Jeff Davis	6	5	1
Jim Hogg	38	15	23
Jim Wells	39	30	9
Karnes	64	31	33
Kenedy	17	11	6
Kent	7	2	5
Kerr	111	48	63
Kimble	13	8	5
King	2	2	0
Kinney	27	20	7
Kleberg	74	26	48
Lamar	75	28	47
Lamb	29	11	18
La Salle	116	21	95
Lavaca	35	15	20
Lee	38	14	24
Leon	46	25	21
Limestone	66	20	46
Llano	49	24	25
Loving	10	7	3
Madison	33	11	22
Marion	24	11	13
Mason	12	6	6
Matagorda	74	70	4
Maverick	91	77	14
McCulloch	8	7	1
McMullen	12	11	1
Menard	11	6	5
Milam	72	24	48
Mills	19	7	12
Montague	32	12	20
Moore	52	20	32
Morris	21	9	12
Motley	1	1	0
Nacogdoches	84	39	45
Navarro	127	42	85
Newton	15	15	0
Nolan	42	16	26
Palo Pinto	56	24	32
Panola	68	41	27
Parmer	20	7	13
Pecos	45	24	21
Polk	109	49	60
Presidio	31	6	25
Rains	35	26	9
Reagan	29	14	15
Real	9	5	4
Red River	35	13	22
Reeves	63	29	34
Refugio	49	18	31
Runnels	30	6	24
Sabine	19	9	10
San Augustine	20	9	11
San Jacinto	66	31	35

Table 80. Full-Time Law Enforcement Employees, by Selected State Metropolitan and Nonmetropolitan Counties, 2020—Continued

(Number.)

State/county	Law enforcement employees	Officers	Civilians
San Saba	5	5	0
Schleicher	9	3	6
Shelby	34	14	20
Somervell	45	23	22
Starr	114	49	65
Sutton	17	7	10
Terrell	7	4	3
Terry	33	10	23
Titus	59	22	37
Trinity	17	15	2
Upton	22	11	11
Uvalde	73	25	48
Val Verde	68	43	25
Van Zandt	64	30	34
Walker	79	40	39
Ward	40	17	23
Washington	60	33	27
Wharton	78	45	33
Wilbarger	18	8	10
Winkler	29	29	0
Yoakum	23	22	1
Young	36	10	26
Zapata	79	69	10
Zavala	41	21	20
UTAH			
Metropolitan Counties			
Box Elder	79	22	57
Cache	144	49	95
Davis	319	90	229
Juab	29	17	12
Morgan	15	13	2
Salt Lake County Unified Police Department	444	368	76
Tooele	89	25	64
Utah	407	166	241
Washington	162	44	118
Nonmetropolitan Counties			
Beaver	74	25	49
Carbon	47	26	21
Daggett	5	4	1
Duchesne	69	21	48
Emery	38	30	8
Garfield	32	15	17
Grand	34	22	12
Iron	84	33	51
Kane	54	24	30
Millard	58	31	27
Piute	4	3	1
Rich	10	4	6
San Juan	34	16	18
Sanpete	62	26	36
Sevier	60	23	37
Summit	105	66	39
Uintah	95	29	66
Wasatch	64	33	31
Wayne	7	6	1
VERMONT			
Metropolitan Counties			
Chittenden	18	15	3
Franklin	12	12	0
Grand Isle	1	1	0
Nonmetropolitan Counties			
Addison	20	13	7
Bennington	14	11	3
Caledonia	8	7	1
Essex	4	4	0
Lamoille	26	14	12
Orange	13	8	5
Orleans	24	22	2
Rutland	22	18	4
Washington	9	7	2
Windham	18	12	6
Windsor	16	14	2
VIRGINIA			
Metropolitan Counties			
Albemarle County Police Department	177	146	31
Amelia	30	19	11
Amherst	51	44	7
Appomattox	23	21	2

Table 80. Full-Time Law Enforcement Employees, by Selected State Metropolitan and Nonmetropolitan Counties, 2020—Continued

(Number.)

State/county	Law enforcement employees	Officers	Civilians
Arlington County Police Department	446	342	104
Augusta	84	74	10
Bedford	92	84	8
Botetourt	118	99	19
Campbell	69	64	5
Charles City	19	13	6
Chesterfield County Police Department	644	523	121
Clarke	28	15	13
Craig	13	8	5
Culpeper	126	113	13
Dinwiddie	63	59	4
Fairfax County Police Department	1,713	1,463	250
Fauquier	181	142	39
Fluvanna	51	37	14
Franklin	104	79	25
Frederick	148	138	10
Giles	38	26	12
Gloucester	105	84	21
Goochland	54	38	16
Greene	34	25	9
Hanover	276	257	19
Henrico County Police Department	829	655	174
Isle of Wight	53	48	5
James City County Police Department	108	102	6
King and Queen	19	12	7
King William	33	21	12
Loudoun	744	575	169
Madison	34	22	12
Mathews	19	11	8
Montgomery	124	118	6
Nelson	25	21	4
New Kent	51	38	13
Powhatan	45	41	4
Prince George County Police Department	73	54	19
Prince William County Police Department	826	659	167
Pulaski	55	53	2
Rappahannock	22	16	6
Roanoke County Police Department	146	132	14
Rockingham	77	62	15
Scott	36	31	5
Southampton	79	64	15
Spotsylvania	310	239	71
Stafford	258	192	66
Sussex	45	21	24
Warren	85	62	23
Washington	85	68	17
York	97	90	7
Nonmetropolitan Counties			
Accomack	63	56	7
Alleghany	64	47	17
Bath	22	15	7
Bland	20	11	9
Brunswick	48	34	14
Buchanan	48	35	13
Buckingham	25	18	7
Caroline	69	47	22
Carroll	43	38	5
Charlotte	38	17	21
Cumberland	24	17	7
Dickenson	41	27	14
Essex	21	15	6
Floyd	36	26	10
Grayson	32	26	6
Greensville	31	20	11
Halifax	45	42	3
Henry	133	120	13
Highland	11	7	4
King George	53	37	16
Lancaster	40	31	9
Lee	36	25	11
Louisa	68	49	19
Lunenburg	15	9	6
Mecklenburg	54	48	6
Middlesex	26	18	8
Northampton	79	64	15
Northumberland	41	27	14
Nottoway	25	16	9
Orange	44	41	3
Page	63	55	8
Patrick	69	53	16
Pittsylvania	127	111	16
Prince Edward	33	26	7

Table 80. Full-Time Law Enforcement Employees, by Selected State Metropolitan and Nonmetropolitan Counties, 2020—Continued

(Number.)

State/county	Law enforcement employees	Officers	Civilians
Richmond	22	15	7
Rockbridge	39	35	4
Russell	52	36	16
Shenandoah	69	63	6
Smyth	56	43	13
Surry	24	15	9
Tazewell	76	53	23
Westmoreland	48	31	17
Wise	70	54	16
Wythe	48	39	9
WASHINGTON			
Metropolitan Counties			
Asotin	31	13	18
Benton	81	68	13
Chelan	68	52	16
Clark	221	132	89
Cowlitz	64	40	24
Douglas	35	29	6
Franklin	84	27	57
King	253	199	54
Kitsap	252	121	131
Pierce	331	272	59
Skagit	136	56	80
Skamania	34	31	3
Snohomish	355	288	67
Spokane	142	118	24
Stevens	64	31	33
Thurston	233	89	144
Walla Walla	36	28	8
Whatcom	186	86	100
Yakima	83	58	25
Nonmetropolitan Counties			
Adams	36	16	20
Clallam	46	38	8
Columbia	8	8	0
Ferry	24	7	17
Garfield	13	6	7
Grant	125	55	70
Grays Harbor	83	60	23
Island	75	42	33
Jefferson	45	23	22
Kittitas	88	38	50
Klickitat	40	19	21
Lewis	103	41	62
Lincoln	28	15	13
Mason	92	48	44
Okanogan	83	30	53
Pacific	45	16	29
Pend Oreille	37	14	23
San Juan	34	20	14
Wahkiakum	20	9	11
Whitman	36	18	18
WEST VIRGINIA			
Metropolitan Counties			
Berkeley	67	60	7
Boone	20	18	2
Brooke	19	19	0
Cabell	55	43	12
Clay	5	5	0
Fayette	44	36	8
Hampshire	25	19	6
Hancock	34	30	4
Jackson	25	17	8
Jefferson	37	31	6
Kanawha	134	103	31
Lincoln	7	6	1
Marshall	33	30	3
Mineral	26	20	6
Monongalia	51	47	4
Morgan	13	12	1
Ohio	38	36	2
Preston	23	20	3
Putnam	68	42	26
Raleigh	75	57	18
Wayne	34	23	11
Wirt	5	3	2
Wood	61	39	22
Nonmetropolitan Counties			
Barbour	11	8	3
Braxton	11	9	2

Table 80. Full-Time Law Enforcement Employees, by Selected State Metropolitan and Nonmetropolitan Counties, 2020—Continued

(Number.)

State/county	Law enforcement employees	Officers	Civilians
Calhoun	6	4	2
Doddridge	10	9	1
Gilmer	6	4	2
Grant	15	12	3
Greenbrier	38	27	11
Hardy	13	11	2
Harrison	57	53	4
Lewis	14	12	2
Logan	25	23	2
Marion	46	29	17
Mason	20	18	2
McDowell	13	11	2
Mercer	36	29	7
Mingo	22	20	2
Monroe	13	10	3
Nicholas	20	20	0
Pendleton	3	3	0
Pleasants	6	5	1
Pocahontas	10	7	3
Randolph	22	15	7
Ritchie	15	10	5
Roane	8	7	1
Summers	8	7	1
Taylor	17	9	8
Tucker	5	5	0
Tyler	18	12	6
Upshur	15	12	3
Webster	6	3	3
Wetzel	17	14	3
Wyoming	18	18	0
WISCONSIN			
Metropolitan Counties			
Brown	368	164	204
Calumet	55	28	27
Chippewa	71	30	41
Columbia	105	43	62
Dane	583	470	113
Douglas	73	29	44
Eau Claire	73	29	44
Fond du Lac	130	60	70
Green	56	43	13
Iowa	40	21	19
Kenosha	321	114	207
Kewaunee	36	34	2
La Crosse	86	40	46
Lincoln	96	31	65
Marathon	189	74	115
Milwaukee	781	326	455
Oconto	67	29	38
Outagamie	192	79	113
Ozaukee	106	77	29
Pierce	59	34	25
Racine	275	158	117
Rock	125	96	29
Sheboygan	190	73	117
St. Croix	111	82	29
Washington	173	76	97
Waukesha	341	163	178
Winnebago	231	137	94
Nonmetropolitan Counties			
Adams	61	30	31
Ashland	47	37	10
Barron	73	29	44
Bayfield	43	20	23
Buffalo	26	12	14
Burnett	35	35	0
Clark	39	28	11
Crawford	29	22	7
Dodge	157	63	94
Door	56	52	4
Dunn	30	26	4
Florence	21	12	9
Forest	45	21	24
Grant	56	29	27
Green Lake	44	20	24
Iron	21	10	11
Jackson	44	21	23
Jefferson	124	96	28
Juneau	55	41	14
Lafayette	29	28	1
Langlade	46	19	27
Manitowoc	99	62	37

Table 80. Full-Time Law Enforcement Employees, by Selected State Metropolitan and Nonmetropolitan Counties, 2020—Continued

(Number.)

State/county	Law enforcement employees	Officers	Civilians
Marinette	63	33	30
Menominee	16	9	7
Monroe	58	28	30
Oneida	83	34	49
Pepin	19	8	11
Polk	75	29	46
Portage	102	47	55
Price	30	19	11
Richland	34	34	0
Rusk	30	27	3
Sauk	129	37	92
Sawyer	49	28	21
Shawano	106	38	68
Taylor	40	19	21
Trempealeau	61	30	31
Vernon	51	23	28
Vilas	71	36	35
Walworth	201	81	120
Washburn	34	17	17
Waupaca	106	50	56
Waushara	58	28	30
Wood	72	42	30
WYOMING			
Metropolitan Counties			
Laramie	181	44	137
Natrona	146	107	39
Nonmetropolitan Counties			
Albany	50	27	23
Big Horn	45	17	28
Campbell	152	58	94
Carbon	52	18	34
Converse	45	24	21
Crook	22	15	7
Fremont	95	33	62
Goshen	26	9	17
Hot Springs	15	5	10
Johnson	32	29	3
Lincoln	48	22	26
Niobrara	16	4	12
Park	55	20	35
Platte	38	25	13
Sheridan	56	19	37
Sublette	69	36	33
Sweetwater	97	39	58
Uinta	48	21	27
Washakie	21	7	14
Weston	8	8	0

1 The employee data presented in this table for Mecklenburg represent only the Mecklenburg County Sheriff's Office employees and exclude the Charlotte-Mecklenburg Police Department employees.

Table 81. Full-Time Law Enforcement Employees, by Selected State and Agency, 2020

(Number.)

State/agency	Law enforcement employees	Officers	Civilians
ALABAMA			
State Agencies			
Alabama Department of Mental Health	4	3	1
Alabama Law Enforcement Agency	1,454	862	592
Department of Corrections Investigations and Intelligence Division	121	101	20
State Fire Marshal	42	34	8
Tannehill Ironworks Historic State Park	1	1	0
Taylor Hardin Secure Medical Facility	17	16	1
Tribal Agencies			
Poarch Creek Tribal	54	46	8
Other Agencies			
Huntsville International Airport	18	17	1
Mobile Regional Airport	22	18	4
Norfolk Southern Railway	6	6	0
Trussville Fire Department Fire and Explosion Investigation Unit	3	3	0
ALASKA			
Tribal Agencies			
Metlakatla Tribal	9	4	5
Other Agencies			
Fairbanks International Airport	30	23	7
Ted Stevens Anchorage International Airport	74	60	14
ARIZONA			
Tribal Agencies			
Ak-Chin Tribal	59	12	47
Cocopah Tribal	24	15	9
Colorado River Tribal	25	15	10
Hualapai Tribal	18	14	4
Navajo Nation	274	189	85
Salt River Tribal	162	122	40
San Carlos Apache	54	30	24
White Mountain Apache Tribal	49	26	23
Yavapai-Apache Nation	17	13	4
Yavapai-Prescott Tribal	14	11	3
Other Agencies			
Tucson Airport Authority	52	22	30
ARKANSAS			
State Agencies			
Camp Robinson	15	8	7
State Capitol Police	23	21	2
CALIFORNIA			
State Agencies			
Atascadero State Hospital	179	166	13
California State Fair	3	2	1
Coalinga State Hospital	263	245	18
Department of Parks and Recreation, Capital	569	516	53
Metropolitan State Hospital	143	131	12
Napa State Hospital	135	122	13
Patton State Hospital	114	97	17
Tribal Agencies			
Hoopa Valley Tribal	16	10	6
Table Mountain Rancheria	25	18	7
Other Agencies			
Baldwin Park Unified School District	14	8	6
Clovis Unified School District	15	14	1
East Bay Regional Park District	94	61	33
Fontana Unified School District	73	15	58
Kern High School District	35	30	5
Port of San Diego Harbor	161	132	29
San Bernardino Unified School District	85	25	60
San Francisco Bay Area Rapid Transit, Contra Costa County	352	222	130
Shasta County Marshal	25	21	4
Stockton Unified School District	46	33	13
Twin Rivers Unified School District	21	16	5
COLORADO			
State Agencies			
Colorado Bureau of Investigation	277	45	232
Colorado Mental Health Institute	115	18	97
Division of Gaming Criminal Enforcement and Investigations Section			
Cripple Creek	19	11	8
Golden	50	16	34
Tribal Agencies			
Southern Ute Tribal	41	20	21
Ute Mountain Tribal	10	5	5

Table 81. Full-Time Law Enforcement Employees, by Selected State and Agency, 2020—Continued

(Number.)

State/agency	Law enforcement employees	Officers	Civilians
Other Agencies			
All Crimes Enforcement Team	2	2	0
Southwest Drug Task Force	3	3	0
CONNECTICUT			
State Agencies			
Department of Energy and Environmental Protection	56	49	7
Department of Motor Vehicles	54	50	4
State Capitol Police	33	21	12
Tribal Agencies			
Mashantucket Pequot Tribal	35	25	10
Mohegan Tribal	27	26	1
Other Agencies			
Metropolitan Transportation Authority	42	42	0
DELAWARE			
State Agencies			
Alcohol and Tobacco Enforcement	14	13	1
Animal Welfare, New Castle County	29	22	7
Attorney General			
Kent County	87	11	76
New Castle County	335	31	304
Sussex County	65	2	63
Environmental Control	14	13	1
Fish and Wildlife	34	28	6
Park Rangers	22	21	1
River and Bay Authority	68	58	10
State Capitol Police	89	68	21
State Fire Marshal	50	20	30
Other Agencies			
Amtrak Police	462	403	59
Wilmington Fire Department	14	9	5
DISTRICT OF COLUMBIA			
Other Agencies			
District of Columbia Fire and Emergency Medical Services, Arson Investigation Unit	16	12	4
Metro Transit Police	493	408	85
FLORIDA			
State Agencies			
Capitol Police	85	66	19
Department of Corrections, Office of the Inspector General, Leon County	147	122	25
Department of Law Enforcement			
Duval County, Jacksonville	121	40	81
Escambia County, Pensacola	89	33	56
Hillsborough County, Tampa	168	57	111
Lee County, Fort Myers	85	38	47
Leon County, Tallahassee	948	109	839
Miami-Dade County, Miami	95	72	23
Orange County, Orlando	172	56	116
Division of Alcoholic Beverages and Tobacco, Leon County	155	89	66
Department of Investigative and Forensic Services, Leon County	293	228	65
Fish and Wildlife Conservation Commission, Leon County	962	793	169
Tribal Agencies			
Miccosukee Tribal	63	44	19
Seminole Tribal	201	132	69
Other Agencies			
Clay County School Board	45	44	1
Duval County Schools	155	97	58
Florida School for the Deaf and Blind	16	9	7
Jackson County School District	15	15	0
Jacksonville Aviation Authority	43	30	13
Lee County Port Authority	63	43	20
Melbourne International Airport	16	14	2
Miami-Dade County Public Schools	497	452	45
Northwest Florida Beaches International Airport	22	15	7
Palm Beach County School District	347	257	90
Sarasota County Schools	63	61	2
Sarasota-Manatee Airport Authority	12	11	1
Tampa International Airport	136	78	58
Volusia County Beach Safety	69	53	16
GEORGIA			
State Agencies			
Georgia Bureau of Investigation, Headquarters	4	4	0
Georgia Department of Transportation, Office of Investigations	6	5	1
Georgia Forestry Commission	178	67	111
Georgia Public Safety Training Center	28	19	9
Georgia World Congress	154	113	41
Ports Authority, Savannah	135	104	31
State Board of Workers Compensation Fraud Investigation Division	9	5	4

Table 81. Full-Time Law Enforcement Employees, by Selected State and Agency, 2020—Continued

(Number.)

State/agency	Law enforcement employees	Officers	Civilians
Other Agencies			
Albany-Dougherty Metropolitan Drug Squad	23	19	4
Atlanta Public Schools	82	80	2
Augusta Board of Education	35	31	4
Bibb County Board of Education	27	21	6
Chatham County Board of Education	96	56	40
Cherokee County Board of Education	25	21	4
Cherokee County Marshal	20	12	8
Cobb County Board of Education	70	67	3
DeKalb County School System	195	67	128
Decatur County Schools	6	5	1
Fayette County Marshal	6	4	2
Forsyth County Fire Investigation Unit	3	3	0
Fulton County Marshal	67	54	13
Fulton County School System	83	81	2
Glynn County School System	25	24	1
Gwinnett County Public Schools	108	98	10
Hall County Marshal	15	13	2
Metropolitan Atlanta Rapid Transit Authority	369	295	74
Muscogee County Schools	24	18	6
Paulding County Marshal	10	9	1
Richmond County Marshal	58	45	13
Stone Mountain Park	21	18	3
Washington County Board of Education	6	6	0
IDAHO			
State Agencies			
Idaho State Lottery Security Division	2	2	0
Tribal Agencies			
Coeur d'Alene Tribal	13	12	1
Fort Hall Tribal	28	14	14
Kootenai Tribal	2	2	0
ILLINOIS			
Other Agencies			
Crystal Lake Park District	1	1	0
Fox Valley Park District	3	2	1
Kane County Forest Preserve	6	6	0
McHenry County Conservation District	11	10	1
Pekin Park District	1	1	0
Rockford Park District	13	12	1
Springfield Park District	7	4	3
Terminal Railroad Association	6	6	0
INDIANA			
State Agencies			
Indiana State Excise Police	82	76	6
Other Agencies			
Indianapolis International Airport	40	39	1
KANSAS			
State Agencies			
Kansas Bureau of Investigation	318	91	227
Kansas Department of Wildlife and Parks	179	177	2
Kansas Lottery Security Division	6	4	2
Kansas Racing Commission, Security Division	68	48	20
Securities Office, Investigation Section	26	9	17
State Fire Marshal	12	11	1
Tribal Agencies			
Iowa Tribal	6	6	0
Kickapoo Tribal	2	2	0
Potawatomi Tribal	19	9	10
Sac and Fox Tribal	5	4	1
Other Agencies			
Blue Valley School District	11	10	1
El Dorado School District	2	2	0
Johnson County Park	30	28	2
Metropolitan Topeka Airport Authority	24	19	5
Shawnee Mission Public Schools	8	8	0
Topeka Fire Department Arson Investigation	3	2	1
Unified School District			
Auburn-Washburn	3	3	0
Bluestem	1	1	0
Goddard	5	5	0
Kansas City	42	30	12
Seaman	4	4	0
KENTUCKY			
State Agencies			
Department of Agriculture Animal Health Enforcement Division	4	4	0
Fish and Wildlife Enforcement	122	119	3
Kentucky Horse Park	9	9	0
Park Security	43	43	0

Table 81. Full-Time Law Enforcement Employees, by Selected State and Agency, 2020—Continued

(Number.)

State/agency	Law enforcement employees	Officers	Civilians
Other Agencies			
Barren County Drug Task Force	3	2	1
Bluegrass Narcotics Task Force	4	4	0
Clark County School System	10	10	0
Fayette County Schools	62	58	4
Greater Hardin County Narcotics Task Force	2	1	1
Jefferson County School District	21	14	7
Lake Cumberland Area Drug Enforcement Task Force	4	3	1
Louisville Regional Airport Authority	36	35	1
McCracken County Public Schools	7	7	0
Metcalfe County Schools	2	2	0
Northern Kentucky Drug Strike Force	3	2	1
Pennyrile Narcotics Task Force	3	2	1
South Central Kentucky Drug Task Force	8	7	1
Warren County Drug Task Force	3	2	1
Woodford County Public Schools	5	5	0
LOUISIANA			
Tribal Agencies			
Chitimacha Tribal	15	15	0
Tunica-Biloxi Tribal	13	12	1
MAINE			
State Agencies			
Bureau of Capitol Police	26	13	13
Drug Enforcement Agency	1	1	0
State Fire Marshal	32	16	16
Tribal Agencies			
Passamaquoddy Indian Township	15	6	9
Passamaquoddy Pleasant Point Tribal	5	5	0
Penobscot Nation	10	6	4
MARYLAND			
State Agencies			
Comptroller of the Treasury, Field Enforcement Division	51	22	29
Department of Public Safety and Correctional Services, Internal Investigation			
Division	89	47	42
General Services			
Annapolis, Anne Arundel County	59	36	23
Baltimore City	82	27	55
Natural Resources Police	324	267	57
State Fire Marshal	72	46	26
Transit Administration	233	168	65
Transportation Authority	574	428	146
Other Agencies			
Maryland-National Capital Park Police			
Montgomery County	113	90	23
Prince George's County	151	124	27
MASSACHUSETTS			
State Agencies			
Massachusetts Bay Transportation Authority, Suffolk County	234	225	9
Tribal Agencies			
Wampanoag Tribe of Gay Head	2	2	0
Other Agencies			
Massachusetts General Hospital	219	64	155
MICHIGAN			
State Agencies			
Department of Natural Resources Law Enforcement Division	262	235	27
Tribal Agencies			
Gun Lake Tribal	19	17	2
Little River Band of Ottawa Indians	14	14	0
Little Traverse Bay Bands of Odawa Indians	14	10	4
Nottawaseppi Huron Band of Potawatomi	20	19	1
Other Agencies			
Bishop International Airport	6	5	1
Capitol Region Airport Authority	15	8	7
Genesee County Parks and Recreation	8	8	0
Gerald R. Ford International Airport	18	16	2
Huron-Clinton Metropolitan Authority			
Hudson Mills Metropark	3	3	0
Kensington Metropark	9	9	0
Lower Huron Metropark	6	6	0
Stony Creek Metropark	10	10	0
Wayne County Airport	125	105	20
MINNESOTA			
State Agencies			
Bureau of Criminal Apprehension	418	75	343
Capitol Security, St. Paul	85	23	62

Table 81. Full-Time Law Enforcement Employees, by Selected State and Agency, 2020—Continued

(Number.)

State/agency	Law enforcement employees	Officers	Civilians
Tribal Agencies			
Fond du Lac Tribal	19	17	2
Mille Lacs Tribal	28	22	6
Upper Sioux Community	6	6	0
White Earth Tribal	32	24	8
Other Agencies			
Metropolitan Transit Commission	166	140	26
Minneapolis-St. Paul International Airport	156	90	66
Three Rivers Park District	12	11	1
MISSISSIPPI			
State Agencies			
State Capitol Police	38	35	3
Tribal Agencies			
Choctaw Tribal	38	35	3
Other Agencies			
Singing River Health System	54	31	23
MISSOURI			
State Agencies			
Department of Conservation	181	178	3
Department of Revenue, Compliance and Investigation Bureau	17	14	3
Department of Social Services, State Technical Assistance Team	23	15	8
Division of Alcohol and Tobacco Control	35	22	13
Gaming Commission, Enforcement Division	114	3	111
State Park Rangers	46	45	1
Other Agencies			
Clay County Drug Task Force	5	5	0
Clay County Park Authority	11	10	1
Jackson County Park Rangers	21	19	2
Lambert-St. Louis International Airport	71	61	10
Logan-Rogersville School District	2	2	0
Springfield-Branson Airport	17	12	5
Terminal Railroad	6	6	0
MONTANA			
State Agencies			
Gambling Investigations Bureau	45	19	26
Tribal Agencies			
Blackfeet Agency	34	25	9
Crow Agency	9	7	2
Fort Belknap Tribal	13	7	6
Fort Peck Assiniboine and Sioux Tribes	27	25	2
Northern Cheyenne Agency	9	7	2
Rocky Boy's Tribal	22	14	8
NEBRASKA			
Tribal Agencies			
Santee Tribal	5	5	0
Winnebago Tribal	8	4	4
NEVADA			
State Agencies			
Attorney General Investigations Division	335	50	285
Capitol Police	19	19	0
Department of Wildlife, Law Enforcement Division	46	34	12
State Fire Marshal	6	5	1
Tribal Agencies			
Eastern Nevada Agency	8	4	4
Ely Shoshone Tribal	2	2	0
Lovelock Paiute Tribal	3	3	0
Moapa Tribal	15	10	5
Pyramid Lake Tribal	11	10	1
Reno-Sparks Indian Colony	15	14	1
Walker River Tribal	5	5	0
Western Shoshone Tribal	2	2	0
Other Agencies			
Clark County School District	205	171	34
Las Vegas Fire and Rescue, Arson Bomb Unit	13	13	0
Reno Municipal Court Marshal	13	11	2
Reno Tahoe Airport Authority	24	23	1
Washoe County School District	44	36	8
NEW HAMPSHIRE			
State Agencies			
Liquor Commission	34	21	13
NEW JERSEY			
State Agencies			
Department of Corrections	7,935	5,936	1,999

Table 81. Full-Time Law Enforcement Employees, by Selected State and Agency, 2020—Continued

(Number.)

State/agency	Law enforcement employees	Officers	Civilians
Department of Human Services	78	61	17
Division of Fish and Wildlife	54	51	3
New Jersey Transit Police	322	260	62
Palisades Interstate Parkway	30	26	4
Port Authority of New York and New Jersey	2,382	2,205	177
State Park Police	83	81	2
Other Agencies			
Park Police			
Morris County	28	27	1
Union County	102	68	34
Prosecutor			
Atlantic County	157	72	85
Bergen County	256	102	154
Burlington County	127	43	84
Camden County	272	186	86
Cape May County	92	43	49
Cumberland County	109	38	71
Essex County	245	120	125
Gloucester County	108	38	70
Hudson County	251	97	154
Hunterdon County	46	24	22
Mercer County	185	64	121
Middlesex County	215	69	146
Monmouth County	281	76	205
Morris County	149	61	88
Ocean County	174	68	106
Passaic County	184	77	107
Salem County	60	21	39
Somerset County	134	55	79
Sussex County	56	37	19
Union County	179	75	104
Warren County	65	22	43
NEW MEXICO			
Tribal Agencies			
Acoma Tribal	21	9	12
Isleta Tribal	54	33	21
Jemez Pueblo	10	8	2
Jicarilla Apache Tribal	40	24	16
Laguna Tribal	38	27	11
Mescalero Tribal	17	11	6
Northern Pueblos Agency	9	8	1
Pojoaque Tribal	23	14	9
Ramah Navajo Tribal	20	8	12
Santa Ana Tribal	27	25	2
Santa Clara Pueblo	12	7	5
Southern Pueblos Agency	20	12	8
Taos Pueblo	10	7	3
Tesuque Pueblo	12	6	6
Zia Pueblo	6	5	1
Zuni Tribal	34	23	11
NEW YORK			
State Agencies			
State Park			
Allegany Region	14	11	3
Central Region	18	15	3
Finger Lakes Region	14	11	3
Genesee Region	16	14	2
Long Island Region	58	53	5
New York City Region	17	14	3
Niagara Region	31	30	1
Palisades Region	32	29	3
Saratoga/Capital Region	39	33	6
Taconic Region	16	15	1
Thousand Island Region	15	14	1
Tribal Agencies			
Oneida Indian Nation	42	36	6
St. Regis Tribal	35	30	5
Other Agencies			
New York City Department of Environmental Protection Police, Ashokan Precinct	267	235	32
New York City Metropolitan Transportation Authority	901	835	66
Niagara Frontier Transportation Authority	83	79	4
Onondaga County Parks	1	1	0
NORTH CAROLINA			
State Agencies			
Cherry Hospital	16	9	7
Department of Health and Human Resources	7	7	0
Department of Wildlife	208	197	11
Division of Alcohol Law Enforcement	108	97	11
Division of Marine Fisheries	60	51	9

Table 81. Full-Time Law Enforcement Employees, by Selected State and Agency, 2020—Continued

(Number.)

State/agency	Law enforcement employees	Officers	Civilians
North Carolina Arboretum	4	4	0
North Carolina State Bureau of Investigation	420	257	163
State Capitol Police	88	55	33
State Fairgrounds	5	1	4
State Park Rangers			
Carolina Beach	6	4	2
Carvers Creek	5	2	3
Chimney Rock	8	5	3
Cliffs of the Neuse	3	3	0
Crowders Mountain	7	7	0
Dismal Swamp	4	2	2
Elk Knob	5	3	2
Eno River	9	6	3
Falls Lake Recreation Area	12	12	0
Fort Fisher	4	4	0
Fort Macon	5	4	1
Goose Creek	8	4	4
Gorges	2	2	0
Grandfather Mountain	5	4	1
Hammocks Beach	4	4	0
Hanging Rock	6	6	0
Haw River	2	2	0
Jockey's Ridge	6	5	1
Jones Lake	5	4	1
Jordan Lake State Recreation Area	17	15	2
Kerr Lake	12	10	2
Lake James	5	5	0
Lake Norman	3	3	0
Lake Waccamaw	5	3	2
Lumber River	8	5	3
Mayo River	4	2	2
Medoc Mountain	2	2	0
Merchants Millpond	5	4	1
Morrow Mountain	5	5	0
Mount Mitchell	8	3	5
New River-Mount Jefferson	8	8	0
Pettigrew	5	3	2
Pilot Mountain	5	5	0
Raven Rock	5	2	3
Singletary Lake	5	2	3
South Mountains	9	8	1
Stone Mountain	6	6	0
Weymouth Woods/Sandhills Nature Preserve	5	3	2
William B. Umstead	6	6	0
Other Agencies			
Asheville Regional Airport	15	15	0
Beaufort County Alcoholic Beverage Control Enforcement	3	1	2
Moore County Schools	13	13	0
Nash County Alcoholic Beverage Control Enforcement	1	1	0
North Carolina General Assembly	39	22	17
North Carolina Museum of Art Park Police	5	5	0
North Carolina State Port Authority, Division [1]	13	12	1
Piedmont Triad International Airport	34	23	11
Raleigh-Durham International Airport	41	40	1
Triad Municipal Alcoholic Beverage Control Law Enforcement	5	5	0
University of North Carolina Hospitals	117	38	79
WakeMed Campus Police	91	48	43
Wilmington International Airport	6	1	5
NORTH DAKOTA			
Tribal Agencies			
Three Affiliated Tribes	40	31	9
Turtle Mountain Agency	* 36	21	15
OHIO			
State Agencies			
Ohio Department of Natural Resources	333	301	32
Other Agencies			
Clark County Park District	1	1	0
Hamilton County Park District	33	31	2
Preservation Parks of Delaware County	6	6	0
Sandusky County Park District	4	4	0
University Hospitals Portage Medical Center	7	7	0
Wood County Park District	6	6	0
OKLAHOMA			
State Agencies			
Capitol Park Police	62	9	53
State Bureau of Investigation	314	93	221
State Park Rangers	43	43	0
Tribal Agencies			
Absentee Shawnee Tribal	13	12	1

Table 81. Full-Time Law Enforcement Employees, by Selected State and Agency, 2020—Continued

(Number.)

State/agency	Law enforcement employees	Officers	Civilians
Anadarko Agency	12	7	5
Cherokee Nation	43	35	8
Chickasaw Nation	76	63	13
Citizen Potawatomi Nation	43	28	15
Comanche Nation	31	22	9
Concho Agency	7	7	0
Eastern Shawnee Tribal	17	16	1
Kaw Tribal	7	7	0
Kickapoo Tribal	14	13	1
Miami Agency	5	5	0
Miami Tribal	10	10	0
Muscogee Nation Tribal	66	55	11
Osage Nation	15	14	1
Otoe-Missouria Tribal	12	7	5
Pawnee Tribal	6	5	1
Ponca Tribal	6	6	0
Sac and Fox Tribal	10	10	0
Seminole Nation Lighthorse	10	9	1
Tonkawa Tribal	8	6	2
Wyandotte Nation	11	9	2
Other Agencies			
Beggs Public Schools	1	1	0
District 1 Narcotics Task Force	5	5	0
District 8 Narcotics Task Force	3	3	0
Jenks Public Schools	8	7	1
Lawton Public Schools	22	21	1
Muskogee City Schools	7	5	2
Putnam City Campus	19	12	7
Victory Life	1	1	0
OREGON			
State Agencies			
Liquor Commission			
Benton County	2	2	0
Clatsop County	2	1	1
Coos County	1	1	0
Deschutes County	8	7	1
Douglas County	2	1	1
Headquarters	3	1	2
Jackson County	20	17	3
Klamath County	1	1	0
Lane County	12	11	1
Lincoln County	2	1	1
Malheur County	4	4	0
Marion County	8	7	1
Multnomah County	30	29	1
Umatilla County	2	2	0
Tribal Agencies			
Coos, Lower Umpqua, and Siuslaw Tribal	5	4	1
Coquille Tribal	2	2	0
Grand Ronde Tribal	9	8	1
Other Agencies			
Hillsboro School District	1	1	0
Port of Portland	70	52	18
PENNSYLVANIA			
State Agencies			
Pennsylvania Fish and Boat Commission	99	88	11
State Capitol Police	108	100	8
State Park Rangers			
Bald Eagle	4	4	0
Beltzville	3	3	0
Bendigo	1	1	0
Black Moshannon	2	2	0
Caledonia	1	1	0
Chapman	1	1	0
Codorus	10	3	7
Colonel Denning	4	1	3
Cook Forest	6	6	0
Cowans Gap	2	2	0
Delaware Canal	5	5	0
Evansburg	3	3	0
Fort Washington	1	1	0
Frances Slocum	2	2	0
French Creek	5	5	0
Gifford Pinchot	4	2	2
Greenwood Furnace	6	2	4
Hickory Run	5	5	0
Hills Creek	2	2	0
Keystone	2	2	0
Kings Gap Environmental Education Center	1	1	0
Laurel Hill	5	5	0

Table 81. Full-Time Law Enforcement Employees, by Selected State and Agency, 2020—Continued

(Number.)

State/agency	Law enforcement employees	Officers	Civilians
Linn Run	1	1	0
Little Buffalo	2	2	0
Little Pine	1	1	0
Lyman Run	2	2	0
Moraine	6	6	0
Mount Pisgah	1	1	0
Neshaminy	3	3	0
Pine Grove Furnace	1	1	0
Point	2	2	0
Presque Isle	6	6	0
Prince Gallitzin	1	1	0
Pymatuning	3	3	0
Raccoon Creek	12	4	8
Raymond B. Winter	1	1	0
Ricketts Glen	4	4	0
Ryerson Station	4	1	3
Shawnee	1	1	0
Sinnemahoning	1	1	0
Sizerville	1	1	0
Tobyhanna	2	2	0
Tuscarora	3	3	0
Worlds End	7	2	5
Yellow Creek	1	1	0
Other Agencies			
Allegheny County Housing Authority	10	9	1
Allegheny County Port Authority	58	45	13
County Detective			
Beaver County	8	8	0
Bucks County	29	23	6
Butler County	4	4	0
Chester County	24	22	2
Dauphin County	12	10	2
Erie County	11	9	2
Lackawanna County	14	14	0
Lawrence County	8	7	1
Lebanon County	6	5	1
Luzerne County	13	13	0
McKean County	8	2	6
Montgomery County	54	39	15
Pike County	4	4	0
Schuylkill County	23	6	17
Warren County	5	3	2
Wayne County	3	3	0
Westmoreland County	59	14	45
Wyoming County	4	4	0
York County	19	16	3
Delaware County District Attorney, Criminal Investigation Division	51	38	13
Delaware County Park	74	73	1
Erie Municipal Airport Authority	4	4	0
Fort Indiantown Gap	23	18	5
Harrisburg International Airport	17	10	7
Lehigh Valley International Airport	11	11	0
Westmoreland County Park	35	34	1
Wyoming Area School District	1	1	0
RHODE ISLAND			
State Agencies			
Department of Environmental Management	42	32	10
T.F. Green Airport	33	26	7
Tribal Agencies			
Narragansett Tribal	3	3	0
SOUTH CAROLINA			
State Agencies			
Department of Mental Health	104	77	27
Department of Natural Resources			
Abbeville County	2	2	0
Aiken County	3	3	0
Allendale County	2	2	0
Anderson County	5	5	0
Bamberg County	2	2	0
Barnwell County	3	3	0
Beaufort County	6	6	0
Berkeley County	7	7	0
Calhoun County	4	4	0
Charleston County	34	34	0
Cherokee County	3	3	0
Chester County	2	2	0
Chesterfield County	3	3	0
Clarendon County	4	4	0
Colleton County	4	4	0
Darlington County	3	3	0
Dillon County	2	2	0

Table 81. Full-Time Law Enforcement Employees, by Selected State and Agency, 2020—Continued

(Number.)

State/agency	Law enforcement employees	Officers	Civilians
Dorchester County	3	3	0
Edgefield County	3	3	0
Fairfield County	2	2	0
Florence County	9	7	2
Georgetown County	6	6	0
Greenville County	2	2	0
Greenwood County	3	3	0
Hampton County	3	3	0
Horry County	7	7	0
Jasper County	4	4	0
Kershaw County	2	2	0
Lancaster County	3	3	0
Laurens County	5	5	0
Lee County	2	2	0
Lexington County	6	6	0
Marion County	3	3	0
Marlboro County	3	3	0
McCormick County	2	2	0
Newberry County	3	3	0
Oconee County	3	3	0
Orangeburg County	3	3	0
Pickens County	7	7	0
Richland County	48	47	1
Saluda County	32	3	29
Spartanburg County	4	4	0
Sumter County	3	3	0
Union County	2	2	0
Williamsburg County	6	6	0
York County	6	4	2
Department of Public Safety, Illegal Immigration Enforcement Unit	7	6	1
Forestry Commission			
Aiken County	1	1	0
Anderson County	2	1	1
Bamberg County	1	1	0
Berkeley County	1	1	0
Cherokee County	1	1	0
Chesterfield County	2	2	0
Colleton County	2	2	0
Darlington County	1	1	0
Dorchester County	1	1	0
Fairfield County	1	1	0
Florence County	1	1	0
Hampton County	2	1	1
Horry County	1	1	0
Kershaw County	2	2	0
Laurens County	1	1	0
Lexington County	3	3	0
Marlboro County	1	1	0
Newberry County	1	1	0
Oconee County	1	1	0
Orangeburg County	3	3	0
Pickens County	1	1	0
Richland County	3	3	0
Spartanburg County	1	1	0
Sumter County	2	2	0
Williamsburg County	1	1	0
Santee Cooper	9	8	1
South Carolina School for the Deaf and Blind	1	1	0
State Museum	4	1	3
State Ports Authority	89	33	56
State Transport Police			
Abbeville County	1	1	0
Aiken County	1	1	0
Barnwell County	1	1	0
Beaufort County	3	3	0
Berkeley County	1	1	0
Charleston County	1	1	0
Chester County	1	1	0
Chesterfield County	2	2	0
Colleton County	1	1	0
Darlington County	1	1	0
Dillon County	1	1	0
Dorchester County	6	5	1
Edgefield County	1	1	0
Florence County	5	4	1
Greenville County	3	3	0
Greenwood County	6	6	0
Hampton County	1	1	0
Horry County	1	1	0
Kershaw County	2	1	1
Laurens County	1	1	0
Lexington County	14	11	3
Marion County	3	3	0
Newberry County	2	2	0
Oconee County	2	2	0

Table 81. Full-Time Law Enforcement Employees, by Selected State and Agency, 2020—Continued

(Number.)

State/agency	Law enforcement employees	Officers	Civilians
Orangeburg County	2	1	1
Richland County	22	3	19
Saluda County	3	3	0
Spartanburg County	6	6	0
Sumter County	2	1	1
Williamsburg County	1	1	0
York County	4	4	0
United States Department of Energy Savannah River Plant	53	41	12
Other Agencies			
15th Circuit Drug Enforcement Unit	4	3	1
Charleston County Aviation Authority	50	36	14
Columbia Metropolitan Airport	16	16	0
Florence Regional Airport	3	3	0
Foxville and Northern Railroad	4	4	0
Greenville Hospital			
Greenville	29	29	0
Laurens	6	6	0
Oconee	6	6	0
Greenville-Spartanburg International Airport	18	17	1
Lexington County Medical Center	58	27	31
SOUTH DAKOTA			
State Agencies			
Division of Criminal Investigation	174	49	125
Tribal Agencies			
Crow Creek Tribal	13	8	5
Flandreau Santee Sioux Tribal	3	3	0
Lower Brule Tribal	13	8	5
Rosebud Tribal	44	31	13
TENNESSEE			
State Agencies			
Alcoholic Beverage Commission	74	44	30
Department of Agriculture, Agricultural Crime Unit	7	7	0
Department of Correction, Internal Affairs	81	37	44
State Park Rangers			
Bicentennial Capitol Mall	4	4	0
Big Hill Pond	2	2	0
Big Ridge	4	4	0
Bledsoe Creek	2	2	0
Booker T. Washington	4	4	0
Burgess Falls Natural Area	5	5	0
Cedars of Lebanon	5	5	0
Chickasaw	4	4	0
Cordell Hull Birthplace	2	2	0
Cove Lake	4	4	0
Cumberland Mountain	4	4	0
Cumberland Trail	10	10	0
Cummins Falls	4	4	0
David Crockett	4	4	0
Davy Crockett Birthplace	3	3	0
Dunbar Cave Natural Area	3	3	0
Edgar Evins	4	4	0
Fall Creek Falls	10	10	0
Fort Loudon State Historic Park	4	4	0
Fort Pillow State Historic Park	2	2	0
Frozen Head Natural Area	5	5	0
Harpeth Scenic Rivers	4	4	0
Harrison Bay	5	5	0
Henry Horton	10	8	2
Hiwassee/Ocoee State Scenic Rivers	7	7	0
Indian Mountain	2	2	0
Johnsonville State Historic Park	3	3	0
Long Hunter	4	4	0
Meeman-Shelby Forest	4	4	0
Montgomery Bell	6	6	0
Mousetail Landing	3	3	0
Natchez Trace	5	5	0
Nathan Bedford Forrest	3	3	0
Norris Dam	4	4	0
Old Stone Fort State Archaeological Park	1	1	0
Panther Creek	4	4	0
Paris Landing	5	5	0
Pickett	5	5	0
Pickwick Landing	5	5	0
Pinson Mounds State Archaeological Park	2	2	0
Radnor Lake Natural Area	6	6	0
Red Clay State Historic Park	2	2	0
Reelfoot Lake	4	4	0
Roan Mountain	4	4	0
Rock Island	5	5	0
Rocky Fork	1	1	0
Seven Islands Birding Park	2	2	0

Table 81. Full-Time Law Enforcement Employees, by Selected State and Agency, 2020—Continued

(Number.)

State/agency	Law enforcement employees	Officers	Civilians
Sgt. Alvin C. York	3	3	0
South Cumberland Recreation Area	10	10	0
Standing Stone	4	4	0
Sycamore Shoals State Historic Park	3	3	0
Tim's Ford	5	5	0
T.O. Fuller	3	3	0
Warrior's Path	5	5	0
TennCare Office of Inspector General	46	20	26
Tennessee Bureau of Investigation	587	388	199
Tennessee Department of Revenue, Special Investigations Unit	43	30	13
Wildlife Resources Agency			
Region 1	45	42	3
Region 2	60	56	4
Region 3	52	49	3
Region 4	52	48	4
Other Agencies			
Chattanooga Housing Authority	6	5	1
Chattanooga Metropolitan Airport	12	10	2
Dickson City Park Ranger Division	2	2	0
Drug Task Force	3	3	0
2nd Judicial District	3	3	0
3rd Judicial District	4	4	0
4th Judicial District	1	1	0
8th Judicial District	3	1	2
9th Judicial District	4	3	1
10th Judicial District	6	6	0
14th Judicial District	2	2	0
15th Judicial District	2	1	1
18th Judicial District	4	3	1
21st Judicial District	2	2	0
22nd Judicial District	1	1	0
23rd Judicial District	6	6	0
24th Judicial District	4	2	2
25th Judicial District	1	1	0
31st Judicial District	2	2	0
Knoxville Metropolitan Airport	45	26	19
Memphis-Shelby County Airport Authority	61	48	13
Metropolitan Nashville Park Police	17	17	0
Nashville International Airport	89	65	24
Tri-Cities Regional Airport	14	14	0
West Tennessee Violent Crime Task Force	7	6	1
TEXAS			
Tribal Agencies			
Ysleta del Sur Pueblo Tribal	19	17	2
Other Agencies			
Amarillo International Airport	13	13	0
Dallas-Fort Worth International Airport	221	208	13
Denton County Water District	17	16	1
Hospital District			
Dallas County	174	110	64
Tarrant County	72	46	26
Houston Metropolitan Transit Authority	283	200	83
Independent School District			
Alief	53	46	7
Alvin	41	33	8
Angleton	18	11	7
Aubrey	3	3	0
Austin	114	81	33
Barbers Hill	7	6	1
Bastrop	18	10	8
Bay City	10	9	1
Brownsboro	2	2	0
Brownsville	150	53	97
Calhoun County	3	3	0
Centerpoint	2	2	0
Columbia-Brazoria	5	5	0
Conroe	109	76	33
Corpus Christi	62	41	21
Corsicana	15	11	4
Duncanville	9	6	3
East Central	17	15	2
Ector County	29	27	2
Edinburg	112	84	28
El Paso	48	39	9
Floresville	7	6	1
Galveston	14	10	4
Gonzales	1	1	0
Hallsville	5	5	0
Houston	229	186	43
Humble	56	41	15
Hutto	6	6	0
Idalou	1	1	0

Table 81. Full-Time Law Enforcement Employees, by Selected State and Agency, 2020—Continued

(Number.)

State/agency	Law enforcement employees	Officers	Civilians
Jonesboro	1	1	0
Judson	22	21	1
Katy	140	65	75
Killeen	26	25	1
Klein	77	53	24
Lancaster	12	9	3
Laredo	113	37	76
Lufkin	16	11	5
Malakoff	3	3	0
Mansfield	63	55	8
McAllen	74	62	12
Midland	18	14	4
Northside	118	98	20
Pasadena	42	34	8
Pflugerville	27	25	2
Raymondville	7	6	1
Roma	10	9	1
Santa Fe	21	11	10
Santa Rosa	5	3	2
Sealy	4	4	0
Socorro	57	49	8
Spring Branch	54	42	12
Taft	2	2	0
Terrell	7	7	0
Trinity	4	4	0
United	233	91	142
Van Vleck	1	1	0
Vensus	1	1	0
Wharton	5	3	2
Port of Brownsville	30	13	17
Port of Houston Authority	51	37	14
UTAH			
State Agencies			
Parks and Recreation	59	58	1
Utah Tax Commission Motor Vehicle Division, Vehicle Investigation Section	31	18	13
Wildlife Resources	86	76	10
Tribal Agencies			
Uintah and Ouray Tribal	20	18	2
Other Agencies			
Cache-Rich Drug Task Force	5	4	1
Granite School District	31	24	7
Unified Fire Authority Investigations Bureau	7	6	1
Utah County Attorney, Investigations Division	5	5	0
Utah Transit Authority	93	72	21
VERMONT			
State Agencies			
Attorney General	81	3	78
Capitol Police	4	4	0
Department of Liquor Control, Division of Enforcement and Licensing	14	10	4
Department of Motor Vehicles	39	25	14
Fish and Wildlife Department, Law Enforcement Division	38	37	1
Secretary of State, Investigations Unit	7	5	2
VIRGINIA			
State Agencies			
Alcoholic Beverage Control Commission	221	91	130
Department of Conservation and Recreation	91	91	0
Department of Game and Inland Fisheries, Enforcement Division	167	147	20
Department of Motor Vehicles	87	76	11
Virginia Marine Resources Commission Law Enforcement Division	80	74	6
Virginia State Capitol	80	68	12
Other Agencies			
Norfolk Airport Authority	43	35	8
Port Authority, Norfolk	50	37	13
Reagan National Airport	279	221	58
Richmond International Airport	31	23	8
WASHINGTON			
State Agencies			
State Gambling Commission, Enforcement Unit	104	58	46
State Insurance Commissioner, Special Investigations Unit	10	8	2
Tribal Agencies			
Chehalis Tribal	31	14	17
Colville Tribal	34	22	12
Elwha Klallam Tribal	19	13	6
Jamestown S'Klallam Tribal	45	37	8
Kalispel Tribal	25	22	3
La Push Tribal	5	5	0
Lummi Tribal	21	19	2

Table 81. Full-Time Law Enforcement Employees, by Selected State and Agency, 2020—Continued

(Number.)

State/agency	Law enforcement employees	Officers	Civilians
Makah Tribal	17	9	8
Muckleshoot Tribal	14	12	2
Nisqually Tribal	24	21	3
Nooksack Tribal	9	9	0
Port Gamble S'Klallam Tribal	12	10	2
Puyallup Tribal	47	26	21
Quinault Indian Nation	19	10	9
Sauk-Suiattle Tribal	9	8	1
Shoalwater Bay Tribal	6	5	1
Skokomish Tribal	9	8	1
Snoqualmie Tribal	3	3	0
Spokane Agency	22	12	10
Squaxin Island Tribal	10	9	1
Stillaguamish Tribal	13	13	0
Suquamish Tribal	16	14	2
Swinomish Tribal	18	11	7
Tulalip Tribal	56	37	19
Upper Skagit Tribal	8	8	0
Yakama Nation	51	34	17
Other Agencies			
Port of Seattle	153	115	38
WEST VIRGINIA			
State Agencies			
Capitol Protective Services	47	26	21
Department of Natural Resources			
Barbour County	1	1	0
Berkeley County	2	2	0
Boone County	1	1	0
Braxton County	2	2	0
Brooke County	2	2	0
Cabell County	2	2	0
Calhoun County	2	2	0
Clay County	1	1	0
Doddridge County	2	2	0
Fayette County	2	2	0
Grant County	2	2	0
Greenbrier County	2	2	0
Hampshire County	7	6	1
Hancock County	1	1	0
Hardy County	2	2	0
Harrison County	1	1	0
Jackson County	2	2	0
Jefferson County	1	1	0
Kanawha County	19	14	5
Lewis County	1	1	0
Lincoln County	3	3	0
Logan County	3	3	0
Marion County	6	5	1
Marshall County	2	2	0
Mason County	2	2	0
McDowell County	2	2	0
Mercer County	2	2	0
Mineral County	1	1	0
Mingo County	2	2	0
Monongalia County	2	2	0
Monroe County	2	2	0
Morgan County	1	1	0
Nicholas County	2	2	0
Ohio County	1	1	0
Pendleton County	2	2	0
Pleasants County	1	1	0
Pocahontas County	2	2	0
Preston County	3	3	0
Putnam County	2	2	0
Raleigh County	6	5	1
Randolph County	3	3	0
Roane County	1	1	0
Summers County	3	3	0
Taylor County	1	1	0
Tucker County	1	1	0
Upshur County	5	4	1
Webster County	2	2	0
Wetzel County	1	1	0
Wirt County	1	1	0
Wood County	6	5	1
Wyoming County	1	1	0
State Fire Marshall, Kanawha County	47	31	16
Other Agencies			
Central West Virginia Drug Task Force	2	1	1
Eastern Panhandle Drug and Violent Crime Task Force	19	19	0
Greenbrier County Drug and Violent Crime Task Force	4	3	1
Hancock/Brooke/Weirton Drug Task Force	6	6	0

Table 81. Full-Time Law Enforcement Employees, by Selected State and Agency, 2020—Continued

(Number.)

State/agency	Law enforcement employees	Officers	Civilians
Harrison County Drug and Violent Crime Task Force	7	7	0
Huntington Drug and Violent Crime Task Force	4	3	1
Kanawha County Parks and Recreation	3	3	0
Logan County Drug and Violent Crime Task Force	3	2	1
Metropolitan Drug Enforcement Network Team	3	3	0
Mon Metro Drug Task Force	11	10	1
Ohio Valley Drug and Violent Crime Task Force	4	4	0
Parkersburg Narcotics and Violent Crime Task Force	8	8	0
Potomac Highlands Drug and Violent Crime Task Force	2	2	0
Southern Regional Drug and Violent Crime Task Force	9	8	1
Three Rivers Drug and Violent Crime Task Force	2	2	0
WISCONSIN			
State Agencies			
Capitol Police	48	37	11
Tribal Agencies			
Lac Courte Oreilles Tribal	10	8	2
Lac du Flambeau Tribal	12	10	2
Menominee Tribal	24	19	5
Oneida Tribal	30	21	9
St. Croix Tribal	11	8	3
WYOMING			
State Agencies			
Wyoming Division of Criminal Investigation	83	37	46
Wind River Agency	22	18	4
Tribal Agencies			
Wind River Agency	22	18	4
PUERTO RICO AND OTHER OUTLYING AREAS			
Puerto Rico	12,721	12,077	644

SECTION VI

HATE CRIMES

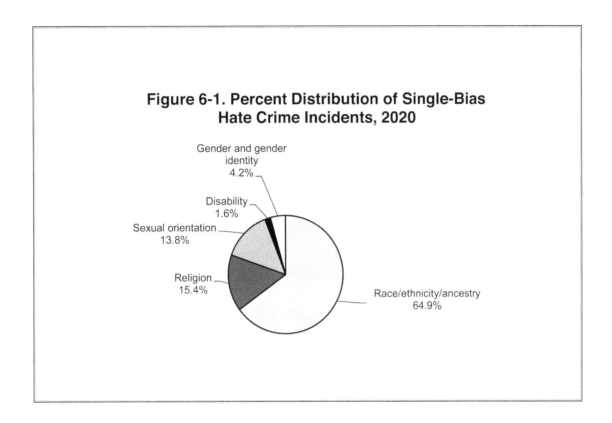

Figure 6-1. Percent Distribution of Single-Bias Hate Crime Incidents, 2020

Gender and gender identity
4.2%

Disability
1.6%

Sexual orientation
13.8%

Religion
15.4%

Race/ethnicity/ancestry
64.9%

The Federal Bureau of Investigation (FBI) began the procedures for implementing, collecting, and managing hate crime data after Congress passed the Hate Crime Statistics Act in 1990. This act required the collection of data "about crimes that manifest evidence of prejudice based on race, religion, sexual orientation, or ethnicity." Beginning in 2013, law enforcement agencies could submit hate crime data in accordance with a number of program modifications. In 1994, the Hate Crime Statistics Act was amended to include bias against persons with disabilities. The Church Arson Prevention Act, which was signed into law in July 1996, removed the sunset clause from the original statute and mandated that the collection of hate crime data become a permanent part of the UCR program. In 2009, Congress further amended the Hate Crime Statistics Act by passing the Matthew Shepard and James Byrd, Jr., Hate Crime Prevention Act. The amendment includes the collection of data for crimes motivated by bias against a particular gender and gender identity, as well as for crimes committed by, and crimes directed against, juveniles. In response to the Shepard/Byrd Act, the FBI modified its data collection so that reporting agencies could indicate whether hate crimes were committed by, or directed against, juveniles.

Definitions

Hate crimes include any crime motivated by bias against race, religion, sexual orientation, ethnicity/national origin, and/or disability. Because motivation is subjective, it is sometimes difficult to know with certainty whether a crime resulted from the offender's bias. Moreover, the presence of bias alone does not necessarily mean that a crime can be considered a hate crime. Only when law enforcement investigation reveals sufficient evidence to lead a reasonable and prudent person to conclude that the offender's actions were motivated, in whole or in part, by his or her bias should an incident be reported as a hate crime.

Data Collection

The UCR (Uniform Crime Reporting) program collects data about both single-bias and multiple-bias hate crimes. A single-bias incident is defined as an incident in which one or more offense types are motivated by the same bias. A multiple-bias incident is defined as an incident in which more than one offense type occurs and at least two offense types are motivated by different biases.

Important Note: Rape Data

In 2013, the UCR Program initiated the collection of rape data under a revised definition and removed the term "forcible" from the offense name. The UCR Program now defines rape as follows:

- **Rape (revised definition):** Penetration, no matter how slight, of the vagina or anus with any body part or object, or oral penetration by a sex organ of another person, without the consent of the victim. (This includes the offenses of rape, sodomy, and sexual assault with an object as converted from data submitted via the National Incident-Based Reporting System.)

- **Rape (legacy definition):** The carnal knowledge of a female forcibly and against her will.

In 2016, the FBI Director approved the recommendation to discontinue the reporting of rape data using the UCR legacy definition beginning in 2017.

The offenses of fondling, incest, and statutory rape are included in the crimes against persons, *other* category.

CRIMES AGAINST PERSONS, PROPERTY, OR SOCIETY

The UCR program's data collection guidelines stipulate that a hate crime may involve multiple offenses, victims, and offenders within one incident; therefore, the Hate Crime Statistics program is incident-based. According to UCR counting guidelines:

- One offense is counted for each victim in *crimes against persons*

- One offense is counted for each offense type in *crimes against property*

- One offense is counted for each offense type in *crimes against society*

VICTIMS

In the UCR program, the victim of a hate crime may be an individual, a business, an institution, or society as a whole.

OFFENDERS

According to the UCR program, the term *known offender* does not imply that the suspect's identity is known; rather, the term indicates that some aspect of the suspect was identified, thus distinguishing the suspect from an unknown offender. Law enforcement agencies specify the number of offenders, and when possible, the race of the offender or offenders as a group.

RACE/ETHNICITY

The UCR program uses the following racial designations in its Hate Crime Statistics program: White; Black; American Indian or Alaskan Native; Asian; Native Hawaiian or Other Pacific Islander; and Multiple Races, Group. In addition, the UCR program uses the ethnic designations of Hispanic or Latino and Not Hispanic or Latino.

The law enforcement agencies that voluntarily participate in the Hate Crime Statistics program collect details about an offender's bias motivation associated with 11 offense types already being reported to the UCR program: murder and nonnegligent manslaughter, rape, aggravated assault, simple assault, and intimidation (crimes against persons); and robbery, burglary, larceny-theft, motor vehicle theft, arson, and destruction/damage/vandalism (crimes against property). The law enforcement agencies that participate in the UCR program via the National Incident-Based Reporting System (NIBRS) collect data about additional offenses for *crimes against persons* and *crimes against property*. These data appear in the category of other. These agencies also collect hate crime data for the category called *crimes against society*, which includes drug or narcotic offenses, gambling offenses, prostitution offenses, and weapon law violations.

NATIONAL VOLUME AND PERCENT DISTRIBUTION

In 2020, 2,172 law enforcement agencies (out of 15,588 participating agencies) reported 8,263 hate crime incidents involving 11,129 offenses. Of these, 8,052 were single-bias offenses. An analysis of the single-bias incidents revealed that 64.9 percent were racially/ethnically/ancestrally motivated, 15.4 percent were motivated by religious bias, 13.8 percent resulted from sexual orientation bias, 4.2 percent were motivated by gender and gender-identity bias, and 1.6 percent were prompted by a disability bias. (Table 82)

The majority of the 5,227 hate crime incidents that were racially motivated resulted from an anti-Black or African American bias (54.9 percent) followed by an anti-White bias (16.6 percent). Bias against people of more than one race accounted for 4.0 percent of offenses, while anti-Asian bias accounted for 5.3 percent of racially motivated offenses, anti-Arab bias accounted for 1.4 percent of these offenses, anti–Native Hawaiian and Other Pacific Islander accounted for 0.3 percent of these offenses, and anti–American Indian or Alaska Native bias accounted for 1.8 percent of these offenses. Approximately 9.9 percent of crimes were classified as an anti–Hispanic or Latino bias. (Table 82)

Hate crimes motivated by religious bias accounted for 1,244 incidents reported by law enforcement. A breakdown of these offenses revealed 54.9 percent were motivated by anti-Jewish bias, 8.8 percent by anti-Islamic (Muslim) bias, 3.2 percent were anti–multiple religions or groups, 5.9 percent had an anti-Catholic bias, 2.4 percent were anti-Protestant, 3.5 percent were anti–Eastern Orthodox (Russian, Greek, or other), 4.0 percent were anti–other Christian, 0.6 percent were anti-atheism/agnosticism/etc., 0.6 percent were anti-Mormon, 0.9 percent were anti-Hindu, 0.7 percent were anti–Jehovah's Witness, 1.2 percent were anti-Buddhist, 7.2 percent were anti-Sikh, and the remainder, 6.1 percent, of offenses were based on a bias against other religions—those not specified. The 2020 numbers for incidents against Buddhists and Sikhs experienced a significant uptick from 2019. (Table 82)

In 2020, 1,110 incidents were committed on the basis of sexual orientation bias. Of the offenses based on sexual orientation, 27.6 percent were classified as having an anti–lesbian, gay, bisexual, or transgender (mixed group) bias; 60.6 percent were classified as having an anti-gay bias; 9.3 percent had an anti-lesbian bias; 1.5 percent had an anti-bisexual bias; and 1.0 percent had an anti-heterosexual bias. (Table 82)

Hate crime incidents committed based on disability totaled 130 incidents. The majority (59.2 percent) were classified as anti–mental disability, with the rest (40.8 percent) classified as anti–physical disability. (Table 82)

Of the 266 gender identity bias incidents reported, 213 (80.1 percent) were anti-transgender and 53 were anti–gender nonconforming. Of the 75 gender bias offenses reported, 50 were anti-female and 25 were anti-male. (Table 82)

CRIMES AGAINST PERSONS

Law enforcement agencies reported 5,201 hate crime incidents against persons in 2020. Approximately 42.1 percent involved intimidation, 35.9 percent involved simple assault, and 20.6 percent involved aggravated assault. There were 20 murders and 21 rapes. (Table 83)

CRIMES AGAINST PROPERTY

In 2020, hate crime incidents against property totaled 3,147. Approximately 74.1 percent of offenses involved destruction/damage or vandalism. The remaining 25.9 percent of crimes against property consisted of robbery, burglary, larceny-theft, motor vehicle theft, arson, and other crimes. (Table 83)

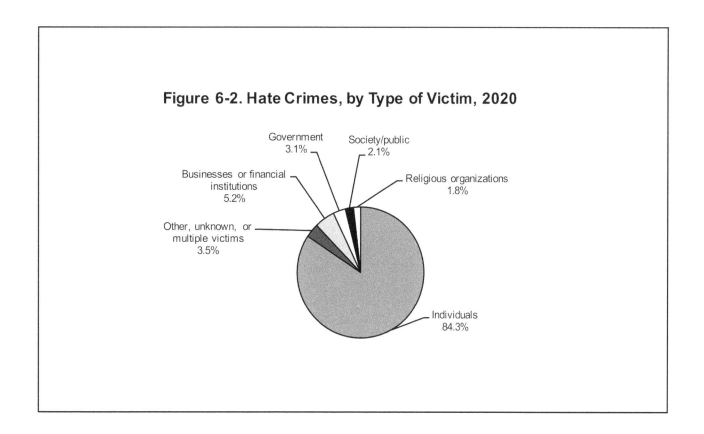

Figure 6-2. Hate Crimes, by Type of Victim, 2020

Table 82. Incidents, Offenses, Victims, and Known Offenders, by Bias Motivation, 2020

(Number.)

Bias motivation	Incidents	Offenses	Victims[1]	Known offenders[2]
Total	8,263	11,129	11,472	6,780
Single-Bias Incidents	8,052	10,790	11,126	6,657
Race/Ethnicity/Ancestry	5,227	6,677	6,880	4,339
Anti-White	869	1,048	1,082	825
Anti-Black or African American	2,871	3,819	3,915	2,302
Anti-American Indian or Alaska Native	96	103	108	74
Anti-Asian	279	330	342	239
Anti-Native Hawaiian or Other Pacific Islander	15	15	18	12
Anti-Multiple Races, Group	211	270	281	114
Anti-Arab	71	85	87	52
Anti-Hispanic or Latino	517	664	693	525
Anti-Other Race/Ethnicity/Ancestry	298	343	354	196
Religion	1,244	1,402	1,481	814
Anti-Jewish	683	794	831	401
Anti-Catholic	73	77	80	47
Anti-Protestant	30	31	32	26
Anti-Islamic (Muslim)	110	126	131	126
Anti-Other Religion	76	85	105	44
Anti-Multiple Religions, Group	40	44	49	19
Anti-Mormon	7	8	8	7
Anti-Jehovah's Witness	9	10	10	3
Anti-Eastern Orthodox (Russian, Greek, Other)	43	43	43	30
Anti-Other Christian	50	56	62	27
Anti-Buddhist	15	16	16	14
Anti-Hindu	11	11	11	6
Anti-Sikh	89	93	94	59
Anti-Atheism/Agnosticism/etc.	8	8	9	5
Sexual Orientation	1,110	2,185	2,229	1,043
Anti-Gay (Male)	673	770	791	680
Anti-Lesbian	103	1,021	1,026	89
Anti-Lesbian, Gay, Bisexual, or Transgender (Mixed Group)	306	363	380	250
Anti-Heterosexual	11	12	13	10
Anti-Bisexual	17	19	19	14
Disability	130	151	152	117
Anti-Physical	53	60	60	47
Anti-Mental	77	91	92	70
Gender	75	81	82	65
Anti-Male	25	25	25	24
Anti-Female	50	56	57	41
Gender Identity	266	294	302	279
Anti-Transgender	213	237	244	226
Anti-Gender Non-Conforming	53	57	58	53
Multiple-Bias Incidents[3]	211	339	346	123

1 The term *victim* may refer to an individual, business/financial institution, government entity, religious organization, or society/public as a whole.   2 The term *known offender* does not imply the suspect's identity is known; rather, the term indicates some aspect of the suspect was identified, thus distinguishing the suspect from an unknown offender.   3 A multiple-bias incident is an incident in which one or more offense types are motivated by two or more biases.

Table 83. Incidents, Offenses, Victims, and Known Offenders, by Offense Type, 2020

(Number.)

Offense type	Incidents[1]	Offenses	Victims[2]	Known offenders[3]
Total	8,263	11,129	11,472	6,780
Crimes Against Persons	5,201	7,750	7,750	5,244
Murder and nonnegligent manslaughter	20	22	22	22
Rape[4]	21	21	21	23
Aggravated assault	1,074	1,390	1,390	1,257
Simple assault	1,867	2,166	2,166	2,061
Intimidation	2,190	4,119	4,119	1,853
Other[5]	29	32	32	28
Crimes Against Property	3,147	3,147	3,490	1,635
Robbery	140	140	155	228
Burglary	132	132	152	94
Larceny-theft	362	362	383	175
Motor vehicle theft	34	34	36	28
Arson	67	67	105	38
Destruction/damage/vandalism	2,333	2,333	2,574	1,031
Other[5]	79	79	85	41
Crimes Against Society[5]	232	232	232	269

1 The actual number of incidents is 8,263. However, the column figures will not add to the total because incidents may include more than one offense type, and these are counted in each appropriate offense type category.   2 The term *victim* may refer to an individual, business/financial institution, government entity, religious organization, or society/public as a whole.   3 The term *known offender* does not imply the suspect's identity is known; rather, the term indicates some aspect of the suspect was identified, thus distinguishing the suspect from an unknown offender. The actual number of known offenders is 6,780. However, the column figures will not add to the total because some offenders are responsible for more than one offense type, and are, therefore, counted more than once in this table.   4 Only the revised Uniform Crime Reporting definition of rape was used for the figures reported in this row.   5 The figures shown include additional offenses collected in the National Incident-Based Reporting System.

Table 84. Offenses, Known Offender's Race and Ethnicity, by Offense Type, 2020

(Number.)

Bias motivation	Total offenses	Known offender's race							Known offender's ethnicity[1]				Unknown offender
		White	Black or African American	American Indian or Alaska Native	Asian	Native Hawaiian or Other Pacific Islander	Group of multiple races	Unknown race	Hispanic or Latino	Not Hispanic or Latino	Group of multiple ethnicities	Unknown ethnicity	
Total	11,129	4,958	1,390	73	75	29	223	947	608	2,625	69	2,915	3,434
Crimes Against Persons	7,750	4,194	1,148	64	60	24	187	583	509	2,150	52	2,342	1,490
Murder and nonnegligent manslaughter	22	8	3	0	0	0	1	5	3	6	0	7	5
Rape [2]	21	9	5	0	0	1	1	3	5	6	0	8	2
Aggravated assault	1,390	746	311	12	15	3	48	119	162	530	19	472	136
Simple assault	2,166	1,136	488	37	27	6	92	155	193	742	26	791	225
Intimidation	4,119	2,277	335	14	17	13	45	301	142	856	7	1,051	1,117
Other[3]	32	18	6	1	1	1	0	0	4	10	0	13	5
Crimes Against Property	3,147	628	182	7	12	5	30	360	94	362	15	482	1,923
Robbery	140	38	47	2	0	2	5	25	23	37	4	41	21
Burglary	132	41	9	1	0	0	4	14	0	27	2	32	63
Larceny-theft	362	99	32	0	0	0	2	11	7	60	1	67	218
Motor vehicle theft	34	11	5	0	0	0	0	3	0	8	0	11	15
Arson	67	23	3	0	0	0	1	4	6	7	0	17	36
Destruction/damage/ vandalism	2,333	390	78	4	12	3	18	302	54	208	8	298	1,526
Other[3]	79	26	8	0	0	0	0	1	4	15	0	16	44
Crimes Against Society[3]	232	136	60	2	3	0	6	4	5	113	2	91	21

1 The sum of offenses by the known offender's ethnicity does not equal the sum of offenses by the known offender's race because not all law enforcement agencies that report offender race data also report offender ethnicity data.   2 Only the revised Uniform Crime Reporting definition of rape was used for the figures reported in this row.   3 The figures shown include additional offenses collected in the National Incident-Based Reporting System.

Table 85. Offenses, Offense Type, by Bias Motivation, 2020

(Number.)

Bias motivation	Total offenses	Crimes against persons					
		Murder and nonnegligent manslaughter	Rape[1]	Aggravated assault	Simple assault	Intimidation	Other[2]
Total	11,129	22	21	1,390	2,166	4,119	32
Single-Bias Incidents	10,790	22	21	1,370	2,131	3,940	32
Race/Ethnicity/Ancestry	6,677	8	10	976	1,455	2,296	20
Anti-White	1,048	1	7	145	317	231	8
Anti-Black or African American	3,819	5	2	530	660	1,577	5
Anti-American Indian or Alaska Native	103	0	1	5	26	14	3
Anti-Asian	330	0	0	47	99	111	0
Anti-Native Hawaiian or Other Pacific Islander	15	0	0	2	2	3	0
Anti-Multiple Races, Group	270	2	0	31	41	77	0
Anti-Arab	85	0	0	9	24	29	0
Anti-Hispanic or Latino	664	0	0	162	215	170	4
Anti-Other Race/Ethnicity/Ancestry	343	0	0	45	71	84	0
Religion	1,402	1	0	73	151	293	0
Anti-Jewish	794	1	0	34	59	209	0
Anti-Catholic	77	0	0	5	5	5	0
Anti-Protestant	31	0	0	2	6	1	0
Anti-Islamic (Muslim)	126	0	0	12	32	43	0
Anti-Other Religion	85	0	0	10	6	10	0
Anti-Multiple Religions, Group	44	0	0	0	6	9	0
Anti-Mormon	8	0	0	1	0	1	0
Anti-Jehovah's Witness	10	0	0	0	1	0	0
Anti-Eastern Orthodox (Russian, Greek, Other)	43	0	0	1	5	1	0
Anti-Other Christian	56	0	0	1	8	6	0
Anti-Buddhist	16	0	0	0	2	0	0
Anti-Hindu	11	0	0	0	3	1	0
Anti-Sikh	93	0	0	5	17	7	0
Anti-Atheism/Agnosticism/etc.	8	0	0	2	1	0	0
Sexual Orientation	2,185	5	6	223	370	1,254	2
Anti-Gay (Male)	770	5	2	157	252	203	2
Anti-Lesbian	1,021	0	2	17	28	940	0
Anti-Lesbian, Gay, Bisexual, or Transgender (Mixed Group)	363	0	2	45	84	102	0
Anti-Heterosexual	12	0	0	0	1	4	0
Anti-Bisexual	19	0	0	4	5	5	0
Disability	151		2	18	41	21	3
Anti-Physical	60	0	0	6	20	8	3
Anti-Mental	91	0	2	12	21	13	0
Gender	81		2	19	24	16	1
Anti-Male	25	0	0	8	6	2	1
Anti-Female	56	0	2	11	18	14	0
Gender Identity	294	8	1	61	90	60	6
Anti-Transgender	237	8	0	57	76	52	2
Anti-Gender Non-Conforming	57	0	1	4	14	8	4
Multiple-Bias Incidents[3]	339	0	0	20	35	179	0

Table 85. Offenses, Offense Type, by Bias Motivation, 2020—Continued

(Number.)

Bias motivation	Robbery	Burglary	Larceny- theft	Motor vehicle theft	Arson	Destruction/ damage/ vandalism	Other[2]	Crimes against society[2]
				Crimes against property				
Total	140	132	362	34	67	2,333	79	232
Single-Bias Incidents	139	130	356	34	63	2,243	78	231
Race/Ethnicity/Ancestry	82	69	166	18	36	1,355	38	148
Anti-White	27	17	56	6	3	150	15	65
Anti-Black or African American	23	32	71	6	25	821	8	54
Anti-American Indian or Alaska Native	1	4	10	2	1	22	5	9
Anti-Asian	7	3	4	2	0	52	0	5
Anti-Native Hawaiian or Other Pacific Islander	0	2	0	0	1	2	3	0
Anti-Multiple Races, Group	1	1	5	0	1	105	3	3
Anti-Arab	0	2	2	0	0	19	0	0
Anti-Hispanic or Latino	18	6	6	0	2	73	2	6
Anti-Other Race/Ethnicity/Ancestry	5	2	12	2	3	111	2	6
Religion	7	34	78	8	18	671	25	43
Anti-Jewish	3	11	9	0	1	460	1	6
Anti-Catholic	0	4	8	2	5	33	5	5
Anti-Protestant	1	2	4	1	0	10	2	2
Anti-Islamic (Muslim)	1	4	7	0	4	23	0	0
Anti-Other Religion	0	2	4	1	3	46	1	2
Anti-Multiple Religions, Group	1	0	5	0	1	19	2	1
Anti-Mormon	0	1	0	0	0	4	0	1
Anti-Jehovah's Witness	0	1	1	0	0	6	0	1
Anti-Eastern Orthodox (Russian, Greek, Other)	0	1	8	2	0	9	3	13
Anti-Other Christian	0	1	3	0	4	33	0	0
Anti-Buddhist	0	0	1	0	0	13	0	0
Anti-Hindu	0	1	0	0	0	5	1	0
Anti-Sikh	1	6	25	2	0	9	9	12
Anti-Atheism/Agnosticism/etc.	0	0	3	0	0	1	1	0
Sexual Orientation	34	17	68	2	9	179	4	12
Anti-Gay (Male)	28	7	15	1	2	87	3	6
Anti-Lesbian	0	1	6	0	2	24	0	1
Anti-Lesbian, Gay, Bisexual, or Transgender (Mixed Group)	6	7	45	1	5	63	0	3
Anti-Heterosexual	0	1	1	0	0	3	0	2
Anti-Bisexual	0	1	1	0	0	2	1	0
Disability	5	5	22	4	0	14	6	10
Anti-Physical	3	2	8	1	0	4	0	5
Anti-Mental	2	3	14	3	0	10	6	5
Gender	1	2	4	0	0	4	2	6
Anti-Male	0	1	3	0	0	1	0	3
Anti-Female	1	1	1	0	0	3	2	3
Gender Identity	10	3	18	2	0	20	3	12
Anti-Transgender	8	3	9	2	0	13	2	5
Anti-Gender Non-Conforming	2	0	9	0	0	7	1	7
Multiple-Bias Incidents[3]	1	2	6	0	4	90	1	1

1 Only the revised Uniform Crime Reporting definition of rape was used for the figures reported in this column.   2 The figures shown include additional offenses collected in the National Incident-Based Reporting System.   3 A multiple-bias incident is an incident in which one or more offense types are motivated by two or more biases.

Table 86. Offenses, Known Offender's Race, by Bias Motivation, 2020

(Number.)

Bias motivation	Total offenses	Known offender's race							Known offender's ethnicity[1]				Unknown offender
		White	Black or African American	American Indian or Alaska Native	Asian	Native Hawaiian or Other Pacific Islander	Group of multiple races	Unknown race	Hispanic or Latino	Not Hispanic or Latino	Group of multiple ethnicities	Unknown ethnicity	
Total	11,129	4,958	1,390	73	75	29	223	947	608	2,625	69	2,915	3,434
Single-Bias Incidents	10,790	4,873	1,377	72	74	29	215	859	600	2,576	68	2,777	3,291
Race/Ethnicity/Ancestry	6,677	2,843	835	60	59	25	133	465	387	1,791	43	1,919	2,257
Anti-White	1,048	175	480	18	7	16	27	46	46	323	9	363	279
Anti-Black or African American	3,819	1,866	87	25	29	6	74	286	218	927	12	1,063	1,446
Anti-American Indian or Alaska Native	103	41	12	8	1	0	2	3	9	31	0	27	36
Anti-Asian	330	128	44	0	6	1	11	58	40	80	3	80	82
Anti-Native Hawaiian or Other Pacific Islander	15	8	1	1	0	0	0	1	1	6	0	4	4
Anti-Multiple Races, Group	270	106	12	1	2	1	6	9	10	62	3	53	133
Anti-Arab	85	38	10	0	0	1	1	3	5	24	0	23	32
Anti-Hispanic or Latino	664	362	144	6	9	0	8	36	43	265	15	212	99
Anti-Other Race/Ethnicity/Ancestry	343	119	45	1	5	0	4	23	15	73	1	94	146
Religion	1,402	430	90	4	6	1	23	235	42	256	5	274	613
Anti-Jewish	794	191	34	2	3	0	14	175	12	121	3	103	375
Anti-Catholic	77	26	5	0	0	0	1	14	2	11	0	21	31
Anti-Protestant	31	14	3	0	0	0	0	1	1	7	0	8	13
Anti-Islamic (Muslim)	126	70	19	0	2	0	3	13	10	34	2	48	19
Anti-Other Religion	85	31	7	0	0	0	1	7	3	9	0	32	39
Anti-Multiple Religions, Group	44	9	2	1	0	0	1	3	1	7	0	8	28
Anti-Mormon	8	0	1	0	0	1	0	2	1	1	0	2	4
Anti-Jehovah's Witness	10	2	0	0	0	0	0	1	0	2	0	0	7
Anti-Eastern Orthodox (Russian, Greek, Other)	43	19	8	0	0	0	0	0	2	18	0	7	16
Anti-Other Christian	56	21	1	0	0	0	0	8	4	10	0	16	26
Anti-Buddhist	16	2	0	0	0	0	2	5	0	4	0	5	7
Anti-Hindu	11	2	0	1	1	0	0	2	1	2	0	1	5
Anti-Sikh	93	39	9	0	0	0	1	4	5	25	0	23	40
Anti-Atheism/Agnosticism/etc.	8	4	1	0	0	0	0	0	0	5	0	0	3
Sexual Orientation	2,185	1,367	322	4	8	2	48	112	118	365	16	403	322
Anti-Gay (Male)	770	284	211	3	4	2	31	82	92	209	10	262	153
Anti-Lesbian	1,021	939	32	0	0	0	4	9	12	34	1	29	37
Anti-Lesbian, Gay, Bisexual, or Transgender (Mixed Group)	363	131	74	1	4	0	13	19	13	109	5	107	121
Anti-Heterosexual	12	7	1	0	0	0	0	0	0	5	0	3	4
Anti-Bisexual	19	6	4	0	0	0	0	2	1	8	0	2	7
Disability	151	79	27	2	1	0	0	6	7	51	0	57	36
Anti-Physical	60	31	8	2	1	0	0	5	1	19	0	27	13
Anti-Mental	91	48	19	0	0	0	0	1	6	32	0	30	23
Gender	81	44	17	1	0	0	1	4	7	32	0	21	14
Anti-Male	25	16	4	0	0	0	0	0	2	5	0	12	5
Anti-Female	56	28	13	1	0	0	1	4	5	27	0	9	9
Gender Identity	294	110	86	1	0	1	10	37	39	81	4	103	49
Anti-Transgender	237	76	78	1	0	0	9	34	33	65	3	82	39
Anti-Gender Non-Conforming	57	34	8	0	0	1	1	3	6	16	1	21	10
Multiple-Bias Incidents[2]	339	85	13	1	1	0	8	88	8	49	1	138	143

1 The aggregate of offenses by the known offender's ethnicity does not equal the aggregate of offenses by the known offender's race because not all law enforcement agencies that report offender race data also report offender ethnicity data.   2 A multiple-bias incident is an incident in which one or more offense types are motivated by two or more biases.

Table 87. Offenses, Victim Type, by Offense Type, 2020

(Number.)

Offense type	Total offenses	Victim type					
		Individual	Business/ financial institution	Government	Religious organization	Society/ public[1]	Other/ unknown/ multiple
Total	11,129	9,376	577	345	204	232	395
Crimes against persons[2]	7,750	7,750	NA	NA	NA	NA	NA
Crimes against property	3,147	1,626	577	345	204	0	395
Robbery	140	129	2	0	0	0	9
Burglary	132	90	24	2	8	0	8
Larceny-theft	362	266	75	2	4	0	15
Motor vehicle theft	34	30	3	0	0	0	1
Arson	67	40	7	4	9	0	7
Destruction/damage/vandalism	2,333	1,007	456	334	183	0	353
Other[2]	79	64	10	3	0	0	2
Crimes against society[2]	232	NA	NA	NA	NA	193	NA

NA = Not available.
1 The victim type *society/public* is collected only in National Incident-Based Reporting System (NIBRS).   2 Includes additional offenses collected in the NIBRS.

Table 88. Victims, Offense Type, by Bias Motivation, 2020

(Number.)

Bias motivation	Total victims[1]	Total number of adult victims[2]	Total number of juvenile victims[2]	Crimes against persons					
				Murder and nonnegligent manslaughter	Rape[3]	Aggravated assault	Simple assault	Intimidation	Other[4]
Total	11,472	7,729	791	22	21	1,390	2,166	4,119	32
Single-Bias Incidents	11,126	7,469	776	22	21	1,370	2,131	3,940	32
Race/Ethnicity/Ancestry	6,880	5,205	589	8	10	976	1,455	2,296	20
Anti-White	1,082	845	64	1	7	145	317	231	8
Anti-Black or African American	3,915	2,932	408	5	2	530	660	1,577	5
Anti-American Indian or Alaska Native	108	85	6	0	1	5	26	14	3
Anti-Asian	342	262	14	0	0	47	99	111	0
Anti-Native Hawaiian or Other Pacific Islander	18	14	0	0	0	2	2	3	0
Anti-Multiple Races, Group	281	160	24	2	0	31	41	77	0
Anti-Arab	87	74	3	0	0	9	24	29	0
Anti-Hispanic or Latino	693	590	61	0	0	162	215	170	4
Anti-Other Race/Ethnicity/Ancestry	354	243	9	0	0	45	71	84	0
Religion	1,481	740	32	1	0	73	151	293	0
Anti-Jewish	831	361	12	1	0	34	59	209	0
Anti-Catholic	80	39	0	0	0	5	5	5	0
Anti-Protestant	32	20	3	0	0	2	6	1	0
Anti-Islamic (Muslim)	131	97	9	0	0	12	32	43	0
Anti-Other Religion	105	55	6	0	0	10	6	10	0
Anti-Multiple Religions, Group	49	26	0	0	0	0	6	9	0
Anti-Mormon	8	2	0	0	0	1	0	1	0
Anti-Jehovah's Witness	10	4	0	0	0	0	1	0	0
Anti-Eastern Orthodox (Russian, Greek, Other)	43	23	0	0	0	1	5	1	0
Anti-Other Christian	62	24	0	0	0	1	8	6	0
Anti-Buddhist	16	5	0	0	0	0	2	0	0
Anti-Hindu	11	5	0	0	0	0	3	1	0
Anti-Sikh	94	71	2	0	0	5	17	7	0
Anti-Atheism/Agnosticism/etc.	9	8	0	0	0	2	1	0	0
Sexual Orientation	2,229	1,090	109	5	6	223	370	1,254	2
Anti-Gay (Male)	791	674	53	5	2	157	252	203	2
Anti-Lesbian	1,026	98	14	0	2	17	28	940	0
Anti-Lesbian, Gay, Bisexual, or Transgender (Mixed Group)	380	294	39	0	2	45	84	102	0
Anti-Heterosexual	13	8	2	0	0	0	1	4	0
Anti-Bisexual	19	16	1	0	0	4	5	5	0
Disability	152	116	19	0	2	18	41	21	3
Anti-Physical	60	48	10	0	0	6	20	8	3
Anti-Mental	92	68	9	0	2	12	21	13	0
Gender	82	64	5	0	2	19	24	16	1
Anti-Male	25	20	1	0	0	8	6	2	1
Anti-Female	57	44	4	0	2	11	18	14	0
Gender Identity	302	254	22	8	1	61	90	60	6
Anti-Transgender	244	209	15	8	0	57	76	52	2
Anti-Gender Non-Conforming	58	45	7	0	1	4	14	8	4
Multiple-Bias Incidents[5]	346	260	15	0	0	20	35	179	0

Table 88. Victims, Offense Type, by Bias Motivation, 2020—Continued

(Number.)

Bias motivation	Crimes against property							Crimes against society[4]
	Robbery	Burglary	Larceny- theft	Motor vehicle theft	Arson	Destruction/ damage/ vandalism	Other[4]	
Total	155	152	383	36	105	2,574	85	232
Single-Bias Incidents	154	150	376	36	100	2,479	84	231
Race/Ethnicity/Ancestry	90	79	181	18	41	1,515	43	148
Anti-White	31	18	63	6	4	168	18	65
Anti-Black or African American	23	38	77	6	27	902	9	54
Anti-American Indian or Alaska Native	1	5	11	2	1	25	5	9
Anti-Asian	8	4	4	2	0	62	0	5
Anti-Native Hawaiian or Other Pacific Islander	0	2	0	0	1	4	4	
Anti-Multiple Races, Group	1	1	6	0	1	115	3	3
Anti-Arab	0	2	2	0	0	21	0	0
Anti-Hispanic or Latino	20	7	6	0	4	97	2	6
Anti-Other Race/Ethnicity/Ancestry	6	2	12	2	3	121	2	6
Religion	7	36	79	8	48	716	26	43
Anti-Jewish	3	12	9	0	2	494	2	6
Anti-Catholic		4	8	2	8	33	5	5
Anti-Protestant	1	2	4	1	0	11	2	2
Anti-Islamic (Muslim)	1	4	7	0	9	23	0	0
Anti-Other Religion	0	2	4	1	22	47	1	2
Anti-Multiple Religions, Group	1	0	5	0	3	22	2	1
Anti-Mormon	0	1	0	0	0	4	0	1
Anti-Jehovah's Witness	0	1	1	0	0	6	0	1
Anti-Eastern Orthodox (Russian, Greek, Other)	0	1	8	2	0	9	3	13
Anti-Other Christian	0	1	3	0	4	39	0	0
Anti-Buddhist	0	0	1	0	0	13	0	0
Anti-Hindu	0	1	0	0	0	5	1	0
Anti-Sikh	1	7	25	2	0	9	9	12
Anti-Atheism/Agnosticism/etc.	0	0	4	0	0	1	1	0
Sexual Orientation	37	25	72	2	11	206	4	12
Anti-Gay (Male)	31	9	16	1	3	101	3	6
Anti-Lesbian	0	1	7	0	2	28	0	1
Anti-Lesbian, Gay, Bisexual, or Transgender (Mixed Group)	6	13	47	1	6	71	0	3
Anti-Heterosexual	0	1	1	0	0	4	0	2
Anti-Bisexual	0	1	1	0	0	2	1	0
Disability	5	5	22	4	0	15	6	10
Anti-Physical	3	2	8	1	0	4	0	5
Anti-Mental	2	3	14	3	0	11	6	5
Gender	1	2	4	0	0	5	2	6
Anti-Male	0	1	3	0	0	1	0	3
Anti-Female	1	1	1	0	0	4	2	3
Gender Identity	14	3	18	4	0	22	3	12
Anti-Transgender	11	3	9	4	0	15	2	5
Anti-Gender Non-Conforming	3		9	0	0	7	1	7
Multiple-Bias Incidents[5]	1	2	7	0	5	95	1	1

NOTE: The aggregate of adult and juvenile individual victims does not equal the total number of victims because total victims include individuals, businesses/financial institutions, government entities, religious organizations, and society/public as a whole. In addition, the aggregate of adult and juvenile individual victims does not equal the aggregate of victims of crimes against persons because not all law enforcement agencies report the ages of individual victims.
1 The term *victim* may refer to an individual, business/financial institution, government entity, religious organization, or society/public as a whole.   2 The figures shown are individual victims only.   3 Only the revised Uniform Crime Reporting definition of rape is used for the figures reported in this column.   4 The figures shown include additional offenses collected in the National Incident-Based Reporting System.   5 A multiple-bias incident is an incident in which one or more offense types are motivated by two or more biases.

Table 89. Incidents, Victim Type, by Bias Motivation, 2020

(Number.)

Bias motivation	Total incidents	Victim type					
		Individual	Business/ financial institution	Government	Religious organization	Society/ public[1]	Other/ unknown/ multiple
Total	8,263	6,546	551	343	200	185	438
Single-Bias Incidents	8,052	6,406	535	321	195	185	410
Race/Ethnicity/Ancestry	5,227	4,345	328	212	20	107	215
Religion	1,244	624	162	91	169	41	157
Sexual Orientation	1,110	1,025	25	14	6	9	31
Disability	130	106	11	1	0	10	2
Gender	75	66	1	1	0	6	1
Gender Identity	266	240	8	2	0	12	4
Multiple-Bias Incidents[2]	211	140	16	22	5	0	28

1 The victim type *society/public* is collected only in the National Incident-Based Reporting System.
2 A multiple-bias incident is an incident in which one or more offense types are motivated by two or more biases.

Table 90. Known Offenders,[1] by Known Offender's Race, Ethnicity, and Age, 2020

(Number.)

Race/ethnicity/age	Total
Race	6,780
White	3,737
Black or African American	1,438
American Indian or Alaska Native	69
Asian	73
Native Hawaiian or Other Pacific Islander	31
Group of multiple races[2]	366
Unknown race	1,066
Ethnicity[3]	6,169
Hispanic or Latino	629
Not Hispanic or Latino	2,424
Group of multiple ethnicities[4]	146
Unknown ethnicity	2,970
Age[3]	6,264
Total known offenders 18 and over	5,581
Total known offenders under 18	683

1 The term *known offender* does not imply the suspect's identity is known; rather, the term indicates some aspect of the suspect was identified, thus distinguishing the suspect from an unknown offender.   2 The term *group of multiple races* is used to describe a group of offenders of varying races.   3 The total number of known offenders by age and the total number of known offenders by ethnicity do not equal the total number of known offenders by race because not all law enforcement agencies report the age and/or ethnicity of the known offenders.   4 The term *group of multiple ethnicities* is used to describe a group of offenders of varying ethnicities.

Table 91. Incidents, Bias Motivation, by Location, 2020

(Number.)

Location	Total incidents	Bias motivation						Multiple bias incidents[1]
		Race/ethnicity/ ancestry	Religion	Sexual orientation	Disability	Gender	Gender identity	
Total	8,263	5,227	1,244	1,110	130	75	266	211
Abandoned/condemned structure	10	6	0	0	0	0	2	2
Air/bus/train terminal	118	77	9	20	2	0	6	4
Amusement park	4	3	0	1	0	0	0	0
Arena/stadium/fairgrounds/coliseum	9	6	3	0	0	0	0	0
Auto dealership new/used	11	6	2	0	0	0	3	0
Bank/savings and loan	25	21	1	0	0	1	2	0
Bar/nightclub	82	43	4	25	2	1	4	3
Camp/campground	12	6	6	0	0	0	0	0
Church/synagogue/temple/mosque	285	50	218	10	0	0	0	7
Commercial office building	183	114	36	21	2	5	1	4
Community center	31	22	5	3	0	0	0	1
Construction site	33	24	8	0	0	0	0	1
Convenience store	192	146	14	21	2	0	5	4
Cyberspace	104	58	19	10	3	2	5	7
Daycare facility	6	5	1	0	0	0	0	0
Department/discount store	107	76	10	13	3	0	4	1
Dock/wharf/freight/modal terminal	5	5	0	0	0	0	0	0
Drug store/doctor's office/hospital	98	70	8	8	2	2	2	6
Farm facility	4	4	0	0	0	0	0	0
Field/woods	61	35	15	9	0	0	0	2
Gambling facility/casino/race track	9	6	2	0	0	0	1	0
Government/public building	122	93	16	6	1	1	2	3
Grocery/supermarket	122	90	12	11	3	1	3	2
Highway/road/alley/street/sidewalk	1,645	1,135	148	240	18	8	66	30
Hotel/motel/etc.	91	65	11	7	1	0	4	3
Industrial site	15	10	3	0	0	0	0	2
Jail/prison/penitentiary/corrections facility	63	45	3	14	0	1	0	0
Lake/waterway/beach	24	16	2	4	0	0	0	2
Liquor store	26	15	6	4	0	1	0	0
Military installation	1	1	0	0	0	0	0	0
Park/playground	294	182	50	33	1	2	11	15
Parking/drop lot/garage	540	396	44	70	4	5	12	9
Rental storage facility	12	6	4	2	0	0	0	0
Residence/home	2,390	1,465	283	397	67	32	92	54
Rest area	8	6	1	0	0	1	0	0
Restaurant	207	152	12	34	1	1	2	5
School/college[2]	27	17	6	3	0	0	0	1
School-college/university	114	67	23	16	0	1	4	3
School-elementary/secondary	209	122	39	24	6	0	3	15
Service/gas station	100	65	10	13	2	2	6	2
Shelter-mission/homeless	25	15	2	3	2	0	3	0
Shopping mall	26	18	2	5	0	0	1	0
Specialty store (TV, fur, etc.)	76	53	9	9	1	0	3	1
Tribal Lands	5	4	0	0	0	0	1	0
Other/unknown	713	392	196	73	7	8	18	19
Multiple locations	19	14	1	1	0	0	0	3

1 A multiple-bias incident is an incident in which one or more offense types are motivated by two or more biases. 2 The location designation *School/college* has been retained for agencies that have not updated their records management systems to include the new location designations of *School—college/university* and *School—elementary/secondary*, which allow for more specificity in reporting.

Table 92. Offenses, Offense Type, by Participating State/Federal, 2020

(Number.)

State	Total offenses	Crimes against persons						Crimes against property							Crimes against society[2]
		Murder and nonnegligent manslaughter	Rape[1]	Aggravated assault	Simple assault	Intimidation	Other[2]	Robbery	Burglary	Larceny-theft	Motor vehicle theft	Arson	Destruction/ damage/ vandalism	Other[2]	
Total	11,129	22	21	1,390	2,166	4,119	32	140	132	362	34	67	2,333	79	232
Alabama	33	0	0	2	3	4	0	0	2	3	0	0	4	1	14
Alaska	10	0	1	5	3	0	0	1	0	0	0	0	0	0	0
Arizona	332	2	0	54	93	99	3	1	5	5	0	3	62	1	4
Arkansas	22	0	0	6	2	7	0	0	0	0	0	0	7	0	0
California	1,537	0	2	331	362	358	1	49	13	8	1	13	399	0	0
Colorado	343	0	0	52	72	105	0	9	9	13	1	3	74	5	0
Connecticut	126	0	0	9	28	53	0	1	0	3	1	0	29	1	1
Delaware	18	0	0	0	2	9	0	1	0	0	0	0	5	1	0
District of Columbia	151	0	0	35	69	24	0	2	0	0	0	0	21	0	0
Florida	112	0	0	28	38	18	0	1	2	0	0	5	20	0	0
Georgia	234	0	0	25	56	89	0	0	1	8	2	3	38	6	6
Hawaii	39	0	0	5	13	16	1	2	0	1	0	0	1	0	0
Idaho	53	0	0	8	18	16	0	1	1	0	0	0	9	0	0
Illinois	75	1	0	21	21	22	0	0	0	0	0	0	10	0	0
Indiana	229	0	0	33	65	61	0	2	4	19	2	1	24	5	13
Iowa	18	0	0	1	7	1	0	1	1	0	0	0	6	0	1
Kansas	156	0	0	24	11	38	1	1	2	9	1	2	49	5	13
Kentucky	229	0	2	12	52	96	1	3	2	3	2	3	50	0	3
Louisiana	53	0	0	17	16	1	0	1	2	1	0	0	7	0	8
Maine	93	0	0	6	12	24	0	0	0	29	0	1	20	0	1
Maryland	45	0	0	10	8	3	0	3	0	0	0	0	21	0	0
Massachusetts	351	0	0	41	65	97	1	0	1	18	0	0	123	2	3
Michigan	453	0	1	52	109	189	2	4	6	17	4	1	45	8	15
Minnesota	232	0	0	44	39	67	1	5	4	12	0	0	57	0	3
Mississippi	16	0	0	1	8	4	0	0	2	0	0	0	1	0	0
Missouri	154	0	0	28	55	34	0	1	2	2	0	3	25	0	4
Montana	29	0	0	3	7	3	2	2	1	1	0	0	10	0	0
Nebraska	985	0	1	16	11	911	0	0	0	3	0	0	27	0	16
Nevada	153	1	0	36	48	15	0	4	2	5	3	0	25	0	14
New Hampshire	24	0	0	2	5	6	0	0	1	0	0	0	10	0	0
New Jersey	389	0	0	12	26	193	0	2	1	4	0	2	149	0	0
New Mexico	78	0	1	14	28	8	0	2	2	2	0	0	19	0	2
New York	466	1	0	32	149	21	0	7	9	10	0	0	237	0	0
North Carolina	243	1	3	34	45	86	1	3	3	7	0	0	53	1	6
North Dakota	29	0	0	3	11	8	1	0	1	1	0	0	3	1	0
Ohio	633	0	4	51	118	166	5	11	19	81	9	3	112	14	40
Oklahoma	9	0	0	1	2	3	0	0	1	0	0	0	1	0	1
Oregon	324	0	0	31	72	92	1	2	6	8	1	0	104	3	4
Pennsylvania	91	0	0	8	7	38	0	1	0	1	1	1	32	1	1
Rhode Island	16	0	0	1	5	1	0	0	1	1	0	0	7	0	0
South Carolina	130	0	1	26	25	21	1	1	3	12	0	0	18	3	19
South Dakota	19	0	0	2	9	4	0	1	0	0	0	0	3	0	0
Tennessee	93	0	0	20	17	38	0	1	1	1	0	0	14	0	1
Texas	467	1	4	88	119	94	3	5	11	17	1	3	106	6	9
Utah	51	0	0	1	13	6	4	0	1	6	0	1	12	4	3
Vermont	64	0	0	4	8	4	1	0	1	12	1	0	31	2	0
Virginia	193	0	1	10	60	36	0	0	0	4	0	1	77	1	3
Washington	526	0	0	52	101	219	0	6	7	20	3	3	106	5	4
West Virginia	58	0	0	4	11	5	1	2	2	10	1	0	6	1	15
Wisconsin	88	2	0	17	22	15	1	0	0	3	0	0	21	2	5
Wyoming	21	0	0	3	9	5	0	0	0	1	0	0	3	0	0
Federal															
Federal Bureau of Investigation, Field Offices	832	13	0	69	11	682	0	1	0	1	0	15	40	0	0
Pentagon Force Protection Agency	3	0	0	0	0	3	0	0	0	0	0	0	0	0	0
United States Marine Corps Law Enforcement	1	0	0	0	0	1	0	0	0	0	0	0	0	0	0

1 Only the revised Uniform Crime Reporting definition of rape was used for the figures shown in this column.   2 The figures shown include additional offenses collected in the National Incident-Based Reporting System.

Table 93. Agency Hate Crime Reporting, by Participating State/Territory and Federal, 2020

(Number.)

State	Number of participating agencies	Population covered	Agencies submitting incident reports	Total number of incidents reported
Total	15,138	306,085,895	2,389	8,263
Alabama	409	4,798,528	17	27
Alaska	32	719,120	4	9
Arizona	81	5,989,615	25	280
Arkansas	281	2,818,360	8	19
California	732	39,361,017	244	1,339
Colorado	227	5,754,151	66	281
Connecticut	107	3,557,006	38	101
Delaware	62	986,809	7	13
District of Columbia	2	712,816	2	133
Florida	452	19,525,021	54	109
Georgia	401	7,938,166	68	195
Hawaii	1	966,438	1	36
Idaho	107	1,819,575	15	43
Illinois	700	11,752,377	26	56
Indiana	174	4,858,228	53	186
Iowa	251	3,083,186	10	15
Kansas	359	2,586,059	61	124
Kentucky	423	4,472,499	67	166
Louisiana	137	3,491,734	18	39
Maine	131	1,350,141	23	83
Maryland	152	6,055,802	14	40
Massachusetts	368	6,835,964	95	310
Michigan	628	9,767,448	168	377
Minnesota	413	5,655,413	61	194
Mississippi	92	1,306,283	11	16
Missouri	549	6,089,883	38	115
Montana	106	1,075,088	12	26
Nebraska	126	1,807,565	13	72
Nevada	48	3,128,688	12	113
New Hampshire	193	1,335,848	16	19
New Jersey	534	8,462,314	182	389
New Mexico	35	1,114,118	8	55
New York	559	19,122,405	78	463
North Carolina	378	9,618,194	65	185
North Dakota	110	765,309	13	21
Ohio	578	10,035,054	136	538
Oklahoma	443	3,980,783	4	8
Oregon	207	4,000,770	67	280
Pennsylvania	734	8,190,948	20	81
Rhode Island	49	1,057,125	9	14
South Carolina	398	5,139,301	46	110
South Dakota	128	848,707	14	17
Tennessee	463	6,886,834	29	78
Texas	1,073	29,247,610	131	406
Utah	126	3,181,559	23	44
Vermont	88	623,347	28	60
Virginia	416	8,589,304	65	170
Washington	243	7,663,709	92	451
West Virginia	251	1,562,004	23	54
Wisconsin	441	5,824,028	48	72
Wyoming	59	573,644	8	18
Federal[1]				
Board of Governors of the Federal Reserve System and the Consumer Financial Protection Bureau, Office of Inpector General	1	0	0	0
Central Intelligence Agency Security Protective Service	1	0	0	0
Corporation for National and Community Service, Office of Inspector General	1	0	0	0
Defense Intelligence Agency	1	0	0	0
Drug Enforcement Administration, Wilmington Resident Office	1	0	0	0
Export-Import Bank of the United States, Office of Inspector General	1	0	0	0
Federal Bureau of Investigation, Field Offices	52	0	51	209
Federal Emergency Management Agency	1	0	0	0
Federal Housing Finance Agency, Office of Inspector General	1	0	0	0
National Institute of Health	1	0	0	0
National Security Agency Police	1	0	0	0
Peace Corps, Office of Inspector General	1	0	0	0
Pension Benefit Guaranty Corporation, Office of Inspector General	1	0	0	0
Pentagon Force Protection Agency	1	0	1	3
Tennessee Valley Authority, Office of Inspector General	1	0	0	0
United States Agency for International Development, Office of Inspector General	1	0	0	0
United States Air Force, Office of Special Investigations	1	0	0	0

Table 93. Agency Hate Crime Reporting, by Participating State/Territory and Federal, 2020—Continued

(Number.)

State	Number of participating agencies	Population covered	Agencies submitting incident reports	Total number of incidents reported
United States Army	1	0	0	0
United States Department of Agriculture, Office of Inspector General	1	0	0	0
United States Department of Defense, Office of Inspector General	1	0	0	0
United States Department of Education, Office of Inspector General	1	0	0	0
United States Department of Justice, Office of Inspector General	1	0	0	0
United States Election Assistance Commission, Office of Inspector General	1	0	0	0
United States Environmental Protection Agency, Office of Inspector General	1	0	0	0
United States Federal Deposit Insurance Corporation, Office of Inspector General	1	0	0	0
United States Marine Corps Law Enforcement	1	0	1	1
United States National Archives and Records Administration, Office of Inspector General	1	0	0	0
United States Navy Law Enforcement	1	0	0	0
United States Nuclear Regulatory Commission, Office of Inspector General	1	0	0	0
United States Office of Personnel Management, Office of the Inspector General	1	0	0	0

1 Population estimates are not attributed to the federal agencies.

Table 94. Hate Crime Incidents Per Bias Motivation and Quarter, by Selected State and Agency and Federal, 2020

(Number.)

State/agency	Number of incidents per bias motivation						Number of incidents per quarter				Population[1]
	Race/ Ethnicity/ Ancestry	Religion	Sexual orientation	Disability	Gender	Gender Identity	1st quarter	2nd quarter	3rd quarter	4th quarter	
ALABAMA											
Total	22	5	1	0	0	0					
Cities	8	5	1	0	0	0					
Bayou La Batre	1	0	0	0	0	0	0	1			2,466
Birmingham	1	1	0	0	0	0	1	1			209,081
Carrollton	1	0	0	0	0	0	0	1			935
Dora	0	1	0	0	0	0	1	0			1,890
Evergreen	1	0	0	0	0	0	0	1			3,482
Fayette	1	0	0	0	0	0	0	1			4,239
Hoover	0	1	0	0	0	0	0	1	0	0	86,321
Linden	0	0	1	0	0	0	0	1			1,856
Margaret	1	0	0	0	0	0	1	0			5,222
Mobile[2]	1	2	0	0	0	0	1	1			243,900
Tuskegee	1	0	0	0	0	0	0	1			7,973
Metropolitan Counties	9	0	0	0	0	0					
Etowah	1	0	0	0	0	0	1	0			
Washington	8	0	0	0	0	0	8	0			
Nonmetropolitan Counties	5	0	0	0	0	0					
Crenshaw	1	0	0	0	0	0	1	0			
Dallas	1	0	0	0	0	0	1	0			
DeKalb	2	0	0	0	0	0	1	1			
Walker	1	0	0	0	0	0	0	1			
ALASKA											
Total	5	0	1	0	2	1					
Cities	5	0	1	0	2	1					
Anchorage	3	0	1	0	1	0	0	2	2	1	286,388
Fairbanks	0	0	0	0	0	1	1		0	0	30,832
Juneau	2	0	0	0	0	0	0	1	1	0	31,925
North Pole	0	0	0	0	1	0	0	1	0	0	2,090
ARIZONA											
Total	202	37	34	2	1	7					
Cities	178	30	32	1	1	6					
Apache Junction	1	0	0	0	0	0	0	0	0	1	43,385
Casa Grande	2	1	0	0	0	0	0	0	2	1	59,822
Chandler	2	2	0	0	0	0	2	0	1	1	264,071
Fredonia	0	0	1	0	0	0	0	0	0	1	1,275
Gilbert	3	2	1	0	0	0	1	1	2	2	259,629
Glendale	6	0	1	0	0	0	2	2	3	0	255,468
Maricopa	0	0	1	0	0	0	1	0	0	0	53,165
Mesa	7	2	0	0	0	1	2	3	5	0	527,361
Page	1	0	0	0	0	0	0	1	0	0	7,546
Payson	1	0	0	0	0	0	0	1	0	0	15,869
Peoria	2	0	0	0	0	0	0	1	0	1	178,486
Phoenix[2]	140	17	28	0	1	3	24	47	65	51	1,708,960
Prescott	1	0	0	0	0	0	0	0	1	0	44,835
San Luis	0	1	0	0	0	1	1	0	0	1	35,574
Scottsdale	1	1	0	0	0	0	0	0	0	2	263,006
Sierra Vista	0	0	0	0	0	1	0	0	0	1	42,800
Somerton	0	1	0	0	0	0	1	0	0	0	16,811
Surprise	3	0	0	0	0	0	0	1	1	1	144,620
Tempe	3	0	0	0	0	0	0	2	1		199,935
Williams	1	0	0	0	0	0			1	0	3,271
Yuma	4	3	0	1	0	0	1	5	1	1	99,096
Metropolitan Counties	24	7	2	1	0	1					
Coconino	1	0	0	0	0	0	0	0	1	0	
Pima[2]	20	4	2	0	0	1	2	6	6	12	
Yavapai	2	1	0	0	0	0	2	1	0		
Yuma	1	2	0	1	0	0	1	1	1	1	
ARKANSAS											
Total	13	2	4	0	0	0					
Cities	12	1	4	0	0	0					
Conway	1	1	0	0	0	0	0	2	0	0	68,599
Fort Smith	5	0	1	0	0	0	1	4	0	1	88,071
Paragould	1	0	1	0	0	0	1	0	0	1	29,288
Rogers	4	0	1	0	0	0	0	1	4	0	70,194
Sherwood	1	0	0	0	0	0	0	0	1	0	31,636
Van Buren	0	0	1	0	0	0	0	0	0	1	23,779
Universities and Colleges	1	0	0	0	0	0					
University of Arkansas, Medical Sciences	1	0	0	0	0	0	0	1	0	0	2,996
Metropolitan Counties	0	1	0	0	0	0					
Sebastian	0	1	0	0	0	0	0	1	0	0	
CALIFORNIA											
Total	882	181	210	5	3	59					
Cities	790	160	188	4	2	57					
Alameda	5	0	0	0	0	0	0	0	4	1	78,047
Albany	3	0	0	0	0	0	0	0	1	2	19,830

Table 94. Hate Crime Incidents Per Bias Motivation and Quarter, by Selected State and Agency and Federal, 2020—Continued

(Number.)

State/agency	Number of incidents per bias motivation						Number of incidents per quarter				Population[1]
	Race/ Ethnicity/ Ancestry	Religion	Sexual orientation	Disability	Gender	Gender Identity	1st quarter	2nd quarter	3rd quarter	4th quarter	
Alhambra	1	0	0	0	0	0	0	1	0	0	83,817
Aliso Viejo	5	1	0	0	0	0	2	1	2	1	51,244
Antioch	0	0	0	0	0	1	0	0	1	0	112,481
Arcadia	2	0	0	0	0	0	0	0	2	0	58,122
Arcata	0	0	1	0	0	0	0	0	0	1	18,516
Atwater	1	0	0	0	0	0	0	0	1	0	29,704
Auburn	1	0	0	0	0	0	0	0	1	0	14,293
Avalon	0	0	1	0	0	0	0	0	1	0	3,676
Azusa	2	0	0	0	0	0	0	1	1	0	50,373
Bakersfield	1	2	3	0	0	0	0	0	2	4	388,265
Bell	1	0	0	0	0	0	0	1	0	0	35,526
Benicia	2	0	0	0	0	0	0	1	1	0	28,374
Berkeley	3	2	1	0	0	1	1	0	3	3	122,346
Beverly Hills	1	2	2	0	0	0	1	0	2	2	33,776
Big Bear	1	0	1	0	0	0	0	0	2	0	5,305
Brawley	0	0	0	0	0	1	0	1	0	0	26,363
Buena Park	0	0	0	1	0	0	0	0	0	1	81,901
Burbank	6	1	0	0	0	0	0	0	2	5	102,419
Calabasas	1	0	0	0	0	0	0	0	1	0	23,897
Calexico	0	0	1	0	0	0	0	0	0	1	39,957
Camarillo	2	0	0	0	0	0	0	0	1	1	70,424
Campbell	3	0	0	0	0	0	0	1	0	2	41,921
Capitola	0	0	0	0	0	1	1	0	0	0	10,020
Carlsbad	2	1	0	1	0	0	1	3	0	0	116,516
Carson	2	0	0	0	0	0	0	1	0	1	91,372
Cathedral City	1	0	1	0	0	2	0	1	3	0	55,417
Central Marin	5	2	0	0	0	0	0	0	3	4	34,593
Cerritos	1	1	0	0	0	0	1	0	1	0	49,952
Chico	2	0	0	0	0	0	0	1	1	0	105,355
Chino	7	0	0	0	0	0	1	3	1	2	96,309
Chula Vista	4	1	0	0	0	0	0	2	1	2	278,027
Citrus Heights	3	1	0	0	0	0	0	0	3	1	88,314
Clearlake	2	0	0	0	0	0	0	0	1	1	15,268
Clovis	2	0	0	0	0	0	0	1	1	0	116,809
Coalinga	1	0	0	0	0	0	0	0	1	0	17,061
Colusa	1	0	0	0	0	0	0	1	0	0	6,042
Costa Mesa	7	0	1	0	0	0	2	1	3	2	113,317
Covina	3	0	0	0	0	0	2	0	1	0	47,413
Crescent City	1	0	0	0	0	0	0	1	0	0	6,706
Culver City	1	0	0	0	0	0	0	0	1	0	39,218
Cupertino	0	1	0	0	0	0	0	1	0	0	59,343
Cypress	1	0	0	0	0	0	0	0	0	1	49,124
Daly City	1	0	0	0	0	0	0	0	1	0	106,855
Dana Point	1	0	0	0	0	0	0	0	1	0	33,604
Davis	11	2	3	0	0	0	4	2	5	5	69,853
Diamond Bar	1	0	0	0	0	0	0	0	0	1	55,735
El Cajon	1	0	1	0	0	1	1	1	1	0	103,035
El Cerrito	4	0	0	0	0	0	1	1	1	1	25,725
Elk Grove	3	2	0	0	0	0	2	0	2	1	177,331
El Monte	2	0	0	0	0	1	0	2	1	0	115,690
Encinitas	2	1	1	0	0	0	1	0	2	1	63,055
Escondido	1	0	0	0	0	0	0	0	0	1	152,446
Eureka	0	0	0	1	0	0	0	0	1	0	26,656
Fairfax	1	2	0	0	0	1	0	1	0	3	7,530
Fairfield	3	0	1	0	0	0	1	1	0	2	118,491
Fontana	1	1	1	0	0	0	0	0	1	2	216,553
Fort Bragg	1	0	0	0	0	0	0	1	0	0	7,289
Foster City	1	0	0	0	0	0	1	0	0	0	34,291
Fountain Valley	1	0	0	0	0	0	0	1	0	0	55,345
Fremont	4	0	0	0	0	0	0	2	2	0	244,259
Fresno	11	0	1	0	0	0	1	3	3	5	535,472
Fullerton	0	0	1	0	0	0	0	0	1	0	139,011
Galt	1	0	0	0	0	0	0	0	0	1	26,867
Gardena	1	0	0	0	0	0	0	0	1	0	59,385
Garden Grove	4	4	1	0	0	0	1	1	2	5	171,698
Grover Beach	1	0	0	0	0	0	0	0	1	0	13,491
Hawaiian Gardens	1	0	0	0	0	0	0	1	0	0	14,146
Hawthorne	0	0	1	0	0	0	0	0	0	1	86,269
Hayward	3	0	1	0	0	0	0	0	2	2	160,891
Healdsburg	0	0	1	0	0	0	0	0	0	1	11,907
Hermosa Beach	0	1	0	0	0	0	0	0	0	1	19,300
Hesperia	0	1	0	0	0	0	0	0	0	1	96,378
Hillsborough	1	0	0	0	0	0	0	1	0	0	11,447
Hollister	0	0	1	0	0	0	0	1	0	0	41,438
Huntington Beach	2	0	2	0	0	0	2	0	1	1	200,128
Indio	0	2	0	0	0	0	0	0	1	1	93,219
Industry	1	0	0	0	0	0	0	0	0	1	201
Irvine	6	1	0	0	0	0	2	3	0	2	297,069
Jurupa Valley	0	0	1	0	0	0	0	0	1	0	111,198

Table 94. Hate Crime Incidents Per Bias Motivation and Quarter, by Selected State and Agency and Federal, 2020—Continued

(Number.)

State/agency	Number of incidents per bias motivation						Number of incidents per quarter				Population[1]
	Race/ Ethnicity/ Ancestry	Religion	Sexual orientation	Disability	Gender	Gender Identity	1st quarter	2nd quarter	3rd quarter	4th quarter	
Laguna Hills	0	0	1	0	0	0	0	1	0	0	31,264
La Habra	0	0	1	0	0	0	0	1	0	0	60,672
Lake Forest	1	0	0	0	0	0	1	0	0	0	86,469
Lakewood	0	0	1	0	0	0	0	1	0	0	79,222
La Mesa	1	0	0	0	0	0	0	1	0	0	59,488
La Mirada	1	0	0	0	0	0	0	0	0	1	48,144
Lancaster	8	0	0	0	0	0	2	3	3	0	157,689
Lodi	1	0	0	0	0	0	0	0	1	0	68,207
Lomita	1	0	0	0	0	0	0	0	1	0	20,327
Long Beach	15	1	2	0	0	0	3	3	3	9	462,654
Los Altos	0	1	0	0	0	0	0	0	0	1	30,203
Los Angeles[2]	187	67	81	1	2	31	69	104	110	85	4,000,587
Los Gatos	1	0	0	0	0	0	0	0	0	1	30,271
Malibu	0	0	1	0	0	0	0	1	0	0	11,736
Manhattan Beach	3	0	0	0	0	0	0	0	2	1	35,190
Martinez	2	0	0	0	0	0	1	0	1	0	38,543
Mendota	1	0	0	0	0	0	0	0	1	0	11,531
Menifee	3	1	0	0	0	0	2	0	1	1	96,837
Merced	2	0	0	0	0	0	0	0	2	0	84,197
Modesto	7	0	4	0	0	0	1	0	3	7	216,560
Montclair	0	1	0	0	0	0	0	0	1	0	40,473
Monterey	4	1	0	0	0	0	1	2	2	0	28,209
Monterey Park	1	0	0	0	0	0	0	0	0	1	59,609
Moorpark	1	0	0	0	0	0	0	0	0	1	36,573
Moreno Valley	1	0	0	0	0	0	0	1	0	0	215,257
Mountain View	1	0	0	0	0	0	0	0	1	0	83,745
National City	2	0	0	0	0	0	0	1	1	0	61,710
Norco	1	0	0	0	0	0	1	0	0	0	26,536
Norwalk	3	0	0	0	0	1	2	0	1	1	103,774
Novato	6	0	0	0	0	0	2	2	2	0	55,926
Oakdale	1	1	0	0	0	0	0	0	0	2	23,926
Oakland	12	1	4	0	0	2	4	6	4	5	437,923
Oceanside	7	0	0	0	0	0	0	2	3	2	176,616
Orange	3	0	1	0	0	0	1	0	1	2	138,846
Oxnard	1	0	0	0	0	0	0	1	0	0	210,064
Pacifica	3	0	0	0	0	0	0	3	0	0	38,677
Pacific Grove	2	0	0	0	0	0	0	0	2	0	15,451
Palmdale	3	0	0	0	0	0	1	0	2	0	155,321
Palm Springs	5	2	3	0	0	0	1	6	1	2	48,952
Palo Alto	4	0	0	0	0	0	1	2	1	0	65,459
Paramount	1	0	0	0	0	0	0	1	0	0	53,939
Pasadena	4	0	0	0	0	1	2	2	1	0	141,473
Perris	1	0	0	0	0	0	0	1	0	0	80,526
Petaluma	5	0	1	0	0	0	1	2	2	1	60,806
Pico Rivera	0	0	0	0	0	1	0	0	1	0	61,925
Pittsburg	1	0	0	0	0	0	0	0	1	0	73,673
Placentia	0	1	0	0	0	0	0	0	1	0	51,260
Pleasanton	1	0	0	0	0	0	0	1	0	0	83,164
Poway	1	1	1	0	0	0	1	1	0	1	49,479
Rancho Cordova	1	0	0	0	0	0	0	0	1	0	76,292
Rancho Cucamonga	4	0	0	0	0	0	2	2	0	0	178,916
Red Bluff	4	0	0	0	0	0	2	0	0	2	14,590
Redding	6	0	0	0	0	0	1	1	4	0	92,895
Redlands	5	1	2	0	0	0	5	1	2	0	71,820
Redondo Beach	1	0	0	0	0	0	0	0	1	0	66,729
Redwood City	2	1	0	0	0	0	0	1	2	0	86,983
Rialto	0	0	2	0	0	0	1	0	1	0	104,004
Richmond	5	0	1	0	0	0	2	1	1	2	111,367
Ridgecrest	1	0	0	0	0	0	0	0	1	0	29,120
Rio Dell	0	1	0	0	0	0	1	0	0	0	3,347
Riverside	9	2	3	0	0	0	7	1	3	3	334,370
Rohnert Park	1	0	0	0	0	0	0	1	0	0	43,572
Rosemead	0	0	2	0	0	0	0	0	1	1	54,087
Roseville	8	1	0	0	0	0	1	4	3	1	144,128
Sacramento	8	0	2	0	0	0	1	6	2	1	519,050
Salinas	1	0	0	0	0	0	0	1	0	0	155,984
San Bernardino	2	1	2	0	0	1	0	0	5	1	216,365
San Bruno	1	0	0	0	0	0	0	1	0	0	42,997
San Clemente	1	0	0	0	0	0	0	1	0	0	64,665
San Diego	17	1	7	0	0	1	6	8	5	7	1,437,608
San Francisco	37	7	8	0	0	2	14	6	18	16	881,514
San Gabriel	0	0	0	0	0	1	0	0	1	0	39,927
San Jose	75	9	9	0	0	1	18	37	23	16	1,029,542
San Leandro	1	0	0	0	0	0	0	1	0	0	89,239
San Luis Obispo	10	0	1	0	0	0	2	3	5	1	47,722
San Marcos	2	1	0	0	0	0	0	0	2	1	98,198
San Mateo	1	0	0	0	0	0	0	1	0	0	105,246
San Pablo	1	0	0	0	0	0	1	0	0	0	31,164
San Rafael	3	1	0	0	0	0	1	2	1	0	58,512

Table 94. Hate Crime Incidents Per Bias Motivation and Quarter, by Selected State and Agency and Federal, 2020—Continued

(Number.)

State/agency	Number of incidents per bias motivation						Number of incidents per quarter				Population[1]
	Race/ Ethnicity/ Ancestry	Religion	Sexual orientation	Disability	Gender	Gender Identity	1st quarter	2nd quarter	3rd quarter	4th quarter	
San Ramon	2	0	0	0	0	0	0	0	2	0	76,502
Santa Ana	5	8	2	0	0	1	0	3	4	9	333,107
Santa Barbara	0	0	0	0	0	1	0	0	0	1	91,692
Santa Clarita	4	0	0	0	0	0	0	0	3	1	221,932
Santa Cruz	3	0	2	0	0	1	0	1	4	1	65,073
Santa Maria	0	1	1	0	0	0	1	0	1	0	108,140
Santa Monica	11	0	1	0	0	0	1	6	3	2	90,474
Santa Rosa	6	4	1	0	0	0	0	0	8	3	176,932
Santee	3	0	0	0	0	0	0	1	1	1	58,598
Sausalito	0	1	0	0	0	0	0	1	0	0	7,080
Sierra Madre	2	0	0	0	0	0	0	2	0	0	10,779
Signal Hill	1	0	0	0	0	0	0	1	0	0	11,467
Simi Valley	4	0	1	0	0	0	2	0	1	2	125,742
South Gate	1	0	1	0	0	0	1	0	1	0	93,336
South Lake Tahoe	1	0	2	0	0	0	0	0	3	0	22,286
South San Francisco	0	0	1	0	0	0	0	0	0	1	68,260
Stockton	5	0	1	0	0	0	2	2	1	1	314,981
Sunnyvale	6	1	0	0	0	1	3	0	4	1	154,133
Tehachapi	1	0	0	0	0	0	0	1	0	0	12,873
Temecula	0	0	0	0	0	1	0	0	1	0	116,442
Thousand Oaks	2	0	0	0	0	0	0	0	2	0	126,823
Torrance	10	0	1	0	0	0	1	5	3	2	143,421
Tracy	1	2	0	0	0	0	0	1	1	1	96,067
Tulare	0	1	0	0	0	0	0	0	1	0	66,207
Turlock	1	1	0	0	0	0	0	0	1	1	74,183
Union City	2	0	0	0	0	0	0	1	1	0	74,625
Vacaville	3	0	0	0	0	0	0	2	0	1	101,616
Vallejo	7	0	0	0	0	0	0	3	3	1	122,326
Ventura	3	0	0	0	0	1	1	0	2	1	109,295
Vernon	0	1	0	0	0	0	1	0	0	0	110
Victorville	2	0	0	0	0	0	1	1	0	0	123,085
Visalia	0	1	0	0	0	0	1	0	0	0	135,733
Vista	4	1	0	0	0	0	0	3	1	1	102,600
Walnut Creek	7	0	2	0	0	0	2	3	3	1	70,849
West Covina	2	0	0	0	0	0	1	0	0	1	104,989
West Hollywood	4	1	2	0	0	0	1	1	2	3	36,719
Westminster	6	0	0	0	0	0	2	2	1	1	90,741
Woodland	1	0	0	0	0	0	0	0	0	1	61,123
Yorba Linda	1	1	0	0	0	0	0	1	1	0	68,017
Yuba City	4	0	0	0	0	0	0	0	3	1	67,165
Yucaipa	0	0	1	0	0	0	0	1	0	0	54,200
Yucca Valley	1	0	0	0	0	0	0	0	0	1	21,901
Universities and Colleges	11	3	0	0	0	0					
California State University, San Marcos	2	0	0	0	0	0	0	1	1	0	17,136
Riverside Community College	1	0	0	0	0	0	1	0	0	0	62,345
Sonoma County Junior College	1	0	0	0	0	0	0	1	0	0	29,046
University of California											
Irvine	3	1	0	0	0	0	2	1	0	1	38,105
Los Angeles	3	2	0	0	0	0	2	1	1	1	47,103
San Diego	1	0	0	0	0	0	0	0	0	1	39,811
Metropolitan Counties	73	15	17	0	1	0					
Alameda	1	0	1	0	0	0	1	0	1	0	
Butte	0	0	1	0	0	0	0	0	1	0	
Contra Costa	1	0	0	0	0	0	0	0	0	1	
El Dorado	1	1	0	0	0	0	2	0	0	0	
Fresno	0	1	0	0	0	0	0	0	1	0	
Kern	1	0	2	0	0	0	0	1	1	1	
Los Angeles	21	1	4	0	0	0	5	5	12	4	
Marin	1	0	0	0	0	0	0	1	0	0	
Monterey	0	1	0	0	0	0	0	1	0	0	
Orange	2	5	0	0	0	0	4	1	2	0	
Sacramento	2	0	0	0	0	0	0	1	0	1	
San Bernardino	6	0	0	0	0	0	0	2	2	2	
San Diego	12	3	3	0	1	0	5	5	4	5	
San Luis Obispo	1	0	0	0	0	0	0	0	0	1	
San Mateo	5	0	2	0	0	0	4	1	1	1	
Santa Barbara	1	0	0	0	0	0	0	1	0	0	
Santa Clara	3	3	0	0	0	0	4	1	1	0	
Santa Cruz	6	0	1	0	0	0	0	0	4	3	
Shasta	0	0	1	0	0	0	0	0	1	0	
Sonoma	4	0	2	0	0	0	1	4	1	0	
Stanislaus	2	0	0	0	0	0	1	1	0	0	
Yolo	1	0	0	0	0	0	0	1	0	0	
Yuba	2	0	0	0	0	0	0	2	0	0	
Nonmetropolitan Counties	2	2	1	0	0	2					
Amador	0	0	1	0	0	2	0	3	0	0	
Lake	1	0	0	0	0	0	0	1	0	0	
Lassen	1	0	0	0	0	0	0	0	0	1	
Nevada	0	1	0	0	0	0	0	0	0	1	

Table 94. Hate Crime Incidents Per Bias Motivation and Quarter, by Selected State and Agency and Federal, 2020—Continued

(Number.)

State/agency	Number of incidents per bias motivation						Number of incidents per quarter				Population[1]
	Race/ Ethnicity/ Ancestry	Religion	Sexual orientation	Disability	Gender	Gender Identity	1st quarter	2nd quarter	3rd quarter	4th quarter	
Tuolumne	0	1	0	0	0	0	0	0	1	0	
Other Agencies	6	1	4	1	0	0					
Department of Parks and Recreation, Bay Area	1	0	0	0	0	0	1	0	0	0	
East Bay Regional Park District	1	0	2	0	0	0	0	1	2	0	
Los Angeles Transportation Services Bureau	2	0	0	0	0	0	0	0	1	1	
Porterville Developmental Center	1	0	0	0	0	0	0	0	1	0	
Port of San Diego Harbor	0	0	1	0	0	0	1	0	0	0	
San Francisco Bay Area Rapid Transit:											
Alameda County	0	0	1	0	0	0	0	1	0	0	
Contra Costa County	0	0	0	1	0	0	0	1	0	0	
Santa Clara Transit District	1	1	0	0	0	0	1	1	0	0	
COLORADO											
Total	184	35	49	5	0	10					
Cities	154	25	39	2	0	6					
Aurora	13	0	1	0	0	0	0	7	4	3	385,720
Avon	1	0	0	0	0	0	0	1	0	0	6,526
Blue River	1	0	0	0	0	0	0	1	0	0	929
Boulder	8	1	1	0	0	0	3	4	2	1	106,598
Brighton	0	1	0	0	0	0	0	0	1	0	42,536
Broomfield	2	1	0	0	0	0	0	0	1	2	71,795
Canon City	3	0	0	0	0	0	1	0	2	0	16,761
Castle Rock	5	0	0	0	0	0	0	3	1	1	71,150
Centennial	8	2	0	0	0	0	2	5	2	1	112,104
Colorado Springs	15	2	3	0	0	0	4	3	11	2	485,083
Craig	0	0	1	0	0	0	1	0	0	0	8,975
Crested Butte	1	0	0	0	0	0	0	0	1	0	1,751
Cripple Creek	1	0	0	0	0	0	0	0	1	0	1,261
Denver	47	7	21	1	0	4	10	21	24	25	737,709
Durango	2	0	1	0	0	0	0	1	1	1	19,220
Empire	1	0	0	0	0	0	1	0	0	0	307
Englewood	1	0	0	0	0	0	0	0	1	0	35,464
Erie	1	1	0	0	0	0	2	0	0	0	28,198
Estes Park	1	0	0	0	0	0	0	0	1	0	6,480
Fort Collins	2	1	0	0	0	0	0	2	1	0	173,274
Fort Morgan	1	0	0	0	0	0	0	1	0	0	11,471
Glendale	0	1	0	0	0	0	0	1	0	0	5,243
Golden	0	0	1	0	0	0	1	0	0	0	20,981
Grand Junction	2	0	1	0	0	0	0	3	0	0	64,149
Greeley	0	0	1	0	0	0	0	0	0	1	110,505
Hudson	3	0	0	0	0	0	0	1	1	1	2,817
Johnstown	1	0	0	0	0	0	0	1	0	0	15,932
Lafayette	0	0	1	0	0	0	0	0	0	1	31,457
Lakewood[2]	3	1	2	0	0	1	1	2	3	0	159,719
Littleton	1	0	0	0	0	0	0	0	1	0	48,805
Longmont	5	0	0	0	0	1	2	1	1	2	98,545
Louisville	1	0	0	0	0	0	0	0	1	0	21,101
Montrose	2	0	0	0	0	0	0	1	1	0	19,864
Monument	0	1	0	0	0	0	0	0	1	0	8,361
Northglenn	0	0	1	0	0	0	0	1	0	0	39,161
Parker	2	0	0	0	0	0	0	2	0	0	59,245
Pueblo	9	0	0	0	0	0	1	0	6	2	113,002
Rifle	1	0	0	0	0	0	1	0	0	0	9,747
Steamboat Springs	0	4	0	0	0	0	2	0	2	0	13,345
Telluride	1	0	0	0	0	0	1	0	0	0	2,508
Thornton	4	1	2	0	0	0	1	2	1	3	144,156
Trinidad	1	0	0	0	0	0	0	1	0	0	8,114
Vail	1	0	0	0	0	0	0	0	1	0	5,450
Westminster	2	1	1	0	0	0	0	1	2	1	113,941
Wheat Ridge	0	0	1	0	0	0	0	0	0	1	31,451
Woodland Park	1	0	0	1	0	0	0	1	0	1	7,969
Universities and Colleges	1	3	1	0	0	0					
University of Colorado, Boulder	1	3	1	0	0	0	1	2	2	0	40,353
Metropolitan Counties	23	6	6	3	0	3					
Adams	4	0	0	0	0	0	1	1	2	0	
Arapahoe	8	3	2	0	0	1	1	3	6	4	
Boulder	2	0	0	0	0	0	0	0	1	1	
Douglas	3	0	1	3	0	0	3	2	2	0	
El Paso	0	0	1	0	0	0	1	0	0	0	
Jefferson[2]	5	2	0	0	0	1	2	3	2	0	
Larimer	1	0	1	0	0	0	0	0	2	0	
Park	0	1	0	0	0	0	1	0	0	0	
Pueblo	0	0	0	0	0	1	0	1	0	0	
Weld	0	0	1	0	0	0	1	0	0	0	
Nonmetropolitan Counties	6	1	3	0	0	1					
Crowley	1	0	0	0	0	0	0	0	1	0	
Custer	0	0	1	0	0	0	1	0	0	0	
Fremont	0	0	1	0	0	0	0	1	0	0	
Garfield	2	0	0	0	0	0	0	0	1	1	

Table 94. Hate Crime Incidents Per Bias Motivation and Quarter, by Selected State and Agency and Federal, 2020—Continued

(Number.)

State/agency	Number of incidents per bias motivation						Number of incidents per quarter				Population[1]
	Race/ Ethnicity/ Ancestry	Religion	Sexual orientation	Disability	Gender	Gender Identity	1st quarter	2nd quarter	3rd quarter	4th quarter	
Gunnison	0	0	1	0	0	0	0	1	0	0	
Las Animas	0	0	0	0	0	1	1	0	0	0	
Montrose	0	1	0	0	0	0	0	1	0	0	
Routt	1	0	0	0	0	0	0	1	0	0	
Summit	2	0	0	0	0	0	0	0	2	0	
CONNECTICUT											
Total	65	18	15	4	0	0					
Cities	63	15	15	4	0	0					
Bethel	1	0	1	0	0	0	0	2	0	0	19,932
Bridgeport	0	0	3	0	0	0	1	0	2	0	144,350
Coventry	2	0	0	0	0	0	1	1	0	0	12,404
Danbury	4	0	0	0	0	0	2	0	0	2	85,080
Derby	1	1	0	0	0	0	1	0	1	0	12,281
East Haven	1	0	0	0	0	0	0	1	0	0	28,498
East Lyme	0	1	0	0	0	0	0	1	0	0	18,391
Enfield	2	0	0	1	0	0	3	0	0	0	43,551
Fairfield	0	0	2	0	0	0	2	0	0	0	62,311
Glastonbury[2]	7	1	0	1	0	0	0	4	0	4	34,487
Groton	1	0	0	0	0	0	0	0	1	0	8,861
Hartford	2	0	0	0	0	0	1	1	0	0	121,749
Manchester	2	1	0	0	0	0	2	1	0	0	57,510
Middletown	1	0	1	0	0	0	0	0	1	1	46,106
Naugatuck	2	1	0	0	0	0	1	2	0	0	31,024
New Britain	8	2	0	1	0	0	1	2	5	3	72,412
New Haven	7	3	1	0	0	0	2	3	4	2	130,299
North Branford	1	0	0	0	0	0	0	1	0	0	14,115
Norwalk	1	0	0	0	0	0	0	0	1	0	89,140
Norwich	3	0	1	0	0	0	0	1	2	1	38,576
Plymouth	1	0	0	0	0	0	1	0	0	0	11,529
Rocky Hill	1	0	0	0	0	0	0	1	1	0	20,160
Seymour	1	0	1	0	0	0	0	2	0	0	16,426
Shelton	2	0	0	0	0	0	0	1	0	1	41,302
Southington	2	0	0	0	0	0	1	0	1	0	43,906
South Windsor	0	0	1	0	0	0	0	0	1	0	26,213
Stamford	5	1	2	0	0	0	1	3	3	1	130,425
Stonington	1	1	0	0	0	0	1	0	1	0	18,563
Stratford	1	0	0	0	0	0	0	0	0	1	51,895
Torrington	1	0	0	0	0	0	0	1	0	0	33,796
Waterbury	0	2	1	0	0	0	0	1	1	1	107,263
Waterford	1	0	0	0	0	0	0	0	1	0	18,664
West Haven	1	0	0	0	0	0	0	1	0	0	54,516
Westport	0	0	0	1	0	0	0	0	0	1	28,728
Woodbridge	0	1	0	0	0	0	0	0	1	0	8,725
Universities and Colleges	1	1	0	0	0	0					
University of Connecticut, Storrs, Avery Point, and Hartford[3]	1	0	0	0	0	0	0	0	0	1	
Yale University	0	1	0	0	0	0	0	0	0	1	14,389
State Police Agencies	1	2	0	0	0	0					
Connecticut State Police	1	2	0	0	0	0	2	0	1	0	
DELAWARE											
Total	7	2	4	0	0	0					
Cities	2	0	2	0	0	0					
Newark	1	0	0	0	0	0	0	1	0	0	33,752
Rehoboth Beach	1	0	0	0	0	0	0	1	0	0	1,573
Wilmington	0	0	2	0	0	0	0	0	2	0	70,100
Universities and Colleges	1	1	2	0	0	0					
University of Delaware	1	1	2	0	0	0	3	1	0	0	25,885
Metropolitan Counties	1	0	0	0	0	0					
New Castle County Police Department	1	0	0	0	0	0	0	1	0	0	
State Police Agencies	3	1	0	0	0	0					
State Police											
New Castle County	1	0	0	0	0	0	0	0	1	0	
Sussex County	2	1	0	0	0	0	1	2	0	0	
DISTRICT OF COLUMBIA											
Total	63	1	41	0	0	28					
Cities	60	1	38	0	0	27					
Washington	60	1	38	0	0	27	31	21	41	33	712,816
Other Agencies	3	0	3	0	0	1					
Metro Transit Police	3	0	3	0	0	1	4	0	1	2	
FLORIDA											
Total	65	20	22	0	0	2					
Cities	47	13	16	0	0	2					
Boca Raton	2	0	0	0	0	0	1	0	1	0	101,583
Chattahoochee	1	0	1	0	0	0	0	0	0	2	3,157
Clearwater	0	0	1	0	0	0	0	0	0	1	117,859
Deerfield Beach	2	0	0	0	0	0	2	0	0	0	81,749

Table 94. Hate Crime Incidents Per Bias Motivation and Quarter, by Selected State and Agency and Federal, 2020—Continued

(Number.)

State/agency	Number of incidents per bias motivation						Number of incidents per quarter				Population[1]
	Race/ Ethnicity/ Ancestry	Religion	Sexual orientation	Disability	Gender	Gender Identity	1st quarter	2nd quarter	3rd quarter	4th quarter	
Doral	1	0	0	0	0	0	0	0	0	1	68,425
Fort Lauderdale	1	0	0	0	0	0	0	1	0	0	184,347
Fort Myers	1	0	0	0	0	0	1	0	0		90,380
Fort Walton Beach	1	0	0	0	0	0	0	1	0	0	22,871
Gainesville	1	1	1	0	0	0	0	2	1		135,076
Hialeah	1	0	1	0	0	0	1	1	0	0	234,235
Hollywood	0	1	0	0	0	0	1	0	0	0	156,434
Homestead	1	1	0	0	0	0		1		1	70,538
Jacksonville	9	0	1	0	0	1	0	4	4	3	920,508
Jacksonville Beach	1	0	0	0	0	0	0	0	1		23,894
Largo	2	0	0	0	0	0	1	1			85,594
Lauderdale Lakes	1	0	0	0	0	0	0	1	0	0	36,587
Melbourne	1	0	0	0	0	0	0	1	0	0	83,806
Miami Beach	3	4	4	0	0	0	2	1	4	4	89,017
Miami Shores	1	0	0	0	0	0	1	0	0		10,358
Milton	1	0	0	0	0	0	0	0		1	10,728
New Port Richey	2	0	0	0	0	0	0	1		1	16,954
New Smyrna Beach	1	0	0	0	0	0	0	0	1		28,380
North Miami Beach	0	2	0	0	0	0	0	1	1		43,273
Ocoee	1	0	0	0	0	0	1	0	0	0	49,877
Orlando	1	0	1	0	0	0	1	0		1	293,363
Palm Bay	0	0	0	0	0	1	1	0	0	0	116,897
Palm Beach Gardens	1	1	0	0	0	0	0	0	1	1	58,629
Pembroke Pines	2	0	0	0	0	0	0	0	1	1	175,757
Pensacola	1	0	0	0	0	0		1	0	0	53,083
Pinellas Park	1	0	1	0	0	0	0	0	0	2	54,114
Port St. Lucie	1	0	0	0	0	0	0	1			206,450
Sarasota	1	2	1	0	0	0	1	2	0	1	59,002
Southwest Ranches	1	1	0	0	0	0	1	1	0		8,025
St. Pete Beach	1	0	1	0	0	0	0	0	2	0	9,616
Tampa	0	0	1	0	0	0	0	0	1	0	407,350
West Palm Beach	2	0	2	0	0	0	0	1	3	0	113,268
Universities and Colleges	2	0	1	0	0	0					
Pensacola State College	2	0	0	0	0	0	1	1	0	0	13,758
Tallahassee Community College	0	0	1	0	0	0	1	0	0	0	16,760
Metropolitan Counties	15	7	5	0	0	0					
Alachua	1	1	0	0	0	0	1	1	0	0	
Collier	3	0	0	0	0	0	0	0	3		
Highlands	0	0	1	0	0	0	0	1	0	0	
Lake	1	0	0	0	0	0	0	1	0	0	
Lee	2	0	0	0	0	0	0	0	2	0	
Marion	1	1	0	0	0	0	1		1	0	
Martin	1	0	0	0	0	0	0	0	1	0	
Miami-Dade	1	1	1	0	0	0	1	1	1		
Orange	1	1	0	0	0	0	1	0	1	0	
Pasco	1	0	2	0	0	0	1	0	0	2	
Pinellas	1	0	0	0	0	0	0	0	0	1	
Santa Rosa	1	0	0	0	0	0	0	0	0	1	
Sarasota	0	3	0	0	0	0	0	1	2		
St. Johns	1	0	0	0	0	0	0	0	1	0	
Sumter	0	0	1	0	0	0				1	
Nonmetropolitan Counties	1	0	0	0	0	0					
Taylor	1	0	0	0	0	0	1				
GEORGIA											
Total	132	26	24	7	3	4					
Cities	68	11	11	2	1	3					
Athens-Clarke County	4	1	0	0	0	2	0	4	2	1	128,152
Atlanta	3	0	1	0	0	0				4	515,945
Brookhaven	3	1	0	0	0	0	0	2	0	2	56,248
Byron	0	1	0	0	0	0	0	0	1	0	5,304
Cedartown	3	0	0	0	0	0	1	1	1	0	10,020
College Park	0	0	1	0	0	0	1	0	0	0	15,204
Dalton	1	0	0	0	0	0				1	33,723
Decatur	0	0	1	0	0	0	0	0	0	1	26,473
Demorest	1	0	0	0	0	0	1	0			2,157
Douglasville	1	0	0	0	0	0	0	0	0	1	34,409
Dunwoody	3	1	0	0	0	0	1	0	3	0	49,687
Eastman	0	0	1	0	0	0	0	0	0	1	5,018
Forest Park	1	0	1	0	0	0	0	0	0	2	20,202
Gainesville	3	1	0	0	0	0	0	2	1	1	44,398
Hiram	1	0	0	0	0	0	0	1	0	0	4,301
Johns Creek	1	0	0	2	0	0	1	2	0	0	85,408
Marietta	7	1	0	0	1	0	1	3	4	1	61,348
Milton	0	0	1	0	0	0	1	0	0	0	40,368
Newington	1	0	0	0	0	0	0	1	0	0	261
Newnan	4	0	0	0	0	0	0	0	1	3	42,658
Peachtree City	1	1	0	0	0	0	1	0	1	0	36,421
Pine Mountain	1	0	0	0	0	0	1	0	0	0	1,430
Rockmart	1	0	0	0	0	0	0	1	0	0	4,458

Table 94. Hate Crime Incidents Per Bias Motivation and Quarter, by Selected State and Agency and Federal, 2020—Continued

(Number.)

State/agency	Number of incidents per bias motivation						Number of incidents per quarter				Population[1]
	Race/Ethnicity/Ancestry	Religion	Sexual orientation	Disability	Gender	Gender Identity	1st quarter	2nd quarter	3rd quarter	4th quarter	
Rome	5	0	0	0	0	0		0	2	3	36,747
Sandy Springs	7	0	0	0	0	1	1	2	3	2	111,219
Smyrna	5	2	2	0	0	0	5	1	0	3	57,317
South Fulton	1	0	0	0	0	0	1	0	0	0	100,658
Sparta	2	0	0	0	0	0	0	2	0	0	1,213
Suwanee	0	1	0	0	0	0	0	0	1	0	21,633
Temple	0	0	1	0	0	0	1	0	0	0	4,832
Thomasville	2	0	1	0	0	0	1	0	1	1	18,512
Toccoa	1	0	0	0	0	0	0	0	1	0	8,312
Villa Rica	1	1	0	0	0	0	0	0	1	1	16,296
Warner Robins	4	0	1	0	0	0	0	4	1	0	78,508
Universities and Colleges	1	0	1	0	0	0					
Georgia Institute of Technology	0	0	1	0	0	0	0	0	0	1	38,951
University of West Georgia	1	0	0	0	0	0	1	0	0	0	16,353
Metropolitan Counties	48	14	9	5	0	0					
Brooks	1	0	0	0	0	0	0	0	1	0	
Catoosa	3	0	0	0	0	0	0	1	2	0	
Cherokee	2	0	1	0	0	0	0	2	0	1	
Clayton County Police Department	3	0	2	0	0	0	1	1	1	2	
Cobb County Police Department[2]	15	7	1	1	0	0	3	6	12	2	
Coweta	2	0	0	0	0	0	0	1	1	0	
DeKalb County Police Department	4	1	2	0	0	0	2	1	3	1	
Floyd County Police Department	1	0	0	0	0	0	0	0	1	0	
Forsyth	3	0	2	0	0	0	0	1	1	3	
Glynn County Police Department	1	1	0	0	0	0	2	0	0	0	
Hall	2	0	1	1	0	0	0	3	1	0	
Haralson	1	0	0	0	0	0	0	0	0	1	
Henry County Police Department	0	2	0	0	0	0	0	0	0	2	
Lee	2	0	0	0	0	0	0	0	2	0	
Long	1	0	0	0	0	0	0	0	0	1	
Lowndes	0	1	0	0	0	0	0	0	0	1	
Madison	0	0	0	1	0	0	0	0	0	1	
Oglethorpe	1	0	0	0	0	0	1	0	0	0	
Paulding	4	1	0	0	0	0	0	0	4	1	
Peach	0	0	0	1	0	0	0	1	0	0	
Pickens	0	1	0	0	0	0	0	1	0	0	
Walton	0	0	0	1	0	0	0	0	1	0	
Whitfield	2	0	0	0	0	0	2	0	0	0	
Nonmetropolitan Counties	14	1	2	0	2	1					
Bulloch	5	0	0	0	1	0	4	2	0		
Coffee	0	0	1	0	0	0	0	1	0	0	
Decatur	2	0	0	0	0	0	1	0	0	1	
Grady	2	1	0	0	0	0	1	1	0	1	
Greene	1	0	0	0	0	0	0	0	1	0	
Jackson	1	0	0	0	0	0	0	0	1	0	
Lumpkin	2	0	1	0	1	1	0	2	2	1	
Thomas	1	0	0	0	0	0	0	0	1	0	
Other Agencies	1	0	1	0	0	0					
Fulton County School System	1	0	1	0	0	0	0	0	1	1	
HAWAII											
Total	31	0	5	0	0	0					
Cities	31	0	5	0	0	0					
Honolulu	31	0	5	0	0	0	7	8	10	11	966,438
IDAHO											
Total	27	7	6	1	1	1					
Cities	25	6	4	0	1	1					
Boise	10	5	2	0	1	1	2	7	4	6	231,223
Chubbuck	1	0	0	0	0	0	0	1	0	0	15,773
Coeur d'Alene	5	0	0	0	0	0	0	2	2	1	53,405
Fruitland	1	0	0	0	0	0	0	1	0	0	5,505
Jerome	1	0	0	0	0	0	0	1	0	0	12,120
Ketchum	1	0	0	0	0	0	1	0	0	0	2,872
Meridian	2	0	0	0	0	0	1	0	1	0	119,203
Pocatello	0	0	1	0	0	0	0	1	0	0	56,900
Rexburg	1	0	0	0	0	0	0	0	0	1	29,865
Twin Falls	3	1	1	0	0	0	0	2	1	2	50,872
Metropolitan Counties	0	1	0	0	0	0					
Bonneville	0	1	0	0	0	0	0	1	0	0	
Nonmetropolitan Counties	2	0	2	1	0	0					
Fremont	0	0	0	1	0	0	0	0	0	1	
Gooding	1	0	1	0	0	0	0	1	1	0	
Lincoln	0	0	1	0	0	0	1	0	0	0	
Teton	1	0	0	0	0	0	0	1	0	0	
ILLINOIS											
Total	38	4	11	0	1	2					
Cities	35	4	10	0	1	2					

Table 94. Hate Crime Incidents Per Bias Motivation and Quarter, by Selected State and Agency and Federal, 2020—Continued

(Number.)

State/agency	Number of incidents per bias motivation						Number of incidents per quarter				Population[1]
	Race/ Ethnicity/ Ancestry	Religion	Sexual orientation	Disability	Gender	Gender Identity	1st quarter	2nd quarter	3rd quarter	4th quarter	
Arlington Heights	2	0	0	0	0	0	0		2	0	74,706
Aurora	1	0	0	0	0	0		0	0	1	197,709
Bolingbrook	1	0	0	0	0	0	1	0	0	0	74,665
Carlyle	1	0	0	0	0	0	0	1	0	0	3,174
Centralia	1	0	0	0	0	0	0	0	0	1	12,123
Chicago	9	3	7	0	0	2	5	7	5	4	2,693,598
Crest Hill	1	0	0	0	0	0	0	0	0	1	20,328
Darien	1	0	0	0	0	0	1	0	0	0	21,590
Decatur	1	0	0	0	0	0	0	1	0	0	70,175
Elgin	0	1	0	0	0	0	1	0	0	0	111,127
Fairmont City	1	0	0	0	0	0	0	1	0	0	2,434
Lombard	1	0	0	0	0	0	0	1	0	0	44,392
New Lenox	1	0	0	0	0	0	1	0	0	0	27,230
Palatine	1	0	0	0	1	0	0	0	2		67,358
Peoria	0	0	2	0	0	0	0	0	1	1	109,924
Plainfield	4	0	0	0	0	0	1	1	2	0	44,817
Quincy	1	0	0	0	0	0	0	1	0	0	39,860
Rockford	1	0	1	0	0	0	0	0	1	1	144,795
Skokie	1	0	0	0	0	0	0	1	0	0	62,462
Springfield	2	0	0	0	0	0	1	0	1	0	113,912
Steger	3	0	0	0	0	0	1	1	0	1	9,184
Winnetka	1	0	0	0	0	0	0		1	0	12,328
Metropolitan Counties	2	0	1	0	0	0					
McLean	1	0	0	0	0	0	0	1	0	0	
Peoria	0	0	1	0	0	0	0	0	1		
Sangamon	1	0	0	0	0	0	0	1	0	0	
Other Agencies	1	0	0	0	0	0					
Cook County Forest Preserve	1	0	0	0	0	0	0	1	0	0	
INDIANA											
Total	124	34	23	2	2	4					
Cities	109	27	21	1	2	1					
Angola	1	0	0	0	2	0	0	2	1	0	8,748
Avon	1	0	0	0	0	0	0	1	0	0	19,377
Bloomington	4	0	0	0	0	0	2	0	0	2	86,347
Brownsburg	2	0	0	0	0	0	0	0	2	0	27,621
Columbus	3	0	2	0	0	0	1	3	1	0	48,505
Danville	0	0	1	0	0	0	0	0	0	1	10,247
East Chicago	1	0	0	0	0	0	1	0			27,616
Edinburgh	1	0	0	0	0	0	1	0	0	0	4,603
Evansville	8	0	2	0	0	0		3	3	4	117,747
Fishers	2	0	0	0	0	0	0	0	0	2	97,481
Fort Wayne	5	1	2	0	0	0	0		0	8	272,270
Franklin[2]	3	1	0	0	0	0	0	0	3	0	25,825
Goshen	0	1	0	0	0	0	1	0	0	0	34,409
Greenfield	1	0	0	0	0	0	0	0	1	0	23,273
Greenwood	2	0	0	0	0	0		1	0	1	60,460
Hammond	6	1	0	0	0	0		0	7	0	74,966
Hobart	3	0	0	0	0	0	0	0	0	3	27,791
Huntington	3	0	1	0	0	0	0	1	2	1	17,096
Indianapolis[2]	18	0	6	0	0	0	4	7	8	4	890,672
Jeffersonville	5	1	0	0	0	0	0	1	5		48,467
Kokomo	0	3	0	0	0	0	2	0	0	1	58,001
Lafayette	2	0	1	0	0	0	1	1	1		72,040
La Porte	0	0	1	0	0	0	0	0	0	1	21,515
Lawrence[2]	1	2	0	0	0	0	0	2	0	0	49,865
Lebanon	2	0	0	0	0	0	0	1	1	0	16,097
McCordsville	1	0	0	0	0	0	1	0	0	0	7,801
Michigan City	2	1	0	0	0	0	1	0	2	0	30,976
Mishawaka	0	1	0	0	0	0	1	0	0	0	50,610
Muncie	1	0	0	0	0	0	0	1	0	0	67,760
Munster	2	0	0	0	0	0	0	1	1	0	22,357
Noblesville	2	0	0	0	0	0	0	0	1	1	66,127
Plainfield	1	0	0	0	0	0	1	0	0	0	36,239
Schererville	2	0	0	0	0	0	1	1	0		28,454
Seymour	2	0	0	0	0	0	0	2	0	0	20,171
Shelbyville	1	1	0	1	0	0			1	2	19,451
South Bend	11	2	2	0	0	1	4	6	4	2	102,119
Terre Haute	4	12	2	0	0	0	0	10	5	3	60,604
Warsaw	1	0	1	0	0	0	1	1	0	0	15,319
Washington	1	0	0	0	0	0	0	0	0	1	12,612
Westfield	4	0	0	0	0	0	0	0	3	1	45,469
Universities and Colleges	2	0	1	0	0	0					
Indiana University, South Bend	2	0	0	0	0	0	2	0	0	0	6,168
Purdue University	0	0	1	0	0	0			1		47,412
Metropolitan Counties	7	2	1	1	0	1					
Hendricks	1	1	0	0	0	0	0	0	2	0	
Johnson	0	0	0	1	0	0	0	1	0	0	
Lake	1	0	0	0	0	0	1	0	0	0	

Table 94. Hate Crime Incidents Per Bias Motivation and Quarter, by Selected State and Agency and Federal, 2020—Continued

(Number.)

State/agency	Number of incidents per bias motivation						Number of incidents per quarter				Population[1]
	Race/ Ethnicity/ Ancestry	Religion	Sexual orientation	Disability	Gender	Gender Identity	1st quarter	2nd quarter	3rd quarter	4th quarter	
Monroe	3	0	1	0	0	0	1	1	2	0	
St. Joseph	0	1	0	0	0	0	1	0	0	0	
Vanderburgh	1	0	0	0	0	0		0	1	0	
Vigo	1	0	0	0	0	1	1	0	1	0	
Nonmetropolitan Counties	1	0	0	0	0	1					
Greene	1	0	0	0	0	0	1	0	0	0	
Steuben	0	0	0	0	0	1	1	0	0	0	
State Police Agencies	5	3	0	0	0	0					
Indiana State Police	5	3	0	0	0	0	2	2	3	1	
Other Agencies	0	2	0	0	0	1					
Indiana Gaming Commission	0	2	0	0	0	1	1	0	2	0	
IOWA											
Total	12	0	3	0	0	0					
Cities	9	0	3	0	0	0					
Adel	1	0	0	0	0	0	0	0	1	0	5,696
Ames	2	0	1	0	0	0	2	1	0	0	67,109
Davenport	1	0	0	0	0	0	0	0	1	0	101,806
Dubuque	0	0	1	0	0	0	1	0	0	0	57,904
Indianola	0	0	1	0	0	0	0	0	0	1	16,154
Iowa City	3	0	0	0	0	0	0	1	2	0	75,964
Marion	1	0	0	0	0	0	0	1	0	0	40,968
Waterloo	1	0	0	0	0	0	0	0	1	0	67,200
Universities and Colleges	2	0	0	0	0	0					
Iowa State University	2	0	0	0	0	0	1	0	1	0	37,944
Nonmetropolitan Counties	1	0	0	0	0	0					
Marshall	1	0	0	0	0	0	1	0	0	0	
KANSAS											
Total	85	28	8	0	3	0					
Cities	62	19	6	0	0	0					
Atchison	1	0	0	0	0	0	0	1	0	0	10,421
Augusta	0	0	1	0	0	0	1	0	0	0	9,339
Bel Aire	2	0	0	0	0	0	0	1	1	0	8,490
Belleville	1	0	0	0	0	0	0	0	0	1	1,869
Beloit	0	0	1	0	0	0	0	0	0	1	3,604
Burlington	0	1	0	0	0	0	0	0	0	1	2,530
Clay Center	16	2	0	0	0	0	3	15	0	0	3,944
Coffeyville	1	1	0	0	0	0	1	0	1	0	9,171
Colby	2	0	0	0	0	0	1	1	0	0	5,365
Concordia	1	1	0	0	0	0	0	1	0	1	4,944
Derby	1	0	0	0	0	0	0	0	1	0	25,229
Dodge City	3	0	0	0	0	0	1	1	0	1	27,066
Edwardsville	1	0	0	0	0	0	0	1	0	0	4,503
El Dorado	1	0	0	0	0	0	1	0	0	0	12,924
Garden City	0	1	0	0	0	0	0	0	1	0	26,360
Goodland	0	1	0	0	0	0	0	1	0	0	4,397
Hays	1	0	0	0	0	0	0	1	0	0	20,769
Hiawatha	0	2	0	0	0	0	0	1	1	0	3,103
Independence	0	0	1	0	0	0	0	0	0	1	8,405
Junction City	2	1	0	0	0	0	0	1	0	2	21,242
Larned	0	1	0	0	0	0	0	0	1	0	3,632
Leavenworth	3	2	1	0	0	0	0	4	1	1	36,023
Leon	1	0	0	0	0	0	0	0	1	0	732
McPherson	1	0	0	0	0	0	1	0	0	0	13,053
Newton	4	1	0	0	0	0	2	2	1	0	18,830
Olathe	1	1	0	0	0	0	0	1	1	0	142,228
Overland Park	5	0	0	0	0	0	0	3	1	1	198,036
Pittsburg	2	0	0	0	0	0	0	0	1	1	20,027
Russell	0	0	1	0	0	0	0	0	1	0	4,412
Salina	2	1	1	0	0	0	0	1	2	1	46,400
Shawnee	3	0	0	0	0	0	0	1	0	2	66,208
Spring Hill	0	1	0	0	0	0	0	0	0	1	7,572
Topeka	1	0	0	0	0	0	0	0	1		125,024
Wellington	0	1	0	0	0	0	0	0	1	0	7,608
Wichita	6	1	0	0	0	0	0	3	3	1	390,746
Universities and Colleges	3	0	0	0	0	0					
Fort Hays State University	1	0	0	0	0	0	0	0	0	1	18,343
Kansas State University	1	0	0	0	0	0	0	0	0	1	24,546
University of Kansas, Medical Center[3]	1	0	0	0	0	0	0	0	0	1	
Metropolitan Counties	10	3	1	0	1	0					
Jefferson	0	2	0	0	0	0	1	0	1	0	
Leavenworth	1	0	1	0	0	0	0	2	0	0	
Pottawatomie	1	0	0	0	0	0	0	0	1	0	
Riley County Police Department	5	1	0	0	0	0	0	2	4	0	
Sedgwick	1	0	0	0	1	0	1	1	0	0	
Shawnee	2	0	0	0	0	0	0	2	0	0	
Nonmetropolitan Counties	10	3	0	0	2	0					
Anderson	1	0	0	0	0	0	0	0	1	0	

Table 94. Hate Crime Incidents Per Bias Motivation and Quarter, by Selected State and Agency and Federal, 2020—Continued

(Number.)

State/agency	Race/Ethnicity/Ancestry	Religion	Sexual orientation	Disability	Gender	Gender Identity	1st quarter	2nd quarter	3rd quarter	4th quarter	Population[1]
Barton	0	1	0	0	0	0	0	0	0	1	
Cherokee	1	0	0	0	0	0	1	0	0	0	
Gray	1	0	0	0	0	0	0	0	1	0	
Kingman	1	0	0	0	0	0	1	0	0	0	
Lyon	1	0	0	0	0	0	0	1	0		
Marion	0	1	0	0	0	0	1	0	0	0	
Marshall	1	0	0	0	0	0	0	0	1	0	
McPherson	1	0	0	0	0	0	0	1	0	0	
Montgomery	1	1	0	0	0	0	0	0	1	1	
Rawlins	0	0	0	0	1	0	0	1	0		
Rush	0	0	0	0	1	0	0	0	1	0	
Russell	1	0	0	0	0	0	1	0	0	0	
Saline	1	0	0	0	0	0	0	0	1	0	
State Police Agencies	0	1	0	0	0	0					
Highway Patrol, Troop F	0	1	0	0	0	0	1	0	0	0	
Tribal Agencies	0	0	1	0	0	0					
Potawatomi Tribal	0	0	1	0	0	0	0	0	0	1	
Other Agencies	0	2	0	0	0	0					
Reno County Drug Enforcement Unit	0	2	0	0	0	0	2	0			
KENTUCKY											
Total	134	18	18	1	2	3					
Cities	99	14	14	0	2	3					
Ashland	3	0	0	0	0	0	0	2	1	0	19,979
Bellevue	1	0	0	0	0	0	0	1	0	0	5,695
Berea	2	0	0	0	0	0	0	0	1	1	16,311
Bowling Green[2]	3	2	0	0	0	0	2	0	1	1	71,861
Covington	1	0	1	0	0	1	1	0	1	1	40,324
Cynthiana	3	0	0	0	0	0	1	2	0	0	6,329
Dayton	1	0	0	0	0	0	1	0	0	0	5,639
Eminence	1	0	0	0	0	0	0	0	1	0	2,591
Falmouth	1	0	0	0	0	0	0	0	1	0	2,091
Florence	1	0	0	0	0	0	0	0	0	1	33,397
Frankfort	1	0	0	0	0	0	1	0	0	0	27,803
Glasgow	1	0	0	0	0	0	0	0	1	0	14,537
Grayson	1	0	0	0	0	0	0	0	1	0	3,870
Hopkinsville	2	0	0	0	0	0	1	0	0	1	30,532
Independence	0	0	1	0	0	0	0	0	1	0	28,957
Indian Hills	1	0	0	0	0	0	1	0	0	0	2,978
Jeffersontown	1	0	0	0	0	0	0	0	0	1	27,700
La Grange	1	0	1	0	0	0	0	1	1	0	9,142
Leitchfield	1	0	0	0	0	0	0	0	1	0	6,880
Lexington[2]	18	5	6	0	0	2	5	7	11	5	325,851
Louisville Metro	27	2	3	0	0	0	3	12	9	8	673,730
Marion	1	0	0	0	0	0	0	0	0	1	2,821
Maysville	0	0	1	0	0	0	0	1	0	0	8,695
Middlesboro	1	0	0	0	0	0	0	0	1	0	8,968
Morehead	1	0	0	0	0	0	0	0	1	0	7,644
Murray	4	0	0	0	0	0	0	3	1	0	19,499
Newport	3	0	0	0	0	0	0	2	1	0	14,874
Owensboro	4	1	0	0	0	0	0	2	2	1	60,430
Paducah[2]	3	1	1	0	1	0	1	2	0	1	24,850
Paris	1	0	0	0	0	0	0	0	1	0	9,655
Radcliff	2	0	0	0	0	0	0	2	0	0	22,950
Richmond[2]	1	1	0	0	1	0	1	0	1	0	36,691
Russell Springs	2	0	0	0	0	0	0	1	1	0	2,661
Scottsville	1	1	0	0	0	0	1	0	0	1	4,576
Shively	1	0	0	0	0	0	0	1	0	0	15,735
St. Matthews	1	1	0	0	0	0	0	0	2	0	18,162
Warsaw	1	0	0	0	0	0	0	0	1	0	1,705
Winchester	1	0	0	0	0	0	0	0	0	1	18,570
Universities and Colleges	6	0	1	0	0	0					
University of Kentucky	1	0	0	0	0	0	0	0	1	0	30,981
University of Louisville	4	0	0	0	0	0	1	0	3	0	24,770
Western Kentucky University[2]	1	0	1	0	0	0	0	0	1	0	23,228
Metropolitan Counties	9	1	3	1	0	0					
Boone[2]	4	1	1	0	0	0	0	1	1	3	
Bullitt	1	0	0	0	0	0	0	0	1	0	
Campbell County Police Department	1	0	0	0	0	0	0	0	0	1	
Carter	1	0	0	0	0	0	1	0	0	0	
Jessamine	1	0	0	0	0	0	0	0	0	1	
Kenton County Police Department	0	0	0	1	0	0	0	0	1	0	
Oldham County Police Department[2]	1	0	1	0	0	0	0	1	0	0	
Warren	0	0	1	0	0	0	0	1	0	0	
Nonmetropolitan Counties	14	3	0	0	0	0					
Barren	1	0	0	0	0	0	0	1	0	0	
Bell	0	1	0	0	0	0	0	1	0	0	
Carroll	1	0	0	0	0	0	0	0	1	0	
Graves	2	0	0	0	0	0	0	1	1	0	

Table 94. Hate Crime Incidents Per Bias Motivation and Quarter, by Selected State and Agency and Federal, 2020—Continued

(Number.)

State/agency	Number of incidents per bias motivation						Number of incidents per quarter				Population[1]
	Race/ Ethnicity/ Ancestry	Religion	Sexual orientation	Disability	Gender	Gender Identity	1st quarter	2nd quarter	3rd quarter	4th quarter	
Knox	1	0	0	0	0	0	0	1	0	0	
Madison	1	0	0	0	0	0	0	0	0	1	
Mason	1	0	0	0	0	0	0	0	1	0	
McCracken	3	0	0	0	0	0	1	2	0	0	
Montgomery	1	0	0	0	0	0	1	0	0	0	
Pulaski	2	0	0	0	0	0	0	1	1	0	
Rockcastle	0	1	0	0	0	0	0	0	1	0	
Rowan	1	0	0	0	0	0	0	1	0	0	
Whitley	0	1	0	0	0	0	0	0	1	0	
State Police Agencies	5	0	0	0	0	0					
State Police											
Bowling Green	2	0	0	0	0	0	0	1	0	1	
Dry Ridge	1	0	0	0	0	0	0	0	0	1	
Hazard	1	0	0	0	0	0	0	0	1	0	
Madisonville	1	0	0	0	0	0	0	1	0	0	
Other Agencies	1	0	0	0	0	0					
Louisville Regional Airport Authority	1	0	0	0	0	0	0	0	1	0	
LOUISIANA											
Total	27	5	6	1	1	0					
Cities	13	1	4	0	1	0					
Alexandria[2]	1	0	1	0	0	0		1			45,986
Baton Rouge	1	0	0	0	0	0	0	0	0	1	219,245
Bossier City	1	0	0	0	0	0	0	0	1	0	68,869
Gonzales	1	0	0	0	0	0	0	0	1	0	11,092
Jennings	0	0	1	0	0	0	0	0	1	0	9,737
Lake Charles	1	0	0	0	0	0	0	0	1	0	79,077
Mansfield	3	1	0	0	1	0			2	3	4,587
New Orleans	3	0	2	0	0	0	0	2	2	1	393,779
Port Allen	1	0	0	0	0	0	0	0	0	1	4,695
Rayne	1	0	0	0	0	0	0		0	1	7,997
Metropolitan Counties	12	3	2	1	0	0					
Ascension	0	0	1	0	0	0	0	1	0	0	
Calcasieu	1	0	0	0	0	0	0	1	0	0	
Lafourche	4	1	0	1	0	0	0	1	3	2	
Rapides	5	1	1	0	0	0	2	3	1	1	
St. James	0	1	0	0	0	0	0	0	1	0	
St. John the Baptist	2	0	0	0	0	0	0	2	0	0	
Nonmetropolitan Counties	2	1	0	0	0	0					
Lincoln	1	1	0	0	0	0			1	1	
Madison	1	0	0	0	0	0	1	0	0	0	
MAINE											
Total	40	7	36	0	0	1					
Cities	29	6	4	0	0	1					
Augusta	3	0	0	0	0	0	0	3	0	0	18,653
Bangor	0	1	0	0	0	0	0	1	0	0	32,179
Bath	1	0	0	0	0	0	0	0	0	1	8,322
Biddeford	1	0	0	0	0	0	0	1	0	0	21,530
Boothbay Harbor	0	1	0	0	0	0	0	0	0	1	2,219
Brunswick	2	0	0	0	0	0	0	0	2	0	20,566
Cumberland	1	0	0	0	0	0	0	0	0	1	8,327
Fryeburg	1	0	0	0	0	0	0	1	0	0	3,452
Kennebunk	2	0	0	0	0	0	0	2	0	0	11,719
Lewiston	0	0	1	0	0	0	1	0	0	0	36,186
Livermore Falls	2	0	0	0	0	0	0	2	0	0	3,154
Mexico	2	0	0	0	0	0	1	1	0	0	2,624
Norway	1	0	0	0	0	0	0	1	0	0	4,989
Portland	3	1	2	0	0	0	1	1	4	0	66,229
Rockland	0	1	1	0	0	1	0	0	2	1	7,151
Saco	5	1	0	0	0	0	0	3	3	0	20,133
Skowhegan	1	0	0	0	0	0	0	1	0	0	8,202
South Portland	1	1	0	0	0	0	1	1	0	0	25,593
Waterville	1	0	0	0	0	0	0	0	0	1	16,654
Windham	2	0	0	0	0	0	1	0	1	0	18,720
Metropolitan Counties	7	1	29	0	0	0					
Cumberland	7	1	29	0	0	0	0	2	22	13	
Nonmetropolitan Counties	1	0	0	0	0	0					
Waldo	1	0	0	0	0	0	0	1	0	0	
State Police Agencies	3	0	3	0	0	0					
State Police[2]	3	0	3	0	0	0	1	1	2	1	
MARYLAND											
Total	27	5	7	0	0	1					
Cities	7	0	3	0	0	0					
Annapolis	1	0	0	0	0	0	1	0	0		39,315
Baltimore	3	0	2	0	0	0	1	1	3		588,594
Bowie	3	0	0	0	0	0	0	1	2	0	59,008
Greenbelt	0	0	1	0	0	0	0	1			23,342

Table 94. Hate Crime Incidents Per Bias Motivation and Quarter, by Selected State and Agency and Federal, 2020—Continued

(Number.)

State/agency	Number of incidents per bias motivation						Number of incidents per quarter				Population[1]
	Race/ Ethnicity/ Ancestry	Religion	Sexual orientation	Disability	Gender	Gender Identity	1st quarter	2nd quarter	3rd quarter	4th quarter	
Universities and Colleges	2	0	0	0	0	0					
St. Mary's College	1	0	0	0	0	0	0	0	1		1,705
University of Maryland, Baltimore County	1	0	0	0	0	0	0	0	1		15,726
Metropolitan Counties	16	5	4	0	0	1					
Anne Arundel County Police Department	1	0	0	0	0	0	0	0	1		
Baltimore County Police Department	7	2	2	0	0	0	0	4	4	3	
Frederick	0	0	0	0	0	1	1	0	0		
Harford	3	0	0	0	0	0	1	0	2		
Montgomery County Police Department	1	3	1	0	0	0	2	2	1	0	
Prince George's County Police Department	4	0	1	0	0	0	0	2	2	1	
State Police Agencies	1	0	0	0	0	0					
State Police, Harford County	1	0	0	0	0	0	1	0	0		
Other Agencies	1	0	0	0	0	0					
Maryland-National Capital Park Police, Montgomery County	1	0	0	0	0	0	1	0	0		
MASSACHUSETTS											
Total	188	69	51	2	2	11					
Cities	180	65	48	2	2	10					
Acton	3	2	0	0	0	0	2	2	0	1	23,728
Adams[2]	1	1	0	0	0	0	0	0	1	0	7,959
Amherst	0	1	0	0	0	0	0	0	0	1	40,061
Andover	1	0	0	0	0	0	1	0	0	0	36,534
Arlington	6	0	0	0	0	0	1	0	5	0	45,582
Attleboro	0	1	0	0	0	0	0	0	0	1	45,181
Ayer	0	0	1	0	0	0	0	0	1	0	8,237
Barnstable	1	0	0	1	0	0	0	1	1	0	44,169
Bedford	0	1	0	0	0	0	0	1	0	0	14,135
Belmont	1	0	0	0	0	0	0	1	0	0	26,136
Berlin	1	0	0	0	0	0	0	0	1	0	3,266
Beverly	1	0	0	0	0	0	0	0	1	0	42,229
Billerica	0	1	0	0	0	0	1	0	0	0	43,473
Boston[2]	11	9	17	0	0	8	19	6	5	14	697,323
Boxford	1	0	0	0	0	0	0	0	1	0	8,328
Braintree	1	0	0	0	0	1	0	1	1	0	37,278
Brockton	1	0	0	0	0	0	0	0	1	0	99,171
Brookline	1	0	1	0	0	0	0	0	0	2	59,057
Cambridge	10	1	4	0	0	0	2	4	7	2	119,938
Chelmsford	5	1	5	0	0	0	0	3	6	2	35,369
Danvers	1	0	0	0	0	0	0	0	1	0	27,517
Dedham	1	0	0	0	0	0	0	0	0	1	25,217
Douglas	1	0	0	0	0	0	0	1	0	0	9,054
Duxbury	1	0	0	0	0	0	0	0	1	0	16,561
Edgartown	0	0	0	1	0	0	0	0	1	0	4,374
Everett	3	0	0	0	0	0	0	1	2	0	46,765
Fall River	0	1	0	0	0	0	0	0	0	1	89,136
Falmouth	1	0	0	0	0	0	0	0	0	1	30,769
Fitchburg	1	0	0	0	0	0	0	0	0	1	40,443
Great Barrington	0	1	0	0	0	0	0	0	1	0	6,928
Greenfield	1	0	0	0	0	0	0	1	0		17,239
Halifax	1	0	0	0	0	0	0	0	1	0	8,207
Haverhill	6	5	0	0	0	0	1	3	4	3	64,015
Holbrook	0	1	0	0	0	0	1	0	0	0	11,035
Holyoke	1	0	0	0	0	0	1	0	0	0	40,002
Ipswich	0	0	0	0	1	0	0	0	0	1	14,097
Leominster	1	0	0	0	0	0	1	0	0	0	41,598
Lowell	1	0	0	0	0	0	1	0	0	0	110,876
Lunenburg	0	0	1	0	0	0	0	0	1	0	11,874
Lynn	13	1	0	0	0	0	2	8	3	1	94,223
Lynnfield	1	0	0	0	0	0	0	0	1	0	13,093
Malden	3	5	0	0	0	1	3	2	4	0	60,231
Manchester-by-the-Sea	1	0	0	0	0	0	0	0	0	1	5,438
Marblehead[2]	1	2	1	0	0	0	0	1	1	1	20,525
Marlborough	1	0	0	0	0	0	0	0	0	1	39,498
Mashpee	1	0	0	0	0	0	0	0	1	0	14,180
Medford	7	3	1	0	0	0	2	0	7	2	57,137
Methuen	2	0	2	0	0	0	0	1	1	0	50,810
Middleton	1	0	0	0	0	0	0	0	1	0	10,189
Monson	1	0	0	0	0	0	0	1	0	0	8,782
Montague[2]	1	1	0	0	0	0	0	1	0	0	8,185
Natick	1	0	0	0	0	0	0	0	0	1	36,200
Newbury	1	0	1	0	0	0	0	0	1	1	7,163
Newburyport	1	0	0	0	0	0	0	1	0	0	18,288
Newton	4	1	0	0	0	0	0	4	0	1	88,281
North Andover	0	0	1	0	0	0	0	0	0	1	31,341
North Attleboro	1	0	0	0	0	0	0	0	1	0	29,280
Norwood	1	0	0	0	0	0	1	0	0	0	29,791
Oakham	1	0	0	0	0	0	0	1	0	0	1,953
Palmer	0	0	1	0	0	0	0	0	1	0	12,200

Table 94. Hate Crime Incidents Per Bias Motivation and Quarter, by Selected State and Agency and Federal, 2020—Continued

(Number.)

State/agency	Number of incidents per bias motivation						Number of incidents per quarter				Population[1]
	Race/ Ethnicity/ Ancestry	Religion	Sexual orientation	Disability	Gender	Gender Identity	1st quarter	2nd quarter	3rd quarter	4th quarter	
Plymouth	1	0	0	0	0	0	0	0	1	0	64,199
Provincetown	4	0	1	0	0	0	0	1	2	2	2,947
Quincy[2]	6	3	6	0	0	0	4	6	3	1	94,519
Randolph	1	0	0	0	0	0	0	1	0	0	32,052
Revere	1	0	0	0	1	0	0	1	0	1	52,930
Salem[2]	6	4	0	0	0	0	2	5	1	0	43,154
Somerville	6	1	3	0	0	0	2	1	2	5	81,552
South Hadley	2	0	0	0	0	0	0	2	0	0	17,613
Spencer	0	1	0	0	0	0	0	1	0	0	11,896
Springfield	14	2	1	0	0	0	1	1	10	5	153,084
Sudbury	1	0	0	0	0	0	0	1	0	0	19,778
Sunderland[2]	1	1	0	0	0	0	1	0	0	0	3,622
Swampscott[2]	3	1	0	0	0	0	0	0	2	1	15,391
Taunton	1	0	1	0	0	0	0	2	0	0	57,338
Tisbury	1	0	0	0	0	0	0	1	0	0	4,108
Uxbridge	1	0	0	0	0	0	0	0	1	0	14,202
Waltham[2]	6	1	0	0	0	0	1	2	1	2	62,339
Wareham	0	0	1	0	0	0	0	0	1	0	23,619
Watertown	3	0	0	0	0	0	0	1	2	0	36,201
Wenham	3	0	0	0	0	0	0	0	3	0	5,296
Westford	0	1	0	0	0	0	0	0	1	0	25,011
Westwood	3	7	0	0	0	0	0	0	9	1	16,578
Winchester	1	0	0	0	0	0	1	0	0	0	22,827
Worcester[2]	2	3	1	0	0	0	1	1	2	1	184,850
Yarmouth[2]	5	1	0	0	0	0	0	4	0	1	23,015
Universities and Colleges	7	4	3	0	0	1					
Boston University	2	1	0	0	0	0	0	1	1	1	42,779
Fitchburg State University	1	0	0	0	0	0	0	0	0	1	11,130
Gordon College	1	0	0	0	0	0	0	0	0	1	2,397
Harvard University	0	1	0	0	0	0	0	1	0	0	41,987
Holyoke Community College[2]	0	0	1	0	0	1	1	0	0	0	6,832
Massachusetts Institute of Technology	0	2	1	0	0	0	0	0	3	0	12,321
Salem State University	0	0	1	0	0	0	1	0	0	0	10,069
University of Massachusetts											
Amherst	1	0	0	0	0	0	1	0	0	0	35,116
Medical Center, Worcester	2	0	0	0	0	0	1	1	0	0	1,227
Other Agencies	1	0	0	0	0	0					
Massachusetts General Hospital	1	0	0	0	0	0	1				
MICHIGAN											
Total	273	33	40	9	9	13					
Cities	227	28	34	9	8	11					
Alpena	0	0	1	0	0	0	1	0	0	0	9,900
Ann Arbor	3	0	0	0	0	1	0	1	3	0	120,647
Auburn Hills	1	0	0	0	0	0	0	0	1	0	25,149
Bangor	1	0	0	0	0	0	0	0	1	0	1,827
Bath Township	1	0	0	0	0	0	0	0	1	0	13,167
Battle Creek	4	0	1	1	0	0	1	1	2	2	60,479
Benton Harbor	0	0	1	0	0	0	0	0	1	0	9,710
Benton Township	1	0	0	1	0	0	0	0	0	2	14,251
Birch Run	1	0	0	0	0	0	0	0	1	0	1,468
Bloomfield Township	1	0	0	0	0	0	0	0	1	0	42,059
Boyne City	0	0	0	1	0	0	1	0	0	0	3,729
Bridgeport Township	2	0	0	0	0	0	0	2	0	0	9,736
Buena Vista Township	1	0	0	0	0	0	0	0	1	0	8,047
Burton	2	2	0	0	0	0	1	1	0	2	28,427
Cadillac	1	0	1	0	0	0	1	0	0	1	10,513
Cambridge Township	1	0	0	0	0	0	1	0	0	0	5,679
Canton Township	2	0	1	0	0	0	1	0	1	1	94,128
Cassopolis	1	0	0	0	1	0	1	0	1	0	1,692
Chesaning	0	1	0	0	0	0	0	0	1	0	2,221
Clawson	1	0	0	0	0	0	1	0	0	0	11,846
Clinton Township	1	0	0	0	0	0	0	0	1	0	100,884
Columbia Township	1	0	0	0	0	0	0	0	0	1	7,350
Commerce Township	1	0	0	0	0	0	0	1	0	0	39,689
Covert Township	1	0	0	0	0	0	0	0	1	0	2,891
Dearborn	1	0	0	0	0	0	0	0	0	1	93,507
Dearborn Heights	3	0	0	0	0	0	0	0	2	1	55,105
Decatur	1	0	0	0	0	0	0	1	0	0	1,724
Denton Township	1	0	0	0	0	0	1	0	0	0	5,421
Detroit	17	1	13	2	2	0	4	9	12	10	659,616
DeWitt	1	0	0	0	0	0	0	0	0	1	4,844
DeWitt Township	1	0	0	0	0	0	0	0	0	1	15,756
Durand	0	0	0	0	0	1	0	0	0	1	3,818
East Grand Rapids	1	0	0	0	0	0	0	0	1	0	12,105
East Lansing	2	0	0	0	0	0	0	2	0	0	48,098
Eastpointe	4	0	1	0	0	0	2	0	2	1	32,046
Eaton Rapids	1	0	0	0	0	1	0	2	0	0	5,248
Ecorse	1	1	0	0	0	0	1	0	1	0	9,576

Table 94. Hate Crime Incidents Per Bias Motivation and Quarter, by Selected State and Agency and Federal, 2020—Continued

(Number.)

State/agency	Number of incidents per bias motivation						Number of incidents per quarter				
	Race/Ethnicity/Ancestry	Religion	Sexual orientation	Disability	Gender	Gender Identity	1st quarter	2nd quarter	3rd quarter	4th quarter	Population[1]
Escanaba	2	0	0	0	1	0	0	1	1	1	12,111
Essexville	1	0	0	0	0	0	0	0	1	0	3,257
Farmington Hills	4	0	0	0	0	0	0	4	0	0	80,708
Ferndale	1	0	0	0	0	0	0	0	0	1	20,048
Flint	1	0	0	0	0	0	0	0	0	1	94,842
Flint Township	1	0	0	0	0	0	0	1	0	0	30,178
Flushing	1	0	0	0	0	0	0	1	0	0	7,827
Flushing Township	0	0	0	0	1	0	0	1	0	0	10,133
Frankenmuth	2	0	0	0	0	0	0	0	2	0	5,595
Fraser	2	0	0	0	0	0	1	0	1	0	14,480
Fremont	0	0	0	0	0	1	0	0	1	0	4,077
Garden City	1	0	0	0	0	0	0	0	0	1	26,282
Gaylord	1	0	0	0	0	0	0	1	0	0	3,692
Gladwin	1	0	0	0	0	0	0	1	0	0	2,887
Grand Blanc Township	1	0	0	0	0	0	0	0	0	1	36,498
Grand Haven	2	0	0	0	0	0	0	1	1	0	11,126
Grand Rapids	1	0	0	0	0	0	1	0	0	0	202,513
Grandville	1	0	0	0	0	0	0	1	0	0	15,913
Greenville	0	0	0	0	0	1	0	0	0	1	8,415
Grosse Pointe	2	0	0	0	0	0	0	0	1	1	5,127
Hamburg Township	0	1	0	0	0	0	0	0	0	1	21,867
Hamtramck	1	2	1	0	0	0	0	3	1	0	21,514
Harper Woods	1	0	0	0	0	0	0	0	1	0	13,679
Highland Park	3	0	1	0	0	0	0	1	0	3	10,680
Houghton	0	0	1	0	0	0	0	0	0	1	7,760
Howell	0	0	1	0	0	0	0	0	0	1	9,620
Huntington Woods	1	1	0	0	0	0	0	0	0	2	6,268
Inkster	4	0	0	0	0	0	0	1	2	1	24,173
Ionia	0	0	1	0	0	0	0	0	1	0	11,153
Jackson	0	1	0	0	0	0	1	0	0	0	32,332
Kalamazoo	1	0	0	0	0	0	0	1	0	0	76,411
Kalamazoo Township	1	0	0	0	0	0	0	0	0	1	24,562
Kentwood	0	1	0	1	0	0	0	0	0	2	52,263
Lansing	7	1	2	0	0	0	2	1	3	4	118,651
Lincoln Park	2	0	0	0	0	0	1	1	0	0	36,140
Livonia	3	0	0	0	0	1	0	0	1	3	93,342
Madison Heights	1	0	0	0	0	0	1	0	0	0	29,906
Manistee	1	0	0	0	0	0	0	1	0	0	6,103
Marshall	0	0	1	0	0	0	0	0	1	0	6,954
Meridian Township	5	0	0	0	0	0	0	2	1	2	43,598
Metro Police Authority of Genesee County	1	0	0	0	0	0	0	0	1	0	19,883
Midland	3	0	0	0	0	0	0	0	3	0	41,682
Montrose Township	1	0	0	0	0	0	0	1	0	0	7,431
Mount Pleasant	2	0	0	0	0	0	1	0	1	0	24,668
Muskegon Township	1	0	0	0	0	0	1	0	0	0	18,022
Negaunee	0	0	0	0	2	0	0	0	0	2	4,520
Niles	1	0	0	0	0	0	0	1	0	0	11,102
Northville Township	1	0	0	0	0	0	1	0	0	0	29,434
Norton Shores	2	0	0	0	0	0	0	0	1	1	24,742
Ontwa Township-Edwardsburg	2	0	0	0	0	0	0	0	1	1	6,602
Ovid	1	0	0	0	0	0	0	0	1	0	1,616
Owosso	5	1	0	0	0	0	1	0	5	0	14,363
Oxford	1	0	0	0	0	0	0	0	1	0	3,570
Paw Paw	0	1	0	0	0	0	0	0	0	1	3,351
Pinckney	2	0	0	0	0	0	1	0	1	0	2,419
Pontiac	3	0	0	0	0	0	0	2	1	0	59,411
Port Huron	1	1	0	0	0	1	0	0	0	3	28,602
Richland Township, Saginaw County	1	0	0	0	0	0	0	0	1	0	3,904
Richmond	0	0	1	0	0	0	0	0	0	1	5,856
River Rouge	0	1	0	0	0	0	0	1	0	0	7,369
Rochester Hills	3	0	0	0	0	0	0	2	1	0	74,913
Rockford	1	0	0	0	0	0	0	1	0	0	6,472
Romeo	1	0	0	0	0	0	0	0	1	0	3,607
Romulus	1	0	1	0	1	1	2	0	1	1	23,533
Roosevelt Park	1	0	0	0	0	0	0	1	0	0	3,793
Roseville	3	0	0	0	0	0	0	1	1	1	46,983
Royal Oak	1	1	0	0	0	1	1	1	0	1	59,506
Saginaw	3	0	0	0	0	0	0	1	1	1	47,767
Saginaw Township	1	0	0	0	0	0	0	1	0	0	38,971
Saline	1	0	0	0	0	0	0	0	1	0	9,400
Shelby	2	0	0	0	0	0	0	1	1	0	2,008
Shelby Township	1	0	0	0	0	0	0	0	1	0	81,416
Southfield	5	0	0	0	0	0	1	0	4	0	72,794
Southgate	1	0	0	0	0	0	0	0	0	1	28,848
South Haven	0	0	0	1	0	0	0	1	0	0	4,341
Spring Arbor Township	1	0	0	0	0	0	1	0	0	0	7,838
Stanton	1	0	0	0	0	0	1	0	0	0	1,423
St. Clair Shores	1	0	0	0	0	0	0	1	0	0	58,898
Sterling Heights	12	3	0	0	0	0	1	4	5	5	132,745

Table 94. Hate Crime Incidents Per Bias Motivation and Quarter, by Selected State and Agency and Federal, 2020—Continued

(Number.)

	Number of incidents per bias motivation						Number of incidents per quarter				
State/agency	Race/ Ethnicity/ Ancestry	Religion	Sexual orientation	Disability	Gender	Gender Identity	1st quarter	2nd quarter	3rd quarter	4th quarter	Population[1]
Sumpter Township	2	0	0	0	0	0	0	1	1	0	9,348
Taylor	1	0	0	0	0	0	0	0	1	0	60,698
Tecumseh	2	0	0	0	0	0	0	1	1	0	8,392
Three Oaks	1	0	1	1	0	0	2	0	0	1	1,537
Three Rivers	1	0	0	0	0	0	1	0	0	0	7,604
Traverse City	1	0	0	0	0	0	0	0	1	0	15,855
Troy	7	0	2	0	0	0	1	4	2	2	84,441
Walker	2	0	0	0	0	0	0	0	1	1	25,020
Warren	10	1	0	0	0	0	0	4	6	1	133,928
Waterford Township	1	0	1	0	0	0	1	0	0	1	72,735
Wayne	2	0	0	0	0	0	0	1	0	1	16,734
West Bloomfield Township	4	5	0	1	0	0	2	4	2	2	65,711
Westland	2	1	1	0	0	0	0	1	2	1	81,244
Wyoming	5	1	0	0	0	2	2	0	4	2	76,071
Universities and Colleges	8	1	0	0	0	1					
Grand Valley State University	1	0	0	0	0	0	0	0	1	0	27,752
Michigan Technological University	0	0	0	0	0	1	0	0	1	0	7,657
Oakland Community College	1	0	0	0	0	0	0	0	0	1	25,217
University of Michigan											
Ann Arbor	5	1	0	0	0	0	1	0	3	2	48,218
Flint	1	0	0	0	0	0	0	1	0	0	8,806
Metropolitan Counties	16	1	5	0	0	1					
Bay	2	0	0	0	0	0	1	1	0	0	
Berrien	0	0	0	0	0	1	0	0	1	0	
Calhoun	1	0	0	0	0	0	0	0	1	0	
Clinton	1	0	0	0	0	0	0	0	0	1	
Genesee	1	1	0	0	0	0	0	0	2	0	
Ingham	2	0	1	0	0	0	0	0	3	0	
Ionia	3	0	0	0	0	0	0	1	1	1	
Kalamazoo	1	0	0	0	0	0	0	1	0	0	
Kent	1	0	1	0	0	0	0	0	0	2	
Oakland	1	0	0	0	0	0	0	1	0	0	
Ottawa	1	0	2	0	0	0	0	0	1	2	
Saginaw	1	0	0	0	0	0	1	0	0	0	
Washtenaw	1	0	1	0	0	0	0	1	1	0	
Nonmetropolitan Counties	12	3	1	0	1	0					
Arenac	2	0	0	0	0	0	0	0	1	1	
Barry	2	0	0	0	0	0	0	1	1	0	
Charlevoix	0	0	1	0	0	0	0	0	0	1	
Dickinson	1	0	0	0	0	0	1	0	0	0	
Grand Traverse	0	1	0	0	0	0	1	0	0	0	
Houghton	1	1	0	0	0	0	0	0	0	2	
Isabella	1	0	0	0	0	0	0	0	1	0	
Lake	1	0	0	0	0	0	0	0	0	1	
Mecosta	2	0	0	0	0	0	0	2	0	0	
Missaukee	0	0	0	0	1	0	0	0	1	0	
Oceana	1	0	0	0	0	0	0	0	0	1	
Ogemaw	1	0	0	0	0	0	0	0	1	0	
Van Buren	0	1	0	0	0	0	0	0	1	0	
State Police Agencies	7	0	0	0	0	0					
State Police											
Lapeer County	1	0	0	0	0	0	0	1	0	0	
Midland County	1	0	0	0	0	0	1	0	0	0	
Saginaw County	1	0	0	0	0	0	0	0	0	1	
Shiawassee County	4	0	0	0	0	0	1	1	0	2	
Tribal Agencies	1	0	0	0	0	0					
Nottawaseppi Huron Band of Potawatomi	1	0	0	0	0	0	0	0	0	1	
Other Agencies	2	0	0	0	0	0					
Department of Natural Resources Law Enforcement Division	1	0	0	0	0	0	0	1	0	0	
Genesee County Parks and Recreation	1	0	0	0	0	0	1	0	0	0	
MINNESOTA											
Total	134	30	27	3	0	2					
Cities	117	23	24	1	0	1					
Alexandria	1	0	0	0	0	0	1	0	0	0	13,978
Blaine	1	0	0	0	0	0	0	0	0	1	66,588
Bloomington	0	0	1	0	0	0	1	0	0	0	85,159
Brainerd	3	0	0	0	0	0	0	1	1	1	13,417
Brooklyn Center	1	0	0	0	0	0	0	0	1	0	30,744
Brooklyn Park	2	0	0	0	0	0	0	1	1	0	80,897
Burnsville	2	0	0	0	0	0	1	1	0	0	61,445
Coon Rapids	1	0	0	0	0	0	0	0	1	0	63,162
Crystal	0	0	1	0	0	0	0	1	0	0	22,987
Dayton	1	0	0	0	0	0	0	0	1	0	6,958
Eden Prairie	2	0	0	0	0	0	0	0	1	1	65,353
Edina	1	0	0	0	0	0	0	0	1	0	53,422
Fairmont	2	0	0	0	0	0	1	1	0	0	9,964

Table 94. Hate Crime Incidents Per Bias Motivation and Quarter, by Selected State and Agency and Federal, 2020—Continued

(Number.)

State/agency	Number of incidents per bias motivation						Number of incidents per quarter				
	Race/ Ethnicity/ Ancestry	Religion	Sexual orientation	Disability	Gender	Gender Identity	1st quarter	2nd quarter	3rd quarter	4th quarter	Population[1]
Goodhue	1	0	0	0	0	0	0	1	0	0	1,177
Hastings	1	1	0	0	0	0	0	1	0	1	22,959
Hopkins	4	0	0	0	0	0	0	0	2	2	18,568
Inver Grove Heights	1	0	0	0	0	0	1	0	0	0	35,861
Janesville	0	1	1	0	0	0	0	0	1	1	2,251
Lakes Area	2	0	0	0	0	0	0	0	1	1	10,000
Lakeville	4	1	0	0	0	0	1	2	1	1	68,688
Mankato	4	1	1	1	0	0	0	3	3	1	43,276
Maple Grove	1	0	0	0	0	0	0	0	0	1	73,939
Maplewood	5	1	0	0	0	0	1	2	2	1	41,096
Minneapolis	18	4	5	0	0	0	9	9	5	4	435,116
Minnetonka	1	1	0	0	0	0	0	2	0	0	54,561
Mountain Lake	0	1	0	0	0	0	0	1	0	0	2,029
Plainview	1	0	0	0	0	0	0	0	1	0	3,293
Plymouth	1	1	1	0	0	0	0	0	2	1	80,843
Prior Lake	1	0	0	0	0	0	0	0	1	0	27,748
Red Wing	2	0	5	0	0	0	1	0	3	3	16,304
Rochester	3	0	0	0	0	0	0	0	1	2	120,336
Roseville	13	0	0	0	0	0	0	6	6	1	36,675
Savage	4	1	0	0	0	0	0	1	3	1	33,020
Sleepy Eye	1	0	0	0	0	0	0	1	0	0	3,331
South Lake Minnetonka	1	0	1	0	0	0	0	0	2	0	12,867
South St. Paul	0	0	1	0	0	0	0	0	0	1	20,053
St. Cloud	2	0	1	0	0	0	1	1	1	0	68,751
Stillwater	1	0	0	0	0	0	0	0	0	1	19,736
St. Louis Park	3	2	0	0	0	0	1	2	2	0	49,058
St. Paul	20	5	6	0	0	1	3	14	7	8	309,859
St. Paul Park	0	1	0	0	0	0	0	0	0	1	5,374
Wayzata	0	1	0	0	0	0	0	0	1	0	6,602
Willmar	2	0	0	0	0	0	0	0	1	1	19,901
Winona	0	1	0	0	0	0	0	0	1	0	26,487
Woodbury	3	0	0	0	0	0	2	0	0	1	74,110
Universities and Colleges	1	0	0	0	0	0					
University of Minnesota, Twin Cities	1	0	0	0	0	0	1	0	0	0	61,787
Metropolitan Counties	9	6	3	2	0	1					
Anoka	0	1	0	0	0	0	0	0	1	0	
Carver	0	1	0	0	0	0	0	1	0	0	
Olmsted	1	0	0	0	0	0	0	1	0	0	
Ramsey[2]	4	3	1	2	0	1	0	2	7	1	
Sherburne	2	0	0	0	0	0	0	0	0	2	
Washington[2]	2	1	1	0	0	0	0	0	0	3	
Wright	0	0	1	0	0	0	1	0	0	0	
Nonmetropolitan Counties	6	1	0	0	0	0					
Brown	1	0	0	0	0	0	0	0	1	0	
Cook	1	0	0	0	0	0	0	0	1	0	
Crow Wing	1	0	0	0	0	0	1	0	0	0	
Itasca	0	1	0	0	0	0	0	1	0	0	
Jackson	1	0	0	0	0	0	0	0	0	1	
Mahnomen	1	0	0	0	0	0	0	0	0	1	
Pine	1	0	0	0	0	0	0	0	1	0	
Other Agencies	1	0	0	0	0	0					
Metropolitan Transit Commission	1	0	0	0	0	0	0	0	1	0	
MISSISSIPPI											
Total	14	2	0	0	0	0					
Cities	9	2	0	0	0	0					
Cleveland	0	1	0	0	0	0	1	0	0	0	10,944
Corinth	1	0	0	0	0	0	0	0	0	1	14,461
Flowood	0	1	0	0	0	0				1	9,564
Gulfport	3	0	0	0	0	0	0	1	1	1	72,142
Kosciusko	1	0	0	0	0	0	0	0	0	1	6,652
Lucedale	1	0	0	0	0	0	0	0	0	1	3,179
Olive Branch	2	0	0	0	0	0	1	1	0	0	39,566
Southaven	1	0	0	0	0	0	0	0	0	1	56,573
Metropolitan Counties	2	0	0	0	0	0					
DeSoto	1	0	0	0	0	0	0	0	1	0	
Stone	1	0	0	0	0	0	0	0	0	1	
Nonmetropolitan Counties	3	0	0	0	0	0					
Jasper	3	0	0	0	0	0	0	0	1	2	
MISSOURI											
Total	78	15	18	2	3	2					
Cities	69	14	14	2	2	2					
Belton	1	0	0	0	0	0	0	1	0	0	23,698
Blue Springs[2]	5	3	1	0	0	0	2	1	2	3	56,193
Cameron	1	0	0	0	0	0	0	0	1	0	9,618
Cape Girardeau	2	1	1	0	1	0	0	4	1	0	40,845
Columbia	1	0	0	0	0	0	0	0	0	1	124,829
Creve Coeur	1	0	0	0	0	0	0	1	0	0	18,716

Table 94. Hate Crime Incidents Per Bias Motivation and Quarter, by Selected State and Agency and Federal, 2020—Continued

(Number.)

State/agency	Number of incidents per bias motivation						Number of incidents per quarter				Population[1]
	Race/ Ethnicity/ Ancestry	Religion	Sexual orientation	Disability	Gender	Gender Identity	1st quarter	2nd quarter	3rd quarter	4th quarter	
Eldon	0	1	0	0	0	0	1	0	0	0	4,721
Harrisonville	1	0	0	0	0	0	0	0	1	0	10,083
Herculaneum	1	0	0	0	0	0	0	0	1	0	4,216
Independence	4	0	0	0	0	0	1	3	0	0	116,648
Jefferson City	1	0	1	0	0	0	0	0	0	2	42,653
Kansas City[2]	34	5	7	0	1	2	4	18	18	7	499,335
Kirksville	2	0	0	0	0	0	0	0	2	0	17,611
Kirkwood	0	1	0	0	0	0	0	0	1	0	27,834
Lee's Summit	2	0	0	0	0	0	0	1	0	1	100,268
Macon	1	0	0	0	0	0	0	0	1	0	5,326
Marceline	0	1	0	0	0	0	0	0	1	0	2,069
North Kansas City	0	0	1	0	0	0	1	0	0	0	4,615
Odessa	1	0	0	0	0	0	0	0	1	0	5,238
Platte City	1	0	0	0	0	0	0	1	0	0	4,987
Potosi	1	2	0	0	0	0	0	0	2	1	2,568
Rolla	0	0	1	2	0	0	0	0	0	3	20,522
Sikeston	2	0	0	0	0	0	0	0	1	1	15,987
Smithville	0	0	1	0	0	0	0	1	0	0	11,097
St. Louis	1	0	0	0	0	0		0	1		298,422
Strafford	1	0	0	0	0	0	0	0	0	1	2,473
Sullivan	1	0	0	0	0	0	0	0	0	1	7,128
Thayer	1	0	1	0	0	0	0	0	1	1	2,121
Union	2	0	0	0	0	0	1	0	1	0	12,195
University City	1	0	0	0	0	0	0	0	0	1	34,045
Metropolitan Counties	5	0	3	0	0	0					
Franklin	0	0	1	0	0	0	0	0	1	0	
Jackson	1	0	0	0	0	0	0	1	0	0	
St. Louis County Police Department	4	0	2	0	0	0	0	1	5	0	
Nonmetropolitan Counties	4	1	1	0	1	0					
Benton	1	0	0	0	0	0	0	1	0	0	
Butler	1	0	0	0	0	0	0	0	1	0	
Camden	2	0	0	0	1	0	0	0	2	1	
Douglas	0	1	0	0	0	0	0	1	0	0	
Phelps	0	0	1	0	0	0	1	0	0	0	
MONTANA											
Total	16	6	3	1	0	0					
Cities	11	5	2	0	0	0					
Billings	4	3	0	0	0	0	1	4	1	1	110,157
Great Falls	5	0	1	0	0	0	0	2	4	0	58,345
Helena	1	0	0	0	0	0	0	1	0	0	33,629
Kalispell	0	2	0	0	0	0	0	0	2	0	25,125
Livingston	0	0	1	0	0	0	0	0	0	1	7,892
Missoula	1	0	0	0	0	0	0	0	1	0	76,468
Universities and Colleges	1	0	0	0	0	0					
Montana State University	1	0	0	0	0	0	0	0	0	1	18,898
Metropolitan Counties	1	0	0	0	0	0					
Missoula	1	0	0	0	0	0	0	1	0	0	
Nonmetropolitan Counties	3	1	1	1	0	0					
Big Horn	0	1	0	1	0	0	0	0	2	0	
Gallatin	2	0	0	0	0	0	0	2	0	0	
Jefferson	0	0	1	0	0	0	1	0	0	0	
Sheridan	1	0	0	0	0	0	0	1	0	0	
NEBRASKA											
Total	52	11	8	1	0	0					
Cities	35	11	7	1	0	0					
Fremont	1	0	1	0	0	0	1	0	1	0	26,381
Grand Island	2	0	0	0	0	0	1	1	0	0	51,547
Kearney	1	0	0	0	0	0	0	1	0	0	34,201
Lincoln	17	5	3	0	0	0		9	8	8	292,600
McCook	10	0	0	0	0	0	5	5	0	0	7,543
Nebraska City	1	0	1	0	0	0	1	0	1	0	7,292
North Platte	1	0	0	0	0	0	0	0	1	0	23,523
Omaha	1	6	2	0	0	0	1	1	3	4	480,297
Scottsbluff	1	0	0	0	0	0	0	1	0	0	15,665
South Sioux City	0	0	0	1	0	0	0	1	0	0	12,746
Metropolitan Counties	2	0	1	0	0	0					
Douglas	1	0	1	0	0	0	1	1	0	0	
Sarpy	1	0	0	0	0	0	0	1	0	0	
Nonmetropolitan Counties	15	0	0	0	0	0					
Keith	15	0	0	0	0	0	1	5	8	1	
NEVADA											
Total	82	14	14	1	2	1					
Cities	72	10	14	1	2	1					
Henderson	7	2	0	0	0	0	0	0	2	7	328,056
Las Vegas Metropolitan Police Department[2]	27	1	9	1	0	1	9	12	6	11	1,693,061
North Las Vegas	3	0	3	0	0	0	2	0	2	2	256,217

Table 94. Hate Crime Incidents Per Bias Motivation and Quarter, by Selected State and Agency and Federal, 2020—Continued

(Number.)

State/agency	Number of incidents per bias motivation						Number of incidents per quarter				Population[1]
	Race/ Ethnicity/ Ancestry	Religion	Sexual orientation	Disability	Gender	Gender Identity	1st quarter	2nd quarter	3rd quarter	4th quarter	
Reno	30	3	1	0	2	0	6	9	15	6	259,168
Sparks	5	4	1	0	0	0	1	3	1	5	106,664
Universities and Colleges	2	0	0	0	0	0					
University Police Services	1	0	0	0	0	0	0	0	1	0	92,407
University of Nevada, Reno	1	0	0	0	0	0	0	1	0	0	24,246
Metropolitan Counties	4	3	0	0	0	0					
Washoe	4	3	0	0	0	0	1	2	1	3	
Nonmetropolitan Counties	1	1	0	0	0	0					
Douglas	1	0	0	0	0	0	0	0	1	0	
Mineral	0	1	0	0	0	0	0	0	0	1	
State Police Agencies	1	0	0	0	0	0					
Highway Patrol, Southern Division	1	0	0	0	0	0	0	0	1	0	
Other Agencies	2	0	0	0	0	0					
Clark County School District	2	0	0	0	0	0	2	0	0	0	
NEW HAMPSHIRE											
Total	9	4	4	1	0	1					
Cities	7	4	4	1	0	1					
Charlestown	0	0	1	0	0	0	0	0	1	0	5,010
Concord	0	2	0	0	0	0	0	0	0	2	43,737
Dunbarton	0	1	0	0	0	0	0	0	1	0	2,894
Hanover	0	1	0	0	0	0	0	0	0	1	11,498
Hudson	1	0	0	0	0	0	0	0	0	1	25,748
Laconia	1	0	0	0	0	0	0	0	1	0	16,669
Londonderry	0	0	1	0	0	0	0	0	1	0	26,812
Manchester	0	0	1	0	0	0	0	0	1	0	113,018
Nashua	0	0	1	0	0	0	0	0	1	0	89,671
New Hampton	1	0	0	0	0	0	0	0	1	0	2,231
New Ipswich	1	0	0	0	0	0	0	1	0	0	5,425
Salem	2	0	0	0	0	1	0	1	0	2	29,943
Seabrook	1	0	0	0	0	0	0	0	1	0	8,871
Somersworth	0	0	0	1	0	0	0	0	0	1	12,005
Universities and Colleges	2	0	0	0	0	0					
Plymouth State University	1	0	0	0	0	0	0	0	1	0	5,868
University of New Hampshire	1	0	0	0	0	0	1	0	0	0	16,673
NEW JERSEY											
Total	267	136	62	4	8	8					
Cities	250	124	55	4	8	8					
Aberdeen Township	1	1	0	0	0	0	1	0	1	0	19,471
Absecon	1	0	0	0	0	0	0	0	1	0	8,856
Asbury Park	1	0	0	0	0	0	0	1	0	0	15,331
Atlantic City[2]	1	0	0	0	1	0	0	1	0	0	37,550
Audubon	1	0	0	0	0	0	0	0	0	1	8,608
Bayonne[2]	3	1	1	0	0	0	1	1	1	0	65,013
Belmar	1	1	0	0	0	0	1	1	0	0	5,518
Bergenfield[2]	1	1	0	0	0	0	0			1	27,347
Berkeley Township[2]	3	1	2	0	0	0			3		42,168
Berlin[2]	1	1	1	1	0	0	1	0	0	0	7,517
Bloomingdale	1	0	0	0	0	0	0	1	0		8,098
Branchburg Township[2]	1	1	0	0	0	0	1	0	0	0	14,526
Brick Township[2]	2	4	2	0	0	0	1	1	0	3	76,326
Bridgewater Township[2]	3	1	1	0	0	0	2	0	2	0	44,006
Brigantine	0	1	0	0	0	0	1	0	0	0	8,566
Byram Township[2]	1	1	0	0	0	0	0	0	1	0	7,880
Camden County Police Department	1	0	0	0	0	0	0	1	0	0	73,127
Cape May	0	0	1	0	0	0	0	0	1	0	3,401
Carlstadt[2]	1	1	0	0	0	0	0	1	0	0	6,126
Cedar Grove Township	0	1	0	0	0	0	0	1	0	0	12,483
Cherry Hill Township[2]	2	3	0	1	0	0	0	0	3	0	71,220
Cinnaminson Township	2	0	0	0	0	0	0	0	2	0	16,429
Clark Township	2	1	0	0	0	0	0	1	2		16,026
Clifton	2	0	0	0	0	0	0	0	1	1	85,058
Clinton Township	0	1	0	0	0	0	0	1		0	12,465
Collingswood[2]	1	1	0	0	0	0	0	1	0	0	13,864
Cranford Township[2]	2	1	0	0	0	0	1	0	1	0	24,186
Delran Township	1	0	0	0	0	0	0	0	1	0	16,444
Deptford Township[2]	1	1	0	0	0	0	0	0	0	1	30,275
Dunellen	0	1	0	0	0	0	1	0	0	0	7,192
East Brunswick Township	1	1	0	0	0	0	1	0	0	1	47,573
East Hanover Township	1	1	0	0	0	0	0	0	1	1	10,881
Eatontown[2]	2	2	0	0	0	0	1	0	2	0	12,124
Edison Township	3	1	0	0	0	0	0	3	0	1	99,584
Egg Harbor City	1	0	0	0	0	0	0	0	1	0	4,031
Egg Harbor Township	1	0	2	0	0	0	1	1	1	0	42,110
Elizabeth	0	0	1	0	0	0	0	0	1		129,518
Englewood[2]	4	1	1	0	0	0	2	0	2	1	28,514
Evesham Township	2	1	0	0	0	0	0	2	0	1	45,148
Ewing Township	1	0	0	0	0	0	0	0	1	0	36,325

Table 94. Hate Crime Incidents Per Bias Motivation and Quarter, by Selected State and Agency and Federal, 2020—Continued

(Number.)

State/agency	Number of incidents per bias motivation						Number of incidents per quarter				Population[1]
	Race/ Ethnicity/ Ancestry	Religion	Sexual orientation	Disability	Gender	Gender Identity	1st quarter	2nd quarter	3rd quarter	4th quarter	
Fair Lawn	1	0	0	0	0	0	0	1	0	0	32,910
Florence Township	1	0	0	0	0	0	0	1	0	0	12,527
Fort Lee	1	1	0	0	0	0	0	1	1	0	38,921
Franklin	1	0	0	0	0	0	1	0		0	4,684
Franklin Township, Gloucester County[2]	2	1	0	0	0	0	1	1	0	0	16,226
Franklin Township, Somerset County	3	0	0	0	0	0	0	3	0	0	66,138
Freehold Borough	0	1	0	0	0	0	1	0	0	0	11,643
Garfield[2]	1	1	0	0	0	0	0	0	0	1	31,908
Garwood[2]	1	1	0	0	0	0	0	0	0	1	4,360
Glen Rock	1	0	0	0	0	0	0	0	0	1	11,705
Gloucester City	0	0	1	0	0	0	0	0	1	0	11,182
Gloucester Township	1	0	0	0	0	0	0	1	0	0	63,755
Hackensack	1	0	0	0	0	0	0	1	0	0	44,264
Hackettstown[2]	1	1	0	0	0	0	1	0	0	0	9,316
Hamburg[2]	1	1	0	0	0	0	0	1	0	0	3,110
Hamilton Township, Mercer County[2]	14	2	1	0	1	0	0	6	7	1	86,805
Hanover Township	1	0	0	0	0	0	0	1	0	0	14,290
Harrison	0	1	1	0	0	0	0	1	1	0	20,937
Hawthorne	0	1	0	0	0	0	0		1	0	18,728
High Bridge	2	0	0	0	0	0	0		2		3,385
Highland Park	1	0	0	0	0	0		0	0	1	13,666
Hightstown	2	1	0	0	0	0	1	0	2	0	5,273
Hillsborough Township	0	1	0	0	0	0	0	1	0	0	40,210
Hillside Township[2]	1	1	1	0	0	0	1	1	0	0	21,995
Hoboken[2]	2	1	0	0	0	0	1	1	0	0	52,902
Holmdel Township	1	1	0	0	0	0	0	2	0	0	16,726
Hopewell Township[2]	3	0	1	1	0	0	1	1	2	0	17,641
Howell Township[2]	1	1	0	0	0	0	0	0	1	0	52,048
Jackson Township	1	2	0	0	0	0	2	0	1	0	58,120
Jefferson Township	1	0	0	0	0	0	0	1	0	0	20,626
Jersey City	1	1	0	0	0	0	1	0	1	0	263,273
Keansburg	2	0	1	0	0	0	1	1	1	0	9,582
Kearny	1	0	0	0	0	1	0	0	2	0	41,037
Lacey Township	1	0	0	0	0	0	0	1		0	29,524
Lakewood Township[2]	3	12	1	0	0	0	6	0	4	4	108,023
Lambertville	1	0	1	0	0	0	0	2	0	0	3,788
Linden	4	0	0	0	0	0	1	1	0	2	42,515
Lodi	0	1	0	0	0	0	0	1	0	0	24,343
Logan Township	1	0	0	0	0	0	0	0	0	1	5,847
Long Branch	0	2	0	0	0	0	0	2	0	0	30,175
Lopatcong Township	1	0	0	0	0	0	1	0	0	0	8,419
Lower Township	3	0	0	0	0	0	1	1	1	0	21,177
Lumberton Township	2	1	1	0	0	0	2	1	1	0	12,153
Madison[2]	1	1	0	0	0	0	0	0	1	0	17,850
Manasquan[2]	1	1	1	0	0	0	0	0		1	5,796
Manchester Township	3	0	0	0	0	0	2	1	0		43,856
Mansfield Township, Burlington County	1	0	0	0	0	0	0	1	0	0	8,527
Mansfield Township, Warren County	1	0	0	0	0	0	0	1	0	0	7,325
Maple Shade Township	3	1	1	0	0	0	2	2	1	0	18,402
Marlboro Township[2]	4	0	2	0	0	0	0	1	1	3	39,593
Medford Township	3	0	3	0	0	0	1	4	0	1	23,433
Middletown Township[2]	4	5	0	0	0	0	0	2	2	3	65,170
Millburn Township	0	1	0	0	0	0	0	1	0	0	20,053
Millville	1	0	0	0	0	0	0	0	0	1	27,272
Monmouth Beach	1	0	0	0	0	0	0	1			3,235
Monroe Township, Gloucester County	1	0	1	0	0	0	0	2	0	0	36,893
Monroe Township, Middlesex County[2]	3	2	1	0	1	0	1	0	2	0	45,653
Montclair[2]	5	3	1	0	0	0	4	3	0	0	38,621
Montgomery Township	2	1	0	0	0	0	2	0	1	0	23,268
Montvale	1	0	0	0	0	0	0	0	0	1	8,643
Montville Township	1	0	0	0	0	0	0	0	1	0	20,982
Mount Laurel Township	4	0	0	0	0	0	0	0	2	2	41,179
Neptune Township	0	0	1	0	0	0	0	1	0	0	27,320
New Brunswick[2]	1	2	3	0	1	1	0	4	1	2	55,701
New Providence	0	1	0	0	0	0	1	0	0	0	13,741
North Bergen Township[2]	1	1	0	0	0	0	0	0	1	0	60,567
Northfield	1	0	0	0	0	0	0	1		0	7,979
North Plainfield	2	0	0	0	0	0	0	1	0	1	21,279
Northvale	1	0	0	0	0	0	0	0	1	0	4,955
Nutley Township[2]	3	3	0	0	0	0	0	1	2	0	28,408
Oakland	0	2	0	0	0	0	1	1	0	0	12,929
Ocean City	1	0	0	0	0	0	0	1	0	0	10,893
Ocean Township, Monmouth County[2]	1	2	0	0	0	0	0	1	1	0	26,462
Old Bridge Township[2]	2	1	0	0	0	0	0	0	2	0	65,537
Paramus[2]	4	1	2	0	1	0	1	1	0	5	26,222
Passaic[2]	1	1	1	0	0	1	1	1	1	0	69,610
Paterson	0	1	0	0	0	0	1	0	0	0	144,947
Pemberton Township	1	0	0	0	0	0	0	0	1	0	26,875
Pennington	1	0	0	0	0	0	0	0	1	0	2,575

Table 94. Hate Crime Incidents Per Bias Motivation and Quarter, by Selected State and Agency and Federal, 2020—Continued

(Number.)

State/agency	Race/ Ethnicity/ Ancestry	Religion	Sexual orientation	Disability	Gender	Gender Identity	1st quarter	2nd quarter	3rd quarter	4th quarter	Population[1]
Pennsauken Township	2	0	0	0	0	0	0	1	1	0	35,698
Pennsville Township	1	0	0	0	0	0	0	0	0	1	12,315
Pequannock Township[2]	0	1	1	0	0	1	0	1		1	14,887
Pine Beach	1	0	0	0	0	0	0	1	0	0	2,192
Piscataway Township[2]	1	1	0	0	0	0	0	0	1	0	56,870
Pitman	1	0	0	0	0	0	0	1		0	8,701
Plainsboro Township	1	0	0	0	0	0	0	1	0	0	22,847
Pohatcong Township	0	0	1	0	0	0	1			0	3,158
Point Pleasant[2]	3	1	0	0	0	0	0	1	1	1	18,842
Princeton	2	0	0	0	0	0	0	2	0	0	31,458
Rahway	2	0	0	0	0	0	1	0	0	1	30,157
Ramsey[2]	0	1	1	0	1	0	0		1	1	14,904
Randolph Township	1	0	0	0	0	0	0	0	0	1	25,311
Raritan	1	0	0	0	0	0	1	0	0	0	7,888
Raritan Township	1	0	0	0	0	1	1	1	0	0	22,402
Red Bank[2]	2	1	0	0	0	0	0	1	0	1	11,929
Ridgewood	0	1	0	0	0	0	0	0	0	1	25,036
River Edge	0	0	0	1	0	0	0	0	1	0	11,431
Riverside Township	0	1	0	0	0	0	1		0	0	7,788
Rockaway Township[2]	2	0	2	0	0	0	2	0	0	0	26,046
Roselle[2]	1	1	0	0	0	0	0	0	0	1	21,867
Saddle River	1	0	0	0	0	0		1			3,170
Scotch Plains Township	1	0	0	0	0	0	0	0	1	0	24,313
Somerville	1	0	0	0	0	0	0	0	0	1	12,084
South Amboy[2]	0	0	1	0	0	1	1	0	0	0	9,235
South Brunswick Township	1	0	0	0	0	0	0	0	0	1	45,877
South Plainfield	2	0	0	0	0	0	0	0	1	1	24,100
Spotswood	1	0	0	0	0	0	0	0	1	0	8,216
Teaneck Township[2]	4	2	0	0	1	0	0	2	2	0	40,290
Toms River Township	1	0	0	0	0	0	0	0	1		94,561
Totowa	0	0	1	0	0	0		1	0		10,777
Trenton	1	0	0	0	0	0	0	1			82,909
Union City[2]	0	0	1	0	0	1	1	0	0	0	68,055
Union Township	0	2	0	0	0	0	0	0	0	2	58,613
Waldwick	0	1	0	0	0	0	0	1	0	0	10,156
Wallington	1	0	0	0	0	0	1	0	0	0	11,499
Warren Township[2]	4	2	0	0	0	0	3	0	1	0	15,689
Washington Township, Bergen County	0	1	0	0	0	0	1				9,171
Washington Township, Gloucester County[2]	2	1	1	0	0	0	1	1	1	0	47,551
Washington Township, Warren County	1	0	0	0	0	0	0	1	0	0	6,323
Wayne Township[2]	12	5	4	0	0	1	1	6	4	4	53,162
Weehawken Township[2]	1	1	0	0	0	0		1	0	0	14,874
Westampton Township	1	0	0	0	0	0	1	0	0	0	8,632
West Amwell Township[2]	2	0	2	0	1	0		1	1		2,728
Westfield	1	1	0	0	0	0	2	0	0	0	29,389
West Milford Township[2]	2	1	0	0	0	0	1	1	0	0	26,310
West New York	1	0	0	0	0	0	0	1	0	0	52,977
Woodbridge Township	2	0	0	0	0	0	0	0	2	0	100,119
Woodbury	4	0	1	0	0	0	0	2	1	2	9,744
Woodcliff Lake[2]	1	1	0	0	0	0				1	5,845
Wyckoff Township	1	0	0	0	0	0	0	1	0	0	16,950
Universities and Colleges	7	3	5	0	0	0					
Monmouth University	1	0	0	0	0	0		1	0	0	6,704
New Jersey Institute of Technology	1	0	0	0	0	0	0	0	1		13,236
Princeton University	1	2	0	0	0	0	1	1	0	1	8,720
Rutgers University											
Camden[2]	1	0	1	0	0	0	0	1	0	0	8,154
Newark	1	0	0	0	0	0	1	0	0	0	15,897
New Brunswick	1	1	4	0	0	0	5	1		0	57,162
The College of New Jersey	1	0	0	0	0	0	0	0	0	1	8,825
Metropolitan Counties	2	2	0	0	0	0					
Bergen[2]	1	1	0	0	0	0	0	0	0	1	
Hudson[2]	1	1	0	0	0	0	0	0	0	1	
Metropolitan Counties	5	4	0	0	0	0					
State Police[2]	5	4	0	0	0	0	2	1	2	2	
Other Agencies	3	3	2	0	0	0					
New Jersey Transit Police[2]	3	2	2	0	0	0	3	0	0	3	
Prosecutor, Hudson County	0	1	0	0	0	0	0	0	1	0	
NEW MEXICO											
Total	35	6	9	1	3	2					
Cities	28	5	9	1	3	2					
Albuquerque[2]	26	3	9	1	2	2	11	9	14	8	562,065
Carlsbad	1	0	0	0	0	0	0	0	0	1	30,233
Farmington	1	0	0	0	1	0	1	0	1	0	44,191
Gallup	0	1	0	0	0	0			1	0	21,460
Sunland Park	0	1	0	0	0	0	0	0	1	0	18,437
Metropolitan Counties	6	1	0	0	0	0					
Bernalillo	5	1	0	0	0	0	1	1	2	2	

Table 94. Hate Crime Incidents Per Bias Motivation and Quarter, by Selected State and Agency and Federal, 2020—Continued

(Number.)

State/agency	Number of incidents per bias motivation						Number of incidents per quarter				Population[1]
	Race/ Ethnicity/ Ancestry	Religion	Sexual orientation	Disability	Gender	Gender Identity	1st quarter	2nd quarter	3rd quarter	4th quarter	
San Juan	1	0	0	0	0	0	0	0	1	0	
State Police Agencies	1	0	0	0	0	0					
New Mexico State Police	1	0	0	0	0	0			1		
NEW YORK											
Total	200	202	40	0	7	14					
Cities	127	155	30	0	7	12					
Albany	0	0	1	0	0	0	1	0	0		96,318
Amherst Town	4	0	0	0	0	0	3	1		0	121,304
Binghamton	0	0	1	0	0	0	0	1	0	0	44,083
Brighton Town	1	1	0	0	0	0	1	0	0	1	35,853
Buffalo	5	0	1	0	0	1	0	1	1	5	254,627
Carmel Town	1	0	0	0	0	0	0	0	0	1	34,093
Cheektowaga Town	1	0	0	0	0	0	0	1	0	0	76,536
Clarkstown Town	0	1	0	0	0	0	0	0	0	1	80,462
Cobleskill Village	0	1	0	0	0	0	0	0	1	0	4,323
Colchester Town	1	0	0	0	0	0	1	0		0	1,947
Goshen Village	0	1	0	0	0	0	1	0	0	0	5,361
Greenburgh Town	0	1	0	0	0	0	1	0	0	0	44,727
Hudson	2	0	0	0	0	0	0	2	0	0	6,004
Hyde Park Town	1	0	0	0	0	0	0	0	1		20,766
Ilion Village	1	0	0	0	0	0	0	1	0	0	7,613
Jamestown	1	0	0	0	0	0	0	0	1		28,842
Middletown	1	0	0	0	0	0	0	0		1	28,194
Monroe Village	0	1	0	0	0	0	0	0	0	1	8,609
Mount Vernon	4	1	1	0	0	0	0	2	3	1	67,339
New Castle Town	4	0	0	0	0	0	1	0	3	0	17,824
New Rochelle	1	1	0	0	0	0	2	0			78,707
New York	84	144	24	0	7	11	86	50	66	68	8,300,377
Oneida	1	0	0	0	0	0	1	0			10,849
Orangetown Town	0	0	1	0	0	0	0	0	1	0	37,320
Plattsburgh City	1	0	0	0	0	0	0	0	0	1	19,460
Port Washington	0	1	0	0	0	0	0	0	0	1	19,391
Poughkeepsie	1	0	0	0	0	0	0	1	0		30,480
Poughkeepsie Town	2	1	0	0	0	0	1	0	1	1	38,934
Riverhead Town	1	0	0	0	0	0	0	1	0	0	33,461
Rochester	1	0	0	0	0	0	0	0	0	1	205,199
Rome	1	0	0	0	0	0	0	0	1	0	31,978
Southampton Town	1	0	0	0	0	0	0	1	0	0	51,162
Vestal Town	1	0	0	0	0	0	0	0	1	0	28,639
White Plains	4	0	1	0	0	0	0	1	1	3	58,240
Yorktown Town	1	1	0	0	0	0	1	0	1	0	36,284
Universities and Colleges	3	3	2	0	0	0					
Cornell University	2	0	0	0	0	0	1	0	1	0	24,189
State University of New York Police											
Maritime	0	2	0	0	0	0	2	0	0	0	1,947
Oneonta	0	0	1	0	0	0	1	0			7,131
Plattsburgh	1	1	1	0	0	0	3	0		0	6,475
Metropolitan Counties	23	20	5	0	0	0					
Broome	0	1	0	0	0	0	1	0	0	0	
Monroe	8	0	0	0	0	0	1	2	5	0	
Nassau	7	17	2	0	0	0	4	6	10	6	
Ontario	1	0	0	0	0	0	0	0	0	1	
Saratoga	2	0	2	0	0	0	0	2	1	1	
Suffolk County Police Department	4	1	1	0	0	0	2	3		1	
Westchester Public Safety	1	1	0	0	0	0	1	1		0	
Nonmetropolitan Counties	2	0	0	0	0	0					
Columbia	2	0	0	0	0	0	0	0	0	2	
State Police Agencies	38	17	3	0	0	2					
State Police											
Albany County	1	0	0	0	0	0	1	0	0	0	
Broome County	1	0	3	0	0	0	0	2	1	1	
Cattaraugus County	1	1	0	0	0	0	1	1	0	0	
Cayuga County	1	2	0	0	0	0	2	1	0	0	
Chautauqua County	0	1	0	0	0	0	1	0		0	
Chemung County	1	0	0	0	0	0	0	0	0	1	
Clinton County	5	0	0	0	0	0	1	2	2	0	
Columbia County	2	2	0	0	0	0	2	0	0	2	
Dutchess County	2	1	0	0	0	0	1	0	2	0	
Essex County	3	0	0	0	0	0	0	1	1	1	
Franklin County	1	1	0	0	0	0	1	1	0	0	
Greene County	1	0	0	0	0	0	0	1		0	
Jefferson County	1	1	0	0	0	0	0	1	0	1	
Madison County	1	0	0	0	0	0	0	1	0	0	
New York County	1	0	0	0	0	0	1	0	0	0	
Niagara County	1	0	0	0	0	0	0	1	0		
Ontario County	0	0	0	0	0	1	0	0		1	
Orange County	0	1	0	0	0	1	1	0	1		
Oswego County	2	0	0	0	0	0	0	0	1	1	

Table 94. Hate Crime Incidents Per Bias Motivation and Quarter, by Selected State and Agency and Federal, 2020—Continued

(Number.)

State/agency	Race/ Ethnicity/ Ancestry	Religion	Sexual orientation	Disability	Gender	Gender Identity	1st quarter	2nd quarter	3rd quarter	4th quarter	Population[1]
Otsego County	0	1	0	0	0	0	1	0	0	0	
Rockland County	1	1	0	0	0	0	0	1	1	0	
Saratoga County	2	1	0	0	0	0	0	0	1	2	
Schoharie County	1	0	0	0	0	0	0	1	0	0	
Steuben County	1	0	0	0	0	0	0	0	0	1	
Ulster County	1	2	0	0	0	0	0	1	1	1	
Warren County	1	0	0	0	0	0	0	0	1	0	
Wayne County	1	0	0	0	0	0	0	0	1	0	
Westchester County	5	2	0	0	0	0	2	1	2	2	
Other Agencies	7	7	0	0	0	0					
New York City Metropolitan Transportation Authority	7	5	0	0	0	0	6	2	3	1	
State Park											
Finger Lakes Region	0	1	0	0	0	0	0	0	1	0	
Long Island Region	0	1	0	0	0	0	0	0	0	1	
NORTH CAROLINA											
Total	148	12	25	0	1	0					
Cities	120	8	17	0	0	0					
Albemarle	0	0	1	0	0	0	0	1	0	0	16,287
Asheville	5	1	0	0	0	0	0	3	3	0	93,980
Boone	2	0	0	0	0	0	0	0	1	1	19,975
Burgaw	1	0	0	0	0	0	0	0	1	0	4,182
Burlington	3	0	0	0	0	0	0	2	0	1	55,003
Carolina Beach	1	0	0	0	0	0	0	0	1	0	6,479
Chapel Hill	2	0	0	0	0	0	1	0	0	1	64,853
Charlotte-Mecklenburg	13	0	5	0	0	0	4	5	8	1	958,358
Conover	0	0	1	0	0	0	1	0	0	0	8,567
Creedmoor	2	0	0	0	0	0	0	0	2	0	4,669
Durham	12	1	2	0	0	0	4	3	8	0	284,925
Elon	0	1	0	0	0	0	0	1	0	0	12,609
Emerald Isle	1	0	0	0	0	0	0	0	1	0	3,698
Fayetteville	13	0	1	0	0	0	1	6	3	4	212,033
Greensboro	11	1	4	0	0	0	3	5	4	4	299,887
Greenville	2	0	0	0	0	0	1	0	1	0	94,372
High Point	2	0	0	0	0	0	0	1	1	0	113,727
Hope Mills	1	0	0	0	0	0	0	0	1	0	15,924
Kannapolis	1	0	0	0	0	0	1	0	0	0	51,837
Knightdale	1	0	0	0	0	0	0	0	1	0	18,735
Lexington	1	0	0	0	0	0	0	1	0	0	18,933
Lincolnton	2	0	1	0	0	0	1	1	1	0	11,300
Matthews	2	2	0	0	0	0	0	0	1	3	33,860
Mebane	1	0	0	0	0	0	0	0	1	0	16,894
Monroe	1	0	0	0	0	0	0	1	0	0	35,836
Mooresville	1	0	0	0	0	0	0	0	1	0	39,692
Morganton	2	0	0	0	0	0	1	0	0	1	16,550
Morrisville	1	0	0	0	0	0	0	1	0	0	30,264
Newport	1	0	0	0	0	0	0	0	1	0	4,646
Oxford	1	0	0	0	0	0	0	0	1	0	8,934
Pittsboro	1	0	0	0	0	0	0	0	0	1	4,440
Raleigh	16	0	1	0	0	0	0	2	8	7	482,264
Reidsville	6	0	0	0	0	0	0	3	1	2	13,936
Rocky Mount	0	1	0	0	0	0	1	0	0	0	53,520
Salisbury	1	0	0	0	0	0	1	0	0	0	34,045
Scotland Neck	1	0	0	0	0	0	0	0	0	1	1,819
Statesville	5	0	0	0	0	0	1	0	2	2	27,879
Taylortown	0	1	0	0	0	0	0	1	0	0	867
Troy	2	0	0	0	0	0	0	0	0	2	3,194
Warsaw	1	0	0	0	0	0	0	0	1	0	3,086
Weldon	1	0	0	0	0	0	0	0	1	0	1,452
Winston-Salem	0	0	1	0	0	0	1	0	0	0	250,021
Universities and Colleges	1	0	0	0	0	0					
Western Carolina University	1	0	0	0	0	0	0	0	0	1	13,342
Metropolitan Counties	17	2	6	0	0	0					
Anson	1	0	0	0	0	0	0	0	1	0	
Cabarrus	3	0	1	0	0	0	0	3	1	0	
Currituck	1	0	0	0	0	0	0	0	1	0	
Durham	0	1	0	0	0	0	0	1	0	0	
Edgecombe	1	0	0	0	0	0	0	0	0	1	
Gaston County Police Department	1	0	0	0	0	0	0	0	1	0	
Guilford	4	0	1	0	0	0	1	2	2	0	
New Hanover	1	0	0	0	0	0	0	0	1	0	
Pamlico	0	0	1	0	0	0	0	0	1	0	
Pitt	1	0	0	0	0	0	0	0	1	0	
Wake	3	1	3	0	0	0	2	0	4	1	
Wayne	1	0	0	0	0	0	0	1	0	0	
Nonmetropolitan Counties	9	2	1	0	1	0					
Carteret[2]	1	0	1	0	0	0	0	1	0	0	
Cleveland	1	0	0	0	0	0	0	0	1	0	
Greene	0	1	0	0	0	0	0	0	1	0	

Table 94. Hate Crime Incidents Per Bias Motivation and Quarter, by Selected State and Agency and Federal, 2020—Continued

(Number.)

State/agency	Number of incidents per bias motivation						Number of incidents per quarter				Population[1]
	Race/ Ethnicity/ Ancestry	Religion	Sexual orientation	Disability	Gender	Gender Identity	1st quarter	2nd quarter	3rd quarter	4th quarter	
Hertford	1	0	0	0	0	0	1	0	0	0	
Jackson	2	1	0	0	0	0	0	2	0	1	
McDowell	1	0	0	0	0	0	1	0	0	0	
Montgomery	2	0	0	0	0	0	1	0	0	1	
Swain	1	0	0	0	1	0	0	2	0	0	
Other Agencies	1	0	1	0	0	0					
University of North Carolina Hospitals	1	0	0	0	0	0	0	0	1	0	
WakeMed Campus Police	0	0	1	0	0	0	0	0	0	1	
NORTH DAKOTA											
Total	17	0	3	0	0	1					
Cities	12	0	3	0	0	1					
Bismarck	1	0	0	0	0	0	0	0	0	1	74,997
Dickinson	2	0	0	0	0	0	0	0	1	1	23,801
Fargo	3	0	1	0	0	1	0	1	3	1	126,927
Grand Forks	1	0	1	0	0	0	0	0	2	0	56,163
Napoleon	1	0	0	0	0	0	0	0	1	0	747
Valley City	2	0	0	0	0	0	1	0	0	1	6,288
Watford City	0	0	1	0	0	0	0	0	0	1	9,309
Williston	2	0	0	0	0	0	1	1	0	0	31,046
Universities and Colleges	1	0	0	0	0	0					
University of North Dakota	1	0	0	0	0	0	0	0	1	0	17,050
Metropolitan Counties	2	0	0	0	0	0					
Burleigh	1	0	0	0	0	0	0	1	0	0	
Morton	1	0	0	0	0	0	0	1	0	0	
Nonmetropolitan Counties	2	0	0	0	0	0					
McKenzie	1	0	0	0	0	0	0	1	0	0	
Ward	1	0	0	0	0	0	0	0	1	0	
OHIO											
Total	304	77	69	54	4	34					
Cities	265	57	59	50	3	31					
Akron	3	1	3	2	0	0	1	1	3	4	197,433
Alliance	1	0	1	0	0	0	1	1	0	0	21,356
Arcanum	0	0	2	0	0	0	0	2	0	0	1,997
Ashland	0	0	0	1	0	0	0	0	0	1	20,247
Austintown	1	0	0	0	0	0	0	0	1	0	34,688
Avon Lake	1	0	0	0	0	0	0	0	1	0	24,724
Barberton	2	0	0	0	0	0	0	0	0	2	25,890
Bath Township, Summit County	0	0	0	1	0	0	1	0	0	0	9,635
Bazetta Township	1	0	0	0	0	0	0	0	0	1	5,494
Beavercreek	0	1	0	0	0	0	0	1	0	0	48,029
Beaver Township	1	0	0	0	0	0	0	0	1	0	6,358
Boardman	1	0	0	0	0	0	0	0	0	1	38,625
Butler Township	1	0	1	0	0	0	0	1	0	1	7,816
Canton	2	0	0	0	0	0	0	1	0	1	70,124
Cedarville	0	0	1	0	0	0	0	0	1	0	4,361
Cheviot	1	0	0	0	0	0	1	0	0	0	8,195
Chillicothe	0	4	0	0	0	3	0	3	3	1	21,700
Cincinnati	29	2	3	2	0	0	3	6	18	9	304,724
Circleville	0	2	0	0	0	0	0	2	0	0	14,113
Cleveland[2]	64	13	14	6	3	19	25	26	39	27	379,121
Colerain Township	2	0	0	1	0	0	0	0	2	1	59,307
Columbus[2]	56	7	16	1	0	6	11	25	27	22	911,383
Copley Township	1	0	0	3	0	0	1	1	1	1	17,280
Dayton	4	0	1	0	0	0	0	3	1	1	140,193
Defiance[2]	1	2	0	0	0	3	0	1	1	3	16,576
Delhi Township	1	0	0	0	0	0	0	0	0	1	29,831
Dublin	1	1	0	0	0	0	0	0	2	0	49,954
Eaton	0	1	0	0	0	0	1	0	0	0	8,118
Elyria	3	0	0	0	0	0	0	0	1	2	53,677
Englewood	3	0	0	0	0	0	0	1	1	1	13,435
Fairfax	0	0	0	1	0	0	0	0	1	0	1,701
Findlay	1	0	0	0	0	0	0	0	1	0	41,237
Gahanna	1	3	0	0	0	0	0	1	0	3	35,738
Garfield Heights	4	0	0	1	0	0		1	4		27,283
Germantown	1	0	0	0	0	0	0	0	1	0	5,517
Green Township	2	0	0	1	0	0	1	0	1	1	59,142
Grove City	1	0	0	0	0	0	0	1	0	0	42,551
Groveport	3	0	0	0	0	0	0	2	0	1	5,649
Hamilton	3	0	0	0	0	0	3				62,053
Hilliard	2	0	0	0	0	0	1	0	0	1	37,585
Huber Heights	0	0	1	6	0	0	1	4	1	1	38,158
Jackson Township, Stark County	2	0	1	0	0	0	0	0	1	2	40,270
Lancaster	3	1	0	0	0	0	1	1	2	0	40,700
Lebanon	2	0	0	0	0	0	1	0	1	0	20,720
Lockland	1	0	0	0	0	0	1	0	0	0	3,440
Lodi	1	0	0	0	0	0	0	0	1	0	2,915
Lyndhurst	1	0	0	0	0	0	0	1	0	0	13,291

Table 94. Hate Crime Incidents Per Bias Motivation and Quarter, by Selected State and Agency and Federal, 2020—Continued

(Number.)

State/agency	Race/ Ethnicity/ Ancestry	Religion	Sexual orientation	Disability	Gender	Gender Identity	1st quarter	2nd quarter	3rd quarter	4th quarter	Population[1]
Madison Township, Franklin County	0	0	0	1	0	0	0	0	1	0	19,828
Marietta	1	0	0	0	0	0	0	0	1	0	13,281
Mason	4	1	0	0	0	0	1	1	2	1	34,218
Maumee	0	0	1	0	0	0	0	0	1	0	13,605
Medina	0	4	0	0	0	0	0	1	3	0	25,882
Medina Township	1	1	0	0	0	0	0	0	2	0	9,105
Mentor	1	0	0	0	0	0	0	1	0	0	47,275
Miamisburg	1	0	1	0	0	0	1	0	1	0	20,140
Miami Township, Montgomery County	1	0	0	0	0	0	0	1	0	0	29,125
Middletown	6	0	0	2	0	0	3	3	2	0	48,814
Monroe	0	1	0	2	0	0	0	0	1	2	16,663
Mount Healthy	1	0	0	0	0	0	0	1	0	0	6,729
Napoleon	0	1	0	0	0	0	0	1	0	0	8,148
New Albany	3	2	0	0	0	0	2	1	2	0	11,330
Newark	2	0	0	0	0	0	0	2	0	0	50,625
New Franklin	1	0	1	0	0	0	0	1	1	0	14,125
North Canton	0	0	3	0	0	0	2	0	1	0	17,142
North College Hill	1	0	0	0	0	0	0	0	1	0	9,269
North Olmsted	1	0	0	0	0	0	0	0	1	0	31,176
Norton	1	0	0	0	0	0	0	0	0	1	11,951
Norwood	0	0	0	1	0	0	1	0	0		19,843
Perrysburg Township	1	0	0	0	0	0	0	1	0	0	13,011
Pickerington	0	1	0	0	0	0	1	0	0	0	22,631
Pierce Township	1	0	0	0	0	0	0	0	0	1	11,789
Portsmouth	1	1	0	1	0	0	0	1	1	1	20,151
Reynoldsburg	1	0	0	0	0	0	1	0	0	0	38,600
Riverside	1	0	1	0	0	0	0	0	2	0	25,128
Rocky River	1	0	0	0	0	0	0	0	1	0	19,951
Sandusky	0	0	3	0	0	0	0	0	2	1	24,422
Shawnee Township	1	0	0	0	0	0	0	0	1	0	12,044
Shelby	0	0	0	1	0	0	0	1	0	0	9,002
Springfield Township, Hamilton County	3	0	0	1	0	0	1	0	2	1	35,947
Springfield Township, Summit County	1	0	0	2	0	0	0	2	1	0	14,507
St. Clair Township	0	0	0	1	0	0	1	0	0	0	7,436
Streetsboro	1	0	0	0	0	0	0	0	1	0	16,527
Sylvania	1	0	0	0	0	0	0	0	1	0	19,337
Toledo	4	0	1	0	0	0	2	3	0	0	271,237
Trotwood	2	0	0	0	0	0	0	1	1	0	24,399
Troy	1	0	0	0	0	0	0	0	1		26,407
Uniontown	1	0	0	0	0	0	0	0	1	0	3,309
Upper Arlington	0	1	0	0	0	0	0	1	0	0	35,557
Urbana	1	0	1	1	0	0	0	2	1	0	11,351
Vandalia	1	0	0	0	0	0			1		14,968
Van Wert	0	1	0	0	0	0	0	0	0	1	10,659
Vienna Township	1	0	0	0	0	0	0	0	0	1	3,761
Walbridge	1	0	0	0	0	0		0	0	1	3,169
Wapakoneta	1	0	1	0	0	0	0	0	1	1	9,680
Washington Court House	0	2	0	0	0	0	1	0	1	0	14,076
Waverly	0	2	0	0	0	0	0	2	0	0	4,217
West Chester Township	0	0	0	1	0	0	1	0	0	0	62,685
Willoughby	0	0	0	1	0	0	1	0	0	0	23,058
Wooster	1	0	0	2	0	0	0	2	1	0	26,424
Worthington	0	1	0	1	0	0	0	0	2	0	14,822
Wyoming	0	0	1	0	0	0	0	0	0	1	8,578
Youngstown	1	0	0	0	0	0	1	0			65,316
Zanesville	4	0	1	6	0	0	0	3	5	3	25,136
Universities and Colleges	4	1	0	0	0	0					
Ohio State University, Columbus	3	1	0	0	0	0	0	0	4	0	66,178
Wright State University	1	0	0	0	0	0	0	0	1	0	16,523
Metropolitan Counties	17	2	2	0	0	2					
Clermont	2	0	0	0	0	0	1	0	0	1	
Delaware	1	0	0	0	0	0	0	0	1	0	
Jefferson	1	0	0	0	0	0	0	0	0	1	
Lawrence	1	1	0	0	0	0	1	0	0	1	
Licking	1	0	0	0	0	0	0	0	1	0	
Lorain	1	0	0	0	0	0	1	0	0	0	
Lucas	1	0	0	0	0	0	0	0	1	0	
Medina	1	1	0	0	0	0	0	0	1	1	
Montgomery	4	0	0	0	0	0	1	0	1	2	
Pickaway	1	0	0	0	0	1	1	1	0	0	
Summit	2	0	1	0	0	0	1	1	1	0	
Trumbull	1	0	0	0	0	0	1	0	0	0	
Union	0	0	1	0	0	0	1	0	0	0	
Warren	0	0	0	0	0	1	0	0	0	1	
Nonmetropolitan Counties	13	16	7	4	1	1					
Ashland	1	0	0	0	0	0	0	1	0	0	
Auglaize	1	0	0	0	0	0	0	0	1	0	
Coshocton	0	1	0	0	0	0	0	0	0	1	
Fayette	1	0	0	0	0	0	0	0	1	0	

Table 94. Hate Crime Incidents Per Bias Motivation and Quarter, by Selected State and Agency and Federal, 2020—Continued

(Number.)

State/agency	Number of incidents per bias motivation						Number of incidents per quarter				Population[1]
	Race/ Ethnicity/ Ancestry	Religion	Sexual orientation	Disability	Gender	Gender Identity	1st quarter	2nd quarter	3rd quarter	4th quarter	
Logan	1	0	0	1	0	0	0	0	2	0	
Marion	1	0	1	0	0	0	0	0	2	0	
Muskingum	3	0	0	0	0	0	0	0	2	1	
Pike	1	1	1	0	0	0	1	2	0	0	
Preble	0	6	0	0	1	1	1	2	3	2	
Putnam	0	1	0	0	0	0	0	0	0	1	
Ross	2	7	2	0	0	0	0	2	7	2	
Shelby	0	0	0	1	0	0	1	0	0	0	
Vinton	1	0	0	0	0	0	0	0	1	0	
Washington	0	0	3	2	0	0	1	0	2	2	
Wayne	1	0	0	0	0	0	0	0	1		
Other Agencies	5	1	1	0	0	0					
Greater Cleveland Regional Transit Authority	3	0	1	0	0	0	3		1		
Ohio Department of Natural Resources	2	1	0	0	0	0	1	1	1	0	
OKLAHOMA											
Total	4	1	2	1	0	0					
Cities	4	1	1	1	0	0					
Konawa	0	0	1	0	0	0	1	0	0	0	1,186
Oklahoma City	3	1	0	1	0	0	4	1	0	0	663,661
Tulsa	1	0	0	0	0	0	1	0	0	0	402,166
Nonmetropolitan Counties	0	0	1	0	0	0					
McIntosh	0	0	1	0	0	0	1	0	0	0	
OREGON											
Total	203	30	34	6	2	11					
Cities	179	27	29	6	2	9					
Albany	1	0	0	0	0	0	0	0	1	0	55,926
Astoria	2	0	2	0	0	0	3	1	0	0	10,076
Beaverton	1	1	0	0	0	0	0	2	0	0	100,085
Bend	5	7	0	1	0	0	4	1	4	4	103,485
Carlton	1	0	0	0	0	0	0	0	1	0	2,202
Central Point	1	0	0	0	0	0	0	1	0	0	19,032
Coos Bay	1	0	1	0	0	0	0	0	2	0	16,403
Corvallis	1	0	0	0	0	0	0	0	1	0	59,375
Cottage Grove	1	0	0	0	0	0	0	0	0	1	10,556
Dallas	2	1	1	0	0	0	2	1	1	0	17,265
Eugene	29	6	3	3	0	2	11	14	14	4	174,513
Forest Grove	2	0	0	0	0	0	1	0	1	0	26,065
Gladstone	2	0	0	0	0	0	0	1	0	1	12,418
Gresham	1	0	0	0	0	0	1	0	0	0	109,767
Hermiston	1	0	0	0	0	0	0	0	1	0	17,896
Hillsboro[2]	6	0	2	0	0	1	3	1	1	3	111,146
Hood River	2	0	0	0	0	0	0	2	0	0	7,863
Hubbard	0	1	0	0	0	1	0	0	0	2	3,615
Keizer	1	0	0	0	0	0	0	1	0	0	40,087
Klamath Falls	2	0	1	0	0	0	2	0	0	1	22,693
La Grande	4	0	0	1	0	1	0	0	2	4	13,674
Lake Oswego	3	0	0	0	0	0	0	0	1	2	40,171
Lincoln City	6	0	0	0	0	0	1	0	4	1	9,275
McMinnville	2	0	1	0	0	0	0	1	2	0	35,040
Medford	1	0	0	0	0	0	0	1	0	0	84,016
Molalla	0	0	1	0	0	0	0	0	0	1	9,351
Monmouth	1	0	0	0	0	0	0	1	0	0	10,708
Mount Angel	1	0	0	0	0	0	0	0	1	0	3,647
Newberg-Dundee	1	0	0	0	0	0	0	0	1	0	24,081
Newport	2	0	0	0	0	0	2	0	0	0	10,950
North Bend[2]	4	0	1	0	0	0	0	3	0	1	9,778
Ontario	2	0	0	0	0	0	0	0	0	2	10,952
Oregon City	5	0	0	0	0	2	1	3	3	0	37,892
Pendleton	0	0	0	1	0	0	0	1	0	0	16,804
Phoenix	1	0	0	0	0	0	1	0	0	0	4,680
Portland[2]	28	2	9	0	1	0	8	10	10	10	662,941
Rainier[2]	1	0	1	0	0	0	0	0	0	1	2,021
Reedsport	1	1	0	0	0	0	0	2	0	0	4,111
Roseburg	1	0	0	0	0	0	0	1	0	0	23,551
Salem[2]	21	2	5	0	0	2	6	9	8	6	176,632
Sherwood	2	0	0	0	0	0	1	1	0	0	20,052
Silverton	1	0	0	0	0	0	0	1	0	0	10,782
Springfield	7	3	0	0	0	0	0	4	3	3	63,666
Sutherlin	1	0	0	0	0	0	0	0	0	1	8,223
Talent	0	1	0	0	0	0	0	0	0	1	6,671
Tigard	11	1	1	0	0	0	2	5	4	2	56,377
Tualatin	4	0	0	0	1	0	3	1	1	3	28,030
Turner	1	0	0	0	0	0	0	0	1	0	2,153
Umatilla	2	0	0	0	0	0	0	0	1	1	7,366
West Linn	2	1	0	0	0	0	0	1	2	1	26,916
Woodburn	1	0	0	0	0	0	0	0	0	1	26,521
Universities and Colleges	1	1	0	0	0	0					

Table 94. Hate Crime Incidents Per Bias Motivation and Quarter, by Selected State and Agency and Federal, 2020—Continued

(Number.)

State/agency	Number of incidents per bias motivation						Number of incidents per quarter				Population[1]
	Race/ Ethnicity/ Ancestry	Religion	Sexual orientation	Disability	Gender	Gender Identity	1st quarter	2nd quarter	3rd quarter	4th quarter	
Portland State University	1	1	0	0	0	0	2	0	0	0	32,445
Metropolitan Counties	15	1	2	0	0	2					
Clackamas	8	0	0	0	0	1	2	0	3	4	
Jackson	1	0	0	0	0	1	1	1	0	0	
Josephine	0	0	2	0	0	0	1	0	1	0	
Linn	1	0	0	0	0	0	0	0	1	0	
Polk	3	0	0	0	0	0	0	3	0	0	
Washington	2	0	0	0	0	0	0	1	0	1	
Yamhill	0	1	0	0	0	0	0	1	0	0	
Nonmetropolitan Counties	5	1	2	0	0	0					
Jefferson	2	0	0	0	0	0	0	0	0	2	
Klamath	2	0	1	0	0	0	0	0	1	2	
Lincoln	1	0	0	0	0	0	1	0	0	0	
Tillamook	0	0	1	0	0	0	0	0	0	1	
Union	0	1	0	0	0	0	0	0	1	0	
State Police Agencies	3	0	1	0	0	0					
State Police											
Benton County	1	0	0	0	0	0	0	1	0	0	
Columbia County	1	0	0	0	0	0	0	1	0	0	
Marion County	1	0	1	0	0	0	0	0	2	0	
PENNSYLVANIA											
Total	62	13	5	0	0	2					
Cities	58	13	4	0	0	2					
Altoona	2	0	0	0	0	0	0	0	1	1	43,090
East Earl Township	1	0	0	0	0	0	1	0	0	0	6,934
East Pennsboro Township	1	1	0	0	0	0	1	1	0	0	21,556
Gettysburg	1	0	0	0	0	0				1	7,738
Johnsonburg	1	0	0	0	0	0	0	1	0	0	2,271
Meadville	2	0	0	0	0	0	0	2	0	0	12,579
New Hope	1	0	0	0	0	0	0	1	0	0	2,530
Philadelphia	36	9	3	0	0	2	19	10	15	6	1,586,666
Pittsburgh	3	2	0	0	0	0	0	2	2	1	298,608
Pocono Mountain Regional	1	0	0	0	0	0	0	1	0	0	43,250
Pottsville	1	0	0	0	0	0			1		13,384
Reading	2	0	0	0	0	0	1	1	0	0	88,412
Southern Chester County Regional	0	1	0	0	0	0	0	0	0	1	16,477
South Greensburg	1	0	0	0	0	0	0	1	0	0	1,983
State College	1	0	0	0	0	0	0	1	0	0	58,471
Upper Darby Township	1	0	0	0	0	0	0	0	0	1	82,947
Upper Moreland Township[2]	3	0	1	0	0	0	0	0	2	1	24,031
Universities and Colleges	4	0	1	0	0	0					
Lehigh University	1	0	0	0	0	0		0	1	0	7,330
Pennsylvania State University, University Park	1	0	1	0	0	0		0	1	1	49,935
Shippensburg University	2	0	0	0	0	0	1	0	1	0	7,138
RHODE ISLAND											
Total	4	4	5	0	0	1					
Cities	4	2	3	0	0	0					
Barrington	0	1	0	0	0	0	0	0	1	0	15,986
Burrillville	0	0	1	0	0	0	1	0	0	0	16,904
Coventry	1	0	0	0	0	0	0	1	0	0	34,740
Cranston	1	0	0	0	0	0	0	1	0	0	81,313
Lincoln	0	1	0	0	0	0	1	0	0	0	22,029
Pawtucket	1	0	1	0	0	0	0	1	0	1	72,017
Providence	1	0	0	0	0	0	0	1	0	0	179,603
Tiverton	0	0	1	0	0	0	0	0	1	0	15,604
Universities and Colleges	0	2	2	0	0	1					
Brown University	0	2	2	0	0	1	4	0	1	0	10,760
SOUTH CAROLINA											
Total	58	31	12	1	4	4					
Cities	35	3	8	1	1	3					
Aiken	0	1	0	0	1	0	0	1	0	1	31,007
Batesburg-Leesville	1	0	0	0	0	0	0	0	1	0	5,419
Calhoun Falls	7	0	0	0	0	0	1	0	1	5	1,892
Cayce	1	0	0	0	0	0	0	0	0	1	14,117
Charleston	5	0	2	0	0	0	1	2	2	2	139,582
Chester	1	0	0	0	0	0	0	0	0	1	5,354
Chesterfield	1	0	0	0	0	0	0	1	0	0	1,409
Columbia	2	0	0	0	0	0	0	1	1	0	131,777
Easley	0	0	0	0	0	1	1	0	0	0	21,512
Florence	1	0	2	0	0	0	0	1	0	2	38,597
Fort Mill	1	0	0	0	0	0	0	1	0	0	23,966
Gaffney	2	0	0	0	0	0	0	0	2	0	12,631
Goose Creek	1	0	0	0	0	0	0	0	0	1	44,522
Hartsville	1	0	1	0	0	0	0	0	1	1	7,519
Lake View	3	0	0	0	0	0	0	0	2	1	752
Landrum	0	0	0	1	0	0	0	0	1	0	2,713

Table 94. Hate Crime Incidents Per Bias Motivation and Quarter, by Selected State and Agency and Federal, 2020—Continued

(Number.)

State/agency	Race/ Ethnicity/ Ancestry	Religion	Sexual orientation	Disability	Gender	Gender Identity	1st quarter	2nd quarter	3rd quarter	4th quarter	Population[1]
Lexington	1	0	0	0	0	0	0	0	1	0	22,592
Mauldin	0	0	0	0	0	1	0	1	0	0	25,662
Moncks Corner	1	1	0	0	0	0	0	1	0	1	12,580
Myrtle Beach	1	0	1	0	0	0	1	0	0	1	35,658
North Myrtle Beach	0	0	1	0	0	1	0	0	1	1	17,183
Orangeburg	1	0	0	0	0	0	1	0	0	0	12,529
Pickens	1	0	0	0	0	0	0	0	0	1	3,177
Port Royal	1	0	0	0	0	0	0	0	0	1	13,553
Rock Hill	0	1	0	0	0	0	0	0	1	0	76,016
Walterboro	0	0	1	0	0	0	1	0	0	0	5,387
Winnsboro	1	0	0	0	0	0	0	0	1	0	3,144
York	1	0	0	0	0	0	1	0	0	0	8,486
Universities and Colleges	1	0	0	0	0	0					
University of South Carolina, Columbia	1	0	0	0	0	0	1	0	0	0	37,510
Metropolitan Counties	12	21	4	0	3	1					
Anderson	1	0	0	0	0	0	0	1	0	0	
Beaufort	2	0	0	0	0	0	0	0	1	1	
Berkeley	0	20	1	0	0	0	5	4	9	3	
Charleston	3	1	0	0	0	0	1	1	2	0	
Laurens	1	0	0	0	0	0	0	0	1	0	
Pickens	2	0	0	0	0	0	0	0	1	1	
Richland	3	0	3	0	3	1	2	4	2	2	
Nonmetropolitan Counties	6	7	0	0	0	0					
Allendale	1	0	0	0	0	0	0	1	0	0	
Bamberg	0	4	0	0	0	0	1	2	0	1	
Chesterfield	1	1	0	0	0	0	2	0	0	0	
Georgetown	2	0	0	0	0	0	1	0	0	1	
Oconee	0	2	0	0	0	0	0	0	1	1	
Orangeburg	2	0	0	0	0	0	0	2	0	0	
State Police Agencies	4	0	0	0	0	0					
Highway Patrol											
Chesterfield County	1	0	0	0	0	0	0	1	0	0	
Lancaster County	1	0	0	0	0	0	0	0	0	1	
Lee County	1	0	0	0	0	0	0	1	0	0	
York County	1	0	0	0	0	0	0	0	1	0	
SOUTH DAKOTA											
Total	15	0	1	0	0	1					
Cities	10	0	1	0	0	1					
Aberdeen	1	0	0	0	0	0	0	0	1	0	28,494
Box Elder	1	0	0	0	0	0	0	0	0	1	10,402
Flandreau	1	0	0	0	0	0	0	0	1	0	2,314
Madison	0	0	1	0	0	0	0	0	1	0	7,357
Mobridge	2	0	0	0	0	0	0	0	1	1	3,442
Rapid City	2	0	0	0	0	1	0	0	2	1	78,492
Sioux Falls	1	0	0	0	0	0	0	0	1	0	187,370
Tea	1	0	0	0	0	0	0	1	0	0	6,340
Watertown	1	0	0	0	0	0	0	0	1	0	22,248
Nonmetropolitan Counties	4	0	0	0	0	0					
Brookings	1	0	0	0	0	0	0	1	0	0	
Brown	1	0	0	0	0	0	1	0	0	0	
Marshall	1	0	0	0	0	0	0	0	1	0	
Roberts	1	0	0	0	0	0	1	0	0	0	
Tribal Agencies	1	0	0	0	0	0					
Sisseton-Wahpeton Tribal	1	0	0	0	0	0	0	0	0	1	
TENNESSEE											
Total	56	4	16	2	0	2					
Cities	43	4	12	2	0	1					
Cleveland	9	0	0	0	0	0	1	3	3	2	45,994
Collierville	1	0	1	0	0	1	1	0	1	1	51,677
Fairview	1	0	0	0	0	0	0	0	1	0	9,300
Franklin	2	1	0	0	0	0	2	1	0	0	85,722
Germantown	2	0	0	0	0	0	0	0	1	1	39,264
Goodlettsville	0	0	1	0	0	0	1	0	0	0	16,896
Hendersonville	0	0	1	0	0	0	0	0	1	0	58,901
Jackson	3	0	1	2	0	0	2	1	1	2	67,234
Knoxville	3	0	2	0	0	0	1	2	2	0	188,672
Lebanon	3	0	0	0	0	0	0	0	2	1	37,832
Manchester	3	0	0	0	0	0	0	1	1	1	11,145
Maryville	1	0	0	0	0	0	0	1	0	0	30,006
Memphis	5	1	4	0	0	0	2	3	2	3	650,937
Metropolitan Nashville Police Department	3	1	2	0	0	0	0	2	2	2	688,013
Murfreesboro	3	0	0	0	0	0	0	1	0	2	151,769
Pigeon Forge	1	0	0	0	0	0	0	1	0	0	6,311
Rogersville	1	0	0	0	0	0	0	0	1	0	4,368
Shelbyville	1	0	0	0	0	0	0	0	0	1	22,306
Spring Hill[2]	1	1	0	0	0	0	1	0	0	0	45,765
Universities and Colleges	1	0	0	0	0	0					

Table 94. Hate Crime Incidents Per Bias Motivation and Quarter, by Selected State and Agency and Federal, 2020—Continued

(Number.)

State/agency	Number of incidents per bias motivation						Number of incidents per quarter				Population[1]
	Race/ Ethnicity/ Ancestry	Religion	Sexual orientation	Disability	Gender	Gender Identity	1st quarter	2nd quarter	3rd quarter	4th quarter	
Vanderbilt University	1	0	0	0	0	0	1	0	0	0	13,634
Metropolitan Counties	11	0	2	0	0	1					
Anderson	1	0	1	0	0	0	0	0	0	2	
Blount	4	0	0	0	0	0	1	2	0	1	
Knox[2]	1	0	0	0	0	1	0	0	1	0	
Montgomery	1	0	0	0	0	0	0	1	0	0	
Rutherford	1	0	0	0	0	0	1	0	0	0	
Shelby	2	0	0	0	0	0	1	1	0	0	
Washington	1	0	1	0	0	0	0	2	0	0	
Nonmetropolitan Counties	1	0	2	0	0	0					
Cocke	0	0	1	0	0	0	0	0	0	1	
Warren	1	0	1	0	0	0	1	0	0	1	
TEXAS											
Total	288	31	70	6	9	7					
Cities	248	27	62	3	8	7					
Abilene[2]	3	3	0	0	0	0	0	0	5	0	124,061
Addison	1	0	0	0	0	0	1	0	0	0	16,778
Amarillo	2	0	0	0	0	0	0	0	1	1	200,296
Anna	1	0	0	0	0	0	0	0	0	1	16,036
Aransas Pass	0	0	1	0	0	0	0	1	0	0	8,414
Arlington	13	0	0	0	0	0	4	6	2	1	402,700
Austin[2]	13	2	8	0	0	2	3	9	4	6	1,000,276
Baird	1	0	0	0	0	0	0	0	1	0	1,485
Balch Springs	0	0	1	0	0	0	0	1	0	0	25,189
Beaumont	0	0	1	0	0	0	0	0	0	1	116,766
Bellmead	0	0	1	0	0	0	1	0	0	0	10,835
Benbrook	1	0	0	0	0	0	0	1	0	0	23,766
Brenham	1	1	0	0	0	1	2	0	1	0	18,106
Burkburnett	1	0	0	0	0	0	0	0	1	0	11,321
Burleson	1	0	0	0	0	0	0	0	0	1	49,660
Caldwell	1	0	0	0	0	0	0	0	0	1	4,403
Carrollton	4	0	1	0	0	0	0	1	1	3	141,745
Cedar Park	2	0	1	0	0	0	0	0	2	1	82,653
Cibolo	1	0	0	0	0	0	0	1	0	0	32,777
Cleburne	0	1	0	0	0	0	1	0	0	0	31,486
Clifton	1	0	0	0	0	0	0	1	0	0	3,446
College Station	1	1	0	0	0	0	0	0	1	1	120,831
Comanche	0	1	0	0	0	0	0	1	0	0	4,183
Coppell	4	0	0	0	0	0	1	3	0	0	41,807
Corpus Christi	2	0	0	0	0	0	0	1	1	0	329,050
Corrigan	1	0	0	0	0	0	0	0	1	0	1,613
Crockett	1	0	0	0	0	0	0	0	1	0	6,327
Crowley	1	0	0	0	0	0	0	0	1	0	16,909
Dallas	24	3	11	0	0	0	5	10	17	6	1,363,028
Deer Park	1	0	0	0	0	0	0	0	1	0	33,631
Denton	8	0	0	0	0	0	1	2	2	3	144,569
Elgin	2	1	0	0	0	0	1	1	0	1	10,567
El Paso	2	0	0	0	5	0	0	0	0	7	685,288
Fort Worth	4	1	5	1	0	0	6	2	2	1	929,509
Galena Park	3	0	0	0	0	0	0	0	1	2	10,740
Garland	3	0	0	0	0	0	0	0	2	1	241,845
Gatesville	0	2	0	0	0	0	0	0	2	0	12,394
Greenville	1	0	0	0	0	0	0	1	0	0	29,209
Hamilton	1	0	0	0	0	0	1	0	0	0	3,005
Hempstead	1	0	0	0	0	0	0	0	1	0	8,699
Henderson	2	0	0	0	0	0	0	0	1	1	13,093
Hewitt	1	1	0	0	0	0	1	0	0	1	15,092
Hollywood Park	1	0	0	0	0	0	0	0	1	0	3,370
Houston	31	1	8	0	0	3	7	23	12	1	2,346,155
Huntsville	0	0	1	0	0	0	0	0	1	0	42,648
Hurst	6	0	0	0	0	0	0	2	4	0	38,796
Irving	1	1	1	0	0	0	2	1	0	0	242,976
Jarrell	1	0	0	0	0	0	0	0	0	1	1,953
Jonestown	1	0	0	0	0	0	0	1	0	0	2,139
Kaufman	0	1	0	0	0	0	0	0	0	1	7,930
Kennedale	1	0	0	0	0	0	0	0	1	0	8,881
Killeen	0	0	1	0	0	0	1	0	0	0	154,417
Kingsville	1	0	0	0	0	0	1	0	0	0	25,195
Kyle	1	0	0	0	0	0	0	0	0	1	51,306
Lacy-Lakeview	1	0	0	0	0	0	0	0	0	1	6,748
Lampasas	1	0	0	0	0	0	0	0	1	0	8,132
Laredo	0	0	1	0	0	0	0	1	0	0	265,515
Leander	2	0	0	0	1	0	0	3	0	0	68,571
Leon Valley	3	1	0	0	0	0	0	0	2	2	12,453
Little Elm	1	0	0	0	0	0	0	0	0	1	57,482
Live Oak	0	0	1	0	0	0	0	0	0	1	16,910
Lockhart	2	0	0	0	0	0	0	0	1	1	14,297
Lubbock	5	0	2	0	0	0	1	0	2	4	262,146

Table 94. Hate Crime Incidents Per Bias Motivation and Quarter, by Selected State and Agency and Federal, 2020—Continued

(Number.)

State/agency	Number of incidents per bias motivation						Number of incidents per quarter				Population[1]
	Race/ Ethnicity/ Ancestry	Religion	Sexual orientation	Disability	Gender	Gender Identity	1st quarter	2nd quarter	3rd quarter	4th quarter	
Lytle	1	0	0	0	0	0	1	0	0	0	3,135
Mansfield	1	0	0	0	0	0	0	0	0	1	74,360
McKinney	5	0	2	0	0	0	1	0	3	3	208,335
Mesquite	0	0	1	0	0	0	0	0	1	0	141,325
Midland	1	0	0	0	0	0	1	0	0	0	150,529
Missouri City	0	0	0	1	1	0	0	1	0	1	76,476
Montgomery	0	0	0	0	1	0	1	0	0	0	1,488
Mount Pleasant	1	0	0	0	0	0	0	0	0	1	15,974
Navasota	1	0	0	0	0	0	0	1	0	0	8,104
New Boston	0	1	0	0	0	0		0	0	1	4,588
New Braunfels	2	0	0	0	0	0	0	1	0	1	94,751
Odessa	0	0	2	0	0	0	0	0	2	0	126,288
Palestine	2	1	0	0	0	0	0	1	1	1	17,625
Pampa	2	0	0	0	0	0	0	1	1	0	16,975
Pasadena	2	0	0	0	0	0	0	1	1	0	151,421
Pelican Bay	0	0	1	0	0	0	0	0	1	0	2,064
Plainview	1	0	1	0	0	0	0	1	0	1	19,926
Plano	1	1	0	0	0	0	0	2	0	0	290,786
Pleasanton	3	0	0	0	0	0	0	0	2	1	11,006
Rio Grande City	4	0	0	1	0	0	1	2	0	2	14,587
Robinson	1	0	0	0	0	0	1	0	0	0	12,087
Rockport	0	0	1	0	0	0	0	0	0	1	10,672
Round Rock	4	0	0	0	0	0	0	0	3	1	137,593
Rowlett	2	0	0	0	0	0	0	2	0	0	68,810
San Antonio	10	2	3	0	0	1	3	8	4	1	1,573,189
San Saba	3	1	0	0	0	0	2	0	2	0	3,164
Seabrook	6	0	0	0	0	0	0	4	2	0	14,415
Sherman	3	0	0	0	0	0	0	0	2	1	44,611
Silsbee	1	0	0	0	0	0	0	0	0	1	6,613
Spur	4	0	0	0	0	0	2	0	2	0	1,186
Stafford	1	0	0	0	0	0	0	0	1	0	17,423
Sugar Land	1	0	0	0	0	0	1	0	0	0	119,671
Sweeny	1	0	0	0	0	0	0	0	0	1	3,716
Texas City	2	0	1	0	0	0	1	0	2	0	50,660
The Colony	4	0	0	0	0	0	0	1	3	0	45,419
Tyler	1	0	3	0	0	0	1	1	0	2	108,139
University Park	1	0	0	0	0	0	0	0	1	0	25,253
Uvalde	2	0	0	0	0	0	0	0	0	2	16,027
Victoria	1	0	0	0	0	0	0	0	1	0	67,407
Waco	1	0	0	0	0	0	0	0	0	1	140,870
Watauga	2	0	0	0	0	0	0	1	1	0	24,588
West[2]	1	0	1	0	0	0	1	0	0	0	3,008
Willis	0	0	1	0	0	0	0	0	0	1	7,166
Universities and Colleges	7	1	3	0	0	0					
Angelo State University	0	1	0	0	0	0	0	0	1	0	11,737
Trinity Valley Community College	4	0	0	0	0	0	1	0	2	1	9,896
University of Texas											
Arlington	1	0	2	0	0	0	0	0	0	3	60,035
Austin	2	0	0	0	0	0	1	0	0	1	55,128
Permian Basin	0	0	1	0	0	0	0	1	0	0	8,165
Metropolitan Counties	26	2	4	3	0	0					
Ellis	4	0	0	1	0	0	0	1	1	3	
Fort Bend	5	0	0	0	0	0	0	4	0	1	
Galveston	1	0	1	0	0	0	0	1	0	1	
Harris	5	1	0	0	0	0	2	2	2	0	
Johnson	1	0	0	0	0	0	0	1	0	0	
Lubbock	1	0	0	2	0	0	0	0	0	3	
Parker	0	0	1	0	0	0	1	0	0	0	
Potter	1	0	0	0	0	0	1	0	0	0	
Tarrant	1	1	0	0	0	0	0	0	1	1	
Travis	5	0	0	0	0	0	3	0	1	1	
Williamson	2	0	2	0	0	0	0	3	1	0	
Nonmetropolitan Counties	5	1	1	0	1	0					
Cherokee	0	0	1	0	0	0	1	0	0	0	
Hill	1	0	0	0	0	0	0	0	0	1	
Moore	1	0	0	0	0	0	0	1	0	0	
San Augustine	0	0	0	0	1	0	0	1	0	0	
Van Zandt	2	0	0	0	0	0	0	1	0	1	
Willacy	1	0	0	0	0	0	0	0	0	1	
Zavala	0	1	0	0	0	0	0	0	0	1	
Other Agencies	2	0	0	0	0	0					
Independent School District											
Barbers Hill	1	0	0	0	0	0	0	0	0	1	
Houston	1	0	0	0	0	0	0	0	0	1	
UTAH											
Total	20	12	6	1	0	7					
Cities	14	6	4	1	0	5					
Ephraim	3	0	0	0	0	0	0	3	0	0	7,450
Layton	1	1	0	0	0	1	0	1	0	2	79,240

Table 94. Hate Crime Incidents Per Bias Motivation and Quarter, by Selected State and Agency and Federal, 2020—Continued

(Number.)

State/agency	Number of incidents per bias motivation						Number of incidents per quarter				Population[1]
	Race/ Ethnicity/ Ancestry	Religion	Sexual orientation	Disability	Gender	Gender Identity	1st quarter	2nd quarter	3rd quarter	4th quarter	
Lindon	0	0	0	0	0	2	0	2	0	0	11,218
North Salt Lake	0	0	1	0	0	0	0	0	0	1	21,540
Ogden	0	0	0	0	0	1	0	0	1	0	88,309
Perry	1	0	0	0	0	0	0	0	1	0	5,335
Price	0	0	0	0	0	1	1	0	0	0	8,291
Roosevelt	2	0	0	0	0	0	0	1	1	0	7,359
Salem	0	1	0	0	0	0	1	0	0	0	8,902
Salt Lake City[2]	1	0	2	0	0	0	0	1	1	0	202,187
Springville	1	0	0	0	0	0	0	0	0	1	33,728
Sunset	0	2	0	0	0	0	0	2	0	0	5,387
Tooele[2]	3	1	0	0	0	0			1	2	36,527
Washington	0	0	1	0	0	0	0	0	0	1	30,622
West Valley	2	1	0	1	0	0	1	1	2	0	135,887
Universities and Colleges	0	0	1	0	0	0					
Dixie State University	0	0	1	0	0	0	0	1	0	0	12,263
Metropolitan Counties	1	4	0	0	0	2					
Davis	1	0	0	0	0	0	0	0	0	1	
Tooele	0	2	0	0	0	2			0	4	
Weber	0	2	0	0	0	0	0	1	0	1	
Nonmetropolitan Counties	0	1	0	0	0	0					
Sanpete	0	1	0	0	0	0	0	1	0	0	
State Police Agencies	1	0	0	0	0	0					
Utah Highway Patrol	1	0	0	0	0	0	0	1	0	0	
Other Agencies	4	1	1	0	0	0					
Parks and Recreation	2	0	0	0	0	0	0	2	0	0	
Utah Transit Authority	2	1	1	0	0	0	1	2	0	1	
VERMONT											
Total	42	9	6	3	0	0					
Cities	24	7	5	3	0	0					
Barre	1	1	0	0	0	0	0	0	1	1	8,471
Bellows Falls	0	0	0	1	0	0	0	0	0	1	2,946
Burlington	1	0	1	0	0	0	0	0	1	1	42,862
Colchester	0	0	1	0	0	0	0	0	1	0	17,129
Dover	0	1	0	0	0	0	0	0	1	0	1,052
Essex	2	0	0	0	0	0	0	0	1	1	22,156
Hartford	0	2	1	0	0	0	1	1	0	1	9,515
Manchester	2	0	0	0	0	0	0	0	1	1	4,206
Middlebury	5	0	0	0	0	0	0	0	3	2	8,813
Milton	2	0	0	1	0	0	0	1	2	0	10,882
Montpelier	1	1	0	0	0	0	0	1	1	0	7,321
Morristown	2	0	0	0	0	0	0	0	2	0	5,532
Norwich	1	0	0	0	0	0	0	0	1	0	3,409
Rutland	1	0	0	0	0	0	1	0	0	0	14,930
South Burlington	2	1	1	0	0	0	0	1	0	3	19,690
St. Albans	1	1	1	1	0	0	1	1	1	1	6,788
Stowe	1	0	0	0	0	0	0	0	1	0	4,444
Winooski	2	0	0	0	0	0	0	0	0	2	7,341
Universities and Colleges	2	0	0	0	0	0					
University of Vermont	2	0	0	0	0	0	1	0	1	0	15,698
Metropolitan Counties	1	0	0	0	0	0					
Grand Isle	1	0	0	0	0	0	0	1	0	0	
Nonmetropolitan Counties	5	0	0	0	0	0					
Lamoille	2	0	0	0	0	0	0	1	1	0	
Rutland	1	0	0	0	0	0	0	0	1	0	
Windham	2	0	0	0	0	0	0	0	2	0	
State Police Agencies	10	2	1	0	0	0					
State Police											
New Haven	1	2	0	0	0	0	1	0	0	2	
Rutland	1	0	0	0	0	0	0	0	1	0	
St. Albans	1	0	0	0	0	0	0	0	1	0	
Westminster	4	0	0	0	0	0	0	0	4	0	
Williston	3	0	1	0	0	0	0	0	3	1	
VIRGINIA											
Total	123	22	23	1	0	1					
Cities	44	8	9	1	0	0					
Alexandria	0	1	1	0	0	0	0	1	0	1	161,525
Bedford	1	0	0	0	0	0	0	1	0	0	6,601
Bristol	0	1	0	0	0	0	0	0	1	0	16,640
Chesapeake	2	0	0	0	0	0	0	1	0	1	247,118
Christiansburg	1	0	0	0	0	0	0	0	0	1	22,643
Front Royal	1	0	0	0	0	0	0	0	1	0	15,387
Hampton	1	0	0	0	0	0	0	0	0	1	134,082
Harrisonburg	0	0	1	0	0	0	1	0	0	0	53,442
Hopewell	1	0	0	0	0	0	0	0	1	0	22,498
Leesburg	18	4	0	0	0	0	0	16	6	0	55,070
Lynchburg	1	0	1	0	0	0	0	0	1	1	82,871
Manassas Park	1	0	0	0	0	0	0	1	0	0	17,839
Marion	1	0	0	0	0	0	0	1	0	0	5,515

Table 94. Hate Crime Incidents Per Bias Motivation and Quarter, by Selected State and Agency and Federal, 2020—Continued

(Number.)

State/agency	Number of incidents per bias motivation						Number of incidents per quarter				Population[1]
	Race/ Ethnicity/ Ancestry	Religion	Sexual orientation	Disability	Gender	Gender Identity	1st quarter	2nd quarter	3rd quarter	4th quarter	
Newport News	2	0	2	0	0	0	3	0	0	1	178,896
Norfolk	1	0	1	0	0	0	0	1	1	0	242,516
Pennington Gap	0	0	1	0	0	0	0	0	1	0	1,705
Portsmouth	1	0	1	0	0	0	1	0	1	0	94,205
Radford	1	0	0	0	0	0	0	0	1	0	18,450
Rich Creek	1	0	0	0	0	0	0	0	0	1	738
Richmond	1	1	0	1	0	0	0	0	1	2	233,350
South Boston	0	0	1	0	0	0	1	0	0	0	7,528
Suffolk	3	0	0	0	0	0	0	2	1	0	92,881
Vienna	1	0	0	0	0	0	1	0	0	0	16,570
Vinton	0	1	0	0	0	0	1	0	0	0	8,117
Virginia Beach	3	0	0	0	0	0	1	2	0	0	450,858
Waynesboro	1	0	0	0	0	0	0	0	0	1	22,801
West Point	1	0	0	0	0	0	0	0	0	1	3,250
Universities and Colleges	8	2	2	0	0	0					
Christopher Newport University	0	0	1	0	0	0	1	0	0	0	5,117
College of William and Mary	1	0	0	0	0	0	1	0	0	0	9,765
George Mason University	0	1	0	0	0	0	1	0	0	0	48,678
James Madison University	1	0	0	0	0	0	0	0	0	1	24,152
Northern Virginia Community College	1	0	0	0	0	0	1	0	0	0	73,642
Old Dominion University	1	0	0	0	0	0	1	0	0	0	28,046
University of Richmond	3	1	0	0	0	0	4	0	0	0	4,602
University of Virginia	0	0	1	0	0	0	0	0	1	0	28,593
Virginia Commonwealth University	1	0	0	0	0	0	0	0	1	0	33,462
Metropolitan Counties	65	10	11	0	0	1					
Albemarle County Police Department	2	0	0	0	0	0	0	0	1	1	
Amherst	1	0	1	0	0	0	1	0	0	1	
Arlington County Police Department	1	1	0	0	0	0	1	0	1	0	
Augusta	1	0	0	0	0	0	0	1	0	0	
Botetourt	1	0	0	0	0	0	0	0	1	0	
Chesterfield County Police Department	5	1	0	0	0	0	1	4	1	0	
Clarke	2	0	0	0	0	0	0	0	2	0	
Fairfax County Police Department	30	4	3	0	0	0	10	11	7	9	
Hanover	3	0	0	0	0	0	0	3	0	0	
Henrico County Police Department	3	0	0	0	0	0	1	0	1	1	
James City County Police Department	1	0	1	0	0	0	1	0	0	1	
Loudoun	6	3	3	U	0	0	3	1	6	2	
Montgomery	1	0	0	0	0	0	0	0	1	0	
Nelson	0	0	1	0	0	0	0	0	1	0	
New Kent	1	0	0	0	0	0	0	1	0	0	
Powhatan	0	1	0	0	0	0	1	0	0	0	
Prince William County Police Department	1	0	0	0	0	1	0	1	1	0	
Rockingham	1	0	0	0	0	0	0	1	0	0	
Spotsylvania	2	0	2	0	0	0	1	0	2	1	
Stafford	3	0	0	0	0	0	2	1	0	0	
Nonmetropolitan Counties	2	1	1	0	0	0					
King George	0	1	0	0	0	0	0	1	0	0	
Louisa	1	0	0	0	0	0	0	0	1	0	
Orange	1	0	0	0	0	0	0	1	0	0	
Patrick	0	0	1	0	0	0	0	0	0	1	
State Police Agencies	4	1	0	0	0	0					
State Police											
Brunswick County	1	0	0	0	0	0	0	1	0	0	
Goochland County	1	0	0	0	0	0	0	0	0	1	
Grayson County	0	1	0	0	0	0	1	0	0	0	
Roanoke	1	0	0	0	0	0	0	0	0	1	
Smyth County	1	0	0	0	0	0	0	1	0	0	
WASHINGTON											
Total	309	52	67	5	6	23					
Cities	258	36	60	4	6	15					
Aberdeen	0	0	0	0	0	1	1	0	0	0	16,744
Airway Heights	1	0	0	0	0	0	0	1	0	0	10,010
Arlington	2	0	0	0	0	0	2	0	0	0	20,825
Auburn	1	1	0	0	0	0	1	1	0	0	82,779
Bainbridge Island	0	0	1	0	0	0	0	0	1	0	25,561
Bellevue	11	2	4	0	0	1	4	3	6	5	150,548
Bellingham	9	2	3	0	0	0	3	7	3	1	93,629
Black Diamond	2	1	0	0	0	0	0	2	1	0	4,858
Blaine	1	0	0	0	0	0	0	1	0	0	5,717
Bothell	1	0	0	0	0	1	0	0	2	0	48,323
Bremerton	2	0	0	0	0	0	0	1	0	1	41,817
Brier	1	0	0	0	0	0	0	1	0	0	7,055
Burien	4	0	3	0	0	0	3	2	2	0	51,879
Carnation	0	1	0	0	0	0	0	0	1	0	2,345
Chehalis	0	0	2	0	0	0	0	1	0	1	7,700
College Place	1	0	0	0	0	0	0	1	0	0	9,374
Des Moines	1	1	0	0	0	0	1	1	0	0	32,652
East Wenatchee	0	0	1	0	0	0	1	0	0	0	14,336

Table 94. Hate Crime Incidents Per Bias Motivation and Quarter, by Selected State and Agency and Federal, 2020—Continued

(Number.)

State/agency	Number of incidents per bias motivation						Number of incidents per quarter				Population[1]
	Race/ Ethnicity/ Ancestry	Religion	Sexual orientation	Disability	Gender	Gender Identity	1st quarter	2nd quarter	3rd quarter	4th quarter	
Edmonds	7	1	0	0	0	0	0	3	2	3	42,934
Ellensburg	2	0	0	0	0	0	0	0	2	0	21,448
Everett	11	0	3	0	1	0	2	7	3	3	112,439
Federal Way	2	0	0	0	0	0	0	1	0	1	97,071
Fife	1	0	0	0	0	0	0	0	1	0	10,301
Fircrest	1	0	0	0	0	0	0	0	0	1	6,869
Granite Falls	2	0	0	0	0	0	1	0	1	0	4,341
Hoquiam	0	1	0	0	0	0	0	0	1	0	8,647
Issaquah	1	1	0	0	0	0	1	0	1	0	40,659
Kent	5	1	1	0	0	0	1	1	3	2	133,883
Kirkland	3	1	0	0	0	0	1	0	2	1	94,470
Lacey	0	0	1	0	0	0	1	0	0	0	53,826
Lake Stevens	0	1	0	0	0	0	0	0	0	1	34,600
Lakewood	1	0	0	0	0	0	0	0	0	1	61,432
Longview	2	0	0	0	0	0	1	1	0	0	38,629
Lynnwood	3	0	1	0	0	0	2	1	0	1	39,517
Maple Valley	1	0	0	0	0	0	0	0	1	0	27,736
Marysville	0	0	0	1	0	0	0	0	0	1	71,522
Mill Creek	0	0	1	0	0	0	0	0	0	1	21,214
Moses Lake	0	1	0	0	0	0	0	1	0	0	24,524
Mount Vernon	1	0	0	0	0	0	0	1	0	0	36,513
Mukilteo	1	1	0	0	0	0	0	1	1	0	21,573
Normandy Park	1	0	0	0	0	0	1	0	0	0	6,633
Olympia	1	0	1	0	0	0	0	0	1	1	53,571
Port Angeles	1	1	0	0	0	0	0	1	1	0	20,364
Port Townsend	1	0	0	0	0	0	0	1	0	0	9,914
Poulsbo	0	1	0	0	0	0	0	0	1	0	11,401
Pullman	2	0	0	0	0	0	1	1	0	0	35,071
Puyallup	1	0	0	0	0	0	0	0	1	0	42,974
Quincy	1	1	0	0	0	0	1	0	1	0	8,183
Redmond	1	0	0	0	0	0	0	0	1	0	74,154
Renton	4	0	0	0	0	0	0	2	0	2	102,856
Richland	4	0	0	0	0	0	0	3	1	0	59,370
Ridgefield	4	1	0	0	0	0	0	4	1	0	9,835
Sammamish[2]	3	1	1	0	0	0	0	2	1	1	66,878
SeaTac	2	1	0	0	0	0	0	2	1	0	29,282
Seattle[2]	100	6	27	3	4	8	28	38	46	28	771,517
Sedro Woolley	2	0	0	0	0	0	0	1	1	0	12,189
Sequim	0	0	0	0	0	1	0	0	0	1	7,768
Shelton	0	0	1	0	0	0	0	1	0	0	10,749
Shoreline	5	3	1	0	0	0	1	2	3	3	57,472
Snohomish	1	0	0	0	0	0	1	0	0	0	10,269
South Bend	1	0	0	0	0	0	0	0	1	0	1,706
Spokane	9	0	1	0	0	2	5	2	4	1	223,524
Spokane Valley	3	0	0	0	0	0	1	1	0	1	102,366
Stanwood	1	0	0	0	0	0	0	0	1	0	7,410
Tacoma	9	0	2	0	0	0	0	3	6	2	220,123
Toppenish	1	0	0	0	0	0	0	0	1	0	8,792
Tukwila	1	1	1	0	0	0	1	1	1	0	20,483
Tumwater	1	0	0	0	0	0	0	1	0	0	24,493
University Place	1	0	0	0	0	0	0	1	0	0	34,339
Vancouver	11	1	3	0	1	0	0	6	2	8	186,440
Walla Walla	2	1	1	0	0	0	1	0	2	1	32,944
Westport	1	0	0	0	0	0	0	1	0	0	2,102
Yakima	2	2	0	0	0	1	1	0	2	2	93,862
Universities and Colleges	1	5	1	0	0	4					
University of Washington	1	5	0	0	0	3	2	1	2	4	56,315
Western Washington University	0	0	1	0	0	1	1	1	0	0	17,966
Metropolitan Counties	37	10	6	1	0	3					
Clark	4	0	1	0	0	0	0	0	2	3	
Cowlitz	0	0	0	1	0	0	0	0	0	1	
King[2]	18	4	5	0	0	1	5	8	9	4	
Pierce	3	0	0	0	0	0	0	1	1	1	
Skagit	2	1	0	0	0	2	0	2	3	0	
Snohomish	4	1	0	0	0	0	3	1	0	1	
Spokane	1	1	0	0	0	0	1	0	0	1	
Stevens	0	1	0	0	0	0	1	0	0	0	
Thurston	1	0	0	0	0	0	0	1	0	0	
Whatcom	2	2	0	0	0	0	2	2	0	0	
Yakima	2	0	0	0	0	0	0	1	1	0	
Nonmetropolitan Counties	9	0	0	0	0	1					
Clallam	4	0	0	0	0	1	1	3	0	1	
Grays Harbor	1	0	0	0	0	0	0	1	0	0	
Island	3	0	0	0	0	0	0	3	0	0	
Okanogan	1	0	0	0	0	0	0	1	0	0	
Tribal Agencies	1	0	0	0	0	0					
Swinomish Tribal	1	0	0	0	0	0	0	0	0	1	
Other Agencies	3	1	0	0	0	0					
Washington State Parks and Recreation Law Enforcement	3	1	0	0	0	0		1	1	2	

Table 94. Hate Crime Incidents Per Bias Motivation and Quarter, by Selected State and Agency and Federal, 2020—Continued

(Number.)

State/agency	Number of incidents per bias motivation						Number of incidents per quarter				Population[1]
	Race/ Ethnicity/ Ancestry	Religion	Sexual orientation	Disability	Gender	Gender Identity	1st quarter	2nd quarter	3rd quarter	4th quarter	
WEST VIRGINIA											
Total	30	16	4	1	2	1					
Cities	18	10	3	0	1	1					
Charleston	3	4	0	0	0	0	0	2	1	4	46,038
Clarksburg	0	1	0	0	0	0	0	0	0	1	15,092
Moorefield	3	0	0	0	0	0	0	0	1	2	2,403
Morgantown	2	0	1	0	0	0	1	1	1	0	30,775
Parkersburg	4	4	2	0	1	1	4	2	4	2	29,096
Princeton	1	0	0	0	0	0	0	1	0	0	5,627
Vienna	0	1	0	0	0	0	0	1	0	0	10,049
Weirton	1	0	0	0	0	0	0	1	0	0	18,111
Wheeling	4	0	0	0	0	0	1	1	2	0	26,222
Universities and Colleges	0	1	0	0	0	0					
Marshall University	0	1	0	0	0	0	1	0	0	0	16,452
Metropolitan Counties	3	2	1	0	1	0					
Berkeley	0	0	1	0	0	0	0	1	0	0	
Brooke	1	1	0	0	0	0	0	1	1	0	
Kanawha	1	0	0	0	0	0	0	0	1	0	
Putnam	0	1	0	0	0	0	0	1	0	0	
Raleigh	1	0	0	0	0	0	1	0	0	0	
Wood	0	0	0	0	1	0	0	1	0	0	
Nonmetropolitan Counties	6	1	0	1	0	0					
Hardy	1	0	0	1	0	0	0	1	0	1	
Mason	3	1	0	0	0	0	3	0	1	0	
McDowell	1	0	0	0	0	0	0	0	0	1	
Randolph	1	0	0	0	0	0	0	0	1	0	
State Police Agencies	2	2	0	0	0	0					
State Police											
Beckley	2	1	0	0	0	0	0	0	3	0	
Union	0	1	0	0	0	0	1	0	0	0	
Other Agencies	1	0	0	0	0	0					
Logan County Drug and Violent Crime Task Force	1	0	0	0	0	0	0	1			
WASHINGTON											
Total	43	10	11	3	3	2					
Cities	30	7	6	3	1	2					
Appleton	0	0	0	0	0	1	1	0	0	0	74,255
Beaver Dam	0	0	0	1	0	0	1	0	0	0	16,426
De Pere	1	0	0	0	0	0	0	1	0	0	25,090
Eau Claire	0	0	1	0	0	0	1	0	0	0	69,086
Elkhart Lake	1	0	0	0	0	0	0	0	1	0	1,022
Fond du Lac	1	0	0	0	0	0	0	0	1	0	43,295
Fox Crossing	0	0	2	0	0	0	0	1	1	0	19,099
Green Bay	2	0	0	1	0	0	0	3	0	0	104,649
Janesville	0	1	0	0	1	0	0	0	2	0	64,682
Kenosha	1	0	0	0	0	0	0	1	0	0	100,005
La Crosse	1	0	0	0	0	0	0	0	0	1	51,211
Lodi	1	0	0	0	0	0	0	0	1	0	3,096
Madison	4	0	1	0	0	0	1	3	1	0	262,736
Marinette	1	0	0	0	0	0	0	0	1	0	10,497
Menomonie	2	1	0	0	0	0	0	2	0	1	16,582
Mequon	0	1	0	0	0	0	0	0	1	0	24,527
Milwaukee	1	1	0	0	0	0	1	0	1	0	589,105
Neenah	1	0	0	0	0	0	0	0	1	0	26,390
New Holstein	1	0	0	0	0	0	0	0	1	0	3,088
Oak Creek	1	0	1	0	0	0	1	0	1	0	36,502
Oshkosh	1	0	1	0	0	0	0	1	0	1	67,080
Palmyra	1	0	0	0	0	0	0	1	0	0	1,753
Pewaukee Village	0	1	0	0	0	0	1	0	0	0	8,102
Platteville	3	0	0	0	0	0	0	2	1	0	12,184
Plover	1	0	0	0	0	0	0	0	1	0	13,201
Rhinelander	1	0	0	0	0	1	0	2	0	0	7,629
Stanley	0	1	0	0	0	0	0	0	0	1	3,722
Stevens Point	1	0	0	0	0	0	0	0	1	0	25,790
Stoughton	0	0	0	1	0	0	0	1	0	0	13,164
Waterloo	0	1	0	0	0	0	0	1	0	0	3,332
Wausau	3	0	0	0	0	0	0	1	1	1	38,492
Universities and Colleges	0	0	1	0	0	0					
University of Wisconsin, Eau Claire	0	0	1	0	0	0	0	0	0	1	12,637
Metropolitan Counties	5	3	3	0	1	0					
Calumet	0	0	1	0	0	0	0	0	0	1	
Chippewa	0	0	1	0	0	0	0	0	0	1	
Dane	1	0	1	0	0	0	1	1	0	0	
Fond du Lac	1	0	0	0	0	0	0	0	1	0	
Lincoln	0	2	0	0	1	0	0	2	0	1	
Marathon	1	0	0	0	0	0	0	0	1	0	
Rock	2	0	0	0	0	0	0	0	0	2	
Waukesha	0	1	0	0	0	0	0	0	1	0	
Nonmetropolitan Counties	7	0	1	0	1	0					
Burnett	2	0	0	0	0	0	0	1	1	0	

Table 94. Hate Crime Incidents Per Bias Motivation and Quarter, by Selected State and Agency and Federal, 2020—Continued

(Number.)

State/agency	Number of incidents per bias motivation						Number of incidents per quarter				Population[1]
	Race/ Ethnicity/ Ancestry	Religion	Sexual orientation	Disability	Gender	Gender Identity	1st quarter	2nd quarter	3rd quarter	4th quarter	
Dunn	0	0	0	0	1	0	1	0	0	0	
Grant	1	0	1	0	0	0	1	0	1	0	
Menominee	1	0	0	0	0	0	0	0	1	0	
Monroe	1	0	0	0	0	0	0	0	1	0	
Oneida	1	0	0	0	0	0	1	0	0	0	
Taylor	1	0	0	0	0	0	0	0	1	0	
Tribal Agencies	1	0	0	0	0	0					
Oneida Tribal	1	0	0	0	0	0	0	0	1	0	
WYOMING											
Total	11	2	2	0	2	1					
Cities	9	2	2	0	2	1					
Cheyenne	1	0	0	0	0	0	0	1	0	0	64,751
Cody	0	0	0	0	1	0	0	1	0	0	9,816
Evanston	2	0	0	0	1	1	1	0	1	2	11,563
Gillette	0	1	0	0	0	0	0	1	0	0	32,093
Laramie	3	0	0	0	0	0	1	1	1	0	32,913
Sheridan	3	1	2	0	0	0	2	0	2	2	17,991
Nonmetropolitan Counties	2	0	0	0	0	0					
Park	1	0	0	0	0	0	0	0	0	1	
Sheridan	1	0	0	0	0	0	0	0	0	1	
FEDERAL											
Federal Agencies	128	60	24	0	1	10					
Federal Bureau of Investigation Field Offices											
Albany	1	0	0	0	0	0		1			
Albuquerque[2]	3	2	1	0	0	0		2	1	1	
Anchorage	0	1	0	0	0	0	1				
Atlanta	4	2	1	0	0	0	2	2	1	2	
Baltimore	4	3	0	0	0	0	2	3	2		
Birmingham	2	1	0	0	0	0		2		1	
Boston	2	1	0	0	0	0		2		1	
Charlotte	0	0	1	0	0	0	1				
Chicago	1	1	1	0	0	2	2	3			
Cincinnati	0	1	0	0	0	0				1	
Cleveland	2	1	0	0	0	0		1	1	1	
Columbia	1	0	0	0	0	0			1		
Denver	3	0	1	0	0	0	1	2	1		
Detroit	5	0	1	0	0	0		2	3	1	
El Paso[2]	8	2	1	0	0	0	3	5	2		
Honolulu	0	0	1	0	0	0		1			
Indianapolis[2]	3	2	0	0	0	0		2	2		
Jackson	1	2	2	0	0	0	1	2		2	
Jacksonville	1	1	0	0	0	0	1		1		
Kansas City	6	1	0	0	0	0		5	2		
Knoxville	1	0	1	0	0	0	1		1		
Las Vegas	2	2	1	0	0	0	2		2	1	
Little Rock	3	1	0	0	0	1		4		1	
Los Angeles[2]	11	6	1	0	0	1	1	7	3	6	
Louisville	1	1	0	0	0	0		1		1	
Memphis	1	0	1	0	0	0			2		
Miami	1	1	0	0	0	0	1		1		
Milwaukee[2]	2	1	0	0	0	0		1	1		
Minneapolis	11	2	1	0	0	0	1	9	4		
Mobile	1	0	0	0	0	0		1			
Newark	2	1	0	0	0	0		2	1		
New Haven	2	1	0	0	1	0		3	1		
New Orleans	1	0	2	0	0	0	1	1		1	
New York[2]	3	7	0	0	0	0	6		2	1	
Norfolk	0	2	0	0	0	0	1	1			
Omaha	4	2	0	0	0	0		3	2	1	
Philadelphia	1	1	0	0	0	1		1	2		
Phoenix	1	1	0	0	0	0	2				
Pittsburgh	0	0	1	0	0	0			1		
Portland	0	0	0	0	0	0		2	3		
Richmond	3	0	0	0	0	0		2	1		
Sacramento[2]	3	1	0	0	0	0	1	2	0	0	
Salt Lake City	1	0	1	0	0	0	2				
San Antonio	1	0	0	0	0	0		1			
San Diego	0	0	1	0	0	1			2		
San Francisco[2]	4	1	1	0	0	0		3	2		
San Juan	0	0	0	0	0	3	1	1		1	
Seattle	5	1	2	0	0	0	1	3	3	1	
St. Louis	2	2	0	0	0	1	1	2	2		
Tampa	4	4	0	0	0	0		4	4		
Washington	2	0	1	0	0	0		1	1	1	
Pentagon Force Protection Agency	2	1	0	0	0	0	0	1	1	1	
United States Marine Corps Law Enforcement	1	0	0	0	0	0	1	0	0	0	

1 Population figures are published only for the cities. The figures listed for the universities and colleges are student enrollment and were provided by the United States Department of Education for the 2019 school year, the most recent available. The enrollment figures include full-time and part-time students.   2 The figures shown include one or more incidents reported with more than one bias motivation.   3 Student enrollment figures were not available.

Table 95. Participation Table, Number of Participating Agencies and Population Covered, by Population Group and Federal, 2020

(Number.)

Population group	Number of participating agencies	Population covered
Total	15,138	306,085,895
Group I (cities 250,000 and over)	89	64,053,353
Group II (cities 100,000-249,999)	226	32,907,848
Group III (cities 50,000-99,999)	487	33,943,172
Group IV (cities 25,000-49,999)	882	30,531,381
Group V (cities 10,000-24,999)	1,787	28,560,177
Group VI1 (cities under 10,000)	7,786	22,084,327
Metropolitan counties[1]	1,654	71,083,178
Nonmetropolitan counties[1]	2,146	22,922,459
Federal[2]	81	0

1 The figures shown include universities and colleges, state police agencies, and/or other agencies to which no population is attributed.   2 Population estimates are not attributed to the federal agencies.

SECTION VII

COVID-19 AND THE INMATE POPULATION

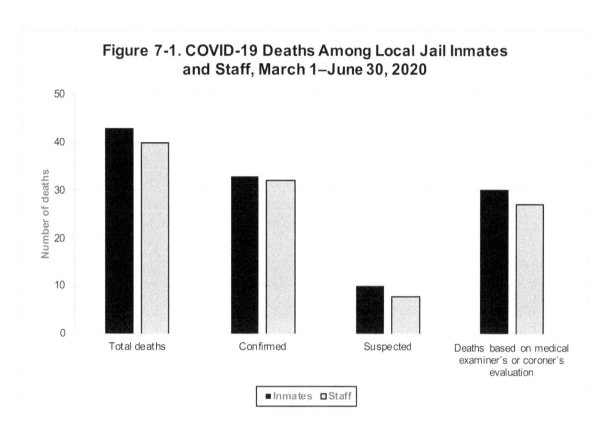

Figure 7-1. COVID-19 Deaths Among Local Jail Inmates and Staff, March 1–June 30, 2020

Tables 96–100 in Section VII are derived from the Bureau of Justice Statistics' *Covid-19 and the Inmate Population* report. This report is one of the first COVID-19 publications concentrating on correctional facilities. It includes data on COVID-19 tests and data on confirmed and suspected deaths due to COVID-19 among jail inmates and staff.

The impact of COVID-19 on local jails began in March 2020, with a drop of 18 percent in the inmate population between the end of February and the end of March, followed by an 11 percent drop by the end of April. From March to June 2020, about 208,500 inmates received expedited release in response to COVID-19.

Findings in this report are based on the 2019 Census of Jails (COJ) and the 2020 Annual Survey of Jails (ASJ). The Bureau of Justice Statistics (BJS) periodically conducts the COJ, collecting a complete enumeration of local jail facilities. In the years between COJ administration, BJS conducts the ASJ, a national survey administered to a sample of 897 jail jurisdictions, to provide nationally representative statistics on the number and characteristics of local jails, inmates, and staff. In response to

the COVID-19 pandemic, BJS added a special addendum to the 2020 and 2021 ASJ to measure the impact of this public health emergency on local jails. In designing the addendum, BJS solicited comments and suggestions from a correctional health expert and jail administrators regarding data availability and reporting capabilities; question design and order; and estimated burden. For more information, please see https://www.bjs.gov/index.cfm?ty=dcdetail&iid=261#Questionnaires.

The COJ and ASJ gather data from jails that hold inmates beyond arraignment, usually for a period exceeding 72 hours. Jail facilities are intended to hold adults, but some also hold juveniles (persons age 17 or younger). The universe of the COJ consists of all local jail jurisdictions (including county, city, regional, and privately operated jail facilities) and BOP detention facilities that function as jails. The universe of the ASJ includes all local jail jurisdictions but excludes BOP detention facilities. In this report, BOP data are excluded. The universe of the COJ and ASJ excludes separate temporary holding facilities (such as drunk tanks and police lockups) that do not hold persons after they have been formally charged in court, unless the temporary holding facilities are operated as part of a local jail. Also excluded are combined jail and prison systems in Alaska, Connecticut, Delaware, Hawaii, Rhode Island, and Vermont. These combined systems are operated by state departments of corrections and included in BJS's National Prisoner Statistics program. However, there are 15 independently operated jails in Alaska that are included in the universe of the COJ and ASJ.

A jail jurisdiction is a legal entity that has responsibility for managing jail facilities. Jail jurisdictions typically operate at the county level, with a sheriff's office or jail administrator managing the local facilities. Most jail jurisdictions consist of a single facility, but some have multiple facilities, or multiple facility operators, called reporting units.

The ASJ uses a stratified probability sampling design based on jail population data collected through the most recent COJ. Jails in the ASJ sample are surveyed annually until the next sample is drawn. The ASJ sample is drawn at the jail jurisdiction level. When a jail jurisdiction with multiple jail operators or facilities is sampled, data are collected from all reporting units within that jail jurisdiction. The most recent sample refresh occurred in the 2020 ASJ, where a sample of 899 jail jurisdictions was selected to represent the approximately 2,850 jail jurisdictions nationwide. In selecting jails, all jurisdictions were grouped into 10 strata based on their inmate population and the presence of juveniles at midyear 2019. In 8 of the 10 strata, a random sample of jail jurisdictions was selected. The remaining two strata were certainty strata, where all jail jurisdictions were selected. For more

information, please see https://bjs.ojp.gov/content/pub/pdf/icljpjj20.pdf.

Definitions: COVID-19

Confirmed death—Deaths where COVID-19 was the cause of death or a significant contributor of death as determined by a positive test for coronavirus before or after death.

County residents' confirmed infection rate—County-level confirmed COVID-19 cases as a percentage of the county population.

COVID-19 test—A viral test for coronavirus disease. This is not a serology or antibody test.

Expedited releases—All inmates released to limit inmate risk and exposure, or due to coronavirus-related under-staffing, court orders, and legislative mandates.

Suspected death—Deaths where coronavirus was the suspected cause of death or a significant contributor to the death, based on the person having symptoms of COVID-19 but no positive test for coronavirus.

Tables 101 and 102 are derived from the Bureau of Prisons' COVID-19 tracker page. Please see https://www.bop.gov/coronavirus/index.jsp for more information.

BJS plans to release a final report that will include results from July to December 2020, but this had not been completed as this book went to press.

Table 96. Number of Inmates Confined in Local Jails on the Last Weekday in June 2019 and the Last Weekday of Each Month, January–June 2020

(Number.)

Last weekday in:	Number
June 2019^	734,500
January 2020[a]	711,900
February 2020[a]	710,300
March 2020[a]	585,900
April 2020[a]	519,500
May 2020[a]	536,600
June 2020[a]	549,100

^ = Comparison year.
[a]Difference with comparison month is significant at the 95% confidence level.

Table 97. Admissions and Expedited Releases, by Size of Jail Jurisdiction, Region, and County COVID-19 Infection Rate, March 1–June 30, 2020

(Number; percent.)

Characteristic	Number of admissions[1]	Expedited releases[2]	
		Number	As a percentage of admissions
Total	2,387,000	208,500	8.7
Jail Jurisdiction Size (ADP)[3]			
Less than 50 inmates	183,000	20,000	11.0
50 to 99 inmates	182,000	24,900	13.7
100 to 249 inmates	425,000	44,000	10.4[a]
250 to 499 inmates	392,000	25,900	6.6
500 to 999 inmates	447,000	36,600	8.2[a]
1,000 to 2,499 inmates	439,000	36,200	8.3[a]
2,500 or more inmates^	320,000	20,800	6.5
Region			
Northeast	121,000	18,800	15.5[a]
Midwest^	551,000	59,900	10.9
South	1,193,000	89,200	7.5
West	521,000	40,600	7.8
County Residents' Confirmed Infection Rate through June 30, 2020[4]			
Less than 0.2%^	430,000	50,000	11.6
0.2% to 0.39%	524,000	33,000	6.3[a]
0.4% to 0.59%	515,000	51,300	10.0
0.6% to 0.99%	552,000	43,200	7.8
1% or more	366,000	30,900	8.5

^ = Comparison year.
[a]Difference with comparison month is significant at the 95% confidence level.
[1]Admissions from March 2020 to June 2020 were estimated based on reported annual admissions from July 1, 2019 to June 30, 2020, and on the confined population on the last weekday in June 2019 and from January 2020 to June 2020.   [2] Expedited releases were granted to limit inmate risk and exposure, or due to coronavirus-related understaffing, court orders, and legislative mandates.   [3] Based on the average daily population (ADP) from July 2019 to June 2020.   [4] County-level cumulative confirmed COVID-19 cases as a percentage of the county population through June 30, 2020.

Table 98. COVID-19 Testing and Positive Cases among Local Jail Inmates, by Size of Jail Jurisdiction, Region, and County Infection Rate, March 1–June 30, 2020

(Number; percent.)

Characteristic	Admissions[1]	Total tests conducted[2]	Number of positive tests[2]	Number of persons who tested positive[3]	Percent of admissions tested	Percent of tests that were positive
Total	2,387,000	215,360	24,550	23,020	9.0	11.4
Jail Jurisdiction Size (ADP)[3]						
Less than 50 inmates	183,000	4,220	320	320	2.3[a]	7.5[a]
50 to 99 inmates	182,000	6,570	250	250	3.6[a]	3.7[a]
100 to 249 inmates	425,000	14,240	1,330	1,320	3.4[a]	9.3[a]
250 to 499 inmates	392,000	23,910	2,420	2,240	6.1[a]	10.1[a]
500 to 999 inmates	447,000	42,080	3,660	3,250	9.4[a]	8.7[a]
1,000 to 2,499 inmates	439,000	53,610	6,630	5,950	12.2[a]	12.4[a]
2,500 or more inmates^	320,000	70,720	9,960	9,690	22.1	14.1
Region						
Northeast	121,000	24,940	2,950	2,940	20.6[a]	11.8[a]
Midwest^	551,000	31,480	2,650	2,440	5.7	8.4
South	1,193,000	88,740	10,990	10,380	7.4[a]	12.4[a]
West	521,000	70,200	7,970	7,260	13.5[a]	11.3[a]
County Residents' Confirmed Infection Rate through June 30, 2020[4]						
Less than 0.2%^	430,000	16,780	270	260	3.9	1.6
0.2% to 0.39%	524,000	40,360	3,830	3,580	7.7[a]	9.5[a]
0.4% to 0.59%	515,000	31,560	3,690	3,300	6.1[a]	11.7[a]
0.6% to 0.99%	552,000	51,060	6,200	5,690	9.2[a]	12.1[a]
1% or more	366,000	75,590	10,560	10,190	20.7[a]	14.0[a]

^ = Comparison year.
a Difference with comparison month is significant at the 95% confidence level.
1 Admissions from March 2020 to June 2020 were estimated based on reported annual admissions from July 1, 2019 to June 30, 2020, and on the confined population on the last weekday in June 2019 and from January 2020 to June 2020.   2 Inmates may be tested more than once and may account for multiple positive tests.   3 Individuals may test positive for COVID-19 multiple times. Multiple positive results for the same individual were counted only once.   4 Based on the average daily population (ADP) from July 2019 to June 2020.

Table 99. Inmate Population Change and Inmate and Staff COVID-19 Testing and Cases in the 50 Largest Local Jail Jurisdictions, March–June 2020

(Number; percent.)

Characteristic	Inmates in custody[1]			Inmate tests[2]				Staff tests[3]	
	Number in 2019	Number in 2020	Percent change	Total tests conducted	Percent of admissions tested	Number of positive tests	Percent of positive tests	Number of positive tests	Percent of positive tests
U.S. Total[4]	734,500	549,100	-25.2	215,360	9.0	24,550	11.4	10,850	4.7
50 Largest Jail Jursidictions									
Estimated[4]	180,700	134,200	-25.7	88,900	18.7	12,670	14.3	4,570	6.7
Reported	173,966	125,949	:	77,087	:	11,471		4,277	:
Los Angeles County, CA	17,385	12,045	-30.7	13,197	57.8	2,640	20.0	292	6.3
Harris County, TX	8,883	8,517	-4.1	4,401	22.4	1,120	25.4	366	6.9
Maricopa County, AZ	7,873	4,501	-42.8	2,837	13.3	804	28.3	131	5.5
New York City, NY	7,341	3,927	-46.5	NR	NR	NR	NR	1,432	14.7
San Diego County, CA	5,959	3,650	-38.7	1,681	9.3	18	1.1	12	0.6
Cook County, IL	5,666	4,617	-18.5	7,477	56.6	776	10.4	382	10.4
San Bernardino County, CA	5,623	4,553	-19.0	409	2.0	159	38.9	33	2.5
Orange County, CA	5,480	3,070	-44.0	2,113	18.4	403	19.1	30	2.0
Dallas County, TX	4,817	5,125	6.4	1,058	6.1	563	53.2	6	0.3
Shelby County, TN	4,776	3,429	-28.2	1,504	17.5	280	18.6	153	12.3
Philadelphia City, PA	4,670	3,872	-17.1	4,540	76.6	229	5.0	199	10.1
Miami-Dade County, FL	4,302	3,271	-24.0	746	5.8	262	35.1	210	7.4
Tarrant County, TX	4,144	4,008	-3.3	565	3.8	215	38.1	67	7.0
Bexar County, TX	3,963	3,620	-8.7	4,164	25.5	518	12.4	86	8.7
Riverside County, CA	3,796	3,140	-17.3	3,418	24.0	271	7.9	NR	NR
Broward County, FL	3,758	2,878	-23.4	294	3.5	56	19.0	13	0.9
Las Vegas, NV	3,749	2,464	-34.3	5,227	26.1	93	1.8	36	2.9
Sacramento County, CA	3,546	2,515	-29.1	1,182	9.8	9	0.8	14	2.0
Hillsborough County, FL[5]	3,302	NR	NR	NR	NR	NR	NR	NR	NR
Santa Clara County, CA	3,200	2,102	-34.3	2,036	33.5	40	2.0	16	1.6
Jacksonville City, FL	3,199	2,791	-12.8	NR	NR	NR	NR	NR	NR
Fresno County, CA	3,090	2,191	-29.1	1,948	26.6	598	30.7	42	7.1
Pinellas County, FL	3,019	2,144	-29.0	63	0.7	15	23.8	28	2.6
Fulton County, GA[5]	2,945	NR	NR	NR	NR	NR	NR	NR	NR
Allegheny County, PA	2,720	1,996	-26.6	205	6.0	46	22.4	17	2.1
Polk County, FL5,[6]	NR	NR	NR	NR	NR	NR	NR	NR	NR
Gwinnett County, GA	2,603	1,872	-28.1	312	4.1	18	5.8	12	1.3
Orange County, FL	2,530	2,149	-15.1	881	8.9	8	0.9	47	2.9
Alameda County, CA	2,458	1,733	-29.5	1,409	15.6	65	4.6	37	8.5
El Paso County, TX	2,279	2,030	-10.9	215	2.6	79	36.7	13	2.0
Marion County, IN	2,204	1,756	-20.3	755	10.8	177	23.4	11	1.4
Southwest Virginia Regional Jail Authority, VA	2,181	1,703	-21.9	0	0.0	0	NR	0	0.0
Cuyahoga County, OH	2,179	1,161	-46.7	1,464	23.1	162	11.1	40	5.4
Davidson County, TN	2,168	1,743	-19.6	981	12.8	218	22.2	40	5.1
Salt Lake County, UT	2,153	1,179	-45.2	147	2.1	23	15.6	34	4.6
Franklin County, OH	2,124	1,673	-21.2	130	2.0	29	22.3	33	5.4
Travis County, TX	2,057	1,778	-13.6	340	3.9	9	2.6	29	2.8
Clayton County, GA	2,055	1,998	-2.8	200	3.0	40	20.0	21	11.5
King County, WA[6]	NR	1,312	NR	235	3.3	8	3.4	16	2.3
Palm Beach County, FL	2,045	1,580	-22.7	207	2.6	58	28.0	36	4.1
Denver County, CO	2,044	974	-52.3	4,692	65.9	648	13.8	58	8.2
Milwaukee County, WI	2,027	1,362	-32.8	1,761	22.0	139	7.9	15	2.6
Cobb County, GA[5]	2,022	NR	NR	NR	NR	NR	NR	NR	NR
Essex County, NJ	2,021	1,778	-12.0	2,422	48.2	499	20.6	102	15.0
El Paso County, CO	2,020	1,316	-34.9	16	0.3	0	0.0	7	1.5
York County, PA	2,013	1,214	-39.7	151	7.1	0	0.0	0	0.0
Dekalb County, GA[6]	NR	1,217	NR	117	1.6	25	21.4	44	8.4
Kern County, CA	1,892	1,769	-6.5	145	1.9	23	15.9	24	5.6
Chatham County, GA	1,857	1,207	-35.0	370	11.0	4	1.1	4	1.0
Delaware County, PA	1,828	1,019	-44.3	1,072	57.8	124	11.6	89	18.6

NR = Not reported.

: = Not calculated because the numerator and denominator are not based on the same jail jurisdictions.

1 Number of inmates confined on the last weekday in June.   2 Inmates may be tested more than once and may account for multiple positive tests.   3 Includes deputies, monitors, and other custody staff who spend more than 50% of their time with the incarcerated population, and administrators, clerical and maintenance staff, educational staff, professional and technical staff, and other unspecified staff who spend more than 50% of their time in the facility. Multiple positive results for the same employee were counted only once. The 2020 Annual Survey of Jails (ASJ) did not capture the number of staff who were tested for COVID-19, due to potential employee testing practices (i.e., tests conducted in jail versus employees who tested during their personal time).   4 Data were adjusted for survey and item non-response.   5 Did not respond or provide complete data to the 2020 ASJ.   6 Did not respond to the 2019 Census of Jails.

Table 100. COVID-19 Deaths Among Local Jail Inmates and Staff, March 1–June 30, 2020

(Number; percent.)

Characteristic	Inmates	Staff[1]
COVID-19 deaths in responding jails[2]		
Total deaths	43	40
Confirmed[3]	33	32
Suspected[4]	10	8
Deaths based on medical examiner's or coroner's evaluation	30	27
Inmate and staff population at midyear 2020 in jails that reported on COVID-19 deaths		
Number of inmates and staff	376,500	160,500
As percentage of of inmate population and staff employed in all jails	68.6	67.8

1 Includes deputies, monitors, and other custody staff who spend more than 50% of their time with the incarcerated population, and administrators, clerical and maintenance staff, educational staff, professional and technical staff, and other unspecified staff who spend more than 50% of their time in the facility.   2 Unweighted and unadjusted for item non-response. The number of deaths are based on 841 jail reporting units that reported data on inmate and staff deaths from March 1 to June 30, 2020, out of a total of 943 jail reporting units that were selected for the 2020 Annual Survey of Jails.   3 COVID-19 was a significant contributor as determined by a positive test for COVID-19 before or after death.   4 COVID-19 was a significant contributor based on the person having symptoms of COVID-19 before death but no positive test to confirm COVID-19.

Table 101. Fully Vaccinated Status Among Staff and Inmates, February 18, 2022

(Number.)

Facility name	Full inmate inoculations completed	Full staff inoculations completed
ALDERSON FPC	531	75
ALICEVILLE FCI	1,295	181
ALLENWOOD FCC	1,991	586
ASHLAND FCI	1,096	197
ATLANTA USP	695	292
ATWATER USP	685	212
BASTROP FCI	1,207	199
BEAUMONT FCC	3,318	494
BECKLEY FCI	1,156	252
BENNETTSVILLE FCI	1,176	192
BERLIN FCI	582	175
BIG SANDY USP	996	219
BIG SPRING FCI	936	101
BROOKLYN MDC	955	332
BRYAN FPC	650	115
BUTNER FCC	3,248	1,151
CANAAN USP	1,217	214
CARSWELL FMC	1,525	395
CENTRAL OFFICE HQ	0	570
CHICAGO MCC	775	181
COLEMAN FCC	5,146	846
CUMBERLAND FCI	1,049	250
DANBURY FCI	859	241
DEVENS FMC	910	455
DUBLIN FCI	1,085	238
DULUTH FPC	241	59
EDGEFIELD FCI	1,444	263
EL RENO FCI	1,031	227
ELKTON FCI	1,467	272
ENGLEWOOD FCI	783	144
ESTILL FCI	101	149
FAIRTON FCI	924	196
FLORENCE FCC	1,889	541
FORREST CITY FCC	2,364	324
FORT DIX FCI	2,662	300
FORT WORTH FMC	1,297	263
GILMER FCI	1,404	200
GLYNCO	0	null
GRAND PRAIRIE	0	334
GREENVILLE FCI	1,151	194
GUAYNABO MDC	1,610	237
HAZELTON FCC	2,817	558
HERLONG FCI	1,051	127
HONOLULU FDC	342	172
HOUSTON FDC	890	147
JESUP FCI	1,168	159
LA TUNA FCI	1,218	229
LEAVENWORTH USP	1,719	212
LEE USP	945	240
LEWISBURG USP	1,014	292
LEXINGTON FMC	1,222	452
LOMPOC FCC	2,070	314
LORETTO FCI	828	183
LOS ANGELES MDC	588	200
MANCHESTER FCI	932	127
MARIANNA FCI	785	166
MARION USP	1,267	192
MCCREARY USP	1,334	199
MCDOWELL FCI	1,147	175
MCKEAN FCI	925	60
MEMPHIS FCI	1,065	210
MENDOTA FCI	1,089	242
MIAMI FCI	783	129
MIAMI FDC	1,098	148
MID-ATLANTIC RO	0	39
MILAN FCI	1,069	210
MONTGOMERY FPC	444	94
MORGANTOWN FCI	399	113
MSTC	0	38
NEW YORK MCC	315	125
NORTH CENTRAL RO	0	62

Table 101. Fully Vaccinated Status Among Staff and Inmates, February 18, 2022—Continued

(Number.)

Facility name	Full inmate inoculations completed	Full staff inoculations completed
OAKDALE FCC	1,861	257
OKLAHOMA CITY FTC	890	204
OTISVILLE FCI	630	160
OXFORD FCI	667	115
PEKIN FCI	966	152
PENSACOLA FPC	363	59
PETERSBURG FCC	2,386	463
PHILADELPHIA FDC	877	240
PHOENIX FCI	1,186	168
POLLOCK FCC	2,334	420
RAY BROOK FCI	539	144
ROCHESTER FMC	622	406
SAFFORD FCI	826	146
SAN DIEGO MCC	1,615	189
SANDSTONE FCI	933	179
SCHUYLKILL FCI	1,062	169
SEAGOVILLE FCI	1,581	201
SEATAC FDC	849	128
SHERIDAN FCI	1,568	249
SOUTH CENTRAL RO	0	71
SOUTHEAST RO	0	55
SPRINGFIELD MCFP	977	530
TALLADEGA FCI	856	167
TALLAHASSEE FCI	967	120
TERMINAL ISLAND FCI	628	242
TERRE HAUTE FCC	2,241	461
TEXARKANA FCI	1,053	171
THOMSON USP	782	378
THREE RIVERS FCI	1,257	177
TUCSON FCC	1,619	501
VICTORVILLE FCC	3,525	551
WASECA FCI	744	133
WESTERN RO	0	65
WILLIAMSBURG FCI	1,448	212
YANKTON FPC	389	91
YAZOO CITY FCC	2,841	466

NOTE: As of February 21, 2022, 327,742 doses have been distributed and 297,835 doses have been administered. The information is compiled from a variety of sources and reviewed by BOP Health Services staff before documented for reporting. The numbers in the table only reflect staff and inmates that have completed both doses (fully inoculated). The figures below do not include any additional booster shots given, although boosters have been offered to inmates. Staff who received their vaccination in the community rather than a BOP facility are not reflected in the numbers below.

Table 102. COVID-19 Cases, Deaths, and Recoveries Among Inmates and Staff, by State, February 18, 2022

(Number.)

Facility name	City	State	Inmate positive cases	Inmate deaths	Inmates recovered	Staff positive cases	Staff deaths	Staff recovered
ALABAMA								
Aliceville FCI	Aliceville	AL	29	0	302	0	0	22
Keeton Corrections, Inc. (Birmingham) (RRC)	Birmingham	AL	0	0	3	0	0	0
Dismas Charities Inc. (RRC)	Montgomery	AL	0	0	10	0	0	0
Montgomery FPC	Montgomery	AL	1	0	75	19	0	16
Keeton Corrections Inc. (RRC)	Spanish Fort	AL	0	1	1	0	0	0
Talladega FCI	Talladega	AL	1	5	317	27	0	71
ALASKA								
Anchorage RRC Cordova Center (RRC)	Anchorage	AK	1	0	2	0	0	0
ARIZONA								
Behavioral Systems Florence (RRC)	Florence	AZ	0	0	1	0	0	0
Behavioral Systems Southwest, Inc. (RRC)	Phoenix	AZ	0	1	0	0	0	0
Phoenix FCI	Phoenix	AZ	12	2	478	11	0	118
Safford FCI	Safford	AZ	4	1	501	18	0	57
Dismas Charities (RRC)	Tucson	AZ	0	0	2	0	0	0
Tucson FCI	Tucson	AZ	0	0	122	2	0	102
Tucson USP	Tucson	AZ	0	11	871	9	0	207
ARKANSAS								
Forrest City Low FCI	Forrest City	AR	3	0	597	16	0	68
Forrest City Medium FCI	Forrest City	AR	1	2	310	13	0	84
CALIFORNIA								
Atwater USP	Atwater	CA	15	0	418	22	0	98
Brawley RRC (RRC)	Brawley	CA	0	1	2	0	0	0
Dublin FCI	Dublin	CA	12	0	271	0	0	44
GEO Group Inc. (RRC)	El Monte	CA	0	0	2	0	0	0
Working Alternatives GG (RRC)	Garden Grove	CA	0	0	6	0	0	0
Herlong FCI	Herlong	CA	8	0	545	8	0	69
Lompoc FCI	Lompoc	CA	9	3	510	1	0	35
Lompoc USP	Lompoc	CA	119	3	272	0	0	79
Behavioral Systems Southwest, Inc. (RRC)	Los Angeles	CA	0	0	1	0	0	0
GEO Reentry Inc (RRC)	Los Angeles	CA	0	0	2	0	0	0
Los Angeles MDC	Los Angeles	CA	9	1	483	7	0	115
Mendota FCI	Mendota	CA	9	2	112	3	0	86
GEO Reentry of Alaska, Inc. (RRC)	Oakland	CA	0	0	7	0	0	0
BEHAVIORAL SYSTEMS S. W. (RRC)	Rubidoux	CA	0	0	16	0	0	0
GEO Care, LLC (RRC)	Sacramento	CA	0	0	1	0	0	0
Correctional Alternatives Inc. (RRC)	San Diego	CA	0	0	5	0	0	0
San Diego MCC	San Diego	CA	9	1	475	0	0	70
GEO-Taylor St. Facility (RRC)	San Francisco	CA	3	0	3	0	0	0
Terminal Island FCI	San Pedro	CA	1	11	549	1	0	116
Western RO	Stockton	CA	0	0	0	2	0	4
Victorville Medium I FCI	Victorville	CA	12	3	563	13	1	123
Victorville Medium II FCI	Victorville	CA	34	1	607	7	0	84
Victorville USP	Victorville	CA	1	1	528	12	0	111
COLORADO								
MSTC	Aurora	CO	0	0	0	2	0	7
RRK Enterprises DBA Independence House (RRC)	Denver	CO	0	1	2	0	0	0
Florence ADMAX USP	Florence	CO	4	0	61	52	0	61
Florence - High USP	Florence	CO	3	2	362	37	0	89
Florence FCI	Florence	CO	6	2	755	37	0	66
Englewood FCI	Littleton	CO	4	1	520	11	0	110
CONNECTICUT								
Community Solutions, Inc. (RRC)	Hartford	CT	0	0	1	0	0	0
Danbury FCI	Danbury	CT	3	1	364	4	0	126
Drapelick Center (RRC)	Hartford	CT	0	0	4	0	0	0
DELAWARE								
Community Solutions, Inc. (RRC)	Wilmington	DE	0	0	2	0	0	0
DISTRICT OF COLUMBIA								
Central Office HQ	Washington	DC	0	0	0	33	0	112
Core DC LLC. (RRC)	Washington	DC	0	0	3	0	0	0
Reynolds and Associates Inc (RRC)	Washington	DC	0	0	1	0	0	0
FLORIDA								
Dismas Charities, Inc. (RRC)	Dania	FL	0	0	17	0	0	0
Salvation Army (RRC)	Fort Myers	FL	0	0	2	0	0	0
BRIDGES REINTEGRATION CENTER (RRC)	Jacksonville	FL	1	0	3	0	0	0
Keeton Corrections Inc. (RRC)	Jacksonville	FL	0	0	3	0	0	0
Marianna FCI	Marianna	FL	4	0	505	15	0	69
Banyan Community Health (RRC)	Miami	FL	0	0	4	0	0	0
Miami FCI	Miami	FL	3	1	236	0	0	66
Miami FDC	Miami	FL	3	2	227	8	0	65
Riverside Christian Ministries (RRC)	Miami	FL	0	0	11	0	0	0
OCALA RESIDENTL REENTRY CENTER (RRC)	Ocala	FL	0	0	6	0	0	0
Dismas Charities Inc. (RRC)	Orlando	FL	0	0	8	0	0	0

Table 102. COVID-19 Cases, Deaths, and Recoveries Among Inmates and Staff, by State, February 18, 2022—Continued

(Number.)

Facility name	City	State	Inmate positive cases	Inmate deaths	Inmates recovered	Staff positive cases	Staff deaths	Staff recovered
Pensacola FPC	Pensacola	FL	0	0	39	6	0	30
Coleman I USP	Sumterville	FL	7	0	128	5	0	131
Coleman II USP	Sumterville	FL	1	1	456	1	0	137
Coleman Low FCI	Sumterville	FL	0	1	453	1	1	101
Coleman Medium FCI	Sumterville	FL	0	5	345	1	1	118
Keeton Corrections Inc (RRC)	Tallahassee	FL	0	0	2	0	0	0
Tallahassee FCI	Tallahassee	FL	5	2	439	0	0	62
Geo Residential Reentry Center (RRC)	Tampa	FL	0	0	8	0	0	0
Hillsborough County RRC (RRC)	Tampa	FL	0	0	4	0	0	0
Salvation Army (RRC)	West Palm Beach	FL	0	1	6	0	0	0
GEORGIA								
Atlanta USP	Atlanta	GA	15	2	294	0	1	29
CSC-Dismas Charities (RRC)	Atlanta	GA	0	0	11	0	0	0
Southeast RO	Atlanta	GA	0	0	0	2	0	23
Dismas Charities Inc. (RRC)	Augusta	GA	0	1	14	0	0	0
Glynco	Glynco	GA	0	0	0	5	0	14
Jesup FCI	Jesup	GA	0	2	441	0	0	23
RRC DISMAS HOUSE OF MACON (RRC)	Macon	GA	0	0	11	0	0	0
Dismas Charities Inc. (RRC)	Savannah	GA	0	1	5	0	0	0
HAWAII								
Honolulu FDC	Honolulu	HI	14	0	166	1	0	37
ILLINOIS								
Central Territorial of the Salvation Army; DBA Salvation Army Correctional Ser (RRC)	Chicago	IL	1	0	21	0	0	0
Chicago MCC	Chicago	IL	1	0	401	14	0	72
Greenville FCI	Greenville	IL	4	0	814	0	0	115
Centerstone of Illinois (RRC)	Marion	IL	0	0	2	0	0	0
Marion USP	Marion	IL	9	2	750	10	0	61
Pekin FCI	Pekin	IL	25	0	845	24	0	91
Human Service Center (RRC)	Peoria	IL	0	0	2	0	0	0
Family guidance Centers Inc. (RRC)	Springfield	IL	0	0	1	0	0	0
Thomson USP	Thomson	IL	5	0	763	1	1	104
INDIANA								
Volunteers of America of IN (RRC)	Evansville	IN	0	0	2	0	0	0
Volunteers of America Inc. (RRC)	Indianapolis	IN	1	0	5	0	0	0
Pact Inc. Pact-Bradley House (RRC)	Michigan City	IN	0	1	2	0	0	0
Terre Haute FCI	Terre Haute	IN	7	4	394	9	0	231
Terre Haute USP	Terre Haute	IN	8	2	707	1	0	34
IOWA								
Dismas Charities Inc. (RRC)	Sioux City	IA	0	0	8	0	0	0
KANSAS								
North Central RO	Kansas City	KS	0	0	0	1	0	4
GEO Reentry, Inc. (RRC)	Leavenworth	KS	0	1	15	0	0	0
Leavenworth USP	Leavenworth	KS	5	3	655	9	0	18
The Mirror Inc. (RRC)	Topeka	KS	0	0	7	0	0	0
Mirror Inc. (RRC)	Wichita	KS	0	0	1	0	0	0
KENTUCKY								
Ashland FCI	Ashland	KY	12	6	343	1	0	153
Big Sandy USP	Inez	KY	19	0	286	3	0	199
Dismas Charities Inc. (RRC)	Lexington	KY	2	0	1	0	0	0
Lexington FMC	Lexington	KY	7	9	616	2	0	181
Dismas Charities Louisville (RRC)	Louisville	KY	0	0	4	0	0	0
Dismas of Manchester (RRC)	Manchester	KY	2	0	12	0	0	0
Manchester FCI	Manchester	KY	3	0	522	3	0	229
McCreary USP	Pine Knot	KY	1	2	287	0	0	145
LOUISIANA								
Oakdale I FCI	Oakdale	LA	160	7	567	18	0	77
Oakdale II FCI	Oakdale	LA	243	2	557	17	0	31
Pollock FCI	Pollock	LA	3	0	757	16	0	33
Pollock USP	Pollock	LA	11	0	583	62	0	149
MARYLAND								
Mid-Atlantic RO	Annapolis Junct	MD	0	0	0	0	0	19
Volunteers of America Inc. (RRC)	Baltimore	MD	1	0	33	0	0	0
Cumberland FCI	Cumberland	MD	1	0	358	2	0	124
MASSACHUSETTS								
Devens FMC	Ayer	MA	11	13	385	14	0	166
Community Resources for Justice, Inc. (RRC)	Boston	MA	0	0	1	0	0	0
MICHIGAN								
Kalamazoo Prob Enhancement Pro (RRC)	Battle Creek	MI	0	0	1	0	0	0
Kalamazoo Prob Enhancement Pro (RRC)	Benton Harbor	MI	0	0	1	0	0	0
Cherry Street Services, Inc. (RRC)	Detroit	MI	0	0	10	0	0	0

Table 102. COVID-19 Cases, Deaths, and Recoveries Among Inmates and Staff, by State, February 18, 2022—Continued

(Number.)

Facility name	City	State	Inmate positive cases	Inmate deaths	Inmates recovered	Staff positive cases	Staff deaths	Staff recovered
Cherry Street Services, Inc. (RRC)	Grand Rapids	MI	0	0	1	0	0	0
Kalamazoo Prob Enhancement Pro (RRC)	Kalamazoo	MI	0	0	2	0	0	0
Milan FCI	Milan	MI	5	3	281	2	0	85
MINNESOTA								
Duluth FPC	Duluth	MN	3	0	118	6	0	45
Volunteers of America, Inc. (Minnesota) (RRC)	Minneapolis	MN	1	0	5	0	0	0
Rochester FMC	Rochester	MN	88	0	309	11	0	162
Volunteers of America of Minnesota (RRC)	Roseville	MN	0	0	3	0	0	0
Sandstone FCI	Sandstone	MN	30	1	555	4	0	58
Waseca FCI	Waseca	MN	15	0	501	7	0	46
MISSISSIPPI								
Dismas Charities (RRC)	Hattiesburg	MS	0	1	0	0	0	0
RRC, JACKSON, MISSISSIPPI (RRC)	Jackson	MS	0	0	6	0	0	0
RRC Tupelo, Mississippi (RRC)	Tupelo	MS	0	0	7	0	0	0
Yazoo City Low FCI	Yazoo City	MS	0	3	205	5	0	14
Yazoo City Medium FCI	Yazoo City	MS	19	0	935	10	0	16
Yazoo City USP	Yazoo City	MS	28	2	462	5	0	19
MISSOURI								
Southeast Missouri Behavioral Health, Inc.; DBA: SEMO CTC (RRC)	Farmington	MO	0	0	6	0	0	0
Cydkam Center LLC (RRC)	Neelyville	MO	0	0	1	0	0	0
Dismas House of St. Louis (RRC)	Saint Louis	MO	2	0	8	0	0	0
Alpha House of Springfield (RRC)	Springfield	MO	1	0	4	0	0	0
MONTANA								
Alternatives Incorporated (RRC)	Billings	MT	0	0	2	0	0	0
Alternatives Incorporated (RRC)	Billings	MT	0	0	1	0	0	0
Great Falls Pre-Release Center (RRC)	Great Falls	MT	0	0	1	0	0	0
NEBRASKA								
Dismas Charities, Inc. (RRC)	Kearney	NE	0	0	4	0	0	0
Dismas Charities Inc. (RRC)	Omaha	NE	1	0	9	0	0	0
NEVADA								
Geo Care (RRC)	Las Vegas	NV	0	0	4	0	0	0
NEW HAMPSHIRE								
Berlin FCI	Berlin	NH	0	0	484	9	0	72
Hampshire House (RRC)	Manchester	NH	4	0	4	0	0	0
NEW JERSEY								
The Kintock Group, Inc. (RRC)	Bridgeton	NJ	0	0	1	0	0	0
Fairton FCI	Fairton	NJ	0	1	234	4	0	126
Fort Dix FCI	Joint Base Mdl	NJ	9	2	1,628	19	0	108
The Klintock Group Inc. (RRC)	Newark	NJ	0	1	6	0	0	0
NEW MEXICO								
Dismas Charities Albuguerque (RRC)	Albuquerque	NM	0	0	16	0	0	0
Dismas Charities (RRC)	Las Cruces	NM	0	0	4	0	0	0
NEW YORK								
Horizon House (RRC)	Albany	NY	0	0	4	0	0	0
GEO Care, Inc. (RRC)	Bronx	NY	0	1	5	0	0	0
Brooklyn MDC	Brooklyn	NY	3	1	700	14	0	128
CORE Services Group, Inc. (RRC)	Brooklyn	NY	0	0	11	0	0	0
Community Resources for Justic (RRC)	Buffalo	NY	0	0	2	0	0	0
New York MCC	New York	NY	0	0	38	3	0	67
Otisville FCI	Otisville	NY	29	0	311	15	0	66
Ray Brook FCI	Ray Brook	NY	1	0	220	22	0	46
Volunteers of America of Western New York, Inc. (RRC)	Rochester	NY	0	0	1	0	0	0
Firetree LTD. (RRC)	Syracuse	NY	0	0	1	0	0	0
NORTH CAROLINA								
Butner FMC	Butner	NC	7	4	183	14	0	185
Butner Low FCI	Butner	NC	5	18	425	11	2	98
Butner Medium I FCI	Butner	NC	3	10	157	14	0	144
Butner Medium II FCI	Butner	NC	2	4	382	0	0	75
Corecivic (RRC)	Raleigh	NC	0	0	12	0	0	0
Dismas Charities (RRC)	Greensboro	NC	1	0	1	0	0	0
NORTH DAKOTA								
COMMUNITY EXTENDED NUCLEAR TRA (RRC)	Fargo	ND	0	0	4	0	0	0
Community Extended Nuclear TRA (RRC)	Fargo	ND	0	0	5	0	0	0
Community Extended Nuclear TRA (RRC)	Mandan	ND	0	0	1	0	0	0
OHIO								
ATalbert House Inc. (RRC)	Cincinnati	OH	0	0	4	0	0	0
Talbert House For Women (RRC)	Cincinnati	OH	0	0	1	0	0	0

Table 102. COVID-19 Cases, Deaths, and Recoveries Among Inmates and Staff, by State, February 18, 2022—Continued

(Number.)

Facility name	City	State	Inmate positive cases	Inmate deaths	Inmates recovered	Staff positive cases	Staff deaths	Staff recovered
Oriana House Inc. (RRC)	Cleveland	OH	0	0	2	0	0	0
Alvis House Inc. (RRC)	Columbus	OH	0	0	3	0	0	0
Elkton FCI	Lisbon	OH	4	9	661	28	0	88
Volunteers of America of Greater Ohio (RRC)	Toledo	OH	0	0	3	0	0	0
Community Corrections Assoc. (RRC)	Youngstown	OH	0	0	1	0	0	0
OKLAHOMA								
El Reno FCI	El Reno	OK	1	1	559	63	0	105
CORECIVIC-OK REENTRY OPP.CTR (RRC)	Oklahoma City	OK	0	0	1	0	0	0
Oklahoma City FTC	Oklahoma City	OK	5	2	711	1	0	82
OREGON								
NW Regional Re-Entry Center (RRC)	Portland	OR	1	0	4	0	0	0
Sheridan FCI	Sheridan	OR	74	2	464	4	0	22
PENNSYLVANIA								
Allenwood Low FCI	Allenwood	PA	0	1	425	2	0	21
Allenwood USP	Allenwood	PA	0	1	298	1	0	49
Guaynabo MDC	Guaynabo	PR	3	0	325	1	0	63
Firetree LTD. (RRC)	Harrisburg	PA	0	0	17	0	0	0
McKean FCI	Lewis Run	PA	12	0	422	25	0	15
Lewisburg USP	Lewisburg	PA	19	1	352	20	0	140
Loretto FCI	Loretto	PA	9	1	792	12	0	69
Schuylkill FCI	Minersville	PA	19	0	524	3	0	73
Community Education Centers; DBA: CEC (RRC)	Philadelphia	PA	0	0	3	0	0	0
Kintock Group, The (RRC)	Philadelphia	PA	1	0	2	0	0	0
Northeast RO	Philadelphia	PA	0	0	0	0	0	3
Philadelphia FDC	Philadelphia	PA	2	0	539	2	0	107
RENEWAL INC FEMALES (RRC)	Pittsburgh	PA	0	0	2	0	0	0
Renewal Inc. (RRC)	Pittsburgh	PA	0	0	6	0	0	0
Scranton Pavilion (RRC)	Scranton	PA	0	0	1	0	0	0
Canaan USP	Waymart	PA	0	0	394	5	0	151
Allenwood Medium FCI	White Deer	PA	2	0	574	0	0	54
PUERTO RICO								
Volunteers of America Inc. (RRC)	San Juan	RQ	0	0	11	0	0	0
RHODE ISLAND								
Community Resources Justice (RRC)	Pawtucket	RI	0	0	1	0	0	0
SOUTH CAROLINA								
Bennettsville FCI	Bennettsville	SC	0	1	171	7	0	109
Alston Wilkes Society (RRC)	Columbia	SC	0	1	1	0	0	0
Edgefield FCI	Edgefield	SC	1	3	281	0	0	37
Estill FCI	Estill	SC	0	0	8	3	0	53
Alston Wilkes Society (RRC)	Florence	SC	1	1	2	0	0	0
Bannum, Inc. (RRC)	Greenville	SC	0	0	2	0	0	0
Williamsburg FCI	Salters	SC	2	3	263	55	0	72
SOUTH DAKOTA								
Community Education Centers (RRC)	Rapid City	SD	0	0	2	0	0	0
Yankton FPC	Yankton	SD	1	0	217	1	0	20
TENNESSEE								
Salvation Army (RRC)	Chattanooga	TN	0	0	15	0	0	0
Midway Rehabilitation Center (RRC)	Knoxville	TN	1	0	13	0	0	0
Dismas Charities (RRC)	Memphis	TN	0	0	3	0	0	0
Memphis FCI	Memphis	TN	7	2	281	0	0	107
Dismas Charities Nashville (RRC)	Nashville	TN	0	0	3	0	0	0
TEXAS								
La Tuna FCI	Anthony	TX	0	2	639	48	0	72
Bastrop FCI	Bastrop	TX	15	1	466	14	0	76
Beaumont Low FCI	Beaumont	TX	3	4	931	22	0	40
Beaumont Medium FCI	Beaumont	TX	0	0	496	19	0	48
Beaumont USP	Beaumont	TX	7	0	275	31	0	68
Big Spring FCI	Big Spring	TX	32	3	696	1	0	19
GEO Care Inc. (RRC)	Brownsville	TX	0	1	9	0	0	0
Bryan FPC	Bryan	TX	4	0	247	3	0	54
Dismas Charities, Inc. (RRC)	Corpus Christi	TX	0	0	3	0	0	0
Dismas Charities (RRC)	Del Rio	TX	0	0	7	0	0	0
ACS Corrections (RRC)	Del Valle	TX	0	1	2	0	0	0
GEO Group Inc. (RRC)	Edinburg	TX	0	0	8	0	0	0
Dismas Charities (RRC)	El Paso	TX	0	0	2	0	0	0
Carswell FMC	Fort Worth	TX	48	8	875	49	0	7
Fort Worth FMC	Fort Worth	TX	9	17	621	22	0	50
Vol. of America Fort Worth Texas (RRC)	Ft. Worth	TX	0	0	1	0	0	0
Grand Prairie	Grand Prairie	TX	0	0	0	34	0	82
South Central RO	Grand Prairie	TX	0	0	0	1	0	10
Houston FDC	Houston	TX	2	0	271	10	0	61
The Geo Group, Inc. (RRC)	Houston	TX	0	2	2	0	0	0

Table 102. COVID-19 Cases, Deaths, and Recoveries Among Inmates and Staff, by State, February 18, 2022—Continued

(Number.)

Facility name	City	State	Inmate positive cases	Inmate deaths	Inmates recovered	Staff positive cases	Staff deaths	Staff recovered
Volunteers of America Texas, Inc. (RRC)	Hutchins	TX	0	1	6	0	0	0
Dismas Laredo (RRC)	Laredo	TX	0	0	7	0	0	0
Dismas Charities (RRC)	Midland	TX	0	0	11	0	0	0
Crosspoint Inc. (RRC)	San Antonio	TX	0	0	6	0	0	0
Seagoville FCI	Seagoville	TX	116	7	1,013	26	0	75
Texarkana FCI	Texarkana	TX	47	2	700	36	0	115
Three Rivers FCI	Three Rivers	TX	7	0	501	32	0	79
County Rehabilitation Center (RRC)	Tyler	TX	0	0	2	0	0	0
Salvation Army (RRC)	Waco	TX	0	1	1	0	0	0
UTAH								
GEO Care Salt Lake City Center (RRC)	Salt Lake City	UT	0	0	3	0	0	0
VIRGINIA								
Petersburg Low FCI	Hopewell	VA	0	0	209	1	0	60
Petersburg Medium FCI	Hopewell	VA	28	1	231	4	0	38
Core Civic (RRC)	Newport News	VA	0	0	2	0	0	0
Corecivic (RRC)	Norfolk	VA	0	0	1	0	0	0
Lee USP	Pennington Gap	VA	1	0	510	2	0	204
WASHINGTON								
Pioneer Human Services; DBA: Pioneer Industries (RRC)	Seattle	WA	0	0	1	0	0	0
SeaTac FDC	Seattle	WA	4	0	253	3	0	73
Pioneer Human Services (RRC)	Spokane	WA	0	0	2	0	0	0
WEST VIRGINIA								
Alderson FPC	Alderson	WV	38	2	295	4	0	65
Beckley FCI	Beaver	WV	2	0	197	0	0	142
Hazelton FCI	Bruceton Mills	WV	3	2	169	2	0	119
Hazelton USP	Bruceton Mills	WV	4	0	82	3	0	264
Dismas Charities (RRC)	Clarksburg	WV	0	0	3	0	0	0
Gilmer FCI	Glenville	WV	3	1	304	3	0	131
Morgantown FCI	Morgantown	WV	1	0	314	0	0	77
Dismas Charities (RRC)	St. Albans	WV	0	0	2	0	0	0
McDowell FCI	Welch	WV	3	0	432	0	0	66
WISCONSIN								
Lutherin Social Services (RRC)	Eau Claire	WI	0	0	1	0	0	0
Rock Valley Comm Programs Inc. (RRC)	Janesville	WI	1	0	14	0	0	0
Wisconsin Community Svs (RRC)	Milwaukee	WI	0	0	3	0	0	0
Oxford FCI	Oxford	WI	1	0	663	13	0	95
WYOMING								
Community Education Centers (RRC)	Mills	WY	0	0	2	0	0	0

NOTE: The positive test numbers are based on the most recently available confirmed lab results involving open cases from across the agency as reported by the BOP's Office of Occupational Safety and Health at 11:00 a.m. each day. BOP field sites may report additional updates throughout the day. Reported staff deaths have been determined to be work-related as defined by 29 CFR 1904 (OSHA Recordkeeping standard). As such, they have been recorded on the respective institution's OSHA 300 injury and illness log as a work-related fatality. The BOP tests inmates in accordance with CDC guidance. The BOP utilizes this information for the management of an outbreak at the relevant, affected facility. The inmate totals listed do not include inmates participating in the Federal Location Monitoring program, inmates supervised under the USPO, or being held in privately-managed prisons or state facilities/jails. References to RRCs include both individuals housed at the RRC and individuals on home confinement under the RRC's supervision.

APPENDIXES

APPENDIX I. METHODOLOGY

Submitting UCR data to the FBI is a collective effort on the part of city, university/college, county, state, tribal, and federal law enforcement agencies to present a nationwide view of crime. Participating agencies throughout the country voluntarily provide reports on crimes known to the police and on persons arrested. For the most part, agencies submit monthly crime reports, using uniform offense definitions, to a centralized repository within their state. The state UCR Program then forwards the data to the FBI's UCR Program. Agencies in states that do not have a state UCR Program submit their data directly to the FBI. Staff members review the information for accuracy and reasonableness. [The FBI distributes the data presentations, special studies, and other publications compiled from the data to all who are interested in knowing about crime in the nation.] The national UCR Program is housed in the Operational Programs (OP) Branch of the FBI's Criminal Justice Information Services (CJIS) Division. Within the OP Branch, four units (the Crime Statistics Management Unit [CSMU], the CJIS Audit Unit, the Multimedia Productions Group [MPG]), and the CJIS Training and Advisory Process [CTAP] Unit), are involved in the day-to-day administration of the program.

Criteria for State UCR programs

The criteria established for state programs ensure consistency and comparability in the data submitted to the national program, as well as regular and timely reporting. These criteria are:

1. A UCR Program must conform to the FBI UCR Program's submission standards, definitions, specifications, and required deadlines.

2. A UCR Program must establish data integrity procedures and have personnel assigned to assist contributing agencies in quality assurance practices and crime reporting procedures. Data integrity procedures should include crime trend assessments, offense classification verification, and technical specification validation.

3. A UCR Program's submissions must cover more than 50 percent of the law enforcement agencies within its established reporting domain and be willing to cover any and all UCR-contributing agencies that wish to use the UCR Program from within its domain. (An agency wishing to become a UCR Program must be willing to report for all of the agencies within the state.)

• A UCR Program must furnish the FBI UCR Program with all of the UCR data collected by the law enforcement agencies within its domain.

These requirements do not prohibit the state from gathering other statistical data beyond the national collection.

Data Completeness and Quality

National program staff members contact the state UCR program in connection with crime-reporting matters and, when necessary and approved by the state, they contact individual contributors within the state. To fulfill its responsibilities in connection with the UCR program, the FBI reviews and edits individual agency reports for completeness and quality. Upon request, they conduct training programs within the state on law enforcement record-keeping and crime-reporting procedures. The FBI conducts an audit of each state's UCR data collection procedures once every three years, in accordance with audit standards established by the federal government. Should circumstances develop in which the state program does not comply with the aforementioned requirements, the national program may institute a direct collection of data from law enforcement agencies within the state.

During a review of publication processes, the UCR Program staff analyzed Web statistics from previous editions of *Crime in the United States* (*CIUS*) to determine the tables that users access the most. Based on these criteria, the UCR Program streamlined the 2016 edition by reducing the number of tables from 81 to 29. The publication, however, still presents the major topics (offenses known, clearances, and persons arrested) that readers have come to expect. On June 30, 2017, the UCR Program launched the Crime Data Explorer (CDE), which provides law enforcement and the general public with crime data at the agency, state, and national levels. Offering multiple pathways to reported crime data, the CDE provides data visualizations of high-level trends and incident data with more detailed perspectives through downloads and a system enabling developers to create software applications. Planned enhancements to the CDE include additional tools to create dynamic data presentations, progressing beyond the static data tables of *CIUS* and the National Incident-Based Reporting System (NIBRS).

Beginning January 1, 2017, the UCR Program discontinued collecting rape data via the SRS according to the legacy definition. Therefore, the 2016 editions of *CIUS* and *Hate Crime Statistics* are the final publications which include the legacy definition of rape. Only rape data submitted under the revised definition will be published for 2017 and subsequent years. This change did not affect agencies that submit rape data via NIBRS.

Reporting Procedures

Offenses known and value of property — Law enforcement agencies tabulate the number of Part I offenses reported based on records of all reports of crime received from victims, officers who discover infractions, or other sources, and submit these reports each month to the FBI directly or through their state UCR programs. Part I offenses include murder and nonnegligent manslaughter, forcible rape, robbery, aggravated assault, burglary, larceny-theft, motor vehicle theft, and arson. Each month, law enforcement agencies also submit to the FBI the value of property stolen and recovered in connection with the offenses and detailed information pertaining to criminal homicide.

Unfounded offenses and clearances — When, through investigation, an agency determines that complaints of crimes are unfounded or false, the agency eliminates that offense from its crime tally through an entry on the monthly report. The report also provides the total number of actual Part I offenses, the number of offenses cleared, and the number of clearances that involve only offenders under the age of 18. (Law enforcement can clear crimes in one of two ways: by the arrest of at least one person who is charged and turned over to the court for prosecution or by exceptional means — when some element beyond law enforcement's control precludes the arrest of a known offender.)

Persons arrested — In addition to reporting Part I offenses each month, law enforcement agencies also provide data on the age, sex, and race of persons arrested for Part I and Part II offenses. Part II offenses encompass all crimes, except traffic violations, that are not classified as Part I offenses.

Officers killed or assaulted — Each month, law enforcement agencies also report information to the UCR program regarding law enforcement officers killed or assaulted, and each year they report the number of full-time sworn and civilian law enforcement personnel employed as of October 31.

Hate crimes — At the end of each quarter, law enforcement agencies report summarized data on hate crimes; that is specific offenses that were motivated by an offender's bias against the perceived race, religion, ethnic or national origin, sexual orientation, or physical or mental disability of the victim. Those agencies participating in the UCR program's National Incident-Based Reporting System (NIBRS) submit hate crime data monthly.

Editing Procedures

The UCR program thoroughly examines each report it receives for arithmetical accuracy and for deviations in crime data from month to month and from present to past years that may indicate errors. UCR staff members compare an agency's monthly reports with its previous submissions and with reports from similar agencies to identify any unusual fluctuations in the agency's crime count. Considerable variations in crime levels may indicate modified records procedures, incomplete reporting, or changes in the jurisdiction's geopolitical structure.

Evaluation of trends — Data reliability is a high priority of the FBI, which brings any deviations or arithmetical adjustments to the attention of state UCR programs or the submitting agencies. Typically, FBI staff members study the monthly reports to evaluate periodic trends prepared for individual reporting units. Any significant increase or decrease becomes the subject of a special inquiry. Changes in crime reporting procedures or annexations that affect an agency's jurisdiction can influence the level of reported crime. When this occurs, the FBI excludes the figures for specific crime categories or totals, if necessary, from the trend tabulations.

Training for contributors — In addition to the evaluation of trends, the FBI provides training seminars and instructional materials on crime reporting procedures to assist contributors in complying with UCR standards. Throughout the country, representatives from the national program coordinate with representatives of state programs and law enforcement personnel and hold training sessions to explain the purpose of the program, the rules of uniform classification and scoring, and the methods of assembling the information for reporting. When an individual agency has specific problems with compiling its crime statistics and its remedial efforts are unsuccessful, personnel from the FBI's Criminal Justice Information Services Division may visit the contributor to aid in resolving the problems.

UCR Handbook — The national UCR program publishes the *Uniform Crime Reporting (UCR) Handbook*, which details procedures for classifying and scoring offenses and serves as the contributing agencies' basic resource for preparing reports. The national staff also produces letters to UCR contributors, state program bulletins, and UCR newsletters as needed. These publications provide policy updates and new information, as well as clarification of reporting issues.

The final responsibility for data submissions rests with the individual contributing law enforcement agency. Although the FBI makes every effort through its editing procedures, training practices, and correspondence to ensure the validity of the data it receives, the accuracy of the statistics depends primarily on the adherence of each contributor to the established standards of reporting. Deviations from these established standards that cannot be resolved by the national UCR program may be brought to the attention of the Criminal Justice Information Systems Committees of the International Association of Chiefs of Police and the National Sheriffs' Association.

NIBRS Conversion

Thirty-three state programs are certified to provide their UCR data in the expanded National Incident-Based Reporting System (NIBRS) format. For presentation in this book, the NIBRS data were converted to the historical Summary Reporting System data. The UCR program staff constructed the NIBRS database to allow for such conversion so that UCR's long-running time series could continue.

Crime Trends

By showing fluctuations from year to year, trend statistics offer the data user an added perspective from which to study crime. Percent change tabulations in this publication are computed only for reporting agencies that provided comparable data for the periods under consideration. The FBI excludes from the trend calculations all figures except those received for common months from common agencies. Also excluded are unusual fluctuations of data that the FBI determines are the result of such variables as improved records procedures, annexations, and so on.

Caution to Users

Data users should exercise care in making any direct comparison between data in this publication and those in prior issues of *Crime in the United States*. Because of differing levels of participation from year to year and reporting problems that require the FBI to estimate crime counts for certain contributors, some data may not be comparable. In addition, this publication may contain updates to data provided in prior years' publications.

Offense Estimation

Some tables in this publication contain statistics for the entire United States. Because not all law enforcement agencies provide data for complete reporting periods, the FBI includes estimated crime numbers in these presentations. The FBI estimates data for three areas: Metropolitan Statistical Areas (MSAs), cities outside MSAs, and nonmetropolitan counties; and computes estimates for participating agencies that do not provide 12 months of complete data. For agencies supplying 3 to 11 months of data, the national UCR program estimates for the missing data by following a standard estimation procedure using the data provided by the agency. If an agency has supplied less than 3 months of data, the FBI computes estimates by using the known crime figures of similar areas within a state and assigning the same proportion of crime volumes to nonreporting agencies. The estimation process considers the following: population size covered by the agency; type of jurisdiction; for example, police department versus sheriff's office; and geographic location.

Estimation of State-Level Data

In response to various circumstances, the FBI calculates estimated offense totals for certain states. For example, some states do not provide forcible rape figures in accordance with UCR guidelines. In addition, problems at the state level have, at times, resulted in no useable data. Also, the conversion of the National Incident-Based Reporting System (NIBRS) data to Summary data has contributed to the need for unique estimation procedures.

APPENDIX II. OFFENSE DEFINITIONS

The Uniform Crime Reporting (UCR) program divides offenses into two groups. Contributing agencies submit information on the number of Part I offenses known to law enforcement; those offenses cleared by arrest or exceptional means; and the age, sex, and race of persons arrested for each of these offenses. Contributors provide only arrest data for Part II offenses. These are definitions of offenses set forth by the UCR.

The UCR program collects data on Part I offenses to measure the level and scope of crime occurring throughout the nation. The program's founders chose these offenses because (1) they are serious crimes, (2) they occur with regularity in all areas of the country, and (3) they are likely to be reported to police.

Part I offenses include criminal homicide, forcible rape, robbery, aggravated assault, burglary, larceny-theft, motor vehicle theft, and arson.

Criminal homicide—a. Murder and nonnegligent manslaughter: the willful (nonnegligent) killing of one human being by another. Deaths caused by negligence, attempts to kill, assaults to kill, suicides, and accidental deaths are excluded. The program classifies justifiable homicides separately and limits the definition to (1) the killing of a felon by a law enforcement officer in the line of duty; or (2) the killing of a felon, during the commission of a felony, by a private citizen. b. Manslaughter by negligence: the killing of another person through gross negligence. Deaths of persons due to their own negligence, accidental deaths not resulting from gross negligence, and traffic fatalities are excluded.

Rape—In 2013, the FBI UCR Program began collecting rape data under a revised definition within the Summary Reporting System. Previously, offense data for forcible rape were collected under the legacy UCR definition: the carnal knowledge of a female forcibly and against her will. Beginning with the 2013 data year, the term "forcible" was removed from the offense title, and the definition was changed. The revised UCR definition of rape is: penetration, no matter how slight, of the vagina or anus with any body part or object, or oral penetration by a sex organ of another person, without the consent of the victim. Attempts or assaults to commit rape are also included in the statistics presented here; however, statutory rape and incest are excluded. In 2016, the FBI director approved the recommendation to discontinue the reporting of rape data using the UCR legacy definition beginning in 2017. However, to maintain the 20-year trend in Table 1, national estimates for rape under the legacy definition are provided along with estimates under the revised definition for 2017. The UCR Program counts one offense for each victim of a rape, attempted rape, or assault with intent to rape, regardless of the victim's age. Non-consensual sexual relations involving a familial member is considered rape, not incest. All other crimes of a sexual nature are considered to be Part II offenses; as such, the UCR Program collects only arrest data for those crimes. The offense of statutory rape, in which no force is used but the female victim is under the age of consent, is included in the arrest total for the sex offenses category.

Robbery—The taking or attempted taking of anything of value from the care, custody, or control of a person or persons by force or threat of force or violence and/or by putting the victim in fear.

Aggravated assault—An unlawful attack by one person upon another for the purpose of inflicting severe or aggravated bodily injury. This type of assault usually is accompanied by the use of a weapon or by means likely to produce death or great bodily harm. Simple assaults are excluded.

Burglary (breaking or entering)—The unlawful entry of a structure to commit a felony or a theft. Attempted forcible entry is included.

Larceny-theft (except motor vehicle theft)—The unlawful taking, carrying, leading, or riding away of property from the possession or constructive possession of another. Examples are thefts of bicycles or automobile parts and accessories, shoplifting, pocket-picking, or the stealing of any property or article that is not taken by force and violence or by fraud. Attempted larcenies are included. Embezzlement, confidence games, forgery, worthless checks, and the like, are excluded.

Motor vehicle theft—The theft or attempted theft of a motor vehicle. A motor vehicle is self-propelled and runs on land surface and not on rails. Motorboats, construction equipment, airplanes, and farming equipment are specifically excluded from this category.

Arson—Any willful or malicious burning or attempt to burn, with or without intent to defraud, a dwelling house, public building, motor vehicle, aircraft, personal property of another, and the like.

The **Part II** offenses for which only arrest data are collected, are:

Other assaults, also known as other assaults (simple)—Assaults and attempted assaults that are not of an aggravated nature and do not result in serious injury to the victim. Included in this category are stalking, intimidation, coercion, and hazing.

Forgery and counterfeiting—The altering, copying, or imitating of something, without authority or right, with the intent to deceive or defraud by passing the copy or thing altered or imitated as that which is original or genuine; or the selling, buying, or possession of an altered, copied, or imitated thing with the intent to deceive or defraud. Attempts are included.

Fraud—The intentional perversion of the truth for the purpose of inducing another person or other entity in reliance upon it to part with something of value or to surrender a legal right. Fraudulent conversion and obtaining of money or property by false pretenses. Confidence games and bad checks, except forgeries and counterfeiting, are included.

Embezzlement—The unlawful misappropriation or misapplication by an offender of money, property, or some other thing of value entrusted to that offender's care, custody, or control.

Stolen property; buying, receiving, possessing—Buying, receiving, possessing, selling, concealing, or transporting any property with the knowledge that it has been unlawfully taken, as by burglary, embezzlement, fraud, larceny, robbery, and the like. Attempts are included.

Vandalism—To willfully or maliciously destroy, injure, disfigure, or deface any public or private property, real or personal, without the consent of the owner or person having custody or control by cutting, tearing, breaking, marking, painting, drawing, covering with filth, or any other such means as may be specified by local law. Attempts are included.

Weapons; carrying, possessing, and the like—The violation of laws or ordinances prohibiting the manufacture, sale, purchase, transportation, possession, concealment, or use of firearms, cutting instruments, explosives, incendiary devices, or other deadly weapons. Attempts are included.

Prostitution and commercialized vice—The unlawful promotion of or participation in sexual activities for profit, including attempts. To solicit customers or transport persons for prostitution purposes; to own, manage, or operate a dwelling or other establishment for the purposes of providing a place where prostitution is performed; or to otherwise assist or promote prostitution.

Sex offenses (except forcible rape, prostitution, and commercialized vice)—Offenses against chastity, common decency, morals, and the like. Incest, indecent exposure, and statutory rape, as well as attempts are included.

Drug abuse violations—The violation of laws prohibiting the production, distribution, and/or use of certain controlled substances. The unlawful cultivation, manufacture, distribution, sale, purchase, use, possession, transportation, or importation of any controlled drug or narcotic substance. Arrests for violations of state and local laws, specifically those relating to the unlawful possession, sale, use, growing, manufacturing, and making of narcotic drugs. The following drug categories are specified: opium or cocaine and their derivatives (morphine, heroin, codeine); marijuana; synthetic narcotics—manufactured narcotics that can cause true addiction (demerol, methadone); and dangerous nonnarcotic drugs (barbiturates, benzedrine).

Gambling—To unlawfully bet or wager money or something else of value; assist, promote, or operate a game of chance for money or some other stake; possess or transmit wagering information; manufacture, sell, purchase, possess, or transport gambling equipment, devices, or goods; or tamper with the outcome of a sporting event or contest to gain a gambling advantage.

Offenses against the family and children—Unlawful nonviolent acts by a family member (or legal guardian) that threaten the physical, mental, or economic well-being or morals of another family member and that are not classifiable as other offenses, such as assault or sex offenses. Attempts are included.

Driving under the influence—Driving or operating a motor vehicle or common carrier while mentally or physically impaired as the result of consuming an alcoholic beverage or using a drug or narcotic.

Liquor laws—The violation of state or local laws or ordinances prohibiting the manufacture, sale, purchase, transportation, possession, or use of alcoholic beverages, not including driving under the influence and drunkenness. Federal violations are excluded.

Drunkenness—To drink alcoholic beverages to the extent that one's mental faculties and physical coordination are substantially impaired. Excludes driving under the influence.

Disorderly conduct—Any behavior that tends to disturb the public peace or decorum, scandalize the community, or shock the public sense of morality.

Vagrancy—The violation of a court order, regulation, ordinance, or law requiring the withdrawal of persons from the streets or other specified areas; prohibiting persons from remaining in an area or place in an idle or aimless manner; or prohibiting persons from going from place to place without visible means of support.

All other offenses—All violations of state or local laws not specifically identified as Part I or Part II offenses, except traffic violations.

Suspicion—Arrested for no specific offense and released without formal charges being placed.

Curfew and loitering laws (persons under 18 years of age)—Violations by juveniles of local curfew or loitering ordinances.

APPENDIX III. GEOGRAPHIC AREA DEFINITIONS

The program collects crime data and supplemental information that make it possible to generate a variety of statistical compilations, including data presented by reporting areas. These statistics enable data users to analyze local crime data in conjunction with those for areas of similar geographic location or population size. The reporting areas that the program uses in its data breakdowns include community types, population groups, and regions and divisions. For community types, the program considers proximity to metropolitan areas using the designations established by the U.S. Office of Management and Budget (OMB). (Generally, sheriffs, county police, and state police report crimes within counties but outside of cities; local police report crimes within city limits.) The number of inhabitants living in a locale (based on the U.S. Census Bureau's figures) determines the population group into which the program places it. For its geographic breakdowns, the program divides the United States into regions and divisions.

Regions and Divisions

The following list shows the nine divisions that make up the four regions of the United States. The program uses this widely recognized geographic organization when compiling the nation's crime data. The regions and divisions are as follows:

NORTHEAST

New England—Connecticut, Maine, Massachusetts, New Hampshire, Rhode Island, and Vermont

Middle Atlantic—New York, New Jersey, and Pennsylvania

MIDWEST

East North Central—Illinois, Indiana, Michigan, Ohio, and Wisconsin

West North Central—Iowa, Kansas, Minnesota, Missouri, Nebraska, North Dakota, and South Dakota

SOUTH

South Atlantic—Delaware, District of Columbia, Florida, Georgia, Maryland, North Carolina, South Carolina, Virginia, and West Virginia

East South Central—Alabama, Kentucky, Mississippi, and Tennessee

West South Central—Arkansas, Louisiana, Oklahoma, and Texas

WEST

Mountain—Arizona, Colorado, Idaho, Montana, Nevada, New Mexico, Utah, and Wyoming

Pacific—Alaska, California, Hawaii, Oregon, and Washington

Community Types

To assist data users who wish to analyze and present uniform statistical data about metropolitan areas, the program uses reporting units that represent major population centers. The program compiles data for the following three types of communities:

Metropolitan Statistical Areas (MSAs)—Each MSA contains a principal city or urbanized area with a population of at least 50,000 inhabitants. MSAs include the principal city, the county in which the city is located, and other adjacent counties that have a high degree of economic and social integration with the principal city and county (as defined by the OMB), which is measured through commuting. In the program, counties within an MSA are considered metropolitan counties. In addition, MSAs may cross state boundaries.

Some presentations in this publication refer to Metropolitan Divisions, which are subdivisions of an MSA that consists of a core with "a population of at least 2.5 million persons. A Metropolitan Division consists of one or more main/secondary counties that represent an employment center or centers, plus adjacent counties associated with the main county or counties through commuting ties," (*Federal Register* 65 [249]). Also, some tables reference suburban areas, which are subdivisions of MSAs that exclude the principal cities but include all the remaining cities (those having fewer than 50,000 inhabitants) and the unincorporated areas of the MSAs.

Because the elements that comprise MSAs, particularly the geographic compositions, are subject to change, the program discourages data users from making year-to-year comparisons of MSA data.

Cities Outside MSAs—Ordinarily, cities outside MSAs are incorporated areas. In 2013, cities outside MSAs made up 6.0 percent of the nation's population.

Nonmetropolitan Counties Outside MSAs—Most nonmetropolitan counties are composed of unincorporated areas.

Metropolitan and nonmetropolitan community types are further illustrated in the following table:

Metropolitan	Nonmetropolitan
Principal cities (50,000+ inhabitants)	Cities outside metropolitan areas
Suburban cities	
Metropolitan counties	Nonmetropolitan counties

The Department of Justice administers two statistical programs to measure the magnitude, nature, and impact of crime in the nation: the Uniform Crime Reporting (UCR) program and the National Crime Victimization Survey (NCVS). Each of these programs produces valuable information about aspects of the nation's crime problem. Because the UCR and NCVS programs are conducted for different purposes, use different methods, and focus on somewhat different aspects of crime, the information they produce together provides a more comprehensive panorama of the nation's crime problem than either could produce alone.

Uniform Crime Reporting (UCR) program

The UCR program, administered by the Federal Bureau of Investigation (FBI), was created in 1929 and collects information on the following crimes reported to law enforcement authorities: murder and nonnegligent manslaughter, forcible rape, robbery, aggravated assault, burglary, larceny-theft, motor vehicle theft, and arson. Law enforcement agencies also report arrest data for 20 additional crime categories.

The UCR program compiles data from monthly law enforcement reports and from individual crime incident records transmitted directly to the FBI or to centralized state agencies that report to the FBI. The program thoroughly examines each report it receives for reasonableness, accuracy, and deviations that may indicate errors. Large variations in crime levels may indicate modified records procedures, incomplete reporting, or changes in a jurisdiction's boundaries. To identify any unusual fluctuations in an agency's crime counts, the program compares monthly reports to previous submissions of the agency and to those for similar agencies.

The FBI annually publishes its findings in a preliminary release in the spring of the following calendar year, followed by a detailed annual report, *Crime in the United States*, issued in the fall. (The printed copy of *Crime in the United States* is now published by Bernan.) In addition to crime counts and trends, this report includes data on crimes cleared, persons arrested (age, sex, and race), law enforcement personnel (including the number of sworn officers killed or assaulted), and the characteristics of homicides (including age, sex, and race of victims and offenders; victim-offender relationships; weapons used; and circumstances surrounding the homicides). Other periodic reports are also available from the UCR program.

The state and local law enforcement agencies participating in the UCR program are continually converting to the more comprehensive and detailed National Incident-Based Reporting System (NIBRS).

The UCR program presents crime counts for the nation as a whole, as well as for regions, states, counties, cities, towns, tribal law enforcement areas, and colleges and universities. This allows for studies among neighboring jurisdictions and among those with similar populations and other common characteristics.

National Crime Victimization Survey

The NCVS, conducted by the Bureau of Justice Statistics (BJS), began in 1973. It provides a detailed picture of crime incidents, victims, and trends. After a substantial period of research, the BJS completed an intensive methodological redesign of the survey in 1993. It conducted this redesign to improve the questions used to uncover crime, update the survey methods, and broaden the scope of crimes measured. The redesigned survey collects detailed information on the frequency and nature of the crimes of rape, sexual assault, personal robbery, aggravated and simple assault, household burglary, theft, and motor vehicle theft. It does not measure homicide or commercial crimes (such as burglaries of stores).

Twice a year, Census Bureau personnel interview household members in a nationally representative sample of approximately 90,000 households (about 160,000 people). Households stay in the sample for 3 years, and new households rotate into the sample on an ongoing basis.

The NCVS collects information on crimes suffered by individuals and households, whether or not those crimes were reported to law enforcement. It estimates the proportion of each crime type reported to law enforcement, and it summarizes the reasons that victims give for reporting or not reporting.

The survey provides information about victims (age, sex, race, ethnicity, marital status, income, and educational level); offenders (sex, race, approximate age, and victim-offender relationship); and crimes (time and place of occurrence, use of weapons, nature of injury, and economic consequences). Questions also cover victims' experiences with the criminal justice system, self-protective measures used by victims, and possible substance abuse by offenders. Supplements are added to the survey periodically to obtain detailed information on specific topics, such as school crime.

The BJS published the first data from the redesigned NCVS in a June 1995 bulletin. The publication of NCVS data includes *Criminal Victimization in the United States*, an annual report that covers the broad range of detailed information collected by the NCVS. The bureau also publishes detailed reports on topics such as crime against women, urban crime, and gun use in crime. The National Archive of Criminal Justice Data at the University of Michigan archives the NCVS data files to help researchers perform independent analyses.

Comparing the UCR program and the NCVS

Because the BJS designed the NCVS to complement the UCR program, the two programs share many similarities. As much as their different collection methods permit, the two measure the same subset of serious crimes with the same definitions. Both programs cover rape, robbery, aggravated assault, burglary, theft, and motor vehicle theft; both define rape, robbery, theft, and motor vehicle theft virtually identically. (Although rape is defined analogously, the UCR program measures the crime against women only, and the NCVS measures it against both sexes.)

There are also significant differences between the two programs. First, the two programs were created to serve different purposes. The UCR program's primary objective is to provide a reliable set of criminal justice statistics for law enforcement administration, operation, and management. The BJS established the NCVS to provide previously unavailable information about crime (including crime not reported to police), victims, and offenders.

Second, the two programs measure an overlapping but nonidentical set of crimes. The NCVS includes crimes both reported and not reported to law enforcement. The NCVS excludes—but the UCR program includes—homicide, arson, commercial crimes, and crimes committed against children under 12 years of age. The UCR program captures crimes reported to law enforcement but collects only arrest data for simple assaults and sexual assaults other than forcible rape.

Third, because of methodology, the NCVS and UCR have different definitions of some crimes. For example, the UCR defines burglary as the unlawful entry or attempted entry of a structure to commit a felony or theft. The NCVS, not wanting to ask victims to ascertain offender motives, defines burglary as the entry or attempted entry of a residence by a person who had no right to be there.

Fourth, for property crimes (burglary, theft, and motor vehicle theft), the two programs calculate crime rates using different bases. The UCR program rates for these crimes are per capita (number of crimes per 100,000 persons), whereas the NCVS rates for these crimes are per household (number of crimes per 1,000 households).

Because the number of households may not grow at the same annual rate as the total population, trend data for rates of property crimes measured by the two programs may not be comparable. In addition, some differences in the data from the two programs may result from sampling variation in the NCVS and from estimating for non-responsiveness in the UCR program.

The BJS derives the NCVS estimates from interviewing a sample and are, therefore, subject to a margin of error. The bureau uses rigorous statistical methods to calculate confidence intervals around all survey estimates, and describes trend data in the NCVS reports as genuine only if there is at least a 90-percent certainty that the measured changes are not the result of sampling variation. The UCR program bases its data on the actual counts of offenses reported by law enforcement agencies. In some circumstances, the UCR program estimates its data for nonparticipating agencies or those reporting partial data. Apparent discrepancies between statistics from the two programs can usually be accounted for by their definitional and procedural differences, or resolved by comparing NCVS sampling variations (confidence intervals) of crimes said to have been reported to police with UCR program statistics.

For most types of crimes measured by both the UCR program and the NCVS, analysts familiar with the programs can exclude those aspects of crime not common to both from analysis. Resulting long-term trend lines can be brought into close concordance. The impact of such adjustments is most striking for robbery, burglary, and motor vehicle theft, whose definitions most closely coincide.

With robbery, the BJS bases the NCVS victimization rates on only those robberies reported to the police. It is also possible to remove UCR program robberies of commercial establishments, such as gas stations, convenience stores, and banks, from analysis. When users compare the resulting NCVS police-reported robbery rates and the UCR program noncommercial robbery rates, the results reveal closely corresponding long-term trends.

Conclusion

Each program has unique strengths. The UCR program provides a measure of the number of crimes reported to law enforcement agencies throughout the country. The program's Supplementary Homicide Reports provide the most reliable, timely data on the extent and nature of homicides in the nation. The NCVS is the primary source of information on the characteristics of criminal victimization and on the number and types of crimes not reported to law enforcement authorities.

By understanding the strengths and limitations of each program, it is possible to use the UCR program and NCVS to achieve a greater understanding of crime trends and the nature of crime in the United States. For example, changes in police procedures, shifting attitudes towards crime and police, and other societal changes can affect the extent to which people report and law enforcement agencies record crime. NCVS and UCR program data can be used in concert to explore why trends in reported and police-recorded crime may differ.

Appendix V. Calculations by Population, Tables 16, 17, 18, 19

Due to a system upgrade in 2019, the FBI calculates rates for each offense based on the individual offenses and population that were published for each agency in tables 8-11. (Previous to 2019, when agencies were published in tables 8-11, but they had one or two offenses removed from publication due to not meeting UCR publication guidelines, the agency's data was not used to calculate rates for this table.) This table provides the rate per 100,000 inhabitants and the number of offenses known to law enforcement for violent crimes (murder and non-negligent manslaughter, rape, robbery, and aggravated assault) and property crimes (burglary, larceny-theft, and motor vehicle theft) nationally and by city and county groupings for law enforcement agencies submitting 12 months of publishable data for 2019. For the 2019 population estimates used in this table, the FBI computed individual rates of growth from one year to the next for every city/town and county using 2010 decennial population counts and 2011 through 2018 population estimates from the U.S. Census Bureau. Each agency's rates of growth were averaged; that average was then applied and added to its 2018 Census population estimate to derive the agency's 2019 population estimate.

The UCR Program does not have sufficient data to publish arson offenses in this table.

Group VI city classifications include universities and colleges to which no population is attributed. The nonmetropolitan counties classification includes state police agencies that report aggregately for the entire state. Metropolitan and nonmetropolitan counties include state police to which no population is attributed. Suburban areas include law enforcement agencies in cities with fewer than 50,000 inhabitants and county law enforcement agencies that are within a Metropolitan Statistical Area. Suburban areas exclude all metropolitan agencies associated with a principal city. The agencies associated with suburban areas also appear in other groups within this The FBI derived the offense rates by first dividing the individual offense counts by the individual populations covered by contributing agencies for which 12 months of publishable data were supplied and then multiplying the resulting figure by 100,000.

Populations Used to Calculate Violent Crime Rates, by Population Group, Beginning in 2019

	Violent crime total		Murder/nonnegligent manslaughter		Rape		Robbery		Aggravated assault	
	Agency count	Population	Agency count	Population	Agency count	Population	Agency count	Population	Agency count	Population
Total	**12,730**	**279,536,935**	12,721	279,321,521	12,709	279,018,775	12,729	279,424,554	12,728	279,497,051
Total, Cities	**9,195**	**194,512,905**	9,192	194,342,817	9,180	194,253,008	9,194	194,400,524	9,193	194,473,021
GROUP I (250,000 and over)	83	60,188,585	83	60,188,585	83	60,188,585	83	60,188,585	83	60,188,585
Cities with 1,000,000 or over	10	26,216,990	10	26,216,990	10	26,216,990	10	26,216,990	10	26,216,990
Cities with 500,000 through 999,999	24	17,433,188	24	17,433,188	24	17,433,188	24	17,433,188	24	17,433,188
Cities with 250,000 through 499,999	49	16,538,407	49	16,538,407	49	16,538,407	49	16,538,407	49	16,538,407
GROUP II (100,000 to 249,999)	212	30,850,549	211	30,740,351	211	30,740,351	211	30,740,351	212	30,850,549
GROUP III (50,000 to 99,999)	458	31,931,708	458	31,931,708	458	31,931,708	458	31,931,708	458	31,931,708
GROUP IV (25,000 to 49,999)	803	27,996,450	803	27,996,450	803	27,996,450	803	27,996,450	803	27,996,450
GROUP V (10,000 to 24,999)	1,563	25,119,823	1,563	25,119,823	1,559	25,059,847	1,563	25,119,823	1,561	25,079,939
GROUP VI (under 10,000)	6,076	18,425,790	6,075	18,416,052	6,066	18,389,166	6,076	18,425,790	6,076	18,425,790
Metropolitan counties	1,608	65,156,789	1,604	65,134,008	1,604	65,134,008	1,608	65,156,789	1,608	65,156,789
Nonmetropolitan counties	1,927	19,867,241	1,925	19,844,696	1,925	19,844,696	1,927	19,867,241	1,927	19,867,241
Suburban areas	6,971	118,340,932	6,967	118,318,151	6,961	118,092,494	6,971	118,340,932	6,970	118,320,268

Populations Used to Calculate Property Crime Rates, by Population Group, Beginning in 2019

	Property crime total		Burglary		Larceny-theft		Motor vehicle theft	
	Agency count	Population	Agency count	Population	Agency count	Population	Agency count	Population
Total	**12,730**	**279,536,935**	12,704	278,387,019	12,720	279,320,446	12,726	278,744,544
Total, Cities	**9,195**	**194,512,905**	9,182	193,726,208	9,187	194,354,748	9,191	193,720,514
GROUP I (250,000 and over)	**83**	**60,188,585**	82	59,626,665	83	60,188,585	82	59,626,665
Cities with 1,000,000 or over	**10**	**26,216,990**	10	26,216,990	10	26,216,990	10	26,216,990
Cities with 500,000 through 999,999	**24**	**17,433,188**	23	16,871,268	24	17,433,188	23	16,871,268
Cities with 250,000 through 499,999	**49**	**16,538,407**	49	16,538,407	49	16,538,407	49	16,538,407
GROUP II (100,000 to 249,999)	**212**	**30,850,549**	211	30,740,351	211	30,740,351	211	30,740,351
GROUP III (50,000 to 99,999)	**458**	**31,931,708**	458	31,931,708	457	31,865,408	457	31,865,408
GROUP IV (25,000 to 49,999)	**803**	**27,996,450**	798	27,827,090	802	27,971,438	803	27,996,450
GROUP V (10,000 to 24,999)	**1,563**	**25,119,823**	1,561	25,1088,221	1,560	25,064,398	1,562	25,1100,993
GROUP VI (under 10,000)	**6,076**	**18,425,790**	6,071	18,401,975	6,073	18,414,370	6,075	18,423,524
Metropolitan counties	**1,608**	**65,156,789**	1,596	64,083,397	1,607	65,112,211	1,608	65,156,789
Nonmetropolitan counties	**1,927**	**19,867,241**	1,926	19,857,414	1,926	19,853,487	1,927	19,867,241
Suburban areas	**6,971**	**118,340,932**	6,952	117,846,365	6,965	118,236,886	6,970	118,322,103